C0-DKM-443

1971

churches & church membership in the united states

an enumeration by region, state and county

douglas w. johnson
paul r. picard
bernard quinn

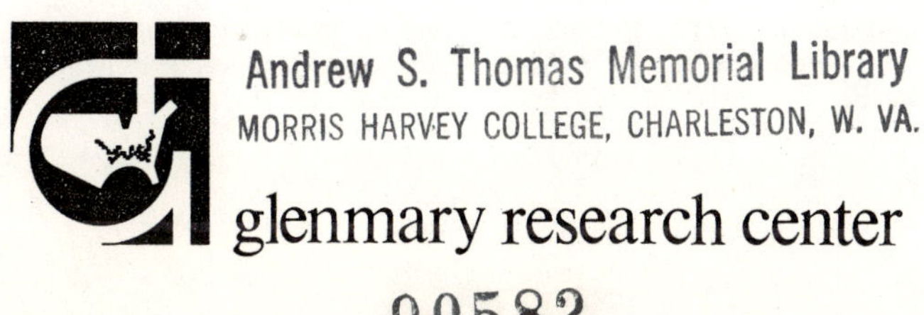

glenmary research center washington, d.c.

GRC A-47/P-233 (89)
International Standard Book Number: 0-914422-01-4
Library of Congress Catalog Card Number: 73-94224
Printed in the United States of America.

Published by the Glenmary Research Center, 4606 East-West Highway, Washington, D.C. 20014. Available also through the National Council of the Churches of Christ in the U.S.A., 475 Riverside Dr., New York, N.Y. 10027. Price: $15.00, including fold-out map, *Ranking Christian Denominations, by Counties of the United States: 1971.* Map is also available separately for $3.00.

ERRATA

The United Methodist data for Allen County, Indiana, through a computer procedure fault, were not properly tabulated. As a result, no data for United Methodists in Allen County were forwarded for inclusion in this publication and no listing appears in the table for Allen County.

The following table presents the data for Allen County with the United Methodist data included. Because of this change in the county data, the Indiana state data were changed and a table has been prepared to reflect this change. All percentages in both tables have been recalculated to reflect the changes made.

PAGE 62

County and Denomination	Number of Churches	Communicant, confirmed, Full members	Total Adherents		
			Number	Percent of total Population	Percent of total Adherents
ALLEN	**179**	**74,237**	**154,101**	**54.9**	**100.0**
019 Amer Bapt Conv	6	2,804	3,505*	1.2	2.2
029 Amer Luth Ch. .	6	2,710	3,698	1.3	2.4
081 Catholic.	24	0	55,737	19.9	36.2
093 Cr Ch (Disc). .	4	1,904	2,380*	0.8	1.5
097 Cr C and C Cr.	8	2,062	2,578*	0.9	1.7
107 Christian Un. .	1	284	355*	0.1	0.2
123 Ch God (Ander)	4	430	1,137	0.4	0.7
127 Ch God (Cleve)	2	143	179*	0.1	0.1
157 Ch of Brethren	3	741	926*	0.3	0.6
165 Ch of Nazarene	11	1,284	2,407	0.9	1.6
193 Episcopal	1	1,255	1,729	0.6	1.1
221 Free Meth C NA	1	88	125	–	0.1
226 Friends–USA. . .	2	25	31*	–	–
281 Luth Ch Amer. .	13	7,847	10,595	3.8	6.9
283 Luth––Mo Synod	28	21,423	29,403	10.5	19.1
285 Mennonite Ch. .	8	793	991*	0.4	0.6
287 Menn Gen Conf.	1	177	221*	0.1	0.1
413 S–D Adventists	2	250	313*	0.1	0.2
419 So Bapt Conv. .	3	480	600*	0.2	0.4
435 Unitarian–Univ	1	225	308	0.1	0.2
443 Un C of Christ	5	3,915	4,894*	1.7	3.2
449 Un Methodist...	35	19,243	24,277	8.7	15.8
453 Un Pres Ch USA	9	6,069	7,587*	2.7	4.9
469 Wisc Evan Luth	1	85	125	–	0.1

PAGE 61

INDIANA STATE TOTAL	**6,127**	**1,230,834**	**2,340,812**	**45.1**	**100.0**

PAGE 5

County and Denomination	Number of Churches	Communicant, confirmed, Full members	Total Adherents		
			Number	Percent of total Population	Percent of total Adherents
INDIANA	**6,127**	**1,230,834**	**2,340,812**	**45,1**	**100.0**
019 Amer Bapt Conv	428	122,937	151,029*	2,9	6.5
029 Amer Luth Ch. .	54	16,143	22,940	0.4	1.0
059 Bapt Miss Assn	4	154	192*	–	–
075 Brethren in Cr.	2	57	71*	–	–
081 Catholic.	513	0	724,115	13.9	30.9
093 Cr.Ch (Disc). .	293	80,284	98,975*	1.9	4.2
097 Cr C and C Cr.	621	127,688	157,753*	3.0	6.7
105 Christian Ref.	13	3,034	5,228	0.1	0.2
107 Christian Un. .	8	1,067	1,330*	–	0.1
121 Ch God (Abr). .	7	321	392*	–	–
123 Ch God (Ander)	144	14,165	37,092	0.7	1.6
127 Ch God (Cleve)	85	5,018	6,204*	0.1	0.3
151 L–D Saints.	0	0	12,186	0.2	0.5
157 Ch of Brethren	107	18,510	22,873*	0.4	1.0
165 Ch of Nazarene	351	30,410	77,017	1.5	3.3
175 Cong Cr Ch. . . .	10	2,310	2,804*	0.1	0.1
185 Cumber Presb. . .	8	1,404	1,696*	–	0.1
193 Episcopal.	80	19,761	30,284	0.6	1.3
197 Evan Ch of NA.201	2	182	226*	–	–
201 Evan Cov Ch Am	5	596	732*	–	–
221 Free Meth C NA	43	3,384	4,791	0.1	0.2
223 Free Will Bapt	20	1,657	2,045*	–	0.1
226 Friends–USA. . .	142	18,708	23,193*	0.4	1.0
231 General Bapt. .	106	10,951	13,513*	0.3	0.6
281 Luth Ch Amer. .	148	44,196	61,161	1.2	2.6
283 Luth––Mo Synod	212	83,955	116,658	2.2	5.0
285 Mennonite Ch. .	77	9,911	12,411*	0.2	0.5
287 Menn Gen Conf.	10	2,501	3,145*	0.1	0.1
293 Morav Ch–North	4	582	927	–	–
313 No Am Bapt GC	1	48	60*	–	–
349 Pent Holiness.	3	72	90*	–	–
353 Ply Brethren. .	11	330	590	–	–
371 Ref Ch in Am. .	10	2,187	3,170	0.1	0.1
381 Ref Pres-Evan.	4	239	308	–	–
403 Salvation Army	39	3,049	16,117	0.3	0.7
413 S–D Adventists	85	7,530	9,292*	0.2	0.4
419 So Bapt Conv. .	230	55,898	68,777*	1.3	3.0
435 Unitarian–Univ	18	2,306	3,224	0.1	0.1
443 Un C of Christ	188	56,110	68,995*	1.3	3.0
449 Un Methodist. .	1,468	369,418	439,817	8.5	18.8
453 Un Pres Ch USA	296	102,986	127,053*	2.4	5.4
467 Wesleyan	274	10,601	12,073	0.2	0.5
469 Wisc Evan Luth	3	174	263	–	–

PAGE 1

THE NATION	**187,900**	**42,422,404**	**100,836,766***	**49.6**	**100.0**

PAGE 2

449 Un Methodist. .	**37,854**	**10,093,206**	**11,535,986**	**5.7**	**11.4**

The authors gratefully acknowledge the generous grant from the members of AID ASSOCIATION FOR LUTHERANS, a fraternal insurance society based in Appleton, Wisconsin. Their generosity has made this study and its publication possible, as well as the distribution of this volume to participating church bodies.

contents

preface

This report contains statistics by region, state and county on Christian churches and church membership for 1971. Fifty-three denominations are included, representing an estimated 80.8 percent of church membership in the United States.

The study on which this report was based was sponsored by the Office of Research, Evaluation and Planning of the National Council of the Churches of Christ in the U.S.A. (New York); the Department of Research and Statistics of the Lutheran Church—Missouri Synod (St. Louis); and the Glenmary Research Center (Washington, D.C.), a Catholic agency.

The authors are Douglas W. Johnson, Staff Associate for Planning and Research, Office of Research, Evaluation and Planning, National Council of the Churches of Christ in the U.S.A.; Paul R. Picard, Director of Research, Lutheran Church—Missouri Synod; and Bernard Quinn, Director, Glenmary Research Center.

A generous grant from the members of Aid Association for Lutherans covered major costs for the study and for the distribution of this report. Additional costs were absorbed by the three sponsoring agencies and the denominational offices that furnished the data.

The authors wish to thank the three members of the study's Advisory Committee: Alan K. Waltz, Assistant General Secretary, General Council on Ministries, The United Methodist Church; Victor B. Streufert, of the Center for Social Research in the Church, Concordia Teachers College, River Forest, Illinois; and Constant H. Jacquet, Jr., Staff Associate for Information Services, Office of Research, Evaluation and Planning, National Council of the Churches of Christ in the U.S.A., and editor of the *Yearbook of American and Canadian Churches.*

Special thanks are also due to denominational staff workers who furnished the data; to the staff of the Center for Social Research in the Church and the Computer Center of Concordia Teachers College, River Forest, Illinois, and in particular to Richard Helmke and William Kammrath for programming and to Carol Gersmehl for supervisory and clerical assistance; and finally, to Patricia Byers, Richard and Diana Ley and Daniel Rojcewicz of the Glenmary Research Center.

Statistics contained in this report are available on computer tape. Church executives and scholars interested in obtaining copies of the tape may address inquiries to the Office of Research, Evaluation and Planning, National Council of the Churches of Christ in the U.S.A., 475 Riverside Drive, New York, N.Y. 10027.

It is hoped that this report, despite its limitations, will facilitate ecumenical and denominational planning, contribute to the study of long-range religious trends in America, and stimulate a more sophisticated study of churches and church membership at the time of the 1980 Census.

introduction

SCOPE OF THE STUDY

This study reports the number of Christian churches and church members by denomination, for each region, state and county of the United States in 1971. Statistics are reported for 53 communions, with a combined membership of 100,812,489; this represents 49.6 percent of the 1970 population and 80.8 percent of the estimated 1971 Christian church membership in the United States.[1]

It is a replication of a similar study entitled *Churches and Church Membership in the United States,* published in 1956 by the National Council of the Churches of Christ in the U.S.A. This earlier study reported 1952 statistics for 109 Christian[2] communions, with a combined membership of 68,999,287; this represented 45.8 percent of the 1950 population and 79.3 percent of the estimated 1952 Christian church membership in the United States.[3]

PARTICIPATING CHURCH BODIES

The following denominations participated in the 1971 study:

Communions with Membership of 1,000,000 or More

1. American Baptist Convention (American Baptist Churches in the U.S.A.)
2. American Lutheran Church
3. Catholic Church
4. Christian Church (Disciples of Christ)
5. Church of Jesus Christ of Latter-Day Saints
6. Episcopal Church
7. Lutheran Church in America
8. Lutheran Church - Missouri Synod
9. Presbyterian Church in the U.S.
10. Southern Baptist Convention
11. United Church of Christ
12. United Methodist Church
13. United Presbyterian Church in the U.S.A.

Communions with Membership of 100,000 to 999,000

14. Baptist Missionary Association of America
15. Christian Churches and Churches of Christ
16. Christian Reformed Church
17. Church of God (Anderson, Indiana)
18. Church of God (Cleveland, Tennesee)
19. Church of the Brethren
20. Church of the Nazarene
21. Congregational Christian Churches, National Association of
22. Cumberland Presbyterian Church
23. Free Will Baptists
24. Friends World Committee, American Section
25. Mennonite Church
26. Reformed Church in America
27. Salvation Army
28. Seventh-Day Adventists
29. Unitarian-Universalist Association
30. Wisconsin Evangelical Lutheran Synod

Communions with Membership of Less than 100,000

31. Associate Reformed Presbyterian Church (General Synod)
32. Brethren in Christ Church
33. Christ Catholic Church (Diocese of Boston)
34. Christian Union
35. Church of God General Conference, Abrahamic Faith (Oregon, Illinois)
36. Evangelical Church of North America
37. Evangelical Congregational Church
38. Evangelical Covenant Church of America
39. Evangelical Mennonite Brethren Conference
40. Free Methodist Church of North America
41. General Baptists (General Association of)
42. Mennonite Church, The General Conference
43. Moravian Church in America, Northern Province
44. Moravian Church in America, Southern Province
45. North American Baptist General Conference
46. North American Old Roman Catholic Church
47. Orthodox Presbyterian Church
48. Pentecostal Holiness Church
49. Plymouth Brethren
50. Reformed Presbyterian Church, Evangelical Synod
51. Seventh-Day Baptist General Conference
52. Unity of the Brethren
53. Wesleyan Church

---

1. The *Yearbook of American Churches 1973* reports 124,829,551 members of Christian churches. For the most part, statistics reported in the 1973 *Yearbook* are for 1971. The census figure for the 1970 U.S. population is 203,211,926.

2. The 1952 study also reported 5,126,175 additional members of 5 non-Christian religious bodies, or a total of 74,125,462 church members. The census figure for the 1950 U.S. population is 150,697,361.

3. The *Yearbook of American Churches 1953* reports 87,027,507 members of Christian churches. For the most part, statistics reported in the 1953 *Yearbook* are for 1952.

INCLUSIVENESS OF THE STUDY

Both the 1952 and 1971 studies include the vast majority of Christian church members in the United States: 79.3 percent in 1952 and 80.8 percent in 1971. This represents 45.8 percent of the nation's population in 1950 and 49.6 percent in 1970. The important omissions are discussed below.

Black Denominations. Black churches were not included in either of the two studies. Unfortunately this means that the majority of blacks were not counted; while some are included among the members of participating communions, the principal concentration of blacks is in the black denominations. It was not possible to secure data because black churches do not have national systems for reporting membership statistics or national agencies that can respond to requests for such information. For the most part, statistics reported to the *Yearbook of American Churches* by black denominations represent estimates rather than actual count; black churches reported 13 million members for 1971.

Eastern Churches. Eastern churches were not included in either of the two studies. For the most part, statistics reported to the *Yearbook of American Churches* by Eastern churches represent estimates rather than actual count; Eastern churches reported 4.2 million members for 1971.

Other Large Churches. The Churches of Christ, with an estimated 1.5 million members in 1952 and 2.4 million in 1971, did not participate in either of the two studies. The Assemblies of God, with 0.5 million members in 1952 and 2.4 million in 1971, participated in 1952 but not in 1971. On the other hand, the Christian Churches and Churches of Christ, with 0.9 million members in 1971, participated in 1971 but not in 1952.

Number of Denominations Participating in 1952 and 1971. Although the percent of Christian church membership included in both studies is approximately the same, there is a substantial difference in the number of denominations participating. In 1952, 109 communions participated, while in 1971 there were 53.

Of the 109 Christian communions that participated in 1952, 53 participated again in 1971. Because of denominational mergers and variation in the method of listing, however, these 53 units are represented by 37 units in the 1971 study.[4]

Of the 109 Christian communions that participated in 1952, 56 did not participate in 1971. It is thought that 6 small denominations have gone out of existence since 1952, since they failed to maintain contact with the *Yearbook of American Churches.* The rest, mostly small denominations, declined to participate in 1971. For comparative purposes, the only large omission in 1971 was the Assemblies of God, a denomination which reported 459,256 members in the 1952 study and 1,078,332

---

4. *The following changes took place between the two studies:* the American Lutheran Church was formed in 1961 from the union of the American Lutheran Church, the Evangelical Lutheran Church and the United Evangelical Lutheran Church; the Evangelical Church of North America was formed in 1968 by a combination of the Holiness Methodist Church and Evangelical United Brethren congregations choosing not to unite with The United Methodist Church; the Lutheran Church in America was formed in 1962 from a union of the American Evangelical Lutheran Church, the Augustana Evangelical Lutheran Church, the Finnish Evangelical Lutheran Church and the United Lutheran Church in America; the Lutheran Church - Missouri Synod aligned itself with the church listed in 1951 as Slovak Evangelical Lutheran Church; the Mennonite Church now includes the Conservative Mennonite Conference; the Unitarian-Universalist Association was formed in 1961 from a union of the Unitarian Churches and the Universalist Church of America; the United Church of Christ was formed in 1961 from a union of the Evangelical and Reformed Church and the General Council of Congregational Christian Churches; The United Methodist Church was formed in 1968 from a union of the Evangelical United Brethren and The Methodist Church; the United Presbyterian Church in the U.S.A. was formed in 1958 from a union of the Presbyterian Church in the U.S.A. and the United Presbyterian Church of North America; and the Wesleyan Church was formed in 1968 from a union of the Pilgrim Holiness Church and the Wesleyan Methodist Church of America. The 1971 listing for Friends World Commitee, American Section includes the following 1952 listings: the Religious Society of Friends (Conservative), the Religious Society of Friends (General Conference), the Five Years Meeting of Friends, the Religious Society of Friends (Philadelphia and vicinity), the Central Yearly Meeting of Friends, the Oregon Yearly Meeting of Friends Church. The two 1971 listings for the Moravian Church in America, Northern Province and the Moravian Church in America, Southern Province were listed as one in 1952, the Moravian Church in America. *The following denominations, not involved in mergers during the interval between the two studies, participated in both studies, although it is to be noted that some have either changed their names or are listed in a different manner:* the American Baptist Convention (as of January 1, 1973, the American Baptist Churches in the U.S.A.); the Baptist Missionary Association of America; the Brethren in Christ Church; the Catholic Church (formerly listed as the Roman Catholic Church); Christian Church, Disciples of Christ (formerly listed as Disciples of Christ, International Convention); Christian Reformed Church; the Church of God, Anderson, Indiana; the Church of God, Cleveland, Tennessee; The Church of Jesus Christ of Latter-Day Saints; the Church of the Brethren; the Church of the Nazarene; the Cumberland Presbyterian Church; The Episcopal Church (formerly listed as the Protestant Episcopal Church); the Evangelical Congregational Church; the Evangelical Covenant Church of America (formerly listed as the Evangelical Mission Covenant Church of America); the Free Methodist Church of North America; the Pentecostal Holiness Church; the Plymouth Brethren; the Presbyterian Church in the U.S.; the Reformed Church in America; Seventh-Day Adventists; the Seventh-Day Baptist General Conference; the Southern Baptist Convention; and the Wisconsin Evangelical Lutheran Synod (formerly listed as the Evangelical Lutheran Joint Synod of Wisconsin and Other States).

for 1971 to the *Yearbook of American Churches.*

There were 16 communions[5] participating in 1971 that did not participate in 1952, making a total of 53 reporting units in 1971. A large addition in 1971 was the Christian Churches and Churches of Christ, with 994,926 members reported.

Summary. Although fewer denominations participated in 1971 than in 1952, the two studies are comparable in the percent of total Christian chuch membership reported.

The 1952 study reports 68,999,287 of the 87,027,507 Christian church members reported to the *Yearbook of American Churches,* or 79.3 percent, representing 45.8 pecent of the total 1950 population of the United States.

The 1971 study reports 100,812,489 of the 124,829,551 Christian church members reported to the *Yearbook of American Churches,* or 80.8 percent, repesenting 49.6 pecent of the total 1970 population of the United States.

Neither study recorded membership in black denominations or Eastern churches, although virtually all of the other large denominations are included in both.

Of the estimated 24 million Christian church members not reported in 1971, approximately 13 million are members of black denominations, 4.2 million are members of Eastern churches, 2.4 million are members of the Churches of Christ and the remaining 4.4 million are members of the smaller churches.

PROBLEMS

Defining Membership. The most critical methodological problem was that of defining church membership. Since there is no generally acceptable definition of church membership, it was felt that the designation of members rested finally with the denominations themselves. In an effort to achieve comparability of data, however, two major categories were established: "communicant, confirmed or full members," and "total adherents."[6]

Since it was planned to use total adherents in computing percent of church membership to total population, in cases where denominations reported only communicant, confirmed or full members, total adherents were estimated by computer according to the following procedure. The total county population was divided by the total county population less children 13 years and under, and the resulting figure was multiplied by the confirmed members.[7] The first count 1970 U.S. Census tapes were used to determine for each county the population 13 years and under. An asterisk after a figure in the tables indicates that total adherents were estimated through use of this procedure.

Locating Members by County. Membership statistics are generally reported for the county in which the church itself is located, rather than for the county in which the member resides. In a majority of cases the county of residence will correspond to the county where the church is located, although modern mobility patterns suggest caution in accepting this assumption in every case. In fact, there are 26 counties in this study with more church members than population; it is very probable that churches in these counties draw heavily on members from other counties. (Excess of 1971 church membership over 1970 county population may also in some instances be explained by high population growth in certain areas since the 1970 Census.)

Alaska and Virginia. Since Alaska has no counties, the census divisions which serve as county equivalents for statistical reporting purposes were employed by this study. A list of census divisions for Alaska will be found in the *Appendix.*

In Virginia there are 38 independent cities which are legally separated from the counties of that state. Since most denominations record location of churches within the counties from which these cities have been separated, it was decided to combine most of these cities with contiguous counties. A list of combinations and exceptions will be found in *Appendix.*

Obtaining a Uniform Reporting Date. Denominations were requested to submit statistics as of December 31, 1971, or as near as possible to this date. Since some denominations collect their statistics in the spring, some in the fall, etc., a variation of some months in the reporting date is to be expected.

Variations in Data Compilation. Most large denominations maintain national offices which receive statistical reports from their individual congregations; these reports were combined to provide the membership data for this study. On the other hand, many smaller denominations, as well as those in which local churches have a great deal of autonomy, only request and do not re-

---

5. *Communions participating in 1971 that did not participate in 1952 are the following:* Associate Reformed Presbyterian Church, General Synod; Christ Catholic Church, Diocese of Boston; Christian Church and Churches of Christ; Christian Union; Church of God General Conference, Abrahamic Faith, Oregon, Illinois; Congregational Christian Churches, National Association of; Evangelical Mennonite Brethren Conference; Free Will Baptists; General Baptists, General Association of; Mennonite Church, the General Conference; North American Baptist General Conference; North American Old Roman Catholic Church; Orthodox Presbyterian Church; Reformed Presbyterian Church, Evangelical Synod; The Salvation Army; and Unity of the Brethren.

6. See *Appendix* for instructions to participating denominations for furnishing the data.

7. Thus the total adherents in a county with population of 1000 and 100 children 13 years and under would be the confirmed members multiplied by 1.11; total adherents in a county with population of 1000 and 300 children would be the confirmed members multiplied by 1.43; and total adherents in a county with population of 1000 and 500 children would be the confirmed members multiplied by 2.00.

quire such reports. This means that data for a few denominations will not be as complete and current as might be desired.

DATA PRESENTATION

This report consists of three tables and a fold-out map. It contains no analysis, but rather provides basic data for denominational planning and for studies of trends in American religion. The information contained in this study is also retained on computer tape and is accessible through a specified procedure to certain persons and groups.[8]

Table 1. The first table, "Churches and Church Membership by Denomination, for the United States: 1971," presents for each denomination, the number of churches, the number of communicant, confirmed or full members, and the total adherents, for the entire United States. It also indicates, for each denomination, what percent of the U.S. population and what percent of the total reported church membership its members comprise.

In all the tables, denominational names are abbreviated. A list of abbreviations will be found on the page facing Table 1.

Table 2. The second table, "Churches and Church Membership by Region, State and Denomination: 1971," presents, for each of the nine census regions of the United States and for each state, the grand total of Christian churches and members as reported. Both communicant, confirmed or full members and total adherents are given, as well as the percent of the regional and state population that the combined Christian church membership represents.

In addition, for each state there is a breakdown of data by denomination, showing for each communion the number of churches, the number of communicant, confirmed or full members, the number of total adherents, and the percent of state population and of total adherents its members comprise.

Table 2 is arranged by regions, and within regions, by states. The *Index* contains a list of regions and states within regions, indicating the page on which information for each region or state can be found.

Table 3. The third table, "Churches and Church Membership by State, County and Denomination: 1971," provides the detailed data on which the totals in Tables 1 and 2 are based.

For each county of the United States, there is given the grand total of Christian churches and members reported. Both communicant, confirmed or full members and total adherents are shown, as well as the percent of the county population that the combined Christian Church membership represents.

In addition, for each county there is a breakdown of data by denomination, showing for each communion the number of churches, the number of communicant, confirmed or full members, the number of total adherents, and the percent of county population and of total adherents its members comprise.

In a few instances, churches were able to provide county breakdowns for some states but not for others. When no county breakdown is available for a given denomination for a given state, the state totals for that denomination are given at the end of the state's county listing, under the heading, "County Data Not Available."

Fold-Out Map. Accompanying this report is a color map, 30" x 42", entitled *Ranking Christian Denominations, by Counties of the United States: 1971*. By means of a color code, this map indicates, for each county of the United States, the Christian group that predominates. For computations, denominations were in some instances grouped into families.[9]

A solid color indicates that a group has 50 percent or more of the church membership in that county, as reported in the present study. When no group has 50 percent, a striped shading indicates the largest group with 25-49 percent of church membership in a county. When no group has 25 percent, the county is left blank.

Percentages on which the map is based are taken from Table 3, Column 5 of this report.

METHODOLOGY

A copy of the letters and instruments used for gathering and recording the data will be found in the

8. Inquiries may be addressed to the Office of Research Evaluation and Planning, National Council of the Churches of Christ in the U.S.A., 475 Riverside Drive, New York, N. Y. 10027.

9. The family groupings are as follows: ADVENTIST: Church of God General Conference, Abrahamic Faith, Oregon, Illinois: Seventh-Day Adventists: BAPTIST: American Baptist Convention; Baptist Missionary Association of America; Free Will Baptists; General Baptists, General Association of; North American Baptist General Conference; Seventh-Day Baptist General Conference; Southern Baptist Convention; MENNONITE: Evangelical Mennonite Brethren; Mennonite Church; Mennonite Church, The General Conference; METHODIST: Free Methodist Church of North America; The United Methodist Church; LUTHERAN: The American Lutheran Church; Lutheran Church in America; Lutheran Church - Missouri Synod; Wisconsin Evangelical Lutheran Synod; MORAVIAN: The Moravian Church in America; Northern Province; The Moravian Church in America, Southern Province; Unity of the Brethren; OLD CATHOLIC: Christ Catholic Church, Diocese of Boston; North American Old Roman Catholic Church; PENTECOSTAL: Church of God, Cleveland, Tennessee; Pentecostal Holiness Church; United Pentecostal Church; PRESBYTERIAN: Associate Reformed Presbyterian Church, General Synod; Cumberland Presbyterian Church; The Orthodox Presbyterian Church; Presbyterian Church in the U.S.; Reformed Presbyterian Church, Evangelical Synod; The United Presbyterian Church in the U.S.A.; REFORMED: Christian Reformed Church; Reformed Church in America.

Appendix. The data collection process itself, though time-consuming, was relatively simple. The sequence was as follows.

Invitation to Participate. On January 10, 1973, all the denominations listed in the *Yearbook of American Churches 1971* were contacted by letter and invited to participate in the study. The letter explained the general purpose of the survey and the connection between it and the 1952 study. A card was enclosed on which the denominational representative could respond affirmatively or negatively or could request further information.

Obtaining the Data. When replies came into the offices of the National Council of Churches, additional information was given those who asked for it and a preliminary letter of instructions was sent to those who indicated a desire to participate.

In the meantime, the computer center at Concordia Teachers College, River Forest, Illinois, prepared a complete set of pre-punched county-coded computer cards, to be used for recording the data.

Since some denominations do not have churches in every state, denominations were asked to indicate whether cards would be neded for every county in the nation, or just for those in certain states.

County-coded cards for the states requested were then sent to participating denominations, along with detailed instructions for recording the data.

This process put the major burden of work on the denominational offices, since they were asked to compile data by county for all their congregations. In some cases, however, denominations were able to furnish information only in the form of yearbooks or other sources. Transferring yearbook information onto county cards then became the responsibility of the authors.

Compiling the Data. The county cards were then returned to the computer center for key punching and verification. During this process the authors were in frequent contact with the participating denominations in working out problems and difficulties.

Information received up to December 31, 1973 was included in the study.

The final step was to run a series of computer edit tests to check for errors and to produce the print-out of tables for this report.

abbreviations

Code	Abbreviation	Name
019	AMER BAPT CONV	AMERICAN BAPTIST CONVENTION (AS OF JANUARY 1, 1973: AMERICAN BAPTIST CHURCHES IN THE USA)
029	AMER LUTH CH..	AMERICAN LUTHERAN CHURCH, THE
055	AS REF PRES CH	ASSOCIATE REFORMED PRESBYTERIAN CHURCH (GENERAL SYNOD)
059	BAPT MISS ASSN	BAPTIST MISSIONARY ASSOCIATION OF AMERICA
075	BRETHREN IN CR	BRETHREN IN CHRIST CHURCH
081	CATHOLIC......	CATHOLIC CHURCH
083	CR CATH CH DOB	CHRIST CATHOLIC CHURCH (DIOCESE OF BOSTON)
093	CR CH (DISC)..	CHRISTIAN CHURCH (DISCIPLES OF CHRIST)
097	CR C AND C CR.	CHRISTIAN CHURCHES AND CHURCHES OF CHRIST
105	CHRISTIAN REF.	CHRISTIAN REFORMED CHURCH
107	CHRISTIAN UN..	CHRISTIAN UNION
121	CH GOD (ABR)..	CHURCH OF GOD GENERAL CONFERENCE (ABRAHAMIC FAITH)
123	CH GOD (ANDER)	CHURCH OF GOD (ANDERSON, INDIANA)
127	CH GOD (CLEVE)	CHURCH OF GOD (CLEVELAND, TENNESSEE)
151	L-D SAINTS....	CHURCH OF JESUS CHRIST OF LATTER-DAY SAINTS, THE
157	CH OF BRETHREN	CHURCH OF THE BRETHREN
165	CH OF NAZARENE	CHURCH OF THE NAZARENE
175	CONG CR CH....	CONGREGATIONAL CHRISTIAN CHURCHES, NATIONAL ASSN OF
185	CUMBER PRESB..	CUMBERLAND PRESBYTERIAN CHURCH
193	EPISCOPAL.....	EPISCOPAL CHURCH, THE
197	EVAN CH OF NA.	EVANGELICAL CHURCH OF NORTH AMERICA
199	EVAN CONG CH..	EVANGELICAL CONGREGATIONAL CHURCH
201	EVAN COV CH AM	EVANGELICAL COVENANT CHURCH OF AMERICA, THE
211	EV MENN BRETH.	EVANGELICAL MENNONITE BRETHREN CONFERENCE
221	FREE METH C NA	FREE METHODIST CHURCH OF NORTH AMERICA
223	FREE WILL BAPT	FREE WILL BAPTISTS
226	FRIENDS-USA...	FRIENDS WORLD COMMITTEE, AMERICAN SECTION
231	GENERAL BAPT..	GENERAL BAPTISTS (GENERAL ASSOCIATION OF)
281	LUTH CH AMER..	LUTHERAN CHURCH IN AMERICA
283	LUTH--MO SYNOD	LUTHERAN CHURCH - MISSOURI SYNOD, THE
285	MENNONITE CH..	MENNONITE CHURCH
287	MENN GEN CONF.	MENNONITE CHURCH, THE GENERAL CONFERENCE
293	MORAV CH-NORTH	MORAVIAN CHURCH IN AMERICA, NORTHERN PROVINCE
295	MORAV CH-SOUTH	MORAVIAN CHURCH IN AMERICA, SOUTHERN PROVINCE
313	NO AM BAPT GC.	NORTH AMERICAN BAPTIST GENERAL CONFERENCE
315	NO AM OLD RC..	NORTH AMERICAN OLD ROMAN CATHOLIC CHURCH
335	ORTH PRESB CH.	ORTHODOX PRESBYTERIAN CHURCH, THE
349	PENT HOLINESS.	PENTECOSTAL HOLINESS CHURCH, INC
353	PLY BRETHREN..	PLYMOUTH BRETHREN
357	PRESB CH US...	PRESBYTERIAN CHURCH IN THE US
371	REF CH IN AM..	REFORMED CHURCH IN AMERICA
381	REF PRES-EVAN.	REFORMED PRESBYTERIAN CHURCH, EVANGELICAL SYNOD
403	SALVATION ARMY	SALVATION ARMY, THE
413	S-D ADVENTISTS	SEVENTH-DAY ADVENTISTS
415	S-D BAPTIST GC	SEVENTH-DAY BAPTIST GENERAL CONFERENCE
419	SO BAPT CONV..	SOUTHERN BAPTIST CONVENTION
435	UNITARIAN-UNIV	UNITARIAN-UNIVERSALIST ASSOCIATION
443	UN C OF CHRIST	UNITED CHURCH OF CHRIST
449	UN METHODIST..	UNITED METHODIST CHURCH, THE
453	UN PRES CH USA	UNITED PRESBYTERIAN CHURCH IN THE USA, THE
461	UNITY OF BRETH	UNITY OF THE BRETHREN
467	WESLEYAN......	WESLEYAN CHURCH, THE
469	WISC EVAN LUTH	WISCONSIN EVANGELICAL LUTHERAN SYNOD

Table 1. Churches and Church Membership by Denomination: 1971

County and Denomination	Number of churches	Communicant, confirmed, full members	Total adherents		
			Number	Percent of total population	Percent of total adherents
THE NATION	187,865	42,403,161	100,812,489*	49.6	100.0
019 AMER BAPT CONV	5,933	1,388,417	1,693,423*	0.8	1.7
029 AMER LUTH CH..	4,821	1,770,773	2,490,537	1.2	2.5
055 AS REF PRES CH	144	28,221	34,625*	-	-
059 BAPT MISS ASSN	1,397	195,388	238,454*	0.1	0.2
075 BRETHREN IN CR	153	9,406	11,458*	-	-
081 CATHOLIC......	22,028	0	44,863,492	22.1	44.5
083 CR CATH CH DOB	5	247	258	-	-
093 CR CH (DISC)..	4,835	951,317	1,158,855*	0.6	1.1
097 CR C AND C CR.	5,187	815,076	994,926*	0.5	1.0
105 CHRISTIAN REF.	514	121,107	208,965	0.1	0.2
107 CHRISTIAN UN..	113	5,655	6,931*	-	-
121 CH GOD (ABR)..	94	4,866	5,949*	-	-
123 CH GOD (ANDER)	2,207	155,424	389,989	0.2	0.4
127 CH GOD (CLEVE)	4,147	301,335	369,989*	0.2	0.4
151 L-D SAINTS....	0	0	2,133,072	1.0	2.1
157 CH OF BRETHREN	1,042	181,106	220,813*	0.1	0.2
165 CH OF NAZARENE	4,640	398,714	869,831	0.4	0.9
175 CONG CR CH....	328	86,667	106,209*	0.1	0.1
185 CUMBER PRESB..	802	85,793	104,070*	0.1	0.1
193 EPISCOPAL.....	6,934	2,051,929	3,032,197	1.5	3.0
197 EVAN CH OF NA.	120	9,922	12,040*	-	-
199 EVAN CONG CH..	160	29,682	35,742*	-	-
201 EVAN COV CH AM	507	67,500	82,453*	-	0.1
211 EV MENN BRETH.	15	1,737	2,097*	-	-
221 FREE METH C NA	1,075	46,514	63,540	-	0.1
223 FREE WILL BAPT	2,701	213,570	270,444*	0.1	0.3
226 FRIENDS-USA...	1,001	107,553	131,771*	0.1	0.1
231 GENERAL BAPT..	789	66,435	82,730*	-	0.1
281 LUTH CH AMER..	5,727	2,153,029	3,010,150	1.5	3.0
283 LUTH--MO SYNOD	5,711	1,957,922	2,772,996	1.4	2.8
285 MENNONITE CH..	997	88,116	108,108*	0.1	0.1
287 MENN GEN CONF.	187	36,771	44,578*	-	-
293 MORAV CH-NORTH	99	26,101	34,555	-	-
295 MORAV CH-SOUTH	48	16,802	22,566	-	-
313 NO AM BAPT GC.	246	41,302	50,583*	-	0.1
315 NO AM OLD RC..	75	22,745	26,837*	-	-
335 ORTH PRESB CH.	122	9,514	14,394	-	-
349 PENT HOLINESS.	1,310	72,720	89,140*	-	0.1

*Total adherents estimated from known number of communicant, confirmed, full members. —Represents a percent less than 0.1.

Table 1. Churches and Church Membership by Denomination: 1971

County and Denomination	Number of churches	Communicant, confirmed, full members	Total adherents		
			Number	Percent of total population	Percent of total adherents
353 PLY BRETHREN..	682	37,479	63,268	-	0.1
357 PRESB CH US...	4,175	936,225	1,147,499*	0.6	1.1
371 REF CH IN AM..	886	261,076	370,509	0.2	0.4
381 REF PRES-EVAN.	135	15,413	19,770	-	-
403 SALVATION ARMY	1,043	74,967	392,299	0.2	0.4
413 S-D ADVENTISTS	3,251	439,020	536,082*	0.3	0.5
415 S-D BAPTIST GC	60	5,042	6,178*	-	-
419 SO BAPT CONV..	34,610	11,814,243	14,488,635*	7.1	14.4
435 UNITARIAN-UNIV	954	145,668	194,733	0.1	0.2
443 UN C OF CHRIST	6,492	1,858,592	2,271,432*	1.1	2.3
449 UN METHODIST..	37,819	10,036,109	11,511,709	5.7	11.4
453 UN PRES CH USA	8,747	2,906,147	3,546,941*	1.7	3.5
461 UNITY OF BRETH	27	3,249	3,945	-	-
467 WESLEYAN......	1,792	76,016	88,802	-	0.1
469 WISC EVAN LUTH	978	274,539	381,920	0.2	0.4

*Total adherents estimated from known number of communicant, confirmed, full members.—Represents a percent less than 0.1.

Table 2. Churches and Church Membership by Region, State and Denomination: 1971

County and Denomination	Number of churches	Communicant, confirmed, full members	Total adherents		
			Number	Percent of total population	Percent of total adherents
NEW ENGLAND					
THE REGION....	6,977	1,204,263	7,150,196*	60.4	100.0
CONNECTICUT	1,422	345,336	1,797,210*	59.3	100.0
019 AMER BAPT CONV	128	25,062	30,716*	1.0	1.7
081 CATHOLIC......	416	0	1,330,957	43.9	74.1
093 CR CH (DISC)..	3	401	488*	-	-
097 CR C AND C CR.	5	188	228*	-	-
105 CHRISTIAN REF.	1	44	98	-	-
123 CH GOD (ANDER)	3	105	290	-	-
127 CH GOD (CLEVE)	9	586	719*	-	-
151 L-D SAINTS....	0	0	3,533	0.1	0.2
165 CH OF NAZARENE	9	684	1,432	-	0.1
175 CONG CR CH....	21	4,094	5,025*	0.2	0.3
193 EPISCOPAL.....	184	71,071	126,303	4.2	7.0
201 EVAN COV CH AM	16	2,434	2,971*	0.1	0.2
226 FRIENDS-USA...	9	755	921*	-	0.1
281 LUTH CH AMER..	64	28,388	38,177	1.3	2.1
283 LUTH--MO SYNOD	46	15,468	21,781	0.7	1.2
313 NO AM BAPT GC.	2	173	211*	-	-
315 NO AM OLD RC..	1	231	282*	-	-
335 ORTH PRESB CH.	1	36	57	-	-
353 PLY BRETHREN..	12	813	1,328	-	0.1
381 REF PRES-EVAN.	1	110	160	-	-
403 SALVATION ARMY	21	1,047	5,807	0.2	0.3
413 S-D ADVENTISTS	23	2,221	2,716*	0.1	0.2
415 S-D BAPTIST GC	1	37	46*	-	-
419 SO BAPT CONV..	9	1,511	1,858*	0.1	0.1
435 UNITARIAN-UNIV	21	4,153	5,737	0.2	0.3
443 UN C OF CHRIST	263	121,046	147,870*	4.9	8.2
449 UN METHODIST..	134	53,963	54,426	1.8	3.0
453 UN PRES CH USA	17	10,647	12,967*	0.4	0.7
469 WISC EVAN LUTH	2	68	106	-	-
MAINE	1,228	130,376	444,794*	44.8	100.0
019 AMER BAPT CONV	273	33,616	41,294*	4.2	9.3
029 AMER LUTH CH..	6	980	1,402	0.1	0.3
081 CATHOLIC......	252	0	271,126	27.3	61.0
097 CR C AND C CR.	2	67	82*	-	-
127 CH GOD (CLEVE)	12	547	668*	0.1	0.2
151 L-D SAINTS....	0	0	3,671	0.4	0.8
165 CH OF NAZARENE	53	3,059	10,270	1.0	2.3
175 CONG CR CH....	24	3,274	3,990*	0.4	0.9
193 EPISCOPAL.....	62	12,788	22,342	2.3	5.0
201 EVAN COV CH AM	3	194	242*	-	0.1
221 FREE METH C NA	2	48	66	-	-
223 FREE WILL BAPT	2	88	108*	-	-
226 FRIENDS-USA...	14	570	699*	0.1	0.2
281 LUTH CH AMER..	7	1,025	1,464	0.1	0.3
283 LUTH--MO SYNOD	3	381	508	0.1	0.1
285 MENNONITE CH..	1	1	1*	-	-
335 ORTH PRESB CH.	5	297	457	-	0.1
353 PLY BRETHREN..	5	100	170	-	-
403 SALVATION ARMY	11	604	3,808	0.4	0.9
413 S-D ADVENTISTS	24	1,938	2,376*	0.2	0.5
419 SO BAPT CONV..	4	454	561*	0.1	0.1
435 UNITARIAN-UNIV	41	4,789	5,818	0.6	1.3
443 UN C OF CHRIST	178	31,571	38,626*	3.9	8.7
449 UN METHODIST..	205	32,246	32,984	3.3	7.4
453 UN PRES CH USA	8	588	727*	0.1	0.2
467 WESLEYAN......	31	1,151	1,334	0.1	0.3
MASSACHUSETTS	2,584	496,959	3,593,205*	63.2	100.0
019 AMER BAPT CONV	272	70,619	86,006*	1.5	2.4
029 AMER LUTH CH..	6	747	1,055	-	-
081 CATHOLIC......	824	0	2,939,175	51.7	81.8
083 CR CATH CH DOB	1	104	104	-	-
093 CR CH (DISC)..	3	343	418*	-	-
097 CR C AND C CR.	4	94	115*	-	-
105 CHRISTIAN REF.	3	789	1,434	-	-
123 CH GOD (ANDER)	2	101	201	-	-
127 CH GOD (CLEVE)	12	559	675*	-	-
151 L-D SAINTS....	0	0	5,071	0.1	0.1
165 CH OF NAZARENE	35	3,165	6,901	0.1	0.2
175 CONG CR CH....	22	9,503	11,513*	0.2	0.3
193 EPISCOPAL.....	224	94,466	156,189	2.7	4.3
201 EVAN COV CH AM	15	3,197	3,894*	0.1	0.1
221 FREE METH C NA	6	112	163	-	-
226 FRIENDS-USA...	16	1,703	2,066*	-	0.1
281 LUTH CH AMER..	52	19,489	26,909	0.5	0.7
283 LUTH--MO SYNOD	39	9,261	13,441	0.2	0.4
285 MENNONITE CH..	2	41	50*	-	-
287 MENN GEN CONF.	1	35	43*	-	-
315 NO AM OLD RC..	3	971	1,154*	-	-
335 ORTH PRESB CH.	2	98	153	-	-
353 PLY BRETHREN..	18	919	1,500	-	-
371 REF CH IN AM..	1	54	78	-	-
403 SALVATION ARMY	34	1,903	10,109	0.2	0.3
413 S-D ADVENTISTS	43	6,009	7,266*	0.1	0.2
419 SO BAPT CONV..	10	1,693	2,061*	-	0.1
435 UNITARIAN-UNIV	170	30,671	39,418	0.7	1.1
443 UN C OF CHRIST	460	153,095	186,477*	3.3	5.2
449 UN METHODIST..	268	79,803	80,524	1.4	2.2
453 UN PRES CH USA	35	7,371	8,978*	0.2	0.2
469 WISC EVAN LUTH	1	44	64	-	-
NEW HAMPSHIRE	650	79,511	370,751*	50.3	100.0
019 AMER BAPT CONV	95	13,362	16,482*	2.2	4.4
029 AMER LUTH CH..	3	346	587	0.1	0.2
081 CATHOLIC......	166	0	265,233	36.0	71.5
097 CR C AND C CR.	3	101	126*	-	-
123 CH GOD (ANDER)	1	28	58	-	-
127 CH GOD (CLEVE)	1	23	29*	-	-
151 L-D SAINTS....	0	0	2,019	0.3	0.5
165 CH OF NAZARENE	8	374	1,045	0.1	0.3
175 CONG CR CH....	13	1,744	2,148*	0.3	0.6
193 EPISCOPAL.....	47	9,984	18,316	2.5	4.9
201 EVAN COV CH AM	1	125	157*	-	-
223 FREE WILL BAPT	3	132	163*	-	-
226 FRIENDS-USA...	7	341	416*	0.1	0.1
281 LUTH CH AMER..	4	856	1,258	0.2	0.3
283 LUTH--MO SYNOD	8	1,416	2,084	0.3	0.6
353 PLY BRETHREN..	1	10	20	-	-
403 SALVATION ARMY	8	372	1,916	0.3	0.5
413 S-D ADVENTISTS	10	684	835*	0.1	0.2
419 SO BAPT CONV..	1	342	434*	0.1	0.1
435 UNITARIAN-UNIV	22	2,377	3,248	0.4	0.9
443 UN C OF CHRIST	137	28,358	34,899*	4.7	9.4
449 UN METHODIST..	103	17,071	17,437	2.4	4.7
453 UN PRES CH USA	8	1,465	1,841*	0.2	0.5
RHODE ISLAND	455	83,997	712,787*	75.3	100.0
019 AMER BAPT CONV	84	21,838	26,386*	2.8	3.7
081 CATHOLIC......	168	0	602,333	63.6	84.5
097 CR C AND C CR.	1	21	25*	-	-
123 CH GOD (ANDER)	4	154	343	-	-
127 CH GOD (CLEVE)	5	215	260*	-	-
151 L-D SAINTS....	0	0	904	0.1	0.1
165 CH OF NAZARENE	6	314	634	0.1	0.1
175 CONG CR CH....	2	225	274*	-	-
193 EPISCOPAL.....	67	29,459	43,390	4.6	6.1
201 EVAN COV CH AM	6	455	547*	0.1	0.1
226 FRIENDS-USA...	5	369	444*	-	0.1
281 LUTH CH AMER..	11	4,456	6,326	0.7	0.9
283 LUTH--MO SYNOD	3	1,082	1,590	0.2	0.2
353 PLY BRETHREN..	5	215	383	-	0.1
403 SALVATION ARMY	1	35	222	-	-
413 S-D ADVENTISTS	4	526	631*	0.1	0.1
415 S-D BAPTIST GC	4	412	506*	0.1	0.1
419 SO BAPT CONV..	4	914	1,113*	0.1	0.2
435 UNITARIAN-UNIV	8	1,585	1,990	0.2	0.3
443 UN C OF CHRIST	28	9,205	11,080*	1.2	1.6
449 UN METHODIST..	28	8,872	8,981	0.9	1.3
453 UN PRES CH USA	11	3,645	4,425*	0.5	0.6
VERMONT	638	68,084	231,449*	52.1	100.0
019 AMER BAPT CONV	69	8,589	10,576*	2.4	4.6
029 AMER LUTH CH..	1	45	49	-	-
081 CATHOLIC......	136	0	145,182	32.7	62.7
097 CR C AND C CR.	4	112	138*	-	0.1
105 CHRISTIAN REF.	1	92	219	-	0.1
123 CH GOD (ANDER)	1	29	106	-	-
151 L-D SAINTS....	0	0	1,744	0.4	0.8
165 CH OF NAZARENE	9	331	856	0.2	0.4
175 CONG CR CH....	3	293	361*	0.1	0.2
193 EPISCOPAL.....	52	7,041	12,966	2.9	5.6
201 EVAN COV CH AM	2	27	33*	-	-
221 FREE METH C NA	1	26	37	-	-
223 FREE WILL BAPT	1	45	56*	-	-
226 FRIENDS-USA...	5	208	258*	0.1	0.1
281 LUTH CH AMER..	4	769	1,101	0.2	0.5
283 LUTH--MO SYNOD	1	223	313	0.1	0.1
285 MENNONITE CH..	3	102	124*	-	0.1
315 NO AM OLD RC..	1	38	47*	-	-
353 PLY BRETHREN..	1	20	30	-	-
403 SALVATION ARMY	3	91	446	0.1	0.2
413 S-D ADVENTISTS	12	555	683*	0.2	0.3
419 SO BAPT CONV..	1	121	153*	-	0.1
435 UNITARIAN-UNIV	20	1,777	2,230	0.5	1.0
443 UN C OF CHRIST	160	23,553	29,073*	6.5	12.6
449 UN METHODIST..	135	22,798	23,202	5.2	10.0

*Total adherents estimated from known number of communicant, confirmed, full members.

—Represents a percent less than 0.1.

Percentages may not total due to rounding.

Table 2. Churches and Church Membership by Region, State and Denomination: 1971

County and Denomination	Number of churches	Communicant, confirmed, full members	Total adherents: Number	Total adherents: Percent of total population	Total adherents: Percent of total adherents
453 UN PRES CH USA	12	1,199	1,466*	0.3	0.6

MIDDLE ATLANTIC

County and Denomination	Number of churches	Communicant, confirmed, full members	Total adherents: Number	Total adherents: Percent of total population	Total adherents: Percent of total adherents
THE REGION....	21,900	4,825,091	19,204,868*	51.6	100.0
NEW JERSEY	3,093	726,408	3,655,469*	51.0	100.0
019 AMER BAPT CONV	211	53,210	64,814*	0.9	1.8
029 AMER LUTH CH..	16	4,053	6,046	0.1	0.2
059 BAPT MISS ASSN	1	53	65*	-	-
081 CATHOLIC......	754	0	2,722,413	38.0	74.5
093 CR CH (DISC)..	3	268	328*	-	-
097 CR C AND C CR.	8	439	536*	-	-
105 CHRISTIAN REF.	23	5,439	8,474	0.1	0.2
123 CH GOD (ANDER)	16	745	1,802	-	-
127 CH GOD (CLEVE)	34	1,570	1,930*	-	0.1
151 L-D SAINTS....	0	0	6,192	0.1	0.2
157 CH OF BRETHREN	1	134	165*	-	-
165 CH OF NAZARENE	31	2,438	5,613	0.1	0.2
175 CONG CR CH....	3	768	945*	-	-
193 EPISCOPAL.....	294	109,866	168,357	2.3	4.6
199 EVAN CONG CH..	1	103	127*	-	-
201 EVAN COV CH AM	4	657	801*	-	-
221 FREE METH C NA	2	44	51	-	-
226 FRIENDS-USA...	33	3,915	4,806*	0.1	0.1
281 LUTH CH AMER..	180	67,805	98,629	1.4	2.7
283 LUTH--MO SYNOD	76	24,657	37,074	0.5	1.0
285 MENNONITE CH..	6	130	161*	-	-
293 MORAV CH-NORTH	4	1,059	1,442	-	-
313 NO AM BAPT GC.	7	743	897*	-	-
315 NO AM OLD RC..	6	340	408*	-	-
335 ORTH PRESB CH.	15	1,698	2,497	-	0.1
349 PENT HOLINESS.	1	67	80*	-	-
353 PLY BRETHREN..	39	2,075	3,640	0.1	0.1
371 REF CH IN AM..	145	48,653	62,735	0.9	1.7
381 REF PRES-EVAN.	7	542	648	-	-
403 SALVATION ARMY	25	1,395	7,716	0.1	0.2
413 S-D ADVENTISTS	64	6,145	7,498*	0.1	0.2
415 S-D BAPTIST GC	4	606	745*	-	-
419 SO BAPT CONV..	25	4,994	6,149*	0.1	0.2
435 UNITARIAN-UNIV	22	4,352	6,086	0.1	0.2
443 UN C OF CHRIST	60	23,414	28,427*	0.4	0.8
449 UN METHODIST..	575	168,307	170,509	2.4	4.7
453 UN PRES CH USA	382	184,950	225,635*	3.1	6.2
467 WESLEYAN......	13	520	638	-	-
469 WISC EVAN LUTH	2	254	390	-	-
NEW YORK	7,880	1,592,333	8,567,413*	47.0	100.0
019 AMER BAPT CONV	574	119,717	146,675*	0.8	1.7
029 AMER LUTH CH..	74	21,997	33,086	0.2	0.4
059 BAPT MISS ASSN	1	26	33*	-	-
075 BRETHREN IN CR	3	159	194*	-	-
081 CATHOLIC......	1,915	0	6,474,465	35.5	75.6
083 CR CATH CH DOB	1	36	36	-	-
093 CR CH (DISC)..	53	8,699	10,543*	0.1	0.1
097 CR C AND C CR.	37	1,844	2,270*	-	-
105 CHRISTIAN REF.	11	1,283	2,381	-	-
123 CH GOD (ANDER)	33	2,172	4,526	-	0.1
127 CH GOD (CLEVE)	67	2,328	2,771*	-	-
151 L-D SAINTS....	0	0	15,972	0.1	0.2
157 CH OF BRETHREN	2	171	209*	-	-
165 CH OF NAZARENE	84	5,932	13,927	0.1	0.2
175 CONG CR CH....	10	4,504	5,436*	-	0.1
193 EPISCOPAL.....	723	224,324	349,797	1.9	4.1
201 EVAN COV CH AM	13	2,345	2,853*	-	-
221 FREE METH C NA	89	3,818	5,047	-	0.1
226 FRIENDS-USA...	52	5,659	6,802*	-	0.1
281 LUTH CH AMER..	360	133,522	191,090	1.0	2.2
283 LUTH--MO SYNOD	238	83,453	129,401	0.7	1.5
285 MENNONITE CH..	23	1,935	2,409*	-	-
293 MORAV CH-NORTH	11	3,109	4,104	-	-
313 NO AM BAPT GC.	10	1,491	1,788*	-	-
315 NO AM OLD RC..	37	17,966	21,055*	0.1	0.2
335 ORTH PRESB CH.	5	534	785	-	-
349 PENT HOLINESS.	1	9	11*	-	-
353 PLY BRETHREN..	46	2,470	4,117	-	-
371 REF CH IN AM..	248	75,308	92,379	0.5	1.1
381 REF PRES-EVAN.	4	294	397	-	-
403 SALVATION ARMY	78	4,542	27,879	0.2	0.3
413 S-D ADVENTISTS	146	22,772	27,398*	0.2	0.3
415 S-D BAPTIST GC	14	977	1,193*	-	-

*Total adherents estimated from known number of communicant, confirmed, full members.

County and Denomination	Number of churches	Communicant, confirmed, full members	Total adherents: Number	Total adherents: Percent of total population	Total adherents: Percent of total adherents
419 SO BAPT CONV..	59	8,369	10,205*	0.1	0.1
435 UNITARIAN-UNIV	72	13,159	16,859	0.1	0.2
443 UN C OF CHRIST	318	84,584	102,979*	0.6	1.2
449 UN METHODIST..	1,534	465,428	529,369	2.9	6.2
453 UN PRES CH USA	803	262,320	320,719*	1.8	3.7
467 WESLEYAN......	131	5,077	6,253	-	0.1
PENNSYLVANIA	10,927	2,506,350	6,981,986*	59.2	100.0
019 AMER BAPT CONV	471	94,398	113,850*	1.0	1.6
029 AMER LUTH CH..	50	19,508	26,686	0.2	0.4
075 BRETHREN IN CR	85	6,362	7,746*	0.1	0.1
081 CATHOLIC......	1,851	0	3,831,066	32.5	54.9
093 CR CH (DISC)..	74	14,360	17,291*	0.1	0.2
097 CR C AND C CR.	119	22,788	27,372*	0.2	0.4
105 CHRISTIAN REF.	2	145	252	-	-
121 CH GOD (ABR)..	1	12	15*	-	-
123 CH GOD (ANDER)	86	6,592	16,428	0.1	0.2
127 CH GOD (CLEVE)	77	5,402	6,538*	0.1	0.1
151 L-D SAINTS....	0	0	11,080	0.1	0.2
157 CH OF BRETHREN	220	53,197	64,544*	0.5	0.9
165 CH OF NAZARENE	159	13,392	30,121	0.3	0.4
175 CONG CR CH....	15	2,073	2,505*	-	-
193 EPISCOPAL.....	420	137,727	193,399	1.6	2.8
197 EVAN CH OF NA.	11	1,038	1,257*	-	-
199 EVAN CONG CH..	134	26,476	31,828*	0.3	0.5
201 EVAN COV CH AM	16	896	1,094*	-	-
221 FREE METH C NA	139	4,193	5,847	-	0.1
226 FRIENDS-USA...	76	12,614	15,351*	0.1	0.2
281 LUTH CH AMER..	1,391	578,689	796,741	6.8	11.4
283 LUTH--MO SYNOD	98	23,175	32,383	0.3	0.5
285 MENNONITE CH..	301	30,065	36,712*	0.3	0.5
287 MENN GEN CONF.	27	4,171	5,102*	-	0.1
293 MORAV CH-NORTH	27	9,785	12,697	0.1	0.2
313 NO AM BAPT GC.	10	1,595	1,918*	-	-
315 NO AM OLD RC..	4	298	360*	-	-
335 ORTH PRESB CH.	16	1,361	2,065	-	-
349 PENT HOLINESS.	16	851	1,034*	-	-
353 PLY BRETHREN..	48	2,783	4,169	-	0.1
357 PRESB CH US...	1	91	113*	-	-
371 REF CH IN AM..	10	4,031	5,458	-	0.1
381 REF PRES-EVAN.	24	3,010	4,243	-	0.1
403 SALVATION ARMY	75	4,647	30,056	0.3	0.4
413 S-D ADVENTISTS	111	10,473	12,642*	0.1	0.2
415 S-D BAPTIST GC	2	108	134*	-	-
419 SO BAPT CONV..	47	6,592	7,976*	0.1	0.1
435 UNITARIAN-UNIV	39	4,715	6,425	0.1	0.1
443 UN C OF CHRIST	846	257,784	310,389*	2.6	4.4
449 UN METHODIST..	2,554	661,043	728,915	6.2	10.4
453 UN PRES CH USA	1,188	476,345	573,905*	4.9	8.2
467 WESLEYAN......	83	3,484	4,170	-	0.1
469 WISC EVAN LUTH	3	81	109	-	-

EAST NORTH CENTRAL

County and Denomination	Number of churches	Communicant, confirmed, full members	Total adherents: Number	Total adherents: Percent of total population	Total adherents: Percent of total adherents
THE REGION....	33,928	7,694,965	20,539,751*	51.0	100.0
ILLINOIS	8,468	1,972,185	6,136,362*	55.2	100.0
019 AMER BAPT CONV	318	89,191	108,334*	1.0	1.8
029 AMER LUTH CH..	211	82,026	115,160	1.0	1.9
059 BAPT MISS ASSN	16	868	1,062*	-	-
075 BRETHREN IN CR	1	25	30*	-	-
081 CATHOLIC......	1,268	0	3,565,785	32.1	58.1
093 CR CH (DISC)..	244	57,221	69,170*	0.6	1.1
097 CR C AND C CR.	489	84,082	101,316*	0.9	1.7
105 CHRISTIAN REF.	39	9,959	16,898	0.2	0.3
121 CH GOD (ABR)..	13	719	869*	-	-
123 CH GOD (ANDER)	113	7,470	19,242	0.2	0.3
127 CH GOD (CLEVE)	115	7,579	9,192*	0.1	0.1
151 L-D SAINTS....	0	0	16,299	0.1	0.3
157 CH OF BRETHREN	42	6,542	8,041*	0.1	0.1
165 CH OF NAZARENE	254	20,310	52,840	0.5	0.9
175 CONG CR CH....	28	4,100	4,987*	-	0.1
185 CUMBER PRESB..	48	3,445	4,076*	-	0.1
193 EPISCOPAL.....	211	60,157	81,957	0.7	1.3
197 EVAN CH OF NA.	3	87	104*	-	-
199 EVAN CONG CH..	11	1,133	1,388*	-	-
201 EVAN COV CH AM	56	12,046	14,864*	0.1	0.2
211 EV MENN BRETH.	1	34	42*	-	-
221 FREE METH C NA	86	4,347	5,728	0.1	0.1
223 FREE WILL BAPT	48	4,047	4,954*	-	0.1
226 FRIENDS-USA...	26	2,004	2,429*	-	-

—Represents a percent less than 0.1.

Percentages may not total due to rounding.

Table 2. Churches and Church Membership by Region, State and Denomination: 1971

County and Denomination	Number of churches	Communicant, confirmed, full members	Total adherents		
			Number	Percent of total population	Percent of total adherents
231 GENERAL BAPT..	139	8,363	10,238*	0.1	0.2
281 LUTH CH AMER..	326	151,664	204,421	1.8	3.3
283 LUTH--MO SYNOD	527	252,332	351,990	3.2	5.7
285 MENNONITE CH..	38	4,615	5,664*	0.1	0.1
287 MENN GEN CONF.	16	2,070	2,531*	-	-
293 MORAV CH-NORTH	1	279	408	-	-
313 NO AM BAPT GC.	12	2,274	2,795*	-	-
315 NO AM OLD RC..	3	852	1,046*	-	-
335 ORTH PRESB CH.	4	266	467	-	-
349 PENT HOLINESS.	5	100	125*	-	-
353 PLY BRETHREN..	34	2,340	3,938	-	0.1
371 REF CH IN AM..	54	14,908	22,431	0.2	0.4
381 REF PRES-EVAN.	6	571	712	-	-
403 SALVATION ARMY	55	4,687	21,943	0.2	0.4
413 S-D ADVENTISTS	87	11,098	13,666*	0.1	0.2
415 S-D BAPTIST GC	3	90	106*	-	-
419 SO BAPT CONV..	893	193,974	233,863*	2.1	3.8
435 UNITARIAN-UNIV	40	8,070	10,579	0.1	0.2
443 UN C OF CHRIST	439	171,484	211,149*	1.9	3.4
449 UN METHODIST..	1,569	486,633	589,975	5.3	9.6
453 UN PRES CH USA	512	191,603	234,465*	2.1	3.8
467 WESLEYAN......	39	1,383	1,738	-	-
469 WISC EVAN LUTH	25	5,137	7,345	0.1	0.1
INDIANA	6,092	1,211,591	2,316,535*	44.6	100.0
019 AMER BAPT CONV	428	122,937	151,029*	2.9	6.5
029 AMER LUTH CH..	54	16,143	22,940	0.4	1.0
059 BAPT MISS ASSN	4	154	192*	-	-
075 BRETHREN IN CR	2	57	71*	-	-
081 CATHOLIC......	513	0	724,115	13.9	31.3
093 CR CH (DISC)..	293	80,284	98,975*	1.9	4.3
097 CR C AND C CR.	621	127,688	157,753*	3.0	6.8
105 CHRISTIAN REF.	13	3,034	5,228	0.1	0.2
107 CHRISTIAN UN..	8	1,067	1,330*	-	0.1
121 CH GOD (ABR)..	7	321	392*	-	-
123 CH GOD (ANDER)	144	14,165	37,092	0.7	1.6
127 CH GOD (CLEVE)	85	5,018	6,204*	0.1	0.3
151 L-D SAINTS....	0	0	12,186	0.2	0.5
157 CH OF BRETHREN	107	18,510	22,873*	0.4	1.0
165 CH OF NAZARENE	351	30,410	77,017	1.5	3.3
175 CONG CR CH....	10	2,310	2,804*	0.1	0.1
185 CUMBER PRESB..	8	1,404	1,696*	-	0.1
193 EPISCOPAL.....	80	19,761	30,284	0.6	1.3
197 EVAN CH OF NA.	2	182	226*	-	-
201 EVAN COV CH AM	5	596	732*	-	-
221 FREE METH C NA	43	3,384	4,791	0.1	0.2
223 FREE WILL BAPT	20	1,657	2,045*	-	0.1
226 FRIENDS-USA...	142	18,708	23,193*	0.4	1.0
231 GENERAL BAPT..	106	10,951	13,513*	0.3	0.6
281 LUTH CH AMER..	148	44,196	61,161	1.2	2.6
283 LUTH--MO SYNOD	212	83,955	116,658	2.2	5.0
285 MENNONITE CH..	77	9,911	12,411*	0.2	0.5
287 MENN GEN CONF.	10	2,501	3,145*	0.1	0.1
293 MORAV CH-NORTH	4	582	927	-	-
313 NO AM BAPT GC.	1	48	60*	-	-
349 PENT HOLINESS.	3	72	90*	-	-
353 PLY BRETHREN..	11	330	590	-	-
371 REF CH IN AM..	10	2,187	3,170	0.1	0.1
381 REF PRES-EVAN.	4	239	308	-	-
403 SALVATION ARMY	39	3,049	16,117	0.3	0.7
413 S-D ADVENTISTS	85	7,530	9,292*	0.2	0.4
419 SO BAPT CONV..	230	55,898	68,777*	1.3	3.0
435 UNITARIAN-UNIV	18	2,306	3,224	0.1	0.1
443 UN C OF CHRIST	188	56,110	68,995*	1.3	3.0
449 UN METHODIST..	1,433	350,175	415,540	8.0	17.9
453 UN PRES CH USA	296	102,986	127,053*	2.4	5.5
467 WESLEYAN......	274	10,601	12,073	0.2	0.5
469 WISC EVAN LUTH	3	174	263	-	-
MICHIGAN	6,257	1,296,349	4,070,237*	45.9	100.0
019 AMER BAPT CONV	194	51,792	64,262*	0.7	1.6
029 AMER LUTH CH..	144	62,107	89,315	1.0	2.2
059 BAPT MISS ASSN	14	1,579	1,989*	-	-
075 BRETHREN IN CR	8	143	178*	-	-
081 CATHOLIC......	970	0	2,252,827	25.4	55.3
093 CR CH (DISC)..	128	10,013	12,453*	0.1	0.3
097 CR C AND C CR.	101	14,791	18,403*	0.2	0.5
105 CHRISTIAN REF.	189	56,881	96,372	1.1	2.4
121 CH GOD (ABR)..	6	479	593*	-	-
123 CH GOD (ANDER)	125	11,000	25,311	0.3	0.6
127 CH GOD (CLEVE)	105	9,215	11,480*	0.1	0.3
151 L-D SAINTS....	0	0	13,434	0.2	0.3
157 CH OF BRETHREN	25	2,843	3,518*	-	0.1
165 CH OF NAZARENE	194	17,157	38,357	0.4	0.9
175 CONG CR CH....	46	14,713	18,234*	0.2	0.4
185 CUMBER PRESB..	3	729	935*	-	-
193 EPISCOPAL.....	246	80,340	116,386	1.3	2.9
197 EVAN CH OF NA.	1	105	134*	-	-
201 EVAN COV CH AM	37	4,029	4,938*	0.1	0.1
211 EV MENN BRETH.	1	19	23*	-	-
221 FREE METH C NA	174	7,959	10,694	0.1	0.3
223 FREE WILL BAPT	453	5,641	7,005*	0.1	0.2
226 FRIENDS-USA...	20	1,638	2,008*	-	-
231 GENERAL BAPT..	44	3,410	4,235*	-	0.1
281 LUTH CH AMER..	204	65,109	95,925	1.1	2.4
283 LUTH--MO SYNOD	380	194,983	283,030	3.2	7.0
285 MENNONITE CH..	50	2,891	3,581*	-	0.1
287 MENN GEN CONF.	2	160	193*	-	-
293 MORAV CH-NORTH	3	664	906	-	-
313 NO AM BAPT GC.	20	6,523	8,165*	0.1	0.2
315 NO AM OLD RC..	3	231	286*	-	-
335 ORTH PRESB CH.	1	43	57	-	-
349 PENT HOLINESS.	4	153	190*	-	-
353 PLY BRETHREN..	48	2,702	4,596	0.1	0.1
371 REF CH IN AM..	162	50,962	77,823	0.9	1.9
381 REF PRES-EVAN.	1	100	100	-	-
403 SALVATION ARMY	55	5,272	24,770	0.3	0.6
413 S-D ADVENTISTS	179	24,155	29,993*	0.3	0.7
415 S-D BAPTIST GC	1	258	317*	-	
419 SO BAPT CONV..	169	35,698	44,501*	0.5	1.1
435 UNITARIAN-UNIV	27	3,849	5,395	0.1	0.1
443 UN C OF CHRIST	219	82,271	102,132*	1.2	2.5
449 UN METHODIST..	941	268,662	348,490	3.9	8.6
453 UN PRES CH USA	291	152,137	188,675*	2.1	4.6
467 WESLEYAN......	149	8,979	9,960	0.1	0.2
469 WISC EVAN LUTH	120	33,964	48,068	0.5	1.2
OHIO	8,932	2,127,682	5,043,970*	47.4	100.0
019 AMER BAPT CONV	333	94,131	115,683*	1.1	2.3
029 AMER LUTH CH..	322	147,000	205,991	1.9	4.1
059 BAPT MISS ASSN	1	125	154*	-	-
075 BRETHREN IN CR	13	604	742*	-	-
081 CATHOLIC......	1,047	0	2,254,410	21.2	44.7
093 CR CH (DISC)..	228	69,072	84,759*	0.8	1.7
097 CR C AND C CR.	456	102,312	125,872*	1.2	2.5
105 CHRISTIAN REF.	9	1,103	1,929	-	-
107 CHRISTIAN UN..	72	2,459	3,038*	-	0.1
121 CH GOD (ABR)..	11	693	855*	-	-
123 CH GOD (ANDER)	204	22,384	58,475	0.5	1.2
127 CH GOD (CLEVE)	210	17,742	21,855*	0.2	0.4
151 L-D SAINTS....	0	0	17,700	0.2	0.4
157 CH OF BRETHREN	110	20,388	25,151*	0.2	0.5
165 CH OF NAZARENE	394	41,686	95,737	0.9	1.9
175 CONG CR CH....	16	4,017	4,922*	-	0.1
193 EPISCOPAL.....	193	72,825	106,983	1.0	2.1
197 EVAN CH OF NA.	1	10	12*	-	-
199 EVAN CONG CH..	13	1,536	1,882*	-	-
201 EVAN COV CH AM	7	1,410	1,709*	-	-
221 FREE METH C NA	55	1,937	2,721	-	0.1
223 FREE WILL BAPT	129	9,278	11,397*	0.1	0.2
226 FRIENDS-USA...	98	10,614	12,982*	0.1	0.3
281 LUTH CH AMER..	348	136,343	189,321	1.8	3.8
283 LUTH--MO SYNOD	188	70,984	99,901	0.9	2.0
285 MENNONITE CH..	114	12,975	16,138*	0.2	0.3
287 MENN GEN CONF.	12	3,136	3,921*	-	0.1
293 MORAV CH-NORTH	8	2,195	2,906	-	0.1
313 NO AM BAPT GC.	8	1,755	2,138*	-	-
315 NO AM OLD RC..	2	84	104*	-	-
335 ORTH PRESB CH.	2	31	55	-	-
349 PENT HOLINESS.	13	480	594*	-	-
353 PLY BRETHREN..	24	1,165	2,040	-	-
357 PRESB CH US...	1	119	147*	-	-
371 REF CH IN AM..	7	1,402	1,980	-	-
381 REF PRES-EVAN.	1	62	81	-	-
403 SALVATION ARMY	58	4,276	30,841	0.3	0.6
413 S-D ADVENTISTS	106	14,063	17,247*	0.2	0.3
415 S-D BAPTIST GC	2	27	34*	-	-
419 SO BAPT CONV..	380	87,739	108,426*	1.0	2.1
435 UNITARIAN-UNIV	40	6,391	8,547	0.1	0.2
443 UN C OF CHRIST	527	191,286	235,720*	2.2	4.7
449 UN METHODIST..	2,335	707,983	845,445	7.9	16.8
453 UN PRES CH USA	656	256,135	313,787*	2.9	6.2
467 WESLEYAN......	163	4,737	5,445	0.1	0.1
469 WISC EVAN LUTH	15	2,988	4,193	-	0.1
WISCONSIN	4,179	1,087,158	2,972,647*	67.3	100.0
019 AMER BAPT CONV	99	19,905	24,566*	0.6	0.8
029 AMER LUTH CH..	541	258,368	360,243	8.2	12.1
075 BRETHREN IN CR	1	10	12*	-	-
081 CATHOLIC......	985	0	1,487,559	33.7	50.0
093 CR CH (DISC)..	3	475	590*	-	-
097 CR C AND C CR.	32	4,474	5,531*	0.1	0.2
105 CHRISTIAN REF.	15	3,330	4,021	0.1	0.2
121 CH GOD (ABR)..	1	35	41*	-	-

*Total adherents estimated from known number of communicant, confirmed, full members.

—Represents a percent less than 0.1.

Percentages may not total due to rounding.

Table 2. Churches and Church Membership by Region, State and Denomination: 1971

County and Denomination	Number of churches	Communicant, confirmed, full members	Total adherents		
			Number	Percent of total population	Percent of total adherents
123 CH GOD (ANDER)	17	995	2,261	0.1	0.1
127 CH GOD (CLEVE)	26	868	1,082*	-	-
151 L-D SAINTS....	0	0	5,040	0.1	0.2
157 CH OF BRETHREN	5	351	437*	-	-
165 CH OF NAZARENE	41	2,214	4,666	0.1	0.2
175 CONG CR CH....	20	9,499	11,764*	0.3	0.4
193 EPISCOPAL.....	130	26,521	36,248	0.8	1.2
201 EVAN COV CH AM	25	1,552	1,898*	-	0.1
221 FREE METH C NA	13	647	825	-	-
226 FRIENDS-USA...	4	298	364*	-	-
281 LUTH CH AMER..	178	86,081	123,181	2.8	4.1
283 LUTH--MO SYNOD	411	190,855	262,783	5.9	8.8
285 MENNONITE CH..	11	324	397*	-	-
293 MORAV CH-NORTH	21	5,607	7,322	0.2	0.2
313 NO AM BAPT GC.	15	2,612	3,233*	0.1	0.1
335 ORTH PRESB CH.	4	850	1,306	-	-
353 PLY BRETHREN..	13	475	705	-	-
371 REF CH IN AM..	25	8,003	12,091	0.3	0.4
381 REF PRES-EVAN.	1	74	92	-	-
403 SALVATION ARMY	20	1,409	6,509	0.1	0.2
413 S-D ADVENTISTS	79	5,853	7,242*	0.2	0.2
415 S-D BAPTIST GC	5	658	825*	-	-
419 SO BAPT CONV..	20	3,076	3,824*	0.1	0.1
435 UNITARIAN-UNIV	18	2,169	3,090	0.1	0.1
443 UN C OF CHRIST	273	84,729	105,025*	2.4	3.5
449 UN METHODIST..	529	148,912	197,427	4.5	6.6
453 UN PRES CH USA	176	54,805	67,681*	1.5	2.3
467 WESLEYAN......	28	1,374	1,561	-	0.1
469 WISC EVAN LUTH	394	159,750	219,205	5.0	7.4

WEST NORTH CENTRAL

County and Denomination	Number of churches	Communicant, confirmed, full members	Total adherents		
			Number	Percent of total population	Percent of total adherents
THE REGION....	23,404	4,952,424	9,691,788*	59.4	100.0
IOWA	4,074	930,154	1,762,704*	62.4	100.0
019 AMER BAPT CONV	145	31,560	38,241*	1.4	2.2
029 AMER LUTH CH..	397	148,661	205,943	7.3	11.7
075 BRETHREN IN CR	2	68	83*	-	-
081 CATHOLIC......	578	0	528,858	18.7	30.0
093 CR CH (DISC)..	199	40,425	48,863*	1.7	2.8
097 CR C AND C CR.	124	16,024	19,428*	0.7	1.1
105 CHRISTIAN REF.	54	11,550	19,986	0.7	1.1
107 CHRISTIAN UN..	9	297	365*	-	-
121 CH GOD (ABR)..	5	171	208*	-	-
123 CH GOD (ANDER)	14	610	1,548	0.1	0.1
127 CH GOD (CLEVE)	16	695	849*	-	-
151 L-D SAINTS....	0	0	5,655	0.2	0.3
157 CH OF BRETHREN	33	4,081	4,974*	0.2	0.3
165 CH OF NAZARENE	80	5,798	15,663	0.6	0.9
175 CONG CR CH....	11	3,331	4,049*	0.1	0.2
185 CUMBER PRESB..	1	178	213*	-	-
193 EPISCOPAL.....	69	14,495	22,174	0.8	1.3
197 EVAN CH OF NA.	3	99	121*	-	-
201 EVAN COV CH AM	23	2,544	3,065*	0.1	0.2
221 FREE METH C NA	30	975	1,350	-	0.1
223 FREE WILL BAPT	1	100	122*	-	-
226 FRIENDS-USA...	54	5,628	6,834*	0.2	0.4
281 LUTH CH AMER..	128	60,948	85,904	3.0	4.9
283 LUTH--MO SYNOD	277	90,344	126,868	4.5	7.2
285 MENNONITE CH..	24	3,376	4,097*	0.1	0.2
287 MENN GEN CONF.	4	669	800*	-	-
313 NO AM BAPT GC.	13	2,698	3,274*	0.1	0.2
335 ORTH PRESB CH.	1	45	56	-	-
353 PLY BRETHREN..	34	1,502	2,304	0.1	0.1
371 REF CH IN AM..	73	20,865	31,425	1.1	1.8
381 REF PRES-EVAN.	2	75	98	-	-
403 SALVATION ARMY	20	1,629	9,094	0.3	0.5
413 S-D ADVENTISTS	62	3,819	4,644*	0.2	0.3
419 SO BAPT CONV..	18	4,002	4,880*	0.2	0.3
435 UNITARIAN-UNIV	10	1,357	1,993	0.1	0.1
443 UN C OF CHRIST	222	51,563	62,887*	2.2	3.6
449 UN METHODIST..	950	298,040	370,513	13.1	21.0
453 UN PRES CH USA	338	98,610	120,634*	4.3	6.8
467 WESLEYAN......	41	2,453	3,268	0.1	0.2
469 WISC EVAN LUTH	9	869	1,373	-	0.1
KANSAS	3,382	696,641	1,184,802*	52.7	100.0
019 AMER BAPT CONV	273	67,321	81,277*	3.6	6.9
029 AMER LUTH CH..	52	10,194	14,179	0.6	1.2
059 BAPT MISS ASSN	8	822	981*	-	0.1
075 BRETHREN IN CR	4	259	306*	-	-
081 CATHOLIC......	390	0	312,952	13.9	26.4
093 CR CH (DISC)..	187	53,951	64,958*	2.9	5.5
097 CR C AND C CR.	203	31,548	37,865*	1.7	3.2
105 CHRISTIAN REF.	2	332	497	-	-
121 CH GOD (ABR)..	1	35	41*	-	-
123 CH GOD (ANDER)	55	3,564	9,279	0.4	0.8
127 CH GOD (CLEVE)	25	1,054	1,268*	0.1	0.1
151 L-D SAINTS....	0	0	6,777	0.3	0.6
157 CH OF BRETHREN	36	4,024	4,848*	0.2	0.4
165 CH OF NAZARENE	135	13,252	26,773	1.2	2.3
175 CONG CR CH....	6	3,364	4,127*	0.2	0.3
193 EPISCOPAL.....	82	19,190	25,140	1.1	2.1
201 EVAN COV CH AM	21	1,885	2,271*	0.1	0.2
221 FREE METH C NA	31	1,475	1,875	0.1	0.2
223 FREE WILL BAPT	14	809	978*	-	0.1
226 FRIENDS-USA...	51	3,603	4,305*	0.2	0.4
281 LUTH CH AMER..	84	22,937	29,942	1.3	2.5
283 LUTH--MO SYNOD	165	44,577	60,835	2.7	5.1
285 MENNONITE CH..	17	2,161	2,576*	0.1	0.2
287 MENN GEN CONF.	41	11,416	13,589*	0.6	1.1
313 NO AM BAPT GC.	13	1,568	1,846*	0.1	0.2
335 ORTH PRESB CH.	1	27	36	-	-
349 PENT HOLINESS.	21	754	904*	-	0.1
353 PLY BRETHREN..	17	510	924	-	0.1
371 REF CH IN AM..	1	195	282	-	-
403 SALVATION ARMY	19	1,341	7,303	0.3	0.6
413 S-D ADVENTISTS	66	4,301	5,163*	0.2	0.4
415 S-D BAPTIST GC	1	95	118*	-	-
419 SO BAPT CONV..	176	50,153	61,098*	2.7	5.2
435 UNITARIAN-UNIV	6	597	898	-	0.1
443 UN C OF CHRIST	88	18,662	22,465*	1.0	1.9
449 UN METHODIST..	793	250,149	290,792	12.9	24.5
453 UN PRES CH USA	224	67,952	82,217*	3.7	6.9
467 WESLEYAN......	68	2,377	2,832	0.1	0.2
469 WISC EVAN LUTH	5	187	285	-	-
MINNESOTA	4,038	1,095,566	2,522,913*	66.3	100.0
019 AMER BAPT CONV	29	7,374	9,012*	0.2	0.4
029 AMER LUTH CH..	817	350,097	492,212	12.9	19.5
081 CATHOLIC......	805	0	995,723	26.2	39.5
093 CR CH (DISC)..	15	3,223	3,975*	0.1	0.2
097 CR C AND C CR.	48	5,202	6,447*	0.2	0.3
105 CHRISTIAN REF.	28	4,944	8,919	0.2	0.4
121 CH GOD (ABR)..	5	263	329*	-	-
123 CH GOD (ANDER)	11	669	1,539	-	0.1
127 CH GOD (CLEVE)	8	201	245*	-	-
151 L-D SAINTS....	0	0	7,277	0.2	0.3
157 CH OF BRETHREN	4	446	542*	-	-
165 CH OF NAZARENE	34	2,303	5,024	0.1	0.2
175 CONG CR CH....	6	3,414	4,209*	0.1	0.2
193 EPISCOPAL.....	119	28,470	42,139	1.1	1.7
197 EVAN CH OF NA.	9	277	339*	-	-
201 EVAN COV CH AM	98	12,508	15,382*	0.4	0.6
211 EV MENN BRETH.	2	294	356*	-	-
221 FREE METH C NA	17	398	491	-	-
223 FREE WILL BAPT	1	26	32*	-	-
226 FRIENDS-USA...	2	315	387*	-	-
281 LUTH CH AMER..	390	192,949	280,262	7.4	11.1
283 LUTH--MO SYNOD	438	162,864	228,276	6.0	9.0
285 MENNONITE CH..	16	315	384*	-	-
287 MENN GEN CONF.	8	1,657	2,012*	0.1	0.1
293 MORAV CH-NORTH	7	1,109	1,405	-	0.1
313 NO AM BAPT GC.	9	1,279	1,610*	-	0.1
353 PLY BRETHREN..	11	490	778	-	-
371 REF CH IN AM..	22	4,915	7,985	0.2	0.3
403 SALVATION ARMY	24	2,083	7,900	0.2	0.3
413 S-D ADVENTISTS	60	4,735	5,819*	0.2	0.2
415 S-D BAPTIST GC	1	134	167*	-	-
419 SO BAPT CONV..	13	1,670	2,100*	0.1	0.1
435 UNITARIAN-UNIV	22	3,228	4,189	0.1	0.2
443 UN C OF CHRIST	163	47,896	59,068*	1.6	2.3
449 UN METHODIST..	446	134,657	179,014	4.7	7.1
453 UN PRES CH USA	217	71,665	88,149*	2.3	3.5
469 WISC EVAN LUTH	133	43,496	59,216	1.6	2.3
MISSOURI	6,627	1,313,154	2,391,454*	51.1	100.0
019 AMER BAPT CONV	20	13,273	15,993*	0.3	0.7
029 AMER LUTH CH..	27	5,099	7,280	0.2	0.3
055 AS REF PRES CH	2	166	204*	-	-
059 BAPT MISS ASSN	95	7,587	9,288*	0.2	0.4
081 CATHOLIC......	581	0	754,946	16.1	31.6
093 CR CH (DISC)..	468	89,712	107,837*	2.3	4.5
097 CR C AND C CR.	390	42,945	51,334*	1.1	2.1
105 CHRISTIAN REF.	2	89	181	-	-
107 CHRISTIAN UN..	16	1,295	1,557*	-	0.1
121 CH GOD (ABR)..	7	247	294*	-	-
123 CH GOD (ANDER)	94	6,162	15,731	0.3	0.7

*Total adherents estimated from known number of communicant, confirmed, full members.

—Represents a percent less than 0.1.

Percentages may not total due to rounding.

Table 2. Churches and Church Membership by Region, State and Denomination: 1971

County and Denomination	Number of churches	Communicant, confirmed, full members	Total adherents: Number	Percent of total population	Percent of total adherents
127 CH GOD (CLEVE)	58	3,580	4,387*	0.1	0.2
151 L-D SAINTS....	0	0	11,454	0.2	0.5
157 CH OF BRETHREN	23	1,474	1,762*	-	0.1
165 CH OF NAZARENE	162	12,824	27,161	0.6	1.1
175 CONG CR CH....	2	470	570*	-	-
185 CUMBER PRESB..	47	3,268	3,897*	0.1	0.2
193 EPISCOPAL.....	103	29,085	40,990	0.9	1.7
197 EVAN CH OF NA.	2	108	126*	-	-
201 EVAN COV CH AM	2	244	296*	-	-
221 FREE METH C NA	21	440	590	-	-
223 FREE WILL BAPT	140	14,409	17,471*	0.4	0.7
226 FRIENDS-USA...	6	255	310*	-	-
231 GENERAL BAPT..	220	15,224	18,459*	0.4	0.8
281 LUTH CH AMER..	39	10,702	14,547	0.3	0.6
283 LUTH--MO SYNOD	295	111,904	153,932	3.3	6.4
285 MENNONITE CH..	13	833	1,010*	-	-
287 MENN GEN CONF.	1	137	163*	-	-
313 NO AM BAPT GC.	1	23	28*	-	-
349 PENT HOLINESS.	16	598	726*	-	-
353 PLY BRETHREN..	17	859	1,356	-	0.1
357 PRESB CH US...	279	35,219	42,656*	0.9	1.8
381 REF PRES-EVAN.	8	837	1,240	-	0.1
403 SALVATION ARMY	25	2,102	11,251	0.2	0.5
413 S-D ADVENTISTS	65	6,917	8,385*	0.2	0.4
415 S-D BAPTIST GC	1	17	21*	-	-
419 SO BAPT CONV..	1,812	519,115	626,279*	13.4	26.2
435 UNITARIAN-UNIV	8	1,717	2,435	0.1	0.1
443 UN C OF CHRIST	187	63,388	77,335*	1.7	3.2
449 UN METHODIST..	1,030	252,196	286,967	6.1	12.0
453 UN PRES CH USA	323	57,755	69,838*	1.5	2.9
467 WESLEYAN......	15	608	747	-	-
469 WISC EVAN LUTH	4	271	420	-	-
NEBRASKA	2,242	460,539	896,127*	60.4	100.0
019 AMER BAPT CONV	76	15,916	19,203*	1.3	2.1
029 AMER LUTH CH..	112	36,146	48,846	3.3	5.5
081 CATHOLIC......	382	0	291,443	19.6	32.5
093 CR CH (DISC)..	66	13,810	16,614*	1.1	1.9
097 CR C AND C CR.	74	8,241	9,936*	0.7	1.1
105 CHRISTIAN REF.	2	121	234	-	-
121 CH GOD (ABR)..	4	167	203*	-	-
123 CH GOD (ANDER)	23	825	2,112	0.1	0.2
127 CH GOD (CLEVE)	11	508	626*	-	0.1
151 L-D SAINTS....	0	0	5,067	0.3	0.6
157 CH OF BRETHREN	5	529	633*	-	0.1
165 CH OF NAZARENE	39	2,101	4,885	0.3	0.5
175 CONG CR CH....	6	606	724*	-	0.1
193 EPISCOPAL.....	70	12,792	17,353	1.2	1.9
197 EVAN CH OF NA.	1	32	41*	-	-
201 EVAN COV CH AM	20	2,474	2,994*	0.2	0.3
211 EV MENN BRETH.	5	431	522*	-	0.1
221 FREE METH C NA	12	237	309	-	-
226 FRIENDS-USA...	8	600	729*	-	0.1
231 GENERAL BAPT..	3	47	57*	-	-
281 LUTH CH AMER..	161	58,154	80,592	5.4	9.0
283 LUTH--MO SYNOD	261	79,726	110,033	7.4	12.3
285 MENNONITE CH..	13	1,427	1,694*	0.1	0.2
287 MENN GEN CONF.	4	2,271	2,709*	0.2	0.3
313 NO AM BAPT GC.	4	349	426*	-	-
335 ORTH PRESB CH.	2	118	159	-	-
353 PLY BRETHREN..	5	178	320	-	-
371 REF CH IN AM..	6	1,037	1,587	0.1	0.2
381 REF PRES-EVAN.	1	76	90	-	-
403 SALVATION ARMY	10	1,028	4,641	0.3	0.5
413 S-D ADVENTISTS	61	5,669	6,849*	0.5	0.8
415 S-D BAPTIST GC	1	229	272*	-	-
419 SO BAPT CONV..	23	5,141	6,538*	0.4	0.7
435 UNITARIAN-UNIV	2	767	1,042	0.1	0.1
443 UN C OF CHRIST	123	26,254	31,699*	2.1	3.5
449 UN METHODIST..	425	120,932	149,148	10.1	16.6
453 UN PRES CH USA	163	56,494	68,858*	4.6	7.7
467 WESLEYAN......	28	598	692	-	0.1
469 WISC EVAN LUTH	30	4,508	6,247	0.4	0.7
NORTH DAKOTA	1,562	220,835	473,332*	76.6	100.0
019 AMER BAPT CONV	22	2,771	3,404*	0.6	0.7
029 AMER LUTH CH..	527	123,610	169,208	27.4	35.7
081 CATHOLIC......	297	0	172,427	27.9	36.4
093 CR CH (DISC)..	1	68	83*	-	-
097 CR C AND C CR.	2	96	117*	-	-
105 CHRISTIAN REF.	1	105	188	-	-
123 CH GOD (ANDER)	4	88	216	-	-
127 CH GOD (CLEVE)	16	549	680*	0.1	0.1
151 L-D SAINTS....	0	0	2,026	0.3	0.4
157 CH OF BRETHREN	4	284	350*	0.1	0.1
165 CH OF NAZARENE	33	1,150	2,240	0.4	0.5
193 EPISCOPAL.....	25	1,995	3,414	0.6	0.7
197 EVAN CH OF NA.	8	290	354*	0.1	0.1
201 EVAN COV CH AM	2	134	162*	-	-
221 FREE METH C NA	4	78	109	-	-
281 LUTH CH AMER..	40	10,526	14,745	2.4	3.1
283 LUTH--MO SYNOD	100	19,815	27,647	4.5	5.8
285 MENNONITE CH..	4	293	368*	0.1	0.1
287 MENN GEN CONF.	4	282	349*	0.1	0.1
293 MORAV CH-NORTH	6	659	821	0.1	0.2
313 NO AM BAPT GC.	35	4,196	5,151*	0.8	1.1
335 ORTH PRESB CH.	3	69	114	-	-
353 PLY BRETHREN..	5	74	128	-	-
371 REF CH IN AM..	5	425	715	0.1	0.2
381 REF PRES-EVAN.	1	59	62	-	-
403 SALVATION ARMY	7	440	2,066	0.3	0.4
413 S-D ADVENTISTS	41	2,435	2,965*	0.5	0.6
419 SO BAPT CONV..	10	1,638	2,038*	0.3	0.4
435 UNITARIAN-UNIV	3	97	129	-	-
443 UN C OF CHRIST	77	9,648	11,840*	1.9	2.5
449 UN METHODIST..	161	23,561	30,067	4.9	6.4
453 UN PRES CH USA	76	13,214	16,258*	2.6	3.4
467 WESLEYAN......	24	795	951	0.2	0.2
469 WISC EVAN LUTH	14	1,391	1,940	0.3	0.4
SOUTH DAKOTA	1,479	235,535	460,456*	69.2	100.0
019 AMER BAPT CONV	47	8,277	10,103*	1.5	2.2
029 AMER LUTH CH..	260	80,979	114,831	17.3	24.9
081 CATHOLIC......	244	0	134,783	20.3	29.3
093 CR CH (DISC)..	5	775	959*	0.1	0.2
097 CR C AND C CR.	13	928	1,135*	0.2	0.2
105 CHRISTIAN REF.	10	2,034	3,545	0.5	0.8
123 CH GOD (ANDER)	5	425	946	0.1	0.2
127 CH GOD (CLEVE)	13	380	470*	0.1	0.1
151 L-D SAINTS....	0	0	3,282	0.5	0.7
165 CH OF NAZARENE	21	674	1,478	0.2	0.3
193 EPISCOPAL.....	108	8,923	14,541	2.2	3.2
201 EVAN COV CH AM	9	479	586*	0.1	0.1
211 EV MENN BRETH.	1	143	168*	-	-
221 FREE METH C NA	8	203	260	-	0.1
226 FRIENDS-USA...	2	41	49*	-	-
281 LUTH CH AMER..	28	5,182	6,820	1.0	1.5
283 LUTH--MO SYNOD	116	25,457	35,071	5.3	7.6
285 MENNONITE CH..	1	20	25*	-	-
287 MENN GEN CONF.	10	2,465	2,946*	0.4	0.6
313 NO AM BAPT GC.	25	3,168	3,868*	0.6	0.8
335 ORTH PRESB CH.	7	302	484	0.1	0.1
371 REF CH IN AM..	27	3,896	6,224	0.9	1.4
381 REF PRES-EVAN.	1	59	74	-	-
403 SALVATION ARMY	5	391	1,523	0.2	0.3
413 S-D ADVENTISTS	26	1,381	1,703*	0.3	0.4
419 SO BAPT CONV..	14	2,366	2,965*	0.4	0.6
435 UNITARIAN-UNIV	3	60	62	-	-
443 UN C OF CHRIST	105	18,181	22,171*	3.3	4.8
449 UN METHODIST..	187	42,843	57,220	8.6	12.4
453 UN PRES CH USA	101	17,467	21,364*	3.2	4.6
467 WESLEYAN......	23	796	953	0.1	0.2
469 WISC EVAN LUTH	54	7,240	9,847	1.5	2.1

SOUTH ATLANTIC

County and Denomination	Number of churches	Communicant, confirmed, full members	Total adherents: Number	Percent of total population	Percent of total adherents
THE REGION....	37,722	9,063,394	13,725,207*	44.7	100.0
DELAWARE	413	101,954	236,868*	43.2	100.0
019 AMER BAPT CONV	9	1,973	2,457*	0.4	1.0
029 AMER LUTH CH..	1	42	69	-	-
081 CATHOLIC......	41	0	102,766	18.7	43.4
093 CR CH (DISC)..	1	122	151*	-	0.1
097 CR C AND C CR.	6	665	819*	0.1	0.3
123 CH GOD (ANDER)	3	107	359	0.1	0.2
127 CH GOD (CLEVE)	12	1,067	1,315*	0.2	0.6
151 L-D SAINTS....	0	0	1,149	0.2	0.5
157 CH OF BRETHREN	2	206	257*	-	0.1
165 CH OF NAZARENE	8	514	1,484	0.3	0.6
193 EPISCOPAL.....	38	12,994	20,000	3.6	8.4
226 FRIENDS-USA...	8	858	1,065*	0.2	0.4
281 LUTH CH AMER..	11	5,498	8,002	1.5	3.4
283 LUTH--MO SYNOD	6	1,364	2,024	0.4	0.9
285 MENNONITE CH..	7	614	759*	0.1	0.3
313 NO AM BAPT GC.	1	70	87*	-	-
335 ORTH PRESB CH.	2	296	426	0.1	0.2
353 PLY BRETHREN..	2	110	150	-	0.1
381 REF PRES-EVAN.	5	1,094	1,403	0.3	0.6
403 SALVATION ARMY	1	110	855	0.2	0.4

*Total adherents estimated from known number of communicant, confirmed, full members.

—Represents a percent less than 0.1.

Percentages may not total due to rounding.

Table 2. Churches and Church Membership by Region, State and Denomination: 1971

County and Denomination	Number of churches	Communicant, confirmed, full members	Total adherents		
			Number	Percent of total population	Percent of total adherents
413 S-D ADVENTISTS	10	973	1,211*	0.2	0.5
419 SO BAPT CONV..	8	3,082	3,846*	0.7	1.6
435 UNITARIAN-UNIV	3	1,000	1,414	0.3	0.6
443 UN C OF CHRIST	2	771	969*	0.2	0.4
449 UN METHODIST..	171	50,633	61,849	11.3	26.1
453 UN PRES CH USA	38	17,191	21,296*	3.9	9.0
467 WESLEYAN......	17	600	686	0.1	0.3
DISTRICT OF COLUMBIA	292	108,509	240,279*	31.8	100.0
019 AMER BAPT CONV	33	19,371	23,167*	3.1	9.6
029 AMER LUTH CH..	3	886	1,115	0.1	0.5
081 CATHOLIC......	44	0	95,508	12.6	39.7
093 CR CH (DISC)..	6	1,743	2,085*	0.3	0.9
097 CR C AND C CR.	8	1,007	1,204*	0.2	0.5
105 CHRISTIAN REF.	2	246	414	0.1	0.2
123 CH GOD (ANDER)	5	565	1,053	0.1	0.4
127 CH GOD (CLEVE)	3	377	451*	0.1	0.2
151 L-D SAINTS....	0	0	5,101	0.7	2.1
157 CH OF BRETHREN	1	413	494*	0.1	0.2
165 CH OF NAZARENE	2	424	630	0.1	0.3
193 EPISCOPAL.....	40	15,280	27,159	3.6	11.3
221 FREE METH C NA	2	104	194	-	0.1
226 FRIENDS-USA...	1	692	828*	0.1	0.3
281 LUTH CH AMER..	8	3,844	4,998	0.7	2.1
283 LUTH--MO SYNOD	7	1,680	2,684	0.4	1.1
285 MENNONITE CH..	1	11	13*	-	-
349 PENT HOLINESS.	3	230	275*	-	0.1
353 PLY BRETHREN..	3	140	210	-	0.1
357 PRESB CH US...	3	771	922*	0.1	0.4
403 SALVATION ARMY	4	307	1,455	0.2	0.6
413 S-D ADVENTISTS	7	2,792	3,339*	0.4	1.4
415 S-D BAPTIST GC	2	56	67*	-	-
419 SO BAPT CONV..	31	22,483	26,889*	3.6	11.2
435 UNITARIAN-UNIV	2	1,445	1,735	0.2	0.7
443 UN C OF CHRIST	9	5,362	6,413*	0.8	2.7
449 UN METHODIST..	43	22,393	24,835	3.3	10.3
453 UN PRES CH USA	19	5,887	7,041*	0.9	2.9
FLORIDA	4,948	1,511,981	2,799,114*	41.2	100.0
019 AMER BAPT CONV	4	224	273*	-	-
029 AMER LUTH CH..	39	13,791	19,364	0.3	0.7
055 AS REF PRES CH	7	1,908	2,324*	-	0.1
059 BAPT MISS ASSN	17	1,669	2,073*	-	0.1
075 BRETHREN IN CR	2	54	64*	-	-
081 CATHOLIC......	347	0	917,459	13.5	32.8
093 CR CH (DISC)..	102	18,755	22,333*	0.3	0.8
097 CR C AND C CR.	124	21,367	25,461*	0.4	0.9
105 CHRISTIAN REF.	8	1,192	1,867	-	0.1
123 CH GOD (ANDER)	84	5,719	13,804	0.2	0.5
127 CH GOD (CLEVE)	340	28,814	34,702*	0.5	1.2
151 L-D SAINTS....	0	0	24,414	0.4	0.9
157 CH OF BRETHREN	13	1,446	1,729*	-	0.1
165 CH OF NAZARENE	141	12,513	25,952	0.4	0.9
175 CONG CR CH....	2	352	426*	-	-
185 CUMBER PRESB..	3	895	1,092*	-	-
193 EPISCOPAL.....	288	106,776	150,542	2.2	5.4
201 EVAN COV CH AM	10	1,516	1,766*	-	0.1
221 FREE METH C NA	17	662	880	-	-
223 FREE WILL BAPT	77	6,175	7,381*	0.1	0.3
226 FRIENDS-USA...	15	520	616*	-	-
281 LUTH CH AMER..	110	33,404	43,510	0.6	1.6
283 LUTH--MO SYNOD	121	36,869	49,950	0.7	1.8
285 MENNONITE CH..	20	1,345	1,556*	-	0.1
295 MORAV CH-SOUTH	3	613	883	-	-
315 NO AM OLD RC..	2	265	313*	-	-
335 ORTH PRESB CH.	5	380	616	-	-
349 PENT HOLINESS.	77	4,136	5,030*	0.1	0.2
353 PLY BRETHREN..	24	1,887	3,715	0.1	0.1
357 PRESB CH US...	235	97,599	116,705*	1.7	4.2
371 REF CH IN AM..	14	2,492	3,039	-	0.1
381 REF PRES-EVAN.	10	1,222	1,438	-	0.1
403 SALVATION ARMY	31	2,635	11,260	0.2	0.4
413 S-D ADVENTISTS	122	18,368	22,129*	0.3	0.8
415 S-D BAPTIST GC	2	86	102*	-	-
419 SO BAPT CONV..	1,471	666,078	806,088*	11.9	28.8
435 UNITARIAN-UNIV	26	3,654	4,680	0.1	0.2
443 UN C OF CHRIST	77	27,656	32,379*	0.5	1.2
449 UN METHODIST..	795	341,571	385,051	5.7	13.8
453 UN PRES CH USA	118	45,463	53,696*	0.8	1.9
467 WESLEYAN......	34	912	1,023	-	-
469 WISC EVAN LUTH	11	998	1,429	-	0.1
GEORGIA	6,255	1,638,773	2,118,091*	46.2	100.0
019 AMER BAPT CONV	1	481	602*	-	-
029 AMER LUTH CH..	5	1,487	2,472	0.1	0.1
055 AS REF PRES CH	11	2,166	2,682*	0.1	0.1
059 BAPT MISS ASSN	1	131	167*	-	-
081 CATHOLIC......	129	0	103,609	2.3	4.9
093 CR CH (DISC)..	101	13,272	16,405*	0.4	0.8
097 CR C AND C CR.	129	24,315	30,090*	0.7	1.4
123 CH GOD (ANDER)	43	1,732	4,052	0.1	0.2
127 CH GOD (CLEVE)	368	34,704	43,161*	0.9	2.0
151 L-D SAINTS....	0	0	13,956	0.3	0.7
165 CH OF NAZARENE	87	6,542	11,630	0.3	0.5
175 CONG CR CH....	3	192	242*	-	-
185 CUMBER PRESB..	4	430	540*	-	-
193 EPISCOPAL.....	131	39,780	54,187	1.2	2.6
221 FREE METH C NA	6	200	297	-	-
223 FREE WILL BAPT	130	11,925	14,806*	0.3	0.7
226 FRIENDS-USA...	2	87	107*	-	-
281 LUTH CH AMER..	45	12,654	17,198	0.4	0.8
283 LUTH--MO SYNOD	33	4,902	7,198	0.2	0.3
285 MENNONITE CH..	4	120	147*	-	-
335 ORTH PRESB CH.	2	158	227	-	-
349 PENT HOLINESS.	51	2,592	3,183*	0.1	0.2
353 PLY BRETHREN..	12	905	1,543	-	0.1
357 PRESB CH US...	308	76,718	94,946*	2.1	4.5
381 REF PRES-EVAN.	2	245	330	-	-
403 SALVATION ARMY	23	1,684	7,208	0.2	0.3
413 S-D ADVENTISTS	69	8,433	10,434*	0.2	0.5
419 SO BAPT CONV..	2,947	1,026,650	1,276,081*	27.8	60.2
435 UNITARIAN-UNIV	12	1,451	2,345	0.1	0.1
443 UN C OF CHRIST	19	2,737	3,363*	0.1	0.2
449 UN METHODIST..	1,522	358,372	390,240	8.5	18.4
453 UN PRES CH USA	24	2,802	3,444*	0.1	0.2
467 WESLEYAN......	30	866	1,127	-	0.1
469 WISC EVAN LUTH	1	40	72	-	-
MARYLAND	2,725	676,054	1,677,329*	42.8	100.0
019 AMER BAPT CONV	46	18,995	23,789*	0.6	1.4
029 AMER LUTH CH..	44	19,146	30,482	0.8	1.8
075 BRETHREN IN CR	2	152	185*	-	-
081 CATHOLIC......	277	0	785,571	20.0	46.8
093 CR CH (DISC)..	34	6,847	8,468*	0.2	0.5
097 CR C AND C CR.	27	3,222	4,014*	0.1	0.2
123 CH GOD (ANDER)	16	1,184	2,988	0.1	0.2
127 CH GOD (CLEVE)	70	5,932	7,264*	0.2	0.4
151 L-D SAINTS....	0	0	8,465	0.2	0.5
157 CH OF BRETHREN	59	12,016	14,703*	0.4	0.9
165 CH OF NAZARENE	31	3,162	7,000	0.2	0.4
175 CONG CR CH....	2	250	304*	-	-
193 EPISCOPAL.....	161	47,954	73,577	1.9	4.4
201 EVAN COV CH AM	1	74	95*	-	-
221 FREE METH C NA	9	430	634	-	-
223 FREE WILL BAPT	20	1,502	1,857*	-	0.1
226 FRIENDS-USA...	12	1,598	1,968*	0.1	0.1
281 LUTH CH AMER..	163	71,198	101,754	2.6	6.1
283 LUTH--MO SYNOD	50	16,720	24,599	0.6	1.5
285 MENNONITE CH..	42	2,347	2,883*	0.1	0.2
293 MORAV CH-NORTH	3	459	685	-	-
315 NO AM OLD RC..	1	87	106*	-	-
335 ORTH PRESB CH.	3	337	494	-	-
349 PENT HOLINESS.	7	572	702*	-	-
353 PLY BRETHREN..	17	812	1,275	-	0.1
357 PRESB CH US...	22	8,039	9,880*	0.3	0.6
381 REF PRES-EVAN.	6	1,042	1,224	-	0.1
403 SALVATION ARMY	13	1,164	5,406	0.1	0.3
413 S-D ADVENTISTS	61	13,469	16,583*	0.4	1.0
419 SO BAPT CONV..	243	92,923	115,390*	2.9	6.9
435 UNITARIAN-UNIV	15	3,331	5,318	0.1	0.3
443 UN C OF CHRIST	79	22,874	28,027*	0.7	1.7
449 UN METHODIST..	1,006	269,973	332,511	8.5	19.8
453 UN PRES CH USA	133	46,179	56,836*	1.4	3.4
467 WESLEYAN......	48	1,974	2,146	0.1	0.1
469 WISC EVAN LUTH	2	90	146	-	-
NORTH CAROLINA	8,985	2,053,652	2,578,641*	50.7	100.0
019 AMER BAPT CONV	10	4,256	5,174*	0.1	0.2
029 AMER LUTH CH..	12	3,465	4,824	0.1	0.2
055 AS REF PRES CH	33	9,187	11,255*	0.2	0.4
059 BAPT MISS ASSN	1	165	200*	-	-
081 CATHOLIC......	157	0	69,133	1.4	2.7
093 CR CH (DISC)..	334	37,816	46,310*	0.9	1.8
097 CR C AND C CR.	141	18,564	22,733*	0.4	0.9
105 CHRISTIAN REF.	1	86	170	-	-
121 CH GOD (ABR)..	2	100	124*	-	-
123 CH GOD (ANDER)	39	1,795	4,515	0.1	0.2
127 CH GOD (CLEVE)	326	26,162	32,140*	0.6	1.2
151 L-D SAINTS....	0	0	15,047	0.3	0.6
157 CH OF BRETHREN	19	2,042	2,469*	-	0.1
165 CH OF NAZARENE	50	3,936	7,795	0.2	0.3
175 CONG CR CH....	3	160	196*	-	-
193 EPISCOPAL.....	223	46,897	65,665	1.3	2.5
221 FREE METH C NA	4	73	114	-	-
223 FREE WILL BAPT	162	24,254	29,714*	0.6	1.2
226 FRIENDS-USA...	73	10,253	12,511*	0.2	0.5

*Total adherents estimated from known number of communicant, confirmed, full members.

—Represents a percent less than 0.1.

Percentages may not total due to rounding.

Table 2. Churches and Church Membership by Region, State and Denomination: 1971

County and Denomination	Number of churches	Communicant, confirmed, full members	Total adherents		
			Number	Percent of total population	Percent of total adherents
281 LUTH CH AMER..	204	58,961	77,656	1.5	3.0
283 LUTH--MO SYNOD	49	10,926	15,704	0.3	0.6
285 MENNONITE CH..	7	127	155*	-	-
295 MORAV CH-SOUTH	43	16,017	21,488	0.4	0.8
335 ORTH PRESB CH.	1	7	8	-	-
349 PENT HOLINESS.	277	18,983	23,334*	0.5	0.9
353 PLY BRETHREN..	28	2,251	4,232	0.1	0.2
357 PRESB CH US...	675	161,082	197,669*	3.9	7.7
381 REF PRES-EVAN.	7	733	801	-	-
403 SALVATION ARMY	37	3,100	17,977	0.4	0.7
413 S-D ADVENTISTS	74	8,739	10,686*	0.2	0.4
419 SO BAPT CONV..	3,441	1,031,095	1,260,919*	24.8	48.9
435 UNITARIAN-UNIV	15	1,402	2,000	-	0.1
443 UN C OF CHRIST	255	44,118	53,839*	1.1	2.1
449 UN METHODIST..	2,014	484,272	534,607	10.5	20.7
453 UN PRES CH USA	113	12,569	15,461*	0.3	0.6
467 WESLEYAN......	155	10,059	12,016	0.2	0.5
SOUTH CAROLINA	4,331	1,053,836	1,356,819*	52.4	100.0
055 AS REF PRES CH	49	8,481	10,458*	0.4	0.8
081 CATHOLIC......	92	0	46,642	1.8	3.4
093 CR CH (DISC)..	43	3,878	4,900*	0.2	0.4
097 CR C AND C CR.	20	1,740	2,208*	0.1	0.2
121 CH GOD (ABR)..	2	261	319*	-	-
123 CH GOD (ANDER)	44	2,450	6,031	0.2	0.4
127 CH GOD (CLEVE)	232	22,338	27,638*	1.1	2.0
151 L-D SAINTS....	0	0	11,153	0.4	0.8
157 CH OF BRETHREN	1	48	59*	-	-
165 CH OF NAZARENE	53	4,468	9,131	0.4	0.7
193 EPISCOPAL.....	137	35,084	47,586	1.8	3.5
223 FREE WILL BAPT	77	9,228	11,463*	0.4	0.8
226 FRIENDS-USA...	1	14	17*	-	-
281 LUTH CH AMER..	149	39,409	52,186	2.0	3.8
283 LUTH--MO SYNOD	8	1,039	1,608	0.1	0.1
285 MENNONITE CH..	2	32	39*	-	-
315 NO AM OLD RC..	2	225	276*	-	-
349 PENT HOLINESS.	207	13,663	17,036*	0.7	1.3
353 PLY BRETHREN..	15	676	1,091	-	0.1
357 PRESB CH US...	333	74,615	92,443*	3.6	6.8
381 REF PRES-EVAN.	8	1,351	1,599	0.1	0.1
403 SALVATION ARMY	13	1,009	5,359	0.2	0.4
413 S-D ADVENTISTS	33	2,703	3,342*	0.1	0.2
419 SO BAPT CONV..	1,597	592,750	734,709*	28.4	54.1
435 UNITARIAN-UNIV	7	311	453	-	-
443 UN C OF CHRIST	1	69	86*	-	-
449 UN METHODIST..	1,076	228,188	256,888	9.9	18.9
453 UN PRES CH USA	57	7,021	8,839*	0.3	0.7
467 WESLEYAN......	71	2,772	3,231	0.1	0.2
469 WISC EVAN LUTH	1	13	29	-	-
VIRGINIA	5,952	1,429,205	2,011,887*	43.3	100.0
019 AMER BAPT CONV	40	5,367	6,491*	0.1	0.3
029 AMER LUTH CH..	19	6,589	10,151	0.2	0.5
055 AS REF PRES CH	10	2,301	2,762*	0.1	0.1
059 BAPT MISS ASSN	4	591	742*	-	-
075 BRETHREN IN CR	4	169	203*	-	-
081 CATHOLIC......	150	0	244,678	5.3	12.2
093 CR CH (DISC)..	292	38,398	46,679*	1.0	2.3
097 CR C AND C CR.	201	27,506	33,646*	0.7	1.7
121 CH GOD (ABR)..	5	171	207*	-	-
123 CH GOD (ANDER)	50	3,044	7,905	0.2	0.4
127 CH GOD (CLEVE)	142	10,339	12,591*	0.3	0.6
151 L-D SAINTS....	0	0	19,756	0.4	1.0
157 CH OF BRETHREN	150	29,048	35,184*	0.8	1.7
165 CH OF NAZARENE	53	4,838	11,735	0.3	0.6
193 EPISCOPAL.....	331	88,913	136,755	2.9	6.8
201 EVAN COV CH AM	2	97	114*	-	-
221 FREE METH C NA	4	147	202	-	-
223 FREE WILL BAPT	91	8,177	10,007*	0.2	0.5
226 FRIENDS-USA...	28	1,929	2,375*	0.1	0.1
281 LUTH CH AMER..	159	34,075	46,075	1.0	2.3
283 LUTH--MO SYNOD	35	8,910	12,780	0.3	0.6
285 MENNONITE CH..	60	4,974	6,015*	0.1	0.3
295 MORAV CH-SOUTH	2	172	195	-	-
335 ORTH PRESB CH.	3	128	234	-	-
349 PENT HOLINESS.	151	9,580	11,607*	0.2	0.6
353 PLY BRETHREN..	17	769	1,253	-	0.1
357 PRESB CH US...	493	118,459	144,057*	3.1	7.2
381 REF PRES-EVAN.	7	649	809	-	-
403 SALVATION ARMY	21	1,424	6,768	0.1	0.3
413 S-D ADVENTISTS	71	7,185	8,727*	0.2	0.4
419 SO BAPT CONV..	1,414	526,340	642,930*	13.8	32.0
435 UNITARIAN-UNIV	18	2,791	4,165	0.1	0.2
443 UN C OF CHRIST	122	22,189	27,182*	0.6	1.4
449 UN METHODIST..	1,677	447,739	497,027	10.7	24.7
453 UN PRES CH USA	70	13,235	16,442*	0.4	0.8

County and Denomination	Number of churches	Communicant, confirmed, full members	Total adherents		
			Number	Percent of total population	Percent of total adherents
467 WESLEYAN......	54	2,775	3,106	0.1	0.2
469 WISC EVAN LUTH	2	187	332	-	-
WEST VIRGINIA	3,821	489,430	706,179*	40.5	100.0
019 AMER BAPT CONV	700	118,593	142,963*	8.2	20.2
029 AMER LUTH CH..	22	3,536	4,861	0.3	0.7
055 AS REF PRES CH	2	239	285*	-	-
075 BRETHREN IN CR	1	6	7*	-	-
081 CATHOLIC......	155	0	98,808	5.7	14.0
093 CR CH (DISC)..	94	14,066	16,954*	1.0	2.4
097 CR C AND C CR.	86	12,180	14,690*	0.8	2.1
123 CH GOD (ANDER)	100	5,928	16,541	0.9	2.3
127 CH GOD (CLEVE)	164	10,795	13,124*	0.8	1.9
151 L-D SAINTS....	0	0	9,222	0.5	1.3
157 CH OF BRETHREN	60	7,137	8,662*	0.5	1.2
165 CH OF NAZARENE	118	10,897	25,073	1.4	3.6
175 CONG CR CH....	1	100	123*	-	-
193 EPISCOPAL.....	85	14,136	19,620	1.1	2.8
199 EVAN CONG CH..	1	434	517*	-	0.1
221 FREE METH C NA	20	455	662	-	0.1
223 FREE WILL BAPT	175	8,347	10,066*	0.6	1.4
226 FRIENDS-USA...	1	6	7*	-	-
281 LUTH CH AMER..	44	9,175	12,326	0.7	1.7
283 LUTH--MO SYNOD	3	365	569	-	0.1
285 MENNONITE CH..	14	435	522*	-	0.1
349 PENT HOLINESS.	35	1,742	2,115*	0.1	0.3
353 PLY BRETHREN..	6	235	560	-	0.1
357 PRESB CH US...	162	30,352	36,489*	2.1	5.2
403 SALVATION ARMY	20	1,390	5,849	0.3	0.8
413 S-D ADVENTISTS	32	2,140	2,580*	0.1	0.4
415 S-D BAPTIST GC	5	345	412*	-	0.1
419 SO BAPT CONV..	67	18,848	22,792*	1.3	3.2
435 UNITARIAN-UNIV	5	130	145	-	-
443 UN C OF CHRIST	9	1,805	2,154*	0.1	0.3
449 UN METHODIST..	1,533	199,538	218,312	12.5	30.9
453 UN PRES CH USA	68	15,303	18,354*	1.1	2.6
467 WESLEYAN......	33	772	815	-	0.1

EAST SOUTH CENTRAL

County and Denomination	Number of churches	Communicant, confirmed, full members	Total adherents		
			Number	Percent of total population	Percent of total adherents
THE REGION....	23,169	4,852,248	6,507,863*	50.8	100.0
ALABAMA	6,078	1,277,309	1,645,794*	47.8	100.0
029 AMER LUTH CH..	6	352	550	-	-
055 AS REF PRES CH	4	320	406*	-	-
059 BAPT MISS ASSN	17	2,469	3,067*	0.1	0.2
081 CATHOLIC......	161	0	85,991	2.5	5.2
093 CR CH (DISC)..	71	8,074	10,008*	0.3	0.6
097 CR C AND C CR.	24	1,819	2,270*	0.1	0.1
123 CH GOD (ANDER)	73	3,573	8,745	0.3	0.5
127 CH GOD (CLEVE)	323	22,167	27,214*	0.8	1.7
151 L-D SAINTS....	0	0	7,586	0.2	0.5
157 CH OF BRETHREN	4	215	268*	-	-
165 CH OF NAZARENE	98	6,769	11,152	0.3	0.7
185 CUMBER PRESB..	66	7,193	8,836*	0.3	0.5
193 EPISCOPAL.....	109	22,454	32,303	0.9	2.0
201 EVAN COV CH AM	2	128	158*	-	-
221 FREE METH C NA	3	36	68	-	-
223 FREE WILL BAPT	195	20,044	24,700*	0.7	1.5
226 FRIENDS-USA...	1	42	52*	-	-
281 LUTH CH AMER..	12	2,759	3,882	0.1	0.2
283 LUTH--MO SYNOD	55	8,338	12,701	0.4	0.8
285 MENNONITE CH..	10	138	171*	-	-
349 PENT HOLINESS.	43	1,912	2,354*	0.1	0.1
353 PLY BRETHREN..	4	67	147	-	-
357 PRESB CH US...	206	37,002	45,551*	1.3	2.8
371 REF CH IN AM..	1	49	65	-	-
381 REF PRES-EVAN.	3	226	330	-	-
403 SALVATION ARMY	16	1,150	5,869	0.2	0.4
413 S-D ADVENTISTS	50	6,086	7,528*	0.2	0.5
415 S-D BAPTIST GC	1	52	64*	-	-
419 SO BAPT CONV..	2,937	857,935	1,054,917*	30.6	64.1
435 UNITARIAN-UNIV	11	558	833	-	0.1
443 UN C OF CHRIST	32	2,965	3,636*	0.1	0.2
449 UN METHODIST..	1,486	254,412	274,531	8.0	16.7
453 UN PRES CH USA	44	7,660	9,452*	0.3	0.6
467 WESLEYAN......	8	286	307	-	-
469 WISC EVAN LUTH	2	59	82	-	-
KENTUCKY	6,101	1,161,357	1,764,374*	54.8	100.0
029 AMER LUTH CH..	3	386	598	-	-

*Total adherents estimated from known number of communicant, confirmed, full members.

—Represents a percent less than 0.1.

Percentages may not total due to rounding.

Table 2. Churches and Church Membership by Region, State and Denomination: 1971

County and Denomination	Number of churches	Communicant, confirmed, full members	Total adherents: Number	Total adherents: Percent of total population	Total adherents: Percent of total adherents
055 AS REF PRES CH	1	98	121*	-	-
075 BRETHREN IN CR	5	109	130*	-	-
081 CATHOLIC......	355	0	339,375	10.5	19.2
093 CR CH (DISC)..	370	59,184	72,276*	2.2	4.1
097 CR C AND C CR.	456	56,912	69,711*	2.2	4.0
123 CH GOD (ANDER)	126	8,467	21,814	0.7	1.2
127 CH GOD (CLEVE)	154	9,974	12,267*	0.4	0.7
151 L-D SAINTS....	0	0	10,635	0.3	0.6
157 CH OF BRETHREN	4	376	485*	-	-
165 CH OF NAZARENE	136	11,560	24,070	0.7	1.4
185 CUMBER PRESB..	132	13,490	16,233*	0.5	0.9
193 EPISCOPAL.....	74	17,504	23,213	0.7	1.3
221 FREE METH C NA	11	281	387	-	-
223 FREE WILL BAPT	125	12,719	15,572*	0.5	0.9
226 FRIENDS-USA...	3	103	126*	-	-
231 GENERAL BAPT..	171	19,811	24,254*	0.8	1.4
281 LUTH CH AMER..	31	7,589	10,341	0.3	0.6
283 LUTH--MO SYNOD	22	3,304	4,827	0.1	0.3
285 MENNONITE CH..	11	166	204*	-	-
349 PENT HOLINESS.	3	141	169*	-	-
353 PLY BRETHREN..	1	5	5	-	-
357 PRESB CH US...	211	22,096	27,052*	0.8	1.5
371 REF CH IN AM..	4	391	408	-	-
403 SALVATION ARMY	15	968	4,077	0.1	0.2
413 S-D ADVENTISTS	44	2,879	3,517*	0.1	0.2
419 SO BAPT CONV..	2,187	672,511	820,739*	25.5	46.5
435 UNITARIAN-UNIV	8	897	1,310	-	0.1
443 UN C OF CHRIST	36	13,334	16,450*	0.5	0.9
449 UN METHODIST..	1,124	201,725	214,322	6.7	12.1
453 UN PRES CH USA	219	22,621	27,720*	0.9	1.6
467 WESLEYAN......	59	1,756	1,966	0.1	0.1
MISSISSIPPI	4,382	856,746	1,132,375*	51.1	100.0
029 AMER LUTH CH..	2	143	244	-	-
055 AS REF PRES CH	4	683	832*	-	0.1
059 BAPT MISS ASSN	173	24,409	30,197*	1.4	2.7
081 CATHOLIC......	155	0	83,043	3.7	7.3
093 CR CH (DISC)..	53	5,262	6,580*	0.3	0.6
097 CR C AND C CR.	27	3,050	3,783*	0.2	0.3
123 CH GOD (ANDER)	52	1,842	4,774	0.2	0.4
127 CH GOD (CLEVE)	135	8,441	10,564*	0.5	0.9
151 L-D SAINTS....	0	0	6,079	0.3	0.5
165 CH OF NAZARENE	56	3,275	6,034	0.3	0.5
185 CUMBER PRESB..	21	1,585	1,966*	0.1	0.2
193 EPISCOPAL.....	83	13,520	17,858	0.8	1.6
223 FREE WILL BAPT	49	5,048	6,324*	0.3	0.6
281 LUTH CH AMER..	13	946	1,249	0.1	0.1
283 LUTH--MO SYNOD	27	2,347	3,473	0.2	0.3
285 MENNONITE CH..	6	184	230*	-	-
349 PENT HOLINESS.	14	552	682*	-	0.1
353 PLY BRETHREN..	3	50	70	-	-
357 PRESB CH US...	245	35,889	44,888*	2.0	4.0
403 SALVATION ARMY	14	817	3,095	0.1	0.3
413 S-D ADVENTISTS	43	3,077	3,847*	0.2	0.3
419 SO BAPT CONV..	1,887	545,422	679,574*	30.7	60.0
435 UNITARIAN-UNIV	5	177	197	-	-
443 UN C OF CHRIST	2	73	91*	-	-
449 UN METHODIST..	1,275	198,242	214,603	9.7	19.0
453 UN PRES CH USA	30	1,426	1,791*	0.1	0.2
467 WESLEYAN......	8	286	307	-	-
TENNESSEE	6,608	1,556,836	1,965,320*	50.1	100.0
029 AMER LUTH CH..	6	770	1,055	-	0.1
055 AS REF PRES CH	13	1,872	2,320*	0.1	0.1
059 BAPT MISS ASSN	11	1,547	1,892*	-	0.1
075 BRETHREN IN CR	3	94	114*	-	-
081 CATHOLIC......	111	0	92,577	2.4	4.7
093 CR CH (DISC)..	88	17,849	21,756*	0.6	1.1
097 CR C AND C CR.	148	22,379	27,104*	0.7	1.4
123 CH GOD (ANDER)	62	4,287	10,768	0.3	0.5
127 CH GOD (CLEVE)	278	23,936	29,189*	0.7	1.5
151 L-D SAINTS....	0	0	7,325	0.2	0.4
157 CH OF BRETHREN	20	1,575	1,902*	-	0.1
165 CH OF NAZARENE	173	11,767	22,946	0.6	1.2
185 CUMBER PRESB..	307	38,246	46,452*	1.2	2.4
193 EPISCOPAL.....	104	30,679	39,284	1.0	2.0
201 EVAN COV CH AM	1	36	43*	-	-
221 FREE METH C NA	8	130	181	-	-
223 FREE WILL BAPT	172	20,801	25,340*	0.6	1.3
226 FRIENDS-USA...	10	468	566*	-	-
231 GENERAL BAPT..	24	3,311	4,034*	0.1	0.2
281 LUTH CH AMER..	42	8,324	11,067	0.3	0.6
283 LUTH--MO SYNOD	41	7,152	10,154	0.3	0.5
285 MENNONITE CH..	5	102	122*	-	-
315 NO AM OLD RC..	2	165	198*	-	-
335 ORTH PRESB CH.	2	105	135	-	-
349 PENT HOLINESS.	24	1,039	1,270*	-	0.1

County and Denomination	Number of churches	Communicant, confirmed, full members	Total adherents: Number	Total adherents: Percent of total population	Total adherents: Percent of total adherents
353 PLY BRETHREN..	4	155	270	-	-
357 PRESB CH US...	235	63,259	77,140*	2.0	3.9
381 REF PRES-EVAN.	3	136	170	-	-
403 SALVATION ARMY	12	1,000	4,571	0.1	0.2
413 S-D ADVENTISTS	84	12,074	14,709*	0.4	0.7
419 SO BAPT CONV..	2,697	900,743	1,095,956*	27.9	55.8
435 UNITARIAN-UNIV	9	1,658	2,520	0.1	0.1
443 UN C OF CHRIST	13	1,741	2,124*	0.1	0.1
449 UN METHODIST..	1,727	360,749	387,529	9.9	19.7
453 UN PRES CH USA	146	18,146	21,936*	0.6	1.1
467 WESLEYAN......	22	534	590	-	-
469 WISC EVAN LUTH	1	7	11	-	-

WEST SOUTH CENTRAL

County and Denomination	Number of churches	Communicant, confirmed, full members	Total adherents: Number	Total adherents: Percent of total population	Total adherents: Percent of total adherents
THE REGION....	22,001	5,935,339	10,763,900*	55.7	100.0
ARKANSAS	3,568	686,386	880,433*	45.8	100.0
029 AMER LUTH CH..	2	298	399	-	-
055 AS REF PRES CH	8	800	976*	0.1	0.1
059 BAPT MISS ASSN	370	48,716	59,024*	3.1	6.7
081 CATHOLIC......	119	0	55,025	2.9	6.2
093 CR CH (DISC)..	82	10,993	13,350*	0.7	1.5
097 CR C AND C CR.	47	4,606	5,558*	0.3	0.6
121 CH GOD (ABR)..	5	205	247*	-	-
123 CH GOD (ANDER)	32	1,435	3,475	0.2	0.4
127 CH GOD (CLEVE)	77	3,252	4,000*	0.2	0.5
151 L-D SAINTS....	0	0	4,538	0.2	0.5
157 CH OF BRETHREN	1	52	66*	-	-
165 CH OF NAZARENE	109	8,357	15,137	0.8	1.7
185 CUMBER PRESB..	72	4,759	5,741*	0.3	0.7
193 EPISCOPAL.....	51	12,293	15,762	0.8	1.8
221 FREE METH C NA	2	35	37	-	-
223 FREE WILL BAPT	211	18,500	22,555*	1.2	2.6
226 FRIENDS-USA...	3	40	49*	-	-
231 GENERAL BAPT..	47	3,277	3,995*	0.2	0.5
281 LUTH CH AMER..	6	852	1,186	0.1	0.1
283 LUTH--MO SYNOD	46	7,723	10,184	0.5	1.2
285 MENNONITE CH..	8	130	154*	-	-
349 PENT HOLINESS.	11	403	490*	-	0.1
353 PLY BRETHREN..	2	7	11	-	-
357 PRESB CH US...	160	19,681	24,026*	1.2	2.7
403 SALVATION ARMY	9	514	2,084	0.1	0.2
413 S-D ADVENTISTS	40	2,931	3,539*	0.2	0.4
419 SO BAPT CONV..	1,187	356,839	435,183*	22.6	49.4
435 UNITARIAN-UNIV	4	238	399	-	-
443 UN C OF CHRIST	4	295	367*	-	-
449 UN METHODIST..	777	172,450	184,724	9.6	21.0
453 UN PRES CH USA	68	6,400	7,776*	0.4	0.9
467 WESLEYAN......	8	305	376	-	-
LOUISIANA	3,125	712,104	2,178,589*	59.8	100.0
019 AMER BAPT CONV	1	86	107*	-	-
029 AMER LUTH CH..	7	1,486	2,114	0.1	0.1
059 BAPT MISS ASSN	48	7,389	9,212*	0.3	0.4
081 CATHOLIC......	614	0	1,280,536	35.2	58.8
093 CR CH (DISC)..	27	4,697	5,852*	0.2	0.3
097 CR C AND C CR.	28	2,678	3,364*	0.1	0.2
121 CH GOD (ABR)..	4	195	244*	-	-
123 CH GOD (ANDER)	68	2,952	7,840	0.2	0.4
127 CH GOD (CLEVE)	48	3,250	4,063*	0.1	0.2
151 L-D SAINTS....	0	0	7,993	0.2	0.4
157 CH OF BRETHREN	1	108	138*	-	-
165 CH OF NAZARENE	56	2,766	4,823	0.1	0.2
185 CUMBER PRESB..	9	709	881*	-	-
193 EPISCOPAL.....	93	31,581	41,348	1.1	1.9
221 FREE METH C NA	17	538	685	-	-
226 FRIENDS-USA...	2	59	73*	-	-
281 LUTH CH AMER..	9	1,316	2,014	0.1	0.1
283 LUTH--MO SYNOD	64	15,545	22,401	0.6	1.0
285 MENNONITE CH..	2	111	146*	-	-
313 NO AM BAPT GC.	1	55	70*	-	-
349 PENT HOLINESS.	1	20	25*	-	-
353 PLY BRETHREN..	6	255	590	-	-
357 PRESB CH US...	131	31,622	39,538*	1.1	1.8
403 SALVATION ARMY	7	869	4,515	0.1	0.2
413 S-D ADVENTISTS	36	4,384	5,449*	0.1	0.3
415 S-D BAPTIST GC	4	104	128*	-	-
419 SO BAPT CONV..	1,310	482,535	602,687*	16.6	27.7
435 UNITARIAN-UNIV	8	747	1,013	-	-
443 UN C OF CHRIST	20	3,450	4,280*	0.1	0.2

*Total adherents estimated from known number of communicant, confirmed, full members.

—Represents a percent less than 0.1.

Percentages may not total due to rounding.

Table 2. Churches and Church Membership by Region, State and Denomination: 1971

County and Denomination	Number of churches	Communicant, confirmed, full members	Total adherents: Number	Total adherents: Percent of total population	Total adherents: Percent of total adherents
449 UN METHODIST..	490	111,864	125,581	3.4	5.8
453 UN PRES CH USA	3	384	482*	-	-
467 WESLEYAN......	8	287	309	-	-
469 WISC EVAN LUTH	2	62	88	-	-
OKLAHOMA	4,085	1,073,997	1,410,323*	55.1	100.0
019 AMER BAPT CONV	11	1,056	1,270*	-	0.1
029 AMER LUTH CH..	13	2,440	3,393	0.1	0.2
059 BAPT MISS ASSN	42	5,360	6,448*	0.3	0.5
075 BRETHREN IN CR	2	112	131*	-	-
081 CATHOLIC......	189	0	100,663	3.9	7.1
093 CR CH (DISC)..	213	51,050	61,376*	2.4	4.4
097 CR C AND C CR.	197	27,742	33,270*	1.3	2.4
107 CHRISTIAN UN..	8	537	641*	-	-
123 CH GOD (ANDER)	74	6,000	14,965	0.6	1.1
127 CH GOD (CLEVE)	62	3,066	3,698*	0.1	0.3
151 L-D SAINTS....	0	0	8,788	0.3	0.6
157 CH OF BRETHREN	8	551	648*	-	-
165 CH OF NAZARENE	215	16,605	35,762	1.4	2.5
175 CONG CR CH....	3	604	740*	-	0.1
185 CUMBER PRESB..	26	1,638	1,960*	0.1	0.1
193 EPISCOPAL.....	77	17,465	23,340	0.9	1.7
211 EV MENN BRETH.	1	72	88*	-	-
221 FREE METH C NA	18	654	919	-	0.1
223 FREE WILL BAPT	231	19,842	23,919*	0.9	1.7
226 FRIENDS-USA...	23	1,502	1,771*	0.1	0.1
231 GENERAL BAPT..	12	1,081	1,303*	0.1	0.1
281 LUTH CH AMER..	11	2,759	3,992	0.2	0.3
283 LUTH--MO SYNOD	77	16,531	22,790	0.9	1.6
285 MENNONITE CH..	4	376	453*	-	-
287 MENN GEN CONF.	17	1,732	2,053*	0.1	0.1
313 NO AM BAPT GC.	6	451	531*	-	-
335 ORTH PRESB CH.	3	107	155	-	-
349 PENT HOLINESS.	151	8,249	9,911*	0.4	0.7
353 PLY BRETHREN..	4	170	250	-	-
357 PRESB CH US...	33	4,966	6,001*	0.2	0.4
371 REF CH IN AM..	2	176	288	-	-
381 REF PRES-EVAN.	3	152	176	-	-
403 SALVATION ARMY	16	1,329	6,893	0.3	0.5
413 S-D ADVENTISTS	62	5,186	6,251*	0.2	0.4
419 SO BAPT CONV..	1,390	560,654	674,280*	26.3	47.8
435 UNITARIAN-UNIV	6	1,385	2,146	0.1	0.2
443 UN C OF CHRIST	18	1,808	2,184*	0.1	0.2
449 UN METHODIST..	704	269,183	296,806	11.6	21.0
453 UN PRES CH USA	136	40,684	49,153*	1.9	3.5
467 WESLEYAN......	15	608	747	-	0.1
469 WISC EVAN LUTH	2	114	170	-	-
TEXAS	11,223	3,462,852	6,294,555*	56.2	100.0
019 AMER BAPT CONV	7	1,465	1,853*	-	-
029 AMER LUTH CH..	250	81,472	105,798	0.9	1.7
059 BAPT MISS ASSN	517	86,108	104,751*	0.9	1.7
081 CATHOLIC......	1,104	0	2,012,355	18.0	32.0
093 CR CH (DISC)..	465	95,379	117,597*	1.1	1.9
097 CR C AND C CR.	128	17,277	21,411*	0.2	0.3
121 CH GOD (ABR)..	3	79	95*	-	-
123 CH GOD (ANDER)	87	4,047	9,948	0.1	0.2
127 CH GOD (CLEVE)	148	9,423	11,526*	0.1	0.2
151 L-D SAINTS....	0	0	42,514	0.4	0.7
157 CH OF BRETHREN	4	389	477*	-	-
165 CH OF NAZARENE	272	21,128	35,982	0.3	0.6
175 CONG CR CH....	2	662	828*	-	-
185 CUMBER PRESB..	50	6,604	8,080*	0.1	0.1
193 EPISCOPAL.....	388	128,657	175,694	1.6	2.8
201 EVAN COV CH AM	2	70	91*	-	-
221 FREE METH C NA	20	607	1,012	-	-
223 FREE WILL BAPT	64	4,000	4,950*	-	0.1
226 FRIENDS-USA...	12	1,264	1,557*	-	-
281 LUTH CH AMER..	94	23,641	32,269	0.3	0.5
283 LUTH--MO SYNOD	290	78,104	109,616	1.0	1.7
285 MENNONITE CH..	7	331	423*	-	-
287 MENN GEN CONF.	1	45	57*	-	-
313 NO AM BAPT GC.	11	772	939*	-	-
335 ORTH PRESB CH.	1	29	37	-	-
349 PENT HOLINESS.	57	1,909	2,400*	-	-
353 PLY BRETHREN..	20	1,004	1,856	-	-
357 PRESB CH US...	441	118,580	147,194*	1.3	2.3
381 REF PRES-EVAN.	4	287	332	-	-
403 SALVATION ARMY	30	2,574	13,640	0.1	0.2
413 S-D ADVENTISTS	144	14,313	17,708*	0.2	0.3
419 SO BAPT CONV..	4,003	1,923,977	2,362,851*	21.1	37.5
435 UNITARIAN-UNIV	33	3,552	5,272	-	0.1
443 UN C OF CHRIST	68	17,627	21,650*	0.2	0.3
449 UN METHODIST..	2,154	763,994	855,733	7.6	13.6
453 UN PRES CH USA	292	49,247	60,698*	0.5	1.0
461 UNITY OF BRETH	27	3,249	3,945	-	0.1
467 WESLEYAN......	10	255	320	-	-
469 WISC EVAN LUTH	13	731	1,096	-	-

MOUNTAIN

County and Denomination	Number of churches	Communicant, confirmed, full members	Total adherents: Number	Total adherents: Percent of total population	Total adherents: Percent of total adherents
THE REGION....	6,440	1,165,860	4,333,407*	52.3	100.0
ARIZONA	1,176	245,630	839,667*	47.4	100.0
019 AMER BAPT CONV	30	7,226	8,938*	0.5	1.1
029 AMER LUTH CH..	29	10,933	15,893	0.9	1.9
059 BAPT MISS ASSN	4	308	381*	-	-
081 CATHOLIC......	222	0	408,996	23.1	48.7
083 CR CATH CH DOB	1	36	37	-	-
093 CR CH (DISC)..	18	4,151	5,094*	0.3	0.6
097 CR C AND C CR.	46	8,070	10,023*	0.6	1.2
105 CHRISTIAN REF.	5	724	1,177	0.1	0.1
121 CH GOD (ABR)..	2	282	348*	-	-
123 CH GOD (ANDER)	12	1,240	2,780	0.2	0.3
127 CH GOD (CLEVE)	41	2,524	3,126*	0.2	0.4
151 L-D SAINTS....	0	0	106,323	6.0	12.7
157 CH OF BRETHREN	4	600	738*	-	0.1
165 CH OF NAZARENE	41	5,344	10,523	0.6	1.3
193 EPISCOPAL.....	60	18,682	23,119	1.3	2.8
201 EVAN COV CH AM	3	345	425*	-	0.1
221 FREE METH C NA	14	636	887	0.1	0.1
223 FREE WILL BAPT	4	474	588*	-	0.1
226 FRIENDS-USA...	7	232	290*	-	-
231 GENERAL BAPT..	3	103	128*	-	-
281 LUTH CH AMER..	24	10,923	15,130	0.9	1.8
283 LUTH--MO SYNOD	33	9,448	13,389	0.8	1.6
285 MENNONITE CH..	8	446	558*	-	0.1
287 MENN GEN CONF.	1	70	86*	-	-
315 NO AM OLD RC..	1	35	45*	-	-
349 PENT HOLINESS.	13	228	283*	-	-
353 PLY BRETHREN..	8	298	696	-	0.1
371 REF CH IN AM..	5	1,426	1,874	0.1	0.2
403 SALVATION ARMY	12	639	5,847	0.3	0.7
413 S-D ADVENTISTS	44	4,978	6,160*	0.3	0.7
419 SO BAPT CONV..	216	68,505	85,173*	4.8	10.1
435 UNITARIAN-UNIV	5	1,162	1,647	0.1	0.2
443 UN C OF CHRIST	26	12,602	15,533*	0.9	1.8
449 UN METHODIST..	96	42,440	53,148	3.0	6.3
453 UN PRES CH USA	84	25,118	31,158*	1.8	3.7
467 WESLEYAN......	13	633	786	-	0.1
469 WISC EVAN LUTH	41	4,769	8,340	0.5	1.0
COLORADO	1,683	373,442	916,743*	41.5	100.0
019 AMER BAPT CONV	81	23,927	29,157*	1.3	3.2
029 AMER LUTH CH..	54	18,557	27,104	1.2	3.0
059 BAPT MISS ASSN	3	160	200*	-	-
075 BRETHREN IN CR	1	55	68*	-	-
081 CATHOLIC......	273	0	377,214	17.1	41.1
093 CR CH (DISC)..	51	13,110	16,053*	0.7	1.8
097 CR C AND C CR.	60	9,292	11,426*	0.5	1.2
105 CHRISTIAN REF.	12	2,389	4,192	0.2	0.5
121 CH GOD (ABR)..	2	49	61*	-	-
123 CH GOD (ANDER)	25	1,588	3,672	0.2	0.4
127 CH GOD (CLEVE)	12	644	801*	-	0.1
151 L-D SAINTS....	0	0	38,256	1.7	4.2
157 CH OF BRETHREN	10	1,240	1,502*	0.1	0.2
165 CH OF NAZARENE	78	7,969	17,773	0.8	1.9
193 EPISCOPAL.....	96	29,695	44,658	2.0	4.9
201 EVAN COV CH AM	6	822	1,012*	-	0.1
221 FREE METH C NA	16	516	657	-	0.1
223 FREE WILL BAPT	2	92	113*	-	-
226 FRIENDS-USA...	21	1,567	1,893*	0.1	0.2
231 GENERAL BAPT..	2	85	104*	-	-
281 LUTH CH AMER..	36	17,019	24,882	1.1	2.7
283 LUTH--MO SYNOD	96	33,358	47,808	2.2	5.2
285 MENNONITE CH..	18	1,120	1,366*	0.1	0.1
287 MENN GEN CONF.	2	108	135*	-	-
313 NO AM BAPT GC.	4	279	344*	-	-
315 NO AM OLD RC..	1	87	104*	-	-
335 ORTH PRESB CH.	3	154	249	-	-
349 PENT HOLINESS.	16	422	513*	-	0.1
353 PLY BRETHREN..	15	1,172	1,794	0.1	0.2
371 REF CH IN AM..	8	1,926	2,710	0.1	0.3
381 REF PRES-EVAN.	3	694	958	-	0.1
403 SALVATION ARMY	8	590	2,554	0.1	0.3
413 S-D ADVENTISTS	68	10,875	13,317*	0.6	1.5
415 S-D BAPTIST GC	2	253	315*	-	-
419 SO BAPT CONV..	122	40,821	50,385*	2.3	5.5

*Total adherents estimated from known number of communicant, confirmed, full members.

—Represents a percent less than 0.1.

Percentages may not total due to rounding.

Table 2. Churches and Church Membership by Region, State and Denomination: 1971

County and Denomination	Number of churches	Communicant, confirmed, full members	Total adherents: Number	Total adherents: Percent of total population	Total adherents: Percent of total adherents
435 UNITARIAN-UNIV	12	1,869	2,684	0.1	0.3
443 UN C OF CHRIST	77	19,042	23,344*	1.1	2.5
449 UN METHODIST..	222	80,454	103,926	4.7	11.3
453 UN PRES CH USA	131	49,710	61,092*	2.8	6.7
467 WESLEYAN......	19	713	833	-	0.1
469 WISC EVAN LUTH	15	1,019	1,514	0.1	0.2
IDAHO	629	93,538	381,760*	53.6	100.0
019 AMER BAPT CONV	40	8,012	9,872*	1.4	2.6
029 AMER LUTH CH..	26	5,800	8,454	1.2	2.2
059 BAPT MISS ASSN	2	115	141*	-	-
081 CATHOLIC......	104	0	59,117	8.3	15.5
093 CR CH (DISC)..	13	4,050	4,991*	0.7	1.3
097 CR C AND C CR.	15	4,178	5,102*	0.7	1.3
105 CHRISTIAN REF.	1	76	184	-	-
123 CH GOD (ANDER)	11	483	1,277	0.2	0.3
127 CH GOD (CLEVE)	18	504	620*	0.1	0.2
151 L-D SAINTS....	0	0	193,405	27.1	50.7
157 CH OF BRETHREN	8	903	1,098*	0.2	0.3
165 CH OF NAZARENE	52	6,535	12,912	1.8	3.4
175 CONG CR CH....	1	73	90*	-	-
193 EPISCOPAL.....	36	6,113	10,099	1.4	2.6
201 EVAN COV CH AM	1	63	82*	-	-
221 FREE METH C NA	6	265	337	-	0.1
223 FREE WILL BAPT	6	243	301*	-	0.1
226 FRIENDS-USA...	13	1,097	1,340*	0.2	0.4
281 LUTH CH AMER..	12	2,667	4,169	0.6	1.1
283 LUTH--MO SYNOD	35	8,161	12,167	1.7	3.2
285 MENNONITE CH..	4	296	362*	0.1	0.1
287 MENN GEN CONF.	1	346	448*	0.1	0.1
313 NO AM BAPT GC.	1	127	160*	-	-
403 SALVATION ARMY	7	378	1,634	0.2	0.4
413 S-D ADVENTISTS	40	4,089	4,997*	0.7	1.3
419 SO BAPT CONV..	28	5,017	6,250*	0.9	1.6
435 UNITARIAN-UNIV	4	164	227	-	0.1
443 UN C OF CHRIST	20	2,975	3,669*	0.5	1.0
449 UN METHODIST..	65	19,247	24,046	3.4	6.3
453 UN PRES CH USA	54	11,418	14,044*	2.0	3.7
467 WESLEYAN......	5	143	165	-	-
MONTANA	995	122,411	323,738*	46.6	100.0
019 AMER BAPT CONV	29	4,829	5,979*	0.9	1.8
029 AMER LUTH CH..	134	33,052	48,504	7.0	15.0
059 BAPT MISS ASSN	1	50	65*	-	-
081 CATHOLIC......	272	0	131,877	19.0	40.7
093 CR CH (DISC)..	19	3,293	4,030*	0.6	1.2
097 CR C AND C CR.	13	1,346	1,662*	0.2	0.5
105 CHRISTIAN REF.	5	858	1,612	0.2	0.5
123 CH GOD (ANDER)	10	351	975	0.1	0.3
127 CH GOD (CLEVE)	9	234	284*	-	0.1
151 L-D SAINTS....	0	0	22,847	3.3	7.1
157 CH OF BRETHREN	2	65	81*	-	-
165 CH OF NAZARENE	21	995	2,342	0.3	0.7
175 CONG CR CH....	4	154	183*	-	0.1
193 EPISCOPAL.....	45	5,842	9,871	1.4	3.0
197 EVAN CH OF NA.	21	1,201	1,463*	0.2	0.5
201 EVAN COV CH AM	4	232	284*	-	0.1
211 EV MENN BRETH.	1	110	138*	-	-
281 LUTH CH AMER..	17	4,874	7,974	1.1	2.5
283 LUTH--MO SYNOD	60	10,304	15,215	2.2	4.7
285 MENNONITE CH..	4	230	286*	-	0.1
287 MENN GEN CONF.	7	500	634*	0.1	0.2
313 NO AM BAPT GC.	4	651	802*	0.1	0.2
353 PLY BRETHREN..	3	70	120	-	-
371 REF CH IN AM..	2	159	247	-	0.1
403 SALVATION ARMY	7	266	1,615	0.2	0.5
413 S-D ADVENTISTS	33	2,544	3,101*	0.4	1.0
419 SO BAPT CONV..	33	4,261	5,257*	0.8	1.6
435 UNITARIAN-UNIV	5	142	142	-	-
443 UN C OF CHRIST	36	8,448	10,383*	1.5	3.2
449 UN METHODIST..	129	23,730	28,790	4.1	8.9
453 UN PRES CH USA	53	12,968	15,948*	2.3	4.9
469 WISC EVAN LUTH	12	652	1,027	0.1	0.3
NEVADA	231	32,975	184,561*	37.8	100.0
019 AMER BAPT CONV	15	2,457	3,038*	0.6	1.6
029 AMER LUTH CH..	3	1,456	2,273	0.5	1.2
059 BAPT MISS ASSN	1	50	63*	-	-
081 CATHOLIC......	39	0	92,100	18.8	49.9
093 CR CH (DISC)..	1	316	397*	0.1	0.2
097 CR C AND C CR.	7	430	534*	0.1	0.3
123 CH GOD (ANDER)	4	257	510	0.1	0.3
127 CH GOD (CLEVE)	7	193	240*	-	0.1
151 L-D SAINTS....	0	0	47,269	9.7	25.6
165 CH OF NAZARENE	16	633	1,986	0.4	1.1
193 EPISCOPAL.....	29	4,219	6,414	1.3	3.5
221 FREE METH C NA	1	5	6	-	-
226 FRIENDS-USA...	2	27	33*	-	-
281 LUTH CH AMER..	3	1,052	1,712	0.4	0.9
283 LUTH--MO SYNOD	17	2,911	4,598	0.9	2.5
353 PLY BRETHREN..	1	10	10	-	-
403 SALVATION ARMY	3	116	502	0.1	0.3
413 S-D ADVENTISTS	11	806	996*	0.2	0.5
419 SO BAPT CONV..	29	7,329	9,141*	1.9	5.0
435 UNITARIAN-UNIV	2	97	107	-	0.1
443 UN C OF CHRIST	3	609	753*	0.2	0.4
449 UN METHODIST..	22	6,544	7,585	1.6	4.1
453 UN PRES CH USA	14	3,437	4,254*	0.9	2.3
469 WISC EVAN LUTH	1	21	40	-	-
NEW MEXICO	1,142	204,049	643,408*	63.3	100.0
019 AMER BAPT CONV	2	1,650	2,092*	0.2	0.3
029 AMER LUTH CH..	4	965	1,425	0.1	0.2
059 BAPT MISS ASSN	12	831	1,037*	0.1	0.2
075 BRETHREN IN CR	2	61	78*	-	-
081 CATHOLIC......	398	0	363,518	35.8	56.5
083 CR CATH CH DOB	2	71	81	-	-
093 CR CH (DISC)..	17	3,287	4,123*	0.4	0.6
097 CR C AND C CR.	27	4,946	6,238*	0.6	1.0
105 CHRISTIAN REF.	5	373	712	0.1	0.1
123 CH GOD (ANDER)	7	356	904	0.1	0.1
127 CH GOD (CLEVE)	31	1,403	1,802*	0.2	0.3
151 L-D SAINTS....	0	0	21,843	2.1	3.4
157 CH OF BRETHREN	2	177	228*	-	-
165 CH OF NAZARENE	36	2,857	5,838	0.6	0.9
185 CUMBER PRESB..	1	489	614*	0.1	0.1
193 EPISCOPAL.....	44	10,432	14,731	1.4	2.3
201 EVAN COV CH AM	1	73	92*	-	-
221 FREE METH C NA	4	55	80	-	-
223 FREE WILL BAPT	9	641	814*	0.1	0.1
226 FRIENDS-USA...	3	122	153*	-	-
281 LUTH CH AMER..	13	4,348	6,652	0.7	1.0
283 LUTH--MO SYNOD	23	4,076	5,788	0.6	0.9
285 MENNONITE CH..	2	53	66*	-	-
315 NO AM OLD RC..	1	27	34*	-	-
349 PENT HOLINESS.	6	120	150*	-	-
353 PLY BRETHREN..	3	143	260	-	-
357 PRESB CH US...	1	66	82*	-	-
371 REF CH IN AM..	2	188	296	-	-
381 REF PRES-EVAN.	2	272	355	-	0.1
403 SALVATION ARMY	6	200	1,126	0.1	0.2
413 S-D ADVENTISTS	32	2,309	2,945*	0.3	0.5
419 SO BAPT CONV..	250	92,917	116,869*	11.5	18.2
435 UNITARIAN-UNIV	6	944	1,273	0.1	0.2
443 UN C OF CHRIST	8	2,021	2,564*	0.3	0.4
449 UN METHODIST..	113	51,890	58,700	5.8	9.1
453 UN PRES CH USA	65	15,605	19,731*	1.9	3.1
467 WESLEYAN......	1	33	41	-	-
469 WISC EVAN LUTH	1	48	73	-	-
UTAH	223	32,865	885,332*	83.6	100.0
019 AMER BAPT CONV	10	2,974	3,838*	0.4	0.4
029 AMER LUTH CH..	4	844	1,375	0.1	0.2
081 CATHOLIC......	47	0	50,581	4.8	5.7
093 CR CH (DISC)..	3	573	727*	0.1	0.1
097 CR C AND C CR.	4	584	745*	0.1	0.1
105 CHRISTIAN REF.	3	230	468	-	0.1
127 CH GOD (CLEVE)	2	42	52*	-	-
151 L-D SAINTS....	0	0	789,419	74.5	89.2
165 CH OF NAZARENE	5	312	559	0.1	0.1
175 CONG CR CH....	1	497	635*	0.1	0.1
193 EPISCOPAL.....	18	4,067	6,372	0.6	0.7
226 FRIENDS-USA...	2	16	20*	-	-
281 LUTH CH AMER..	7	1,693	2,510	0.2	0.3
283 LUTH--MO SYNOD	12	2,539	3,868	0.4	0.4
353 PLY BRETHREN..	2	60	120	-	-
403 SALVATION ARMY	2	109	442	-	-
413 S-D ADVENTISTS	9	811	1,055*	0.1	0.1
419 SO BAPT CONV..	40	5,559	7,148*	0.7	0.8
435 UNITARIAN-UNIV	1	406	621	0.1	0.1
443 UN C OF CHRIST	9	1,752	2,258*	0.2	0.3
449 UN METHODIST..	16	4,624	5,956	0.6	0.7
453 UN PRES CH USA	26	5,173	6,563*	0.6	0.7
WYOMING	361	60,950	158,198*	47.6	100.0
019 AMER BAPT CONV	26	5,937	7,291*	2.2	4.6
029 AMER LUTH CH..	9	1,938	3,011	0.9	1.9
081 CATHOLIC......	67	0	45,917	13.8	29.0
093 CR CH (DISC)..	4	2,251	2,765*	0.8	1.7
097 CR C AND C CR.	14	1,265	1,571*	0.5	1.0
123 CH GOD (ANDER)	5	166	411	0.1	0.3
127 CH GOD (CLEVE)	2	137	170*	0.1	0.1
151 L-D SAINTS....	0	0	28,954	8.7	18.3
165 CH OF NAZARENE	18	1,000	2,344	0.7	1.5
175 CONG CR CH....	3	1,444	1,792*	0.5	1.1

*Total adherents estimated from known number of communicant, confirmed, full members.

—Represents a percent less than 0.1.

Percentages may not total due to rounding.

Table 2. Churches and Church Membership by Region, State and Denomination: 1971

County and Denomination	Number of churches	Communicant, confirmed, full members	Total adherents: Number	Total adherents: Percent of total population	Total adherents: Percent of total adherents
193 EPISCOPAL.....	39	7,145	12,569	3.8	7.9
201 EVAN COV CH AM	1	27	34*	-	-
221 FREE METH C NA	1	16	23	-	-
223 FREE WILL BAPT	1	45	55*	-	-
281 LUTH CH AMER..	6	1,975	2,886	0.9	1.8
283 LUTH--MO SYNOD	37	6,061	8,830	2.7	5.6
353 PLY BRETHREN..	1	2	2	-	-
403 SALVATION ARMY	4	145	636	0.2	0.4
413 S-D ADVENTISTS	22	1,605	1,964*	0.6	1.2
419 SO BAPT CONV..	23	4,575	5,647*	1.7	3.6
435 UNITARIAN-UNIV	3	73	92	-	0.1
443 UN C OF CHRIST	13	3,033	3,688*	1.1	2.3
449 UN METHODIST..	34	12,929	16,283	4.9	10.3
453 UN PRES CH USA	28	9,181	11,263*	3.4	7.1

PACIFIC

County and Denomination	Number of churches	Communicant, confirmed, full members	Total adherents: Number	Total adherents: Percent of total population	Total adherents: Percent of total adherents
THE REGION....	12,324	2,709,577	8,895,509*	33.5	100.0
ALASKA	326	37,055	111,252*	37.0	100.0
019 AMER BAPT CONV	3	372	483*	0.2	0.4
029 AMER LUTH CH..	13	2,795	4,738	1.6	4.3
059 BAPT MISS ASSN	2	66	85*	-	0.1
081 CATHOLIC......	82	0	49,187	16.4	44.2
093 CR CH (DISC)..	1	230	297*	0.1	0.3
097 CR C AND C CR.	5	140	180*	0.1	0.2
105 CHRISTIAN REF.	1	89	139	-	0.1
123 CH GOD (ANDER)	9	460	1,138	0.4	1.0
127 CH GOD (CLEVE)	11	296	382*	0.1	0.3
151 L-D SAINTS....	0	0	6,630	2.2	6.0
165 CH OF NAZARENE	13	794	2,127	0.7	1.9
175 CONG CR CH....	2	405	545*	0.2	0.5
193 EPISCOPAL.....	26	3,235	5,084	1.7	4.6
201 EVAN COV CH AM	1	55	71*	-	0.1
221 FREE METH C NA	1	34	53	-	-
223 FREE WILL BAPT	2	89	115*	-	0.1
226 FRIENDS-USA...	14	2,493	3,510*	1.2	3.2
281 LUTH CH AMER..	3	935	1,457	0.5	1.3
283 LUTH--MO SYNOD	7	1,399	2,187	0.7	2.0
349 PENT HOLINESS.	5	89	122*	-	0.1
353 PLY BRETHREN..	4	97	275	0.1	0.2
403 SALVATION ARMY	14	626	2,914	1.0	2.6
413 S-D ADVENTISTS	12	937	1,193*	0.4	1.1
419 SO BAPT CONV..	36	12,404	15,995*	5.3	14.4
435 UNITARIAN-UNIV	4	357	417	0.1	0.4
449 UN METHODIST..	23	4,198	5,996	2.0	5.4
453 UN PRES CH USA	31	4,405	5,802*	1.9	5.2
469 WISC EVAN LUTH	1	55	130	-	0.1
CALIFORNIA	7,552	1,808,346	6,692,785*	33.5	100.0
019 AMER BAPT CONV	491	150,867	184,052*	0.9	2.8
029 AMER LUTH CH..	248	97,959	143,150	0.7	2.1
059 BAPT MISS ASSN	23	3,654	4,474*	-	0.1
075 BRETHREN IN CR	9	820	1,012*	-	-
081 CATHOLIC......	1,208	0	3,939,752	19.7	58.9
093 CR CH (DISC)..	209	55,581	67,719*	0.3	1.0
097 CR C AND C CR.	239	42,277	51,857*	0.3	0.8
105 CHRISTIAN REF.	37	8,404	15,297	0.1	0.2
121 CH GOD (ABR)..	5	222	273*	-	-
123 CH GOD (ANDER)	114	9,242	22,390	0.1	0.3
127 CH GOD (CLEVE)	149	9,291	11,512*	0.1	0.2
151 L-D SAINTS....	0	0	367,521	1.8	5.5
157 CH OF BRETHREN	33	6,612	8,061*	-	0.1
165 CH OF NAZARENE	349	40,059	85,742	0.4	1.3
175 CONG CR CH....	25	7,719	9,379*	-	0.1
185 CUMBER PRESB..	4	731	858*	-	-
193 EPISCOPAL.....	365	136,285	199,685	1.0	3.0
201 EVAN COV CH AM	54	9,201	11,199*	0.1	0.2
211 EV MENN BRETH.	1	55	68*	-	-
221 FREE METH C NA	69	4,269	6,051	-	0.1
223 FREE WILL BAPT	78	4,805	14,998*	0.1	0.2
226 FRIENDS-USA...	61	6,972	8,525*	-	0.1
231 GENERAL BAPT..	18	772	2,410*	-	-
281 LUTH CH AMER..	218	67,329	99,459	0.5	1.5
283 LUTH--MO SYNOD	380	118,600	172,030	0.9	2.6
285 MENNONITE CH..	7	475	584*	-	-
287 MENN GEN CONF.	7	1,467	1,793*	-	-
293 MORAV CH-NORTH	4	594	932	-	-
313 NO AM BAPT GC.	13	4,925	6,069*	-	0.1
315 NO AM OLD RC..	5	843	1,019*	-	-
335 ORTH PRESB CH.	23	1,685	2,510	-	-
349 PENT HOLINESS.	64	2,609	3,195*	-	-
353 PLY BRETHREN..	50	4,231	6,469	-	0.1
371 REF CH IN AM..	44	15,595	23,887	0.1	0.4
381 REF PRES-EVAN.	3	160	271	-	-
403 SALVATION ARMY	64	5,117	24,970	0.1	0.4
413 S-D ADVENTISTS	392	105,073	128,080*	0.6	1.9
415 S-D BAPTIST GC	3	449	547*	-	-
419 SO BAPT CONV..	861	256,726	314,217*	1.6	4.7
435 UNITARIAN-UNIV	74	12,955	15,982	0.1	0.2
443 UN C OF CHRIST	251	37,445	45,502*	0.2	0.7
449 UN METHODIST..	716	307,741	361,116	1.8	5.4
453 UN PRES CH USA	513	261,642	318,858*	1.6	4.8
467 WESLEYAN......	42	3,940	4,628	-	0.1
469 WISC EVAN LUTH	29	2,948	4,682	-	0.1
HAWAII	353	51,912	291,471*	37.9	100.0
019 AMER BAPT CONV	4	526	656*	0.1	0.2
029 AMER LUTH CH..	5	752	1,016	0.1	0.3
081 CATHOLIC......	66	0	195,046	25.4	66.9
093 CR CH (DISC)..	5	802	1,000*	0.1	0.3
097 CR C AND C CR.	9	541	674*	0.1	0.2
105 CHRISTIAN REF.	1	79	137	-	-
123 CH GOD (ANDER)	2	101	213	-	0.1
127 CH GOD (CLEVE)	10	328	407*	0.1	0.1
151 L-D SAINTS....	0	0	25,214	3.3	8.7
165 CH OF NAZARENE	11	716	1,628	0.2	0.6
175 CONG CR CH....	5	271	337*	-	0.1
193 EPISCOPAL.....	40	7,688	12,157	1.6	4.2
223 FREE WILL BAPT	1	122	152*	-	0.1
226 FRIENDS-USA...	1	80	100*	-	-
281 LUTH CH AMER..	5	600	888	0.1	0.3
283 LUTH--MO SYNOD	9	1,425	2,270	0.3	0.8
353 PLY BRETHREN..	2	150	416	0.1	0.1
403 SALVATION ARMY	9	608	2,858	0.4	1.0
413 S-D ADVENTISTS	20	2,975	3,698*	0.5	1.3
419 SO BAPT CONV..	33	9,452	11,767*	1.5	4.0
435 UNITARIAN-UNIV	2	243	319	-	0.1
443 UN C OF CHRIST	79	16,440	20,438*	2.7	7.0
449 UN METHODIST..	30	6,832	8,615	1.1	3.0
453 UN PRES CH USA	3	1,149	1,410*	0.2	0.5
469 WISC EVAN LUTH	1	32	55	-	-
OREGON	1,721	317,405	691,085*	33.0	100.0
019 AMER BAPT CONV	50	14,509	17,428*	0.8	2.5
029 AMER LUTH CH..	66	23,053	32,231	1.5	4.7
059 BAPT MISS ASSN	4	225	277*	-	-
075 BRETHREN IN CR	3	87	104*	-	-
081 CATHOLIC......	217	0	212,583	10.2	30.8
093 CR CH (DISC)..	58	15,001	18,161*	0.9	2.6
097 CR C AND C CR.	157	24,769	29,995*	1.4	4.3
105 CHRISTIAN REF.	3	272	510	-	0.1
123 CH GOD (ANDER)	48	3,895	9,635	0.5	1.4
127 CH GOD (CLEVE)	32	1,446	1,751*	0.1	0.3
151 L-D SAINTS....	0	0	59,178	2.8	8.6
157 CH OF BRETHREN	6	612	738*	-	0.1
165 CH OF NAZARENE	89	10,401	20,758	1.0	3.0
175 CONG CR CH....	1	250	306*	-	-
193 EPISCOPAL.....	93	26,691	38,558	1.8	5.6
197 EVAN CH OF NA.	45	5,246	6,342*	0.3	0.9
201 EVAN COV CH AM	8	925	1,103*	0.1	0.2
211 EV MENN BRETH.	2	579	692*	-	0.1
221 FREE METH C NA	36	1,568	2,212	0.1	0.3
226 FRIENDS-USA...	34	4,039	4,861*	0.2	0.7
281 LUTH CH AMER..	41	14,023	20,661	1.0	3.0
283 LUTH--MO SYNOD	85	20,518	30,258	1.4	4.4
285 MENNONITE CH..	28	2,505	3,050*	0.1	0.4
287 MENN GEN CONF.	5	1,003	1,212*	0.1	0.2
313 NO AM BAPT GC.	9	2,079	2,485*	0.1	0.4
335 ORTH PRESB CH.	4	320	497	-	0.1
349 PENT HOLINESS.	7	245	295*	-	-
353 PLY BRETHREN..	11	732	1,126	0.1	0.2
403 SALVATION ARMY	12	674	3,007	0.1	0.4
413 S-D ADVENTISTS	108	21,834	26,320*	1.3	3.8
419 SO BAPT CONV..	75	15,208	18,404*	0.9	2.7
435 UNITARIAN-UNIV	14	1,941	2,457	0.1	0.4
443 UN C OF CHRIST	45	10,614	12,768*	0.6	1.8
449 UN METHODIST..	176	48,773	58,731	2.8	8.5
453 UN PRES CH USA	129	42,374	50,941*	2.4	7.4
467 WESLEYAN......	14	359	414	-	0.1
469 WISC EVAN LUTH	6	635	1,036	-	0.1
WASHINGTON	2,372	494,859	1,108,916*	32.5	100.0
019 AMER BAPT CONV	129	28,405	34,547*	1.0	3.1
029 AMER LUTH CH..	172	68,274	98,815	2.9	8.9
059 BAPT MISS ASSN	4	161	194*	-	-
081 CATHOLIC......	291	0	366,087	10.7	33.0
093 CR CH (DISC)..	87	18,187	22,114*	0.6	2.0
097 CR C AND C CR.	58	6,224	7,554*	0.2	0.7

*Total adherents estimated from known number of communicant, confirmed, full members.

—Represents a percent less than 0.1.

Percentages may not total due to rounding.

Table 2. Churches and Church Membership by Region, State and Denomination: 1971

County and Denomination	Number of churches	Communicant, confirmed, full members	Total adherents		
			Number	Percent of total population	Percent of total adherents
105 CHRISTIAN REF.	25	4,815	9,230	0.3	0.8
121 CH GOD (ABR)..	3	160	191*	-	-
123 CH GOD (ANDER)	47	3,875	9,001	0.3	0.8
127 CH GOD (CLEVE)	36	1,637	2,007*	0.1	0.2
151 L-D SAINTS....	C	0	66,109	1.9	6.0
157 CH OF BRETHREN	13	2,301	2,779*	0.1	0.3
165 CH OF NAZARENE	121	12,010	26,323	0.8	2.4
175 CONG CR CH....	6	1,232	1,496*	-	0.1
193 EPISCOPAL.....	121	38,588	56,319	1.7	5.1
197 EVAN CH OF NA.	13	1,247	1,521*	-	0.1
201 EVAN COV CH AM	29	3,605	4,395*	0.1	0.4
221 FREE METH C NA	53	4,477	6,008	0.2	0.5
223 FREE WILL BAPT	7	265	323*	-	-
226 FRIENDS-USA...	18	1,635	2,005*	0.1	0.2
281 LUTH CH AMER..	84	29,397	43,549	1.3	3.9
283 LUTH--MO SYNOD	101	30,391	45,727	1.3	4.1
285 MENNONITE CH..	2	33	42*	-	-
287 MENN GEN CONF.	6	530	657*	-	0.1
313 NO AM BAPT GC.	11	1,398	1,688*	-	0.2
335 ORTH PRESB CH.	1	33	58	-	-
349 PENT HOLINESS.	7	200	245*	-	-
353 PLY BRETHREN..	20	986	1,716	0.1	0.2
371 REF CH IN AM..	8	1,833	11,332	0.3	1.0
381 REF PRES-EVAN.	7	1,042	1,269	-	0.1
403 SALVATION ARMY	20	1,112	5,396	0.2	0.5
413 S-D ADVENTISTS	124	21,173	25,664*	0.8	2.3
415 S-D BAPTIST GC	1	49	59*	-	-
419 SO BAPT CONV..	129	25,144	30,752*	0.9	2.8
435 UNITARIAN-UNIV	23	2,402	3,426	0.1	0.3
443 UN C OF CHRIST	98	20,655	25,032*	0.7	2.3
449 UN METHODIST..	268	97,135	116,723	3.4	10.5
453 UN PRES CH USA	201	62,396	75,818*	2.2	6.8
467 WESLEYAN......	8	215	248	-	-
469 WISC EVAN LUTH	20	1,637	2,497	0.1	0.2

County and Denomination	Number of churches	Communicant, confirmed, full members	Total adherents		
			Number	Percent of total population	Percent of total adherents

*Total adherents estimated from known number of communicant, confirmed, full members.

—Represents a percent less than 0.1.

Percentages may not total due to rounding.

Table 3. Churches and Church Membership by State, County and Denomination: 1971

County and Denomination	Number of churches	Communicant, confirmed, full members	Total adherents: Number	Total adherents: Percent of total population	Total adherents: Percent of total adherents
ALABAMA					
THE STATE.....	6,078	1,277,309	1,645,794*	47.8	100.0
AUTAUGA	40	7,550	9,814*	40.1	100.0
081 CATHOLIC......	1	0	455	1.9	4.6
093 CR CH (DISC)..	1	20	26*	0.1	0.3
097 CR C AND C CR.	1	81	104*	0.4	1.1
123 CH GOD (ANDER)	1	25	60	0.2	0.6
127 CH GOD (CLEVE)	3	142	183*	0.7	1.9
193 EPISCOPAL.....	1	107	151	0.6	1.5
283 LUTH--MO SYNOD	1	77	125	0.5	1.3
357 PRESB CH US...	2	384	494*	2.0	5.0
419 SO BAPT CONV..	20	5,190	6,678*	27.3	68.0
449 UN METHODIST..	9	1,524	1,538	6.3	15.7
BALDWIN	118	20,281	28,151*	47.4	100.0
081 CATHOLIC......	11	C	3,153	5.3	11.2
093 CR CH (DISC)..	3	328	406*	0.7	1.4
127 CH GOD (CLEVE)	11	607	751*	1.3	2.7
165 CH OF NAZARENE	1	38	83	0.1	0.3
193 EPISCOPAL.....	7	910	1,304	2.2	4.6
201 EVAN COV CH AM	2	128	158*	0.3	0.6
226 FRIENDS-USA...	1	42	52*	0.1	0.2
281 LUTH CH AMER..	1	34	42	0.1	0.1
283 LUTH--MO SYNOD	5	874	1,259	2.1	4.5
349 PENT HOLINESS.	5	265	328*	0.6	1.2
357 PRESB CH US...	9	1,238	1,531*	2.6	5.4
413 S-D ADVENTISTS	1	16	20*	-	0.1
419 SO BAPT CONV..	41	12,223	15,121*	25.5	53.7
435 UNITARIAN-UNIV	1	10	10	-	-
449 UN METHODIST..	19	3,568	3,933	6.6	14.0
BARBOUR	56	9,075	11,081*	49.2	100.0
081 CATHOLIC......	1	0	135	0.6	1.2
127 CH GOD (CLEVE)	1	41	51*	0.2	0.5
193 EPISCOPAL.....	2	1,339	1,765	7.8	15.9
357 PRESB CH US...	8	664	824*	3.7	7.4
419 SO BAPT CONV..	25	4,965	6,161*	27.3	55.6
443 UN C OF CHRIST	1	42	52*	0.2	0.5
449 UN METHODIST..	18	2,024	2,093	9.3	18.9
BIBB	53	6,290	7,770*	56.3	100.0
081 CATHOLIC......	1	0	37	0.3	0.5
127 CH GOD (CLEVE)	1	24	30*	0.2	0.4
165 CH OF NAZARENE	2	70	125	0.9	1.6
185 CUMBER PRESB..	1	69	86*	0.6	1.1
357 PRESB CH US...	2	184	230*	1.7	3.0
419 SO BAPT CONV..	35	5,099	6,361*	46.1	81.9
449 UN METHODIST..	10	827	880	6.4	11.3
453 UN PRES CH USA	1	17	21*	0.2	0.3
BLOUNT	107	15,503	18,320*	68.2	100.0
127 CH GOD (CLEVE)	3	178	216*	0.8	1.2
157 CH OF BRETHREN	1	45	55*	0.2	0.3
165 CH OF NAZARENE	3	146	181	0.7	1.0
185 CUMBER PRESB..	3	220	267*	1.0	1.5
419 SO BAPT CONV..	68	11,754	14,292*	53.2	78.0
449 UN METHODIST..	29	3,160	3,309	12.3	18.1
BULLOCK	19	2,335	2,859*	24.2	100.0
081 CATHOLIC......	1	0	18	0.2	0.6
349 PENT HOLINESS.	1	16	20*	0.2	0.7
357 PRESB CH US...	2	149	188*	1.6	6.6
419 SO BAPT CONV..	8	1,727	2,178*	18.4	76.2
449 UN METHODIST..	7	443	455	3.8	15.9
BUTLER	68	8,372	9,974*	45.3	100.0
081 CATHOLIC......	1	0	59	0.3	0.6
093 CR CH (DISC)..	1	25	31*	0.1	0.3
127 CH GOD (CLEVE)	2	91	112*	0.5	1.1
193 EPISCOPAL.....	1	106	145	0.7	1.5
349 PENT HOLINESS.	5	107	131*	0.6	1.3
357 PRESB CH US...	2	234	287*	1.3	2.9
413 S-D ADVENTISTS	1	31	38*	0.2	0.4
419 SO BAPT CONV..	33	5,789	7,099*	32.3	71.2
449 UN METHODIST..	22	1,989	2,072	9.4	20.8
CALHOUN	152	41,580	51,410*	49.9	100.0
029 AMER LUTH CH..	1	65	120	0.1	0.2
081 CATHOLIC......	4	0	960	0.9	1.9
093 CR CH (DISC)..	1	160	195*	0.2	0.4
097 CR C AND C CR.	2	184	225*	0.2	0.4
123 CH GOD (ANDER)	3	64	183	0.2	0.4
127 CH GOD (CLEVE)	10	907	1,107*	1.1	2.2
165 CH OF NAZARENE	1	51	123	0.1	0.2
193 EPISCOPAL.....	2	490	576	0.6	1.1
281 LUTH CH AMER..	1	117	139	0.1	0.3
349 PENT HOLINESS.	1	87	106*	0.1	0.2
357 PRESB CH US...	7	1,331	1,625*	1.6	3.2
403 SALVATION ARMY	1	133	771	0.7	1.5
413 S-D ADVENTISTS	1	38	46*	-	0.1
419 SO BAPT CONV..	85	30,275	36,957*	35.8	71.9
449 UN METHODIST..	31	7,562	8,135	7.9	15.8
453 UN PRES CH USA	1	116	142*	0.1	0.3
CHAMBERS	96	18,053	22,052*	60.7	100.0
081 CATHOLIC......	1	0	126	0.3	0.6
093 CR CH (DISC)..	6	563	692*	1.9	3.1
097 CR C AND C CR.	1	130	160*	0.4	0.7
123 CH GOD (ANDER)	3	152	369	1.0	1.7
127 CH GOD (CLEVE)	1	96	118*	0.3	0.5
165 CH OF NAZARENE	6	654	1,198	3.3	5.4
357 PRESB CH US...	3	46	57*	0.2	0.3
419 SO BAPT CONV..	37	10,214	12,556*	34.5	56.9
443 UN C OF CHRIST	4	787	967*	2.7	4.4
449 UN METHODIST..	34	5,411	5,809	16.0	26.3
CHEROKEE	78	8,862	10,272*	65.8	100.0
127 CH GOD (CLEVE)	1	37	44*	0.3	0.4
357 PRESB CH US...	1	48	58*	0.4	0.6
419 SO BAPT CONV..	48	6,444	7,735*	49.6	75.3
449 UN METHODIST..	28	2,333	2,435	15.6	23.7
CHILTON	80	13,746	16,561*	65.8	100.0
081 CATHOLIC......	1	0	59	0.2	0.4
123 CH GOD (ANDER)	1	30	80	0.3	0.5
127 CH GOD (CLEVE)	6	413	501*	2.0	3.0
165 CH OF NAZARENE	1	9	22	0.1	0.1
193 EPISCOPAL.....	1	13	14	0.1	0.1
283 LUTH--MO SYNOD	1	2	5	-	-
357 PRESB CH US...	1	71	86*	0.3	0.5
413 S-D ADVENTISTS	1	104	126*	0.5	0.8
419 SO BAPT CONV..	53	11,748	14,238*	56.5	86.0
449 UN METHODIST..	14	1,356	1,430	5.7	8.6
CHOCTAW	61	5,183	6,357*	38.3	100.0
081 CATHOLIC......	1	C	140	0.8	2.2
123 CH GOD (ANDER)	1	5	9	0.1	0.1
127 CH GOD (CLEVE)	1	72	91*	0.5	1.4
165 CH OF NAZARENE	1	12	18	0.1	0.3
283 LUTH--MO SYNOD	1	34	46	0.3	0.7
349 PENT HOLINESS.	2	43	55*	0.3	0.9
357 PRESB CH US...	1	37	47*	0.3	0.7
413 S-D ADVENTISTS	1	35	44*	0.3	0.7
419 SO BAPT CONV..	29	3,543	4,492*	27.1	70.7
449 UN METHODIST..	23	1,402	1,415	8.5	22.3
CLARKE	78	11,244	14,091*	52.7	100.0
081 CATHOLIC......	3	0	187	0.7	1.3
123 CH GOD (ANDER)	1	15	36	0.1	0.3
127 CH GOD (CLEVE)	1	71	91*	0.3	0.6
165 CH OF NAZARENE	1	34	60	0.2	0.4
193 EPISCOPAL.....	1	46	52	0.2	0.4
283 LUTH--MO SYNOD	1	20	45	0.2	0.3
357 PRESB CH US...	1	81	103*	0.4	0.7
413 S-D ADVENTISTS	1	9	11*	-	0.1
419 SO BAPT CONV..	45	8,598	10,972*	41.1	77.9
449 UN METHODIST..	23	2,370	2,534	9.5	18.0
CLAY	64	7,930	9,415*	74.5	100.0
127 CH GOD (CLEVE)	1	25	31*	0.2	0.3
193 EPISCOPAL.....	1	19	29	0.2	0.3
349 PENT HOLINESS.	1	20	24*	0.2	0.3
419 SO BAPT CONV..	44	5,915	7,244*	57.3	76.9
449 UN METHODIST..	17	1,951	2,087	16.5	22.2
CLEBURNE	53	7,569	9,063*	82.4	100.0
127 CH GOD (CLEVE)	2	70	86*	0.8	0.9
419 SO BAPT CONV..	37	6,149	7,569*	68.8	83.5
449 UN METHODIST..	14	1,350	1,408	12.8	15.5
COFFEE	67	16,743	20,602*	59.1	100.0
081 CATHOLIC......	1	0	400	1.1	1.9
127 CH GOD (CLEVE)	2	116	143*	0.4	0.7
193 EPISCOPAL.....	1	135	185	0.5	0.9
283 LUTH--MO SYNOD	1	103	152	0.4	0.7
357 PRESB CH US...	2	247	305*	0.9	1.5
419 SO BAPT CONV..	46	13,172	16,269*	46.7	79.0
449 UN METHODIST..	14	2,970	3,148	9.0	15.3
COLBERT	78	19,042	23,642*	47.6	100.0
059 BAPT MISS ASSN	1	110	136*	0.3	0.6
081 CATHOLIC......	1	0	656	1.3	2.8
093 CR CH (DISC)..	1	120	149*	0.3	0.6
123 CH GOD (ANDER)	1	105	225	0.5	1.0
127 CH GOD (CLEVE)	4	223	276*	0.6	1.2
165 CH OF NAZARENE	4	329	568	1.1	2.4
185 CUMBER PRESB..	7	490	607*	1.2	2.6
193 EPISCOPAL.....	1	193	230	0.5	1.0
283 LUTH--MO SYNOD	1	58	80	0.2	0.3
357 PRESB CH US...	2	555	688*	1.4	2.9
381 REF PRES-EVAN.	1	22	22	-	0.1
413 S-D ADVENTISTS	1	78	97*	0.2	0.4
419 SO BAPT CONV..	34	12,333	15,290*	30.8	64.7
449 UN METHODIST..	17	4,277	4,433	8.9	18.8
453 UN PRES CH USA	2	149	185*	0.4	0.8
CONECUH	54	5,720	6,744*	43.1	100.0

*Total adherents estimated from known number of communicant, confirmed, full members.

—Represents a percent less than 0.1.

Percentages may not total due to rounding.

Table 3. Churches and Church Membership by State, County and Denomination: 1971

County and Denomination	Number of churches	Communicant, confirmed, full members	Total adherents		
			Number	Percent of total population	Percent of total adherents
059 BAPT MISS ASSN	1	10	12*	0.1	0.2
349 PENT HOLINESS.	3	81	101*	0.6	1.5
357 PRESB CH US...	1	69	86*	0.5	1.3
419 SO BAPT CONV..	28	3,868	4,800*	30.7	71.2
449 UN METHODIST..	21	1,692	1,745	11.2	25.9
COOSA	49	5,278	6,265*	58.8	100.0
059 BAPT MISS ASSN	1	16	20*	0.2	0.3
123 CH GOD (ANDER)	1	19	64	0.6	1.0
127 CH GOD (CLEVE)	2	134	166*	1.6	2.6
357 PRESB CH US...	5	204	253*	2.4	4.0
419 SO BAPT CONV..	22	3,114	3,855*	36.2	61.5
449 UN METHODIST..	18	1,791	1,907	17.9	30.4
COVINGTON	92	17,487	20,765*	60.9	100.0
055 AS REF PRES CH	1	98	118*	0.3	0.6
081 CATHOLIC......	1	0	111	0.3	0.5
127 CH GOD (CLEVE)	6	179	215*	0.6	1.0
193 EPISCOPAL.....	1	40	41	0.1	0.2
283 LUTH--MO SYNOD	1	33	39	0.1	0.2
349 PENT HOLINESS.	2	48	58*	0.2	0.3
357 PRESB CH US...	2	310	373*	1.1	1.8
413 S-D ADVENTISTS	1	36	43*	0.1	0.2
419 SO BAPT CONV..	59	14,125	16,993*	49.9	81.8
443 UN C OF CHRIST	2	139	167*	0.5	0.8
449 UN METHODIST..	16	2,479	2,607	7.6	12.6
CRENSHAW	49	5,335	6,169*	46.8	100.0
093 CR CH (DISC)..	1	23	28*	0.2	0.5
127 CH GOD (CLEVE)	2	43	52*	0.4	0.8
419 SO BAPT CONV..	29	3,941	4,727*	35.8	76.6
443 UN C OF CHRIST	2	15	18*	0.1	0.3
449 UN METHODIST..	15	1,313	1,344	10.2	21.8
CULLMAN	167	30,196	37,693*	71.9	100.0
081 CATHOLIC......	2	0	1,233	2.4	3.3
093 CR CH (DISC)..	1	61	74*	0.1	0.2
097 CR C AND C CR.	1	13	16*	-	-
123 CH GOD (ANDER)	1	100	254	0.5	0.7
127 CH GOD (CLEVE)	9	604	736*	1.4	2.0
165 CH OF NAZARENE	1	168	236	0.4	0.6
185 CUMBER PRESB..	8	636	775*	1.5	2.1
193 EPISCOPAL.....	1	112	147	0.3	0.4
281 LUTH CH AMER..	1	168	248	0.5	0.7
283 LUTH--MO SYNOD	2	862	1,140	2.2	3.0
357 PRESB CH US...	1	182	222*	0.4	0.6
413 S-D ADVENTISTS	1	73	89*	0.2	0.2
419 SO BAPT CONV..	104	22,847	27,829*	53.1	73.8
443 UN C OF CHRIST	3	504	614*	1.2	1.6
449 UN METHODIST..	31	3,866	4,080	7.8	10.8
DALE	67	13,944	17,004*	32.1	100.0
081 CATHOLIC......	1	0	456	0.9	2.7
127 CH GOD (CLEVE)	1	57	71*	0.1	0.4
165 CH OF NAZARENE	1	49	65	0.1	0.4
193 EPISCOPAL.....	1	60	81	0.2	0.5
283 LUTH--MO SYNOD	1	83	112	0.2	0.7
357 PRESB CH US...	2	231	286*	0.5	1.7
413 S-D ADVENTISTS	1	75	93*	0.2	0.5
419 SO BAPT CONV..	32	9,600	11,905*	22.5	70.0
435 UNITARIAN-UNIV	1	30	30	0.1	0.2
449 UN METHODIST..	26	3,759	3,905	7.4	23.0
DALLAS	63	14,170	18,716*	33.8	100.0
055 AS REF PRES CH	1	44	56*	0.1	0.3
081 CATHOLIC......	2	0	754	1.4	4.0
093 CR CH (DISC)..	1	109	139*	0.3	0.7
097 CR C AND C CR.	3	500	638*	1.2	3.4
123 CH GOD (ANDER)	1	27	77	0.1	0.4
127 CH GOD (CLEVE)	4	137	175*	0.3	0.9
165 CH OF NAZARENE	1	130	266	0.5	1.4
193 EPISCOPAL.....	2	494	618	1.1	3.3
283 LUTH--MO SYNOD	3	264	400	0.7	2.1
357 PRESB CH US...	10	1,312	1,673*	3.0	8.9
403 SALVATION ARMY	1	53	213	0.4	1.1
413 S-D ADVENTISTS	2	171	218*	0.4	1.2
419 SO BAPT CONV..	20	8,629	11,002*	19.9	58.8
449 UN METHODIST..	12	2,300	2,487	4.5	13.3
DE KALB	134	21,322	24,996*	59.5	100.0
081 CATHOLIC......	1	0	60	0.1	0.2
123 CH GOD (ANDER)	1	27	72	0.2	0.3
127 CH GOD (CLEVE)	15	855	1,028*	2.4	4.1
193 EPISCOPAL.....	1	39	69	0.2	0.3
357 PRESB CH US...	3	103	124*	0.3	0.5
419 SO BAPT CONV..	72	15,716	18,902*	45.0	75.6
449 UN METHODIST..	41	4,582	4,741	11.3	19.0
ELMORE	73	13,632	16,379*	48.8	100.0
059 BAPT MISS ASSN	1	83	103*	0.3	0.6
081 CATHOLIC......	1	0	51	0.2	0.3
123 CH GOD (ANDER)	1	15	35	0.1	0.2
127 CH GOD (CLEVE)	3	167	207*	0.6	1.3
193 EPISCOPAL.....	2	95	135	0.4	0.8
357 PRESB CH US...	3	245	303*	0.9	1.8
419 SO BAPT CONV..	39	10,034	12,422*	37.0	75.8
449 UN METHODIST..	23	2,993	3,123	9.3	19.1

County and Denomination	Number of churches	Communicant, confirmed, full members	Total adherents		
			Number	Percent of total population	Percent of total adherents
ESCAMBIA	79	11,944	16,283*	46.6	100.0
081 CATHOLIC......	3	0	485	1.4	3.0
127 CH GOD (CLEVE)	4	127	157*	0.4	1.0
165 CH OF NAZARENE	2	96	203	0.6	1.2
193 EPISCOPAL.....	3	234	323	0.9	2.0
283 LUTH--MO SYNOD	1	112	226	0.6	1.4
285 MENNONITE CH..	7	108	133*	0.4	0.8
349 PENT HOLINESS.	7	299	369*	1.1	2.3
357 PRESB CH US...	2	298	368*	1.1	2.3
371 REF CH IN AM..	1	49	65	0.2	0.4
413 S-D ADVENTISTS	1	57	70*	0.2	0.4
419 SO BAPT CONV..	33	8,241	10,167*	29.1	62.4
435 UNITARIAN-UNIV	1	44	54	0.2	0.3
449 UN METHODIST..	14	2,279	3,663	10.5	22.5
ETOWAH	168	48,239	58,242*	61.9	100.0
081 CATHOLIC......	2	0	913	1.0	1.6
093 CR CH (DISC)..	1	101	122*	0.1	0.2
123 CH GOD (ANDER)	1	30	61	0.1	0.1
127 CH GOD (CLEVE)	15	1,221	1,479*	1.6	2.5
165 CH OF NAZARENE	1	88	144	0.2	0.2
185 CUMBER PRESB..	4	846	1,025*	1.1	1.8
193 EPISCOPAL.....	2	323	395	0.4	0.7
283 LUTH--MO SYNOD	2	163	252	0.3	0.4
357 PRESB CH US...	4	958	1,160*	1.2	2.0
403 SALVATION ARMY	1	76	340	0.4	0.6
413 S-D ADVENTISTS	2	130	157*	0.2	0.3
419 SO BAPT CONV..	94	34,249	41,483*	44.1	71.2
449 UN METHODIST..	39	10,054	10,711	11.4	18.4
FAYETTE	52	6,070	7,112*	43.8	100.0
127 CH GOD (CLEVE)	2	156	188*	1.2	2.6
165 CH OF NAZARENE	3	87	173	1.1	2.4
193 EPISCOPAL.....	1	10	14	0.1	0.2
419 SO BAPT CONV..	34	4,344	5,234*	32.2	73.6
449 UN METHODIST..	12	1,473	1,503	9.2	21.1
FRANKLIN	50	8,204	9,639*	40.3	100.0
127 CH GOD (CLEVE)	2	137	165*	0.7	1.7
165 CH OF NAZARENE	1	53	82	0.3	0.9
185 CUMBER PRESB..	1	26	31*	0.1	0.3
357 PRESB CH US...	1	96	116*	0.5	1.2
413 S-D ADVENTISTS	1	24	29*	0.1	0.3
419 SO BAPT CONV..	32	6,459	7,781*	32.5	80.7
449 UN METHODIST..	11	1,392	1,415	5.9	14.7
453 UN PRES CH USA	1	17	20*	0.1	0.2
GENEVA	62	10,952	12,890*	58.8	100.0
127 CH GOD (CLEVE)	1	100	121*	0.6	0.9
357 PRESB CH US...	3	124	150*	0.7	1.2
419 SO BAPT CONV..	37	8,173	9,911*	45.2	76.9
449 UN METHODIST..	21	2,555	2,708	12.4	21.0
GREENE	30	2,528	3,066*	28.8	100.0
081 CATHOLIC......	1	0	53	0.5	1.7
093 CR CH (DISC)..	3	135	170*	1.6	5.5
123 CH GOD (ANDER)	1	35	70	0.7	2.3
185 CUMBER PRESB..	2	183	231*	2.2	7.5
193 EPISCOPAL.....	3	121	143	1.3	4.7
357 PRESB CH US...	2	79	100*	0.9	3.3
419 SO BAPT CONV..	6	1,024	1,292*	12.1	42.1
449 UN METHODIST..	12	951	1,007	9.5	32.8
HALE	45	4,672	5,700*	35.9	100.0
081 CATHOLIC......	1	0	38	0.2	0.7
123 CH GOD (ANDER)	3	38	96	0.6	1.7
165 CH OF NAZARENE	2	35	65	0.4	1.1
193 EPISCOPAL.....	1	82	134	0.8	2.4
357 PRESB CH US...	6	443	557*	3.5	9.8
419 SO BAPT CONV..	15	2,560	3,219*	20.3	56.5
449 UN METHODIST..	17	1,514	1,591	10.0	27.9
HENRY	28	5,880	6,936*	52.3	100.0
419 SO BAPT CONV..	22	4,761	5,765*	43.5	83.1
449 UN METHODIST..	6	1,119	1,171	8.8	16.9
HOUSTON	80	25,077	31,391*	55.5	100.0
081 CATHOLIC......	1	0	812	1.4	2.6
093 CR CH (DISC)..	1	83	103*	0.2	0.3
123 CH GOD (ANDER)	1	30	85	0.2	0.3
127 CH GOD (CLEVE)	3	136	169*	0.3	0.5
165 CH OF NAZARENE	1	56	134	0.2	0.4
193 EPISCOPAL.....	1	412	515	0.9	1.6
283 LUTH--MO SYNOD	1	93	132	0.2	0.4
357 PRESB CH US...	4	788	977*	1.7	3.1
403 SALVATION ARMY	1	81	268	0.5	0.9
413 S-D ADVENTISTS	2	259	321*	0.6	1.0
419 SO BAPT CONV..	44	18,239	22,612*	40.0	72.0
449 UN METHODIST..	20	4,900	5,263	9.3	16.8
JACKSON	108	14,558	16,541*	42.2	100.0
081 CATHOLIC......	1	0	160	0.4	1.0
127 CH GOD (CLEVE)	8	568	694*	1.8	4.2
165 CH OF NAZARENE	3	95	190	0.5	1.1
185 CUMBER PRESB..	4	521	636*	1.6	3.8

*Total adherents estimated from known number of communicant, confirmed, full members.

—Represents a percent less than 0.1.

Percentages may not total due to rounding.

Table 3. Churches and Church Membership by State, County and Denomination: 1971

County and Denomination	Number of churches	Communicant, confirmed, full members	Total adherents: Number	Total adherents: Percent of total population	Total adherents: Percent of total adherents
193 EPISCOPAL.....	1	32	54	0.1	0.3
283 LUTH--MO SYNOD	1	52	98	0.2	0.6
413 S-D ADVENTISTS	2	252	308*	0.8	1.9
415 S-D BAPTIST GC	1	52	64*	0.2	0.4
419 SO BAPT CONV..	57	10,068	12,299*	31.4	74.4
449 UN METHODIST..	29	2,903	2,020	5.2	12.2
453 UN PRES CH USA	1	15	18*	-	0.1
JEFFERSON	602	212,725	285,950*	44.3	100.0
029 AMER LUTH CH..	2	143	225	-	0.1
059 BAPT MISS ASSN	2	187	226*	-	0.1
081 CATHOLIC......	37	0	24,159	3.7	8.4
093 CR CH (DISC)..	9	1,708	2,068*	0.3	0.7
097 CR C AND C CR.	4	138	167*	-	0.1
123 CH GOD (ANDER)	17	1,117	2,594	0.4	0.9
127 CH GOD (CLEVE)	50	4,029	4,878*	0.8	1.7
157 CH OF BRETHREN	1	35	42*	-	-
165 CH OF NAZARENE	10	1,192	1,680	0.3	0.6
185 CUMBER PRESB..	9	1,555	1,883*	0.3	0.7
193 EPISCOPAL.....	16	6,145	9,368	1.5	3.3
221 FREE METH C NA	1	5	10	-	-
281 LUTH CH AMER..	2	630	860	0.1	0.3
283 LUTH--MO SYNOD	9	1,481	2,179	0.3	0.8
285 MENNONITE CH..	1	4	5*	-	-
349 PENT HOLINESS.	6	488	591*	0.1	0.2
353 PLY BRETHREN..	1	40	80	-	-
357 PRESB CH US...	28	10,312	12,485*	1.9	4.4
403 SALVATION ARMY	3	254	1,054	0.2	0.4
413 S-D ADVENTISTS	7	1,642	1,988*	0.3	0.7
419 SO BAPT CONV..	269	151,377	183,279*	28.4	64.1
435 UNITARIAN-UNIV	1	175	305	-	0.1
443 UN C OF CHRIST	2	284	344*	0.1	0.1
449 UN METHODIST..	99	25,365	30,126	4.7	10.5
453 UN PRES CH USA	15	4,377	5,299*	0.8	1.9
469 WISC EVAN LUTH	1	42	55	-	-
LAMAR	56	5,452	6,215*	43.4	100.0
059 BAPT MISS ASSN	1	83	100*	0.7	1.6
127 CH GOD (CLEVE)	6	203	245*	1.7	3.9
165 CH OF NAZARENE	2	48	58	0.4	0.9
185 CUMBER PRESB..	1	105	127*	0.9	2.0
419 SO BAPT CONV..	24	3,093	3,733*	26.0	60.1
449 UN METHODIST..	22	1,920	1,952	13.6	31.4
LAUDERDALE	100	21,542	26,742*	39.3	100.0
081 CATHOLIC......	2	0	1,344	2.0	5.0
093 CR CH (DISC)..	1	174	214*	0.3	0.8
123 CH GOD (ANDER)	1	24	56	0.1	0.2
127 CH GOD (CLEVE)	2	65	80*	0.1	0.3
165 CH OF NAZARENE	3	289	508	0.7	1.9
185 CUMBER PRESB..	10	1,090	1,338*	2.0	5.0
193 EPISCOPAL.....	2	525	689	1.0	2.6
281 LUTH CH AMER..	1	82	127	0.2	0.5
283 LUTH--MO SYNOD	1	81	104	0.2	0.4
357 PRESB CH US...	2	863	1,060*	1.6	4.0
403 SALVATION ARMY	1	52	188	0.3	0.7
413 S-D ADVENTISTS	1	15	18*	-	0.1
419 SO BAPT CONV..	34	10,150	12,463*	18.3	46.6
435 UNITARIAN-UNIV	1	19	32	-	0.1
449 UN METHODIST..	35	8,065	8,462	12.4	31.6
453 UN PRES CH USA	3	48	59*	0.1	0.2
LAWRENCE	51	9,109	11,157*	40.9	100.0
127 CH GOD (CLEVE)	1	132	168*	0.6	1.5
165 CH OF NAZARENE	1	55	88	0.3	0.8
185 CUMBER PRESB..	1	25	32*	0.1	0.3
357 PRESB CH US...	1	76	97*	0.4	0.9
419 SO BAPT CONV..	28	6,712	8,550*	31.3	76.6
443 UN C OF CHRIST	1	140	178*	0.7	1.6
449 UN METHODIST..	17	1,882	1,933	7.1	17.3
453 UN PRES CH USA	1	87	111*	0.4	1.0
LEE	69	18,545	22,673*	37.0	100.0
081 CATHOLIC......	2	0	852	1.4	3.8
093 CR CH (DISC)..	2	211	257*	0.4	1.1
123 CH GOD (ANDER)	2	53	116	0.2	0.5
127 CH GOD (CLEVE)	2	83	101*	0.2	0.4
165 CH OF NAZARENE	2	74	117	0.2	0.5
193 EPISCOPAL.....	3	422	572	0.9	2.5
283 LUTH--MO SYNOD	1	170	249	0.4	1.1
357 PRESB CH US...	2	904	1,103*	1.8	4.9
381 REF PRES-EVAN.	1	43	48	0.1	0.2
413 S-D ADVENTISTS	1	17	21*	-	0.1
419 SO BAPT CONV..	28	10,539	12,855*	21.0	56.7
435 UNITARIAN-UNIV	1	15	33	0.1	0.1
449 UN METHODIST..	22	6,014	6,349	10.4	28.0
LIMESTONE	60	10,982	13,969*	33.5	100.0
081 CATHOLIC......	2	0	217	0.5	1.6
093 CR CH (DISC)..	1	225	284*	0.7	2.0
123 CH GOD (ANDER)	3	291	728	1.7	5.2
127 CH GOD (CLEVE)	2	66	83*	0.2	0.6
165 CH OF NAZARENE	1	20	29	0.1	0.2
193 EPISCOPAL.....	1	143	198	0.5	1.4
413 S-D ADVENTISTS	1	55	69*	0.2	0.5
419 SO BAPT CONV..	25	6,660	8,394*	20.1	60.1
449 UN METHODIST..	20	3,087	3,419	8.2	24.5
453 UN PRES CH USA	4	435	548*	1.3	3.9
LOWNDES	36	2,192	2,722*	21.1	100.0
081 CATHOLIC......	1	0	47	0.4	1.7
093 CR CH (DISC)..	12	411	545*	4.2	20.0
193 EPISCOPAL.....	1	33	52	0.4	1.9
357 PRESB CH US...	3	124	164*	1.3	6.0
419 SO BAPT CONV..	9	841	1,115*	8.6	41.0
449 UN METHODIST..	10	783	799	6.2	29.4
MACON	29	3,633	4,713*	19.0	100.0
081 CATHOLIC......	1	0	558	2.2	11.8
093 CR CH (DISC)..	1	111	134*	0.5	2.8
193 EPISCOPAL.....	1	151	219	0.9	4.6
357 PRESB CH US...	5	321	386*	1.6	8.2
413 S-D ADVENTISTS	1	34	41*	0.2	0.9
419 SO BAPT CONV..	7	1,392	1,675*	6.7	35.5
449 UN METHODIST..	13	1,624	1,700	6.8	36.1
MADISON	164	55,912	78,822*	42.3	100.0
059 BAPT MISS ASSN	1	126	161*	0.1	0.2
081 CATHOLIC......	4	0	7,618	4.1	9.7
093 CR CH (DISC)..	2	735	937*	0.5	1.2
123 CH GOD (ANDER)	3	269	703	0.4	0.9
127 CH GOD (CLEVE)	7	824	1,051*	0.6	1.3
165 CH OF NAZARENE	3	305	560	0.3	0.7
185 CUMBER PRESB..	7	973	1,241*	0.7	1.6
193 EPISCOPAL.....	5	1,530	2,349	1.3	3.0
221 FREE METH C NA	1	24	38	-	-
281 LUTH CH AMER..	3	999	1,476	0.8	1.9
283 LUTH--MO SYNOD	2	600	960	0.5	1.2
349 PENT HOLINESS.	1	103	131*	0.1	0.2
353 PLY BRETHREN..	1	12	31	-	-
357 PRESB CH US...	6	2,391	3,050*	1.6	3.9
381 REF PRES-EVAN.	1	161	260	0.1	0.3
403 SALVATION ARMY	1	73	311	0.2	0.4
413 S-D ADVENTISTS	3	978	1,247*	0.7	1.6
419 SO BAPT CONV..	63	29,926	38,170*	20.5	48.4
435 UNITARIAN-UNIV	1	100	140	0.1	0.2
443 UN C OF CHRIST	1	93	119*	0.1	0.2
449 UN METHODIST..	41	14,133	16,278	8.7	20.7
453 UN PRES CH USA	6	1,540	1,964*	1.1	2.5
469 WISC EVAN LUTH	1	17	27	-	-
MARENGO	58	7,912	9,830*	41.3	100.0
081 CATHOLIC......	1	0	174	0.7	1.8
093 CR CH (DISC)..	1	60	76*	0.3	0.8
127 CH GOD (CLEVE)	3	77	97*	0.4	1.0
193 EPISCOPAL.....	2	225	260	1.1	2.6
353 PLY BRETHREN..	1	10	20	0.1	0.2
357 PRESB CH US...	4	162	205*	0.9	2.1
419 SO BAPT CONV..	29	5,582	7,062*	29.6	71.8
449 UN METHODIST..	16	1,776	1,911	8.0	19.4
453 UN PRES CH USA	1	20	25*	0.1	0.3
MARION	47	7,202	8,359*	35.1	100.0
059 BAPT MISS ASSN	2	133	161*	0.7	1.9
081 CATHOLIC......	1	0	75	0.3	0.9
127 CH GOD (CLEVE)	5	196	237*	1.0	2.8
419 SO BAPT CONV..	22	4,466	5,389*	22.7	64.5
449 UN METHODIST..	17	2,407	2,497	10.5	29.9
MARSHALL	123	27,514	32,853*	60.6	100.0
081 CATHOLIC......	1	0	190	0.4	0.6
123 CH GOD (ANDER)	1	31	102	0.2	0.3
127 CH GOD (CLEVE)	8	688	838*	1.5	2.6
165 CH OF NAZARENE	1	159	188	0.3	0.6
193 EPISCOPAL.....	1	151	215	0.4	0.7
221 FREE METH C NA	1	7	20	-	0.1
357 PRESB CH US...	2	480	585*	1.1	1.8
419 SO BAPT CONV..	77	20,640	25,150*	46.4	76.6
449 UN METHODIST..	31	5,358	5,565	10.3	16.9
MOBILE	259	89,735	140,866*	44.4	100.0
029 AMER LUTH CH..	1	91	123	-	0.1
059 BAPT MISS ASSN	6	1,195	1,497*	0.5	1.1
081 CATHOLIC......	37	0	28,054	8.8	19.9
093 CR CH (DISC)..	4	836	1,047*	0.3	0.7
097 CR C AND C CR.	4	110	138*	-	0.1
123 CH GOD (ANDER)	4	174	427	0.1	0.3
127 CH GOD (CLEVE)	20	2,316	2,902*	0.9	2.1
157 CH OF BRETHREN	1	93	117*	-	0.1
165 CH OF NAZARENE	6	405	727	0.2	0.5
193 EPISCOPAL.....	14	3,207	5,020	1.6	3.6
281 LUTH CH AMER..	2	358	475	0.1	0.3
283 LUTH--MO SYNOD	7	1,472	2,317	0.7	1.6
285 MENNONITE CH..	1	2	3*	-	-
349 PENT HOLINESS.	2	98	123*	-	0.1
353 PLY BRETHREN..	1	5	16	-	-
403 SALVATION ARMY	2	170	893	0.3	0.6
413 S-D ADVENTISTS	4	918	1,150*	0.4	0.8
419 SO BAPT CONV..	92	62,238	77,977*	24.6	55.4
435 UNITARIAN-UNIV	1	45	45	-	-
449 UN METHODIST..	50	16,002	17,815	5.6	12.6
MONROE	50	8,309	10,250*	49.1	100.0
081 CATHOLIC......	1	0	89	0.4	0.9
127 CH GOD (CLEVE)	1	9	11*	0.1	0.1
165 CH OF NAZARENE	2	54	91	0.4	0.9

*Total adherents estimated from known number of communicant, confirmed, full members.

—Represents a percent less than 0.1.

Percentages may not total due to rounding.

Table 3. Churches and Church Membership by State, County and Denomination: 1971

County and Denomination	Number of churches	Communicant, confirmed, full members	Total adherents: Number	Total adherents: Percent of total population	Total adherents: Percent of total adherents
193 EPISCOPAL.....	1	53	71	0.3	0.7
283 LUTH--MO SYNOD	1	144	245	1.2	2.4
357 PRESB CH US...	2	184	233*	1.1	2.3
419 SO BAPT CONV..	27	6,201	7,841*	37.5	76.5
449 UN METHODIST..	15	1,664	1,669	8.0	16.3
MONTGOMERY	126	52,971	71,125*	42.4	100.0
059 BAPT MISS ASSN	1	526	651*	0.4	0.9
081 CATHOLIC......	7	0	5,890	3.5	8.3
093 CR CH (DISC)..	5	836	1,034*	0.6	1.5
097 CR C AND C CR.	2	139	172*	0.1	0.2
123 CH GOD (ANDER)	2	100	217	0.1	0.3
127 CH GOD (CLEVE)	4	331	410*	0.2	0.6
165 CH OF NAZARENE	2	59	123	0.1	0.2
193 EPISCOPAL.....	6	2,344	3,052	1.8	4.3
281 LUTH CH AMER..	1	371	515	0.3	0.7
283 LUTH--MO SYNOD	4	567	853	0.5	1.2
349 PENT HOLINESS.	2	36	45*	-	0.1
357 PRESB CH US...	9	4,359	5,393*	3.2	7.6
403 SALVATION ARMY	2	93	1,095	0.7	1.5
413 S-D ADVENTISTS	2	585	724*	0.4	1.0
419 SO BAPT CONV..	40	29,652	36,686*	21.9	51.6
435 UNITARIAN-UNIV	1	47	66	-	0.1
443 UN C OF CHRIST	1	68	84*	0.1	0.1
449 UN METHODIST..	35	12,858	14,115	8.4	19.8
MORGAN	127	35,084	44,470*	57.5	100.0
081 CATHOLIC......	1	0	1,496	1.9	3.4
093 CR CH (DISC)..	5	489	614*	0.8	1.4
097 CR C AND C CR.	2	225	283*	0.4	0.6
123 CH GOD (ANDER)	3	225	533	0.7	1.2
127 CH GOD (CLEVE)	7	594	746*	1.0	1.7
165 CH OF NAZARENE	3	251	494	0.6	1.1
193 EPISCOPAL.....	1	529	646	0.8	1.5
283 LUTH--MO SYNOD	1	310	395	0.5	0.9
357 PRESB CH US...	4	718	902*	1.2	2.0
403 SALVATION ARMY	1	52	207	0.3	0.5
413 S-D ADVENTISTS	2	71	89*	0.1	0.2
419 SO BAPT CONV..	62	21,545	27,067*	35.0	60.9
449 UN METHODIST..	33	9,527	10,310	13.3	23.2
453 UN PRES CH USA	2	548	688*	0.9	1.5
PERRY	35	4,365	5,326*	34.6	100.0
097 CR C AND C CR.	1	150	187*	1.2	3.5
127 CH GOD (CLEVE)	3	74	92*	0.6	1.7
165 CH OF NAZARENE	1	53	68	0.4	1.3
193 EPISCOPAL.....	2	72	122	0.8	2.3
357 PRESB CH US...	2	287	358*	2.3	6.7
419 SO BAPT CONV..	16	2,841	3,547*	23.1	66.6
443 UN C OF CHRIST	1	18	22*	0.1	0.4
449 UN METHODIST..	9	870	930	6.0	17.5
PICKENS	61	7,903	9,357*	46.0	100.0
127 CH GOD (CLEVE)	3	90	111*	0.5	1.2
165 CH OF NAZARENE	1	38	38	0.2	0.4
357 PRESB CH US...	6	411	508*	2.5	5.4
419 SO BAPT CONV..	35	5,220	6,451*	31.7	68.9
449 UN METHODIST..	16	2,144	2,249	11.1	24.0
PIKE	58	10,229	12,154*	48.5	100.0
081 CATHOLIC......	1	0	118	0.5	1.0
127 CH GOD (CLEVE)	2	169	204*	0.8	1.7
193 EPISCOPAL.....	1	81	124	0.5	1.0
357 PRESB CH US...	3	303	365*	1.5	3.0
419 SO BAPT CONV..	34	7,773	9,364*	37.4	77.0
449 UN METHODIST..	17	1,903	1,979	7.9	16.3
RANDOLPH	86	10,195	11,558*	63.1	100.0
081 CATHOLIC......	1	0	30	0.2	0.3
093 CR CH (DISC)..	3	113	137*	0.7	1.2
097 CR C AND C CR.	3	149	180*	1.0	1.6
123 CH GOD (ANDER)	1	25	65	0.4	0.6
127 CH GOD (CLEVE)	3	170	206*	1.1	1.8
165 CH OF NAZARENE	2	58	111	0.6	1.0
193 EPISCOPAL.....	1	19	22	0.1	0.2
419 SO BAPT CONV..	32	4,847	5,865*	32.0	50.7
443 UN C OF CHRIST	8	503	609*	3.3	5.3
449 UN METHODIST..	32	4,311	4,333	23.6	37.5
RUSSELL	54	12,210	15,738*	34.7	100.0
081 CATHOLIC......	3	0	595	1.3	3.8
127 CH GOD (CLEVE)	2	85	107*	0.2	0.7
193 EPISCOPAL.....	1	13	18	-	0.1
357 PRESB CH US...	1	72	91*	0.2	0.6
403 SALVATION ARMY	1	33	201	0.4	1.3
413 S-D ADVENTISTS	1	37	47*	0.1	0.3
419 SO BAPT CONV..	28	9,576	12,078*	26.6	76.7
443 UN C OF CHRIST	2	128	161*	0.4	1.0
449 UN METHODIST..	15	2,266	2,440	5.4	15.5
ST CLAIR	98	14,601	17,842*	63.8	100.0
081 CATHOLIC......	1	0	45	0.2	0.3
127 CH GOD (CLEVE)	10	318	396*	1.4	2.2
165 CH OF NAZARENE	1	42	79	0.3	0.4
185 CUMBER PRESB..	3	171	213*	0.8	1.2
285 MENNONITE CH..	1	24	30*	0.1	0.2
357 PRESB CH US...	1	23	29*	0.1	0.2
413 S-D ADVENTISTS	2	77	96*	0.3	0.5
419 SO BAPT CONV..	63	11,845	14,740*	52.7	82.6
449 UN METHODIST..	14	2,007	2,097	7.5	11.8
453 UN PRES CH USA	2	94	117*	0.4	0.7
SHELBY	89	14,928	18,362*	48.3	100.0
081 CATHOLIC......	1	0	184	0.5	1.0
123 CH GOD (ANDER)	3	162	426	1.1	2.3
127 CH GOD (CLEVE)	9	395	490*	1.3	2.7
165 CH OF NAZARENE	1	78	123	0.3	0.7
185 CUMBER PRESB..	3	132	164*	0.4	0.9
193 EPISCOPAL.....	1	52	60	0.2	0.3
349 PENT HOLINESS.	1	33	41*	0.1	0.2
357 PRESB CH US...	2	148	184*	0.5	1.0
413 S-D ADVENTISTS	1	19	24*	0.1	0.1
419 SO BAPT CONV..	48	10,939	13,582*	35.7	74.0
449 UN METHODIST..	19	2,970	3,084	8.1	16.8
SUMTER	45	3,512	4,255*	25.1	100.0
081 CATHOLIC......	1	0	60	0.4	1.4
123 CH GOD (ANDER)	1	11	31	0.2	0.7
193 EPISCOPAL.....	1	55	83	0.5	2.0
357 PRESB CH US...	12	634	788*	4.6	18.5
419 SO BAPT CONV..	13	1,719	2,136*	12.6	50.2
449 UN METHODIST..	17	1,093	1,157	6.8	27.2
TALLADEGA	122	27,235	33,382*	51.1	100.0
081 CATHOLIC......	3	0	257	0.4	0.8
123 CH GOD (ANDER)	2	153	411	0.6	1.2
127 CH GOD (CLEVE)	12	780	974*	1.5	2.9
165 CH OF NAZARENE	3	292	393	0.6	1.2
193 EPISCOPAL.....	4	236	304	0.5	0.9
357 PRESB CH US...	4	864	1,079*	1.7	3.2
413 S-D ADVENTISTS	1	80	100*	0.2	0.3
419 SO BAPT CONV..	64	18,730	23,383*	35.8	70.0
443 UN C OF CHRIST	2	134	167*	0.3	0.5
449 UN METHODIST..	26	5,931	6,270	9.6	18.8
453 UN PRES CH USA	1	35	44*	0.1	0.1
TALLAPOOSA	86	16,436	19,486*	57.6	100.0
081 CATHOLIC......	1	0	125	0.4	0.6
093 CR CH (DISC)..	1	63	77*	0.2	0.4
123 CH GOD (ANDER)	2	30	85	0.3	0.4
127 CH GOD (CLEVE)	2	128	156*	0.5	0.8
165 CH OF NAZARENE	1	19	26	0.1	0.1
193 EPISCOPAL.....	1	86	106	0.3	0.5
357 PRESB CH US...	5	496	605*	1.8	3.1
419 SO BAPT CONV..	46	10,979	13,387*	39.6	68.7
435 UNITARIAN-UNIV	1	53	98	0.3	0.5
443 UN C OF CHRIST	2	110	134*	0.4	0.7
449 UN METHODIST..	24	4,472	4,687	13.9	24.1
TUSCALOOSA	161	42,317	52,399*	45.2	100.0
081 CATHOLIC......	2	0	2,030	1.7	3.9
093 CR CH (DISC)..	2	270	323*	0.3	0.6
123 CH GOD (ANDER)	2	67	159	0.1	0.3
127 CH GOD (CLEVE)	7	574	686*	0.6	1.3
165 CH OF NAZARENE	6	628	1,016	0.9	1.9
185 CUMBER PRESB..	2	151	180*	0.2	0.3
193 EPISCOPAL.....	3	869	1,434	1.2	2.7
283 LUTH--MO SYNOD	3	289	389	0.3	0.7
357 PRESB CH US...	6	1,872	2,237*	1.9	4.3
403 SALVATION ARMY	1	80	328	0.3	0.6
413 S-D ADVENTISTS	2	152	182*	0.2	0.3
419 SO BAPT CONV..	86	28,828	34,445*	29.7	65.7
435 UNITARIAN-UNIV	1	20	20	-	-
449 UN METHODIST..	38	8,517	8,970	7.7	17.1
WALKER	137	20,964	25,272*	44.9	100.0
029 AMER LUTH CH..	1	35	57	0.1	0.2
081 CATHOLIC......	1	0	125	0.2	0.5
093 CR CH (DISC)..	1	104	126*	0.2	0.5
123 CH GOD (ANDER)	3	116	278	0.5	1.1
127 CH GOD (CLEVE)	14	1,481	1,796*	3.2	7.1
165 CH OF NAZARENE	9	435	651	1.2	2.6
193 EPISCOPAL.....	1	64	74	0.1	0.3
413 S-D ADVENTISTS	1	18	22*	-	0.1
419 SO BAPT CONV..	80	15,343	18,604*	33.1	73.6
449 UN METHODIST..	26	3,368	3,539	6.3	14.0
WASHINGTON	59	6,128	7,556*	46.5	100.0
081 CATHOLIC......	1	0	45	0.3	0.6
127 CH GOD (CLEVE)	4	147	189*	1.2	2.5
157 CH OF BRETHREN	1	42	54*	0.3	0.7
357 PRESB CH US...	1	104	134*	0.8	1.8
419 SO BAPT CONV..	32	4,246	5,465*	33.6	72.3
449 UN METHODIST..	20	1,589	1,669	10.3	22.1
WILCOX	44	3,901	5,307*	32.6	100.0
055 AS REF PRES CH	2	178	232*	1.4	4.4
081 CATHOLIC......	1	0	40	0.2	0.8
123 CH GOD (ANDER)	1	8	38	0.2	0.7
127 CH GOD (CLEVE)	3	79	103*	0.6	1.9
283 LUTH--MO SYNOD	3	394	899	5.5	16.9
357 PRESB CH US...	3	183	239*	1.5	4.5
419 SO BAPT CONV..	14	2,011	2,625*	16.1	49.5

*Total adherents estimated from known number of communicant, confirmed, full members.

—Represents a percent less than 0.1.

Percentages may not total due to rounding.

Table 3. Churches and Church Membership by State, County and Denomination: 1971

County and Denomination	Number of churches	Communicant, confirmed, full members	Total adherents: Number	Total adherents: Percent of total population	Total adherents: Percent of total adherents
449 UN METHODIST..	14	886	920	5.6	17.3
453 UN PRES CH USA	3	162	211*	1.3	4.0
WINSTON	61	8,473	10,204*	61.3	100.0
029 AMER LUTH CH..	1	18	25	0.2	0.2
081 CATHOLIC......	1	0	63	0.4	0.6
127 CH GOD (CLEVE)	4	330	403*	2.4	3.9
165 CH OF NAZARENE	1	15	48	0.3	0.5
349 PENT HOLINESS.	1	28	34*	0.2	0.3
419 SO BAPT CONV..	43	6,894	8,429*	50.6	82.6
449 UN METHODIST..	10	1,188	1,202	7.2	11.8
CO DATA NOT AVAIL	207	20,527	32,915*	N/A	N/A
151 L-D SAINTS....	0	0	7,586	N/A	N/A
193 EPISCOPAL.....	1	37	125	N/A	N/A
223 FREE WILL BAPT	195	20,044	24,700*	N/A	N/A
349 PENT HOLINESS.	3	160	197*	N/A	N/A
467 WESLEYAN......	8	286	307	N/A	N/A

ALASKA

County and Denomination	Number of churches	Communicant, confirmed, full members	Total adherents: Number	Total adherents: Percent of total population	Total adherents: Percent of total adherents
THE STATE.....	326	37,055	111,252*	37.0	100.0
ALEUTIAN ISLANDS	2	0	1,000	12.4	100.0
081 CATHOLIC......	2	0	1,000	12.4	100.0
ANCHORAGE	77	16,566	51,929*	41.7	100.0
019 AMER BAPT CONV	1	142	184*	0.1	0.4
029 AMER LUTH CH..	3	1,145	1,885	1.5	3.6
059 BAPT MISS ASSN	2	66	85*	0.1	0.2
081 CATHOLIC......	11	0	28,494	22.9	54.9
093 CR CH (DISC)..	1	230	297*	0.2	0.6
105 CHRISTIAN REF.	1	89	139	0.1	0.3
123 CH GOD (ANDER)	2	234	517	0.4	1.0
127 CH GOD (CLEVE)	5	145	188*	0.2	0.4
165 CH OF NAZARENE	4	383	843	0.7	1.6
175 CONG CR CH....	1	175	226*	0.2	0.4
193 EPISCOPAL.....	3	710	867	0.7	1.7
201 EVAN COV CH AM	1	55	71*	0.1	0.1
221 FREE METH C NA	1	34	53	-	0.1
226 FRIENDS-USA...	2	272	352*	0.3	0.7
281 LUTH CH AMER..	1	488	780	0.6	1.5
283 LUTH--MO SYNOD	3	876	1,311	1.1	2.5
349 PENT HOLINESS.	1	31	40*	-	0.1
353 PLY BRETHREN..	2	42	110	0.1	0.2
403 SALVATION ARMY	1	48	333	0.3	0.6
413 S-D ADVENTISTS	2	349	451*	0.4	0.9
419 SO BAPT CONV..	15	7,681	9,934*	8.0	19.1
435 UNITARIAN-UNIV	1	300	360	0.3	0.7
449 UN METHODIST..	8	2,058	3,040	2.4	5.9
453 UN PRES CH USA	4	958	1,239*	1.0	2.4
469 WISC EVAN LUTH	1	55	130	0.1	0.3
ANGOON	3	147	414*	82.3	100.0
081 CATHOLIC......	0	0	9	1.8	2.2
403 SALVATION ARMY	2	118	368	73.2	88.9
453 UN PRES CH USA	1	29	37*	7.4	8.9
BARROW	4	820	1,219*	45.8	100.0
081 CATHOLIC......	1	0	50	1.9	4.1
453 UN PRES CH USA	3	820	1,169*	43.9	95.9
BETHEL	6	46	1,856*	24.5	100.0
081 CATHOLIC......	5	0	1,789	23.6	96.4
349 PENT HOLINESS.	1	46	67*	0.9	3.6
BRISTOL BAY BOROUGH	4	148	253*	22.1	100.0
081 CATHOLIC......	2	0	75	6.5	29.6
413 S-D ADVENTISTS	2	148	178*	15.5	70.4
BRISTOL BAY DIVISION	2	0	75	2.2	100.0
081 CATHOLIC......	2	0	75	2.2	100.0
CORDOVA-MC CARTHY	3	86	338*	18.2	100.0
019 AMER BAPT CONV	1	65	83*	4.5	24.6
081 CATHOLIC......	1	0	160	8.6	47.3
193 EPISCOPAL.....	1	21	95	5.1	28.1
FAIRBANKS	29	5,873	12,763*	27.8	100.0
029 AMER LUTH CH..	1	413	637	1.4	5.0
081 CATHOLIC......	2	0	4,500	9.8	35.3
097 CR C AND C CR.	1	50	64*	0.1	0.5
123 CH GOD (ANDER)	1	33	73	0.2	0.6
127 CH GOD (CLEVE)	1	22	28*	0.1	0.2
165 CH OF NAZARENE	2	170	471	1.0	3.7

County and Denomination	Number of churches	Communicant, confirmed, full members	Total adherents: Number	Total adherents: Percent of total population	Total adherents: Percent of total adherents
193 EPISCOPAL.....	1	520	520	1.1	4.1
226 FRIENDS-USA...	2	260	331*	0.7	2.6
283 LUTH--MO SYNOD	1	222	316	0.7	2.5
349 PENT HOLINESS.	1	8	10*	-	0.1
353 PLY BRETHREN..	1	50	160	0.3	1.3
403 SALVATION ARMY	1	23	383	0.8	3.0
413 S-D ADVENTISTS	1	71	90*	0.2	0.7
419 SO BAPT CONV..	9	2,999	3,814*	8.3	29.9
435 UNITARIAN-UNIV	1	23	23	0.1	0.2
449 UN METHODIST..	1	652	889	1.9	7.0
453 UN PRES CH USA	2	357	454*	1.0	3.6
HAINES	4	175	342*	22.7	100.0
081 CATHOLIC......	1	0	30	2.0	8.8
403 SALVATION ARMY	1	37	137	9.1	40.1
453 UN PRES CH USA	2	138	175*	11.6	51.2
JUNEAU	18	2,006	4,566*	33.7	100.0
081 CATHOLIC......	3	0	1,656	12.2	36.3
123 CH GOD (ANDER)	1	39	81	0.6	1.8
165 CH OF NAZARENE	1	27	81	0.6	1.8
193 EPISCOPAL.....	1	290	350	2.6	7.7
281 LUTH CH AMER..	2	447	677	5.0	14.8
283 LUTH--MO SYNOD	1	68	126	0.9	2.8
403 SALVATION ARMY	1	52	203	1.5	4.4
413 S-D ADVENTISTS	1	61	78*	0.6	1.7
419 SO BAPT CONV..	2	242	309*	2.3	6.8
435 UNITARIAN-UNIV	1	19	19	0.1	0.4
449 UN METHODIST..	2	341	449	3.3	9.8
453 UN PRES CH USA	2	420	537*	4.0	11.8
KENAI-COOK INLET	19	638	1,771*	12.4	100.0
081 CATHOLIC......	5	0	708	5.0	40.0
097 CR C AND C CR.	2	65	85*	0.6	4.8
123 CH GOD (ANDER)	1	24	89	0.6	5.0
127 CH GOD (CLEVE)	1	4	5*	-	0.3
165 CH OF NAZARENE	1	41	116	0.8	6.5
283 LUTH--MO SYNOD	1	99	195	1.4	11.0
449 UN METHODIST..	8	405	573	4.0	32.4
KETCHIKAN	14	1,689	3,563*	35.5	100.0
029 AMER LUTH CH..	1	256	424	4.2	11.9
081 CATHOLIC......	1	0	653	6.5	18.3
127 CH GOD (CLEVE)	2	91	117*	1.2	3.3
165 CH OF NAZARENE	1	27	100	1.0	2.8
193 EPISCOPAL.....	1	153	383	3.8	10.7
403 SALVATION ARMY	2	87	458	4.6	12.9
413 S-D ADVENTISTS	2	165	212*	2.1	6.0
419 SO BAPT CONV..	1	310	398*	4.0	11.2
449 UN METHODIST..	1	385	542	5.4	15.2
453 UN PRES CH USA	2	215	276*	2.7	7.7
KOBUK	16	2,695	4,249*	95.8	100.0
081 CATHOLIC......	1	0	214	4.8	5.0
193 EPISCOPAL.....	3	384	703	15.9	16.5
226 FRIENDS-USA...	10	1,961	2,827*	63.8	66.5
419 SO BAPT CONV..	2	350	505*	11.4	11.9
KODIAK	6	382	1,081*	11.5	100.0
019 AMER BAPT CONV	1	165	216*	2.3	20.0
029 AMER LUTH CH..	1	49	102	1.1	9.4
081 CATHOLIC......	1	0	450	4.8	41.6
123 CH GOD (ANDER)	1	30	80	0.9	7.4
193 EPISCOPAL.....	1	75	150	1.6	13.9
419 SO BAPT CONV..	1	63	83*	0.9	7.7
KUSKOKWIM	5	65	900	39.0	100.0
081 CATHOLIC......	4	0	745	32.3	82.8
193 EPISCOPAL.....	1	65	155	6.7	17.2
MATANUSKA-SUSITNA	12	578	2,042*	31.4	100.0
081 CATHOLIC......	3	0	1,126	17.3	55.1
097 CR C AND C CR.	2	25	31*	0.5	1.5
123 CH GOD (ANDER)	2	80	220	3.4	10.8
127 CH GOD (CLEVE)	1	22	28*	0.4	1.4
283 LUTH--MO SYNOD	1	134	239	3.7	11.7
413 S-D ADVENTISTS	1	52	65*	1.0	3.2
453 UN PRES CH USA	2	265	333*	5.1	16.3
NOME	15	1,130	2,942*	51.2	100.0
029 AMER LUTH CH..	4	468	997	17.3	33.9
081 CATHOLIC......	5	0	999	17.4	34.0
165 CH OF NAZARENE	1	28	66	1.1	2.2
353 PLY BRETHREN..	1	5	5	0.1	0.2
413 S-D ADVENTISTS	1	19	26*	0.5	0.9
449 UN METHODIST..	1	145	219	3.8	7.4
453 UN PRES CH USA	2	465	630*	11.0	21.4
OUTER KETCHIKAN	3	255	519*	31.0	100.0
175 CONG CR CH....	1	230	319*	19.0	61.5
403 SALVATION ARMY	2	25	200	11.9	38.5
PRINCE OF WALES	3	126	164*	7.8	100.0
127 CH GOD (CLEVE)	1	12	16*	0.8	9.8

*Total adherents estimated from known number of communicant, confirmed, full members.

—Represents a percent less than 0.1.

Percentages may not total due to rounding.

Table 3. Churches and Church Membership by State, County and Denomination: 1971

County and Denomination	Number of churches	Communicant, confirmed, full members	Total adherents: Number	Total adherents: Percent of total population	Total adherents: Percent of total adherents
453 UN PRES CH USA	2	114	148*	7.0	90.2
SEWARD	8	737	1,274*	54.5	100.0
029 AMER LUTH CH..	2	234	395	16.9	31.0
081 CATHOLIC......	1	0	100	4.3	7.8
165 CH OF NAZARENE	1	26	154	6.6	12.1
193 EPISCOPAL.....	1	18	50	2.1	3.9
419 SO BAPT CONV..	2	353	433*	18.5	34.0
449 UN METHODIST..	1	106	142	6.1	11.1
SITKA	9	655	1,540*	25.2	100.0
081 CATHOLIC......	2	0	500	8.2	32.5
165 CH OF NAZARENE	1	68	175	2.9	11.4
403 SALVATION ARMY	1	29	138	2.3	9.0
413 S-D ADVENTISTS	1	50	65*	1.1	4.2
419 SO BAPT CONV..	1	176	230*	3.8	14.9
435 UNITARIAN-UNIV	1	15	15	0.2	1.0
449 UN METHODIST..	1	106	142	2.3	9.2
453 UN PRES CH USA	1	211	275*	4.5	17.9
SKAGWAY-YAKUTAT	5	134	275*	12.7	100.0
081 CATHOLIC......	2	0	100	4.6	36.4
453 UN PRES CH USA	3	134	175*	8.1	63.6
SOUTHEAST FAIRBANKS	8	342	935*	22.4	100.0
081 CATHOLIC......	2	0	400	9.6	42.8
193 EPISCOPAL.....	2	135	275	6.6	29.4
349 PENT HOLINESS.	2	4	5*	0.1	0.5
419 SO BAPT CONV..	1	157	197*	4.7	21.1
453 UN PRES CH USA	1	46	58*	1.4	6.2
UPPER YUKON	5	456	778*	46.2	100.0
193 EPISCOPAL.....	4	419	733	43.5	94.2
453 UN PRES CH USA	1	37	45*	2.7	5.8
VALDEZ-CHITINA-WHITT	5	89	329*	10.6	100.0
081 CATHOLIC......	3	0	202	6.5	61.4
193 EPISCOPAL.....	1	37	62	2.0	18.8
419 SO BAPT CONV..	1	52	65*	2.1	19.8
WADE HAMPTON	12	38	3,425	87.4	100.0
081 CATHOLIC......	11	0	3,330	85.0	97.2
193 EPISCOPAL.....	1	38	95	2.4	2.8
WRANGELL-PETERSBURG	13	789	1,919*	39.1	100.0
029 AMER LUTH CH..	1	230	298	6.1	15.5
081 CATHOLIC......	2	0	450	9.2	23.4
123 CH GOD (ANDER)	1	20	78	1.6	4.1
193 EPISCOPAL.....	1	93	93	1.9	4.8
403 SALVATION ARMY	3	207	694	14.1	36.2
413 S-D ADVENTISTS	1	22	28*	0.6	1.5
419 SO BAPT CONV..	1	21	27*	0.5	1.4
453 UN PRES CH USA	3	196	251*	5.1	13.1
YUKON-KOYUKUK	14	301	2,046	43.1	100.0
081 CATHOLIC......	9	0	1,372	28.9	67.1
165 CH OF NAZARENE	1	24	121	2.5	5.9
193 EPISCOPAL.....	4	277	553	11.6	27.0
CO DATA NOT AVAIL	2	89	6,745*	N/A	N/A
151 L-D SAINTS....	0	0	6,630	N/A	N/A
223 FREE WILL BAPT	2	89	115*	N/A	N/A

ARIZONA

County and Denomination	Number of churches	Communicant, confirmed, full members	Total adherents: Number	Total adherents: Percent of total population	Total adherents: Percent of total adherents
THE STATE.....	1,176	245,630	839,667*	47.4	100.0
APACHE	30	1,631	14,225*	44.0	100.0
029 AMER LUTH CH..	1	45	95	0.3	0.7
081 CATHOLIC......	9	0	11,471	35.5	80.6
097 CR C AND C CR.	2	87	122*	0.4	0.9
193 EPISCOPAL.....	1	132	531	1.6	3.7
226 FRIENDS-USA...	1	21	30*	0.1	0.2
285 MENNONITE CH..	2	44	62*	0.2	0.4
353 PLY BRETHREN..	1	30	65	0.2	0.5
413 S-D ADVENTISTS	1	22	31*	0.1	0.2
419 SO BAPT CONV..	5	601	845*	2.6	5.9
449 UN METHODIST..	1	27	60	0.2	0.4
453 UN PRES CH USA	5	610	858*	2.7	6.0
469 WISC EVAN LUTH	1	12	55	0.2	0.4
COCHISE	76	7,199	26,817*	43.3	100.0
029 AMER LUTH CH..	3	506	719	1.2	2.7
081 CATHOLIC......	15	0	17,074	27.6	63.7
093 CR CH (DISC)..	2	149	185*	0.3	0.7
097 CR C AND C CR.	1	90	112*	0.2	0.4
127 CH GOD (CLEVE)	4	122	152*	0.2	0.6
165 CH OF NAZARENE	4	172	534	0.9	2.0
193 EPISCOPAL.....	5	478	764	1.2	2.8
349 PENT HOLINESS.	1	8	10*	-	-
403 SALVATION ARMY	1	9	113	0.2	0.4
413 S-D ADVENTISTS	4	118	147*	0.2	0.5
419 SO BAPT CONV..	18	3,261	4,053*	6.5	15.1
443 UN C OF CHRIST	3	333	414*	0.7	1.5
449 UN METHODIST..	9	1,302	1,723	2.8	6.4
453 UN PRES CH USA	3	506	629*	1.0	2.3
469 WISC EVAN LUTH	3	145	188	0.3	0.7
COCONINO	44	4,846	17,992*	37.2	100.0
081 CATHOLIC......	7	0	11,644	24.1	64.7
097 CR C AND C CR.	3	235	300*	0.6	1.7
127 CH GOD (CLEVE)	1	48	61*	0.1	0.3
165 CH OF NAZARENE	2	70	204	0.4	1.1
193 EPISCOPAL.....	3	635	792	1.6	4.4
226 FRIENDS-USA...	1	13	17*	-	0.1
281 LUTH CH AMER..	1	126	200	0.4	1.1
283 LUTH--MO SYNOD	2	158	248	0.5	1.4
315 NO AM OLD RC..	1	35	45*	0.1	0.3
353 PLY BRETHREN..	1	5	10	-	0.1
403 SALVATION ARMY	1	15	137	0.3	0.8
413 S-D ADVENTISTS	2	134	171*	0.4	1.0
419 SO BAPT CONV..	7	1,549	1,979*	4.1	11.0
435 UNITARIAN-UNIV	1	47	83	0.2	0.5
443 UN C OF CHRIST	2	287	367*	0.8	2.0
449 UN METHODIST..	5	932	1,008	2.1	5.6
453 UN PRES CH USA	3	416	532*	1.1	3.0
469 WISC EVAN LUTH	1	141	194	0.4	1.1
GILA	40	3,778	13,986*	47.8	100.0
019 AMER BAPT CONV	2	254	323*	1.1	2.3
081 CATHOLIC......	8	0	8,440	28.8	60.3
093 CR CH (DISC)..	1	71	90*	0.3	0.6
097 CR C AND C CR.	1	50	64*	0.2	0.5
165 CH OF NAZARENE	2	86	240	0.8	1.7
193 EPISCOPAL.....	2	224	224	0.8	1.6
281 LUTH CH AMER..	2	289	450	1.5	3.2
403 SALVATION ARMY	1	51	256	0.9	1.8
413 S-D ADVENTISTS	2	49	62*	0.2	0.4
419 SO BAPT CONV..	7	1,501	1,908*	6.5	13.6
449 UN METHODIST..	4	468	478	1.6	3.4
453 UN PRES CH USA	5	387	492*	1.7	3.5
469 WISC EVAN LUTH	3	348	959	3.3	6.9
GRAHAM	11	1,308	5,361*	32.3	100.0
081 CATHOLIC......	2	0	3,531	21.3	65.9
193 EPISCOPAL.....	2	187	250	1.5	4.7
413 S-D ADVENTISTS	1	74	94*	0.6	1.8
419 SO BAPT CONV..	3	424	540*	3.3	10.1
449 UN METHODIST..	1	395	470	2.8	8.8
469 WISC EVAN LUTH	2	228	476	2.9	8.9
GREENLEE	12	1,353	7,590*	73.5	100.0
019 AMER BAPT CONV	1	83	104*	1.0	1.4
059 BAPT MISS ASSN	1	138	173*	1.7	2.3
081 CATHOLIC......	3	0	5,875	56.9	77.4
193 EPISCOPAL.....	1	79	118	1.1	1.6
419 SO BAPT CONV..	3	681	853*	8.3	11.2
449 UN METHODIST..	1	59	59	0.6	0.8
453 UN PRES CH USA	1	289	362*	3.5	4.8
469 WISC EVAN LUTH	1	24	46	0.4	0.6
MARICOPA	477	147,167	374,595*	38.7	100.0
019 AMER BAPT CONV	20	6,099	7,529*	0.8	2.0
029 AMER LUTH CH..	15	7,845	11,532	1.2	3.1
059 BAPT MISS ASSN	2	91	112*	-	-
081 CATHOLIC......	62	0	181,906	18.8	48.6
083 CR CATH CH DOB	1	36	37	-	-
093 CR CH (DISC)..	8	2,096	2,588*	0.3	0.7
097 CR C AND C CR.	26	5,796	7,155*	0.7	1.9
105 CHRISTIAN REF.	3	559	983	0.1	0.3
121 CH GOD (ABR)..	2	282	348*	-	0.1
123 CH GOD (ANDER)	5	896	1,976	0.2	0.5
127 CH GOD (CLEVE)	23	1,660	2,049*	0.2	0.5
157 CH OF BRETHREN	3	456	563*	0.1	0.2
165 CH OF NAZARENE	18	3,529	6,259	0.6	1.7
193 EPISCOPAL.....	20	10,825	12,409	1.3	3.3
201 EVAN COV CH AM	2	263	325*	-	0.1
221 FREE METH C NA	9	501	685	0.1	0.2
226 FRIENDS-USA...	3	106	131*	-	-
281 LUTH CH AMER..	15	7,855	10,855	1.1	2.9
283 LUTH--MO SYNOD	17	5,986	8,629	0.9	2.3
285 MENNONITE CH..	6	402	496*	0.1	0.1
287 MENN GEN CONF.	1	70	86*	-	-
349 PENT HOLINESS.	7	158	195*	-	0.1
353 PLY BRETHREN..	3	155	255	-	0.1
371 REF CH IN AM..	4	1,104	1,476	0.2	0.4
403 SALVATION ARMY	5	349	4,096	0.4	1.1
413 S-D ADVENTISTS	16	3,013	3,720*	0.4	1.0
419 SO BAPT CONV..	82	34,483	42,570*	4.4	11.4
435 UNITARIAN-UNIV	2	677	966	0.1	0.3
443 UN C OF CHRIST	12	9,729	12,011*	1.2	3.2
449 UN METHODIST..	42	26,957	33,457	3.5	8.9
453 UN PRES CH USA	31	13,333	16,460*	1.7	4.4
469 WISC EVAN LUTH	12	1,856	2,736	0.3	0.7

*Total adherents estimated from known number of communicant, confirmed, full members.

—Represents a percent less than 0.1.

Percentages may not total due to rounding.

Table 3. Churches and Church Membership by State, County and Denomination: 1971

County and Denomination	Number of churches	Communicant, confirmed, full members	Total adherents		
			Number	Percent of total population	Percent of total adherents
MOHAVE	28	2,882	10,241*	39.6	100.0
029 AMER LUTH CH..	2	420	600	2.3	5.9
081 CATHOLIC......	3	0	6,525	25.2	63.7
097 CR C AND C CR.	2	71	87*	0.3	0.8
123 CH GOD (ANDER)	1	18	47	0.2	0.5
165 CH OF NAZARENE	1	17	32	0.1	0.3
193 EPISCOPAL.....	4	210	302	1.2	2.9
353 PLY BRETHREN..	1	6	20	0.1	0.2
413 S-D ADVENTISTS	4	123	151*	0.6	1.5
419 SO BAPT CONV..	5	981	1,201*	4.6	11.7
449 UN METHODIST..	2	690	851	3.3	8.3
453 UN PRES CH USA	2	338	414*	1.6	4.0
469 WISC EVAN LUTH	1	8	11	-	0.1
NAVAJO	50	4,273	11,974*	25.1	100.0
019 AMER BAPT CONV	3	142	196*	0.4	1.6
029 AMER LUTH CH..	2	129	162	0.3	1.4
081 CATHOLIC......	10	0	5,263	11.0	44.0
097 CR C AND C CR.	1	190	262*	0.5	2.2
127 CH GOD (CLEVE)	1	9	12*	-	0.1
193 EPISCOPAL.....	4	202	252	0.5	2.1
353 PLY BRETHREN..	1	12	66	0.1	0.6
413 S-D ADVENTISTS	3	137	189*	0.4	1.6
419 SO BAPT CONV..	10	2,188	3,019*	6.3	25.2
449 UN METHODIST..	3	521	660	1.4	5.5
453 UN PRES CH USA	4	242	334*	0.7	2.8
469 WISC EVAN LUTH	8	501	1,559	3.3	13.0
PIMA	196	49,380	163,363*	46.5	100.0
019 AMER BAPT CONV	3	595	724*	0.2	0.4
029 AMER LUTH CH..	4	1,630	2,324	0.7	1.4
059 BAPT MISS ASSN	1	79	96*	-	0.1
081 CATHOLIC......	58	0	99,273	28.2	60.8
093 CR CH (DISC)..	5	1,670	2,033*	0.6	1.2
097 CR C AND C CR.	6	849	1,033*	0.3	0.6
105 CHRISTIAN REF.	2	165	194	0.1	0.1
123 CH GOD (ANDER)	4	199	458	0.1	0.3
127 CH GOD (CLEVE)	6	391	476*	0.1	0.3
157 CH OF BRETHREN	1	144	175*	-	0.1
165 CH OF NAZARENE	6	777	1,539	0.4	0.9
193 EPISCOPAL.....	10	5,063	6,512	1.9	4.0
201 EVAN COV CH AM	1	82	100*	-	0.1
221 FREE METH C NA	2	50	81	-	-
226 FRIENDS-USA...	2	92	112*	-	0.1
281 LUTH CH AMER..	5	2,468	3,382	1.0	2.1
283 LUTH--MO SYNOD	7	2,452	3,296	0.9	2.0
349 PENT HOLINESS.	1	15	18*	-	-
353 PLY BRETHREN..	1	90	280	0.1	0.2
371 REF CH IN AM..	1	322	398	0.1	0.2
403 SALVATION ARMY	2	145	811	0.2	0.5
413 S-D ADVENTISTS	3	787	958*	0.3	0.6
419 SO BAPT CONV..	33	13,378	16,282*	4.6	10.0
435 UNITARIAN-UNIV	1	423	583	0.2	0.4
443 UN C OF CHRIST	3	1,511	1,839*	0.5	1.1
449 UN METHODIST..	13	8,685	11,271	3.2	6.9
453 UN PRES CH USA	10	6,173	7,513*	2.1	4.6
469 WISC EVAN LUTH	5	1,145	1,602	0.5	1.0
PINAL	88	9,406	35,655*	52.5	100.0
081 CATHOLIC......	20	0	23,036	33.9	64.6
093 CR CH (DISC)..	1	32	41*	0.1	0.1
097 CR C AND C CR.	2	252	325*	0.5	0.9
127 CH GOD (CLEVE)	5	211	272*	0.4	0.8
165 CH OF NAZARENE	3	282	771	1.1	2.2
193 EPISCOPAL.....	5	412	686	1.0	1.9
283 LUTH--MO SYNOD	2	175	243	0.4	0.7
349 PENT HOLINESS.	3	34	44*	0.1	0.1
413 S-D ADVENTISTS	3	48	62*	0.1	0.2
419 SO BAPT CONV..	24	5,216	6,720*	9.9	18.8
443 UN C OF CHRIST	1	81	104*	0.2	0.3
449 UN METHODIST..	5	940	1,104	1.6	3.1
453 UN PRES CH USA	12	1,615	2,081*	3.1	5.8
469 WISC EVAN LUTH	2	108	166	0.2	0.5
SANTA CRUZ	12	628	9,430*	67.5	100.0
081 CATHOLIC......	4	0	8,591	61.5	91.1
193 EPISCOPAL.....	1	155	197	1.4	2.1
221 FREE METH C NA	1	31	54	0.4	0.6
283 LUTH--MO SYNOD	1	23	41	0.3	0.4
413 S-D ADVENTISTS	2	69	88*	0.6	0.9
443 UN C OF CHRIST	1	[illegible]	250*	1.8	2.7
449 UN METHODIST..	2	154	209	1.5	2.2
YAVAPAI	51	3,780	20,418*	55.6	100.0
019 AMER BAPT CONV	1	53	62*	0.2	0.3
029 AMER LUTH CH..	2	358	[illegible]	1.3	2.3
081 CATHOLIC......	14	0	[illegible]	41.4	74.6
093 CR CH (DISC)..	1	133	[illegible]	0.4	0.8
123 CH GOD (ANDER)	1	90	[illegible]	0.5	1.0
165 CH OF NAZARENE	1	79	258	0.7	1.3
193 EPISCOPAL.....	1	50	50	0.1	0.2
221 FREE METH C NA	2	54	67	0.2	0.3
283 LUTH--MO SYNOD	1	54	71	0.2	0.3
403 SALVATION ARMY	1	51	265	0.7	1.3
413 S-D ADVENTISTS	2	251	296*	0.8	1.4
419 SO BAPT CONV..	12	1,404	1,655*	4.5	8.1
443 UN C OF CHRIST	4	465	548*	1.5	2.7
449 UN METHODIST..	4	109	328	0.9	[illegible]
453 UN PRES CH USA	3	401	473*	1.3	2.3
469 WISC EVAN LUTH	1	228	307	0.8	1.5
YUMA	41	6,789	20,195*	33.2	100.0
081 CATHOLIC......	7	0	11,142	18.3	55.2
097 CR C AND C CR.	2	450	563*	0.9	2.8
123 CH GOD (ANDER)	1	37	104	0.2	0.5
127 CH GOD (CLEVE)	1	83	104*	0.2	0.5
165 CH OF NAZARENE	4	332	686	1.1	3.4
193 EPISCOPAL.....	1	30	32	0.1	0.2
281 LUTH CH AMER..	1	185	243	0.4	1.2
283 LUTH--MO SYNOD	3	600	861	1.4	4.3
349 PENT HOLINESS.	1	13	16*	-	0.1
403 SALVATION ARMY	1	19	169	0.3	0.8
413 S-D ADVENTISTS	1	153	191*	0.3	0.9
419 SO BAPT CONV..	7	2,838	3,548*	5.8	17.6
435 UNITARIAN-UNIV	1	15	15	-	0.1
449 UN METHODIST..	4	1,201	1,470	2.4	7.3
453 UN PRES CH USA	5	808	1,010*	1.7	5.0
469 WISC EVAN LUTH	1	25	41	0.1	0.2
CO DATA NOT AVAIL	20	1,210	107,825*	N/A	N/A
151 L-D SAINTS....	0	0	106,323	N/A	N/A
223 FREE WILL BAPT	4	474	588*	N/A	N/A
231 GENERAL BAPT..	3	103	128*	N/A	N/A
467 WESLEYAN......	13	633	786	N/A	N/A

ARKANSAS

County and Denomination	Number of churches	Communicant, confirmed, full members	Total adherents		
			Number	Percent of total population	Percent of total adherents
THE STATE.....	3,568	686,386	880,433*	45.8	100.0
ARKANSAS	44	9,591	12,012*	51.4	100.0
029 AMER LUTH CH..	1	204	254	1.1	2.1
059 BAPT MISS ASSN	8	417	512*	2.2	4.3
081 CATHOLIC......	2	0	560	2.4	4.7
093 CR CH (DISC)..	1	296	364*	1.6	3.0
097 CR C AND C CR.	2	335	412*	1.8	3.4
165 CH OF NAZARENE	2	68	87	0.4	0.7
193 EPISCOPAL.....	1	114	130	0.6	1.1
226 FRIENDS-USA...	1	25	31*	0.1	0.3
283 LUTH--MO SYNOD	3	903	1,177	5.0	9.8
357 PRESB CH US...	1	176	216*	0.9	1.8
419 SO BAPT CONV..	11	3,852	4,732*	20.3	39.4
449 UN METHODIST..	11	3,201	3,537	15.1	29.4
ASHLEY	42	9,362	11,806*	47.3	100.0
059 BAPT MISS ASSN	2	287	362*	1.4	3.1
081 CATHOLIC......	1	0	165	0.7	1.4
123 CH GOD (ANDER)	1	55	173	0.7	1.5
193 EPISCOPAL.....	1	153	184	0.7	1.6
283 LUTH--MO SYNOD	1	25	33	0.1	0.3
357 PRESB CH US...	2	171	215*	0.9	1.8
419 SO BAPT CONV..	26	7,287	9,179*	36.8	77.7
449 UN METHODIST..	8	1,384	1,495	6.0	12.7
BAXTER	33	5,296	6,711*	43.8	100.0
059 BAPT MISS ASSN	2	52	60*	0.4	0.9
081 CATHOLIC......	1	0	604	3.9	9.0
093 CR CH (DISC)..	1	195	225*	1.5	3.4
097 CR C AND C CR.	1	198	228*	1.5	3.4
127 CH GOD (CLEVE)	2	61	70*	0.5	1.0
165 CH OF NAZARENE	2	70	124	0.8	1.8
185 CUMBER PRESB..	1	107	123*	0.8	1.8
193 EPISCOPAL.....	1	70	142	0.9	2.1
283 LUTH--MO SYNOD	1	505	595	3.9	8.9
285 MENNONITE CH..	1	11	13*	0.1	0.2
357 PRESB CH US...	3	395	455*	3.0	6.8
413 S-D ADVENTISTS	1	43	50*	0.3	0.7
419 SO BAPT CONV..	12	2,467	2,842*	18.6	42.3
449 UN METHODIST..	4	1,122	1,180	7.7	17.6
BENTON	101	17,688	22,420*	44.4	100.0
059 BAPT MISS ASSN	14	1,029	1,238*	2.5	5.5
081 CATHOLIC......	2	0	1,120	2.2	5.0
093 CR CH (DISC)..	4	668	804*	1.6	3.6
097 CR C AND C CR.	5	445	535*	1.1	2.4
127 CH GOD (CLEVE.	1	17	20*	-	0.1
165 CH OF NAZARENE	6	518	1,038	2.1	4.6
193 EPISCOPAL.....	1	225	326	0.6	1.5
221 FREE METH C NA	1	20	22	-	0.1
281 LUTH CH AMER..	1	127	167	0.3	0.7
283 LUTH--MO SYNOD	2	233	309	0.6	1.4
349 PENT HOLINESS.	4	138	166*	0.3	0.7
357 PRESB CH US...	6	521	627*	1.2	2.8
413 S-D ADVENTISTS	6	707	851*	1.7	3.8
419 SO BAPT CONV..	26	8,557	10,297*	20.4	45.9
449 UN METHODIST..	16	3,950	4,259	8.4	19.0
453 UN PRES CH USA	6	533	641*	1.3	2.9
BOONE	49	7,157	8,956*	47.0	100.0

*Total adherents estimated from known number of communicant, confirmed, full members.

—Represents a percent less than 0.1.

Percentages may not total due to rounding.

Table 3. Churches and Church Membership by State, County and Denomination: 1971

County and Denomination	Number of churches	Communicant, confirmed, full members	Total adherents: Number	Percent of total population	Percent of total adherents
081 CATHOLIC......	1	0	375	2.0	4.2
093 CR CH (DISC)..	3	439	523*	2.7	5.8
123 CH GOD (ANDER)	2	88	258	1.4	2.9
127 CH GOD (CLEVE)	1	35	42*	0.2	0.5
165 CH OF NAZARENE	1	60	114	0.6	1.3
185 CUMBER PRESB..	1	33	39*	0.2	0.4
193 EPISCOPAL.....	1	172	234	1.2	2.6
283 LUTH--MO SYNOD	1	75	101	0.5	1.1
353 PLY BRETHREN..	1	5	6	-	0.1
357 PRESB CH US...	2	271	323*	1.7	3.6
413 S-D ADVENTISTS	1	111	132*	0.7	1.5
419 SO BAPT CONV..	24	4,350	5,178*	27.1	57.8
449 UN METHODIST..	8	1,236	1,295	6.8	14.5
453 UN PRES CH USA	2	282	336*	1.8	3.8
BRADLEY	33	5,603	6,661*	52.1	100.0
055 AS REF PRES CH	1	48	58*	0.5	0.9
059 BAPT MISS ASSN	7	881	1,058*	8.3	15.9
081 CATHOLIC......	1	0	120	0.9	1.8
127 CH GOD (CLEVE)	2	84	101*	0.8	1.5
357 PRESB CH US...	3	391	470*	3.7	7.1
419 SO BAPT CONV..	13	3,258	3,913*	30.6	58.7
449 UN METHODIST..	6	941	941	7.4	14.1
CALHOUN	18	1,906	2,189*	39.3	100.0
059 BAPT MISS ASSN	8	482	573*	10.3	26.2
185 CUMBER PRESB..	1	248	295*	5.3	13.5
419 SO BAPT CONV..	5	768	913*	16.4	41.7
449 UN METHODIST..	4	408	408	7.3	18.6
CARROLL	27	3,545	4,395*	35.7	100.0
059 BAPT MISS ASSN	1	25	29*	0.2	0.7
081 CATHOLIC......	2	0	309	2.5	7.0
093 CR CH (DISC)..	1	126	148*	1.2	3.4
097 CR C AND C CR.	2	60	70*	0.6	1.6
165 CH OF NAZARENE	2	34	129	1.0	2.9
193 EPISCOPAL.....	1	105	119	1.0	2.7
353 PLY BRETHREN..	1	2	5	-	0.1
357 PRESB CH US...	2	79	93*	0.8	2.1
419 SO BAPT CONV..	8	2,024	2,376*	19.3	54.1
449 UN METHODIST..	5	1,035	1,052	8.6	23.9
453 UN PRES CH USA	2	55	65*	0.5	1.5
CHICOT	25	4,839	6,620*	36.4	100.0
059 BAPT MISS ASSN	2	208	262*	1.4	4.0
081 CATHOLIC......	2	0	680	3.7	10.3
127 CH GOD (CLEVE)	1	32	40*	0.2	0.6
193 EPISCOPAL.....	1	72	86	0.5	1.3
357 PRESB CH US...	3	216	272*	1.5	4.1
419 SO BAPT CONV..	12	3,584	4,520*	24.9	68.3
449 UN METHODIST..	4	727	760	4.2	11.5
CLARK	59	9,697	11,384*	52.9	100.0
059 BAPT MISS ASSN	5	712	831*	3.9	7.3
081 CATHOLIC......	1	0	103	0.5	0.9
093 CR CH (DISC)..	3	179	209*	1.0	1.8
123 CH GOD (ANDER)	2	50	130	0.6	1.1
165 CH OF NAZARENE	2	76	196	0.9	1.7
193 EPISCOPAL.....	1	52	63	0.3	0.6
283 LUTH--MO SYNOD	1	19	19	0.1	0.2
357 PRESB CH US...	4	448	523*	2.4	4.6
419 SO BAPT CONV..	28	5,890	6,877*	31.9	60.4
449 UN METHODIST..	11	2,255	2,414	11.2	21.2
453 UN PRES CH USA	1	16	19*	0.1	0.2
CLAY	49	6,735	8,118*	43.2	100.0
059 BAPT MISS ASSN	5	291	346*	1.8	4.3
081 CATHOLIC......	3	0	293	1.6	3.6
097 CR C AND C CR.	2	285	339*	1.8	4.2
123 CH GOD (ANDER)	1	65	174	0.9	2.1
165 CH OF NAZARENE	1	14	40	0.2	0.5
283 LUTH--MO SYNOD	1	64	92	0.5	1.1
419 SO BAPT CONV..	20	3,770	4,480*	23.9	55.2
449 UN METHODIST..	16	2,246	2,354	12.5	29.0
CLEBURNE	35	4,336	5,100*	49.3	100.0
059 BAPT MISS ASSN	6	465	543*	5.2	10.6
081 CATHOLIC......	1	0	102	1.0	2.0
123 CH GOD (ANDER)	1	18	70	0.7	1.4
127 CH GOD (CLEVE)	2	52	61*	0.6	1.2
165 CH OF NAZARENE	2	43	70	0.7	1.4
357 PRESB CH US...	1	114	133*	1.3	2.6
419 SO BAPT CONV..	15	2,543	2,970*	28.7	58.2
449 UN METHODIST..	7	1,101	1,151	11.1	22.6
CLEVELAND	22	2,206	2,569*	38.9	100.0
055 AS REF PRES CH	1	19	23*	0.3	0.9
059 BAPT MISS ASSN	8	779	944*	14.3	36.7
123 CH GOD (ANDER)	1	32	84	1.3	3.3
127 CH GOD (CLEVE)	1	20	24*	0.4	0.9
357 PRESB CH US...	1	14	17*	0.3	0.7
419 SO BAPT CONV..	2	575	697*	10.6	27.1
449 UN METHODIST..	8	767	780	11.8	30.4
COLUMBIA	57	10,773	12,609*	48.6	100.0
059 BAPT MISS ASSN	23	4,069	4,898*	18.9	38.8

County and Denomination	Number of churches	Communicant, confirmed, full members	Total adherents: Number	Percent of total population	Percent of total adherents
081 CATHOLIC......	1	0	151	0.6	1.2
093 CR CH (DISC)..	1	5	6*	-	-
123 CH GOD (ANDER)	1	23	46	0.2	0.4
165 CH OF NAZARENE	1	36	69	0.3	0.5
185 CUMBER PRESB..	2	106	128*	0.5	1.0
193 EPISCOPAL.....	1	44	50	0.2	0.4
283 LUTH--MO SYNOD	1	49	71	0.3	0.6
357 PRESB CH US...	1	245	295*	1.1	2.3
419 SO BAPT CONV..	6	2,684	3,231*	12.4	25.6
449 UN METHODIST..	19	3,512	3,664	14.1	29.1
CONWAY	33	3,954	5,844*	34.8	100.0
059 BAPT MISS ASSN	8	942	1,149*	6.8	19.7
081 CATHOLIC......	4	0	1,275	7.6	21.8
165 CH OF NAZARENE	1	77	122	0.7	2.1
185 CUMBER PRESB..	2	137	167*	1.0	2.9
283 LUTH--MO SYNOD	1	12	12	0.1	0.2
357 PRESB CH US...	2	131	160*	1.0	2.7
419 SO BAPT CONV..	3	1,020	1,244*	7.4	21.3
449 UN METHODIST..	10	1,503	1,554	9.2	26.6
453 UN PRES CH USA	2	132	161*	1.0	2.8
CRAIGHEAD	98	24,058	29,980*	57.6	100.0
059 BAPT MISS ASSN	23	3,477	4,170*	8.0	13.9
081 CATHOLIC......	2	0	1,345	2.6	4.5
093 CR CH (DISC)..	2	390	468*	0.9	1.6
097 CR C AND C CR.	3	242	290*	0.6	1.0
127 CH GOD (CLEVE)	3	105	126*	0.2	0.4
165 CH OF NAZARENE	3	309	558	1.1	1.9
193 EPISCOPAL.....	1	246	344	0.7	1.1
283 LUTH--MO SYNOD	1	93	125	0.2	0.4
357 PRESB CH US...	2	460	552*	1.1	1.8
403 SALVATION ARMY	1	64	222	0.4	0.7
413 S-D ADVENTISTS	1	77	92*	0.2	0.3
419 SO BAPT CONV..	34	12,937	15,517*	29.8	51.8
435 UNITARIAN-UNIV	1	13	13	-	-
449 UN METHODIST..	21	5,645	6,158	11.8	20.5
CRAWFORD	45	7,666	9,312*	36.3	100.0
081 CATHOLIC......	1	0	202	0.8	2.2
093 CR CH (DISC)..	3	203	248*	1.0	2.7
097 CR C AND C CR.	1	36	44*	0.2	0.5
127 CH GOD (CLEVE)	1	19	23*	0.1	0.2
165 CH OF NAZARENE	2	168	315	1.2	3.4
185 CUMBER PRESB..	1	13	16*	0.1	0.2
193 EPISCOPAL.....	1	128	135	0.5	1.4
357 PRESB CH US...	3	190	232*	0.9	2.5
413 S-D ADVENTISTS	2	165	202*	0.8	2.2
419 SO BAPT CONV..	15	4,679	5,715*	22.3	61.4
449 UN METHODIST..	12	1,865	1,936	7.5	20.8
453 UN PRES CH USA	3	200	244*	1.0	2.6
CRITTENDEN	33	10,055	13,982*	29.1	100.0
059 BAPT MISS ASSN	3	199	261*	0.5	1.9
081 CATHOLIC......	3	0	1,021	2.1	7.3
093 CR CH (DISC)..	1	35	46*	0.1	0.3
127 CH GOD (CLEVE)	2	122	160*	0.3	1.1
165 CH OF NAZARENE	2	159	455	0.9	3.3
193 EPISCOPAL.....	1	159	191	0.4	1.4
283 LUTH--MO SYNOD	1	55	75	0.2	0.5
357 PRESB CH US...	3	627	821*	1.7	5.9
413 S-D ADVENTISTS	1	45	59*	0.1	0.4
419 SO BAPT CONV..	10	6,363	8,334*	17.3	59.6
449 UN METHODIST..	6	2,291	2,559	5.3	18.3
CROSS	38	7,000	8,697*	44.0	100.0
059 BAPT MISS ASSN	4	415	526*	2.7	6.0
081 CATHOLIC......	1	0	300	1.5	3.4
093 CR CH (DISC)..	1	25	32*	0.2	0.4
127 CH GOD (CLEVE)	5	179	227*	1.1	2.6
157 CH OF BRETHREN	1	52	66*	0.3	0.8
193 EPISCOPAL.....	1	16	23	0.1	0.3
357 PRESB CH US...	2	280	355*	1.8	4.1
419 SO BAPT CONV..	13	3,849	4,883*	24.7	56.1
449 UN METHODIST..	10	2,184	2,285	11.6	26.3
DALLAS	37	4,072	4,714*	47.0	100.0
059 BAPT MISS ASSN	6	661	792*	7.9	16.8
165 CH OF NAZARENE	1	23	53	0.5	1.1
357 PRESB CH US...	3	143	171*	1.7	3.6
419 SO BAPT CONV..	12	2,030	2,433*	24.3	51.6
449 UN METHODIST..	15	1,215	1,265	12.6	26.8
DESHA	27	6,418	7,984*	42.6	100.0
059 BAPT MISS ASSN	3	378	477*	2.5	6.0
081 CATHOLIC......	2	0	164	0.9	2.1
097 CR C AND C CR.	1	135	170*	0.9	2.1
165 CH OF NAZARENE	1	38	62	0.3	0.8
193 EPISCOPAL.....	2	23	30	0.2	0.4
357 PRESB CH US...	1	179	226*	1.2	2.8
419 SO BAPT CONV..	12	4,124	5,208*	27.8	65.2
449 UN METHODIST..	5	1,541	1,647	8.8	20.6
DREW	32	5,397	6,371*	4[illegible].0	100.0
055 AS REF PRES CH	1	104	126*	0.8	2.0
059 BAPT MISS ASSN	1	186	226*	1.5	3.5
185 CUMBER PRESB..	1	114	138*	0.9	2.2

*Total adherents estimated from known number of communicant, confirmed, full members.

—Represents a percent less than 0.1.

Percentages may not total due to rounding.

Table 3. Churches and Church Membership by State, County and Denomination: 1971

County and Denomination	Number of churches	Communicant, confirmed, full members	Total adherents		
			Number	Percent of total population	Percent of total adherents
193 EPISCOPAL.....	1	43	52	0.3	0.8
357 PRESB CH US...	3	273	331*	2.2	5.2
413 S-D ADVENTISTS	1	25	30*	0.2	0.5
419 SO BAPT CONV..	14	3,573	4,334*	28.6	68.0
449 UN METHODIST..	9	1,046	1,094	7.2	17.2
453 UN PRES CH USA	1	33	40*	0.3	0.6
FAULKNER	69	11,623	15,980*	50.6	100.0
059 BAPT MISS ASSN	20	3,086	3,660*	11.6	22.9
081 CATHOLIC......	1	0	2,225	7.0	13.9
093 CR CH (DISC)..	1	39	46*	0.1	0.3
121 CH GOD (ABR)..	1	75	89*	0.3	0.6
165 CH OF NAZARENE	7	593	897	2.8	5.6
193 EPISCOPAL.....	1	111	126	0.4	0.8
283 LUTH--MO SYNOD	1	92	127	0.4	0.8
357 PRESB CH US...	2	107	127*	0.4	0.8
419 SO BAPT CONV..	21	5,019	5,952*	18.9	37.2
449 UN METHODIST..	12	2,390	2,599	8.2	16.3
453 UN PRES CH USA	2	111	132*	0.4	0.8
FRANKLIN	31	4,028	5,602*	49.6	100.0
081 CATHOLIC......	2	0	970	8.6	17.3
093 CR CH (DISC)..	1	112	134*	1.2	2.4
165 CH OF NAZARENE	2	48	124	1.1	2.2
185 CUMBER PRESB..	1	48	57*	0.5	1.0
221 FREE METH C NA	1	15	15	0.1	0.3
357 PRESB CH US...	1	67	80*	0.7	1.4
419 SO BAPT CONV..	8	2,017	2,408*	21.3	43.0
449 UN METHODIST..	11	1,571	1,635	14.5	29.2
453 UN PRES CH USA	4	150	179*	1.6	3.2
FULTON	22	2,044	2,295*	29.8	100.0
059 BAPT MISS ASSN	1	32	37*	0.5	1.6
093 CR CH (DISC)..	1	58	67*	0.9	2.9
127 CH GOD (CLEVE)	2	30	35*	0.5	1.5
185 CUMBER PRESB..	1	39	45*	0.6	2.0
357 PRESB CH US...	1	43	50*	0.6	2.2
413 S-D ADVENTISTS	1	32	37*	0.5	1.6
419 SO BAPT CONV..	11	1,236	1,433*	18.6	62.4
449 UN METHODIST..	4	574	591	7.7	25.8
GARLAND	59	19,627	25,615*	47.3	100.0
081 CATHOLIC......	2	0	2,505	4.6	9.8
093 CR CH (DISC)..	2	767	927*	1.7	3.6
121 CH GOD (ABR)..	1	45	53*	0.1	0.2
127 CH GOD (CLEVE)	1	39	46*	0.1	0.2
165 CH OF NAZARENE	3	432	683	1.3	2.7
193 EPISCOPAL.....	1	521	631	1.2	2.5
281 LUTH CH AMER..	1	179	217	0.4	0.8
283 LUTH--MO SYNOD	1	248	297	0.5	1.2
357 PRESB CH US...	4	1,178	1,387*	2.6	5.4
403 SALVATION ARMY	1	74	303	0.6	1.2
413 S-D ADVENTISTS	2	232	273*	0.5	1.1
419 SO BAPT CONV..	29	11,486	13,525*	25.0	52.8
435 UNITARIAN-UNIV	1	20	20	-	0.1
449 UN METHODIST..	10	4,386	4,748	8.8	18.5
GRANT	16	2,194	2,547*	26.2	100.0
059 BAPT MISS ASSN	1	122	147*	1.5	5.8
081 CATHOLIC......	1	0	70	0.7	2.7
093 CR CH (DISC)..	2	93	112*	1.2	4.4
127 CH GOD (CLEVE)	1	30	36*	0.4	1.4
419 SO BAPT CONV..	4	895	1,080*	11.1	42.4
449 UN METHODIST..	7	1,054	1,102	11.3	43.3
GREENE	64	11,019	13,381*	54.0	100.0
059 BAPT MISS ASSN	2	184	220*	0.9	1.6
081 CATHOLIC......	1	0	505	2.0	3.8
093 CR CH (DISC)..	1	18	22*	0.1	0.2
097 CR C AND C CR.	1	50	60*	0.2	0.4
123 CH GOD (ANDER)	1	78	168	0.7	1.3
127 CH GOD (CLEVE)	1	43	51*	0.2	0.4
165 CH OF NAZARENE	2	86	160	0.6	1.2
193 EPISCOPAL.....	1	66	105	0.4	0.8
283 LUTH--MO SYNOD	2	179	221	0.9	1.7
357 PRESB CH US...	1	85	102*	0.4	0.8
419 SO BAPT CONV..	38	7,427	8,885*	35.9	66.4
449 UN METHODIST..	13	2,803	2,882	11.6	21.5
HEMPSTEAD	50	7,609	9,106*	47.2	100.0
059 BAPT MISS ASSN	15	2,593	3,120*	16.2	34.3
081 CATHOLIC......	1	0	117	0.6	1.3
093 CR CH (DISC)..	1	81	97*	0.5	1.1
123 CH GOD (ANDER)	2	46	105	0.5	1.2
165 CH OF NAZARENE	3	122	235	1.2	2.6
193 EPISCOPAL.....	1	51	67	0.3	0.7
357 PRESB CH US...	2	231	278*	1.4	3.1
419 SO BAPT CONV..	12	2,522	3,034*	15.7	33.3
449 UN METHODIST..	13	1,963	2,053	10.6	22.5
HOT SPRING	28	4,005	5,093*	23.2	100.0
059 BAPT MISS ASSN	2	125	149*	0.7	2.9
081 CATHOLIC......	1	0	94	0.4	1.8
123 CH GOD (ANDER)	5	346	786	3.6	15.4
127 CH GOD (CLEVE)	1	77	92*	0.4	1.8
165 CH OF NAZARENE	1	23	86	0.4	1.7
283 LUTH--MO SYNOD	1	49	79	0.4	1.6
357 PRESB CH US...	1	161	192*	0.9	3.8
413 S-D ADVENTISTS	1	91	109*	0.5	2.1
419 SO BAPT CONV..	6	1,372	1,637*	7.5	32.1
449 UN METHODIST..	9	1,761	1,869	8.5	36.7
HOWARD	36	4,657	5,478*	48.0	100.0
059 BAPT MISS ASSN	15	1,689	2,026*	17.8	37.0
081 CATHOLIC......	1	0	75	0.7	1.4
093 CR CH (DISC)..	2	97	116*	1.0	2.1
097 CR C AND C CR.	2	64	77*	0.7	1.4
123 CH GOD (ANDER)	1	40	90	0.8	1.6
419 SO BAPT CONV..	5	1,575	1,889*	16.6	34.5
449 UN METHODIST..	10	1,192	1,205	10.6	22.0
INDEPENDENCE	63	9,447	11,343*	49.9	100.0
059 BAPT MISS ASSN	6	862	1,023*	4.5	9.0
081 CATHOLIC......	1	0	505	2.2	4.5
123 CH GOD (ANDER)	1	14	37	0.2	0.3
127 CH GOD (CLEVE)	1	22	26*	0.1	0.2
165 CH OF NAZARENE	1	128	197	0.9	1.7
185 CUMBER PRESB..	3	107	127*	0.6	1.1
193 EPISCOPAL.....	1	152	225	1.0	2.0
357 PRESB CH US...	2	267	317*	1.4	2.8
413 S-D ADVENTISTS	1	69	82*	0.4	0.7
419 SO BAPT CONV..	18	4,305	5,109*	22.5	45.0
449 UN METHODIST..	28	3,521	3,695	16.3	32.6
IZARD	34	3,178	3,696*	50.1	100.0
059 BAPT MISS ASSN	1	89	103*	1.4	2.8
081 CATHOLIC......	1	0	130	1.8	3.5
185 CUMBER PRESB..	5	269	312*	4.2	8.4
285 MENNONITE CH..	3	54	63*	0.9	1.7
357 PRESB CH US...	1	49	57*	0.8	1.5
419 SO BAPT CONV..	15	1,824	2,114*	28.6	57.2
449 UN METHODIST..	8	893	917	12.4	24.8
JACKSON	29	5,197	6,249*	30.6	100.0
059 BAPT MISS ASSN	3	317	384*	1.9	6.1
081 CATHOLIC......	1	0	75	0.4	1.2
093 CR CH (DISC)..	1	124	150*	0.7	2.4
123 CH GOD (ANDER)	1	8	26	0.1	0.4
127 CH GOD (CLEVE)	1	6	7*	-	0.1
165 CH OF NAZARENE	1	79	81	0.4	1.3
193 EPISCOPAL.....	1	233	354	1.7	5.7
357 PRESB CH US...	1	105	127*	0.6	2.0
413 S-D ADVENTISTS	1	39	47*	0.2	0.8
419 SO BAPT CONV..	11	2,934	3,555*	17.4	56.9
449 UN METHODIST..	7	1,352	1,443	7.1	23.1
JEFFERSON	73	24,746	32,808*	38.4	100.0
029 AMER LUTH CH..	1	94	145	0.2	0.4
059 BAPT MISS ASSN	8	894	1,117*	1.3	3.4
081 CATHOLIC......	3	0	2,090	2.4	6.4
093 CR CH (DISC)..	2	501	626*	0.7	1.9
097 CR C AND C CR.	1	80	100*	0.1	0.3
123 CH GOD (ANDER)	3	41	101	0.1	0.3
127 CH GOD (CLEVE)	2	100	125*	0.1	0.4
165 CH OF NAZARENE	2	197	359	0.4	1.1
185 CUMBER PRESB..	2	265	331*	0.4	1.0
193 EPISCOPAL.....	2	524	983	1.2	3.0
283 LUTH--MO SYNOD	1	252	340	0.4	1.0
357 PRESB CH US...	5	1,663	2,079*	2.4	6.3
403 SALVATION ARMY	1	34	132	0.2	0.4
413 S-D ADVENTISTS	1	43	54*	0.1	0.2
419 SO BAPT CONV..	25	14,081	17,600*	20.6	53.6
449 UN METHODIST..	14	5,977	6,626	7.8	20.2
JOHNSON	33	4,320	5,434*	39.9	100.0
059 BAPT MISS ASSN	1	52	61*	0.4	1.1
081 CATHOLIC......	2	0	453	3.3	8.3
097 CR C AND C CR.	1	15	18*	0.1	0.3
165 CH OF NAZARENE	1	41	171	1.3	3.1
185 CUMBER PRESB..	1	4	5*	-	0.1
283 LUTH--MO SYNOD	1	45	54	0.4	1.0
357 PRESB CH US...	4	292	344*	2.5	6.3
419 SO BAPT CONV..	13	2,080	2,448*	18.0	45.0
449 UN METHODIST..	5	1,512	1,552	11.4	28.6
453 UN PRES CH USA	4	279	328*	2.4	6.0
LAFAYETTE	26	4,019	4,725*	47.2	100.0
059 BAPT MISS ASSN	9	1,010	1,245*	12.4	26.3
093 CR CH (DISC)..	1	12	15*	0.1	0.3
357 PRESB CH US...	2	37	46*	0.5	1.0
419 SO BAPT CONV..	6	1,830	2,257*	22.5	47.8
449 UN METHODIST..	8	1,130	1,162	11.6	24.6
LAWRENCE	30	4,270	5,248*	32.2	100.0
059 BAPT MISS ASSN	2	224	264*	1.6	5.0
081 CATHOLIC......	1	0	274	1.7	5.2
165 CH OF NAZARENE	1	40	120	0.7	2.3
185 CUMBER PRESB..	1	30	35*	0.2	0.7
357 PRESB CH US...	1	72	85*	0.5	1.6
419 SO BAPT CONV..	13	2,889	3,408*	20.9	64.9
449 UN METHODIST..	11	1,015	1,062	6.5	20.2
LEE	18	3,371	4,284*	22.7	100.0

*Total adherents estimated from known number of communicant, confirmed, full members.

—Represents a percent less than 0.1.

Percentages may not total due to rounding.

Table 3. Churches and Church Membership by State, County and Denomination: 1971

County and Denomination	Number of churches	Communicant, confirmed, full members	Total adherents: Number	Total adherents: Percent of total population	Total adherents: Percent of total adherents
059 BAPT MISS ASSN	2	250	321*	1.7	7.5
081 CATHOLIC......	1	0	120	0.6	2.8
093 CR CH (DISC)..	1	146	187*	1.0	4.4
097 CR C AND C CR.	1	150	193*	1.0	4.5
127 CH GOD (CLEVE)	1	18	23*	0.1	0.5
193 EPISCOPAL.....	1	90	134	0.7	3.1
357 PRESB CH US...	1	132	170*	0.9	4.0
413 S-D ADVENTISTS	1	2	3*	-	0.1
419 SO BAPT CONV..	5	1,862	2,391*	12.7	55.8
449 UN METHODIST..	4	721	742	3.9	17.3
LINCOLN	22	3,352	4,032*	31.2	100.0
081 CATHOLIC......	1	0	60	0.5	1.5
093 CR CH (DISC)..	1	70	86*	0.7	2.1
127 CH GOD (CLEVE)	1	20	25*	0.2	0.6
185 CUMBER PRESB..	1	41	51*	0.4	1.3
357 PRESB CH US...	2	243	299*	2.3	7.4
419 SO BAPT CONV..	10	2,301	2,834*	21.9	70.3
449 UN METHODIST..	6	677	677	5.2	16.8
LITTLE RIVER	27	3,555	4,372*	39.1	100.0
059 BAPT MISS ASSN	3	475	595*	5.3	13.6
081 CATHOLIC......	1	0	50	0.4	1.1
097 CR C AND C CR.	1	45	56*	0.5	1.3
165 CH OF NAZARENE	1	28	93	0.8	2.1
185 CUMBER PRESB..	3	97	122*	1.1	2.8
193 EPISCOPAL.....	1	69	87	0.8	2.0
357 PRESB CH US...	1	90	113*	1.0	2.6
419 SO BAPT CONV..	8	1,876	2,351*	21.0	53.8
449 UN METHODIST..	8	875	905	8.1	20.7
LOGAN	46	6,029	9,174*	54.6	100.0
059 BAPT MISS ASSN	1	39	47*	0.3	0.5
081 CATHOLIC......	7	0	2,277	13.6	24.8
093 CR CH (DISC)..	1	116	139*	0.8	1.5
127 CH GOD (CLEVE)	1	13	16*	0.1	0.2
185 CUMBER PRESB..	7	345	413*	2.5	4.5
357 PRESB CH US...	1	26	31*	0.2	0.3
413 S-D ADVENTISTS	1	19	23*	0.1	0.3
419 SO BAPT CONV..	14	3,366	4,025*	24.0	43.9
449 UN METHODIST..	12	2,079	2,172	12.9	23.7
453 UN PRES CH USA	1	26	31*	0.2	0.3
LONOKE	65	10,467	12,816*	48.8	100.0
059 BAPT MISS ASSN	9	1,346	1,665*	6.3	13.0
081 CATHOLIC......	1	0	247	0.9	1.9
093 CR CH (DISC)..	4	65	80*	0.3	0.6
165 CH OF NAZARENE	4	122	283	1.1	2.2
185 CUMBER PRESB..	1	38	47*	0.2	0.4
357 PRESB CH US...	3	261	323*	1.2	2.5
419 SO BAPT CONV..	23	5,794	7,167*	27.3	55.9
449 UN METHODIST..	20	2,841	3,004	11.4	23.4
MADISON	15	1,012	1,284*	13.6	100.0
059 BAPT MISS ASSN	1	128	152*	1.6	11.8
081 CATHOLIC......	1	0	125	1.3	9.7
357 PRESB CH US...	2	33	39*	0.4	3.0
413 S-D ADVENTISTS	1	51	61*	0.6	4.8
419 SO BAPT CONV..	5	526	626*	6.6	48.8
449 UN METHODIST..	3	245	247	2.6	19.2
453 UN PRES CH USA	2	29	34*	0.4	2.6
MARION	19	2,359	2,701*	38.6	100.0
093 CR CH (DISC)..	1	80	93*	1.3	3.4
097 CR C AND C CR.	2	205	239*	3.4	8.8
127 CH GOD (CLEVE)	1	32	37*	0.5	1.4
357 PRESB CH US...	2	191	222*	3.2	8.2
419 SO BAPT CONV..	8	1,418	1,651*	23.6	61.1
449 UN METHODIST..	4	390	409	5.8	15.1
453 UN PRES CH USA	1	43	50*	0.7	1.9
MILLER	52	11,755	15,278*	45.8	100.0
059 BAPT MISS ASSN	2	158	194*	0.6	1.3
081 CATHOLIC......	1	0	1,065	3.2	7.0
093 CR CH (DISC)..	1	540	665*	2.0	4.4
165 CH OF NAZARENE	1	136	263	0.8	1.7
357 PRESB CH US...	2	402	495*	1.5	3.2
413 S-D ADVENTISTS	1	120	148*	0.4	1.0
419 SO BAPT CONV..	28	8,066	9,929*	29.7	65.0
443 UN C OF CHRIST	1	30	37*	0.1	0.2
449 UN METHODIST..	14	2,288	2,464	7.4	16.1
453 UN PRES CH USA	1	15	18*	0.1	0.1
MISSISSIPPI	87	23,164	29,196*	47.0	100.0
059 BAPT MISS ASSN	8	1,201	1,511*	2.4	5.2
081 CATHOLIC......	2	0	750	1.2	2.6
093 CR CH (DISC)..	2	337	424*	0.7	1.5
127 CH GOD (CLEVE)	8	362	455*	0.7	1.6
165 CH OF NAZARENE	2	200	319	0.5	1.1
193 EPISCOPAL.....	2	235	269	0.4	0.9
283 LUTH--MO SYNOD	1	124	187	0.3	0.6
349 PENT HOLINESS.	1	46	58*	0.1	0.2
357 PRESB CH US...	3	631	794*	1.3	2.7
419 SO BAPT CONV..	44	15,428	19,405*	31.3	66.5
449 UN METHODIST..	14	4,600	5,024	8.1	17.2
MONROE	19	3,612	4,469*	28.5	100.0
059 BAPT MISS ASSN	4	274	343*	2.2	7.7
081 CATHOLIC......	1	0	180	1.1	4.0
283 LUTH--MO SYNOD	1	100	133	0.8	3.0
357 PRESB CH US...	3	301	377*	2.4	8.4
419 SO BAPT CONV..	4	1,798	2,249*	14.4	50.3
449 UN METHODIST..	6	1,139	1,187	7.6	26.6
MONTGOMERY	23	1,922	2,253*	38.7	100.0
081 CATHOLIC......	1	0	33	0.6	1.5
185 CUMBER PRESB..	1	47	55*	0.9	2.4
357 PRESB CH US...	3	138	163*	2.8	7.2
419 SO BAPT CONV..	14	1,428	1,682*	28.9	74.7
449 UN METHODIST..	4	309	320	5.5	14.2
NEVADA	32	4,080	4,746*	46.9	100.0
059 BAPT MISS ASSN	17	2,080	2,464*	24.4	51.9
093 CR CH (DISC)..	1	58	69*	0.7	1.5
123 CH GOD (ANDER)	1	20	55	0.5	1.2
165 CH OF NAZARENE	2	129	189	1.9	4.0
185 CUMBER PRESB..	2	18	21*	0.2	0.4
357 PRESB CH US...	1	131	155*	1.5	3.3
419 SO BAPT CONV..	3	800	948*	9.4	20.0
449 UN METHODIST..	5	844	845	8.4	17.8
NEWTON	9	753	893*	15.3	100.0
093 CR CH (DISC)..	1	80	96*	1.6	10.8
097 CR C AND C CR.	1	150	180*	3.1	20.2
127 CH GOD (CLEVE)	1	37	44*	0.8	4.9
419 SO BAPT CONV..	5	347	417*	7.1	46.7
449 UN METHODIST..	1	139	156	2.7	17.5
OUACHITA	62	11,959	14,091*	45.6	100.0
059 BAPT MISS ASSN	6	950	1,140*	3.7	8.1
081 CATHOLIC......	1	0	262	0.8	1.9
093 CR CH (DISC)..	1	93	112*	0.4	0.8
123 CH GOD (ANDER)	1	20	36	0.1	0.3
165 CH OF NAZARENE	1	49	88	0.3	0.6
185 CUMBER PRESB..	5	306	367*	1.2	2.6
193 EPISCOPAL.....	1	137	182	0.6	1.3
283 LUTH--MO SYNOD	1	10	24	0.1	0.2
357 PRESB CH US...	4	439	527*	1.7	3.7
413 S-D ADVENTISTS	1	32	38*	0.1	0.3
419 SO BAPT CONV..	19	5,879	7,052*	22.8	50.0
449 UN METHODIST..	19	4,015	4,228	13.7	30.0
453 UN PRES CH USA	2	29	35*	0.1	0.2
PERRY	22	1,775	2,361*	41.9	100.0
081 CATHOLIC......	1	0	245	4.3	10.4
349 PENT HOLINESS.	2	87	106*	1.9	4.5
413 S-D ADVENTISTS	1	26	32*	0.6	1.4
419 SO BAPT CONV..	12	1,318	1,607*	28.5	68.1
449 UN METHODIST..	6	344	371	6.6	15.7
PHILLIPS	37	10,283	13,676*	34.2	100.0
059 BAPT MISS ASSN	6	840	1,077*	2.7	7.9
081 CATHOLIC......	2	0	813	2.0	5.9
097 CR C AND C CR.	1	52	67*	0.2	0.5
127 CH GOD (CLEVE)	2	98	126*	0.3	0.9
165 CH OF NAZARENE	1	99	175	0.4	1.3
193 EPISCOPAL.....	1	308	397	1.0	2.9
283 LUTH--MO SYNOD	1	35	51	0.1	0.4
357 PRESB CH US...	3	510	654*	1.6	4.8
413 S-D ADVENTISTS	1	28	36*	0.1	0.3
419 SO BAPT CONV..	11	5,920	7,590*	19.0	55.5
443 UN C OF CHRIST	1	72	92*	0.2	0.7
449 UN METHODIST..	7	2,321	2,598	6.5	19.0
PIKE	19	1,989	2,261*	26.0	100.0
059 BAPT MISS ASSN	1	54	64*	0.7	2.8
093 CR CH (DISC)..	2	43	51*	0.6	2.3
097 CR C AND C CR.	3	330	392*	4.5	17.3
413 S-D ADVENTISTS	1	90	107*	1.2	4.7
419 SO BAPT CONV..	5	784	932*	10.7	41.2
449 UN METHODIST..	7	688	715	8.2	31.6
POINSETT	57	10,442	12,746*	47.5	100.0
059 BAPT MISS ASSN	3	358	443*	1.7	3.5
081 CATHOLIC......	2	0	220	0.8	1.7
093 CR CH (DISC)..	3	145	179*	0.7	1.4
097 CR C AND C CR.	1	75	93*	0.3	0.7
127 CH GOD (CLEVE)	4	262	324*	1.2	2.5
283 LUTH--MO SYNOD	1	149	200	0.7	1.6
357 PRESB CH US...	1	36	45*	0.2	0.4
419 SO BAPT CONV..	31	7,088	8,765*	32.7	68.8
449 UN METHODIST..	11	2,329	2,477	9.2	19.4
POLK	46	5,951	7,146*	53.7	100.0
059 BAPT MISS ASSN	1	50	59*	0.4	0.8
081 CATHOLIC......	1	0	220	1.7	3.1
097 CR C AND C CR.	3	575	684*	5.1	9.6
127 CH GOD (CLEVE)	2	52	62*	0.5	0.9
165 CH OF NAZARENE	3	102	174	1.3	2.4
193 EPISCOPAL.....	1	48	60	0.5	0.8
283 LUTH--MO SYNOD	1	48	64	0.5	0.9
357 PRESB CH US...	3	212	252*	1.9	3.5
419 SO BAPT CONV..	19	3,615	4,297*	32.3	60.1

*Total adherents estimated from known number of communicant, confirmed, full members.

–Represents a percent less than 0.1.

Percentages may not total due to rounding.

Table 3. Churches and Church Membership by State, County and Denomination: 1971

County and Denomination	Number of churches	Communicant, confirmed, full members	Total adherents: Number	Total adherents: Percent of total population	Total adherents: Percent of total adherents
449 UN METHODIST..	10	1,224	1,244	9.4	17.4
453 UN PRES CH USA	2	25	30*	0.2	0.4
POPE	50	7,761	10,018*	35.0	100.0
055 AS REF PRES CH	2	169	204*	0.7	2.0
059 BAPT MISS ASSN	1	74	89*	0.3	0.9
081 CATHOLIC......	2	0	754	2.6	7.5
093 CR CH (DISC)..	2	191	230*	0.8	2.3
127 CH GOD (CLEVE)	1	19	23*	0.1	0.2
165 CH OF NAZARENE	1	46	62	0.2	0.6
185 CUMBER PRESB..	8	875	1,055*	3.7	10.5
193 EPISCOPAL.....	1	123	178	0.6	1.8
283 LUTH--MO SYNOD	2	332	432	1.5	4.3
357 PRESB CH US...	3	314	379*	1.3	3.8
413 S-D ADVENTISTS	1	31	37*	0.1	0.4
419 SO BAPT CONV..	15	3,489	4,208*	14.7	42.0
449 UN METHODIST..	9	1,832	2,046	7.2	20.4
453 UN PRES CH USA	2	266	321*	1.1	3.2
PRAIRIE	21	2,915	3,843*	37.5	100.0
059 BAPT MISS ASSN	1	68	84*	0.8	2.2
081 CATHOLIC......	2	0	357	3.5	9.3
093 CR CH (DISC)..	1	24	30*	0.3	0.8
193 EPISCOPAL.....	1	151	246	2.4	6.4
283 LUTH--MO SYNOD	1	221	308	3.0	8.0
357 PRESB CH US...	1	36	44*	0.4	1.1
413 S-D ADVENTISTS	1	14	17*	0.2	0.4
419 SO BAPT CONV..	5	1,287	1,582*	15.4	41.2
449 UN METHODIST..	8	1,114	1,175	11.5	30.6
PULASKI	236	102,454	139,195*	48.5	100.0
055 AS REF PRES CH	2	405	499*	0.2	0.4
059 BAPT MISS ASSN	19	4,360	5,367*	1.9	3.9
081 CATHOLIC......	14	0	14,888	5.2	10.7
093 CR CH (DISC)..	10	2,426	2,986*	1.0	2.1
097 CR C AND C CR.	3	179	220*	0.1	0.2
121 CH GOD (ABR)..	3	85	105*	-	0.1
123 CH GOD (ANDER)	2	197	424	0.1	0.3
127 CH GOD (CLEVE)	5	188	231*	0.1	0.2
165 CH OF NAZARENE	15	2,347	3,953	1.4	2.8
185 CUMBER PRESB..	3	292	359*	0.1	0.3
193 EPISCOPAL.....	7	4,819	6,026	2.1	4.3
226 FRIENDS-USA...	1	13	16*	-	-
281 LUTH CH AMER..	2	226	335	0.1	0.2
283 LUTH--MO SYNOD	6	1,883	2,453	0.9	1.8
357 PRESB CH US...	12	2,528	3,112*	1.1	2.2
403 SALVATION ARMY	2	126	640	0.2	0.5
413 S-D ADVENTISTS	2	315	388*	0.1	0.3
419 SO BAPT CONV..	75	50,415	62,062*	21.6	44.6
435 UNITARIAN-UNIV	1	153	284	0.1	0.2
443 UN C OF CHRIST	2	193	238*	0.1	0.2
449 UN METHODIST..	39	28,851	31,589	11.0	22.7
453 UN PRES CH USA	11	2,453	3,020*	1.1	2.2
RANDOLPH	23	3,084	4,784*	37.8	100.0
059 BAPT MISS ASSN	1	162	193*	1.5	4.0
081 CATHOLIC......	2	0	1,220	9.6	25.5
357 PRESB CH US...	1	21	25*	0.2	0.5
413 S-D ADVENTISTS	1	30	36*	0.3	0.8
419 SO BAPT CONV..	11	2,123	2,535*	20.0	53.0
449 UN METHODIST..	7	748	775	6.1	16.2
ST FRANCIS	46	9,520	12,151*	39.5	100.0
059 BAPT MISS ASSN	3	527	677*	2.2	5.6
081 CATHOLIC......	1	0	366	1.2	3.0
093 CR CH (DISC)..	1	63	81*	0.3	0.7
127 CH GOD (CLEVE)	3	202	260*	0.8	2.1
165 CH OF NAZARENE	1	55	97	0.3	0.8
185 CUMBER PRESB..	1	125	161*	0.5	1.3
193 EPISCOPAL.....	2	211	243	0.8	2.0
283 LUTH--MO SYNOD	1	40	68	0.2	0.6
357 PRESB CH US...	4	447	575*	1.9	4.7
419 SO BAPT CONV..	17	5,468	7,028*	22.8	57.8
449 UN METHODIST..	12	2,382	2,595	8.4	21.4
SALINE	42	9,330	11,687*	32.4	100.0
059 BAPT MISS ASSN	2	230	281*	0.8	2.4
081 CATHOLIC......	1	0	404	1.1	3.5
093 CR CH (DISC)..	1	56	68*	0.2	0.6
123 CH GOD (ANDER)	2	87	231	0.6	2.0
127 CH GOD (CLEVE)	4	247	302*	0.8	2.6
165 CH OF NAZARENE	1	68	161	0.4	1.4
193 EPISCOPAL.....	1	73	98	0.3	0.8
283 LUTH--MO SYNOD	2	224	318	0.9	2.7
357 PRESB CH US...	1	86	105*	0.3	0.9
413 S-D ADVENTISTS	1	51	62*	0.2	0.5
419 SO BAPT CONV..	16	5,416	6,622*	18.3	56.7
449 UN METHODIST..	9	2,710	2,935	8.1	25.1
453 UN PRES CH USA	1	82	100*	0.3	0.9
SCOTT	32	3,486	4,311*	52.5	100.0
081 CATHOLIC......	1	0	50	0.6	1.2
165 CH OF NAZARENE	2	170	350	4.3	8.1
185 CUMBER PRESB..	2	135	162*	2.0	3.8
419 SO BAPT CONV..	21	2,673	3,212*	39.1	74.5
449 UN METHODIST..	6	508	537	6.5	12.5
SEARCY	12	1,518	1,746*	22.6	100.0
127 CH GOD (CLEVE)	1	23	27*	0.3	1.5
413 S-D ADVENTISTS	1	42	50*	0.6	2.9
419 SO BAPT CONV..	7	1,101	1,304*	16.9	74.7
449 UN METHODIST..	3	352	365	4.7	20.9
SEBASTIAN	102	36,319	50,226*	63.4	100.0
059 BAPT MISS ASSN	2	230	282*	0.4	0.6
081 CATHOLIC......	6	0	6,215	7.8	12.4
093 CR CH (DISC)..	1	651	798*	1.0	1.6
097 CR C AND C CR.	3	445	546*	0.7	1.1
123 CH GOD (ANDER)	1	145	320	0.4	0.6
127 CH GOD (CLEVE)	1	39	48*	0.1	0.1
165 CH OF NAZARENE	4	324	542	0.7	1.1
185 CUMBER PRESB..	1	175	215*	0.3	0.4
193 EPISCOPAL.....	3	1,085	1,359	1.7	2.7
281 LUTH CH AMER..	1	209	286	0.4	0.6
283 LUTH--MO SYNOD	3	911	1,239	1.6	2.5
349 PENT HOLINESS.	1	40	49*	0.1	0.1
357 PRESB CH US...	6	619	759*	1.0	1.5
403 SALVATION ARMY	1	136	430	0.5	0.9
419 SO BAPT CONV..	40	20,936	25,678*	32.4	51.1
449 UN METHODIST..	22	9,507	10,397	13.1	20.7
453 UN PRES CH USA	6	867	1,063*	1.3	2.1
SEVIER	35	4,536	5,560*	49.3	100.0
059 BAPT MISS ASSN	2	349	423*	3.8	7.6
081 CATHOLIC......	1	0	214	1.9	3.8
093 CR CH (DISC)..	1	72	87*	0.8	1.6
165 CH OF NAZARENE	2	57	108	1.0	1.9
185 CUMBER PRESB..	6	223	270*	2.4	4.9
357 PRESB CH US...	1	105	127*	1.1	2.3
413 S-D ADVENTISTS	1	176	213*	1.9	3.8
419 SO BAPT CONV..	10	2,430	2,947*	26.1	53.0
449 UN METHODIST..	11	1,124	1,171	10.4	21.1
SHARP	32	2,768	3,296*	40.0	100.0
059 BAPT MISS ASSN	4	244	284*	3.4	8.6
081 CATHOLIC......	1	0	182	2.2	5.5
093 CR CH (DISC)..	1	7	8*	0.1	0.2
127 CH GOD (CLEVE)	1	25	29*	0.4	0.9
165 CH OF NAZARENE	1	11	16	0.2	0.5
185 CUMBER PRESB..	1	31	36*	0.4	1.1
193 EPISCOPAL.....	1	56	89	1.1	2.7
283 LUTH--MO SYNOD	1	146	177	2.1	5.4
357 PRESB CH US...	1	144	167*	2.0	5.1
419 SO BAPT CONV..	10	1,154	1,341*	16.3	40.7
449 UN METHODIST..	10	950	967	11.7	29.3
STONE	13	1,197	1,443*	21.1	100.0
081 CATHOLIC......	1	0	60	0.9	4.2
097 CR C AND C CR.	1	60	71*	1.0	4.9
285 MENNONITE CH..	2	26	31*	0.5	2.1
419 SO BAPT CONV..	7	849	1,010*	14.8	70.0
449 UN METHODIST..	2	262	271	4.0	18.8
UNION	82	23,106	27,920*	61.5	100.0
059 BAPT MISS ASSN	10	1,574	1,899*	4.2	6.8
081 CATHOLIC......	1	0	550	1.2	2.0
093 CR CH (DISC)..	1	248	299*	0.7	1.1
123 CH GOD (ANDER)	1	58	150	0.3	0.5
165 CH OF NAZARENE	2	136	197	0.4	0.7
185 CUMBER PRESB..	1	113	136*	0.3	0.5
193 EPISCOPAL.....	1	512	619	1.4	2.2
283 LUTH--MO SYNOD	1	102	133	0.3	0.5
285 MENNONITE CH..	1	20	24*	0.1	0.1
357 PRESB CH US...	5	1,023	1,234*	2.7	4.4
403 SALVATION ARMY	1	48	207	0.5	0.7
413 S-D ADVENTISTS	1	49	59*	0.1	0.2
419 SO BAPT CONV..	35	13,388	16,155*	35.6	57.9
449 UN METHODIST..	21	5,835	6,258	13.8	22.4
VAN BUREN	23	2,856	3,376*	40.8	100.0
059 BAPT MISS ASSN	2	80	94*	1.1	2.8
081 CATHOLIC......	2	0	135	1.6	4.0
165 CH OF NAZARENE	1	25	37	0.4	1.1
419 SO BAPT CONV..	17	2,003	2,355*	28.5	69.8
449 UN METHODIST..	1	748	755	9.1	22.4
WASHINGTON	119	24,097	32,264*	41.7	100.0
059 BAPT MISS ASSN	14	2,418	2,899*	3.7	9.0
081 CATHOLIC......	5	0	3,514	4.5	10.9
093 CR CH (DISC)..	5	799	958*	1.2	3.0
097 CR C AND C CR.	5	395	474*	0.6	1.5
123 CH GOD (ANDER)	1	4	11	-	-
127 CH GOD (CLEVE)	4	99	119*	0.2	0.4
165 CH OF NAZARENE	5	365	787	1.0	2.4
185 CUMBER PRESB..	1	61	73*	0.1	0.2
193 EPISCOPAL.....	2	1,033	1,085	1.4	3.4
226 FRIENDS-USA...	1	2	2*	-	-
281 LUTH CH AMER..	1	111	181	0.2	0.6
283 LUTH--MO SYNOD	2	500	670	0.9	2.1
349 PENT HOLINESS.	2	53	64*	0.1	0.2
357 PRESB CH US...	10	691	828*	1.1	2.6
403 SALVATION ARMY	2	32	150	0.2	0.5
413 S-D ADVENTISTS	3	176	211*	0.3	0.7
419 SO BAPT CONV..	29	10,380	12,444*	16.1	38.6
435 UNITARIAN-UNIV	1	52	82	0.1	0.3
449 UN METHODIST..	16	6,223	6,869	8.9	21.3

*Total adherents estimated from known number of communicant, confirmed, full members.

—Represents a percent less than 0.1.

Percentages may not total due to rounding.

Table 3. Churches and Church Membership by State, County and Denomination: 1971

County and Denomination	Number of churches	Communicant, confirmed, full members	Total adherents: Number	Total adherents: Percent of total population	Total adherents: Percent of total adherents
453 UN PRES CH USA	10	703	843*	1.1	2.6
WHITE	89	13,096	15,576*	39.7	100.0
059 BAPT MISS ASSN	15	2,371	2,838*	7.2	18.2
081 CATHOLIC......	3	0	297	0.8	1.9
093 CR CH (DISC)..	3	200	239*	0.6	1.5
127 CH GOD (CLEVE)	3	217	260*	0.7	1.7
165 CH OF NAZARENE	4	311	493	1.3	3.2
185 CUMBER PRESB..	4	192	230*	0.6	1.5
193 EPISCOPAL.....	1	63	90	0.2	0.6
349 PENT HOLINESS.	1	39	47*	0.1	0.3
357 PRESB CH US...	2	152	182*	0.5	1.2
419 SO BAPT CONV..	27	5,949	7,121*	18.1	45.7
449 UN METHODIST..	26	3,602	3,779	9.6	24.3
WOODRUFF	28	4,711	5,663*	49.0	100.0
059 BAPT MISS ASSN	3	488	602*	5.2	10.6
081 CATHOLIC......	1	0	75	0.6	1.3
127 CH GOD (CLEVE)	1	190	234*	2.0	4.1
165 CH OF NAZARENE	1	83	160	1.4	2.8
357 PRESB CH US...	2	58	72*	0.6	1.3
419 SO BAPT CONV..	11	2,322	2,863*	24.8	50.6
449 UN METHODIST..	8	1,549	1,631	14.1	28.8
453 UN PRES CH USA	1	21	26*	0.2	0.5
YELL	39	4,364	5,074*	35.7	100.0
055 AS REF PRES CH	1	55	66*	0.5	1.3
059 BAPT MISS ASSN	2	104	124*	0.9	2.4
081 CATHOLIC......	1	0	100	0.7	2.0
127 CH GOD (CLEVE)	1	36	43*	0.3	0.8
165 CH OF NAZARENE	1	12	45	0.3	0.9
185 CUMBER PRESB..	1	125	150*	1.1	3.0
419 SO BAPT CONV..	10	2,166	2,591*	18.2	51.1
449 UN METHODIST..	21	1,816	1,895	13.3	37.3
453 UN PRES CH USA	1	50	60*	0.4	1.2
CO DATA NOT AVAIL	267	22,101	31,487*	N/A	N/A
151 L-D SAINTS....	0	0	4,538	N/A	N/A
223 FREE WILL BAPT	211	18,500	22,555*	N/A	N/A
231 GENERAL BAPT..	47	3,277	3,995*	N/A	N/A
285 MENNONITE CH..	1	19	23*	N/A	N/A
467 WESLEYAN......	8	305	376	N/A	N/A
CALIFORNIA					
THE STATE.....	7,552	1,808,346	6,692,785*	33.5	100.0
ALAMEDA	331	79,361	322,577*	30.1	100.0
019 AMER BAPT CONV	22	6,945	8,361*	0.8	2.6
029 AMER LUTH CH..	10	3,270	4,580	0.4	1.4
059 BAPT MISS ASSN	4	490	590*	0.1	0.2
081 CATHOLIC......	51	0	221,415	20.6	68.6
093 CR CH (DISC)..	10	1,618	1,948*	0.2	0.6
097 CR C AND C CR.	9	803	967*	0.1	0.3
105 CHRISTIAN REF.	2	249	452	-	0.1
123 CH GOD (ANDER)	5	274	779	0.1	0.2
127 CH GOD (CLEVE)	4	111	134*	-	-
157 CH OF BRETHREN	1	71	85*	-	-
165 CH OF NAZARENE	13	1,096	2,602	0.2	0.8
175 CONG CR CH....	1	241	290*	-	0.1
193 EPISCOPAL.....	20	7,484	10,018	0.9	3.1
201 EVAN COV CH AM	3	705	849*	0.1	0.3
221 FREE METH C NA	2	235	348	-	0.1
226 FRIENDS-USA...	3	347	418*	-	0.1
281 LUTH CH AMER..	12	4,525	7,062	0.7	2.2
283 LUTH--MO SYNOD	20	6,673	9,477	0.9	2.9
335 ORTH PRESB CH.	1	42	57	-	-
349 PENT HOLINESS.	3	211	254*	-	0.1
353 PLY BRETHREN..	6	623	1,422	0.1	0.4
371 REF CH IN AM..	1	113	132	-	-
403 SALVATION ARMY	3	282	847	0.1	0.3
413 S-D ADVENTISTS	10	2,872	3,458*	0.3	1.1
419 SO BAPT CONV..	36	9,182	11,055*	1.0	3.4
435 UNITARIAN-UNIV	4	619	749	0.1	0.2
443 UN C OF CHRIST	16	5,107	6,149*	0.6	1.9
449 UN METHODIST..	32	10,926	10,926	1.0	3.4
453 UN PRES CH USA	27	14,247	17,153*	1.6	5.3
ALPINE	0	0	0	-	-
AMADOR	14	635	2,796*	23.7	100.0
081 CATHOLIC......	6	0	1,987	16.8	71.1
127 CH GOD (CLEVE)	1	7	8*	0.1	0.3
165 CH OF NAZARENE	1	24	116	1.0	4.1
193 EPISCOPAL.....	1	129	145	1.2	5.2
221 FREE METH C NA	1	32	39	0.3	1.4
413 S-D ADVENTISTS	1	75	87*	0.7	3.1
449 UN METHODIST..	3	368	414	3.5	14.8
BUTTE	63	11,510	23,971*	23.5	100.0
019 AMER BAPT CONV	3	758	894*	0.9	3.7
029 AMER LUTH CH..	2	531	752	0.7	3.1
081 CATHOLIC......	6	0	9,147	9.0	38.2
093 CR CH (DISC)..	2	447	527*	0.5	2.2
097 CR C AND C CR.	4	351	414*	0.4	1.7
123 CH GOD (ANDER)	1	110	257	0.3	1.1
127 CH GOD (CLEVE)	2	42	50*	-	0.2
157 CH OF BRETHREN	2	135	159*	0.2	0.7
165 CH OF NAZARENE	5	478	1,250	1.2	5.2
193 EPISCOPAL.....	4	597	855	0.8	3.6
221 FREE METH C NA	2	43	54	0.1	0.2
283 LUTH--MO SYNOD	4	796	1,075	1.1	4.5
353 PLY BRETHREN..	1	20	40	-	0.2
403 SALVATION ARMY	1	42	163	0.2	0.7
413 S-D ADVENTISTS	4	1,683	1,984*	1.9	8.3
419 SO BAPT CONV..	7	1,621	1,911*	1.9	8.0
435 UNITARIAN-UNIV	1	55	55	0.1	0.2
443 UN C OF CHRIST	2	429	506*	0.5	2.1
449 UN METHODIST..	7	2,192	2,487	2.4	10.4
453 UN PRES CH USA	3	1,180	1,391*	1.4	5.8
CALAVERAS	22	949	3,003*	22.1	100.0
081 CATHOLIC......	6	0	1,760	13.0	58.6
123 CH GOD (ANDER)	1	36	76	0.6	2.5
165 CH OF NAZARENE	1	14	23	0.2	0.8
193 EPISCOPAL.....	1	124	224	1.6	7.5
201 EVAN COV CH AM	4	218	252*	1.9	8.4
281 LUTH CH AMER..	1	66	100	0.7	3.3
413 S-D ADVENTISTS	2	70	81*	0.6	2.7
419 SO BAPT CONV..	4	255	295*	2.2	9.8
443 UN C OF CHRIST	2	166	192*	1.4	6.4
COLUSA	20	1,742	5,087*	40.9	100.0
019 AMER BAPT CONV	3	155	187*	1.5	3.7
081 CATHOLIC......	5	0	3,000	24.1	59.0
093 CR CH (DISC)..	1	45	54*	0.4	1.1
165 CH OF NAZARENE	1	13	41	0.3	0.8
193 EPISCOPAL.....	1	188	286	2.3	5.6
283 LUTH--MO SYNOD	1	72	88	0.7	1.7
419 SO BAPT CONV..	1	205	247*	2.0	4.9
449 UN METHODIST..	6	946	1,042	8.4	20.5
453 UN PRES CH USA	1	118	142*	1.1	2.8
CONTRA COSTA	224	56,696	183,702*	32.9	100.0
019 AMER BAPT CONV	19	3,823	4,707*	0.8	2.6
029 AMER LUTH CH..	4	1,266	1,927	0.3	1.0
081 CATHOLIC......	35	0	110,285	19.8	60.0
093 CR CH (DISC)..	6	1,011	1,245*	0.2	0.7
097 CR C AND C CR.	5	275	339*	0.1	0.2
105 CHRISTIAN REF.	1	110	255	-	0.1
123 CH GOD (ANDER)	1	47	125	-	0.1
127 CH GOD (CLEVE)	4	442	544*	0.1	0.3
165 CH OF NAZARENE	7	728	1,447	0.3	0.8
193 EPISCOPAL.....	17	5,619	8,255	1.5	4.5
201 EVAN COV CH AM	2	231	284*	0.1	0.2
221 FREE METH C NA	1	39	71	-	-
226 FRIENDS-USA...	1	79	97*	-	0.1
281 LUTH CH AMER..	12	4,842	7,254	1.3	3.9
283 LUTH--MO SYNOD	14	3,936	6,094	1.1	3.3
349 PENT HOLINESS.	4	265	326*	0.1	0.2
353 PLY BRETHREN..	3	297	500	0.1	0.3
371 REF CH IN AM..	1	161	218	-	0.1
403 SALVATION ARMY	1	112	393	0.1	0.2
413 S-D ADVENTISTS	7	1,568	1,931*	0.3	1.1
415 S-D BAPTIST GC	1	19	23*	-	-
419 SO BAPT CONV..	31	9,788	12,052*	2.2	6.6
435 UNITARIAN-UNIV	3	1,126	1,321	0.2	0.7
443 UN C OF CHRIST	10	3,528	4,344*	0.8	2.4
449 UN METHODIST..	19	8,095	8,172	1.5	4.4
453 UN PRES CH USA	14	9,217	11,349*	2.0	6.2
469 WISC EVAN LUTH	1	72	144	-	0.1
DEL NORTE	13	1,867	3,447*	23.6	100.0
081 CATHOLIC......	2	0	1,100	7.5	31.9
097 CR C AND C CR.	1	50	61*	0.4	1.8
127 CH GOD (CLEVE)	1	5	6*	-	0.2
193 EPISCOPAL.....	1	108	123	0.8	3.6
283 LUTH--MO SYNOD	1	203	404	2.8	11.7
413 S-D ADVENTISTS	1	229	281*	1.9	8.2
419 SO BAPT CONV..	3	792	970*	6.7	28.1
449 UN METHODIST..	3	480	502	3.4	14.6
EL DORADO	26	3,053	7,943*	18.1	100.0
019 AMER BAPT CONV	2	266	317*	0.7	4.0
081 CATHOLIC......	3	0	3,810	8.7	48.0
127 CH GOD (CLEVE)	1	5	6*	-	0.1
165 CH OF NAZARENE	2	105	222	0.5	2.8
193 EPISCOPAL.....	1	224	336	0.8	4.2
281 LUTH CH AMER..	1	85	130	0.3	1.6
283 LUTH--MO SYNOD	2	440	803	1.8	10.1
413 S-D ADVENTISTS	3	684	814*	1.9	10.2
419 SO BAPT CONV..	5	508	605*	1.4	7.6
443 UN C OF CHRIST	2	136	162*	0.4	2.0
449 UN METHODIST..	2	180	238	0.5	3.0
453 UN PRES CH USA	2	420	500*	1.1	6.3
FRESNO	248	46,885	158,093*	38.3	100.0
019 AMER BAPT CONV	18	4,989	6,156*	1.5	3.9
029 AMER LUTH CH..	8	1,903	2,504	0.6	1.6

*Total adherents estimated from known number of communicant, confirmed, full members.

—Represents a percent less than 0.1.

Percentages may not total due to rounding.

Table 3. Churches and Church Membership by State, County and Denomination: 1971

County and Denomination	Number of churches	Communicant, confirmed, full members	Total adherents: Number	Total adherents: Percent of total population	Total adherents: Percent of total adherents
059 BAPT MISS ASSN	1	134	165*	-	0.1
081 CATHOLIC......	40	0	98,000	23.7	62.0
093 CR CH (DISC)..	6	1,254	1,547*	0.4	1.0
097 CR C AND C CR.	5	488	602*	0.1	0.4
105 CHRISTIAN REF.	1	69	145	-	0.1
123 CH GOD (ANDER)	8	383	1,090	0.3	0.7
127 CH GOD (CLEVE)	9	649	801*	0.2	0.5
157 CH OF BRETHREN	3	819	1,011*	0.2	0.6
165 CH OF NAZARENE	12	1,183	2,521	0.6	1.6
185 CUMBER PRESB..	1	89	110*	-	0.1
193 EPISCOPAL.....	8	2,072	2,909	0.7	1.8
201 EVAN COV CH AM	4	658	812*	0.2	0.5
211 EV MENN BRETH.	1	55	68*	-	-
221 FREE METH C NA	2	61	84	-	0.1
226 FRIENDS-USA...	2	101	125*	-	0.1
281 LUTH CH AMER..	10	2,561	3,777	0.9	2.4
283 LUTH--MO SYNOD	6	1,820	2,366	0.6	1.5
287 MENN GEN CONF.	2	684	844*	0.2	0.5
349 PENT HOLINESS.	7	267	329*	0.1	0.2
353 PLY BRETHREN..	1	60	80	-	0.1
403 SALVATION ARMY	1	111	326	0.1	0.2
413 S-D ADVENTISTS	11	2,517	3,106*	0.8	2.0
419 SO BAPT CONV..	33	9,215	11,370*	2.8	7.2
435 UNITARIAN-UNIV	1	156	211	0.1	0.1
443 UN C OF CHRIST	6	2,137	2,637*	0.6	1.7
449 UN METHODIST..	25	7,160	7,866	1.9	5.0
453 UN PRES CH USA	15	5,251	6,479*	1.6	4.1
469 WISC EVAN LUTH	1	39	52	-	-
GLENN	23	2,516	6,081*	34.7	100.0
019 AMER BAPT CONV	3	651	779*	4.4	12.8
029 AMER LUTH CH..	1	284	376	2.1	6.2
081 CATHOLIC......	3	0	3,000	17.1	49.3
093 CR CH (DISC)..	1	20	24*	0.1	0.4
097 CR C AND C CR.	2	125	150*	0.9	2.5
165 CH OF NAZARENE	1	49	147	0.8	2.4
193 EPISCOPAL.....	2	183	234	1.3	3.8
226 FRIENDS-USA...	1	49	59*	0.3	1.0
283 LUTH--MO SYNOD	2	174	217	1.2	3.6
413 S-D ADVENTISTS	2	155	186*	1.1	3.1
419 SO BAPT CONV..	2	255	305*	1.7	5.0
449 UN METHODIST..	2	496	514	2.9	8.5
453 UN PRES CH USA	1	75	90*	0.5	1.5
HUMBOLDT	94	13,055	31,079*	31.2	100.0
019 AMER BAPT CONV	3	1,725	2,083*	2.1	6.7
029 AMER LUTH CH..	5	1,101	1,622	1.6	5.2
081 CATHOLIC......	15	0	13,208	13.2	42.5
093 CR CH (DISC)..	2	208	251*	0.3	0.8
097 CR C AND C CR.	3	215	260*	0.3	0.8
127 CH GOD (CLEVE)	4	181	219*	0.2	0.7
165 CH OF NAZARENE	8	639	1,987	2.0	6.4
193 EPISCOPAL.....	5	1,450	1,911	1.9	6.1
201 EVAN COV CH AM	1	152	184*	0.2	0.6
281 LUTH CH AMER..	2	116	159	0.2	0.5
283 LUTH--MO SYNOD	4	531	793	0.8	2.6
349 PENT HOLINESS.	1	50	60*	0.1	0.2
403 SALVATION ARMY	1	54	247	0.2	0.8
413 S-D ADVENTISTS	5	1,204	1,454*	1.5	4.7
419 SO BAPT CONV..	16	2,299	2,777*	2.8	8.9
435 UNITARIAN-UNIV	1	150	170	0.2	0.5
443 UN C OF CHRIST	2	229	277*	0.3	0.9
449 UN METHODIST..	4	1,311	1,678	1.7	5.4
453 UN PRES CH USA	12	1,440	1,739*	1.7	5.6
IMPERIAL	50	6,178	28,030*	37.6	100.0
019 AMER BAPT CONV	5	919	1,176*	1.6	4.2
081 CATHOLIC......	14	0	18,537	24.9	66.1
093 CR CH (DISC)..	1	138	177*	0.2	0.6
097 CR C AND C CR.	2	375	480*	0.6	1.7
123 CH GOD (ANDER)	1	6	25	-	0.1
127 CH GOD (CLEVE)	1	25	32*	-	0.1
165 CH OF NAZARENE	3	169	308	0.4	1.1
226 FRIENDS-USA...	1	28	36*	-	0.1
283 LUTH--MO SYNOD	4	598	906	1.2	3.2
403 SALVATION ARMY	1	22	1,342	1.8	4.8
413 S-D ADVENTISTS	4	402	515*	0.7	1.8
419 SO BAPT CONV..	6	1,420	1,817*	2.4	6.5
449 UN METHODIST..	4	1,372	1,778	2.4	6.3
453 UN PRES CH USA	3	704	901*	1.2	3.2
INYO	19	1,513	4,675*	30.0	100.0
081 CATHOLIC......	5	0	2,500	16.1	53.5
097 CR C AND C CR.	1	35	42*	0.3	0.9
165 CH OF NAZARENE	2	132	349	2.2	7.5
193 EPISCOPAL.....	2	189	378	2.4	8.1
283 LUTH--MO SYNOD	1	130	183	1.2	3.9
413 S-D ADVENTISTS	2	157	187*	1.2	4.0
419 SO BAPT CONV..	1	13	15*	0.1	0.3
449 UN METHODIST..	3	542	646	4.1	13.8
453 UN PRES CH USA	2	315	375*	2.4	8.0
KERN	223	41,762	119,640*	36.3	100.0
019 AMER BAPT CONV	16	4,928	6,133*	1.9	5.1
029 AMER LUTH CH..	4	1,065	1,570	0.5	1.3
059 BAPT MISS ASSN	2	142	177*	0.1	0.1
081 CATHOLIC......	30	0	65,000	19.7	54.3
093 CR CH (DISC)..	3	888	1,105*	0.3	0.9
097 CR C AND C CR.	10	1,441	1,793*	0.5	1.5
105 CHRISTIAN REF.	1	61	131	-	0.1
123 CH GOD (ANDER)	2	115	350	0.1	0.3
127 CH GOD (CLEVE)	14	1,085	1,350*	0.4	1.1
157 CH OF BRETHREN	2	368	458*	0.1	0.4
165 CH OF NAZARENE	17	1,361	4,000	1.2	3.3
193 EPISCOPAL.....	8	1,416	1,934	0.6	1.6
221 FREE METH C NA	1	25	31	-	-
281 LUTH CH AMER..	2	422	595	0.2	0.5
283 LUTH--MO SYNOD	10	1,419	2,058	0.6	1.7
349 PENT HOLINESS.	7	250	311*	0.1	0.3
403 SALVATION ARMY	1	65	218	0.1	0.2
413 S-D ADVENTISTS	11	2,254	2,805*	0.9	2.3
419 SO BAPT CONV..	49	14,036	17,467*	5.3	14.6
435 UNITARIAN-UNIV	2	88	120	-	0.1
443 UN C OF CHRIST	7	1,296	1,613*	0.5	1.3
449 UN METHODIST..	18	5,574	6,111	1.9	5.1
453 UN PRES CH USA	6	3,463	4,310*	1.3	3.6
KINGS	53	6,015	22,224*	34.4	100.0
019 AMER BAPT CONV	6	781	994*	1.5	4.5
081 CATHOLIC......	8	0	14,000	21.7	63.0
093 CR CH (DISC)..	1	200	254*	0.4	1.1
097 CR C AND C CR.	1	35	45*	0.1	0.2
105 CHRISTIAN REF.	1	314	572	0.9	2.6
127 CH GOD (CLEVE)	1	74	94*	0.1	0.4
165 CH OF NAZARENE	3	194	307	0.5	1.4
193 EPISCOPAL.....	4	344	633	1.0	2.8
281 LUTH CH AMER..	1	172	246	0.4	1.1
283 LUTH--MO SYNOD	2	191	353	0.5	1.6
349 PENT HOLINESS.	1	16	20*	-	0.1
403 SALVATION ARMY	2	45	189	0.3	0.9
413 S-D ADVENTISTS	5	688	875*	1.4	3.9
419 SO BAPT CONV..	7	941	1,197*	1.9	5.4
449 UN METHODIST..	6	1,046	1,206	1.9	5.4
453 UN PRES CH USA	4	974	1,239*	1.9	5.6
LAKE	39	2,457	4,660*	23.8	100.0
019 AMER BAPT CONV	2	211	240*	1.2	5.2
081 CATHOLIC......	13	0	1,730	8.9	37.1
093 CR CH (DISC)..	1	72	82*	0.4	1.8
097 CR C AND C CR.	1	35	40*	0.2	0.9
165 CH OF NAZARENE	1	38	91	0.5	2.0
193 EPISCOPAL.....	1	137	261	1.3	5.6
281 LUTH CH AMER..	1	66	78	0.4	1.7
283 LUTH--MO SYNOD	2	119	185	0.9	4.0
413 S-D ADVENTISTS	4	379	431*	2.2	9.2
419 SO BAPT CONV..	3	320	364*	1.9	7.8
449 UN METHODIST..	7	689	713	3.6	15.3
453 UN PRES CH USA	3	391	445*	2.3	9.5
LASSEN	19	2,126	5,737*	38.3	100.0
019 AMER BAPT CONV	2	262	314*	2.1	5.5
081 CATHOLIC......	4	0	3,081	20.6	53.7
123 CH GOD (ANDER)	1	33	57	0.4	1.0
127 CH GOD (CLEVE)	1	16	19*	0.1	0.3
165 CH OF NAZARENE	1	22	48	0.3	0.8
193 EPISCOPAL.....	1	88	124	0.8	2.2
283 LUTH--MO SYNOD	2	188	276	1.8	4.8
413 S-D ADVENTISTS	2	159	191*	1.3	3.3
419 SO BAPT CONV..	4	1,027	1,232*	8.2	21.5
449 UN METHODIST..	1	331	395	2.6	6.9
LOS ANGELES	1,838	564,382	2,080,207*	29.6	100.0
019 AMER BAPT CONV	144	58,729	71,193*	1.0	3.4
029 AMER LUTH CH..	73	35,601	51,338	0.7	2.5
059 BAPT MISS ASSN	4	1,476	1,789*	-	0.1
081 CATHOLIC......	255	0	1,343,679	19.1	64.6
093 CR CH (DISC)..	79	24,058	29,164*	0.4	1.4
097 CR C AND C CR.	78	13,655	16,553*	0.2	0.8
105 CHRISTIAN REF.	12	3,041	5,204	0.1	0.3
123 CH GOD (ANDER)	27	2,790	6,671	0.1	0.3
127 CH GOD (CLEVE)	23	2,013	2,440*	-	0.1
157 CH OF BRETHREN	13	3,187	3,863*	0.1	0.2
165 CH OF NAZARENE	80	11,650	21,551	0.3	1.0
175 CONG CR CH....	14	5,855	7,098*	0.1	0.3
185 CUMBER PRESB..	1	121	147*	-	-
193 EPISCOPAL.....	93	49,074	71,745	1.0	3.4
201 EVAN COV CH AM	11	2,448	2,968*	-	0.1
221 FREE METH C NA	20	1,665	2,430	-	0.1
226 FRIENDS-USA...	23	3,416	4,141*	0.1	0.2
281 LUTH CH AMER..	67	20,170	29,464	0.4	1.4
283 LUTH--MO SYNOD	92	33,725	48,714	0.7	2.3
285 MENNONITE CH..	3	176	213*	-	-
287 MENN GEN CONF.	2	287	348*	-	-
293 MORAV CH-NORTH	2	423	645	-	-
313 NO AM BAPT GC.	1	45	55*	-	-
315 NO AM OLD RC..	2	420	509*	-	-
335 ORTH PRESB CH.	7	858	1,256	-	0.1
349 PENT HOLINESS.	10	436	529*	-	-
353 PLY BRETHREN..	19	1,552	1,954	-	0.1
371 REF CH IN AM..	13	5,208	7,989	0.1	0.4
381 REF PRES-EVAN.	2	143	250	-	-
403 SALVATION ARMY	19	1,906	7,907	0.1	0.4
413 S-D ADVENTISTS	83	26,814	32,505*	0.5	1.6
415 S-D BAPTIST GC	1	151	183*	-	-
419 SO BAPT CONV..	154	57,832	70,105*	1.0	3.4
435 UNITARIAN-UNIV	19	3,622	4,617	0.1	0.2
443 UN C OF CHRIST	62	0	0*	-	-
449 UN METHODIST..	179	106,217	127,071	1.8	6.1
453 UN PRES CH USA	144	85,086	103,143*	1.5	5.0
469 WISC EVAN LUTH	7	532	776	-	-

*Total adherents estimated from known number of communicant, confirmed, full members.

—Represents a percent less than 0.1.

Percentages may not total due to rounding.

Table 3. Churches and Church Membership by State, County and Denomination: 1971

County and Denomination	Number of churches	Communicant, confirmed, full members	Total adherents: Number	Percent of total population	Percent of total adherents
MADERA	36	4,423	15,777*	38.0	100.0
019 AMER BAPT CONV	4	395	485*	1.2	3.1
029 AMER LUTH CH..	1	201	275	0.7	1.7
081 CATHOLIC......	6	0	10,000	24.1	63.4
093 CR CH (DISC)..	1	117	144*	0.3	0.9
097 CR C AND C CR.	1	120	147*	0.4	0.9
123 CH GOD (ANDER)	2	164	397	1.0	2.5
127 CH GOD (CLEVE)	1	58	71*	0.2	0.5
165 CH OF NAZARENE	2	157	293	0.7	1.9
193 EPISCOPAL.....	1	175	275	0.7	1.7
283 LUTH--MO SYNOD	1	57	77	0.2	0.5
349 PENT HOLINESS.	1	11	14*	-	0.1
413 S-D ADVENTISTS	4	639	785*	1.9	5.0
419 SO BAPT CONV..	6	1,138	1,398*	3.4	8.9
443 UN C OF CHRIST	1	19	23*	0.1	0.1
449 UN METHODIST..	2	678	786	1.9	5.0
453 UN PRES CH USA	2	494	607*	1.5	3.8
MARIN	90	15,563	66,847*	32.4	100.0
019 AMER BAPT CONV	6	1,139	1,373*	0.7	2.1
029 AMER LUTH CH..	6	1,394	2,063	1.0	3.1
081 CATHOLIC......	19	0	46,250	22.4	69.2
097 CR C AND C CR.	1	80	96*	-	0.1
123 CH GOD (ANDER)	4	188	467	0.2	0.7
165 CH OF NAZARENE	1	53	118	0.1	0.2
193 EPISCOPAL.....	11	2,672	3,913	1.9	5.9
201 EVAN COV CH AM	1	52	63*	-	0.1
226 FRIENDS-USA...	1	27	33*	-	-
281 LUTH CH AMER..	1	270	401	0.2	0.6
283 LUTH--MO SYNOD	4	1,071	1,565	0.8	2.3
335 ORTH PRESB CH.	1	19	36	-	0.1
353 PLY BRETHREN..	1	20	30	-	-
413 S-D ADVENTISTS	2	188	227*	0.1	0.3
419 SO BAPT CONV..	5	1,534	1,849*	0.9	2.8
435 UNITARIAN-UNIV	1	408	458	0.2	0.7
443 UN C OF CHRIST	4	644	776*	0.4	1.2
449 UN METHODIST..	5	1,331	1,738	0.8	2.6
453 UN PRES CH USA	16	4,473	5,391*	2.6	8.1
MARIPOSA	9	406	1,088*	18.1	100.0
081 CATHOLIC......	3	0	600	10.0	55.1
193 EPISCOPAL.....	1	46	69	1.1	6.3
413 S-D ADVENTISTS	2	155	181*	3.0	16.6
449 UN METHODIST..	3	205	238	4.0	21.9
MENDOCINO	56	7,875	13,971*	27.3	100.0
019 AMER BAPT CONV	3	706	848*	1.7	6.1
029 AMER LUTH CH..	1	125	197	0.4	1.4
081 CATHOLIC......	16	0	3,845	7.5	27.5
093 CR CH (DISC)..	2	2,322	2,788*	5.5	20.0
165 CH OF NAZARENE	3	87	290	0.6	2.1
193 EPISCOPAL.....	2	343	585	1.1	4.2
281 LUTH CH AMER..	1	146	267	0.5	1.9
283 LUTH--MO SYNOD	3	310	446	0.9	3.2
413 S-D ADVENTISTS	5	787	945*	1.8	6.8
419 SO BAPT CONV..	7	1,246	1,496*	2.9	10.7
449 UN METHODIST..	8	905	1,186	2.3	8.5
453 UN PRES CH USA	5	898	1,078*	2.1	7.7
MERCED	72	10,954	44,511*	42.5	100.0
019 AMER BAPT CONV	4	970	1,221*	1.2	2.7
081 CATHOLIC......	19	0	30,000	28.7	67.4
093 CR CH (DISC)..	2	235	296*	0.3	0.7
097 CR C AND C CR.	1	150	189*	0.2	0.4
123 CH GOD (ANDER)	3	184	449	0.4	1.0
127 CH GOD (CLEVE)	1	7	9*	-	-
165 CH OF NAZARENE	3	276	517	0.5	1.2
193 EPISCOPAL.....	2	385	649	0.6	1.5
201 EVAN COV CH AM	1	332	418*	0.4	0.9
281 LUTH CH AMER..	2	434	622	0.6	1.4
283 LUTH--MO SYNOD	4	652	958	0.9	2.2
285 MENNONITE CH..	1	85	107*	0.1	0.2
287 MENN GEN CONF.	1	74	93*	0.1	0.2
353 PLY BRETHREN..	1	50	60	0.1	0.1
403 SALVATION ARMY	1	20	141	0.1	0.3
413 S-D ADVENTISTS	3	310	390*	0.4	0.9
419 SO BAPT CONV..	13	3,489	4,391*	4.2	9.9
435 UNITARIAN-UNIV	1	18	38	-	0.1
449 UN METHODIST..	6	2,133	2,516	2.4	5.7
453 UN PRES CH USA	3	1,150	1,447*	1.4	3.3
MODOC	12	663	1,271*	17.0	100.0
081 CATHOLIC......	2	0	400	5.4	31.5
165 CH OF NAZARENE	1	8	66	0.9	5.2
193 EPISCOPAL.....	1	91	136	1.8	10.7
413 S-D ADVENTISTS	2	46	55*	0.7	4.3
419 SO BAPT CONV..	1	195	231*	3.1	18.2
443 UN C OF CHRIST	5	323	383*	5.1	30.1
MONO	7	78	230*	5.7	100.0
081 CATHOLIC......	3	0	140	3.5	60.9
419 SO BAPT CONV..	1	15	18*	0.4	7.8
449 UN METHODIST..	1	15	15	0.4	6.5
453 UN PRES CH USA	2	48	57*	1.4	24.8
MONTEREY	99	18,032	68,820*	27.5	100.0
019 AMER BAPT CONV	4	385	467*	0.2	0.7
029 AMER LUTH CH..	4	820	1,157	0.5	1.7
059 BAPT MISS ASSN	1	45	55*	-	0.1
081 CATHOLIC......	19	0	45,128	18.0	65.6
093 CR CH (DISC)..	1	117	142*	0.1	0.2
097 CR C AND C CR.	1	250	303*	0.1	0.4
123 CH GOD (ANDER)	1	70	245	0.1	0.4
127 CH GOD (CLEVE)	3	99	120*	-	0.2
165 CH OF NAZARENE	2	204	532	0.2	0.8
193 EPISCOPAL.....	10	2,072	2,902	1.2	4.2
201 EVAN COV CH AM	1	38	46*	-	0.1
226 FRIENDS-USA...	1	26	32*	-	-
281 LUTH CH AMER..	3	1,023	1,540	0.6	2.2
283 LUTH--MO SYNOD	3	832	1,157	0.5	1.7
353 PLY BRETHREN..	1	10	15	-	-
403 SALVATION ARMY	2	104	392	0.2	0.6
413 S-D ADVENTISTS	4	568	689*	0.3	1.0
419 SO BAPT CONV..	16	4,984	6,049*	2.4	8.8
435 UNITARIAN-UNIV	2	171	201	0.1	0.3
443 UN C OF CHRIST	1	108	131*	0.1	0.2
449 UN METHODIST..	11	3,075	3,838	1.5	5.6
453 UN PRES CH USA	8	3,031	3,679*	1.5	5.3
NAPA	45	12,308	26,728*	33.8	100.0
019 AMER BAPT CONV	2	692	821*	1.0	3.1
029 AMER LUTH CH..	1	227	332	0.4	1.2
081 CATHOLIC......	11	0	11,292	14.3	42.2
097 CR C AND C CR.	2	585	694*	0.9	2.6
123 CH GOD (ANDER)	2	81	168	0.2	0.6
165 CH OF NAZARENE	1	192	411	0.5	1.5
193 EPISCOPAL.....	3	649	1,088	1.4	4.1
281 LUTH CH AMER..	1	181	276	0.3	1.0
283 LUTH--MO SYNOD	2	793	1,116	1.4	4.2
353 PLY BRETHREN..	1	89	140	0.2	0.5
403 SALVATION ARMY	1	16	140	0.2	0.5
413 S-D ADVENTISTS	7	4,825	5,727*	7.2	21.4
419 SO BAPT CONV..	5	1,460	1,733*	2.2	6.5
449 UN METHODIST..	3	1,064	1,064	1.3	4.0
453 UN PRES CH USA	3	1,454	1,726*	2.2	6.5
NEVADA	24	2,776	6,981*	26.5	100.0
019 AMER BAPT CONV	1	126	147*	0.6	2.1
029 AMER LUTH CH..	1	170	248	0.9	3.6
081 CATHOLIC......	4	0	3,242	12.3	46.4
097 CR C AND C CR.	1	40	47*	0.2	0.7
123 CH GOD (ANDER)	1	85	85	0.3	1.2
127 CH GOD (CLEVE)	1	15	18*	0.1	0.3
165 CH OF NAZARENE	1	55	104	0.4	1.5
193 EPISCOPAL.....	2	523	956	3.6	13.7
226 FRIENDS-USA...	1	20	23*	0.1	0.3
283 LUTH--MO SYNOD	2	32	44	0.2	0.6
413 S-D ADVENTISTS	2	397	464*	1.8	6.6
419 SO BAPT CONV..	2	336	393*	1.5	5.6
449 UN METHODIST..	4	823	1,030	3.9	14.8
453 UN PRES CH USA	1	154	180*	0.7	2.6
ORANGE	391	157,379	489,233*	34.4	100.0
019 AMER BAPT CONV	21	8,031	10,000*	0.7	2.0
029 AMER LUTH CH..	25	12,055	17,951	1.3	3.7
059 BAPT MISS ASSN	4	974	1,213*	0.1	0.2
081 CATHOLIC......	44	0	277,413	19.5	56.7
093 CR CH (DISC)..	11	4,612	5,743*	0.4	1.2
097 CR C AND C CR.	17	6,086	7,578*	0.5	1.5
105 CHRISTIAN REF.	2	327	658	-	0.1
123 CH GOD (ANDER)	3	381	999	0.1	0.2
127 CH GOD (CLEVE)	8	690	859*	0.1	0.2
157 CH OF BRETHREN	1	199	248*	-	0.1
165 CH OF NAZARENE	17	3,370	7,009	0.5	1.4
175 CONG CR CH....	4	733	913*	0.1	0.2
193 EPISCOPAL.....	18	10,478	16,627	1.2	3.4
201 EVAN COV CH AM	2	182	227*	-	-
221 FREE METH C NA	7	374	510	-	0.1
226 FRIENDS-USA...	8	1,660	2,067*	0.1	0.4
281 LUTH CH AMER..	14	5,904	8,754	0.6	1.8
283 LUTH--MO SYNOD	26	13,996	21,204	1.5	4.3
293 MORAV CH-NORTH	1	60	104	-	-
313 NO AM BAPT GC.	6	2,435	3,032*	0.2	0.6
335 ORTH PRESB CH.	1	115	164	-	-
349 PENT HOLINESS.	2	100	125*	-	-
353 PLY BRETHREN..	2	475	492	-	0.1
371 REF CH IN AM..	13	6,758	10,042	0.7	2.1
403 SALVATION ARMY	2	231	760	0.1	0.2
413 S-D ADVENTISTS	12	3,976	4,951*	0.3	1.0
419 SO BAPT CONV..	36	18,286	22,768*	1.6	4.7
435 UNITARIAN-UNIV	6	478	673	-	0.1
443 UN C OF CHRIST	11	2,549	3,174*	0.2	0.6
449 UN METHODIST..	37	26,137	30,758	2.2	6.3
453 UN PRES CH USA	28	25,226	31,410*	2.2	6.4
469 WISC EVAN LUTH	2	501	807	0.1	0.2
PLACER	64	7,500	22,260*	28.8	100.0
019 AMER BAPT CONV	1	163	195*	0.3	0.9
029 AMER LUTH CH..	4	799	1,096	1.4	4.9
081 CATHOLIC......	11	0	12,360	16.0	55.5
097 CR C AND C CR.	1	21	25*	-	0.1
127 CH GOD (CLEVE)	1	29	35*	-	0.2
165 CH OF NAZARENE	4	323	751	1.0	3.4
193 EPISCOPAL.....	4	481	802	1.0	3.6
281 LUTH CH AMER..	2	294	445	0.6	2.0
283 LUTH--MO SYNOD	1	158	241	0.3	1.1
353 PLY BRETHREN..	1	70	107	0.1	0.5
413 S-D ADVENTISTS	7	845	1,010*	1.3	4.5

*Total adherents estimated from known number of communicant, confirmed, full members.

—Represents a percent less than 0.1.

Percentages may not total due to rounding.

Table 3. Churches and Church Membership by State, County and Denomination: 1971

County and Denomination	Number of churches	Communicant, confirmed, full members	Total adherents		
			Number	Percent of total population	Percent of total adherents
419 SO BAPT CONV..	14	1,858	2,221*	2.9	10.0
443 UN C OF CHRIST	3	345	412*	0.5	1.9
449 UN METHODIST..	9	1,523	1,854	2.4	8.3
453 UN PRES CH USA	1	591	706*	0.9	3.2
PLUMAS	19	1,377	2,808*	24.0	100.0
081 CATHOLIC......	4	0	1,153	9.8	41.1
165 CH OF NAZARENE	1	22	75	0.6	2.7
283 LUTH--MO SYNOD	4	178	232	2.0	8.3
413 S-D ADVENTISTS	1	22	26*	0.2	0.9
419 SO BAPT CONV..	4	658	781*	6.7	27.8
449 UN METHODIST..	5	497	541	4.6	19.3
RIVERSIDE	241	54,374	147,621*	32.2	100.0
019 AMER BAPT CONV	16	3,607	4,405*	1.0	3.0
029 AMER LUTH CH..	5	1,610	2,228	0.5	1.5
075 BRETHREN IN CR	2	49	60*	-	-
081 CATHOLIC......	35	0	77,237	16.8	52.3
093 CR CH (DISC)..	6	2,028	2,477*	0.5	1.7
097 CR C AND C CR.	8	1,092	1,334*	0.3	0.9
105 CHRISTIAN REF.	1	55	107	-	0.1
121 CH GOD (ABR)..	3	170	208*	-	0.1
123 CH GOD (ANDER)	5	455	968	0.2	0.7
127 CH GOD (CLEVE)	6	376	459*	0.1	0.3
165 CH OF NAZARENE	14	1,331	3,224	0.7	2.2
193 EPISCOPAL.....	5	1,296	2,084	0.5	1.4
221 FREE METH C NA	2	136	177	-	0.1
226 FRIENDS-USA...	1	10	12*	-	-
281 LUTH CH AMER..	6	2,531	3,562	0.8	2.4
283 LUTH--MO SYNOD	12	2,900	3,897	0.8	2.6
293 MORAV CH-NORTH	1	111	183	-	0.1
349 PENT HOLINESS.	3	106	129*	-	0.1
353 PLY BRETHREN..	1	85	190	-	0.1
371 REF CH IN AM..	3	481	872	0.2	0.6
403 SALVATION ARMY	1	67	568	0.1	0.4
413 S-D ADVENTISTS	23	8,238	10,061*	2.2	6.8
415 S-D BAPTIST GC	1	279	341*	0.1	0.2
419 SO BAPT CONV..	37	9,229	11,271*	2.5	7.6
435 UNITARIAN-UNIV	4	353	403	0.1	0.3
443 UN C OF CHRIST	7	2,211	2,700*	0.6	1.8
449 UN METHODIST..	21	9,248	10,729	2.3	7.3
453 UN PRES CH USA	11	6,275	7,664*	1.7	5.2
469 WISC EVAN LUTH	1	45	71	-	-
SACRAMENTO	248	67,264	196,581*	31.1	100.0
019 AMER BAPT CONV	15	6,128	7,509*	1.2	3.8
029 AMER LUTH CH..	11	4,352	6,380	1.0	3.2
059 BAPT MISS ASSN	1	99	121*	-	0.1
081 CATHOLIC......	35	0	107,819	17.1	54.8
093 CR CH (DISC)..	6	1,386	1,698*	0.3	0.9
097 CR C AND C CR.	4	892	1,093*	0.2	0.6
105 CHRISTIAN REF.	1	96	188	-	0.1
123 CH GOD (ANDER)	4	511	1,155	0.2	0.6
127 CH GOD (CLEVE)	3	250	306*	-	0.2
157 CH OF BRETHREN	2	191	234*	-	0.1
165 CH OF NAZARENE	13	1,830	4,368	0.7	2.2
193 EPISCOPAL.....	12	4,675	6,523	1.0	3.3
201 EVAN COV CH AM	4	574	703*	0.1	0.4
221 FREE METH C NA	2	126	230	-	0.1
226 FRIENDS-USA...	3	269	330*	0.1	0.2
281 LUTH CH AMER..	9	3,412	4,919	0.8	2.5
283 LUTH--MO SYNOD	12	4,289	6,165	1.0	3.1
313 NO AM BAPT GC.	3	722	885*	0.1	0.5
349 PENT HOLINESS.	3	234	287*	-	0.1
353 PLY BRETHREN..	1	40	140	-	0.1
371 REF CH IN AM..	4	565	862	0.1	0.4
403 SALVATION ARMY	1	178	615	0.1	0.3
413 S-D ADVENTISTS	11	3,181	3,898*	0.6	2.0
419 SO BAPT CONV..	33	11,201	13,724*	2.2	7.0
435 UNITARIAN-UNIV	2	603	813	0.1	0.4
443 UN C OF CHRIST	7	1,963	2,405*	0.4	1.2
449 UN METHODIST..	31	10,178	11,674	1.8	5.9
453 UN PRES CH USA	14	9,126	11,182*	1.8	5.7
469 WISC EVAN LUTH	1	193	355	0.1	0.2
SAN BENITO	9	905	4,495*	24.7	100.0
081 CATHOLIC......	3	0	3,281	18.0	73.0
127 CH GOD (CLEVE)	1	42	53*	0.3	1.2
193 EPISCOPAL.....	1	119	204	1.1	4.5
413 S-D ADVENTISTS	1	118	148*	0.8	3.3
419 SO BAPT CONV..	1	75	94*	0.5	2.1
449 UN METHODIST..	1	316	420	2.3	9.3
453 UN PRES CH USA	1	235	295*	1.6	6.6
SAN BERNARDINO	354	79,978	240,856*	35.2	100.0
019 AMER BAPT CONV	25	7,215	8,927*	1.3	3.7
029 AMER LUTH CH..	8	2,960	4,278	0.6	1.8
059 BAPT MISS ASSN	1	57	71*	-	-
075 BRETHREN IN CR	4	739	914*	0.1	0.4
081 CATHOLIC......	52	0	133,541	19.5	55.4
093 CR CH (DISC)..	11	2,368	2,930*	0.4	1.2
097 CR C AND C CR.	16	4,489	5,554*	0.8	2.3
105 CHRISTIAN REF.	5	1,717	3,197	0.5	1.3
123 CH GOD (ANDER)	8	509	1,377	0.2	0.6
127 CH GOD (CLEVE)	10	454	562*	0.1	0.2
165 CH OF NAZARENE	18	3,207	6,863	1.0	2.8
185 CUMBER PRESB..	1	70	87*	-	-
193 EPISCOPAL.....	15	3,514	4,801	0.7	2.0
221 FREE METH C NA	10	543	736	0.1	0.3
226 FRIENDS-USA...	1	17	21*	-	-
281 LUTH CH AMER..	7	1,615	2,458	0.4	1.0
283 LUTH--MO SYNOD	21	4,579	6,727	1.0	2.8
285 MENNONITE CH..	1	180	223*	-	0.1
287 MENN GEN CONF.	1	224	277*	-	0.1
349 PENT HOLINESS.	2	108	134*	-	0.1
353 PLY BRETHREN..	2	53	95	-	-
371 REF CH IN AM..	2	1,003	1,729	0.3	0.7
381 REF PRES-EVAN.	1	17	21	-	-
403 SALVATION ARMY	3	177	952	0.1	0.4
413 S-D ADVENTISTS	27	11,534	14,270*	2.1	5.9
419 SO BAPT CONV..	43	14,308	17,702*	2.6	7.3
435 UNITARIAN-UNIV	2	275	339	-	0.1
443 UN C OF CHRIST	14	0	0*	-	-
449 UN METHODIST..	25	12,077	14,677	2.1	6.1
453 UN PRES CH USA	16	5,911	7,313*	1.1	3.0
469 WISC EVAN LUTH	2	58	80	-	-
SAN DIEGO	433	125,363	452,300*	33.3	100.0
019 AMER BAPT CONV	27	7,852	9,479*	0.7	2.1
029 AMER LUTH CH..	21	8,694	13,094	1.0	2.9
081 CATHOLIC......	77	0	288,581	21.3	63.8
093 CR CH (DISC)..	14	4,175	5,040*	0.4	1.1
097 CR C AND C CR.	10	2,287	2,761*	0.2	0.6
105 CHRISTIAN REF.	3	546	1,002	0.1	0.2
123 CH GOD (ANDER)	7	741	1,685	0.1	0.4
127 CH GOD (CLEVE)	7	256	309*	-	0.1
157 CH OF BRETHREN	2	232	280*	-	0.1
165 CH OF NAZARENE	13	1,863	3,500	0.3	0.8
175 CONG CR CH....	2	143	173*	-	-
201 EVAN COV CH AM	3	609	735*	0.1	0.2
221 FREE METH C NA	4	267	369	-	0.1
226 FRIENDS-USA...	4	265	320*	-	0.1
281 LUTH CH AMER..	13	4,792	6,731	0.5	1.5
283 LUTH--MO SYNOD	28	10,802	15,185	1.1	3.4
285 MENNONITE CH..	1	30	36*	-	-
335 ORTH PRESB CH.	4	228	334	-	0.1
349 PENT HOLINESS.	3	67	81*	-	-
353 PLY BRETHREN..	3	377	519	-	0.1
371 REF CH IN AM..	2	347	506	-	0.1
403 SALVATION ARMY	4	385	3,159	0.2	0.7
413 S-D ADVENTISTS	25	6,190	7,472*	0.6	1.7
419 SO BAPT CONV..	54	21,133	25,511*	1.9	5.6
435 UNITARIAN-UNIV	3	977	1,189	0.1	0.3
443 UN C OF CHRIST	23	6,359	7,676*	0.6	1.7
449 UN METHODIST..	40	23,196	29,147	2.1	6.4
453 UN PRES CH USA	31	22,135	26,721*	2.0	5.9
469 WISC EVAN LUTH	5	415	705	0.1	0.2
SAN FRANCISCO	192	30,574	234,380*	32.7	100.0
019 AMER BAPT CONV	15	2,531	2,883*	0.4	1.2
029 AMER LUTH CH..	6	1,069	1,594	0.2	0.7
075 BRETHREN IN CR	2	21	24*	-	-
081 CATHOLIC......	58	0	195,922	27.4	83.6
093 CR CH (DISC)..	2	561	639*	0.1	0.3
127 CH GOD (CLEVE)	1	121	138*	-	0.1
157 CH OF BRETHREN	1	155	177*	-	0.1
185 CUMBER PRESB..	1	451	514*	0.1	0.2
193 EPISCOPAL.....	14	4,723	5,943	0.8	2.5
201 EVAN COV CH AM	2	352	401*	0.1	0.2
226 FRIENDS-USA...	1	78	89*	-	-
281 LUTH CH AMER..	6	1,185	1,760	0.2	0.8
283 LUTH--MO SYNOD	10	2,938	4,054	0.6	1.7
315 NO AM OLD RC..	1	93	106*	-	-
335 ORTH PRESB CH.	1	45	57	-	-
349 PENT HOLINESS.	1	21	24*	-	-
353 PLY BRETHREN..	2	60	100	-	-
371 REF CH IN AM..	1	100	117	-	-
403 SALVATION ARMY	5	521	1,972	0.3	0.8
413 S-D ADVENTISTS	8	1,526	1,738*	0.2	0.7
419 SO BAPT CONV..	12	1,454	1,656*	0.2	0.7
435 UNITARIAN-UNIV	1	727	767	0.1	0.3
443 UN C OF CHRIST	7	1,185	1,350*	0.2	0.6
449 UN METHODIST..	17	4,496	5,338	0.7	2.3
453 UN PRES CH USA	17	6,161	7,017*	1.0	3.0
SAN JOAQUIN	144	31,325	101,824*	35.1	100.0
019 AMER BAPT CONV	7	1,091	1,328*	0.5	1.3
029 AMER LUTH CH..	3	1,623	2,388	0.8	2.3
059 BAPT MISS ASSN	1	82	100*	-	0.1
081 CATHOLIC......	19	0	60,440	20.8	59.4
093 CR CH (DISC)..	5	1,005	1,223*	0.4	1.2
097 CR C AND C CR.	3	80	97*	-	0.1
105 CHRISTIAN REF.	3	1,010	1,840	0.6	1.8
123 CH GOD (ANDER)	3	291	636	0.2	0.6
127 CH GOD (CLEVE)	4	257	313*	0.1	0.3
165 CH OF NAZARENE	6	815	1,614	0.6	1.6
193 EPISCOPAL.....	6	1,237	2,328	0.8	2.3
201 EVAN COV CH AM	4	416	506*	0.2	0.5
221 FREE METH C NA	2	73	114	-	0.1
226 FRIENDS-USA...	1	27	33*	-	-
281 LUTH CH AMER..	4	931	1,288	0.4	1.3
283 LUTH--MO SYNOD	6	2,433	3,331	1.1	3.3
285 MENNONITE CH..	1	4	5*	-	-
313 NO AM BAPT GC.	3	1,723	2,097*	0.7	2.1
335 ORTH PRESB CH.	1	25	35	-	-
349 PENT HOLINESS.	2	99	120*	-	0.1
371 REF CH IN AM..	1	510	865	0.3	0.8
403 SALVATION ARMY	1	78	196	0.1	0.2
413 S-D ADVENTISTS	8	2,781	3,385*	1.2	3.3
419 SO BAPT CONV..	21	4,303	5,237*	1.8	5.1
435 UNITARIAN-UNIV	1	283	333	0.1	0.3
443 UN C OF CHRIST	5	2,091	2,545*	0.9	2.5

*Total adherents estimated from known number of communicant, confirmed, full members.

—Represents a percent less than 0.1.

Percentages may not total due to rounding.

Table 3. Churches and Church Membership by State, County and Denomination: 1971

County and Denomination	Number of churches	Communicant, confirmed, full members	Total adherents: Number	Total adherents: Percent of total population	Total adherents: Percent of total adherents
449 UN METHODIST..	14	5,613	6,475	2.2	6.4
453 UN PRES CH USA	8	2,197	2,674*	0.9	2.6
469 WISC EVAN LUTH	1	247	278	0.1	0.3
SAN LUIS OBISPO	75	11,370	33,440*	31.6	100.0
019 AMER BAPT CONV	2	552	644*	0.6	1.9
029 AMER LUTH CH..	1	348	490	0.5	1.5
081 CATHOLIC......	12	0	19,024	18.0	56.9
093 CR CH (DISC)..	3	235	274*	0.3	0.8
097 CR C AND C CR.	2	190	222*	0.2	0.7
123 CH GOD (ANDER)	1	37	87	0.1	0.3
127 CH GOD (CLEVE)	2	92	107*	0.1	0.3
165 CH OF NAZARENE	5	425	960	0.9	2.9
193 EPISCOPAL.....	6	1,013	1,359	1.3	4.1
281 LUTH CH AMER..	3	224	295	0.3	0.9
283 LUTH--MO SYNOD	4	1,005	1,293	1.2	3.9
287 MENN GEN CONF.	1	198	231*	0.2	0.7
353 PLY BRETHREN..	1	200	360	0.3	1.1
403 SALVATION ARMY	1	16	56	0.1	0.2
413 S-D ADVENTISTS	4	541	631*	0.6	1.9
419 SO BAPT CONV..	8	1,637	1,910*	1.8	5.7
435 UNITARIAN-UNIV	1	45	45	-	0.1
443 UN C OF CHRIST	3	730	852*	0.8	2.5
449 UN METHODIST..	8	1,834	2,211	2.1	6.6
453 UN PRES CH USA	7	2,048	2,389*	2.3	7.1
SAN MATEO	175	38,786	187,642*	33.7	100.0
019 AMER BAPT CONV	18	4,955	5,963*	1.1	3.2
029 AMER LUTH CH..	8	2,086	3,090	0.6	1.6
081 CATHOLIC......	42	0	136,455	24.5	72.7
093 CR CH (DISC)..	2	170	205*	-	0.1
097 CR C AND C CR.	4	490	590*	0.1	0.3
123 CH GOD (ANDER)	5	352	907	0.2	0.5
127 CH GOD (CLEVE)	1	31	37*	-	-
165 CH OF NAZARENE	7	513	1,093	0.2	0.6
193 EPISCOPAL.....	13	7,033	10,209	1.8	5.4
201 EVAN COV CH AM	2	470	566*	0.1	0.3
221 FREE METH C NA	3	127	185	-	0.1
281 LUTH CH AMER..	5	1,562	2,700	0.5	1.4
283 LUTH--MO SYNOD	9	3,400	4,594	0.8	2.4
335 ORTH PRESB CH.	1	37	76	-	-
353 PLY BRETHREN..	1	60	100	-	0.1
403 SALVATION ARMY	1	25	205	-	0.1
413 S-D ADVENTISTS	3	445	536*	0.1	0.3
419 SO BAPT CONV..	12	2,682	3,228*	0.6	1.7
435 UNITARIAN-UNIV	3	494	581	0.1	0.3
443 UN C OF CHRIST	10	0	0*	-	-
449 UN METHODIST..	13	6,238	7,125	1.3	3.8
453 UN PRES CH USA	11	7,546	9,082*	1.6	4.8
469 WISC EVAN LUTH	1	70	115	-	0.1
SANTA BARBARA	100	27,210	85,780*	32.5	100.0
019 AMER BAPT CONV	6	1,070	1,296*	0.5	1.5
029 AMER LUTH CH..	5	2,401	3,677	1.4	4.3
081 CATHOLIC......	14	0	50,378	19.1	58.7
093 CR CH (DISC)..	3	1,095	1,326*	0.5	1.5
097 CR C AND C CR.	2	280	339*	0.1	0.4
123 CH GOD (ANDER)	1	70	182	0.1	0.2
127 CH GOD (CLEVE)	2	130	157*	0.1	0.2
165 CH OF NAZARENE	5	495	931	0.4	1.1
193 EPISCOPAL.....	7	3,558	5,170	2.0	6.0
201 EVAN COV CH AM	1	136	165*	0.1	0.2
221 FREE METH C NA	1	22	35	-	-
281 LUTH CH AMER..	4	1,371	1,855	0.7	2.2
283 LUTH--MO SYNOD	6	1,660	2,325	0.9	2.7
335 ORTH PRESB CH.	1	71	115	-	0.1
353 PLY BRETHREN..	1	20	25	-	-
403 SALVATION ARMY	2	81	386	0.1	0.4
413 S-D ADVENTISTS	4	659	798*	0.3	0.9
419 SO BAPT CONV..	11	2,904	3,517*	1.3	4.1
435 UNITARIAN-UNIV	1	476	526	0.2	0.6
443 UN C OF CHRIST	3	654	792*	0.3	0.9
449 UN METHODIST..	8	4,457	5,000	1.9	5.8
453 UN PRES CH USA	11	5,592	6,773*	2.6	7.9
469 WISC EVAN LUTH	1	8	12	-	-
SANTA CLARA	276	78,829	335,674*	31.5	100.0
019 AMER BAPT CONV	13	3,750	4,698*	0.4	1.4
029 AMER LUTH CH..	10	5,324	7,954	0.7	2.4
059 BAPT MISS ASSN	2	47	59*	-	-
081 CATHOLIC......	50	0	230,405	21.6	68.6
093 CR CH (DISC)..	3	688	862*	0.1	0.3
097 CR C AND C CR.	13	3,165	3,965*	0.4	1.2
105 CHRISTIAN REF.	2	279	563	0.1	0.2
121 CH GOD (ABR)..	1	32	40*	-	-
123 CH GOD (ANDER)	2	280	651	0.1	0.2
127 CH GOD (CLEVE)	5	232	291*	-	0.1
165 CH OF NAZARENE	14	1,468	3,213	0.3	1.0
175 CONG CR CH....	1	278	348*	-	0.1
193 EPISCOPAL.....	16	9,096	13,395	1.3	4.0
201 EVAN COV CH AM	3	694	869*	0.1	0.3
221 FREE METH C NA	1	104	131	-	-
226 FRIENDS-USA...	2	197	247*	-	0.1
281 LUTH CH AMER..	13	4,509	6,836	0.6	2.0
283 LUTH--MO SYNOD	12	5,159	7,683	0.7	2.3
315 NO AM OLD RC..	1	210	263*	-	0.1
335 ORTH PRESB CH.	2	133	208	-	0.1
349 PENT HOLINESS.	2	52	65*	-	-
353 PLY BRETHREN..	1	70	100	-	-
371 REF CH IN AM..	1	125	189	-	0.1
403 SALVATION ARMY	1	199	1,008	0.1	0.3
413 S-D ADVENTISTS	16	4,329	5,423*	0.5	1.6
419 SO BAPT CONV..	30	10,275	12,872*	1.2	3.8
435 UNITARIAN-UNIV	4	1,052	1,363	0.1	0.4
443 UN C OF CHRIST	11	0	0*	-	-
449 UN METHODIST..	28	15,381	17,072	1.6	5.1
453 UN PRES CH USA	13	11,305	14,163*	1.3	4.2
469 WISC EVAN LUTH	3	396	738	0.1	0.2
SANTA CRUZ	72	12,315	38,582*	31.2	100.0
019 AMER BAPT CONV	2	353	416*	0.3	1.1
029 AMER LUTH CH..	1	203	305	0.2	0.8
081 CATHOLIC......	12	0	22,282	18.0	57.8
093 CR CH (DISC)..	2	663	782*	0.6	2.0
097 CR C AND C CR.	2	278	328*	0.3	0.9
123 CH GOD (ANDER)	1	36	84	0.1	0.2
127 CH GOD (CLEVE)	2	36	42*	-	0.1
165 CH OF NAZARENE	2	362	713	0.6	1.8
175 CONG CR CH....	1	343	404*	0.3	1.0
193 EPISCOPAL.....	3	981	1,565	1.3	4.1
221 FREE METH C NA	3	127	172	0.1	0.4
226 FRIENDS-USA...	1	20	24*	-	0.1
281 LUTH CH AMER..	3	820	1,283	1.0	3.3
283 LUTH--MO SYNOD	3	552	905	0.7	2.3
315 NO AM OLD RC..	1	120	141*	0.1	0.4
335 ORTH PRESB CH.	1	45	58	-	0.2
349 PENT HOLINESS.	2	56	66*	0.1	0.2
403 SALVATION ARMY	2	100	558	0.5	1.4
413 S-D ADVENTISTS	3	947	1,116*	0.9	2.9
419 SO BAPT CONV..	8	1,678	1,978*	1.6	5.1
435 UNITARIAN-UNIV	1	140	140	0.1	0.4
443 UN C OF CHRIST	2	715	843*	0.7	2.2
449 UN METHODIST..	7	1,796	2,085	1.7	5.4
453 UN PRES CH USA	7	1,944	2,292*	1.9	5.9
SHASTA	42	6,336	15,088*	19.4	100.0
019 AMER BAPT CONV	2	594	727*	0.9	4.8
081 CATHOLIC......	5	0	6,550	8.4	43.4
093 CR CH (DISC)..	1	17	21*	-	0.1
097 CR C AND C CR.	2	100	122*	0.2	0.8
123 CH GOD (ANDER)	1	20	62	0.1	0.4
165 CH OF NAZARENE	4	310	669	0.9	4.4
193 EPISCOPAL.....	2	407	716	0.9	4.7
281 LUTH CH AMER..	1	170	260	0.3	1.7
283 LUTH--MO SYNOD	2	353	610	0.8	4.0
403 SALVATION ARMY	1	25	105	0.1	0.7
413 S-D ADVENTISTS	3	632	773*	1.0	5.1
419 SO BAPT CONV..	7	1,359	1,663*	2.1	11.0
435 UNITARIAN-UNIV	2	35	35	-	0.2
443 UN C OF CHRIST	1	263	322*	0.4	2.1
449 UN METHODIST..	4	1,178	1,297	1.7	8.6
453 UN PRES CH USA	2	536	656*	0.8	4.3
469 WISC EVAN LUTH	2	337	500	0.6	3.3
SIERRA	6	230	394*	16.7	100.0
019 AMER BAPT CONV	1	170	200*	8.5	50.8
081 CATHOLIC......	3	0	134	5.7	34.0
449 UN METHODIST..	2	60	60	2.5	15.2
SISKIYOU	48	3,793	10,294*	31.0	100.0
019 AMER BAPT CONV	3	306	366*	1.1	3.6
029 AMER LUTH CH..	1	97	129	0.4	1.3
081 CATHOLIC......	14	0	5,617	16.9	54.6
097 CR C AND C CR.	3	156	186*	0.6	1.8
165 CH OF NAZARENE	3	83	281	0.8	2.7
193 EPISCOPAL.....	3	345	346	1.0	3.4
281 LUTH CH AMER..	1	258	369	1.1	3.6
283 LUTH--MO SYNOD	1	90	128	0.4	1.2
413 S-D ADVENTISTS	2	117	140*	0.4	1.4
419 SO BAPT CONV..	7	754	901*	2.7	8.8
449 UN METHODIST..	7	1,106	1,256	3.8	12.2
453 UN PRES CH USA	3	481	575*	1.7	5.6
SOLANO	66	15,514	48,961*	28.8	100.0
019 AMER BAPT CONV	8	2,426	3,014*	1.8	6.2
029 AMER LUTH CH..	2	766	1,155	0.7	2.4
059 BAPT MISS ASSN	1	65	81*	-	0.2
081 CATHOLIC......	9	0	27,892	16.4	57.0
093 CR CH (DISC)..	2	271	337*	0.2	0.7
127 CH GOD (CLEVE)	3	130	161*	0.1	0.3
165 CH OF NAZARENE	5	330	981	0.6	2.0
193 EPISCOPAL.....	4	1,267	1,967	1.2	4.0
281 LUTH CH AMER..	1	427	785	0.5	1.6
283 LUTH--MO SYNOD	3	739	1,082	0.6	2.2
349 PENT HOLINESS.	1	8	10*	-	-
403 SALVATION ARMY	1	57	197	0.1	0.4
413 S-D ADVENTISTS	4	472	586*	0.3	1.2
419 SO BAPT CONV..	9	4,551	5,654*	3.3	11.5
443 UN C OF CHRIST	3	339	421*	0.2	0.9
449 UN METHODIST..	6	1,720	2,221	1.3	4.5
453 UN PRES CH USA	4	1,946	2,417*	1.4	4.9
SONOMA	110	18,547	57,139*	27.9	100.0
019 AMER BAPT CONV	1	571	692*	0.3	1.2
029 AMER LUTH CH..	2	681	1,159	0.6	2.0
081 CATHOLIC......	24	0	32,993	16.1	57.7
093 CR CH (DISC)..	1	80	97*	-	0.2
097 CR C AND C CR.	6	918	1,112*	0.5	1.9
123 CH GOD (ANDER)	1	36	66	-	0.1
127 CH GOD (CLEVE)	1	12	15*	-	-

*Total adherents estimated from known number of communicant, confirmed, full members.

—Represents a percent less than 0.1.

Percentages may not total due to rounding.

Table 3. Churches and Church Membership by State, County and Denomination: 1971

County and Denomination	Number of churches	Communicant, confirmed, full members	Total adherents: Number	Percent of total population	Percent of total adherents
165 CH OF NAZARENE	4	406	804	0.4	1.4
175 CONG CR CH....	2	126	153*	0.1	0.3
193 EPISCOPAL.....	7	1,894	2,637	1.3	4.6
226 FRIENDS-USA...	1	12	15*	-	-
281 LUTH CH AMER..	1	238	366	0.2	0.6
283 LUTH--MO SYNOD	7	1,854	2,587	1.3	4.5
371 REF CH IN AM..	1	72	133	0.1	0.2
403 SALVATION ARMY	1	59	293	0.1	0.5
413 S-D ADVENTISTS	8	1,499	1,816*	0.9	3.2
419 SO BAPT CONV..	12	3,027	3,668*	1.8	6.4
435 UNITARIAN-UNIV	1	60	90	-	0.2
443 UN C OF CHRIST	9	1,367	1,656*	0.8	2.9
449 UN METHODIST..	11	2,975	3,564	1.7	6.2
453 UN PRES CH USA	9	2,660	3,223*	1.6	5.6
STANISLAUS	123	26,495	64,706*	33.3	100.0
019 AMER BAPT CONV	6	2,313	2,842*	1.5	4.4
029 AMER LUTH CH..	2	534	729	0.4	1.1
059 BAPT MISS ASSN	1	43	53*	-	0.1
081 CATHOLIC......	13	0	28,568	14.7	44.2
093 CR CH (DISC)..	4	954	1,172*	0.6	1.8
097 CR C AND C CR.	2	480	590*	0.3	0.9
105 CHRISTIAN REF.	1	388	682	0.4	1.1
121 CH GOD (ABR)..	1	20	25*	-	-
123 CH GOD (ANDER)	2	190	435	0.2	0.7
127 CH GOD (CLEVE)	3	256	315*	0.2	0.5
157 CH OF BRETHREN	3	920	1,131*	0.6	1.7
165 CH OF NAZARENE	9	866	2,446	1.3	3.8
193 EPISCOPAL.....	4	997	1,707	0.9	2.6
201 EVAN COV CH AM	3	668	821*	0.4	1.3
221 FREE METH C NA	3	235	299	0.2	0.5
226 FRIENDS-USA...	1	163	200*	0.1	0.3
281 LUTH CH AMER..	2	944	1,242	0.6	1.9
283 LUTH--MO SYNOD	5	1,267	2,023	1.0	3.1
335 ORTH PRESB CH.	1	34	59	-	0.1
349 PENT HOLINESS.	4	98	120*	0.1	0.2
371 REF CH IN AM..	1	152	233	0.1	0.4
403 SALVATION ARMY	1	92	1,258	0.6	1.9
413 S-D ADVENTISTS	7	2,338	2,873*	1.5	4.4
419 SO BAPT CONV..	23	5,600	6,882*	3.5	10.6
435 UNITARIAN-UNIV	1	114	194	0.1	0.3
443 UN C OF CHRIST	2	376	462*	0.2	0.7
449 UN METHODIST..	9	4,199	4,575	2.4	7.1
453 UN PRES CH USA	9	2,254	2,770*	1.4	4.3
SUTTER	25	4,050	10,502*	25.0	100.0
081 CATHOLIC......	3	0	5,213	12.4	49.6
093 CR CH (DISC)..	1	85	105*	0.3	1.0
097 CR C AND C CR.	2	250	309*	0.7	2.9
123 CH GOD (ANDER)	1	65	138	0.3	1.3
157 CH OF BRETHREN	2	198	245*	0.6	2.3
165 CH OF NAZARENE	3	200	442	1.1	4.2
283 LUTH--MO SYNOD	1	298	494	1.2	4.7
349 PENT HOLINESS.	1	34	42*	0.1	0.4
413 S-D ADVENTISTS	1	284	351*	0.8	3.3
419 SO BAPT CONV..	5	1,279	1,581*	3.8	15.1
449 UN METHODIST..	4	965	1,097	2.6	10.4
453 UN PRES CH USA	1	392	485*	1.2	4.6
TEHAMA	26	3,224	7,008*	23.7	100.0
019 AMER BAPT CONV	3	650	793*	2.7	11.3
081 CATHOLIC......	3	0	2,875	9.7	41.0
093 CR CH (DISC)..	2	258	315*	1.1	4.5
127 CH GOD (CLEVE)	1	22	27*	0.1	0.4
165 CH OF NAZARENE	2	170	378	1.3	5.4
193 EPISCOPAL.....	2	169	216	0.7	3.1
283 LUTH--MO SYNOD	2	116	179	0.6	2.6
413 S-D ADVENTISTS	2	212	259*	0.9	3.7
419 SO BAPT CONV..	3	359	438*	1.5	6.3
449 UN METHODIST..	4	769	919	3.1	13.1
453 UN PRES CH USA	2	499	609*	2.1	8.7
TRINITY	9	234	789*	10.4	100.0
081 CATHOLIC......	3	0	329	4.3	41.7
097 CR C AND C CR.	1	50	60*	0.8	7.6
165 CH OF NAZARENE	1	57	226	3.0	28.6
193 EPISCOPAL.....	1	22	48	0.6	6.1
443 UN C OF CHRIST	3	105	126*	1.7	16.0
TULARE	151	25,092	72,786*	38.6	100.0
019 AMER BAPT CONV	9	3,078	3,823*	2.0	5.3
029 AMER LUTH CH..	3	582	856	0.5	1.2
075 BRETHREN IN CR	1	11	14*	-	-
081 CATHOLIC......	20	0	39,000	20.7	53.6
093 CR CH (DISC)..	4	740	919*	0.5	1.3
097 CR C AND C CR.	4	275	342*	0.2	0.5
105 CHRISTIAN REF.	1	142	301	0.2	0.4
123 CH GOD (ANDER)	7	642	1,563	0.8	2.1
127 CH GOD (CLEVE)	10	780	969*	0.5	1.3
157 CH OF BRETHREN	1	137	170*	0.1	0.2
165 CH OF NAZARENE	13	1,577	3,582	1.9	4.9
193 EPISCOPAL.....	5	1,144	1,780	0.9	2.4
221 FREE METH C NA	1	17	17	-	-
226 FRIENDS-USA...	1	45	56*	-	0.1
283 LUTH--MO SYNOD	6	1,413	1,966	1.0	2.7
349 PENT HOLINESS.	3	97	120*	0.1	0.2
413 S-D ADVENTISTS	10	1,515	1,882*	1.0	2.6
419 SO BAPT CONV..	22	4,408	5,475*	2.9	7.5
435 UNITARIAN-UNIV	2	40	40	-	0.1
443 UN C OF CHRIST	2	568	706*	0.4	1.0
449 UN METHODIST..	14	4,160	4,583	2.4	6.3
453 UN PRES CH USA	12	3,721	4,622*	2.5	6.4
TUOLUMNE	25	1,987	4,545*	20.5	100.0
019 AMER BAPT CONV	1	134	157*	0.7	3.5
081 CATHOLIC......	10	0	1,890	8.5	41.6
165 CH OF NAZARENE	1	42	85	0.4	1.9
193 EPISCOPAL.....	1	139	420	1.9	9.2
281 LUTH CH AMER..	1	83	117	0.5	2.6
283 LUTH--MO SYNOD	1	159	219	1.0	4.8
335 ORTH PRESB CH.	1	33	55	0.2	1.2
413 S-D ADVENTISTS	1	362	424*	1.9	9.3
419 SO BAPT CONV..	3	364	426*	1.9	9.4
449 UN METHODIST..	4	377	408	1.8	9.0
453 UN PRES CH USA	1	294	344*	1.6	7.6
VENTURA	150	40,870	133,780*	35.5	100.0
019 AMER BAPT CONV	12	3,463	4,416*	1.2	3.3
029 AMER LUTH CH..	7	3,116	4,729	1.3	3.5
081 CATHOLIC......	16	0	77,745	20.7	58.1
093 CR CH (DISC)..	3	592	755*	0.2	0.6
097 CR C AND C CR.	8	1,590	2,028*	0.5	1.5
123 CH GOD (ANDER)	1	37	90	-	0.1
127 CH GOD (CLEVE)	3	123	157*	-	0.1
165 CH OF NAZARENE	8	696	1,442	0.4	1.1
193 EPISCOPAL.....	9	4,033	5,866	1.6	4.4
201 EVAN COV CH AM	1	117	149*	-	0.1
221 FREE METH C NA	1	18	19	-	-
226 FRIENDS-USA...	1	93	119*	-	0.1
281 LUTH CH AMER..	4	871	1,302	0.3	1.0
283 LUTH--MO SYNOD	9	2,796	4,489	1.2	3.4
349 PENT HOLINESS.	1	23	29*	-	-
403 SALVATION ARMY	2	47	377	0.1	0.3
413 S-D ADVENTISTS	10	2,097	2,674*	0.7	2.0
419 SO BAPT CONV..	19	6,889	8,786*	2.3	6.6
435 UNITARIAN-UNIV	3	201	272	0.1	0.2
443 UN C OF CHRIST	3	715	912*	0.2	0.7
449 UN METHODIST..	17	7,852	10,404	2.8	7.8
453 UN PRES CH USA	11	5,466	6,971*	1.9	5.2
469 WISC EVAN LUTH	1	35	49	-	-
YOLO	47	7,973	35,065*	38.2	100.0
019 AMER BAPT CONV	3	170	206*	0.2	0.6
029 AMER LUTH CH..	1	292	375	0.4	1.1
081 CATHOLIC......	10	0	24,507	26.7	69.9
093 CR CH (DISC)..	2	471	571*	0.6	1.6
123 CH GOD (ANDER)	1	23	64	0.1	0.2
127 CH GOD (CLEVE)	1	41	50*	0.1	0.1
165 CH OF NAZARENE	2	174	384	0.4	1.1
193 EPISCOPAL.....	2	764	1,326	1.4	3.8
201 EVAN COV CH AM	1	149	181*	0.2	0.5
226 FRIENDS-USA...	1	23	28*	-	0.1
281 LUTH CH AMER..	1	109	161	0.2	0.5
283 LUTH--MO SYNOD	3	704	1,062	1.2	3.0
413 S-D ADVENTISTS	1	147	178*	0.2	0.5
419 SO BAPT CONV..	6	1,011	1,226*	1.3	3.5
435 UNITARIAN-UNIV	1	189	239	0.3	0.7
443 UN C OF CHRIST	2	788	955*	1.0	2.7
449 UN METHODIST..	4	915	1,124	1.2	3.2
453 UN PRES CH USA	5	2,003	2,428*	2.6	6.9
YUBA	23	4,098	9,341*	20.9	100.0
019 AMER BAPT CONV	2	139	177*	0.4	1.9
029 AMER LUTH CH..	1	409	552	1.2	5.9
081 CATHOLIC......	4	0	4,012	9.0	43.0
093 CR CH (DISC)..	2	377	480*	1.1	5.1
127 CH GOD (CLEVE)	1	40	51*	0.1	0.5
165 CH OF NAZARENE	3	197	367	0.8	3.9
193 EPISCOPAL.....	2	518	702	1.6	7.5
413 S-D ADVENTISTS	2	241	307*	0.7	3.3
419 SO BAPT CONV..	3	1,338	1,705*	3.8	18.3
449 UN METHODIST..	2	324	332	0.7	3.6
453 UN PRES CH USA	1	515	656*	1.5	7.0
CO DATA NOT AVAIL	139	9,574	389,735*	N/A	N/A
127 CH GOD (CLEVE)	1	57	178*	N/A	N/A
151 L-D SAINTS....	0	0	367,521	N/A	N/A
223 FREE WILL BAPT	78	4,805	14,998*	N/A	N/A
231 GENERAL BAPT..	18	772	2,410*	N/A	N/A
467 WESLEYAN......	42	3,940	4,628	N/A	N/A

COLORADO

County and Denomination	Number of churches	Communicant, confirmed, full members	Total adherents: Number	Percent of total population	Percent of total adherents
THE STATE.....	1,683	373,442	916,743*	41.5	100.0
ADAMS	86	24,591	81,184*	43.7	100.0
019 AMER BAPT CONV	3	742	966*	0.5	1.2
029 AMER LUTH CH..	3	1,284	1,921	1.0	2.4
081 CATHOLIC......	11	0	45,500	24.5	56.0
093 CR CH (DISC)..	4	1,006	1,309*	0.7	1.6

*Total adherents estimated from known number of communicant, confirmed, full members.

—Represents a percent less than 0.1.

Percentages may not total due to rounding.

Table 3. Churches and Church Membership by State, County and Denomination: 1971

County and Denomination	Number of churches	Communicant, confirmed, full members	Total adherents		
			Number	Percent of total population	Percent of total adherents
097 CR C AND C CR.	5	888	1,156*	0.6	1.4
123 CH GOD (ANDER)	1	49	114	0.1	0.1
127 CH GOD (CLEVE)	3	155	202*	0.1	0.2
165 CH OF NAZARENE	5	291	718	0.4	0.9
193 EPISCOPAL.....	4	1,087	2,366	1.3	2.9
201 EVAN COV CH AM	1	233	303*	0.2	0.4
221 FREE METH C NA	1	38	42	-	0.1
281 LUTH CH AMER..	4	1,513	2,641	1.4	3.3
283 LUTH--MO SYNOD	4	3,164	4,882	2.6	6.0
313 NO AM BAPT GC.	1	17	22*	-	-
335 ORTH PRESB CH.	1	49	90	-	0.1
413 S-D ADVENTISTS	3	899	1,170*	0.6	1.4
419 SO BAPT CONV..	9	3,983	5,184*	2.8	6.4
443 UN C OF CHRIST	7	939	1,222*	0.7	1.5
449 UN METHODIST..	8	3,908	5,719	3.1	7.0
453 UN PRES CH USA	8	4,346	5,657*	3.0	7.0
ALAMOSA	11	1,968	5,677*	49.7	100.0
019 AMER BAPT CONV	1	99	121*	1.1	2.1
081 CATHOLIC......	1	0	3,000	26.3	52.8
093 CR CH (DISC)..	1	161	197*	1.7	3.5
105 CHRISTIAN REF.	1	126	230	2.0	4.1
193 EPISCOPAL.....	1	137	301	2.6	5.3
283 LUTH--MO SYNOD	1	180	260	2.3	4.6
413 S-D ADVENTISTS	1	83	102*	0.9	1.8
419 SO BAPT CONV..	1	308	378*	3.3	6.7
449 UN METHODIST..	2	528	664	5.8	11.7
453 UN PRES CH USA	1	346	424*	3.7	7.5
ARAPAHOE	78	25,086	58,494*	36.1	100.0
019 AMER BAPT CONV	4	660	825*	0.5	1.4
029 AMER LUTH CH..	6	2,231	3,549	2.2	6.1
059 BAPT MISS ASSN	2	115	144*	0.1	0.2
081 CATHOLIC......	6	0	22,500	13.9	38.5
093 CR CH (DISC)..	1	381	476*	0.3	0.8
097 CR C AND C CR.	3	327	409*	0.3	0.7
121 CH GOD (ABR)..	1	34	42*	-	0.1
123 CH GOD (ANDER)	6	576	1,225	0.8	2.1
165 CH OF NAZARENE	5	1,257	3,071	1.9	5.3
193 EPISCOPAL.....	4	1,528	2,053	1.3	3.5
221 FREE METH C NA	3	182	230	0.1	0.4
226 FRIENDS-USA...	1	59	74*	-	0.1
281 LUTH CH AMER..	2	1,602	2,455	1.5	4.2
283 LUTH--MO SYNOD	5	2,889	4,138	2.6	7.1
349 PENT HOLINESS.	2	57	71*	-	0.1
353 PLY BRETHREN..	2	250	350	0.2	0.6
403 SALVATION ARMY	1	55	223	0.1	0.4
413 S-D ADVENTISTS	3	737	921*	0.6	1.6
419 SO BAPT CONV..	6	3,399	4,246*	2.6	7.3
443 UN C OF CHRIST	3	453	566*	0.3	1.0
449 UN METHODIST..	5	5,440	7,360	4.5	12.6
453 UN PRES CH USA	7	2,854	3,566*	2.2	6.1
ARCHULETA	7	298	1,408*	51.5	100.0
081 CATHOLIC......	4	0	1,023	37.4	72.7
413 S-D ADVENTISTS	1	6	8*	0.3	0.6
419 SO BAPT CONV..	1	158	205*	7.5	14.6
449 UN METHODIST..	1	134	172	6.3	12.2
BACA	14	934	1,365*	24.1	100.0
081 CATHOLIC......	2	0	239	4.2	17.5
123 CH GOD (ANDER)	2	57	133	2.3	9.7
226 FRIENDS-USA...	3	125	150*	2.6	11.0
349 PENT HOLINESS.	2	50	60*	1.1	4.4
413 S-D ADVENTISTS	1	39	47*	0.8	3.4
449 UN METHODIST..	4	663	736	13.0	53.9
BENT	13	1,379	3,266*	50.3	100.0
019 AMER BAPT CONV	1	270	322*	5.0	9.9
081 CATHOLIC......	1	0	1,600	24.6	49.0
093 CR CH (DISC)..	1	140	167*	2.6	5.1
165 CH OF NAZARENE	1	30	58	0.9	1.8
193 EPISCOPAL.....	1	13	25	0.4	0.8
226 FRIENDS-USA...	2	122	145*	2.2	4.4
413 S-D ADVENTISTS	1	41	49*	0.8	1.5
449 UN METHODIST..	3	536	624	9.6	19.1
453 UN PRES CH USA	1	216	257*	4.0	7.9
469 WISC EVAN LUTH	1	11	19	0.3	0.6
BOULDER	86	29,290	55,993*	42.5	100.0
019 AMER BAPT CONV	3	1,194	1,463*	1.1	2.6
029 AMER LUTH CH..	3	1,368	2,152	1.6	3.8
081 CATHOLIC......	9	0	16,600	12.6	29.6
093 CR CH (DISC)..	2	161	197*	0.1	0.4
097 CR C AND C CR.	3	1,332	1,633*	1.2	2.9
105 CHRISTIAN REF.	1	80	154	0.1	0.3
127 CH GOD (CLEVE)	1	37	45*	-	0.1
165 CH OF NAZARENE	6	496	1,098	0.8	2.0
193 EPISCOPAL.....	6	2,507	3,510	2.7	6.3
221 FREE METH C NA	2	42	62	-	0.1
226 FRIENDS-USA...	1	82	101*	0.1	0.2
281 LUTH CH AMER..	3	2,300	3,415	2.6	6.1
283 LUTH--MO SYNOD	6	2,187	3,115	2.4	5.6
349 PENT HOLINESS.	1	20	25*	-	-
353 PLY BRETHREN..	3	193	368	0.3	0.7
413 S-D ADVENTISTS	1	1,064	1,304*	1.0	2.3
415 S-D BAPTIST GC	1	91	112*	0.1	0.2
419 SO BAPT CONV..	6	1,378	1,689*	1.3	3.0
435 UNITARIAN-UNIV	1	351	531	0.4	0.9
443 UN C OF CHRIST	6	2,018	2,473*	1.9	4.4
449 UN METHODIST..	12	7,852	10,375	7.9	18.5
453 UN PRES CH USA	8	4,460	5,466*	4.1	9.8
469 WISC EVAN LUTH	1	77	105	0.1	0.2
CHAFFEE	15	1,811	4,375*	43.1	100.0
081 CATHOLIC......	2	0	2,062	20.3	47.1
093 CR CH (DISC)..	1	121	149*	1.5	3.4
097 CR C AND C CR.	1	50	62*	0.6	1.4
127 CH GOD (CLEVE)	1	35	43*	0.4	1.0
165 CH OF NAZARENE	1	31	53	0.5	1.2
193 EPISCOPAL.....	2	276	375	3.7	8.6
283 LUTH--MO SYNOD	1	96	170	1.7	3.9
413 S-D ADVENTISTS	1	18	22*	0.2	0.5
419 SO BAPT CONV..	2	543	668*	6.6	15.3
443 UN C OF CHRIST	1	140	172*	1.7	3.9
449 UN METHODIST..	1	355	419	4.1	9.6
453 UN PRES CH USA	1	146	180*	1.8	4.1
CHEYENNE	9	709	1,473*	61.5	100.0
029 AMER LUTH CH..	1	29	31	1.3	2.1
081 CATHOLIC......	2	0	625	26.1	42.4
097 CR C AND C CR.	2	225	272*	11.4	18.5
283 LUTH--MO SYNOD	2	116	146	6.1	9.9
449 UN METHODIST..	2	339	399	16.7	27.1
CLEAR CREEK	10	422	1,261*	26.2	100.0
081 CATHOLIC......	3	0	700	14.5	55.5
193 EPISCOPAL.....	2	46	105	2.2	8.3
281 LUTH CH AMER..	1	56	84	1.7	6.7
413 S-D ADVENTISTS	1	36	45*	0.9	3.6
449 UN METHODIST..	1	119	119	2.5	9.4
453 UN PRES CH USA	2	165	208*	4.3	16.5
CONEJOS	14	144	4,197*	53.5	100.0
081 CATHOLIC......	11	0	4,010	51.1	95.5
285 MENNONITE CH..	1	12	16*	0.2	0.4
453 UN PRES CH USA	2	132	171*	2.2	4.1
COSTILLA	14	97	2,169*	70.2	100.0
081 CATHOLIC......	11	0	2,040	66.0	94.1
413 S-D ADVENTISTS	1	25	31*	1.0	1.4
449 UN METHODIST..	1	48	68	2.2	3.1
453 UN PRES CH USA	1	24	30*	1.0	1.4
CROWLEY	10	591	1,611*	52.2	100.0
029 AMER LUTH CH..	1	69	61	2.0	3.8
081 CATHOLIC......	2	0	967	31.3	60.0
093 CR CH (DISC)..	1	3	4*	0.1	0.2
226 FRIENDS-USA...	1	15	18*	0.6	1.1
283 LUTH--MO SYNOD	1	62	81	2.6	5.0
413 S-D ADVENTISTS	1	12	14	0.5	0.9
449 UN METHODIST..	2	410	437	14.2	27.1
469 WISC EVAN LUTH	1	20	29	0.9	1.8
CUSTER	5	405	580*	51.8	100.0
081 CATHOLIC......	1		79	7.1	13.6
193 EPISCOPAL.....	1	67	101	9.0	17.4
283 LUTH--MO SYNOD	1	118	135	12.1	23.3
419 SO BAPT CONV..	1	56	64*	5.7	11.0
449 UN METHODIST..	1	164	201	17.9	34.7
DELTA	27	2,683	5,387*	35.2	100.0
019 AMER BAPT CONV	4	788	924*	6.0	17.2
081 CATHOLIC......	4	0	2,039	13.3	37.9
123 CH GOD (ANDER)	2	95	231	1.5	4.3
165 CH OF NAZARENE	2	137	246	1.6	4.6
193 EPISCOPAL.....	2	192	251	1.6	4.7
226 FRIENDS-USA...	1	174	204*	1.3	3.8
283 LUTH--MO SYNOD	2	167	237	1.6	4.4
413 S-D ADVENTISTS	3	224	263*	1.7	4.9
419 SO BAPT CONV..	1	53	62*	0.4	1.2
449 UN METHODIST..	4	620	657	4.3	12.2
453 UN PRES CH USA	2	233	273*	1.8	5.1
DENVER	215	68,799	189,475*	36.8	100.0
019 AMER BAPT CONV	15	5,862	7,037*	1.4	3.7
029 AMER LUTH CH..	11	3,587	5,132	1.0	2.7
081 CATHOLIC......	34	0	94,275	18.3	49.8
093 CR CH (DISC)..	9	2,801	3,362*	0.7	1.8
097 CR C AND C CR.	3	296	355*	0.1	0.2
105 CHRISTIAN REF.	7	1,909	3,329	0.6	1.8
127 CH GOD (CLEVE)	1	21	25*	-	-
157 CH OF BRETHREN	2	473	568*	0.1	0.3
193 EPISCOPAL.....	19	11,472	17,370	3.4	9.2
201 EVAN COV CH AM	1	244	293*	0.1	0.2
226 FRIENDS-USA...	3	212	254*	-	0.1
281 LUTH CH AMER..	7	4,982	6,819	1.3	3.6
283 LUTH--MO SYNOD	11	7,772	11,345	2.2	6.0
285 MENNONITE CH..	3	380	456*	0.1	0.2
315 NO AM OLD RC..	1	87	104*	-	0.1
335 ORTH PRESB CH.	1	84	122	-	0.1
349 PENT HOLINESS.	1	69	83*	-	-
353 PLY BRETHREN..	2	310	375	0.1	0.2
371 REF CH IN AM..	8	1,926	2,710	0.5	1.4
403 SALVATION ARMY	2	158	692	0.1	0.4

*Total adherents estimated from known number of communicant, confirmed, full members.

—Represents a percent less than 0.1.

Percentages may not total due to rounding.

Table 3. Churches and Church Membership by State, County and Denomination: 1971

County and Denomination	Number of churches	Communicant, confirmed, full members	Total adherents: Number	Total adherents: Percent of total population	Total adherents: Percent of total adherents
413 S-D ADVENTISTS	4	1,994	2,394*	0.5	1.3
419 SO BAPT CONV..	11	6,568	7,884*	1.5	4.2
435 UNITARIAN-UNIV	3	720	937	0.2	0.5
443 UN C OF CHRIST	12	4,212	5,056*	1.0	2.7
449 UN METHODIST..	25	1,664	5,205	1.0	2.7
453 UN PRES CH USA	17	10,608	12,734*	2.5	6.7
469 WISC EVAN LUTH	2	388	559	0.1	0.3
DOLORES	4	288	356*	21.7	100.0
413 S-D ADVENTISTS	1	32	39*	2.4	11.0
419 SO BAPT CONV..	1	163	198*	12.1	55.6
449 UN METHODIST..	1	78	101	6.2	28.4
453 UN PRES CH USA	1	15	18*	1.1	5.1
DOUGLAS	11	1,378	2,613*	31.1	100.0
029 AMER LUTH CH..	1	49	84	1.0	3.2
081 CATHOLIC......	1	0	825	9.8	31.6
193 EPISCOPAL.....	2	276	412	4.9	15.8
283 LUTH--MO SYNOD	1	206	311	3.7	11.9
413 S-D ADVENTISTS	1	45	55*	0.7	2.1
443 UN C OF CHRIST	1	119	147*	1.7	5.6
449 UN METHODIST..	2	513	569	6.8	21.8
453 UN PRES CH USA	2	170	210*	2.5	8.0
EAGLE	9	357	860*	11.5	100.0
081 CATHOLIC......	4	0	450	6.0	52.3
449 UN METHODIST..	3	278	309	4.1	35.9
453 UN PRES CH USA	2	79	101*	1.3	11.7
ELBERT	9	740	1,042*	26.7	100.0
019 AMER BAPT CONV	1	226	271*	6.9	26.0
081 CATHOLIC......	2	0	100	2.6	9.6
097 CR C AND C CR.	1	70	84*	2.2	8.1
165 CH OF NAZARENE	1	20	58	1.5	5.6
449 UN METHODIST..	2	192	251	6.4	24.1
453 UN PRES CH USA	2	232	278*	7.1	26.7
EL PASO	122	46,006	88,516*	37.5	100.0
019 AMER BAPT CONV	6	2,321	2,872*	1.2	3.2
029 AMER LUTH CH..	5	1,976	2,900	1.2	3.3
075 BRETHREN IN CR	1	55	68*	-	0.1
081 CATHOLIC......	14	0	25,700	10.9	29.0
093 CR CH (DISC)..	3	1,557	1,926*	0.8	2.2
097 CR C AND C CR.	5	1,113	1,377*	0.6	1.6
105 CHRISTIAN REF.	1	136	259	0.1	0.3
121 CH GOD (ABR)..	1	15	19*	-	-
123 CH GOD (ANDER)	2	183	424	0.2	0.5
127 CH GOD (CLEVE)	2	126	156*	0.1	0.2
157 CH OF BRETHREN	1	99	122*	0.1	0.1
165 CH OF NAZARENE	8	1,826	4,742	2.0	5.4
193 EPISCOPAL.....	6	2,916	4,479	1.9	5.1
221 FREE METH C NA	2	64	80	-	0.1
226 FRIENDS-USA...	1	147	182*	0.1	0.2
281 LUTH CH AMER..	6	1,754	2,464	1.0	2.8
283 LUTH--MO SYNOD	4	2,531	3,537	1.5	4.0
285 MENNONITE CH..	2	196	243*	0.1	0.3
349 PENT HOLINESS.	1	14	17*	-	-
353 PLY BRETHREN..	2	259	436	0.2	0.5
381 REF PRES-EVAN.	2	642	900	0.4	1.0
403 SALVATION ARMY	1	130	496	0.2	0.6
413 S-D ADVENTISTS	1	413	511*	0.2	0.6
419 SO BAPT CONV..	15	9,720	12,026*	5.1	13.6
435 UNITARIAN-UNIV	2	172	256	0.1	0.3
443 UN C OF CHRIST	5	2,312	2,861*	1.2	3.2
449 UN METHODIST..	16	10,787	13,823	5.9	15.6
453 UN PRES CH USA	6	4,343	5,373*	2.3	6.1
469 WISC EVAN LUTH	1	199	267	0.1	0.3
FREMONT	29	4,710	10,258*	46.8	100.0
019 AMER BAPT CONV	2	761	895*	4.1	8.7
081 CATHOLIC......	4	0	4,266	19.4	41.6
093 CR CH (DISC)..	1	263	309*	1.4	3.0
097 CR C AND C CR.	2	247	291*	1.3	2.8
123 CH GOD (ANDER)	1	13	32	0.1	0.3
165 CH OF NAZARENE	3	224	539	2.5	5.3
193 EPISCOPAL.....	1	277	393	1.8	3.8
221 FREE METH C NA	1	28	43	0.2	0.4
226 FRIENDS-USA...	1	60	71*	0.3	0.7
281 LUTH CH AMER..	1	106	163	0.7	1.6
283 LUTH--MO SYNOD	1	204	263	1.2	2.6
349 PENT HOLINESS.	1	23	27*	0.1	0.3
413 S-D ADVENTISTS	2	226	266*	1.2	2.6
419 SO BAPT CONV..	3	685	806*	3.7	7.9
449 UN METHODIST..	2	947	1,134	5.2	11.1
453 UN PRES CH USA	3	646	760*	3.5	7.4
GARFIELD	27	2,575	4,429*	29.9	100.0
019 AMER BAPT CONV	1	118	142*	1.0	3.2
081 CATHOLIC......	5	0	1,150	7.8	26.0
097 CR C AND C CR.	2	325	392*	2.6	8.9
165 CH OF NAZARENE	2	64	141	1.0	3.2
193 EPISCOPAL.....	2	121	250	1.7	5.6
281 LUTH CH AMER..	1	184	313	2.1	7.1
283 LUTH--MO SYNOD	2	163	243	1.6	5.5
285 MENNONITE CH..	1	41	49*	0.3	1.1
349 PENT HOLINESS.	1	4	5*	-	0.1
413 S-D ADVENTISTS	2	155	187*	1.3	4.2
419 SO BAPT CONV..	1	69	83*	0.6	1.9

County and Denomination	Number of churches	Communicant, confirmed, full members	Total adherents: Number	Total adherents: Percent of total population	Total adherents: Percent of total adherents
443 UN C OF CHRIST	2	95	114*	0.8	2.6
449 UN METHODIST..	4	1,115	1,214	8.2	27.4
453 UN PRES CH USA	1	121	146*	1.0	3.3
GILPIN	2	45	56	4.4	100.0
193 EPISCOPAL.....	1	8	19	1.5	33.9
449 UN METHODIST..	1	37	37	2.9	66.1
GRAND	8	419	802*	19.5	100.0
081 CATHOLIC......	2	0	300	7.3	37.4
193 EPISCOPAL.....	2	85	103	2.5	12.8
419 SO BAPT CONV..	1	84	100*	2.4	12.5
453 UN PRES CH USA	3	250	299*	7.3	37.3
GUNNISON	7	359	1,289*	17.0	100.0
081 CATHOLIC......	3	0	845	11.2	65.6
193 EPISCOPAL.....	1	107	136	1.8	10.6
283 LUTH--MO SYNOD	1	49	73	1.0	5.7
419 SO BAPT CONV..	1	197	228*	3.0	17.7
443 UN C OF CHRIST	1	6	7*	0.1	0.5
HINSDALE	1	27	31*	15.3	100.0
453 UN PRES CH USA	1	27	31*	15.3	100.0
HUERFANO	12	743	4,110*	62.4	100.0
019 AMER BAPT CONV	2	149	179*	2.7	4.4
081 CATHOLIC......	3	0	3,225	48.9	78.5
285 MENNONITE CH..	1	19	23*	0.3	0.6
413 S-D ADVENTISTS	1	19	23*	0.3	0.6
419 SO BAPT CONV..	2	191	229*	3.5	5.6
449 UN METHODIST..	3	365	431	6.5	10.5
JACKSON	2	201	361	19.9	100.0
081 CATHOLIC......	1	0	150	8.3	41.6
449 UN METHODIST..	1	201	211	11.7	58.4
JEFFERSON	93	34,438	89,523*	38.4	100.0
019 AMER BAPT CONV	2	330	414*	0.2	0.5
029 AMER LUTH CH..	4	1,588	2,410	1.0	2.7
081 CATHOLIC......	11	0	41,700	17.9	46.6
093 CR CH (DISC)..	4	847	1,063*	0.5	1.2
097 CR C AND C CR.	5	900	1,130*	0.5	1.3
123 CH GOD (ANDER)	1	56	131	0.1	0.1
127 CH GOD (CLEVE)	1	79	99*	-	0.1
165 CH OF NAZARENE	10	1,071	2,134	0.9	2.4
193 EPISCOPAL.....	7	2,565	4,282	1.8	4.8
201 EVAN COV CH AM	1	29	36*	-	-
281 LUTH CH AMER..	4	2,365	3,520	1.5	3.9
283 LUTH--MO SYNOD	6	4,326	6,206	2.7	6.9
287 MENN GEN CONF.	1	91	114*	-	0.1
381 REF PRES-EVAN.	1	52	58	-	0.1
413 S-D ADVENTISTS	3	665	835*	0.4	0.9
415 S-D BAPTIST GC	1	162	203*	0.1	0.2
419 SO BAPT CONV..	7	3,040	3,817*	1.6	4.3
435 UNITARIAN-UNIV	1	310	544	0.2	0.6
443 UN C OF CHRIST	5	1,286	1,615*	0.7	1.8
449 UN METHODIST..	10	9,049	12,147	5.2	13.6
453 UN PRES CH USA	8	5,627	7,065*	3.0	7.9
KIOWA	6	592	707*	34.8	100.0
097 CR C AND C CR.	1	110	133*	6.6	18.8
226 FRIENDS-USA...	1	46	56*	2.8	7.9
419 SO BAPT CONV..	1	120	145*	7.1	20.5
449 UN METHODIST..	3	316	373	18.4	52.8
KIT CARSON	25	2,646	4,420*	58.7	100.0
019 AMER BAPT CONV	1	269	333*	4.4	7.5
029 AMER LUTH CH..	2	345	480	6.4	10.9
081 CATHOLIC......	3	0	1,000	13.3	22.6
093 CR CH (DISC)..	1	226	280*	3.7	6.3
097 CR C AND C CR.	2	50	62*	0.8	1.4
123 CH GOD (ANDER)	1	45	129	1.7	2.9
165 CH OF NAZARENE	2	32	72	1.0	1.6
283 LUTH--MO SYNOD	3	378	504	6.7	11.4
287 MENN GEN CONF.	1	17	21*	0.3	0.5
353 PLY BRETHREN..	1	30	60	0.8	1.4
413 S-D ADVENTISTS	2	21	26*	0.3	0.6
419 SO BAPT CONV..	1	219	271*	3.6	6.1
443 UN C OF CHRIST	2	245	303*	4.0	6.9
449 UN METHODIST..	3	769	879	11.7	19.9
LAKE	7	642	4,834*	58.4	100.0
081 CATHOLIC......	2	0	3,900	47.1	80.7
193 EPISCOPAL.....	1	68	135	1.6	2.8
283 LUTH--MO SYNOD	1	111	189	2.3	3.9
413 S-D ADVENTISTS	1	39	51*	0.6	1.1
419 SO BAPT CONV..	1	233	307*	3.7	6.4
453 UN PRES CH USA	1	191	252*	3.0	5.2
LA PLATA	20	2,238	6,253*	32.6	100.0
081 CATHOLIC......	3	0	3,580	18.6	57.3
097 CR C AND C CR.	1	91	110*	0.6	1.8
165 CH OF NAZARENE	1	38	62	0.3	1.0
221 FREE METH C NA	2	30	41	0.2	0.7

*Total adherents estimated from known number of communicant, confirmed, full members.

—Represents a percent less than 0.1.

Percentages may not total due to rounding.

Table 3. Churches and Church Membership by State, County and Denomination: 1971

County and Denomination	Number of churches	Communicant, confirmed, full members	Total adherents		
			Number	Percent of total population	Percent of total adherents
283 LUTH--MO SYNOD	1	130	171	0.9	2.7
413 S-D ADVENTISTS	1	96	116*	0.6	1.9
419 SO BAPT CONV..	3	437	526*	2.7	8.4
435 UNITARIAN-UNIV	1	11	11	0.1	0.2
449 UN METHODIST..	2	652	730	3.8	11.7
453 UN PRES CH USA	5	753	906*	4.7	14.5
LARIMER	61	22,856	34,209*	38.1	100.0
019 AMER BAPT CONV	2	971	1,163*	1.3	3.4
029 AMER LUTH CH..	3	2,387	3,376	3.8	9.9
081 CATHOLIC......	4	0	5,100	5.7	14.9
093 CR CH (DISC)..	2	1,207	1,446*	1.6	4.2
097 CR C AND C CR.	1	89	107*	0.1	0.3
105 CHRISTIAN REF.	1	96	145	0.2	0.4
123 CH GOD (ANDER)	1	62	129	0.1	0.4
165 CH OF NAZARENE	2	311	569	0.6	1.7
193 EPISCOPAL.....	3	1,365	1,415	1.6	4.1
201 EVAN COV CH AM	1	91	109*	0.1	0.3
221 FREE METH C NA	2	62	75	0.1	0.2
226 FRIENDS-USA...	1	150	180*	0.2	0.5
281 LUTH CH AMER..	2	820	1,215	1.4	3.6
283 LUTH--MO SYNOD	6	1,959	2,785	3.1	8.1
353 PLY BRETHREN..	1	50	70	0.1	0.2
403 SALVATION ARMY	1	53	274	0.3	0.8
413 S-D ADVENTISTS	4	1,141	1,367*	1.5	4.0
419 SO BAPT CONV..	5	1,071	1,283*	1.4	3.8
435 UNITARIAN-UNIV	1	201	261	0.3	0.8
443 UN C OF CHRIST	3	884	1,059*	1.2	3.1
449 UN METHODIST..	5	5,084	6,318	7.0	18.5
453 UN PRES CH USA	9	4,753	5,694*	6.3	16.6
469 WISC EVAN LUTH	1	49	69	0.1	0.2
LAS ANIMAS	28	1,437	7,920*	50.3	100.0
019 AMER BAPT CONV	1	151	179*	1.1	2.3
081 CATHOLIC......	16	0	6,219	39.5	78.5
093 CR CH (DISC)..	1	159	189*	1.2	2.4
165 CH OF NAZARENE	1	27	31	0.2	0.4
193 EPISCOPAL.....	1	101	114	0.7	1.4
281 LUTH CH AMER..	1	78	121	0.8	1.5
413 S-D ADVENTISTS	1	22	26*	0.2	0.3
419 SO BAPT CONV..	3	391	464*	2.9	5.9
449 UN METHODIST..	1	381	426	2.7	5.4
453 UN PRES CH USA	2	127	151*	1.0	1.9
LINCOLN	23	2,495	3,696*	76.4	100.0
019 AMER BAPT CONV	1	155	187*	3.9	5.1
029 AMER LUTH CH..	2	135	186	3.8	5.0
081 CATHOLIC......	3	0	600	12.4	16.2
097 CR C AND C CR.	1	20	24*	0.5	0.6
157 CH OF BRETHREN	1	45	54*	1.1	1.5
165 CH OF NAZARENE	2	56	149	3.1	4.0
193 EPISCOPAL.....	1	43	43	0.9	1.2
283 LUTH--MO SYNOD	3	160	236	4.9	6.4
285 MENNONITE CH..	1	13	16*	0.3	0.4
353 PLY BRETHREN..	1	30	50	1.0	1.4
413 S-D ADVENTISTS	1	19	23*	0.5	0.6
443 UN C OF CHRIST	1	140	169*	3.5	4.6
449 UN METHODIST..	4	731	815	16.9	22.1
453 UN PRES CH USA	1	948	1,144*	23.7	31.0
LOGAN	28	5,812	11,293*	59.9	100.0
019 AMER BAPT CONV	2	434	527*	2.8	4.7
029 AMER LUTH CH..	1	245	365	1.9	3.2
081 CATHOLIC......	5	0	3,850	20.4	34.1
093 CR CH (DISC)..	1	247	300*	1.6	2.7
165 CH OF NAZARENE	1	81	192	1.0	1.7
193 EPISCOPAL.....	1	181	275	1.5	2.4
283 LUTH--MO SYNOD	3	839	1,130	6.0	10.0
413 S-D ADVENTISTS	1	106	129*	0.7	1.1
419 SO BAPT CONV..	1	263	319*	1.7	2.8
443 UN C OF CHRIST	2	289	351*	1.9	3.1
449 UN METHODIST..	8	2,237	2,774	14.7	24.6
453 UN PRES CH USA	2	890	1,081*	5.7	9.6
MESA	42	8,824	16,160*	29.7	100.0
019 AMER BAPT CONV	4	1,029	1,227*	2.3	7.6
029 AMER LUTH CH..	1	446	588	1.1	3.6
081 CATHOLIC......	4	0	5,498	10.1	34.0
093 CR CH (DISC)..	1	287	342*	0.6	2.1
097 CR C AND C CR.	5	773	922*	1.7	5.7
123 CH GOD (ANDER)	1	74	189	0.3	1.2
127 CH GOD (CLEVE)	1	88	105*	0.2	0.6
157 CH OF BRETHREN	1	115	137*	0.3	0.8
165 CH OF NAZARENE	2	211	330	0.6	2.0
193 EPISCOPAL.....	1	638	712	1.3	4.4
226 FRIENDS-USA...	1	103	123*	0.2	0.8
283 LUTH--MO SYNOD	1	370	510	0.9	3.2
335 ORTH PRESB CH.	1	21	37	0.1	0.2
349 PENT HOLINESS.	2	86	103*	0.2	0.6
403 SALVATION ARMY	1	66	215	0.4	1.3
413 S-D ADVENTISTS	3	647	772*	1.4	4.8
419 SO BAPT CONV..	2	640	763*	1.4	4.7
435 UNITARIAN-UNIV	1	13	13	-	0.1
443 UN C OF CHRIST	2	941	1,122*	2.1	6.9
449 UN METHODIST..	6	2,261	2,421	4.5	15.0
469 WISC EVAN LUTH	1	15	31	0.1	0.2
MINERAL	2	55	126*	16.0	100.0
193 EPISCOPAL.....	1	13	71	9.0	56.3
443 UN C OF CHRIST	1	42	55*	7.0	43.7
MOFFAT	10	958	1,566*	24.0	100.0
081 CATHOLIC......	1	0	300	4.6	19.2
097 CR C AND C CR.	1	350	435*	6.7	27.8
165 CH OF NAZARENE	1	17	41	0.6	2.6
193 EPISCOPAL.....	1	37	75	1.1	4.8
283 LUTH--MO SYNOD	1	58	99	1.5	6.3
413 S-D ADVENTISTS	1	45	56*	0.9	3.6
419 SO BAPT CONV..	2	199	247*	3.8	15.8
443 UN C OF CHRIST	2	252	313*	4.8	20.0
MONTEZUMA	22	2,787	5,055*	39.0	100.0
019 AMER BAPT CONV	2	508	634*	4.9	12.5
059 BAPT MISS ASSN	1	45	56*	0.4	1.1
081 CATHOLIC......	3	0	1,511	11.7	29.9
097 CR C AND C CR.	1	70	87*	0.7	1.7
165 CH OF NAZARENE	1	51	82	0.6	1.6
193 EPISCOPAL.....	2	303	477	3.7	9.4
283 LUTH--MO SYNOD	1	92	141	1.1	2.8
413 S-D ADVENTISTS	1	218	272*	2.1	5.4
419 SO BAPT CONV..	3	621	775*	6.0	15.3
449 UN METHODIST..	4	653	738	5.7	14.6
453 UN PRES CH USA	3	226	282*	2.2	5.6
MONTROSE	24	4,194	7,810*	42.5	100.0
019 AMER BAPT CONV	2	813	1,009*	5.5	12.9
081 CATHOLIC......	2	0	2,588	14.1	33.1
097 CR C AND C CR.	1	600	745*	4.1	9.5
165 CH OF NAZARENE	1	99	157	0.9	2.0
193 EPISCOPAL.....	2	182	232	1.3	3.0
283 LUTH--MO SYNOD	1	185	250	1.4	3.2
413 S-D ADVENTISTS	2	266	330*	1.8	4.2
419 SO BAPT CONV..	4	865	1,074*	5.8	13.8
443 UN C OF CHRIST	4	187	232*	1.3	3.0
449 UN METHODIST..	2	714	810	4.4	10.4
453 UN PRES CH USA	2	254	315*	1.7	4.0
469 WISC EVAN LUTH	1	29	68	0.4	0.9
MORGAN	31	6,515	11,033*	54.9	100.0
019 AMER BAPT CONV	1	366	455*	2.3	4.1
029 AMER LUTH CH..	3	684	913	4.5	8.3
081 CATHOLIC......	3	0	2,700	13.4	24.5
093 CR CH (DISC)..	1	335	417*	2.1	3.8
097 CR C AND C CR.	1	14	17*	0.1	0.2
165 CH OF NAZARENE	2	165	412	2.0	3.7
193 EPISCOPAL.....	1	231	240	1.2	2.2
226 FRIENDS-USA...	1	50	62*	0.3	0.6
283 LUTH--MO SYNOD	1	347	526	2.6	4.8
413 S-D ADVENTISTS	1	61	76*	0.4	0.7
419 SO BAPT CONV..	2	354	440*	2.2	4.0
443 UN C OF CHRIST	3	1,077	1,340*	6.7	12.1
449 UN METHODIST..	5	1,539	1,816	9.0	16.5
453 UN PRES CH USA	4	1,186	1,476*	7.3	13.4
469 WISC EVAN LUTH	2	106	143	0.7	1.3
OTERO	49	6,687	13,334*	56.7	100.0
019 AMER BAPT CONV	3	784	968*	4.1	7.3
029 AMER LUTH CH..	1	248	354	1.5	2.7
081 CATHOLIC......	7	0	4,789	20.4	35.9
093 CR CH (DISC)..	4	560	692*	2.9	5.2
097 CR C AND C CR.	2	17	21*	0.1	0.2
123 CH GOD (ANDER)	2	90	240	1.0	1.8
127 CH GOD (CLEVE)	1	34	42*	0.2	0.3
157 CH OF BRETHREN	1	175	216*	0.9	1.6
165 CH OF NAZARENE	4	292	546	2.3	4.1
193 EPISCOPAL.....	1	206	247	1.1	1.9
221 FREE METH C NA	1	11	12	0.1	0.1
226 FRIENDS-USA...	1	58	72*	0.3	0.5
283 LUTH--MO SYNOD	2	211	277	1.2	2.1
285 MENNONITE CH..	4	320	395*	1.7	3.0
413 S-D ADVENTISTS	2	129	159*	0.7	1.2
419 SO BAPT CONV..	3	605	747*	3.2	5.6
443 UN C OF CHRIST	1	77	95*	0.4	0.7
449 UN METHODIST..	6	2,103	2,512	10.7	18.8
453 UN PRES CH USA	2	751	928*	3.9	7.0
469 WISC EVAN LUTH	1	16	22	0.1	0.2
OURAY	4	204	639*	41.3	100.0
081 CATHOLIC......	1	0	380	24.6	59.5
193 EPISCOPAL.....	1	17	26	1.7	4.1
419 SO BAPT CONV..	1	65	81*	5.2	12.7
453 UN PRES CH USA	1	122	152*	9.8	23.8
PARK	2	31	38*	1.7	100.0
413 S-D ADVENTISTS	1	4	5*	0.2	13.2
453 UN PRES CH USA	1	27	33*	1.5	86.8
PHILLIPS	15	1,921	2,841*	68.8	100.0
019 AMER BAPT CONV	1	121	142*	3.4	5.0
081 CATHOLIC......	2	0	500	12.1	17.6
097 CR C AND C CR.	2	400	469*	11.4	16.5
157 CH OF BRETHREN	1	94	110*	2.7	3.9
165 CH OF NAZARENE	1	42	62	1.5	2.2
201 EVAN COV CH AM	1	81	95*	2.3	3.3
283 LUTH--MO SYNOD	3	651	826	20.0	29.1
353 PLY BRETHREN..	1	10	20	0.5	0.7

*Total adherents estimated from known number of communicant, confirmed, full members.

—Represents a percent less than 0.1.

Percentages may not total due to rounding.

Table 3. Churches and Church Membership by State, County and Denomination: 1971

County and Denomination	Number of churches	Communicant, confirmed, full members	Total adherents: Number	Total adherents: Percent of total population	Total adherents: Percent of total adherents
413 S-D ADVENTISTS	1	38	45*	1.1	1.6
419 SO BAPT CONV..	1	27	32*	0.8	1.1
449 UN METHODIST..	1	457	540	13.1	19.0
PITKIN	6	438	700*	11.3	100.0
081 CATHOLIC......	1	0	150	2.4	21.4
193 EPISCOPAL.....	1	150	181	2.9	25.9
283 LUTH--MO SYNOD	1	32	46	0.7	6.6
285 MENNONITE CH..	1	8	10*	0.2	1.4
449 UN METHODIST..	2	248	313	5.1	44.7
PROWERS	24	3,385	6,744*	50.9	100.0
019 AMER BAPT CONV	2	813	1,012*	7.6	15.0
081 CATHOLIC......	4	0	2,195	16.6	32.5
097 CR C AND C CR.	2	50	62*	0.5	0.9
123 CH GOD (ANDER)	2	85	240	1.8	3.6
157 CH OF BRETHREN	1	100	125*	0.9	1.9
165 CH OF NAZARENE	2	94	321	2.4	4.8
193 EPISCOPAL.....	1	56	118	0.9	1.7
283 LUTH--MO SYNOD	1	98	141	1.1	2.1
413 S-D ADVENTISTS	1	45	56*	0.4	0.8
419 SO BAPT CONV..	1	364	453*	3.4	6.7
449 UN METHODIST..	5	1,437	1,718	13.0	25.5
453 UN PRES CH USA	2	243	303*	2.3	4.5
PUEBLO	78	16,477	58,680*	49.6	100.0
019 AMER BAPT CONV	5	2,263	2,769*	2.3	4.7
081 CATHOLIC......	21	0	37,614	31.8	64.1
093 CR CH (DISC)..	4	1,234	1,510*	1.3	2.6
097 CR C AND C CR.	2	246	301*	0.3	0.5
123 CH GOD (ANDER)	1	56	148	0.1	0.3
127 CH GOD (CLEVE)	1	69	84*	0.1	0.1
157 CH OF BRETHREN	1	119	146*	0.1	0.2
165 CH OF NAZARENE	3	464	814	0.7	1.4
193 EPISCOPAL.....	2	1,024	1,563	1.3	2.7
221 FREE METH C NA	1	33	42	-	0.1
226 FRIENDS-USA...	1	117	143*	0.1	0.2
281 LUTH CH AMER..	2	611	829	0.7	1.4
283 LUTH--MO SYNOD	3	670	1,005	0.8	1.7
285 MENNONITE CH..	1	53	65*	0.1	0.1
349 PENT HOLINESS.	1	22	27*	-	-
353 PLY BRETHREN..	1	10	15	-	-
403 SALVATION ARMY	1	59	204	0.2	0.3
413 S-D ADVENTISTS	3	498	609*	0.5	1.0
419 SO BAPT CONV..	6	1,723	2,109*	1.8	3.6
435 UNITARIAN-UNIV	1	42	67	0.1	0.1
443 UN C OF CHRIST	2	380	465*	0.4	0.8
449 UN METHODIST..	12	5,175	6,129	5.2	10.4
453 UN PRES CH USA	2	1,547	1,893*	1.6	3.2
469 WISC EVAN LUTH	1	62	129	0.1	0.2
RIO BLANCO	10	994	1,703*	35.2	100.0
019 AMER BAPT CONV	1	190	230*	4.8	13.5
081 CATHOLIC......	2	0	500	10.3	29.4
097 CR C AND C CR.	2	134	163*	3.4	9.6
193 EPISCOPAL.....	2	280	341	7.0	20.0
283 LUTH--MO SYNOD	1	23	39	0.8	2.3
419 SO BAPT CONV..	1	200	243*	5.0	14.3
449 UN METHODIST..	1	167	187	3.9	11.0
RIO GRANDE	22	2,643	5,691*	54.2	100.0
019 AMER BAPT CONV	1	152	189*	1.8	3.3
081 CATHOLIC......	5	0	2,470	23.5	43.4
093 CR CH (DISC)..	1	153	190*	1.8	3.3
165 CH OF NAZARENE	1	57	95	0.9	1.7
193 EPISCOPAL.....	2	172	254	2.4	4.5
226 FRIENDS-USA...	1	47	58*	0.6	1.0
283 LUTH--MO SYNOD	1	175	242	2.3	4.3
313 NO AM BAPT GC.	1	39	49*	0.5	0.9
413 S-D ADVENTISTS	1	70	87*	0.8	1.5
419 SO BAPT CONV..	2	278	346*	3.3	6.1
449 UN METHODIST..	3	969	1,048	10.0	18.4
453 UN PRES CH USA	2	515	641*	6.1	11.3
469 WISC EVAN LUTH	1	16	22	0.2	0.4
ROUTT	9	741	1,623*	24.6	100.0
081 CATHOLIC......	2	0	600	9.1	37.0
165 CH OF NAZARENE	1	5	19	0.3	1.2
193 EPISCOPAL.....	1	72	140	2.1	8.6
283 LUTH--MO SYNOD	1	86	131	2.0	8.1
413 S-D ADVENTISTS	1	23	28*	0.4	1.7
443 UN C OF CHRIST	1	154	188*	2.9	11.6
449 UN METHODIST..	2	401	517	7.8	31.9
SAGUACHE	9	769	1,925*	50.3	100.0
019 AMER BAPT CONV	1	120	151*	3.9	7.8
081 CATHOLIC......	4	0	1,000	26.1	51.9
193 EPISCOPAL.....	1	31	57	1.5	3.0
419 SO BAPT CONV..	1	129	162*	4.2	8.4
449 UN METHODIST..	2	489	555	14.5	28.8
SAN JUAN	2	69	85*	10.2	100.0
419 SO BAPT CONV..	1	16	20*	2.4	23.5
443 UN C OF CHRIST	1	53	65*	7.8	76.5
SAN MIGUEL	4	168	221*	11.3	100.0
349 PENT HOLINESS.	1	11	14*	0.7	6.3
419 SO BAPT CONV..	1	54	67*	3.4	30.3
449 UN METHODIST..	1	51	75	3.8	33.9
453 UN PRES CH USA	1	52	65*	3.3	29.4
SEDGWICK	9	1,415	2,704*	79.4	100.0
081 CATHOLIC......	1	0	1,000	29.4	37.0
093 CR CH (DISC)..	1	188	220*	6.5	8.1
097 CR C AND C CR.	1	220	258*	7.6	9.5
283 LUTH--MO SYNOD	1	241	301	8.8	11.1
285 MENNONITE CH..	1	25	29*	0.9	1.1
413 S-D ADVENTISTS	1	33	39*	1.1	1.4
449 UN METHODIST..	2	600	730	21.4	27.0
453 UN PRES CH USA	1	108	127*	3.7	4.7
SUMMIT	3	75	197	7.4	100.0
081 CATHOLIC......	1	0	100	3.8	50.8
193 EPISCOPAL.....	1	25	32	1.2	16.2
449 UN METHODIST..	1	50	65	2.4	33.0
TELLER	9	570	1,118*	33.7	100.0
019 AMER BAPT CONV	1	57	68*	2.1	6.1
081 CATHOLIC......	3	0	400	12.1	35.8
193 EPISCOPAL.....	1	14	20	0.6	1.8
283 LUTH--MO SYNOD	1	149	197	5.9	17.6
353 PLY BRETHREN..	1	30	50	1.5	4.5
419 SO BAPT CONV..	1	305	365*	11.0	32.6
443 UN C OF CHRIST	1	15	18*	0.5	1.6
WASHINGTON	13	1,953	2,770*	49.9	100.0
029 AMER LUTH CH..	2	270	360	6.5	13.0
081 CATHOLIC......	1	0	400	7.2	14.4
165 CH OF NAZARENE	1	18	29	0.5	1.0
283 LUTH--MO SYNOD	1	148	184	3.3	6.6
285 MENNONITE CH..	1	23	27*	0.5	1.0
413 S-D ADVENTISTS	1	19	23*	0.4	0.8
449 UN METHODIST..	3	994	1,175	21.2	42.4
453 UN PRES CH USA	3	481	572*	10.3	20.6
WELD	90	18,215	35,597*	39.9	100.0
019 AMER BAPT CONV	5	1,211	1,483*	1.7	4.2
029 AMER LUTH CH..	4	1,616	2,242	2.5	6.3
081 CATHOLIC......	13	0	11,600	13.0	32.6
093 CR CH (DISC)..	5	897	1,099*	1.2	3.1
097 CR C AND C CR.	2	285	349*	0.4	1.0
105 CHRISTIAN REF.	1	42	75	0.1	0.2
123 CH GOD (ANDER)	2	147	307	0.3	0.9
157 CH OF BRETHREN	1	20	24*	-	0.1
165 CH OF NAZARENE	2	310	624	0.7	1.8
193 EPISCOPAL.....	3	806	1,359	1.5	3.8
201 EVAN COV CH AM	1	144	176*	0.2	0.5
221 FREE METH C NA	1	26	30	-	0.1
281 LUTH CH AMER..	2	648	843	0.9	2.4
283 LUTH--MO SYNOD	7	1,447	1,969	2.2	5.5
285 MENNONITE CH..	1	30	37*	-	0.1
313 NO AM BAPT GC.	2	223	273*	0.3	0.8
349 PENT HOLINESS.	3	66	81*	0.1	0.2
403 SALVATION ARMY	1	69	450	0.5	1.3
413 S-D ADVENTISTS	3	556	681*	0.8	1.9
419 SO BAPT CONV..	4	946	1,159*	1.3	3.3
435 UNITARIAN-UNIV	1	49	64	0.1	0.2
443 UN C OF CHRIST	7	2,626	3,217*	3.6	9.0
449 UN METHODIST..	13	4,586	5,648	6.3	15.9
453 UN PRES CH USA	5	1,434	1,756*	2.0	4.9
469 WISC EVAN LUTH	1	31	51	0.1	0.1
YUMA	23	2,253	3,584*	41.9	100.0
081 CATHOLIC......	2	0	700	8.2	19.5
093 CR CH (DISC)..	1	176	209*	2.4	5.8
165 CH OF NAZARENE	3	152	308	3.6	8.6
283 LUTH--MO SYNOD	2	568	767	9.0	21.4
413 S-D ADVENTISTS	1	46	55*	0.6	1.5
419 SO BAPT CONV..	2	101	120*	1.4	3.3
443 UN C OF CHRIST	1	100	119*	1.4	3.3
449 UN METHODIST..	8	1,048	1,232	14.4	34.4
453 UN PRES CH USA	3	62	74*	0.9	2.1
CO DATA NOT AVAIL	23	890	39,306*	N/A	N/A
151 L-D SAINTS....	0	0	38,256	N/A	N/A
223 FREE WILL BAPT	2	92	113*	N/A	N/A
231 GENERAL BAPT..	2	85	104*	N/A	N/A
467 WESLEYAN......	19	713	833	N/A	N/A

CONNECTICUT

County and Denomination	Number of churches	Communicant, confirmed, full members	Total adherents: Number	Total adherents: Percent of total population	Total adherents: Percent of total adherents
THE STATE.....	1,422	345,336	1,797,210*	59.3	100.0
FAIRFIELD	320	88,817	455,387*	57.4	100.0

*Total adherents estimated from known number of communicant, confirmed, full members.

—Represents a percent less than 0.1.

Percentages may not total due to rounding.

Table 3. Churches and Church Membership by State, County and Denomination: 1971

County and Denomination	Number of churches	Communicant, confirmed, full members	Total adherents		
			Number	Percent of total population	Percent of total adherents
019 AMER BAPT CONV	26	3,456	4,204*	0.5	0.9
081 CATHOLIC......	100	0	328,049	41.4	72.0
093 CR CH (DISC)..	2	378	460*	0.1	0.1
097 CR C AND C CR.	1	30	36*	-	-
127 CH GOD (CLEVE)	2	56	68*	-	-
165 CH OF NAZARENE	2	110	241	-	0.1
175 CONG CR CH....	1	87	106*	-	-
193 EPISCOPAL.....	46	19,329	43,962	5.5	9.7
201 EVAN COV CH AM	4	436	530*	0.1	0.1
226 FRIENDS-USA...	2	287	349*	-	0.1
281 LUTH CH AMER..	15	6,231	8,442	1.1	1.9
283 LUTH--MO SYNOD	10	4,397	5,971	0.8	1.3
313 NO AM BAPT GC.	1	100	122*	-	-
353 PLY BRETHREN..	4	125	200	-	-
403 SALVATION ARMY	5	149	961	0.1	0.2
413 S-D ADVENTISTS	5	512	623*	0.1	0.1
419 SO BAPT CONV..	3	478	581*	0.1	0.1
435 UNITARIAN-UNIV	5	1,348	1,945	0.2	0.4
443 UN C OF CHRIST	43	24,662	29,999*	3.8	6.6
449 UN METHODIST..	33	18,563	18,701	2.4	4.1
453 UN PRES CH USA	9	8,065	9,810*	1.2	2.2
469 WISC EVAN LUTH	1	18	27	-	-
HARTFORD	325	103,416	522,745*	64.0	100.0
019 AMER BAPT CONV	24	6,484	7,908*	1.0	1.5
081 CATHOLIC......	97	0	390,587	47.8	74.7
097 CR C AND C CR.	2	52	63*	-	-
105 CHRISTIAN REF.	1	44	98	-	-
123 CH GOD (ANDER)	1	50	100	-	-
127 CH GOD (CLEVE)	3	204	249*	-	-
165 CH OF NAZARENE	3	347	751	0.1	0.1
175 CONG CR CH....	1	1,737	2,118*	0.3	0.4
193 EPISCOPAL.....	36	18,565	27,707	3.4	5.3
201 EVAN COV CH AM	5	967	1,179*	0.1	0.2
226 FRIENDS-USA...	1	259	316*	-	0.1
281 LUTH CH AMER..	15	9,952	13,414	1.6	2.6
283 LUTH--MO SYNOD	16	6,211	8,628	1.1	1.7
315 NO AM OLD RC..	1	231	282*	-	0.1
353 PLY BRETHREN..	4	263	335	-	0.1
381 REF PRES-EVAN.	1	110	160	-	-
403 SALVATION ARMY	6	521	2,071	0.3	0.4
413 S-D ADVENTISTS	4	600	732*	0.1	0.1
419 SO BAPT CONV..	2	343	418*	0.1	0.1
435 UNITARIAN-UNIV	6	1,789	2,403	0.3	0.5
443 UN C OF CHRIST	57	36,325	44,301*	5.4	8.5
449 UN METHODIST..	34	16,394	16,507	2.0	3.2
453 UN PRES CH USA	4	1,918	2,339*	0.3	0.4
469 WISC EVAN LUTH	1	50	79	-	-
LITCHFIELD	125	23,809	91,128*	63.2	100.0
019 AMER BAPT CONV	5	1,002	1,224*	0.8	1.3
081 CATHOLIC......	28	0	60,461	42.0	66.3
175 CONG CR CH....	3	478	584*	0.4	0.6
193 EPISCOPAL.....	23	6,448	9,905	6.9	10.9
201 EVAN COV CH AM	2	317	387*	0.3	0.4
226 FRIENDS-USA...	2	33	40*	-	-
281 LUTH CH AMER..	5	1,756	2,256	1.6	2.5
283 LUTH--MO SYNOD	3	493	686	0.5	0.8
353 PLY BRETHREN..	1	25	40	-	-
403 SALVATION ARMY	1	18	143	0.1	0.2
413 S-D ADVENTISTS	1	43	53*	-	0.1
443 UN C OF CHRIST	36	9,454	11,553*	8.0	12.7
449 UN METHODIST..	15	3,742	3,796	2.6	4.2
MIDDLESEX	78	15,104	65,517*	57.1	100.0
019 AMER BAPT CONV	6	800	981*	0.9	1.5
081 CATHOLIC......	18	0	44,981	39.2	68.7
175 CONG CR CH....	2	144	177*	0.2	0.3
193 EPISCOPAL.....	12	3,245	5,922	5.2	9.0
201 EVAN COV CH AM	2	238	292*	0.3	0.4
226 FRIENDS-USA...	1	39	48*	-	0.1
281 LUTH CH AMER..	7	1,984	2,699	2.4	4.1
283 LUTH--MO SYNOD	1	300	444	0.4	0.7
403 SALVATION ARMY	1	21	177	0.2	0.3
413 S-D ADVENTISTS	1	50	61*	0.1	0.1
435 UNITARIAN-UNIV	1	33	63	0.1	0.1
443 UN C OF CHRIST	18	6,217	7,623*	6.6	11.6
449 UN METHODIST..	8	2,033	2,049	1.8	3.1
NEW HAVEN	302	72,029	452,957*	60.8	100.0
019 AMER BAPT CONV	25	5,719	6,950*	0.9	1.5
081 CATHOLIC......	103	0	357,313	48.0	78.9
093 CR CH (DISC)..	1	23	28*	-	-
097 CR C AND C CR.	2	106	129*	-	-
123 CH GOD (ANDER)	2	55	190	-	-
127 CH GOD (CLEVE)	2	134	163*	-	-
165 CH OF NAZARENE	2	75	133	-	-
175 CONG CR CH....	2	353	429*	0.1	0.1
193 EPISCOPAL.....	44	16,973	27,408	3.7	6.1
201 EVAN COV CH AM	2	282	343*	-	0.1
226 FRIENDS-USA...	1	58	70*	-	-
281 LUTH CH AMER..	16	6,662	8,808	1.2	1.9
283 LUTH--MO SYNOD	8	2,397	3,457	0.5	0.8
313 NO AM BAPT GC.	1	73	89*	-	-
335 ORTH PRESB CH.	1	36	57	-	-
353 PLY BRETHREN..	2	200	453	0.1	0.1
403 SALVATION ARMY	5	241	1,785	0.2	0.4
413 S-D ADVENTISTS	4	559	679*	0.1	0.1
435 UNITARIAN-UNIV	4	588	823	0.1	0.2
443 UN C OF CHRIST	50	27,821	33,810*	4.5	7.5
449 UN METHODIST..	23	9,378	9,480	1.3	2.1
453 UN PRES CH USA	2	296	360*		0.1
NEW LONDON	129	21,282	104,452*	45.3	100.0
019 AMER BAPT CONV	23	4,974	6,197*	2.7	5.9
081 CATHOLIC......	34	0	75,729	32.9	72.5
127 CH GOD (CLEVE)	2	192	239*	0.1	0.2
165 CH OF NAZARENE	1	54	142	0.1	0.1
175 CONG CR CH....	8	1,022	1,273*	0.6	1.2
193 EPISCOPAL.....	11	3,634	6,025	2.6	5.8
226 FRIENDS-USA...	1	17	21*	-	-
281 LUTH CH AMER..	2	820	1,295	0.6	1.2
283 LUTH--MO SYNOD	5	1,109	1,769	0.8	1.7
353 PLY BRETHREN..	1	200	300	0.1	0.3
403 SALVATION ARMY	2	75	542	0.2	0.5
413 S-D ADVENTISTS	4	261	325*	0.1	0.3
415 S-D BAPTIST GC	1	37	46*	-	-
419 SO BAPT CONV..	2	560	698*	0.3	0.7
435 UNITARIAN-UNIV	2	242	322	0.1	0.3
443 UN C OF CHRIST	19	5,413	6,744*	2.9	6.5
449 UN METHODIST..	9	2,304	2,327	1.0	2.2
453 UN PRES CH USA	2	368	458*	0.2	0.4
TOLLAND	55	11,819	43,905*	42.4	100.0
019 AMER BAPT CONV	5	813	1,011*	1.0	2.3
081 CATHOLIC......	10	0	28,427	27.5	64.7
175 CONG CR CH....	1	48	60*	0.1	0.1
193 EPISCOPAL.....	4	1,443	2,566	2.5	5.8
226 FRIENDS-USA...	1	62	77*	0.1	0.2
281 LUTH CH AMER..	2	701	886	0.9	2.0
283 LUTH--MO SYNOD	3	561	826	0.8	1.9
413 S-D ADVENTISTS	1	52	65*	0.1	0.1
419 SO BAPT CONV..	1	58	72*	0.1	0.2
435 UNITARIAN-UNIV	2	113	133	0.1	0.3
443 UN C OF CHRIST	21	7,449	9,263*	9.0	21.1
449 UN METHODIST..	4	519	519	0.5	1.2
WINDHAM	88	9,060	57,586*	68.1	100.0
019 AMER BAPT CONV	14	1,814	2,241*	2.7	3.9
081 CATHOLIC......	26	0	45,410	53.7	78.9
165 CH OF NAZARENE	1	98	165	0.2	0.3
175 CONG CR CH....	3	225	278*	0.3	0.5
193 EPISCOPAL.....	8	1,434	2,808	3.3	4.9
201 EVAN COV CH AM	1	194	240*	0.3	0.4
281 LUTH CH AMER..	2	282	377	0.4	0.7
403 SALVATION ARMY	1	22	128	0.2	0.2
413 S-D ADVENTISTS	3	144	178*	0.2	0.3
419 SO BAPT CONV..	1	72	89*	0.1	0.2
435 UNITARIAN-UNIV	1	40	48	0.1	0.1
443 UN C OF CHRIST	19	3,705	4,577*	5.4	7.9
449 UN METHODIST..	8	1,030	1,047	1.2	1.8
CO DATA NOT AVAIL	0	0	3,533	N/A	N/A
151 L-D SAINTS....	0	0	3,533	N/A	N/A

DELAWARE

County and Denomination	Number of churches	Communicant, confirmed, full members	Number	Percent of total population	Percent of total adherents
THE STATE.....	413	101,954	236,868*	43.2	100.0
KENT	70	14,348	23,920*	29.2	100.0
019 AMER BAPT CONV	2	705	886*	1.1	3.7
081 CATHOLIC......	4	0	5,091	6.2	21.3
097 CR C AND C CR.	1	25	31*	-	0.1
123 CH GOD (ANDER)	1	25	62	0.1	0.3
127 CH GOD (CLEVE)	2	8	10*	-	-
157 CH OF BRETHREN	1	84	106*	0.1	0.4
165 CH OF NAZARENE	3	197	541	0.7	2.3
193 EPISCOPAL.....	4	1,070	1,699	2.1	7.1
226 FRIENDS-USA...	2	89	112*	0.1	0.5
281 LUTH CH AMER..	1	426	683	0.8	2.9
283 LUTH--MO SYNOD	1	351	491	0.6	2.1
285 MENNONITE CH..	3	100	126*	0.2	0.5
353 PLY BRETHREN..	1	40	60	0.1	0.3
413 S-D ADVENTISTS	4	418	525*	0.6	2.2
419 SO BAPT CONV..	4	1,797	2,259*	2.8	9.4
435 UNITARIAN-UNIV	1	14	14	-	0.1
443 UN C OF CHRIST	1	747	939*	1.1	3.9
449 UN METHODIST..	32	7,544	9,395	11.5	39.3
453 UN PRES CH USA	2	708	890*	1.1	3.7
NEW CASTLE	198	65,562	182,689*	47.3	100.0
019 AMER BAPT CONV	7	1,268	1,571*	0.4	0.9
029 AMER LUTH CH..	1	42	69	-	-
081 CATHOLIC......	32	0	95,883	24.8	52.5
093 CR CH (DISC)..	1	122	151*	-	0.1
097 CR C AND C CR.	2	58	72*	-	-
123 CH GOD (ANDER)	2	82	297	0.1	0.2
127 CH GOD (CLEVE)	3	198	245*	0.1	0.1
157 CH OF BRETHREN	1	122	151*	-	0.1
165 CH OF NAZARENE	2	175	547	0.1	0.3
193 EPISCOPAL.....	24	10,191	15,519	4.0	8.5

*Total adherents estimated from known number of communicant, confirmed, full members.

—Represents a percent less than 0.1.

Percentages may not total due to rounding.

Table 3. Churches and Church Membership by State, County and Denomination: 1971

County and Denomination	Number of churches	Communicant, confirmed, full members	Total adherents: Number	Total adherents: Percent of total population	Total adherents: Percent of total adherents
226 FRIENDS-USA...	6	769	953*	0.2	0.5
281 LUTH CH AMER..	9	4,896	7,086	1.8	3.9
283 LUTH--MO SYNOD	3	818	1,254	0.3	0.7
285 MENNONITE CH..	2	73	90*	-	-
313 NO AM BAPT GC.	1	70	87*	-	-
335 ORTH PRESB CH.	2	296	426	0.1	0.2
353 PLY BRETHREN..	1	70	90	-	-
381 REF PRES-EVAN.	5	1,094	1,403	0.4	0.8
403 SALVATION ARMY	1	110	855	0.2	0.5
413 S-D ADVENTISTS	3	377	467*	0.1	0.3
419 SO BAPT CONV..	2	743	920*	0.2	0.5
435 UNITARIAN-UNIV	2	986	1,400	0.4	0.8
449 UN METHODIST..	59	27,937	34,492	8.9	18.9
453 UN PRES CH USA	27	15,065	18,661*	4.8	10.2
SUSSEX	127	21,429	28,378*	35.3	100.0
081 CATHOLIC......	5	0	1,792	2.2	6.3
097 CR C AND C CR.	3	582	716*	0.9	2.5
127 CH GOD (CLEVE)	7	861	1,060*	1.3	3.7
165 CH OF NAZARENE	3	142	396	0.5	1.4
193 EPISCOPAL.....	9	1,718	2,736	3.4	9.6
281 LUTH CH AMER..	1	176	233	0.3	0.8
283 LUTH--MO SYNOD	2	195	279	0.3	1.0
285 MENNONITE CH..	2	441	543*	0.7	1.9
413 S-D ADVENTISTS	3	178	219*	0.3	0.8
419 SO BAPT CONV..	2	542	667*	0.8	2.4
443 UN C OF CHRIST	1	24	30*	-	0.1
449 UN METHODIST..	80	15,152	17,962	22.4	63.3
453 UN PRES CH USA	9	1,418	1,745*	2.2	6.1
CO DATA NOT AVAIL	18	615	1,881	N/A	N/A
151 L-D SAINTS....	0	0	1,149	N/A	N/A
193 EPISCOPAL.....	1	15	46	N/A	N/A
467 WESLEYAN......	17	600	686	N/A	N/A

DISTRICT OF COLUMBIA

County and Denomination	Number of churches	Communicant, confirmed, full members	Total adherents: Number	Total adherents: Percent of total population	Total adherents: Percent of total adherents
THE DISTRICT..	292	108,509	240,279*	31.8	100.0
019 AMER BAPT CONV	33	19,371	23,167*	3.1	9.6
029 AMER LUTH CH..	3	886	1,115	0.1	0.5
081 CATHOLIC......	44	0	95,508	12.6	39.7
093 CR CH (DISC)..	6	1,743	2,085*	0.3	0.9
097 CR C AND C CR.	8	1,007	1,204*	0.2	0.5
105 CHRISTIAN REF.	2	246	414	0.1	0.2
123 CH GOD (ANDER)	5	565	1,053	0.1	0.4
127 CH GOD (CLEVE)	3	377	451*	0.1	0.2
151 L-D SAINTS....	0	0	5,101	0.7	2.1
157 CH OF BRETHREN	1	413	494*	0.1	0.2
165 CH OF NAZARENE	2	424	630	0.1	0.3
193 EPISCOPAL.....	40	15,280	27,159	3.6	11.3
221 FREE METH C NA	2	104	194	-	0.1
226 FRIENDS-USA...	1	692	828*	0.1	0.3
281 LUTH CH AMER..	8	3,844	4,998	0.7	2.1
283 LUTH--MO SYNOD	7	1,680	2,684	0.4	1.1
285 MENNONITE CH..	1	11	13*	-	-
349 PENT HOLINESS.	3	230	275*	-	0.1
353 PLY BRETHREN..	3	140	210	-	0.1
357 PRESB CH US...	3	771	922*	0.1	0.4
403 SALVATION ARMY	4	307	1,455	0.2	0.6
413 S-D ADVENTISTS	7	2,792	3,339*	0.4	1.4
415 S-D BAPTIST GC	2	56	67*	-	-
419 SO BAPT CONV..	31	22,483	26,889*	3.6	11.2
435 UNITARIAN-UNIV	2	1,445	1,735	0.2	0.7
443 UN C OF CHRIST	9	5,362	6,413*	0.8	2.7
449 UN METHODIST..	43	22,393	24,835	3.3	10.3
453 UN PRES CH USA	19	5,887	7,041*	0.9	2.9

FLORIDA

County and Denomination	Number of churches	Communicant, confirmed, full members	Total adherents: Number	Total adherents: Percent of total population	Total adherents: Percent of total adherents
THE STATE.....	4,948	1,511,981	2,799,114*	41.2	100.0
ALACHUA	123	28,052	39,818*	38.0	100.0
059 BAPT MISS ASSN	1	26	31*	-	0.1
081 CATHOLIC......	4	0	6,553	6.3	16.5
093 CR CH (DISC)..	1	98	119*	0.1	0.3
097 CR C AND C CR.	1	58	70*	0.1	0.2
127 CH GOD (CLEVE)	6	343	415*	0.4	1.0
165 CH OF NAZARENE	5	433	903	0.9	2.3
193 EPISCOPAL.....	9	1,400	1,786	1.7	4.5
226 FRIENDS-USA...	1	11	13*	-	-
281 LUTH CH AMER..	2	299	439	0.4	1.1

County and Denomination	Number of churches	Communicant, confirmed, full members	Total adherents: Number	Total adherents: Percent of total population	Total adherents: Percent of total adherents
283 LUTH--MO SYNOD	1	415	594	0.6	1.5
349 PENT HOLINESS.	3	125	151*	0.1	0.4
357 PRESB CH US...	8	2,683	3,246*	3.1	8.2
403 SALVATION ARMY	1	37	155	0.1	0.4
413 S-D ADVENTISTS	2	217	263*	0.3	0.7
419 SO BAPT CONV..	38	14,354	17,368*	16.6	43.6
435 UNITARIAN-UNIV	1	145	145	0.1	0.4
443 UN C OF CHRIST	1	85	103*	0.1	0.3
449 UN METHODIST..	37	7,292	7,426	7.1	18.6
453 UN PRES CH USA	1	31	38*	-	0.1
BAKER	10	1,503	1,918*	20.8	100.0
081 CATHOLIC......	1	0	57	0.6	3.0
127 CH GOD (CLEVE)	3	221	275*	3.0	14.3
193 EPISCOPAL.....	1	41	60	0.6	3.1
419 SO BAPT CONV..	3	1,004	1,248*	13.5	65.1
449 UN METHODIST..	2	237	278	3.0	14.5
BAY	61	22,972	29,217*	38.8	100.0
029 AMER LUTH CH..	1	137	213	0.3	0.7
081 CATHOLIC......	4	0	1,750	2.3	6.0
093 CR CH (DISC)..	1	30	37*	-	0.1
097 CR C AND C CR.	1	150	186*	0.2	0.6
123 CH GOD (ANDER)	1	38	83	0.1	0.3
127 CH GOD (CLEVE)	2	153	190*	0.3	0.7
165 CH OF NAZARENE	2	159	337	0.4	1.2
193 EPISCOPAL.....	3	779	1,015	1.3	3.5
283 LUTH--MO SYNOD	3	454	270	0.4	0.9
349 PENT HOLINESS.	1	28	35*	-	0.1
357 PRESB CH US...	5	1,517	1,886*	2.5	6.5
403 SALVATION ARMY	1	67	197	0.3	0.7
413 S-D ADVENTISTS	1	245	305*	0.4	1.0
419 SO BAPT CONV..	23	14,384	17,882*	23.8	61.2
449 UN METHODIST..	12	4,831	4,831	6.4	16.5
BRADFORD	32	4,981	6,220*	42.5	100.0
059 BAPT MISS ASSN	1	58	70*	0.5	1.1
081 CATHOLIC......	1	0	127	0.9	2.0
093 CR CH (DISC)..	1	96	116*	0.8	1.9
097 CR C AND C CR.	2	230	278*	1.9	4.5
127 CH GOD (CLEVE)	2	141	171*	1.2	2.7
193 EPISCOPAL.....	1	101	189	1.3	3.0
357 PRESB CH US...	2	260	315*	2.2	5.1
413 S-D ADVENTISTS	2	396	479*	3.3	7.7
419 SO BAPT CONV..	16	3,083	3,732*	25.5	60.0
449 UN METHODIST..	4	616	743	5.1	11.9
BREVARD	145	49,581	90,392*	39.3	100.0
029 AMER LUTH CH..	4	1,074	1,580	0.7	1.7
059 BAPT MISS ASSN	1	68	86*	-	0.1
081 CATHOLIC......	10	0	25,212	11.0	27.9
093 CR CH (DISC)..	3	371	467*	0.2	0.5
097 CR C AND C CR.	8	1,291	1,624*	0.7	1.8
105 CHRISTIAN REF.	1	37	69	-	0.1
123 CH GOD (ANDER)	2	125	345	0.1	0.4
127 CH GOD (CLEVE)	11	891	1,121*	0.5	1.2
165 CH OF NAZARENE	4	420	723	0.3	0.8
193 EPISCOPAL.....	11	4,224	5,889	2.6	6.5
226 FRIENDS-USA...	1	22	28*	-	-
281 LUTH CH AMER..	4	616	922	0.4	1.0
283 LUTH--MO SYNOD	6	1,756	2,651	1.2	2.9
335 ORTH PRESB CH.	1	22	34	-	-
349 PENT HOLINESS.	1	41	52*	-	0.1
353 PLY BRETHREN..	1	80	255	0.1	0.3
357 PRESB CH US...	5	2,138	2,690*	1.2	3.0
403 SALVATION ARMY	3	51	552	0.2	0.6
413 S-D ADVENTISTS	5	417	525*	0.2	0.6
419 SO BAPT CONV..	31	20,818	26,195*	11.4	29.0
435 UNITARIAN-UNIV	2	85	97	-	0.1
443 UN C OF CHRIST	4	579	729*	0.3	0.8
449 UN METHODIST..	19	12,505	16,055	7.0	17.8
453 UN PRES CH USA	6	1,903	2,395*	1.0	2.6
469 WISC EVAN LUTH	1	47	96	-	0.1
BROWARD	217	85,534	252,304*	40.7	100.0
029 AMER LUTH CH..	4	972	1,476	0.2	0.6
081 CATHOLIC......	34	0	147,980	23.9	58.7
093 CR CH (DISC)..	7	2,220	2,605*	0.4	1.0
097 CR C AND C CR.	5	1,000	1,173*	0.2	0.5
105 CHRISTIAN REF.	1	175	271	-	0.1
123 CH GOD (ANDER)	3	235	518	0.1	0.2
127 CH GOD (CLEVE)	11	1,121	1,315*	0.2	0.5
157 CH OF BRETHREN	1	58	68*	-	-
165 CH OF NAZARENE	5	769	1,697	0.3	0.7
193 EPISCOPAL.....	16	6,569	8,557	1.4	3.4
281 LUTH CH AMER..	9	4,519	5,963	1.0	2.4
283 LUTH--MO SYNOD	10	4,294	5,860	0.9	2.3
295 MORAV CH-SOUTH	1	239	373	0.1	0.1
335 ORTH PRESB CH.	1	83	136	-	0.1
349 PENT HOLINESS.	1	17	20*	-	-
353 PLY BRETHREN..	3	360	660	0.1	0.3
357 PRESB CH US...	9	5,925	6,953*	1.1	2.8
371 REF CH IN AM..	2	468	546	0.1	0.2
403 SALVATION ARMY	1	101	422	0.1	0.2
413 S-D ADVENTISTS	8	451	529*	0.1	0.2
419 SO BAPT CONV..	35	21,721	25,488*	4.1	10.1
435 UNITARIAN-UNIV	1	157	199	-	0.1
443 UN C OF CHRIST	5	1,627	1,909*	0.3	0.8
449 UN METHODIST..	27	22,223	25,560	4.1	10.1
453 UN PRES CH USA	16	10,078	11,826*	1.9	4.7

*Total adherents estimated from known number of communicant, confirmed, full members.

—Represents a percent less than 0.1.

Percentages may not total due to rounding.

Table 3. Churches and Church Membership by State, County and Denomination: 1971

County and Denomination	Number of churches	Communicant, confirmed, full members	Total adherents: Number	Percent of total population	Percent of total adherents
469 WISC EVAN LUTH	1	152	200	-	0.1
CALHOUN	22	3,004	3,605*	47.3	100.0
081 CATHOLIC......	0	0	15	0.2	0.4
093 CR CH (DISC)..	1	15	19*	0.2	0.5
127 CH GOD (CLEVE)	1	29	36*	0.5	1.0
285 MENNONITE CH..	3	156	193*	2.5	5.4
349 PENT HOLINESS.	4	248	306*	4.0	8.5
357 PRESB CH US...	1	30	37*	0.5	1.0
419 SO BAPT CONV..	9	2,007	2,480*	32.5	68.8
449 UN METHODIST..	3	519	519	6.8	14.4
CHARLOTTE	32	7,046	11,586*	42.0	100.0
081 CATHOLIC......	2	0	3,288	11.9	28.4
093 CR CH (DISC)..	1	19	21*	0.1	0.2
097 CR C AND C CR.	1	525	581*	2.1	5.0
127 CH GOD (CLEVE)	3	133	147*	0.5	1.3
165 CH OF NAZARENE	1	55	153	0.6	1.3
193 EPISCOPAL.....	2	551	1,032	3.7	8.9
281 LUTH CH AMER..	2	425	490	1.8	4.2
283 LUTH--MO SYNOD	2	369	446	1.6	3.8
357 PRESB CH US...	2	798	883*	3.2	7.6
381 REF PRES-EVAN.	1	73	76	0.3	0.7
413 S-D ADVENTISTS	1	102	113*	0.4	1.0
419 SO BAPT CONV..	5	1,675	1,853*	6.7	16.0
435 UNITARIAN-UNIV	1	49	53	0.2	0.5
443 UN C OF CHRIST	1	32	35*	0.1	0.3
449 UN METHODIST..	6	2,024	2,176	7.9	18.8
453 UN PRES CH USA	1	216	239*	0.9	2.1
CITRUS	30	4,336	7,230*	37.7	100.0
081 CATHOLIC......	3	0	2,165	11.3	29.9
093 CR CH (DISC)..	2	30	34*	0.2	0.5
127 CH GOD (CLEVE)	3	160	182*	0.9	2.5
165 CH OF NAZARENE	1	52	110	0.6	1.5
193 EPISCOPAL.....	2	300	337	1.8	4.7
281 LUTH CH AMER..	1	93	102	0.5	1.4
283 LUTH--MO SYNOD	1	121	210	1.1	2.9
357 PRESB CH US...	1	305	347*	1.8	4.8
413 S-D ADVENTISTS	1	125	142*	0.7	2.0
419 SO BAPT CONV..	8	1,757	2,000*	10.4	27.7
449 UN METHODIST..	5	1,191	1,371	7.1	19.0
453 UN PRES CH USA	2	202	230*	1.2	3.2
CLAY	44	9,175	13,567*	42.3	100.0
029 AMER LUTH CH..	1	259	384	1.2	2.8
081 CATHOLIC......	3	0	1,502	4.7	11.1
123 CH GOD (ANDER)	7	374	837	2.6	6.2
127 CH GOD (CLEVE)	2	143	183*	0.6	1.3
157 CH OF BRETHREN	1	75	96*	0.3	0.7
193 EPISCOPAL.....	4	755	1,029	3.2	7.6
349 PENT HOLINESS.	1	45	58*	0.2	0.4
353 PLY BRETHREN..	1	100	120	0.4	0.9
357 PRESB CH US...	1	505	647*	2.0	4.8
419 SO BAPT CONV..	17	5,148	6,597*	20.6	48.6
449 UN METHODIST..	5	1,657	1,968	6.1	14.5
453 UN PRES CH USA	1	114	146*	0.5	1.1
COLLIER	39	7,783	14,979*	39.4	100.0
081 CATHOLIC......	3	0	5,104	13.4	34.1
093 CR CH (DISC)..	1	135	162*	0.4	1.1
097 CR C AND C CR.	2	20	24*	0.1	0.2
127 CH GOD (CLEVE)	5	432	519*	1.4	3.5
165 CH OF NAZARENE	1	27	99	0.3	0.7
193 EPISCOPAL.....	5	804	1,322	3.5	8.8
281 LUTH CH AMER..	1	381	513	1.3	3.4
283 LUTH--MO SYNOD	2	230	307	0.8	2.0
285 MENNONITE CH..	1	33	40*	0.1	0.3
357 PRESB CH US...	2	496	596*	1.6	4.0
381 REF PRES-EVAN.	1	131	177	0.5	1.2
413 S-D ADVENTISTS	1	77	92*	0.2	0.6
419 SO BAPT CONV..	5	2,251	2,704*	7.1	18.1
443 UN C OF CHRIST	1	156	187*	0.5	1.2
449 UN METHODIST..	6	1,581	1,897	5.0	12.7
453 UN PRES CH USA	2	1,029	1,236*	3.2	8.3
COLUMBIA	43	8,600	11,174*	44.3	100.0
081 CATHOLIC......	1	0	520	2.1	4.7
097 CR C AND C CR.	1	200	249*	1.0	2.2
127 CH GOD (CLEVE)	3	292	364*	1.4	3.3
165 CH OF NAZARENE	1	111	168	0.7	1.5
193 EPISCOPAL.....	1	141	243	1.0	2.2
281 LUTH CH AMER..	2	240	284	1.1	2.5
283 LUTH--MO SYNOD	1	44	77	0.3	0.7
349 PENT HOLINESS.	1	45	56*	0.2	0.5
357 PRESB CH US...	2	691	861*	3.4	7.7
413 S-D ADVENTISTS	1	65	81*	0.3	0.7
419 SO BAPT CONV..	19	5,170	6,441*	25.5	57.6
449 UN METHODIST..	10	1,601	1,830	7.2	16.4
DADE	367	149,811	483,726*	38.2	100.0
019 AMER BAPT CONV	3	56	66*	-	-
029 AMER LUTH CH..	9	4,613	6,836	0.5	1.4
081 CATHOLIC......	53	0	300,245	23.7	62.1
093 CR CH (DISC)..	10	2,293	2,705*	0.2	0.6
097 CR C AND C CR.	6	423	499*	-	0.1
105 CHRISTIAN REF.	2	263	430	-	0.1
123 CH GOD (ANDER)	8	560	1,398	0.1	0.3
127 CH GOD (CLEVE)	12	1,236	1,458*	0.1	0.3
157 CH OF BRETHREN	2	62	73*	-	-
165 CH OF NAZARENE	17	1,647	3,528	0.3	0.7
193 EPISCOPAL.....	27	14,672	19,044	1.5	3.9
201 EVAN COV CH AM	2	337	398*	-	0.1
221 FREE METH C NA	2	48	60	-	-
226 FRIENDS-USA...	2	212	250*	-	0.1
281 LUTH CH AMER..	13	3,741	5,379	0.4	1.1
283 LUTH--MO SYNOD	13	3,227	4,673	0.4	1.0
285 MENNONITE CH..	3	64	76*	-	-
315 NO AM OLD RC..	2	265	313*	-	0.1
335 ORTH PRESB CH.	2	227	372	-	0.1
349 PENT HOLINESS.	2	47	55*	-	-
353 PLY BRETHREN..	5	242	476	-	0.1
357 PRESB CH US...	22	11,724	13,832*	1.1	2.9
371 REF CH IN AM..	2	275	358	-	0.1
403 SALVATION ARMY	2	273	761	0.1	0.2
413 S-D ADVENTISTS	5	1,231	1,452*	0.1	0.3
419 SO BAPT CONV..	73	60,915	71,868*	5.7	14.9
435 UNITARIAN-UNIV	2	633	906	0.1	0.2
443 UN C OF CHRIST	13	7,043	8,309*	0.7	1.7
449 UN METHODIST..	42	29,814	33,570	2.6	6.9
453 UN PRES CH USA	10	3,634	4,287*	0.3	0.9
469 WISC EVAN LUTH	1	34	40	-	-
DE SOTO	25	4,225	5,329*	40.8	100.0
081 CATHOLIC......	1	0	284	2.2	5.3
097 CR C AND C CR.	1	65	78*	0.6	1.5
127 CH GOD (CLEVE)	3	261	313*	2.4	5.9
157 CH OF BRETHREN	1	35	42*	0.3	0.8
165 CH OF NAZARENE	1	92	196	1.5	3.7
193 EPISCOPAL.....	1	305	309	2.4	5.8
357 PRESB CH US...	1	207	248*	1.9	4.7
413 S-D ADVENTISTS	1	42	50*	0.4	0.9
419 SO BAPT CONV..	10	2,299	2,754*	21.1	51.7
449 UN METHODIST..	5	919	1,055	8.1	19.8
DIXIE	20	1,911	2,434*	44.4	100.0
059 BAPT MISS ASSN	1	95	120*	2.2	4.9
081 CATHOLIC......	1	0	65	1.2	2.7
127 CH GOD (CLEVE)	2	90	114*	2.1	4.7
193 EPISCOPAL.....	1	15	15	0.3	0.6
349 PENT HOLINESS.	1	60	76*	1.4	3.1
413 S-D ADVENTISTS	1	36	46*	0.8	1.9
419 SO BAPT CONV..	10	1,306	1,654*	30.2	68.0
449 UN METHODIST..	3	309	344	6.3	14.1
DUVAL	323	141,807	206,736*	39.1	100.0
019 AMER BAPT CONV	1	168	207*	-	0.1
029 AMER LUTH CH..	4	761	1,077	0.2	0.5
059 BAPT MISS ASSN	3	275	338*	0.1	0.2
081 CATHOLIC......	20	0	30,513	5.8	14.8
093 CR CH (DISC)..	12	2,290	2,815*	0.5	1.4
097 CR C AND C CR.	6	1,346	1,655*	0.3	0.8
127 CH GOD (CLEVE)	24	2,479	3,048*	0.6	1.5
157 CH OF BRETHREN	1	28	34*	-	-
165 CH OF NAZARENE	11	1,086	2,249	0.4	1.1
193 EPISCOPAL.....	23	11,131	16,355	3.1	7.9
226 FRIENDS-USA...	1	16	20*	-	-
281 LUTH CH AMER..	7	2,521	3,298	0.6	1.6
283 LUTH--MO SYNOD	7	1,301	1,872	0.4	0.9
349 PENT HOLINESS.	5	462	568*	0.1	0.3
353 PLY BRETHREN..	1	45	58	-	-
357 PRESB CH US...	21	11,248	13,829*	2.6	6.7
403 SALVATION ARMY	1	140	488	0.1	0.2
413 S-D ADVENTISTS	3	1,174	1,443*	0.3	0.7
419 SO BAPT CONV..	111	74,474	91,561*	17.3	44.3
435 UNITARIAN-UNIV	1	414	579	0.1	0.3
443 UN C OF CHRIST	2	552	679*	0.1	0.3
449 UN METHODIST..	54	28,885	32,772	6.2	15.9
453 UN PRES CH USA	3	977	1,201*	0.2	0.6
469 WISC EVAN LUTH	1	34	77	-	-
ESCAMBIA	148	53,697	82,707*	40.3	100.0
059 BAPT MISS ASSN	6	492	609*	0.3	0.7
081 CATHOLIC......	15	0	16,681	8.1	20.2
093 CR CH (DISC)..	6	788	975*	0.5	1.2
097 CR C AND C CR.	1	35	43*	-	0.1
127 CH GOD (CLEVE)	4	283	350*	0.2	0.4
165 CH OF NAZARENE	3	371	762	0.4	0.9
193 EPISCOPAL.....	6	2,899	4,383	2.1	5.3
281 LUTH CH AMER..	1	320	510	0.2	0.6
283 LUTH--MO SYNOD	6	1,662	2,277	1.1	2.8
285 MENNONITE CH..	1	11	14*	-	-
349 PENT HOLINESS.	4	298	369*	0.2	0.4
357 PRESB CH US...	7	2,723	3,370*	1.6	4.1
403 SALVATION ARMY	1	81	937	0.5	1.1
413 S-D ADVENTISTS	2	273	338*	0.2	0.4
419 SO BAPT CONV..	59	32,025	39,631*	19.3	47.9
449 UN METHODIST..	26	11,436	11,458	5.6	13.9
FLAGLER	8	1,126	1,991*	44.7	100.0
081 CATHOLIC......	3	0	681	15.3	34.2
349 PENT HOLINESS.	1	25	30*	0.7	1.5
419 SO BAPT CONV..	2	673	816*	18.3	41.0
449 UN METHODIST..	2	428	464	10.4	23.3
FRANKLIN	13	1,731	2,605*	36.9	100.0
081 CATHOLIC......	3	0	500	7.1	19.2

*Total adherents estimated from known number of communicant, confirmed, full members.

—Represents a percent less than 0.1.

Percentages may not total due to rounding.

Table 3. Churches and Church Membership by State, County and Denomination: 1971

County and Denomination	Number of churches	Communicant, confirmed, full members	Total adherents: Number	Total adherents: Percent of total population	Total adherents: Percent of total adherents
193 EPISCOPAL.....	2	141	236	3.3	9.1
349 PENT HOLINESS.	2	75	92*	1.3	3.5
419 SO BAPT CONV..	3	1,013	1,244*	17.6	47.8
449 UN METHODIST..	3	502	533	7.5	20.5
GADSDEN	36	9,046	11,046*	28.2	100.0
081 CATHOLIC......	1	0	30	0.1	0.3
093 CR CH (DISC)..	1	12	15*	-	0.1
127 CH GOD (CLEVE)	1	49	61*	0.2	0.6
193 EPISCOPAL.....	2	165	277	0.7	2.5
349 PENT HOLINESS.	3	214	267*	0.7	2.4
357 PRESB CH US...	6	741	925*	2.4	8.4
419 SO BAPT CONV..	14	5,581	6,964*	17.8	63.0
449 UN METHODIST..	8	2,284	2,507	6.4	22.7
GILCHRIST	11	1,477	1,816*	51.1	100.0
081 CATHOLIC......	0	0	15	0.4	0.8
127 CH GOD (CLEVE)	2	92	113*	3.2	6.2
413 S-D ADVENTISTS	1	26	32*	0.9	1.8
419 SO BAPT CONV..	7	1,282	1,574*	44.3	86.7
449 UN METHODIST..	1	77	82	2.3	4.5
GLADES	7	802	1,185*	32.3	100.0
081 CATHOLIC......	1	0	205	5.6	17.3
097 CR C AND C CR.	1	56	71*	1.9	6.0
127 CH GOD (CLEVE)	1	32	41*	1.1	3.5
419 SO BAPT CONV..	3	576	730*	19.9	61.6
449 UN METHODIST..	1	138	138	3.8	11.6
GULF	21	2,949	3,780*	37.4	100.0
081 CATHOLIC......	1	0	215	2.1	5.7
127 CH GOD (CLEVE)	3	116	145*	1.4	3.8
165 CH OF NAZARENE	1	25	72	0.7	1.9
193 EPISCOPAL.....	2	129	151	1.5	4.0
349 PENT HOLINESS.	1	50	62*	0.6	1.6
357 PRESB CH US...	3	91	113*	1.1	3.0
419 SO BAPT CONV..	5	1,775	2,214*	21.9	58.6
449 UN METHODIST..	5	763	808	8.0	21.4
HAMILTON	22	2,488	3,069*	39.4	100.0
093 CR CH (DISC)..	1	124	155*	2.0	5.1
127 CH GOD (CLEVE)	4	130	163*	2.1	5.3
165 CH OF NAZARENE	1	40	85	1.1	2.8
357 PRESB CH US...	2	89	111*	1.4	3.6
419 SO BAPT CONV..	8	1,550	1,942*	24.9	63.3
449 UN METHODIST..	6	555	613	7.9	20.0
HARDEE	33	6,847	8,653*	58.1	100.0
081 CATHOLIC......	1	0	98	0.7	1.1
097 CR C AND C CR.	1	146	185*	1.2	2.1
123 CH GOD (ANDER)	1	31	76	0.5	0.9
127 CH GOD (CLEVE)	5	194	245*	1.6	2.8
165 CH OF NAZARENE	1	25	30	0.2	0.3
193 EPISCOPAL.....	1	42	67	0.4	0.8
283 LUTH--MO SYNOD	1	38	52	0.3	0.6
357 PRESB CH US...	1	241	305*	2.0	3.5
413 S-D ADVENTISTS	1	13	16*	0.1	0.2
419 SO BAPT CONV..	17	5,147	6,513*	43.7	75.3
449 UN METHODIST..	3	970	1,066	7.2	12.3
HENDRY	22	3,091	5,498*	46.4	100.0
081 CATHOLIC......	2	0	1,587	13.4	28.9
093 CR CH (DISC)..	1	46	59*	0.5	1.1
097 CR C AND C CR.	2	60	77*	0.6	1.4
123 CH GOD (ANDER)	1	20	60	0.5	1.1
127 CH GOD (CLEVE)	3	156	201*	1.7	3.7
193 EPISCOPAL.....	1	180	223	1.9	4.1
349 PENT HOLINESS.	1	18	23*	0.2	0.4
413 S-D ADVENTISTS	1	18	23*	0.2	0.4
419 SO BAPT CONV..	7	1,965	2,527*	21.3	46.0
449 UN METHODIST..	2	507	562	4.7	10.2
453 UN PRES CH USA	1	121	156*	1.3	2.8
HERNANDO	31	5,393	7,997*	47.0	100.0
081 CATHOLIC......	3	0	1,438	8.5	18.0
097 CR C AND C CR.	2	90	108*	0.6	1.4
123 CH GOD (ANDER)	1	8	28	0.2	0.4
127 CH GOD (CLEVE)	1	47	57*	0.3	0.7
165 CH OF NAZARENE	2	92	204	1.2	2.6
193 EPISCOPAL.....	1	117	217	1.3	2.7
281 LUTH CH AMER..	2	223	248	1.5	3.1
283 LUTH--MO SYNOD	2	207	274	1.6	3.4
357 PRESB CH US...	1	207	249*	1.5	3.1
413 S-D ADVENTISTS	1	194	234*	1.4	2.9
419 SO BAPT CONV..	9	2,469	2,975*	17.5	37.2
449 UN METHODIST..	5	1,242	1,366	8.0	17.1
453 UN PRES CH USA	1	497	599*	3.5	7.5
HIGHLANDS	41	10,147	13,613*	46.1	100.0
055 AS REF PRES CH	2	278	332*	1.1	2.4
081 CATHOLIC......	2	0	1,220	4.1	9.0
093 CR CH (DISC)..	1	159	190*	0.6	1.4
097 CR C AND C CR.	1	60	72*	0.2	0.5
123 CH GOD (ANDER)	1	46	109	0.4	0.8
127 CH GOD (CLEVE)	6	528	631*	2.1	4.6
157 CH OF BRETHREN	2	478	571*	1.9	4.2
165 CH OF NAZARENE	2	156	494	1.7	3.6
193 EPISCOPAL.....	3	422	515	1.7	3.8
226 FRIENDS-USA...	1	11	13*	-	0.1
281 LUTH CH AMER..	2	179	194	0.7	1.4
283 LUTH--MO SYNOD	1	208	259	0.9	1.9
357 PRESB CH US...	1	214	256*	0.9	1.9
403 SALVATION ARMY	1	42	259	0.9	1.9
413 S-D ADVENTISTS	1	369	441*	1.5	3.2
419 SO BAPT CONV..	8	4,306	5,143*	17.4	37.8
443 UN C OF CHRIST	1	286	342*	1.2	2.5
449 UN METHODIST..	5	2,405	2,572	8.7	18.9
HILLSBOROUGH	315	115,685	193,342*	39.4	100.0
055 AS REF PRES CH	1	298	363*	0.1	0.2
081 CATHOLIC......	21	0	49,738	10.1	25.7
093 CR CH (DISC)..	7	1,019	1,243*	0.3	0.6
097 CR C AND C CR.	9	1,764	2,152*	0.4	1.1
123 CH GOD (ANDER)	11	797	2,001	0.4	1.0
127 CH GOD (CLEVE)	20	2,391	2,916*	0.6	1.5
157 CH OF BRETHREN	1	88	107*	-	0.1
165 CH OF NAZARENE	10	905	1,800	0.4	0.9
185 CUMBER PRESB..	3	895	1,092*	0.2	0.6
193 EPISCOPAL.....	15	5,575	8,343	1.7	4.3
221 FREE METH C NA	2	98	148	-	0.1
281 LUTH CH AMER..	8	1,949	2,783	0.6	1.4
283 LUTH--MO SYNOD	7	1,662	2,320	0.5	1.2
285 MENNONITE CH..	2	121	148*	-	0.1
349 PENT HOLINESS.	5	223	272*	0.1	0.1
353 PLY BRETHREN..	0	58	106	-	0.1
357 PRESB CH US...	15	7,489	9,134*	1.9	4.7
371 REF CH IN AM..	1	191	287	0.1	0.1
381 REF PRES-EVAN.	1	183	218	-	0.1
403 SALVATION ARMY	2	241	749	0.2	0.4
413 S-D ADVENTISTS	7	1,501	1,831*	0.4	0.9
419 SO BAPT CONV..	112	62,255	75,932*	15.5	39.3
435 UNITARIAN-UNIV	1	90	110	-	0.1
443 UN C OF CHRIST	2	971	1,184*	0.2	0.6
449 UN METHODIST..	48	24,379	27,668	5.6	14.3
453 UN PRES CH USA	3	432	527*	0.1	0.3
469 WISC EVAN LUTH	1	110	170	-	0.1
HOLMES	42	5,438	6,456*	60.2	100.0
127 CH GOD (CLEVE)	2	64	76*	0.7	1.2
165 CH OF NAZARENE	1	36	90	0.8	1.4
357 PRESB CH US...	1	21	25*	0.2	0.4
413 S-D ADVENTISTS	1	21	25*	0.2	0.4
419 SO BAPT CONV..	30	4,684	5,579*	52.0	86.4
443 UN C OF CHRIST	1	38	45*	0.4	0.7
449 UN METHODIST..	6	574	616	5.7	9.5
INDIAN RIVER	35	9,375	14,846*	41.2	100.0
081 CATHOLIC......	1	0	3,270	9.1	22.0
093 CR CH (DISC)..	1	47	57*	0.2	0.4
097 CR C AND C CR.	2	57	69*	0.2	0.5
123 CH GOD (ANDER)	1	45	137	0.4	0.9
127 CH GOD (CLEVE)	7	605	729*	2.0	4.9
165 CH OF NAZARENE	1	18	40	0.1	0.3
193 EPISCOPAL.....	1	653	1,046	2.9	7.0
201 EVAN COV CH AM	1	120	145*	0.4	1.0
281 LUTH CH AMER..	1	189	241	0.7	1.6
283 LUTH--MO SYNOD	1	51	68	0.2	0.5
413 S-D ADVENTISTS	1	56	67*	0.2	0.5
419 SO BAPT CONV..	9	4,267	5,140*	14.3	34.6
449 UN METHODIST..	7	2,526	2,944	8.2	19.8
453 UN PRES CH USA	1	741	893*	2.5	6.0
JACKSON	75	12,361	14,630*	42.5	100.0
081 CATHOLIC......	1	0	150	0.4	1.0
093 CR CH (DISC)..	1	46	55*	0.2	0.4
127 CH GOD (CLEVE)	5	218	261*	0.8	1.8
165 CH OF NAZARENE	1	114	177	0.5	1.2
193 EPISCOPAL.....	2	272	322	0.9	2.2
283 LUTH--MO SYNOD	1	31	33	0.1	0.2
349 PENT HOLINESS.	4	166	199*	0.6	1.4
357 PRESB CH US...	1	377	452*	1.3	3.1
413 S-D ADVENTISTS	1	28	34*	0.1	0.2
419 SO BAPT CONV..	41	8,595	10,294*	29.9	70.4
435 UNITARIAN-UNIV	1	13	17	-	0.1
449 UN METHODIST..	16	2,501	2,636	7.7	18.0
JEFFERSON	19	2,386	2,948*	33.6	100.0
081 CATHOLIC......	1	0	98	1.1	3.3
127 CH GOD (CLEVE)	1	27	34*	0.4	1.2
193 EPISCOPAL.....	1	73	112	1.3	3.8
349 PENT HOLINESS.	2	120	149*	1.7	5.1
357 PRESB CH US...	1	125	155*	1.8	5.3
419 SO BAPT CONV..	6	1,358	1,686*	19.2	57.2
449 UN METHODIST..	7	683	714	8.1	24.2
LAFAYETTE	16	1,579	1,928*	66.7	100.0
081 CATHOLIC......	0	0	10	0.3	0.5
127 CH GOD (CLEVE)	2	91	112*	3.9	5.8
193 EPISCOPAL.....	1	21	32	1.1	1.7
419 SO BAPT CONV..	11	1,279	1,569*	54.3	81.4
449 UN METHODIST..	2	188	205	7.1	10.6
LAKE	93	23,226	30,483*	44.0	100.0
081 CATHOLIC......	3	0	2,766	4.0	9.1

*Total adherents estimated from known number of communicant, confirmed, full members.

—Represents a percent less than 0.1.

Percentages may not total due to rounding.

Table 3. Churches and Church Membership by State, County and Denomination: 1971

County and Denomination	Number of churches	Communicant, confirmed, full members	Total adherents: Number	Total adherents: Percent of total population	Total adherents: Percent of total adherents
093 CR CH (DISC)..	2	267	315*	0.5	1.0
097 CR C AND C CR.	3	718	846*	1.2	2.8
123 CH GOD (ANDER)	4	252	594	0.9	1.9
127 CH GOD (CLEVE)	14	832	980*	1.4	3.2
165 CH OF NAZARENE	2	125	190	0.3	0.6
175 CONG CR CH....	1	196	231*	0.3	0.8
193 EPISCOPAL.....	5	1,605	2,349	3.4	7.7
281 LUTH CH AMER..	4	437	530	0.8	1.7
283 LUTH--MO SYNOD	2	471	564	0.8	1.9
357 PRESB CH US...	1	193	227*	0.3	0.7
413 S-D ADVENTISTS	4	254	299*	0.4	1.0
419 SO BAPT CONV..	27	10,012	11,794*	17.0	38.7
443 UN C OF CHRIST	1	249	293*	0.4	1.0
449 UN METHODIST..	15	6,002	6,605	9.5	21.7
453 UN PRES CH USA	5	1,613	1,900*	2.7	6.2
LEE	94	25,167	43,904*	41.7	100.0
081 CATHOLIC......	10	0	12,828	12.2	29.2
093 CR CH (DISC)..	2	232	274*	0.3	0.6
097 CR C AND C CR.	4	696	821*	0.8	1.9
123 CH GOD (ANDER)	2	90	206	0.2	0.5
127 CH GOD (CLEVE)	8	674	795*	0.8	1.8
157 CH OF BRETHREN	1	53	63*	0.1	0.1
165 CH OF NAZARENE	4	110	332	0.3	0.8
193 EPISCOPAL.....	7	1,843	3,017	2.9	6.9
281 LUTH CH AMER..	4	1,337	1,575	1.5	3.6
283 LUTH--MO SYNOD	3	986	1,326	1.3	3.0
357 PRESB CH US...	3	1,194	1,408*	1.3	3.2
403 SALVATION ARMY	1	93	421	0.4	1.0
413 S-D ADVENTISTS	2	271	320*	0.3	0.7
419 SO BAPT CONV..	17	8,185	9,653*	9.2	22.0
435 UNITARIAN-UNIV	1	109	109	0.1	0.2
443 UN C OF CHRIST	2	189	223*	0.2	0.5
449 UN METHODIST..	16	6,763	7,771	7.4	17.7
453 UN PRES CH USA	6	2,326	2,743*	2.6	6.2
469 WISC EVAN LUTH	1	16	19	-	-
LEON	66	26,668	38,733*	37.6	100.0
081 CATHOLIC......	2	0	6,290	6.1	16.2
093 CR CH (DISC)..	1	33	40*	-	0.1
097 CR C AND C CR.	2	465	562*	0.5	1.5
123 CH GOD (ANDER)	1	12	21	-	0.1
127 CH GOD (CLEVE)	2	255	308*	0.3	0.8
165 CH OF NAZARENE	1	169	259	0.3	0.7
193 EPISCOPAL.....	5	2,181	2,966	2.9	7.7
281 LUTH CH AMER..	1	335	455	0.4	1.2
283 LUTH--MO SYNOD	1	249	360	0.3	0.9
285 MENNONITE CH..	1	14	17*	-	-
349 PENT HOLINESS.	5	650	786*	0.8	2.0
357 PRESB CH US...	5	2,377	2,875*	2.8	7.4
403 SALVATION ARMY	1	42	259	0.3	0.7
413 S-D ADVENTISTS	2	338	409*	0.4	1.1
419 SO BAPT CONV..	20	13,245	16,018*	15.5	41.4
435 UNITARIAN-UNIV	1	135	165	0.2	0.4
449 UN METHODIST..	14	6,066	6,820	6.6	17.6
453 UN PRES CH USA	1	102	123*	0.1	0.3
LEVY	27	4,539	5,433*	42.6	100.0
081 CATHOLIC......	1	0	70	0.5	1.3
127 CH GOD (CLEVE)	3	160	196*	1.5	3.6
193 EPISCOPAL.....	2	102	154	1.2	2.8
357 PRESB CH US...	1	72	88*	0.7	1.6
419 SO BAPT CONV..	12	3,065	3,753*	29.4	69.1
449 UN METHODIST..	8	1,140	1,172	9.2	21.6
LIBERTY	12	1,124	1,348*	39.9	100.0
081 CATHOLIC......	0	0	10	0.3	0.7
097 CR C AND C CR.	1	75	91*	2.7	6.8
127 CH GOD (CLEVE)	1	70	85*	2.5	6.3
349 PENT HOLINESS.	1	80	97*	2.9	7.2
357 PRESB CH US...	1	15	18*	0.5	1.3
419 SO BAPT CONV..	6	739	899*	26.6	66.7
449 UN METHODIST..	2	145	148	4.4	11.0
MADISON	37	5,101	6,219*	46.1	100.0
081 CATHOLIC......	1	0	112	0.8	1.8
127 CH GOD (CLEVE)	2	72	88*	0.7	1.4
165 CH OF NAZARENE	1	15	31	0.2	0.5
357 PRESB CH US...	2	185	226*	1.7	3.6
413 S-D ADVENTISTS	1	7	9*	0.1	0.1
419 SO BAPT CONV..	22	3,559	4,345*	32.2	69.9
449 UN METHODIST..	8	1,263	1,408	10.4	22.6
MANATEE	79	23,341	34,558*	35.6	100.0
029 AMER LUTH CH..	1	188	237	0.2	0.7
081 CATHOLIC......	6	0	5,591	5.8	16.2
093 CR CH (DISC)..	1	410	469*	0.5	1.4
097 CR C AND C CR.	3	242	277*	0.3	0.8
105 CHRISTIAN REF.	1	240	343	0.4	1.0
123 CH GOD (ANDER)	1	215	465	0.5	1.3
127 CH GOD (CLEVE)	5	452	517*	0.5	1.5
165 CH OF NAZARENE	3	356	1,068	1.1	3.1
193 EPISCOPAL.....	4	2,064	3,374	3.5	9.8
201 EVAN COV CH AM	1	203	232*	0.2	0.7
281 LUTH CH AMER..	2	723	955	1.0	2.8
283 LUTH--MO SYNOD	1	386	472	0.5	1.4
349 PENT HOLINESS.	1	47	54*	0.1	0.2
357 PRESB CH US...	3	1,846	2,111*	2.2	6.1
371 REF CH IN AM..	1	396	431	0.4	1.2
381 REF PRES-EVAN.	1	33	36	-	0.1
403 SALVATION ARMY	1	97	333	0.3	1.0
413 S-D ADVENTISTS	2	389	445*	0.5	1.3
419 SO BAPT CONV..	23	8,176	9,348*	9.6	27.1
435 UNITARIAN-UNIV	1	60	66	0.1	0.2
443 UN C OF CHRIST	1	510	583*	0.6	1.7
449 UN METHODIST..	13	5,639	6,361	6.5	18.4
453 UN PRES CH USA	2	553	632*	0.7	1.8
469 WISC EVAN LUTH	1	116	158	0.2	0.5
MARION	92	21,908	29,176*	42.3	100.0
081 CATHOLIC......	2	0	2,790	4.0	9.6
093 CR CH (DISC)..	4	647	788*	1.1	2.7
097 CR C AND C CR.	3	330	402*	0.6	1.4
123 CH GOD (ANDER)	1	45	99	0.1	0.3
127 CH GOD (CLEVE)	4	354	431*	0.6	1.5
165 CH OF NAZARENE	1	153	182	0.3	0.6
193 EPISCOPAL.....	3	1,010	1,486	2.2	5.1
281 LUTH CH AMER..	2	265	340	0.5	1.2
283 LUTH--MO SYNOD	2	407	594	0.9	2.0
349 PENT HOLINESS.	1	61	74*	0.1	0.3
357 PRESB CH US...	6	1,507	1,835*	2.7	6.3
403 SALVATION ARMY	1	70	262	0.4	0.9
413 S-D ADVENTISTS	2	493	600*	0.9	2.1
419 SO BAPT CONV..	31	10,498	12,786*	18.5	43.8
443 UN C OF CHRIST	1	17	21*	-	0.1
449 UN METHODIST..	26	5,754	6,124	8.9	21.0
453 UN PRES CH USA	2	297	362*	0.5	1.2
MARTIN	27	6,219	12,281*	43.8	100.0
081 CATHOLIC......	3	0	4,639	16.5	37.8
097 CR C AND C CR.	1	55	65*	0.2	0.5
127 CH GOD (CLEVE)	6	201	236*	0.8	1.9
193 EPISCOPAL.....	4	969	1,447	5.2	11.8
283 LUTH--MO SYNOD	1	276	351	1.3	2.9
419 SO BAPT CONV..	6	2,425	2,851*	10.2	23.2
443 UN C OF CHRIST	1	139	163*	0.6	1.3
449 UN METHODIST..	3	1,279	1,500	5.4	12.2
453 UN PRES CH USA	2	875	1,029*	3.7	8.4
MONROE	47	8,453	26,264*	49.9	100.0
081 CATHOLIC......	6	0	15,150	28.8	57.7
127 CH GOD (CLEVE)	3	137	166*	0.3	0.6
193 EPISCOPAL.....	6	1,403	2,316	4.4	8.8
281 LUTH CH AMER..	1	100	140	0.3	0.5
283 LUTH--MO SYNOD	3	379	732	1.4	2.8
353 PLY BRETHREN..	1	40	60	0.1	0.2
357 PRESB CH US...	1	280	339*	0.6	1.3
403 SALVATION ARMY	1	51	221	0.4	0.8
413 S-D ADVENTISTS	3	101	122*	0.2	0.5
419 SO BAPT CONV..	8	2,829	3,423*	6.5	13.0
443 UN C OF CHRIST	2	301	364*	0.7	1.4
449 UN METHODIST..	10	2,642	3,001	5.7	11.4
453 UN PRES CH USA	2	190	230*	0.4	0.9
NASSAU	38	7,121	9,590*	46.5	100.0
081 CATHOLIC......	2	0	565	2.7	5.9
097 CR C AND C CR.	1	10	13*	0.1	0.1
127 CH GOD (CLEVE)	6	324	408*	2.0	4.3
193 EPISCOPAL.....	2	226	448	2.2	4.7
281 LUTH CH AMER..	1	79	110	0.5	1.1
357 PRESB CH US...	1	247	311*	1.5	3.2
419 SO BAPT CONV..	18	5,182	6,531*	31.7	68.1
449 UN METHODIST..	7	1,053	1,204	5.8	12.6
OKALOOSA	72	21,460	30,564*	34.7	100.0
059 BAPT MISS ASSN	1	405	514*	0.6	1.7
081 CATHOLIC......	3	0	3,403	3.9	11.1
097 CR C AND C CR.	2	127	161*	0.2	0.5
123 CH GOD (ANDER)	1	37	73	0.1	0.2
127 CH GOD (CLEVE)	2	95	120*	0.1	0.4
165 CH OF NAZARENE	1	100	260	0.3	0.9
193 EPISCOPAL.....	4	1,094	1,682	1.9	5.5
281 LUTH CH AMER..	1	299	427	0.5	1.4
283 LUTH--MO SYNOD	2	328	491	0.6	1.6
285 MENNONITE CH..	1	12	15*	-	-
357 PRESB CH US...	5	874	1,108*	1.3	3.6
381 REF PRES-EVAN.	2	293	333	0.4	1.1
403 SALVATION ARMY	1	16	114	0.1	0.4
413 S-D ADVENTISTS	2	74	94*	0.1	0.3
419 SO BAPT CONV..	34	13,463	17,071*	19.4	55.9
435 UNITARIAN-UNIV	1	30	30	-	0.1
449 UN METHODIST..	9	4,213	4,668	5.3	15.3
OKEECHOBEE	12	4,252	5,902*	52.5	100.0
081 CATHOLIC......	1	0	377	3.4	6.4
127 CH GOD (CLEVE)	1	209	265*	2.4	4.5
165 CH OF NAZARENE	1	43	96	0.9	1.6
193 EPISCOPAL.....	3	1,447	1,897	16.9	32.1
283 LUTH--MO SYNOD	1	27	44	0.4	0.7
413 S-D ADVENTISTS	1	69	88*	0.8	1.5
419 SO BAPT CONV..	3	2,021	2,564*	22.8	43.4
449 UN METHODIST..	1	436	571	5.1	9.7
ORANGE	229	95,058	152,164*	44.2	100.0
029 AMER LUTH CH..	3	1,140	1,515	0.4	1.0
059 BAPT MISS ASSN	1	196	239*	0.1	0.2
075 BRETHREN IN CR	1	32	39*	-	-

*Total adherents estimated from known number of communicant, confirmed, full members.

—Represents a percent less than 0.1.

Percentages may not total due to rounding.

Table 3. Churches and Church Membership by State, County and Denomination: 1971

County and Denomination	Number of churches	Communicant, confirmed, full members	Total adherents		
			Number	Percent of total population	Percent of total adherents
081 CATHOLIC......	11	0	32,759	9.5	21.5
093 CR CH (DISC)..	4	1,404	1,711*	0.[illegible]	1.1
097 CR C AND C CR.	12	2,432	2,965*	0.9	1.9
105 CHRISTIAN REF.	1	63	125	-	0.1
123 CH GOD (ANDER)	2	337	868	0.3	0.6
127 CH GOD (CLEVE)	17	2,044	2,492*	0.7	1.6
157 CH OF BRETHREN	2	355	433*	0.1	0.3
165 CH OF NAZARENE	12	1,441	2,776	0.8	1.8
193 EPISCOPAL.....	11	5,275	7,881	2.3	5.2
201 EVAN COV CH AM	1	98	119*	-	0.1
221 FREE METH C NA	2	60	73	-	-
226 FRIENDS-USA...	2	72	88*	-	0.1
281 LUTH CH AMER..	4	1,974	2,555	0.7	1.7
283 LUTH--MO SYNOD	7	2,656	3,820	1.1	2.5
335 ORTH PRESB CH.	1	48	74	-	-
349 PENT HOLINESS.	3	134	163*	-	0.1
353 PLY BRETHREN..	4	225	509	0.1	0.3
357 PRESB CH US...	17	11,606	14,148*	4.1	9.3
371 REF CH IN AM..	2	295	418	0.1	0.3
381 REF PRES-EVAN.	1	48	66	-	-
403 SALVATION ARMY	1	282	975	0.3	0.6
413 S-D ADVENTISTS	12	3,159	3,851*	1.1	2.5
419 SO BAPT CONV..	57	35,681	43,495*	12.6	28.6
435 UNITARIAN-UNIV	2	355	448	0.1	0.3
443 UN C OF CHRIST	4	1,456	1,775*	0.5	1.2
449 UN METHODIST..	31	22,107	25,653	7.5	16.9
469 WISC EVAN LUTH	1	83	131	-	0.1
OSCEOLA	30	7,582	10,816*	42.8	100.0
029 AMER LUTH CH..	1	247	292	1.2	2.7
081 CATHOLIC......	2	0	1,670	6.6	15.4
097 CR C AND C CR.	3	1,045	1,236*	4.9	11.4
123 CH GOD (ANDER)	1	44	109	0.4	1.0
127 CH GOD (CLEVE)	5	201	238*	0.9	2.2
165 CH OF NAZARENE	3	181	354	1.4	3.3
193 EPISCOPAL.....	2	488	738	2.9	6.8
221 FREE METH C NA	1	33	41	0.2	0.4
283 LUTH--MO SYNOD	1	133	168	0.7	1.6
413 S-D ADVENTISTS	2	85	101*	0.4	0.9
419 SO BAPT CONV..	4	2,699	3,193*	12.6	29.5
449 UN METHODIST..	3	1,980	2,148	8.5	19.9
453 UN PRES CH USA	2	446	528*	2.1	4.9
PALM BEACH	195	65,918	178,711*	51.2	100.0
029 AMER LUTH CH..	2	803	1,124	0.3	0.6
081 CATHOLIC......	22	0	95,806	27.5	53.6
093 CR CH (DISC)..	4	868	1,030*	0.3	0.6
097 CR C AND C CR.	4	464	551*	0.2	0.3
105 CHRISTIAN REF.	1	291	452	0.1	0.3
123 CH GOD (ANDER)	5	443	1,074	0.3	0.6
127 CH GOD (CLEVE)	16	1,398	1,659*	0.5	0.9
165 CH OF NAZARENE	7	483	922	0.3	0.5
193 EPISCOPAL.....	20	8,108	11,145	3.2	6.2
201 EVAN COV CH AM	3	293	348*	0.1	0.2
221 FREE METH C NA	3	80	107	-	0.1
226 FRIENDS-USA...	1	28	33*	-	-
281 LUTH CH AMER..	6	2,018	2,591	0.7	1.4
283 LUTH--MO SYNOD	6	2,491	3,544	1.0	2.0
295 MORAV CH-SOUTH	1	128	201	0.1	0.1
349 PENT HOLINESS.	2	179	212*	0.1	0.1
353 PLY BRETHREN..	1	368	789	0.2	0.4
357 PRESB CH US...	6	1,715	2,036*	0.6	1.1
371 REF CH IN AM..	1	108	151	-	0.1
403 SALVATION ARMY	2	172	912	0.3	0.5
413 S-D ADVENTISTS	7	900	1,068*	0.3	0.6
419 SO BAPT CONV..	32	21,978	26,086*	7.5	14.6
435 UNITARIAN-UNIV	2	234	276	0.1	0.2
443 UN C OF CHRIST	7	2,588	3,072*	0.9	1.7
449 UN METHODIST..	22	13,708	16,315	4.7	9.1
453 UN PRES CH USA	12	6,072	7,207*	2.1	4.0
PASCO	72	16,664	28,694*	37.8	100.0
081 CATHOLIC......	8	0	9,552	12.6	33.3
093 CR CH (DISC)..	1	253	285*	0.4	1.0
097 CR C AND C CR.	1	200	225*	0.3	0.8
123 CH GOD (ANDER)	2	84	164	0.2	0.6
127 CH GOD (CLEVE)	6	374	421*	0.6	1.5
165 CH OF NAZARENE	2	157	407	0.5	1.4
193 EPISCOPAL.....	3	864	1,300	1.7	4.5
221 FREE METH C NA	1	24	27	-	0.1
281 LUTH CH AMER..	3	693	752	1.0	2.6
283 LUTH--MO SYNOD	2	793	871	1.1	3.0
353 PLY BRETHREN..	1	40	60	0.1	0.2
357 PRESB CH US...	4	1,130	1,272*	1.7	4.4
413 S-D ADVENTISTS	3	305	343*	0.5	1.2
419 SO BAPT CONV..	22	6,788	7,640*	10.1	26.6
443 UN C OF CHRIST	2	605	681*	0.9	2.4
449 UN METHODIST..	9	4,042	4,320	5.7	15.1
453 UN PRES CH USA	1	248	279*	0.4	1.0
469 WISC EVAN LUTH	1	64	95	0.1	0.3
PINELLAS	234	119,319	202,192*	38.7	100.0
029 AMER LUTH CH..	4	2,426	3,115	0.6	1.5
081 CATHOLIC......	23	0	61,182	11.7	30.3
093 CR CH (DISC)..	6	1,611	1,823*	0.3	0.9
097 CR C AND C CR.	6	3,848	4,354*	0.8	2.2
105 CHRISTIAN REF.	1	123	177	-	0.1
123 CH GOD (ANDER)	1	82	177	-	0.1
127 CH GOD (CLEVE)	11	2,004	2,267*	0.4	1.1
157 CH OF BRETHREN	1	214	242*	-	0.1
165 CH OF NAZARENE	6	743	1,342	0.3	0.7
193 EPISCOPAL.....	19	11,265	15,662	3.0	7.7
201 EVAN COV CH AM	1	214	242*	-	0.1
221 FREE METH C NA	3	212	281	0.1	0.1
226 FRIENDS-USA...	2	82	93*	-	-
281 LUTH CH AMER..	11	5,177	6,292	1.2	3.1
283 LUTH--MO SYNOD	6	4,914	6,200	1.2	3.1
285 MENNONITE CH..	1	23	26*	-	-
349 PENT HOLINESS.	2	37	42*	-	-
353 PLY BRETHREN..	2	80	130	-	0.1
357 PRESB CH US...	17	9,368	10,599*	2.0	5.2
371 REF CH IN AM..	2	431	491	0.1	0.2
381 REF PRES-EVAN.	1	54	69	-	-
403 SALVATION ARMY	3	399	1,479	0.3	0.7
413 S-D ADVENTISTS	4	1,149	1,300*	0.2	0.6
419 SO BAPT CONV..	32	23,552	26,646*	5.1	13.2
435 UNITARIAN-UNIV	3	624	834	0.2	0.4
443 UN C OF CHRIST	10	5,560	6,290*	1.2	3.1
449 UN METHODIST..	42	39,263	44,156	8.5	21.8
453 UN PRES CH USA	12	5,522	6,247*	1.2	3.1
469 WISC EVAN LUTH	2	342	434	0.1	0.2
POLK	236	76,358	105,283*	46.3	100.0
029 AMER LUTH CH..	1	252	367	0.2	0.3
055 AS REF PRES CH	4	1,332	1,629*	0.7	1.5
059 BAPT MISS ASSN	1	31	38*	-	-
081 CATHOLIC......	6	0	10,889	4.8	10.3
093 CR CH (DISC)..	4	893	1,092*	0.5	1.0
097 CR C AND C CR.	6	1,033	1,263*	0.6	1.2
123 CH GOD (ANDER)	9	550	1,320	0.6	1.3
127 CH GOD (CLEVE)	24	2,922	3,573*	1.6	3.4
165 CH OF NAZARENE	9	864	1,563	0.7	1.5
193 EPISCOPAL.....	9	3,545	4,883	2.1	4.6
221 FREE METH C NA	2	90	114	0.1	0.1
226 FRIENDS-USA...	2	28	34*	-	-
281 LUTH CH AMER..	2	622	775	0.3	0.7
283 LUTH--MO SYNOD	5	2,390	3,229	1.4	3.1
349 PENT HOLINESS.	1	11	13*	-	-
357 PRESB CH US...	9	2,291	2,801*	1.2	2.7
381 REF PRES-EVAN.	1	287	317	0.1	0.3
403 SALVATION ARMY	2	144	516	0.2	0.5
413 S-D ADVENTISTS	6	575	703*	0.3	0.7
419 SO BAPT CONV..	92	40,515	49,535*	21.8	47.0
435 UNITARIAN-UNIV	1	73	88	-	0.1
449 UN METHODIST..	34	15,083	17,085	7.5	16.2
453 UN PRES CH USA	6	2,827	3,456*	1.5	3.3
PUTNAM	65	11,715	15,736*	43.4	100.0
059 BAPT MISS ASSN	1	23	28*	0.1	0.2
081 CATHOLIC......	3	0	1,088	3.0	6.9
123 CH GOD (ANDER)	3	102	263	0.7	1.7
127 CH GOD (CLEVE)	3	230	284*	0.8	1.8
193 EPISCOPAL.....	6	482	669	1.8	4.3
281 LUTH CH AMER..	1	85	113	0.3	0.7
349 PENT HOLINESS.	2	70	87*	0.2	0.6
357 PRESB CH US...	2	577	714*	2.0	4.5
413 S-D ADVENTISTS	2	188	232*	0.6	1.5
415 S-D BAPTIST GC	1	26	32*	0.1	0.2
419 SO BAPT CONV..	28	7,517	9,295*	25.6	59.1
443 UN C OF CHRIST	2	175	216*	0.6	1.4
449 UN METHODIST..	10	2,149	2,602	7.2	16.5
453 UN PRES CH USA	1	91	113*	0.3	0.7
ST JOHNS	35	8,171	13,596*	44.2	100.0
081 CATHOLIC......	6	0	3,697	12.0	27.2
097 CR C AND C CR.	1	70	84*	0.3	0.6
123 CH GOD (ANDER)	2	45	135	0.4	1.0
127 CH GOD (CLEVE)	1	10	12*	-	0.1
165 CH OF NAZARENE	1	77	206	0.7	1.5
193 EPISCOPAL.....	2	799	1,083	3.5	8.0
281 LUTH CH AMER..	1	155	210	0.7	1.5
283 LUTH--MO SYNOD	1	11	11	-	0.1
349 PENT HOLINESS.	3	100	121*	0.4	0.9
413 S-D ADVENTISTS	2	126	152*	0.5	1.1
419 SO BAPT CONV..	8	3,862	4,655*	15.1	34.2
449 UN METHODIST..	6	2,335	2,530	8.2	18.6
453 UN PRES CH USA	1	581	700*	2.3	5.1
ST LUCIE	40	11,161	19,202*	37.8	100.0
029 AMER LUTH CH..	1	157	190	0.4	1.0
081 CATHOLIC......	3	0	5,053	9.9	26.3
093 CR CH (DISC)..	1	145	177*	0.3	0.9
097 CR C AND C CR.	2	355	435*	0.9	2.3
123 CH GOD (ANDER)	1	40	80	0.2	0.4
127 CH GOD (CLEVE)	3	244	299*	0.6	1.6
165 CH OF NAZARENE	1	100	167	0.3	0.9
193 EPISCOPAL.....	3	785	1,323	2.6	6.9
281 LUTH CH AMER..	1	89	108	0.2	0.6
283 LUTH--MO SYNOD	1	303	363	0.7	1.9
353 PLY BRETHREN..	2	119	285	0.6	1.5
357 PRESB CH US...	1	328	401*	0.8	2.1
403 SALVATION ARMY	1	54	184	0.4	1.0
413 S-D ADVENTISTS	2	318	389*	0.8	2.0
419 SO BAPT CONV..	7	4,605	5,636*	11.1	29.4
435 UNITARIAN-UNIV	1	38	38	0.1	0.2
449 UN METHODIST..	6	2,608	3,005	5.9	15.6
453 UN PRES CH USA	3	873	1,069*	2.1	5.6
SANTA ROSA	49	10,499	14,924*	39.5	100.0
081 CATHOLIC......	2	0	2,000	5.3	13.4
123 CH GOD (ANDER)	1	46	126	0.3	0.8

*Total adherents estimated from known number of communicant, confirmed, full members.

—Represents a percent less than 0.1.

Percentages may not total due to rounding.

Table 3. Churches and Church Membership by State, County and Denomination: 1971

County and Denomination	Number of churches	Communicant, confirmed, full members	Total adherents: Number	Total adherents: Percent of total population	Total adherents: Percent of total adherents
193 EPISCOPAL.....	2	337	561	1.5	3.8
283 LUTH--MO SYNOD	2	185	258	0.7	1.7
285 MENNONITE CH..	1	18	22*	0.1	0.1
357 PRESB CH US...	1	373	464*	1.2	3.1
419 SO BAPT CONV..	27	7,411	9,213*	24.4	61.7
435 UNITARIAN-UNIV	1	58	88	0.2	0.6
449 UN METHODIST..	12	2,071	2,192	5.8	14.7
SARASOTA	91	32,149	47,994*	39.9	100.0
029 AMER LUTH CH..	3	762	958	0.8	2.0
075 BRETHREN IN CR	1	22	25*	-	0.1
081 CATHOLIC......	6	0	9,717	8.1	20.2
093 CR CH (DISC)..	3	782	880*	0.7	1.8
097 CR C AND C CR.	5	222	250*	0.2	0.5
123 CH GOD (ANDER)	2	327	722	0.6	1.5
127 CH GOD (CLEVE)	5	304	342*	0.3	0.7
165 CH OF NAZARENE	3	121	358	0.3	0.7
193 EPISCOPAL.....	5	3,578	4,874	4.0	10.2
201 EVAN COV CH AM	1	251	282*	0.2	0.6
226 FRIENDS-USA...	1	20	23*	-	-
281 LUTH CH AMER..	3	1,622	1,978	1.6	4.1
283 LUTH--MO SYNOD	2	1,317	1,577	1.3	3.3
285 MENNONITE CH..	6	893	1,005*	0.8	2.1
353 PLY BRETHREN..	1	40	67	0.1	0.1
357 PRESB CH US...	7	4,460	5,018*	4.2	10.5
371 REF CH IN AM..	3	328	357	0.3	0.7
381 REF PRES-EVAN.	1	120	146	0.1	0.3
403 SALVATION ARMY	1	43	518	0.4	1.1
413 S-D ADVENTISTS	2	270	304*	0.3	0.6
419 SO BAPT CONV..	11	6,960	7,831*	6.5	16.3
435 UNITARIAN-UNIV	1	225	280	0.2	0.6
443 UN C OF CHRIST	4	1,644	1,850*	1.5	3.9
449 UN METHODIST..	11	6,278	6,877	5.7	14.3
453 UN PRES CH USA	3	1,560	1,755*	1.5	3.7
SEMINOLE	64	18,385	33,606*	40.2	100.0
081 CATHOLIC......	5	0	10,290	12.3	30.6
093 CR CH (DISC)..	1	82	102*	0.1	0.3
097 CR C AND C CR.	3	309	386*	0.5	1.1
123 CH GOD (ANDER)	1	10	45	0.1	0.1
127 CH GOD (CLEVE)	4	470	587*	0.7	1.7
165 CH OF NAZARENE	5	300	717	0.9	2.1
175 CONG CR CH....	1	156	195*	0.2	0.6
193 EPISCOPAL.....	1	759	850	1.0	2.5
221 FREE METH C NA	1	17	29	-	0.1
281 LUTH CH AMER..	2	321	446	0.5	1.3
283 LUTH--MO SYNOD	3	1,156	1,490	1.8	4.4
295 MORAV CH-SOUTH	1	246	309	0.4	0.9
357 PRESB CH US...	2	1,003	1,252*	1.5	3.7
403 SALVATION ARMY	1	80	262	0.3	0.8
413 S-D ADVENTISTS	5	1,822	2,274*	2.7	6.8
419 SO BAPT CONV..	16	7,722	9,638*	11.5	28.7
443 UN C OF CHRIST	1	212	265*	0.3	0.8
449 UN METHODIST..	8	3,408	4,080	4.9	12.1
453 UN PRES CH USA	3	312	389*	0.5	1.2
SUMTER	35	5,138	6,023*	40.6	100.0
093 CR CH (DISC)..	1	33	40*	0.3	0.7
127 CH GOD (CLEVE)	7	344	414*	2.8	6.9
193 EPISCOPAL.....	1	46	51	0.3	0.8
357 PRESB CH US...	2	169	203*	1.4	3.4
419 SO BAPT CONV..	13	3,314	3,988*	26.9	66.2
449 UN METHODIST..	10	1,172	1,255	8.5	20.8
453 UN PRES CH USA	1	60	72*	0.5	1.2
SUWANNEE	48	7,266	9,048*	58.2	100.0
081 CATHOLIC......	1	0	86	0.6	1.0
093 CR CH (DISC)..	1	26	32*	0.2	0.4
097 CR C AND C CR.	3	177	217*	1.4	2.4
123 CH GOD (ANDER)	1	35	85	0.5	0.9
127 CH GOD (CLEVE)	3	218	268*	1.7	3.0
165 CH OF NAZARENE	1	41	107	0.7	1.2
193 EPISCOPAL.....	1	127	151	1.0	1.7
357 PRESB CH US...	2	189	232*	1.5	2.6
419 SO BAPT CONV..	29	5,708	7,013*	45.1	77.5
449 UN METHODIST..	6	745	857	5.5	9.5
TAYLOR	30	5,660	7,078*	51.9	100.0
081 CATHOLIC......	1	0	118	0.9	1.7
123 CH GOD (ANDER)	1	38	104	0.8	1.5
127 CH GOD (CLEVE)	1	268	331*	2.4	4.7
165 CH OF NAZARENE	1	17	19	0.1	0.3
193 EPISCOPAL.....	1	160	171	1.3	2.4
283 LUTH--MO SYNOD	1	15	23	0.2	0.3
349 PENT HOLINESS.	2	34	42*	0.3	0.6
357 PRESB CH US...	1	242	299*	2.2	4.2
413 S-D ADVENTISTS	1	20	25*	0.2	0.4
419 SO BAPT CONV..	14	4,027	4,981*	36.5	70.4
449 UN METHODIST..	6	839	965	7.1	13.6
UNION	9	1,366	1,583*	19.5	100.0
081 CATHOLIC......	0	0	20	0.2	1.3
097 CR C AND C CR.	1	120	138*	1.7	8.7
127 CH GOD (CLEVE)	1	72	83*	1.0	5.2
419 SO BAPT CONV..	4	1,014	1,168*	14.4	73.8
449 UN METHODIST..	3	160	174	2.1	11.0
VOLUSIA	154	46,039	72,461*	42.8	100.0
081 CATHOLIC......	9	0	17,350	10.2	23.9
093 CR CH (DISC)..	7	1,231	1,426*	0.8	2.0
097 CR C AND C CR.	4	798	925*	0.5	1.3
123 CH GOD (ANDER)	5	606	1,482	0.9	2.0
127 CH GOD (CLEVE)	11	613	710*	0.4	1.0
165 CH OF NAZARENE	4	284	679	0.4	0.9
193 EPISCOPAL.....	9	3,608	4,756	2.8	6.6
226 FRIENDS-USA...	1	18	21*	-	-
281 LUTH CH AMER..	5	1,378	1,792	1.1	2.5
283 LUTH--MO SYNOD	3	926	1,219	0.7	1.7
349 PENT HOLINESS.	6	316	366*	0.2	0.5
353 PLY BRETHREN..	1	90	140	0.1	0.2
357 PRESB CH US...	7	3,853	4,465*	2.6	6.2
403 SALVATION ARMY	1	59	284	0.2	0.4
413 S-D ADVENTISTS	5	349	404*	0.2	0.6
415 S-D BAPTIST GC	1	60	70*	-	0.1
419 SO BAPT CONV..	36	17,732	20,547*	12.1	28.4
435 UNITARIAN-UNIV	1	127	152	0.1	0.2
443 UN C OF CHRIST	8	2,642	3,061*	1.8	4.2
449 UN METHODIST..	25	10,409	11,523	6.8	15.9
453 UN PRES CH USA	5	940	1,089*	0.6	1.5
WAKULLA	13	1,717	2,120*	33.6	100.0
081 CATHOLIC......	0	0	10	0.2	0.5
127 CH GOD (CLEVE)	1	43	54*	0.9	2.5
349 PENT HOLINESS.	1	10	13*	0.2	0.6
419 SO BAPT CONV..	8	1,382	1,730*	27.4	81.6
449 UN METHODIST..	3	282	313	5.0	14.8
WALTON	49	6,513	7,690*	47.8	100.0
081 CATHOLIC......	1	0	95	0.6	1.2
127 CH GOD (CLEVE)	2	38	45*	0.3	0.6
193 EPISCOPAL.....	1	37	74	0.5	1.0
357 PRESB CH US...	6	508	604*	3.8	7.9
419 SO BAPT CONV..	25	4,587	5,451*	33.9	70.9
449 UN METHODIST..	14	1,343	1,421	8.8	18.5
WASHINGTON	31	3,569	4,404*	38.5	100.0
081 CATHOLIC......	1	0	170	1.5	3.9
127 CH GOD (CLEVE)	2	34	42*	0.4	1.0
193 EPISCOPAL.....	1	35	43	0.4	1.0
349 PENT HOLINESS.	1	28	34*	0.3	0.8
357 PRESB CH US...	1	152	186*	1.6	4.2
413 S-D ADVENTISTS	1	29	36*	0.3	0.8
419 SO BAPT CONV..	15	2,459	3,013*	26.3	68.4
449 UN METHODIST..	9	832	880	7.7	20.0
CO DATA NOT AVAIL	115	7,216	32,989*	N/A	N/A
151 L-D SAINTS....	0	0	24,414	N/A	N/A
193 EPISCOPAL.....	1	57	85	N/A	N/A
223 FREE WILL BAPT	77	6,175	7,381*	N/A	N/A
349 PENT HOLINESS.	3	72	86*	N/A	N/A
467 WESLEYAN......	34	912	1,023	N/A	N/A

GEORGIA

County and Denomination	Number of churches	Communicant, confirmed, full members	Total adherents: Number	Total adherents: Percent of total population	Total adherents: Percent of total adherents
THE STATE.....	6,255	1,638,773	2,118,091*	46.2	100.0
APPLING	36	6,993	8,646*	67.9	100.0
081 CATHOLIC......	1	0	30	0.2	0.3
127 CH GOD (CLEVE)	4	560	709*	5.6	8.2
413 S-D ADVENTISTS	1	45	57*	0.4	0.7
419 SO BAPT CONV..	19	4,950	6,269*	49.3	72.5
449 UN METHODIST..	11	1,438	1,581	12.4	18.3
ATKINSON	15	1,398	1,715*	29.2	100.0
081 CATHOLIC......	1	0	40	0.7	2.3
127 CH GOD (CLEVE)	1	33	42*	0.7	2.4
419 SO BAPT CONV..	6	804	1,027*	17.5	59.9
449 UN METHODIST..	7	561	606	10.3	35.3
BACON	21	3,318	4,000*	48.6	100.0
081 CATHOLIC......	0	0	10	0.1	0.3
127 CH GOD (CLEVE)	4	548	682*	8.3	17.1
413 S-D ADVENTISTS	1	24	30*	0.4	0.8
419 SO BAPT CONV..	11	1,997	2,484*	30.2	62.1
449 UN METHODIST..	5	749	794	9.6	19.9
BAKER	13	1,304	1,610*	41.5	100.0
127 CH GOD (CLEVE)	1	110	138*	3.6	8.6
357 PRESB CH US...	1	40	50*	1.3	3.1
419 SO BAPT CONV..	8	1,034	1,293*	33.4	80.3
449 UN METHODIST..	3	120	129	3.3	8.0
BALDWIN	29	8,074	9,835*	28.7	100.0
081 CATHOLIC......	1	C	508	1.5	5.2
097 CR C AND C CR.	2	431	506*	1.5	5.1

*Total adherents estimated from known number of communicant, confirmed, full members.

—Represents a percent less than 0.1.

Percentages may not total due to rounding.

Table 3. Churches and Church Membership by State, County and Denomination: 1971

County and Denomination	Number of churches	Communicant, confirmed, full members	Total adherents		
			Number	Percent of total population	Percent of total adherents
127 CH GOD (CLEVE)	1	47	55*	0.2	0.6
193 EPISCOPAL.....	1	226	277	0.8	2.8
283 LUTH--MO SYNOD	2	51	90	0.3	0.9
357 PRESB CH US...	1	440	516*	1.5	5.2
413 S-D ADVENTISTS	1	53	62*	0.2	0.6
419 SO BAPT CONV..	11	5,088	5,971*	17.4	60.7
449 UN METHODIST..	9	1,738	1,850	5.4	18.8
BANKS	28	4,679	5,671*	83.0	100.0
097 CR C AND C CR.	2	225	275*	4.0	4.8
127 CH GOD (CLEVE)	2	173	212*	3.1	3.7
357 PRESB CH US...	1	62	76*	1.1	1.3
419 SO BAPT CONV..	17	3,843	4,705*	68.9	83.0
449 UN METHODIST..	6	376	403	5.9	7.1
BARROW	37	7,518	8,942*	53.0	100.0
081 CATHOLIC......	1	0	125	0.7	1.4
093 CR CH (DISC)..	4	554	678*	4.0	7.6
127 CH GOD (CLEVE)	1	3	4*	-	-
193 EPISCOPAL.....	1	52	69	0.4	0.8
357 PRESB CH US...	2	247	302*	1.8	3.4
419 SO BAPT CONV..	13	4,191	5,127*	30.4	57.3
435 UNITARIAN-UNIV	1	10	10	0.1	0.1
449 UN METHODIST..	14	2,461	2,627	15.6	29.4
BARTOW	64	14,237	17,627*	54.0	100.0
081 CATHOLIC......	1	0	217	0.7	1.2
097 CR C AND C CR.	4	575	722*	2.2	4.1
127 CH GOD (CLEVE)	4	306	384*	1.2	2.2
193 EPISCOPAL.....	1	170	206	0.6	1.2
357 PRESB CH US...	2	439	551*	1.7	3.1
419 SO BAPT CONV..	38	10,286	12,920*	39.6	73.3
449 UN METHODIST..	14	2,461	2,627	8.0	14.9
BEN HILL	28	6,102	7,332*	55.7	100.0
081 CATHOLIC......	1	0	75	0.6	1.0
093 CR CH (DISC)..	1	29	35*	0.3	0.5
097 CR C AND C CR.	1	130	157*	1.2	2.1
127 CH GOD (CLEVE)	1	178	214*	1.6	2.9
165 CH OF NAZARENE	1	188	264	2.0	3.6
193 EPISCOPAL.....	1	51	61	0.5	0.8
357 PRESB CH US...	1	101	122*	0.9	1.7
413 S-D ADVENTISTS	2	69	83*	0.6	1.1
419 SO BAPT CONV..	14	4,242	5,108*	38.8	69.7
449 UN METHODIST..	5	1,114	1,213	9.2	16.5
BERRIEN	20	3,414	4,154*	35.9	100.0
081 CATHOLIC......	2	0	50	0.4	1.2
093 CR CH (DISC)..	1	26	32*	0.3	0.8
127 CH GOD (CLEVE)	3	169	209*	1.8	5.0
165 CH OF NAZARENE	1	45	100	0.9	2.4
175 CONG CR CH....	1	65	80*	0.7	1.9
419 SO BAPT CONV..	7	2,304	2,850*	24.7	68.6
449 UN METHODIST..	5	805	833	7.2	20.1
BIBB	111	56,032	71,845*	50.1	100.0
081 CATHOLIC......	3	0	4,294	3.0	6.0
093 CR CH (DISC)..	4	790	973*	0.7	1.4
097 CR C AND C CR.	2	231	284*	0.2	0.4
123 CH GOD (ANDER)	1	140	325	0.2	0.5
127 CH GOD (CLEVE)	5	550	677*	0.5	0.9
165 CH OF NAZARENE	3	175	376	0.3	0.5
193 EPISCOPAL.....	6	1,664	2,042	1.4	2.8
221 FREE METH C NA	1	54	59	-	0.1
281 LUTH CH AMER..	1	409	568	0.4	0.8
283 LUTH--MO SYNOD	1	82	113	0.1	0.2
349 PENT HOLINESS.	2	87	107*	0.1	0.1
353 PLY BRETHREN..	1	40	50	-	0.1
357 PRESB CH US...	6	2,619	3,224*	2.2	4.5
403 SALVATION ARMY	1	125	393	0.3	0.5
413 S-D ADVENTISTS	2	296	364*	0.3	0.5
419 SO BAPT CONV..	44	33,858	41,686*	29.1	58.0
449 UN METHODIST..	27	14,829	16,208	11.3	22.6
453 UN PRES CH USA	1	83	102*	0.1	0.1
BLECKLEY	18	4,649	5,504*	53.5	100.0
127 CH GOD (CLEVE)	1	90	109*	1.1	2.0
165 CH OF NAZARENE	1	37	39	0.4	0.7
193 EPISCOPAL.....	1	64	80	0.8	1.5
419 SO BAPT CONV..	12	3,706	4,485*	43.6	81.5
449 UN METHODIST..	3	752	791	7.7	14.4
BRANTLEY	16	2,299	2,873*	48.4	100.0
127 CH GOD (CLEVE)	2	102	128*	2.2	4.5
165 CH OF NAZARENE	1	29	49	0.8	1.7
419 SO BAPT CONV..	11	2,055	2,575*	43.4	89.6
449 UN METHODIST..	2	113	121	2.0	4.2
BROOKS	36	5,058	6,144*	44.7	100.0
081 CATHOLIC......	0	0	10	0.1	0.2
127 CH GOD (CLEVE)	2	65	81*	0.6	1.3
165 CH OF NAZARENE	1	46	90	0.7	1.5
193 EPISCOPAL.....	1	11	11	0.1	0.2
357 PRESB CH US...	1	105	131*	1.0	2.1
413 S-D ADVENTISTS	2	60	75*	0.5	1.2
419 SO BAPT CONV..	19	3,554	4,445*	32.4	72.3
449 UN METHODIST..	10	1,217	1,301	9.5	21.2
BRYAN	17	2,543	3,141*	48.0	100.0
081 CATHOLIC......	1	0	30	0.5	1.0
093 CR CH (DISC)..	1	106	135*	2.1	4.3
127 CH GOD (CLEVE)	1	10	13*	0.2	0.4
357 PRESB CH US...	1	20	26*	0.4	0.8
419 SO BAPT CONV..	10	1,800	2,301*	35.2	73.3
449 UN METHODIST..	3	607	636	9.7	20.2
BULLOCH	40	8,064	10,094*	32.0	100.0
081 CATHOLIC......	1	0	304	1.0	3.0
123 CH GOD (ANDER)	3	59	189	0.6	1.9
127 CH GOD (CLEVE)	2	125	155*	0.5	1.5
193 EPISCOPAL.....	1	89	129	0.4	1.3
283 LUTH--MO SYNOD	1	74	118	0.4	1.2
357 PRESB CH US...	1	177	220*	0.7	2.2
419 SO BAPT CONV..	20	5,086	6,308*	20.0	62.5
449 UN METHODIST..	11	2,454	2,671	8.5	26.5
BURKE	28	4,495	5,469*	30.0	100.0
093 CR CH (DISC)..	1	32	41*	0.2	0.7
127 CH GOD (CLEVE)	2	151	194*	1.1	3.5
193 EPISCOPAL.....	1	86	112	0.6	2.0
353 PLY BRETHREN..	1	50	80	0.4	1.5
357 PRESB CH US...	1	115	148*	0.8	2.7
419 SO BAPT CONV..	10	2,638	3,384*	18.5	61.9
449 UN METHODIST..	10	1,310	1,365	7.5	25.0
453 UN PRES CH USA	2	113	145*	0.8	2.7
BUTTS	21	3,931	4,820*	45.6	100.0
081 CATHOLIC......	1	0	80	0.8	1.7
093 CR CH (DISC)..	1	47	59*	0.6	1.2
097 CR C AND C CR.	2	62	77*	0.7	1.6
165 CH OF NAZARENE	1	103	141	1.3	2.9
419 SO BAPT CONV..	11	2,909	3,629*	34.4	75.3
449 UN METHODIST..	5	810	834	7.9	17.3
CALHOUN	12	2,026	2,471*	37.4	100.0
357 PRESB CH US...	1	29	37*	0.6	1.5
419 SO BAPT CONV..	6	1,485	1,880*	28.5	76.1
449 UN METHODIST..	5	512	554	8.4	22.4
CAMDEN	27	2,962	3,747*	33.1	100.0
081 CATHOLIC......	2	0	75	0.7	2.0
127 CH GOD (CLEVE)	7	369	484*	4.3	12.9
193 EPISCOPAL.....	2	83	138	1.2	3.7
357 PRESB CH US...	1	111	145*	1.3	3.9
419 SO BAPT CONV..	7	1,095	1,435*	12.7	38.3
449 UN METHODIST..	8	1,304	1,470	13.0	39.2
CANDLER	14	1,971	2,446*	38.1	100.0
081 CATHOLIC......	1	0	50	0.8	2.0
123 CH GOD (ANDER)	1	10	30	0.5	1.2
127 CH GOD (CLEVE)	2	96	119*	1.9	4.9
357 PRESB CH US...	1	73	91*	1.4	3.7
419 SO BAPT CONV..	7	1,422	1,767*	27.6	72.2
449 UN METHODIST..	2	370	389	6.1	15.9
CARROLL	82	18,342	22,510*	49.6	100.0
081 CATHOLIC......	1	0	425	0.9	1.9
093 CR CH (DISC)..	1	53	65*	0.1	0.3
097 CR C AND C CR.	10	1,130	1,389*	3.1	6.2
127 CH GOD (CLEVE)	5	387	476*	1.0	2.1
193 EPISCOPAL.....	1	162	299	0.7	1.3
349 PENT HOLINESS.	1	45	55*	0.1	0.2
357 PRESB CH US...	2	409	503*	1.1	2.2
419 SO BAPT CONV..	36	12,436	15,290*	33.7	67.9
449 UN METHODIST..	25	3,720	4,008	8.8	17.8
CATOOSA	38	11,401	14,674*	51.9	100.0
081 CATHOLIC......	1	0	821	2.9	5.6
127 CH GOD (CLEVE)	2	224	280*	1.0	1.9
165 CH OF NAZARENE	1	75	83	0.3	0.6
357 PRESB CH US...	2	143	179*	0.6	1.2
413 S-D ADVENTISTS	1	129	161*	0.6	1.1
419 SO BAPT CONV..	24	9,248	11,568*	40.9	78.8
449 UN METHODIST..	7	1,582	1,582	5.6	10.8
CHARLTON	17	2,109	2,607*	45.9	100.0
081 CATHOLIC......	1	0	25	0.4	1.0
127 CH GOD (CLEVE)	3	110	142*	2.5	5.4
419 SO BAPT CONV..	8	1,391	1,800*	31.7	69.0
449 UN METHODIST..	5	608	640	11.3	24.5
CHATHAM	137	53,936	78,537*	41.8	100.0
081 CATHOLIC......	11	0	12,000	6.4	15.3
093 CR CH (DISC)..	4	898	1,109*	0.6	1.4
097 CR C AND C CR.	6	1,150	1,420*	0.8	1.8
123 CH GOD (ANDER)	1	90	200	0.1	0.3
127 CH GOD (CLEVE)	5	1,031	1,273*	0.7	1.6
165 CH OF NAZARENE	3	311	411	0.2	0.5
193 EPISCOPAL.....	12	4,480	6,259	3.3	8.0
221 FREE METH C NA	1	36	69	-	0.1

*Total adherents estimated from known number of communicant, confirmed, full members.

—Represents a percent less than 0.1.

Percentages may not total due to rounding.

Table 3. Churches and Church Membership by State, County and Denomination: 1971

County and Denomination	Number of churches	Communicant, confirmed, full members	Total adherents		
			Number	Percent of total population	Percent of total adherents
281 LUTH CH AMER..	7	2,521	3,463	1.8	4.4
283 LUTH--MO SYNOD	1	114	183	0.1	0.2
349 PENT HOLINESS.	2	119	147*	0.1	0.2
357 PRESB CH US...	7	1,863	2,301*	1.2	2.9
381 REF PRES-EVAN.	1	68	91	-	0.1
403 SALVATION ARMY	1	91	325	0.2	0.4
413 S-D ADVENTISTS	2	807	997*	0.5	1.3
419 SO BAPT CONV..	44	28,102	34,705*	18.5	44.2
435 UNITARIAN-UNIV	1	45	60	-	0.1
443 UN C OF CHRIST	1	104	128*	0.1	0.2
449 UN METHODIST..	24	11,749	12,955	6.9	16.5
453 UN PRES CH USA	3	357	441*	0.2	0.6
CHATTAHOOCHEE	2	435	462*	1.8	100.0
419 SO BAPT CONV..	1	237	264*	1.0	57.1
449 UN METHODIST..	1	198	198	0.8	42.9
CHATTOOGA	54	8,988	10,830*	52.7	100.0
081 CATHOLIC......	1	0	15	0.1	0.1
127 CH GOD (CLEVE)	3	330	403*	2.0	3.7
165 CH OF NAZARENE	2	66	112	0.5	1.0
193 EPISCOPAL.....	1	28	34	0.2	0.3
357 PRESB CH US...	6	551	673*	3.3	6.2
419 SO BAPT CONV..	33	7,002	8,547*	41.6	78.9
449 UN METHODIST..	8	1,011	1,046	5.1	9.7
CHEROKEE	58	12,362	15,234*	49.0	100.0
081 CATHOLIC......	1	0	105	0.3	0.7
093 CR CH (DISC)..	1	88	111*	0.4	0.7
097 CR C AND C CR.	1	125	158*	0.5	1.0
127 CH GOD (CLEVE)	2	277	349*	1.1	2.3
349 PENT HOLINESS.	1	19	24*	0.1	0.2
357 PRESB CH US...	2	89	112*	0.4	0.7
419 SO BAPT CONV..	32	9,357	11,793*	38.0	77.4
449 UN METHODIST..	18	2,407	2,582	8.3	16.9
CLARKE	44	18,465	23,845*	36.6	100.0
081 CATHOLIC......	1	0	1,838	2.8	7.7
093 CR CH (DISC)..	2	340	405*	0.6	1.7
097 CR C AND C CR.	1	95	113*	0.2	0.5
165 CH OF NAZARENE	1	62	116	0.2	0.5
193 EPISCOPAL.....	2	1,034	1,305	2.0	5.5
281 LUTH CH AMER..	1	153	231	0.4	1.0
283 LUTH--MO SYNOD	2	143	165	0.3	0.7
349 PENT HOLINESS.	1	147	175*	0.3	0.7
357 PRESB CH US...	5	1,587	1,888*	2.9	7.9
403 SALVATION ARMY	1	60	262	0.4	1.1
413 S-D ADVENTISTS	1	43	51*	0.1	0.2
419 SO BAPT CONV..	14	9,060	10,781*	16.5	45.2
435 UNITARIAN-UNIV	1	105	192	0.3	0.8
449 UN METHODIST..	10	5,579	6,255	9.6	26.2
453 UN PRES CH USA	1	57	68*	0.1	0.3
CLAY	14	1,367	1,573*	43.3	100.0
357 PRESB CH US...	1	28	34*	0.9	2.2
419 SO BAPT CONV..	7	851	1,043*	28.7	66.3
449 UN METHODIST..	6	488	496	13.6	31.5
CLAYTON	65	30,270	41,376*	42.2	100.0
081 CATHOLIC......	1	0	2,200	2.2	5.3
093 CR CH (DISC)..	1	73	96*	0.1	0.2
097 CR C AND C CR.	4	925	1,216*	1.2	2.9
127 CH GOD (CLEVE)	4	388	510*	0.5	1.2
165 CH OF NAZARENE	1	71	213	0.2	0.5
193 EPISCOPAL.....	1	268	466	0.5	1.1
281 LUTH CH AMER..	2	459	665	0.7	1.6
283 LUTH--MO SYNOD	1	168	266	0.3	0.6
353 PLY BRETHREN..	1	40	60	0.1	0.1
357 PRESB CH US...	5	1,340	1,761*	1.8	4.3
413 S-D ADVENTISTS	1	97	127*	0.1	0.3
419 SO BAPT CONV..	33	21,877	28,750*	29.3	69.5
443 UN C OF CHRIST	1	165	217*	0.2	0.5
449 UN METHODIST..	9	4,399	4,829	4.9	11.7
CLINCH	8	1,248	1,537*	24.0	100.0
127 CH GOD (CLEVE)	2	218	281*	4.4	18.3
419 SO BAPT CONV..	3	665	856*	13.4	55.7
449 UN METHODIST..	3	365	400	6.2	26.0
COBB	166	73,574	99,224*	50.4	100.0
029 AMER LUTH CH..	1	261	495	0.3	0.5
081 CATHOLIC......	3	0	6,913	3.5	7.0
093 CR CH (DISC)..	1	190	241*	0.1	0.2
097 CR C AND C CR.	8	780	989*	0.5	1.0
123 CH GOD (ANDER)	1	18	49	-	-
127 CH GOD (CLEVE)	5	918	1,164*	0.6	1.2
165 CH OF NAZARENE	2	236	503	0.3	0.5
193 EPISCOPAL.....	3	1,551	2,024	1.0	2.0
221 FREE METH C NA	1	18	37	-	-
281 LUTH CH AMER..	1	293	445	0.2	0.4
283 LUTH--MO SYNOD	1	523	819	0.4	0.8
349 PENT HOLINESS.	1	33	42*	-	-
353 PLY BRETHREN..	1	50	80	-	0.1
357 PRESB CH US...	10	3,653	4,634*	2.4	4.7
403 SALVATION ARMY	1	30	581	0.3	0.6
413 S-D ADVENTISTS	3	368	467*	0.2	0.5
419 SO BAPT CONV..	90	50,463	64,011*	32.5	64.5
449 UN METHODIST..	33	14,189	15,730	8.0	15.9
COFFEE	39	7,133	9,274*	40.6	100.0
081 CATHOLIC......	1	0	540	2.4	5.8
127 CH GOD (CLEVE)	4	481	602*	2.6	6.5
165 CH OF NAZARENE	1	30	70	0.3	0.8
193 EPISCOPAL.....	1	71	89	0.4	1.0
357 PRESB CH US...	1	111	139*	0.6	1.5
419 SO BAPT CONV..	21	5,007	6,271*	27.5	67.6
443 UN C OF CHRIST	1	52	65*	0.3	0.7
449 UN METHODIST..	9	1,381	1,498	6.6	16.2
COLQUITT	58	17,117	20,993*	65.2	100.0
127 CH GOD (CLEVE)	2	229	286*	0.9	1.4
165 CH OF NAZARENE	2	186	335	1.0	1.6
193 EPISCOPAL.....	1	79	102	0.3	0.5
283 LUTH--MO SYNOD	1	20	39	0.1	0.2
357 PRESB CH US...	1	446	556*	1.7	2.6
413 S-D ADVENTISTS	1	48	60*	0.2	0.3
419 SO BAPT CONV..	40	14,012	17,474*	54.3	83.2
449 UN METHODIST..	10	2,097	2,141	6.6	10.2
COLUMBIA	26	5,220	6,501*	29.1	100.0
097 CR C AND C CR.	1	76	98*	0.4	1.5
193 EPISCOPAL.....	1	49	73	0.3	1.1
357 PRESB CH US...	2	149	192*	0.9	3.0
419 SO BAPT CONV..	12	3,669	4,734*	21.2	72.8
449 UN METHODIST..	10	1,277	1,404	6.3	21.6
COOK	24	4,717	5,729*	47.2	100.0
081 CATHOLIC......	1	0	25	0.2	0.4
127 CH GOD (CLEVE)	2	222	279*	2.3	4.9
165 CH OF NAZARENE	1	25	25	0.2	0.4
357 PRESB CH US...	1	19	24*	0.2	0.4
419 SO BAPT CONV..	13	3,315	4,174*	34.4	72.9
449 UN METHODIST..	6	1,136	1,202	9.9	21.0
COWETA	58	12,825	16,076*	49.8	100.0
055 AS REF PRES CH	1	169	211*	0.7	1.3
081 CATHOLIC......	1	0	444	1.4	2.8
093 CR CH (DISC)..	1	31	39*	0.1	0.2
097 CR C AND C CR.	2	348	435*	1.3	2.7
127 CH GOD (CLEVE)	1	17	21*	0.1	0.1
193 EPISCOPAL.....	1	106	106	0.3	0.7
281 LUTH CH AMER..	1	39	57	0.2	0.4
283 LUTH--MO SYNOD	1	55	74	0.2	0.5
349 PENT HOLINESS.	1	115	144*	0.4	0.9
357 PRESB CH US...	2	284	355*	1.1	2.2
419 SO BAPT CONV..	27	8,711	10,883*	33.7	67.7
435 UNITARIAN-UNIV	1	12	12	-	0.1
449 UN METHODIST..	17	2,907	3,256	10.1	20.3
453 UN PRES CH USA	1	31	39*	0.1	0.2
CRAWFORD	12	1,485	1,796*	31.2	100.0
175 CONG CR CH....	1	60	77*	1.3	4.3
419 SO BAPT CONV..	4	970	1,241*	21.6	69.1
449 UN METHODIST..	7	455	478	8.3	26.6
CRISP	28	4,898	5,906*	32.7	100.0
081 CATHOLIC......	1	0	30	0.2	0.5
127 CH GOD (CLEVE)	1	14	18*	0.1	0.3
193 EPISCOPAL.....	1	55	82	0.5	1.4
357 PRESB CH US...	1	49	62*	0.3	1.0
419 SO BAPT CONV..	15	3,288	4,135*	22.9	70.0
449 UN METHODIST..	8	1,465	1,545	8.5	26.2
453 UN PRES CH USA	1	27	34*	0.2	0.6
DADE	26	2,664	3,144*	31.7	100.0
127 CH GOD (CLEVE)	4	155	192*	1.9	6.1
381 REF PRES-EVAN.	1	177	239	2.4	7.6
413 S-D ADVENTISTS	3	326	404*	4.1	12.8
419 SO BAPT CONV..	8	1,075	1,331*	13.4	42.3
449 UN METHODIST..	10	931	978	9.9	31.1
DAWSON	17	2,963	3,527*	96.9	100.0
127 CH GOD (CLEVE)	1	58	70*	1.9	2.0
419 SO BAPT CONV..	12	2,578	3,128*	86.0	88.7
449 UN METHODIST..	4	327	329	9.0	9.3
DECATUR	44	8,481	10,387*	46.6	100.0
093 CR CH (DISC)..	1	38	47*	0.2	0.5
097 CR C AND C CR.	1	263	327*	1.5	3.1
123 CH GOD (ANDER)	2	18	43	0.2	0.4
127 CH GOD (CLEVE)	4	294	365*	1.6	3.5
165 CH OF NAZARENE	1	88	145	0.6	1.4
193 EPISCOPAL.....	1	58	91	0.4	0.9
357 PRESB CH US...	1	274	340*	1.5	3.3
413 S-D ADVENTISTS	1	39	48*	0.2	0.5
419 SO BAPT CONV..	22	5,782	7,178*	32.2	69.1
449 UN METHODIST..	10	1,627	1,803	8.1	17.4
DE KALB	196	133,785	185,318*	44.6	100.0
029 AMER LUTH CH..	3	1,040	1,696	0.4	0.9
055 AS REF PRES CH	2	607	757*	0.2	0.4

*Total adherents estimated from known number of communicant, confirmed, full members.

—Represents a percent less than 0.1.

Percentages may not total due to rounding.

Table 3. Churches and Church Membership by State, County and Denomination: 1971

County and Denomination	Number of churches	Communicant, confirmed, full members	Total adherents: Number	Percent of total population	Percent of total adherents
081 CATHOLIC......	7	0	20,355	4.9	11.0
093 CR CH (DISC)..	4	1,822	2,271*	0.5	1.2
097 CR C AND C CR.	6	6,150	7,667*	1.8	4.1
123 CH GOD (ANDER)	5	458	1,015	0.2	0.5
127 CH GOD (CLEVE)	5	997	1,243*	0.3	0.7
165 CH OF NAZARENE	1	118	263	0.1	0.1
185 CUMBER PRESB..	1	121	151*	-	0.1
193 EPISCOPAL.....	3	1,671	2,243	0.5	1.2
226 FRIENDS-USA...	1	45	56*	-	-
281 LUTH CH AMER..	4	1,007	1,388	0.3	0.7
283 LUTH--MO SYNOD	3	1,025	1,475	0.4	0.8
335 ORTH PRESB CH.	1	41	64	-	-
349 PENT HOLINESS.	1	42	52*	-	-
357 PRESB CH US...	29	15,682	19,550*	4.7	10.5
413 S-D ADVENTISTS	2	829	1,033*	0.2	0.6
419 SO BAPT CONV..	74	66,005	82,285*	19.8	44.4
435 UNITARIAN-UNIV	1	990	1,686	0.4	0.9
449 UN METHODIST..	42	35,052	39,965	9.6	21.6
453 UN PRES CH USA	1	83	103*	-	0.1
DODGE	58	9,081	11,036*	70.5	100.0
093 CR CH (DISC)..	2	81	100*	0.6	0.9
097 CR C AND C CR.	1	100	123*	0.8	1.1
127 CH GOD (CLEVE)	3	148	183*	1.2	1.7
165 CH OF NAZARENE	1	15	37	0.2	0.3
193 EPISCOPAL.....	1	12	21	0.1	0.2
349 PENT HOLINESS.	1	52	64*	0.4	0.6
357 PRESB CH US...	2	243	300*	1.9	2.7
419 SO BAPT CONV..	39	7,219	8,912*	56.9	80.8
449 UN METHODIST..	8	1,211	1,296	8.3	11.7
DOOLY	30	5,825	6,975*	67.0	100.0
127 CH GOD (CLEVE)	1	25	31*	0.3	0.4
419 SO BAPT CONV..	18	4,321	5,427*	52.2	77.8
449 UN METHODIST..	10	1,460	1,493	14.4	21.4
453 UN PRES CH USA	1	19	24*	0.2	0.3
DOUGHERTY	54	23,939	33,188*	37.0	100.0
081 CATHOLIC......	1	0	3,000	3.3	9.0
093 CR CH (DISC)..	1	148	190*	0.2	0.6
097 CR C AND C CR.	2	40	51*	0.1	0.2
127 CH GOD (CLEVE)	3	585	750*	0.8	2.3
165 CH OF NAZARENE	1	120	215	0.2	0.6
193 EPISCOPAL.....	4	1,080	1,398	1.6	4.2
281 LUTH CH AMER..	1	180	262	0.3	0.8
283 LUTH--MO SYNOD	1	105	170	0.2	0.5
285 MENNONITE CH..	1	10	13*	-	-
349 PENT HOLINESS.	1	22	28*	-	0.1
353 PLY BRETHREN..	1	145	350	0.4	1.1
357 PRESB CH US...	5	1,444	1,850*	2.1	5.6
403 SALVATION ARMY	1	79	390	0.4	1.2
413 S-D ADVENTISTS	2	206	264*	0.3	0.8
419 SO BAPT CONV..	20	13,870	17,774*	19.8	53.6
449 UN METHODIST..	8	5,875	6,445	7.2	19.4
453 UN PRES CH USA	1	30	38*	-	0.1
DOUGLAS	32	9,414	11,643*	40.6	100.0
097 CR C AND C CR.	2	110	140*	0.5	1.2
127 CH GOD (CLEVE)	3	221	282*	1.0	2.4
283 LUTH--MO SYNOD	1	30	59	0.2	0.5
357 PRESB CH US...	1	113	144*	0.5	1.2
413 S-D ADVENTISTS	1	134	171*	0.6	1.5
419 SO BAPT CONV..	18	7,211	9,187*	32.1	78.9
449 UN METHODIST..	6	1,595	1,660	5.8	14.3
EARLY	27	3,757	4,636*	36.6	100.0
123 CH GOD (ANDER)	2	34	72	0.6	1.6
127 CH GOD (CLEVE)	1	52	67*	0.5	1.4
193 EPISCOPAL.....	1	20	23	0.2	0.5
357 PRESB CH US...	1	43	55*	0.4	1.2
413 S-D ADVENTISTS	1	41	53*	0.4	1.1
419 SO BAPT CONV..	14	2,614	3,356*	26.5	72.4
449 UN METHODIST..	7	953	1,010	8.0	21.8
ECHOLS	4	411	494*	25.7	100.0
127 CH GOD (CLEVE)	1	28	35*	1.8	7.1
419 SO BAPT CONV..	2	250	317*	16.5	64.2
449 UN METHODIST..	1	133	142	7.4	28.7
EFFINGHAM	37	6,127	7,326*	53.7	100.0
093 CR CH (DISC)..	2	124	158*	1.2	2.2
097 CR C AND C CR.	3	69	88*	0.6	1.2
123 CH GOD (ANDER)	1	20	65	0.5	0.9
127 CH GOD (CLEVE)	1	36	46*	0.3	0.6
281 LUTH CH AMER..	7	1,042	1,259	9.2	17.2
419 SO BAPT CONV..	12	2,850	3,632*	26.6	49.6
449 UN METHODIST..	11	1,986	2,078	15.2	28.4
ELBERT	47	10,544	12,781*	74.0	100.0
081 CATHOLIC......	1	0	75	0.4	0.6
097 CR C AND C CR.	1	100	123*	0.7	1.0
127 CH GOD (CLEVE)	2	99	122*	0.7	1.0
193 EPISCOPAL.....	1	79	115	0.7	0.9
281 LUTH CH AMER..	1	90	101	0.6	0.8
349 PENT HOLINESS.	3	217	267*	1.5	2.1
357 PRESB CH US...	3	390	479*	2.8	3.7
403 SALVATION ARMY	1	21	269	1.6	2.1
419 SO BAPT CONV..	20	6,659	8,181*	47.4	64.0
449 UN METHODIST..	14	2,889	3,049	17.7	23.9
EMANUEL	44	6,271	7,559*	41.6	100.0
081 CATHOLIC......	1	0	130	0.7	1.7
123 CH GOD (ANDER)	1	8	8	-	0.1
127 CH GOD (CLEVE)	4	185	229*	1.3	3.0
165 CH OF NAZARENE	1	46	73	0.4	1.0
193 EPISCOPAL.....	1	39	68	0.4	0.9
349 PENT HOLINESS.	1	15	19*	0.1	0.3
357 PRESB CH US...	1	85	105*	0.6	1.4
419 SO BAPT CONV..	19	3,851	4,765*	26.2	63.0
449 UN METHODIST..	15	2,042	2,162	11.9	28.6
EVANS	15	2,348	2,788*	38.2	100.0
081 CATHOLIC......	1	0	75	1.0	2.7
127 CH GOD (CLEVE)	1	7	9*	0.1	0.3
165 CH OF NAZARENE	1	80	100	1.4	3.6
419 SO BAPT CONV..	5	1,071	1,344*	18.4	48.2
449 UN METHODIST..	7	1,190	1,260	17.3	45.2
FANNIN	53	9,273	11,006*	82.4	100.0
081 CATHOLIC......	1	0	50	0.4	0.5
127 CH GOD (CLEVE)	3	206	246*	1.8	2.2
221 FREE METH C NA	1	9	9	0.1	0.1
413 S-D ADVENTISTS	1	37	44*	0.3	0.4
419 SO BAPT CONV..	41	8,290	9,904*	74.1	90.0
449 UN METHODIST..	6	731	753	5.6	6.8
FAYETTE	31	5,854	7,163*	63.0	100.0
093 CR CH (DISC)..	2	53	67*	0.6	0.9
097 CR C AND C CR.	3	52	66*	0.6	0.9
127 CH GOD (CLEVE)	1	45	57*	0.5	0.8
357 PRESB CH US...	2	261	332*	2.9	4.6
419 SO BAPT CONV..	15	3,914	4,974*	43.8	69.4
449 UN METHODIST..	8	1,529	1,667	14.7	23.3
FLOYD	107	35,690	44,378*	60.2	100.0
081 CATHOLIC......	1	0	1,400	1.9	3.2
093 CR CH (DISC)..	1	125	152*	0.2	0.3
097 CR C AND C CR.	1	225	274*	0.4	0.6
127 CH GOD (CLEVE)	6	1,046	1,276*	1.7	2.9
165 CH OF NAZARENE	1	40	55	0.1	0.1
193 EPISCOPAL.....	2	743	878	1.2	2.0
281 LUTH CH AMER..	1	52	74	0.1	0.2
283 LUTH--MO SYNOD	1	84	159	0.2	0.4
357 PRESB CH US...	5	1,331	1,623*	2.2	3.7
403 SALVATION ARMY	1	67	247	0.3	0.6
413 S-D ADVENTISTS	2	90	110*	0.1	0.2
419 SO BAPT CONV..	62	26,509	32,326*	43.8	72.8
449 UN METHODIST..	22	5,363	5,786	7.8	13.0
453 UN PRES CH USA	1	15	18*	-	-
FORSYTH	46	13,726	17,157*	101.4#	100.0
127 CH GOD (CLEVE)	1	136	172*	1.0	1.0
357 PRESB CH US...	1	89	113*	0.7	0.7
419 SO BAPT CONV..	35	12,470	15,767*	93.1	91.9
449 UN METHODIST..	9	1,031	1,105	6.5	6.4
FRANKLIN	53	8,997	10,626*	83.1	100.0
097 CR C AND C CR.	2	115	139*	1.1	1.3
127 CH GOD (CLEVE)	6	515	623*	4.9	5.9
349 PENT HOLINESS.	4	391	473*	3.7	4.5
357 PRESB CH US...	4	138	167*	1.3	1.6
419 SO BAPT CONV..	25	6,144	7,430*	58.1	69.9
449 UN METHODIST..	12	1,694	1,794	14.0	16.9
FULTON	326	189,041	254,337*	41.9	100.0
029 AMER LUTH CH..	1	186	281	-	0.1
055 AS REF PRES CH	2	747	906*	0.1	0.4
081 CATHOLIC......	14	0	25,608	4.2	10.1
093 CR CH (DISC)..	10	2,581	3,131*	0.5	1.2
097 CR C AND C CR.	21	6,943	8,423*	1.4	3.3
127 CH GOD (CLEVE)	17	3,509	4,257*	0.7	1.7
165 CH OF NAZARENE	4	678	1,036	0.2	0.4
193 EPISCOPAL.....	19	15,468	20,651	3.4	8.1
221 FREE METH C NA	1	45	69	-	-
281 LUTH CH AMER..	7	3,721	4,888	0.8	1.9
283 LUTH--MO SYNOD	5	1,115	1,539	0.3	0.6
285 MENNONITE CH..	1	46	56*	-	-
353 PLY BRETHREN..	3	200	330	0.1	0.1
357 PRESB CH US...	27	18,757	22,756*	3.7	8.9
403 SALVATION ARMY	5	549	1,691	0.3	0.7
413 S-D ADVENTISTS	4	2,058	2,497*	0.4	1.0
419 SO BAPT CONV..	109	87,360	105,987*	17.4	41.7
435 UNITARIAN-UNIV	3	115	155	-	0.1
443 UN C OF CHRIST	3	1,428	1,732*	0.3	0.7
449 UN METHODIST..	65	42,276	46,793	7.7	18.4
453 UN PRES CH USA	4	1,219	1,479*	0.2	0.6
469 WISC EVAN LUTH	1	40	72	-	-
GILMER	27	4,273	5,163*	57.6	100.0
081 CATHOLIC......	1	0	10	0.1	0.2
127 CH GOD (CLEVE)	1	88	107*	1.2	2.1
413 S-D ADVENTISTS	1	95	116*	1.3	2.2
419 SO BAPT CONV..	19	3,686	4,482*	50.0	86.8

*Total adherents estimated from known number of communicant, confirmed, full members.

—Represents a percent less than 0.1.

Percentages may not total due to rounding.

#See Introduction for explanation of why total adherents reported by churches exceed the 1970 population figure.

Table 3. Churches and Church Membership by State, County and Denomination: 1971

County and Denomination	Number of churches	Communicant, confirmed, full members	Total adherents: Number	Total adherents: Percent of total population	Total adherents: Percent of total adherents
449 UN METHODIST..	5	404	448	5.0	8.7
GLASCOCK	14	1,596	1,892*	83.0	100.0
123 CH GOD (ANDER)	1	18	43	1.9	2.3
127 CH GOD (CLEVE)	2	59	72*	3.2	3.8
419 SO BAPT CONV..	7	1,144	1,402*	61.5	74.1
449 UN METHODIST..	4	375	375	16.4	19.8
GLYNN	57	17,481	22,795*	45.1	100.0
081 CATHOLIC......	2	0	1,100	2.2	4.8
093 CR CH (DISC)..	1	56	70*	0.1	0.3
097 CR C AND C CR.	1	15	19*	-	0.1
127 CH GOD (CLEVE)	4	722	899*	1.8	3.9
165 CH OF NAZARENE	2	185	374	0.7	1.6
193 EPISCOPAL.....	7	1,255	1,746	3.5	7.7
281 LUTH CH AMER..	1	198	269	0.5	1.2
283 LUTH--MO SYNOD	1	104	157	0.3	0.7
357 PRESB CH US...	4	1,069	1,332*	2.6	5.8
403 SALVATION ARMY	1	40	140	0.3	0.6
413 S-D ADVENTISTS	2	150	187*	0.4	0.8
419 SO BAPT CONV..	20	9,493	11,826*	23.4	51.9
449 UN METHODIST..	10	4,162	4,636	9.2	20.3
453 UN PRES CH USA	1	32	40*	0.1	0.2
GORDON	55	10,294	12,722*	54.0	100.0
081 CATHOLIC......	1	0	105	0.4	0.8
127 CH GOD (CLEVE)	4	575	718*	3.0	5.6
185 CUMBER PRESB..	1	36	45*	0.2	0.4
357 PRESB CH US...	1	53	66*	0.3	0.5
413 S-D ADVENTISTS	2	174	217*	0.9	1.7
419 SO BAPT CONV..	32	8,074	10,077*	42.8	79.2
449 UN METHODIST..	14	1,382	1,494	6.3	11.7
GRADY	37	7,350	8,906*	50.0	100.0
093 CR CH (DISC)..	1	31	38*	0.2	0.4
127 CH GOD (CLEVE)	1	110	137*	0.8	1.5
165 CH OF NAZARENE	1	32	80	0.4	0.9
357 PRESB CH US...	1	152	189*	1.1	2.1
419 SO BAPT CONV..	23	5,730	7,111*	39.9	79.8
443 UN C OF CHRIST	1	35	43*	0.2	0.5
449 UN METHODIST..	9	1,260	1,308	7.3	14.7
GREENE	26	4,031	4,769*	46.7	100.0
127 CH GOD (CLEVE)	1	38	47*	0.5	1.0
193 EPISCOPAL.....	1	42	49	0.5	1.0
357 PRESB CH US...	5	197	243*	2.4	5.1
419 SO BAPT CONV..	12	2,681	3,308*	32.4	69.4
449 UN METHODIST..	7	1,073	1,122	11.0	23.5
GWINNETT	88	25,462	33,335*	46.1	100.0
081 CATHOLIC......	2	0	1,650	2.3	4.9
093 CR CH (DISC)..	2	365	469*	0.6	1.4
097 CR C AND C CR.	4	80	103*	0.1	0.3
127 CH GOD (CLEVE)	8	1,316	1,691*	2.3	5.1
193 EPISCOPAL.....	1	108	147	0.2	0.4
281 LUTH CH AMER..	1	193	325	0.4	1.0
357 PRESB CH US...	6	617	793*	1.1	2.4
413 S-D ADVENTISTS	1	126	162*	0.2	0.5
419 SO BAPT CONV..	35	16,138	20,738*	28.7	62.2
449 UN METHODIST..	28	6,519	7,257	10.0	21.8
HABERSHAM	50	10,901	13,105*	63.3	100.0
081 CATHOLIC......	1	0	129	0.6	1.0
097 CR C AND C CR.	2	265	319*	1.5	2.4
127 CH GOD (CLEVE)	2	238	286*	1.4	2.2
193 EPISCOPAL.....	1	171	216	1.0	1.6
357 PRESB CH US...	3	266	320*	1.5	2.4
419 SO BAPT CONV..	32	8,704	10,462*	50.6	79.8
443 UN C OF CHRIST	1	45	54*	0.3	0.4
449 UN METHODIST..	8	1,212	1,319	6.4	10.1
HALL	84	26,670	33,463*	56.3	100.0
081 CATHOLIC......	1	0	600	1.0	1.8
093 CR CH (DISC)..	1	65	81*	0.1	0.2
127 CH GOD (CLEVE)	3	150	187*	0.3	0.6
165 CH OF NAZARENE	2	197	379	0.6	1.1
193 EPISCOPAL.....	1	480	600	1.0	1.8
221 FREE METH C NA	1	38	54	0.1	0.2
283 LUTH--MO SYNOD	1	89	138	0.2	0.4
357 PRESB CH US...	3	860	1,070*	1.8	3.2
403 SALVATION ARMY	1	47	241	0.4	0.7
413 S-D ADVENTISTS	1	76	95*	0.2	0.3
419 SO BAPT CONV..	50	20,976	26,102*	43.9	78.0
449 UN METHODIST..	19	3,692	3,916	6.6	11.7
HANCOCK	21	2,168	2,637*	29.2	100.0
093 CR CH (DISC)..	1	23	29*	0.3	1.1
193 EPISCOPAL.....	1	94	119	1.3	4.5
357 PRESB CH US...	1	20	26*	0.3	1.0
419 SO BAPT CONV..	14	1,496	1,916*	21.2	72.7
449 UN METHODIST..	4	535	547	6.1	20.7
HARALSON	44	8,488	10,247*	64.3	100.0
097 CR C AND C CR.	3	194	238*	1.5	2.3
127 CH GOD (CLEVE)	3	257	316*	2.0	3.1
349 PENT HOLINESS.	1	25	31*	0.2	0.3
357 PRESB CH US...	2	79	97*	0.6	0.9
419 SO BAPT CONV..	25	6,591	8,098*	50.8	79.0
449 UN METHODIST..	10	1,342	1,467	9.2	14.3
HARRIS	32	3,693	4,367*	37.9	100.0
081 CATHOLIC......	1	0	40	0.3	0.9
127 CH GOD (CLEVE)	2	146	180*	1.6	4.1
413 S-D ADVENTISTS	1	82	101*	0.9	2.3
419 SO BAPT CONV..	17	2,159	2,660*	23.1	60.9
443 UN C OF CHRIST	1	104	128*	1.1	2.9
449 UN METHODIST..	10	1,202	1,258	10.9	28.8
HART	39	7,900	9,518*	60.2	100.0
081 CATHOLIC......	1	0	52	0.3	0.5
127 CH GOD (CLEVE)	5	469	582*	3.7	6.1
193 EPISCOPAL.....	1	49	66	0.4	0.7
349 PENT HOLINESS.	3	77	96*	0.6	1.0
357 PRESB CH US...	2	145	180*	1.1	1.9
419 SO BAPT CONV..	17	5,520	6,852*	43.3	72.0
435 UNITARIAN-UNIV	1	15	15	0.1	0.2
449 UN METHODIST..	9	1,625	1,675	10.6	17.6
HEARD	23	2,051	2,384*	44.5	100.0
093 CR CH (DISC)..	2	115	141*	2.6	5.9
127 CH GOD (CLEVE)	3	90	111*	2.1	4.7
419 SO BAPT CONV..	9	1,242	1,527*	28.5	64.1
449 UN METHODIST..	9	604	605	11.3	25.4
HENRY	42	8,967	11,007*	46.4	100.0
081 CATHOLIC......	1	0	80	0.3	0.7
093 CR CH (DISC)..	1	140	178*	0.8	1.6
097 CR C AND C CR.	2	327	415*	1.7	3.8
127 CH GOD (CLEVE)	2	121	154*	0.6	1.4
175 CONG CR CH....	1	67	85*	0.4	0.8
357 PRESB CH US...	5	688	874*	3.7	7.9
419 SO BAPT CONV..	16	4,975	6,317*	26.6	57.4
449 UN METHODIST..	14	2,649	2,904	12.2	26.4
HOUSTON	55	19,845	25,030*	39.8	100.0
059 BAPT MISS ASSN	1	131	167*	0.3	0.7
081 CATHOLIC......	1	0	197	0.3	0.8
093 CR CH (DISC)..	1	122	156*	0.2	0.6
097 CR C AND C CR.	1	40	51*	0.1	0.2
127 CH GOD (CLEVE)	5	475	607*	1.0	2.4
165 CH OF NAZARENE	2	158	268	0.4	1.1
193 EPISCOPAL.....	1	326	376	0.6	1.5
281 LUTH CH AMER..	1	333	484	0.8	1.9
349 PENT HOLINESS.	1	16	20*	-	0.1
357 PRESB CH US...	3	658	841*	1.3	3.4
403 SALVATION ARMY	1	16	131	0.2	0.5
413 S-D ADVENTISTS	1	43	55*	0.1	0.2
419 SO BAPT CONV..	24	13,045	16,667*	26.5	66.6
435 UNITARIAN-UNIV	1	14	18	-	0.1
449 UN METHODIST..	10	4,348	4,839	7.7	19.3
453 UN PRES CH USA	1	120	153*	0.2	0.6
IRWIN	14	2,322	2,850*	35.5	100.0
081 CATHOLIC......	1	C	25	0.3	0.9
127 CH GOD (CLEVE)	1	41	51*	0.6	1.8
419 SO BAPT CONV..	10	1,879	2,333*	29.0	81.9
449 UN METHODIST..	2	402	441	5.5	15.5
JACKSON	58	9,873	11,814*	56.0	100.0
093 CR CH (DISC)..	3	198	244*	1.2	2.1
097 CR C AND C CR.	3	409	504*	2.4	4.3
127 CH GOD (CLEVE)	2	83	102*	0.5	0.9
349 PENT HOLINESS.	1	6	7*	-	0.1
357 PRESB CH US...	6	278	342*	1.6	2.9
419 SO BAPT CONV..	27	6,917	8,519*	40.4	72.1
443 UN C OF CHRIST	1	50	62*	0.3	0.5
449 UN METHODIST..	15	1,932	2,034	9.6	17.2
JASPER	19	2,196	2,610*	45.3	100.0
127 CH GOD (CLEVE)	2	84	103*	1.8	3.9
357 PRESB CH US...	1	123	151*	2.6	5.8
419 SO BAPT CONV..	10	1,381	1,696*	29.4	65.0
449 UN METHODIST..	6	608	660	11.5	25.3
JEFF DAVIS	21	5,140	6,302*	66.9	100.0
127 CH GOD (CLEVE)	3	586	732*	7.8	11.6
413 S-D ADVENTISTS	1	67	84*	0.9	1.3
419 SO BAPT CONV..	14	3,744	4,674*	49.6	74.2
449 UN METHODIST..	3	743	812	8.6	12.9
JEFFERSON	41	6,243	7,677*	44.7	100.0
055 AS REF PRES CH	4	382	485*	2.8	6.3
081 CATHOLIC......	1	0	35	0.2	0.5
123 CH GOD (ANDER)	2	86	188	1.1	2.4
127 CH GOD (CLEVE)	2	123	156*	0.9	2.0
165 CH OF NAZARENE	2	77	190	1.1	2.5
185 CUMBER PRESB..	1	104	132*	C.8	1.7
353 PLY BRETHREN..	1	20	30	0.2	0.4
419 SO BAPT CONV..	15	3,344	4,243*	24.7	55.3
449 UN METHODIST..	13	2,107	2,218	12.9	28.9

*Total adherents estimated from known number of communicant, confirmed, full members.

—Represents a percent less than 0.1.

Percentages may not total due to rounding.

Table 3. Churches and Church Membership by State, County and Denomination: 1971

County and Denomination	Number of churches	Communicant, confirmed, full members	Total adherents Number	Percent of total population	Percent of total adherents
JENKINS	17	3,527	4,343*	52.1	100.0
081 CATHOLIC......	1	0	25	0.3	0.6
123 CH GOD (ANDER)	1	16	46	0.6	1.1
127 CH GOD (CLEVE)	1	55	69*	0.8	1.6
419 SO BAPT CONV..	10	2,758	3,474*	41.7	80.0
449 UN METHODIST..	4	698	729	8.7	16.8
JOHNSON	34	3,855	4,666*	60.4	100.0
097 CR C AND C CR.	1	147	182*	2.4	3.9
127 CH GOD (CLEVE)	2	149	185*	2.4	4.0
165 CH OF NAZARENE	4	252	468	6.1	10.0
349 PENT HOLINESS.	1	36	45*	0.6	1.0
419 SO BAPT CONV..	13	1,959	2,428*	31.4	52.0
449 UN METHODIST..	13	1,312	1,358	17.6	29.1
JONES	14	2,361	2,889*	23.6	100.0
357 PRESB CH US...	1	47	60*	0.5	2.1
419 SO BAPT CONV..	9	1,708	2,172*	17.8	75.2
449 UN METHODIST..	4	606	657	5.4	22.7
LAMAR	22	3,670	4,477*	41.9	100.0
081 CATHOLIC......	1	0	52	0.5	1.2
127 CH GOD (CLEVE)	1	23	28*	0.3	0.6
165 CH OF NAZARENE	1	105	174	1.6	3.9
349 PENT HOLINESS.	3	115	142*	1.3	3.2
357 PRESB CH US...	1	73	90*	0.8	2.0
419 SO BAPT CONV..	7	2,380	2,947*	27.6	65.8
443 UN C OF CHRIST	1	63	78*	0.7	1.7
449 UN METHODIST..	7	911	966	9.0	21.6
LANIER	9	1,725	2,132*	42.4	100.0
081 CATHOLIC......	1	0	40	0.8	1.9
127 CH GOD (CLEVE)	2	66	84*	1.7	3.9
413 S-D ADVENTISTS	1	42	53*	1.1	2.5
419 SO BAPT CONV..	3	998	1,267*	25.2	59.4
449 UN METHODIST..	2	619	688	13.7	32.3
LAURENS	78	14,056	17,376*	53.1	100.0
081 CATHOLIC......	1	0	327	1.0	1.9
093 CR CH (DISC)..	3	141	175*	0.5	1.0
123 CH GOD (ANDER)	3	80	171	0.5	1.0
127 CH GOD (CLEVE)	2	102	126*	0.4	0.7
165 CH OF NAZARENE	5	300	417	1.3	2.4
193 EPISCOPAL.....	1	143	215	0.7	1.2
283 LUTH--MO SYNOD	1	29	49	0.1	0.3
357 PRESB CH US...	2	348	431*	1.3	2.5
413 S-D ADVENTISTS	1	62	77*	0.2	0.4
419 SO BAPT CONV..	39	9,570	11,863*	36.2	68.3
449 UN METHODIST..	20	3,281	3,525	10.8	20.3
LEE	8	1,589	1,963*	27.9	100.0
357 PRESB CH US...	1	16	20*	0.3	1.0
419 SO BAPT CONV..	5	1,192	1,520*	21.6	77.4
449 UN METHODIST..	2	381	423	6.0	21.5
LIBERTY	21	3,443	4,333*	24.7	100.0
081 CATHOLIC......	1	0	30	0.2	0.7
123 CH GOD (ANDER)	1	13	65	0.4	1.5
127 CH GOD (CLEVE)	2	157	199*	1.1	4.6
193 EPISCOPAL.....	1	29	79	0.4	1.8
357 PRESB CH US...	5	424	537*	3.1	12.4
419 SO BAPT CONV..	6	1,794	2,273*	12.9	52.5
443 UN C OF CHRIST	1	89	113*	0.6	2.6
449 UN METHODIST..	3	781	839	4.8	19.4
453 UN PRES CH USA	1	156	198*	1.1	4.6
LINCOLN	16	2,426	2,894*	49.1	100.0
349 PENT HOLINESS.	1	17	21*	0.4	0.7
357 PRESB CH US...	1	19	24*	0.4	0.8
419 SO BAPT CONV..	8	1,718	2,147*	36.4	74.2
449 UN METHODIST..	6	672	702	11.9	24.3
LONG	8	1,508	1,853*	49.5	100.0
127 CH GOD (CLEVE)	1	39	49*	1.3	2.6
419 SO BAPT CONV..	5	1,281	1,605*	42.8	86.6
449 UN METHODIST..	2	188	199	5.3	10.7
LOWNDES	59	15,931	20,333*	36.9	100.0
081 CATHOLIC......	1	0	700	1.3	3.4
093 CR CH (DISC)..	4	114	143*	0.3	0.7
097 CR C AND C CR.	1	32	40*	0.1	0.2
127 CH GOD (CLEVE)	7	594	747*	1.4	3.7
165 CH OF NAZARENE	1	141	206	0.4	1.0
193 EPISCOPAL.....	1	282	599	1.1	2.9
283 LUTH--MO SYNOD	1	166	247	0.4	1.2
335 ORTH PRESB CH.	1	117	163	0.3	0.8
357 PRESB CH US...	3	625	786*	1.4	3.9
403 SALVATION ARMY	1	70	266	0.5	1.3
413 S-D ADVENTISTS	2	129	162*	0.3	0.8
419 SO BAPT CONV..	21	8,525	10,716*	19.4	52.7
435 UNITARIAN-UNIV	1	17	29	0.1	0.1
449 UN METHODIST..	14	5,119	5,529	10.0	27.2
LUMPKIN	11	1,656	2,211*	25.3	100.0

County and Denomination	Number of churches	Communicant, confirmed, full members	Total adherents Number	Percent of total population	Percent of total adherents
081 CATHOLIC......	1	0	260	3.0	11.8
127 CH GOD (CLEVE)	1	122	147*	1.7	6.6
357 PRESB CH US...	1	57	69*	0.8	3.1
419 SO BAPT CONV..	4	1,071	1,288*	14.8	58.3
449 UN METHODIST..	4	406	447	5.1	20.2
MC DUFFIE	21	5,178	6,559*	42.9	100.0
081 CATHOLIC......	1	0	220	1.4	3.4
127 CH GOD (CLEVE)	2	101	129*	0.8	2.0
193 EPISCOPAL.....	1	43	80	0.5	1.2
357 PRESB CH US...	1	135	172*	1.1	2.6
419 SO BAPT CONV..	11	3,480	4,442*	29.1	67.7
449 UN METHODIST..	5	1,419	1,516	9.9	23.1
MC INTOSH	15	1,549	2,062*	28.0	100.0
081 CATHOLIC......	1	0	25	0.3	1.2
127 CH GOD (CLEVE)	2	172	224*	3.0	10.9
193 EPISCOPAL.....	2	113	226	3.1	11.0
357 PRESB CH US...	2	167	217*	2.9	10.5
419 SO BAPT CONV..	6	894	1,164*	15.8	56.5
449 UN METHODIST..	2	203	206	2.8	10.0
MACON	21	3,389	4,077*	31.5	100.0
081 CATHOLIC......	1	0	20	0.2	0.5
193 EPISCOPAL.....	1	36	39	0.3	1.0
281 LUTH CH AMER..	1	142	181	1.4	4.4
413 S-D ADVENTISTS	1	30	38*	0.3	0.9
419 SO BAPT CONV..	10	2,179	2,778*	21.5	68.1
449 UN METHODIST..	7	1,002	1,021	7.9	25.0
MADISON	34	6,368	7,729*	57.2	100.0
093 CR CH (DISC)..	1	60	75*	0.6	1.0
097 CR C AND C CR.	1	75	93*	0.7	1.2
349 PENT HOLINESS.	1	14	17*	0.1	0.2
357 PRESB CH US...	3	184	229*	1.7	3.0
419 SO BAPT CONV..	21	4,904	6,108*	45.2	79.0
449 UN METHODIST..	7	1,131	1,207	8.9	15.6
MARION	17	1,580	1,839*	36.1	100.0
127 CH GOD (CLEVE)	2	104	131*	2.6	7.1
419 SO BAPT CONV..	9	844	1,067*	20.9	58.0
449 UN METHODIST..	6	632	641	12.6	34.9
MERIWETHER	50	7,078	8,784*	45.1	100.0
081 CATHOLIC......	2	0	73	0.4	0.8
127 CH GOD (CLEVE)	3	130	163*	0.8	1.9
165 CH OF NAZARENE	2	124	334	1.7	3.8
357 PRESB CH US...	2	120	150*	0.8	1.7
419 SO BAPT CONV..	23	4,768	5,965*	30.7	67.9
443 UN C OF CHRIST	1	132	165*	0.8	1.9
449 UN METHODIST..	17	1,804	1,934	9.9	22.0
MILLER	14	1,770	2,092*	32.7	100.0
127 CH GOD (CLEVE)	5	124	154*	2.4	7.4
285 MENNONITE CH..	1	18	22*	0.3	1.1
419 SO BAPT CONV..	5	995	1,236*	19.3	59.1
449 UN METHODIST..	3	633	680	10.6	32.5
MITCHELL	32	6,697	8,398*	44.3	100.0
127 CH GOD (CLEVE)	2	59	76*	0.4	0.9
193 EPISCOPAL.....	1	26	37	0.2	0.4
357 PRESB CH US...	2	86	110*	0.6	1.3
419 SO BAPT CONV..	19	5,818	7,467*	39.4	88.9
449 UN METHODIST..	8	708	708	3.7	8.4
MONROE	27	3,382	4,049*	36.8	100.0
081 CATHOLIC......	1	0	40	0.4	1.0
357 PRESB CH US...	1	70	86*	0.8	2.1
419 SO BAPT CONV..	16	2,469	3,047*	27.7	75.3
449 UN METHODIST..	9	843	876	8.0	21.6
MONTGOMERY	21	2,388	2,833*	46.5	100.0
127 CH GOD (CLEVE)	2	64	79*	1.3	2.8
357 PRESB CH US...	2	86	106*	1.7	3.7
419 SO BAPT CONV..	10	1,713	2,104*	34.5	74.3
449 UN METHODIST..	7	525	544	8.9	19.2
MORGAN	25	3,552	4,335*	43.8	100.0
081 CATHOLIC......	1	0	75	0.8	1.7
097 CR C AND C CR.	1	21	27*	0.3	0.6
127 CH GOD (CLEVE)	1	50	63*	0.6	1.5
193 EPISCOPAL.....	1	47	47	0.5	1.1
357 PRESB CH US...	1	66	84*	0.8	1.9
413 S-D ADVENTISTS	2	81	103*	1.0	2.4
419 SO BAPT CONV..	9	2,196	2,784*	28.1	64.2
449 UN METHODIST..	9	1,091	1,152	11.6	26.6
MURRAY	26	4,802	5,929*	45.7	100.0
081 CATHOLIC......	0	0	50	0.4	0.8
127 CH GOD (CLEVE)	3	111	139*	1.1	2.3
185 CUMBER PRESB..	1	169	212*	1.6	3.6
419 SO BAPT CONV..	14	3,826	4,801*	37.0	81.0
449 UN METHODIST..	8	696	727	5.6	12.3

*Total adherents estimated from known number of communicant, confirmed, full members.

—Represents a percent less than 0.1.

Percentages may not total due to rounding.

Table 3. Churches and Church Membership by State, County and Denomination: 1971

County and Denomination	Number of churches	Communicant, confirmed, full members	Total adherents: Number	Total adherents: Percent of total population	Total adherents: Percent of total adherents
MUSCOGEE	103	48,846	63,755*	38.1	100.0
019 AMER BAPT CONV	1	481	602*	0.4	0.9
081 CATHOLIC......	1	0	3,658	2.2	5.7
093 CR CH (DISC)..	1	235	294*	0.2	0.5
097 CR C AND C CR.	2	196	245*	0.1	0.4
123 CH GOD (ANDER)	1	102	214	0.1	0.3
127 CH GOD (CLEVE)	5	600	751*	0.4	1.2
165 CH OF NAZARENE	4	356	534	0.3	0.8
193 EPISCOPAL.....	3	1,244	1,490	0.9	2.3
281 LUTH CH AMER..	2	316	464	0.3	0.7
283 LUTH--MO SYNOD	3	493	733	0.4	1.1
357 PRESB CH US...	7	2,444	3,060*	1.8	4.8
403 SALVATION ARMY	1	97	428	0.3	0.7
413 S-D ADVENTISTS	2	413	517*	0.3	0.8
419 SO BAPT CONV..	44	29,623	37,087*	22.2	58.2
443 UN C OF CHRIST	2	93	116*	0.1	0.2
449 UN METHODIST..	23	12,111	13,509	8.1	21.2
453 UN PRES CH USA	1	42	53*	-	0.1
NEWTON	45	9,529	11,696*	44.5	100.0
055 AS REF PRES CH	1	108	137*	0.5	1.2
081 CATHOLIC......	1	0	268	1.0	2.3
097 CR C AND C CR.	1	80	102*	0.4	0.9
127 CH GOD (CLEVE)	1	63	80*	0.3	0.7
165 CH OF NAZARENE	1	26	53	0.2	0.5
193 EPISCOPAL.....	1	109	150	0.6	1.3
357 PRESB CH US...	6	639	811*	3.1	6.9
413 S-D ADVENTISTS	1	29	37*	0.1	0.3
419 SO BAPT CONV..	15	5,144	6,528*	24.8	55.8
449 UN METHODIST..	17	3,331	3,530	13.4	30.2
OCONEE	24	3,426	4,062*	51.3	100.0
093 CR CH (DISC)..	6	469	578*	7.3	14.2
349 PENT HOLINESS.	1	17	21*	0.3	0.5
357 PRESB CH US...	1	193	238*	3.0	5.9
419 SO BAPT CONV..	8	1,906	2,349*	29.7	57.8
449 UN METHODIST..	8	841	876	11.1	21.6
OGLETHORPE	28	2,814	3,315*	43.6	100.0
093 CR CH (DISC)..	1	55	69*	0.9	2.1
357 PRESB CH US...	2	24	30*	0.4	0.9
419 SO BAPT CONV..	15	1,938	2,419*	31.8	73.0
449 UN METHODIST..	10	797	797	10.5	24.0
PAULDING	33	7,144	8,776*	50.1	100.0
097 CR C AND C CR.	1	400	501*	2.9	5.7
127 CH GOD (CLEVE)	1	46	58*	0.3	0.7
419 SO BAPT CONV..	21	5,775	7,236*	41.3	82.5
449 UN METHODIST..	10	923	981	5.6	11.2
PEACH	15	3,730	4,483*	28.0	100.0
081 CATHOLIC......	1	0	40	0.3	0.9
127 CH GOD (CLEVE)	1	41	51*	0.3	1.1
165 CH OF NAZARENE	1	129	227	1.4	5.1
193 EPISCOPAL.....	2	217	245	1.5	5.5
357 PRESB CH US...	1	178	222*	1.4	5.0
413 S-D ADVENTISTS	1	43	54*	0.3	1.2
419 SO BAPT CONV..	4	1,768	2,208*	13.8	49.3
449 UN METHODIST..	4	1,354	1,436	9.0	32.0
PICKENS	12	2,868	3,499*	36.4	100.0
093 CR CH (DISC)..	1	113	139*	1.4	4.0
127 CH GOD (CLEVE)	1	129	159*	1.7	4.5
419 SO BAPT CONV..	7	2,250	2,777*	28.9	79.4
449 UN METHODIST..	3	376	424	4.4	12.1
PIERCE	24	4,567	5,558*	59.9	100.0
127 CH GOD (CLEVE)	2	210	260*	2.8	4.7
357 PRESB CH US...	1	149	185*	2.0	3.3
419 SO BAPT CONV..	15	3,589	4,447*	47.9	80.0
449 UN METHODIST..	6	619	666	7.2	12.0
PIKE	28	3,398	4,099*	56.0	100.0
093 CR CH (DISC)..	2	47	59*	0.8	1.4
127 CH GOD (CLEVE)	1	34	43*	0.6	1.0
349 PENT HOLINESS.	1	29	36*	0.5	0.9
357 PRESB CH US...	1	34	43*	0.6	1.0
419 SO BAPT CONV..	14	2,486	3,111*	42.5	75.9
449 UN METHODIST..	9	768	807	11.0	19.7
POLK	49	13,988	17,157*	57.9	100.0
081 CATHOLIC......	1	0	143	0.5	0.8
127 CH GOD (CLEVE)	4	413	511*	1.7	3.0
193 EPISCOPAL.....	1	92	121	0.4	0.7
357 PRESB CH US...	2	402	497*	1.7	2.9
413 S-D ADVENTISTS	1	61	75*	0.3	0.4
419 SO BAPT CONV..	33	11,369	14,055*	47.4	81.9
449 UN METHODIST..	7	1,651	1,755	5.9	10.2
PULASKI	16	4,216	5,052*	62.6	100.0
127 CH GOD (CLEVE)	1	18	22*	0.3	0.4
193 EPISCOPAL.....	1	57	80	1.0	1.6
349 PENT HOLINESS.	1	40	49*	0.6	1.0
419 SO BAPT CONV..	12	3,584	4,384*	54.4	86.8
449 UN METHODIST..	1	517	517	6.4	10.2
PUTNAM	19	2,562	3,053*	36.4	100.0
123 CH GOD (ANDER)	1	45	95	1.1	3.1
127 CH GOD (CLEVE)	2	59	75*	0.9	2.5
349 PENT HOLINESS.	1	30	38*	0.5	1.2
357 PRESB CH US...	1	49	62*	0.7	2.0
419 SO BAPT CONV..	4	1,266	1,599*	19.0	52.4
449 UN METHODIST..	10	1,113	1,184	14.1	38.8
QUITMAN	4	332	391*	17.9	100.0
081 CATHOLIC......	0	0	10	0.5	2.6
419 SO BAPT CONV..	2	162	201*	9.2	51.4
449 UN METHODIST..	2	170	180	8.3	46.0
RABUN	42	4,440	5,240*	62.9	100.0
081 CATHOLIC......	1	0	26	0.3	0.5
127 CH GOD (CLEVE)	4	227	271*	3.3	5.2
193 EPISCOPAL.....	1	34	34	0.4	0.6
357 PRESB CH US...	6	187	223*	2.7	4.3
419 SO BAPT CONV..	24	3,403	4,061*	48.8	77.5
449 UN METHODIST..	6	589	625	7.5	11.9
RANDOLPH	24	3,171	3,714*	42.5	100.0
357 PRESB CH US...	1	102	124*	1.4	3.3
419 SO BAPT CONV..	14	2,340	2,841*	32.5	76.5
449 UN METHODIST..	9	729	749	8.6	20.2
RICHMOND	109	51,129	68,893*	42.4	100.0
055 AS REF PRES CH	1	153	186*	0.1	0.3
081 CATHOLIC......	4	0	6,000	3.7	8.7
093 CR CH (DISC)..	3	757	919*	0.6	1.3
097 CR C AND C CR.	2	135	164*	0.1	0.2
123 CH GOD (ANDER)	1	25	62	-	0.1
127 CH GOD (CLEVE)	6	784	952*	0.6	1.4
165 CH OF NAZARENE	1	145	341	0.2	0.5
193 EPISCOPAL.....	8	2,563	3,793	2.3	5.5
226 FRIENDS-USA...	1	42	51*	-	0.1
281 LUTH CH AMER..	3	1,363	1,900	1.2	2.8
283 LUTH--MO SYNOD	1	335	450	0.3	0.7
285 MENNONITE CH..	1	46	56*	-	0.1
349 PENT HOLINESS.	4	245	297*	0.2	0.4
353 PLY BRETHREN..	2	260	363	0.2	0.5
357 PRESB CH US...	8	3,310	4,019*	2.5	5.8
403 SALVATION ARMY	1	146	666	0.4	1.0
413 S-D ADVENTISTS	2	345	419*	0.3	0.6
419 SO BAPT CONV..	36	29,814	36,199*	22.3	52.5
435 UNITARIAN-UNIV	1	128	168	0.1	0.2
449 UN METHODIST..	21	10,142	11,413	7.0	16.6
453 UN PRES CH USA	2	391	475*	0.3	0.7
ROCKDALE	18	4,724	6,116*	33.7	100.0
081 CATHOLIC......	2	0	328	1.8	5.4
097 CR C AND C CR.	3	380	489*	2.7	8.0
127 CH GOD (CLEVE)	1	23	30*	0.2	0.5
357 PRESB CH US...	2	603	775*	4.3	12.7
419 SO BAPT CONV..	5	2,411	3,100*	17.1	50.7
449 UN METHODIST..	5	1,307	1,394	7.7	22.8
SCHLEY	7	1,038	1,199*	38.7	100.0
419 SO BAPT CONV..	2	462	590*	19.1	49.2
449 UN METHODIST..	5	576	609	19.7	50.8
SCREVEN	47	6,530	7,840*	62.3	100.0
081 CATHOLIC......	1	0	132	1.0	1.7
093 CR CH (DISC)..	2	74	91*	0.7	1.2
097 CR C AND C CR.	2	148	182*	1.4	2.3
123 CH GOD (ANDER)	2	51	107	0.8	1.4
127 CH GOD (CLEVE)	1	31	38*	0.3	0.5
357 PRESB CH US...	1	65	80*	0.6	1.0
419 SO BAPT CONV..	22	3,889	4,772*	37.9	60.9
449 UN METHODIST..	16	2,272	2,438	19.4	31.1
SEMINOLE	13	2,115	2,620*	37.1	100.0
127 CH GOD (CLEVE)	3	200	251*	3.6	9.6
165 CH OF NAZARENE	1	49	90	1.3	3.4
357 PRESB CH US...	1	191	240*	3.4	9.2
419 SO BAPT CONV..	4	1,150	1,445*	20.5	55.2
449 UN METHODIST..	4	525	594	8.4	22.7
SPALDING	51	15,785	20,484*	51.8	100.0
081 CATHOLIC......	1	0	1,154	2.9	5.6
093 CR CH (DISC)..	3	372	462*	1.2	2.3
097 CR C AND C CR.	1	125	155*	0.4	0.8
127 CH GOD (CLEVE)	2	593	736*	1.9	3.6
165 CH OF NAZARENE	1	46	93	0.2	0.5
193 EPISCOPAL.....	2	432	482	1.2	2.4
349 PENT HOLINESS.	1	29	36*	0.1	0.2
357 PRESB CH US...	1	382	474*	1.2	2.3
403 SALVATION ARMY	1	52	279	0.7	1.4
413 S-D ADVENTISTS	1	42	52*	0.1	0.3
419 SO BAPT CONV..	26	10,551	13,096*	33.1	63.9
449 UN METHODIST..	11	3,161	3,465	8.8	16.9
STEPHENS	35	9,085	11,385*	56.0	100.0

*Total adherents estimated from known number of communicant, confirmed, full members.

—Represents a percent less than 0.1.

Percentages may not total due to rounding.

Table 3. Churches and Church Membership by State, County and Denomination: 1971

County and Denomination	Number of churches	Communicant, confirmed, full members	Total adherents: Number	Total adherents: Percent of total population	Total adherents: Percent of total adherents
081 CATHOLIC......	1	0	160	0.8	1.4
123 CH GOD (ANDER)	1	54	122	0.6	1.1
127 CH GOD (CLEVE)	2	238	288*	1.4	2.5
165 CH OF NAZARENE	1	20	64	0.3	0.6
193 EPISCOPAL.....	1	101	138	0.7	1.2
283 LUTH--MO SYNOD	1	10	15	0.1	0.1
349 PENT HOLINESS.	1	95	115*	0.6	1.0
357 PRESB CH US...	1	315	382*	1.9	3.4
403 SALVATION ARMY	1	43	213	1.0	1.9
419 SO BAPT CONV..	22	7,880	9,550*	47.0	83.9
449 UN METHODIST..	3	329	338	1.7	3.0
STEWART	17	1,488	1,811*	27.8	100.0
419 SO BAPT CONV..	9	971	1,254*	19.3	69.2
443 UN C OF CHRIST	1	16	21*	0.3	1.2
449 UN METHODIST..	7	501	536	8.2	29.6
SUMTER	37	8,907	11,075*	41.1	100.0
081 CATHOLIC......	1	0	388	1.4	3.5
093 CR CH (DISC)..	1	49	61*	0.2	0.6
165 CH OF NAZARENE	1	12	21	0.1	0.2
193 EPISCOPAL.....	1	177	373	1.4	3.4
281 LUTH CH AMER..	1	68	81	0.3	0.7
357 PRESB CH US...	2	294	369*	1.4	3.3
413 S-D ADVENTISTS	1	39	49*	0.2	0.4
419 SO BAPT CONV..	18	5,377	6,743*	25.0	60.9
449 UN METHODIST..	11	2,891	2,990	11.1	27.0
TALBOT	19	1,491	1,710*	25.8	100.0
357 PRESB CH US...	1	14	17*	0.3	1.0
419 SO BAPT CONV..	6	714	891*	13.4	52.1
449 UN METHODIST..	12	763	802	12.1	46.9
TALIAFERRO	13	978	1,173*	48.4	100.0
081 CATHOLIC......	1	0	25	1.0	2.1
357 PRESB CH US...	2	61	74*	3.1	6.3
419 SO BAPT CONV..	6	720	873*	36.0	74.4
449 UN METHODIST..	4	197	201	8.3	17.1
TATTNALL	32	4,789	5,647*	34.1	100.0
081 CATHOLIC......	1	0	30	0.2	0.5
093 CR CH (DISC)..	1	184	220*	1.3	3.9
123 CH GOD (ANDER)	2	39	111	0.7	2.0
127 CH GOD (CLEVE)	2	90	107*	0.6	1.9
349 PENT HOLINESS.	1	33	39*	0.2	0.7
419 SO BAPT CONV..	15	3,093	3,690*	22.3	65.3
449 UN METHODIST..	10	1,350	1,450	8.8	25.7
TAYLOR	19	2,230	2,638*	33.5	100.0
127 CH GOD (CLEVE)	1	66	83*	1.1	3.1
165 CH OF NAZARENE	1	26	29	0.4	1.1
419 SO BAPT CONV..	9	1,324	1,662*	21.1	63.0
449 UN METHODIST..	8	814	864	11.0	32.8
TELFAIR	39	4,777	5,695*	50.0	100.0
081 CATHOLIC......	1	0	60	0.5	1.1
127 CH GOD (CLEVE)	6	289	360*	3.2	6.3
357 PRESB CH US...	1	98	122*	1.1	2.1
419 SO BAPT CONV..	16	2,682	3,344*	29.4	58.7
449 UN METHODIST..	15	1,708	1,809	15.9	31.8
TERRELL	22	3,506	4,252*	37.2	100.0
127 CH GOD (CLEVE)	1	36	46*	0.4	1.1
193 EPISCOPAL.....	1	73	95	0.8	2.2
357 PRESB CH US...	1	124	159*	1.4	3.7
419 SO BAPT CONV..	11	2,089	2,686*	23.5	63.2
449 UN METHODIST..	8	1,184	1,266	11.1	29.8
THOMAS	63	13,739	17,797*	51.6	100.0
081 CATHOLIC......	1	0	740	2.1	4.2
093 CR CH (DISC)..	2	40	50*	0.1	0.3
097 CR C AND C CR.	2	180	225*	0.7	1.3
127 CH GOD (CLEVE)	6	334	418*	1.2	2.3
165 CH OF NAZARENE	1	129	181	0.5	1.0
193 EPISCOPAL.....	2	347	683	2.0	3.8
283 LUTH--MO SYNOD	1	18	26	0.1	0.1
349 PENT HOLINESS.	1	51	64*	0.2	0.4
357 PRESB CH US...	6	883	1,105*	3.2	6.2
403 SALVATION ARMY	1	39	202	0.6	1.1
413 S-D ADVENTISTS	2	127	159*	0.5	0.9
419 SO BAPT CONV..	23	8,664	10,841*	31.4	60.9
443 UN C OF CHRIST	1	49	61*	0.2	0.3
449 UN METHODIST..	14	2,878	3,042	8.8	17.1
TIFT	38	10,569	13,078*	47.9	100.0
081 CATHOLIC......	1	0	100	0.4	0.8
127 CH GOD (CLEVE)	4	492	619*	2.3	4.7
165 CH OF NAZARENE	1	124	230	0.8	1.8
193 EPISCOPAL.....	1	96	131	0.5	1.0
283 LUTH--MO SYNOD	1	69	114	0.4	0.9
357 PRESB CH US...	1	219	276*	1.0	2.1
413 S-D ADVENTISTS	1	31	39*	0.1	0.3
419 SO BAPT CONV..	16	7,185	9,044*	33.1	69.2
449 UN METHODIST..	12	2,353	2,525	9.3	19.3

County and Denomination	Number of churches	Communicant, confirmed, full members	Total adherents: Number	Total adherents: Percent of total population	Total adherents: Percent of total adherents
TOOMBS	41	8,422	10,380*	54.2	100.0
081 CATHOLIC......	1	0	135	0.7	1.3
093 CR CH (DISC)..	1	45	57*	0.3	0.5
127 CH GOD (CLEVE)	5	309	389*	2.0	3.7
165 CH OF NAZARENE	1	68	158	0.8	1.5
193 EPISCOPAL.....	1	55	97	0.5	0.9
357 PRESB CH US...	2	343	432*	2.3	4.2
419 SO BAPT CONV..	19	5,425	6,835*	35.7	65.8
449 UN METHODIST..	11	2,177	2,277	11.9	21.9
TOWNS	19	3,273	3,863*	84.6	100.0
127 CH GOD (CLEVE)	2	54	64*	1.4	1.7
419 SO BAPT CONV..	14	2,906	3,465*	75.9	89.7
449 UN METHODIST..	3	313	334	7.3	8.6
TREUTLEN	9	1,355	1,612*	28.5	100.0
165 CH OF NAZARENE	1	8	15	0.3	0.9
419 SO BAPT CONV..	5	980	1,204*	21.3	74.7
449 UN METHODIST..	3	367	393	7.0	24.4
TROUP	82	19,669	23,921*	53.8	100.0
081 CATHOLIC......	1	0	304	0.7	1.3
097 CR C AND C CR.	1	80	97*	0.2	0.4
123 CH GOD (ANDER)	1	92	222	0.5	0.9
127 CH GOD (CLEVE)	6	433	527*	1.2	2.2
165 CH OF NAZARENE	1	12	30	0.1	0.1
193 EPISCOPAL.....	2	463	625	1.4	2.6
349 PENT HOLINESS.	1	46	56*	0.1	0.2
357 PRESB CH US...	7	1,125	1,370*	3.1	5.7
413 S-D ADVENTISTS	1	54	66*	0.1	0.3
419 SO BAPT CONV..	37	12,219	14,880*	33.5	62.2
443 UN C OF CHRIST	2	312	380*	0.9	1.6
449 UN METHODIST..	22	4,833	5,364	12.1	22.4
TURNER	20	4,190	5,096*	58.0	100.0
419 SO BAPT CONV..	14	3,411	4,288*	48.8	84.1
449 UN METHODIST..	6	779	808	9.2	15.9
TWIGGS	16	2,609	3,192*	38.8	100.0
419 SO BAPT CONV..	9	1,956	2,523*	30.7	79.0
449 UN METHODIST..	7	653	669	8.1	21.0
UNION	35	4,580	5,498*	80.7	100.0
081 CATHOLIC......	1	0	30	0.4	0.5
127 CH GOD (CLEVE)	1	82	98*	1.4	1.8
165 CH OF NAZARENE	1	33	110	1.6	2.0
419 SO BAPT CONV..	23	3,822	4,576*	67.2	83.2
449 UN METHODIST..	9	643	684	10.0	12.4
UPSON	41	9,979	12,015*	51.1	100.0
081 CATHOLIC......	1	0	90	0.4	0.7
127 CH GOD (CLEVE)	1	300	365*	1.6	3.0
165 CH OF NAZARENE	4	117	225	1.0	1.9
349 PENT HOLINESS.	1	19	23*	0.1	0.2
357 PRESB CH US...	1	293	357*	1.5	3.0
413 S-D ADVENTISTS	1	53	65*	0.3	0.5
419 SO BAPT CONV..	25	7,264	8,849*	37.6	73.6
449 UN METHODIST..	7	1,933	2,041	8.7	17.0
WALKER	97	18,455	22,653*	44.7	100.0
123 CH GOD (ANDER)	4	151	358	0.7	1.6
127 CH GOD (CLEVE)	11	1,071	1,318*	2.6	5.8
165 CH OF NAZARENE	5	373	695	1.4	3.1
281 LUTH CH AMER..	1	75	93	0.2	0.4
357 PRESB CH US...	4	394	485*	1.0	2.1
413 S-D ADVENTISTS	1	96	118*	0.2	0.5
419 SO BAPT CONV..	54	13,256	16,318*	32.2	72.0
449 UN METHODIST..	17	3,039	3,268	6.4	14.4
WALTON	40	8,152	10,311*	44.1	100.0
081 CATHOLIC......	1	0	400	1.7	3.9
093 CR CH (DISC)..	4	604	766*	3.3	7.4
097 CR C AND C CR.	1	470	596*	2.5	5.8
127 CH GOD (CLEVE)	2	176	223*	1.0	2.2
193 EPISCOPAL.....	1	56	93	0.4	0.9
349 PENT HOLINESS.	1	70	89*	0.4	0.9
357 PRESB CH US...	1	118	150*	0.6	1.5
419 SO BAPT CONV..	17	4,408	5,591*	23.9	54.2
449 UN METHODIST..	12	2,250	2,403	10.3	23.3
WARE	46	13,029	16,064*	47.9	100.0
081 CATHOLIC......	1	0	240	0.7	1.5
093 CR CH (DISC)..	1	365	450*	1.3	2.8
127 CH GOD (CLEVE)	5	395	487*	1.5	3.0
165 CH OF NAZARENE	1	98	173	0.5	1.1
193 EPISCOPAL.....	1	278	389	1.2	2.4
349 PENT HOLINESS.	3	257	317*	0.9	2.0
357 PRESB CH US...	1	346	426*	1.3	2.7
403 SALVATION ARMY	1	74	250	0.7	1.6
413 S-D ADVENTISTS	1	63	78*	0.2	0.5
419 SO BAPT CONV..	19	7,713	9,507*	28.4	59.2
449 UN METHODIST..	12	3,440	3,747	11.2	23.3
WARREN	15	1,863	2,204*	33.0	100.0

*Total adherents estimated from known number of communicant, confirmed, full members.

—Represents a percent less than 0.1.

Percentages may not total due to rounding.

Table 3. Churches and Church Membership by State, County and Denomination: 1971

County and Denomination	Number of churches	Communicant, confirmed, full members	Total adherents		
			Number	Percent of total population	Percent of total adherents
419 SO BAPT CONV..	8	1,143	1,447*	21.7	65.7
449 UN METHODIST..	7	720	757	11.4	34.3
WASHINGTON	50	6,741	8,282*	47.4	100.0
081 CATHOLIC......	1	0	45	0.3	0.5
093 CR CH (DISC)..	4	204	256*	1.5	3.1
097 CR C AND C CR.	3	50	63*	0.4	0.8
123 CH GOD (ANDER)	1	15	62	0.4	0.7
127 CH GOD (CLEVE)	4	136	170*	1.0	2.1
165 CH OF NAZARENE	1	200	372	2.1	4.5
193 EPISCOPAL.....	1	52	70	0.4	0.8
357 PRESB CH US...	1	18	23*	0.1	0.3
419 SO BAPT CONV..	23	4,289	5,375*	30.7	64.9
449 UN METHODIST..	11	1,777	1,846	10.6	22.3
WAYNE	40	7,200	9,191*	51.5	100.0
081 CATHOLIC......	1	0	235	1.3	2.6
123 CH GOD (ANDER)	1	50	80	0.4	0.9
127 CH GOD (CLEVE)	7	863	1,086*	6.1	11.8
193 EPISCOPAL.....	1	220	362	2.0	3.9
357 PRESB CH US...	2	85	107*	0.6	1.2
419 SO BAPT CONV..	21	4,801	6,039*	33.8	65.7
449 UN METHODIST..	7	1,181	1,282	7.2	13.9
WEBSTER	9	1,100	1,332*	56.4	100.0
357 PRESB CH US...	1	19	24*	1.0	1.8
419 SO BAPT CONV..	5	826	1,043*	44.2	78.3
449 UN METHODIST..	3	255	265	11.2	19.9
WHEELER	18	2,091	2,482*	54.0	100.0
123 CH GOD (ANDER)	2	40	110	2.4	4.4
127 CH GOD (CLEVE)	2	80	98*	2.1	3.9
419 SO BAPT CONV..	7	1,211	1,479*	32.2	59.6
449 UN METHODIST..	7	760	795	17.3	32.0
WHITE	23	3,140	3,770*	48.7	100.0
081 CATHOLIC......	1	0	70	0.9	1.9
357 PRESB CH US...	2	112	136*	1.8	3.6
413 S-D ADVENTISTS	1	81	98*	1.3	2.6
419 SO BAPT CONV..	12	2,291	2,781*	35.9	73.8
449 UN METHODIST..	7	656	685	8.8	18.2
WHITFIELD	73	19,464	24,980*	45.3	100.0
081 CATHOLIC......	1	0	550	1.0	2.2
097 CR C AND C CR.	1	16	20*	-	0.1
127 CH GOD (CLEVE)	5	727	918*	1.7	3.7
165 CH OF NAZARENE	2	130	248	0.5	1.0
193 EPISCOPAL.....	1	246	539	1.0	2.2
357 PRESB CH US...	3	784	989*	1.8	4.0
403 SALVATION ARMY	1	38	234	0.4	0.9
419 SO BAPT CONV..	41	13,813	17,433*	31.6	69.8
449 UN METHODIST..	17	3,683	4,015	7.3	16.1
453 UN PRES CH USA	1	27	34*	0.1	0.1
WILCOX	33	4,211	4,988*	71.3	100.0
127 CH GOD (CLEVE)	5	179	216*	3.1	4.3
419 SO BAPT CONV..	21	3,387	4,096*	58.5	82.1
449 UN METHODIST..	7	645	676	9.7	13.6
WILKES	29	4,393	5,547*	54.5	100.0
081 CATHOLIC......	1	0	286	2.8	5.2
127 CH GOD (CLEVE)	1	6	7*	0.1	0.1
193 EPISCOPAL.....	1	75	104	1.0	1.9
353 PLY BRETHREN..	1	100	200	2.0	3.6
357 PRESB CH US...	2	186	226*	2.2	4.1
419 SO BAPT CONV..	15	3,047	3,706*	36.4	66.8
449 UN METHODIST..	8	979	1,018	10.0	18.4
WILKINSON	22	2,806	3,488*	37.1	100.0
081 CATHOLIC......	1	0	30	0.3	0.9
419 SO BAPT CONV..	14	2,209	2,793*	29.7	80.1
449 UN METHODIST..	7	597	665	7.1	19.1
WORTH	37	5,775	7,082*	47.9	100.0
127 CH GOD (CLEVE)	1	6	8*	0.1	0.1
349 PENT HOLINESS.	1	21	27*	0.2	0.4
357 PRESB CH US...	1	58	73*	0.5	1.0
419 SO BAPT CONV..	27	4,684	5,923*	40.1	83.6
449 UN METHODIST..	7	1,006	1,051	7.1	14.8
CO DATA NOT AVAIL	160	12,791	29,889*	N/A	N/A
151 L-D SAINTS....	0	0	13,956	N/A	N/A
223 FREE WILL BAPT	130	11,925	14,806*	N/A	N/A
467 WESLEYAN......	30	866	1,127	N/A	N/A

HAWAII

County and Denomination	Number of churches	Communicant, confirmed, full members	Total adherents		
			Number	Percent of total population	Percent of total adherents
THE STATE.....	353	51,912	291,471*	37.9	100.0
HAWAII	55	4,506	29,359*	46.3	100.0
081 CATHOLIC......	15	0	22,376	35.3	76.2
127 CH GOD (CLEVE)	1	9	11*	-	-
165 CH OF NAZARENE	1	36	118	0.2	0.4
193 EPISCOPAL.....	7	566	1,198	1.9	4.1
283 LUTH--MO SYNOD	2	112	165	0.3	0.6
403 SALVATION ARMY	3	132	890	1.4	3.0
413 S-D ADVENTISTS	4	340	417*	0.7	1.4
419 SO BAPT CONV..	2	435	534*	0.8	1.8
443 UN C OF CHRIST	13	1,328	1,630*	2.6	5.6
449 UN METHODIST..	4	399	610	1.0	2.1
453 UN PRES CH USA	3	1,149	1,410*	2.2	4.8
HONOLULU	206	41,523	206,300*	32.8	100.0
019 AMER BAPT CONV	4	526	656*	0.1	0.3
029 AMER LUTH CH..	5	752	1,016	0.2	0.5
081 CATHOLIC......	32	0	150,701	24.0	73.0
093 CR CH (DISC)..	5	802	1,000*	0.2	0.5
097 CR C AND C CR.	9	541	674*	0.1	0.3
105 CHRISTIAN REF.	1	79	137	-	0.1
123 CH GOD (ANDER)	2	101	213	-	0.1
127 CH GOD (CLEVE)	6	221	275*	-	0.1
165 CH OF NAZARENE	8	587	1,357	0.2	0.7
175 CONG CR CH....	3	150	187*	-	0.1
193 EPISCOPAL.....	23	6,243	9,476	1.5	4.6
226 FRIENDS-USA...	1	80	100*	-	-
281 LUTH CH AMER..	4	518	771	0.1	0.4
283 LUTH--MO SYNOD	6	1,255	1,995	0.3	1.0
353 PLY BRETHREN..	2	150	416	0.1	0.2
403 SALVATION ARMY	3	287	951	0.2	0.5
413 S-D ADVENTISTS	11	2,280	2,842*	0.5	1.4
419 SO BAPT CONV..	25	8,419	10,494*	1.7	5.1
435 UNITARIAN-UNIV	2	243	319	0.1	0.2
443 UN C OF CHRIST	33	12,322	15,359*	2.4	7.4
449 UN METHODIST..	20	5,935	7,306	1.2	3.5
469 WISC EVAN LUTH	1	32	55	-	-
KAUAI	36	2,460	11,231*	37.7	100.0
081 CATHOLIC......	5	0	7,125	23.9	63.4
127 CH GOD (CLEVE)	1	17	21*	0.1	0.2
165 CH OF NAZARENE	1	52	108	0.4	1.0
175 CONG CR CH....	2	121	150*	0.5	1.3
193 EPISCOPAL.....	6	268	652	2.2	5.8
281 LUTH CH AMER..	1	82	117	0.4	1.0
403 SALVATION ARMY	2	141	769	2.6	6.8
413 S-D ADVENTISTS	2	129	160*	0.5	1.4
419 SO BAPT CONV..	2	288	357*	1.2	3.2
443 UN C OF CHRIST	11	1,130	1,401*	4.7	12.5
449 UN METHODIST..	3	232	371	1.2	3.3
MAUI	55	3,301	19,215*	41.6	100.0
081 CATHOLIC......	14	0	14,844	32.2	77.3
127 CH GOD (CLEVE)	2	81	100*	0.2	0.5
165 CH OF NAZARENE	1	41	45	0.1	0.2
193 EPISCOPAL.....	4	611	831	1.8	4.3
283 LUTH--MO SYNOD	1	58	110	0.2	0.6
403 SALVATION ARMY	1	48	248	0.5	1.3
413 S-D ADVENTISTS	3	226	279*	0.6	1.5
419 SO BAPT CONV..	4	310	382*	0.8	2.0
443 UN C OF CHRIST	22	1,660	2,048*	4.4	10.7
449 UN METHODIST..	3	266	328	0.7	1.7
CO DATA NOT AVAIL	1	122	25,366*	N/A	N/A
151 L-D SAINTS....	0	0	25,214	N/A	N/A
223 FREE WILL BAPT	1	122	152*	N/A	N/A

IDAHO

County and Denomination	Number of churches	Communicant, confirmed, full members	Number	Percent of total population	Percent of total adherents
IDAHO	629	93,538	381,760*	53.6	100.0
ADA	68	17,973	37,756*	33.6	100.0
019 AMER BAPT CONV	4	1,625	1,993*	1.8	5.3
059 BAPT MISS ASSN	1	42	52*	-	0.1
081 CATHOLIC......	8	0	12,303	11.0	32.6
093 CR CH (DISC)..	2	1,661	2,037*	1.8	5.4
097 CR C AND C CR.	5	727	892*	0.8	2.4
123 CH GOD (ANDER)	3	131	365	0.3	1.0
127 CH GOD (CLEVE)	2	75	92*	0.1	0.2
157 CH OF BRETHREN	2	144	177*	0.2	0.5
165 CH OF NAZARENE	6	975	1,765	1.6	4.7
193 EPISCOPAL.....	4	1,810	3,281	2.9	8.7
226 FRIENDS-USA...	3	251	308*	0.3	0.8
281 LUTH CH AMER..	3	934	1,556	1.4	4.1
283 LUTH--MO SYNOD	3	966	1,435	1.3	3.8
403 SALVATION ARMY	2	152	621	0.6	1.6
413 S-D ADVENTISTS	3	668	819*	0.7	2.2
419 SO BAPT CONV..	3	703	862*	0.8	2.3
435 UNITARIAN-UNIV	1	90	125	0.1	0.3

*Total adherents estimated from known number of communicant, confirmed, full members.

—Represents a percent less than 0.1.

Percentages may not total due to rounding.

Table 3. Churches and Church Membership by State, County and Denomination: 1971

County and Denomination	Number of churches	Communicant, confirmed, full members	Total adherents: Number	Percent of total population	Percent of total adherents
443 UN C OF CHRIST	2	814	998*	0.9	2.6
449 UN METHODIST..	8	3,813	5,141	4.6	13.6
453 UN PRES CH USA	3	2,392	2,934*	2.6	7.8
ADAMS	6	230	459*	16.0	100.0
081 CATHOLIC......	1	0	118	4.1	25.7
165 CH OF NAZARENE	1	58	130	4.5	28.3
175 CONG CR CH....	1	73	90*	3.1	19.6
226 FRIENDS-USA...	1	22	27*	0.9	5.9
413 S-D ADVENTISTS	1	37	46*	1.6	10.0
449 UN METHODIST..	1	40	48	1.7	10.5
BANNOCK	21	4,444	11,346*	21.7	100.0
019 AMER BAPT CONV	1	419	523*	1.0	4.6
081 CATHOLIC......	4	0	4,961	9.5	43.7
093 CR CH (DISC)..	1	402	502*	1.0	4.4
123 CH GOD (ANDER)	1	17	47	0.1	0.4
127 CH GOD (CLEVE)	1	35	44*	0.1	0.4
165 CH OF NAZARENE	1	53	112	0.2	1.0
193 EPISCOPAL.....	1	415	615	1.2	5.4
281 LUTH CH AMER..	1	346	517	1.0	4.6
283 LUTH--MO SYNOD	2	598	984	1.9	8.7
403 SALVATION ARMY	1	47	262	0.5	2.3
413 S-D ADVENTISTS	1	142	177*	0.3	1.6
419 SO BAPT CONV..	1	368	460*	0.9	4.1
435 UNITARIAN-UNIV	1	23	43	0.1	0.4
443 UN C OF CHRIST	2	267	334*	0.6	2.9
449 UN METHODIST..	1	803	1,129	2.2	10.0
453 UN PRES CH USA	1	509	636*	1.2	5.6
BEAR LAKE	2	34	148*	2.6	100.0
081 CATHOLIC......	1	0	106	1.8	71.6
453 UN PRES CH USA	1	34	42*	0.7	28.4
BENEWAH	9	564	2,033*	32.6	100.0
029 AMER LUTH CH..	1	164	242	3.9	11.9
081 CATHOLIC......	3	0	1,239	19.9	60.9
165 CH OF NAZARENE	1	74	151	2.4	7.4
221 FREE METH C NA	1	15	18	0.3	0.9
413 S-D ADVENTISTS	1	35	43*	0.7	2.1
419 SO BAPT CONV..	1	57	70*	1.1	3.4
453 UN PRES CH USA	1	219	270*	4.3	13.3
BINGHAM	15	1,786	3,992*	13.7	100.0
019 AMER BAPT CONV	1	279	361*	1.2	9.0
081 CATHOLIC......	2	0	1,494	5.1	37.4
193 EPISCOPAL.....	2	173	315	1.1	7.9
281 LUTH CH AMER..	2	207	354	1.2	8.9
283 LUTH--MO SYNOD	1	96	140	0.5	3.5
287 MENN GEN CONF.	1	346	448*	1.5	11.2
413 S-D ADVENTISTS	1	14	18*	0.1	0.5
419 SO BAPT CONV..	1	98	127*	0.4	3.2
449 UN METHODIST..	3	538	690	2.4	17.3
453 UN PRES CH USA	1	35	45*	0.2	1.1
BLAINE	7	279	765*	13.3	100.0
019 AMER BAPT CONV	1	136	164*	2.9	21.4
081 CATHOLIC......	3	0	442	7.7	57.8
193 EPISCOPAL.....	2	84	88	1.5	11.5
453 UN PRES CH USA	1	59	71*	1.2	9.3
BOISE	3	34	120	6.8	100.0
081 CATHOLIC......	2	0	76	4.3	63.3
281 LUTH CH AMER..	1	34	44	2.5	36.7
BONNER	22	2,170	3,678*	23.6	100.0
019 AMER BAPT CONV	2	249	300*	1.9	8.2
029 AMER LUTH CH..	2	345	515	3.3	14.0
081 CATHOLIC......	4	0	866	5.6	23.5
097 CR C AND C CR.	1	178	214*	1.4	5.8
123 CH GOD (ANDER)	1	24	59	0.4	1.6
127 CH GOD (CLEVE)	1	54	65*	0.4	1.8
165 CH OF NAZARENE	1	41	72	0.5	2.0
193 EPISCOPAL.....	1	65	121	0.8	3.3
221 FREE METH C NA	1	19	27	0.2	0.7
413 S-D ADVENTISTS	2	287	345*	2.2	9.4
443 UN C OF CHRIST	2	194	233*	1.5	6.3
449 UN METHODIST..	3	432	522	3.4	14.2
453 UN PRES CH USA	1	282	339*	2.2	9.2
BONNEVILLE	19	5,620	11,682*	22.8	100.0
019 AMER BAPT CONV	1	694	901*	1.8	7.7
081 CATHOLIC......	2	0	3,721	7.3	31.9
093 CR CH (DISC)..	1	152	197*	0.4	1.7
127 CH GOD (CLEVE)	1	9	12*	-	0.1
165 CH OF NAZARENE	1	73	137	0.3	1.2
193 EPISCOPAL.....	1	459	831	1.6	7.1
201 EVAN COV CH AM	1	63	82*	0.2	0.7
281 LUTH CH AMER..	1	500	733	1.4	6.3
283 LUTH--MO SYNOD	2	754	1,192	2.3	10.2
403 SALVATION ARMY	1	65	250	0.5	2.1
413 S-D ADVENTISTS	1	62	81*	0.2	0.7
419 SO BAPT CONV..	1	353	459*	0.9	3.9
435 UNITARIAN-UNIV	1	26	26	0.1	0.2
449 UN METHODIST..	2	1,315	1,638	3.2	14.0
453 UN PRES CH USA	2	1,095	1,422*	2.8	12.2
BOUNDARY	9	1,211	2,103*	33.0	100.0
029 AMER LUTH CH..	1	430	684	10.7	32.5
081 CATHOLIC......	1	0	451	7.1	21.4
193 EPISCOPAL.....	1	22	41	0.6	1.9
221 FREE METH C NA	1	16	18	0.3	0.9
413 S-D ADVENTISTS	1	58	71*	1.1	3.4
419 SO BAPT CONV..	2	335	412*	6.5	19.6
449 UN METHODIST..	1	338	411	6.5	19.5
453 UN PRES CH USA	1	12	15*	0.2	0.7
BUTTE	3	250	510*	17.4	100.0
019 AMER BAPT CONV	1	245	310*	10.6	60.8
081 CATHOLIC......	1	0	195	6.7	38.2
193 EPISCOPAL.....	1	5	5	0.2	1.0
CAMAS	1	0	19	2.6	100.0
081 CATHOLIC......	1	0	19	2.6	100.0
CANYON	62	13,894	25,164*	41.1	100.0
019 AMER BAPT CONV	4	522	635*	1.0	2.5
081 CATHOLIC......	4	0	5,764	9.4	22.9
093 CR CH (DISC)..	2	949	1,155*	1.9	4.6
097 CR C AND C CR.	1	971	1,182*	1.9	4.7
123 CH GOD (ANDER)	1	90	205	0.3	0.8
127 CH GOD (CLEVE)	3	97	118*	0.2	0.5
157 CH OF BRETHREN	2	431	524*	0.9	2.1
165 CH OF NAZARENE	11	2,902	5,150	8.4	20.5
193 EPISCOPAL.....	2	317	761	1.2	3.0
221 FREE METH C NA	2	181	229	0.4	0.9
226 FRIENDS-USA...	5	656	798*	1.3	3.2
281 LUTH CH AMER..	2	451	671	1.1	2.7
283 LUTH--MO SYNOD	3	882	1,351	2.2	5.4
285 MENNONITE CH..	2	160	195*	0.3	0.8
403 SALVATION ARMY	1	56	238	0.4	0.9
413 S-D ADVENTISTS	4	760	925*	1.5	3.7
419 SO BAPT CONV..	2	462	562*	0.9	2.2
443 UN C OF CHRIST	1	241	293*	0.5	1.2
449 UN METHODIST..	5	2,007	2,267	3.7	9.0
453 UN PRES CH USA	5	1,759	2,141*	3.5	8.5
CARIBOU	4	224	475*	7.3	100.0
081 CATHOLIC......	1	0	173	2.6	36.4
283 LUTH--MO SYNOD	1	14	30	0.5	6.3
419 SO BAPT CONV..	1	54	70*	1.1	14.7
453 UN PRES CH USA	1	156	202*	3.1	42.5
CASSIA	8	1,687	3,029*	17.8	100.0
081 CATHOLIC......	1	0	725	4.3	23.9
093 CR CH (DISC)..	1	250	320*	1.9	10.6
165 CH OF NAZARENE	1	26	72	0.4	2.4
193 EPISCOPAL.....	1	60	88	0.5	2.9
283 LUTH--MO SYNOD	1	273	399	2.3	13.2
419 SO BAPT CONV..	1	208	266*	1.6	8.8
449 UN METHODIST..	1	538	734	4.3	24.2
453 UN PRES CH USA	1	332	425*	2.5	14.0
CLARK	1	53	67*	9.0	100.0
019 AMER BAPT CONV	1	53	67*	9.0	100.0
CLEARWATER	13	934	1,957*	18.0	100.0
029 AMER LUTH CH..	2	234	386	3.6	19.7
081 CATHOLIC......	2	0	528	4.9	27.0
123 CH GOD (ANDER)	1	42	127	1.2	6.5
165 CH OF NAZARENE	2	73	202	1.9	10.3
413 S-D ADVENTISTS	2	114	143*	1.3	7.3
419 SO BAPT CONV..	1	115	144*	1.3	7.4
449 UN METHODIST..	2	346	414	3.8	21.2
453 UN PRES CH USA	1	10	13*	0.1	0.7
CUSTER	3	55	277*	9.3	100.0
081 CATHOLIC......	2	0	210	7.1	75.8
443 UN C OF CHRIST	1	55	67*	2.3	24.2
ELMORE	16	1,833	3,462*	19.8	100.0
019 AMER BAPT CONV	1	173	223*	1.3	6.4
081 CATHOLIC......	2	0	982	5.6	28.4
093 CR CH (DISC)..	1	97	125*	0.7	3.6
127 CH GOD (CLEVE)	1	26	33*	0.2	1.0
165 CH OF NAZARENE	2	57	121	0.7	3.5
193 EPISCOPAL.....	2	170	255	1.5	7.4
283 LUTH--MO SYNOD	1	142	220	1.3	6.4
413 S-D ADVENTISTS	1	71	91*	0.5	2.6
419 SO BAPT CONV..	2	742	955*	5.5	27.6
443 UN C OF CHRIST	1	186	239*	1.4	6.9
449 UN METHODIST..	1	116	150	0.9	4.3
453 UN PRES CH USA	1	53	68*	0.4	2.0
FRANKLIN	2	32	85*	1.2	100.0
081 CATHOLIC......	1	0	45	0.6	52.9
453 UN PRES CH USA	1	32	40*	0.5	47.1
FREMONT	4	630	1,021*	11.7	100.0
081 CATHOLIC......	1	0	160	1.8	15.7

*Total adherents estimated from known number of communicant, confirmed, full members.

—Represents a percent less than 0.1.

Percentages may not total due to rounding.

Table 3. Churches and Church Membership by State, County and Denomination: 1971

County and Denomination	Number of churches	Communicant, confirmed, full members	Total adherents		
			Number	Percent of total population	Percent of total adherents
283 LUTH--MO SYNOD	1	314	481	5.5	47.1
449 UN METHODIST..	1	183	212	2.4	20.8
453 UN PRES CH USA	1	133	168*	1.9	16.5
GEM	14	1,723	2,783*	29.6	100.0
019 AMER BAPT CONV	1	203	249*	2.7	8.9
081 CATHOLIC......	1	0	449	4.8	16.1
097 CR C AND C CR.	1	400	490*	5.2	17.6
127 CH GOD (CLEVE)	1	27	33*	0.4	1.2
165 CH OF NAZARENE	2	151	306	3.3	11.0
193 EPISCOPAL.....	1	154	250	2.7	9.0
226 FRIENDS-USA...	1	12	15*	0.2	0.5
283 LUTH--MO SYNOD	1	186	283	3.0	10.2
413 S-D ADVENTISTS	1	48	59*	0.6	2.1
449 UN METHODIST..	3	403	479	5.1	17.2
453 UN PRES CH USA	1	139	170*	1.8	6.1
GOODING	17	1,604	2,589*	29.9	100.0
019 AMER BAPT CONV	1	126	151*	1.7	5.8
081 CATHOLIC......	3	0	530	6.1	20.5
093 CR CH (DISC)..	1	18	22*	0.3	0.8
097 CR C AND C CR.	2	250	299*	3.5	11.5
165 CH OF NAZARENE	1	47	148	1.7	5.7
193 EPISCOPAL.....	1	64	102	1.2	3.9
283 LUTH--MO SYNOD	2	149	175	2.0	6.8
413 S-D ADVENTISTS	1	29	35*	0.4	1.4
419 SO BAPT CONV..	1	77	92*	1.1	3.6
449 UN METHODIST..	3	669	825	9.5	31.9
453 UN PRES CH USA	1	175	210*	2.4	8.1
IDAHO	24	1,108	4,574*	35.5	100.0
019 AMER BAPT CONV	1	96	119*	0.9	2.6
081 CATHOLIC......	6	0	3,011	23.4	65.8
105 CHRISTIAN REF.	1	76	184	1.4	4.0
127 CH GOD (CLEVE)	2	43	53*	0.4	1.2
165 CH OF NAZARENE	1	78	199	1.5	4.4
193 EPISCOPAL.....	1	54	54	0.4	1.2
283 LUTH--MO SYNOD	1	117	169	1.3	3.7
413 S-D ADVENTISTS	3	66	82*	0.6	1.8
419 SO BAPT CONV..	2	86	107*	0.8	2.3
449 UN METHODIST..	3	438	529	4.1	11.6
453 UN PRES CH USA	3	54	67*	0.5	1.5
JEFFERSON	4	64	157*	1.4	100.0
019 AMER BAPT CONV	2	64	82*	0.7	52.2
081 CATHOLIC......	2	0	75	0.6	47.8
JEROME	13	1,671	2,784*	27.2	100.0
019 AMER BAPT CONV	1	266	319*	3.1	11.5
081 CATHOLIC......	2	0	520	5.1	18.7
093 CR CH (DISC)..	1	120	144*	1.4	5.2
123 CH GOD (ANDER)	1	58	144	1.4	5.2
165 CH OF NAZARENE	1	76	125	1.2	4.5
193 EPISCOPAL.....	1	64	100	1.0	3.6
283 LUTH--MO SYNOD	2	348	515	5.0	18.5
413 S-D ADVENTISTS	1	43	51*	0.5	1.8
449 UN METHODIST..	1	241	321	3.1	11.5
453 UN PRES CH USA	2	455	545*	5.3	19.6
KOOTENAI	26	4,119	9,591*	27.1	100.0
019 AMER BAPT CONV	1	46	56*	0.2	0.6
029 AMER LUTH CH..	4	1,023	1,441	4.1	15.0
081 CATHOLIC......	7	0	3,747	10.6	39.1
123 CH GOD (ANDER)	1	73	182	0.5	1.9
127 CH GOD (CLEVE)	1	28	34*	0.1	0.4
165 CH OF NAZARENE	2	212	509	1.4	5.3
193 EPISCOPAL.....	1	348	409	1.2	4.3
226 FRIENDS-USA...	1	65	79*	0.2	0.8
283 LUTH--MO SYNOD	1	579	997	2.8	10.4
413 S-D ADVENTISTS	1	338	411*	1.2	4.3
449 UN METHODIST..	3	578	718	2.0	7.5
453 UN PRES CH USA	3	829	1,008*	2.9	10.5
LATAH	31	3,735	8,549*	34.3	100.0
019 AMER BAPT CONV	1	250	297*	1.2	3.5
029 AMER LUTH CH..	6	1,036	1,444	5.8	16.9
081 CATHOLIC......	5	0	3,133	12.6	36.6
097 CR C AND C CR.	1	30	36*	0.1	0.4
123 CH GOD (ANDER)	1	30	80	0.3	0.9
165 CH OF NAZARENE	4	347	991	4.0	11.6
193 EPISCOPAL.....	1	178	269	1.1	3.1
281 LUTH CH AMER..	2	195	294	1.2	3.4
413 S-D ADVENTISTS	4	283	336*	1.3	3.9
419 SO BAPT CONV..	1	148	176*	0.7	2.1
449 UN METHODIST..	2	764	930	3.7	10.9
453 UN PRES CH USA	3	474	563*	2.3	6.6
LEMHI	6	543	1,001*	18.0	100.0
081 CATHOLIC......	2	0	219	3.9	21.9
193 EPISCOPAL.....	1	72	147	2.6	14.7
413 S-D ADVENTISTS	1	89	109*	2.0	10.9
449 UN METHODIST..	1	342	477	8.6	47.7
453 UN PRES CH USA	1	40	49*	0.9	4.9
LEWIS	17	804	1,582*	40.9	100.0
019 AMER BAPT CONV	1	108	131*	3.4	8.3
029 AMER LUTH CH..	3	234	342	8.8	21.6
081 CATHOLIC......	3	0	559	14.5	35.3
157 CH OF BRETHREN	1	9	11*	0.3	0.7
226 FRIENDS-USA...	1	22	27*	0.7	1.7
419 SO BAPT CONV..	1	7	8*	0.2	0.5
449 UN METHODIST..	1	90	99	2.6	6.3
453 UN PRES CH USA	6	334	405*	10.5	25.6
LINCOLN	6	389	811*	26.5	100.0
019 AMER BAPT CONV	1	146	174*	5.7	21.5
081 CATHOLIC......	2	0	249	8.1	30.7
193 EPISCOPAL.....	1	59	116	3.8	14.3
449 UN METHODIST..	2	184	272	8.9	33.5
MADISON	3	133	204*	1.5	100.0
081 CATHOLIC......	1	0	44	0.3	21.6
453 UN PRES CH USA	2	133	160*	1.2	78.4
MINIDOKA	11	2,158	4,142*	26.3	100.0
019 AMER BAPT CONV	1	106	134*	0.9	3.2
081 CATHOLIC......	1	0	1,400	8.9	33.8
097 CR C AND C CR.	1	450	567*	3.6	13.7
127 CH GOD (CLEVE)	1	9	11*	0.1	0.3
165 CH OF NAZARENE	1	74	167	1.1	4.0
193 EPISCOPAL.....	1	123	170	1.1	4.1
283 LUTH--MO SYNOD	1	532	653	4.2	15.8
313 NO AM BAPT GC.	1	127	160*	1.0	3.9
413 S-D ADVENTISTS	1	37	47*	0.3	1.1
449 UN METHODIST..	2	700	833	5.3	20.1
NEZ PERCE	26	4,005	8,184*	26.9	100.0
019 AMER BAPT CONV	1	154	190*	0.6	2.3
029 AMER LUTH CH..	3	902	1,271	4.2	15.5
081 CATHOLIC......	4	0	2,646	8.7	32.3
123 CH GOD (ANDER)	1	18	68	0.2	0.8
127 CH GOD (CLEVE)	1	41	50*	0.2	0.6
165 CH OF NAZARENE	2	265	585	1.9	7.1
193 EPISCOPAL.....	1	470	676	2.2	8.3
283 LUTH--MO SYNOD	1	97	185	0.6	2.3
403 SALVATION ARMY	1	22	92	0.3	1.1
413 S-D ADVENTISTS	1	222	273*	0.9	3.3
419 SO BAPT CONV..	1	488	601*	2.0	7.3
435 UNITARIAN-UNIV	1	25	33	0.1	0.4
443 UN C OF CHRIST	1	64	79*	0.3	1.0
449 UN METHODIST..	4	801	898	3.0	11.0
453 UN PRES CH USA	3	436	537*	1.8	6.6
ONEIDA	2	48	83*	2.9	100.0
081 CATHOLIC......	1	0	26	0.9	31.3
453 UN PRES CH USA	1	48	57*	2.0	68.7
OWYHEE	14	51[illegible]	1,591*	24.8	100.0
081 CATHOLIC......	4	0	792	12.3	49.8
093 CR CH (DISC)..	1	59	74*	1.2	4.7
165 CH OF NAZARENE	2	83	243	3.8	15.3
226 FRIENDS-USA...	1	69	86*	1.3	5.4
283 LUTH--MO SYNOD	1	57	88	1.4	5.5
285 MENNONITE CH..	1	58	72*	1.1	4.5
413 S-D ADVENTISTS	1	41	51*	0.8	3.2
443 UN C OF CHRIST	2	67	84*	1.3	5.3
453 UN PRES CH USA	1	81	101*	1.6	6.3
PAYETTE	19	2,122	3,423*	27.6	100.0
019 AMER BAPT CONV	2	279	338*	2.7	9.9
081 CATHOLIC......	2	0	641	5.2	18.7
097 CR C AND C CR.	1	175	212*	1.7	6.2
127 CH GOD (CLEVE)	1	8	10*	0.1	0.3
157 CH OF BRETHREN	1	173	209*	1.7	6.1
165 CH OF NAZARENE	2	167	357	2.9	10.4
193 EPISCOPAL.....	1	135	215	1.7	6.3
221 FREE METH C NA	1	34	45	0.4	1.3
283 LUTH--MO SYNOD	1	85	114	0.9	3.3
413 S-D ADVENTISTS	2	202	245*	2.0	7.2
419 SO BAPT CONV..	1	77	93*	0.7	2.7
443 UN C OF CHRIST	2	158	191*	1.5	5.6
449 UN METHODIST..	2	629	753	6.1	22.0
POWER	7	886	1,402*	28.8	100.0
019 AMER BAPT CONV	1	156	196*	4.0	14.0
029 AMER LUTH CH..	1	421	593	12.2	42.3
081 CATHOLIC......	1	0	250	5.1	17.8
193 EPISCOPAL.....	1	26	36	0.7	2.6
443 UN C OF CHRIST	2	106	133*	2.7	9.5
449 UN METHODIST..	1	177	194	4.0	13.8
SHOSHONE	18	2,533	5,636*	28.6	100.0
019 AMER BAPT CONV	1	83	105*	0.5	1.9
029 AMER LUTH CH..	2	758	1,138	5.8	20.2
081 CATHOLIC......	3	0	1,993	10.1	35.4
127 CH GOD (CLEVE)	1	30	38*	0.2	0.7
165 CH OF NAZARENE	1	116	343	1.7	6.1
193 EPISCOPAL.....	2	240	340	1.7	6.0
283 LUTH--MO SYNOD	2	230	337	1.7	6.0
413 S-D ADVENTISTS	1	52	66*	0.3	1.2
419 SO BAPT CONV..	1	216	273*	1.4	4.8
443 UN C OF CHRIST	2	431	546*	2.8	9.7

*Total adherents estimated from known number of communicant, confirmed, full members.

—Represents a percent less than 0.1.

Percentages may not total due to rounding.

Table 3. Churches and Church Membership by State, County and Denomination: 1971

County and Denomination	Number of churches	Communicant, confirmed, full members	Total adherents: Number	Total adherents: Percent of total population	Total adherents: Percent of total adherents
449 UN METHODIST..	2	377	457	2.3	8.1
TETON	0	0	0	-	-
TWIN FALLS	39	8,541	14,603*	34.9	100.0
019 AMER BAPT CONV	4	1,077	1,307*	3.1	9.0
029 AMER LUTH CH..	1	253	398	1.0	2.7
059 BAPT MISS ASSN	1	73	89*	0.2	0.6
081 CATHOLIC......	3	0	3,380	8.1	23.1
093 CR CH (DISC)..	2	342	415*	1.0	2.8
097 CR C AND C CR.	1	932	1,131*	2.7	7.7
127 CH GOD (CLEVE)	1	22	27*	0.1	0.2
157 CH OF BRETHREN	1	126	153*	0.4	1.0
165 CH OF NAZARENE	4	458	790	1.9	5.4
193 EPISCOPAL.....	2	425	652	1.6	4.5
283 LUTH--MO SYNOD	5	1,631	2,237	5.4	15.3
285 MENNONITE CH..	1	78	95*	0.2	0.7
403 SALVATION ARMY	1	36	171	0.4	1.2
413 S-D ADVENTISTS	2	280	340*	0.8	2.3
419 SO BAPT CONV..	4	423	513*	1.2	3.5
449 UN METHODIST..	6	2,385	2,905	6.9	19.9
VALLEY	10	1,321	1,881*	52.1	100.0
081 CATHOLIC......	2	0	240	6.7	12.8
097 CR C AND C CR.	1	65	79*	2.2	4.2
165 CH OF NAZARENE	1	22	49	1.4	2.6
193 EPISCOPAL.....	1	74	74	2.1	3.9
283 LUTH--MO SYNOD	1	44	86	2.4	4.6
443 UN C OF CHRIST	1	164	199*	5.5	10.6
453 UN PRES CH USA	3	952	1,154*	32.0	61.4
WASHINGTON	13	1,193	2,171*	28.4	100.0
019 AMER BAPT CONV	3	457	547*	7.2	25.2
081 CATHOLIC......	2	0	635	8.3	29.2
157 CH OF BRETHREN	1	20	24*	0.3	1.1
165 CH OF NAZARENE	1	107	188	2.5	8.7
193 EPISCOPAL.....	1	47	88	1.2	4.1
283 LUTH--MO SYNOD	1	67	96	1.3	4.4
413 S-D ADVENTISTS	2	111	133*	1.7	6.1
443 UN C OF CHRIST	1	228	273*	3.6	12.6
453 UN PRES CH USA	1	156	187*	2.4	8.6
CO DATA NOT AVAIL	11	386	193,871*	N/A	N/A
151 L-D SAINTS....	0	0	193,405	N/A	N/A
223 FREE WILL BAPT	6	243	301*	N/A	N/A
467 WESLEYAN......	5	143	165	N/A	N/A

ILLINOIS

County and Denomination	Number of churches	Communicant, confirmed, full members	Total adherents: Number	Total adherents: Percent of total population	Total adherents: Percent of total adherents
THE STATE.....	8,468	1,972,185	6,136,362*	55.2	100.0
ADAMS	91	20,717	44,829*	63.3	100.0
019 AMER BAPT CONV	6	1,897	2,296*	3.2	5.1
029 AMER LUTH CH..	2	521	708	1.0	1.6
081 CATHOLIC......	11	0	18,451	26.0	41.2
093 CR CH (DISC)..	8	1,126	1,363*	1.9	3.0
097 CR C AND C CR.	10	1,734	2,099*	3.0	4.7
157 CH OF BRETHREN	1	57	69*	0.1	0.2
165 CH OF NAZARENE	1	145	425	0.6	0.9
193 EPISCOPAL.....	1	427	475	0.7	1.1
221 FREE METH C NA	1	14	19	-	-
226 FRIENDS-USA...	1	7	8*	-	-
281 LUTH CH AMER..	6	2,238	2,973	4.2	6.6
283 LUTH--MO SYNOD	5	2,121	2,847	4.0	6.4
403 SALVATION ARMY	1	108	776	1.1	1.7
413 S-D ADVENTISTS	1	8	10*	-	-
419 SO BAPT CONV..	1	348	421*	0.6	0.9
435 UNITARIAN-UNIV	1	82	112	0.2	0.2
443 UN C OF CHRIST	7	3,599	4,357*	6.1	9.7
449 UN METHODIST..	23	5,347	6,285	8.9	14.0
453 UN PRES CH USA	4	938	1,135*	1.6	2.5
ALEXANDER	28	3,689	5,121*	42.6	100.0
019 AMER BAPT CONV	1	564	669*	5.6	13.1
081 CATHOLIC......	3	0	705	5.9	13.8
093 CR CH (DISC)..	1	95	113*	0.9	2.2
127 CH GOD (CLEVE)	1	31	37*	0.3	0.7
193 EPISCOPAL.....	1	120	238	2.0	4.6
281 LUTH CH AMER..	1	131	154	1.3	3.0
413 S-D ADVENTISTS	1	7	8*	0.1	0.2
419 SO BAPT CONV..	10	1,853	2,198*	18.3	42.9
443 UN C OF CHRIST	1	35	42*	0.3	0.8
449 UN METHODIST..	7	657	725	6.0	14.2
453 UN PRES CH USA	1	196	232*	1.9	4.5
BOND	42	5,281	7,634*	54.5	100.0
019 AMER BAPT CONV	1	254	302*	2.2	4.0
081 CATHOLIC......	3	0	1,301	9.3	17.0
093 CR CH (DISC)..	1	56	67*	0.5	0.9

County and Denomination	Number of churches	Communicant, confirmed, full members	Total adherents: Number	Total adherents: Percent of total population	Total adherents: Percent of total adherents
097 CR C AND C CR.	7	1,029	1,223*	8.7	16.0
157 CH OF BRETHREN	1	52	62*	0.4	0.8
185 CUMBER PRESB..	2	137	163*	1.2	2.1
221 FREE METH C NA	3	351	456	3.3	6.0
283 LUTH--MO SYNOD	1	179	285	2.0	3.7
419 SO BAPT CONV..	12	1,537	1,826*	13.0	23.9
443 UN C OF CHRIST	1	105	125*	0.9	1.6
449 UN METHODIST..	7	995	1,128	8.1	14.8
453 UN PRES CH USA	3	586	696*	5.0	9.1
BOONE	23	7,316	12,813*	50.4	100.0
019 AMER BAPT CONV	1	374	472*	1.9	3.7
029 AMER LUTH CH..	1	233	331	1.3	2.6
081 CATHOLIC......	1	0	3,388	13.3	26.4
165 CH OF NAZARENE	1	22	69	0.3	0.5
193 EPISCOPAL.....	1	183	218	0.9	1.7
201 EVAN COV CH AM	1	216	273*	1.1	2.1
221 FREE METH C NA	1	21	22	0.1	0.2
281 LUTH CH AMER..	1	641	958	3.8	7.5
283 LUTH--MO SYNOD	1	1,405	1,959	7.7	15.3
403 SALVATION ARMY	1	32	139	0.5	1.1
419 SO BAPT CONV..	1	52	66*	0.3	0.5
443 UN C OF CHRIST	3	612	773*	3.0	6.0
449 UN METHODIST..	6	2,050	2,244	8.8	17.5
453 UN PRES CH USA	2	1,397	1,764*	6.9	13.8
469 WISC EVAN LUTH	1	78	137	0.5	1.1
BROWN	19	1,808	3,285*	58.8	100.0
019 AMER BAPT CONV	2	326	390*	7.0	11.9
081 CATHOLIC......	2	0	1,014	18.2	30.9
093 CR CH (DISC)..	2	331	396*	7.1	12.1
097 CR C AND C CR.	4	362	433*	7.8	13.2
121 CH GOD (ABR)..	1	92	110*	2.0	3.3
165 CH OF NAZARENE	1	40	153	2.7	4.7
283 LUTH--MO SYNOD	1	62	88	1.6	2.7
419 SO BAPT CONV..	2	116	139*	2.5	4.2
449 UN METHODIST..	1	288	333	6.0	10.1
453 UN PRES CH USA	3	191	229*	4.1	7.0
BUREAU	70	10,467	22,665*	58.8	100.0
019 AMER BAPT CONV	5	866	1,059*	2.7	4.7
029 AMER LUTH CH..	5	1,025	1,381	3.6	6.1
081 CATHOLIC......	18	0	9,768	25.3	43.1
093 CR CH (DISC)..	3	548	670*	1.7	3.0
165 CH OF NAZARENE	2	43	156	0.4	0.7
175 CONG CR CH....	3	311	380*	1.0	1.7
193 EPISCOPAL.....	2	156	182	0.5	0.8
201 EVAN COV CH AM	1	315	385*	1.0	1.7
281 LUTH CH AMER..	3	1,609	2,089	5.4	9.2
283 LUTH--MO SYNOD	1	60	109	0.3	0.5
285 MENNONITE CH..	1	124	152*	0.4	0.7
287 MENN GEN CONF.	1	45	55*	0.1	0.2
413 S-D ADVENTISTS	1	21	26*	0.1	0.1
419 SO BAPT CONV..	1	152	186*	0.5	0.8
443 UN C OF CHRIST	8	1,632	1,996*	5.2	8.8
449 UN METHODIST..	12	3,062	3,462	9.0	15.3
453 UN PRES CH USA	3	498	609*	1.6	2.7
CALHOUN	19	925	3,947*	69.6	100.0
081 CATHOLIC......	7	0	2,707	47.7	68.6
165 CH OF NAZARENE	2	30	66	1.2	1.7
281 LUTH CH AMER..	1	69	71	1.3	1.8
283 LUTH--MO SYNOD	3	428	578	10.2	14.6
449 UN METHODIST..	3	174	253	4.5	6.4
453 UN PRES CH USA	3	224	272*	4.8	6.9
CARROLL	31	5,883	9,381*	48.7	100.0
019 AMER BAPT CONV	2	191	231*	1.2	2.5
081 CATHOLIC......	3	0	2,019	10.5	21.5
157 CH OF BRETHREN	3	515	622*	3.2	6.6
193 EPISCOPAL.....	1	78	111	0.6	1.2
281 LUTH CH AMER..	4	1,171	1,635	8.5	17.4
371 REF CH IN AM..	1	69	93	0.5	1.0
413 S-D ADVENTISTS	1	9	11*	0.1	0.1
419 SO BAPT CONV..	1	57	69*	0.4	0.7
443 UN C OF CHRIST	1	266	321*	1.7	3.4
449 UN METHODIST..	10	2,828	3,356	17.4	35.8
453 UN PRES CH USA	2	296	357*	1.9	3.8
469 WISC EVAN LUTH	2	403	556	2.9	5.9
CASS	36	6,707	9,705*	68.3	100.0
019 AMER BAPT CONV	3	348	422*	3.0	4.3
081 CATHOLIC......	5	0	1,160	8.2	12.0
093 CR CH (DISC)..	2	199	241*	1.7	2.5
097 CR C AND C CR.	3	447	542*	3.8	5.6
165 CH OF NAZARENE	1	78	295	2.1	3.0
185 CUMBER PRESB..	1	89	108*	0.8	1.1
281 LUTH CH AMER..	4	1,153	1,518	10.7	15.6
283 LUTH--MO SYNOD	4	1,153	1,521	10.7	15.7
419 SO BAPT CONV..	4	707	857*	6.0	8.8
443 UN C OF CHRIST	1	216	262*	1.8	2.7
449 UN METHODIST..	6	2,021	2,420	17.0	24.9
453 UN PRES CH USA	2	296	359*	2.5	3.7
CHAMPAIGN	122	37,242	67,055*	41.1	100.0
019 AMER BAPT CONV	6	1,578	1,891*	1.2	2.8
029 AMER LUTH CH..	8	3,944	5,487	3.4	8.2
081 CATHOLIC......	16	0	19,898	12.2	29.7

*Total adherents estimated from known number of communicant, confirmed, full members.

—Represents a percent less than 0.1.

Percentages may not total due to rounding.

Table 3. Churches and Church Membership by State, County and Denomination: 1971

County and Denomination	Number of churches	Communicant, confirmed, full members	Total adherents: Number	Total adherents: Percent of total population	Total adherents: Percent of total adherents
093 CR CH (DISC)..	3	1,190	1,426*	0.9	2.1
097 CR C AND C CR.	10	3,269	3,916*	2.4	5.8
105 CHRISTIAN REF.	1	33	47	-	0.1
123 CH GOD (ANDER)	1	48	136	0.1	0.2
127 CH GOD (CLEVE)	1	122	146*	0.1	0.2
157 CH OF BRETHREN	1	87	104*	0.1	0.2
165 CH OF NAZARENE	9	690	1,925	1.2	2.9
193 EPISCOPAL.....	3	908	1,054	0.6	1.6
221 FREE METH C NA	1	84	106	0.1	0.2
226 FRIENDS-USA...	1	102	122*	0.1	0.2
281 LUTH CH AMER..	1	440	568	0.3	0.8
283 LUTH--MO SYNOD	6	2,376	3,377	2.1	5.0
285 MENNONITE CH..	3	482	577*	0.4	0.9
287 MENN GEN CONF.	1	50	60*	-	0.1
353 PLY BRETHREN..	1	150	250	0.2	0.4
403 SALVATION ARMY	1	110	358	0.2	0.5
413 S-D ADVENTISTS	1	110	132*	0.1	0.2
419 SO BAPT CONV..	7	2,539	3,042*	1.9	4.5
435 UNITARIAN-UNIV	1	352	520	0.3	0.8
443 UN C OF CHRIST	3	1,239	1,484*	0.9	2.2
449 UN METHODIST..	28	13,637	15,994	9.8	23.9
453 UN PRES CH USA	8	3,702	4,435*	2.7	6.6
CHRISTIAN	54	10,918	20,849*	58.0	100.0
019 AMER BAPT CONV	5	677	821*	2.3	3.9
081 CATHOLIC......	6	0	6,805	18.9	32.6
093 CR CH (DISC)..	3	908	1,101*	3.1	5.3
097 CR C AND C CR.	4	955	1,158*	3.2	5.6
127 CH GOD (CLEVE)	1	104	126*	0.4	0.6
165 CH OF NAZARENE	5	391	937	2.6	4.5
221 FREE METH C NA	2	84	110	0.3	0.5
283 LUTH--MO SYNOD	4	1,055	1,519	4.2	7.3
419 SO BAPT CONV..	3	349	423*	1.2	2.0
443 UN C OF CHRIST	1	352	427*	1.2	2.0
449 UN METHODIST..	15	4,521	5,576	15.5	26.7
453 UN PRES CH USA	5	1,522	1,846*	5.1	8.9
CLARK	48	6,100	7,877*	48.6	100.0
081 CATHOLIC......	2	0	582	3.6	7.4
093 CR CH (DISC)..	1	215	255*	1.6	3.2
097 CR C AND C CR.	6	876	1,040*	6.4	13.2
121 CH GOD (ABR)..	2	42	50*	0.3	0.6
165 CH OF NAZARENE	3	141	318	2.0	4.0
185 CUMBER PRESB..	3	183	217*	1.3	2.8
283 LUTH--MO SYNOD	2	83	111	0.7	1.4
419 SO BAPT CONV..	14	1,897	2,252*	13.9	28.6
443 UN C OF CHRIST	1	102	121*	0.7	1.5
449 UN METHODIST..	13	2,441	2,789	17.2	35.4
453 UN PRES CH USA	1	120	142*	0.9	1.8
CLAY	50	7,501	10,242*	69.5	100.0
019 AMER BAPT CONV	1	291	345*	2.3	3.4
081 CATHOLIC......	2	0	1,128	7.7	11.0
097 CR C AND C CR.	15	2,532	3,004*	20.4	29.3
123 CH GOD (ANDER)	1	110	290	2.0	2.8
127 CH GOD (CLEVE)	2	38	45*	0.3	0.4
165 CH OF NAZARENE	1	114	348	2.4	3.4
283 LUTH--MO SYNOD	1	80	112	0.8	1.1
419 SO BAPT CONV..	10	1,466	1,740*	11.8	17.0
443 UN C OF CHRIST	1	57	68*	0.5	0.7
449 UN METHODIST..	15	2,671	2,994	20.3	29.2
453 UN PRES CH USA	1	142	168*	1.1	1.6
CLINTON	47	4,468	21,270*	75.1	100.0
019 AMER BAPT CONV	1	111	138*	0.5	0.6
081 CATHOLIC......	17	0	15,458	54.6	72.7
097 CR C AND C CR.	2	50	62*	0.2	0.3
283 LUTH--MO SYNOD	4	1,100	1,468	5.2	6.9
313 NO AM BAPT GC.	1	113	141*	0.5	0.7
413 S-D ADVENTISTS	1	29	36*	0.1	0.2
419 SO BAPT CONV..	4	467	582*	2.1	2.7
443 UN C OF CHRIST	5	1,029	1,283*	4.5	6.0
449 UN METHODIST..	11	1,560	2,091	7.4	9.8
453 UN PRES CH USA	1	9	11*	-	0.1
COLES	57	14,279	20,711*	43.3	100.0
019 AMER BAPT CONV	4	1,890	2,213*	4.6	10.7
029 AMER LUTH CH..	1	122	172	0.4	0.8
081 CATHOLIC......	2	0	3,123	6.5	15.1
093 CR CH (DISC)..	4	2,564	3,002*	6.3	14.5
097 CR C AND C CR.	6	1,270	1,487*	3.1	7.2
123 CH GOD (ANDER)	1	56	176	0.4	0.8
165 CH OF NAZARENE	3	250	635	1.3	3.1
185 CUMBER PRESB..	2	113	132*	0.3	0.6
193 EPISCOPAL.....	1	110	228	0.5	1.1
221 FREE METH C NA	1	78	114	0.2	0.6
281 LUTH CH AMER..	1	91	133	0.3	0.6
283 LUTH--MO SYNOD	3	1,300	1,745	3.6	8.4
403 SALVATION ARMY	1	68	298	0.6	1.4
413 S-D ADVENTISTS	1	48	56*	0.1	0.3
419 SO BAPT CONV..	6	765	896*	1.9	4.3
435 UNITARIAN-UNIV	1	36	36	0.1	0.2
449 UN METHODIST..	12	3,815	4,271	8.9	20.6
453 UN PRES CH USA	7	1,703	1,994*	4.2	9.6
COOK	1,705	475,328	3,041,249*	55.4	100.0
019 AMER BAPT CONV	64	18,061	22,066*	0.4	0.7
029 AMER LUTH CH..	61	30,355	42,952	0.8	1.4
059 BAPT MISS ASSN	3	136	166*	-	-
081 CATHOLIC......	443	0	2,409,465	43.9	79.2
093 CR CH (DISC)..	24	6,116	7,472*	0.1	0.2
097 CR C AND C CR.	15	1,724	2,106*	-	0.1
105 CHRISTIAN REF.	30	8,488	14,284	0.3	0.5
121 CH GOD (ABR)..	1	45	55*	-	-
123 CH GOD (ANDER)	14	2,036	3,890	0.1	0.1
127 CH GOD (CLEVE)	30	2,215	2,706*	-	0.1
157 CH OF BRETHREN	3	281	343*	-	-
165 CH OF NAZARENE	19	2,241	4,523	0.1	0.1
175 CONG CR CH....	5	1,035	1,265*	-	-
193 EPISCOPAL.....	81	26,379	35,657	0.6	1.2
199 EVAN CONG CH..	3	170	208*	-	-
201 EVAN COV CH AM	29	5,651	6,904*	0.1	0.2
211 EV MENN BRETH.	1	34	42*	-	-
221 FREE METH C NA	5	371	501	-	-
226 FRIENDS-USA...	5	471	575*	-	-
281 LUTH CH AMER..	111	48,907	67,535	1.2	2.2
283 LUTH--MO SYNOD	166	97,146	137,316	2.5	4.5
285 MENNONITE CH..	3	286	349*	-	-
287 MENN GEN CONF.	3	181	221*	-	-
313 NO AM BAPT GC.	6	1,107	1,352*	-	-
315 NO AM OLD RC..	2	731	893*	-	-
335 ORTH PRESB CH.	3	158	304	-	-
349 PENT HOLINESS.	2	39	48*	-	-
353 PLY BRETHREN..	19	1,392	2,325	-	0.1
371 REF CH IN AM..	26	8,572	12,892	0.2	0.4
403 SALVATION ARMY	18	1,768	8,227	0.1	0.3
413 S-D ADVENTISTS	31	5,746	7,020*	0.1	0.2
415 S-D BAPTIST GC	1	5	6*	-	-
419 SO BAPT CONV..	58	9,708	11,861*	0.2	0.4
435 UNITARIAN-UNIV	13	3,911	4,847	0.1	0.2
443 UN C OF CHRIST	123	55,781	68,151*	1.2	2.2
449 UN METHODIST..	162	76,326	91,904	1.7	3.0
453 UN PRES CH USA	115	56,309	68,796*	1.3	2.3
469 WISC EVAN LUTH	7	1,446	2,022	-	0.1
CRAWFORD	66	8,622	10,702*	54.0	100.0
019 AMER BAPT CONV	2	887	1,044*	5.3	9.8
081 CATHOLIC......	2	0	814	4.1	7.6
093 CR CH (DISC)..	2	565	665*	3.4	6.2
097 CR C AND C CR.	8	1,485	1,749*	8.8	16.3
127 CH GOD (CLEVE)	1	58	68*	0.3	0.6
157 CH OF BRETHREN	1	42	49*	0.2	0.5
165 CH OF NAZARENE	1	37	75	0.4	0.7
185 CUMBER PRESB..	2	111	131*	0.7	1.2
193 EPISCOPAL.....	1	47	47	0.2	0.4
197 EVAN CH OF NA.	1	60	71*	0.4	0.7
221 FREE METH C NA	2	38	60	0.3	0.6
226 FRIENDS-USA...	1	99	117*	0.6	1.1
419 SO BAPT CONV..	9	1,109	1,306*	6.6	12.2
435 UNITARIAN-UNIV	1	30	40	0.2	0.4
443 UN C OF CHRIST	3	166	195*	1.0	1.8
449 UN METHODIST..	27	3,411	3,709	18.7	34.7
453 UN PRES CH USA	2	477	562*	2.8	5.3
CUMBERLAND	29	2,309	3,460*	35.4	100.0
081 CATHOLIC......	3	0	807	8.3	23.3
093 CR CH (DISC)..	2	51	62*	0.6	1.8
097 CR C AND C CR.	4	565	686*	7.0	19.8
221 FREE METH C NA	2	54	68	0.7	2.0
226 FRIENDS-USA...	2	89	108*	1.1	3.1
419 SO BAPT CONV..	7	456	554*	5.7	16.0
449 UN METHODIST..	7	716	716	7.3	20.7
453 UN PRES CH USA	2	378	459*	4.7	13.3
DE KALB	64	19,484	42,095*	58.7	100.0
019 AMER BAPT CONV	4	1,304	1,543*	2.2	3.7
029 AMER LUTH CH..	3	869	1,126	1.6	2.7
081 CATHOLIC......	6	0	17,124	23.9	40.7
097 CR C AND C CR.	1	120	142*	0.2	0.3
127 CH GOD (CLEVE)	1	67	79*	0.1	0.2
165 CH OF NAZARENE	2	183	565	0.8	1.3
193 EPISCOPAL.....	2	387	528	0.7	1.3
201 EVAN COV CH AM	1	107	127*	0.2	0.3
226 FRIENDS-USA...	1	11	13*	-	-
281 LUTH CH AMER..	5	3,007	4,056	5.7	9.6
283 LUTH--MO SYNOD	4	1,993	2,786	3.9	6.6
403 SALVATION ARMY	1	76	276	0.4	0.7
419 SO BAPT CONV..	4	614	726*	1.0	1.7
435 UNITARIAN-UNIV	2	674	849	1.2	2.0
443 UN C OF CHRIST	8	2,608	3,085*	4.3	7.3
449 UN METHODIST..	15	6,640	8,095	11.3	19.2
453 UN PRES CH USA	4	824	975*	1.4	2.3
DE WITT	34	5,896	8,307*	48.9	100.0
081 CATHOLIC......	3	0	1,320	7.8	15.9
097 CR C AND C CR.	9	2,018	2,431*	14.3	29.3
123 CH GOD (ANDER)	1	15	35	0.2	0.4
127 CH GOD (CLEVE)	2	96	116*	0.7	1.4
165 CH OF NAZARENE	2	189	562	3.3	6.8
185 CUMBER PRESB..	2	106	128*	0.8	1.5
193 EPISCOPAL.....	1	4	4	-	-
221 FREE METH C NA	1	24	27	0.2	0.3
283 LUTH--MO SYNOD	1	116	180	1.1	2.2
419 SO BAPT CONV..	2	317	382*	2.3	4.6
435 UNITARIAN-UNIV	1	63	73	0.4	0.9
449 UN METHODIST..	8	2,631	2,667	15.7	32.1
453 UN PRES CH USA	1	317	382*	2.3	4.6
DOUGLAS	39	6,716	10,215*	53.8	100.0

*Total adherents estimated from known number of communicant, confirmed, full members.

—Represents a percent less than 0.1.

Percentages may not total due to rounding.

Table 3. Churches and Church Membership by State, County and Denomination: 1971

County and Denomination	Number of churches	Communicant, confirmed, full members	Total adherents		
			Number	Percent of total population	Percent of total adherents
019 AMER BAPT CONV	4	498	604*	3.2	5.9
081 CATHOLIC......	3	0	1,855	9.8	18.2
093 CR CH (DISC)..	4	602	730*	3.8	7.1
097 CR C AND C CR.	4	1,031	1,251*	6.6	12.2
123 CH GOD (ANDER)	2	48	144	0.8	1.4
165 CH OF NAZARENE	3	176	548	2.9	5.4
221 FREE METH C NA	1	32	49	0.3	0.5
283 LUTH--MO SYNOD	1	318	443	2.3	4.3
419 SO BAPT CONV..	2	169	205*	1.1	2.0
443 UN C OF CHRIST	1	145	176*	0.9	1.7
449 UN METHODIST..	11	3,372	3,816	20.1	37.4
453 UN PRES CH USA	3	325	394*	2.1	3.9
DU PAGE	218	91,902	298,902*	60.8	100.0
019 AMER BAPT CONV	5	749	950*	0.2	0.3
029 AMER LUTH CH..	3	1,704	2,433	0.5	0.8
081 CATHOLIC......	40	0	180,370	36.7	60.3
093 CR CH (DISC)..	2	316	401*	0.1	0.1
097 CR C AND C CR.	5	535	679*	0.1	0.2
105 CHRISTIAN REF.	3	654	1,182	0.2	0.4
157 CH OF BRETHREN	2	565	717*	0.1	0.2
165 CH OF NAZARENE	2	211	371	0.1	0.1
175 CONG CR CH....	3	459	582*	0.1	0.2
193 EPISCOPAL.....	12	6,250	8,146	1.7	2.7
201 EVAN COV CH AM	4	1,122	1,423*	0.3	0.5
226 FRIENDS-USA...	1	54	68*	-	-
281 LUTH CH AMER..	18	9,851	9,851	2.0	3.3
283 LUTH--MO SYNOD	25	18,596	27,309	5.6	9.1
285 MENNONITE CH..	1	100	127*	-	-
313 NO AM BAPT GC.	1	152	193*	-	0.1
335 ORTH PRESB CH.	1	108	163	-	0.1
353 PLY BRETHREN..	3	363	668	0.1	0.2
371 REF CH IN AM..	2	296	522	0.1	0.2
403 SALVATION ARMY	2	154	757	0.2	0.3
413 S-D ADVENTISTS	5	1,787	2,266*	0.5	0.8
419 SO BAPT CONV..	9	1,481	1,878*	0.4	0.6
435 UNITARIAN-UNIV	2	438	610	0.1	0.2
443 UN C OF CHRIST	25	15,106	19,158*	3.9	6.4
449 UN METHODIST..	28	19,767	24,021	4.9	8.0
453 UN PRES CH USA	14	11,084	14,057*	2.9	4.7
EDGAR	51	7,367	10,703*	49.6	100.0
019 AMER BAPT CONV	2	540	639*	3.0	6.0
081 CATHOLIC......	4	0	1,809	8.4	16.9
093 CR CH (DISC)..	4	929	1,100*	5.1	10.3
097 CR C AND C CR.	12	1,403	1,661*	7.7	15.5
165 CH OF NAZARENE	3	231	630	2.9	5.9
193 EPISCOPAL.....	1	96	110	0.5	1.0
226 FRIENDS-USA...	1	133	157*	0.7	1.5
283 LUTH--MO SYNOD	1	267	376	1.7	3.5
413 S-D ADVENTISTS	1	26	31*	0.1	0.3
419 SO BAPT CONV..	2	108	128*	0.6	1.2
449 UN METHODIST..	17	3,076	3,401	15.8	31.8
453 UN PRES CH USA	3	558	661*	3.1	6.2
EDWARDS	34	4,344	5,051*	71.2	100.0
093 CR CH (DISC)..	1	265	310*	4.4	6.1
097 CR C AND C CR.	6	1,082	1,267*	17.9	25.1
165 CH OF NAZARENE	1	10	23	0.3	0.5
175 CONG CR CH....	2	175	205*	2.9	4.1
193 EPISCOPAL.....	1	33	43	0.6	0.9
221 FREE METH C NA	3	69	73	1.0	1.4
293 MORAV CH-NORTH	1	279	408	5.8	8.1
419 SO BAPT CONV..	3	808	946*	13.3	18.7
443 UN C OF CHRIST	1	72	84*	1.2	1.7
449 UN METHODIST..	11	1,273	1,366	19.3	27.0
453 UN PRES CH USA	4	278	326*	4.6	6.5
EFFINGHAM	65	8,585	21,025*	85.4	100.0
029 AMER LUTH CH..	2	447	576	2.3	2.7
081 CATHOLIC......	11	0	9,845	40.0	46.8
093 CR CH (DISC)..	2	264	330*	1.3	1.6
097 CR C AND C CR.	8	712	889*	3.6	4.2
123 CH GOD (ANDER)	2	162	333	1.4	1.6
165 CH OF NAZARENE	2	88	398	1.6	1.9
185 CUMBER PRESB..	1	52	65*	0.3	0.3
193 EPISCOPAL.....	1	36	65	0.3	0.3
221 FREE METH C NA	1	51	55	0.2	0.3
283 LUTH--MO SYNOD	9	2,488	3,481	14.1	16.6
419 SO BAPT CONV..	6	1,688	2,107*	8.6	10.0
443 UN C OF CHRIST	2	132	165*	0.7	0.8
449 UN METHODIST..	16	2,118	2,283	9.3	10.9
453 UN PRES CH USA	2	347	433*	1.8	2.1
FAYETTE	65	9,512	12,517*	60.3	100.0
081 CATHOLIC......	4	0	834	4.0	6.7
093 CR CH (DISC)..	2	301	355*	1.7	2.8
097 CR C AND C CR.	8	790	931*	4.5	7.4
123 CH GOD (ANDER)	4	146	723	3.5	5.8
157 CH OF BRETHREN	1	96	113*	0.5	0.9
221 FREE METH C NA	2	143	173	0.8	1.4
281 LUTH CH AMER..	2	394	485	2.3	3.9
283 LUTH--MO SYNOD	4	1,587	1,982	9.6	15.8
415 S-D BAPTIST GC	1	50	59*	0.3	0.5
419 SO BAPT CONV..	18	3,640	4,289*	20.7	34.3
435 UNITARIAN-UNIV	1	25	25	0.1	0.2
443 UN C OF CHRIST	1	105	124*	0.6	1.0
449 UN METHODIST..	16	2,036	2,190	10.6	17.5
453 UN PRES CH USA	1	199	234*	1.1	1.9
FORD	42	9,565	13,861*	84.6	100.0
029 AMER LUTH CH..	5	1,059	1,449	8.8	10.5
081 CATHOLIC......	6	0	2,000	12.2	14.4
093 CR CH (DISC)..	2	405	487*	3.0	3.5
097 CR C AND C CR.	1	300	360*	2.2	2.6
127 CH GOD (CLEVE)	1	18	22*	0.1	0.2
165 CH OF NAZARENE	3	72	185	1.1	1.3
201 EVAN COV CH AM	1	290	348*	2.1	2.5
281 LUTH CH AMER..	1	576	715	4.4	5.2
419 SO BAPT CONV..	2	513	616*	3.8	4.4
443 UN C OF CHRIST	2	158	190*	1.2	1.4
449 UN METHODIST..	15	5,504	6,684	40.8	48.2
453 UN PRES CH USA	3	670	805*	4.9	5.8
FRANKLIN	108	18,678	30,808*	80.4	100.0
019 AMER BAPT CONV	6	1,406	1,642*	4.3	5.3
081 CATHOLIC......	6	0	2,623	6.8	8.5
093 CR CH (DISC)..	1	459	536*	1.4	1.7
097 CR C AND C CR.	12	2,149	2,509*	6.5	8.1
123 CH GOD (ANDER)	4	580	1,909	5.0	6.2
127 CH GOD (CLEVE)	5	570	665*	1.7	2.2
165 CH OF NAZARENE	3	173	636	1.7	2.1
185 CUMBER PRESB..	1	115	134*	0.3	0.4
193 EPISCOPAL.....	1	103	154	0.4	0.5
283 LUTH--MO SYNOD	1	106	137	0.4	0.4
403 SALVATION ARMY	1	37	161	0.4	0.5
413 S-D ADVENTISTS	1	53	62*	0.2	0.2
419 SO BAPT CONV..	44	10,557	12,326*	32.2	40.0
449 UN METHODIST..	21	2,262	7,188	18.8	23.3
453 UN PRES CH USA	1	108	126*	0.3	0.4
FULTON	79	11,859	18,225*	43.5	100.0
019 AMER BAPT CONV	2	1,119	1,345*	3.2	7.4
081 CATHOLIC......	4	0	3,134	7.5	17.2
093 CR CH (DISC)..	6	1,198	1,440*	3.4	7.9
097 CR C AND C CR.	6	600	721*	1.7	4.0
157 CH OF BRETHREN	3	444	534*	1.3	2.9
165 CH OF NAZARENE	9	363	1,130	2.7	6.2
193 EPISCOPAL.....	2	154	284	0.7	1.6
221 FREE METH C NA	2	73	84	0.2	0.5
281 LUTH CH AMER..	2	406	547	1.3	3.0
371 REF CH IN AM..	1	308	332	0.8	1.8
403 SALVATION ARMY	1	73	248	0.6	1.4
413 S-D ADVENTISTS	1	61	73*	0.2	0.4
419 SO BAPT CONV..	1	195	234*	0.6	1.3
435 UNITARIAN-UNIV	1	86	86	0.2	0.5
443 UN C OF CHRIST	3	543	653*	1.6	3.6
449 UN METHODIST..	31	5,121	6,039	14.4	33.1
453 UN PRES CH USA	4	1,115	1,341*	3.2	7.4
GALLATIN	27	1,592	3,100*	41.8	100.0
081 CATHOLIC......	4	0	1,160	15.6	37.4
123 CH GOD (ANDER)	1	13	31	0.4	1.0
127 CH GOD (CLEVE)	3	64	77*	1.0	2.5
165 CH OF NAZARENE	1	34	90	1.2	2.9
185 CUMBER PRESB..	2	45	54*	0.7	1.7
419 SO BAPT CONV..	4	672	813*	11.0	26.2
449 UN METHODIST..	7	500	555	7.5	17.9
453 UN PRES CH USA	5	264	320*	4.3	10.3
GREENE	42	7,616	11,006*	64.7	100.0
019 AMER BAPT CONV	10	2,851	3,440*	20.2	31.3
081 CATHOLIC......	3	0	1,904	11.2	17.3
093 CR CH (DISC)..	2	336	405*	2.4	3.7
097 CR C AND C CR.	1	35	42*	0.2	0.4
283 LUTH--MO SYNOD	1	118	163	1.0	1.5
419 SO BAPT CONV..	16	2,487	3,001*	17.6	27.3
449 UN METHODIST..	6	1,411	1,595	9.4	14.5
453 UN PRES CH USA	3	378	456*	2.7	4.1
GRUNDY	28	7,072	17,175*	64.7	100.0
019 AMER BAPT CONV	1	441	550*	2.1	3.2
029 AMER LUTH CH..	3	1,928	2,619	9.9	15.2
081 CATHOLIC......	6	0	8,000	30.1	46.6
097 CR C AND C CR.	1	81	101*	0.4	0.6
165 CH OF NAZARENE	1	65	210	0.8	1.2
193 EPISCOPAL.....	1	110	156	0.6	0.9
221 FREE METH C NA	1	50	70	0.3	0.4
283 LUTH--MO SYNOD	1	96	152	0.6	0.9
419 SO BAPT CONV..	2	333	415*	1.6	2.4
443 UN C OF CHRIST	1	290	362*	1.4	2.1
449 UN METHODIST..	7	2,480	3,046	11.5	17.7
453 UN PRES CH USA	3	1,198	1,494*	5.6	8.7
HAMILTON	46	4,038	5,679*	65.5	100.0
081 CATHOLIC......	3	0	1,078	12.4	19.0
093 CR CH (DISC)..	3	113	131*	1.5	2.3
097 CR C AND C CR.	5	210	243*	2.8	4.3
127 CH GOD (CLEVE)	1	18	21*	0.2	0.4
175 CONG CR CH....	1	65	75*	0.9	1.3
185 CUMBER PRESB..	1	63	73*	0.8	1.3
193 EPISCOPAL.....	1	16	21	0.2	0.4
283 LUTH--MO SYNOD	1	44	48	0.6	0.8
419 SO BAPT CONV..	20	2,877	3,335*	38.5	58.7
449 UN METHODIST..	10	632	654	7.5	11.5
HANCOCK	62	8,874	12,735*	53.9	100.0

*Total adherents estimated from known number of communicant, confirmed, full members.

—Represents a percent less than 0.1.

Percentages may not total due to rounding.

Table 3. Churches and Church Membership by State, County and Denomination: 1971

County and Denomination	Number of churches	Communicant, confirmed, full members	Total adherents		
			Number	Percent of total population	Percent of total adherents
019 AMER BAPT CONV	3	489	585*	2.5	4.6
029 AMER LUTH CH..	3	530	751	3.2	5.9
081 CATHOLIC......	6	0	1,986	8.4	15.6
093 CR CH (DISC)..	6	932	1,115*	4.7	8.8
097 CR C AND C CR.	9	1,034	1,237*	5.2	9.7
165 CH OF NAZARENE	1	46	46	0.2	0.4
193 EPISCOPAL.....	2	112	201	0.9	1.6
221 FREE METH C NA	1	32	44	0.2	0.3
281 LUTH CH AMER..	1	345	448	1.9	3.5
283 LUTH--MO SYNOD	2	311	378	1.6	3.0
413 S-D ADVENTISTS	2	35	42*	0.2	0.3
443 UN C OF CHRIST	3	613	733*	3.1	5.8
449 UN METHODIST..	16	3,177	3,712	15.7	29.1
453 UN PRES CH USA	7	1,218	1,457*	6.2	11.4
HARDIN	13	1,194	1,599*	32.5	100.0
081 CATHOLIC......	1	0	164	3.3	10.3
093 CR CH (DISC)..	1	31	37*	0.8	2.3
097 CR C AND C CR.	3	286	341*	6.9	21.3
123 CH GOD (ANDER)	1	22	83	1.7	5.2
419 SO BAPT CONV..	4	556	662*	13.5	41.4
449 UN METHODIST..	3	299	312	6.3	19.5
HENDERSON	19	2,799	3,874*	45.8	100.0
019 AMER BAPT CONV	1	217	266*	3.1	6.9
081 CATHOLIC......	2	0	300	3.5	7.7
093 CR CH (DISC)..	1	160	196*	2.3	5.1
097 CR C AND C CR.	1	343	421*	5.0	10.9
165 CH OF NAZARENE	1	58	80	0.9	2.1
281 LUTH CH AMER..	1	157	219	2.6	5.7
371 REF CH IN AM..	1	71	98	1.2	2.5
449 UN METHODIST..	8	1,282	1,667	19.7	43.0
453 UN PRES CH USA	3	511	627*	7.4	16.2
HENRY	73	18,333	34,461*	64.8	100.0
019 AMER BAPT CONV	6	1,811	2,218*	4.2	6.4
029 AMER LUTH CH..	1	85	139	0.3	0.4
059 BAPT MISS ASSN	1	37	45*	0.1	0.1
081 CATHOLIC......	12	0	10,955	20.6	31.8
097 CR C AND C CR.	1	350	429*	0.8	1.2
127 CH GOD (CLEVE)	2	69	84*	0.2	0.2
165 CH OF NAZARENE	3	196	495	0.9	1.4
193 EPISCOPAL.....	2	224	299	0.6	0.9
199 EVAN CONG CH..	1	83	102*	0.2	0.3
201 EVAN COV CH AM	1	134	164*	0.3	0.5
221 FREE METH C NA	1	16	17	-	-
281 LUTH CH AMER..	8	3,721	5,018	9.4	14.6
283 LUTH--MO SYNOD	3	1,499	2,121	4.0	6.2
403 SALVATION ARMY	1	70	329	0.6	1.0
413 S-D ADVENTISTS	1	56	69*	0.1	0.2
419 SO BAPT CONV..	1	185	227*	0.4	0.7
443 UN C OF CHRIST	7	1,906	2,334*	4.4	6.8
449 UN METHODIST..	18	6,748	8,016	15.1	23.3
453 UN PRES CH USA	3	1,143	1,400*	2.6	4.1
IROQUOIS	76	13,542	22,115*	66.0	100.0
029 AMER LUTH CH..	8	2,373	3,251	9.7	14.7
081 CATHOLIC......	10	0	5,000	14.9	22.6
093 CR CH (DISC)..	2	352	428*	1.3	1.9
097 CR C AND C CR.	11	1,479	1,799*	5.4	8.1
123 CH GOD (ANDER)	1	45	115	0.3	0.5
165 CH OF NAZARENE	4	123	370	1.1	1.7
175 CONG CR CH....	1	160	195*	0.6	0.9
193 EPISCOPAL.....	1	53	65	0.2	0.3
226 FRIENDS-USA...	1	78	95*	0.3	0.4
283 LUTH--MO SYNOD	9	2,806	3,731	11.1	16.9
371 REF CH IN AM..	1	182	262	0.8	1.2
419 SO BAPT CONV..	2	130	158*	0.5	0.7
443 UN C OF CHRIST	3	611	743*	2.2	3.4
449 UN METHODIST..	19	4,797	5,474	16.3	24.8
453 UN PRES CH USA	3	353	429*	1.3	1.9
JACKSON	84	16,215	22,870*	41.6	100.0
019 AMER BAPT CONV	10	2,234	2,576*	4.7	11.3
081 CATHOLIC......	6	0	2,874	5.2	12.6
093 CR CH (DISC)..	1	346	399*	0.7	1.7
097 CR C AND C CR.	4	1,175	1,355*	2.5	5.9
123 CH GOD (ANDER)	4	88	218	0.4	1.0
127 CH GOD (CLEVE)	1	21	24*	-	0.1
165 CH OF NAZARENE	2	219	563	1.0	2.5
185 CUMBER PRESB..	1	24	28*	0.1	0.1
193 EPISCOPAL.....	1	244	275	0.5	1.2
226 FRIENDS-USA...	1	16	18*	-	0.1
281 LUTH CH AMER..	5	1,254	1,760	3.2	7.7
283 LUTH--MO SYNOD	5	1,475	2,116	3.8	9.3
353 PLY BRETHREN..	1	10	15	-	0.1
381 REF PRES-EVAN.	1	15	28	0.1	0.1
419 SO BAPT CONV..	17	4,762	5,492*	10.0	24.0
435 UNITARIAN-UNIV	1	50	50	0.1	0.2
443 UN C OF CHRIST	2	211	243*	0.4	1.1
449 UN METHODIST..	16	3,096	3,712	6.7	16.2
453 UN PRES CH USA	5	975	1,124*	2.0	4.9
JASPER	32	2,856	6,232*	58.0	100.0
019 AMER BAPT CONV	1	268	325*	3.0	5.2
081 CATHOLIC......	3	0	2,510	23.4	40.3
097 CR C AND C CR.	6	711	862*	8.0	13.8
175 CONG CR CH....	1	50	61*	0.6	1.0
185 CUMBER PRESB..	1	25	30*	0.3	0.5
221 FREE METH C NA	1	48	70	0.7	1.1
281 LUTH CH AMER..	1	63	71	0.7	1.1
419 SO BAPT CONV..	6	471	571*	5.3	9.2
443 UN C OF CHRIST	2	180	218*	2.0	3.5
449 UN METHODIST..	9	907	1,353	12.6	21.7
453 UN PRES CH USA	1	133	161*	1.5	2.6
JEFFERSON	81	13,577	17,976*	57.2	100.0
019 AMER BAPT CONV	1	385	463*	1.5	2.6
029 AMER LUTH CH..	1	123	188	0.6	1.0
081 CATHOLIC......	3	0	1,252	4.0	7.0
097 CR C AND C CR.	11	1,403	1,686*	5.4	9.4
123 CH GOD (ANDER)	4	115	358	1.1	2.0
127 CH GOD (CLEVE)	1	96	115*	0.4	0.6
165 CH OF NAZARENE	3	149	341	1.1	1.9
193 EPISCOPAL.....	1	117	204	0.6	1.1
221 FREE METH C NA	1	26	27	0.1	0.2
283 LUTH--MO SYNOD	1	209	267	0.8	1.5
413 S-D ADVENTISTS	1	26	31*	0.1	0.2
419 SO BAPT CONV..	33	7,517	9,034*	28.7	50.3
435 UNITARIAN-UNIV	1	50	65	0.2	0.4
449 UN METHODIST..	17	2,395	2,784	8.9	15.5
453 UN PRES CH USA	2	966	1,161*	3.7	6.5
JERSEY	24	3,755	7,964*	43.1	100.0
019 AMER BAPT CONV	4	1,312	1,603*	8.7	20.1
081 CATHOLIC......	5	0	3,220	17.4	40.4
097 CR C AND C CR.	1	50	61*	0.3	0.8
165 CH OF NAZARENE	1	58	214	1.2	2.7
283 LUTH--MO SYNOD	1	153	234	1.3	2.9
419 SO BAPT CONV..	5	558	682*	3.7	8.6
443 UN C OF CHRIST	2	364	445*	2.4	5.6
449 UN METHODIST..	4	816	962	5.2	12.1
453 UN PRES CH USA	1	444	543*	2.9	6.8
JO DAVIESS	41	5,889	16,636*	76.4	100.0
029 AMER LUTH CH..	9	1,932	2,663	12.2	16.0
081 CATHOLIC......	10	0	9,005	41.4	54.1
165 CH OF NAZARENE	1	37	116	0.5	0.7
193 EPISCOPAL.....	1	38	48	0.2	0.3
283 LUTH--MO SYNOD	1	186	255	1.2	1.5
435 UNITARIAN-UNIV	1	164	217	1.0	1.3
449 UN METHODIST..	10	2,369	2,884	13.3	17.3
453 UN PRES CH USA	7	1,084	1,348*	6.2	8.1
469 WISC EVAN LUTH	1	79	100	0.5	0.6
JOHNSON	24	3,094	3,683*	48.8	100.0
019 AMER BAPT CONV	1	94	111*	1.5	3.0
081 CATHOLIC......	2	0	100	1.3	2.7
097 CR C AND C CR.	1	112	132*	1.7	3.6
123 CH GOD (ANDER)	1	12	43	0.6	1.2
185 CUMBER PRESB..	4	216	254*	3.4	6.9
419 SO BAPT CONV..	13	1,771	2,082*	27.6	56.5
449 UN METHODIST..	2	889	961	12.7	26.1
KANE	167	60,041	146,562*	58.4	100.0
019 AMER BAPT CONV	9	3,286	4,113*	1.6	2.8
029 AMER LUTH CH..	4	1,984	2,788	1.1	1.9
081 CATHOLIC......	27	0	67,403	26.9	46.0
097 CR C AND C CR.	3	833	1,043*	0.4	0.7
123 CH GOD (ANDER)	1	51	128	0.1	0.1
127 CH GOD (CLEVE)	3	299	374*	0.1	0.3
157 CH OF BRETHREN	2	732	916*	0.4	0.6
165 CH OF NAZARENE	5	315	830	0.3	0.6
193 EPISCOPAL.....	6	2,543	3,137	1.2	2.1
201 EVAN COV CH AM	2	251	314*	0.1	0.2
221 FREE METH C NA	3	189	243	0.1	0.2
281 LUTH CH AMER..	11	7,602	11,076	4.4	7.6
283 LUTH--MO SYNOD	18	11,535	15,923	6.3	10.9
349 PENT HOLINESS.	2	39	49*	-	-
353 PLY BRETHREN..	2	170	270	0.1	0.2
381 REF PRES-EVAN.	1	113	167	0.1	0.1
403 SALVATION ARMY	1	72	251	0.1	0.2
413 S-D ADVENTISTS	4	458	573*	0.2	0.4
419 SO BAPT CONV..	14	2,783	3,483*	1.4	2.4
435 UNITARIAN-UNIV	2	203	258	0.1	0.2
443 UN C OF CHRIST	16	7,804	9,767*	3.9	6.7
449 UN METHODIST..	23	15,059	18,783	7.5	12.8
453 UN PRES CH USA	7	3,674	4,598*	1.8	3.1
469 WISC EVAN LUTH	1	46	75	-	0.1
KANKAKEE	85	20,796	56,120*	57.7	100.0
019 AMER BAPT CONV	2	761	938*	1.0	1.7
029 AMER LUTH CH..	2	605	890	0.9	1.6
081 CATHOLIC......	17	0	28,000	28.8	49.9
093 CR CH (DISC)..	2	616	760*	0.8	1.4
097 CR C AND C CR.	1	181	223*	0.2	0.4
105 CHRISTIAN REF.	1	112	192	0.2	0.3
123 CH GOD (ANDER)	2	62	148	0.2	0.3
127 CH GOD (CLEVE)	2	218	269*	0.3	0.5
165 CH OF NAZARENE	10	1,713	3,456	3.6	6.2
193 EPISCOPAL.....	2	431	699	0.7	1.2
283 LUTH--MO SYNOD	8	3,827	5,219	5.4	9.3
285 MENNONITE CH..	1	107	132*	0.1	0.2
313 NO AM BAPT GC.	1	574	708*	0.7	1.3
371 REF CH IN AM..	3	509	767	0.8	1.4
403 SALVATION ARMY	1	90	279	0.3	0.5
413 S-D ADVENTISTS	2	101	125*	0.1	0.2
419 SO BAPT CONV..	4	1,048	1,292*	1.3	2.3

*Total adherents estimated from known number of communicant, confirmed, full members.

—Represents a percent less than 0.1.

Percentages may not total due to rounding.

Table 3. Churches and Church Membership by State, County and Denomination: 1971

County and Denomination	Number of churches	Communicant, confirmed, full members	Total adherents		
			Number	Percent of total population	Percent of total adherents
443 UN C OF CHRIST	3	1,180	1,455*	1.5	2.6
449 UN METHODIST..	16	7,282	8,836	9.1	15.7
453 UN PRES CH USA	3	1,095	1,350*	1.4	2.4
469 WISC EVAN LUTH	2	284	382	0.4	0.7
KENDALL	30	7,118	13,785*	52.3	100.0
019 AMER BAPT CONV	1	333	427*	1.6	3.1
029 AMER LUTH CH..	7	2,382	3,368	12.8	24.4
059 BAPT MISS ASSN	1	50	64*	0.2	0.5
081 CATHOLIC......	3	0	4,000	15.2	29.0
097 CR C AND C CR.	1	35	45*	0.2	0.3
157 CH OF BRETHREN	1	248	318*	1.2	2.3
283 LUTH--MO SYNOD	2	775	1,144	4.3	8.3
419 SO BAPT CONV..	2	183	235*	0.9	1.7
443 UN C OF CHRIST	1	460	590*	2.2	4.3
449 UN METHODIST..	9	1,738	2,422	9.2	17.6
453 UN PRES CH USA	2	914	1,172*	4.4	8.5
KNOX	46	15,932	26,621*	43.4	100.0
019 AMER BAPT CONV	1	742	885*	1.4	3.3
081 CATHOLIC......	6	0	6,388	10.4	24.0
093 CR CH (DISC)..	3	1,522	1,815*	3.0	6.8
097 CR C AND C CR.	2	80	95*	0.2	0.4
123 CH GOD (ANDER)	1	120	270	0.4	1.0
127 CH GOD (CLEVE)	1	59	70*	0.1	0.3
165 CH OF NAZARENE	2	174	644	1.1	2.4
175 CONG CR CH....	4	896	1,069*	1.7	4.0
193 EPISCOPAL.....	1	128	195	0.3	0.7
201 EVAN COV CH AM	1	438	522*	0.9	2.0
226 FRIENDS-USA...	1	19	23*	-	0.1
281 LUTH CH AMER..	6	3,383	4,373	7.1	16.4
283 LUTH--MO SYNOD	1	267	350	0.6	1.3
403 SALVATION ARMY	1	50	273	0.4	1.0
413 S-D ADVENTISTS	1	87	104*	0.2	0.4
419 SO BAPT CONV..	1	193	230*	0.4	0.9
443 UN C OF CHRIST	2	408	487*	0.8	1.8
449 UN METHODIST..	6	5,410	6,495	10.6	24.4
453 UN PRES CH USA	5	1,956	2,333*	3.8	8.8
LAKE	143	51,564	178,501*	46.7	100.0
019 AMER BAPT CONV	3	2,458	3,046*	0.8	1.7
029 AMER LUTH CH..	4	1,754	2,660	0.7	1.5
081 CATHOLIC......	25	0	106,154	27.7	59.5
093 CR CH (DISC)..	3	1,156	1,433*	0.4	0.8
097 CR C AND C CR.	3	315	390*	0.1	0.2
127 CH GOD (CLEVE)	3	358	444*	0.1	0.2
165 CH OF NAZARENE	3	196	449	0.1	0.3
193 EPISCOPAL.....	10	5,251	7,272	1.9	4.1
199 EVAN CONG CH..	1	162	201*	0.1	0.1
221 FREE METH C NA	1	40	67	-	-
226 FRIENDS-USA...	1	78	97*	-	0.1
281 LUTH CH AMER..	11	6,388	9,454	2.5	5.3
283 LUTH--MO SYNOD	9	3,713	5,479	1.4	3.1
313 NO AM BAPT GC.	1	33	41*	-	-
353 PLY BRETHREN..	1	60	100	-	0.1
403 SALVATION ARMY	1	53	250	0.1	0.1
413 S-D ADVENTISTS	1	232	288*	0.1	0.2
419 SO BAPT CONV..	14	3,552	4,402*	1.2	2.5
435 UNITARIAN-UNIV	1	425	675	0.2	0.4
443 UN C OF CHRIST	16	6,019	7,460*	1.9	4.2
449 UN METHODIST..	20	10,182	16,516	4.3	9.3
453 UN PRES CH USA	8	8,033	9,956*	2.6	5.6
469 WISC EVAN LUTH	3	1,106	1,667	0.4	0.9
LA SALLE	127	25,379	75,450*	67.7	100.0
019 AMER BAPT CONV	3	1,099	1,338*	1.2	1.8
029 AMER LUTH CH..	14	5,580	7,879	7.1	10.4
081 CATHOLIC......	32	0	41,539	37.3	55.1
097 CR C AND C CR.	3	1,063	1,294*	1.2	1.7
123 CH GOD (ANDER)	2	73	189	0.2	0.3
127 CH GOD (CLEVE)	1	25	30*	-	-
165 CH OF NAZARENE	7	572	1,533	1.4	2.0
193 EPISCOPAL.....	3	598	934	0.8	1.2
197 EVAN CH OF NA.	1	12	15*	-	-
281 LUTH CH AMER..	3	410	534	0.5	0.7
283 LUTH--MO SYNOD	3	1,365	1,885	1.7	2.5
403 SALVATION ARMY	2	108	423	0.4	0.6
413 S-D ADVENTISTS	3	142	173*	0.2	0.2
419 SO BAPT CONV..	8	543	661*	0.6	0.9
443 UN C OF CHRIST	7	2,681	3,265*	2.9	4.3
449 UN METHODIST..	27	8,468	10,543	9.5	14.0
453 UN PRES CH USA	8	2,640	3,215*	2.9	4.3
LAWRENCE	51	6,984	9,144*	52.2	100.0
081 CATHOLIC......	3	0	859	4.9	9.4
093 CR CH (DISC)..	1	515	613*	3.5	6.7
097 CR C AND C CR.	8	1,508	1,796*	10.2	19.6
123 CH GOD (ANDER)	1	35	80	0.5	0.9
127 CH GOD (CLEVE)	3	177	211*	1.2	2.3
157 CH OF BRETHREN	1	93	111*	0.6	1.2
165 CH OF NAZARENE	1	17	44	0.3	0.5
221 FREE METH C NA	6	344	482	2.8	5.3
283 LUTH--MO SYNOD	1	154	201	1.1	2.2
419 SO BAPT CONV..	2	674	803*	4.6	8.8
443 UN C OF CHRIST	2	104	124*	0.7	1.4
449 UN METHODIST..	18	2,808	3,159	18.0	34.5
453 UN PRES CH USA	4	555	661*	3.8	7.2
LEE	52	10,482	21,762*	57.3	100.0
019 AMER BAPT CONV	2	635	769*	2.0	3.5
029 AMER LUTH CH..	7	2,314	3,170	8.4	14.6
081 CATHOLIC......	9	0	8,181	21.6	37.6
093 CR CH (DISC)..	1	182	220*	0.6	1.0
097 CR C AND C CR.	1	55	67*	0.2	0.3
121 CH GOD (ABR)..	1	50	61*	0.2	0.3
123 CH GOD (ANDER)	1	54	180	0.5	0.8
157 CH OF BRETHREN	2	412	499*	1.3	2.3
165 CH OF NAZARENE	1	53	220	0.6	1.0
193 EPISCOPAL.....	1	277	323	0.9	1.5
199 EVAN CONG CH..	3	412	499*	1.3	2.3
281 LUTH CH AMER..	2	1,249	1,723	4.5	7.9
419 SO BAPT CONV..	3	295	357*	0.9	1.6
443 UN C OF CHRIST	3	319	386*	1.0	1.8
449 UN METHODIST..	12	3,242	3,977	10.5	18.3
453 UN PRES CH USA	3	933	1,130*	3.0	5.2
LIVINGSTON	77	14,575	25,306*	62.2	100.0
019 AMER BAPT CONV	5	1,109	1,342*	3.3	5.3
029 AMER LUTH CH..	9	2,677	3,647	9.0	14.4
081 CATHOLIC......	13	0	6,220	15.3	24.6
093 CR CH (DISC)..	5	484	586*	1.4	2.3
097 CR C AND C CR.	2	265	321*	0.8	1.3
123 CH GOD (ANDER)	1	32	104	0.3	0.4
127 CH GOD (CLEVE)	1	30	36*	0.1	0.1
165 CH OF NAZARENE	4	181	588	1.4	2.3
193 EPISCOPAL.....	2	170	247	0.6	1.0
221 FREE METH C NA	1	12	12	-	-
281 LUTH CH AMER..	1	437	575	1.4	2.3
283 LUTH--MO SYNOD	2	590	822	2.0	3.2
285 MENNONITE CH..	1	210	254*	0.6	1.0
287 MENN GEN CONF.	2	285	345*	0.8	1.4
403 SALVATION ARMY	1	28	218	0.5	0.9
419 SO BAPT CONV..	1	59	71*	0.2	0.3
443 UN C OF CHRIST	3	595	720*	1.8	2.8
449 UN METHODIST..	21	6,111	7,625	18.7	30.1
453 UN PRES CH USA	2	1,300	1,573*	3.9	6.2
LOGAN	54	13,942	20,518*	61.2	100.0
019 AMER BAPT CONV	1	233	276*	0.8	1.3
029 AMER LUTH CH..	3	1,639	2,158	6.4	10.5
059 BAPT MISS ASSN	1	16	19*	0.1	0.1
081 CATHOLIC......	6	0	3,374	10.1	16.4
093 CR CH (DISC)..	2	116	137*	0.4	0.7
097 CR C AND C CR.	12	3,826	4,533*	13.5	22.1
127 CH GOD (CLEVE)	1	47	56*	0.2	0.3
165 CH OF NAZARENE	1	51	138	0.4	0.7
185 CUMBER PRESB..	2	294	348*	1.0	1.7
193 EPISCOPAL.....	1	178	235	0.7	1.1
221 FREE METH C NA	1	49	67	0.2	0.3
281 LUTH CH AMER..	1	319	389	1.2	1.9
283 LUTH--MO SYNOD	5	2,004	2,595	7.7	12.6
403 SALVATION ARMY	1	44	177	0.5	0.9
413 S-D ADVENTISTS	1	18	21*	0.1	0.1
419 SO BAPT CONV..	1	254	301*	0.9	1.5
443 UN C OF CHRIST	1	506	600*	1.8	2.9
449 UN METHODIST..	12	3,843	4,496	13.4	21.9
453 UN PRES CH USA	1	505	598*	1.8	2.9
MC DONOUGH	46	10,295	16,100*	43.9	100.0
019 AMER BAPT CONV	4	1,380	1,586*	4.3	9.9
059 BAPT MISS ASSN	1	29	33*	0.1	0.2
081 CATHOLIC......	4	0	3,720	10.1	23.1
093 CR CH (DISC)..	5	860	988*	2.7	6.1
097 CR C AND C CR.	5	755	868*	2.4	5.4
121 CH GOD (ABR)..	1	124	143*	0.4	0.9
123 CH GOD (ANDER)	1	12	37	0.1	0.2
165 CH OF NAZARENE	2	104	266	0.7	1.7
193 EPISCOPAL.....	1	136	180	0.5	1.1
221 FREE METH C NA	1	30	45	0.1	0.3
281 LUTH CH AMER..	1	188	253	0.7	1.6
283 LUTH--MO SYNOD	1	147	228	0.6	1.4
403 SALVATION ARMY	1	57	221	0.6	1.4
419 SO BAPT CONV..	1	146	168*	0.5	1.0
435 UNITARIAN-UNIV	1	37	52	0.1	0.3
449 UN METHODIST..	9	4,429	5,173	14.1	32.1
453 UN PRES CH USA	7	1,861	2,139*	5.8	13.3
MC HENRY	78	27,503	71,486*	64.1	100.0
019 AMER BAPT CONV	2	334	418*	0.4	0.6
029 AMER LUTH CH..	1	650	978	0.9	1.4
081 CATHOLIC......	14	0	33,879	30.4	47.4
097 CR C AND C CR.	1	152	190*	0.2	0.3
127 CH GOD (CLEVE)	1	8	10*	-	-
165 CH OF NAZARENE	1	55	111	0.1	0.2
193 EPISCOPAL.....	4	712	1,127	1.0	1.6
201 EVAN COV CH AM	1	53	66*	0.1	0.1
221 FREE METH C NA	1	103	123	0.1	0.2
281 LUTH CH AMER..	7	5,147	7,904	7.1	11.1
283 LUTH--MO SYNOD	10	7,580	10,551	9.5	14.8
419 SO BAPT CONV..	6	1,035	1,297*	1.2	1.8
435 UNITARIAN-UNIV	1	140	174	0.2	0.2
443 UN C OF CHRIST	7	3,518	4,407*	4.0	6.2
449 UN METHODIST..	16	6,193	7,967	7.1	11.1
453 UN PRES CH USA	5	1,823	2,284*	2.0	3.2
MC LEAN	113	33,249	57,853*	55.4	100.0
019 AMER BAPT CONV	6	1,265	1,513*	1.4	2.6
029 AMER LUTH CH..	4	1,010	1,399	1.3	2.4
081 CATHOLIC......	11	0	16,113	15.4	27.9

*Total adherents estimated from known number of communicant, confirmed, full members.

—Represents a percent less than 0.1.

Percentages may not total due to rounding.

Table 3. Churches and Church Membership by State, County and Denomination: 1971

County and Denomination	Number of churches	Communicant, confirmed, full members	Total adherents: Number	Total adherents: Percent of total population	Total adherents: Percent of total adherents
093 CR CH (DISC)..	14	3,188	3,813*	3.7	6.6
097 CR C AND C CR.	10	2,145	2,566*	2.5	4.4
123 CH GOD (ANDER)	4	230	632	0.6	1.1
127 CH GOD (CLEVE)	1	65	78*	0.1	0.1
165 CH OF NAZARENE	2	187	429	0.4	0.7
193 EPISCOPAL.....	2	886	1,078	1.0	1.9
221 FREE METH C NA	1	40	60	0.1	0.1
281 LUTH CH AMER..	1	1,117	1,576	1.5	2.7
283 LUTH--MO SYNOD	7	3,789	5,119	4.9	8.8
285 MENNONITE CH..	1	40	48*	-	0.1
287 MENN GEN CONF.	3	579	693*	0.7	1.2
403 SALVATION ARMY	1	147	551	0.5	1.0
413 S-D ADVENTISTS	1	24	29*	-	0.1
419 SO BAPT CONV..	4	784	938*	0.9	1.6
435 UNITARIAN-UNIV	1	229	398	0.4	0.7
443 UN C OF CHRIST	2	429	513*	0.5	0.9
449 UN METHODIST..	28	12,311	14,585	14.0	25.2
453 UN PRES CH USA	9	4,784	5,722*	5.5	9.9
MACON	102	35,107	62,251*	49.8	100.0
019 AMER BAPT CONV	1	1,002	1,234*	1.0	2.0
059 BAPT MISS ASSN	1	43	53*	-	0.1
081 CATHOLIC......	7	0	17,247	13.8	27.7
093 CR CH (DISC)..	10	3,899	4,802*	3.8	7.7
097 CR C AND C CR.	3	900	1,108*	0.9	1.8
123 CH GOD (ANDER)	5	435	1,095	0.9	1.8
127 CH GOD (CLEVE)	1	99	122*	0.1	0.2
157 CH OF BRETHREN	2	220	271*	0.2	0.4
165 CH OF NAZARENE	5	959	2,296	1.8	3.7
193 EPISCOPAL.....	1	701	912	0.7	1.5
221 FREE METH C NA	1	178	234	0.2	0.4
226 FRIENDS-USA...	1	18	22*	-	-
281 LUTH CH AMER..	3	1,445	1,913	1.5	3.1
283 LUTH--MO SYNOD	7	4,844	6,366	5.1	10.2
403 SALVATION ARMY	1	142	639	0.5	1.0
413 S-D ADVENTISTS	1	138	170*	0.1	0.3
419 SO BAPT CONV..	12	3,318	4,087*	3.3	6.6
435 UNITARIAN-UNIV	1	50	75	0.1	0.1
443 UN C OF CHRIST	2	578	712*	0.6	1.1
449 UN METHODIST..	30	12,181	14,019	11.2	22.5
453 UN PRES CH USA	7	3,957	4,874*	3.9	7.8
MACOUPIN	104	15,268	26,433*	59.3	100.0
019 AMER BAPT CONV	5	909	1,090*	2.4	4.1
029 AMER LUTH CH..	5	971	1,286	2.9	4.9
081 CATHOLIC......	16	0	7,384	16.6	27.9
093 CR CH (DISC)..	4	653	783*	1.8	3.0
097 CR C AND C CR.	8	640	767*	1.7	2.9
157 CH OF BRETHREN	2	317	380*	0.9	1.4
165 CH OF NAZARENE	2	128	322	0.7	1.2
193 EPISCOPAL.....	2	128	158	0.4	0.6
221 FREE METH C NA	2	17	23	0.1	0.1
283 LUTH--MO SYNOD	6	2,198	2,990	6.7	11.3
419 SO BAPT CONV..	25	3,409	4,087*	9.2	15.5
443 UN C OF CHRIST	4	1,143	1,370*	3.1	5.2
449 UN METHODIST..	19	4,233	5,167	11.6	19.5
453 UN PRES CH USA	4	522	626*	1.4	2.4
MADISON	218	64,904	131,202*	52.3	100.0
019 AMER BAPT CONV	16	5,882	7,234*	2.9	5.5
029 AMER LUTH CH..	1	250	324	0.1	0.2
081 CATHOLIC......	29	0	46,568	18.6	35.5
093 CR CH (DISC)..	3	810	996*	0.4	0.8
097 CR C AND C CR.	9	1,775	2,183*	0.9	1.7
123 CH GOD (ANDER)	6	355	961	0.4	0.7
127 CH GOD (CLEVE)	6	436	536*	0.2	0.4
165 CH OF NAZARENE	7	930	2,760	1.1	2.1
175 CONG CR CH....	1	241	296*	0.1	0.2
193 EPISCOPAL.....	6	329	1,127	0.4	0.9
221 FREE METH C NA	2	123	150	0.1	0.1
281 LUTH CH AMER..	2	137	205	0.1	0.2
283 LUTH--MO SYNOD	23	10,031	14,122	5.6	10.8
381 REF PRES-EVAN.	1	62	87	-	0.1
403 SALVATION ARMY	2	176	717	0.3	0.5
413 S-D ADVENTISTS	2	169	208*	0.1	0.2
419 SO BAPT CONV..	37	15,811	19,445*	7.7	14.8
435 UNITARIAN-UNIV	1	100	110	-	0.1
443 UN C OF CHRIST	17	10,015	12,317*	4.9	9.4
449 UN METHODIST..	29	9,819	11,690	4.7	8.9
453 UN PRES CH USA	18	7,453	9,166*	3.7	7.0
MARION	89	16,596	22,900*	58.7	100.0
019 AMER BAPT CONV	1	1,533	1,844*	4.7	8.1
059 BAPT MISS ASSN	2	99	119*	0.3	0.5
081 CATHOLIC......	5	0	2,669	6.8	11.7
093 CR CH (DISC)..	3	693	834*	2.1	3.6
097 CR C AND C CR.	15	2,398	2,884*	7.4	12.6
123 CH GOD (ANDER)	2	96	302	0.8	1.3
127 CH GOD (CLEVE)	2	144	173*	0.4	0.8
157 CH OF BRETHREN	1	50	60*	0.2	0.3
165 CH OF NAZARENE	2	108	342	0.9	1.5
193 EPISCOPAL.....	1	55	92	0.2	0.4
221 FREE METH C NA	2	136	188	0.5	0.8
281 LUTH CH AMER..	1	194	249	0.6	1.1
283 LUTH--MO SYNOD	3	1,160	1,524	3.9	6.7
403 SALVATION ARMY	1	65	220	0.6	1.0
419 SO BAPT CONV..	22	5,098	6,132*	15.7	26.8
443 UN C OF CHRIST	2	529	636*	1.6	2.8
449 UN METHODIST..	20	3,632	3,903	10.0	17.0
453 UN PRES CH USA	4	606	729*	1.9	3.2

*Total adherents estimated from known number of communicant, confirmed, full members.

County and Denomination	Number of churches	Communicant, confirmed, full members	Total adherents: Number	Total adherents: Percent of total population	Total adherents: Percent of total adherents
MARSHALL	29	4,530	8,961*	67.4	100.0
029 AMER LUTH CH..	2	609	873	6.6	9.7
081 CATHOLIC......	7	0	3,259	24.5	36.4
093 CR CH (DISC)..	1	144	174*	1.3	1.9
097 CR C AND C CR.	2	391	473*	3.6	5.3
165 CH OF NAZARENE	1	41	144	1.1	1.6
193 EPISCOPAL.....	1	41	41	0.3	0.5
281 LUTH CH AMER..	1	176	208	1.6	2.3
283 LUTH--MO SYNOD	3	538	673	5.1	7.5
443 UN C OF CHRIST	1	176	213*	1.6	2.4
449 UN METHODIST..	6	1,675	2,009	15.1	22.4
453 UN PRES CH USA	4	739	894*	6.7	10.0
MASON	31	7,039	9,754*	60.4	100.0
019 AMER BAPT CONV	4	912	1,105*	6.8	11.3
081 CATHOLIC......	3	0	962	6.0	9.9
093 CR CH (DISC)..	2	715	867*	5.4	8.9
097 CR C AND C CR.	2	375	454*	2.8	4.7
165 CH OF NAZARENE	2	95	380	2.4	3.9
193 EPISCOPAL.....	1	166	177	1.1	1.8
283 LUTH--MO SYNOD	7	1,791	2,411	14.9	24.7
419 SO BAPT CONV..	4	646	783*	4.8	8.0
449 UN METHODIST..	5	2,037	2,249	13.9	23.1
453 UN PRES CH USA	1	302	366*	2.3	3.8
MASSAC	35	7,138	9,055*	65.2	100.0
029 AMER LUTH CH..	3	459	602	4.3	6.6
081 CATHOLIC......	1	0	400	2.9	4.4
093 CR CH (DISC)..	2	203	240*	1.7	2.7
097 CR C AND C CR.	3	200	237*	1.7	2.6
123 CH GOD (ANDER)	1	113	321	2.3	3.5
127 CH GOD (CLEVE)	2	79	93*	0.7	1.0
165 CH OF NAZARENE	1	36	118	0.8	1.3
185 CUMBER PRESB..	1	100	118*	0.8	1.3
281 LUTH CH AMER..	1	352	412	3.0	4.5
413 S-D ADVENTISTS	1	17	20*	0.1	0.2
419 SO BAPT CONV..	11	4,122	4,877*	35.1	53.9
443 UN C OF CHRIST	2	314	371*	2.7	4.1
449 UN METHODIST..	5	1,022	1,103	7.9	12.2
453 UN PRES CH USA	1	121	143*	1.0	1.6
MENARD	25	4,620	6,353*	65.6	100.0
081 CATHOLIC......	3	0	758	7.8	11.9
093 CR CH (DISC)..	2	286	346*	3.6	5.4
097 CR C AND C CR.	3	700	848*	8.8	13.3
185 CUMBER PRESB..	1	90	109*	1.1	1.7
283 LUTH--MO SYNOD	2	572	722	7.5	11.4
413 S-D ADVENTISTS	1	12	15*	0.2	0.2
419 SO BAPT CONV..	2	622	753*	7.8	11.9
443 UN C OF CHRIST	1	309	374*	3.9	5.9
449 UN METHODIST..	3	764	896	9.3	14.1
453 UN PRES CH USA	7	1,265	1,532*	15.8	24.1
MERCER	34	6,458	9,846*	56.9	100.0
019 AMER BAPT CONV	1	411	503*	2.9	5.1
081 CATHOLIC......	5	0	1,553	9.0	15.8
093 CR CH (DISC)..	1	138	169*	1.0	1.7
165 CH OF NAZARENE	1	39	131	0.8	1.3
193 EPISCOPAL.....	1	52	58	0.3	0.6
281 LUTH CH AMER..	5	1,192	1,596	9.2	16.2
413 S-D ADVENTISTS	1	41	50*	0.3	0.5
419 SO BAPT CONV..	1	53	65*	0.4	0.7
449 UN METHODIST..	7	2,294	2,981	17.2	30.3
453 UN PRES CH USA	11	2,238	2,740*	15.8	27.8
MONROE	26	6,005	13,079*	69.5	100.0
081 CATHOLIC......	8	0	5,490	29.2	42.0
127 CH GOD (CLEVE)	1	8	10*	0.1	0.1
283 LUTH--MO SYNOD	4	1,163	1,602	8.5	12.2
419 SO BAPT CONV..	3	799	985*	5.2	7.5
443 UN C OF CHRIST	9	3,965	4,890*	26.0	37.4
449 UN METHODIST..	1	70	102	0.5	0.8
MONTGOMERY	78	11,790	19,999*	66.1	100.0
019 AMER BAPT CONV	2	440	531*	1.8	2.7
081 CATHOLIC......	9	0	5,313	17.6	26.6
093 CR CH (DISC)..	6	813	982*	3.2	4.9
097 CR C AND C CR.	4	385	465*	1.5	2.3
123 CH GOD (ANDER)	1	140	329	1.1	1.6
165 CH OF NAZARENE	1	4	30	0.1	0.2
221 FREE METH C NA	4	70	82	0.3	0.4
281 LUTH CH AMER..	8	1,366	1,750	5.8	8.8
283 LUTH--MO SYNOD	5	1,907	2,583	8.5	12.9
419 SO BAPT CONV..	17	2,817	3,403*	11.2	17.0
443 UN C OF CHRIST	1	101	122*	0.4	0.6
449 UN METHODIST..	13	2,667	3,104	10.3	15.5
453 UN PRES CH USA	7	1,080	1,305*	4.3	6.5
MORGAN	66	12,593	20,328*	56.2	100.0
019 AMER BAPT CONV	3	1,280	1,519*	4.2	7.5
081 CATHOLIC......	6	0	4,499	12.4	22.1
093 CR CH (DISC)..	7	1,612	1,913*	5.3	9.4
097 CR C AND C CR.	3	458	544*	1.5	2.7
123 CH GOD (ANDER)	1	28	80	0.2	0.4
127 CH GOD (CLEVE)	1	11	13*	-	0.1
165 CH OF NAZARENE	2	126	256	0.7	1.3
193 EPISCOPAL.....	1	202	251	0.7	1.2

—Represents a percent less than 0.1.

Percentages may not total due to rounding.

Table 3. Churches and Church Membership by State, County and Denomination: 1971

County and Denomination	Number of churches	Communicant, confirmed, full members	Total adherents: Number	Percent of total population	Percent of total adherents
281 LUTH CH AMER..	3	425	562	1.6	2.8
283 LUTH--MO SYNOD	4	1,492	2,057	5.7	10.1
403 SALVATION ARMY	1	78	459	1.3	2.3
419 SO BAPT CONV..	10	1,391	1,651*	4.6	8.1
443 UN C OF CHRIST	2	353	419*	1.2	2.1
449 UN METHODIST..	18	4,191	4,983	13.8	24.5
453 UN PRES CH USA	3	932	1,106*	3.1	5.4
469 WISC EVAN LUTH	1	14	16	-	0.1
MOULTRIE	35	5,079	6,961*	52.5	100.0
019 AMER BAPT CONV	2	529	636*	4.8	9.1
081 CATHOLIC......	4	0	600	4.5	8.6
093 CR CH (DISC)..	7	1,412	1,698*	12.8	24.4
097 CR C AND C CR.	2	235	283*	2.1	4.1
123 CH GOD (ANDER)	2	121	465	3.5	6.7
185 CUMBER PRESB..	1	228	274*	2.1	3.9
221 FREE METH C NA	1	49	62	0.5	0.9
283 LUTH--MO SYNOD	1	88	140	1.1	2.0
285 MENNONITE CH..	4	426	512*	3.9	7.4
419 SO BAPT CONV..	3	443	533*	4.0	7.7
443 UN C OF CHRIST	1	103	124*	0.9	1.8
449 UN METHODIST..	5	1,229	1,374	10.4	19.7
453 UN PRES CH USA	2	216	260*	2.0	3.7
OGLE	64	14,229	22,170*	51.7	100.0
029 AMER LUTH CH..	4	826	1,214	2.8	5.5
081 CATHOLIC......	4	0	4,400	10.3	19.8
093 CR CH (DISC)..	2	173	215*	0.5	1.0
097 CR C AND C CR.	5	276	344*	0.8	1.6
121 CH GOD (ABR)..	3	208	259*	0.6	1.2
123 CH GOD (ANDER)	1	40	80	0.2	0.4
127 CH GOD (CLEVE)	1	166	207*	0.5	0.9
157 CH OF BRETHREN	3	997	1,241*	2.9	5.6
165 CH OF NAZARENE	2	132	326	0.8	1.5
193 EPISCOPAL.....	2	183	253	0.6	1.1
201 EVAN COV CH AM	1	70	87*	0.2	0.4
281 LUTH CH AMER..	4	1,813	2,446	5.7	11.0
283 LUTH--MO SYNOD	2	1,093	1,441	3.4	6.5
371 REF CH IN AM..	4	806	1,197	2.8	5.4
419 SO BAPT CONV..	3	454	565*	1.3	2.5
443 UN C OF CHRIST	2	762	949*	2.2	4.3
449 UN METHODIST..	14	4,550	4,854	11.3	21.9
453 UN PRES CH USA	7	1,680	2,092*	4.9	9.4
PEORIA	143	44,251	90,551*	46.4	100.0
019 AMER BAPT CONV	5	2,008	2,445*	1.3	2.7
029 AMER LUTH CH..	7	4,283	5,835	3.0	6.4
059 BAPT MISS ASSN	1	23	28*	-	-
081 CATHOLIC......	26	0	33,346	17.1	36.8
093 CR CH (DISC)..	5	1,900	2,313*	1.2	2.6
097 CR C AND C CR.	4	385	469*	0.2	0.5
121 CH GOD (ABR)..	1	31	38*	-	-
123 CH GOD (ANDER)	3	365	1,102	0.6	1.2
127 CH GOD (CLEVE)	1	98	119*	0.1	0.1
157 CH OF BRETHREN	1	128	156*	0.1	0.2
165 CH OF NAZARENE	8	517	1,971	1.0	2.2
193 EPISCOPAL.....	5	1,305	1,610	0.8	1.8
201 EVAN COV CH AM	1	74	90*	-	0.1
221 FREE METH C NA	3	260	346	0.2	0.4
281 LUTH CH AMER..	3	1,288	1,749	0.9	1.9
283 LUTH--MO SYNOD	7	4,525	6,227	3.2	6.9
285 MENNONITE CH..	3	262	319*	0.2	0.4
287 MENN GEN CONF.	1	114	139*	0.1	0.2
313 NO AM BAPT GC.	1	181	220*	0.1	0.2
353 PLY BRETHREN..	1	5	5	-	-
371 REF CH IN AM..	1	96	137	0.1	0.2
403 SALVATION ARMY	1	144	300	0.2	0.3
413 S-D ADVENTISTS	2	403	491*	0.3	0.5
419 SO BAPT CONV..	7	2,122	2,584*	1.3	2.9
435 UNITARIAN-UNIV	1	289	367	0.2	0.4
443 UN C OF CHRIST	8	2,094	2,550*	1.3	2.8
449 UN METHODIST..	24	13,792	16,374	8.4	18.1
453 UN PRES CH USA	11	7,530	9,169*	4.7	10.1
469 WISC EVAN LUTH	1	29	52	-	0.1
PERRY	45	9,032	14,115*	71.4	100.0
019 AMER BAPT CONV	2	242	289*	1.5	2.0
081 CATHOLIC......	5	0	3,399	17.2	24.1
093 CR CH (DISC)..	1	577	689*	3.5	4.9
097 CR C AND C CR.	3	54	65*	0.3	0.5
165 CH OF NAZARENE	1	35	54	0.3	0.4
283 LUTH--MO SYNOD	3	299	364	1.8	2.6
381 REF PRES-EVAN.	1	27	43	0.2	0.3
413 S-D ADVENTISTS	1	39	47*	0.2	0.3
419 SO BAPT CONV..	18	5,266	6,290*	31.8	44.6
443 UN C OF CHRIST	2	804	960*	4.9	6.8
449 UN METHODIST..	3	953	1,036	5.2	7.3
453 UN PRES CH USA	5	736	879*	4.4	6.2
PIATT	32	6,791	9,177*	59.2	100.0
019 AMER BAPT CONV	1	189	229*	1.5	2.5
081 CATHOLIC......	2	0	896	5.8	9.8
093 CR CH (DISC)..	1	205	248*	1.6	2.7
097 CR C AND C CR.	2	655	793*	5.1	8.6
123 CH GOD (ANDER)	1	26	48	0.3	0.5
157 CH OF BRETHREN	2	354	429*	2.8	4.7
165 CH OF NAZARENE	2	132	394	2.5	4.3
419 SO BAPT CONV..	6	487	590*	3.8	6.4
443 UN C OF CHRIST	4	766	927*	6.0	10.1
449 UN METHODIST..	9	3,482	4,024	25.9	43.8

County and Denomination	Number of churches	Communicant, confirmed, full members	Total adherents: Number	Percent of total population	Percent of total adherents
453 UN PRES CH USA	2	495	599*	3.9	6.5
PIKE	57	7,167	9,668*	50.4	100.0
019 AMER BAPT CONV	3	347	413*	2.2	4.3
081 CATHOLIC......	3	0	853	4.4	8.8
093 CR CH (DISC)..	5	716	851*	4.4	8.8
097 CR C AND C CR.	12	1,515	1,801*	9.4	18.6
165 CH OF NAZARENE	5	338	873	4.6	9.0
193 EPISCOPAL.....	1	60	82	0.4	0.8
283 LUTH--MO SYNOD	1	117	162	0.8	1.7
419 SO BAPT CONV..	6	775	921*	4.8	9.5
443 UN C OF CHRIST	1	68	81*	0.4	0.8
449 UN METHODIST..	18	3,171	3,560	18.6	36.8
453 UN PRES CH USA	2	60	71*	0.4	0.7
POPE	26	1,675	1,932*	50.1	100.0
123 CH GOD (ANDER)	1	12	44	1.1	2.3
127 CH GOD (CLEVE)	1	4	5*	0.1	0.3
185 CUMBER PRESB..	1	30	34*	0.9	1.8
283 LUTH--MO SYNOD	1	41	46	1.2	2.4
419 SO BAPT CONV..	17	1,225	1,407*	36.5	72.8
449 UN METHODIST..	4	315	341	8.8	17.7
453 UN PRES CH USA	1	48	55*	1.4	2.8
PULASKI	31	4,680	6,375*	72.9	100.0
081 CATHOLIC......	3	0	367	4.2	5.8
093 CR CH (DISC)..	1	61	73*	0.8	1.1
097 CR C AND C CR.	2	115	138*	1.6	2.2
193 EPISCOPAL.....	1	22	33	0.4	0.5
283 LUTH--MO SYNOD	1	99	116	1.3	1.8
419 SO BAPT CONV..	8	1,562	1,878*	21.5	29.5
443 UN C OF CHRIST	2	118	142*	1.6	2.2
449 UN METHODIST..	13	2,703	3,628	41.5	56.9
PUTNAM	13	1,247	2,627*	52.5	100.0
081 CATHOLIC......	3	0	960	19.2	36.5
097 CR C AND C CR.	1	70	86*	1.7	3.3
226 FRIENDS-USA...	1	88	108*	2.2	4.1
281 LUTH CH AMER..	2	311	447	8.9	17.0
443 UN C OF CHRIST	1	285	350*	7.0	13.3
449 UN METHODIST..	5	493	676	13.5	25.7
RANDOLPH	72	16,056	26,735*	85.2	100.0
019 AMER BAPT CONV	1	209	250*	0.8	0.9
059 BAPT MISS ASSN	1	65	78*	0.2	0.3
081 CATHOLIC......	15	0	6,354	20.2	23.8
165 CH OF NAZARENE	3	69	239	0.8	0.9
193 EPISCOPAL.....	5	2,437	3,408	10.9	12.7
281 LUTH CH AMER..	5	1,546	1,973	6.3	7.4
283 LUTH--MO SYNOD	9	4,996	6,449	20.6	24.1
353 PLY BRETHREN..	1	30	50	0.2	0.2
381 REF PRES-EVAN.	2	354	387	1.2	1.4
419 SO BAPT CONV..	11	2,297	2,751*	8.8	10.3
443 UN C OF CHRIST	2	629	753*	2.4	2.8
449 UN METHODIST..	8	1,428	1,652	5.3	6.2
453 UN PRES CH USA	9	1,996	2,391*	7.6	8.9
RICHLAND	41	6,289	9,593*	57.0	100.0
019 AMER BAPT CONV	1	408	492*	2.9	5.1
081 CATHOLIC......	2	0	2,026	12.0	21.1
093 CR CH (DISC)..	2	155	187*	1.1	1.9
097 CR C AND C CR.	7	740	892*	5.3	9.3
127 CH GOD (CLEVE)	1	60	72*	0.4	0.8
157 CH OF BRETHREN	1	49	59*	0.4	0.6
165 CH OF NAZARENE	1	199	529	3.1	5.5
193 EPISCOPAL.....	1	84	111	0.7	1.2
221 FREE METH C NA	1	118	148	0.9	1.5
281 LUTH CH AMER..	1	391	513	3.0	5.3
413 S-D ADVENTISTS	1	55	66*	0.4	0.7
419 SO BAPT CONV..	4	463	558*	3.3	5.8
443 UN C OF CHRIST	2	183	221*	1.3	2.3
449 UN METHODIST..	15	3,047	3,313	19.7	34.5
453 UN PRES CH USA	1	337	406*	2.4	4.2
ROCK ISLAND	103	37,617	78,080*	46.8	100.0
019 AMER BAPT CONV	5	1,574	1,939*	1.2	2.5
081 CATHOLIC......	19	0	28,170	16.9	36.1
093 CR CH (DISC)..	5	2,957	3,643*	2.2	4.7
097 CR C AND C CR.	1	95	117*	0.1	0.1
165 CH OF NAZARENE	3	282	922	0.6	1.2
193 EPISCOPAL.....	3	1,035	1,448	0.9	1.9
201 EVAN COV CH AM	2	650	801*	0.5	1.0
221 FREE METH C NA	1	44	72	-	0.1
281 LUTH CH AMER..	13	7,494	10,419	6.2	13.3
283 LUTH--MO SYNOD	7	3,964	5,580	3.3	7.1
403 SALVATION ARMY	2	150	690	0.4	0.9
413 S-D ADVENTISTS	1	173	213*	0.1	0.3
419 SO BAPT CONV..	3	332	409*	0.2	0.5
443 UN C OF CHRIST	5	3,072	3,785*	2.3	4.8
449 UN METHODIST..	20	9,575	12,151	7.3	15.6
453 UN PRES CH USA	12	6,003	7,395*	4.4	9.5
469 WISC EVAN LUTH	1	217	326	0.2	0.4
ST CLAIR	198	47,844	118,099*	41.4	100.0
019 AMER BAPT CONV	4	971	1,210*	0.4	1.0
059 BAPT MISS ASSN	1	170	212*	0.1	0.2
081 CATHOLIC......	55	0	56,241	19.7	47.6

*Total adherents estimated from known number of communicant, confirmed, full members.

—Represents a percent less than 0.1.

Percentages may not total due to rounding.

Table 3. Churches and Church Membership by State, County and Denomination: 1971

County and Denomination	Number of churches	Communicant, confirmed, full members	Total adherents: Number	Percent of total population	Percent of total adherents
093 CR CH (DISC)..	3	464	578*	0.2	0.5
097 CR C AND C CR.	6	976	1,216*	0.4	1.0
123 CH GOD (ANDER)	6	318	755	0.3	0.6
127 CH GOD (CLEVE)	4	265	330*	0.1	0.3
165 CH OF NAZARENE	7	443	1,115	0.4	0.9
193 EPISCOPAL.....	2	755	820	0.3	0.7
221 FREE METH C NA	1	23	38	-	-
226 FRIENDS-USA...	1	13	16*	-	-
281 LUTH CH AMER..	2	545	782	0.3	0.7
283 LUTH--MO SYNOD	14	5,340	7,284	2.6	6.2
287 MENN GEN CONF.	1	30	37*	-	-
353 PLY BRETHREN..	1	30	50	-	-
403 SALVATION ARMY	1	123	1,071	0.4	0.9
413 S-D ADVENTISTS	1	108	135*	-	0.1
419 SO BAPT CONV..	37	16,617	20,707*	7.3	17.5
443 UN C OF CHRIST	24	11,392	14,196*	5.0	12.0
449 UN METHODIST..	23	7,094	8,606	3.0	7.3
453 UN PRES CH USA	4	2,167	2,700*	0.9	2.3
SALINE	74	13,232	17,079*	66.4	100.0
019 AMER BAPT CONV	1	203	238*	0.9	1.4
029 AMER LUTH CH..	1	59	94	0.4	0.6
081 CATHOLIC......	3	0	1,247	4.8	7.3
097 CR C AND C CR.	2	535	626*	2.4	3.7
121 CH GOD (ABR)..	1	61	71*	0.3	0.4
123 CH GOD (ANDER)	3	134	350	1.4	2.0
127 CH GOD (CLEVE)	3	374	438*	1.7	2.6
165 CH OF NAZARENE	4	76	251	1.0	1.5
185 CUMBER PRESB..	4	263	308*	1.2	1.8
221 FREE METH C NA	1	26	28	0.1	0.2
415 S-D BAPTIST GC	1	35	41*	0.2	0.2
419 SO BAPT CONV..	37	9,059	10,607*	41.2	62.1
449 UN METHODIST..	11	1,820	2,093	8.1	12.3
453 UN PRES CH USA	2	587	687*	2.7	4.0
SANGAMON	141	44,133	94,337*	58.5	100.0
019 AMER BAPT CONV	9	3,537	4,320*	2.7	4.6
029 AMER LUTH CH..	1	118	192	0.1	0.2
081 CATHOLIC......	20	0	38,073	23.6	40.4
093 CR CH (DISC)..	4	1,236	1,510*	0.9	1.6
097 CR C AND C CR.	15	5,982	7,306*	4.5	7.7
123 CH GOD (ANDER)	4	246	692	0.4	0.7
127 CH GOD (CLEVE)	2	9	11*	-	-
157 CH OF BRETHREN	1	182	222*	0.1	0.2
165 CH OF NAZARENE	4	544	1,380	0.9	1.5
193 EPISCOPAL.....	3	1,811	2,545	1.6	2.7
221 FREE METH C NA	1	93	111	0.1	0.1
226 FRIENDS-USA...	1	5	6*	-	-
281 LUTH CH AMER..	4	3,041	3,041	1.9	3.2
283 LUTH--MO SYNOD	11	4,708	6,493	4.0	6.9
353 PLY BRETHREN..	1	50	85	0.1	0.1
403 SALVATION ARMY	1	103	750	0.5	0.8
413 S-D ADVENTISTS	2	79	96*	0.1	0.1
419 SO BAPT CONV..	8	2,077	2,537*	1.6	2.7
435 UNITARIAN-UNIV	1	62	97	0.1	0.1
443 UN C OF CHRIST	1	718	877*	0.5	0.9
449 UN METHODIST..	35	13,038	16,062	10.0	17.0
453 UN PRES CH USA	12	6,494	7,931*	4.9	8.4
SCHUYLER	22	2,716	3,597*	44.2	100.0
019 AMER BAPT CONV	1	53	63*	0.8	1.8
081 CATHOLIC......	1	0	325	4.0	9.0
093 CR CH (DISC)..	2	433	511*	6.3	14.2
165 CH OF NAZARENE	1	31	98	1.2	2.7
221 FREE METH C NA	1	112	148	1.8	4.1
283 LUTH--MO SYNOD	1	73	103	1.3	2.9
419 SO BAPT CONV..	1	74	87*	1.1	2.4
449 UN METHODIST..	13	1,701	1,980	24.3	55.0
453 UN PRES CH USA	1	239	282*	3.5	7.8
SCOTT	24	3,521	4,568*	74.9	100.0
019 AMER BAPT CONV	4	1,023	1,223*	20.1	26.8
081 CATHOLIC......	2	0	372	6.1	8.1
093 CR CH (DISC)..	2	241	288*	4.7	6.3
281 LUTH CH AMER..	1	267	309	5.1	6.8
283 LUTH--MO SYNOD	2	400	528	8.7	11.6
419 SO BAPT CONV..	8	876	1,047*	17.2	22.9
449 UN METHODIST..	5	714	801	13.1	17.5
SHELBY	63	8,623	12,473*	55.2	100.0
019 AMER BAPT CONV	1	154	186*	0.8	1.5
029 AMER LUTH CH..	2	272	394	1.7	3.2
081 CATHOLIC......	5	0	1,608	7.1	12.9
093 CR CH (DISC)..	2	541	653*	2.9	5.2
097 CR C AND C CR.	11	1,961	2,367*	10.5	19.0
165 CH OF NAZARENE	1	209	696	3.1	5.6
221 FREE METH C NA	4	179	246	1.1	2.0
283 LUTH--MO SYNOD	5	1,374	1,735	7.7	13.9
285 MENNONITE CH..	1	41	49*	0.2	0.4
419 SO BAPT CONV..	6	501	605*	2.7	4.9
443 UN C OF CHRIST	1	54	65*	0.3	0.5
449 UN METHODIST..	22	3,142	3,634	16.1	29.1
453 UN PRES CH USA	2	195	235*	1.0	1.9
STARK	16	2,631	4,359*	58.0	100.0
019 AMER BAPT CONV	1	319	386*	5.1	8.9
029 AMER LUTH CH..	1	113	161	2.1	3.7
081 CATHOLIC......	3	C	1,130	15.0	25.9
165 CH OF NAZARENE	1	38	134	1.8	3.1
175 CONG CR CH....	1	246	297*	4.0	6.8
413 S-D ADVENTISTS	1	18	22*	0.3	0.5
419 SO BAPT CONV..	1	82	99*	1.3	2.3
443 UN C OF CHRIST	1	228	276*	3.7	6.3
449 UN METHODIST..	5	1,375	1,598	21.3	36.7
453 UN PRES CH USA	1	212	256*	3.4	5.9
STEPHENSON	76	16,866	28,964*	59.3	100.0
081 CATHOLIC......	6	0	7,516	15.4	25.9
105 CHRISTIAN REF.	1	94	162	0.3	0.6
121 CH GOD (ABR)..	1	15	18*	-	0.1
123 CH GOD (ANDER)	1	15	75	0.2	0.3
157 CH OF BRETHREN	3	270	331*	0.7	1.1
165 CH OF NAZARENE	1	133	241	0.5	0.8
193 EPISCOPAL.....	1	416	485	1.0	1.7
199 EVAN CONG CH..	2	214	263*	0.5	0.9
221 FREE METH C NA	3	66	85	0.2	0.3
281 LUTH CH AMER..	8	2,427	3,348	6.9	11.6
283 LUTH--MO SYNOD	3	1,238	1,643	3.4	5.7
285 MENNONITE CH..	2	203	249*	0.5	0.9
313 NO AM BAPT GC.	1	114	140*	0.3	0.5
371 REF CH IN AM..	2	437	666	1.4	2.3
403 SALVATION ARMY	1	49	158	0.3	0.5
413 S-D ADVENTISTS	1	50	61*	0.1	0.2
443 UN C OF CHRIST	6	2,312	2,839*	5.8	9.8
449 UN METHODIST..	28	7,209	8,687	17.8	30.0
453 UN PRES CH USA	3	1,525	1,872*	3.8	6.5
469 WISC EVAN LUTH	2	79	125	0.3	0.4
TAZEWELL	101	29,476	51,060*	43.0	100.0
019 AMER BAPT CONV	4	878	1,099*	0.9	2.2
029 AMER LUTH CH..	1	393	595	0.5	1.2
059 BAPT MISS ASSN	1	80	100*	0.1	0.2
081 CATHOLIC......	8	0	12,830	10.8	25.1
093 CR CH (DISC)..	4	1,235	1,547*	1.3	3.0
097 CR C AND C CR.	8	2,085	2,611*	2.2	5.1
123 CH GOD (ANDER)	3	130	357	0.3	0.7
165 CH OF NAZARENE	4	467	1,382	1.2	2.7
193 EPISCOPAL.....	2	296	324	0.3	0.6
221 FREE METH C NA	1	26	41	-	0.1
281 LUTH CH AMER..	3	1,677	2,300	1.9	4.5
283 LUTH--MO SYNOD	8	3,671	5,175	4.4	10.1
285 MENNONITE CH..	8	886	1,109*	0.9	2.2
287 MENN GEN CONF.	3	626	784*	0.7	1.5
371 REF CH IN AM..	2	424	595	0.5	1.2
403 SALVATION ARMY	1	84	400	0.3	0.8
419 SO BAPT CONV..	12	2,391	2,994*	2.5	5.9
443 UN C OF CHRIST	6	3,076	3,852*	3.2	7.5
449 UN METHODIST..	15	9,703	11,277	9.5	22.1
453 UN PRES CH USA	7	1,348	1,688*	1.4	3.3
UNION	47	8,848	11,041*	68.7	100.0
019 AMER BAPT CONV	2	213	249*	1.5	2.3
081 CATHOLIC......	3	0	606	3.8	5.5
097 CR C AND C CR.	3	249	291*	1.8	2.6
165 CH OF NAZARENE	1	105	259	1.6	2.3
175 CONG CR CH....	1	60	70*	0.4	0.6
185 CUMBER PRESB..	2	91	106*	0.7	1.0
193 EPISCOPAL.....	1	21	28	0.2	0.3
281 LUTH CH AMER..	4	702	865	5.4	7.8
283 LUTH--MO SYNOD	1	145	192	1.2	1.7
285 MENNONITE CH..	1	31	36*	0.2	0.3
419 SO BAPT CONV..	21	6,204	7,246*	45.1	65.6
449 UN METHODIST..	5	746	765	4.8	6.9
453 UN PRES CH USA	2	281	328*	2.0	3.0
VERMILION	137	27,302	43,923*	45.3	100.0
019 AMER BAPT CONV	5	780	945*	1.0	2.2
081 CATHOLIC......	9	0	8,951	9.2	20.4
093 CR CH (DISC)..	6	1,881	2,278*	2.3	5.2
097 CR C AND C CR.	25	5,915	7,163*	7.4	16.3
123 CH GOD (ANDER)	4	145	353	0.4	0.8
127 CH GOD (CLEVE)	4	231	280*	0.3	0.6
165 CH OF NAZARENE	18	1,607	3,607	3.7	8.2
175 CONG CR CH....	2	216	262*	0.3	0.6
185 CUMBER PRESB..	2	69	84*	0.1	0.2
193 EPISCOPAL.....	1	242	316	0.3	0.7
197 EVAN CH OF NA.	1	15	18*	-	-
221 FREE METH C NA	1	92	118	0.1	0.3
226 FRIENDS-USA...	4	702	850*	0.9	1.9
281 LUTH CH AMER..	2	526	710	0.7	1.6
283 LUTH--MO SYNOD	3	2,224	2,939	3.0	6.7
403 SALVATION ARMY	1	45	383	0.4	0.9
413 S-D ADVENTISTS	1	76	92*	0.1	0.2
419 SO BAPT CONV..	1	154	187*	0.2	0.4
435 UNITARIAN-UNIV	1	60	60	0.1	0.1
443 UN C OF CHRIST	4	1,065	1,290*	1.3	2.9
449 UN METHODIST..	37	9,321	10,692	11.0	24.3
453 UN PRES CH USA	5	1,936	2,345*	2.4	5.3
WABASH	30	4,249	6,803*	53.0	100.0
081 CATHOLIC......	2	0	1,547	12.0	22.7
093 CR CH (DISC)..	3	863	1,025*	8.0	15.1
097 CR C AND C CR.	8	600	712*	5.5	10.5
123 CH GOD (ANDER)	1	135	336	2.6	4.9
165 CH OF NAZARENE	1	56	145	1.1	2.1
193 EPISCOPAL.....	1	40	40	0.3	0.6
221 FREE METH C NA	1	110	146	1.1	2.1
281 LUTH CH AMER..	1	276	355	2.8	5.2
283 LUTH--MO SYNOD	1	80	161	1.3	2.4

*Total adherents estimated from known number of communicant, confirmed, full members.

—Represents a percent less than 0.1.

Percentages may not total due to rounding.

Table 3. Churches and Church Membership by State, County and Denomination: 1971

County and Denomination	Number of churches	Communicant, confirmed, full members	Total adherents		
			Number	Percent of total population	Percent of total adherents
419 SO BAPT CONV..	1	376	446*	3.5	6.6
449 UN METHODIST..	10	1,713	1,890	14.7	27.8
WARREN	32	8,224	11,674*	54.1	100.0
019 AMER BAPT CONV	3	540	648*	3.0	5.6
081 CATHOLIC......	2	0	1,426	6.6	12.2
093 CR CH (DISC)..	3	557	668*	3.1	5.7
097 CR C AND C CR.	2	900	1,080*	5.0	9.3
165 CH OF NAZARENE	3	100	313	1.4	2.7
193 EPISCOPAL.....	1	56	115	0.5	1.0
281 LUTH CH AMER..	1	779	983	4.6	8.4
413 S-D ADVENTISTS	2	25	30*	0.1	0.3
449 UN METHODIST..	9	3,061	3,764	17.4	32.2
453 UN PRES CH USA	6	2,206	2,647*	12.3	22.7
WASHINGTON	44	6,500	11,037*	80.1	100.0
019 AMER BAPT CONV	2	134	159*	1.2	1.4
075 BRETHREN IN CR	1	25	30*	0.2	0.3
081 CATHOLIC......	6	0	3,255	23.6	29.5
097 CR C AND C CR.	2	60	71*	0.5	0.6
283 LUTH--MO SYNOD	7	2,274	2,839	20.6	25.7
419 SO BAPT CONV..	5	720	852*	6.2	7.7
443 UN C OF CHRIST	11	2,043	2,418*	17.5	21.9
449 UN METHODIST..	8	991	1,114	8.1	10.1
453 UN PRES CH USA	2	253	299*	2.2	2.7
WAYNE	64	7,600	9,242*	54.4	100.0
019 AMER BAPT CONV	1	39	46*	0.3	0.5
081 CATHOLIC......	1	0	265	1.6	2.9
093 CR CH (DISC)..	3	139	164*	1.0	1.8
097 CR C AND C CR.	11	1,639	1,940*	11.4	21.0
123 CH GOD (ANDER)	2	31	77	0.5	0.8
127 CH GOD (CLEVE)	1	75	89*	0.5	1.0
157 CH OF BRETHREN	1	19	22*	0.1	0.2
165 CH OF NAZARENE	2	105	209	1.2	2.3
175 CONG CR CH....	1	50	59*	0.3	0.6
185 CUMBER PRESB..	5	552	653*	3.8	7.1
283 LUTH--MO SYNOD	1	48	64	0.4	0.7
419 SO BAPT CONV..	22	3,281	3,883*	22.8	42.0
449 UN METHODIST..	13	1,622	1,771	10.4	19.2
WHITE	61	7,709	9,573*	55.3	100.0
081 CATHOLIC......	3	0	595	3.4	6.2
093 CR CH (DISC)..	1	70	82*	0.5	0.9
097 CR C AND C CR.	7	920	1,076*	6.2	11.2
123 CH GOD (ANDER)	1	6	12	0.1	0.1
127 CH GOD (CLEVE)	3	147	172*	1.0	1.8
165 CH OF NAZARENE	1	99	210	1.2	2.2
185 CUMBER PRESB..	6	449	525*	3.0	5.5
221 FREE METH C NA	1	12	12	0.1	0.1
283 LUTH--MO SYNOD	1	59	72	0.4	0.8
419 SO BAPT CONV..	13	2,877	3,365*	19.4	35.2
449 UN METHODIST..	20	2,439	2,714	15.7	28.4
453 UN PRES CH USA	4	631	738*	4.3	7.7
WHITESIDE	87	22,514	43,653*	69.4	100.0
019 AMER BAPT CONV	3	521	649*	1.0	1.5
029 AMER LUTH CH..	2	1,714	2,398	3.8	5.5
081 CATHOLIC......	9	0	12,488	19.9	28.6
093 CR CH (DISC)..	3	641	799*	1.3	1.8
097 CR C AND C CR.	6	740	922*	1.5	2.1
105 CHRISTIAN REF.	3	578	1,031	1.6	2.4
165 CH OF NAZARENE	3	449	1,456	2.3	3.3
193 EPISCOPAL.....	2	249	284	0.5	0.7
199 EVAN CONG CH..	1	92	115*	0.2	0.3
221 FREE METH C NA	1	36	62	0.1	0.1
281 LUTH CH AMER..	4	2,395	3,114	5.0	7.1
283 LUTH--MO SYNOD	4	1,546	2,089	3.3	4.8
285 MENNONITE CH..	4	457	570*	0.9	1.3
371 REF CH IN AM..	8	2,903	4,455	7.1	10.2
403 SALVATION ARMY	1	70	385	0.6	0.9
413 S-D ADVENTISTS	2	64	80*	0.1	0.2
419 SO BAPT CONV..	5	1,153	1,437*	2.3	3.3
443 UN C OF CHRIST	4	1,335	1,664*	2.6	3.8
449 UN METHODIST..	17	5,847	7,506	11.9	17.2
453 UN PRES CH USA	5	1,724	2,149*	3.4	4.9
WILL	163	38,752	147,784*	59.2	100.0
019 AMER BAPT CONV	6	1,792	2,265*	0.9	1.5
029 AMER LUTH CH..	2	566	850	0.3	0.6
081 CATHOLIC......	39	0	95,500	38.3	64.6
097 CR C AND C CR.	6	1,244	1,573*	0.6	1.1
123 CH GOD (ANDER)	2	157	396	0.2	0.3
127 CH GOD (CLEVE)	2	34	43*	-	-
165 CH OF NAZARENE	7	489	1,216	0.5	0.8
175 CONG CR CH....	1	111	140*	0.1	0.1
193 EPISCOPAL.....	3	476	770	0.3	0.5
201 EVAN COV CH AM	2	400	506*	0.2	0.3
221 FREE METH C NA	1	8	9	-	-
281 LUTH CH AMER..	6	3,584	5,033	2.0	3.4
283 LUTH--MO SYNOD	15	6,298	9,150	3.7	6.2
315 NO AM OLD RC..	1	121	153*	0.1	0.1
349 PENT HOLINESS.	1	22	28*	-	-
353 PLY BRETHREN..	1	20	30	-	-
371 REF CH IN AM..	1	107	188	0.1	0.1
403 SALVATION ARMY	1	56	360	0.1	0.2
413 S-D ADVENTISTS	1	128	162*	0.1	0.1
419 SO BAPT CONV..	14	3,497	4,421*	1.8	3.0
435 UNITARIAN-UNIV	1	102	124	-	0.1
443 UN C OF CHRIST	11	4,568	5,774*	2.3	3.9
449 UN METHODIST..	26	9,693	12,255	4.9	8.3
453 UN PRES CH USA	11	3,948	4,991*	2.0	3.4
469 WISC EVAN LUTH	2	1,331	1,847	0.7	1.2
WILLIAMSON	98	18,235	25,378*	51.8	100.0
019 AMER BAPT CONV	9	1,332	1,585*	3.2	6.2
059 BAPT MISS ASSN	1	79	94*	0.2	0.4
081 CATHOLIC......	5	0	3,284	6.7	12.9
093 CR CH (DISC)..	1	339	403*	0.8	1.6
097 CR C AND C CR.	8	1,189	1,415*	2.9	5.6
123 CH GOD (ANDER)	4	224	657	1.3	2.6
127 CH GOD (CLEVE)	5	216	257*	0.5	1.0
165 CH OF NAZARENE	3	140	388	0.8	1.5
193 EPISCOPAL.....	1	60	73	0.1	0.3
221 FREE METH C NA	3	65	68	0.1	0.3
283 LUTH--MO SYNOD	1	104	151	0.3	0.6
413 S-D ADVENTISTS	1	58	69*	0.1	0.3
419 SO BAPT CONV..	32	10,130	12,055*	24.6	47.5
443 UN C OF CHRIST	2	564	671*	1.4	2.6
449 UN METHODIST..	18	3,170	3,536	7.2	13.9
453 UN PRES CH USA	4	565	672*	1.4	2.6
WINNEBAGO	137	52,206	113,150*	45.9	100.0
019 AMER BAPT CONV	2	605	759*	0.3	0.7
029 AMER LUTH CH..	5	2,661	3,963	1.6	3.5
059 BAPT MISS ASSN	1	41	51*	-	-
081 CATHOLIC......	15	0	41,763	16.9	36.9
093 CR CH (DISC)..	2	43	54*	-	-
097 CR C AND C CR.	4	1,120	1,405*	0.6	1.2
121 CH GOD (ABR)..	1	51	64*	-	0.1
123 CH GOD (ANDER)	2	33	103	-	0.1
127 CH GOD (CLEVE)	3	233	292*	0.1	0.3
157 CH OF BRETHREN	1	198	248*	0.1	0.2
165 CH OF NAZARENE	5	349	1,077	0.4	1.0
175 CONG CR CH....	1	25	31*	-	-
193 EPISCOPAL.....	4	1,207	2,110	0.9	1.9
201 EVAN COV CH AM	8	2,275	2,854*	1.2	2.5
221 FREE METH C NA	1	38	67	-	0.1
226 FRIENDS-USA...	1	21	26*	-	-
281 LUTH CH AMER..	17	14,851	20,478	8.3	18.1
283 LUTH--MO SYNOD	8	4,112	5,627	2.3	5.0
353 PLY BRETHREN..	2	60	90	-	0.1
371 REF CH IN AM..	1	128	227	0.1	0.2
403 SALVATION ARMY	2	257	1,199	0.5	1.1
413 S-D ADVENTISTS	1	361	453*	0.2	0.4
419 SO BAPT CONV..	9	2,264	2,840*	1.2	2.5
435 UNITARIAN-UNIV	1	412	659	0.3	0.6
443 UN C OF CHRIST	8	4,089	5,129*	2.1	4.5
449 UN METHODIST..	24	11,805	15,341	6.2	13.6
453 UN PRES CH USA	7	4,942	6,200*	2.5	5.5
469 WISC EVAN LUTH	1	25	40	-	-
WOODFORD	50	9,259	16,356*	58.4	100.0
019 AMER BAPT CONV	3	554	681*	2.4	4.2
029 AMER LUTH CH..	3	887	1,216	4.3	7.4
081 CATHOLIC......	7	0	4,445	15.9	27.2
093 CR CH (DISC)..	3	804	989*	3.5	6.0
097 CR C AND C CR.	1	85	105*	0.4	0.6
157 CH OF BRETHREN	2	134	165*	0.6	1.0
165 CH OF NAZARENE	2	179	370	1.3	2.3
193 EPISCOPAL.....	1	33	46	0.2	0.3
283 LUTH--MO SYNOD	5	1,058	1,460	5.2	8.9
285 MENNONITE CH..	4	960	1,181*	4.2	7.2
287 MENN GEN CONF.	1	160	197*	0.7	1.2
419 SO BAPT CONV..	3	593	729*	2.6	4.5
443 UN C OF CHRIST	4	1,415	1,740*	6.2	10.6
449 UN METHODIST..	8	1,912	2,436	8.7	14.9
453 UN PRES CH USA	3	485	596*	2.1	3.6
CO DATA NOT AVAIL	227	13,810	33,250*	N/A	N/A
127 CH GOD (CLEVE)	1	17	21*	N/A	N/A
151 L-D SAINTS....	0	0	16,299	N/A	N/A
223 FREE WILL BAPT	48	4,047	4,954*	N/A	N/A
231 GENERAL BAPT..	139	8,363	10,238*	N/A	N/A
467 WESLEYAN......	39	1,383	1,738	N/A	N/A

INDIANA

County and Denomination	Number of churches	Communicant, confirmed, full members	Number	Percent of total population	Percent of total adherents
THE STATE.....	6,092	1,211,591	2,316,535*	44.6	100.0
ADAMS	42	9,853	17,162*	63.9	100.0
019 AMER BAPT CONV	2	315	398*	1.5	2.3
081 CATHOLIC......	2	0	3,854	14.3	22.5
093 CR CH (DISC)..	1	90	114*	0.4	0.7
097 CR C AND C CR.	3	98	124*	0.5	0.7
123 CH GOD (ANDER)	1	225	595	2.2	3.5
157 CH OF BRETHREN	1	242	306*	1.1	1.8
165 CH OF NAZARENE	4	346	880	3.3	5.1
226 FRIENDS-USA...	1	24	30*	0.1	0.2
283 LUTH--MO SYNOD	7	2,539	3,553	13.2	20.7

*Total adherents estimated from known number of communicant, confirmed, full members.

—Represents a percent less than 0.1.

Percentages may not total due to rounding.

Table 3. Churches and Church Membership by State, County and Denomination: 1971

County and Denomination	Number of churches	Communicant, confirmed, full members	Total adherents		
			Number	Percent of total population	Percent of total adherents
285 MENNONITE CH..	1	12	15*	0.1	0.1
287 MENN GEN CONF.	1	1,227	1,549*	5.8	9.0
349 PENT HOLINESS.	1	31	39*	0.1	0.2
443 UN C OF CHRIST	4	1,590	2,007*	7.5	11.7
449 UN METHODIST..	12	2,855	3,371	12.5	19.6
453 UN PRES CH USA	1	259	327*	1.2	1.9
ALLEN	144	54,994	129,824*	46.3	100.0
019 AMER BAPT CONV	6	2,804	3,505*	1.2	2.7
029 AMER LUTH CH..	6	2,710	3,698	1.3	2.8
081 CATHOLIC......	24	0	55,737	19.9	42.9
093 CR CH (DISC)..	4	1,904	2,380*	0.8	1.8
097 CR C AND C CR.	8	2,062	2,578*	0.9	2.0
107 CHRISTIAN UN..	1	284	355*	0.1	0.3
123 CH GOD (ANDER)	4	430	1,137	0.4	0.9
127 CH GOD (CLEVE)	2	143	179*	0.1	0.1
157 CH OF BRETHREN	3	741	926*	0.3	0.7
165 CH OF NAZARENE	11	1,284	2,407	0.9	1.9
193 EPISCOPAL.....	1	1,255	1,729	0.6	1.3
221 FREE METH C NA	1	88	125	-	0.1
226 FRIENDS-USA...	2	25	31*	-	-
281 LUTH CH AMER..	13	7,847	10,595	3.8	8.2
283 LUTH--MO SYNOD	28	21,423	29,403	10.5	22.6
285 MENNONITE CH..	8	793	991*	0.4	0.8
287 MENN GEN CONF.	1	177	221*	0.1	0.2
413 S-D ADVENTISTS	2	250	313*	0.1	0.2
419 SO BAPT CONV..	3	480	600*	0.2	0.5
435 UNITARIAN-UNIV	1	225	308	0.1	0.2
443 UN C OF CHRIST	5	3,915	4,894*	1.7	3.8
453 UN PRES CH USA	9	6,069	7,587*	2.7	5.8
469 WISC EVAN LUTH	1	85	125	-	0.1
BARTHOLOMEW	67	20,322	29,813*	52.3	100.0
019 AMER BAPT CONV	5	2,744	3,497*	6.1	11.7
081 CATHOLIC......	2	0	2,941	5.2	9.9
093 CR CH (DISC)..	3	637	812*	1.4	2.7
097 CR C AND C CR.	11	4,774	6,084*	10.7	20.4
107 CHRISTIAN UN..	2	142	181*	0.3	0.6
123 CH GOD (ANDER)	1	25	89	0.2	0.3
127 CH GOD (CLEVE)	1	62	79*	0.1	0.3
165 CH OF NAZARENE	3	371	1,002	1.8	3.4
193 EPISCOPAL.....	1	179	329	0.6	1.1
221 FREE METH C NA	1	135	214	0.4	0.7
226 FRIENDS-USA...	1	195	249*	0.4	0.8
281 LUTH CH AMER..	1	277	370	0.6	1.2
283 LUTH--MO SYNOD	7	3,330	4,546	8.0	15.2
293 MORAV CH-NORTH	1	269	457	0.8	1.5
413 S-D ADVENTISTS	1	93	119*	0.2	0.4
419 SO BAPT CONV..	3	329	419*	0.7	1.4
435 UNITARIAN-UNIV	1	21	33	0.1	0.1
449 UN METHODIST..	19	5,669	7,028	12.3	23.6
453 UN PRES CH USA	3	1,070	1,364*	2.4	4.6
BENTON	28	3,664	8,905*	79.1	100.0
081 CATHOLIC......	6	0	4,292	38.1	48.2
093 CR CH (DISC)..	1	109	134*	1.2	1.5
097 CR C AND C CR.	6	946	1,166*	10.4	13.1
121 CH GOD (ABR)..	1	26	32*	0.3	0.4
165 CH OF NAZARENE	1	39	54	0.5	0.6
221 FREE METH C NA	1	12	14	0.1	0.2
419 SO BAPT CONV..	2	187	230*	2.0	2.6
449 UN METHODIST..	7	1,830	2,348	20.8	26.4
453 UN PRES CH USA	3	515	635*	5.6	7.1
BLACKFORD	29	4,203	7,518*	47.3	100.0
019 AMER BAPT CONV	1	219	272*	1.7	3.6
029 AMER LUTH CH..	1	490	699	4.4	9.3
081 CATHOLIC......	2	0	1,425	9.0	19.0
093 CR CH (DISC)..	1	364	452*	2.8	6.0
097 CR C AND C CR.	2	125	155*	1.0	2.1
123 CH GOD (ANDER)	1	11	43	0.3	0.6
157 CH OF BRETHREN	1	115	143*	0.9	1.9
165 CH OF NAZARENE	4	283	1,121	7.1	14.9
226 FRIENDS-USA...	1	16	20*	0.1	0.3
413 S-D ADVENTISTS	1	22	27*	0.2	0.4
419 SO BAPT CONV..	2	137	170*	1.1	2.3
449 UN METHODIST..	11	2,157	2,663	16.8	35.4
453 UN PRES CH USA	1	264	328*	2.1	4.4
BOONE	45	9,958	13,800*	44.7	100.0
019 AMER BAPT CONV	5	1,424	1,746*	5.7	12.7
081 CATHOLIC......	2	0	1,650	5.3	12.0
093 CR CH (DISC)..	3	1,353	1,659*	5.4	12.0
097 CR C AND C CR.	8	1,711	2,097*	6.8	15.2
123 CH GOD (ANDER)	1	11	64	0.2	0.5
165 CH OF NAZARENE	1	44	142	0.5	1.0
193 EPISCOPAL.....	2	122	204	0.7	1.5
226 FRIENDS-USA...	1	45	55*	0.2	0.4
281 LUTH CH AMER..	2	326	519	1.7	3.8
443 UN C OF CHRIST	5	713	874*	2.8	6.3
449 UN METHODIST..	12	3,319	3,699	12.0	26.8
453 UN PRES CH USA	3	890	1,091*	3.5	7.9
BROWN	13	990	1,459*	16.1	100.0
081 CATHOLIC......	1	0	209	2.3	14.3
093 CR CH (DISC)..	2	56	69*	0.8	4.7
097 CR C AND C CR.	2	400	493*	5.4	33.8
165 CH OF NAZARENE	1	70	158	1.7	10.8
283 LUTH--MO SYNOD	1	74	102	1.1	7.0
449 UN METHODIST..	6	390	428	4.7	29.3
CARROLL	35	6,282	8,530*	48.1	100.0
019 AMER BAPT CONV	3	511	626*	3.5	7.3
081 CATHOLIC......	1	0	648	3.7	7.6
093 CR CH (DISC)..	3	498	610*	3.4	7.2
097 CR C AND C CR.	2	520	637*	3.6	7.5
157 CH OF BRETHREN	5	862	1,056*	6.0	12.4
281 LUTH CH AMER..	3	519	754	4.3	8.8
419 SO BAPT CONV..	3	223	273*	1.5	3.2
443 UN C OF CHRIST	1	93	114*	0.6	1.3
449 UN METHODIST..	8	1,788	2,258	12.7	26.5
453 UN PRES CH USA	6	1,268	1,554*	8.8	18.2
CASS	62	11,250	18,997*	47.0	100.0
019 AMER BAPT CONV	5	1,626	1,970*	4.9	10.4
081 CATHOLIC......	4	0	4,812	11.9	25.3
093 CR CH (DISC)..	5	1,184	1,434*	3.5	7.5
097 CR C AND C CR.	5	436	528*	1.3	2.8
123 CH GOD (ANDER)	1	110	369	0.9	1.9
127 CH GOD (CLEVE)	1	125	151*	0.4	0.8
157 CH OF BRETHREN	1	138	167*	0.4	0.9
165 CH OF NAZARENE	1	137	347	0.9	1.8
193 EPISCOPAL.....	1	128	216	0.5	1.1
281 LUTH CH AMER..	3	675	902	2.2	4.7
283 LUTH--MO SYNOD	1	435	550	1.4	2.9
353 PLY BRETHREN..	1	30	40	0.1	0.2
403 SALVATION ARMY	1	58	358	0.9	1.9
413 S-D ADVENTISTS	1	72	87*	0.2	0.5
419 SO BAPT CONV..	1	80	97*	0.2	0.5
443 UN C OF CHRIST	3	335	406*	1.0	2.1
449 UN METHODIST..	22	4,372	4,977	12.3	26.2
453 UN PRES CH USA	5	1,309	1,586*	3.9	8.3
CLARK	95	17,546	34,801*	45.9	100.0
019 AMER BAPT CONV	9	1,535	1,911*	2.5	5.5
081 CATHOLIC......	8	0	12,417	16.4	35.7
093 CR CH (DISC)..	6	1,552	1,932*	2.5	5.6
097 CR C AND C CR.	16	1,339	1,667*	2.2	4.8
123 CH GOD (ANDER)	3	523	1,099	1.4	3.2
127 CH GOD (CLEVE)	2	95	118*	0.2	0.3
165 CH OF NAZARENE	4	144	298	0.4	0.9
193 EPISCOPAL.....	1	207	508	0.7	1.5
281 LUTH CH AMER..	1	187	252	0.3	0.7
283 LUTH--MO SYNOD	1	170	248	0.3	0.7
413 S-D ADVENTISTS	2	68	85*	0.1	0.2
419 SO BAPT CONV..	11	4,133	5,146*	6.8	14.8
443 UN C OF CHRIST	2	546	680*	0.9	2.0
449 UN METHODIST..	22	5,708	6,773	8.9	19.5
453 UN PRES CH USA	7	1,339	1,667*	2.2	4.8
CLAY	56	8,287	10,789*	45.1	100.0
019 AMER BAPT CONV	6	1,229	1,469*	6.1	13.6
081 CATHOLIC......	1	0	601	2.5	5.6
093 CR CH (DISC)..	2	49	59*	0.2	0.5
097 CR C AND C CR.	6	1,500	1,793*	7.5	16.6
127 CH GOD (CLEVE)	1	23	27*	0.1	0.3
165 CH OF NAZARENE	5	448	915	3.8	8.5
175 CONG CR CH....	2	364	435*	1.8	4.0
221 FREE METH C NA	1	30	34	0.1	0.3
283 LUTH--MO SYNOD	1	209	277	1.2	2.6
419 SO BAPT CONV..	1	113	135*	0.6	1.3
443 UN C OF CHRIST	4	698	834*	3.5	7.7
449 UN METHODIST..	24	3,232	3,741	15.6	34.7
453 UN PRES CH USA	2	392	469*	2.0	4.3
CLINTON	49	11,586	15,309*	50.1	100.0
019 AMER BAPT CONV	4	1,662	2,020*	6.6	13.2
081 CATHOLIC......	1	0	1,053	3.4	6.9
093 CR CH (DISC)..	2	884	1,075*	3.5	7.0
097 CR C AND C CR.	7	2,086	2,536*	8.3	16.6
123 CH GOD (ANDER)	2	47	144	0.5	0.9
157 CH OF BRETHREN	1	133	162*	0.5	1.1
165 CH OF NAZARENE	2	347	692	2.3	4.5
281 LUTH CH AMER..	2	440	619	2.0	4.0
403 SALVATION ARMY	1	34	184	0.6	1.2
413 S-D ADVENTISTS	1	57	69*	0.2	0.5
419 SO BAPT CONV..	1	47	57*	0.2	0.4
443 UN C OF CHRIST	4	525	638*	2.1	4.2
449 UN METHODIST..	16	3,938	4,375	14.3	28.6
453 UN PRES CH USA	5	1,386	1,685*	5.5	11.0
CRAWFORD	42	2,665	3,254*	40.5	100.0
019 AMER BAPT CONV	3	280	339*	4.2	10.4
075 BRETHREN IN CR	1	9	11*	0.1	0.3
081 CATHOLIC......	1	0	62	0.8	1.9
093 CR CH (DISC)..	5	350	424*	5.3	13.0
097 CR C AND C CR.	13	775	939*	11.7	28.9
165 CH OF NAZARENE	2	52	147	1.8	4.5
221 FREE METH C NA	1	24	27	0.3	0.8
419 SO BAPT CONV..	2	72	87*	1.1	2.7
449 UN METHODIST..	12	896	967	12.0	29.7
453 UN PRES CH USA	2	207	251*	3.1	7.7
DAVIESS	51	8,112	15,604*	58.7	100.0
019 AMER BAPT CONV	2	55	67*	0.3	0.4
029 AMER LUTH CH..	1	145	219	0.8	1.4
081 CATHOLIC......	6	0	5,492	20.6	35.2

*Total adherents estimated from known number of communicant, confirmed, full members.

—Represents a percent less than 0.1.

Percentages may not total due to rounding.

Table 3. Churches and Church Membership by State, County and Denomination: 1971

County and Denomination	Number of churches	Communicant, confirmed, full members	Total adherents: Number	Total adherents: Percent of total population	Total adherents: Percent of total adherents
093 CR CH (DISC)..	3	804	982*	3.7	6.3
097 CR C AND C CR.	6	2,783	3,401*	12.8	21.8
123 CH GOD (ANDER)	1	30	82	0.3	0.5
165 CH OF NAZARENE	2	99	198	0.7	1.3
185 CUMBER PRESB..	1	40	49*	0.2	0.3
193 EPISCOPAL.....	2	154	316	1.2	2.0
221 FREE METH C NA	1	134	187	0.7	1.2
285 MENNONITE CH..	5	463	566*	2.1	3.6
413 S-D ADVENTISTS	1	23	28*	0.1	0.2
419 SO BAPT CONV..	1	166	203*	0.8	1.3
449 UN METHODIST..	18	2,932	3,467	13.0	22.2
453 UN PRES CH USA	1	284	347*	1.3	2.2
DEARBORN	54	9,132	15,984*	54.3	100.0
019 AMER BAPT CONV	10	2,114	2,632*	8.9	16.5
029 AMER LUTH CH..	3	541	720	2.4	4.5
081 CATHOLIC......	6	0	4,630	15.7	29.0
097 CR C AND C CR.	7	1,605	1,998*	6.8	12.5
123 CH GOD (ANDER)	1	18	39	0.1	0.2
193 EPISCOPAL.....	1	30	74	0.3	0.5
281 LUTH CH AMER..	1	262	344	1.2	2.2
283 LUTH--MO SYNOD	4	1,086	1,396	4.7	8.7
419 SO BAPT CONV..	1	102	127*	0.4	0.8
435 UNITARIAN-UNIV	1	45	85	0.3	0.5
443 UN C OF CHRIST	2	364	453*	1.5	2.8
449 UN METHODIST..	13	2,362	2,735	9.3	17.1
453 UN PRES CH USA	4	603	751*	2.6	4.7
DECATUR	52	8,169	14,067*	61.9	100.0
019 AMER BAPT CONV	11	3,001	3,785*	16.6	26.9
081 CATHOLIC......	5	0	3,789	16.7	26.9
093 CR CH (DISC)..	3	770	971*	4.3	6.9
097 CR C AND C CR.	7	1,248	1,574*	6.9	11.2
123 CH GOD (ANDER)	1	75	167	0.7	1.2
127 CH GOD (CLEVE)	1	52	66*	0.3	0.5
165 CH OF NAZARENE	1	25	122	0.5	0.9
221 FREE METH C NA	1	33	49	0.2	0.3
281 LUTH CH AMER..	2	172	243	1.1	1.7
283 LUTH--MO SYNOD	1	91	128	0.6	0.9
419 SO BAPT CONV..	2	120	151*	0.7	1.1
449 UN METHODIST..	13	1,970	2,250	9.9	16.0
453 UN PRES CH USA	4	612	772*	3.4	5.5
DE KALB	54	9,328	20,926*	67.9	100.0
019 AMER BAPT CONV	2	281	350*	1.1	1.7
075 BRETHREN IN CR	1	48	60*	0.2	0.3
081 CATHOLIC......	3	0	3,058	9.9	14.6
093 CR CH (DISC)..	1	375	468*	1.5	2.2
097 CR C AND C CR.	7	1,176	1,466*	4.8	7.0
123 CH GOD (ANDER)	4	398	1,122	3.6	5.4
157 CH OF BRETHREN	4	484	603*	2.0	2.9
165 CH OF NAZARENE	5	455	1,219	4.0	5.8
281 LUTH CH AMER..	5	848	1,153	3.7	5.5
283 LUTH--MO SYNOD	3	682	958	3.1	4.6
449 UN METHODIST..	17	3,530	9,159	29.7	43.8
453 UN PRES CH USA	2	1,051	1,310*	4.2	6.3
DELAWARE	99	23,365	39,901*	30.9	100.0
019 AMER BAPT CONV	3	1,750	2,141*	1.7	5.4
029 AMER LUTH CH..	1	67	127	0.1	0.3
081 CATHOLIC......	3	0	7,547	5.8	18.9
093 CR CH (DISC)..	5	1,459	1,785*	1.4	4.5
097 CR C AND C CR.	4	450	550*	0.4	1.4
123 CH GOD (ANDER)	6	354	1,060	0.8	2.7
127 CH GOD (CLEVE)	1	44	54*	-	0.1
157 CH OF BRETHREN	3	274	335*	0.3	0.8
165 CH OF NAZARENE	16	1,854	4,625	3.6	11.6
193 EPISCOPAL.....	1	204	252	0.2	0.6
221 FREE METH C NA	1	15	19	-	-
226 FRIENDS-USA...	2	482	590*	0.5	1.5
281 LUTH CH AMER..	2	621	1,005	0.8	2.5
283 LUTH--MO SYNOD	2	494	700	0.5	1.8
381 REF PRES-EVAN.	1	62	73	0.1	0.2
403 SALVATION ARMY	1	48	278	0.2	0.7
413 S-D ADVENTISTS	2	85	104*	0.1	0.3
419 SO BAPT CONV..	6	1,161	1,420*	1.1	3.6
435 UNITARIAN-UNIV	1	276	356	0.3	0.9
443 UN C OF CHRIST	5	1,029	1,259*	1.0	3.2
449 UN METHODIST..	31	10,804	13,380	10.4	33.5
453 UN PRES CH USA	2	1,832	2,241*	1.7	5.6
DUBOIS	41	5,472	28,657*	92.6	100.0
029 AMER LUTH CH..	5	1,247	1,635	5.3	5.7
081 CATHOLIC......	13	0	21,619	69.9	75.4
093 CR CH (DISC)..	1	40	51*	0.2	0.2
097 CR C AND C CR.	5	375	480*	1.6	1.7
165 CH OF NAZARENE	1	34	100	0.3	0.3
281 LUTH CH AMER..	2	699	962	3.1	3.4
419 SO BAPT CONV..	2	174	223*	0.7	0.8
443 UN C OF CHRIST	6	1,573	2,015*	6.5	7.0
449 UN METHODIST..	4	1,152	1,344	4.3	4.7
453 UN PRES CH USA	2	178	228*	0.7	0.8
ELKHART	134	34,791	54,700*	43.2	100.0
029 AMER LUTH CH..	1	368	516	0.4	0.9
081 CATHOLIC......	5	0	8,257	6.5	15.1
093 CR CH (DISC)..	2	1,053	1,311*	1.0	2.4
097 CR C AND C CR.	1	90	112*	0.1	0.2
105 CHRISTIAN REF.	1	136	253	0.2	0.5
123 CH GOD (ANDER)	4	455	1,525	1.2	2.8
127 CH GOD (CLEVE)	3	166	207*	0.2	0.4
157 CH OF BRETHREN	17	4,610	5,740*	4.5	10.5
165 CH OF NAZARENE	8	747	2,003	1.6	3.7
193 EPISCOPAL.....	4	1,457	1,998	1.6	3.7
221 FREE METH C NA	1	56	78	0.1	0.1
281 LUTH CH AMER..	9	2,720	3,695	2.9	6.8
283 LUTH--MO SYNOD	1	980	1,284	1.0	2.3
285 MENNONITE CH..	31	5,778	7,194*	5.7	13.2
287 MENN GEN CONF.	6	875	1,089*	0.9	2.0
353 PLY BRETHREN..	1	15	50	-	0.1
403 SALVATION ARMY	2	172	733	0.6	1.3
413 S-D ADVENTISTS	2	152	189*	0.1	0.3
419 SO BAPT CONV..	1	146	182*	0.1	0.3
435 UNITARIAN-UNIV	1	85	130	0.1	0.2
443 UN C OF CHRIST	7	1,663	2,071*	1.6	3.8
449 UN METHODIST..	23	10,795	13,254	10.5	24.2
453 UN PRES CH USA	3	2,272	2,829*	2.2	5.2
FAYETTE	32	5,002	10,118*	38.6	100.0
081 CATHOLIC......	1	0	3,615	13.8	35.7
093 CR CH (DISC)..	5	887	1,101*	4.2	10.9
097 CR C AND C CR.	6	620	769*	2.9	7.6
123 CH GOD (ANDER)	1	105	280	1.1	2.8
127 CH GOD (CLEVE)	1	30	37*	0.1	0.4
165 CH OF NAZARENE	2	149	260	1.0	2.6
193 EPISCOPAL.....	1	90	146	0.6	1.4
281 LUTH CH AMER..	2	288	384	1.5	3.8
283 LUTH--MO SYNOD	1	98	143	0.5	1.4
403 SALVATION ARMY	1	57	255	1.0	2.5
413 S-D ADVENTISTS	1	35	43*	0.2	0.4
449 UN METHODIST..	9	2,187	2,519	9.6	24.9
453 UN PRES CH USA	1	456	566*	2.2	5.6
FLOYD	56	15,671	32,736*	58.9	100.0
019 AMER BAPT CONV	4	2,387	2,921*	5.3	8.9
081 CATHOLIC......	6	0	12,339	22.2	37.7
093 CR CH (DISC)..	7	1,576	1,929*	3.5	5.9
097 CR C AND C CR.	4	743	909*	1.6	2.8
123 CH GOD (ANDER)	1	250	675	1.2	2.1
127 CH GOD (CLEVE)	1	41	50*	0.1	0.2
165 CH OF NAZARENE	4	390	1,154	2.1	3.5
193 EPISCOPAL.....	1	260	297	0.5	0.9
283 LUTH--MO SYNOD	2	515	743	1.3	2.3
403 SALVATION ARMY	1	60	402	0.7	1.2
413 S-D ADVENTISTS	1	164	201*	0.4	0.6
419 SO BAPT CONV..	5	2,003	2,451*	4.4	7.5
443 UN C OF CHRIST	1	1,056	1,292*	2.3	3.9
449 UN METHODIST..	16	5,276	6,210	11.2	19.0
453 UN PRES CH USA	2	950	1,163*	2.1	3.6
FOUNTAIN	44	4,736	6,592*	36.1	100.0
081 CATHOLIC......	2	0	669	3.7	10.1
093 CR CH (DISC)..	3	312	384*	2.1	5.8
097 CR C AND C CR.	13	1,070	1,317*	7.2	20.0
123 CH GOD (ANDER)	1	55	180	1.0	2.7
127 CH GOD (CLEVE)	1	41	50*	0.3	0.8
165 CH OF NAZARENE	5	162	387	2.1	5.9
221 FREE METH C NA	1	59	79	0.4	1.2
281 LUTH CH AMER..	2	199	264	1.4	4.0
283 LUTH--MO SYNOD	1	203	266	1.5	4.0
413 S-D ADVENTISTS	1	9	11*	0.1	0.2
419 SO BAPT CONV..	1	133	164*	0.9	2.5
443 UN C OF CHRIST	2	154	190*	1.0	2.9
449 UN METHODIST..	9	2,057	2,284	12.5	34.6
453 UN PRES CH USA	2	282	347*	1.9	5.3
FRANKLIN	36	3,594	9,518*	56.2	100.0
029 AMER LUTH CH..	1	94	117	0.7	1.2
081 CATHOLIC......	7	0	4,956	29.3	52.1
093 CR CH (DISC)..	1	35	44*	0.3	0.5
097 CR C AND C CR.	6	324	407*	2.4	4.3
165 CH OF NAZARENE	2	43	195	1.2	2.0
281 LUTH CH AMER..	1	258	334	2.0	3.5
413 S-D ADVENTISTS	1	9	11*	0.1	0.1
419 SO BAPT CONV..	4	1,239	1,555*	9.2	16.3
443 UN C OF CHRIST	1	54	68*	0.4	0.7
449 UN METHODIST..	11	1,467	1,742	10.3	18.3
453 UN PRES CH USA	1	71	89*	0.5	0.9
FULTON	28	4,615	6,989*	41.2	100.0
019 AMER BAPT CONV	2	457	554*	3.3	7.9
081 CATHOLIC......	2	0	852	5.0	12.2
093 CR CH (DISC)..	1	292	354*	2.1	5.1
097 CR C AND C CR.	1	100	121*	0.7	1.7
123 CH GOD (ANDER)	3	398	1,133	6.7	16.2
157 CH OF BRETHREN	1	88	107*	0.6	1.5
165 CH OF NAZARENE	1	62	93	0.5	1.3
419 SO BAPT CONV..	1	179	217*	1.3	3.1
449 UN METHODIST..	15	2,842	3,319	19.5	47.5
453 UN PRES CH USA	1	197	239*	1.4	3.4
GIBSON	54	6,335	14,250*	46.8	100.0
081 CATHOLIC......	6	0	5,427	17.8	38.1
093 CR CH (DISC)..	2	434	522*	1.7	3.7
097 CR C AND C CR.	4	451	543*	1.8	3.8
123 CH GOD (ANDER)	1	111	290	1.0	2.0
165 CH OF NAZARENE	7	590	1,442	4.7	10.1
185 CUMBER PRESB..	1	90	108*	0.4	0.8

*Total adherents estimated from known number of communicant, confirmed, full members.

—Represents a percent less than 0.1.

Percentages may not total due to rounding.

Table 3. Churches and Church Membership by State, County and Denomination: 1971

County and Denomination	Number of churches	Communicant, confirmed, full members	Total adherents: Number	Total adherents: Percent of total population	Total adherents: Percent of total adherents
281 LUTH CH AMER..	1	129	197	0.6	1.4
403 SALVATION ARMY	1	49	435	1.4	3.1
413 S-D ADVENTISTS	1	16	19*	0.1	0.1
419 SO BAPT CONV..	3	212	255*	0.8	1.8
443 UN C OF CHRIST	3	277	333*	1.1	2.3
449 UN METHODIST..	18	3,032	3,543	11.6	24.9
453 UN PRES CH USA	6	944	1,136*	3.7	8.0
GRANT	89	15,374	26,959*	32.1	100.0
019 AMER BAPT CONV	5	801	993*	1.2	3.7
029 AMER LUTH CH..	1	517	717	0.9	2.7
081 CATHOLIC......	2	0	6,532	7.8	24.2
093 CR CH (DISC)..	7	2,061	2,554*	3.0	9.5
097 CR C AND C CR.	3	150	186*	0.2	0.7
123 CH GOD (ANDER)	4	226	677	0.8	2.5
127 CH GOD (CLEVE)	1	25	31*	-	0.1
157 CH OF BRETHREN	2	197	244*	0.3	0.9
165 CH OF NAZARENE	8	523	1,693	2.0	6.3
193 EPISCOPAL.....	2	471	570	0.7	2.1
226 FRIENDS-USA...	13	1,833	2,272*	2.7	8.4
281 LUTH CH AMER..	1	67	96	0.1	0.4
283 LUTH--MO SYNOD	1	332	478	0.6	1.8
403 SALVATION ARMY	1	125	320	0.4	1.2
413 S-D ADVENTISTS	2	146	181*	0.2	0.7
419 SO BAPT CONV..	2	345	428*	0.5	1.6
443 UN C OF CHRIST	2	381	472*	0.6	1.8
449 UN METHODIST..	29	5,965	7,017	8.4	26.0
453 UN PRES CH USA	3	1,209	1,498*	1.8	5.6
GREENE	65	14,910	18,540*	68.9	100.0
019 AMER BAPT CONV	12	9,087	10,893*	40.5	58.8
029 AMER LUTH CH..	1	108	159	0.6	0.9
081 CATHOLIC......	3	0	587	2.2	3.2
093 CR CH (DISC)..	7	861	1,032*	3.8	5.6
097 CR C AND C CR.	10	1,227	1,471*	5.5	7.9
123 CH GOD (ANDER)	2	77	235	0.9	1.3
127 CH GOD (CLEVE)	3	188	225*	0.8	1.2
165 CH OF NAZARENE	3	105	227	0.8	1.2
221 FREE METH C NA	1	34	44	0.2	0.2
403 SALVATION ARMY	1	25	120	0.4	0.6
413 S-D ADVENTISTS	1	66	79*	0.3	0.4
443 UN C OF CHRIST	1	299	358*	1.3	1.9
449 UN METHODIST..	19	2,750	3,011	11.2	16.2
453 UN PRES CH USA	1	83	99*	0.4	0.5
HAMILTON	70	15,954	25,137*	46.1	100.0
019 AMER BAPT CONV	1	149	186*	0.3	0.7
081 CATHOLIC......	3	0	4,226	7.7	16.8
093 CR CH (DISC)..	7	1,877	2,349*	4.3	9.3
097 CR C AND C CR.	11	2,115	2,647*	4.9	10.5
123 CH GOD (ANDER)	4	255	750	1.4	3.0
127 CH GOD (CLEVE)	1	43	54*	0.1	0.2
157 CH OF BRETHREN	1	116	145*	0.3	0.6
165 CH OF NAZARENE	2	167	323	0.6	1.3
193 EPISCOPAL.....	2	467	764	1.4	3.0
226 FRIENDS-USA...	10	2,002	2,506*	4.6	10.0
281 LUTH CH AMER..	2	615	962	1.8	3.8
283 LUTH--MO SYNOD	3	879	1,226	2.2	4.9
413 S-D ADVENTISTS	2	388	486*	0.9	1.9
419 SO BAPT CONV..	2	183	229*	0.4	0.9
449 UN METHODIST..	17	5,054	6,226	11.4	24.8
453 UN PRES CH USA	2	1,644	2,058*	3.8	8.2
HANCOCK	51	9,604	14,482*	41.3	100.0
081 CATHOLIC......	2	0	1,365	3.9	9.4
093 CR CH (DISC)..	4	890	1,121*	3.2	7.7
097 CR C AND C CR.	7	1,961	2,470*	7.0	17.1
123 CH GOD (ANDER)	1	110	250	0.7	1.7
127 CH GOD (CLEVE)	1	153	193*	0.5	1.3
165 CH OF NAZARENE	7	410	1,223	3.5	8.4
226 FRIENDS-USA...	2	329	414*	1.2	2.9
281 LUTH CH AMER..	1	150	267	0.8	1.8
283 LUTH--MO SYNOD	2	550	860	2.5	5.9
413 S-D ADVENTISTS	1	43	54*	0.2	0.4
419 SO BAPT CONV..	2	266	335*	1.0	2.3
443 UN C OF CHRIST	1	227	286*	0.8	2.0
449 UN METHODIST..	19	4,302	5,376	15.3	37.1
453 UN PRES CH USA	1	213	268*	0.8	1.9
HARRISON	64	5,519	9,848*	48.2	100.0
081 CATHOLIC......	6	0	3,088	15.1	31.4
093 CR CH (DISC)..	1	374	461*	2.3	4.7
097 CR C AND C CR.	5	40	49*	0.2	0.5
165 CH OF NAZARENE	2	139	326	1.6	3.3
281 LUTH CH AMER..	2	315	406	2.0	4.1
283 LUTH--MO SYNOD	1	522	710	3.5	7.2
413 S-D ADVENTISTS	1	26	32*	0.2	0.3
419 SO BAPT CONV..	5	546	674*	3.3	6.8
443 UN C OF CHRIST	1	15	19*	0.1	0.2
449 UN METHODIST..	35	3,084	3,518	17.2	35.7
453 UN PRES CH USA	5	458	565*	2.8	5.7
HENDRICKS	67	12,635	19,818*	36.7	100.0
019 AMER BAPT CONV	6	1,652	2,071*	3.8	10.5
081 CATHOLIC......	3	0	3,638	6.7	18.4
093 CR CH (DISC)..	8	1,340	1,680*	3.1	8.5
097 CR C AND C CR.	12	3,294	4,130*	7.7	20.8
123 CH GOD (ANDER)	1	37	82	0.2	0.4
127 CH GOD (CLEVE)	1	28	35*	0.1	0.2
165 CH OF NAZARENE	6	208	592	1.1	3.0
193 EPISCOPAL.....	1	110	170	0.3	0.9
226 FRIENDS-USA...	6	939	1,177*	2.2	5.9
281 LUTH CH AMER..	1	213	364	0.7	1.8
283 LUTH--MO SYNOD	1	219	333	0.6	1.7
413 S-D ADVENTISTS	1	88	110*	0.2	0.6
419 SO BAPT CONV..	2	534	670*	1.2	3.4
449 UN METHODIST..	13	3,410	4,060	7.5	20.5
453 UN PRES CH USA	5	563	706*	1.3	3.6
HENRY	77	12,190	18,859*	35.9	100.0
019 AMER BAPT CONV	1	672	828*	1.6	4.4
081 CATHOLIC......	2	0	1,660	3.2	8.8
093 CR CH (DISC)..	4	1,235	1,522*	2.9	8.1
097 CR C AND C CR.	10	1,700	2,095*	4.0	11.1
123 CH GOD (ANDER)	2	371	894	1.7	4.7
127 CH GOD (CLEVE)	1	111	137*	0.3	0.7
157 CH OF BRETHREN	4	305	376*	0.7	2.0
165 CH OF NAZARENE	10	863	2,503	4.8	13.3
193 EPISCOPAL.....	1	120	169	0.3	0.9
221 FREE METH C NA	1	34	54	0.1	0.3
226 FRIENDS-USA...	11	1,533	1,889*	3.6	10.0
281 LUTH CH AMER..	1	265	385	0.7	2.0
403 SALVATION ARMY	1	39	412	0.8	2.2
413 S-D ADVENTISTS	1	30	37*	0.1	0.2
419 SO BAPT CONV..	6	664	818*	1.6	4.3
443 UN C OF CHRIST	2	372	458*	0.9	2.4
449 UN METHODIST..	16	2,971	3,507	6.7	18.6
453 UN PRES CH USA	3	905	1,115*	2.1	5.9
HOWARD	82	20,460	35,565*	42.7	100.0
019 AMER BAPT CONV	5	1,439	1,814*	2.2	5.1
081 CATHOLIC......	2	0	7,637	9.2	21.5
093 CR CH (DISC)..	5	1,561	1,967*	2.4	5.5
097 CR C AND C CR.	9	2,405	3,031*	3.6	8.5
121 CH GOD (ABR)..	1	44	55*	0.1	0.2
123 CH GOD (ANDER)	1	98	346	0.4	1.0
127 CH GOD (CLEVE)	2	216	272*	0.3	0.8
157 CH OF BRETHREN	2	284	358*	0.4	1.0
165 CH OF NAZARENE	4	491	1,409	1.7	4.0
193 EPISCOPAL.....	1	429	653	0.8	1.8
221 FREE METH C NA	1	98	131	0.2	0.4
226 FRIENDS-USA...	13	1,849	2,330*	2.8	6.6
281 LUTH CH AMER..	2	493	755	0.9	2.1
283 LUTH--MO SYNOD	2	659	930	1.1	2.6
285 MENNONITE CH..	3	389	490*	0.6	1.4
403 SALVATION ARMY	1	183	1,176	1.4	3.3
413 S-D ADVENTISTS	1	176	222*	0.3	0.6
419 SO BAPT CONV..	4	620	781*	0.9	2.2
443 UN C OF CHRIST	4	696	877*	1.1	2.5
449 UN METHODIST..	17	6,645	8,207	9.9	23.1
453 UN PRES CH USA	2	1,685	2,124*	2.6	6.0
HUNTINGTON	54	11,477	19,742*	56.5	100.0
019 AMER BAPT CONV	2	340	416*	1.2	2.1
029 AMER LUTH CH..	1	17	18	0.1	0.1
081 CATHOLIC......	2	0	4,849	13.9	24.6
093 CR CH (DISC)..	4	908	1,110*	3.2	5.6
097 CR C AND C CR.	4	795	972*	2.8	4.9
123 CH GOD (ANDER)	1	230	454	1.3	2.3
157 CH OF BRETHREN	6	938	1,147*	3.3	5.8
165 CH OF NAZARENE	5	561	1,029	2.9	5.2
193 EPISCOPAL.....	1	95	191	0.5	1.0
283 LUTH--MO SYNOD	1	783	1,128	3.2	5.7
403 SALVATION ARMY	1	64	414	1.2	2.1
413 S-D ADVENTISTS	1	10	12*	-	0.1
443 UN C OF CHRIST	6	1,664	2,035*	5.8	10.3
449 UN METHODIST..	18	4,474	5,236	15.0	26.5
453 UN PRES CH USA	1	598	731*	2.1	3.7
JACKSON	80	15,104	21,252*	64.0	100.0
019 AMER BAPT CONV	9	2,194	2,705*	8.2	12.7
029 AMER LUTH CH..	1	284	401	1.2	1.9
081 CATHOLIC......	2	0	1,413	4.3	6.6
093 CR CH (DISC)..	3	893	1,101*	3.3	5.2
097 CR C AND C CR.	20	3,046	3,755*	11.3	17.7
123 CH GOD (ANDER)	1	55	110	0.3	0.5
127 CH GOD (CLEVE)	1	84	104*	0.3	0.5
157 CH OF BRETHREN	1	52	64*	0.2	0.3
165 CH OF NAZARENE	7	959	2,053	6.2	9.7
193 EPISCOPAL.....	1	70	96	0.3	0.5
221 FREE METH C NA	1	15	28	0.1	0.1
283 LUTH--MO SYNOD	9	4,033	5,407	16.3	25.4
413 S-D ADVENTISTS	1	40	49*	0.1	0.2
419 SO BAPT CONV..	2	418	515*	1.6	2.4
443 UN C OF CHRIST	2	241	297*	0.9	1.4
449 UN METHODIST..	16	2,016	2,286	6.9	10.8
453 UN PRES CH USA	3	704	868*	2.6	4.1
JASPER	37	5,350	10,853*	53.1	100.0
019 AMER BAPT CONV	2	230	285*	1.4	2.6
081 CATHOLIC......	5	0	3,774	18.5	34.8
093 CR CH (DISC)..	4	485	601*	2.9	5.5
097 CR C AND C CR.	1	125	155*	0.8	1.4
105 CHRISTIAN REF.	2	553	982	4.8	9.0
123 CH GOD (ANDER)	1	12	47	0.2	0.4
165 CH OF NAZARENE	2	119	365	1.8	3.4
193 EPISCOPAL.....	1	24	29	0.1	0.3
283 LUTH--MO SYNOD	3	420	615	3.0	5.7
285 MENNONITE CH..	1	45	56*	0.3	0.5

*Total adherents estimated from known number of communicant, confirmed, full members

—Represents a percent less than 0.1.

Percentages may not total due to rounding.

Table 3. Churches and Church Membership by State, County and Denomination: 1971

County and Denomination	Number of churches	Communicant, confirmed, full members	Total adherents: Number	Total adherents: Percent of total population	Total adherents: Percent of total adherents
371 REF CH IN AM..	2	856	1,273	6.2	11.7
413 S-D ADVENTISTS	1	18	22*	0.1	0.2
419 SO BAPT CONV..	1	84	104*	0.5	1.0
449 UN METHODIST..	9	1,966	2,033	10.0	18.7
453 UN PRES CH USA	2	413	512*	2.5	4.7
JAY	52	5,920	9,157*	38.8	100.0
019 AMER BAPT CONV	1	191	236*	1.0	2.6
029 AMER LUTH CH..	1	100	114	0.5	1.2
081 CATHOLIC......	3	0	1,386	5.9	15.1
093 CR CH (DISC)..	1	24	30*	0.1	0.3
097 CR C AND C CR.	4	645	796*	3.4	8.7
123 CH GOD (ANDER)	1	25	105	0.4	1.1
157 CH OF BRETHREN	2	109	134*	0.6	1.5
165 CH OF NAZARENE	5	357	812	3.4	8.9
221 FREE METH C NA	1	3	3	-	-
226 FRIENDS-USA...	4	144	178*	0.8	1.9
281 LUTH CH AMER..	2	529	746	3.2	8.1
413 S-D ADVENTISTS	1	21	26*	0.1	0.3
419 SO BAPT CONV..	1	155	191*	0.8	2.1
443 UN C OF CHRIST	4	297	366*	1.6	4.0
449 UN METHODIST..	20	2,828	3,427	14.5	37.4
453 UN PRES CH USA	1	492	607*	2.6	6.6
JEFFERSON	61	8,957	13,109*	48.5	100.0
019 AMER BAPT CONV	21	4,702	5,715*	21.2	43.6
081 CATHOLIC......	4	0	1,932	7.2	14.7
093 CR CH (DISC)..	2	311	378*	1.4	2.9
097 CR C AND C CR.	4	455	553*	2.0	4.2
123 CH GOD (ANDER)	1	21	61	0.2	0.5
127 CH GOD (CLEVE)	1	56	68*	0.3	0.5
165 CH OF NAZARENE	3	110	360	1.3	2.7
193 EPISCOPAL.....	1	104	160	0.6	1.2
281 LUTH CH AMER..	1	118	182	0.7	1.4
283 LUTH--MO SYNOD	1	75	93	0.3	0.7
403 SALVATION ARMY	1	49	182	0.7	1.4
413 S-D ADVENTISTS	1	16	19*	0.1	0.1
419 SO BAPT CONV..	1	200	243*	0.9	1.9
443 UN C OF CHRIST	1	75	91*	0.3	0.7
449 UN METHODIST..	14	1,878	2,115	7.8	16.1
453 UN PRES CH USA	4	787	957*	3.5	7.3
JENNINGS	42	5,073	8,576*	44.1	100.0
019 AMER BAPT CONV	12	2,247	2,802*	14.4	32.7
081 CATHOLIC......	4	0	1,923	9.9	22.4
097 CR C AND C CR.	4	945	1,179*	6.1	13.7
123 CH GOD (ANDER)	3	124	405	2.1	4.7
127 CH GOD (CLEVE)	1	34	42*	0.2	0.5
165 CH OF NAZARENE	1	120	348	1.8	4.1
413 S-D ADVENTISTS	1	43	54*	0.3	0.6
419 SO BAPT CONV..	1	115	143*	0.7	1.7
449 UN METHODIST..	10	1,065	1,206	6.2	14.1
453 UN PRES CH USA	5	380	474*	2.4	5.5
JOHNSON	67	15,785	23,398*	38.3	100.0
019 AMER BAPT CONV	6	2,002	2,523*	4.1	10.8
081 CATHOLIC......	3	0	3,193	5.2	13.6
093 CR CH (DISC)..	11	2,121	2,673*	4.4	11.4
097 CR C AND C CR.	13	3,995	5,034*	8.2	21.5
123 CH GOD (ANDER)	1	45	120	0.2	0.5
127 CH GOD (CLEVE)	2	122	154*	0.3	0.7
165 CH OF NAZARENE	4	282	699	1.1	3.0
193 EPISCOPAL.....	1	64	88	0.1	0.4
281 LUTH CH AMER..	3	375	538	0.9	2.3
283 LUTH--MO SYNOD	2	377	583	1.0	2.5
419 SO BAPT CONV..	4	984	1,240*	2.0	5.3
443 UN C OF CHRIST	1	99	125*	0.2	0.5
449 UN METHODIST..	10	3,617	4,283	7.0	18.3
453 UN PRES CH USA	6	1,702	2,145*	3.5	9.2
KNOX	76	13,526	25,040*	60.3	100.0
019 AMER BAPT CONV	5	1,386	1,646*	4.0	6.6
081 CATHOLIC......	6	0	7,319	17.6	29.2
093 CR CH (DISC)..	6	1,248	1,482*	3.6	5.9
097 CR C AND C CR.	10	1,519	1,803*	4.3	7.2
123 CH GOD (ANDER)	2	275	674	1.6	2.7
127 CH GOD (CLEVE)	1	25	30*	0.1	0.1
165 CH OF NAZARENE	3	327	916	2.2	3.7
185 CUMBER PRESB..	1	150	178*	0.4	0.7
193 EPISCOPAL.....	1	123	163	0.4	0.7
221 FREE METH C NA	1	200	274	0.7	1.1
281 LUTH CH AMER..	1	125	184	0.4	0.7
283 LUTH--MO SYNOD	2	790	1,136	2.7	4.5
381 REF PRES-EVAN.	1	23	45	0.1	0.2
403 SALVATION ARMY	1	94	593	1.4	2.4
413 S-D ADVENTISTS	1	65	77*	0.2	0.3
419 SO BAPT CONV..	1	309	367*	0.9	1.5
443 UN C OF CHRIST	3	1,494	1,774*	4.3	7.1
449 UN METHODIST..	23	4,361	5,177	12.5	20.7
453 UN PRES CH USA	7	1,012	1,202*	2.9	4.8
KOSCIUSKO	63	11,652	17,032*	35.4	100.0
019 AMER BAPT CONV	1	138	171*	0.4	1.0
081 CATHOLIC......	3	0	1,948	4.0	11.4
093 CR CH (DISC)..	2	109	135*	0.3	0.8
097 CR C AND C CR.	3	400	495*	1.0	2.9
123 CH GOD (ANDER)	2	350	903	1.9	5.3
157 CH OF BRETHREN	10	1,532	1,895*	3.9	11.1
165 CH OF NAZARENE	2	55	153	0.3	0.9
193 EPISCOPAL.....	2	215	278	0.6	1.6
221 FREE METH C NA	1	250	317	0.7	1.9
281 LUTH CH AMER..	1	220	293	0.6	1.7
283 LUTH--MO SYNOD	1	373	534	1.1	3.1
285 MENNONITE CH..	2	345	427*	0.9	2.5
403 SALVATION ARMY	1	60	281	0.6	1.6
443 UN C OF CHRIST	1	60	74*	0.2	0.4
449 UN METHODIST..	28	6,454	7,778	16.2	45.7
453 UN PRES CH USA	3	1,091	1,350*	2.8	7.9
LAGRANGE	37	5,075	7,432*	35.6	100.0
019 AMER BAPT CONV	2	168	221*	1.1	3.0
081 CATHOLIC......	1	0	498	2.4	6.7
097 CR C AND C CR.	2	375	493*	2.4	6.6
123 CH GOD (ANDER)	2	156	422	2.0	5.7
157 CH OF BRETHREN	1	102	134*	0.6	1.8
165 CH OF NAZARENE	2	107	253	1.2	3.4
193 EPISCOPAL.....	1	106	125	0.6	1.7
281 LUTH CH AMER..	1	348	475	2.3	6.4
283 LUTH--MO SYNOD	1	196	308	1.5	4.1
285 MENNONITE CH..	7	1,078	1,417*	6.8	19.1
287 MENN GEN CONF.	1	160	210*	1.0	2.8
449 UN METHODIST..	14	1,775	2,214	10.6	29.8
453 UN PRES CH USA	2	504	662*	3.2	8.9
LAKE	330	72,460	240,588*	44.0	100.0
019 AMER BAPT CONV	12	3,460	4,324*	0.8	1.8
029 AMER LUTH CH..	2	897	1,380	0.3	0.6
059 BAPT MISS ASSN	3	87	109*	-	-
081 CATHOLIC......	85	0	145,887	26.7	60.6
093 CR CH (DISC)..	5	1,393	1,741*	0.3	0.7
097 CR C AND C CR.	24	5,918	7,397*	1.4	3.1
105 CHRISTIAN REF.	6	1,666	2,925	0.5	1.2
123 CH GOD (ANDER)	10	571	1,491	0.3	0.6
127 CH GOD (CLEVE)	14	709	886*	0.2	0.4
165 CH OF NAZARENE	18	1,995	5,306	1.0	2.2
175 CONG CR CH....	2	512	640*	0.1	0.3
193 EPISCOPAL.....	6	1,524	2,174	0.4	0.9
201 EVAN COV CH AM	2	233	291*	0.1	0.1
221 FREE METH C NA	2	122	187	-	0.1
281 LUTH CH AMER..	10	3,901	5,362	1.0	2.2
283 LUTH--MO SYNOD	26	10,763	15,172	2.8	6.3
349 PENT HOLINESS.	1	15	19*	-	-
371 REF CH IN AM..	4	848	1,160	0.2	0.5
403 SALVATION ARMY	3	201	793	0.1	0.3
413 S-D ADVENTISTS	5	948	1,185*	0.2	0.5
419 SO BAPT CONV..	30	10,081	12,600*	2.3	5.2
435 UNITARIAN-UNIV	1	126	181	-	0.1
443 UN C OF CHRIST	9	2,249	2,811*	0.5	1.2
449 UN METHODIST..	28	14,932	14,932	2.7	6.2
453 UN PRES CH USA	22	9,309	11,635*	2.1	4.8
LA PORTE	87	22,002	54,698*	51.9	100.0
019 AMER BAPT CONV	3	1,372	1,695*	1.6	3.1
029 AMER LUTH CH..	3	2,098	3,271	3.1	6.0
059 BAPT MISS ASSN	1	67	83*	0.1	0.2
081 CATHOLIC......	19	0	25,671	24.4	46.9
093 CR CH (DISC)..	3	779	962*	0.9	1.8
097 CR C AND C CR.	7	1,652	2,041*	1.9	3.7
123 CH GOD (ANDER)	2	75	190	0.2	0.3
127 CH GOD (CLEVE)	2	64	79*	0.1	0.1
157 CH OF BRETHREN	2	159	196*	0.2	0.4
165 CH OF NAZARENE	2	87	150	0.1	0.3
175 CONG CR CH....	1	97	120*	0.1	0.2
193 EPISCOPAL.....	3	926	1,150	1.1	2.1
221 FREE METH C NA	3	126	185	0.2	0.3
281 LUTH CH AMER..	2	877	1,177	1.1	2.2
283 LUTH--MO SYNOD	9	3,192	4,209	4.0	7.7
349 PENT HOLINESS.	1	26	32*	-	0.1
403 SALVATION ARMY	2	233	643	0.6	1.2
413 S-D ADVENTISTS	2	158	195*	0.2	0.4
419 SO BAPT CONV..	2	284	351*	0.3	0.6
443 UN C OF CHRIST	3	2,351	2,904*	2.8	5.3
449 UN METHODIST..	12	5,176	6,673	6.3	12.2
453 UN PRES CH USA	3	2,203	2,721*	2.6	5.0
LAWRENCE	75	13,251	19,291*	50.7	100.0
019 AMER BAPT CONV	16	4,752	5,804*	15.3	30.1
081 CATHOLIC......	2	0	1,430	3.8	7.4
093 CR CH (DISC)..	3	891	1,088*	2.9	5.6
097 CR C AND C CR.	18	2,977	3,636*	9.6	18.8
123 CH GOD (ANDER)	5	444	1,068	2.8	5.5
127 CH GOD (CLEVE)	2	59	72*	0.2	0.4
165 CH OF NAZARENE	5	532	1,369	3.6	7.1
193 EPISCOPAL.....	1	169	227	0.6	1.2
221 FREE METH C NA	1	370	475	1.2	2.5
283 LUTH--MO SYNOD	2	238	401	1.1	2.1
403 SALVATION ARMY	1	82	489	1.3	2.5
413 S-D ADVENTISTS	1	93	114*	0.3	0.6
419 SO BAPT CONV..	1	65	79*	0.2	0.4
449 UN METHODIST..	15	2,168	2,537	6.7	13.2
453 UN PRES CH USA	2	411	502*	1.3	2.6
MADISON	114	31,280	55,123*	39.8	100.0
019 AMER BAPT CONV	9	4,057	5,016*	3.6	9.1
081 CATHOLIC......	4	0	10,117	7.3	18.4
093 CR CH (DISC)..	10	3,837	4,744*	3.4	8.6
097 CR C AND C CR.	7	2,371	2,931*	2.1	5.3
123 CH GOD (ANDER)	14	3,258	7,879	5.7	14.3
127 CH GOD (CLEVE)	2	117	145*	0.1	0.3

*Total adherents estimated from known number of communicant, confirmed, full members.

—Represents a percent less than 0.1.

Percentages may not total due to rounding.

Table 3. Churches and Church Membership by State, County and Denomination: 1971

County and Denomination	Number of churches	Communicant, confirmed, full members	Total adherents		
			Number	Percent of total population	Percent of total adherents
157 CH OF BRETHREN	2	547	676*	0.5	1.2
165 CH OF NAZARENE	10	1,500	3,703	2.7	6.7
193 EPISCOPAL.....	2	445	694	0.5	1.3
197 EVAN CH OF NA.	1	139	172*	0.1	0.3
221 FREE METH C NA	1	44	68	-	0.1
226 FRIENDS-USA...	5	409	506*	0.4	0.9
281 LUTH CH AMER..	3	777	1,133	0.8	2.1
283 LUTH--MO SYNOD	2	616	931	0.7	1.7
403 SALVATION ARMY	2	180	742	0.5	1.3
413 S-D ADVENTISTS	4	308	381*	0.3	0.7
419 SO BAPT CONV..	3	204	252*	0.2	0.5
443 UN C OF CHRIST	1	334	413*	0.3	0.7
449 UN METHODIST..	29	10,302	12,351	8.9	22.4
453 UN PRES CH USA	3	1,835	2,269*	1.6	4.1
MARION	408	153,848	290,438*	36.7	100.0
019 AMER BAPT CONV	33	14,803	18,354*	2.3	6.3
029 AMER LUTH CH..	5	1,542	2,176	0.3	0.7
081 CATHOLIC......	43	0	91,820	11.6	31.6
093 CR CH (DISC)..	32	15,778	19,563*	2.5	6.7
097 CR C AND C CR.	36	20,346	25,227*	3.2	8.7
105 CHRISTIAN REF.	1	88	176	-	0.1
123 CH GOD (ANDER)	11	1,354	3,629	0.5	1.2
127 CH GOD (CLEVE)	7	656	813*	0.1	0.3
157 CH OF BRETHREN	1	233	289*	-	0.1
165 CH OF NAZARENE	29	3,081	7,129	0.9	2.5
185 CUMBER PRESB..	1	125	155*	-	0.1
193 EPISCOPAL.....	10	5,187	8,882	1.1	3.1
221 FREE METH C NA	8	945	1,484	0.2	0.5
226 FRIENDS-USA...	8	2,024	2,510*	0.3	0.9
281 LUTH CH AMER..	15	4,827	6,536	0.8	2.3
283 LUTH--MO SYNOD	16	6,905	9,954	1.3	3.4
285 MENNONITE CH..	1	120	149*	-	0.1
293 MORAV CH-NORTH	3	313	470	0.1	0.2
313 NO AM BAPT GC.	1	48	60*	-	-
353 PLY BRETHREN..	1	50	70	-	-
371 REF CH IN AM..	2	197	297	-	0.1
381 REF PRES-EVAN.	2	154	190	-	0.1
403 SALVATION ARMY	3	287	1,254	0.2	0.4
413 S-D ADVENTISTS	5	1,581	1,960*	0.2	0.7
419 SO BAPT CONV..	20	4,937	6,121*	0.8	2.1
435 UNITARIAN-UNIV	3	951	1,386	0.2	0.5
443 UN C OF CHRIST	17	7,423	9,204*	1.2	3.2
449 UN METHODIST..	68	40,192	46,124	5.8	15.9
453 UN PRES CH USA	25	19,637	24,348*	3.1	8.4
469 WISC EVAN LUTH	1	64	108	-	-
MARSHALL	49	9,033	13,975*	39.9	100.0
019 AMER BAPT CONV	1	97	119*	0.3	0.9
081 CATHOLIC......	3	0	2,582	7.4	18.5
093 CR CH (DISC)..	2	81	100*	0.3	0.7
097 CR C AND C CR.	1	130	160*	0.5	1.1
121 CH GOD (ABR)..	2	88	108*	0.3	0.8
123 CH GOD (ANDER)	2	79	281	0.8	2.0
157 CH OF BRETHREN	6	1,005	1,237*	3.5	8.9
165 CH OF NAZARENE	1	67	117	0.3	0.8
193 EPISCOPAL.....	1	263	368	1.1	2.6
201 EVAN COV CH AM	1	89	110*	0.3	0.8
281 LUTH CH AMER..	1	269	345	1.0	2.5
283 LUTH--MO SYNOD	3	838	1,175	3.4	8.4
285 MENNONITE CH..	1	61	75*	0.2	0.5
413 S-D ADVENTISTS	1	40	49*	0.1	0.4
443 UN C OF CHRIST	4	1,229	1,513*	4.3	10.8
449 UN METHODIST..	18	4,329	5,183	14.8	37.1
453 UN PRES CH USA	1	368	453*	1.3	3.2
MARTIN	26	2,084	5,545*	50.6	100.0
029 AMER LUTH CH..	1	250	335	3.1	6.0
081 CATHOLIC......	4	0	2,950	26.9	53.2
093 CR CH (DISC)..	1	23	29*	0.3	0.5
097 CR C AND C CR.	3	580	728*	6.6	13.1
165 CH OF NAZARENE	2	41	79	0.7	1.4
283 LUTH--MO SYNOD	1	38	38	0.3	0.7
285 MENNONITE CH..	1	21	26*	0.2	0.5
413 S-D ADVENTISTS	1	19	24*	0.2	0.4
419 SO BAPT CONV..	1	30	38*	0.3	0.7
449 UN METHODIST..	11	1,082	1,298	11.8	23.4
MIAMI	48	11,976	17,984*	45.8	100.0
019 AMER BAPT CONV	7	2,520	3,148*	8.0	17.5
081 CATHOLIC......	1	0	2,673	6.8	14.9
093 CR CH (DISC)..	1	754	942*	2.4	5.2
097 CR C AND C CR.	5	2,164	2,703*	6.9	15.0
123 CH GOD (ANDER)	1	80	200	0.5	1.1
127 CH GOD (CLEVE)	1	38	47*	0.1	0.3
157 CH OF BRETHREN	3	818	1,022*	2.6	5.7
165 CH OF NAZARENE	1	170	250	0.6	1.4
193 EPISCOPAL.....	1	153	365	0.9	2.0
226 FRIENDS-USA...	1	491	613*	1.6	3.4
283 LUTH--MO SYNOD	1	658	942	2.4	5.2
285 MENNONITE CH..	1	62	77*	0.2	0.4
403 SALVATION ARMY	1	39	209	0.5	1.2
419 SO BAPT CONV..	1	292	365*	0.9	2.0
449 UN METHODIST..	21	3,239	3,806	9.7	21.2
453 UN PRES CH USA	1	498	622*	1.6	3.5
MONROE	59	14,151	26,711*	31.5	100.0
019 AMER BAPT CONV	10	3,134	3,705*	4.4	13.9
081 CATHOLIC......	3	0	8,853	10.4	33.1
093 CR CH (DISC)..	4	1,738	2,055*	2.4	7.7
097 CR C AND C CR.	10	1,571	1,857*	2.2	7.0
123 CH GOD (ANDER)	1	160	332	0.4	1.2
165 CH OF NAZARENE	5	545	1,078	1.3	4.0
193 EPISCOPAL.....	1	377	622	0.7	2.3
221 FREE METH C NA	1	190	242	0.3	0.9
226 FRIENDS-USA...	1	95	112*	0.1	0.4
281 LUTH CH AMER..	1	155	234	0.3	0.9
283 LUTH--MO SYNOD	1	205	289	0.3	1.1
403 SALVATION ARMY	1	77	316	0.4	1.2
413 S-D ADVENTISTS	1	169	200*	0.2	0.7
419 SO BAPT CONV..	2	515	609*	0.7	2.3
435 UNITARIAN-UNIV	1	187	257	0.3	1.0
443 UN C OF CHRIST	1	54	64*	0.1	0.2
449 UN METHODIST..	13	4,075	4,817	5.7	18.0
453 UN PRES CH USA	2	904	1,069*	1.3	4.0
MONTGOMERY	58	11,841	16,291*	48.0	100.0
019 AMER BAPT CONV	6	1,965	2,397*	7.1	14.7
081 CATHOLIC......	2	0	1,656	4.9	10.2
093 CR CH (DISC)..	4	1,363	1,663*	4.9	10.2
097 CR C AND C CR.	15	2,400	2,928*	8.6	18.0
107 CHRISTIAN UN..	1	132	161*	0.5	1.0
123 CH GOD (ANDER)	1	47	125	0.4	0.8
127 CH GOD (CLEVE)	1	13	16*	-	0.1
157 CH OF BRETHREN	1	11	13*	-	0.1
165 CH OF NAZARENE	2	245	630	1.9	3.9
193 EPISCOPAL.....	1	140	212	0.6	1.3
281 LUTH CH AMER..	1	208	289	0.9	1.8
283 LUTH--MO SYNOD	1	121	182	0.5	1.1
413 S-D ADVENTISTS	1	9	11*	-	0.1
419 SO BAPT CONV..	1	46	56*	0.2	0.3
443 UN C OF CHRIST	1	85	104*	0.3	0.6
449 UN METHODIST..	15	3,911	4,451	13.1	27.3
453 UN PRES CH USA	4	1,145	1,397*	4.1	8.6
MORGAN	67	9,610	13,823*	31.3	100.0
019 AMER BAPT CONV	7	954	1,211*	2.7	8.8
081 CATHOLIC......	2	0	1,161	2.6	8.4
093 CR CH (DISC)..	6	1,437	1,825*	4.1	13.2
097 CR C AND C CR.	19	2,385	3,029*	6.9	21.9
123 CH GOD (ANDER)	3	225	600	1.4	4.3
165 CH OF NAZARENE	5	291	804	1.8	5.8
193 EPISCOPAL.....	1	57	99	0.2	0.7
221 FREE METH C NA	1	52	78	0.2	0.6
226 FRIENDS-USA...	3	670	851*	1.9	6.2
283 LUTH--MO SYNOD	1	112	159	0.4	1.2
285 MENNONITE CH..	2	45	57*	0.1	0.4
413 S-D ADVENTISTS	1	35	44*	0.1	0.3
419 SO BAPT CONV..	6	1,075	1,365*	3.1	9.9
449 UN METHODIST..	9	1,977	2,165	4.9	15.7
453 UN PRES CH USA	1	295	375*	0.8	2.7
NEWTON	25	3,747	6,090*	52.5	100.0
019 AMER BAPT CONV	2	155	191*	1.6	3.1
081 CATHOLIC......	3	0	1,716	14.8	28.2
093 CR CH (DISC)..	2	475	585*	5.0	9.6
097 CR C AND C CR.	2	267	329*	2.8	5.4
123 CH GOD (ANDER)	1	10	40	0.3	0.7
283 LUTH--MO SYNOD	1	94	131	1.1	2.2
287 MENN GEN CONF.	1	62	76*	0.7	1.2
419 SO BAPT CONV..	1	178	219*	1.9	3.6
449 UN METHODIST..	8	2,128	2,337	20.1	38.4
453 UN PRES CH USA	4	378	466*	4.0	7.7
NOBLE	49	7,796	12,510*	39.9	100.0
019 AMER BAPT CONV	1	43	54*	0.2	0.4
081 CATHOLIC......	6	0	2,546	8.1	20.4
093 CR CH (DISC)..	1	333	415*	1.3	3.3
097 CR C AND C CR.	2	190	237*	0.8	1.9
157 CH OF BRETHREN	1	108	135*	0.4	1.1
165 CH OF NAZARENE	3	139	352	1.1	2.8
197 EVAN CH OF NA.	1	43	54*	0.2	0.4
281 LUTH CH AMER..	4	579	937	3.0	7.5
283 LUTH--MO SYNOD	3	1,123	1,582	5.0	12.6
285 MENNONITE CH..	1	24	30*	0.1	0.2
413 S-D ADVENTISTS	2	50	62*	0.2	0.5
443 UN C OF CHRIST	1	165	206*	0.7	1.6
449 UN METHODIST..	19	4,313	5,045	16.1	40.3
453 UN PRES CH USA	4	686	855*	2.7	6.8
OHIO	11	1,903	2,422*	56.5	100.0
019 AMER BAPT CONV	1	451	559*	13.0	23.1
029 AMER LUTH CH..	1	124	157	3.7	6.5
097 CR C AND C CR.	1	300	372*	8.7	15.4
107 CHRISTIAN UN..	1	128	159*	3.7	6.6
165 CH OF NAZARENE	1	71	197	4.6	8.1
443 UN C OF CHRIST	1	195	242*	5.6	10.0
449 UN METHODIST..	4	576	664	15.5	27.4
453 UN PRES CH USA	1	58	72*	1.7	3.0
ORANGE	46	6,211	8,260*	48.7	100.0
019 AMER BAPT CONV	4	1,175	1,430*	8.4	17.3
081 CATHOLIC......	2	0	604	3.6	7.3
093 CR CH (DISC)..	2	250	304*	1.8	3.7
097 CR C AND C CR.	11	2,041	2,484*	14.6	30.1
165 CH OF NAZARENE	3	181	489	2.9	5.9
226 FRIENDS-USA...	4	411	500*	2.9	6.1
413 S-D ADVENTISTS	1	35	43*	0.3	0.5
419 SO BAPT CONV..	1	157	191*	1.1	2.3

*Total adherents estimated from known number of communicant, confirmed, full members.

—Represents a percent less than 0.1.

Percentages may not total due to rounding.

Table 3. Churches and Church Membership by State, County and Denomination: 1971

County and Denomination	Number of churches	Communicant, confirmed, full members	Total adherents: Number	Total adherents: Percent of total population	Total adherents: Percent of total adherents
449 UN METHODIST..	17	1,814	2,036	12.0	24.6
453 UN PRES CH USA	1	147	179*	1.1	2.2
OWEN	45	4,683	6,256*	51.4	100.0
019 AMER BAPT CONV	11	1,843	2,256*	18.5	36.1
029 AMER LUTH CH..	2	76	97	0.8	1.6
081 CATHOLIC......	1	0	198	1.6	3.2
093 CR CH (DISC)..	2	317	388*	3.2	6.2
097 CR C AND C CR.	5	300	367*	3.0	5.9
165 CH OF NAZARENE	6	412	974	8.0	15.6
413 S-D ADVENTISTS	1	11	13*	0.1	0.2
443 UN C OF CHRIST	1	24	29*	0.2	0.5
449 UN METHODIST..	13	1,393	1,558	12.8	24.9
453 UN PRES CH USA	3	307	376*	3.1	6.0
PARKE	36	4,062	5,338*	36.6	100.0
019 AMER BAPT CONV	8	588	708*	4.8	13.3
081 CATHOLIC......	3	0	300	2.1	5.6
093 CR CH (DISC)..	2	141	170*	1.2	3.2
097 CR C AND C CR.	5	1,107	1,333*	9.1	25.0
165 CH OF NAZARENE	4	147	422	2.9	7.9
226 FRIENDS-USA...	4	583	702*	4.8	13.2
449 UN METHODIST..	8	1,067	1,186	8.1	22.2
453 UN PRES CH USA	2	429	517*	3.5	9.7
PERRY	30	3,293	10,966*	57.5	100.0
019 AMER BAPT CONV	4	789	979*	5.1	8.9
081 CATHOLIC......	10	0	6,715	35.2	61.2
093 CR CH (DISC)..	4	183	227*	1.2	2.1
165 CH OF NAZARENE	1	82	282	1.5	2.6
193 EPISCOPAL.....	1	32	51	0.3	0.5
283 LUTH--MO SYNOD	1	192	263	1.4	2.4
413 S-D ADVENTISTS	1	44	55*	0.3	0.5
443 UN C OF CHRIST	2	1,093	1,356*	7.1	12.4
449 UN METHODIST..	6	878	1,038	5.4	9.5
PIKE	31	2,312	3,574*	29.1	100.0
019 AMER BAPT CONV	1	219	262*	2.1	7.3
081 CATHOLIC......	1	0	333	2.7	9.3
093 CR CH (DISC)..	1	60	72*	0.6	2.0
097 CR C AND C CR.	4	235	281*	2.3	7.9
123 CH GOD (ANDER)	5	[illegible]91	599	4.9	16.8
165 CH OF NAZARENE	2	108	278	2.3	7.8
185 CUMBER PRESB..	1	10	12*	0.1	0.3
221 FREE METH C NA	2	90	103	0.8	2.9
413 S-D ADVENTISTS	1	16	19*	0.2	0.5
419 SO BAPT CONV..	1	83	99*	0.8	2.8
449 UN METHODIST..	10	1,042	1,207	9.8	33.8
453 UN PRES CH USA	2	258	309*	2.5	8.6
PORTER	64	16,558	38,256*	43.9	100.0
019 AMER BAPT CONV	2	1,306	1,652*	1.9	4.3
029 AMER LUTH CH..	2	520	830	1.0	2.2
081 CATHOLIC......	8	0	14,719	16.9	38.5
093 CR CH (DISC)..	2	691	874*	1.0	2.3
097 CR C AND C CR.	8	1,143	1,446*	1.7	3.8
123 CH GOD (ANDER)	1	36	114	0.1	0.3
127 CH GOD (CLEVE)	1	92	116*	0.1	0.3
165 CH OF NAZARENE	4	617	2,268	2.6	5.9
193 EPISCOPAL.....	2	175	240	0.3	0.6
281 LUTH CH AMER..	4	1,923	2,721	3.1	7.1
283 LUTH--MO SYNOD	6	3,262	4,539	5.2	11.9
285 MENNONITE CH..	2	335	424*	0.5	1.1
353 PLY BRETHREN..	1	10	15	-	-
413 S-D ADVENTISTS	1	54	68*	0.1	0.2
419 SO BAPT CONV..	6	906	1,146*	1.3	3.0
435 UNITARIAN-UNIV	1	50	50	0.1	0.1
443 UN C OF CHRIST	1	219	277*	0.3	0.7
449 UN METHODIST..	7	3,615	4,728	5.4	12.4
453 UN PRES CH USA	5	1,604	2,029*	2.3	5.3
POSEY	45	5,917	12,217*	56.2	100.0
081 CATHOLIC......	5	0	4,669	21.5	38.2
093 CR CH (DISC)..	2	230	285*	1.3	2.3
097 CR C AND C CR.	4	776	961*	4.4	7.9
127 CH GOD (CLEVE)	2	38	47*	0.2	0.4
165 CH OF NAZARENE	4	174	527	2.4	4.3
193 EPISCOPAL.....	2	162	213	1.0	1.7
221 FREE METH C NA	1	4	4	-	-
413 S-D ADVENTISTS	1	22	27*	0.1	0.2
419 SO BAPT CONV..	2	532	658*	3.0	5.4
443 UN C OF CHRIST	6	1,538	1,904*	8.8	15.6
449 UN METHODIST..	14	2,293	2,739	12.6	22.4
453 UN PRES CH USA	2	148	183*	0.8	1.5
PULASKI	27	3,797	6,801*	54.3	100.0
019 AMER BAPT CONV	1	47	58*	0.5	0.9
081 CATHOLIC......	5	0	2,037	16.3	30.0
093 CR CH (DISC)..	2	261	323*	2.6	4.7
097 CR C AND C CR.	3	975	1,206*	9.6	17.7
165 CH OF NAZARENE	1	126	253	2.0	3.7
283 LUTH--MO SYNOD	3	374	503	4.0	7.4
353 PLY BRETHREN..	1	20	30	0.2	0.4
443 UN C OF CHRIST	3	254	314*	2.5	4.6
449 UN METHODIST..	6	1,420	1,681	13.4	24.7
453 UN PRES CH USA	2	320	396*	3.2	5.8
PUTNAM	40	6,179	8,104*	30.1	100.0
019 AMER BAPT CONV	6	1,150	1,368*	5.1	16.9
081 CATHOLIC......	2	0	460	1.7	5.7
093 CR CH (DISC)..	5	1,181	1,405*	5.2	17.3
097 CR C AND C CR.	6	483	575*	2.1	7.1
127 CH GOD (CLEVE)	1	73	87*	0.3	1.1
165 CH OF NAZARENE	3	256	720	2.7	8.9
175 CONG CR CH....	1	103	123*	0.5	1.5
193 EPISCOPAL.....	1	94	135	0.5	1.7
283 LUTH--MO SYNOD	1	128	181	0.7	2.2
419 SO BAPT CONV..	1	173	206*	0.8	2.5
443 UN C OF CHRIST	1	172	205*	0.8	2.5
449 UN METHODIST..	9	1,847	2,021	7.5	24.9
453 UN PRES CH USA	3	519	618*	2.3	7.6
RANDOLPH	62	7,977	12,193*	42.2	100.0
029 AMER LUTH CH..	1	241	342	1.2	2.8
081 CATHOLIC......	2	0	1,123	3.9	9.2
093 CR CH (DISC)..	4	1,150	1,409*	4.9	11.6
097 CR C AND C CR.	3	820	1,004*	3.5	8.2
123 CH GOD (ANDER)	2	128	371	1.3	3.0
165 CH OF NAZARENE	7	821	2,097	7.3	17.2
175 CONG CR CH....	1	50	61*	0.2	0.5
226 FRIENDS-USA...	17	1,285	1,574*	5.4	12.9
281 LUTH CH AMER..	1	80	143	0.5	1.2
419 SO BAPT CONV..	1	31	38*	0.1	0.3
443 UN C OF CHRIST	1	94	115*	0.4	0.9
449 UN METHODIST..	20	2,935	3,497	12.1	28.7
453 UN PRES CH USA	2	342	419*	1.4	3.4
RIPLEY	49	8,323	15,972*	75.6	100.0
019 AMER BAPT CONV	12	2,855	3,537*	16.7	22.1
029 AMER LUTH CH..	2	629	867	4.1	5.4
081 CATHOLIC......	8	0	5,574	26.4	34.9
097 CR C AND C CR.	6	398	493*	2.3	3.1
165 CH OF NAZARENE	1	70	159	0.8	1.0
281 LUTH CH AMER..	5	1,387	1,767	8.4	11.1
283 LUTH--MO SYNOD	1	177	270	1.3	1.7
419 SO BAPT CONV..	2	194	240*	1.1	1.5
443 UN C OF CHRIST	1	744	922*	4.4	5.8
449 UN METHODIST..	11	1,869	2,143	10.1	13.4
RUSH	46	7,617	11,521*	56.6	100.0
019 AMER BAPT CONV	1	572	708*	3.5	6.1
081 CATHOLIC......	1	0	1,900	9.3	16.5
093 CR CH (DISC)..	8	1,605	1,987*	9.8	17.2
097 CR C AND C CR.	10	2,178	2,696*	13.2	23.4
107 CHRISTIAN UN..	1	106	131*	0.6	1.1
123 CH GOD (ANDER)	1	70	184	0.9	1.6
165 CH OF NAZARENE	3	130	293	1.4	2.5
193 EPISCOPAL.....	1	42	54	0.3	0.5
226 FRIENDS-USA...	4	404	500*	2.5	4.3
403 SALVATION ARMY	1	42	215	1.1	1.9
419 SO BAPT CONV..	2	228	282*	1.4	2.4
435 UNITARIAN-UNIV	1	20	20	0.1	0.2
449 UN METHODIST..	8	1,613	1,800	8.8	15.6
453 UN PRES CH USA	4	607	751*	3.7	6.5
ST JOSEPH	149	36,810	115,234*	47.0	100.0
019 AMER BAPT CONV	3	695	844*	0.3	0.7
029 AMER LUTH CH..	1	244	418	0.2	0.4
081 CATHOLIC......	30	0	66,788	27.3	58.0
093 CR CH (DISC)..	6	1,606	1,950*	0.8	1.7
097 CR C AND C CR.	10	2,022	2,455*	1.0	2.1
105 CHRISTIAN REF.	1	60	103	-	0.1
121 CH GOD (ABR)..	2	113	137*	0.1	0.1
123 CH GOD (ANDER)	3	537	1,325	0.5	1.1
127 CH GOD (CLEVE)	3	189	229*	0.1	0.2
157 CH OF BRETHREN	5	1,146	1,391*	0.6	1.2
165 CH OF NAZARENE	4	407	1,082	0.4	0.9
175 CONG CR CH....	1	751	912*	0.4	0.8
193 EPISCOPAL.....	4	1,402	1,748	0.7	1.5
201 EVAN COV CH AM	1	125	152*	0.1	0.1
281 LUTH CH AMER..	6	2,458	3,461	1.4	3.0
283 LUTH--MO SYNOD	8	3,075	4,349	1.8	3.8
285 MENNONITE CH..	6	247	300*	0.1	0.3
353 PLY BRETHREN..	1	45	115	-	0.1
403 SALVATION ARMY	2	158	1,266	0.5	1.1
413 S-D ADVENTISTS	2	610	741*	0.3	0.6
419 SO BAPT CONV..	1	119	144*	0.1	0.1
435 UNITARIAN-UNIV	1	80	120	-	0.1
443 UN C OF CHRIST	6	1,761	2,138*	0.9	1.9
449 UN METHODIST..	33	14,028	17,079	7.0	14.8
453 UN PRES CH USA	8	4,907	5,957*	2.4	5.2
469 WISC EVAN LUTH	1	25	30	-	-
SCOTT	33	5,315	6,850*	40.0	100.0
019 AMER BAPT CONV	8	1,708	2,167*	12.6	31.6
081 CATHOLIC......	1	0	265	1.5	3.9
097 CR C AND C CR.	6	1,979	2,510*	14.6	36.6
127 CH GOD (CLEVE)	3	249	316*	1.8	4.6
165 CH OF NAZARENE	1	34	81	0.5	1.2
283 LUTH--MO SYNOD	1	55	84	0.5	1.2
285 MENNONITE CH..	1	10	13*	0.1	0.2
413 S-D ADVENTISTS	1	67	85*	0.5	1.2
419 SO BAPT CONV..	2	228	289*	1.7	4.2
449 UN METHODIST..	7	783	784	4.6	11.4
453 UN PRES CH USA	2	202	256*	1.5	3.7
SHELBY	62	10,301	16,707*	44.2	100.0

*Total adherents estimated from known number of communicant, confirmed, full members.

—Represents a percent less than 0.1.

Percentages may not total due to rounding.

Table 3. Churches and Church Membership by State, County and Denomination: 1971

County and Denomination	Number of churches	Communicant, confirmed, full members	Total adherents Number	Percent of total population	Percent of total adherents
019 AMER BAPT CONV	9	2,422	3,022*	8.0	18.1
081 CATHOLIC......	2	0	3,405	9.0	20.4
093 CR CH (DISC)..	4	943	1,177*	3.1	7.0
097 CR C AND C CR.	9	905	1,129*	3.0	6.8
107 CHRISTIAN UN..	2	275	343*	0.9	2.1
123 CH GOD (ANDER)	1	60	125	0.3	0.7
127 CH GOD (CLEVE)	1	77	96*	0.3	0.6
165 CH OF NAZARENE	4	360	802	2.1	4.8
193 EPISCOPAL.....	1	71	132	0.3	0.8
226 FRIENDS-USA...	1	63	79*	0.2	0.5
281 LUTH CH AMER..	1	90	141	0.4	0.8
283 LUTH--MO SYNOD	1	150	207	0.5	1.2
403 SALVATION ARMY	1	36	279	0.7	1.7
413 S-D ADVENTISTS	2	102	127*	0.3	0.8
419 SO BAPT CONV..	1	141	176*	0.5	1.1
443 UN C OF CHRIST	2	416	519*	1.4	3.1
449 UN METHODIST..	19	3,679	4,310	11.4	25.8
453 UN PRES CH USA	1	511	638*	1.7	3.8
SPENCER	54	4,396	11,753*	68.6	100.0
019 AMER BAPT CONV	4	432	530*	3.1	4.5
081 CATHOLIC......	9	0	6,425	37.5	54.7
093 CR CH (DISC)..	1	34	42*	0.2	0.4
097 CR C AND C CR.	4	200	246*	1.4	2.1
127 CH GOD (CLEVE)	1	9	11*	0.1	0.1
165 CH OF NAZARENE	3	142	389	2.3	3.3
281 LUTH CH AMER..	2	162	224	1.3	1.9
283 LUTH--MO SYNOD	1	286	363	2.1	3.1
419 SO BAPT CONV..	3	328	403*	2.4	3.4
443 UN C OF CHRIST	4	442	543*	3.2	4.6
449 UN METHODIST..	21	2,322	2,529	14.8	21.5
453 UN PRES CH USA	1	39	48*	0.3	0.4
STARKE	21	2,655	6,018*	31.2	100.0
081 CATHOLIC......	5	0	2,430	12.6	40.4
097 CR C AND C CR.	1	370	463*	2.4	7.7
165 CH OF NAZARENE	1	24	143	0.7	2.4
283 LUTH--MO SYNOD	3	964	1,349	7.0	22.4
285 MENNONITE CH..	2	72	90*	0.5	1.5
353 PLY BRETHREN..	3	90	130	0.7	2.2
413 S-D ADVENTISTS	1	46	58*	0.3	1.0
443 UN C OF CHRIST	1	145	181*	0.9	3.0
449 UN METHODIST..	4	944	1,174	6.1	19.5
STEUBEN	30	4,691	7,473*	37.1	100.0
019 AMER BAPT CONV	2	207	250*	1.2	3.3
029 AMER LUTH CH..	1	368	550	2.7	7.4
081 CATHOLIC......	1	0	1,198	5.9	16.0
093 CR CH (DISC)..	1	74	89*	0.4	1.2
097 CR C AND C CR.	4	1,115	1,347*	6.7	18.0
165 CH OF NAZARENE	3	181	432	2.1	5.8
193 EPISCOPAL.....	1	95	192	1.0	2.6
283 LUTH--MO SYNOD	1	157	192	1.0	2.6
413 S-D ADVENTISTS	1	42	51*	0.3	0.7
443 UN C OF CHRIST	2	305	368*	1.8	4.9
449 UN METHODIST..	12	1,950	2,566	12.7	34.3
453 UN PRES CH USA	1	197	238*	1.2	3.2
SULLIVAN	50	6,514	7,843*	39.4	100.0
019 AMER BAPT CONV	8	1,831	2,173*	10.9	27.7
081 CATHOLIC......	2	0	257	1.3	3.3
093 CR CH (DISC)..	1	65	77*	0.4	1.0
097 CR C AND C CR.	4	1,425	1,691*	8.5	21.6
127 CH GOD (CLEVE)	3	146	173*	0.9	2.2
165 CH OF NAZARENE	2	86	175	0.9	2.2
226 FRIENDS-USA...	2	53	63*	0.3	0.8
413 S-D ADVENTISTS	2	16	19*	0.1	0.2
419 SO BAPT CONV..	1	26	31*	0.2	0.4
449 UN METHODIST..	22	2,539	2,796	14.1	35.6
453 UN PRES CH USA	3	327	388*	2.0	4.9
SWITZERLAND	23	1,977	2,420*	38.4	100.0
019 AMER BAPT CONV	11	1,436	1,721*	27.3	71.1
081 CATHOLIC......	1	0	50	0.8	2.1
097 CR C AND C CR.	3	85	102*	1.6	4.2
165 CH OF NAZARENE	1	17	60	1.0	2.5
449 UN METHODIST..	5	309	331	5.2	13.7
453 UN PRES CH USA	2	130	156*	2.5	6.4
TIPPECANOE	77	25,183	50,129*	45.8	100.0
019 AMER BAPT CONV	2	1,689	2,032*	1.9	4.1
081 CATHOLIC......	6	0	18,138	16.6	36.2
093 CR CH (DISC)..	3	2,102	2,529*	2.3	5.0
097 CR C AND C CR.	4	1,038	1,249*	1.1	2.5
105 CHRISTIAN REF.	1	476	696	0.6	1.4
121 CH GOD (ABR)..	1	50	60*	0.1	0.1
123 CH GOD (ANDER)	2	159	361	0.3	0.7
127 CH GOD (CLEVE)	1	40	48*	-	0.1
157 CH OF BRETHREN	1	119	143*	0.1	0.3
165 CH OF NAZARENE	2	214	444	0.4	0.9
193 EPISCOPAL.....	2	339	612	0.6	1.2
201 EVAN COV CH AM	1	149	179*	0.2	0.4
221 FREE METH C NA	1	59	72	0.1	0.1
226 FRIENDS-USA...	2	86	103*	0.1	0.2
281 LUTH CH AMER..	5	1,168	1,599	1.5	3.2
283 LUTH--MO SYNOD	3	1,309	2,035	1.9	4.1
353 PLY BRETHREN..	1	30	70	0.1	0.1
371 REF CH IN AM..	2	286	440	0.4	0.9
403 SALVATION ARMY	1	61	264	0.2	0.5

County and Denomination	Number of churches	Communicant, confirmed, full members	Total adherents Number	Percent of total population	Percent of total adherents
413 S-D ADVENTISTS	1	156	188*	0.2	0.4
419 SO BAPT CONV..	4	1,194	1,437*	1.3	2.9
435 UNITARIAN-UNIV	1	107	130	0.1	0.3
443 UN C OF CHRIST	1	940	1,131*	1.0	2.3
449 UN METHODIST..	21	9,057	10,929	10.0	21.8
453 UN PRES CH USA	8	4,355	5,240*	4.8	10.5
TIPTON	26	4,605	6,970*	41.9	100.0
019 AMER BAPT CONV	2	272	334*	2.0	4.8
081 CATHOLIC......	2	0	1,299	7.8	18.6
093 CR CH (DISC)..	2	1,486	1,823*	10.9	26.2
097 CR C AND C CR.	6	681	836*	5.0	12.0
127 CH GOD (CLEVE)	1	53	65*	0.4	0.9
157 CH OF BRETHREN	1	77	94*	0.6	1.3
165 CH OF NAZARENE	1	64	137	0.8	2.0
226 FRIENDS-USA...	2	110	135*	0.8	1.9
283 LUTH--MO SYNOD	1	291	392	2.4	5.6
419 SO BAPT CONV..	1	62	76*	0.5	1.1
449 UN METHODIST..	6	1,307	1,531	9.2	22.0
453 UN PRES CH USA	1	202	248*	1.5	3.6
UNION	14	1,845	2,676*	40.7	100.0
081 CATHOLIC......	1	0	297	4.5	11.1
097 CR C AND C CR.	1	350	434*	6.6	16.2
157 CH OF BRETHREN	1	66	82*	1.2	3.1
165 CH OF NAZARENE	2	75	284	4.3	10.6
226 FRIENDS-USA...	1	62	77*	1.2	2.9
443 UN C OF CHRIST	1	120	149*	2.3	5.6
449 UN METHODIST..	6	982	1,117	17.0	41.7
453 UN PRES CH USA	1	190	236*	3.6	8.8
VANDERBURGH	141	49,656	93,646*	55.5	100.0
019 AMER BAPT CONV	4	2,360	2,831*	1.7	3.0
029 AMER LUTH CH..	3	876	1,190	0.7	1.3
081 CATHOLIC......	25	0	31,098	18.4	33.2
093 CR CH (DISC)..	3	1,333	1,599*	0.9	1.7
097 CR C AND C CR.	4	1,845	2,213*	1.3	2.4
123 CH GOD (ANDER)	2	115	305	0.2	0.3
127 CH GOD (CLEVE)	2	113	136*	0.1	0.1
165 CH OF NAZARENE	6	547	1,385	0.8	1.5
185 CUMBER PRESB..	1	710	852*	0.5	0.9
193 EPISCOPAL.....	2	765	1,111	0.7	1.2
221 FREE METH C NA	1	66	90	0.1	0.1
226 FRIENDS-USA...	1	4	5*	-	-
281 LUTH CH AMER..	3	872	1,224	0.7	1.3
283 LUTH--MO SYNOD	10	3,478	4,509	2.7	4.8
403 SALVATION ARMY	2	224	1,930	1.1	2.1
413 S-D ADVENTISTS	2	193	232*	0.1	0.2
419 SO BAPT CONV..	27	13,797	16,550*	9.8	17.7
435 UNITARIAN-UNIV	1	64	64	-	0.1
443 UN C OF CHRIST	15	8,650	10,376*	6.1	11.1
449 UN METHODIST..	18	10,105	11,701	6.9	12.5
453 UN PRES CH USA	9	3,539	4,245*	2.5	4.5
VERMILLION	31	3,162	4,940*	29.4	100.0
019 AMER BAPT CONV	4	431	515*	3.1	10.4
081 CATHOLIC......	2	0	965	5.7	19.5
093 CR CH (DISC)..	2	314	375*	2.2	7.6
097 CR C AND C CR.	2	250	299*	1.8	6.1
123 CH GOD (ANDER)	1	16	36	0.2	0.7
127 CH GOD (CLEVE)	1	25	30*	0.2	0.6
165 CH OF NAZARENE	3	216	545	3.2	11.0
185 CUMBER PRESB..	1	69	82*	0.5	1.7
226 FRIENDS-USA...	2	156	186*	1.1	3.8
449 UN METHODIST..	11	1,406	1,574	9.4	31.9
453 UN PRES CH USA	2	279	333*	2.0	6.7
VIGO	85	18,521	33,004*	28.8	100.0
019 AMER BAPT CONV	9	2,775	3,285*	2.9	10.0
029 AMER LUTH CH..	1	172	237	0.2	0.7
081 CATHOLIC......	10	0	9,675	8.4	29.3
093 CR CH (DISC)..	1	467	553*	0.5	1.7
097 CR C AND C CR.	7	2,748	3,253*	2.8	9.9
105 CHRISTIAN REF.	1	55	93	0.1	0.3
123 CH GOD (ANDER)	2	87	212	0.2	0.6
127 CH GOD (CLEVE)	1	90	107*	0.1	0.3
165 CH OF NAZARENE	5	382	1,011	0.9	3.1
175 CONG CR CH....	2	433	513*	0.4	1.6
193 EPISCOPAL.....	2	537	973	0.8	2.9
221 FREE METH C NA	1	33	39	-	0.1
226 FRIENDS-USA...	1	46	54*	-	0.2
281 LUTH CH AMER..	2	446	650	0.6	2.0
283 LUTH--MO SYNOD	2	483	613	0.5	1.9
353 PLY BRETHREN..	1	40	70	0.1	0.2
403 SALVATION ARMY	1	48	328	0.3	1.0
413 S-D ADVENTISTS	2	190	225*	0.2	0.7
419 SO BAPT CONV..	1	274	324*	0.3	1.0
435 UNITARIAN-UNIV	2	58	93	0.1	0.3
443 UN C OF CHRIST	2	648	767*	0.7	2.3
449 UN METHODIST..	26	7,336	8,541	7.5	25.9
453 UN PRES CH USA	3	1,173	1,388*	1.2	4.2
WABASH	53	10,055	14,558*	40.9	100.0
029 AMER LUTH CH..	1	149	254	0.7	1.7
081 CATHOLIC......	3	0	1,754	4.9	12.0
093 CR CH (DISC)..	2	506	621*	1.7	4.3
097 CR C AND C CR.	6	865	1,061*	3.0	7.3
123 CH GOD (ANDER)	1	75	239	0.7	1.6
127 CH GOD (CLEVE)	1	21	26*	0.1	0.2

*Total adherents estimated from known number of communicant, confirmed, full members.

—Represents a percent less than 0.1.

Percentages may not total due to rounding.

Table 3. Churches and Church Membership by State, County and Denomination: 1971

County and Denomination	Number of churches	Communicant, confirmed, full members	Total adherents Number	Total adherents Percent of total population	Total adherents Percent of total adherents
157 CH OF BRETHREN	6	1,557	1,910*	5.4	13.1
165 CH OF NAZARENE	2	158	629	1.8	4.3
226 FRIENDS-USA...	1	329	404*	1.1	2.8
281 LUTH CH AMER..	1	193	266	0.7	1.8
283 LUTH--MO SYNOD	1	221	300	0.8	2.1
413 S-D ADVENTISTS	1	40	49*	0.1	0.3
443 UN C OF CHRIST	4	995	1,220*	3.4	8.4
449 UN METHODIST..	21	4,083	4,766	13.4	32.7
453 UN PRES CH USA	2	863	1,059*	3.0	7.3
WARREN	22	2,842	3,471*	39.9	100.0
019 AMER BAPT CONV	1	73	90*	1.0	2.6
093 CR CH (DISC)..	1	48	59*	0.7	1.7
097 CR C AND C CR.	6	1,166	1,435*	16.5	41.3
165 CH OF NAZARENE	2	74	167	1.9	4.8
221 FREE METH C NA	1	15	23	0.3	0.7
449 UN METHODIST..	9	1,264	1,448	16.6	41.7
453 UN PRES CH USA	2	202	249*	2.9	7.2
WARRICK	44	6,053	10,859*	38.8	100.0
019 AMER BAPT CONV	2	206	255*	0.9	2.3
029 AMER LUTH CH..	1	23	31	0.1	0.3
081 CATHOLIC......	2	0	3,123	11.2	28.8
093 CR CH (DISC)..	1	112	139*	0.5	1.3
165 CH OF NAZARENE	3	165	517	1.8	4.8
185 CUMBER PRESB..	1	210	260*	0.9	2.4
221 FREE METH C NA	1	32	40	0.1	0.4
283 LUTH--MO SYNOD	2	144	196	0.7	1.8
419 SO BAPT CONV..	5	1,123	1,393*	5.0	12.8
443 UN C OF CHRIST	6	1,521	1,886*	6.7	17.4
449 UN METHODIST..	18	2,000	2,378	8.5	21.9
453 UN PRES CH USA	2	517	641*	2.3	5.9
WASHINGTON	53	6,049	7,683*	39.9	100.0
019 AMER BAPT CONV	9	1,716	2,119*	11.0	27.6
081 CATHOLIC......	1	0	209	1.1	2.7
093 CR CH (DISC)..	1	709	875*	4.5	11.4
097 CR C AND C CR.	18	1,586	1,958*	10.2	25.5
123 CH GOD (ANDER)	1	30	90	0.5	1.2
127 CH GOD (CLEVE)	1	25	31*	0.2	0.4
165 CH OF NAZARENE	2	84	232	1.2	3.0
226 FRIENDS-USA...	1	68	84*	0.4	1.1
283 LUTH--MO SYNOD	1	34	52	0.3	0.7
285 MENNONITE CH..	1	11	14*	0.1	0.2
413 S-D ADVENTISTS	1	23	28*	0.1	0.4
419 SO BAPT CONV..	1	177	219*	1.1	2.9
449 UN METHODIST..	13	1,377	1,514	7.9	19.7
453 UN PRES CH USA	2	209	258*	1.3	3.4
WAYNE	93	19,114	31,445*	39.7	100.0
019 AMER BAPT CONV	3	1,304	1,606*	2.0	5.1
029 AMER LUTH CH..	2	957	1,213	1.5	3.9
081 CATHOLIC......	4	0	6,059	7.7	19.3
093 CR CH (DISC)..	4	1,331	1,639*	2.1	5.2
097 CR C AND C CR.	10	1,693	2,085*	2.6	6.6
123 CH GOD (ANDER)	1	80	183	0.2	0.6
127 CH GOD (CLEVE)	1	202	249*	0.3	0.8
157 CH OF BRETHREN	2	321	395*	0.5	1.3
165 CH OF NAZARENE	7	792	2,099	2.7	6.7
193 EPISCOPAL.....	1	312	485	0.6	1.5
226 FRIENDS-USA...	12	1,914	2,358*	3.0	7.5
281 LUTH CH AMER..	5	1,677	2,222	2.8	7.1
283 LUTH--MO SYNOD	1	38	70	0.1	0.2
403 SALVATION ARMY	1	138	624	0.8	2.0
413 S-D ADVENTISTS	1	141	174*	0.2	0.6
419 SO BAPT CONV..	9	1,559	1,920*	2.4	6.1
435 UNITARIAN-UNIV	1	11	11	-	-
443 UN C OF CHRIST	2	373	459*	0.6	1.5
449 UN METHODIST..	21	4,787	5,766	7.3	18.3
453 UN PRES CH USA	5	1,484	1,828*	2.3	5.8
WELLS	48	7,630	11,003*	46.2	100.0
019 AMER BAPT CONV	3	842	1,041*	4.4	9.5
029 AMER LUTH CH..	1	289	452	1.9	4.1
081 CATHOLIC......	1	0	1,153	4.8	10.5
097 CR C AND C CR.	4	300	371*	1.6	3.4
127 CH GOD (CLEVE)	1	13	16*	0.1	0.1
165 CH OF NAZARENE	2	193	584	2.5	5.3
226 FRIENDS-USA...	2	29	36*	0.2	0.3
281 LUTH CH AMER..	2	465	698	2.9	6.3
283 LUTH--MO SYNOD	1	378	515	2.2	4.7
413 S-D ADVENTISTS	1	17	21*	0.1	0.2
443 UN C OF CHRIST	3	946	1,169*	4.9	10.6
449 UN METHODIST..	25	3,444	4,065	17.1	36.9
453 UN PRES CH USA	2	714	882*	3.7	8.0
WHITE	40	7,531	10,689*	50.9	100.0
019 AMER BAPT CONV	9	1,855	2,254*	10.7	21.1
081 CATHOLIC......	2	0	1,324	6.3	12.4
093 CR CH (DISC)..	2	721	876*	4.2	8.2
097 CR C AND C CR.	3	300	365*	1.7	3.4
157 CH OF BRETHREN	4	377	458*	2.2	4.3
165 CH OF NAZARENE	1	63	201	1.0	1.9
193 EPISCOPAL.....	1	10	20	0.1	0.2
283 LUTH--MO SYNOD	2	612	895	4.3	8.4
413 S-D ADVENTISTS	2	64	78*	0.4	0.7
443 UN C OF CHRIST	1	120	146*	0.7	1.4
449 UN METHODIST..	9	2,458	2,916	13.9	27.3
453 UN PRES CH USA	4	951	1,156*	5.5	10.8

County and Denomination	Number of churches	Communicant, confirmed, full members	Total adherents Number	Total adherents Percent of total population	Total adherents Percent of total adherents
WHITLEY	40	7,079	11,398*	48.7	100.0
019 AMER BAPT CONV	3	584	717*	3.1	6.3
081 CATHOLIC......	2	0	1,590	6.8	13.9
093 CR CH (DISC)..	2	117	144*	0.6	1.3
097 CR C AND C CR.	2	59	72*	0.3	0.6
123 CH GOD (ANDER)	2	180	485	2.1	4.3
157 CH OF BRETHREN	5	644	790*	3.4	6.9
165 CH OF NAZARENE	2	166	447	1.9	3.9
221 FREE METH C NA	1	16	24	0.1	0.2
281 LUTH CH AMER..	3	1,382	1,787	7.6	15.7
283 LUTH--MO SYNOD	3	707	978	4.2	8.6
403 SALVATION ARMY	1	126	622	2.7	5.5
449 UN METHODIST..	12	2,654	3,197	13.7	28.0
453 UN PRES CH USA	2	444	545*	2.3	4.8
CO DATA NOT AVAIL	400	23,209	39,817*	N/A	N/A
151 L-D SAINTS....	0	0	12,186	N/A	N/A
223 FREE WILL BAPT	20	1,657	2,045*	N/A	N/A
231 GENERAL BAPT..	106	10,951	13,513*	N/A	N/A
467 WESLEYAN......	274	10,601	12,073	N/A	N/A

IOWA

County and Denomination	Number of churches	Communicant, confirmed, full members	Total adherents Number	Total adherents Percent of total population	Total adherents Percent of total adherents
THE STATE.....	4,074	930,154	1,762,704*	62.4	100.0
ADAIR	26	4,155	5,945*	62.7	100.0
029 AMER LUTH CH..	1	554	755	8.0	12.7
081 CATHOLIC......	5	0	776	8.2	13.1
093 CR CH (DISC)..	1	40	47*	0.5	0.8
283 LUTH--MO SYNOD	2	761	1,010	10.6	17.0
413 S-D ADVENTISTS	1	16	19*	0.2	0.3
443 UN C OF CHRIST	3	129	153*	1.6	2.6
449 UN METHODIST..	11	2,187	2,630	27.7	44.2
453 UN PRES CH USA	2	468	555*	5.9	9.3
ADAMS	22	2,728	4,283*	67.7	100.0
019 AMER BAPT CONV	1	169	198*	3.1	4.6
081 CATHOLIC......	1	0	837	13.2	19.5
093 CR CH (DISC)..	2	182	213*	3.4	5.0
105 CHRISTIAN REF.	1	158	305	4.8	7.1
157 CH OF BRETHREN	2	65	76*	1.2	1.8
281 LUTH CH AMER..	1	58	68	1.1	1.6
283 LUTH--MO SYNOD	1	117	196	3.1	4.6
353 PLY BRETHREN..	1	66	90	1.4	2.1
443 UN C OF CHRIST	1	106	124*	2.0	2.9
449 UN METHODIST..	10	1,533	1,855	29.3	43.3
453 UN PRES CH USA	1	274	321*	5.1	7.5
ALLAMAKEE	36	6,390	13,305*	88.9	100.0
029 AMER LUTH CH..	6	1,649	2,229	14.9	16.8
081 CATHOLIC......	12	0	5,080	33.9	38.2
281 LUTH CH AMER..	1	1,369	1,827	12.2	13.7
413 S-D ADVENTISTS	2	77	94*	0.6	0.7
443 UN C OF CHRIST	4	1,132	1,389*	9.3	10.4
449 UN METHODIST..	5	663	845	5.6	6.4
453 UN PRES CH USA	6	1,500	1,841*	12.3	13.8
APPANOOSE	46	4,603	6,866*	45.8	100.0
019 AMER BAPT CONV	3	721	848*	5.7	12.4
081 CATHOLIC......	4	0	1,386	9.2	20.2
093 CR CH (DISC)..	9	841	989*	6.6	14.4
097 CR C AND C CR.	6	120	141*	0.9	2.1
127 CH GOD (CLEVE)	1	93	109*	0.7	1.6
157 CH OF BRETHREN	1	124	146*	1.0	2.1
165 CH OF NAZARENE	3	145	284	1.9	4.1
193 EPISCOPAL.....	1	57	75	0.5	1.1
201 EVAN COV CH AM	1	61	72*	0.5	1.0
281 LUTH CH AMER..	1	232	318	2.1	4.6
353 PLY BRETHREN..	1	90	120	0.8	1.7
413 S-D ADVENTISTS	1	57	67*	0.4	1.0
419 SO BAPT CONV..	1	50	59*	0.4	0.9
449 UN METHODIST..	12	1,802	2,005	13.4	29.2
453 UN PRES CH USA	1	210	247*	1.6	3.6
AUDUBON	21	5,244	7,459*	77.7	100.0
019 AMER BAPT CONV	1	120	144*	1.5	1.9
029 AMER LUTH CH..	5	2,140	2,876	30.0	38.6
081 CATHOLIC......	2	0	614	6.4	8.2
093 CR CH (DISC)..	1	280	336*	3.5	4.5
097 CR C AND C CR.	1	90	108*	1.1	1.4
281 LUTH CH AMER..	2	651	847	8.8	11.4
283 LUTH--MO SYNOD	2	421	619	6.5	8.3
413 S-D ADVENTISTS	2	67	80*	0.8	1.1
443 UN C OF CHRIST	1	94	113*	1.2	1.5
449 UN METHODIST..	3	916	1,163	12.1	15.6
453 UN PRES CH USA	1	465	559*	5.8	7.5
BENTON	49	8,555	14,639*	64.0	100.0

*Total adherents estimated from known number of communicant, confirmed, full members.

—Represents a percent less than 0.1.

Percentages may not total due to rounding.

Table 3. Churches and Church Membership by State, County and Denomination: 1971

County and Denomination	Number of churches	Communicant, confirmed, full members	Total adherents: Number	Total adherents: Percent of total population	Total adherents: Percent of total adherents
019 AMER BAPT CONV	2	246	304*	1.3	2.1
029 AMER LUTH CH..	1	154	242	1.1	1.7
081 CATHOLIC......	8	0	3,780	16.5	25.8
093 CR CH (DISC)..	4	382	472*	2.1	3.2
097 CR C AND C CR.	1	30	37*	0.2	0.3
121 CH GOD (ABR)..	1	22	27*	0.1	0.2
157 CH OF BRETHREN	1	39	48*	0.2	0.3
221 FREE METH C NA	1	14	19	0.1	0.1
281 LUTH CH AMER..	1	211	285	1.2	1.9
283 LUTH--MO SYNOD	11	3,404	4,590	20.1	31.4
443 UN C OF CHRIST	1	299	369*	1.6	2.5
449 UN METHODIST..	11	2,471	2,882	12.6	19.7
453 UN PRES CH USA	6	1,283	1,584*	6.9	10.8
BLACK HAWK	102	39,672	77,935*	58.6	100.0
019 AMER BAPT CONV	4	1,613	1,993*	1.5	2.6
029 AMER LUTH CH..	15	9,192	13,020	9.8	16.7
081 CATHOLIC......	11	0	24,508	18.4	31.4
093 CR CH (DISC)..	2	723	894*	0.7	1.1
097 CR C AND C CR.	1	129	159*	0.1	0.2
105 CHRISTIAN REF.	1	72	143	0.1	0.2
121 CH GOD (ABR)..	1	52	64*	-	0.1
123 CH GOD (ANDER)	1	12	12	-	-
157 CH OF BRETHREN	2	701	866*	0.7	1.1
165 CH OF NAZARENE	2	114	253	0.2	0.3
193 EPISCOPAL.....	2	1,005	1,347	1.0	1.7
201 EVAN COV CH AM	1	44	54*	-	0.1
221 FREE METH C NA	1	82	135	0.1	0.2
281 LUTH CH AMER..	4	1,707	2,341	1.8	3.0
283 LUTH--MO SYNOD	7	3,778	5,450	4.1	7.0
313 NO AM BAPT GC.	1	121	150*	0.1	0.2
335 ORTH PRESB CH.	1	45	56	-	0.1
353 PLY BRETHREN..	5	220	360	0.3	0.5
371 REF CH IN AM..	3	529	817	0.6	1.0
403 SALVATION ARMY	1	176	886	0.7	1.1
413 S-D ADVENTISTS	1	115	142*	0.1	0.2
419 SO BAPT CONV..	2	375	463*	0.3	0.6
435 UNITARIAN-UNIV	1	70	100	0.1	0.1
443 UN C OF CHRIST	3	1,616	1,997*	1.5	2.6
449 UN METHODIST..	19	11,232	14,373	10.8	18.4
453 UN PRES CH USA	10	5,949	7,352*	5.5	9.4
BOONE	43	9,752	15,012*	56.7	100.0
019 AMER BAPT CONV	2	861	1,020*	3.9	6.8
081 CATHOLIC......	5	0	2,576	9.7	17.2
093 CR CH (DISC)..	2	798	945*	3.6	6.3
123 CH GOD (ANDER)	1	59	132	0.5	0.9
157 CH OF BRETHREN	1	42	50*	0.2	0.3
165 CH OF NAZARENE	1	24	83	0.3	0.6
193 EPISCOPAL.....	1	77	149	0.6	1.0
201 EVAN COV CH AM	1	12	14*	0.1	0.1
221 FREE METH C NA	2	32	39	0.1	0.3
281 LUTH CH AMER..	5	1,881	2,575	9.7	17.2
283 LUTH--MO SYNOD	3	1,484	1,915	7.2	12.8
403 SALVATION ARMY	1	48	140	0.5	0.9
413 S-D ADVENTISTS	1	44	52*	0.2	0.3
443 UN C OF CHRIST	2	264	313*	1.2	2.1
449 UN METHODIST..	14	3,559	4,338	16.4	28.9
453 UN PRES CH USA	1	567	671*	2.5	4.5
BREMER	43	12,634	19,210*	84.5	100.0
019 AMER BAPT CONV	1	173	211*	0.9	1.1
029 AMER LUTH CH..	14	6,676	9,126	40.1	47.5
081 CATHOLIC......	4	0	2,293	10.1	11.9
193 EPISCOPAL.....	1	108	134	0.6	0.7
197 EVAN CH OF NA.	1	46	56*	0.2	0.3
283 LUTH--MO SYNOD	8	1,863	2,579	11.3	13.4
313 NO AM BAPT GC.	1	84	102*	0.4	0.5
443 UN C OF CHRIST	5	1,355	1,652*	7.3	8.6
449 UN METHODIST..	8	2,329	3,057	13.4	15.9
BUCHANAN	38	6,542	14,927*	68.6	100.0
019 AMER BAPT CONV	4	445	562*	2.6	3.8
029 AMER LUTH CH..	4	1,481	2,069	9.5	13.9
081 CATHOLIC......	8	0	6,507	29.9	43.6
097 CR C AND C CR.	1	139	176*	0.8	1.2
193 EPISCOPAL.....	1	72	97	0.4	0.6
283 LUTH--MO SYNOD	2	504	672	3.1	4.5
353 PLY BRETHREN..	1	30	40	0.2	0.3
443 UN C OF CHRIST	1	138	174*	0.8	1.2
449 UN METHODIST..	10	2,497	3,069	14.1	20.6
453 UN PRES CH USA	6	1,236	1,561*	7.2	10.5
BUENA VISTA	40	11,325	17,091*	82.6	100.0
019 AMER BAPT CONV	2	315	377*	1.8	2.2
029 AMER LUTH CH..	6	1,471	1,962	9.5	11.5
081 CATHOLIC......	2	0	2,704	13.1	15.8
097 CR C AND C CR.	1	211	252*	1.2	1.5
121 CH GOD (ABR)..	1	20	24*	0.1	0.1
165 CH OF NAZARENE	1	19	65	0.3	0.4
193 EPISCOPAL.....	1	36	78	0.4	0.5
201 EVAN COV CH AM	1	169	202*	1.0	1.2
281 LUTH CH AMER..	4	1,642	2,059	10.0	12.0
283 LUTH--MO SYNOD	7	2,328	3,137	15.2	18.4
443 UN C OF CHRIST	3	385	460*	2.2	2.7
449 UN METHODIST..	8	3,386	4,166	20.1	24.4
453 UN PRES CH USA	3	1,343	1,605*	7.8	9.4
BUTLER	42	8,848	12,680*	74.8	100.0

County and Denomination	Number of churches	Communicant, confirmed, full members	Total adherents: Number	Total adherents: Percent of total population	Total adherents: Percent of total adherents
029 AMER LUTH CH..	6	2,629	3,645	21.5	28.7
081 CATHOLIC......	3	0	843	5.0	6.6
097 CR C AND C CR.	3	95	115*	0.7	0.9
105 CHRISTIAN REF.	2	296	498	2.9	3.9
157 CH OF BRETHREN	1	62	75*	0.4	0.6
175 CONG CR CH....	1	248	300*	1.8	2.4
283 LUTH--MO SYNOD	1	120	160	0.9	1.3
313 NO AM BAPT GC.	2	479	579*	3.4	4.6
353 PLY BRETHREN..	1	15	30	0.2	0.2
371 REF CH IN AM..	6	1,353	1,960	11.6	15.5
443 UN C OF CHRIST	3	773	935*	5.5	7.4
449 UN METHODIST..	8	1,904	2,483	14.6	19.6
453 UN PRES CH USA	5	874	1,057*	6.2	8.3
CALHOUN	38	8,007	12,397*	86.8	100.0
019 AMER BAPT CONV	1	213	253*	1.8	2.0
029 AMER LUTH CH..	3	1,632	2,293	16.0	18.5
081 CATHOLIC......	5	0	2,272	15.9	18.3
093 CR CH (DISC)..	2	386	459*	3.2	3.7
097 CR C AND C CR.	1	135	161*	1.1	1.3
165 CH OF NAZARENE	1	13	22	0.2	0.2
201 EVAN COV CH AM	1	187	222*	1.6	1.8
281 LUTH CH AMER..	2	445	591	4.1	4.8
283 LUTH--MO SYNOD	6	1,438	1,874	13.1	15.1
413 S-D ADVENTISTS	1	31	37*	0.3	0.3
443 UN C OF CHRIST	3	392	466*	3.3	3.8
449 UN METHODIST..	10	2,456	2,939	20.6	23.7
453 UN PRES CH USA	2	679	808*	5.7	6.5
CARROLL	37	6,347	22,989*	100.3#	100.0
029 AMER LUTH CH..	2	377	506	2.2	2.2
081 CATHOLIC......	14	0	15,035	65.6	65.4
093 CR CH (DISC)..	1	181	227*	1.0	1.0
193 EPISCOPAL.....	1	53	66	0.3	0.3
221 FREE METH C NA	1	10	10	-	-
226 FRIENDS-USA...	2	53	67*	0.3	0.3
283 LUTH--MO SYNOD	5	2,251	3,020	13.2	13.1
449 UN METHODIST..	6	2,402	2,777	12.1	12.1
453 UN PRES CH USA	5	1,020	1,281*	5.6	5.6
CASS	47	8,439	12,544*	73.8	100.0
019 AMER BAPT CONV	1	223	267*	1.6	2.1
029 AMER LUTH CH..	1	914	1,267	7.4	10.1
081 CATHOLIC......	6	0	1,833	10.8	14.6
093 CR CH (DISC)..	3	287	344*	2.0	2.7
097 CR C AND C CR.	5	187	224*	1.3	1.8
165 CH OF NAZARENE	1	34	99	0.6	0.8
193 EPISCOPAL.....	1	19	34	0.2	0.3
281 LUTH CH AMER..	1	124	163	1.0	1.3
283 LUTH--MO SYNOD	3	1,363	1,919	11.3	15.3
353 PLY BRETHREN..	4	245	300	1.8	2.4
413 S-D ADVENTISTS	1	53	63*	0.4	0.5
443 UN C OF CHRIST	5	780	934*	5.5	7.4
449 UN METHODIST..	13	3,479	4,222	24.8	33.7
453 UN PRES CH USA	2	731	875*	5.1	7.0
CEDAR	31	7,400	11,110*	62.9	100.0
019 AMER BAPT CONV	1	71	86*	0.5	0.8
029 AMER LUTH CH..	1	216	316	1.8	2.8
081 CATHOLIC......	3	0	1,648	9.3	14.8
157 CH OF BRETHREN	1	24	29*	0.2	0.3
193 EPISCOPAL.....	1	109	152	0.9	1.4
226 FRIENDS-USA...	2	205	249*	1.4	2.2
281 LUTH CH AMER..	2	519	770	4.4	6.9
283 LUTH--MO SYNOD	3	1,047	1,329	7.5	12.0
443 UN C OF CHRIST	4	2,135	2,588*	14.7	23.3
449 UN METHODIST..	9	2,652	3,431	19.4	30.9
453 UN PRES CH USA	4	422	512*	2.9	4.6
CERRO GORDO	53	18,986	33,711*	68.3	100.0
019 AMER BAPT CONV	3	629	754*	1.5	2.2
029 AMER LUTH CH..	6	6,318	8,755	17.7	26.0
081 CATHOLIC......	9	0	9,094	18.4	27.0
093 CR CH (DISC)..	3	660	791*	1.6	2.3
097 CR C AND C CR.	2	22	26*	0.1	0.1
105 CHRISTIAN REF.	1	51	103	0.2	0.3
165 CH OF NAZARENE	1	71	169	0.3	0.5
175 CONG CR CH....	2	537	644*	1.3	1.9
193 EPISCOPAL.....	2	241	416	0.8	1.2
201 EVAN COV CH AM	1	86	103*	0.2	0.3
221 FREE METH C NA	1	51	75	0.2	0.2
281 LUTH CH AMER..	1	561	739	1.5	2.2
283 LUTH--MO SYNOD	2	978	1,292	2.6	3.8
353 PLY BRETHREN..	1	40	50	0.1	0.1
371 REF CH IN AM..	1	246	446	0.9	1.3
403 SALVATION ARMY	1	88	374	0.8	1.1
413 S-D ADVENTISTS	1	82	98*	0.2	0.3
435 UNITARIAN-UNIV	1	21	31	0.1	0.1
443 UN C OF CHRIST	1	752	902*	1.8	2.7
449 UN METHODIST..	11	6,924	8,065	16.3	23.9
453 UN PRES CH USA	1	572	686*	1.4	2.0
469 WISC EVAN LUTH	1	56	98	0.2	0.3
CHEROKEE	29	7,329	12,665*	73.3	100.0
019 AMER BAPT CONV	2	185	225*	1.3	1.8
081 CATHOLIC......	4	0	3,243	18.8	25.6
093 CR CH (DISC)..	2	71	86*	0.5	0.7
097 CR C AND C CR.	1	575	700*	4.1	5.5
281 LUTH CH AMER..	2	1,025	1,389	8.0	11.0

*Total adherents estimated from known number of communicant, confirmed, full members.　—Represents a percent less than 0.1.　Percentages may not total due to rounding.

#See Introduction for explanation of why total adherents reported by churches exceed the 1970 population figure.

Table 3. Churches and Church Membership by State, County and Denomination: 1971

County and Denomination	Number of churches	Communicant, confirmed, full members	Total adherents: Number	Total adherents: Percent of total population	Total adherents: Percent of total adherents
283 LUTH--MO SYNOD	6	1,552	2,120	12.3	16.7
413 S-D ADVENTISTS	1	31	38*	0.2	0.3
443 UN C OF CHRIST	1	140	170*	1.0	1.3
449 UN METHODIST..	7	2,864	3,615	20.9	28.5
453 UN PRES CH USA	3	886	1,079*	6.2	8.5
CHICKASAW	33	4,404	12,115*	80.9	100.0
019 AMER BAPT CONV	2	231	290*	1.9	2.4
029 AMER LUTH CH..	8	1,709	2,315	15.5	19.1
081 CATHOLIC......	9	0	6,419	42.9	53.0
093 CR CH (DISC)..	1	88	111*	0.7	0.9
157 CH OF BRETHREN	1	109	137*	0.9	1.1
283 LUTH--MO SYNOD	1	256	340	2.3	2.8
443 UN C OF CHRIST	5	835	1,049*	7.0	8.7
449 UN METHODIST..	6	1,176	1,454	9.7	12.0
CLARKE	15	2,425	3,191*	42.1	100.0
081 CATHOLIC......	2	0	363	4.8	11.4
093 CR CH (DISC)..	3	611	718*	9.5	22.5
097 CR C AND C CR.	2	500	588*	7.8	18.4
107 CHRISTIAN UN..	1	24	28*	0.4	0.9
283 LUTH--MO SYNOD	1	230	357	4.7	11.2
413 S-D ADVENTISTS	1	51	60*	0.8	1.9
449 UN METHODIST..	4	923	976	12.9	30.6
453 UN PRES CH USA	1	86	101*	1.3	3.2
CLAY	31	7,585	12,319*	66.7	100.0
029 AMER LUTH CH..	3	1,518	2,068	11.2	16.8
081 CATHOLIC......	3	0	2,143	11.6	17.4
093 CR CH (DISC)..	1	374	451*	2.4	3.7
175 CONG CR CH....	2	806	973*	5.3	7.9
193 EPISCOPAL.....	1	43	97	0.5	0.8
226 FRIENDS-USA...	1	92	111*	0.6	0.9
281 LUTH CH AMER..	1	261	403	2.2	3.3
283 LUTH--MO SYNOD	3	934	1,396	7.6	11.3
371 REF CH IN AM..	2	287	462	2.5	3.8
413 S-D ADVENTISTS	1	66	80*	0.4	0.6
443 UN C OF CHRIST	3	281	339*	1.8	2.8
449 UN METHODIST..	10	2,923	3,796	20.6	30.8
CLAYTON	47	7,625	15,529*	75.4	100.0
029 AMER LUTH CH..	17	4,263	5,785	28.1	37.3
081 CATHOLIC......	11	0	5,474	26.6	35.3
281 LUTH CH AMER..	3	798	1,046	5.1	6.7
283 LUTH--MO SYNOD	2	254	368	1.8	2.4
443 UN C OF CHRIST	4	834	1,016*	4.9	6.5
449 UN METHODIST..	9	1,440	1,796	8.7	11.6
453 UN PRES CH USA	1	36	44*	0.2	0.3
CLINTON	66	17,839	36,825*	64.9	100.0
019 AMER BAPT CONV	2	559	690*	1.2	1.9
029 AMER LUTH CH..	11	4,242	5,934	10.5	16.1
081 CATHOLIC......	16	0	12,725	22.4	34.6
097 CR C AND C CR.	1	250	309*	0.5	0.8
123 CH GOD (ANDER)	2	80	242	0.4	0.7
165 CH OF NAZARENE	1	66	135	0.2	0.4
193 EPISCOPAL.....	2	582	931	1.6	2.5
281 LUTH CH AMER..	4	1,663	2,371	4.2	6.4
283 LUTH--MO SYNOD	5	2,833	3,867	6.8	10.5
371 REF CH IN AM..	1	109	158	0.3	0.4
403 SALVATION ARMY	1	65	223	0.4	0.6
419 SO BAPT CONV..	1	324	400*	0.7	1.1
443 UN C OF CHRIST	4	1,595	1,970*	3.5	5.3
449 UN METHODIST..	11	4,060	5,127	9.0	13.9
453 UN PRES CH USA	4	1,411	1,743*	3.1	4.7
CRAWFORD	35	8,072	14,392*	76.6	100.0
019 AMER BAPT CONV	1	185	229*	1.2	1.6
081 CATHOLIC......	6	0	3,671	19.5	25.5
097 CR C AND C CR.	1	32	40*	0.2	0.3
193 EPISCOPAL.....	1	59	86	0.5	0.6
281 LUTH CH AMER..	1	140	191	1.0	1.3
283 LUTH--MO SYNOD	12	4,561	6,324	33.7	43.9
443 UN C OF CHRIST	3	536	663*	3.5	4.6
449 UN METHODIST..	6	1,476	1,849	9.8	12.8
453 UN PRES CH USA	4	1,083	1,339*	7.1	9.3
DALLAS	45	9,015	14,655*	56.2	100.0
029 AMER LUTH CH..	2	382	566	2.2	3.9
075 BRETHREN IN CR	1	49	60*	0.2	0.4
081 CATHOLIC......	5	0	3,415	13.1	23.3
093 CR CH (DISC)..	6	1,402	1,719*	6.6	11.7
097 CR C AND C CR.	2	170	208*	0.8	1.4
127 CH GOD (CLEVE)	1	17	21*	0.1	0.1
157 CH OF BRETHREN	2	515	632*	2.4	4.3
193 EPISCOPAL.....	1	112	132	0.5	0.9
283 LUTH--MO SYNOD	3	782	1,033	4.0	7.0
353 PLY BRETHREN..	1	34	85	0.3	0.6
413 S-D ADVENTISTS	1	19	23*	0.1	0.2
449 UN METHODIST..	17	4,930	6,022	23.1	41.1
453 UN PRES CH USA	3	603	739*	2.8	5.0
DAVIS	18	2,622	3,224*	39.3	100.0
019 AMER BAPT CONV	1	130	153*	1.9	4.7
029 AMER LUTH CH..	1	87	110	1.3	3.4
081 CATHOLIC......	1	0	156	1.9	4.8
093 CR CH (DISC)..	6	906	1,067*	13.0	33.1

County and Denomination	Number of churches	Communicant, confirmed, full members	Total adherents: Number	Total adherents: Percent of total population	Total adherents: Percent of total adherents
165 CH OF NAZARENE	1	70	147	1.8	4.6
287 MENN GEN CONF.	1	156	184*	2.2	5.7
413 S-D ADVENTISTS	1	12	14*	0.2	0.4
449 UN METHODIST..	6	1,261	1,393	17.0	43.2
DECATUR	21	1,574	2,094*	21.5	100.0
019 AMER BAPT CONV	4	167	191*	2.0	9.1
081 CATHOLIC......	2	0	277	2.8	13.2
093 CR CH (DISC)..	2	266	305*	3.1	14.6
165 CH OF NAZARENE	1	19	29	0.3	1.4
419 SO BAPT CONV..	1	110	126*	1.3	6.0
449 UN METHODIST..	8	738	852	8.8	40.7
453 UN PRES CH USA	3	274	314*	3.2	15.0
DELAWARE	36	4,432	13,561*	72.2	100.0
029 AMER LUTH CH..	6	1,236	1,756	9.4	12.9
081 CATHOLIC......	12	0	7,706	41.1	56.8
283 LUTH--MO SYNOD	2	264	371	2.0	2.7
353 PLY BRETHREN..	1	30	40	0.2	0.3
443 UN C OF CHRIST	3	421	539*	2.9	4.0
449 UN METHODIST..	10	2,081	2,637	14.0	19.4
453 UN PRES CH USA	2	400	512*	2.7	3.8
DES MOINES	56	15,046	27,225*	57.9	100.0
019 AMER BAPT CONV	4	772	943*	2.0	3.5
029 AMER LUTH CH..	2	412	623	1.3	2.3
081 CATHOLIC......	8	0	7,839	16.7	28.8
093 CR CH (DISC)..	1	637	778*	1.7	2.9
097 CR C AND C CR.	1	70	85*	0.2	0.3
127 CH GOD (CLEVE)	1	22	27*	0.1	0.1
165 CH OF NAZARENE	2	244	654	1.4	2.4
175 CONG CR CH....	1	463	565*	1.2	2.1
193 EPISCOPAL.....	1	343	429	0.9	1.6
221 FREE METH C NA	3	130	182	0.4	0.7
281 LUTH CH AMER..	4	2,466	3,466	7.4	12.7
283 LUTH--MO SYNOD	1	86	245	0.5	0.9
313 NO AM BAPT GC.	1	772	943*	2.0	3.5
403 SALVATION ARMY	1	43	210	0.4	0.8
413 S-D ADVENTISTS	1	89	109*	0.2	0.4
435 UNITARIAN-UNIV	1	55	74	0.2	0.3
443 UN C OF CHRIST	7	1,927	2,354*	5.0	8.6
449 UN METHODIST..	12	5,076	5,941	12.6	21.8
453 UN PRES CH USA	4	1,439	1,758*	3.7	6.5
DICKINSON	23	5,243	8,617*	68.6	100.0
019 AMER BAPT CONV	1	58	69*	0.5	0.8
029 AMER LUTH CH..	3	802	1,146	9.1	13.3
081 CATHOLIC......	2	0	1,912	15.2	22.2
193 EPISCOPAL.....	1	60	78	0.6	0.9
226 FRIENDS-USA...	1	93	110*	0.9	1.3
283 LUTH--MO SYNOD	3	957	1,228	9.8	14.3
413 S-D ADVENTISTS	1	18	21*	0.2	0.2
443 UN C OF CHRIST	1	235	278*	2.2	3.2
449 UN METHODIST..	8	2,477	3,132	24.9	36.3
453 UN PRES CH USA	2	543	643*	5.1	7.5
DUBUQUE	58	9,396	75,111*	82.9	100.0
019 AMER BAPT CONV	1	90	116*	0.1	0.2
029 AMER LUTH CH..	5	2,005	3,106	3.4	4.1
081 CATHOLIC......	23	0	61,566	67.9	82.0
165 CH OF NAZARENE	1	36	140	0.2	0.2
193 EPISCOPAL.....	1	332	473	0.5	0.6
226 FRIENDS-USA...	1	11	14*	-	-
281 LUTH CH AMER..	1	231	300	0.3	0.4
283 LUTH--MO SYNOD	3	848	1,349	1.5	1.8
353 PLY BRETHREN..	1	20	40	-	0.1
403 SALVATION ARMY	1	47	456	0.5	0.6
413 S-D ADVENTISTS	1	31	40*	-	0.1
443 UN C OF CHRIST	5	1,128	1,449*	1.6	1.9
449 UN METHODIST..	9	2,733	3,642	4.0	4.8
453 UN PRES CH USA	5	1,884	2,420*	2.7	3.2
EMMET	27	7,315	11,707*	83.6	100.0
029 AMER LUTH CH..	9	2,953	4,111	29.3	35.1
081 CATHOLIC......	2	0	1,912	13.6	16.3
093 CR CH (DISC)..	1	301	366*	2.6	3.1
165 CH OF NAZARENE	1	33	112	0.8	1.0
193 EPISCOPAL.....	1	42	64	0.5	0.5
221 FREE METH C NA	1	25	34	0.2	0.3
281 LUTH CH AMER..	2	416	527	3.8	4.5
283 LUTH--MO SYNOD	1	488	673	4.8	5.7
413 S-D ADVENTISTS	1	27	33*	0.2	0.3
449 UN METHODIST..	4	1,563	2,090	14.9	17.9
453 UN PRES CH USA	4	1,467	1,785*	12.7	15.2
FAYETTE	55	11,104	21,026*	78.2	100.0
019 AMER BAPT CONV	2	47	57*	0.2	0.3
029 AMER LUTH CH..	15	4,998	6,868	25.5	32.7
081 CATHOLIC......	7	0	6,407	23.8	30.5
093 CR CH (DISC)..	1	104	127*	0.5	0.6
097 CR C AND C CR.	2	230	281*	1.0	1.3
165 CH OF NAZARENE	1	34	64	0.2	0.3
193 EPISCOPAL.....	2	55	71	0.3	0.3
283 LUTH--MO SYNOD	3	723	1,015	3.8	4.8
313 NO AM BAPT GC.	1	172	210*	0.8	1.0
353 PLY BRETHREN..	1	20	40	0.1	0.2
413 S-D ADVENTISTS	1	45	55*	0.2	0.3
443 UN C OF CHRIST	1	9	11*	-	0.1

*Total adherents estimated from known number of communicant, confirmed, full members.

—Represents a percent less than 0.1.

Percentages may not total due to rounding.

Table 3. Churches and Church Membership by State, County and Denomination: 1971

County and Denomination	Number of churches	Communicant, confirmed, full members	Total adherents		
			Number	Percent of total population	Percent of total adherents
449 UN METHODIST..	14	3,359	4,224	15.7	20.1
453 UN PRES CH USA	4	1,308	1,596*	5.9	7.6
FLOYD	25	8,020	13,065*	65.8	100.0
019 AMER BAPT CONV	2	347	424*	2.1	3.2
029 AMER LUTH CH..	5	2,704	3,654	18.4	28.0
081 CATHOLIC......	3	0	2,655	13.4	20.3
093 CR CH (DISC)..	2	310	378*	1.9	2.9
193 EPISCOPAL.....	1	76	130	0.7	1.0
413 S-D ADVENTISTS	1	17	21*	0.1	0.2
443 UN C OF CHRIST	2	664	811*	4.1	6.2
449 UN METHODIST..	7	3,615	4,609	23.2	35.3
453 UN PRES CH USA	1	175	214*	1.1	1.6
469 WISC EVAN LUTH	1	112	169	0.9	1.3
FRANKLIN	32	7,261	9,503*	71.7	100.0
019 AMER BAPT CONV	2	159	188*	1.4	2.0
029 AMER LUTH CH..	3	1,024	1,379	10.4	14.5
081 CATHOLIC......	2	0	589	4.4	6.2
093 CR CH (DISC)..	1	163	193*	1.5	2.0
097 CR C AND C CR.	1	306	362*	2.7	3.8
157 CH OF BRETHREN	1	28	33*	0.2	0.3
281 LUTH CH AMER..	1	183	209	1.6	2.2
283 LUTH--MO SYNOD	2	1,090	1,303	9.8	13.7
313 NO AM BAPT GC.	1	148	175*	1.3	1.8
371 REF CH IN AM..	2	402	561	4.2	5.9
413 S-D ADVENTISTS	1	47	56*	0.4	0.6
443 UN C OF CHRIST	3	1,014	1,201*	9.1	12.6
449 UN METHODIST..	12	2,697	3,254	24.5	34.2
FREMONT	29	2,986	4,329*	46.6	100.0
019 AMER BAPT CONV	1	303	357*	3.8	8.2
081 CATHOLIC......	2	0	649	7.0	15.0
093 CR CH (DISC)..	2	111	131*	1.4	3.0
097 CR C AND C CR.	4	160	189*	2.0	4.4
165 CH OF NAZARENE	1	79	227	2.4	5.2
221 FREE METH C NA	1	21	37	0.4	0.9
281 LUTH CH AMER..	1	92	115	1.2	2.7
413 S-D ADVENTISTS	1	18	21*	0.2	0.5
443 UN C OF CHRIST	4	128	151*	1.6	3.5
449 UN METHODIST..	9	1,783	2,109	22.7	48.7
453 UN PRES CH USA	3	291	343*	3.7	7.9
GREENE	29	5,641	8,887*	69.9	100.0
019 AMER BAPT CONV	2	582	701*	5.5	7.9
081 CATHOLIC......	6	0	2,172	17.1	24.4
093 CR CH (DISC)..	1	446	537*	4.2	6.0
097 CR C AND C CR.	2	147	177*	1.4	2.0
127 CH GOD (CLEVE)	1	42	51*	0.4	0.6
226 FRIENDS-USA...	1	61	73*	0.6	0.8
283 LUTH--MO SYNOD	2	516	740	5.8	8.3
449 UN METHODIST..	10	3,279	3,752	29.5	42.2
453 UN PRES CH USA	4	568	684*	5.4	7.7
GRUNDY	29	7,827	10,370*	73.4	100.0
029 AMER LUTH CH..	2	394	550	3.9	5.3
081 CATHOLIC......	1	0	291	2.1	2.8
105 CHRISTIAN REF.	3	560	768	5.4	7.4
157 CH OF BRETHREN	1	331	398*	2.8	3.8
281 LUTH CH AMER..	2	586	782	5.5	7.5
283 LUTH--MO SYNOD	2	327	448	3.2	4.3
371 REF CH IN AM..	3	766	1,136	8.0	11.0
443 UN C OF CHRIST	2	663	798*	5.7	7.7
449 UN METHODIST..	6	2,159	2,743	19.4	26.5
453 UN PRES CH USA	7	2,041	2,456*	17.4	23.7
GUTHRIE	35	4,737	7,395*	60.4	100.0
081 CATHOLIC......	6	0	1,763	14.4	23.8
093 CR CH (DISC)..	4	674	801*	6.5	10.8
097 CR C AND C CR.	5	283	336*	2.7	4.5
157 CH OF BRETHREN	1	170	202*	1.6	2.7
226 FRIENDS-USA...	1	27	32*	0.3	0.4
283 LUTH--MO SYNOD	3	516	708	5.8	9.6
413 S-D ADVENTISTS	1	38	45*	0.4	0.6
443 UN C OF CHRIST	2	317	377*	3.1	5.1
449 UN METHODIST..	11	2,595	2,992	24.4	40.5
453 UN PRES CH USA	1	117	139*	1.1	1.9
HAMILTON	36	9,461	14,078*	76.6	100.0
019 AMER BAPT CONV	1	576	694*	3.8	4.9
029 AMER LUTH CH..	7	2,004	2,684	14.6	19.1
081 CATHOLIC......	2	0	1,816	9.9	12.9
093 CR CH (DISC)..	1	146	176*	1.0	1.3
097 CR C AND C CR.	3	700	843*	4.6	6.0
121 CH GOD (ABR)..	1	35	42*	0.2	0.3
127 CH GOD (CLEVE)	1	5	6*	-	-
193 EPISCOPAL.....	1	34	83	0.5	0.6
201 EVAN COV CH AM	1	8	10*	0.1	0.1
281 LUTH CH AMER..	2	1,169	1,683	9.2	12.0
283 LUTH--MO SYNOD	1	532	743	4.0	5.3
435 UNITARIAN-UNIV	1	30	36	0.2	0.3
443 UN C OF CHRIST	3	790	951*	5.2	6.8
449 UN METHODIST..	10	3,023	3,818	20.8	27.1
453 UN PRES CH USA	1	409	493*	2.7	3.5
HANCOCK	33	6,926	11,324*	85.6	100.0
019 AMER BAPT CONV	1	90	109*	0.8	1.0
029 AMER LUTH CH..	7	1,549	2,142	16.2	18.9
081 CATHOLIC......	4	0	2,309	17.5	20.4
105 CHRISTIAN REF.	4	561	883	6.7	7.8
165 CH OF NAZARENE	1	112	163	1.2	1.4
283 LUTH--MO SYNOD	2	554	729	5.5	6.4
443 UN C OF CHRIST	3	869	1,050*	7.9	9.3
449 UN METHODIST..	9	2,887	3,572	27.0	31.5
453 UN PRES CH USA	2	304	367*	2.8	3.2
HARDIN	48	10,493	15,513*	69.7	100.0
019 AMER BAPT CONV	1	182	215*	1.0	1.4
029 AMER LUTH CH..	3	580	839	3.8	5.4
081 CATHOLIC......	4	0	1,941	8.7	12.5
093 CR CH (DISC)..	3	286	339*	1.5	2.2
097 CR C AND C CR.	2	195	231*	1.0	1.5
105 CHRISTIAN REF.	2	155	243	1.1	1.6
123 CH GOD (ANDER)	1	37	117	0.5	0.8
165 CH OF NAZARENE	1	28	63	0.3	0.4
193 EPISCOPAL.....	1	39	103	0.5	0.7
226 FRIENDS-USA...	2	448	530*	2.4	3.4
281 LUTH CH AMER..	1	303	423	1.9	2.7
283 LUTH--MO SYNOD	5	1,952	2,649	11.9	17.1
313 NO AM BAPT GC.	1	246	291*	1.3	1.9
353 PLY BRETHREN..	1	30	50	0.2	0.3
371 REF CH IN AM..	1	232	347	1.6	2.2
443 UN C OF CHRIST	6	1,692	2,003*	9.0	12.9
449 UN METHODIST..	11	3,720	4,693	21.1	30.3
453 UN PRES CH USA	2	368	436*	2.0	2.8
HARRISON	37	4,930	8,968*	55.2	100.0
019 AMER BAPT CONV	1	78	94*	0.6	1.0
081 CATHOLIC......	8	0	2,731	16.8	30.5
093 CR CH (DISC)..	1	193	232*	1.4	2.6
097 CR C AND C CR.	5	875	1,053*	6.5	11.7
165 CH OF NAZARENE	1	42	85	0.5	0.9
281 LUTH CH AMER..	3	554	819	5.0	9.1
283 LUTH--MO SYNOD	4	815	1,146	7.1	12.8
413 S-D ADVENTISTS	1	12	14*	0.1	0.2
449 UN METHODIST..	10	2,018	2,381	14.7	26.5
453 UN PRES CH USA	3	343	413*	2.5	4.6
HENRY	35	7,740	10,500*	58.0	100.0
019 AMER BAPT CONV	3	705	842*	4.6	8.0
081 CATHOLIC......	1	0	1,038	5.7	9.9
097 CR C AND C CR.	2	140	167*	0.9	1.6
165 CH OF NAZARENE	1	39	189	1.0	1.8
175 CONG CR CH....	1	81	97*	0.5	0.9
185 CUMBER PRESB..	1	178	213*	1.2	2.0
193 EPISCOPAL.....	1	177	240	1.3	2.3
226 FRIENDS-USA...	2	250	299*	1.7	2.8
281 LUTH CH AMER..	1	400	502	2.8	4.8
283 LUTH--MO SYNOD	1	208	317	1.8	3.0
285 MENNONITE CH..	3	691	826*	4.6	7.9
287 MENN GEN CONF.	2	333	398*	2.2	3.8
443 UN C OF CHRIST	1	173	207*	1.1	2.0
449 UN METHODIST..	12	3,318	3,914	21.6	37.3
453 UN PRES CH USA	3	1,047	1,251*	6.9	11.9
HOWARD	29	3,753	10,734*	93.8	100.0
019 AMER BAPT CONV	1	125	152*	1.3	1.4
029 AMER LUTH CH..	5	1,768	2,367	20.7	22.1
081 CATHOLIC......	10	0	5,898	51.5	54.9
193 EPISCOPAL.....	1	8	9	0.1	0.1
283 LUTH--MO SYNOD	1	155	242	2.1	2.3
413 S-D ADVENTISTS	1	10	12*	0.1	0.1
443 UN C OF CHRIST	1	155	188*	1.6	1.8
449 UN METHODIST..	7	1,324	1,613	14.1	15.0
453 UN PRES CH USA	2	208	253*	2.2	2.4
HUMBOLDT	24	6,889	10,073*	80.5	100.0
019 AMER BAPT CONV	1	100	121*	1.0	1.2
029 AMER LUTH CH..	8	2,910	3,877	31.0	38.5
081 CATHOLIC......	2	0	1,182	9.4	11.7
283 LUTH--MO SYNOD	2	614	891	7.1	8.8
413 S-D ADVENTISTS	1	36	43*	0.3	0.4
443 UN C OF CHRIST	1	414	500*	4.0	5.0
449 UN METHODIST..	7	2,754	3,385	27.0	33.6
453 UN PRES CH USA	2	61	74*	0.6	0.7
IDA	13	5,011	7,283*	79.2	100.0
029 AMER LUTH CH..	1	823	1,164	12.7	16.0
081 CATHOLIC......	2	0	911	9.9	12.5
283 LUTH--MO SYNOD	3	1,632	2,211	24.1	30.4
449 UN METHODIST..	5	1,863	2,170	23.6	29.8
453 UN PRES CH USA	2	693	827*	9.0	11.4
IOWA	32	6,034	10,811*	70.1	100.0
029 AMER LUTH CH..	1	119	145	0.9	1.3
081 CATHOLIC......	5	0	2,280	14.8	21.1
093 CR CH (DISC)..	1	203	247*	1.6	2.3
121 CH GOD (ABR)..	1	42	51*	0.3	0.5
165 CH OF NAZARENE	1	53	116	0.8	1.1
226 FRIENDS-USA...	1	45	55*	0.4	0.5
283 LUTH--MO SYNOD	8	2,207	3,806	24.7	35.2
285 MENNONITE CH..	2	380	463*	3.0	4.3
313 NO AM BAPT GC.	1	90	110*	0.7	1.0
443 UN C OF CHRIST	1	204	248*	1.6	2.3
449 UN METHODIST..	8	2,026	2,480	16.1	22.9

*Total adherents estimated from known number of communicant, confirmed, full members.

—Represents a percent less than 0.1.

Percentages may not total due to rounding.

Table 3. Churches and Church Membership by State, County and Denomination: 1971

County and Denomination	Number of churches	Communicant, confirmed, full members	Total adherents: Number	Percent of total population	Percent of total adherents
453 UN PRES CH USA	2	665	810*	5.3	7.5
JACKSON	36	5,557	16,395*	78.7	100.0
019 AMER BAPT CONV	1	138	174*	0.8	1.1
029 AMER LUTH CH..	8	3,020	4,146	19.9	25.3
081 CATHOLIC......	14	0	8,950	42.9	54.6
193 EPISCOPAL.....	1	153	250	1.2	1.5
443 UN C OF CHRIST	2	402	508*	2.4	3.1
449 UN METHODIST..	6	1,175	1,522	7.3	9.3
453 UN PRES CH USA	4	669	845*	4.1	5.2
JASPER	53	12,540	18,776*	53.0	100.0
019 AMER BAPT CONV	1	357	434*	1.2	2.3
029 AMER LUTH CH..	2	197	266	0.8	1.4
081 CATHOLIC......	3	0	2,023	5.7	10.8
093 CR CH (DISC)..	7	1,135	1,379*	3.9	7.3
105 CHRISTIAN REF.	3	794	1,528	4.3	8.1
157 CH OF BRETHREN	1	119	145*	0.4	0.8
165 CH OF NAZARENE	1	142	217	0.6	1.2
193 EPISCOPAL.....	1	201	273	0.8	1.5
221 FREE METH C NA	1	5	5	-	-
226 FRIENDS-USA...	2	203	247*	0.7	1.3
281 LUTH CH AMER..	2	1,049	1,483	4.2	7.9
283 LUTH--MO SYNOD	1	192	307	0.9	1.6
371 REF CH IN AM..	3	825	1,303	3.7	6.9
403 SALVATION ARMY	1	74	374	1.1	2.0
413 S-D ADVENTISTS	1	48	58*	0.2	0.3
443 UN C OF CHRIST	5	1,172	1,424*	4.0	7.6
449 UN METHODIST..	13	4,468	5,399	15.2	28.8
453 UN PRES CH USA	4	1,502	1,825*	5.2	9.7
469 WISC EVAN LUTH	1	57	86	0.2	0.5
JEFFERSON	35	5,494	8,631*	54.7	100.0
019 AMER BAPT CONV	3	518	616*	3.9	7.1
029 AMER LUTH CH..	1	184	257	1.6	3.0
081 CATHOLIC......	2	0	1,786	11.3	20.7
093 CR CH (DISC)..	2	458	544*	3.4	6.3
097 CR C AND C CR.	2	25	30*	0.2	0.3
157 CH OF BRETHREN	1	61	73*	0.5	0.8
165 CH OF NAZARENE	1	94	204	1.3	2.4
193 EPISCOPAL.....	1	53	72	0.5	0.8
221 FREE METH C NA	2	100	153	1.0	1.8
226 FRIENDS-USA...	4	455	541*	3.4	6.3
281 LUTH CH AMER..	2	755	1,007	6.4	11.7
283 LUTH--MO SYNOD	1	79	112	0.7	1.3
353 PLY BRETHREN..	1	30	40	0.3	0.5
413 S-D ADVENTISTS	1	63	75*	0.5	0.9
443 UN C OF CHRIST	1	53	63*	0.4	0.7
449 UN METHODIST..	9	2,087	2,489	15.8	28.8
453 UN PRES CH USA	1	479	569*	3.6	6.6
JOHNSON	52	11,420	31,878*	44.2	100.0
019 AMER BAPT CONV	1	405	488*	0.7	1.5
029 AMER LUTH CH..	2	972	1,357	1.9	4.3
081 CATHOLIC......	16	0	16,194	22.5	50.8
093 CR CH (DISC)..	1	338	408*	0.6	1.3
097 CR C AND C CR.	2	43	52*	0.1	0.2
105 CHRISTIAN REF.	1	98	157	0.2	0.5
165 CH OF NAZARENE	1	106	316	0.4	1.0
193 EPISCOPAL.....	1	525	870	1.2	2.7
221 FREE METH C NA	1	41	59	0.1	0.2
226 FRIENDS-USA...	1	61	74*	0.1	0.2
281 LUTH CH AMER..	1	1,041	1,512	2.1	4.7
283 LUTH--MO SYNOD	2	659	1,001	1.4	3.1
285 MENNONITE CH..	3	259	312*	0.4	1.0
413 S-D ADVENTISTS	1	20	24*	-	0.1
435 UNITARIAN-UNIV	1	204	332	0.5	1.0
443 UN C OF CHRIST	3	535	645*	0.9	2.0
449 UN METHODIST..	10	4,040	5,577	7.7	17.5
453 UN PRES CH USA	4	2,073	2,500*	3.5	7.8
JONES	36	6,737	13,019*	65.5	100.0
019 AMER BAPT CONV	1	122	150*	0.8	1.2
029 AMER LUTH CH..	6	2,631	3,673	18.5	28.2
081 CATHOLIC......	7	0	4,013	20.2	30.8
097 CR C AND C CR.	1	105	129*	0.6	1.0
165 CH OF NAZARENE	1	42	91	0.5	0.7
193 EPISCOPAL.....	1	27	43	0.2	0.3
281 LUTH CH AMER..	1	137	197	1.0	1.5
283 LUTH--MO SYNOD	1	321	431	2.2	3.3
419 SO BAPT CONV..	1	128	157*	0.8	1.2
443 UN C OF CHRIST	3	586	719*	3.6	5.5
449 UN METHODIST..	8	1,680	2,240	11.3	17.2
453 UN PRES CH USA	5	958	1,176*	5.9	9.0
KEOKUK	50	4,523	8,371*	60.0	100.0
019 AMER BAPT CONV	6	461	549*	3.9	6.6
029 AMER LUTH CH..	1	85	111	0.8	1.3
081 CATHOLIC......	8	0	2,912	20.9	34.8
093 CR CH (DISC)..	9	613	730*	5.2	8.7
097 CR C AND C CR.	1	28	33*	0.2	0.4
157 CH OF BRETHREN	2	225	268*	1.9	3.2
226 FRIENDS-USA...	2	81	96*	0.7	1.1
283 LUTH--MO SYNOD	1	40	79	0.6	0.9
285 MENNONITE CH..	2	53	63*	0.5	0.8
413 S-D ADVENTISTS	1	3	4*	-	-
449 UN METHODIST..	12	2,370	2,854	20.5	34.1
453 UN PRES CH USA	5	564	672*	4.8	8.0

County and Denomination	Number of churches	Communicant, confirmed, full members	Total adherents: Number	Percent of total population	Percent of total adherents
KOSSUTH	44	9,215	19,315*	84.2	100.0
019 AMER BAPT CONV	1	109	135*	0.6	0.7
029 AMER LUTH CH..	4	958	1,294	5.6	6.7
081 CATHOLIC......	8	0	7,398	32.3	38.3
165 CH OF NAZARENE	1	18	40	0.2	0.2
193 EPISCOPAL.....	1	81	122	0.5	0.6
281 LUTH CH AMER..	3	801	1,062	4.6	5.5
283 LUTH--MO SYNOD	7	2,363	3,160	13.8	16.4
371 REF CH IN AM..	1	355	505	2.2	2.6
443 UN C OF CHRIST	2	555	687*	3.0	3.6
449 UN METHODIST..	11	2,785	3,438	15.0	17.8
453 UN PRES CH USA	5	1,190	1,474*	6.4	7.6
LEE	56	11,610	25,132*	58.5	100.0
019 AMER BAPT CONV	2	1,233	1,495*	3.5	5.9
081 CATHOLIC......	10	0	10,132	23.6	40.3
093 CR CH (DISC)..	3	997	1,209*	2.8	4.8
097 CR C AND C CR.	1	82	99*	0.2	0.4
165 CH OF NAZARENE	3	250	719	1.7	2.9
193 EPISCOPAL.....	2	371	645	1.5	2.6
281 LUTH CH AMER..	2	652	832	1.9	3.3
283 LUTH--MO SYNOD	2	166	248	0.6	1.0
287 MENN GEN CONF.	1	180	218*	0.5	0.9
403 SALVATION ARMY	1	55	312	0.7	1.2
413 S-D ADVENTISTS	2	83	101*	0.2	0.4
419 SO BAPT CONV..	1	169	205*	0.5	0.8
443 UN C OF CHRIST	6	1,895	2,297*	5.3	9.1
449 UN METHODIST..	11	3,780	4,563	10.6	18.2
453 UN PRES CH USA	9	1,697	2,057*	4.8	8.2
LINN	119	38,460	87,883*	53.8	100.0
019 AMER BAPT CONV	3	686	863*	0.5	1.0
029 AMER LUTH CH..	5	2,047	3,256	2.0	3.7
081 CATHOLIC......	10	0	34,147	20.9	38.9
093 CR CH (DISC)..	7	1,380	1,736*	1.1	2.0
097 CR C AND C CR.	4	224	282*	0.2	0.3
123 CH GOD (ANDER)	1	100	250	0.2	0.3
127 CH GOD (CLEVE)	1	22	28*	-	-
157 CH OF BRETHREN	2	181	228*	0.1	0.3
165 CH OF NAZARENE	3	492	1,636	1.0	1.9
175 CONG CR CH....	1	140	176*	0.1	0.2
193 EPISCOPAL.....	3	1,197	1,699	1.0	1.9
201 EVAN COV CH AM	1	67	84*	0.1	0.1
221 FREE METH C NA	4	115	170	0.1	0.2
226 FRIENDS-USA...	2	152	191*	0.1	0.2
281 LUTH CH AMER..	6	3,776	5,695	3.5	6.5
283 LUTH--MO SYNOD	8	4,703	7,175	4.4	8.2
313 NO AM BAPT GC.	1	13	16*	-	-
371 REF CH IN AM..	1	175	306	0.2	0.3
381 REF PRES-EVAN.	2	75	98	0.1	0.1
403 SALVATION ARMY	1	90	425	0.3	0.5
413 S-D ADVENTISTS	1	209	263*	0.2	0.3
419 SO BAPT CONV..	1	500	629*	0.4	0.7
435 UNITARIAN-UNIV	1	260	335	0.2	0.4
443 UN C OF CHRIST	4	1,280	1,610*	1.0	1.8
449 UN METHODIST..	30	12,568	16,488	10.1	18.8
453 UN PRES CH USA	15	7,893	9,927*	6.1	11.3
469 WISC EVAN LUTH	1	115	170	0.1	0.2
LOUISA	16	3,247	4,429*	41.5	100.0
081 CATHOLIC......	2	0	340	3.2	7.7
165 CH OF NAZARENE	1	33	107	1.0	2.4
283 LUTH--MO SYNOD	1	54	80	0.7	1.8
449 UN METHODIST..	7	2,134	2,645	24.8	59.7
453 UN PRES CH USA	5	1,026	1,257*	11.8	28.4
LUCAS	19	3,069	4,323*	42.5	100.0
019 AMER BAPT CONV	2	598	705*	6.9	16.3
081 CATHOLIC......	1	0	575	5.7	13.3
093 CR CH (DISC)..	3	404	477*	4.7	11.0
107 CHRISTIAN UN..	2	50	59*	0.6	1.4
165 CH OF NAZARENE	1	159	361	3.6	8.4
193 EPISCOPAL.....	1	72	78	0.8	1.8
281 LUTH CH AMER..	1	194	303	3.0	7.0
449 UN METHODIST..	6	1,295	1,415	13.9	32.7
453 UN PRES CH USA	2	297	350*	3.4	8.1
LYON	33	6,209	9,947*	74.6	100.0
029 AMER LUTH CH..	5	1,543	1,993	14.9	20.0
081 CATHOLIC......	3	0	1,381	10.4	13.9
093 CR CH (DISC)..	1	111	137*	1.0	1.4
105 CHRISTIAN REF.	3	458	864	6.5	8.7
201 EVAN COV CH AM	1	54	67*	0.5	0.7
283 LUTH--MO SYNOD	2	386	536	4.0	5.4
313 NO AM BAPT GC.	2	370	457*	3.4	4.6
371 REF CH IN AM..	6	1,263	2,069	15.5	20.8
443 UN C OF CHRIST	2	333	411*	3.1	4.1
449 UN METHODIST..	4	718	831	6.2	8.4
453 UN PRES CH USA	4	973	1,201*	9.0	12.1
MADISON	31	4,696	6,401*	55.4	100.0
029 AMER LUTH CH..	1	165	238	2.1	3.7
081 CATHOLIC......	2	0	655	5.7	10.2
093 CR CH (DISC)..	4	541	644*	5.6	10.1
097 CR C AND C CR.	1	80	95*	0.8	1.5
107 CHRISTIAN UN..	1	35	42*	0.4	0.7
165 CH OF NAZARENE	1	24	60	0.5	0.9
193 EPISCOPAL.....	1	17	28	0.2	0.4

*Total adherents estimated from known number of communicant, confirmed, full members.

—Represents a percent less than 0.1.

Percentages may not total due to rounding.

Table 3. Churches and Church Membership by State, County and Denomination: 1971

County and Denomination	Number of churches	Communicant, confirmed, full members	Total adherents		
			Number	Percent of total population	Percent of total adherents
226 FRIENDS-USA...	3	492	586*	5.1	9.2
283 LUTH--MO SYNOD	1	340	492	4.3	7.7
413 S-D ADVENTISTS	1	57	68*	0.6	1.1
419 SO BAPT CONV..	1	155	184*	1.6	2.9
443 UN C OF CHRIST	1	111	132*	1.1	2.1
449 UN METHODIST..	9	2,151	2,549	22.1	39.8
453 UN PRES CH USA	4	528	628*	5.4	9.8
MAHASKA	37	7,821	11,590*	52.3	100.0
019 AMER BAPT CONV	2	282	333*	1.5	2.9
081 CATHOLIC......	1	0	785	3.5	6.8
093 CR CH (DISC)..	4	1,195	1,412*	6.4	12.2
105 CHRISTIAN REF.	5	1,027	1,806	8.1	15.6
165 CH OF NAZARENE	2	319	732	3.3	6.3
193 EPISCOPAL.....	1	115	270	1.2	2.3
221 FREE METH C NA	1	45	57	0.3	0.5
226 FRIENDS-USA...	2	388	458*	2.1	4.0
283 LUTH--MO SYNOD	1	240	357	1.6	3.1
353 PLY BRETHREN..	1	30	50	0.2	0.4
371 REF CH IN AM..	2	752	1,060	4.8	9.1
403 SALVATION ARMY	1	65	225	1.0	1.9
413 S-D ADVENTISTS	1	15	18*	0.1	0.2
443 UN C OF CHRIST	2	312	369*	1.7	3.2
449 UN METHODIST..	8	2,455	2,923	13.2	25.2
453 UN PRES CH USA	2	521	615*	2.8	5.3
469 WISC EVAN LUTH	1	60	120	0.5	1.0
MARION	45	11,304	16,773*	63.6	100.0
019 AMER BAPT CONV	2	798	954*	3.6	5.7
081 CATHOLIC......	4	0	1,617	6.1	9.6
093 CR CH (DISC)..	2	381	456*	1.7	2.7
097 CR C AND C CR.	4	1,261	1,508*	5.7	9.0
105 CHRISTIAN REF.	5	1,622	2,657	10.1	15.8
127 CH GOD (CLEVE)	1	99	118*	0.4	0.7
165 CH OF NAZARENE	1	92	314	1.2	1.9
221 FREE METH C NA	1	47	55	0.2	0.3
283 LUTH--MO SYNOD	3	425	633	2.4	3.8
371 REF CH IN AM..	6	2,924	4,178	15.9	24.9
413 S-D ADVENTISTS	1	76	91*	0.3	0.5
449 UN METHODIST..	14	3,361	3,931	14.9	23.4
453 UN PRES CH USA	1	218	261*	1.0	1.6
MARSHALL	60	14,388	24,880*	60.6	100.0
019 AMER BAPT CONV	1	830	1,019*	2.5	4.1
029 AMER LUTH CH..	3	1,305	1,823	4.4	7.3
081 CATHOLIC......	8	0	5,141	12.5	20.7
093 CR CH (DISC)..	3	922	1,132*	2.8	4.5
097 CR C AND C CR.	2	397	488*	1.2	2.0
123 CH GOD (ANDER)	1	8	16	-	0.1
157 CH OF BRETHREN	1	159	195*	0.5	0.8
165 CH OF NAZARENE	1	153	460	1.1	1.8
175 CONG CR CH....	2	966	1,187*	2.9	4.8
193 EPISCOPAL.....	1	242	376	0.9	1.5
197 EVAN CH OF NA.	1	26	32*	0.1	0.1
226 FRIENDS-USA...	4	819	1,006*	2.4	4.0
281 LUTH CH AMER..	1	372	541	1.3	2.2
283 LUTH--MO SYNOD	4	1,395	1,961	4.8	7.9
403 SALVATION ARMY	1	85	580	1.4	2.3
413 S-D ADVENTISTS	1	84	103*	0.3	0.4
443 UN C OF CHRIST	8	1,143	1,404*	3.4	5.6
449 UN METHODIST..	14	4,607	6,341	15.4	25.5
453 UN PRES CH USA	3	875	1,075*	2.6	4.3
MILLS	23	4,200	5,645*	48.6	100.0
019 AMER BAPT CONV	3	828	991*	8.5	17.6
029 AMER LUTH CH..	1	368	490	4.2	8.7
081 CATHOLIC......	1	0	316	2.7	5.6
093 CR CH (DISC)..	1	249	298*	2.6	5.3
165 CH OF NAZARENE	1	46	177	1.5	3.1
193 EPISCOPAL.....	1	10	11	0.1	0.2
283 LUTH--MO SYNOD	2	405	527	4.5	9.3
413 S-D ADVENTISTS	1	14	17*	0.1	0.3
443 UN C OF CHRIST	1	100	120*	1.0	2.1
449 UN METHODIST..	10	2,138	2,648	22.8	46.9
453 UN PRES CH USA	1	42	50*	0.4	0.9
MITCHELL	29	5,821	11,981*	91.4	100.0
019 AMER BAPT CONV	3	244	299*	2.3	2.5
029 AMER LUTH CH..	7	2,658	3,635	27.7	30.3
081 CATHOLIC......	6	0	4,193	32.0	35.0
221 FREE METH C NA	1	27	27	0.2	0.2
283 LUTH--MO SYNOD	4	1,283	1,806	13.8	15.1
443 UN C OF CHRIST	3	433	531*	4.1	4.4
449 UN METHODIST..	4	1,156	1,465	11.2	12.2
453 UN PRES CH USA	1	20	25*	0.2	0.2
MONONA	30	4,893	7,558*	62.6	100.0
029 AMER LUTH CH..	4	1,322	1,725	14.3	22.8
081 CATHOLIC......	4	0	1,314	10.9	17.4
093 CR CH (DISC)..	1	144	171*	1.4	2.3
097 CR C AND C CR.	5	733	870*	7.2	11.5
193 EPISCOPAL.....	1	12	16	0.1	0.2
283 LUTH--MO SYNOD	2	975	1,386	11.5	18.3
413 S-D ADVENTISTS	2	55	65*	0.5	0.9
443 UN C OF CHRIST	6	720	855*	7.1	11.3
449 UN METHODIST..	5	932	1,156	9.6	15.3
MONROE	20	1,782	4,282*	45.8	100.0
019 AMER BAPT CONV	2	46	54*	0.6	1.3
081 CATHOLIC......	5	0	2,155	23.0	50.3
093 CR CH (DISC)..	1	488	576*	6.2	13.5
157 CH OF BRETHREN	1	66	78*	0.8	1.8
165 CH OF NAZARENE	1	31	114	1.2	2.7
193 EPISCOPAL.....	1	50	63	0.7	1.5
281 LUTH CH AMER..	1	114	152	1.6	3.5
353 PLY BRETHREN..	1	32	35	0.4	0.8
413 S-D ADVENTISTS	1	43	51*	0.5	1.2
419 SO BAPT CONV..	1	107	126*	1.3	2.9
449 UN METHODIST..	4	692	745	8.0	17.4
453 UN PRES CH USA	1	113	133*	1.4	3.1
MONTGOMERY	28	6,356	8,569*	67.0	100.0
019 AMER BAPT CONV	1	336	395*	3.1	4.6
081 CATHOLIC......	3	0	640	5.0	7.5
093 CR CH (DISC)..	2	387	455*	3.6	5.3
165 CH OF NAZARENE	1	52	176	1.4	2.1
201 EVAN COV CH AM	2	382	449*	3.5	5.2
281 LUTH CH AMER..	3	1,416	1,717	13.4	20.0
283 LUTH--MO SYNOD	2	180	247	1.9	2.9
403 SALVATION ARMY	1	51	204	1.6	2.4
443 UN C OF CHRIST	1	153	180*	1.4	2.1
449 UN METHODIST..	8	2,500	3,050	23.9	35.6
453 UN PRES CH USA	4	899	1,056*	8.3	12.3
MUSCATINE	49	10,337	17,711*	47.6	100.0
019 AMER BAPT CONV	1	699	869*	2.3	4.9
029 AMER LUTH CH..	3	1,144	1,605	4.3	9.1
081 CATHOLIC......	5	0	4,508	12.1	25.5
093 CR CH (DISC)..	3	366	455*	1.2	2.6
097 CR C AND C CR.	1	30	37*	0.1	0.2
127 CH GOD (CLEVE)	1	44	55*	0.1	0.3
165 CH OF NAZARENE	1	48	113	0.3	0.6
193 EPISCOPAL.....	1	256	410	1.1	2.3
226 FRIENDS-USA...	2	153	190*	0.5	1.1
281 LUTH CH AMER..	2	1,106	1,493	4.0	8.4
283 LUTH--MO SYNOD	2	562	316	0.8	1.8
285 MENNONITE CH..	1	8	10*	-	0.1
353 PLY BRETHREN..	1	20	40	0.1	0.2
403 SALVATION ARMY	1	39	282	0.8	1.6
413 S-D ADVENTISTS	1	207	257*	0.7	1.5
443 UN C OF CHRIST	4	491	610*	1.6	3.4
449 UN METHODIST..	14	3,866	4,848	13.0	27.4
453 UN PRES CH USA	5	1,298	1,613*	4.3	9.1
OBRIEN	39	9,796	15,389*	87.8	100.0
029 AMER LUTH CH..	3	969	1,389	7.9	9.0
081 CATHOLIC......	5	0	1,959	11.2	12.7
097 CR C AND C CR.	3	315	379*	2.2	2.5
105 CHRISTIAN REF.	3	820	1,477	8.4	9.6
226 FRIENDS-USA...	1	131	158*	0.9	1.0
283 LUTH--MO SYNOD	5	1,975	2,710	15.5	17.6
371 REF CH IN AM..	5	1,660	2,546	14.5	16.5
443 UN C OF CHRIST	4	886	1,067*	6.1	6.9
449 UN METHODIST..	8	2,471	3,019	17.2	19.6
453 UN PRES CH USA	2	569	685*	3.9	4.5
OSCEOLA	20	4,265	7,146*	83.5	100.0
029 AMER LUTH CH..	2	758	1,040	12.2	14.6
081 CATHOLIC......	2	0	1,375	16.1	19.2
105 CHRISTIAN REF.	2	354	646	7.6	9.0
283 LUTH--MO SYNOD	4	752	961	11.2	13.4
371 REF CH IN AM..	3	496	804	9.4	11.3
443 UN C OF CHRIST	1	155	187*	2.2	2.6
449 UN METHODIST..	4	1,149	1,409	16.5	19.7
453 UN PRES CH USA	2	601	724*	8.5	10.1
PAGE	42	8,873	11,874*	64.2	100.0
019 AMER BAPT CONV	2	388	451*	2.4	3.8
081 CATHOLIC......	2	0	1,071	5.8	9.0
093 CR CH (DISC)..	3	863	1,002*	5.4	8.4
165 CH OF NAZARENE	2	148	367	2.0	3.1
193 EPISCOPAL.....	1	161	259	1.4	2.2
201 EVAN COV CH AM	3	232	269*	1.5	2.3
221 FREE METH C NA	2	37	45	0.2	0.4
281 LUTH CH AMER..	4	916	1,158	6.3	9.8
283 LUTH--MO SYNOD	4	1,335	1,772	9.6	14.9
419 SO BAPT CONV..	1	152	177*	1.0	1.5
443 UN C OF CHRIST	1	175	203*	1.1	1.7
449 UN METHODIST..	11	2,965	3,357	18.1	28.3
453 UN PRES CH USA	6	1,501	1,743*	9.4	14.7
PALO ALTO	30	5,809	12,418*	93.4	100.0
029 AMER LUTH CH..	5	1,851	2,487	18.7	20.0
081 CATHOLIC......	6	0	4,737	35.6	38.1
157 CH OF BRETHREN	1	34	41*	0.3	0.3
193 EPISCOPAL.....	1	47	71	0.5	0.6
283 LUTH--MO SYNOD	5	1,142	1,592	12.0	12.8
353 PLY BRETHREN..	1	30	40	0.3	0.3
413 S-D ADVENTISTS	1	39	47*	0.4	0.4
443 UN C OF CHRIST	1	115	140*	1.1	1.1
449 UN METHODIST..	8	2,465	3,159	23.8	25.4
453 UN PRES CH USA	1	86	104*	0.8	0.8
PLYMOUTH	50	8,928	19,835*	81.6	100.0
019 AMER BAPT CONV	2	256	312*	1.3	1.6
029 AMER LUTH CH..	8	3,019	4,110	16.9	20.7

*Total adherents estimated from known number of communicant, confirmed, full members.

—Represents a percent less than 0.1.

Percentages may not total due to rounding.

Table 3. Churches and Church Membership by State, County and Denomination: 1971

County and Denomination	Number of churches	Communicant, confirmed, full members	Total adherents		
			Number	Percent of total population	Percent of total adherents
081 CATHOLIC......	11	0	8,023	33.0	40.4
097 CR C AND C CR.	3	205	250*	1.0	1.3
105 CHRISTIAN REF.	1	101	193	0.8	1.0
157 CH OF BRETHREN	1	86	105*	0.4	0.5
165 CH OF NAZARENE	1	33	94	0.4	0.5
193 EPISCOPAL.....	1	39	42	0.2	0.2
221 FREE METH C NA	1	18	19	0.1	0.1
281 LUTH CH AMER..	2	565	784	3.2	4.0
283 LUTH--MO SYNOD	4	1,458	1,962	8.1	9.9
443 UN C OF CHRIST	3	298	364*	1.5	1.8
449 UN METHODIST..	9	2,327	2,939	12.1	14.8
453 UN PRES CH USA	3	523	638*	2.6	3.2
POCAHONTAS	28	5,090	10,962*	86.1	100.0
019 AMER BAPT CONV	1	61	74*	0.6	0.7
029 AMER LUTH CH..	5	1,634	2,226	17.5	20.3
081 CATHOLIC......	8	0	4,310	33.9	39.3
093 CR CH (DISC)..	1	173	211*	1.7	1.9
281 LUTH CH AMER..	2	341	518	4.1	4.7
283 LUTH--MO SYNOD	1	73	93	0.7	0.8
443 UN C OF CHRIST	1	140	171*	1.3	1.6
449 UN METHODIST..	6	2,162	2,742	21.5	25.0
453 UN PRES CH USA	3	506	617*	4.8	5.6
POLK	178	71,191	139,524*	48.8	100.0
019 AMER BAPT CONV	5	1,769	2,171*	0.8	1.6
029 AMER LUTH CH..	9	4,130	6,033	2.1	4.3
075 BRETHREN IN CR	1	19	23*	-	-
081 CATHOLIC......	18	0	43,455	15.2	31.1
093 CR CH (DISC)..	20	8,635	10,595*	3.7	7.6
097 CR C AND C CR.	9	1,328	1,629*	0.6	1.2
105 CHRISTIAN REF.	1	103	190	0.1	0.1
123 CH GOD (ANDER)	1	73	138	-	0.1
127 CH GOD (CLEVE)	4	167	205*	0.1	0.1
157 CH OF BRETHREN	2	379	465*	0.2	0.3
165 CH OF NAZARENE	5	561	1,547	0.5	1.1
193 EPISCOPAL.....	4	2,643	4,249	1.5	3.0
201 EVAN COV CH AM	2	384	471*	0.2	0.3
226 FRIENDS-USA...	3	311	382*	0.1	0.3
281 LUTH CH AMER..	12	9,816	14,696	5.1	10.5
283 LUTH--MO SYNOD	9	3,151	4,713	1.6	3.4
285 MENNONITE CH..	1	42	52*	-	-
353 PLY BRETHREN..	3	260	383	0.1	0.3
371 REF CH IN AM..	4	645	1,049	0.4	0.8
403 SALVATION ARMY	2	260	1,524	0.5	1.1
413 S-D ADVENTISTS	1	508	623*	0.2	0.4
419 SO BAPT CONV..	1	616	756*	0.3	0.5
435 UNITARIAN-UNIV	1	351	495	0.2	0.4
443 UN C OF CHRIST	6	3,744	4,594*	1.6	3.3
449 UN METHODIST..	37	21,144	26,590	9.3	19.1
453 UN PRES CH USA	16	10,011	12,284*	4.3	8.8
469 WISC EVAN LUTH	1	141	212	0.1	0.2
POTTAWATTAMIE	77	22,488	41,831*	48.1	100.0
019 AMER BAPT CONV	4	905	1,132*	1.3	2.7
029 AMER LUTH CH..	7	3,153	4,616	5.3	11.0
081 CATHOLIC......	9	0	11,063	12.7	26.4
093 CR CH (DISC)..	2	472	590*	0.7	1.4
097 CR C AND C CR.	4	2,434	3,045*	3.5	7.3
127 CH GOD (CLEVE)	1	17	21*	-	0.1
157 CH OF BRETHREN	1	150	188*	0.2	0.4
165 CH OF NAZARENE	3	421	1,260	1.4	3.0
193 EPISCOPAL.....	2	847	1,190	1.4	2.8
281 LUTH CH AMER..	2	1,112	1,568	1.8	3.7
283 LUTH--MO SYNOD	5	1,793	2,615	3.0	6.3
403 SALVATION ARMY	1	91	341	0.4	0.8
413 S-D ADVENTISTS	1	94	118*	0.1	0.3
443 UN C OF CHRIST	9	2,513	3,143*	3.6	7.5
449 UN METHODIST..	13	5,209	6,785	7.8	16.2
453 UN PRES CH USA	12	3,191	3,991*	4.6	9.5
469 WISC EVAN LUTH	1	86	165	0.2	0.4
POWESHIEK	38	6,560	10,389*	55.3	100.0
019 AMER BAPT CONV	1	366	438*	2.3	4.2
029 AMER LUTH CH..	2	694	1,050	5.6	10.1
081 CATHOLIC......	2	0	2,095	11.1	20.2
093 CR CH (DISC)..	2	91	109*	0.6	1.0
097 CR C AND C CR.	3	524	627*	3.3	6.0
127 CH GOD (CLEVE)	1	32	38*	0.2	0.4
157 CH OF BRETHREN	1	59	71*	0.4	0.7
165 CH OF NAZARENE	2	29	146	0.8	1.4
193 EPISCOPAL.....	1	56	112	0.6	1.1
226 FRIENDS-USA...	4	207	248*	1.3	2.4
283 LUTH--MO SYNOD	1	157	235	1.2	2.3
353 PLY BRETHREN..	1	30	50	0.3	0.5
413 S-D ADVENTISTS	1	18	22*	0.1	0.2
443 UN C OF CHRIST	3	698	835*	4.4	8.0
449 UN METHODIST..	7	2,600	3,118	16.6	30.0
453 UN PRES CH USA	6	999	1,195*	6.4	11.5
RINGGOLD	23	2,461	2,973*	46.6	100.0
019 AMER BAPT CONV	1	209	240*	3.8	8.1
081 CATHOLIC......	2	0	125	2.0	4.2
093 CR CH (DISC)..	4	485	558*	8.8	18.8
221 FREE METH C NA	1	36	53	0.8	1.8
283 LUTH--MO SYNOD	1	49	89	1.4	3.0
413 S-D ADVENTISTS	1	29	33*	0.5	1.1
449 UN METHODIST..	10	1,479	1,675	26.3	56.3
453 UN PRES CH USA	3	174	200*	3.1	6.7

County and Denomination	Number of churches	Communicant, confirmed, full members	Total adherents		
			Number	Percent of total population	Percent of total adherents
SAC	38	7,633	13,306*	85.4	100.0
019 AMER BAPT CONV	1	254	304*	2.0	2.3
029 AMER LUTH CH..	1	421	540	3.5	4.1
081 CATHOLIC......	6	0	3,357	21.6	25.2
093 CR CH (DISC)..	1	372	445*	2.9	3.3
201 EVAN COV CH AM	1	39	47*	0.3	0.4
221 FREE METH C NA	1	24	35	0.2	0.3
281 LUTH CH AMER..	1	235	335	2.2	2.5
283 LUTH--MO SYNOD	9	2,508	3,441	22.1	25.9
443 UN C OF CHRIST	2	316	378*	2.4	2.8
449 UN METHODIST..	7	1,711	2,327	14.9	17.5
453 UN PRES CH USA	8	1,753	2,097*	13.5	15.8
SCOTT	82	28,725	70,974*	49.7	100.0
019 AMER BAPT CONV	2	682	861*	0.6	1.2
029 AMER LUTH CH..	2	1,037	1,536	1.1	2.2
081 CATHOLIC......	17	0	30,094	21.1	42.4
093 CR CH (DISC)..	3	931	1,175*	0.8	1.7
097 CR C AND C CR.	2	155	196*	0.1	0.3
105 CHRISTIAN REF.	1	49	84	0.1	0.1
123 CH GOD (ANDER)	1	50	115	0.1	0.2
127 CH GOD (CLEVE)	2	135	170*	0.1	0.2
165 CH OF NAZARENE	2	207	692	0.5	1.0
193 EPISCOPAL.....	3	1,409	2,044	1.4	2.9
226 FRIENDS-USA...	1	126	159*	0.1	0.2
281 LUTH CH AMER..	11	8,797	12,951	9.1	18.2
283 LUTH--MO SYNOD	5	2,796	4,106	2.9	5.8
285 MENNONITE CH..	1	35	44*	-	0.1
353 PLY BRETHREN..	1	70	175	0.1	0.2
403 SALVATION ARMY	1	88	383	0.3	0.5
413 S-D ADVENTISTS	1	213	269*	0.2	0.4
419 SO BAPT CONV..	3	622	785*	0.6	1.1
435 UNITARIAN-UNIV	1	189	270	0.2	0.4
443 UN C OF CHRIST	3	917	1,157*	0.8	1.6
449 UN METHODIST..	8	5,455	7,686	5.4	10.8
453 UN PRES CH USA	10	4,692	5,922*	4.2	8.3
469 WISC EVAN LUTH	1	70	100	0.1	0.1
SHELBY	27	5,185	12,359*	79.6	100.0
019 AMER BAPT CONV	2	459	569*	3.7	4.6
029 AMER LUTH CH..	5	2,343	3,149	20.3	25.5
081 CATHOLIC......	6	0	5,709	36.8	46.2
097 CR C AND C CR.	2	184	228*	1.5	1.8
165 CH OF NAZARENE	1	16	50	0.3	0.4
193 EPISCOPAL.....	1	60	82	0.5	0.7
413 S-D ADVENTISTS	1	33	41*	0.3	0.3
443 UN C OF CHRIST	1	289	358*	2.3	2.9
449 UN METHODIST..	7	1,644	1,978	12.7	16.0
453 UN PRES CH USA	1	157	195*	1.3	1.6
SIOUX	59	14,887	25,702*	91.8	100.0
019 AMER BAPT CONV	1	256	316*	1.1	1.2
029 AMER LUTH CH..	7	1,108	1,576	5.6	6.1
081 CATHOLIC......	6	0	3,161	11.3	12.3
105 CHRISTIAN REF.	13	4,137	7,186	25.7	28.0
157 CH OF BRETHREN	1	58	72*	0.3	0.3
283 LUTH--MO SYNOD	4	814	1,035	3.7	4.0
371 REF CH IN AM..	18	6,970	10,405	37.2	40.5
413 S-D ADVENTISTS	1	24	30*	0.1	0.1
443 UN C OF CHRIST	1	83	103*	0.4	0.4
449 UN METHODIST..	3	773	998	3.6	3.9
453 UN PRES CH USA	4	664	820*	2.9	3.2
STORY	62	21,606	33,060*	52.7	100.0
019 AMER BAPT CONV	1	360	425*	0.7	1.3
029 AMER LUTH CH..	15	7,055	9,591	15.3	29.0
081 CATHOLIC......	7	0	4,617	7.4	14.0
093 CR CH (DISC)..	5	937	1,107*	1.8	3.3
105 CHRISTIAN REF.	1	55	96	0.2	0.3
123 CH GOD (ANDER)	1	18	43	0.1	0.1
157 CH OF BRETHREN	1	37	44*	0.1	0.1
165 CH OF NAZARENE	1	80	211	0.3	0.6
193 EPISCOPAL.....	1	672	1,284	2.0	3.9
226 FRIENDS-USA...	1	26	31*	-	0.1
281 LUTH CH AMER..	1	898	1,249	2.0	3.8
283 LUTH--MO SYNOD	2	674	1,022	1.6	3.1
353 PLY BRETHREN..	1	20	26	-	0.1
413 S-D ADVENTISTS	2	388	458*	0.7	1.4
419 SO BAPT CONV..	1	238	281*	0.4	0.8
435 UNITARIAN-UNIV	1	80	190	0.3	0.6
443 UN C OF CHRIST	2	739	873*	1.4	2.6
449 UN METHODIST..	13	7,407	9,242	14.7	28.0
453 UN PRES CH USA	5	1,922	2,270*	3.6	6.9
TAMA	35	6,376	11,695*	58.0	100.0
029 AMER LUTH CH..	4	1,150	1,638	8.1	14.0
081 CATHOLIC......	7	0	3,527	17.5	30.2
093 CR CH (DISC)..	1	55	66*	0.3	0.6
283 LUTH--MO SYNOD	1	74	101	0.5	0.9
413 S-D ADVENTISTS	1	11	13*	0.1	0.1
443 UN C OF CHRIST	4	1,028	1,240*	6.2	10.6
449 UN METHODIST..	12	3,144	4,007	19.9	34.3
453 UN PRES CH USA	5	914	1,103*	5.5	9.4
TAYLOR	27	4,290	5,427*	61.7	100.0
019 AMER BAPT CONV	2	651	754*	8.6	13.9
081 CATHOLIC......	2	0	425	4.8	7.8
093 CR CH (DISC)..	4	540	626*	7.1	11.5

*Total adherents estimated from known number of communicant, confirmed, full members.

—Represents a percent less than 0.1.

Percentages may not total due to rounding.

Table 3. Churches and Church Membership by State, County and Denomination: 1971

County and Denomination	Number of churches	Communicant, confirmed, full members	Total adherents: Number	Total adherents: Percent of total population	Total adherents: Percent of total adherents
097 CR C AND C CR.	5	430	498*	5.7	9.2
165 CH OF NAZARENE	1	14	52	0.6	1.0
283 LUTH--MO SYNOD	1	61	96	1.1	1.8
449 UN METHODIST..	9	2,172	2,487	28.3	45.8
453 UN PRES CH USA	3	422	489*	5.6	9.0
UNION	27	4,552	7,519*	55.5	100.0
019 AMER BAPT CONV	1	84	101*	0.7	1.3
081 CATHOLIC......	3	0	1,762	13.0	23.4
093 CR CH (DISC)..	2	566	678*	5.0	9.0
123 CH GOD (ANDER)	1	14	32	0.2	0.4
165 CH OF NAZARENE	1	36	87	0.6	1.2
193 EPISCOPAL.....	1	61	111	0.8	1.5
281 LUTH CH AMER..	1	277	370	2.7	4.9
283 LUTH--MO SYNOD	1	333	538	4.0	7.2
353 PLY BRETHREN..	1	30	40	0.3	0.5
413 S-D ADVENTISTS	1	17	20*	0.1	0.3
443 UN C OF CHRIST	3	447	535*	3.9	7.1
449 UN METHODIST..	9	2,147	2,599	19.2	34.6
453 UN PRES CH USA	2	540	646*	4.8	8.6
VAN BUREN	28	3,272	4,089*	47.3	100.0
019 AMER BAPT CONV	2	303	361*	4.2	8.8
081 CATHOLIC......	2	0	185	2.1	4.5
097 CR C AND C CR.	4	530	632*	7.3	15.5
165 CH OF NAZARENE	2	62	109	1.3	2.7
221 FREE METH C NA	1	17	17	0.2	0.4
443 UN C OF CHRIST	1	88	105*	1.2	2.6
449 UN METHODIST..	13	2,131	2,512	29.1	61.4
453 UN PRES CH USA	3	141	168*	1.9	4.1
WAPELLO	53	9,912	17,567*	41.7	100.0
019 AMER BAPT CONV	3	727	867*	2.1	4.9
029 AMER LUTH CH..	1	211	318	0.8	1.8
081 CATHOLIC......	6	0	4,384	10.4	25.0
093 CR CH (DISC)..	8	1,901	2,268*	5.4	12.9
107 CHRISTIAN UN..	2	29	35*	0.1	0.2
123 CH GOD (ANDER)	2	139	399	0.9	2.3
157 CH OF BRETHREN	1	172	205*	0.5	1.2
165 CH OF NAZARENE	3	279	696	1.7	4.0
193 EPISCOPAL.....	1	294	349	0.8	2.0
221 FREE METH C NA	1	57	74	0.2	0.4
281 LUTH CH AMER..	2	1,177	1,592	3.8	9.1
283 LUTH--MO SYNOD	1	312	436	1.0	2.5
371 REF CH IN AM..	1	35	41	0.1	0.2
403 SALVATION ARMY	1	71	616	1.5	3.5
413 S-D ADVENTISTS	1	91	109*	0.3	0.6
419 SO BAPT CONV..	1	197	235*	0.6	1.3
443 UN C OF CHRIST	3	250	298*	0.7	1.7
449 UN METHODIST..	12	2,872	3,335	7.9	19.0
453 UN PRES CH USA	3	1,098	1,310*	3.1	7.5
WARREN	47	7,658	12,462*	45.4	100.0
019 AMER BAPT CONV	1	905	1,143*	4.2	9.2
029 AMER LUTH CH..	3	410	640	2.3	5.1
081 CATHOLIC......	7	0	2,603	9.5	20.9
093 CR CH (DISC)..	7	539	681*	2.5	5.5
107 CHRISTIAN UN..	3	159	201*	0.7	1.6
165 CH OF NAZARENE	2	122	261	1.0	2.1
226 FRIENDS-USA...	6	625	790*	2.9	6.3
283 LUTH--MO SYNOD	2	427	658	2.4	5.3
413 S-D ADVENTISTS	1	64	81*	0.3	0.6
449 UN METHODIST..	12	3,772	4,602	16.8	36.9
453 UN PRES CH USA	3	635	802*	2.9	6.4
WASHINGTON	41	8,067	12,776*	67.4	100.0
019 AMER BAPT CONV	4	625	762*	4.0	6.0
029 AMER LUTH CH..	1	269	393	2.1	3.1
081 CATHOLIC......	4	0	2,851	15.0	22.3
093 CR CH (DISC)..	2	491	599*	3.2	4.7
097 CR C AND C CR.	1	35	43*	0.2	0.3
165 CH OF NAZARENE	1	30	111	0.6	0.9
226 FRIENDS-USA...	1	27	33*	0.2	0.3
283 LUTH--MO SYNOD	1	53	73	0.4	0.6
285 MENNONITE CH..	10	1,859	2,267*	12.0	17.7
413 S-D ADVENTISTS	1	27	33*	0.2	0.3
449 UN METHODIST..	9	3,240	3,890	20.5	30.4
453 UN PRES CH USA	6	1,411	1,721*	9.1	13.5
WAYNE	21	3,017	3,419*	40.7	100.0
019 AMER BAPT CONV	4	683	783*	9.3	22.9
093 CR CH (DISC)..	4	355	407*	4.8	11.9
165 CH OF NAZARENE	1	8	9	0.1	0.3
419 SO BAPT CONV..	1	259	297*	3.5	8.7
449 UN METHODIST..	10	1,651	1,853	22.0	54.2
453 UN PRES CH USA	1	61	70*	0.8	2.0
WEBSTER	66	17,857	33,673*	69.6	100.0
019 AMER BAPT CONV	3	703	862*	1.8	2.6
029 AMER LUTH CH..	7	2,941	4,065	8.4	12.1
081 CATHOLIC......	12	0	9,291	19.2	27.6
093 CR CH (DISC)..	2	350	429*	0.9	1.3
097 CR C AND C CR.	1	50	61*	0.1	0.2
123 CH GOD (ANDER)	1	20	52	0.1	0.2
157 CH OF BRETHREN	1	85	104*	0.2	0.3
165 CH OF NAZARENE	1	103	264	0.5	0.8
193 EPISCOPAL.....	1	327	453	0.9	1.3
201 EVAN COV CH AM	3	456	559*	1.2	1.7
281 LUTH CH AMER..	5	2,076	2,791	5.8	8.3
283 LUTH--MO SYNOD	6	3,388	4,784	9.9	14.2
285 MENNONITE CH..	1	49	60*	0.1	0.2
353 PLY BRETHREN..	2	80	130	0.3	0.4
403 SALVATION ARMY	1	62	478	1.0	1.4
413 S-D ADVENTISTS	1	10	12*	-	-
443 UN C OF CHRIST	2	555	681*	1.4	2.0
449 UN METHODIST..	13	5,241	6,927	14.3	20.6
453 UN PRES CH USA	3	1,361	1,670*	3.5	5.0
WINNEBAGO	25	7,637	11,812*	90.9	100.0
029 AMER LUTH CH..	13	5,483	7,502	57.8	63.5
081 CATHOLIC......	4	0	1,533	11.8	13.0
175 CONG CR CH....	1	90	107*	0.8	0.9
313 NO AM BAPT GC.	1	203	241*	1.9	2.0
371 REF CH IN AM..	1	359	449	3.5	3.8
413 S-D ADVENTISTS	1	13	15*	0.1	0.1
449 UN METHODIST..	4	1,489	1,965	15.1	16.6
WINNESHIEK	36	7,886	16,861*	77.5	100.0
029 AMER LUTH CH..	20	6,694	8,961	41.2	53.1
081 CATHOLIC......	8	0	6,386	29.4	37.9
193 EPISCOPAL.....	1	31	31	0.1	0.2
226 FRIENDS-USA...	1	86	104*	0.5	0.6
443 UN C OF CHRIST	1	173	210*	1.0	1.2
449 UN METHODIST..	4	758	994	4.6	5.9
453 UN PRES CH USA	1	144	175*	0.8	1.0
WOODBURY	104	31,933	65,254*	63.3	100.0
019 AMER BAPT CONV	3	612	746*	0.7	1.1
029 AMER LUTH CH..	8	4,345	6,094	5.9	9.3
081 CATHOLIC......	16	0	21,622	21.0	33.1
093 CR CH (DISC)..	4	508	619*	0.6	0.9
097 CR C AND C CR.	4	565	688*	0.7	1.1
105 CHRISTIAN REF.	1	79	159	0.2	0.2
165 CH OF NAZARENE	4	254	714	0.7	1.1
193 EPISCOPAL.....	3	727	1,197	1.2	1.8
197 EVAN CH OF NA.	1	27	33*	-	0.1
201 EVAN COV CH AM	3	363	442*	0.4	0.7
221 FREE METH C NA	1	41	50	-	0.1
281 LUTH CH AMER..	5	3,115	4,426	4.3	6.8
283 LUTH--MO SYNOD	11	4,299	6,284	6.1	9.6
353 PLY BRETHREN..	1	30	50	-	0.1
371 REF CH IN AM..	1	224	413	0.4	0.6
403 SALVATION ARMY	1	131	1,061	1.0	1.6
413 S-D ADVENTISTS	1	154	188*	0.2	0.3
435 UNITARIAN-UNIV	1	97	130	0.1	0.2
443 UN C OF CHRIST	6	1,471	1,792*	1.7	2.7
449 UN METHODIST..	21	10,984	13,743	13.3	21.1
453 UN PRES CH USA	7	3,735	4,550*	4.4	7.0
469 WISC EVAN LUTH	1	172	253	0.2	0.4
WORTH	19	5,362	7,613*	84.9	100.0
029 AMER LUTH CH..	12	3,594	4,888	54.5	64.2
081 CATHOLIC......	1	0	545	6.1	7.2
097 CR C AND C CR.	1	150	179*	2.0	2.4
281 LUTH CH AMER..	1	523	663	7.4	8.7
449 UN METHODIST..	4	1,095	1,338	14.9	17.6
WRIGHT	34	8,244	13,069*	75.6	100.0
019 AMER BAPT CONV	1	142	169*	1.0	1.3
029 AMER LUTH CH..	9	2,908	3,982	23.0	30.5
081 CATHOLIC......	3	0	2,179	12.6	16.7
097 CR C AND C CR.	2	320	382*	2.2	2.9
165 CH OF NAZARENE	1	19	57	0.3	0.4
283 LUTH--MO SYNOD	2	209	317	1.8	2.4
371 REF CH IN AM..	2	258	410	2.4	3.1
443 UN C OF CHRIST	4	835	996*	5.8	7.6
449 UN METHODIST..	7	2,892	3,789	21.9	29.0
453 UN PRES CH USA	3	661	788*	4.6	6.0
CO DATA NOT AVAIL	42	2,553	9,045*	N/A	N/A
151 L-D SAINTS....	0	0	5,655	N/A	N/A
223 FREE WILL BAPT	1	100	122*	N/A	N/A
467 WESLEYAN......	41	2,453	3,268	N/A	N/A

KANSAS

County and Denomination	Number of churches	Communicant, confirmed, full members	Total adherents: Number	Total adherents: Percent of total population	Total adherents: Percent of total adherents
THE STATE.....	3,382	696,641	1,184,802*	52.7	100.0
ALLEN	34	5,476	7,633*	50.7	100.0
019 AMER BAPT CONV	2	629	739*	4.9	9.7
081 CATHOLIC......	2	0	1,213	8.1	15.9
093 CR CH (DISC)..	1	278	327*	2.2	4.3
097 CR C AND C CR.	5	453	532*	3.5	7.0
165 CH OF NAZARENE	2	217	284	1.9	3.7
193 EPISCOPAL.....	1	64	77	0.5	1.0
201 EVAN COV CH AM	1	78	92*	0.6	1.2
281 LUTH CH AMER..	1	138	188	1.2	2.5

*Total adherents estimated from known number of communicant, confirmed, full members.

—Represents a percent less than 0.1.

Percentages may not total due to rounding.

Table 3. Churches and Church Membership by State, County and Denomination: 1971

County and Denomination	Number of churches	Communicant, confirmed, full members	Total adherents: Number	Total adherents: Percent of total population	Total adherents: Percent of total adherents
283 LUTH--MO SYNOD	2	468	631	4.2	8.3
413 S-D ADVENTISTS	1	89	105*	0.7	1.4
419 SO BAPT CONV..	1	71	83*	0.6	1.1
449 UN METHODIST..	11	2,434	2,708	18.0	35.5
453 UN PRES CH USA	4	557	654*	4.3	8.6
ANDERSON	26	2,501	5,498*	64.7	100.0
019 AMER BAPT CONV	3	453	539*	6.3	9.8
081 CATHOLIC......	5	0	2,550	30.0	46.4
097 CR C AND C CR.	3	525	624*	7.3	11.3
157 CH OF BRETHREN	1	28	33*	0.4	0.6
165 CH OF NAZARENE	1	39	127	1.5	2.3
285 MENNONITE CH..	1	23	27*	0.3	0.5
353 PLY BRETHREN..	1	20	40	0.5	0.7
449 UN METHODIST..	10	1,302	1,426	16.8	25.9
453 UN PRES CH USA	1	111	132*	1.6	2.4
ATCHISON	32	5,163	12,076*	63.0	100.0
019 AMER BAPT CONV	1	437	526*	2.7	4.4
081 CATHOLIC......	7	0	5,290	27.6	43.8
093 CR CH (DISC)..	4	1,072	1,290*	6.7	10.7
097 CR C AND C CR.	4	205	247*	1.3	2.0
165 CH OF NAZARENE	1	28	107	0.6	0.9
193 EPISCOPAL.....	1	190	335	1.7	2.8
281 LUTH CH AMER..	2	578	733	3.8	6.1
283 LUTH--MO SYNOD	1	576	854	4.5	7.1
353 PLY BRETHREN..	1	20	40	0.2	0.3
403 SALVATION ARMY	1	71	246	1.3	2.0
413 S-D ADVENTISTS	1	55	66*	0.3	0.5
419 SO BAPT CONV..	1	60	72*	0.4	0.6
443 UN C OF CHRIST	1	182	219*	1.1	1.8
449 UN METHODIST..	4	1,206	1,470	7.7	12.2
453 UN PRES CH USA	2	483	581*	3.0	4.8
BARBER	22	3,621	4,965*	70.8	100.0
019 AMER BAPT CONV	1	88	103*	1.5	2.1
081 CATHOLIC......	3	0	791	11.3	15.9
093 CR CH (DISC)..	1	61	71*	1.0	1.4
097 CR C AND C CR.	2	1,139	1,332*	19.0	26.8
165 CH OF NAZARENE	1	12	12	0.2	0.2
193 EPISCOPAL.....	1	27	48	0.7	1.0
283 LUTH--MO SYNOD	1	104	151	2.2	3.0
349 PENT HOLINESS.	1	20	23*	0.3	0.5
413 S-D ADVENTISTS	1	15	18*	0.3	0.4
443 UN C OF CHRIST	2	270	316*	4.5	6.4
449 UN METHODIST..	5	1,700	1,884	26.9	37.9
453 UN PRES CH USA	3	185	216*	3.1	4.4
BARTON	51	11,441	23,081*	75.3	100.0
019 AMER BAPT CONV	1	598	729*	2.4	3.2
029 AMER LUTH CH..	1	88	109	0.4	0.5
081 CATHOLIC......	10	0	8,869	28.9	38.4
093 CR CH (DISC)..	2	962	1,173*	3.8	5.1
097 CR C AND C CR.	2	125	152*	0.5	0.7
123 CH GOD (ANDER)	1	21	52	0.2	0.2
165 CH OF NAZARENE	2	277	617	2.0	2.7
193 EPISCOPAL.....	1	159	303	1.0	1.3
226 FRIENDS-USA...	2	72	88*	0.3	0.4
281 LUTH CH AMER..	2	481	623	2.0	2.7
283 LUTH--MO SYNOD	4	1,684	2,107	6.9	9.1
287 MENN GEN CONF.	1	217	265*	0.9	1.1
313 NO AM BAPT GC.	2	226	276*	0.9	1.2
413 S-D ADVENTISTS	1	68	83*	0.3	0.4
419 SO BAPT CONV..	5	910	1,110*	3.6	4.8
443 UN C OF CHRIST	3	997	1,216*	4.0	5.3
449 UN METHODIST..	10	3,992	4,621	15.1	20.0
453 UN PRES CH USA	1	564	688*	2.2	3.0
BOURBON	30	4,558	6,950*	45.7	100.0
019 AMER BAPT CONV	5	874	1,014*	6.7	14.6
059 BAPT MISS ASSN	1	84	97*	0.6	1.4
081 CATHOLIC......	3	0	1,465	9.6	21.1
093 CR CH (DISC)..	2	491	570*	3.7	8.2
157 CH OF BRETHREN	1	43	50*	0.3	0.7
165 CH OF NAZARENE	1	153	310	2.0	4.5
193 EPISCOPAL.....	1	133	233	1.5	3.4
283 LUTH--MO SYNOD	1	55	75	0.5	1.1
413 S-D ADVENTISTS	1	33	38*	0.2	0.5
419 SO BAPT CONV..	1	145	168*	1.1	2.4
449 UN METHODIST..	12	2,033	2,334	15.3	33.6
453 UN PRES CH USA	1	514	596*	3.9	8.6
BROWN	34	5,802	7,909*	67.7	100.0
019 AMER BAPT CONV	4	714	833*	7.1	10.5
029 AMER LUTH CH..	3	506	652	5.6	8.2
075 BRETHREN IN CR	1	27	32*	0.3	0.4
081 CATHOLIC......	2	0	1,250	10.7	15.8
093 CR CH (DISC)..	3	669	781*	6.7	9.9
097 CR C AND C CR.	3	185	216*	1.8	2.7
157 CH OF BRETHREN	1	141	165*	1.4	2.1
283 LUTH--MO SYNOD	3	524	656	5.6	8.3
413 S-D ADVENTISTS	1	26	30*	0.3	0.4
443 UN C OF CHRIST	2	345	403*	3.4	5.1
449 UN METHODIST..	10	2,376	2,554	21.9	32.3
453 UN PRES CH USA	1	289	337*	2.9	4.3
BUTLER	64	13,210	18,329*	47.4	100.0
019 AMER BAPT CONV	10	2,944	3,553*	9.2	19.4
059 BAPT MISS ASSN	1	39	47*	0.1	0.3
081 CATHOLIC......	2	0	1,909	4.9	10.4
093 CR CH (DISC)..	7	1,842	2,223*	5.8	12.1
097 CR C AND C CR.	5	397	479*	1.2	2.6
123 CH GOD (ANDER)	1	121	303	0.8	1.7
127 CH GOD (CLEVE)	1	24	29*	0.1	0.2
165 CH OF NAZARENE	3	272	650	1.7	3.5
193 EPISCOPAL.....	1	309	375	1.0	2.0
226 FRIENDS-USA...	1	37	45*	0.1	0.2
283 LUTH--MO SYNOD	2	399	574	1.5	3.1
287 MENN GEN CONF.	1	186	225*	0.6	1.2
349 PENT HOLINESS.	1	25	30*	0.1	0.2
403 SALVATION ARMY	1	48	226	0.6	1.2
413 S-D ADVENTISTS	1	23	28*	0.1	0.2
419 SO BAPT CONV..	6	1,018	1,229*	3.2	6.7
443 UN C OF CHRIST	2	382	461*	1.2	2.5
449 UN METHODIST..	15	4,560	5,238	13.5	28.6
453 UN PRES CH USA	3	584	705*	1.8	3.8
CHASE	15	1,455	1,817*	53.3	100.0
081 CATHOLIC......	1	0	215	6.3	11.8
093 CR CH (DISC)..	1	55	64*	1.9	3.5
097 CR C AND C CR.	3	36	42*	1.2	2.3
226 FRIENDS-USA...	1	39	45*	1.3	2.5
283 LUTH--MO SYNOD	1	71	94	2.8	5.2
419 SO BAPT CONV..	1	137	158*	4.6	8.7
449 UN METHODIST..	6	850	890	26.1	49.0
453 UN PRES CH USA	1	267	309*	9.1	17.0
CHAUTAUQUA	18	1,844	2,121*	45.7	100.0
019 AMER BAPT CONV	2	607	688*	14.8	32.4
081 CATHOLIC......	2	0	29	0.6	1.4
093 CR CH (DISC)..	1	139	158*	3.4	7.4
097 CR C AND C CR.	2	140	159*	3.4	7.5
193 EPISCOPAL.....	2	112	179	3.9	8.4
413 S-D ADVENTISTS	1	42	48*	1.0	2.3
419 SO BAPT CONV..	1	140	159*	3.4	7.5
449 UN METHODIST..	7	664	701	15.1	33.1
CHEROKEE	53	6,808	9,598*	44.5	100.0
019 AMER BAPT CONV	1	307	366*	1.7	3.8
059 BAPT MISS ASSN	1	366	436*	2.0	4.5
081 CATHOLIC......	6	0	1,397	6.5	14.6
093 CR CH (DISC)..	4	944	1,126*	5.2	11.7
097 CR C AND C CR.	5	683	814*	3.8	8.5
165 CH OF NAZARENE	4	165	343	1.6	3.6
193 EPISCOPAL.....	2	53	92	0.4	1.0
226 FRIENDS-USA...	4	207	247*	1.1	2.6
413 S-D ADVENTISTS	1	58	69*	0.3	0.7
419 SO BAPT CONV..	11	2,042	2,435*	11.3	25.4
449 UN METHODIST..	10	1,470	1,661	7.7	17.3
453 UN PRES CH USA	4	513	612*	2.8	6.4
CHEYENNE	12	1,595	2,307*	54.2	100.0
029 AMER LUTH CH..	3	778	1,070	25.1	46.4
081 CATHOLIC......	2	0	273	6.4	11.8
093 CR CH (DISC)..	1	361	426*	10.0	18.5
226 FRIENDS-USA...	2	21	25*	0.6	1.1
413 S-D ADVENTISTS	1	33	39*	0.9	1.7
449 UN METHODIST..	3	402	474	11.1	20.5
CLARK	10	1,485	2,156*	74.4	100.0
019 AMER BAPT CONV	2	77	90*	3.1	4.2
081 CATHOLIC......	1	0	300	10.4	13.9
097 CR C AND C CR.	3	467	543*	18.8	25.2
123 CH GOD (ANDER)	1	45	168	5.8	7.8
449 UN METHODIST..	2	723	854	29.5	39.6
453 UN PRES CH USA	1	173	201*	6.9	9.3
CLAY	25	5,011	6,482*	65.5	100.0
019 AMER BAPT CONV	1	267	312*	3.2	4.8
081 CATHOLIC......	1	0	549	5.6	8.5
093 CR CH (DISC)..	1	75	88*	0.9	1.4
097 CR C AND C CR.	2	298	348*	3.5	5.4
193 EPISCOPAL.....	2	164	192	1.9	3.0
201 EVAN COV CH AM	1	54	63*	0.6	1.0
281 LUTH CH AMER..	1	129	155	1.6	2.4
283 LUTH--MO SYNOD	1	531	736	7.4	11.4
443 UN C OF CHRIST	1	92	107*	1.1	1.7
449 UN METHODIST..	10	2,182	2,509	25.4	38.7
453 UN PRES CH USA	4	1,219	1,423*	14.4	22.0
CLOUD	28	4,484	8,855*	65.8	100.0
019 AMER BAPT CONV	2	615	723*	5.4	8.2
029 AMER LUTH CH..	1	201	257	1.9	2.9
081 CATHOLIC......	8	0	3,536	26.3	39.9
097 CR C AND C CR.	3	570	670*	5.0	7.6
165 CH OF NAZARENE	1	27	27	0.2	0.3
193 EPISCOPAL.....	1	151	160	1.2	1.8
201 EVAN COV CH AM	1	144	169*	1.3	1.9
281 LUTH CH AMER..	1	179	218	1.6	2.5
449 UN METHODIST..	7	2,062	2,466	18.3	27.8
453 UN PRES CH USA	3	535	629*	4.7	7.1
COFFEY	21	3,645	4,488*	60.7	100.0
019 AMER BAPT CONV	1	163	189*	2.6	4.2
081 CATHOLIC......	1	[illegible]	[illegible]	[illegible]	[illegible]

*Total adherents estimated from known number of communicant, confirmed, full members.

—Represents a percent less than 0.1.

Table 3. Churches and Church Membership by State, County and Denomination: 1971

County and Denomination	Number of churches	Communicant, confirmed, full members	Total adherents Number	Total adherents Percent of total population	Total adherents Percent of total adherents
097 CR C AND C CR.	5	972	1,128*	15.2	25.1
157 CH OF BRETHREN	2	48	56*	0.8	1.2
165 CH OF NAZARENE	1	34	75	1.0	1.7
283 LUTH--MO SYNOD	2	207	273	3.7	6.1
419 SO BAPT CONV..	1	78	90*	1.2	2.0
449 UN METHODIST..	7	2,115	2,345	31.7	52.3
453 UN PRES CH USA	1	28	32*	0.4	0.7
COMANCHE	12	2,057	2,356*	87.2	100.0
019 AMER BAPT CONV	2	265	306*	11.3	13.0
093 CR CH (DISC)..	2	307	355*	13.1	15.1
097 CR C AND C CR.	2	390	451*	16.7	19.1
226 FRIENDS-USA...	1	33	38*	1.4	1.6
285 MENNONITE CH..	1	100	115*	4.3	4.9
449 UN METHODIST..	3	824	931	34.5	39.5
453 UN PRES CH USA	1	138	159*	5.9	6.7
COWLEY	61	13,174	18,608*	53.1	100.0
019 AMER BAPT CONV	4	1,617	1,909*	5.5	10.3
081 CATHOLIC......	2	0	1,935	5.5	10.4
093 CR CH (DISC)..	5	1,577	1,862*	5.3	10.0
097 CR C AND C CR.	3	265	313*	0.9	1.7
121 CH GOD (ABR)..	1	35	41*	0.1	0.2
123 CH GOD (ANDER)	3	114	310	0.9	1.7
127 CH GOD (CLEVE)	2	37	44*	0.1	0.2
165 CH OF NAZARENE	3	250	578	1.7	3.1
193 EPISCOPAL.....	2	403	662	1.9	3.6
221 FREE METH C NA	1	37	55	0.2	0.3
226 FRIENDS-USA...	2	86	102*	0.3	0.5
283 LUTH--MO SYNOD	2	906	1,248	3.6	6.7
403 SALVATION ARMY	1	65	522	1.5	2.8
413 S-D ADVENTISTS	2	62	73*	0.2	0.4
419 SO BAPT CONV..	7	1,603	1,893*	5.4	10.2
443 UN C OF CHRIST	1	63	74*	0.2	0.4
449 UN METHODIST..	15	4,348	4,972	14.2	26.7
453 UN PRES CH USA	5	1,706	2,015*	5.8	10.8
CRAWFORD	64	11,032	20,072*	53.0	100.0
019 AMER BAPT CONV	4	1,428	1,648*	4.4	8.2
029 AMER LUTH CH..	1	307	423	1.1	2.1
059 BAPT MISS ASSN	2	86	99*	0.3	0.5
081 CATHOLIC......	10	0	6,839	18.1	34.1
093 CR CH (DISC)..	4	1,283	1,480*	3.9	7.4
097 CR C AND C CR.	7	585	675*	1.8	3.4
127 CH GOD (CLEVE)	1	116	134*	0.4	0.7
157 CH OF BRETHREN	1	114	132*	0.3	0.7
165 CH OF NAZARENE	3	209	358	0.9	1.8
193 EPISCOPAL.....	1	231	281	0.7	1.4
283 LUTH--MO SYNOD	4	716	928	2.5	4.6
403 SALVATION ARMY	1	69	316	0.8	1.6
413 S-D ADVENTISTS	2	145	167*	0.4	0.8
419 SO BAPT CONV..	4	704	812*	2.1	4.0
449 UN METHODIST..	14	3,896	4,461	11.8	22.2
453 UN PRES CH USA	5	1,143	1,319*	3.5	6.6
DECATUR	19	2,156	2,898*	58.1	100.0
019 AMER BAPT CONV	1	178	208*	4.2	7.2
029 AMER LUTH CH..	2	167	225	4.5	7.8
081 CATHOLIC......	1	0	272	5.5	9.4
093 CR CH (DISC)..	2	128	149*	3.0	5.1
165 CH OF NAZARENE	1	25	50	1.0	1.7
201 EVAN COV CH AM	2	119	139*	2.8	4.8
283 LUTH--MO SYNOD	1	216	314	6.3	10.8
413 S-D ADVENTISTS	1	14	16*	0.3	0.6
419 SO BAPT CONV..	1	70	82*	1.6	2.8
449 UN METHODIST..	6	1,108	1,290	25.9	44.5
453 UN PRES CH USA	1	131	153*	3.1	5.3
DICKINSON	57	9,673	13,841*	69.2	100.0
019 AMER BAPT CONV	5	622	735*	3.7	5.3
029 AMER LUTH CH..	2	437	604	3.0	4.4
075 BRETHREN IN CR	3	232	274*	1.4	2.0
081 CATHOLIC......	5	0	1,984	9.9	14.3
093 CR CH (DISC)..	1	139	164*	0.8	1.2
097 CR C AND C CR.	3	745	880*	4.4	6.4
123 CH GOD (ANDER)	1	40	139	0.7	1.0
157 CH OF BRETHREN	2	115	136*	0.7	1.0
165 CH OF NAZARENE	2	51	155	0.8	1.1
193 EPISCOPAL.....	1	44	44	0.2	0.3
281 LUTH CH AMER..	2	526	652	3.3	4.7
283 LUTH--MO SYNOD	4	938	1,217	6.1	8.8
313 NO AM BAPT GC.	2	212	250*	1.3	1.8
353 PLY BRETHREN..	1	20	40	0.2	0.3
413 S-D ADVENTISTS	2	175	207*	1.0	1.5
419 SO BAPT CONV..	1	25	30*	0.2	0.2
443 UN C OF CHRIST	2	388	458*	2.3	3.3
449 UN METHODIST..	13	4,064	4,809	24.1	34.7
453 UN PRES CH USA	5	900	1,063*	5.3	7.7
DONIPHAN	28	3,266	5,406*	59.4	100.0
019 AMER BAPT CONV	6	965	1,160*	12.7	21.5
081 CATHOLIC......	5	0	1,460	16.0	27.0
093 CR CH (DISC)..	3	325	391*	4.3	7.2
097 CR C AND C CR.	3	200	240*	2.6	4.4
281 LUTH CH AMER..	1	259	327	3.6	6.0
283 LUTH--MO SYNOD	1	184	216	2.4	4.0
413 S-D ADVENTISTS	1	35	42*	0.5	0.8
443 UN C OF CHRIST	1	161	193*	2.1	3.6
449 UN METHODIST..	6	1,014	1,229	13.5	22.7

County and Denomination	Number of churches	Communicant, confirmed, full members	Total adherents Number	Total adherents Percent of total population	Total adherents Percent of total adherents
453 UN PRES CH USA	1	123	148*	1.6	2.7
DOUGLAS	54	13,021	19,450*	33.6	100.0
019 AMER BAPT CONV	2	652	762*	1.3	3.9
029 AMER LUTH CH..	1	98	151	0.3	0.8
081 CATHOLIC......	4	0	3,600	6.2	18.5
093 CR CH (DISC)..	3	707	826*	1.4	4.2
097 CR C AND C CR.	2	250	292*	0.5	1.5
123 CH GOD (ANDER)	1	50	120	0.2	0.6
157 CH OF BRETHREN	2	179	209*	0.4	1.1
165 CH OF NAZARENE	2	249	426	0.7	2.2
193 EPISCOPAL.....	1	507	685	1.2	3.5
221 FREE METH C NA	1	78	87	0.2	0.4
226 FRIENDS-USA...	3	179	209*	0.4	1.1
281 LUTH CH AMER..	1	1,103	1,398	2.4	7.2
283 LUTH--MO SYNOD	2	466	645	1.1	3.3
349 PENT HOLINESS.	1	33	39*	0.1	0.2
353 PLY BRETHREN..	1	50	80	0.1	0.4
403 SALVATION ARMY	1	58	230	0.4	1.2
413 S-D ADVENTISTS	1	42	49*	0.1	0.3
419 SO BAPT CONV..	4	1,243	1,452*	2.5	7.5
435 UNITARIAN-UNIV	1	160	220	0.4	1.1
443 UN C OF CHRIST	3	1,161	1,356*	2.3	7.0
449 UN METHODIST..	14	4,472	5,114	8.8	26.3
453 UN PRES CH USA	3	1,284	1,500*	2.6	7.7
EDWARDS	17	1,788	3,328*	72.6	100.0
019 AMER BAPT CONV	2	88	104*	2.3	3.1
081 CATHOLIC......	4	0	1,230	26.9	37.0
093 CR CH (DISC)..	2	190	224*	4.9	6.7
165 CH OF NAZARENE	1	35	88	1.9	2.6
193 EPISCOPAL.....	1	51	59	1.3	1.8
283 LUTH--MO SYNOD	1	174	210	4.6	6.3
443 UN C OF CHRIST	1	217	256*	5.6	7.7
449 UN METHODIST..	5	1,033	1,157	25.3	34.8
ELK	15	1,813	2,196*	56.9	100.0
019 AMER BAPT CONV	3	399	452*	11.7	20.6
081 CATHOLIC......	1	0	215	5.6	9.8
093 CR CH (DISC)..	1	49	56*	1.5	2.6
097 CR C AND C CR.	4	387	439*	11.4	20.0
449 UN METHODIST..	5	932	982	25.5	44.7
453 UN PRES CH USA	1	46	52*	1.3	2.4
ELLIS	26	3,665	16,607*	67.2	100.0
019 AMER BAPT CONV	2	283	341*	1.4	2.1
029 AMER LUTH CH..	1	183	250	1.0	1.5
081 CATHOLIC......	12	0	11,956	48.3	72.0
097 CR C AND C CR.	1	56	67*	0.3	0.4
165 CH OF NAZARENE	1	71	187	0.8	1.1
193 EPISCOPAL.....	2	199	242	1.0	1.5
281 LUTH CH AMER..	2	548	744	3.0	4.5
283 LUTH--MO SYNOD	1	183	267	1.1	1.6
419 SO BAPT CONV..	1	146	176*	0.7	1.1
449 UN METHODIST..	2	1,507	1,788	7.2	10.8
453 UN PRES CH USA	1	489	589*	2.4	3.5
ELLSWORTH	18	2,932	4,860*	79.1	100.0
029 AMER LUTH CH..	1	182	238	3.9	4.9
081 CATHOLIC......	4	0	1,257	20.5	25.9
193 EPISCOPAL.....	1	46	52	0.8	1.1
281 LUTH CH AMER..	1	58	66	1.1	1.4
283 LUTH--MO SYNOD	3	858	1,182	19.2	24.3
313 NO AM BAPT GC.	1	270	313*	5.1	6.4
443 UN C OF CHRIST	1	225	261*	4.2	5.4
449 UN METHODIST..	4	739	849	13.8	17.5
453 UN PRES CH USA	2	554	642*	10.4	13.2
FINNEY	21	5,8[illegible]	12,097*	63.8	100.0
019 AMER BAPT CONV	1	478	610*	3.2	5.0
029 AMER LUTH CH..	1	217	350	1.8	2.9
081 CATHOLIC......	2	0	4,310	22.7	35.6
093 CR CH (DISC)..	1	530	677*	3.6	5.6
097 CR C AND C CR.	3	225	287*	1.5	2.4
123 CH GOD (ANDER)	1	47	157	0.8	1.3
157 CH OF BRETHREN	1	165	211*	1.1	1.7
165 CH OF NAZARENE	2	275	641	3.4	5.3
193 EPISCOPAL.....	1	162	246	1.3	2.0
283 LUTH--MO SYNOD	1	375	540	2.9	4.5
413 S-D ADVENTISTS	1	54	69*	0.4	0.6
419 SO BAPT CONV..	1	300	383*	2.0	3.2
443 UN C OF CHRIST	1	390	498*	2.6	4.1
449 UN METHODIST..	2	2,146	2,535	13.4	21.0
453 UN PRES CH USA	2	457	583*	3.1	4.8
FORD	32	7,776	15,803*	70.0	100.0
019 AMER BAPT CONV	1	1,299	1,588*	7.0	10.0
029 AMER LUTH CH..	1	314	462	2.0	2.9
081 CATHOLIC......	6	0	5,501	24.4	34.8
097 CR C AND C CR.	4	1,490	1,821*	8.1	11.5
123 CH GOD (ANDER)	1	63	174	0.8	1.1
165 CH OF NAZARENE	2	264	572	2.5	3.6
193 EPISCOPAL.....	1	313	417	1.8	2.6
221 FREE METH C NA	1	32	38	0.2	0.2
283 LUTH--MO SYNOD	3	493	646	2.9	4.1
349 PENT HOLINESS.	1	39	48*	0.2	0.3
403 SALVATION ARMY	1	37	215	1.0	1.4
413 S-D ADVENTISTS	1	21	26*	0.1	0.2

*Total adherents estimated from known number of communicant, confirmed, full members.

—Represents a percent less than 0.1.

Percentages may not total due to rounding.

Table 3. Churches and Church Membership by State, County and Denomination: 1971

County and Denomination	Number of churches	Communicant, confirmed, full members	Total adherents: Number	Total adherents: Percent of total population	Total adherents: Percent of total adherents
419 SO BAPT CONV..	1	158	193*	0.9	1.2
443 UN C OF CHRIST	1	78	95*	0.4	0.6
449 UN METHODIST..	3	2,290	2,925	12.9	18.5
453 UN PRES CH USA	4	885	1,082*	4.8	6.8
FRANKLIN	36	7,375	10,404*	52.0	100.0
019 AMER BAPT CONV	9	2,143	2,561*	12.8	24.6
081 CATHOLIC......	2	0	1,475	7.4	14.2
093 CR CH (DISC)..	3	479	572*	2.9	5.5
157 CH OF BRETHREN	2	166	198*	1.0	1.9
165 CH OF NAZARENE	1	98	127	0.6	1.2
193 EPISCOPAL.....	1	172	259	1.3	2.5
221 FREE METH C NA	2	40	46	0.2	0.4
283 LUTH--MO SYNOD	1	249	416	2.1	4.0
353 PLY BRETHREN..	1	20	30	0.1	0.3
413 S-D ADVENTISTS	1	55	66*	0.3	0.6
449 UN METHODIST..	10	3,468	4,074	20.4	39.2
453 UN PRES CH USA	3	485	580*	2.9	5.6
GEARY	22	5,631	10,203*	36.3	100.0
081 CATHOLIC......	2	0	2,920	10.4	28.6
097 CR C AND C CR.	1	650	778*	2.8	7.6
123 CH GOD (ANDER)	1	42	122	0.4	1.2
127 CH GOD (CLEVE)	1	17	20*	0.1	0.2
165 CH OF NAZARENE	1	55	252	0.9	2.5
193 EPISCOPAL.....	1	327	511	1.8	5.0
221 FREE METH C NA	1	20	48	0.2	0.5
281 LUTH CH AMER..	1	94	140	0.5	1.4
283 LUTH--MO SYNOD	2	584	828	2.9	8.1
313 NO AM BAPT GC.	1	27	32*	0.1	0.3
403 SALVATION ARMY	1	43	145	0.5	1.4
413 S-D ADVENTISTS	2	42	50*	0.2	0.5
419 SO BAPT CONV..	1	799	957*	3.4	9.4
443 UN C OF CHRIST	3	477	571*	2.0	5.6
449 UN METHODIST..	2	1,698	1,924	6.8	18.9
453 UN PRES CH USA	1	756	905*	3.2	8.9
GOVE	8	1,026	2,804*	71.2	100.0
081 CATHOLIC......	3	0	1,527	38.8	54.5
157 CH OF BRETHREN	1	351	437*	11.1	15.6
449 UN METHODIST..	4	675	840	21.3	30.0
GRAHAM	13	1,473	2,639*	55.5	100.0
081 CATHOLIC......	2	0	789	16.6	29.9
097 CR C AND C CR.	1	400	484*	10.2	18.3
123 CH GOD (ANDER)	1	30	70	1.5	2.7
283 LUTH--MO SYNOD	1	64	100	2.1	3.8
419 SO BAPT CONV..	1	140	169*	3.6	6.4
449 UN METHODIST..	6	726	890	18.7	33.7
453 UN PRES CH USA	1	113	137*	2.9	5.2
GRANT	9	1,999	3,459*	58.0	100.0
019 AMER BAPT CONV	1	415	528*	8.9	15.3
081 CATHOLIC......	1	0	775	13.0	22.4
093 CR CH (DISC)..	1	198	252*	4.2	7.3
123 CH GOD (ANDER)	1	60	185	3.1	5.3
165 CH OF NAZARENE	1	28	62	1.0	1.8
193 EPISCOPAL.....	1	71	147	2.5	4.2
283 LUTH--MO SYNOD	1	86	138	2.3	4.0
419 SO BAPT CONV..	1	315	401*	6.7	11.6
449 UN METHODIST..	1	826	971	16.3	28.1
GRAY	10	1,416	2,106*	46.6	100.0
081 CATHOLIC......	1	0	385	8.5	18.3
093 CR CH (DISC)..	1	109	131*	2.9	6.2
097 CR C AND C CR.	1	80	96*	2.1	4.6
165 CH OF NAZARENE	1	94	169	3.7	8.0
287 MENN GEN CONF.	1	31	37*	0.8	1.8
419 SO BAPT CONV..	1	91	110*	2.4	5.2
449 UN METHODIST..	4	1,011	1,178	26.1	55.9
GREELEY	5	860	1,251*	68.8	100.0
019 AMER BAPT CONV	1	299	366*	20.1	29.3
081 CATHOLIC......	1	0	204	11.2	16.3
281 LUTH CH AMER..	1	104	146	8.0	11.7
449 UN METHODIST..	1	335	385	21.2	30.8
453 UN PRES CH USA	1	122	150*	8.2	12.0
GREENWOOD	28	3,592	4,544*	49.7	100.0
081 CATHOLIC......	3	0	380	4.2	8.4
093 CR CH (DISC)..	3	539	620*	6.8	13.6
097 CR C AND C CR.	3	73	84*	0.9	1.8
123 CH GOD (ANDER)	1	25	40	0.4	0.9
165 CH OF NAZARENE	2	112	192	2.1	4.2
281 LUTH CH AMER..	1	291	343	3.8	7.5
413 S-D ADVENTISTS	1	54	62*	0.7	1.4
419 SO BAPT CONV..	3	447	514*	5.6	11.3
443 UN C OF CHRIST	1	184	212*	2.3	4.7
449 UN METHODIST..	9	1,780	1,997	21.8	43.9
453 UN PRES CH USA	1	87	100*	1.1	2.2
HAMILTON	7	1,141	1,598*	58.2	100.0
019 AMER BAPT CONV	1	38	46*	1.7	2.9
081 CATHOLIC......	1	0	262	9.5	16.4
097 CR C AND C CR.	1	225	270*	9.8	16.9
449 UN METHODIST..	2	573	654	23.8	40.9
453 UN PRES CH USA	2	305	366*	13.3	22.9
HARPER	30	4,501	6,132*	77.9	100.0
019 AMER BAPT CONV	3	734	842*	10.7	13.7
081 CATHOLIC......	3	0	910	11.6	14.8
093 CR CH (DISC)..	2	504	578*	7.3	9.4
097 CR C AND C CR.	4	702	806*	10.2	13.1
123 CH GOD (ANDER)	1	30	95	1.2	1.5
165 CH OF NAZARENE	1	49	88	1.1	1.4
193 EPISCOPAL.....	1	29	35	0.4	0.6
285 MENNONITE CH..	2	256	294*	3.7	4.8
413 S-D ADVENTISTS	1	50	57*	0.7	0.9
419 SO BAPT CONV..	1	51	59*	0.7	1.0
443 UN C OF CHRIST	1	137	157*	2.0	2.6
449 UN METHODIST..	6	1,543	1,734	22.0	28.3
453 UN PRES CH USA	4	416	477*	6.1	7.8
HARVEY	47	12,576	18,527*	68.0	100.0
019 AMER BAPT CONV	2	944	1,129*	4.1	6.1
081 CATHOLIC......	3	0	3,257	12.0	17.6
093 CR CH (DISC)..	3	699	836*	3.1	4.5
097 CR C AND C CR.	1	200	239*	0.9	1.3
123 CH GOD (ANDER)	1	30	115	0.4	0.6
127 CH GOD (CLEVE)	1	16	19*	0.1	0.1
157 CH OF BRETHREN	1	74	89*	0.3	0.5
165 CH OF NAZARENE	1	298	474	1.7	2.6
193 EPISCOPAL.....	1	214	252	0.9	1.4
221 FREE METH C NA	1	65	101	0.4	0.5
283 LUTH--MO SYNOD	1	508	711	2.6	3.8
285 MENNONITE CH..	3	805	963*	3.5	5.2
287 MENN GEN CONF.	9	3,508	4,196*	15.4	22.6
403 SALVATION ARMY	1	40	185	0.7	1.0
413 S-D ADVENTISTS	1	29	35*	0.1	0.2
419 SO BAPT CONV..	2	119	142*	0.5	0.8
443 UN C OF CHRIST	3	446	534*	2.0	2.9
449 UN METHODIST..	9	3,756	4,263	15.7	23.0
453 UN PRES CH USA	2	807	965*	3.5	5.2
469 WISC EVAN LUTH	1	18	22	0.1	0.1
HASKELL	9	1,584	2,374*	64.7	100.0
019 AMER BAPT CONV	1	66	82*	2.2	3.5
081 CATHOLIC......	1	0	220	6.0	9.3
097 CR C AND C CR.	1	275	343*	9.3	14.4
123 CH GOD (ANDER)	1	85	243	6.6	10.2
165 CH OF NAZARENE	1	113	211	5.7	8.9
419 SO BAPT CONV..	2	285	356*	9.7	15.0
449 UN METHODIST..	2	760	919	25.0	38.7
HODGEMAN	10	1,008	1,657*	62.2	100.0
019 AMER BAPT CONV	2	177	211*	7.9	12.7
081 CATHOLIC......	3	0	388	14.6	23.4
283 LUTH--MO SYNOD	1	46	73	2.7	4.4
287 MENN GEN CONF.	1	46	55*	2.1	3.3
449 UN METHODIST..	2	492	636	23.9	38.4
453 UN PRES CH USA	1	247	294*	11.0	17.7
JACKSON	31	4,378	6,572*	63.5	100.0
019 AMER BAPT CONV	4	586	707*	6.8	10.8
081 CATHOLIC......	3	0	1,450	14.0	22.1
093 CR CH (DISC)..	5	701	845*	8.2	12.9
097 CR C AND C CR.	3	50	60*	0.6	0.9
165 CH OF NAZARENE	1	6	21	0.2	0.3
193 EPISCOPAL.....	1	25	27	0.3	0.4
283 LUTH--MO SYNOD	2	326	451	4.4	6.9
449 UN METHODIST..	10	2,276	2,519	24.4	38.3
453 UN PRES CH USA	2	408	492*	4.8	7.5
JEFFERSON	32	4,372	6,924*	58.0	100.0
019 AMER BAPT CONV	2	144	178*	1.5	2.6
081 CATHOLIC......	5	0	1,500	12.6	21.7
097 CR C AND C CR.	4	600	742*	6.2	10.7
123 CH GOD (ANDER)	2	150	335	2.8	4.8
165 CH OF NAZARENE	1	19	85	0.7	1.2
226 FRIENDS-USA...	1	24	30*	0.3	0.4
281 LUTH CH AMER..	1	88	115	1.0	1.7
283 LUTH--MO SYNOD	1	189	244	2.0	3.5
287 MENN GEN CONF.	1	71	88*	0.7	1.3
415 S-D BAPTIST GC	1	95	118*	1.0	1.7
419 SO BAPT CONV..	1	159	197*	1.6	2.8
449 UN METHODIST..	11	2,663	3,082	25.8	44.5
453 UN PRES CH USA	1	170	210*	1.8	3.0
JEWELL	23	2,936	3,828*	62.8	100.0
029 AMER LUTH CH..	1	85	133	2.2	3.5
081 CATHOLIC......	2	0	450	7.4	11.8
093 CR CH (DISC)..	1	163	188*	3.1	4.9
097 CR C AND C CR.	3	371	428*	7.0	11.2
165 CH OF NAZARENE	1	62	73	1.2	1.9
226 FRIENDS-USA...	1	119	137*	2.2	3.6
413 S-D ADVENTISTS	2	370	427*	7.0	11.2
419 SO BAPT CONV..	1	83	96*	1.6	2.5
449 UN METHODIST..	11	1,683	1,896	31.1	49.5
JOHNSON	104	55,021	112,199*	51.5	100.0
019 AMER BAPT CONV	12	4,604	5,762*	2.6	5.1
029 AMER LUTH CH..	5	1,831	2,819	1.3	2.5
081 CATHOLIC......	10	0	40,200	18.5	35.8

*Total adherents estimated from known number of communicant, confirmed, full members.

—Represents a percent less than 0.1.

Percentages may not total due to rounding.

Table 3. Churches and Church Membership by State, County and Denomination: 1971

County and Denomination	Number of churches	Communicant, confirmed, full members	Total adherents: Number	Total adherents: Percent of total population	Total adherents: Percent of total adherents
093 CR CH (DISC)..	7	4,936	6,177*	2.8	5.5
097 CR C AND C CR.	3	365	457*	0.2	0.4
157 CH OF BRETHREN	1	36	45*	-	-
165 CH OF NAZARENE	8	1,572	3,453	1.6	3.1
193 EPISCOPAL.....	5	4,118	5,120	2.4	4.6
201 EVAN COV CH AM	1	392	491*	0.2	0.4
226 FRIENDS-USA...	1	51	64*	-	0.1
281 LUTH CH AMER..	4	1,765	2,364	1.1	2.1
283 LUTH--MO SYNOD	5	3,720	5,207	2.4	4.6
349 PENT HOLINESS.	1	3	4*	-	-
353 PLY BRETHREN..	2	70	110	0.1	0.1
419 SO BAPT CONV..	9	3,991	4,995*	2.3	4.5
435 UNITARIAN-UNIV	1	140	271	0.1	0.2
443 UN C OF CHRIST	2	900	1,126*	0.5	1.0
449 UN METHODIST..	15	12,893	16,436	7.6	14.6
453 UN PRES CH USA	11	13,564	16,975*	7.8	15.1
469 WISC EVAN LUTH	1	70	123	0.1	0.1
KEARNY	8	997	1,650*	54.2	100.0
019 AMER BAPT CONV	1	84	103*	3.4	6.2
081 CATHOLIC......	2	0	435	14.3	26.4
093 CR CH (DISC)..	1	41	51*	1.7	3.1
283 LUTH--MO SYNOD	1	156	219	7.2	13.3
449 UN METHODIST..	2	571	663	21.8	40.2
453 UN PRES CH USA	1	145	179*	5.9	10.8
KINGMAN	25	3,108	6,189*	69.6	100.0
019 AMER BAPT CONV	1	122	144*	1.6	2.3
081 CATHOLIC......	7	0	2,543	28.6	41.1
093 CR CH (DISC)..	2	571	675*	7.6	10.9
165 CH OF NAZARENE	1	66	171	1.9	2.8
193 EPISCOPAL.....	1	36	61	0.7	1.0
283 LUTH--MO SYNOD	2	203	245	2.8	4.0
287 MENN GEN CONF.	2	208	246*	2.8	4.0
449 UN METHODIST..	8	1,690	1,853	20.9	29.9
453 UN PRES CH USA	1	212	251*	2.8	4.1
KIOWA	8	2,276	2,652*	64.9	100.0
081 CATHOLIC......	1	0	106	2.6	4.0
093 CR CH (DISC)..	1	245	280*	6.8	10.6
226 FRIENDS-USA...	1	391	446*	10.9	16.8
283 LUTH--MO SYNOD	1	43	60	1.5	2.3
285 MENNONITE CH..	1	88	100*	2.4	3.8
449 UN METHODIST..	3	1,509	1,660	40.6	62.6
LABETTE	54	8,848	12,865*	49.9	100.0
019 AMER BAPT CONV	6	1,230	1,468*	5.7	11.4
081 CATHOLIC......	4	0	2,120	8.2	16.5
093 CR CH (DISC)..	2	778	929*	3.6	7.2
097 CR C AND C CR.	6	649	775*	3.0	6.0
123 CH GOD (ANDER)	1	10	31	0.1	0.2
127 CH GOD (CLEVE)	3	119	142*	0.6	1.1
157 CH OF BRETHREN	1	144	172*	0.7	1.3
165 CH OF NAZARENE	2	207	429	1.7	3.3
193 EPISCOPAL.....	1	243	288	1.1	2.2
283 LUTH--MO SYNOD	2	274	407	1.6	3.2
413 S-D ADVENTISTS	2	57	68*	0.3	0.5
419 SO BAPT CONV..	4	881	1,052*	4.1	8.2
449 UN METHODIST..	17	3,607	4,209	16.3	32.7
453 UN PRES CH USA	3	649	775*	3.0	6.0
LANE	9	1,464	2,089*	77.2	100.0
019 AMER BAPT CONV	1	26	31*	1.1	1.5
081 CATHOLIC......	1	0	303	11.2	14.5
093 CR CH (DISC)..	1	510	609*	22.5	29.2
283 LUTH--MO SYNOD	1	47	78	2.9	3.7
413 S-D ADVENTISTS	1	9	11*	0.4	0.5
419 SO BAPT CONV..	1	42	50*	1.8	2.4
449 UN METHODIST..	3	830	1,007	37.2	48.2
LEAVENWORTH	48	8,828	22,080*	41.4	100.0
019 AMER BAPT CONV	6	1,317	1,602*	3.0	7.3
081 CATHOLIC......	10	0	10,800	20.2	48.9
093 CR CH (DISC)..	1	624	759*	1.4	3.4
097 CR C AND C CR.	3	367	446*	0.8	2.0
123 CH GOD (ANDER)	1	12	12	-	0.1
165 CH OF NAZARENE	1	68	185	0.3	0.8
193 EPISCOPAL.....	2	531	869	1.6	3.9
226 FRIENDS-USA...	2	99	120*	0.2	0.5
283 LUTH--MO SYNOD	3	1,134	1,459	2.7	6.6
403 SALVATION ARMY	1	62	285	0.5	1.3
413 S-D ADVENTISTS	2	87	106*	0.2	0.5
419 SO BAPT CONV..	2	427	519*	1.0	2.4
443 UN C OF CHRIST	2	278	338*	0.6	1.5
449 UN METHODIST..	11	3,195	3,817	7.2	17.3
453 UN PRES CH USA	1	627	763*	1.4	3.5
LINCOLN	17	2,444	3,158*	68.9	100.0
019 AMER BAPT CONV	1	154	175*	3.8	5.5
081 CATHOLIC......	1	0	228	5.0	7.2
093 CR CH (DISC)..	1	40	46*	1.0	1.5
097 CR C AND C CR.	1	75	85*	1.9	2.7
281 LUTH CH AMER..	1	67	76	1.7	2.4
283 LUTH--MO SYNOD	3	1,027	1,313	28.7	41.6
443 UN C OF CHRIST	1	22	25*	0.5	0.8
449 UN METHODIST..	4	655	750	16.4	23.7
453 UN PRES CH USA	4	404	460*	10.0	14.6
LINN	22	2,756	3,351*	43.1	100.0
019 AMER BAPT CONV	2	366	425*	5.5	12.7
081 CATHOLIC......	1	0	200	2.6	6.0
093 CR CH (DISC)..	5	751	873*	11.2	26.1
097 CR C AND C CR.	3	200	232*	3.0	6.9
165 CH OF NAZARENE	1	35	72	0.9	2.1
413 S-D ADVENTISTS	1	26	30*	0.4	0.9
443 UN C OF CHRIST	1	107	124*	1.6	3.7
449 UN METHODIST..	7	1,172	1,280	16.5	38.2
453 UN PRES CH USA	1	99	115*	1.5	3.4
LOGAN	10	1,375	2,790*	73.2	100.0
081 CATHOLIC......	1	0	1,160	30.4	41.6
097 CR C AND C CR.	1	325	400*	10.5	14.3
165 CH OF NAZARENE	1	31	63	1.7	2.3
193 EPISCOPAL.....	1	39	44	1.2	1.6
221 FREE METH C NA	1	52	66	1.7	2.4
281 LUTH CH AMER..	1	56	76	2.0	2.7
283 LUTH--MO SYNOD	1	137	199	5.2	7.1
449 UN METHODIST..	2	712	754	19.8	27.0
453 UN PRES CH USA	1	23	28*	0.7	1.0
LYON	39	8,530	15,677*	48.9	100.0
019 AMER BAPT CONV	2	548	637*	2.0	4.1
081 CATHOLIC......	6	0	5,000	15.6	31.9
093 CR CH (DISC)..	1	720	837*	2.6	5.3
097 CR C AND C CR.	1	50	58*	0.2	0.4
123 CH GOD (ANDER)	1	40	95	0.3	0.6
157 CH OF BRETHREN	1	63	73*	0.2	0.5
165 CH OF NAZARENE	1	161	368	1.1	2.3
193 EPISCOPAL.....	1	190	230	0.7	1.5
221 FREE METH C NA	2	90	96	0.3	0.6
226 FRIENDS-USA...	2	138	160*	0.5	1.0
281 LUTH CH AMER..	1	468	656	2.0	4.2
283 LUTH--MO SYNOD	1	499	838	2.6	5.3
403 SALVATION ARMY	1	38	216	0.7	1.4
413 S-D ADVENTISTS	1	17	20*	0.1	0.1
419 SO BAPT CONV..	2	372	432*	1.3	2.8
449 UN METHODIST..	12	4,008	4,650	14.5	29.7
453 UN PRES CH USA	3	1,128	1,311*	4.1	8.4
MC PHERSON	52	12,775	16,605*	67.0	100.0
019 AMER BAPT CONV	2	935	1,100*	4.4	6.6
081 CATHOLIC......	1	0	986	4.0	5.9
093 CR CH (DISC)..	3	685	806*	3.3	4.9
097 CR C AND C CR.	1	125	147*	0.6	0.9
123 CH GOD (ANDER)	1	69	198	0.8	1.2
157 CH OF BRETHREN	2	491	578*	2.3	3.5
165 CH OF NAZARENE	1	84	217	0.9	1.3
193 EPISCOPAL.....	1	47	70	0.3	0.4
201 EVAN COV CH AM	4	398	468*	1.9	2.8
221 FREE METH C NA	1	311	376	1.5	2.3
281 LUTH CH AMER..	7	2,704	3,391	13.7	20.4
283 LUTH--MO SYNOD	3	485	703	2.8	4.2
285 MENNONITE CH..	2	109	128*	0.5	0.8
287 MENN GEN CONF.	9	2,682	3,156*	12.7	19.0
353 PLY BRETHREN..	1	25	40	0.2	0.2
419 SO BAPT CONV..	2	58	68*	0.3	0.4
443 UN C OF CHRIST	1	256	301*	1.2	1.8
449 UN METHODIST..	8	2,826	3,301	13.3	19.9
453 UN PRES CH USA	2	485	571*	2.3	3.4
MARION	43	6,653	9,046*	64.9	100.0
019 AMER BAPT CONV	1	91	106*	0.8	1.2
029 AMER LUTH CH..	1	55	72	0.5	0.8
081 CATHOLIC......	4	0	1,185	8.5	13.1
093 CR CH (DISC)..	2	433	505*	3.6	5.6
097 CR C AND C CR.	1	100	117*	0.8	1.3
123 CH GOD (ANDER)	1	35	100	0.7	1.1
165 CH OF NAZARENE	1	10	30	0.2	0.3
281 LUTH CH AMER..	1	91	110	0.8	1.2
283 LUTH--MO SYNOD	6	1,044	1,265	9.1	14.0
287 MENN GEN CONF.	7	2,144	2,502*	18.0	27.7
313 NO AM BAPT GC.	3	390	455*	3.3	5.0
413 S-D ADVENTISTS	2	43	50*	0.4	0.6
449 UN METHODIST..	11	2,039	2,341	16.8	25.9
453 UN PRES CH USA	2	178	208*	1.5	2.3
MARSHALL	42	5,796	9,170*	69.8	100.0
019 AMER BAPT CONV	1	190	223*	1.7	2.4
081 CATHOLIC......	8	0	2,250	17.1	24.5
093 CR CH (DISC)..	1	285	334*	2.5	3.6
097 CR C AND C CR.	2	375	439*	3.3	4.8
157 CH OF BRETHREN	1	56	66*	0.5	0.7
193 EPISCOPAL.....	2	81	128	1.0	1.4
201 EVAN COV CH AM	1	50	59*	0.4	0.6
221 FREE METH C NA	1	9	10	0.1	0.1
281 LUTH CH AMER..	3	652	778	5.9	8.5
283 LUTH--MO SYNOD	6	905	1,222	9.3	13.3
413 S-D ADVENTISTS	1	10	12*	0.1	0.1
419 SO BAPT CONV..	1	144	169*	1.3	1.8
443 UN C OF CHRIST	1	369	432*	3.3	4.7
449 UN METHODIST..	8	1,877	2,119	16.1	23.1
453 UN PRES CH USA	5	793	929*	7.1	10.1
MEADE	17	2,183	3,344*	68.1	100.0
019 AMER BAPT CONV	2	308	365*	7.4	10.9
081 CATHOLIC......	3	0	733	14.9	21.9

*Total adherents estimated from known number of communicant, confirmed, full members.

—Represents a percent less than 0.1.

Percentages may not total due to rounding.

Table 3. Churches and Church Membership by State, County and Denomination: 1971

County and Denomination	Number of churches	Communicant, confirmed, full members	Total adherents: Number	Total adherents: Percent of total population	Total adherents: Percent of total adherents
097 CR C AND C CR.	3	244	289*	5.9	8.6
165 CH OF NAZARENE	1	113	179	3.6	5.4
193 EPISCOPAL.....	1	23	37	0.8	1.1
226 FRIENDS-USA...	2	151	179*	3.6	5.4
283 LUTH--MO SYNOD	1	201	261	5.3	7.8
449 UN METHODIST..	3	1,051	1,192	24.3	35.6
453 UN PRES CH USA	1	92	109*	2.2	3.3
MIAMI	33	6,072	10,038*	52.1	100.0
019 AMER BAPT CONV	6	1,409	1,692*	8.8	16.9
081 CATHOLIC......	4	0	2,650	13.8	26.4
093 CR CH (DISC)..	3	488	586*	3.0	5.8
097 CR C AND C CR.	1	80	96*	0.5	1.0
165 CH OF NAZARENE	1	97	222	1.2	2.2
226 FRIENDS-USA...	1	26	31*	0.2	0.3
283 LUTH--MO SYNOD	2	864	1,141	5.9	11.4
419 SO BAPT CONV..	1	92	110*	0.6	1.1
449 UN METHODIST..	9	2,207	2,539	13.2	25.3
453 UN PRES CH USA	5	809	971*	5.0	9.7
MITCHELL	25	3,604	6,992*	87.3	100.0
019 AMER BAPT CONV	3	316	374*	4.7	5.3
081 CATHOLIC......	3	0	2,790	34.8	39.9
093 CR CH (DISC)..	1	284	336*	4.2	4.8
097 CR C AND C CR.	2	205	242*	3.0	3.5
193 EPISCOPAL.....	1	17	20	0.2	0.3
221 FREE METH C NA	2	26	27	0.3	0.4
226 FRIENDS-USA...	1	68	80*	1.0	1.1
281 LUTH CH AMER..	1	364	485	6.1	6.9
283 LUTH--MO SYNOD	1	121	159	2.0	2.3
313 NO AM BAPT GC.	1	79	93*	1.2	1.3
449 UN METHODIST..	6	1,790	1,991	24.9	28.5
453 UN PRES CH USA	3	334	395*	4.9	5.6
MONTGOMERY	80	16,190	22,364*	56.0	100.0
019 AMER BAPT CONV	4	2,152	2,542*	6.4	11.4
059 BAPT MISS ASSN	1	50	59*	0.1	0.3
081 CATHOLIC......	5	0	2,753	6.9	12.3
093 CR CH (DISC)..	5	1,945	2,297*	5.7	10.3
097 CR C AND C CR.	6	952	1,124*	2.8	5.0
123 CH GOD (ANDER)	2	105	314	0.8	1.4
127 CH GOD (CLEVE)	3	176	208*	0.5	0.9
157 CH OF BRETHREN	1	115	136*	0.3	0.6
165 CH OF NAZARENE	6	640	1,200	3.0	5.4
193 EPISCOPAL.....	2	484	555	1.4	2.5
226 FRIENDS-USA...	3	68	80*	0.2	0.4
283 LUTH--MO SYNOD	3	1,024	1,396	3.5	6.2
335 ORTH PRESB CH.	1	27	36	0.1	0.2
349 PENT HOLINESS.	5	173	204*	0.5	0.9
403 SALVATION ARMY	1	56	206	0.5	0.9
413 S-D ADVENTISTS	4	144	170*	0.4	0.8
419 SO BAPT CONV..	10	2,212	2,612*	6.5	11.7
443 UN C OF CHRIST	1	66	78*	0.2	0.3
449 UN METHODIST..	14	4,602	4,978	12.5	22.3
453 UN PRES CH USA	3	1,199	1,416*	3.5	6.3
MORRIS	19	2,896	3,667*	57.0	100.0
019 AMER BAPT CONV	1	199	232*	3.6	6.3
081 CATHOLIC......	1	0	301	4.7	8.2
093 CR CH (DISC)..	1	395	461*	7.2	12.6
097 CR C AND C CR.	3	235	274*	4.3	7.5
281 LUTH CH AMER..	2	247	309	4.8	8.4
283 LUTH--MO SYNOD	2	185	236	3.7	6.4
443 UN C OF CHRIST	1	138	161*	2.5	4.4
449 UN METHODIST..	7	1,366	1,540	23.9	42.0
453 UN PRES CH USA	1	131	153*	2.4	4.2
MORTON	12	1,594	2,330*	65.2	100.0
019 AMER BAPT CONV	1	131	163*	4.6	7.0
081 CATHOLIC......	1	0	210	5.9	9.0
097 CR C AND C CR.	1	140	174*	4.9	7.5
123 CH GOD (ANDER)	1	92	244	6.8	10.5
157 CH OF BRETHREN	1	79	98*	2.7	4.2
165 CH OF NAZARENE	1	102	173	4.8	7.4
283 LUTH--MO SYNOD	1	97	140	3.9	6.0
349 PENT HOLINESS.	1	18	22*	0.6	0.9
419 SO BAPT CONV..	1	221	274*	7.7	11.8
449 UN METHODIST..	3	714	832	23.3	35.7
NEMAHA	27	3,314	7,503*	63.5	100.0
019 AMER BAPT CONV	3	353	431*	3.6	5.7
081 CATHOLIC......	8	0	3,550	30.0	47.3
157 CH OF BRETHREN	3	161	197*	1.7	2.6
175 CONG CR CH....	1	492	601*	5.1	8.0
283 LUTH--MO SYNOD	1	106	157	1.3	2.1
443 UN C OF CHRIST	3	540	660*	5.6	8.8
449 UN METHODIST..	8	1,662	1,907	16.1	25.4
NEOSHO	43	6,287	10,148*	53.9	100.0
019 AMER BAPT CONV	4	916	1,093*	5.8	10.8
081 CATHOLIC......	4	0	2,514	13.4	24.8
093 CR CH (DISC)..	3	743	887*	4.7	8.7
097 CR C AND C CR.	4	395	471*	2.5	4.6
123 CH GOD (ANDER)	1	31	106	0.6	1.0
127 CH GOD (CLEVE)	1	60	72*	0.4	0.7
165 CH OF NAZARENE	2	177	265	1.4	2.6
193 EPISCOPAL.....	1	278	349	1.9	3.4
226 FRIENDS-USA...	1	18	21*	0.1	0.2
281 LUTH CH AMER..	1	28	38	0.2	0.4
283 LUTH--MO SYNOD	1	443	609	3.2	6.0
349 PENT HOLINESS.	1	12	14*	0.1	0.1
413 S-D ADVENTISTS	2	94	112*	0.6	1.1
419 SO BAPT CONV..	1	242	289*	1.5	2.8
449 UN METHODIST..	13	2,376	2,742	14.6	27.0
453 UN PRES CH USA	3	474	566*	3.0	5.6
NESS	18	2,353	4,179*	87.2	100.0
019 AMER BAPT CONV	2	239	282*	5.9	6.7
029 AMER LUTH CH..	1	103	121	2.5	2.9
081 CATHOLIC......	2	0	1,371	28.6	32.8
093 CR CH (DISC)..	1	98	116*	2.4	2.8
283 LUTH--MO SYNOD	1	136	180	3.8	4.3
287 MENN GEN CONF.	1	149	176*	3.7	4.2
353 PLY BRETHREN..	1	20	30	0.6	0.7
413 S-D ADVENTISTS	1	41	48*	1.0	1.1
443 UN C OF CHRIST	1	63	74*	1.5	1.8
449 UN METHODIST..	7	1,504	1,781	37.2	42.6
NORTON	20	2,147	4,126*	56.7	100.0
019 AMER BAPT CONV	1	156	185*	2.5	4.5
081 CATHOLIC......	3	0	1,300	17.9	31.5
097 CR C AND C CR.	2	155	183*	2.5	4.4
123 CH GOD (ANDER)	2	105	310	4.3	7.5
165 CH OF NAZARENE	1	15	16	0.2	0.4
175 CONG CR CH....	1	129	153*	2.1	3.7
193 EPISCOPAL.....	1	80	132	1.8	3.2
221 FREE METH C NA	1	19	23	0.3	0.6
283 LUTH--MO SYNOD	1	120	175	2.4	4.2
413 S-D ADVENTISTS	1	12	14*	0.2	0.3
443 UN C OF CHRIST	1	147	174*	2.4	4.2
449 UN METHODIST..	5	1,209	1,461	20.1	35.4
OSAGE	25	3,439	4,724*	35.4	100.0
081 CATHOLIC......	2	0	700	5.2	14.8
097 CR C AND C CR.	1	66	79*	0.6	1.7
123 CH GOD (ANDER)	1	46	136	1.0	2.9
201 EVAN COV CH AM	3	115	138*	1.0	2.9
221 FREE METH C NA	1	23	26	0.2	0.6
226 FRIENDS-USA...	1	37	44*	0.3	0.9
281 LUTH CH AMER..	1	127	154	1.2	3.3
283 LUTH--MO SYNOD	1	215	264	2.0	5.6
419 SO BAPT CONV..	1	93	111*	0.8	2.3
443 UN C OF CHRIST	1	196	234*	1.8	5.0
449 UN METHODIST..	10	2,209	2,465	18.5	52.2
453 UN PRES CH USA	2	312	373*	2.8	7.9
OSBORNE	26	2,739	3,805*	59.3	100.0
019 AMER BAPT CONV	1	76	87*	1.4	2.3
029 AMER LUTH CH..	1	117	168	2.6	4.4
081 CATHOLIC......	2	0	561	8.7	14.7
093 CR CH (DISC)..	1	157	181*	2.8	4.8
097 CR C AND C CR.	1	100	115*	1.8	3.0
157 CH OF BRETHREN	1	28	32*	0.5	0.8
165 CH OF NAZARENE	1	39	77	1.2	2.0
221 FREE METH C NA	1	44	63	1.0	1.7
226 FRIENDS-USA...	1	49	56*	0.9	1.5
283 LUTH--MO SYNOD	2	387	493	7.7	13.0
443 UN C OF CHRIST	2	290	334*	5.2	8.8
449 UN METHODIST..	10	1,350	1,521	23.7	40.0
453 UN PRES CH USA	2	102	117*	1.8	3.1
OTTAWA	23	2,229	3,200*	51.8	100.0
019 AMER BAPT CONV	2	196	230*	3.7	7.2
029 AMER LUTH CH..	1	145	180	2.9	5.6
081 CATHOLIC......	3	0	524	8.5	16.4
165 CH OF NAZARENE	1	14	56	0.9	1.8
193 EPISCOPAL.....	1	32	33	0.5	1.0
221 FREE METH C NA	2	63	84	1.4	2.6
349 PENT HOLINESS.	1	16	19*	0.3	0.6
449 UN METHODIST..	8	1,273	1,500	24.3	46.9
453 UN PRES CH USA	4	490	574*	9.3	17.9
PAWNEE	17	3,334	4,851*	57.2	100.0
019 AMER BAPT CONV	2	312	361*	4.3	7.4
081 CATHOLIC......	2	0	929	11.0	19.2
093 CR CH (DISC)..	1	350	405*	4.8	8.3
165 CH OF NAZARENE	1	48	112	1.3	2.3
193 EPISCOPAL.....	1	22	32	0.4	0.7
281 LUTH CH AMER..	1	54	75	0.9	1.5
283 LUTH--MO SYNOD	1	310	412	4.9	8.5
349 PENT HOLINESS.	1	77	89*	1.0	1.8
419 SO BAPT CONV..	1	43	50*	0.6	1.0
449 UN METHODIST..	5	1,763	1,975	23.3	40.7
453 UN PRES CH USA	1	355	411*	4.8	8.5
PHILLIPS	26	3,528	4,885*	61.9	100.0
019 AMER BAPT CONV	1	136	161*	2.0	3.3
029 AMER LUTH CH..	4	667	832	10.5	17.0
081 CATHOLIC......	2	0	468	5.9	9.6
093 CR CH (DISC)..	1	280	332*	4.2	6.8
097 CR C AND C CR.	2	120	142*	1.8	2.9
105 CHRISTIAN REF.	1	200	297	3.8	6.1
123 CH GOD (ANDER)	1	35	90	1.1	1.8
165 CH OF NAZARENE	2	81	115	1.5	2.4
221 FREE METH C NA	1	8	9	0.1	0.2
283 LUTH--MO SYNOD	1	123	160	2.0	3.3

*Total adherents estimated from known number of communicant, confirmed, full members.

—Represents a percent less than 0.1.

Percentages may not total due to rounding.

Table 3. Churches and Church Membership by State, County and Denomination: 1971

County and Denomination	Number of churches	Communicant, confirmed, full members	Total adherents: Number	Total adherents: Percent of total population	Total adherents: Percent of total adherents
371 REF CH IN AM..	1	195	282	3.6	5.8
413 S-D ADVENTISTS	1	33	39*	0.5	0.8
449 UN METHODIST..	7	1,388	1,647	20.9	33.7
453 UN PRES CH USA	1	262	311*	3.9	6.4
POTTAWATOMIE	33	3,640	8,125*	69.1	100.0
019 AMER BAPT CONV	3	359	431*	3.7	5.3
029 AMER LUTH CH..	1	29	37	0.3	0.5
081 CATHOLIC......	7	0	3,700	31.5	45.5
097 CR C AND C CR.	2	100	120*	1.0	1.5
193 EPISCOPAL.....	1	91	101	0.9	1.2
281 LUTH CH AMER..	2	170	197	1.7	2.4
283 LUTH--MO SYNOD	2	705	909	7.7	11.2
443 UN C OF CHRIST	4	449	539*	4.6	6.6
449 UN METHODIST..	10	1,539	1,853	15.8	22.8
453 UN PRES CH USA	1	198	238*	2.0	2.9
PRATT	28	4,705	6,315*	62.8	100.0
019 AMER BAPT CONV	3	632	734*	7.3	11.6
081 CATHOLIC......	1	0	784	7.8	12.4
093 CR CH (DISC)..	2	604	702*	7.0	11.1
123 CH GOD (ANDER)	1	30	75	0.7	1.2
127 CH GOD (CLEVE)	1	14	16*	0.2	0.3
165 CH OF NAZARENE	1	85	138	1.4	2.2
193 EPISCOPAL.....	1	35	50	0.5	0.8
221 FREE METH C NA	1	49	60	0.6	1.0
226 FRIENDS-USA...	3	105	122*	1.2	1.9
283 LUTH--MO SYNOD	2	414	545	5.4	8.6
349 PENT HOLINESS.	1	42	49*	0.5	0.8
419 SO BAPT CONV..	1	28	33*	0.3	0.5
449 UN METHODIST..	9	2,276	2,553	25.4	40.4
453 UN PRES CH USA	1	391	454*	4.5	7.2
RAWLINS	12	1,631	3,264*	74.3	100.0
081 CATHOLIC......	4	0	1,320	30.0	40.4
093 CR CH (DISC)..	1	210	251*	5.7	7.7
165 CH OF NAZARENE	1	12	14	0.3	0.4
201 EVAN COV CH AM	1	69	82*	1.9	2.5
283 LUTH--MO SYNOD	2	270	328	7.5	10.0
419 SO BAPT CONV..	1	258	308*	7.0	9.4
443 UN C OF CHRIST	1	126	150*	3.4	4.6
449 UN METHODIST..	1	686	811	18.5	24.8
RENO	78	21,112	31,645*	52.1	100.0
019 AMER BAPT CONV	4	1,419	1,713*	2.8	5.4
081 CATHOLIC......	6	0	5,197	8.6	16.4
093 CR CH (DISC)..	6	1,788	2,158*	3.6	6.8
097 CR C AND C CR.	2	60	72*	0.1	0.2
123 CH GOD (ANDER)	1	138	353	0.6	1.1
127 CH GOD (CLEVE)	1	35	42*	0.1	0.1
157 CH OF BRETHREN	2	375	453*	0.7	1.4
165 CH OF NAZARENE	5	1,097	2,051	3.4	6.5
175 CONG CR CH....	1	300	362*	0.6	1.1
193 EPISCOPAL.....	1	495	600	1.0	1.9
221 FREE METH C NA	1	28	39	0.1	0.1
226 FRIENDS-USA...	1	59	71*	0.1	0.2
281 LUTH CH AMER..	2	645	861	1.4	2.7
283 LUTH--MO SYNOD	3	1,166	1,597	2.6	5.0
285 MENNONITE CH..	3	578	698*	1.1	2.2
287 MENN GEN CONF.	4	1,468	1,772*	2.9	5.6
349 PENT HOLINESS.	1	71	86*	0.1	0.3
353 PLY BRETHREN..	1	40	110	0.2	0.3
403 SALVATION ARMY	1	74	201	0.3	0.6
413 S-D ADVENTISTS	1	225	272*	0.4	0.9
419 SO BAPT CONV..	3	852	1,029*	1.7	3.3
435 UNITARIAN-UNIV	1	20	20	-	0.1
443 UN C OF CHRIST	4	601	726*	1.2	2.3
449 UN METHODIST..	19	7,881	9,113	15.0	28.8
453 UN PRES CH USA	4	1,697	2,049*	3.4	6.5
REPUBLIC	27	3,210	4,638*	54.6	100.0
019 AMER BAPT CONV	2	134	155*	1.8	3.3
029 AMER LUTH CH..	2	213	330	3.9	7.1
081 CATHOLIC......	3	0	830	9.8	17.9
097 CR C AND C CR.	2	35	40*	0.5	0.9
193 EPISCOPAL.....	1	8	8	0.1	0.2
201 EVAN COV CH AM	1	23	27*	0.3	0.6
226 FRIENDS-USA...	1	28	32*	0.4	0.7
281 LUTH CH AMER..	2	413	499	5.9	10.8
413 S-D ADVENTISTS	1	16	18*	0.2	0.4
449 UN METHODIST..	8	1,771	2,043	24.0	44.0
453 UN PRES CH USA	4	569	656*	7.7	14.1
RICE	30	5,659	7,818*	63.5	100.0
019 AMER BAPT CONV	5	701	817*	6.6	10.5
081 CATHOLIC......	4	0	1,173	9.5	15.0
093 CR CH (DISC)..	1	373	435*	3.5	5.6
097 CR C AND C CR.	1	60	70*	0.6	0.9
165 CH OF NAZARENE	2	70	155	1.3	2.0
193 EPISCOPAL.....	1	24	41	0.3	0.5
283 LUTH--MO SYNOD	1	225	301	2.4	3.9
419 SO BAPT CONV..	2	232	270*	2.2	3.5
443 UN C OF CHRIST	1	243	283*	2.3	3.6
449 UN METHODIST..	8	2,975	3,392	27.5	43.4
453 UN PRES CH USA	4	756	881*	7.2	11.3
RILEY	37	10,793	18,526*	32.6	100.0
019 AMER BAPT CONV	1	528	614*	1.1	3.3
081 CATHOLIC......	3	0	5,405	9.5	29.2
093 CR CH (DISC)..	1	686	798*	1.4	4.3
097 CR C AND C CR.	3	238	277*	0.5	1.5
123 CH GOD (ANDER)	1	6	31	0.1	0.2
165 CH OF NAZARENE	1	46	95	0.2	0.5
193 EPISCOPAL.....	1	613	701	1.2	3.8
201 EVAN COV CH AM	1	64	74*	0.1	0.4
221 FREE METH C NA	1	24	25	-	0.1
226 FRIENDS-USA...	1	27	31*	0.1	0.2
281 LUTH CH AMER..	3	1,007	1,552	2.7	8.4
283 LUTH--MO SYNOD	1	587	789	1.4	4.3
413 S-D ADVENTISTS	1	48	56*	0.1	0.3
419 SO BAPT CONV..	1	401	467*	0.8	2.5
435 UNITARIAN-UNIV	1	58	98	0.2	0.5
443 UN C OF CHRIST	1	295	343*	0.6	1.9
449 UN METHODIST..	10	4,116	4,786	8.4	25.8
453 UN PRES CH USA	5	2,049	2,384*	4.2	12.9
ROOKS	20	2,610	5,365*	70.3	100.0
019 AMER BAPT CONV	1	74	88*	1.2	1.6
081 CATHOLIC......	4	0	2,189	28.7	40.8
097 CR C AND C CR.	2	565	675*	8.8	12.6
123 CH GOD (ANDER)	1	33	82	1.1	1.5
127 CH GOD (CLEVE)	1	9	11*	0.1	0.2
165 CH OF NAZARENE	2	123	189	2.5	3.5
283 LUTH--MO SYNOD	1	57	78	1.0	1.5
413 S-D ADVENTISTS	1	34	41*	0.5	0.8
443 UN C OF CHRIST	1	255	305*	4.0	5.7
449 UN METHODIST..	5	1,405	1,637	21.5	30.5
469 WISC EVAN LUTH	1	55	70	0.9	1.3
RUSH	20	2,371	4,178*	81.6	100.0
029 AMER LUTH CH..	4	700	834	16.3	20.0
081 CATHOLIC......	5	0	1,502	29.4	36.0
097 CR C AND C CR.	1	138	160*	3.1	3.8
313 NO AM BAPT GC.	1	59	68*	1.3	1.6
413 S-D ADVENTISTS	3	125	145*	2.8	3.5
449 UN METHODIST..	6	1,349	1,469	28.7	35.2
RUSSELL	27	4,766	7,058*	74.9	100.0
019 AMER BAPT CONV	2	200	234*	2.5	3.3
029 AMER LUTH CH..	2	335	406	4.3	5.8
081 CATHOLIC......	3	0	1,358	14.4	19.2
097 CR C AND C CR.	1	100	117*	1.2	1.7
165 CH OF NAZARENE	1	35	53	0.6	0.8
193 EPISCOPAL.....	1	29	41	0.4	0.6
281 LUTH CH AMER..	2	1,122	1,376	14.6	19.5
283 LUTH--MO SYNOD	1	133	189	2.0	2.7
419 SO BAPT CONV..	1	214	250*	2.7	3.5
443 UN C OF CHRIST	2	352	411*	4.4	5.8
449 UN METHODIST..	10	2,220	2,586	27.4	36.6
469 WISC EVAN LUTH	1	26	37	0.4	0.5
SALINE	49	14,682	27,086*	58.1	100.0
019 AMER BAPT CONV	2	601	748*	1.6	2.8
081 CATHOLIC......	5	0	7,452	16.0	27.5
093 CR CH (DISC)..	2	760	946*	2.0	3.5
097 CR C AND C CR.	1	56	70*	0.2	0.3
123 CH GOD (ANDER)	2	34	143	0.3	0.5
165 CH OF NAZARENE	3	221	849	1.8	3.1
193 EPISCOPAL.....	2	690	808	1.7	3.0
201 EVAN COV CH AM	2	216	269*	0.6	1.0
221 FREE METH C NA	1	53	79	0.2	0.3
281 LUTH CH AMER..	7	2,593	3,383	7.3	12.5
283 LUTH--MO SYNOD	3	962	1,388	3.0	5.1
353 PLY BRETHREN..	1	30	50	0.1	0.2
403 SALVATION ARMY	1	59	557	1.2	2.1
413 S-D ADVENTISTS	1	79	98*	0.2	0.4
419 SO BAPT CONV..	3	1,078	1,342*	2.9	5.0
443 UN C OF CHRIST	1	183	228*	0.5	0.8
449 UN METHODIST..	9	5,182	6,329	13.6	23.4
453 UN PRES CH USA	3	1,885	2,347*	5.0	8.7
SCOTT	11	2,688	3,974*	70.9	100.0
019 AMER BAPT CONV	1	561	697*	12.4	17.5
081 CATHOLIC......	1	0	552	9.8	13.9
093 CR CH (DISC)..	1	422	524*	9.3	13.2
097 CR C AND C CR.	1	175	217*	3.9	5.5
157 CH OF BRETHREN	1	85	106*	1.9	2.7
165 CH OF NAZARENE	1	67	170	3.0	4.3
193 EPISCOPAL.....	1	42	84	1.5	2.1
283 LUTH--MO SYNOD	1	301	412	7.3	10.4
285 MENNONITE CH..	1	52	65*	1.2	1.6
419 SO BAPT CONV..	1	87	108*	1.9	2.7
449 UN METHODIST..	1	896	1,039	18.5	26.1
SEDGWICK	263	98,037	166,408*	47.5	100.0
019 AMER BAPT CONV	25	7,148	8,810*	2.5	5.3
029 AMER LUTH CH..	2	382	557	0.2	0.3
059 BAPT MISS ASSN	1	70	86*	-	0.1
081 CATHOLIC......	28	0	40,801	11.6	24.5
093 CR CH (DISC)..	18	6,979	8,602*	2.5	5.2
097 CR C AND C CR.	12	6,507	8,020*	2.3	4.8
123 CH GOD (ANDER)	6	937	2,279	0.6	1.4
127 CH GOD (CLEVE)	4	332	409*	0.1	0.2
157 CH OF BRETHREN	1	445	548*	0.2	0.3
165 CH OF NAZARENE	13	2,109	3,952	1.1	2.4
175 CONG CR CH....	3	2,443	3,011*	0.9	1.8
193 EPISCOPAL.....	9	3,208	4,240	1.2	2.5

*Total adherents estimated from known number of communicant, confirmed, full members.

—Represents a percent less than 0.1.

Percentages may not total due to rounding.

Table 3. Churches and Church Membership by State, County and Denomination: 1971

County and Denomination	Number of churches	Communicant, confirmed, full members	Total adherents: Number	Total adherents: Percent of total population	Total adherents: Percent of total adherents
201 EVAN COV CH AM	1	61	75*	-	-
221 FREE METH C NA	2	211	258	0.1	0.2
226 FRIENDS-USA...	3	989	1,219*	0.3	0.7
281 LUTH CH AMER..	5	1,847	2,502	0.7	1.5
283 LUTH--MO SYNOD	12	4,567	6,361	1.8	3.8
285 MENNONITE CH..	1	31	38*	-	-
287 MENN GEN CONF.	1	484	597*	0.2	0.4
313 NO AM BAPT GC.	1	105	129*	-	0.1
349 PENT HOLINESS.	2	178	219*	0.1	0.1
353 PLY BRETHREN..	2	80	130	-	0.1
403 SALVATION ARMY	4	456	2,725	0.8	1.6
413 S-D ADVENTISTS	2	708	873*	0.2	0.5
419 SO BAPT CONV..	32	18,373	22,645*	6.5	13.6
435 UNITARIAN-UNIV	1	168	223	0.1	0.1
443 UN C OF CHRIST	7	1,281	1,579*	0.5	0.9
449 UN METHODIST..	46	29,331	34,901	10.0	21.0
453 UN PRES CH USA	18	8,589	10,586*	3.0	6.4
469 WISC EVAN LUTH	1	18	33	-	-
SEWARD	24	5,081	7,914*	50.3	100.0
019 AMER BAPT CONV	2	963	1,213*	7.7	15.3
029 AMER LUTH CH..	1	106	169	1.1	2.1
081 CATHOLIC......	1	0	1,100	7.0	13.9
093 CR CH (DISC)..	1	402	506*	3.2	6.4
097 CR C AND C CR.	1	190	239*	1.5	3.0
123 CH GOD (ANDER)	3	274	676	4.3	8.5
165 CH OF NAZARENE	1	125	222	1.4	2.8
193 EPISCOPAL.....	1	194	297	1.9	3.8
226 FRIENDS-USA...	3	144	181*	1.1	2.3
283 LUTH--MO SYNOD	1	261	398	2.5	5.0
287 MENN GEN CONF.	1	52	65*	0.4	0.8
349 PENT HOLINESS.	1	16	20*	0.1	0.3
413 S-D ADVENTISTS	1	22	28*	0.2	0.4
419 SO BAPT CONV..	2	560	705*	4.5	8.9
449 UN METHODIST..	3	1,468	1,712	10.9	21.6
453 UN PRES CH USA	1	304	383*	2.4	4.8
SHAWNEE	105	38,896	69,069*	44.5	100.0
019 AMER BAPT CONV	11	4,031	4,936*	3.2	7.1
029 AMER LUTH CH..	1	357	572	0.4	0.8
081 CATHOLIC......	8	0	20,100	12.9	29.1
093 CR CH (DISC)..	7	2,694	3,299*	2.1	4.8
097 CR C AND C CR.	6	818	1,002*	0.6	1.5
127 CH GOD (CLEVE)	1	27	33*	-	-
157 CH OF BRETHREN	1	127	156*	0.1	0.2
165 CH OF NAZARENE	4	630	1,127	0.7	1.6
193 EPISCOPAL.....	3	2,231	2,837	1.8	4.1
201 EVAN COV CH AM	1	102	125*	0.1	0.2
221 FREE METH C NA	1	75	115	0.1	0.2
226 FRIENDS-USA...	1	60	73*	-	0.1
281 LUTH CH AMER..	3	1,074	1,443	0.9	2.1
283 LUTH--MO SYNOD	6	2,831	4,054	2.6	5.9
349 PENT HOLINESS.	1	13	16*	-	-
353 PLY BRETHREN..	1	5	8	-	-
403 SALVATION ARMY	1	74	569	0.4	0.8
413 S-D ADVENTISTS	2	325	398*	0.3	0.6
419 SO BAPT CONV..	6	2,258	2,765*	1.8	4.0
435 UNITARIAN-UNIV	1	51	66	-	0.1
443 UN C OF CHRIST	5	2,857	3,498*	2.3	5.1
449 UN METHODIST..	21	12,825	15,227	9.8	22.0
453 UN PRES CH USA	13	5,431	6,650*	4.3	9.6
SHERIDAN	13	1,220	3,398*	88.1	100.0
019 AMER BAPT CONV	2	212	259*	6.7	7.6
081 CATHOLIC......	5	0	1,897	49.2	55.8
093 CR CH (DISC)..	1	149	182*	4.7	5.4
283 LUTH--MO SYNOD	1	151	202	5.2	5.9
449 UN METHODIST..	3	450	543	14.1	16.0
453 UN PRES CH USA	1	258	315*	8.2	9.3
SHERMAN	12	2,343	3,834*	49.2	100.0
019 AMER BAPT CONV	1	115	142*	1.8	3.7
029 AMER LUTH CH..	1	441	615	7.9	16.0
081 CATHOLIC......	1	0	765	9.8	20.0
093 CR CH (DISC)..	1	225	277*	3.6	7.2
165 CH OF NAZARENE	1	61	166	2.1	4.3
193 EPISCOPAL.....	1	90	130	1.7	3.4
283 LUTH--MO SYNOD	1	18	27	0.3	0.7
353 PLY BRETHREN..	1	10	24	0.3	0.6
413 S-D ADVENTISTS	1	46	57*	0.7	1.5
419 SO BAPT CONV..	1	71	87*	1.1	2.3
449 UN METHODIST..	2	1,266	1,544	19.8	40.3
SMITH	25	3,370	4,322*	64.0	100.0
019 AMER BAPT CONV	1	13	15*	0.2	0.3
029 AMER LUTH CH..	3	798	1,081	16.0	25.0
081 CATHOLIC......	2	0	198	2.9	4.6
093 CR CH (DISC)..	3	453	520*	7.7	12.0
097 CR C AND C CR.	2	97	111*	1.6	2.6
105 CHRISTIAN REF.	1	132	200	3.0	4.6
165 CH OF NAZARENE	2	120	227	3.4	5.3
283 LUTH--MO SYNOD	1	136	152	2.2	3.5
443 UN C OF CHRIST	3	321	368*	5.4	8.5
449 UN METHODIST..	6	1,119	1,242	18.4	28.7
453 UN PRES CH USA	1	181	208*	3.1	4.8
STAFFORD	22	3,020	3,840*	64.6	100.0
019 AMER BAPT CONV	2	327	376*	6.3	9.8
081 CATHOLIC......	2	0	365	6.1	9.5
093 CR CH (DISC)..	2	402	462*	7.8	12.0
157 CH OF BRETHREN	1	131	151*	2.5	3.9
165 CH OF NAZARENE	1	45	93	1.6	2.4
221 FREE METH C NA	1	21	22	0.4	0.6
226 FRIENDS-USA...	1	42	48*	0.8	1.3
313 NO AM BAPT GC.	1	200	230*	3.9	6.0
419 SO BAPT CONV..	1	72	83*	1.4	2.2
443 UN C OF CHRIST	2	333	383*	6.4	10.0
449 UN METHODIST..	6	1,295	1,452	24.4	37.8
453 UN PRES CH USA	2	152	175*	2.9	4.6
STANTON	4	756	1,043	45.6	100.0
081 CATHOLIC......	1	0	111	4.9	10.6
165 CH OF NAZARENE	1	68	116	5.1	11.1
449 UN METHODIST..	2	688	816	35.7	78.2
STEVENS	12	2,125	3,051*	72.7	100.0
019 AMER BAPT CONV	2	287	347*	8.3	11.4
081 CATHOLIC......	1	0	250	6.0	8.2
097 CR C AND C CR.	1	652	789*	18.8	25.9
123 CH GOD (ANDER)	1	103	273	6.5	8.9
165 CH OF NAZARENE	1	39	104	2.5	3.4
226 FRIENDS-USA...	1	73	88*	2.1	2.9
283 LUTH--MO SYNOD	1	65	101	2.4	3.3
349 PENT HOLINESS.	1	18	22*	0.5	0.7
419 SO BAPT CONV..	1	61	74*	1.8	2.4
449 UN METHODIST..	2	827	1,003	23.9	32.9
SUMNER	51	10,178	15,193*	64.5	100.0
019 AMER BAPT CONV	6	1,294	1,537*	6.5	10.1
081 CATHOLIC......	6	0	3,258	13.8	21.4
093 CR CH (DISC)..	7	1,315	1,562*	6.6	10.3
123 CH GOD (ANDER)	1	60	135	0.6	0.9
165 CH OF NAZARENE	2	144	234	1.0	1.5
221 FREE METH C NA	1	20	22	0.1	0.1
226 FRIENDS-USA...	1	135	160*	0.7	1.1
281 LUTH CH AMER..	1	132	186	0.8	1.2
283 LUTH--MO SYNOD	2	288	388	1.6	2.6
419 SO BAPT CONV..	6	916	1,088*	4.6	7.2
449 UN METHODIST..	13	4,984	5,566	23.6	36.6
453 UN PRES CH USA	5	890	1,057*	4.5	7.0
THOMAS	12	2,308	4,085*	54.5	100.0
019 AMER BAPT CONV	2	257	312*	4.2	7.6
029 AMER LUTH CH..	1	100	139	1.9	3.4
081 CATHOLIC......	1	0	1,305	17.4	31.9
093 CR CH (DISC)..	1	148	180*	2.4	4.4
165 CH OF NAZARENE	1	3	3	-	0.1
193 EPISCOPAL.....	1	64	67	0.9	1.6
283 LUTH--MO SYNOD	1	209	285	3.8	7.0
449 UN METHODIST..	3	1,313	1,534	20.5	37.6
453 UN PRES CH USA	1	214	260*	3.5	6.4
TREGO	13	1,703	3,234*	72.9	100.0
029 AMER LUTH CH..	1	102	122	2.8	3.8
081 CATHOLIC......	2	0	1,104	24.9	34.1
097 CR C AND C CR.	1	80	95*	2.1	2.9
123 CH GOD (ANDER)	1	26	71	1.6	2.2
165 CH OF NAZARENE	1	19	46	1.0	1.4
281 LUTH CH AMER..	3	680	866	19.5	26.8
413 S-D ADVENTISTS	1	7	8*	0.2	0.2
449 UN METHODIST..	2	420	485	10.9	15.0
453 UN PRES CH USA	1	369	437*	9.9	13.5
WABAUNSEE	20	2,653	3,850*	60.2	100.0
019 AMER BAPT CONV	1	150	179*	2.8	4.6
081 CATHOLIC......	3	0	650	10.2	16.9
097 CR C AND C CR.	1	75	89*	1.4	2.3
283 LUTH--MO SYNOD	3	874	1,150	18.0	29.9
419 SO BAPT CONV..	1	37	44*	0.7	1.1
443 UN C OF CHRIST	3	444	529*	8.3	13.7
449 UN METHODIST..	7	933	1,042	16.3	27.1
453 UN PRES CH USA	1	140	167*	2.6	4.3
WALLACE	8	706	1,368*	61.8	100.0
019 AMER BAPT CONV	2	78	98*	4.4	7.2
081 CATHOLIC......	2	0	560	25.3	40.9
281 LUTH CH AMER..	2	186	244	11.0	17.8
449 UN METHODIST..	2	442	466	21.0	34.1
WASHINGTON	40	4,741	7,667*	82.9	100.0
019 AMER BAPT CONV	1	101	119*	1.3	1.6
029 AMER LUTH CH..	1	150	201	2.2	2.6
081 CATHOLIC......	7	0	1,828	19.8	23.8
093 CR CH (DISC)..	1	43	51*	0.6	0.7
097 CR C AND C CR.	5	470	554*	6.0	7.2
157 CH OF BRETHREN	1	30	35*	0.4	0.5
226 FRIENDS-USA...	1	28	33*	0.4	0.4
281 LUTH CH AMER..	7	856	1,076	11.6	14.0
283 LUTH--MO SYNOD	6	1,383	1,862	20.1	24.3
449 UN METHODIST..	7	1,105	1,230	13.3	16.0
453 UN PRES CH USA	3	575	678*	7.3	8.8
WICHITA	9	953	1,954*	59.7	100.0
019 AMER BAPT CONV	1	293	375*	11.5	19.2
081 CATHOLIC......	2	0	775	23.7	39.7

*Total adherents estimated from known number of communicant, confirmed, full members.

—Represents a percent less than 0.1.

Percentages may not total due to rounding.

Table 3. Churches and Church Membership by State, County and Denomination: 1971

County and Denomination	Number of churches	Communicant, confirmed, full members	Total adherents: Number	Percent of total population	Percent of total adherents
165 CH OF NAZARENE	1	28	35	1.1	1.8
449 UN METHODIST..	3	428	508	15.5	26.0
453 UN PRES CH USA	2	204	261*	8.0	13.4
WILSON	29	3,471	4,750*	42.0	100.0
019 AMER BAPT CONV	2	299	346*	3.1	7.3
081 CATHOLIC......	2	0	542	4.8	11.4
093 CR CH (DISC)..	2	857	991*	8.8	20.9
097 CR C AND C CR.	5	35	40*	0.4	0.8
123 CH GOD (ANDER)	1	39	130	1.1	2.7
157 CH OF BRETHREN	1	35	40*	0.4	0.8
165 CH OF NAZARENE	3	186	392	3.5	8.3
193 EPISCOPAL.....	1	79	92	0.8	1.9
287 MENN GEN CONF.	1	14	16*	0.1	0.3
449 UN METHODIST..	9	1,664	1,857	16.4	39.1
453 UN PRES CH USA	2	263	304*	2.7	6.4
WOODSON	14	1,908	2,676*	55.9	100.0
081 CATHOLIC......	2	0	524	10.9	19.6
093 CR CH (DISC)..	2	508	584*	12.2	21.8
193 EPISCOPAL.....	1	36	47	1.0	1.8
413 S-D ADVENTISTS	1	23	26*	0.5	1.0
419 SO BAPT CONV..	1	208	239*	5.0	8.9
449 UN METHODIST..	5	902	991	20.7	37.0
453 UN PRES CH USA	2	231	265*	5.5	9.9
WYANDOTTE	141	37,198	76,081*	40.7	100.0
019 AMER BAPT CONV	24	7,385	9,131*	4.9	12.0
059 BAPT MISS ASSN	1	127	157*	0.1	0.2
081 CATHOLIC......	18	0	29,100	15.6	38.2
093 CR CH (DISC)..	11	3,998	4,943*	2.6	6.5
097 CR C AND C CR.	3	1,360	1,682*	0.9	2.2
123 CH GOD (ANDER)	4	351	767	0.4	1.0
127 CH GOD (CLEVE)	4	72	89*	-	0.1
157 CH OF BRETHREN	1	199	246*	0.1	0.3
165 CH OF NAZARENE	6	772	1,578	0.8	2.1
193 EPISCOPAL.....	3	884	1,115	0.6	1.5
221 FREE METH C NA	2	77	100	0.1	0.1
281 LUTH CH AMER..	3	1,013	1,397	0.7	1.8
283 LUTH--MO SYNOD	8	2,788	3,796	2.0	5.0
285 MENNONITE CH..	2	119	147*	0.1	0.2
287 MENN GEN CONF.	1	156	193*	0.1	0.3
353 PLY BRETHREN..	2	100	192	0.1	0.3
403 SALVATION ARMY	1	91	459	0.2	0.6
413 S-D ADVENTISTS	2	480	593*	0.3	0.8
419 SO BAPT CONV..	14	4,290	5,304*	2.8	7.0
443 UN C OF CHRIST	5	1,355	1,675*	0.9	2.2
449 UN METHODIST..	18	9,636	11,012	5.9	14.5
453 UN PRES CH USA	8	1,945	2,405*	1.3	3.2
CO DATA NOT AVAIL	82	3,186	10,587*	N/A	N/A
151 L-D SAINTS....	0	0	6,777	N/A	N/A
223 FREE WILL BAPT	14	809	978*	N/A	N/A
467 WESLEYAN......	68	2,377	2,832	N/A	N/A

KENTUCKY

County and Denomination	Number of churches	Communicant, confirmed, full members	Total adherents: Number	Percent of total population	Percent of total adherents
THE STATE.....	6,101	1,161,357	1,764,374*	54.8	100.0
ADAIR	71	7,603	8,826*	67.7	100.0
075 BRETHREN IN CR	4	99	118*	0.9	1.3
081 CATHOLIC......	1	0	21	0.2	0.2
093 CR CH (DISC)..	4	147	175*	1.3	2.0
097 CR C AND C CR.	12	1,376	1,635*	12.5	18.5
123 CH GOD (ANDER)	1	40	80	0.6	0.9
127 CH GOD (CLEVE)	1	44	52*	0.4	0.6
165 CH OF NAZARENE	3	232	564	4.3	6.4
185 CUMBER PRESB..	2	61	72*	0.6	0.8
357 PRESB CH US...	1	63	75*	0.6	0.8
413 S-D ADVENTISTS	1	32	38*	0.3	0.4
419 SO BAPT CONV..	19	2,468	2,932*	22.5	33.2
449 UN METHODIST..	21	2,977	2,988	22.9	33.9
453 UN PRES CH USA	1	64	76*	0.6	0.9
ALLEN	35	5,379	6,228*	49.4	100.0
081 CATHOLIC......	1	0	32	0.3	0.5
165 CH OF NAZARENE	1	49	137	1.1	2.2
221 FREE METH C NA	1	24	29	0.2	0.5
419 SO BAPT CONV..	19	3,486	4,129*	32.8	66.3
449 UN METHODIST..	13	1,820	1,901	15.1	30.5
ANDERSON	30	5,827	7,190*	76.8	100.0
081 CATHOLIC......	1	0	126	1.3	1.8
093 CR CH (DISC)..	5	821	1,005*	10.7	14.0
097 CR C AND C CR.	4	720	882*	9.4	12.3
127 CH GOD (CLEVE)	1	22	27*	0.3	0.4
193 EPISCOPAL.....	1	38	53	0.6	0.7
357 PRESB CH US...	1	57	70*	0.7	1.0
413 S-D ADVENTISTS	1	10	12*	0.1	0.2

County and Denomination	Number of churches	Communicant, confirmed, full members	Total adherents: Number	Percent of total population	Percent of total adherents
419 SO BAPT CONV..	12	3,606	4,416*	47.2	61.4
449 UN METHODIST..	3	505	540	5.8	7.5
453 UN PRES CH USA	1	48	59*	0.6	0.8
BALLARD	31	5,552	6,588*	79.6	100.0
081 CATHOLIC......	1	0	238	2.9	3.6
093 CR CH (DISC)..	3	176	208*	2.5	3.2
185 CUMBER PRESB..	2	313	370*	4.5	5.6
419 SO BAPT CONV..	17	3,825	4,527*	54.7	68.7
449 UN METHODIST..	8	1,238	1,245	15.0	18.9
BARREN	61	12,505	15,103*	52.7	100.0
081 CATHOLIC......	1	0	328	1.1	2.2
093 CR CH (DISC)..	2	538	649*	2.3	4.3
097 CR C AND C CR.	3	329	397*	1.4	2.6
123 CH GOD (ANDER)	1	21	51	0.2	0.3
127 CH GOD (CLEVE)	2	85	102*	0.4	0.7
165 CH OF NAZARENE	2	167	340	1.2	2.3
185 CUMBER PRESB..	3	574	692*	2.4	4.6
193 EPISCOPAL.....	1	36	56	0.2	0.4
357 PRESB CH US...	1	114	137*	0.5	0.9
413 S-D ADVENTISTS	1	10	12*	-	0.1
419 SO BAPT CONV..	25	7,688	9,268*	32.3	61.4
449 UN METHODIST..	18	2,823	2,926	10.2	19.4
453 UN PRES CH USA	1	120	145*	0.5	1.0
BATH	40	2,553	3,886*	42.1	100.0
081 CATHOLIC......	1	0	25	0.3	0.6
093 CR CH (DISC)..	10	1,035	1,263*	13.7	32.5
097 CR C AND C CR.	10	470	573*	6.2	14.7
123 CH GOD (ANDER)	10	476	1,376	14.9	35.4
357 PRESB CH US...	1	12	15*	0.2	0.4
419 SO BAPT CONV..	2	194	237*	2.6	6.1
449 UN METHODIST..	4	327	349	3.8	9.0
453 UN PRES CH USA	2	39	48*	0.5	1.2
BELL	86	15,219	19,267*	62.0	100.0
081 CATHOLIC......	2	0	280	0.9	1.5
093 CR CH (DISC)..	2	235	290*	0.9	1.5
127 CH GOD (CLEVE)	4	217	268*	0.9	1.4
165 CH OF NAZARENE	3	96	362	1.2	1.9
193 EPISCOPAL.....	1	108	138	0.4	0.7
357 PRESB CH US...	2	142	175*	0.6	0.9
403 SALVATION ARMY	1	30	142	0.5	0.7
413 S-D ADVENTISTS	1	10	12*	-	0.1
419 SO BAPT CONV..	63	13,358	16,492*	53.1	85.6
449 UN METHODIST..	5	861	908	2.9	4.7
453 UN PRES CH USA	2	162	200*	0.6	1.0
BOONE	45	10,847	18,314*	55.8	100.0
081 CATHOLIC......	4	0	4,500	13.7	24.6
093 CR CH (DISC)..	7	988	1,264*	3.9	6.9
097 CR C AND C CR.	3	820	1,049*	3.2	5.7
127 CH GOD (CLEVE)	1	37	47*	0.1	0.3
157 CH OF BRETHREN	1	113	145*	0.4	0.8
165 CH OF NAZARENE	1	102	203	0.6	1.1
193 EPISCOPAL.....	1	210	327	1.0	1.8
281 LUTH CH AMER..	2	698	988	3.0	5.4
357 PRESB CH US...	2	86	110*	0.3	0.6
419 SO BAPT CONV..	14	6,357	8,135*	24.8	44.4
449 UN METHODIST..	7	1,352	1,438	4.4	7.9
453 UN PRES CH USA	2	84	108*	0.3	0.6
BOURBON	36	7,846	10,241*	55.4	100.0
081 CATHOLIC......	1	0	550	3.0	5.4
093 CR CH (DISC)..	9	1,753	2,129*	11.5	20.8
097 CR C AND C CR.	3	650	790*	4.3	7.7
123 CH GOD (ANDER)	1	185	375	2.0	3.7
165 CH OF NAZARENE	4	150	339	1.8	3.3
193 EPISCOPAL.....	1	161	180	1.0	1.8
357 PRESB CH US...	3	249	302*	1.6	2.9
419 SO BAPT CONV..	5	2,859	3,473*	18.8	33.9
449 UN METHODIST..	7	1,605	1,819	9.8	17.8
453 UN PRES CH USA	2	234	284*	1.5	2.8
BOYD	73	20,905	28,802*	55.0	100.0
029 AMER LUTH CH..	1	119	170	0.3	0.6
081 CATHOLIC......	3	0	2,000	3.8	6.9
093 CR CH (DISC)..	2	798	960*	1.8	3.3
097 CR C AND C CR.	4	590	710*	1.4	2.5
123 CH GOD (ANDER)	3	395	1,123	2.1	3.9
127 CH GOD (CLEVE)	2	174	209*	0.4	0.7
165 CH OF NAZARENE	8	1,198	2,831	5.4	9.8
193 EPISCOPAL.....	1	730	861	1.6	3.0
283 LUTH--MO SYNOD	1	323	462	0.9	1.6
357 PRESB CH US...	4	686	825*	1.6	2.9
403 SALVATION ARMY	1	48	187	0.4	0.6
413 S-D ADVENTISTS	1	100	120*	0.2	0.4
419 SO BAPT CONV..	20	9,608	11,561*	22.1	40.1
449 UN METHODIST..	18	5,436	5,941	11.3	20.6
453 UN PRES CH USA	4	700	842*	1.6	2.9
BOYLE	45	12,249	15,714*	74.5	100.0
081 CATHOLIC......	3	0	799	3.8	5.1
093 CR CH (DISC)..	5	1,150	1,383*	6.6	8.8
097 CR C AND C CR.	4	453	545*	2.6	3.5
123 CH GOD (ANDER)	1	140	340	1.6	2.2

*Total adherents estimated from known number of communicant, confirmed, full members.

—Represents a percent less than 0.1.

Percentages may not total due to rounding.

Table 3. Churches and Church Membership by State, County and Denomination: 1971

County and Denomination	Number of churches	Communicant, confirmed, full members	Total adherents: Number	Percent of total population	Percent of total adherents
127 CH GOD (CLEVE)	4	214	257*	1.2	1.6
165 CH OF NAZARENE	1	76	137	0.6	0.9
193 EPISCOPAL.....	1	177	237	1.1	1.5
283 LUTH--MO SYNOD	1	14	34	0.2	0.2
357 PRESB CH US...	2	388	467*	2.2	3.0
403 SALVATION ARMY	1	56	187	0.9	1.2
419 SO BAPT CONV..	16	7,815	9,396*	44.6	59.8
449 UN METHODIST..	4	1,385	1,474	7.0	9.4
453 UN PRES CH USA	2	381	458*	2.2	2.9
BRACKEN	41	4,080	5,727*	79.2	100.0
029 AMER LUTH CH..	1	81	135	1.9	2.4
081 CATHOLIC......	2	0	800	11.1	14.0
093 CR CH (DISC)..	2	166	201*	2.8	3.5
097 CR C AND C CR.	14	1,476	1,789*	24.8	31.2
165 CH OF NAZARENE	1	96	209	2.9	3.6
357 PRESB CH US...	2	82	99*	1.4	1.7
419 SO BAPT CONV..	7	1,123	1,362*	18.8	23.8
449 UN METHODIST..	10	973	1,031	14.3	18.0
453 UN PRES CH USA	2	83	101*	1.4	1.8
BREATHITT	29	1,936	2,641*	18.6	100.0
081 CATHOLIC......	1	0	50	0.4	1.9
093 CR CH (DISC)..	3	179	224*	1.6	8.5
097 CR C AND C CR.	1	200	251*	1.8	9.5
123 CH GOD (ANDER)	2	147	395	2.8	15.0
127 CH GOD (CLEVE)	1	45	56*	0.4	2.1
221 FREE METH C NA	2	65	92	0.6	3.5
285 MENNONITE CH..	4	41	51*	0.4	1.9
357 PRESB CH US...	4	135	169*	1.2	6.4
419 SO BAPT CONV..	3	629	789*	5.5	29.9
449 UN METHODIST..	4	362	397	2.8	15.0
453 UN PRES CH USA	4	133	167*	1.2	6.3
BRECKINRIDGE	65	7,991	11,243*	76.0	100.0
081 CATHOLIC......	5	0	2,049	13.9	18.2
123 CH GOD (ANDER)	1	20	75	0.5	0.7
185 CUMBER PRESB..	10	740	903*	6.1	8.0
419 SO BAPT CONV..	20	4,284	5,228*	35.4	46.5
449 UN METHODIST..	28	2,923	2,959	20.0	26.3
453 UN PRES CH USA	1	24	29*	0.2	0.3
BULLITT	41	9,429	15,352*	58.8	100.0
081 CATHOLIC......	4	0	3,203	12.3	20.9
093 CR CH (DISC)..	2	184	244*	0.9	1.6
097 CR C AND C CR.	2	285	378*	1.4	2.5
127 CH GOD (CLEVE)	2	78	104*	0.4	0.7
357 PRESB CH US...	1	62	82*	0.3	0.5
419 SO BAPT CONV..	21	7,249	9,623*	36.9	62.7
449 UN METHODIST..	8	1,513	1,641	6.3	10.7
453 UN PRES CH USA	1	58	77*	0.3	0.5
BUTLER	43	5,377	6,455*	66.4	100.0
081 CATHOLIC......	1	0	42	0.4	0.7
093 CR CH (DISC)..	1	12	14*	0.1	0.2
185 CUMBER PRESB..	3	115	139*	1.4	2.2
285 MENNONITE CH..	1	9	11*	0.1	0.2
357 PRESB CH US...	1	49	59*	0.6	0.9
419 SO BAPT CONV..	24	4,620	5,582*	57.4	86.5
449 UN METHODIST..	9	486	504	5.2	7.8
453 UN PRES CH USA	3	86	104*	1.1	1.6
CALDWELL	44	9,140	10,844*	82.3	100.0
081 CATHOLIC......	1	0	200	1.5	1.8
093 CR CH (DISC)..	2	246	291*	2.2	2.7
097 CR C AND C CR.	1	139	164*	1.2	1.5
185 CUMBER PRESB..	7	501	593*	4.5	5.5
357 PRESB CH US...	1	105	124*	0.9	1.1
413 S-D ADVENTISTS	1	10	12*	0.1	0.1
419 SO BAPT CONV..	25	6,915	8,179*	62.1	75.4
449 UN METHODIST..	5	1,124	1,163	8.8	10.7
453 UN PRES CH USA	1	100	118*	0.9	1.1
CALLOWAY	53	12,005	13,873*	50.1	100.0
081 CATHOLIC......	1	0	341	1.2	2.5
093 CR CH (DISC)..	1	298	344*	1.2	2.5
097 CR C AND C CR.	1	1[illegible]	21*	0.1	0.2
185 CUMBER PRESB..	3	131	151*	0.5	1.1
193 EPISCOPAL.....	1	62	115	0.4	0.8
283 LUTH--MO SYNOD	1	149	201	0.7	1.4
357 PRESB CH US...	1	101	117*	0.4	0.8
413 S-D ADVENTISTS	1	19	22*	0.1	0.2
419 SO BAPT CONV..	26	7,794	9,[illegible]*	32.5	64.9
449 UN METHODIST..	16	3,324	3,43[illegible]	12.4	24.7
453 UN PRES CH USA	1	109	12[illegible]	0.5	0.9
CAMPBELL	98	20,632	53,171*	60.1	100.0
081 CATHOLIC......	22	0	26,500	29.9	49.8
093 CR CH (DISC)..	3	412	510*	0.6	1.0
097 CR C AND C CR.	5	690	854*	1.0	1.6
127 CH GOD (CLEVE)	4	371	459*	0.5	0.9
165 CH OF NAZARENE	7	1,194	2,577	2.9	4.8
193 EPISCOPAL.....	4	809	1,250	1.4	2.4
281 LUTH CH AMER..	4	703	951	1.1	1.[illegible]
285 MENNONITE CH..	1	14	17*	-	-
357 PRESB CH US...	1	327	405*	0.5	0.8
403 SALVATION ARMY	1	49	228	0.3	0.4

County and Denomination	Number of churches	Communicant, confirmed, full members	Total adherents: Number	Percent of total population	Percent of total adherents
419 SO BAPT CONV..	20	8,435	10,446*	11.8	19.6
443 UN C OF CHRIST	8	3,443	4,264*	4.8	8.0
449 UN METHODIST..	15	3,653	4,051	4.6	7.6
453 UN PRES CH USA	3	532	659*	0.7	1.2
CARLISLE	23	3,472	4,163*	77.8	100.0
081 CATHOLIC......	1	0	183	3.4	4.4
093 CR CH (DISC)..	2	215	252*	4.7	6.1
097 CR C AND C CR.	2	100	117*	2.2	2.8
419 SO BAPT CONV..	12	2,554	2,993*	55.9	71.9
449 UN METHODIST..	6	603	618	11.5	14.8
CARROLL	23	3,875	5,019*	58.9	100.0
081 CATHOLIC......	1	0	350	4.1	7.0
093 CR CH (DISC)..	5	397	486*	5.7	9.7
097 CR C AND C CR.	2	93	114*	1.3	2.3
281 LUTH CH AMER..	1	86	122	1.4	2.4
357 PRESB CH US...	1	21	26*	0.3	0.5
419 SO BAPT CONV..	9	2,704	3,310*	38.8	65.9
449 UN METHODIST..	3	552	584	6.9	11.6
453 UN PRES CH USA	1	22	27*	0.3	0.5
CARTER	43	4,033	5,200*	26.2	100.0
081 CATHOLIC......	1	0	25	0.1	0.5
093 CR CH (DISC)..	4	154	190*	1.0	3.7
097 CR C AND C CR.	11	1,311	1,617*	8.1	31.1
123 CH GOD (ANDER)	1	40	139	0.7	2.7
165 CH OF NAZARENE	3	137	415	2.1	8.0
357 PRESB CH US...	1	41	51*	0.3	1.0
419 SO BAPT CONV..	11	1,541	1,901*	9.6	36.6
449 UN METHODIST..	10	768	811	4.1	15.6
453 UN PRES CH USA	1	41	51*	0.3	1.0
CASEY	44	4,652	6,037*	46.7	100.0
081 CATHOLIC......	1	0	530	4.1	8.8
093 CR CH (DISC)..	3	294	354*	2.7	5.9
097 CR C AND C CR.	10	571	688*	5.3	11.4
123 CH GOD (ANDER)	3	79	233	1.8	3.9
127 CH GOD (CLEVE)	1	14	17*	0.1	0.3
165 CH OF NAZARENE	2	56	113	0.9	1.9
419 SO BAPT CONV..	13	2,180	2,626*	20.3	43.5
449 UN METHODIST..	11	1,458	1,476	11.4	24.4
CHRISTIAN	87	17,598	21,919*	39.0	100.0
081 CATHOLIC......	2	0	768	1.4	3.5
093 CR CH (DISC)..	9	1,185	1,435*	2.6	6.5
097 CR C AND C CR.	1	75	91*	0.2	0.4
123 CH GOD (ANDER)	1	22	59	0.1	0.3
127 CH GOD (CLEVE)	2	82	99*	0.2	0.5
165 CH OF NAZARENE	1	18	65	0.1	0.3
185 CUMBER PRESB..	4	585	708*	1.3	3.2
193 EPISCOPAL.....	1	254	317	0.6	1.4
283 LUTH--MO SYNOD	1	54	93	0.2	0.4
357 PRESB CH US...	5	324	392*	0.7	1.8
403 SALVATION ARMY	1	105	406	0.7	1.9
413 S-D ADVENTISTS	1	38	46*	0.1	0.2
419 SO BAPT CONV..	34	11,492	13,913*	24.7	63.5
435 UNITARIAN-UNIV	1	74	82	0.1	0.4
449 UN METHODIST..	18	2,962	3,048	5.4	13.9
453 UN PRES CH USA	5	328	397*	0.7	1.8
CLARK	36	9,446	12,527*	52.0	100.0
081 CATHOLIC......	1	0	600	2.5	4.8
093 CR CH (DISC)..	6	997	1,234*	5.1	9.9
097 CR C AND C CR.	5	744	921*	3.8	7.4
123 CH GOD (ANDER)	2	445	898	3.7	7.2
127 CH GOD (CLEVE)	1	275	340*	1.4	2.7
165 CH OF NAZARENE	1	81	290	1.2	2.3
357 PRESB CH US...	2	181	224*	0.9	1.8
419 SO BAPT CONV..	10	[illegible],682	5,794*	24.1	46.3
449 UN METHODIST..	6	[illegible],844	1,982	8.2	15.8
453 UN PRES CH USA	2	197	244*	1.0	1.9
CLAY	42	5,975	7,707*	41.7	100.0
081 CATHOLIC......	1	0	40	0.2	0.5
093 CR CH (DISC)..	1	140	182*	1.0	2.4
097 CR C AND C CR.	2	150	195*	1.1	2.5
127 CH GOD (CLEVE)	3	126	163*	0.9	2.1
157 CH OF BRETHREN	1	219	284*	1.5	3.7
357 PRESB CH US...	3	53	69*	0.4	0.9
413 S-D ADVENTISTS	1	89	115*	0.6	1.5
419 SO BAPT CONV..	23	4,857	6,301*	34.1	81.8
449 UN METHODIST..	4	283	283	1.5	3.7
453 UN PRES CH USA	[illegible]	58	75*	0.4	1.0
CLINTON	30	3,589	4,150*	50.8	100.0
081 CATHOLIC......	1	0	28	0.3	0.7
093 CR CH (DISC)..	2	132	162*	2.0	3.9
097 CR C AND C CR.	3	39	48*	0.6	1.2
165 CH OF NAZARENE	3	178	362	4.4	8.7
419 SO BAPT CONV..	6	1,277	1,567*	19.2	37.8
449 UN METHODIST..	15	1,963	1,983	24.3	47.8
CRITTENDEN	42	4,731	5,547*	65.3	100.0
081 CATHOLIC......	1	0	65	0.8	1.2
093 CR CH (DISC)..	2	53	63*	0.7	1.1

*Total adherents estimated from known number of communicant, confirmed, full members.

—Represents a percent less than 0.1.

Percentages may not total due to rounding.

Table 3. Churches and Church Membership by State, County and Denomination: 1971

County and Denomination	Number of churches	Communicant, confirmed, full members	Total adherents: Number	Total adherents: Percent of total population	Total adherents: Percent of total adherents
123 CH GOD (ANDER)	1	103	174	2.0	3.1
185 CUMBER PRESB..	6	587	694*	8.2	12.5
357 PRESB CH US...	3	72	85*	1.0	1.5
419 SO BAPT CONV..	18	2,762	3,263*	38.4	58.8
449 UN METHODIST..	8	1,085	1,121	13.2	20.2
453 UN PRES CH USA	3	69	82*	1.0	1.5
CUMBERLAND	29	2,493	2,736*	39.9	100.0
081 CATHOLIC......	1	0	12	0.2	0.4
093 CR CH (DISC)..	1	131	156*	2.3	5.7
097 CR C AND C CR.	3	245	291*	4.2	10.6
165 CH OF NAZARENE	1	48	110	1.6	4.0
185 CUMBER PRESB..	2	32	38*	0.6	1.4
357 PRESB CH US...	1	28	33*	0.5	1.2
419 SO BAPT CONV..	4	398	473*	6.9	17.3
449 UN METHODIST..	16	1,611	1,623	23.7	59.3
DAVIESS	112	32,098	59,802*	75.2	100.0
081 CATHOLIC......	18	0	20,112	25.3	33.6
093 CR CH (DISC)..	4	1,210	1,512*	1.9	2.5
097 CR C AND C CR.	2	464	580*	0.7	1.0
123 CH GOD (ANDER)	1	32	102	0.1	0.2
127 CH GOD (CLEVE)	3	63	79*	0.1	0.1
165 CH OF NAZARENE	2	191	314	0.4	0.5
185 CUMBER PRESB..	4	604	755*	0.9	1.3
193 EPISCOPAL.....	1	306	425	0.5	0.7
221 FREE METH C NA	1	9	16	-	-
281 LUTH CH AMER..	1	137	224	0.3	0.4
283 LUTH--MO SYNOD	1	54	79	0.1	0.1
357 PRESB CH US...	2	529	661*	0.8	1.1
403 SALVATION ARMY	1	107	324	0.4	0.5
413 S-D ADVENTISTS	1	65	81*	0.1	0.1
419 SO BAPT CONV..	45	21,921	27,393*	34.5	45.8
435 UNITARIAN-UNIV	1	16	28	-	-
443 UN C OF CHRIST	1	377	471*	0.6	0.8
449 UN METHODIST..	21	5,461	5,956	7.5	10.0
453 UN PRES CH USA	2	552	690*	0.9	1.2
EDMONSON	18	2,529	3,170*	36.2	100.0
081 CATHOLIC......	2	0	140	1.6	4.4
419 SO BAPT CONV..	14	2,366	2,867*	32.8	90.4
449 UN METHODIST..	2	163	163	1.9	5.1
ELLIOTT	4	341	394*	6.6	100.0
419 SO BAPT CONV..	1	110	137*	2.3	34.8
449 UN METHODIST..	3	231	257	4.3	65.2
ESTILL	43	4,049	5,534*	43.4	100.0
081 CATHOLIC......	1	0	65	0.5	1.2
093 CR CH (DISC)..	2	332	413*	3.2	7.5
097 CR C AND C CR.	11	619	771*	6.0	13.9
123 CH GOD (ANDER)	4	185	545	4.3	9.8
127 CH GOD (CLEVE)	2	167	208*	1.6	3.8
165 CH OF NAZARENE	3	184	450	3.5	8.1
221 FREE METH C NA	1	21	32	0.3	0.6
419 SO BAPT CONV..	14	1,983	2,470*	19.4	44.6
449 UN METHODIST..	5	558	580	4.5	10.5
FAYETTE	134	57,818	88,264*	50.6	100.0
029 AMER LUTH CH..	1	186	293	0.2	0.3
081 CATHOLIC......	6	0	16,800	9.6	19.0
093 CR CH (DISC)..	12	5,718	6,976*	4.0	7.9
097 CR C AND C CR.	15	9,228	11,258*	6.5	12.8
123 CH GOD (ANDER)	3	343	823	0.5	0.9
127 CH GOD (CLEVE)	3	587	716*	0.4	0.8
165 CH OF NAZARENE	6	960	1,626	0.9	1.8
185 CUMBER PRESB..	1	132	161*	0.1	0.2
193 EPISCOPAL.....	8	2,290	3,128	1.8	3.5
221 FREE METH C NA	1	19	24	-	-
226 FRIENDS-USA...	1	13	16*	-	-
281 LUTH CH AMER..	1	659	900	0.5	1.0
283 LUTH--MO SYNOD	3	398	553	0.3	0.6
357 PRESB CH US...	11	2,198	2,681*	1.5	3.0
403 SALVATION ARMY	1	98	427	0.2	0.5
413 S-D ADVENTISTS	2	301	367*	0.2	0.4
419 SO BAPT CONV..	28	22,943	27,989*	16.1	31.7
435 UNITARIAN-UNIV	2	213	384	0.2	0.4
443 UN C OF CHRIST	1	71	87*	-	0.1
449 UN METHODIST..	16	9,274	10,387	6.0	11.8
453 UN PRES CH USA	12	2,187	2,668*	1.5	3.0
FLEMING	46	3,847	4,743*	41.7	100.0
081 CATHOLIC......	1	0	216	1.9	4.6
093 CR CH (DISC)..	5	667	805*	7.1	17.0
097 CR C AND C CR.	14	460	555*	4.9	11.7
123 CH GOD (ANDER)	3	133	328	2.9	6.9
357 PRESB CH US...	2	61	74*	0.7	1.6
419 SO BAPT CONV..	6	749	904*	8.0	19.1
449 UN METHODIST..	13	1,722	1,795	15.8	37.8
453 UN PRES CH USA	2	55	66*	0.6	1.4
FLOYD	50	4,877	6,000*	16.7	100.0
081 CATHOLIC......	3	0	200	0.6	3.3
093 CR CH (DISC)..	6	460	566*	1.6	9.4
097 CR C AND C CR.	4	235	289*	0.8	4.8
123 CH GOD (ANDER)	2	82	192	0.5	3.2
127 CH GOD (CLEVE)	3	61	75*	0.2	1.3
165 CH OF NAZARENE	1	66	66	0.2	1.1
193 EPISCOPAL.....	1	18	27	0.1	0.5
357 PRESB CH US...	2	100	123*	0.3	2.1
413 S-D ADVENTISTS	1	10	12*	-	0.2
419 SO BAPT CONV..	8	2,207	2,715*	7.6	45.3
449 UN METHODIST..	17	1,538	1,612	4.5	26.9
453 UN PRES CH USA	2	100	123*	0.3	2.1
FRANKLIN	50	16,658	23,388*	67.8	100.0
081 CATHOLIC......	1	0	2,800	8.1	12.0
093 CR CH (DISC)..	4	1,819	2,193*	6.4	9.4
097 CR C AND C CR.	4	665	802*	2.3	3.4
123 CH GOD (ANDER)	1	47	127	0.4	0.5
127 CH GOD (CLEVE)	1	66	80*	0.2	0.3
165 CH OF NAZARENE	2	280	510	1.5	2.2
193 EPISCOPAL.....	1	426	539	1.6	2.3
281 LUTH CH AMER..	1	73	112	0.3	0.5
357 PRESB CH US...	2	425	512*	1.5	2.2
403 SALVATION ARMY	1	30	396	1.1	1.7
413 S-D ADVENTISTS	1	53	64*	0.2	0.3
419 SO BAPT CONV..	25	10,732	12,939*	37.5	55.3
449 UN METHODIST..	4	1,606	1,788	5.2	7.6
453 UN PRES CH USA	2	436	526*	1.5	2.2
FULTON	30	6,105	7,530*	73.9	100.0
081 CATHOLIC......	2	0	310	3.0	4.1
093 CR CH (DISC)..	1	129	155*	1.5	2.1
097 CR C AND C CR.	2	143	172*	1.7	2.3
123 CH GOD (ANDER)	1	116	286	2.8	3.8
185 CUMBER PRESB..	2	380	457*	4.5	6.1
193 EPISCOPAL.....	2	104	126	1.2	1.7
419 SO BAPT CONV..	12	3,278	3,940*	38.7	52.3
449 UN METHODIST..	8	1,955	2,084	20.5	27.7
GALLATIN	15	2,286	2,908*	70.3	100.0
081 CATHOLIC......	1	0	125	3.0	4.3
093 CR CH (DISC)..	2	133	164*	4.0	5.6
097 CR C AND C CR.	3	50	62*	1.5	2.1
419 SO BAPT CONV..	7	1,879	2,320*	56.1	79.8
449 UN METHODIST..	2	224	237	5.7	8.1
GARRARD	37	5,042	6,445*	68.2	100.0
081 CATHOLIC......	1	0	200	2.1	3.1
093 CR CH (DISC)..	4	517	619*	6.5	9.6
097 CR C AND C CR.	4	125	150*	1.6	2.3
123 CH GOD (ANDER)	1	165	315	3.3	4.9
127 CH GOD (CLEVE)	1	66	79*	0.8	1.2
165 CH OF NAZARENE	1	145	345	3.6	5.4
357 PRESB CH US...	2	118	141*	1.5	2.2
419 SO BAPT CONV..	13	2,988	3,580*	37.9	55.5
449 UN METHODIST..	8	792	865	9.1	13.4
453 UN PRES CH USA	2	126	151*	1.6	2.3
GRANT	38	5,884	7,390*	73.9	100.0
081 CATHOLIC......	1	0	160	1.6	2.2
093 CR CH (DISC)..	2	280	344*	3.4	4.7
097 CR C AND C CR.	11	865	1,061*	10.6	14.4
123 CH GOD (ANDER)	1	80	160	1.6	2.2
357 PRESB CH US...	1	4	5*	0.1	0.1
419 SO BAPT CONV..	18	4,281	5,252*	52.5	71.1
449 UN METHODIST..	3	369	402	4.0	5.4
453 UN PRES CH USA	1	5	6*	0.1	0.1
GRAVES	79	15,297	20,131*	65.1	100.0
081 CATHOLIC......	2	0	2,305	7.5	11.5
093 CR CH (DISC)..	2	448	531*	1.7	2.6
097 CR C AND C CR.	2	68	81*	0.3	0.4
127 CH GOD (CLEVE)	2	92	109*	0.4	0.5
165 CH OF NAZARENE	1	113	222	0.7	1.1
185 CUMBER PRESB..	8	630	747*	2.4	3.7
193 EPISCOPAL.....	1	30	39	0.1	0.2
349 PENT HOLINESS.	2	115	136*	0.4	0.7
357 PRESB CH US...	1	147	174*	0.6	0.9
419 SO BAPT CONV..	39	10,627	12,597*	40.7	62.6
449 UN METHODIST..	18	2,878	3,013	9.7	15.0
453 UN PRES CH USA	1	149	177*	0.6	0.9
GRAYSON	51	5,053	8,007*	48.7	100.0
081 CATHOLIC......	7	0	2,099	12.8	26.2
093 CR CH (DISC)..	1	102	123*	0.7	1.5
097 CR C AND C CR.	4	384	465*	2.8	5.8
165 CH OF NAZARENE	1	49	58	0.4	0.7
185 CUMBER PRESB..	6	313	379*	2.3	4.7
413 S-D ADVENTISTS	1	23	28*	0.2	0.3
419 SO BAPT CONV..	21	3,013	3,647*	22.2	45.5
449 UN METHODIST..	10	1,169	1,208	7.3	15.1
GREEN	41	7,166	8,363*	80.8	100.0
081 CATHOLIC......	1	0	50	0.5	0.6
097 CR C AND C CR.	2	100	119*	1.1	1.4
165 CH OF NAZARENE	1	102	173	1.7	2.1
185 CUMBER PRESB..	3	568	677*	6.5	8.1
357 PRESB CH US...	2	103	123*	1.2	1.5
419 SO BAPT CONV..	21	4,682	5,577*	53.9	66.7
449 UN METHODIST..	9	1,506	1,519	14.7	18.2
453 UN PRES CH USA	2	105	125*	1.2	1.5

*Total adherents estimated from known number of communicant, confirmed, full members.

—Represents a percent less than 0.1.

Percentages may not total due to rounding.

Table 3. Churches and Church Membership by State, County and Denomination: 1971

County and Denomination	Number of churches	Communicant, confirmed, full members	Total adherents: Number	Total adherents: Percent of total population	Total adherents: Percent of total adherents
GREENUP	45	6,721	9,140*	27.5	100.0
081 CATHOLIC......	1	0	150	0.5	1.6
097 CR C AND C CR.	11	1,720	2,150*	6.5	23.5
123 CH GOD (ANDER)	2	175	544	1.6	6.0
127 CH GOD (CLEVE)	4	170	213*	0.6	2.3
165 CH OF NAZARENE	6	434	1,161	3.5	12.7
419 SO BAPT CONV..	8	2,144	2,681*	8.1	29.3
449 UN METHODIST..	12	2,048	2,203	6.6	24.1
453 UN PRES CH USA	1	30	38*	0.1	0.4
HANCOCK	25	3,723	5,222*	73.8	100.0
081 CATHOLIC......	3	0	698	9.9	13.4
185 CUMBER PRESB..	1	31	39*	0.6	0.7
349 PENT HOLINESS.	1	26	33*	0.5	0.6
419 SO BAPT CONV..	12	2,715	3,419*	48.3	65.5
449 UN METHODIST..	8	951	1,033	14.6	19.8
HARDIN	83	19,678	28,130*	35.9	100.0
081 CATHOLIC......	7	0	5,135	6.5	18.3
093 CR CH (DISC)..	1	66	78*	0.1	0.3
097 CR C AND C CR.	8	1,445	1,711*	2.2	6.1
127 CH GOD (CLEVE)	2	32	38*	-	0.1
165 CH OF NAZARENE	3	85	242	0.3	0.9
185 CUMBER PRESB..	1	29	34*	-	0.1
193 EPISCOPAL.....	1	108	163	0.2	0.6
281 LUTH CH AMER..	1	102	153	0.2	0.5
283 LUTH--MO SYNOD	1	34	74	0.1	0.3
357 PRESB CH US...	1	181	214*	0.3	0.8
413 S-D ADVENTISTS	1	50	59*	0.1	0.2
419 SO BAPT CONV..	36	13,060	15,465*	19.7	55.0
449 UN METHODIST..	19	4,336	4,586	5.8	16.3
453 UN PRES CH USA	1	150	178*	0.2	0.6
HARLAN	98	15,548	19,094*	51.1	100.0
081 CATHOLIC......	3	0	400	1.1	2.1
093 CR CH (DISC)..	4	335	409*	1.1	2.1
097 CR C AND C CR.	7	400	488*	1.3	2.6
123 CH GOD (ANDER)	1	78	218	0.6	1.1
127 CH GOD (CLEVE)	15	919	1,121*	3.0	5.9
165 CH OF NAZARENE	2	41	82	0.2	0.4
193 EPISCOPAL.....	1	115	144	0.4	0.8
357 PRESB CH US...	2	139	170*	0.5	0.9
413 S-D ADVENTISTS	1	13	16*	-	0.1
419 SO BAPT CONV..	48	11,166	13,618*	36.4	71.3
449 UN METHODIST..	11	2,202	2,257	6.0	11.8
453 UN PRES CH USA	3	140	171*	0.5	0.9
HARRISON	53	6,372	8,027*	56.7	100.0
081 CATHOLIC......	1	0	425	3.0	5.3
093 CR CH (DISC)..	5	839	1,013*	7.2	12.6
097 CR C AND C CR.	14	575	694*	4.9	8.6
123 CH GOD (ANDER)	1	130	395	2.8	4.9
165 CH OF NAZARENE	1	54	59	0.4	0.7
193 EPISCOPAL.....	1	34	83	0.6	1.0
357 PRESB CH US...	2	137	165*	1.2	2.1
413 S-D ADVENTISTS	1	35	42*	0.3	0.5
419 SO BAPT CONV..	8	1,992	2,405*	17.0	30.0
449 UN METHODIST..	17	2,439	2,581	18.2	32.2
453 UN PRES CH USA	2	137	165*	1.2	2.1
HART	58	8,204	9,811*	70.2	100.0
081 CATHOLIC......	1	0	116	0.8	1.2
097 CR C AND C CR.	1	85	104*	0.7	1.1
127 CH GOD (CLEVE)	1	44	54*	0.4	0.6
185 CUMBER PRESB..	4	438	534*	3.8	5.4
357 PRESB CH US...	1	10	12*	0.1	0.1
419 SO BAPT CONV..	35	6,175	7,530*	53.9	76.8
449 UN METHODIST..	14	1,442	1,449	10.4	14.8
453 UN PRES CH USA	1	10	12*	0.1	0.1
HENDERSON	55	15,197	21,434*	59.5	100.0
081 CATHOLIC......	2	0	2,985	8.3	13.9
093 CR CH (DISC)..	1	433	536*	1.5	2.5
097 CR C AND C CR.	4	317	392*	1.1	1.8
165 CH OF NAZARENE	2	163	343	1.0	1.6
193 EPISCOPAL.....	1	239	314	0.9	1.5
283 LUTH--MO SYNOD	1	94	119	0.3	0.6
357 PRESB CH US...	2	229	283*	0.8	1.3
403 SALVATION ARMY	1	57	212	0.6	1.0
413 S-D ADVENTISTS	1	56	69*	0.2	0.3
419 SO BAPT CONV..	25	9,609	11,889*	33.0	55.5
443 UN C OF CHRIST	1	64	79*	0.2	0.4
449 UN METHODIST..	12	3,710	3,933	10.9	18.3
453 UN PRES CH USA	2	226	280*	0.8	1.3
HENRY	43	6,768	7,944*	72.8	100.0
081 CATHOLIC......	1	0	40	0.4	0.5
093 CR CH (DISC)..	12	1,045	1,249*	11.4	15.7
097 CR C AND C CR.	1	54	65*	0.6	0.8
127 CH GOD (CLEVE)	1	27	32*	0.3	0.4
357 PRESB CH US...	1	42	50*	0.5	0.6
419 SO BAPT CONV..	15	4,130	4,936*	45.2	62.1
449 UN METHODIST..	11	1,428	1,522	14.0	19.2
453 UN PRES CH USA	1	42	50*	0.5	0.6
HICKMAN	26	3,591	4,212*	67.2	100.0
081 CATHOLIC......	1	0	157	2.5	3.7
093 CR CH (DISC)..	1	63	75*	1.2	1.8
419 SO BAPT CONV..	12	1,992	2,379*	38.0	56.5
449 UN METHODIST..	12	1,536	1,601	25.6	38.0
HOPKINS	76	17,271	21,352*	55.9	100.0
081 CATHOLIC......	3	0	720	1.9	3.4
093 CR CH (DISC)..	6	1,226	1,479*	3.9	6.9
097 CR C AND C CR.	6	655	790*	2.1	3.7
123 CH GOD (ANDER)	1	106	306	0.8	1.4
127 CH GOD (CLEVE)	2	86	104*	0.3	0.5
165 CH OF NAZARENE	1	19	55	0.1	0.3
185 CUMBER PRESB..	3	323	390*	1.0	1.8
193 EPISCOPAL.....	1	176	282	0.7	1.3
357 PRESB CH US...	1	165	199*	0.5	0.9
413 S-D ADVENTISTS	1	34	41*	0.1	0.2
419 SO BAPT CONV..	33	11,087	13,376*	35.0	62.6
449 UN METHODIST..	17	3,219	3,399	8.9	15.9
453 UN PRES CH USA	1	175	211*	0.6	1.0
JACKSON	34	3,406	4,234*	42.3	100.0
081 CATHOLIC......	1	0	50	0.5	1.2
093 CR CH (DISC)..	3	298	368*	3.7	8.7
123 CH GOD (ANDER)	1	50	115	1.1	2.7
127 CH GOD (CLEVE)	1	35	43*	0.4	1.0
371 REF CH IN AM..	4	391	408	4.1	9.6
419 SO BAPT CONV..	24	2,632	3,250*	32.5	76.8
JEFFERSON	471	178,949	375,905*	54.1	100.0
055 AS REF PRES CH	1	98	121*	-	-
081 CATHOLIC......	82	0	156,430	22.5	41.6
093 CR CH (DISC)..	17	7,340	9,033*	1.3	2.4
097 CR C AND C CR.	23	6,089	7,493*	1.1	2.0
123 CH GOD (ANDER)	5	676	1,551	0.2	0.4
127 CH GOD (CLEVE)	12	1,334	1,642*	0.2	0.4
165 CH OF NAZARENE	17	1,563	2,592	0.4	0.7
185 CUMBER PRESB..	2	517	636*	0.1	0.2
193 EPISCOPAL.....	18	8,017	9,978	1.4	2.7
221 FREE METH C NA	1	29	43	-	-
226 FRIENDS-USA...	1	70	86*	-	-
281 LUTH CH AMER..	14	4,185	5,573	0.8	1.5
283 LUTH--MO SYNOD	6	1,485	2,239	0.3	0.6
353 PLY BRETHREN..	1	5	5	-	-
357 PRESB CH US...	34	8,111	9,982*	1.4	2.7
403 SALVATION ARMY	3	205	792	0.1	0.2
413 S-D ADVENTISTS	4	795	978*	0.1	0.3
419 SO BAPT CONV..	118	95,052	116,976*	16.8	31.1
435 UNITARIAN-UNIV	3	579	801	0.1	0.2
443 UN C OF CHRIST	20	8,268	10,175*	1.5	2.7
449 UN METHODIST..	55	26,517	28,917	4.2	7.7
453 UN PRES CH USA	34	8,014	9,862*	1.4	2.6
JESSAMINE	30	4,836	5,935*	34.1	100.0
081 CATHOLIC......	1	0	180	1.0	3.0
093 CR CH (DISC)..	6	409	506*	2.9	8.5
127 CH GOD (CLEVE)	1	90	111*	0.6	1.9
165 CH OF NAZARENE	1	89	169	1.0	2.8
193 EPISCOPAL.....	1	33	35	0.2	0.6
221 FREE METH C NA	1	47	68	0.4	1.1
357 PRESB CH US...	3	122	151*	0.9	2.5
419 SO BAPT CONV..	4	2,159	2,671*	15.3	45.0
449 UN METHODIST..	8	1,760	1,887	10.8	31.8
453 UN PRES CH USA	4	127	157*	0.9	2.6
JOHNSON	19	2,036	2,690*	15.3	100.0
081 CATHOLIC......	2	0	170	1.0	6.3
097 CR C AND C CR.	5	175	211*	1.2	7.8
123 CH GOD (ANDER)	4	159	403	2.3	15.0
419 SO BAPT CONV..	3	793	954*	5.4	35.5
449 UN METHODIST..	5	909	952	5.4	35.4
KENTON	124	31,961	76,374*	59.0	100.0
081 CATHOLIC......	28	0	36,305	28.0	47.5
093 CR CH (DISC)..	8	2,231	2,781*	2.1	3.6
097 CR C AND C CR.	11	2,899	3,614*	2.8	4.7
123 CH GOD (ANDER)	4	347	929	0.7	1.2
127 CH GOD (CLEVE)	3	242	302*	0.2	0.4
165 CH OF NAZARENE	1	53	252	0.2	0.3
193 EPISCOPAL.....	2	629	984	0.8	1.3
281 LUTH CH AMER..	2	360	503	0.4	0.7
283 LUTH--MO SYNOD	1	140	220	0.2	0.3
357 PRESB CH US...	3	606	756*	0.6	1.0
403 SALVATION ARMY	1	53	208	0.2	0.3
413 S-D ADVENTISTS	2	273	340*	0.3	0.4
419 SO BAPT CONV..	27	16,292	20,311*	15.7	26.6
443 UN C OF CHRIST	4	908	1,132*	0.9	1.5
449 UN METHODIST..	22	5,879	6,429	5.0	8.4
453 UN PRES CH USA	5	1,049	1,308*	1.0	1.7
KNOTT	7	1,016	1,248*	8.5	100.0
285 MENNONITE CH..	1	13	16*	0.1	1.3
419 SO BAPT CONV..	5	888	1,117*	7.6	89.5
449 UN METHODIST..	1	115	115	0.8	9.2
KNOX	72	11,591	14,462*	61.0	100.0
081 CATHOLIC......	1	0	70	0.3	0.5
093 CR CH (DISC)..	1	98	122*	0.5	0.8

*Total adherents estimated from known number of communicant, confirmed, full members.

—Represents a percent less than 0.1.

Percentages may not total due to rounding.

Table 3. Churches and Church Membership by State, County and Denomination: 1971

County and Denomination	Number of churches	Communicant, confirmed, full members	Total adherents: Number	Percent of total population	Percent of total adherents
127 CH GOD (CLEVE)	2	89	110*	0.5	0.8
165 CH OF NAZARENE	1	98	210	0.9	1.5
193 EPISCOPAL.....	1	35	54	0.2	0.4
419 SO BAPT CONV..	60	10,770	13,361*	56.4	92.4
449 UN METHODIST..	6	501	535	2.3	3.7
LARUE	26	6,031	7,441*	69.7	100.0
081 CATHOLIC......	1	0	250	2.3	3.4
093 CR CH (DISC)..	1	93	113*	1.1	1.5
097 CR C AND C CR.	2	325	394*	3.7	5.3
127 CH GOD (CLEVE)	1	38	46*	0.4	0.6
185 CUMBER PRESB..	1	223	270*	2.5	3.6
419 SO BAPT CONV..	16	4,565	5,534*	51.9	74.4
449 UN METHODIST..	4	787	834	7.8	11.2
LAUREL	70	9,996	12,558*	45.9	100.0
081 CATHOLIC......	3	0	200	0.7	1.6
093 CR CH (DISC)..	6	627	780*	2.8	6.2
097 CR C AND C CR.	10	665	828*	3.0	6.6
123 CH GOD (ANDER)	1	35	80	0.3	0.6
127 CH GOD (CLEVE)	1	80	100*	0.4	0.8
165 CH OF NAZARENE	1	43	113	0.4	0.9
357 PRESB CH US...	1	58	72*	0.3	0.6
413 S-D ADVENTISTS	1	86	107*	0.4	0.9
419 SO BAPT CONV..	38	7,544	9,388*	34.3	74.8
449 UN METHODIST..	7	792	808	3.0	6.4
453 UN PRES CH USA	1	66	82*	0.3	0.7
LAWRENCE	23	1,515	1,727*	16.1	100.0
081 CATHOLIC......	1	C	20	0.2	1.2
093 CR CH (DISC)..	1	99	120*	1.1	6.9
097 CR C AND C CR.	2	80	97*	0.9	5.6
419 SO BAPT CONV..	4	524	635*	5.9	36.8
449 UN METHODIST..	15	812	855	8.0	49.5
LEE	31	2,251	3,285*	49.9	100.0
081 CATHOLIC......	2	0	120	1.8	3.7
093 CR CH (DISC)..	8	704	862*	13.1	26.2
097 CR C AND C CR.	2	200	245*	3.7	7.5
123 CH GOD (ANDER)	6	211	679	10.3	20.7
127 CH GOD (CLEVE)	1	69	84*	1.3	2.6
165 CH OF NAZARENE	1	39	56	0.9	1.7
193 EPISCOPAL.....	1	51	60	0.9	1.8
357 PRESB CH US...	2	79	97*	1.5	3.0
419 SO BAPT CONV..	5	744	911*	13.8	27.7
449 UN METHODIST..	1	78	78	1.2	2.4
453 UN PRES CH USA	2	76	93*	1.4	2.8
LESLIE	24	1,639	2,044*	17.6	100.0
081 CATHOLIC......	1	0	20	0.2	1.0
093 CR CH (DISC)..	2	256	329*	2.8	16.1
127 CH GOD (CLEVE)	2	118	151*	1.3	7.4
357 PRESB CH US...	3	97	124*	1.1	6.1
419 SO BAPT CONV..	7	753	966*	8.3	47.3
449 UN METHODIST..	6	316	327	2.8	16.0
453 UN PRES CH USA	3	99	127*	1.1	6.2
LETCHER	31	2,513	3,168*	13.7	100.0
081 CATHOLIC......	3	C	150	0.6	4.7
097 CR C AND C CR.	1	55	68*	0.3	2.1
123 CH GOD (ANDER)	1	47	113	0.5	3.6
127 CH GOD (CLEVE)	5	168	207*	0.9	6.5
357 PRESB CH US...	4	130	160*	0.7	5.1
413 S-D ADVENTISTS	1	6	7*	-	0.2
419 SO BAPT CONV..	6	1,356	1,673*	7.2	52.8
449 UN METHODIST..	6	623	632	2.7	19.9
453 UN PRES CH USA	4	128	158*	0.7	5.0
LEWIS	40	2,495	3,134*	25.4	100.0
081 CATHOLIC......	1	0	90	0.7	2.9
093 CR CH (DISC)..	2	82	104*	0.8	3.3
097 CR C AND C CR.	14	680	859*	7.0	27.4
127 CH GOD (CLEVE)	1	140	177*	1.4	5.6
165 CH OF NAZARENE	1	42	118	1.0	3.8
357 PRESB CH US...	2	6	8*	0.1	0.3
419 SO BAPT CONV..	6	715	903*	7.3	28.8
449 UN METHODIST..	11	825	869	7.0	27.7
453 UN PRES CH USA	2	5	6*	-	0.2
LINCOLN	67	8,921	11,297*	67.8	100.0
081 CATHOLIC......	2	C	95	0.6	0.8
093 CR CH (DISC)..	5	438	535*	3.2	4.7
097 CR C AND C CR.	9	480	586*	3.5	5.2
123 CH GOD (ANDER)	8	436	940	5.6	8.3
127 CH GOD (CLEVE)	3	156	190*	1.1	1.7
165 CH OF NAZARENE	2	77	174	1.0	1.5
283 LUTH--MO SYNOD	1	35	35	0.2	0.3
357 PRESB CH US...	1	85	104*	0.6	0.9
413 S-D ADVENTISTS	1	38	46*	0.3	0.4
419 SO BAPT CONV..	26	6,148	7,505*	45.0	66.4
449 UN METHODIST..	8	946	987	5.9	8.7
453 UN PRES CH USA	1	82	100*	0.6	0.9
LIVINGSTON	39	5,040	5,762*	75.9	100.0
093 CR CH (DISC)..	1	39	46*	0.6	0.8
185 CUMBER PRESB..	2	89	106*	1.4	1.8
419 SO BAPT CONV..	23	3,541	4,207*	55.4	73.0
449 UN METHODIST..	13	1,371	1,403	18.5	24.3
LOGAN	61	12,407	14,936*	68.5	100.0
081 CATHOLIC......	1	0	306	1.4	2.0
093 CR CH (DISC)..	3	348	422*	1.9	2.8
185 CUMBER PRESB..	4	313	380*	1.7	2.5
193 EPISCOPAL.....	1	95	117	0.5	0.8
357 PRESB CH US...	2	119	144*	0.7	1.0
419 SO BAPT CONV..	33	9,152	11,109*	51.0	74.4
449 UN METHODIST..	15	2,265	2,318	10.6	15.5
453 UN PRES CH USA	2	115	140*	0.6	0.9
LYON	17	3,118	3,524*	63.4	100.0
081 CATHOLIC......	1	0	30	0.5	0.9
419 SO BAPT CONV..	11	2,408	2,746*	49.4	77.9
449 UN METHODIST..	5	710	748	13.4	21.2
MC CRACKEN	83	27,142	36,657*	62.9	100.0
081 CATHOLIC......	4	0	4,401	7.6	12.0
093 CR CH (DISC)..	4	697	830*	1.4	2.3
097 CR C AND C CR.	2	82	98*	0.2	0.3
123 CH GOD (ANDER)	3	78	217	0.4	0.6
127 CH GOD (CLEVE)	1	29	35*	0.1	0.1
165 CH OF NAZARENE	1	78	152	0.3	0.4
185 CUMBER PRESB..	5	1,614	1,923*	3.3	5.2
193 EPISCOPAL.....	1	706	873	1.5	2.4
281 LUTH CH AMER..	2	425	585	1.0	1.6
283 LUTH--MO SYNOD	1	359	484	0.8	1.3
357 PRESB CH US...	3	435	518*	0.9	1.4
403 SALVATION ARMY	1	67	367	0.6	1.0
413 S-D ADVENTISTS	2	137	163*	0.3	0.4
419 SO BAPT CONV..	31	15,916	18,961*	32.5	51.7
443 UN C OF CHRIST	1	203	242*	0.4	0.7
449 UN METHODIST..	18	5,886	6,296	10.8	17.2
453 UN PRES CH USA	3	430	512*	0.9	1.4
MC CREARY	21	3,073	3,850*	30.7	100.0
081 CATHOLIC......	0	0	17	0.1	0.4
093 CR CH (DISC)..	2	56	71*	0.6	1.8
097 CR C AND C CR.	2	95	120*	1.0	3.1
127 CH GOD (CLEVE)	1	21	26*	0.2	0.7
413 S-D ADVENTISTS	1	69	87*	0.7	2.3
419 SO BAPT CONV..	12	2,623	3,305*	26.3	85.8
449 UN METHODIST..	3	209	224	1.8	5.8
MC LEAN	33	4,925	5,842*	64.5	100.0
081 CATHOLIC......	2	0	170	1.9	2.9
093 CR CH (DISC)..	1	62	75*	0.8	1.3
097 CR C AND C CR.	2	175	210*	2.3	3.6
185 CUMBER PRESB..	3	342	411*	4.5	7.0
221 FREE METH C NA	1	3	3	-	0.1
357 PRESB CH US...	1	19	23*	0.3	0.4
419 SO BAPT CONV..	12	2,634	3,166*	34.9	54.2
449 UN METHODIST..	10	1,671	1,761	19.4	30.1
453 UN PRES CH USA	1	19	23*	0.3	0.4
MADISON	79	14,679	18,135*	42.4	100.0
081 CATHOLIC......	2	0	475	1.1	2.6
093 CR CH (DISC)..	10	1,802	2,138*	5.0	11.8
097 CR C AND C CR.	11	663	787*	1.8	4.3
123 CH GOD (ANDER)	1	50	140	0.3	0.8
127 CH GOD (CLEVE)	3	240	285*	0.7	1.6
165 CH OF NAZARENE	4	465	787	1.8	4.3
193 EPISCOPAL.....	1	99	149	0.3	0.8
226 FRIENDS-USA...	1	20	24*	0.1	0.1
283 LUTH--MO SYNOD	1	2	2	-	-
357 PRESB CH US...	3	238	282*	0.7	1.6
413 S-D ADVENTISTS	1	31	37*	0.1	0.2
419 SO BAPT CONV..	30	9,586	11,376*	26.6	62.7
449 UN METHODIST..	8	1,237	1,361	3.2	7.5
453 UN PRES CH USA	3	246	292*	0.7	1.6
MAGOFFIN	5	607	728*	7.0	100.0
097 CR C AND C CR.	1	100	129*	1.2	17.7
419 SO BAPT CONV..	3	321	413*	4.0	56.7
449 UN METHODIST..	1	186	186	1.8	25.5
MARION	36	4,932	13,907*	83.2	100.0
081 CATHOLIC......	8	0	7,753	46.4	55.7
093 CR CH (DISC)..	1	130	167*	1.0	1.2
097 CR C AND C CR.	4	74	95*	0.6	0.7
123 CH GOD (ANDER)	1	6	18	0.1	0.1
357 PRESB CH US...	2	32	41*	0.2	0.3
419 SO BAPT CONV..	10	3,660	4,698*	28.1	33.8
449 UN METHODIST..	7	910	981	5.9	7.1
453 UN PRES CH USA	3	120	154*	0.9	1.1
MARSHALL	45	9,094	10,771*	52.8	100.0
081 CATHOLIC......	2	0	247	1.2	2.3
093 CR CH (DISC)..	1	80	95*	0.5	0.9
165 CH OF NAZARENE	1	27	65	0.3	0.6
185 CUMBER PRESB..	4	468	557*	2.7	5.2
193 EPISCOPAL.....	1	28	55	0.3	0.5
357 PRESB CH US...	1	59	70*	0.3	0.6
419 SO BAPT CONV..	21	6,189	7,364*	36.1	68.4

*Total adherents estimated from known number of communicant, confirmed, full members.

—Represents a percent less than 0.1.

Percentages may not total due to rounding.

Table 3. Churches and Church Membership by State, County and Denomination: 1971

County and Denomination	Number of churches	Communicant, confirmed, full members	Total adherents		
			Number	Percent of total population	Percent of total adherents
449 UN METHODIST..	13	2,185	2,249	11.0	20.9
453 UN PRES CH USA	1	58	69*	0.3	0.6
MARTIN	11	604	945*	10.1	100.0
081 CATHOLIC......	1	0	20	0.2	2.1
127 CH GOD (CLEVE)	1	55	71*	0.8	7.5
157 CH OF BRETHREN	1	17	22*	0.2	2.3
165 CH OF NAZARENE	2	74	277	3.0	29.3
357 PRESB CH US...	1	4	5*	0.1	0.5
419 SO BAPT CONV..	2	332	427*	4.6	45.2
449 UN METHODIST..	2	117	117	1.2	12.4
453 UN PRES CH USA	1	5	6*	0.1	0.6
MASON	56	8,451	11,099*	64.3	100.0
081 CATHOLIC......	3	0	1,230	7.1	11.1
093 CR CH (DISC)..	9	1,419	1,724*	10.0	15.5
097 CR C AND C CR.	5	524	637*	3.7	5.7
165 CH OF NAZARENE	1	237	336	1.9	3.0
193 EPISCOPAL.....	1	107	185	1.1	1.7
283 LUTH--MO SYNOD	1	39	54	0.3	0.5
357 PRESB CH US...	3	201	244*	1.4	2.2
419 SO BAPT CONV..	8	1,888	2,294*	13.3	20.7
449 UN METHODIST..	22	3,838	4,154	24.0	37.4
453 UN PRES CH USA	3	198	241*	1.4	2.2
MEADE	32	4,950	9,953*	53.0	100.0
081 CATHOLIC......	5	0	3,478	18.5	34.9
097 CR C AND C CR.	2	135	181*	1.0	1.8
165 CH OF NAZARENE	1	73	163	0.9	1.6
193 EPISCOPAL.....	1	36	42	0.2	0.4
357 PRESB CH US...	1	37	50*	0.3	0.5
419 SO BAPT CONV..	15	3,851	5,154*	27.4	51.8
449 UN METHODIST..	6	783	838	4.5	8.4
453 UN PRES CH USA	1	35	47*	0.3	0.5
MENIFEE	9	360	670*	16.5	100.0
093 CR CH (DISC)..	1	88	111*	2.7	16.6
123 CH GOD (ANDER)	2	45	275	6.8	41.0
127 CH GOD (CLEVE)	1	26	33*	0.8	4.9
357 PRESB CH US...	1	38	48*	1.2	7.2
419 SO BAPT CONV..	2	115	145*	3.6	21.6
449 UN METHODIST..	1	10	10	0.2	1.5
453 UN PRES CH USA	1	38	48*	1.2	7.2
MERCER	44	10,026	12,385*	77.6	100.0
081 CATHOLIC......	1	0	420	2.6	3.4
093 CR CH (DISC)..	5	937	1,131*	7.1	9.1
097 CR C AND C CR.	4	475	573*	3.6	4.6
127 CH GOD (CLEVE)	1	145	175*	1.1	1.4
185 CUMBER PRESB..	2	247	298*	1.9	2.4
193 EPISCOPAL.....	1	41	47	0.3	0.4
357 PRESB CH US...	3	184	222*	1.4	1.8
419 SO BAPT CONV..	17	6,937	8,374*	52.5	67.6
449 UN METHODIST..	7	881	929	5.8	7.5
453 UN PRES CH USA	3	179	216*	1.4	1.7
METCALFE	31	3,459	4,032*	49.3	100.0
081 CATHOLIC......	C	0	8	0.1	0.2
097 CR C AND C CR.	1	107	130*	1.6	3.2
185 CUMBER PRESB..	8	630	764*	9.3	18.9
357 PRESB CH US...	1	14	17*	0.2	0.4
419 SO BAPT CONV..	11	1,800	2,183*	26.7	54.1
449 UN METHODIST..	8	866	879	10.7	21.8
453 UN PRES CH USA	2	42	51*	0.6	1.3
MONROE	17	2,826	3,380*	29.0	100.0
081 CATHOLIC......	1	C	16	0.1	0.5
419 SO BAPT CONV..	11	2,498	3,024*	26.0	89.5
449 UN METHODIST..	5	328	340	2.9	10.1
MONTGOMERY	27	4,525	6,715*	43.7	100.0
081 CATHOLIC......	1	0	275	1.8	4.1
093 CR CH (DISC)..	4	1,184	1,455*	9.5	21.7
097 CR C AND C CR.	2	160	197*	1.3	2.9
123 CH GOD (ANDER)	6	621	1,558	10.1	23.2
127 CH GOD (CLEVE)	1	33	41*	0.3	0.6
165 CH OF NAZARENE	1	147	396	2.6	5.9
193 EPISCOPAL.....	1	83	124	0.8	1.8
357 PRESB CH US...	1	117	144*	0.9	2.1
419 SO BAPT CONV..	6	1,338	1,644*	10.7	24.5
449 UN METHODIST..	3	737	752	4.9	11.2
453 UN PRES CH USA	1	105	129*	0.8	1.9
MORGAN	19	1,529	2,133*	21.3	100.0
081 CATHOLIC......	1	0	50	0.5	2.3
093 CR CH (DISC)..	6	459	562*	5.6	26.3
097 CR C AND C CR.	1	240	294*	2.9	13.8
123 CH GOD (ANDER)	3	148	446	4.5	20.9
127 CH GOD (CLEVE)	1	92	113*	1.1	5.3
285 MENNONITE CH..	2	46	56*	0.6	2.6
357 PRESB CH US...	1	51	62*	0.6	2.9
419 SO BAPT CONV..	1	203	249*	2.5	11.7
449 UN METHODIST..	2	240	240	2.4	11.3
453 UN PRES CH USA	1	50	61*	0.6	2.9
MUHLENBERG	82	15,751	18,873*	68.5	100.0
081 CATHOLIC......	1	0	312	1.1	1.7
093 CR CH (DISC)..	2	384	461*	1.7	2.4
097 CR C AND C CR.	1	272	327*	1.2	1.7
127 CH GOD (CLEVE)	1	26	31*	0.1	0.2
165 CH OF NAZARENE	1	54	120	0.4	0.6
185 CUMBER PRESB..	4	409	491*	1.8	2.6
357 PRESB CH US...	6	248	298*	1.1	1.6
413 S-D ADVENTISTS	1	27	32*	0.1	0.2
419 SO BAPT CONV..	44	11,625	13,959*	50.7	74.0
449 UN METHODIST..	15	2,471	2,560	9.3	13.6
453 UN PRES CH USA	6	235	282*	1.0	1.5
NELSON	45	6,852	16,638*	70.9	100.0
081 CATHOLIC......	10	C	8,053	34.3	48.4
093 CR CH (DISC)..	5	653	838*	3.6	5.0
097 CR C AND C CR.	3	200	257*	1.1	1.5
127 CH GOD (CLEVE)	1	111	143*	0.6	0.9
357 PRESB CH US...	3	116	149*	0.6	0.9
419 SO BAPT CONV..	14	4,854	6,232*	26.5	37.5
449 UN METHODIST..	7	844	871	3.7	5.2
453 UN PRES CH USA	2	74	95*	0.4	0.6
NICHOLAS	23	2,982	3,561*	54.7	100.0
081 CATHOLIC......	1	0	120	1.8	3.4
093 CR CH (DISC)..	4	280	339*	5.2	9.5
097 CR C AND C CR.	5	950	1,152*	17.7	32.4
357 PRESB CH US...	1	50	61*	0.9	1.7
419 SO BAPT CONV..	3	619	750*	11.5	21.1
449 UN METHODIST..	8	1,031	1,076	16.5	30.2
453 UN PRES CH USA	1	52	63*	1.0	1.8
OHIO	78	10,738	12,803*	68.1	100.0
081 CATHOLIC......	2	0	180	1.0	1.4
093 CR CH (DISC)..	2	112	135*	0.7	1.1
097 CR C AND C CR.	3	360	434*	2.3	3.4
123 CH GOD (ANDER)	1	45	115	0.6	0.9
127 CH GOD (CLEVE)	2	160	193*	1.0	1.5
185 CUMBER PRESB..	3	103	124*	0.7	1.0
357 PRESB CH US...	1	19	23*	0.1	0.2
413 S-D ADVENTISTS	1	28	34*	0.2	0.3
419 SO BAPT CONV..	42	7,924	9,544*	50.8	74.5
449 UN METHODIST..	20	1,968	1,998	10.6	15.6
453 UN PRES CH USA	1	19	23*	0.1	0.2
OLDHAM	26	5,540	8,005*	54.5	100.0
081 CATHOLIC......	2	0	1,475	10.0	18.4
093 CR CH (DISC)..	3	514	621*	4.2	7.8
193 EPISCOPAL.....	1	90	93	0.6	1.2
357 PRESB CH US...	2	139	168*	1.1	2.1
413 S-D ADVENTISTS	1	154	186*	1.3	2.3
419 SO BAPT CONV..	9	3,352	4,048*	27.6	50.6
449 UN METHODIST..	6	1,169	1,267	8.6	15.8
453 UN PRES CH USA	2	122	147*	1.0	1.8
OWEN	38	5,913	6,978*	93.4	100.0
081 CATHOLIC......	1	C	50	0.7	0.7
093 CR CH (DISC)..	4	274	324*	4.3	4.6
097 CR C AND C CR.	1	120	142*	1.9	2.0
413 S-D ADVENTISTS	1	1C	12*	0.2	0.2
419 SO BAPT CONV..	26	5,160	6,100*	81.7	87.4
449 UN METHODIST..	5	349	350	4.7	5.0
OWSLEY	16	1,010	1,200*	23.9	100.0
081 CATHOLIC......	1	C	20	0.4	1.7
127 CH GOD (CLEVE)	1	41	51*	1.0	4.3
357 PRESB CH US...	3	80	99*	2.0	8.3
419 SO BAPT CONV..	5	486	604*	12.0	50.3
449 UN METHODIST..	3	314	315	6.3	26.3
453 UN PRES CH USA	3	89	111*	2.2	9.3
PENDLETON	40	6,328	7,977*	80.2	100.0
081 CATHOLIC......	2	0	250	2.5	3.1
093 CR CH (DISC)..	6	678	839*	8.4	10.5
097 CR C AND C CR.	7	1,037	1,283*	12.9	16.1
165 CH OF NAZARENE	1	28	75	0.8	0.9
419 SO BAPT CONV..	18	3,670	4,541*	45.6	56.9
449 UN METHODIST..	6	915	989	9.9	12.4
PERRY	53	6,644	8,430*	32.8	100.0
081 CATHOLIC......	1	0	164	0.6	1.9
093 CR CH (DISC)..	6	453	573*	2.2	6.8
127 CH GOD (CLEVE)	8	455	576*	2.2	6.8
193 EPISCOPAL.....	1	37	49	0.2	0.6
285 MENNONITE CH..	1	13	16*	0.1	0.2
357 PRESB CH US...	5	390	494*	1.9	5.9
419 SO BAPT CONV..	22	4,390	5,556*	21.6	65.9
449 UN METHODIST..	4	546	546	2.1	6.5
453 UN PRES CH USA	5	360	456*	1.8	5.4
PIKE	77	8,790	11,254*	18.4	100.0
081 CATHOLIC......	1	C	172	0.3	1.5
093 CR CH (DISC)..	7	562	699*	1.1	6.2
097 CR C AND C CR.	19	1,310	1,629*	2.7	14.5
123 CH GOD (ANDER)	5	153	482	0.8	4.3
127 CH GOD (CLEVE)	7	433	538*	0.9	4.8
157 CH OF BRETHREN	1	27	34*	0.1	0.3

*Total adherents estimated from known number of communicant, confirmed, full members.

—Represents a percent less than 0.1.

Percentages may not total due to rounding.

Table 3. Churches and Church Membership by State, County and Denomination: 1971

County and Denomination	Number of churches	Communicant, confirmed, full members	Total adherents: Number	Total adherents: Percent of total population	Total adherents: Percent of total adherents
165 CH OF NAZARENE	1	88	207	0.3	1.8
193 EPISCOPAL.....	1	79	108	0.2	1.0
357 PRESB CH US...	5	257	320*	0.5	2.8
413 S-D ADVENTISTS	1	20	25*	-	0.2
419 SO BAPT CONV..	13	4,254	5,290*	8.7	47.0
449 UN METHODIST..	11	1,363	1,447	2.4	12.9
453 UN PRES CH USA	5	244	303*	0.5	2.7
POWELL	22	2,038	3,055*	39.7	100.0
093 CR CH (DISC)..	3	243	308*	4.0	10.1
097 CR C AND C CR.	1	150	190*	2.5	6.2
123 CH GOD (ANDER)	8	584	1,285	16.7	42.1
127 CH GOD (CLEVE)	1	81	103*	1.3	3.4
357 PRESB CH US...	1	82	104*	1.3	3.4
419 SO BAPT CONV..	3	530	672*	8.7	22.0
449 UN METHODIST..	4	281	283	3.7	9.3
453 UN PRES CH USA	1	87	110*	1.4	3.6
PULASKI	99	17,791	22,166*	62.9	100.0
081 CATHOLIC......	1	0	400	1.1	1.8
093 CR CH (DISC)..	2	480	580*	1.6	2.6
097 CR C AND C CR.	5	320	387*	1.1	1.7
123 CH GOD (ANDER)	2	97	253	0.7	1.1
127 CH GOD (CLEVE)	3	240	290*	0.8	1.3
165 CH OF NAZARENE	6	499	1,059	3.0	4.8
193 EPISCOPAL.....	1	69	123	0.3	0.6
281 LUTH CH AMER..	1	84	119	0.3	0.5
357 PRESB CH US...	2	162	196*	0.6	0.9
413 S-D ADVENTISTS	1	10	12*	-	0.1
419 SO BAPT CONV..	54	13,224	15,990*	45.4	72.1
449 UN METHODIST..	19	2,466	2,588	7.3	11.7
453 UN PRES CH USA	2	140	169*	0.5	0.8
ROBERTSON	6	790	892*	41.2	100.0
097 CR C AND C CR.	3	460	545*	25.2	61.1
449 UN METHODIST..	3	330	347	16.0	38.9
ROCKCASTLE	35	5,315	6,734*	54.7	100.0
081 CATHOLIC......	1	0	50	0.4	0.7
093 CR CH (DISC)..	1	25	31*	0.3	0.5
097 CR C AND C CR.	8	555	696*	5.7	10.3
127 CH GOD (CLEVE)	1	78	98*	0.8	1.5
165 CH OF NAZARENE	1	16	42	0.3	0.6
419 SO BAPT CONV..	23	4,641	5,817*	47.3	86.4
ROWAN	16	2,244	4,164*	24.5	100.0
081 CATHOLIC......	1	0	750	4.4	18.0
093 CR CH (DISC)..	1	252	295*	1.7	7.1
123 CH GOD (ANDER)	6	440	1,252	7.4	30.1
127 CH GOD (CLEVE)	1	58	68*	0.4	1.6
165 CH OF NAZARENE	1	30	89	0.5	2.1
193 EPISCOPAL.....	1	23	39	0.2	0.9
357 PRESB CH US...	1	32	38*	0.2	0.9
419 SO BAPT CONV..	2	922	1,081*	6.4	26.0
449 UN METHODIST..	1	456	516	3.0	12.4
453 UN PRES CH USA	1	31	36*	0.2	0.9
RUSSELL	36	4,140	4,833*	45.8	100.0
081 CATHOLIC......	1	0	53	0.5	1.1
097 CR C AND C CR.	5	608	732*	6.9	15.1
127 CH GOD (CLEVE)	2	95	114*	1.1	2.4
165 CH OF NAZARENE	2	71	106	1.0	2.2
413 S-D ADVENTISTS	1	46	55*	0.5	1.1
419 SO BAPT CONV..	15	1,987	2,394*	22.7	49.5
449 UN METHODIST..	10	1,333	1,379	13.1	28.5
SCOTT	45	7,888	9,930*	55.3	100.0
081 CATHOLIC......	2	0	260	1.4	2.6
093 CR CH (DISC)..	5	972	1,186*	6.6	11.9
097 CR C AND C CR.	8	820	1,001*	5.6	10.1
123 CH GOD (ANDER)	1	70	171	1.0	1.7
127 CH GOD (CLEVE)	1	117	143*	0.8	1.4
165 CH OF NAZARENE	2	365	480	2.7	4.8
193 EPISCOPAL.....	1	156	184	1.0	1.9
357 PRESB CH US...	4	144	176*	1.0	1.8
419 SO BAPT CONV..	9	4,061	4,957*	27.6	49.9
449 UN METHODIST..	8	1,031	1,186	6.6	11.9
453 UN PRES CH USA	4	152	186*	1.0	1.9
SHELBY	43	11,174	13,795*	72.6	100.0
081 CATHOLIC......	1	0	360	1.9	2.6
093 CR CH (DISC)..	6	393	476*	2.5	3.5
097 CR C AND C CR.	2	305	369*	1.9	2.7
127 CH GOD (CLEVE)	1	36	44*	0.2	0.3
165 CH OF NAZARENE	1	34	49	0.3	0.4
193 EPISCOPAL.....	1	39	51	0.3	0.4
357 PRESB CH US...	1	158	191*	1.0	1.4
419 SO BAPT CONV..	23	9,151	11,085*	58.3	80.4
449 UN METHODIST..	6	900	979	5.2	7.1
453 UN PRES CH USA	1	158	191*	1.0	1.4
SIMPSON	26	4,801	5,914*	45.3	100.0
081 CATHOLIC......	1	0	173	1.3	2.9
165 CH OF NAZARENE	1	23	34	0.3	0.6
185 CUMBER PRESB..	1	25	31*	0.2	0.5
193 EPISCOPAL.....	1	34	44	0.3	0.7

County and Denomination	Number of churches	Communicant, confirmed, full members	Total adherents: Number	Total adherents: Percent of total population	Total adherents: Percent of total adherents
281 LUTH CH AMER..	1	77	111	0.9	1.9
357 PRESB CH US...	2	132	162*	1.2	2.7
419 SO BAPT CONV..	10	3,451	4,233*	32.4	71.6
449 UN METHODIST..	7	929	967	7.4	16.4
453 UN PRES CH USA	2	130	159*	1.2	2.7
SPENCER	17	4,555	5,771*	105.2#	100.0
081 CATHOLIC......	1	0	110	2.0	1.9
093 CR CH (DISC)..	2	243	303*	5.5	5.3
097 CR C AND C CR.	3	670	835*	15.2	14.5
127 CH GOD (CLEVE)	1	28	35*	0.6	0.6
419 SO BAPT CONV..	9	3,511	4,377*	79.8	75.8
449 UN METHODIST..	1	103	111	2.0	1.9
TAYLOR	55	11,068	13,865*	80.9	100.0
075 BRETHREN IN CR	1	10	12*	0.1	0.1
081 CATHOLIC......	2	0	647	3.8	4.7
097 CR C AND C CR.	4	585	708*	4.1	5.1
123 CH GOD (ANDER)	3	193	573	3.3	4.1
165 CH OF NAZARENE	1	31	66	0.4	0.5
185 CUMBER PRESB..	5	569	689*	4.0	5.0
357 PRESB CH US...	1	130	157*	0.9	1.1
419 SO BAPT CONV..	20	6,485	7,852*	45.8	56.6
449 UN METHODIST..	17	2,937	3,006	17.5	21.7
453 UN PRES CH USA	1	128	155*	0.9	1.1
TODD	36	5,499	6,584*	60.8	100.0
081 CATHOLIC......	2	0	135	1.2	2.1
093 CR CH (DISC)..	4	270	328*	3.0	5.0
165 CH OF NAZARENE	1	72	128	1.2	1.9
185 CUMBER PRESB..	3	161	195*	1.8	3.0
357 PRESB CH US...	1	22	27*	0.2	0.4
419 SO BAPT CONV..	13	3,528	4,282*	39.6	65.0
449 UN METHODIST..	11	1,428	1,467	13.6	22.3
453 UN PRES CH USA	1	18	22*	0.2	0.3
TRIGG	30	4,846	5,781*	67.1	100.0
081 CATHOLIC......	1	0	81	0.9	1.4
093 CR CH (DISC)..	2	124	151*	1.8	2.6
419 SO BAPT CONV..	17	3,663	4,452*	51.6	77.0
449 UN METHODIST..	10	1,059	1,097	12.7	19.0
TRIMBLE	18	2,665	3,213*	60.1	100.0
081 CATHOLIC......	1	0	40	0.7	1.2
093 CR CH (DISC)..	1	168	208*	3.9	6.5
097 CR C AND C CR.	3	420	519*	9.7	16.2
419 SO BAPT CONV..	8	1,438	1,778*	33.2	55.3
449 UN METHODIST..	5	639	668	12.5	20.8
UNION	37	6,000	10,760*	67.7	100.0
081 CATHOLIC......	6	0	3,650	23.0	33.9
093 CR CH (DISC)..	4	319	383*	2.4	3.6
097 CR C AND C CR.	3	576	692*	4.4	6.4
185 CUMBER PRESB..	3	102	122*	0.8	1.1
193 EPISCOPAL.....	1	24	37	0.2	0.3
357 PRESB CH US...	2	92	110*	0.7	1.0
419 SO BAPT CONV..	13	4,079	4,897*	30.8	45.5
449 UN METHODIST..	3	712	754	4.7	7.0
453 UN PRES CH USA	2	96	115*	0.7	1.1
WARREN	92	20,169	27,349*	47.6	100.0
081 CATHOLIC......	3	0	3,312	5.8	12.1
093 CR CH (DISC)..	4	983	1,171*	2.0	4.3
097 CR C AND C CR.	3	275	327*	0.6	1.2
123 CH GOD (ANDER)	1	25	68	0.1	0.2
127 CH GOD (CLEVE)	1	64	76*	0.1	0.3
165 CH OF NAZARENE	3	189	427	0.7	1.6
185 CUMBER PRESB..	2	297	354*	0.6	1.3
193 EPISCOPAL.....	1	341	575	1.0	2.1
221 FREE METH C NA	2	64	80	0.1	0.3
283 LUTH--MO SYNOD	1	124	178	0.3	0.7
357 PRESB CH US...	6	495	589*	1.0	2.2
403 SALVATION ARMY	1	63	201	0.3	0.7
413 S-D ADVENTISTS	3	177	211*	0.4	0.8
419 SO BAPT CONV..	35	12,225	14,558*	25.3	53.2
435 UNITARIAN-UNIV	1	15	15	-	0.1
449 UN METHODIST..	21	4,390	4,681	8.2	17.1
453 UN PRES CH USA	4	442	526*	0.9	1.9
WASHINGTON	31	5,717	10,715*	99.9	100.0
081 CATHOLIC......	6	0	3,653	34.1	34.1
097 CR C AND C CR.	5	1,020	1,271*	11.8	11.9
127 CH GOD (CLEVE)	1	77	96*	0.9	0.9
357 PRESB CH US...	2	99	123*	1.1	1.1
419 SO BAPT CONV..	12	4,090	5,098*	47.5	47.6
449 UN METHODIST..	3	332	351	3.3	3.3
453 UN PRES CH USA	2	99	123*	1.1	1.1
WAYNE	35	7,605	9,375*	65.7	100.0
081 CATHOLIC......	1	0	16	0.1	0.2
097 CR C AND C CR.	1	320	391*	2.7	4.2
123 CH GOD (ANDER)	2	66	202	1.4	2.2
127 CH GOD (CLEVE)	1	30	37*	0.3	0.4
165 CH OF NAZARENE	1	137	393	2.8	4.2
419 SO BAPT CONV..	20	5,578	6,809*	47.7	72.6
449 UN METHODIST..	9	1,474	1,527	10.7	16.3

*Total adherents estimated from known number of communicant, confirmed, full members.

—Represents a percent less than 0.1.

Percentages may not total due to rounding.

#See Introduction for explanation of why total adherents reported by churches exceed the 1970 population figure.

Table 3. Churches and Church Membership by State, County and Denomination: 1971

County and Denomination	Number of churches	Communicant, confirmed, full members	Total adherents: Number	Total adherents: Percent of total population	Total adherents: Percent of total adherents
WEBSTER	39	5,983	6,883*	51.8	100.0
093 CR CH (DISC)..	3	271	322*	2.4	4.7
185 CUMBER PRESB..	5	294	349*	2.6	5.1
419 SO BAPT CONV..	20	3,786	4,494*	33.8	65.3
449 UN METHODIST..	11	1,632	1,718	12.9	25.0
WHITLEY	88	16,980	20,195*	83.6	100.0
081 CATHOLIC......	2	0	50	0.2	0.2
093 CR CH (DISC)..	3	767	917*	3.8	4.5
097 CR C AND C CR.	9	477	571*	2.4	2.8
127 CH GOD (CLEVE)	3	215	257*	1.1	1.3
357 PRESB CH US...	1	102	122*	0.5	0.6
419 SO BAPT CONV..	63	14,228	17,018*	70.5	84.3
449 UN METHODIST..	7	1,191	1,260	5.2	6.2
WOLFE	9	834	1,148*	20.3	100.0
093 CR CH (DISC)..	4	254	307*	5.4	26.7
123 CH GOD (ANDER)	1	100	290	5.1	25.3
127 CH GOD (CLEVE)	1	27	33*	0.6	2.9
419 SO BAPT CONV..	1	257	311*	5.5	27.1
449 UN METHODIST..	2	196	207	3.7	18.0
WOODFORD	38	8,188	10,947*	75.8	100.0
081 CATHOLIC......	1	0	700	4.8	6.4
093 CR CH (DISC)..	5	876	1,093*	7.6	10.0
097 CR C AND C CR.	2	423	528*	3.7	4.8
165 CH OF NAZARENE	2	54	175	1.2	1.6
193 EPISCOPAL.....	1	221	403	2.8	3.7
357 PRESB CH US...	5	339	423*	2.9	3.9
413 S-D ADVENTISTS	1	14	17*	0.1	0.2
419 SO BAPT CONV..	11	4,826	6,022*	41.7	55.0
449 UN METHODIST..	5	1,073	1,134	7.9	10.4
453 UN PRES CH USA	5	362	452*	3.1	4.1
CO DATA NOT AVAIL	360	34,554	52,755*	N/A	N/A
127 CH GOD (CLEVE)	4	238	291*	N/A	N/A
151 L-D SAINTS....	0	0	10,635	N/A	N/A
223 FREE WILL BAPT	125	12,719	15,572*	N/A	N/A
231 GENERAL BAPT..	171	19,811	24,254*	N/A	N/A
285 MENNONITE CH..	1	30	37*	N/A	N/A
467 WESLEYAN......	59	1,756	1,966	N/A	N/A

LOUISIANA

County and Denomination	Number of churches	Communicant, confirmed, full members	Total adherents: Number	Total adherents: Percent of total population	Total adherents: Percent of total adherents
THE STATE.....	3,125	712,104	2,178,589*	59.8	100.0
ACADIA	54	5,081	46,748*	89.7	100.0
081 CATHOLIC......	24	0	40,429	77.6	86.5
093 CR CH (DISC)..	1	96	122*	0.2	0.3
097 CR C AND C CR.	3	280	357*	0.7	0.8
165 CH OF NAZARENE	3	200	333	0.6	0.7
193 EPISCOPAL.....	1	98	108	0.2	0.2
283 LUTH--MO SYNOD	2	115	170	0.3	0.4
313 NO AM BAPT GC.	1	55	70*	0.1	0.1
357 PRESB CH US...	1	212	270*	0.5	0.6
419 SO BAPT CONV..	9	2,478	3,161*	6.1	6.8
449 UN METHODIST..	9	1,547	1,728	3.3	3.7
ALLEN	31	5,803	11,508*	55.3	100.0
081 CATHOLIC......	7	0	4,256	20.5	37.0
193 EPISCOPAL.....	1	18	30	0.1	0.3
357 PRESB CH US...	1	70	89*	0.4	0.8
419 SO BAPT CONV..	17	5,073	6,452*	31.0	56.1
449 UN METHODIST..	5	642	681	3.3	5.9
ASCENSION	25	2,868	25,391*	68.5	100.0
081 CATHOLIC......	9	0	21,689	58.5	85.4
193 EPISCOPAL.....	1	13	15	-	0.1
283 LUTH--MO SYNOD	1	16	32	0.1	0.1
413 S-D ADVENTISTS	1	88	116*	0.3	0.5
419 SO BAPT CONV..	7	2,360	3,114*	8.4	12.3
449 UN METHODIST..	6	391	425	1.1	1.7
ASSUMPTION	13	432	13,180*	67.1	100.0
081 CATHOLIC......	8	0	12,669	64.5	96.1
193 EPISCOPAL.....	1	18	32	0.2	0.2
419 SO BAPT CONV..	1	169	225*	1.1	1.7
449 UN METHODIST..	3	245	254	1.3	1.9
AVOYELLES	53	3,423	26,396*	69.9	100.0
081 CATHOLIC......	29	0	22,141	58.7	83.9
097 CR C AND C CR.	1	20	25*	0.1	0.1
165 CH OF NAZARENE	1	66	90	0.2	0.3
193 EPISCOPAL.....	1	64	85	0.2	0.3
283 LUTH--MO SYNOD	1	80	119	0.3	0.5
419 SO BAPT CONV..	16	2,757	3,467*	9.2	13.1

*Total adherents estimated from known number of communicant, confirmed, full members.

County and Denomination	Number of churches	Communicant, confirmed, full members	Total adherents: Number	Total adherents: Percent of total population	Total adherents: Percent of total adherents
449 UN METHODIST..	4	436	469	1.2	1.8
BEAUREGARD	40	6,694	8,965*	39.2	100.0
081 CATHOLIC......	2	0	670	2.9	7.5
093 CR CH (DISC)..	1	13	16*	0.1	0.2
123 CH GOD (ANDER)	1	20	45	0.2	0.5
165 CH OF NAZARENE	1	76	106	0.5	1.2
193 EPISCOPAL.....	1	105	149	0.7	1.7
283 LUTH--MO SYNOD	1	51	68	0.3	0.8
357 PRESB CH US...	1	121	151*	0.7	1.7
413 S-D ADVENTISTS	1	39	49*	0.2	0.5
419 SO BAPT CONV..	29	5,248	6,563*	28.7	73.2
449 UN METHODIST..	2	1,021	1,148	5.0	12.8
BIENVILLE	37	6,840	8,310*	51.9	100.0
059 BAPT MISS ASSN	2	234	289*	1.8	3.5
081 CATHOLIC......	1	0	30	0.2	0.4
185 CUMBER PRESB..	2	35	43*	0.3	0.5
419 SO BAPT CONV..	23	5,528	6,822*	42.6	82.1
449 UN METHODIST..	9	1,043	1,126	7.0	13.5
BOSSIER	59	17,845	25,699*	39.8	100.0
059 BAPT MISS ASSN	6	684	882*	1.4	3.4
081 CATHOLIC......	4	0	2,928	4.5	11.4
093 CR CH (DISC)..	1	123	159*	0.2	0.6
127 CH GOD (CLEVE)	1	39	50*	0.1	0.2
165 CH OF NAZARENE	2	95	209	0.3	0.8
193 EPISCOPAL.....	1	237	323	0.5	1.3
281 LUTH CH AMER..	1	96	162	0.3	0.6
283 LUTH--MO SYNOD	1	189	306	0.5	1.2
357 PRESB CH US...	6	709	914*	1.4	3.6
413 S-D ADVENTISTS	2	199	257*	0.4	1.0
419 SO BAPT CONV..	23	12,727	16,408*	25.4	63.8
449 UN METHODIST..	11	2,747	3,101	4.8	12.1
CADDO	167	84,927	122,942*	53.4	100.0
029 AMER LUTH CH..	2	367	510	0.2	0.4
059 BAPT MISS ASSN	3	489	604*	0.3	0.5
081 CATHOLIC......	11	0	17,901	7.8	14.6
093 CR CH (DISC)..	3	1,453	1,793*	0.8	1.5
097 CR C AND C CR.	5	655	808*	0.4	0.7
123 CH GOD (ANDER)	5	363	995	0.4	0.8
127 CH GOD (CLEVE)	1	110	136*	0.1	0.1
165 CH OF NAZARENE	9	578	963	0.4	0.8
185 CUMBER PRESB..	1	55	68*	-	0.1
193 EPISCOPAL.....	5	5,221	6,100	2.7	5.0
221 FREE METH C NA	2	120	198	0.1	0.2
281 LUTH CH AMER..	1	88	146	0.1	0.1
283 LUTH--MO SYNOD	5	704	1,064	0.5	0.9
357 PRESB CH US...	12	4,550	5,616*	2.4	4.6
403 SALVATION ARMY	1	206	1,449	0.6	1.2
413 S-D ADVENTISTS	3	448	553*	0.2	0.4
419 SO BAPT CONV..	62	52,773	65,139*	28.3	53.0
435 UNITARIAN-UNIV	1	84	134	0.1	0.1
449 UN METHODIST..	35	16,663	18,765	8.2	15.3
CALCASIEU	111	36,295	100,434*	69.1	100.0
081 CATHOLIC......	21	0	55,029	37.8	54.8
093 CR CH (DISC)..	2	480	607*	0.4	0.6
097 CR C AND C CR.	4	600	758*	0.5	0.8
123 CH GOD (ANDER)	3	266	712	0.5	0.7
165 CH OF NAZARENE	7	337	518	0.4	0.5
193 EPISCOPAL.....	4	1,473	1,736	1.2	1.7
281 LUTH CH AMER..	1	101	136	0.1	0.1
283 LUTH--MO SYNOD	3	461	714	0.5	0.7
357 PRESB CH US...	3	1,244	1,572*	1.1	1.6
403 SALVATION ARMY	1	134	393	0.3	0.4
413 S-D ADVENTISTS	2	229	289*	0.2	0.3
419 SO BAPT CONV..	42	23,396	29,570*	20.3	29.4
443 UN C OF CHRIST	1	83	105*	0.1	0.1
449 UN METHODIST..	17	7,491	8,295	5.7	8.3
CALDWELL	26	3,537	4,469*	47.8	100.0
081 CATHOLIC......	2	0	115	1.2	2.6
123 CH GOD (ANDER)	2	45	108	1.2	2.4
127 CH GOD (CLEVE)	2	61	75*	0.8	1.7
221 FREE METH C NA	1	8	12	0.1	0.3
419 SO BAPT CONV..	15	2,987	3,677*	39.3	82.3
449 UN METHODIST..	4	436	482	5.2	10.8
CAMERON	19	965	5,585*	68.2	100.0
081 CATHOLIC......	11	0	4,388	53.6	78.6
419 SO BAPT CONV..	5	755	979*	11.9	17.5
449 UN METHODIST..	3	210	218	2.7	3.9
CATAHOULA	31	4,447	5,596*	47.5	100.0
081 CATHOLIC......	2	0	62	0.5	1.1
123 CH GOD (ANDER)	2	63	138	1.2	2.5
357 PRESB CH US...	1	63	79*	0.7	1.4
419 SO BAPT CONV..	21	3,650	4,595*	39.0	82.1
449 UN METHODIST..	5	671	722	6.1	12.9
CLAIBORNE	35	6,205	7,380*	43.4	100.0
059 BAPT MISS ASSN	1	38	46*	0.3	0.6
081 CATHOLIC......	2	0	103	0.6	1.4
357 PRESB CH US...	3	278	339*	2.0	4.6

—Represents a percent less than 0.1.

Percentages may not total due to rounding.

Table 3. Churches and Church Membership by State, County and Denomination: 1971

County and Denomination	Number of churches	Communicant, confirmed, full members	Total adherents: Number	Total adherents: Percent of total population	Total adherents: Percent of total adherents
419 SO BAPT CONV..	17	4,195	5,119*	30.1	69.4
449 UN METHODIST..	12	1,694	1,773	10.4	24.0
CONCORDIA	34	5,921	8,331*	36.9	100.0
059 BAPT MISS ASSN	1	319	410*	1.8	4.9
081 CATHOLIC......	2	0	589	2.6	7.1
093 CR CH (DISC)..	2	43	55*	0.2	0.7
097 CR C AND C CR.	3	120	154*	0.7	1.8
123 CH GOD (ANDER)	4	151	449	2.0	5.4
127 CH GOD (CLEVE)	1	38	49*	0.2	0.6
221 FREE METH C NA	1	9	9	-	0.1
357 PRESB CH US...	2	137	176*	0.8	2.1
419 SO BAPT CONV..	15	4,265	5,476*	24.3	65.7
449 UN METHODIST..	3	839	964	4.3	11.6
DE SOTO	52	7,571	10,893*	47.9	100.0
081 CATHOLIC......	5	0	1,680	7.4	15.4
093 CR CH (DISC)..	1	16	20*	0.1	0.2
185 CUMBER PRESB..	1	38	47*	0.2	0.4
193 EPISCOPAL.....	1	129	162	0.7	1.5
357 PRESB CH US...	5	272	335*	1.5	3.1
413 S-D ADVENTISTS	1	22	27*	0.1	0.2
419 SO BAPT CONV..	29	6,030	7,438*	32.7	68.3
449 UN METHODIST..	9	1,064	1,184	5.2	10.9
EAST BATON ROUGE	129	57,990	143,451*	50.3	100.0
019 AMER BAPT CONV	1	86	107*	-	0.1
059 BAPT MISS ASSN	4	1,017	1,270*	0.4	0.9
081 CATHOLIC......	21	0	69,720	24.4	48.6
093 CR CH (DISC)..	1	403	503*	0.2	0.4
097 CR C AND C CR.	3	415	518*	0.2	0.4
121 CH GOD (ABR)..	1	30	37*	-	-
123 CH GOD (ANDER)	3	142	468	0.2	0.3
127 CH GOD (CLEVE)	5	454	567*	0.2	0.4
165 CH OF NAZARENE	2	152	284	0.1	0.2
193 EPISCOPAL.....	7	4,330	6,120	2.1	4.3
226 FRIENDS-USA...	1	24	30*	-	-
281 LUTH CH AMER..	1	263	389	0.1	0.3
283 LUTH--MO SYNOD	7	1,067	1,505	0.5	1.0
349 PENT HOLINESS.	1	20	25*	-	-
357 PRESB CH US...	10	5,229	6,528*	2.3	4.6
403 SALVATION ARMY	1	198	513	0.2	0.4
413 S-D ADVENTISTS	2	766	956*	0.3	0.7
419 SO BAPT CONV..	49	41,849	52,246*	18.3	36.4
435 UNITARIAN-UNIV	1	194	244	0.1	0.2
449 UN METHODIST..	8	1,351	1,421	0.5	1.0
EAST CARROLL	13	3,205	4,663*	36.2	100.0
081 CATHOLIC......	1	0	465	3.6	10.0
193 EPISCOPAL.....	1	99	125	1.0	2.7
357 PRESB CH US...	1	64	85*	0.7	1.8
419 SO BAPT CONV..	9	2,685	3,566*	27.7	76.5
449 UN METHODIST..	1	357	422	3.3	9.0
EAST FELICIANA	18	3,281	5,130*	29.1	100.0
081 CATHOLIC......	2	0	1,080	6.1	21.1
193 EPISCOPAL.....	1	95	95	0.5	1.9
283 LUTH--MO SYNOD	1	106	158	0.9	3.1
357 PRESB CH US...	3	124	151*	0.9	2.9
419 SO BAPT CONV..	10	2,910	3,542*	20.1	69.0
449 UN METHODIST..	1	46	104	0.6	2.0
EVANGELINE	28	2,333	23,451*	73.4	100.0
081 CATHOLIC......	13	0	20,505	64.2	87.4
097 CR C AND C CR.	1	100	128*	0.4	0.5
419 SO BAPT CONV..	10	2,088	2,664*	8.3	11.4
449 UN METHODIST..	4	145	154	0.5	0.7
FRANKLIN	50	10,545	13,470*	56.3	100.0
081 CATHOLIC......	2	0	265	1.1	2.0
165 CH OF NAZARENE	2	19	68	0.3	0.5
193 EPISCOPAL.....	1	19	22	0.1	0.2
221 FREE METH C NA	2	55	70	0.3	0.5
353 PLY BRETHREN..	1	20	30	0.1	0.2
357 PRESB CH US...	3	101	128*	0.5	1.0
419 SO BAPT CONV..	33	9,417	11,894*	49.7	88.3
449 UN METHODIST..	6	914	993	4.1	7.4
GRANT	40	6,679	8,542*	62.5	100.0
081 CATHOLIC......	3	0	356	2.6	4.2
123 CH GOD (ANDER)	1	18	54	0.4	0.6
127 CH GOD (CLEVE)	1	24	30*	0.2	0.4
165 CH OF NAZARENE	1	17	26	0.2	0.3
419 SO BAPT CONV..	25	6,035	7,434*	54.4	87.0
449 UN METHODIST..	9	585	642	4.7	7.5
IBERIA	32	4,216	48,836*	85.1	100.0
081 CATHOLIC......	15	0	43,517	75.8	89.1
165 CH OF NAZARENE	1	4	8	-	-
193 EPISCOPAL.....	1	281	360	0.6	0.7
357 PRESB CH US...	2	165	215*	0.4	0.4
413 S-D ADVENTISTS	1	28	36*	0.1	0.1
419 SO BAPT CONV..	4	2,049	2,668*	4.6	5.5
443 UN C OF CHRIST	3	153	199*	0.3	0.4
449 UN METHODIST..	5	1,536	1,833	3.2	3.8
IBERVILLE	24	1,442	13,560*	44.1	100.0
081 CATHOLIC......	11	C	11,714	38.1	86.4
193 EPISCOPAL.....	1	31	55	0.2	0.4
419 SO BAPT CONV..	8	1,209	1,565*	5.1	11.5
449 UN METHODIST..	4	202	226	0.7	1.7
JACKSON	41	6,930	8,622*	54.0	100.0
081 CATHOLIC......	1	0	193	1.2	2.2
123 CH GOD (ANDER)	2	115	265	1.7	3.1
165 CH OF NAZARENE	1	19	32	0.2	0.4
185 CUMBER PRESB..	1	92	112*	0.7	1.3
413 S-D ADVENTISTS	1	23	28*	0.2	0.3
419 SO BAPT CONV..	24	5,396	6,596*	41.3	76.5
449 UN METHODIST..	11	1,285	1,396	8.7	16.2
JEFFERSON	94	27,197	219,748*	65.1	100.0
059 BAPT MISS ASSN	2	348	447*	0.1	0.2
081 CATHOLIC......	35	0	183,595	54.4	83.5
093 CR CH (DISC)..	1	317	408*	0.1	0.2
097 CR C AND C CR.	1	86	111*	-	0.1
127 CH GOD (CLEVE)	3	122	157*	-	0.1
185 CUMBER PRESB..	1	244	314*	0.1	0.1
193 EPISCOPAL.....	3	1,727	3,258	1.0	1.5
283 LUTH--MO SYNOD	5	2,303	3,445	1.0	1.6
357 PRESB CH US...	8	3,017	3,879*	1.1	1.8
413 S-D ADVENTISTS	1	32	41*	-	-
419 SO BAPT CONV..	23	13,389	17,216*	5.1	7.8
443 UN C OF CHRIST	2	713	917*	0.3	0.4
449 UN METHODIST..	9	4,899	5,960	1.8	2.7
JEFFERSON DAVIS	34	4,226	22,301*	75.5	100.0
081 CATHOLIC......	14	0	17,103	57.9	76.7
093 CR CH (DISC)..	1	25	32*	0.1	0.1
097 CR C AND C CR.	3	220	281*	1.0	1.3
157 CH OF BRETHREN	1	108	138*	0.5	0.6
193 EPISCOPAL.....	1	34	42	0.1	0.2
283 LUTH--MO SYNOD	1	70	85	0.3	0.4
413 S-D ADVENTISTS	1	31	40*	0.1	0.2
419 SO BAPT CONV..	5	2,265	2,897*	9.8	13.0
449 UN METHODIST..	7	1,473	1,683	5.7	7.5
LAFAYETTE	50	14,918	99,052*	90.3	100.0
081 CATHOLIC......	28	0	80,451	73.3	81.2
093 CR CH (DISC)..	1	169	216*	0.2	0.2
165 CH OF NAZARENE	1	31	60	0.1	0.1
193 EPISCOPAL.....	2	1,080	1,565	1.4	1.6
281 LUTH CH AMER..	1	120	196	0.2	0.2
283 LUTH--MO SYNOD	1	150	264	0.2	0.3
353 PLY BRETHREN..	1	50	80	0.1	0.1
357 PRESB CH US...	2	1,056	1,351*	1.2	1.4
403 SALVATION ARMY	1	37	160	0.1	0.2
419 SO BAPT CONV..	7	6,073	7,767*	7.1	7.8
435 UNITARIAN-UNIV	1	14	14	-	-
449 UN METHODIST..	4	6,138	6,928	6.3	7.0
LAFOURCHE	31	3,141	66,528*	96.5	100.0
081 CATHOLIC......	17	0	62,520	90.7	94.0
193 EPISCOPAL.....	1	126	213	0.3	0.3
357 PRESB CH US...	4	478	631*	0.9	0.9
419 SO BAPT CONV..	5	1,858	2,451*	3.6	3.7
449 UN METHODIST..	3	645	668	1.0	1.0
453 UN PRES CH USA	1	34	45*	0.1	0.1
LA SALLE	50	8,506	10,464*	78.7	100.0
081 CATHOLIC......	2	0	221	1.7	2.1
127 CH GOD (CLEVE)	2	110	134*	1.0	1.3
165 CH OF NAZARENE	2	47	77	0.6	0.7
221 FREE METH C NA	4	100	124	0.9	1.2
413 S-D ADVENTISTS	1	10	12*	0.1	0.1
419 SO BAPT CONV..	32	7,485	9,090*	68.4	86.9
449 UN METHODIST..	7	754	806	6.1	7.7
LINCOLN	45	11,624	13,054*	38.6	100.0
059 BAPT MISS ASSN	1	88	103*	0.3	0.8
081 CATHOLIC......	2	0	465	1.4	3.6
123 CH GOD (ANDER)	1	75	225	0.7	1.7
165 CH OF NAZARENE	1	41	85	0.3	0.7
185 CUMBER PRESB..	1	66	78*	0.2	0.6
193 EPISCOPAL.....	1	225	271	0.8	2.1
283 LUTH--MO SYNOD	1	67	111	0.3	0.9
357 PRESB CH US...	3	693	815*	2.4	6.2
413 S-D ADVENTISTS	1	10	12*	-	0.1
419 SO BAPT CONV..	21	7,739	9,097*	26.9	69.7
435 UNITARIAN-UNIV	1	14	14	-	0.1
449 UN METHODIST..	11	2,606	1,778	5.3	13.6
LIVINGSTON	64	15,643	23,376*	64.0	100.0
059 BAPT MISS ASSN	3	330	427*	1.2	1.8
081 CATHOLIC......	8	0	3,348	9.2	14.3
127 CH GOD (CLEVE)	1	24	31*	0.1	0.1
193 EPISCOPAL.....	1	116	150	0.4	0.6
357 PRESB CH US...	2	182	235*	0.6	1.0
413 S-D ADVENTISTS	1	42	54*	0.1	0.2
419 SO BAPT CONV..	37	14,063	18,179*	49.8	77.8
449 UN METHODIST..	11	886	952	2.6	4.1

*Total adherents estimated from known number of communicant, confirmed, full members.

—Represents a percent less than 0.1.

Percentages may not total due to rounding.

Table 3. Churches and Church Membership by State, County and Denomination: 1971

County and Denomination	Number of churches	Communicant, confirmed, full members	Total adherents		
			Number	Percent of total population	Percent of total adherents
MADISON	14	3,717	4,941*	32.8	100.0
081 CATHOLIC......	1	0	250	1.7	5.1
193 EPISCOPAL.....	1	115	150	1.0	3.0
357 PRESB CH US...	1	110	143*	0.9	2.9
419 SO BAPT CONV..	10	2,938	3,814*	25.3	77.2
449 UN METHODIST..	1	554	584	3.9	11.8
MOREHOUSE	51	10,585	14,160*	43.6	100.0
059 BAPT MISS ASSN	1	164	208*	0.6	1.5
081 CATHOLIC......	3	0	620	1.9	4.4
123 CH GOD (ANDER)	6	286	745	2.3	5.3
193 EPISCOPAL.....	3	341	492	1.5	3.5
357 PRESB CH US...	2	279	354*	1.1	2.5
419 SO BAPT CONV..	27	7,895	10,023*	30.9	70.8
449 UN METHODIST..	9	1,620	1,718	5.3	12.1
NATCHITOCHES	74	10,295	17,525*	49.8	100.0
059 BAPT MISS ASSN	1	115	139*	0.4	0.8
081 CATHOLIC......	15	0	4,912	13.9	28.0
123 CH GOD (ANDER)	1	27	62	0.2	0.4
165 CH OF NAZARENE	3	157	238	0.7	1.4
193 EPISCOPAL.....	1	206	340	1.0	1.9
221 FREE METH C NA	1	16	16	-	0.1
283 LUTH--MO SYNOD	1	42	60	0.2	0.3
357 PRESB CH US...	1	119	144*	0.4	0.8
413 S-D ADVENTISTS	1	22	27*	0.1	0.2
419 SO BAPT CONV..	37	8,044	9,730*	27.6	55.5
449 UN METHODIST..	12	1,547	1,857	5.3	10.6
ORLEANS	238	68,067	336,051*	56.6	100.0
029 AMER LUTH CH..	5	1,119	1,604	0.3	0.5
081 CATHOLIC......	66	0	250,724	42.2	74.6
093 CR CH (DISC)..	3	574	700*	0.1	0.2
097 CR C AND C CR.	2	120	146*	-	-
121 CH GOD (ABR)...	1	15	18*	-	-
123 CH GOD (ANDER)	2	110	233	-	0.1
127 CH GOD (CLEVE)	3	466	569*	0.1	0.2
165 CH OF NAZARENE	6	243	521	0.1	0.2
193 EPISCOPAL.....	15	8,740	10,606	1.8	3.2
226 FRIENDS-USA...	1	35	43*	-	-
281 LUTH CH AMER..	3	554	843	0.1	0.3
283 LUTH--MO SYNOD	21	8,336	11,744	2.0	3.5
353 PLY BRETHREN..	3	165	440	0.1	0.1
357 PRESB CH US...	14	6,284	7,667*	1.3	2.3
403 SALVATION ARMY	1	63	212	-	0.1
413 S-D ADVENTISTS	5	1,539	1,878*	0.3	0.6
415 S-D BAPTIST GC	2	69	84*	-	-
419 SO BAPT CONV..	36	24,116	29,425*	5.0	8.8
435 UNITARIAN-UNIV	2	407	573	0.1	0.2
443 UN C OF CHRIST	10	2,294	2,799*	0.5	0.8
449 UN METHODIST..	36	12,562	14,910	2.5	4.4
453 UN PRES CH USA	1	256	312*	0.1	0.1
OUACHITA	110	44,640	61,687*	53.5	100.0
059 BAPT MISS ASSN	2	318	398*	0.3	0.6
081 CATHOLIC......	7	0	6,192	5.4	10.0
093 CR CH (DISC)..	2	368	460*	0.4	0.7
123 CH GOD (ANDER)	7	325	885	0.8	1.4
127 CH GOD (CLEVE)	3	294	368*	0.3	0.6
165 CH OF NAZARENE	2	228	374	0.3	0.6
193 EPISCOPAL.....	4	1,314	1,742	1.5	2.8
221 FREE METH C NA	2	67	72	0.1	0.1
281 LUTH CH AMER..	1	94	142	0.1	0.2
283 LUTH--MO SYNOD	1	118	187	0.2	0.3
357 PRESB CH US...	6	1,725	2,157*	1.9	3.5
403 SALVATION ARMY	1	114	310	0.3	0.5
413 S-D ADVENTISTS	2	177	221*	0.2	0.4
419 SO BAPT CONV..	47	31,618	39,545*	34.3	64.1
435 UNITARIAN-UNIV	1	17	17	-	-
443 UN C OF CHRIST	1	88	110*	0.1	0.2
449 UN METHODIST..	21	7,775	8,507	7.4	13.8
PLAQUEMINES	24	2,675	16,973*	67.3	100.0
081 CATHOLIC......	11	0	13,493	53.5	79.5
357 PRESB CH US...	2	89	117*	0.5	0.7
419 SO BAPT CONV..	8	2,413	3,161*	12.5	18.6
449 UN METHODIST..	3	173	202	0.8	1.2
POINTE COUPEE	13	817	11,595*	52.7	100.0
081 CATHOLIC......	5	0	10,477	47.6	90.4
193 EPISCOPAL.....	2	150	263	1.2	2.3
419 SO BAPT CONV..	6	667	855*	3.9	7.4
RAPIDES	165	37,848	67,628*	57.3	100.0
059 BAPT MISS ASSN	1	27	34*	-	0.1
081 CATHOLIC......	24	0	19,203	16.3	28.4
093 CR CH (DISC)..	1	151	189*	0.2	0.3
097 CR C AND C CR.	2	62	78*	0.1	0.1
123 CH GOD (ANDER)	8	215	502	0.4	0.7
127 CH GOD (CLEVE)	1	36	45*	-	0.1
165 CH OF NAZARENE	4	198	371	0.3	0.5
193 EPISCOPAL.....	7	1,921	2,293	1.9	3.4
221 FREE METH C NA	3	119	135	0.1	0.2
283 LUTH--MO SYNOD	2	253	361	0.3	0.5
357 PRESB CH US...	3	703	879*	0.7	1.3
403 SALVATION ARMY	1	117	1,478	1.3	2.2
413 S-D ADVENTISTS	2	295	369*	0.3	0.5
419 SO BAPT CONV..	86	28,818	36,033*	30.5	53.3
435 UNITARIAN-UNIV	1	17	17	-	-
449 UN METHODIST..	19	4,916	5,641	4.8	8.3
RED RIVER	20	3,575	4,415*	47.9	100.0
059 BAPT MISS ASSN	1	166	205*	2.2	4.6
081 CATHOLIC......	1	0	25	0.3	0.6
123 CH GOD (ANDER)	1	21	71	0.8	1.6
127 CH GOD (CLEVE)	1	83	103*	1.1	2.3
413 S-D ADVENTISTS	1	59	73*	0.8	1.7
419 SO BAPT CONV..	10	2,688	3,326*	36.1	75.3
449 UN METHODIST..	5	558	612	6.6	13.9
RICHLAND	51	9,918	12,398*	56.9	100.0
059 BAPT MISS ASSN	1	23	29*	0.1	0.2
081 CATHOLIC......	2	0	185	0.8	1.5
123 CH GOD (ANDER)	2	19	67	0.3	0.5
127 CH GOD (CLEVE)	4	157	196*	0.9	1.6
193 EPISCOPAL.....	1	101	131	0.6	1.1
357 PRESB CH US...	4	186	232*	1.1	1.9
419 SO BAPT CONV..	30	8,218	10,233*	47.0	82.5
449 UN METHODIST..	7	1,214	1,325	6.1	10.7
SABINE	68	7,983	12,808*	68.7	100.0
081 CATHOLIC......	6	0	2,899	15.6	22.6
123 CH GOD (ANDER)	1	15	76	0.4	0.6
165 CH OF NAZARENE	2	100	157	0.8	1.2
185 CUMBER PRESB..	1	45	56*	0.3	0.4
419 SO BAPT CONV..	49	7,163	8,897*	47.7	69.5
449 UN METHODIST..	9	660	723	3.9	5.6
ST BERNARD	19	2,428	38,688*	75.6	100.0
059 BAPT MISS ASSN	1	73	93*	0.2	0.2
081 CATHOLIC......	7	0	35,526	69.4	91.8
193 EPISCOPAL.....	1	172	294	0.6	0.8
283 LUTH--MO SYNOD	1	398	537	1.0	1.4
357 PRESB CH US...	2	191	242*	0.5	0.6
419 SO BAPT CONV..	5	995	1,262*	2.5	3.3
449 UN METHODIST..	2	599	734	1.4	1.9
ST CHARLES	19	3,575	23,518*	79.6	100.0
081 CATHOLIC......	7	0	18,800	63.6	79.9
285 MENNONITE CH..	1	90	120*	0.4	0.5
357 PRESB CH US...	2	199	264*	0.9	1.1
419 SO BAPT CONV..	6	2,755	3,660*	12.4	15.6
449 UN METHODIST..	2	437	549	1.9	2.3
453 UN PRES CH USA	1	94	125*	0.4	0.5
ST HELENA	23	3,718	4,780*	48.1	100.0
059 BAPT MISS ASSN	1	113	150*	1.5	3.1
081 CATHOLIC......	1	0	70	0.7	1.5
419 SO BAPT CONV..	12	2,639	3,499*	35.2	73.2
449 UN METHODIST..	9	966	1,061	10.7	22.2
ST JAMES	12	204	14,977*	75.9	100.0
081 CATHOLIC......	8	0	14,709	74.5	98.2
419 SO BAPT CONV..	1	130	172*	0.9	1.1
449 UN METHODIST..	3	74	96	0.5	0.6
ST JOHN THE BAPTIST	8	517	16,293*	68.4	100.0
081 CATHOLIC......	5	0	15,609	65.5	95.8
193 EPISCOPAL.....	1	45	52	0.2	0.3
419 SO BAPT CONV..	1	451	603*	2.5	3.7
449 UN METHODIST..	1	21	29	0.1	0.2
ST LANDRY	61	4,404	59,849*	74.5	100.0
081 CATHOLIC......	31	0	54,112	67.3	90.4
123 CH GOD (ANDER)	1	25	85	0.1	0.1
193 EPISCOPAL.....	2	167	245	0.3	0.4
283 LUTH--MO SYNOD	1	14	22	-	-
357 PRESB CH US...	2	83	107*	0.1	0.2
419 SO BAPT CONV..	15	3,717	4,772*	5.9	8.0
449 UN METHODIST..	9	398	506	0.6	0.8
ST MARTIN	9	390	29,008*	89.4	100.0
081 CATHOLIC......	6	0	28,457	87.7	98.1
419 SO BAPT CONV..	2	301	394*	1.2	1.4
449 UN METHODIST..	1	89	157	0.5	0.5
ST MARY	45	6,652	38,583*	63.5	100.0
081 CATHOLIC......	17	0	29,804	49.1	77.2
123 CH GOD (ANDER)	1	7	22	-	0.1
193 EPISCOPAL.....	2	351	449	0.7	1.2
283 LUTH--MO SYNOD	1	66	89	0.1	0.2
357 PRESB CH US...	3	287	382*	0.6	1.0
419 SO BAPT CONV..	9	3,898	5,194*	8.5	13.5
449 UN METHODIST..	12	2,043	2,643	4.4	6.9
ST TAMMANY	65	11,715	35,398*	55.7	100.0
059 BAPT MISS ASSN	1	151	193*	0.3	0.5
081 CATHOLIC......	13	0	20,240	31.8	57.2
093 CR CH (DISC)..	1	75	96*	0.2	0.3
123 CH GOD (ANDER)	2	60	182	0.3	0.5

*Total adherents estimated from known number of communicant, confirmed, full members.

—Represents a percent less than 0.1

Percentages may not total due to rounding.

Table 3. Churches and Church Membership by State, County and Denomination: 1971

County and Denomination	Number of churches	Communicant, confirmed, full members	Total adherents		
			Number	Percent of total population	Percent of total adherents
127 CH GOD (CLEVE)	5	602	768*	1.2	2.2
165 CH OF NAZARENE	1	73	165	0.3	0.5
193 EPISCOPAL.....	2	625	885	1.4	2.5
283 LUTH--MO SYNOD	2	413	621	1.0	1.8
357 PRESB CH US...	3	903	1,152*	1.8	3.3
413 S-D ADVENTISTS	2	65	83*	0.1	0.2
419 SO BAPT CONV..	23	7,574	9,659*	15.2	27.3
449 UN METHODIST..	8	1,112	1,266	2.0	3.6
469 WISC EVAN LUTH	2	62	88	0.1	0.2
TANGIPAHOA	77	16,317	29,728*	45.1	100.0
059 BAPT MISS ASSN	2	176	221*	0.3	0.7
081 CATHOLIC......	9	0	9,513	14.4	32.0
093 CR CH (DISC)..	1	180	226*	0.3	0.8
121 CH GOD (ABR)..	2	150	189*	0.3	0.6
123 CH GOD (ANDER)	2	108	268	0.4	0.9
127 CH GOD (CLEVE)	5	206	259*	0.4	0.9
193 EPISCOPAL.....	3	424	513	0.8	1.7
283 LUTH--MO SYNOD	1	130	177	0.3	0.6
285 MENNONITE CH..	1	21	26*	-	0.1
357 PRESB CH US...	3	487	612*	0.9	2.1
413 S-D ADVENTISTS	2	206	259*	0.4	0.9
415 S-D BAPTIST GC	2	35	44*	0.1	0.1
419 SO BAPT CONV..	33	11,824	14,862*	22.6	50.0
449 UN METHODIST..	11	2,370	2,559	3.9	8.6
TENSAS	21	2,409	3,144*	32.3	100.0
081 CATHOLIC......	3	0	172	1.8	5.5
123 CH GOD (ANDER)	1	8	23	0.2	0.7
193 EPISCOPAL.....	2	79	87	0.9	2.8
357 PRESB CH US...	3	103	129*	1.3	4.1
419 SO BAPT CONV..	8	1,832	2,301*	23.6	73.2
449 UN METHODIST..	4	387	432	4.4	13.7
TERREBONNE	37	6,447	29,355*	38.6	100.0
081 CATHOLIC......	21	0	20,721#	27.2	70.6
127 CH GOD (CLEVE)	1	19	25*	-	0.1
193 EPISCOPAL.....	1	345	650	0.9	2.2
283 LUTH--MO SYNOD	1	156	261	0.3	0.9
353 PLY BRETHREN..	1	20	40	0.1	0.1
357 PRESB CH US...	1	238	317*	0.4	1.1
413 S-D ADVENTISTS	1	27	36*	-	0.1
419 SO BAPT CONV..	5	4,177	5,561*	7.3	18.9
449 UN METHODIST..	5	1,465	1,744	2.3	5.9
UNION	53	9,395	11,381*	61.7	100.0
059 BAPT MISS ASSN	5	627	765*	4.1	6.7
081 CATHOLIC......	1	0	53	0.3	0.5
419 SO BAPT CONV..	38	7,893	9,633*	52.2	84.6
449 UN METHODIST..	9	875	930	5.0	8.2
VERMILION	32	2,445	33,922*	78.8	100.0
081 CATHOLIC......	16	0	30,910	71.8	91.1
193 EPISCOPAL.....	1	65	70	0.2	0.2
357 PRESB CH US...	1	76	96*	0.2	0.3
419 SO BAPT CONV..	5	1,118	1,413*	3.3	4.2
443 UN C OF CHRIST	3	119	150*	0.3	0.4
449 UN METHODIST..	6	1,067	1,283	3.0	3.8
VERNON	64	13,247	16,762*	31.2	100.0
081 CATHOLIC......	1	0	1,500	2.8	8.9
093 CR CH (DISC)..	1	78	89*	0.2	0.5
123 CH GOD (ANDER)	3	127	307	0.6	1.8
193 EPISCOPAL.....	1	23	39	0.1	0.2
283 LUTH--MO SYNOD	1	72	100	0.2	0.6
419 SO BAPT CONV..	52	12,312	14,058*	26.1	83.9
449 UN METHODIST..	5	635	669	1.2	4.0
WASHINGTON	50	14,639	19,221*	45.8	100.0
059 BAPT MISS ASSN	2	293	363*	0.9	1.9
081 CATHOLIC......	1	0	1,250	3.0	6.5
127 CH GOD (CLEVE)	2	99	123*	0.3	0.6
193 EPISCOPAL.....	1	147	162	0.4	0.8
283 LUTH--MO SYNOD	1	168	201	0.5	1.0
357 PRESB CH US...	1	266	330*	0.8	1.7
419 SO BAPT CONV..	29	11,595	14,364*	34.2	74.7
449 UN METHODIST..	13	2,071	2,428	5.8	12.6
WEBSTER	59	16,457	20,126*	50.4	100.0
059 BAPT MISS ASSN	6	1,596	1,936*	4.8	9.6
081 CATHOLIC......	3	0	585	1.5	2.9
093 CR CH (DISC)..	2	127	154*	0.4	0.8
123 CH GOD (ANDER)	1	14	41	0.1	0.2
127 CH GOD (CLEVE)	1	36	44*	0.1	0.2
165 CH OF NAZARENE	2	53	72	0.2	0.4
185 CUMBER PRESB..	1	134	163*	0.4	0.8
193 EPISCOPAL.....	1	195	230	0.6	1.1
357 PRESB CH US...	2	310	376*	0.9	1.9
413 S-D ADVENTISTS	1	27	33*	0.1	0.2
419 SO BAPT CONV..	23	10,665	12,940*	32.4	64.3
449 UN METHODIST..	16	3,300	3,552	8.9	17.6
WEST BATON ROUGE	9	1,080	9,359*	55.5	100.0
081 CATHOLIC......	3	0	7,913	46.9	84.5
357 PRESB CH US...	1	112	148*	0.9	1.6
419 SO BAPT CONV..	4	802	1,059*	6.3	11.3

County and Denomination	Number of churches	Communicant, confirmed, full members	Total adherents		
			Number	Percent of total population	Percent of total adherents
449 UN METHODIST..	1	166	239	1.4	2.6
WEST CARROLL	32	6,042	7,894*	60.6	100.0
081 CATHOLIC......	1	0	130	1.0	1.6
123 CH GOD (ANDER)	5	327	812	6.2	10.3
127 CH GOD (CLEVE)	3	131	161*	1.2	2.0
221 FREE METH C NA	1	44	49	0.4	0.6
419 SO BAPT CONV..	16	4,981	6,140*	47.1	77.8
449 UN METHODIST..	6	559	602	4.6	7.6
WEST FELICIANA	5	639	1,910*	16.8	100.0
081 CATHOLIC......	2	0	1,190	10.5	62.3
193 EPISCOPAL.....	1	200	220	1.9	11.5
419 SO BAPT CONV..	2	439	500*	4.4	26.2
WINN	57	7,851	9,634*	58.9	100.0
081 CATHOLIC......	2	0	95	0.6	1.0
093 CR CH (DISC)..	1	6	7*	-	0.1
127 CH GOD (CLEVE)	1	37	45*	0.3	0.5
165 CH OF NAZARENE	2	32	66	0.4	0.7
193 EPISCOPAL.....	1	22	46	0.3	0.5
357 PRESB CH US...	1	107	131*	0.8	1.4
419 SO BAPT CONV..	42	6,958	8,522*	52.1	88.5
449 UN METHODIST..	7	689	722	4.4	7.5
CO DATA NOT AVAIL	10	683	8,803*	N/A	N/A
127 CH GOD (CLEVE)	1	102	128*	N/A	N/A
151 L-D SAINTS....	0	0	7,993	N/A	N/A
193 EPISCOPAL.....	1	294	373	N/A	N/A
467 WESLEYAN......	8	287	309	N/A	N/A

MAINE

County and Denomination	Number of churches	Communicant, confirmed, full members	Total adherents		
			Number	Percent of total population	Percent of total adherents
THE STATE.....	1,228	130,376	444,794*	44.8	100.0
ANDROSCOGGIN	74	7,870	55,648*	61.0	100.0
019 AMER BAPT CONV	11	2,570	3,175*	3.5	5.7
081 CATHOLIC......	25	0	44,991	49.3	80.8
165 CH OF NAZARENE	6	301	1,059	1.2	1.9
175 CONG CR CH....	1	50	62*	0.1	0.1
193 EPISCOPAL.....	3	572	811	0.9	1.5
226 FRIENDS-USA...	1	137	169*	0.2	0.3
283 LUTH--MO SYNOD	1	186	227	0.2	0.4
335 ORTH PRESB CH.	1	28	45	-	0.1
403 SALVATION ARMY	1	108	623	0.7	1.1
413 S-D ADVENTISTS	1	124	153*	0.2	0.3
435 UNITARIAN-UNIV	4	306	405	0.4	0.7
443 UN C OF CHRIST	6	1,391	1,718*	1.9	3.1
449 UN METHODIST..	10	1,791	1,832	2.0	3.3
453 UN PRES CH USA	3	306	378*	0.4	0.7
AROOSTOOK	117	10,487	51,551*	55.8	100.0
019 AMER BAPT CONV	26	4,420	5,598*	6.1	10.9
081 CATHOLIC......	48	0	38,522	41.7	74.7
165 CH OF NAZARENE	2	72	130	0.1	0.3
175 CONG CR CH....	2	150	190*	0.2	0.4
193 EPISCOPAL.....	7	914	1,496	1.6	2.9
201 EVAN COV CH AM	1	93	118*	0.1	0.2
281 LUTH CH AMER..	3	437	583	0.6	1.1
335 ORTH PRESB CH.	1	32	56	0.1	0.1
403 SALVATION ARMY	1	29	132	0.1	0.3
413 S-D ADVENTISTS	2	62	79*	0.1	0.2
419 SO BAPT CONV..	1	147	186*	0.2	0.4
435 UNITARIAN-UNIV	3	215	272	0.3	0.5
443 UN C OF CHRIST	8	872	1,104*	1.2	2.1
449 UN METHODIST..	12	3,044	3,085	3.3	6.0
CUMBERLAND	168	28,585	88,642*	46.0	100.0
019 AMER BAPT CONV	22	3,896	4,754*	2.5	5.4
029 AMER LUTH CH..	4	716	1,016	0.5	1.1
081 CATHOLIC......	36	0	50,765	26.4	57.3
097 CR C AND C CR.	2	67	82*	-	0.1
127 CH GOD (CLEVE)	1	92	112*	0.1	0.1
165 CH OF NAZARENE	9	696	1,753	0.9	2.0
175 CONG CR CH....	2	625	763*	0.4	0.9
193 EPISCOPAL.....	7	3,138	5,586	2.9	6.3
221 FREE METH C NA	1	28	42	-	-
226 FRIENDS-USA...	3	138	168*	0.1	0.2
281 LUTH CH AMER..	1	207	291	0.2	0.3
283 LUTH--MO SYNOD	1	124	171	0.1	0.2
285 MENNONITE CH..	1	1	1*	-	-
335 ORTH PRESB CH.	1	151	211	0.1	0.2
353 PLY BRETHREN..	2	40	70	-	0.1
403 SALVATION ARMY	2	116	1,370	0.7	1.5
413 S-D ADVENTISTS	4	716	874*	0.5	1.0
419 SO BAPT CONV..	2	243	297*	0.2	0.3

*Total adherents estimated from known number of communicant, confirmed, full members.

—Represents a percent less than 0.1.

Percentages may not total due to rounding.

#The corrected Catholic population of Terrebonne County is 50,721

Table 3. Churches and Church Membership by State, County and Denomination: 1971

County and Denomination	Number of churches	Communicant, confirmed, full members	Total adherents		
			Number	Percent of total population	Percent of total adherents
435 UNITARIAN-UNIV	7	1,001	1,230	0.6	1.4
443 UN C OF CHRIST	34	10,951	13,363*	6.9	15.1
449 UN METHODIST..	26	5,639	5,723	3.0	6.5
FRANKLIN	42	3,320	8,865*	39.5	100.0
019 AMER BAPT CONV	10	712	885*	3.9	10.0
081 CATHOLIC......	9	0	4,510	20.1	50.9
165 CH OF NAZARENE	2	150	320	1.4	3.6
193 EPISCOPAL.....	2	464	860	3.8	9.7
413 S-D ADVENTISTS	1	40	50*	0.2	0.6
435 UNITARIAN-UNIV	1	22	22	0.1	0.2
443 UN C OF CHRIST	7	897	1,115*	5.0	12.6
449 UN METHODIST..	8	923	964	4.3	10.9
453 UN PRES CH USA	2	112	139*	0.6	1.6
HANCOCK	90	6,070	10,813*	31.3	100.0
019 AMER BAPT CONV	25	1,442	1,740*	5.0	16.1
081 CATHOLIC......	12	0	2,648	7.7	24.5
127 CH GOD (CLEVE)	1	8	10*	-	0.1
165 CH OF NAZARENE	1	35	196	0.6	1.8
175 CONG CR CH....	1	250	302*	0.9	2.8
193 EPISCOPAL.....	10	1,126	2,179	6.3	20.2
435 UNITARIAN-UNIV	2	125	175	0.5	1.6
443 UN C OF CHRIST	19	2,074	2,502*	7.2	23.1
449 UN METHODIST..	19	1,010	1,061	3.1	9.8
KENNEBEC	101	12,774	43,620*	45.8	100.0
019 AMER BAPT CONV	27	3,776	4,633*	4.9	10.6
029 AMER LUTH CH..	1	233	333	0.3	0.8
081 CATHOLIC......	19	0	26,518	27.8	60.8
127 CH GOD (CLEVE)	2	94	115*	0.1	0.3
165 CH OF NAZARENE	3	307	1,059	1.1	2.4
193 EPISCOPAL.....	6	1,711	3,315	3.5	7.6
221 FREE METH C NA	1	20	24	-	0.1
226 FRIENDS-USA...	4	190	233*	0.2	0.5
283 LUTH--MO SYNOD	1	71	110	0.1	0.3
353 PLY BRETHREN..	1	30	50	0.1	0.1
403 SALVATION ARMY	2	50	388	0.4	0.9
413 S-D ADVENTISTS	2	138	169*	0.2	0.4
435 UNITARIAN-UNIV	4	518	563	0.6	1.3
443 UN C OF CHRIST	9	1,821	2,234*	2.3	5.1
449 UN METHODIST..	19	3,815	3,876	4.1	8.9
KNOX	48	5,158	8,628*	29.7	100.0
019 AMER BAPT CONV	19	1,980	2,366*	8.2	27.4
081 CATHOLIC......	5	0	1,856	6.4	21.5
165 CH OF NAZARENE	3	176	848	2.9	9.8
175 CONG CR CH....	1	185	221*	0.8	2.6
193 EPISCOPAL.....	3	632	796	2.7	9.2
226 FRIENDS-USA...	1	24	29*	0.1	0.3
281 LUTH CH AMER..	1	91	119	0.4	1.4
353 PLY BRETHREN..	1	15	30	0.1	0.3
403 SALVATION ARMY	1	50	163	0.6	1.9
413 S-D ADVENTISTS	1	108	129*	0.4	1.5
435 UNITARIAN-UNIV	1	240	279	1.0	3.2
443 UN C OF CHRIST	3	567	678*	2.3	7.9
449 UN METHODIST..	8	1,090	1,114	3.8	12.9
LINCOLN	38	3,279	5,025*	24.5	100.0
019 AMER BAPT CONV	12	719	866*	4.2	17.2
081 CATHOLIC......	4	0	1,049	5.1	20.9
127 CH GOD (CLEVE)	1	37	45*	0.2	0.9
165 CH OF NAZARENE	1	16	96	0.5	1.9
193 EPISCOPAL.....	3	619	858	4.2	17.1
226 FRIENDS-USA...	1	10	12*	0.1	0.2
443 UN C OF CHRIST	8	946	1,140*	5.6	22.7
449 UN METHODIST..	8	932	959	4.7	19.1
OXFORD	61	5,279	16,736*	38.5	100.0
019 AMER BAPT CONV	8	597	735*	1.7	4.4
081 CATHOLIC......	8	0	10,122	23.3	60.5
165 CH OF NAZARENE	3	157	551	1.3	3.3
175 CONG CR CH....	2	413	508*	1.2	3.0
193 EPISCOPAL.....	2	291	310	0.7	1.9
281 LUTH CH AMER..	1	138	248	0.6	1.5
413 S-D ADVENTISTS	4	284	349*	0.8	2.1
435 UNITARIAN-UNIV	7	304	431	1.0	2.6
443 UN C OF CHRIST	16	1,520	1,870*	4.3	11.2
449 UN METHODIST..	9	1,527	1,553	3.6	9.3
453 UN PRES CH USA	1	48	59*	0.1	0.4
PENOBSCOT	117	15,723	51,914*	41.4	100.0
019 AMER BAPT CONV	28	4,126	5,048*	4.0	9.7
081 CATHOLIC......	23	0	32,478	25.9	62.6
127 CH GOD (CLEVE)	4	172	210*	0.2	0.4
165 CH OF NAZARENE	4	283	744	0.6	1.4
175 CONG CR CH....	2	395	483*	0.4	0.9
193 EPISCOPAL.....	1	1,252	2,094	1.7	4.0
201 EVAN COV CH AM	2	101	124*	0.1	0.2
226 FRIENDS-USA...	1	6	7*	-	-
281 LUTH CH AMER..	1	152	223	0.2	0.4
335 ORTH PRESB CH.	1	61	109	0.1	0.2
403 SALVATION ARMY	1	51	237	0.2	0.5
413 S-D ADVENTISTS	2	102	125*	0.1	0.2
419 SO BAPT CONV..	1	64	78*	0.1	0.2
435 UNITARIAN-UNIV	4	1,159	1,294	1.0	2.5
443 UN C OF CHRIST	19	3,429	4,195*	3.3	8.1
449 UN METHODIST..	23	4,370	4,465	3.6	8.6
PISCATAQUIS	28	2,997	4,968*	30.5	100.0
019 AMER BAPT CONV	4	663	797*	4.9	16.0
081 CATHOLIC......	6	0	1,392	8.5	28.0
165 CH OF NAZARENE	2	31	182	1.1	3.7
193 EPISCOPAL.....	2	85	152	0.9	3.1
435 UNITARIAN-UNIV	2	52	97	0.6	2.0
443 UN C OF CHRIST	5	735	883*	5.4	17.8
449 UN METHODIST..	7	1,431	1,465	9.0	29.5
SAGADAHOC	30	3,059	7,116*	30.3	100.0
019 AMER BAPT CONV	10	1,032	1,282*	5.5	18.0
081 CATHOLIC......	3	0	2,135	9.1	30.0
165 CH OF NAZARENE	5	176	661	2.8	9.3
193 EPISCOPAL.....	1	353	1,158	4.9	16.3
403 SALVATION ARMY	1	29	166	0.7	2.3
413 S-D ADVENTISTS	2	106	132*	0.6	1.9
443 UN C OF CHRIST	3	870	1,081*	4.6	15.2
449 UN METHODIST..	5	493	501	2.1	7.0
SOMERSET	54	4,325	15,799*	38.9	100.0
019 AMER BAPT CONV	8	1,524	1,888*	4.7	12.0
081 CATHOLIC......	10	0	9,246	22.8	58.5
127 CH GOD (CLEVE)	1	31	38*	0.1	0.2
165 CH OF NAZARENE	6	416	1,775	4.4	11.2
175 CONG CR CH....	2	147	182*	0.4	1.2
193 EPISCOPAL.....	3	129	265	0.7	1.7
226 FRIENDS-USA...	1	19	24*	0.1	0.2
335 ORTH PRESB CH.	1	25	36	0.1	0.2
353 PLY BRETHREN..	1	15	20	-	0.1
413 S-D ADVENTISTS	1	135	167*	0.4	1.1
435 UNITARIAN-UNIV	1	178	202	0.5	1.3
443 UN C OF CHRIST	7	660	818*	2.0	5.2
449 UN METHODIST..	10	924	987	2.4	6.2
453 UN PRES CH USA	2	122	151*	0.4	1.0
WALDO	32	2,725	4,454*	19.1	100.0
019 AMER BAPT CONV	8	502	615*	2.6	13.8
081 CATHOLIC......	3	0	1,023	4.4	23.0
127 CH GOD (CLEVE)	1	88	108*	0.5	2.4
165 CH OF NAZARENE	1	89	184	0.8	4.1
175 CONG CR CH....	2	75	92*	0.4	2.1
193 EPISCOPAL.....	1	234	371	1.6	8.3
413 S-D ADVENTISTS	1	29	36*	0.2	0.8
435 UNITARIAN-UNIV	1	306	456	2.0	10.2
443 UN C OF CHRIST	7	623	763*	3.3	17.1
449 UN METHODIST..	7	779	806	3.5	18.1
WASHINGTON	76	4,994	9,221*	30.9	100.0
019 AMER BAPT CONV	19	1,511	1,818*	6.1	19.7
081 CATHOLIC......	13	0	3,102	10.4	33.6
127 CH GOD (CLEVE)	1	25	30*	0.1	0.3
165 CH OF NAZARENE	2	31	153	0.5	1.7
175 CONG CR CH....	8	874	1,052*	3.5	11.4
193 EPISCOPAL.....	4	389	689	2.3	7.5
413 S-D ADVENTISTS	2	70	84*	0.3	0.9
435 UNITARIAN-UNIV	1	18	18	0.1	0.2
443 UN C OF CHRIST	9	674	811*	2.7	8.8
449 UN METHODIST..	17	1,402	1,464	4.9	15.9
YORK	119	12,492	56,681*	50.8	100.0
019 AMER BAPT CONV	36	4,146	5,094*	4.6	9.0
029 AMER LUTH CH..	1	31	53	-	0.1
081 CATHOLIC......	28	0	40,769	36.5	71.9
165 CH OF NAZARENE	3	123	559	0.5	1.0
175 CONG CR CH....	1	110	135*	0.1	0.2
193 EPISCOPAL.....	7	879	1,402	1.3	2.5
226 FRIENDS-USA...	2	46	57*	0.1	0.1
403 SALVATION ARMY	2	171	729	0.7	1.3
413 S-D ADVENTISTS	1	24	29*	-	0.1
435 UNITARIAN-UNIV	3	345	374	0.3	0.7
443 UN C OF CHRIST	18	3,541	4,351*	3.9	7.7
449 UN METHODIST..	17	3,076	3,129	2.8	5.5
CO DATA NOT AVAIL	33	1,239	5,113*	N/A	N/A
151 L-D SAINTS....	0	0	3,671	N/A	N/A
223 FREE WILL BAPT	2	88	108*	N/A	N/A
467 WESLEYAN......	31	1,151	1,334	N/A	N/A

MARYLAND

County and Denomination	Number of churches	Communicant, confirmed, full members	Number	Percent of total population	Percent of total adherents
THE STATE.....	2,725	676,054	1,677,329*	42.8	100.0
ALLEGANY	123	25,225	48,747*	58.0	100.0
081 CATHOLIC......	9	0	17,525	20.9	36.0
093 CR CH (DISC)..	1	156	186*	0.2	0.4
097 CR C AND C CR.	1	49	59*	0.1	0.1
123 CH GOD (ANDER)	1	80	140	0.2	0.3
127 CH GOD (CLEVE)	3	165	197*	0.2	0.4

*Total adherents estimated from known number of communicant, confirmed, full members.

—Represents a percent less than 0.1.

Percentages may not total due to rounding.

Table 3. Churches and Church Membership by State, County and Denomination: 1971

County and Denomination	Number of churches	Communicant, confirmed, full members	Total adherents: Number	Total adherents: Percent of total population	Total adherents: Percent of total adherents
157 CH OF BRETHREN	6	944	1,129*	1.3	2.3
165 CH OF NAZARENE	4	376	814	1.0	1.7
175 CONG CR CH....	1	125	149*	0.2	0.3
193 EPISCOPAL.....	6	1,340	1,758	2.1	3.6
281 LUTH CH AMER..	6	3,551	4,517	5.4	9.3
283 LUTH--MO SYNOD	1	268	268	0.3	0.5
285 MENNONITE CH..	4	258	308*	0.4	0.6
349 PENT HOLINESS.	2	91	109*	0.1	0.2
353 PLY BRETHREN..	2	50	90	0.1	0.2
357 PRESB CH US...	1	37	44*	0.1	0.1
403 SALVATION ARMY	1	109	357	0.4	0.7
413 S-D ADVENTISTS	2	197	236*	0.3	0.5
419 SO BAPT CONV..	10	3,268	3,907*	4.6	8.0
443 UN C OF CHRIST	7	1,105	1,321*	1.6	2.7
449 UN METHODIST..	49	11,500	13,773	16.4	28.3
453 UN PRES CH USA	6	1,556	1,860*	2.2	3.8
ANNE ARUNDEL	156	46,019	119,813*	40.3	100.0
029 AMER LUTH CH..	4	1,421	2,376	0.8	2.0
081 CATHOLIC......	15	0	56,084	18.8	46.8
097 CR C AND C CR.	3	130	162*	0.1	0.1
123 CH GOD (ANDER)	2	135	349	0.1	0.3
127 CH GOD (CLEVE)	7	412	513*	0.2	0.4
157 CH OF BRETHREN	1	143	178*	0.1	0.1
165 CH OF NAZARENE	3	300	781	0.3	0.7
193 EPISCOPAL.....	14	5,208	8,707	2.9	7.3
226 FRIENDS-USA...	1	38	47*	-	-
281 LUTH CH AMER..	8	4,404	7,022	2.4	5.9
283 LUTH--MO SYNOD	5	2,360	3,799	1.3	3.2
353 PLY BRETHREN..	1	40	50	-	-
381 REF PRES-EVAN.	1	220	264	0.1	0.2
403 SALVATION ARMY	2	66	396	0.1	0.3
413 S-D ADVENTISTS	5	515	641*	0.2	0.5
419 SO BAPT CONV..	21	7,078	8,807*	3.0	7.4
435 UNITARIAN-UNIV	1	160	260	0.1	0.2
443 UN C OF CHRIST	1	128	159*	0.1	0.1
449 UN METHODIST..	56	20,541	25,834	8.7	21.6
453 UN PRES CH USA	5	2,720	3,384*	1.1	2.8
BALTIMORE	270	88,561	246,103*	39.6	100.0
019 AMER BAPT CONV	2	627	761*	0.1	0.3
029 AMER LUTH CH..	5	1,982	3,560	0.6	1.4
081 CATHOLIC......	26	0	127,581	20.5	51.8
093 CR CH (DISC)..	10	1,531	1,857*	0.3	0.8
097 CR C AND C CR.	1	286	347*	0.1	0.1
127 CH GOD (CLEVE)	5	481	584*	0.1	0.2
157 CH OF BRETHREN	6	755	916*	0.1	0.4
193 EPISCOPAL.....	18	7,632	11,825	1.9	4.8
226 FRIENDS-USA...	1	44	53*	-	-
281 LUTH CH AMER..	43	24,760	36,146	5.8	14.7
283 LUTH--MO SYNOD	14	5,652	8,014	1.3	3.3
285 MENNONITE CH..	1	33	40*	-	-
315 NO AM OLD RC..	1	87	106*	-	-
349 PENT HOLINESS.	2	244	296*	-	0.1
353 PLY BRETHREN..	8	478	745	0.1	0.3
357 PRESB CH US...	2	2,205	2,675*	0.4	1.1
381 REF PRES-EVAN.	2	437	553	0.1	0.2
413 S-D ADVENTISTS	8	2,010	2,439*	0.4	1.0
419 SO BAPT CONV..	5	926	1,123*	0.2	0.5
435 UNITARIAN-UNIV	1	317	612	0.1	0.2
443 UN C OF CHRIST	1	327	397*	0.1	0.2
449 UN METHODIST..	87	27,556	33,109	5.3	13.5
453 UN PRES CH USA	21	10,191	12,364*	2.0	5.0
BALTIMORE CITY	406	135,816	389,735*	43.0	100.0
019 AMER BAPT CONV	11	2,279	2,782*	0.3	0.7
029 AMER LUTH CH..	20	9,583	15,142	1.7	3.9
075 BRETHREN IN CR	1	55	67*	-	-
081 CATHOLIC......	68	0	212,198	23.4	54.4
097 CR C AND C CR.	6	444	542*	0.1	0.1
123 CH GOD (ANDER)	5	485	1,276	0.1	0.3
127 CH GOD (CLEVE)	11	1,373	1,676*	0.2	0.4
165 CH OF NAZARENE	4	504	1,074	0.1	0.3
193 EPISCOPAL.....	44	19,208	28,786	3.2	7.4
221 FREE METH C NA	3	159	228	-	0.1
226 FRIENDS-USA...	2	620	757*	0.1	0.2
281 LUTH CH AMER..	1	124	184	-	-
283 LUTH--MO SYNOD	1	344	491	0.1	0.1
335 ORTH PRESB CH.	1	41	55	-	-
357 PRESB CH US...	7	1,824	2,227*	0.2	0.6
381 REF PRES-EVAN.	2	363	378	-	0.1
403 SALVATION ARMY	4	398	1,408	0.2	0.4
413 S-D ADVENTISTS	2	489	597*	0.1	0.2
419 SO BAPT CONV..	54	25,238	30,809*	3.4	7.9
435 UNITARIAN-UNIV	1	471	471	0.1	0.1
443 UN C OF CHRIST	18	6,263	7,646*	0.8	2.0
449 UN METHODIST..	114	53,969	66,787	7.4	17.1
453 UN PRES CH USA	25	11,524	14,068*	1.6	3.6
469 WISC EVAN LUTH	1	58	86	-	-
CALVERT	25	3,456	6,344*	30.7	100.0
081 CATHOLIC......	3	0	1,621	7.8	25.6
193 EPISCOPAL.....	3	518	866	4.2	13.7
413 S-D ADVENTISTS	2	48	62*	0.3	1.0
449 UN METHODIST..	17	2,890	3,795	18.3	59.8
CAROLINE	43	5,835	8,222*	41.6	100.0
081 CATHOLIC......	3	0	779	3.9	9.5
123 CH GOD (ANDER)	1	86	190	1.0	2.3
127 CH GOD (CLEVE)	2	120	146*	0.7	1.8
157 CH OF BRETHREN	2	232	282*	1.4	3.4
165 CH OF NAZARENE	1	41	122	0.6	1.5
193 EPISCOPAL.....	2	239	307	1.6	3.7
283 LUTH--MO SYNOD	1	344	491	2.5	6.0
413 S-D ADVENTISTS	1	42	51*	0.3	0.6
419 SO BAPT CONV..	2	167	203*	1.0	2.5
449 UN METHODIST..	28	4,564	5,651	28.6	68.7
CARROLL	118	22,903	35,096*	50.9	100.0
081 CATHOLIC......	4	0	5,672	8.2	16.2
127 CH GOD (CLEVE)	2	159	193*	0.3	0.5
157 CH OF BRETHREN	6	1,444	1,757*	2.5	5.0
165 CH OF NAZARENE	2	62	205	0.3	0.6
193 EPISCOPAL.....	4	523	898	1.3	2.6
221 FREE METH C NA	1	13	27	-	0.1
226 FRIENDS-USA...	1	17	21*	-	0.1
281 LUTH CH AMER..	21	6,742	9,105	13.2	25.9
285 MENNONITE CH..	2	27	33*	-	0.1
357 PRESB CH US...	2	188	229*	0.3	0.7
413 S-D ADVENTISTS	3	220	268*	0.4	0.8
419 SO BAPT CONV..	7	1,149	1,398*	2.0	4.0
443 UN C OF CHRIST	10	2,714	3,303*	4.8	9.4
449 UN METHODIST..	47	9,096	11,319	16.4	32.3
453 UN PRES CH USA	6	549	668*	1.0	1.9
CECIL	69	10,262	17,181*	32.2	100.0
029 AMER LUTH CH..	1	127	165	0.3	1.0
081 CATHOLIC......	7	0	3,196	6.0	18.6
127 CH GOD (CLEVE)	3	153	192*	0.4	1.1
157 CH OF BRETHREN	1	49	61*	0.1	0.4
165 CH OF NAZARENE	3	170	442	0.8	2.6
193 EPISCOPAL.....	4	698	1,197	2.2	7.0
226 FRIENDS-USA...	1	20	25*	-	0.1
285 MENNONITE CH..	2	47	59*	0.1	0.3
381 REF PRES-EVAN.	1	22	29	0.1	0.2
413 S-D ADVENTISTS	3	333	417*	0.8	2.4
419 SO BAPT CONV..	7	2,521	3,159*	5.9	18.4
449 UN METHODIST..	30	5,129	6,995	13.1	40.7
453 UN PRES CH USA	6	993	1,244*	2.3	7.2
CHARLES	41	5,146	25,183*	52.8	100.0
081 CATHOLIC......	12	0	18,342	38.5	72.8
123 CH GOD (ANDER)	1	64	162	0.3	0.6
165 CH OF NAZARENE	1	90	301	0.6	1.2
283 LUTH--MO SYNOD	2	249	415	0.9	1.6
413 S-D ADVENTISTS	2	68	91*	0.2	0.4
419 SO BAPT CONV..	9	2,388	3,210*	6.7	12.7
449 UN METHODIST..	14	2,287	2,662	5.6	10.6
DORCHESTER	70	8,727	11,850*	40.3	100.0
081 CATHOLIC......	3	0	1,022	3.5	8.6
097 CR C AND C CR.	1	46	55*	0.2	0.5
127 CH GOD (CLEVE)	2	143	171*	0.6	1.4
165 CH OF NAZARENE	1	72	142	0.5	1.2
193 EPISCOPAL.....	5	688	1,012	3.4	8.5
283 LUTH--MO SYNOD	1	94	130	0.4	1.1
403 SALVATION ARMY	1	87	304	1.0	2.6
413 S-D ADVENTISTS	2	81	97*	0.3	0.8
419 SO BAPT CONV..	3	838	1,005*	3.4	8.5
443 UN C OF CHRIST	1	263	315*	1.1	2.7
449 UN METHODIST..	50	6,415	7,597	25.8	64.1
FREDERICK	151	30,733	57,022*	67.1	100.0
081 CATHOLIC......	11	0	13,605	16.0	23.9
097 CR C AND C CR.	1	90	111*	0.1	0.2
127 CH GOD (CLEVE)	4	245	301*	0.4	0.5
157 CH OF BRETHREN	11	3,129	3,848*	4.5	6.7
165 CH OF NAZARENE	1	119	270	0.3	0.5
193 EPISCOPAL.....	10	1,420	2,999	3.5	5.3
281 LUTH CH AMER..	31	10,356	14,705	17.3	25.8
293 MORAV CH-NORTH	1	211	295	0.3	0.5
403 SALVATION ARMY	1	115	464	0.5	0.8
413 S-D ADVENTISTS	2	340	418*	0.5	0.7
419 SO BAPT CONV..	4	1,640	2,017*	2.4	3.5
435 UNITARIAN-UNIV	1	40	66	0.1	0.1
443 UN C OF CHRIST	16	3,786	4,656*	5.5	8.2
449 UN METHODIST..	55	8,604	12,482	14.7	21.9
453 UN PRES CH USA	2	638	785*	0.9	1.4
GARRETT	72	7,494	10,415*	48.5	100.0
081 CATHOLIC......	3	0	965	4.5	9.3
093 CR CH (DISC)..	1	60	75*	0.3	0.7
123 CH GOD (ANDER)	1	35	157	0.7	1.5
127 CH GOD (CLEVE)	3	130	161*	0.7	1.5
157 CH OF BRETHREN	9	1,118	1,389*	6.5	13.3
165 CH OF NAZARENE	1	79	134	0.6	1.3
175 CONG CR CH....	1	125	155*	0.7	1.5
193 EPISCOPAL.....	1	68	186	0.9	1.8
281 LUTH CH AMER..	9	1,534	1,969	9.2	18.9
283 LUTH--MO SYNOD	2	341	469	2.2	4.5
285 MENNONITE CH..	7	386	480*	2.2	4.6
353 PLY BRETHREN..	1	10	20	0.1	0.2
413 S-D ADVENTISTS	1	88	109*	0.5	1.0
419 SO BAPT CONV..	3	309	384*	1.8	3.7
443 UN C OF CHRIST	2	254	316*	1.5	3.0
449 UN METHODIST..	27	2,957	3,446	16.0	33.1
HARFORD	95	22,749	47,408*	41.1	100.0

*Total adherents estimated from known number of communicant, confirmed, full members.

—Represents a percent less than 0.1.

Percentages may not total due to rounding.

Table 3. Churches and Church Membership by State, County and Denomination: 1971

County and Denomination	Number of churches	Communicant, confirmed, full members	Total adherents: Number	Total adherents: Percent of total population	Total adherents: Percent of total adherents
029 AMER LUTH CH..	3	1,490	2,406	2.1	5.1
081 CATHOLIC......	8	0	17,539	15.2	37.0
097 CR C AND C CR.	4	1,155	1,465*	1.3	3.1
127 CH GOD (CLEVE)	1	99	126*	0.1	0.3
165 CH OF NAZARENE	1	252	531	0.5	1.1
193 EPISCOPAL.....	10	1,820	2,272	2.0	4.8
226 FRIENDS-USA...	2	144	183*	0.2	0.4
281 LUTH CH AMER..	1	414	649	0.6	1.4
283 LUTH--MO SYNOD	1	446	757	0.7	1.6
349 PENT HOLINESS.	1	67	85*	0.1	0.2
403 SALVATION ARMY	1	59	215	0.2	0.5
419 SO BAPT CONV..	14	4,694	5,955*	5.2	12.6
435 UNITARIAN-UNIV	1	23	36	-	0.1
443 UN C OF CHRIST	1	111	141*	0.1	0.3
449 UN METHODIST..	34	8,052	10,071	8.7	21.2
453 UN PRES CH USA	12	3,923	4,977*	4.3	10.5
HOWARD	74	15,172	31,284*	50.5	100.0
029 AMER LUTH CH..	3	1,098	1,566	2.5	5.0
081 CATHOLIC......	5	0	11,306	18.3	36.1
093 CR CH (DISC)..	1	70	89*	0.1	0.3
123 CH GOD (ANDER)	2	40	140	0.2	0.4
157 CH OF BRETHREN	1	113	143*	0.2	0.5
193 EPISCOPAL.....	6	1,769	2,545	4.1	8.1
281 LUTH CH AMER..	1	854	1,154	1.9	3.7
283 LUTH--MO SYNOD	1	128	242	0.4	0.8
285 MENNONITE CH..	2	49	62*	0.1	0.2
353 PLY BRETHREN..	1	115	180	0.3	0.6
357 PRESB CH US...	2	910	1,152*	1.9	3.7
413 S-D ADVENTISTS	3	263	333*	0.5	1.1
419 SO BAPT CONV..	8	1,968	2,492*	4.0	8.0
435 UNITARIAN-UNIV	1	80	139	0.2	0.4
443 UN C OF CHRIST	2	867	1,098*	1.8	3.5
449 UN METHODIST..	31	5,580	7,037	11.4	22.5
453 UN PRES CH USA	4	1,268	1,606*	2.6	5.1
KENT	46	4,957	8,036*	49.8	100.0
081 CATHOLIC......	4	0	1,433	8.9	17.8
165 CH OF NAZARENE	1	39	140	0.9	1.7
193 EPISCOPAL.....	5	837	1,292	8.0	16.1
283 LUTH--MO SYNOD	1	130	180	1.1	2.2
285 MENNONITE CH..	2	70	84*	0.5	1.0
413 S-D ADVENTISTS	3	257	308*	1.9	3.8
449 UN METHODIST..	30	3,624	4,599	28.5	57.2
MONTGOMERY	220	86,290	234,463*	44.8	100.0
019 AMER BAPT CONV	10	6,447	7,929*	1.5	3.4
029 AMER LUTH CH..	4	1,690	2,372	0.5	1.0
081 CATHOLIC......	25	0	126,512	24.2	54.0
093 CR CH (DISC)..	6	1,441	1,772*	0.3	0.8
097 CR C AND C CR.	1	151	186*	-	0.1
123 CH GOD (ANDER)	1	150	365	0.1	0.2
127 CH GOD (CLEVE)	6	421	518*	0.1	0.2
157 CH OF BRETHREN	2	271	333*	0.1	0.1
165 CH OF NAZARENE	1	127	306	0.1	0.1
221 FREE METH C NA	4	247	347	0.1	0.1
226 FRIENDS-USA...	2	446	549*	0.1	0.2
281 LUTH CH AMER..	8	5,385	8,166	1.6	3.5
283 LUTH--MO SYNOD	5	2,135	3,043	0.6	1.3
285 MENNONITE CH..	2	57	70*	-	-
335 ORTH PRESB CH.	2	296	439	0.1	0.2
349 PENT HOLINESS.	1	104	128*	-	0.1
353 PLY BRETHREN..	1	14	20	-	-
357 PRESB CH US...	4	2,121	2,609*	0.5	1.1
413 S-D ADVENTISTS	7	6,042	7,431*	1.4	3.2
419 SO BAPT CONV..	34	15,927	19,589*	3.7	8.4
435 UNITARIAN-UNIV	4	1,688	2,812	0.5	1.2
443 UN C OF CHRIST	4	2,328	2,863*	0.5	1.2
449 UN METHODIST..	62	33,088	39,076	7.5	16.7
453 UN PRES CH USA	24	5,714	7,028*	1.3	3.0
PRINCE GEORGES	212	70,104	231,977*	35.1	100.0
019 AMER BAPT CONV	22	9,577	12,238*	1.9	5.3
029 AMER LUTH CH..	4	1,755	2,895	0.4	1.2
081 CATHOLIC......	35	0	139,746	21.2	60.2
093 CR CH (DISC)..	8	1,942	2,482*	0.4	1.1
097 CR C AND C CR.	1	395	505*	0.1	0.2
123 CH GOD (ANDER)	1	100	200	-	0.1
127 CH GOD (CLEVE)	5	385	492*	0.1	0.2
157 CH OF BRETHREN	1	351	449*	0.1	0.2
165 CH OF NAZARENE	2	252	478	0.1	0.2
193 EPISCOPAL.....	1	114	152	-	0.1
201 EVAN COV CH AM	1	74	95*	-	-
221 FREE METH C NA	1	11	32	-	-
226 FRIENDS-USA...	1	139	178*	-	0.1
281 LUTH CH AMER..	9	3,492	5,413	0.8	2.3
283 LUTH--MO SYNOD	8	3,229	4,809	0.7	2.1
285 MENNONITE CH..	2	138	176*	-	0.1
293 MORAV CH-NORTH	2	248	390	0.1	0.2
349 PENT HOLINESS.	1	66	84*	-	-
353 PLY BRETHREN..	2	75	120	-	0.1
357 PRESB CH US...	1	409	523*	0.1	0.2
403 SALVATION ARMY	1	126	512	0.1	0.2
413 S-D ADVENTISTS	6	1,236	1,579*	0.2	0.7
419 SO BAPT CONV..	36	17,557	22,435*	3.4	9.7
435 UNITARIAN-UNIV	2	485	835	0.1	0.4
443 UN C OF CHRIST	5	833	1,064*	0.2	0.5
449 UN METHODIST..	46	23,519	29,481	4.5	12.7
453 UN PRES CH USA	7	3,564	4,554*	0.7	2.0
469 WISC EVAN LUTH	1	32	60	-	-
QUEEN ANNES	42	4,702	7,710*	41.9	100.0
081 CATHOLIC......	4	0	1,525	8.3	19.8
127 CH GOD (CLEVE)	3	110	133*	0.7	1.7
193 EPISCOPAL.....	3	454	704	3.8	9.1
283 LUTH--MO SYNOD	1	80	122	0.7	1.6
285 MENNONITE CH..	1	19	23*	0.1	0.3
413 S-D ADVENTISTS	1	101	122*	0.7	1.6
419 SO BAPT CONV..	1	73	88*	0.5	1.1
449 UN METHODIST..	27	3,697	4,790	26.0	62.1
453 UN PRES CH USA	1	168	203*	1.1	2.6
ST MARYS	37	3,244	21,197*	44.7	100.0
081 CATHOLIC......	16	0	16,865	35.6	79.6
097 CR C AND C CR.	1	36	48*	0.1	0.2
127 CH GOD (CLEVE)	1	24	32*	0.1	0.2
165 CH OF NAZARENE	1	136	214	0.5	1.0
283 LUTH--MO SYNOD	2	318	547	1.2	2.6
285 MENNONITE CH..	1	89	118*	0.2	0.6
419 SO BAPT CONV..	2	1,011	1,335*	2.8	6.3
449 UN METHODIST..	12	1,558	1,943	4.1	9.2
453 UN PRES CH USA	1	72	95*	0.2	0.4
SOMERSET	55	7,298	9,252*	48.9	100.0
081 CATHOLIC......	1	0	80	0.4	0.9
093 CR CH (DISC)..	1	25	30*	0.2	0.3
127 CH GOD (CLEVE)	2	366	440*	2.3	4.8
157 CH OF BRETHREN	1	100	120*	0.6	1.3
193 EPISCOPAL.....	3	241	358	1.9	3.9
285 MENNONITE CH..	1	70	84*	0.4	0.9
419 SO BAPT CONV..	4	1,264	1,519*	8.0	16.4
449 UN METHODIST..	40	4,895	6,216	32.8	67.2
453 UN PRES CH USA	2	337	405*	2.1	4.4
TALBOT	48	7,132	10,037*	42.4	100.0
081 CATHOLIC......	3	0	1,325	5.6	13.2
127 CH GOD (CLEVE)	1	210	251*	1.1	2.5
157 CH OF BRETHREN	2	290	347*	1.5	3.5
193 EPISCOPAL.....	7	1,342	1,846	7.8	18.4
226 FRIENDS-USA...	1	130	155*	0.7	1.5
281 LUTH CH AMER..	2	430	603	2.5	6.0
283 LUTH--MO SYNOD	1	149	180	0.8	1.8
413 S-D ADVENTISTS	2	51	61*	0.3	0.6
419 SO BAPT CONV..	2	509	609*	2.6	6.1
435 UNITARIAN-UNIV	1	14	14	0.1	0.1
449 UN METHODIST..	25	3,746	4,334	18.3	43.2
453 UN PRES CH USA	1	261	312*	1.3	3.1
WASHINGTON	137	36,428	53,269*	51.3	100.0
019 AMER BAPT CONV	1	65	79*	0.1	0.1
075 BRETHREN IN CR	1	97	118*	0.1	0.2
081 CATHOLIC......	7	0	7,781	7.5	14.6
093 CR CH (DISC)..	5	1,557	1,898*	1.8	3.6
097 CR C AND C CR.	2	190	232*	0.2	0.4
127 CH GOD (CLEVE)	5	523	638*	0.6	1.2
157 CH OF BRETHREN	10	3,077	3,751*	3.6	7.0
165 CH OF NAZARENE	3	301	507	0.5	1.0
193 EPISCOPAL.....	5	1,210	1,810	1.7	3.4
281 LUTH CH AMER..	22	9,054	11,979	11.5	22.5
283 LUTH--MO SYNOD	2	193	273	0.3	0.5
285 MENNONITE CH..	13	1,053	1,284*	1.2	2.4
353 PLY BRETHREN..	1	30	50	-	0.1
357 PRESB CH US...	3	345	421*	0.4	0.8
403 SALVATION ARMY	1	151	481	0.5	0.9
413 S-D ADVENTISTS	3	729	889*	0.9	1.7
419 SO BAPT CONV..	5	1,760	2,146*	2.1	4.0
435 UNITARIAN-UNIV	1	35	46	-	0.1
443 UN C OF CHRIST	11	3,895	4,748*	4.6	8.9
449 UN METHODIST..	34	11,076	12,813	12.3	24.1
453 UN PRES CH USA	2	1,087	1,325*	1.3	2.5
WICOMICO	82	15,440	22,867*	42.2	100.0
081 CATHOLIC......	2	0	2,298	4.2	10.0
097 CR C AND C CR.	3	205	247*	0.5	1.1
123 CH GOD (ANDER)	1	9	9	-	-
127 CH GOD (CLEVE)	2	347	419*	0.8	1.8
165 CH OF NAZARENE	1	242	539	1.0	2.4
193 EPISCOPAL.....	4	1,529	2,577	4.8	11.3
281 LUTH CH AMER..	1	98	142	0.3	0.6
283 LUTH--MO SYNOD	1	260	369	0.7	1.6
285 MENNONITE CH..	1	13	16*	-	0.1
403 SALVATION ARMY	1	53	1,269	2.3	5.5
413 S-D ADVENTISTS	2	318	384*	0.7	1.7
419 SO BAPT CONV..	5	1,093	1,319*	2.4	5.8
435 UNITARIAN-UNIV	1	18	27	-	0.1
449 UN METHODIST..	56	10,618	12,483	23.0	54.6
453 UN PRES CH USA	1	637	769*	1.4	3.4
WORCESTER	62	8,341	10,932*	44.7	100.0
081 CATHOLIC......	3	0	571	2.3	5.2
093 CR CH (DISC)..	1	65	79*	0.3	0.7
097 CR C AND C CR.	2	45	55*	0.2	0.5
127 CH GOD (CLEVE)	1	31	38*	0.2	0.3
193 EPISCOPAL.....	4	587	805	3.3	7.4
285 MENNONITE CH..	1	38	46*	0.2	0.4
413 S-D ADVENTISTS	1	41	50*	0.2	0.5
419 SO BAPT CONV..	7	1,545	1,881*	7.7	17.2
449 UN METHODIST..	35	5,012	6,218	25.4	56.9
453 UN PRES CH USA	7	977	1,189*	4.9	10.9

*Total adherents estimated from known number of communicant, confirmed, full members.

—Represents a percent less than 0.1.

Percentages may not total due to rounding.

Table 3. Churches and Church Membership by State, County and Denomination: 1971

County and Denomination	Number of churches	Communicant, confirmed, full members	Total adherents: Number	Percent of total population	Percent of total adherents
CO DATA NOT AVAIL	71	4,020	13,186*	N/A	N/A
127 CH GOD (CLEVE)	1	35	43*	N/A	N/A
151 L-D SAINTS....	0	0	8,465	N/A	N/A
193 EPISCOPAL.....	2	509	675	N/A	N/A
223 FREE WILL BAPT	20	1,502	1,857*	N/A	N/A
467 WESLEYAN......	48	1,974	2,146	N/A	N/A
MASSACHUSETTS					
THE STATE.....	2,584	496,959	3,593,205*	63.2	100.0
BARNSTABLE	79	13,632	48,260*	49.9	100.0
019 AMER BAPT CONV	6	923	1,104*	1.1	2.3
081 CATHOLIC......	16	0	30,000	31.0	62.2
165 CH OF NAZARENE	1	33	71	0.1	0.1
175 CONG CR CH....	1	367	439*	0.5	0.9
193 EPISCOPAL.....	10	3,323	6,193	6.4	12.8
226 FRIENDS-USA...	2	22	26*	-	0.1
281 LUTH CH AMER..	1	416	572	0.6	1.2
283 LUTH--MO SYNOD	1	82	102	0.1	0.2
413 S-D ADVENTISTS	1	64	77*	0.1	0.2
419 SO BAPT CONV..	1	132	158*	0.2	0.3
435 UNITARIAN-UNIV	6	764	1,029	1.1	2.1
443 UN C OF CHRIST	17	4,754	5,685*	5.9	11.8
449 UN METHODIST..	16	2,752	2,804	2.9	5.8
BERKSHIRE	110	19,327	97,209*	65.1	100.0
019 AMER BAPT CONV	12	3,452	4,189*	2.8	4.3
081 CATHOLIC......	37	0	71,873	48.1	73.9
165 CH OF NAZARENE	2	104	192	0.1	0.2
175 CONG CR CH....	3	631	766*	0.5	0.8
193 EPISCOPAL.....	11	3,495	6,186	4.1	6.4
281 LUTH CH AMER..	1	841	1,203	0.8	1.2
371 REF CH IN AM..	1	54	78	0.1	0.1
403 SALVATION ARMY	2	73	510	0.3	0.5
413 S-D ADVENTISTS	1	111	135*	0.1	0.1
435 UNITARIAN-UNIV	2	226	296	0.2	0.3
443 UN C OF CHRIST	24	6,467	7,847*	5.3	8.1
449 UN METHODIST..	13	3,829	3,870	2.6	4.0
469 WISC EVAN LUTH	1	44	64	-	0.1
BRISTOL	218	29,017	305,502*	68.8	100.0
019 AMER BAPT CONV	20	4,138	5,029*	1.1	1.6
029 AMER LUTH CH..	1	281	395	0.1	0.1
081 CATHOLIC......	92	0	266,675	60.0	87.3
127 CH GOD (CLEVE)	1	68	83*	-	-
165 CH OF NAZARENE	5	452	1,241	0.3	0.4
175 CONG CR CH....	6	1,810	2,200*	0.5	0.7
193 EPISCOPAL.....	19	7,980	12,518	2.8	4.1
201 EVAN COV CH AM	2	411	499*	0.1	0.2
221 FREE METH C NA	2	28	47	-	-
226 FRIENDS-USA...	6	411	499*	0.1	0.2
281 LUTH CH AMER..	2	883	1,275	0.3	0.4
283 LUTH--MO SYNOD	1	72	161	-	0.1
335 ORTH PRESB CH.	1	32	50	-	-
353 PLY BRETHREN..	2	150	325	0.1	0.1
403 SALVATION ARMY	2	105	484	0.1	0.2
413 S-D ADVENTISTS	5	579	704*	0.2	0.2
435 UNITARIAN-UNIV	11	1,915	2,279	0.5	0.7
443 UN C OF CHRIST	19	5,303	6,445*	1.5	2.1
449 UN METHODIST..	18	3,899	3,985	0.9	1.3
453 UN PRES CH USA	3	500	608*	0.1	0.2
DUKES	16	1,308	3,237*	52.9	100.0
019 AMER BAPT CONV	3	243	284*	4.6	8.8
081 CATHOLIC......	3	0	1,500	24.5	46.3
193 EPISCOPAL.....	2	340	691	11.3	21.3
435 UNITARIAN-UNIV	1	57	57	0.9	1.8
443 UN C OF CHRIST	1	119	139*	2.3	4.3
449 UN METHODIST..	6	549	566	9.3	17.5
ESSEX	294	60,359	443,431*	69.5	100.0
019 AMER BAPT CONV	29	7,675	9,354*	1.5	2.1
081 CATHOLIC......	85	0	361,701	56.7	81.6
093 CR CH (DISC)..	2	210	256*	-	0.1
127 CH GOD (CLEVE)	2	88	107*	-	-
165 CH OF NAZARENE	5	412	941	0.1	0.2
175 CONG CR CH....	1	200	244*	-	0.1
193 EPISCOPAL.....	28	13,763	24,407	3.8	5.5
201 EVAN COV CH AM	1	193	235*	-	0.1
221 FREE METH C NA	1	53	70	-	-
226 FRIENDS-USA...	2	108	132*	-	-
281 LUTH CH AMER..	6	1,606	2,365	0.4	0.5
283 LUTH--MO SYNOD	3	630	916	0.1	0.2
335 ORTH PRESB CH.	1	66	103	-	-
353 PLY BRETHREN..	3	150	245	-	0.1
403 SALVATION ARMY	6	266	1,799	0.3	0.4
413 S-D ADVENTISTS	5	268	327*	0.1	0.1
435 UNITARIAN-UNIV	16	3,013	3,843	0.6	0.9
443 UN C OF CHRIST	56	19,959	24,326*	3.8	5.5
449 UN METHODIST..	37	10,604	10,725	1.7	2.4
453 UN PRES CH USA	5	1,095	1,335*	0.2	0.3
FRANKLIN	77	8,014	29,488*	49.8	100.0
019 AMER BAPT CONV	10	764	913*	1.5	3.1
081 CATHOLIC......	17	0	19,585	33.1	66.4
193 EPISCOPAL.....	1	843	1,084	1.8	3.7
201 EVAN COV CH AM	1	46	55*	0.1	0.2
281 LUTH CH AMER..	2	436	620	1.0	2.1
403 SALVATION ARMY	1	35	283	0.5	1.0
413 S-D ADVENTISTS	1	16	19*	-	0.1
435 UNITARIAN-UNIV	7	449	614	1.0	2.1
443 UN C OF CHRIST	28	4,543	5,430*	9.2	18.4
449 UN METHODIST..	9	882	885	1.5	3.0
HAMPDEN	188	34,432	286,592*	62.4	100.0
019 AMER BAPT CONV	19	5,197	6,329*	1.4	2.2
081 CATHOLIC......	76	0	242,902	52.9	84.8
127 CH GOD (CLEVE)	2	79	96*	-	-
165 CH OF NAZARENE	1	100	168	-	0.1
175 CONG CR CH....	1	389	474*	0.1	0.2
193 EPISCOPAL.....	7	3,406	5,272	1.1	1.8
201 EVAN COV CH AM	1	209	255*	0.1	0.1
221 FREE METH C NA	1	11	19	-	-
281 LUTH CH AMER..	3	963	1,280	0.3	0.4
283 LUTH--MO SYNOD	5	2,288	3,364	0.7	1.2
353 PLY BRETHREN..	2	60	80	-	-
403 SALVATION ARMY	1	25	159	-	0.1
413 S-D ADVENTISTS	3	400	487*	0.1	0.2
419 SO BAPT CONV..	1	233	284*	0.1	0.1
435 UNITARIAN-UNIV	3	459	606	0.1	0.2
443 UN C OF CHRIST	40	18,470	22,493*	4.9	7.8
449 UN METHODIST..	18	1,526	1,573	0.3	0.5
453 UN PRES CH USA	4	617	751*	0.2	0.3
HAMPSHIRE	79	12,524	64,156*	51.7	100.0
019 AMER BAPT CONV	3	439	514*	0.4	0.8
081 CATHOLIC......	26	0	48,512	39.1	75.6
175 CONG CR CH....	1	1,033	1,210*	1.0	1.9
193 EPISCOPAL.....	5	1,320	2,059	1.7	3.2
226 FRIENDS-USA...	1	197	231*	0.2	0.4
283 LUTH--MO SYNOD	4	908	1,304	1.1	2.0
403 SALVATION ARMY	1	120	646	0.5	1.0
413 S-D ADVENTISTS	1	35	41*	-	0.1
435 UNITARIAN-UNIV	3	238	279	0.2	0.4
443 UN C OF CHRIST	28	6,534	7,652*	6.2	11.9
449 UN METHODIST..	6	1,700	1,708	1.4	2.7
MIDDLESEX	511	131,806	800,381*	57.3	100.0
019 AMER BAPT CONV	68	22,416	27,417*	2.0	3.4
029 AMER LUTH CH..	2	145	220	-	-
081 CATHOLIC......	143	0	629,639	45.1	78.7
097 CR C AND C CR.	3	85	104*	-	-
105 CHRISTIAN REF.	1	92	195	-	-
165 CH OF NAZARENE	9	966	1,944	0.1	0.2
193 EPISCOPAL.....	52	25,283	42,384	3.0	5.3
201 EVAN COV CH AM	3	436	533*	-	0.1
226 FRIENDS-USA...	2	646	790*	0.1	0.1
281 LUTH CH AMER..	10	3,373	4,830	0.3	0.6
283 LUTH--MO SYNOD	6	1,376	2,103	0.2	0.3
285 MENNONITE CH..	1	35	43*	-	-
287 MENN GEN CONF.	1	35	43*	-	-
353 PLY BRETHREN..	3	172	240	-	-
403 SALVATION ARMY	7	427	2,098	0.2	0.3
413 S-D ADVENTISTS	4	263	322*	-	-
419 SO BAPT CONV..	4	798	976*	0.1	0.1
435 UNITARIAN-UNIV	45	9,186	12,421	0.9	1.6
443 UN C OF CHRIST	82	33,026	40,395*	2.9	5.0
449 UN METHODIST..	56	30,865	31,016	2.2	3.9
453 UN PRES CH USA	9	2,181	2,668*	0.2	0.3
NANTUCKET	6	1,138	3,099*	82.1	100.0
019 AMER BAPT CONV	1	91	110*	2.9	3.5
081 CATHOLIC......	1	0	1,500	39.7	48.4
175 CONG CR CH....	1	409	494*	13.1	15.9
193 EPISCOPAL.....	1	371	670	17.8	21.6
419 SO BAPT CONV..	1	200	242*	6.4	7.8
435 UNITARIAN-UNIV	1	67	83	2.2	2.7
NORFOLK	221	56,594	404,374*	66.8	100.0
019 AMER BAPT CONV	21	6,059	7,404*	1.2	1.8
029 AMER LUTH CH..	1	112	176	-	-
081 CATHOLIC......	63	0	330,105	54.6	81.6
165 CH OF NAZARENE	3	471	773	0.1	0.2
175 CONG CR CH....	2	915	1,118*	0.2	0.3
193 EPISCOPAL.....	31	13,031	21,012	3.5	5.2
201 EVAN COV CH AM	1	223	273*	-	0.1
226 FRIENDS-USA...	1	155	189*	-	-
281 LUTH CH AMER..	6	1,879	2,615	0.4	0.6
283 LUTH--MO SYNOD	5	975	1,434	0.2	0.4
353 PLY BRETHREN..	4	227	375	0.1	0.1
403 SALVATION ARMY	1	57	206	-	0.1
413 S-D ADVENTISTS	1	59	72*	-	-
419 SO BAPT CONV..	1	69	84*	-	-
435 UNITARIAN-UNIV	20	4,679	6,121	1.0	1.5
443 UN C OF CHRIST	38	19,759	24,145*	4.0	6.0
449 UN METHODIST..	18	6,543	6,584	1.1	1.6
453 UN PRES CH USA	4	1,381	1,688*	0.3	0.4

*Total adherents estimated from known number of communicant, confirmed, full members.

—Represents a percent less than 0.1.

Percentages may not total due to rounding.

Table 3. Churches and Church Membership by State, County and Denomination: 1971

County and Denomination	Number of churches	Communicant, confirmed, full members	Total adherents		
			Number	Percent of total population	Percent of total adherents
PLYMOUTH	160	30,303	238,064*	71.4	100.0
019 AMER BAPT CONV	17	3,153	4,012*	1.2	1.7
081 CATHOLIC......	40	0	196,944	59.1	82.7
165 CH OF NAZARENE	4	331	841	0.3	0.4
175 CONG CR CH....	5	1,346	1,713*	0.5	0.7
193 EPISCOPAL.....	12	5,966	10,209	3.1	4.3
201 EVAN COV CH AM	1	265	337*	0.1	0.1
221 FREE METH C NA	1	5	5	-	-
281 LUTH CH AMER..	4	2,023	2,687	0.8	1.1
283 LUTH--MO SYNOD	3	638	1,059	0.3	0.4
353 PLY BRETHREN..	2	65	85	-	-
403 SALVATION ARMY	2	104	380	0.1	0.2
413 S-D ADVENTISTS	2	109	139*	-	0.1
435 UNITARIAN-UNIV	15	3,055	3,848	1.2	1.6
443 UN C OF CHRIST	28	9,144	11,636*	3.5	4.9
449 UN METHODIST..	23	3,997	4,039	1.2	1.7
453 UN PRES CH USA	1	102	130*	-	0.1
SUFFOLK	225	31,765	435,045*	59.2	100.0
019 AMER BAPT CONV	31	6,706	7,969*	1.1	1.8
029 AMER LUTH CH..	1	97	129	-	-
081 CATHOLIC......	86	0	393,632	53.5	90.5
083 CR CATH CH DOB	1	104	104	-	-
123 CH GOD (ANDER)	2	101	201	-	-
127 CH GOD (CLEVE)	3	186	221*	-	0.1
165 CH OF NAZARENE	2	92	259	-	0.1
175 CONG CR CH....	1	2,403	2,855*	0.4	0.7
193 EPISCOPAL.....	24	8,209	12,113	1.6	2.8
201 EVAN COV CH AM	1	411	488*	0.1	0.1
281 LUTH CH AMER..	4	940	1,354	0.2	0.3
283 LUTH--MO SYNOD	5	967	1,178	0.2	0.3
285 MENNONITE CH..	1	6	7*	-	-
315 NO AM OLD RC..	3	971	1,154*	0.2	0.3
403 SALVATION ARMY	5	381	1,649	0.2	0.4
413 S-D ADVENTISTS	7	1,664	1,977*	0.3	0.5
435 UNITARIAN-UNIV	11	1,886	2,154	0.3	0.5
443 UN C OF CHRIST	20	4,361	5,182*	0.7	1.2
449 UN METHODIST..	11	1,582	1,590	0.2	0.4
453 UN PRES CH USA	6	698	829*	0.1	0.2
WORCESTER	400	66,740	429,296*	67.3	100.0
019 AMER BAPT CONV	32	9,363	11,378*	1.8	2.7
029 AMER LUTH CH..	1	112	135	-	-
081 CATHOLIC......	139	0	344,607	54.0	80.3
093 CR CH (DISC)..	1	133	162*	-	-
097 CR C AND C CR.	1	9	11*	-	-
105 CHRISTIAN REF.	2	697	1,239	0.2	0.3
127 CH GOD (CLEVE)	4	138	168*	-	-
165 CH OF NAZARENE	3	204	471	0.1	0.1
193 EPISCOPAL.....	21	7,136	11,391	1.8	2.7
201 EVAN COV CH AM	4	1,003	1,219*	0.2	0.3
221 FREE METH C NA	1	15	22	-	-
226 FRIENDS-USA...	2	164	199*	-	-
281 LUTH CH AMER..	13	6,129	8,108	1.3	1.9
283 LUTH--MO SYNOD	6	1,325	1,820	0.3	0.4
353 PLY BRETHREN..	2	95	150	-	-
403 SALVATION ARMY	6	310	1,895	0.3	0.4
413 S-D ADVENTISTS	12	2,441	2,966*	0.5	0.7
419 SO BAPT CONV..	2	261	317*	-	0.1
435 UNITARIAN-UNIV	29	4,677	5,788	0.9	1.3
443 UN C OF CHRIST	79	20,656	25,102*	3.9	5.8
449 UN METHODIST..	37	11,075	11,179	1.8	2.6
453 UN PRES CH USA	3	797	969*	0.2	0.2
CO DATA NOT AVAIL	0	0	5,071	N/A	N/A
151 L-D SAINTS....	0	0	5,071	N/A	N/A

MICHIGAN

County and Denomination	Number of churches	Communicant, confirmed, full members	Total adherents		
			Number	Percent of total population	Percent of total adherents
THE STATE.....	6,257	1,296,349	4,070,237*	45.9	100.0
ALCONA	18	800	1,838*	25.8	100.0
019 AMER BAPT CONV	2	41	49*	0.7	2.7
029 AMER LUTH CH..	2	214	284	4.0	15.5
081 CATHOLIC......	3	0	800	11.2	43.5
193 EPISCOPAL.....	1	56	71	1.0	3.9
221 FREE METH C NA	1	17	17	0.2	0.9
283 LUTH--MO SYNOD	1	38	52	0.7	2.8
413 S-D ADVENTISTS	1	23	28*	0.4	1.5
449 UN METHODIST..	4	118	144	2.0	7.8
453 UN PRES CH USA	2	210	251*	3.5	13.7
469 WISC EVAN LUTH	1	83	142	2.0	7.7
ALGER	17	1,555	4,944*	57.7	100.0
081 CATHOLIC......	4	0	2,896	33.8	58.6
193 EPISCOPAL.....	1	75	128	1.5	2.6
221 FREE METH C NA	1	4	4	-	0.1
281 LUTH CH AMER..	4	651	886	10.3	17.9
283 LUTH--MO SYNOD	1	230	329	3.8	6.7
285 MENNONITE CH..	1	9	11*	0.1	0.2
413 S-D ADVENTISTS	1	68	83*	1.0	1.7
449 UN METHODIST..	3	431	501	5.8	10.1
453 UN PRES CH USA	1	87	106*	1.2	2.1
ALLEGAN	155	10,664	23,734*	35.7	100.0
019 AMER BAPT CONV	1	68	86*	0.1	0.4
081 CATHOLIC......	11	0	7,597	11.4	32.0
093 CR CH (DISC)..	80	57	72*	0.1	0.3
105 CHRISTIAN REF.	10	2,686	4,582	6.9	19.3
123 CH GOD (ANDER)	2	242	676	1.0	2.8
127 CH GOD (CLEVE)	2	40	50*	0.1	0.2
165 CH OF NAZARENE	1	54	140	0.2	0.6
175 CONG CR CH....	2	393	494*	0.7	2.1
193 EPISCOPAL.....	3	565	949	1.4	4.0
221 FREE METH C NA	1	8	10	-	-
281 LUTH CH AMER..	1	126	181	0.3	0.8
371 REF CH IN AM..	9	1,844	2,820	4.2	11.9
413 S-D ADVENTISTS	3	184	231*	0.3	1.0
443 UN C OF CHRIST	2	290	365*	0.5	1.5
449 UN METHODIST..	21	3,028	4,008	6.0	16.9
453 UN PRES CH USA	2	458	576*	0.9	2.4
469 WISC EVAN LUTH	4	621	897	1.3	3.8
ALPENA	35	8,054	23,751*	77.3	100.0
019 AMER BAPT CONV	2	305	387*	1.3	1.6
029 AMER LUTH CH..	6	2,744	3,902	12.7	16.4
081 CATHOLIC......	7	0	12,040	39.2	50.7
123 CH GOD (ANDER)	1	45	120	0.4	0.5
165 CH OF NAZARENE	1	74	156	0.5	0.7
193 EPISCOPAL.....	2	823	1,711	5.6	7.2
221 FREE METH C NA	1	62	78	0.3	0.3
283 LUTH--MO SYNOD	3	1,651	2,330	7.6	9.8
285 MENNONITE CH..	1	19	24*	0.1	0.1
313 NO AM BAPT GC.	1	197	250*	0.8	1.1
353 PLY BRETHREN..	1	40	60	0.2	0.3
413 S-D ADVENTISTS	1	114	144*	0.5	0.6
443 UN C OF CHRIST	2	560	710*	2.3	3.0
449 UN METHODIST..	5	1,176	1,530	5.0	6.4
453 UN PRES CH USA	1	244	309*	1.0	1.3
ANTRIM	27	2,231	4,292*	34.0	100.0
029 AMER LUTH CH..	1	78	142	1.1	3.3
081 CATHOLIC......	3	0	1,229	9.7	28.6
105 CHRISTIAN REF.	2	241	417	3.3	9.7
165 CH OF NAZARENE	1	23	66	0.5	1.5
175 CONG CR CH....	1	250	309*	2.5	7.2
193 EPISCOPAL.....	1	49	138	1.1	3.2
221 FREE METH C NA	2	28	31	0.2	0.7
283 LUTH--MO SYNOD	2	127	174	1.4	4.1
285 MENNONITE CH..	1	17	21*	0.2	0.5
371 REF CH IN AM..	1	187	298	2.4	6.9
413 S-D ADVENTISTS	2	63	78*	0.6	1.8
449 UN METHODIST..	9	1,011	1,195	9.5	27.8
453 UN PRES CH USA	1	157	194*	1.5	4.5
ARENAC	24	2,003	6,004*	53.9	100.0
081 CATHOLIC......	5	0	3,326	29.8	55.4
193 EPISCOPAL.....	2	96	190	1.7	3.2
221 FREE METH C NA	3	39	59	0.5	1.0
283 LUTH--MO SYNOD	2	499	757	6.8	12.6
285 MENNONITE CH..	1	120	149*	1.3	2.5
313 NO AM BAPT GC.	2	247	306*	2.7	5.1
443 UN C OF CHRIST	1	65	81*	0.7	1.3
449 UN METHODIST..	5	750	903	8.1	15.0
453 UN PRES CH USA	1	43	53*	0.5	0.9
469 WISC EVAN LUTH	2	144	180	1.6	3.0
BARAGA	15	1,140	3,787*	48.6	100.0
081 CATHOLIC......	3	0	2,284	29.3	60.3
121 CH GOD (ABR)..	1	35	43*	0.6	1.1
193 EPISCOPAL.....	1	28	44	0.6	1.2
281 LUTH CH AMER..	5	590	812	10.4	21.4
283 LUTH--MO SYNOD	1	177	246	3.2	6.5
413 S-D ADVENTISTS	1	35	43*	0.6	1.1
449 UN METHODIST..	3	275	315	4.0	8.3
BARRY	38	5,338	9,584*	25.1	100.0
029 AMER LUTH CH..	1	259	411	1.1	4.3
081 CATHOLIC......	5	0	2,296	6.0	24.0
093 CR CH (DISC)..	1	57	71*	0.2	0.7
105 CHRISTIAN REF.	1	113	201	0.5	2.1
123 CH GOD (ANDER)	1	50	114	0.3	1.2
157 CH OF BRETHREN	1	78	97*	0.3	1.0
165 CH OF NAZARENE	2	141	328	0.9	3.4
193 EPISCOPAL.....	1	334	520	1.4	5.4
221 FREE METH C NA	2	59	79	0.2	0.8
283 LUTH--MO SYNOD	1	259	381	1.0	4.0
371 REF CH IN AM..	1	218	404	1.1	4.2
413 S-D ADVENTISTS	3	180	223*	0.6	2.3
449 UN METHODIST..	17	2,940	3,652	9.6	38.1
453 UN PRES CH USA	1	650	807*	2.1	8.4
BAY	73	21,613	81,728*	69.7	100.0
019 AMER BAPT CONV	3	1,072	1,352*	1.2	1.7
081 CATHOLIC......	21	0	52,394	44.7	64.1
123 CH GOD (ANDER)	3	258	665	0.6	0.8
127 CH GOD (CLEVE)	1	16	20*	-	-
165 CH OF NAZARENE	2	171	345	0.3	0.4
193 EPISCOPAL.....	2	1,258	1,610	1.4	2.0

*Total adherents estimated from known number of communicant, confirmed, full members.

—Represents a percent less than 0.1.

Percentages may not total due to rounding.

Table 3. Churches and Church Membership by State, County and Denomination: 1971

County and Denomination	Number of churches	Communicant, confirmed, full members	Total adherents: Number	Total adherents: Percent of total population	Total adherents: Percent of total adherents
221 FREE METH C NA	1	79	107	0.1	0.1
281 LUTH CH AMER..	2	716	1,039	0.9	1.3
283 LUTH--MO SYNOD	12	8,135	11,398	9.7	13.9
313 NO AM BAPT GC.	1	217	274*	0.2	0.3
403 SALVATION ARMY	1	68	272	0.2	0.3
413 S-D ADVENTISTS	1	79	100*	0.1	0.1
419 SO BAPT CONV..	1	71	90*	0.1	0.1
443 UN C OF CHRIST	2	426	537*	0.5	0.7
449 UN METHODIST..	11	3,684	4,475	3.8	5.5
453 UN PRES CH USA	4	2,427	3,060*	2.6	3.7
469 WISC EVAN LUTH	5	2,936	3,990	3.4	4.9
BENZIE	16	1,755	3,099*	36.1	100.0
029 AMER LUTH CH..	1	278	428	5.0	13.8
059 BAPT MISS ASSN	1	37	45*	0.5	1.5
081 CATHOLIC......	1	C	800	9.3	25.8
093 CR CH (DISC)..	1	127	156*	1.8	5.0
097 CR C AND C CR.	1	15	18*	0.2	0.6
175 CONG CR CH....	1	100	123*	1.4	4.0
193 EPISCOPAL.....	1	112	151	1.8	4.9
221 FREE METH C NA	1	3	5	0.1	0.2
283 LUTH--MO SYNOD	1	142	228	2.7	7.4
413 S-D ADVENTISTS	1	23	28*	0.3	0.9
443 UN C OF CHRIST	3	568	696*	8.1	22.5
449 UN METHODIST..	3	350	421	4.9	13.6
BERRIEN	133	40,446	73,035*	44.6	100.0
019 AMER BAPT CONV	3	720	896*	0.5	1.2
029 AMER LUTH CH..	1	299	509	0.3	0.7
081 CATHOLIC......	14	0	18,786	11.5	25.7
093 CR CH (DISC)..	1	232	289*	0.2	0.4
097 CR C AND C CR.	4	1,418	1,764*	1.1	2.4
105 CHRISTIAN REF.	1	81	153	0.1	0.2
123 CH GOD (ANDER)	7	696	1,505	0.9	2.1
127 CH GOD (CLEVE)	5	430	535*	0.3	0.7
165 CH OF NAZARENE	4	345	820	0.5	1.1
175 CONG CR CH....	1	282	351*	0.2	0.5
193 EPISCOPAL.....	3	1,136	1,670	1.0	2.3
221 FREE METH C NA	4	190	237	0.1	0.3
283 LUTH--MO SYNOD	9	6,997	9,685	5.9	13.3
313 NO AM BAPT GC.	4	1,573	1,957*	1.2	2.7
349 PENT HOLINESS.	1	24	30*	-	-
371 REF CH IN AM..	1	125	190	0.1	0.3
403 SALVATION ARMY	2	251	1,199	0.7	1.6
413 S-D ADVENTISTS	10	4,784	5,952*	3.6	8.1
419 SO BAPT CONV..	4	773	962*	0.6	1.3
435 UNITARIAN-UNIV	2	83	133	0.1	0.2
443 UN C OF CHRIST	14	5,670	7,054*	4.3	9.7
449 UN METHODIST..	27	7,949	9,873	6.0	13.5
453 UN PRES CH USA	5	2,606	3,242*	2.0	4.4
469 WISC EVAN LUTH	6	3,782	5,243	3.2	7.2
BRANCH	30	5,248	10,912*	28.8	100.0
019 AMER BAPT CONV	2	836	1,027*	2.7	9.4
081 CATHOLIC......	2	C	3,886	10.3	35.6
097 CR C AND C CR.	3	131	161*	0.4	1.5
123 CH GOD (ANDER)	1	20	70	0.2	0.6
165 CH OF NAZARENE	1	65	217	0.6	2.0
175 CONG CR CH....	1	88	108*	0.3	1.0
193 EPISCOPAL.....	1	550	729	1.9	6.7
221 FREE METH C NA	2	115	165	0.4	1.5
283 LUTH--MO SYNOD	2	619	848	2.2	7.8
353 PLY BRETHREN..	1	34	74	0.2	0.7
413 S-D ADVENTISTS	1	117	144*	0.4	1.3
443 UN C OF CHRIST	3	560	688*	1.8	6.3
449 UN METHODIST..	8	1,584	2,145	5.7	19.7
453 UN PRES CH USA	2	529	650*	1.7	6.0
CALHOUN	99	24,651	46,827*	33.0	100.0
019 AMER BAPT CONV	8	1,495	1,837*	1.3	3.9
059 BAPT MISS ASSN	2	70	86*	0.1	0.2
081 CATHOLIC......	7	0	13,101	9.2	28.0
093 CR CH (DISC)..	1	92	113*	0.1	0.2
097 CR C AND C CR.	3	650	799*	0.6	1.7
105 CHRISTIAN REF.	2	483	919	0.6	2.0
123 CH GOD (ANDER)	6	392	1,026	0.7	2.2
127 CH GOD (CLEVE)	3	116	143*	0.1	0.3
157 CH OF BRETHREN	1	151	186*	0.1	0.4
165 CH OF NAZARENE	5	406	1,568	1.1	3.3
193 EPISCOPAL.....	5	2,004	2,887	2.0	6.2
221 FREE METH C NA	2	158	227	0.2	0.5
226 FRIENDS-USA...	1	193	237*	0.2	0.5
283 LUTH--MO SYNOD	6	2,909	4,246	3.0	9.1
285 MENNONITE CH..	1	27	33*	-	0.1
353 PLY BRETHREN..	1	20	40	-	0.1
371 REF CH IN AM..	2	149	258	0.2	0.6
403 SALVATION ARMY	1	111	484	0.3	1.0
413 S-D ADVENTISTS	4	1,372	1,686*	1.2	3.6
415 S-D BAPTIST GC	1	258	317*	0.2	0.7
419 SO BAPT CONV..	5	1,132	1,391*	1.0	3.0
443 UN C OF CHRIST	5	2,829	3,476*	2.4	7.4
449 UN METHODIST..	20	5,994	7,262	5.1	15.5
453 UN PRES CH USA	6	3,492	4,290*	3.0	9.2
469 WISC EVAN LUTH	1	148	215	0.2	0.5
CASS	42	4,278	9,141*	21.1	100.0
019 AMER BAPT CONV	3	338	418*	1.0	4.6
059 BAPT MISS ASSN	2	144	178*	0.4	1.9
075 BRETHREN IN CR	1	13	16*	-	0.2
081 CATHOLIC......	6	0	3,737	8.6	40.9
093 CR CH (DISC)..	1	231	286*	0.7	3.1
097 CR C AND C CR.	2	175	216*	0.5	2.4
123 CH GOD (ANDER)	4	143	355	0.8	3.9
127 CH GOD (CLEVE)	1	5	6*	-	0.1
193 EPISCOPAL.....	1	251	309	0.7	3.4
226 FRIENDS-USA...	1	61	75*	0.2	0.8
283 LUTH--MO SYNOD	1	69	93	0.2	1.0
285 MENNONITE CH..	1	2	2*	-	-
413 S-D ADVENTISTS	3	281	348*	0.8	3.8
419 SO BAPT CONV..	1	44	54*	0.1	0.6
443 UN C OF CHRIST	2	404	500*	1.2	5.5
449 UN METHODIST..	9	1,423	1,655	3.8	18.1
453 UN PRES CH USA	2	404	500*	1.2	5.5
469 WISC EVAN LUTH	1	290	393	0.9	4.3
CHARLEVOIX	29	2,918	6,467*	39.1	100.0
019 AMER BAPT CONV	1	101	127*	0.8	2.0
029 AMER LUTH CH..	1	166	252	1.5	3.9
081 CATHOLIC......	5	0	2,525	15.3	39.0
123 CH GOD (ANDER)	1	118	252	1.5	3.9
165 CH OF NAZARENE	2	49	118	0.7	1.8
193 EPISCOPAL.....	1	85	158	1.0	2.4
221 FREE METH C NA	2	58	73	0.4	1.1
283 LUTH--MO SYNOD	2	348	458	2.8	7.1
371 REF CH IN AM..	1	182	252	1.5	3.9
413 S-D ADVENTISTS	1	63	79*	0.5	1.2
443 UN C OF CHRIST	2	587	735*	4.4	11.4
449 UN METHODIST..	8	729	897	5.4	13.9
453 UN PRES CH USA	2	432	541*	3.3	8.4
CHEBOYGAN	23	2,339	9,212*	55.6	100.0
029 AMER LUTH CH..	1	535	835	5.0	9.1
081 CATHOLIC......	6	0	5,924	35.7	64.3
093 CR CH (DISC)..	1	130	163*	1.0	1.8
193 EPISCOPAL.....	2	269	390	2.4	4.2
201 EVAN COV CH AM	1	68	85*	0.5	0.9
221 FREE METH C NA	2	34	60	0.4	0.7
283 LUTH--MO SYNOD	1	159	256	1.5	2.8
403 SALVATION ARMY	1	26	131	0.8	1.4
413 S-D ADVENTISTS	1	34	43*	0.3	0.5
443 UN C OF CHRIST	2	210	263*	1.6	2.9
449 UN METHODIST..	3	748	904	5.5	9.8
453 UN PRES CH USA	2	126	158*	1.0	1.7
CHIPPEWA	46	4,737	13,268*	40.9	100.0
019 AMER BAPT CONV	1	315	391*	1.2	2.9
081 CATHOLIC......	13	0	6,649	20.5	50.1
097 CR C AND C CR.	1	200	248*	0.8	1.9
105 CHRISTIAN REF.	1	125	221	0.7	1.7
127 CH GOD (CLEVE)	2	16	20*	0.1	0.2
165 CH OF NAZARENE	2	116	217	0.7	1.6
193 EPISCOPAL.....	2	345	570	1.8	4.3
221 FREE METH C NA	2	45	59	0.2	0.4
285 MENNONITE CH..	1	29	36*	0.1	0.3
353 PLY BRETHREN..	1	70	90	0.3	0.7
403 SALVATION ARMY	1	64	496	1.5	3.7
413 S-D ADVENTISTS	1	21	26*	0.1	0.2
419 SO BAPT CONV..	3	417	517*	1.6	3.9
443 UN C OF CHRIST	1	44	55*	0.2	0.4
449 UN METHODIST..	5	1,249	1,496	4.6	11.3
453 UN PRES CH USA	8	1,491	1,849*	5.7	13.9
469 WISC EVAN LUTH	1	190	328	1.0	2.5
CLARE	15	2,060	4,523*	27.1	100.0
081 CATHOLIC......	2	0	1,580	9.5	34.9
097 CR C AND C CR.	2	247	301*	1.8	6.7
123 CH GOD (ANDER)	1	50	110	0.7	2.4
165 CH OF NAZARENE	2	77	359	2.2	7.9
283 LUTH--MO SYNOD	1	216	304	1.8	6.7
285 MENNONITE CH..	1	12	15*	0.1	0.3
413 S-D ADVENTISTS	1	34	41*	0.2	0.9
443 UN C OF CHRIST	2	489	597*	3.6	13.2
449 UN METHODIST..	2	733	918	5.5	20.3
469 WISC EVAN LUTH	1	202	298	1.8	6.6
CLINTON	47	6,354	18,038*	37.2	100.0
019 AMER BAPT CONV	4	321	417*	0.9	2.3
081 CATHOLIC......	5	0	9,555	19.7	53.0
097 CR C AND C CR.	3	309	401*	0.8	2.2
123 CH GOD (ANDER)	1	75	155	0.3	0.9
165 CH OF NAZARENE	1	100	238	0.5	1.3
175 CONG CR CH....	1	600	780*	1.6	4.3
193 EPISCOPAL.....	2	213	332	0.7	1.8
221 FREE METH C NA	4	117	180	0.4	1.0
283 LUTH--MO SYNOD	4	1,090	1,538	3.2	8.5
353 PLY BRETHREN..	1	40	50	0.1	0.3
413 S-D ADVENTISTS	2	155	201*	0.4	1.1
443 UN C OF CHRIST	3	653	848*	1.7	4.7
449 UN METHODIST..	16	2,681	3,343	6.9	18.5
CRAWFORD	9	933	2,063*	31.8	100.0
081 CATHOLIC......	1	0	776	12.0	37.6
123 CH GOD (ANDER)	1	17	52	0.8	2.5
193 EPISCOPAL.....	1	76	148	2.3	7.2
221 FREE METH C NA	1	18	23	0.4	1.1
281 LUTH CH AMER..	1	112	136	2.1	6.6
283 LUTH--MO SYNOD	1	175	241	3.7	11.7
413 S-D ADVENTISTS	1	11	14*	0.2	0.7
449 UN METHODIST..	1	512	652	10.1	31.6

*Total adherents estimated from known number of communicant, confirmed, full members.

—Represents a percent less than 0.1.

Percentages may not total due to rounding.

Table 3. Churches and Church Membership by State, County and Denomination: 1971

County and Denomination	Number of churches	Communicant, confirmed, full members	Total adherents		
			Number	Percent of total population	Percent of total adherents
469 WISC EVAN LUTH	1	12	21	0.3	1.0
DELTA	52	3,999	25,533*	71.1	100.0
029 AMER LUTH CH..	1	512	693	1.9	2.7
081 CATHOLIC......	14	0	16,871	47.0	66.1
097 CR C AND C CR.	2	114	141*	0.4	0.6
127 CH GOD (CLEVE)	1	17	21*	0.1	0.1
193 EPISCOPAL.....	3	318	370	1.0	1.4
201 EVAN COV CH AM	2	151	187*	0.5	0.7
221 FREE METH C NA	1	8	11	-	-
281 LUTH CH AMER..	9	259	3,571	9.9	14.0
285 MENNONITE CH..	1	15	19*	0.1	0.1
353 PLY BRETHREN..	1	30	120	0.3	0.5
403 SALVATION ARMY	1	88	328	0.9	1.3
413 S-D ADVENTISTS	2	111	138*	0.4	0.5
419 SO BAPT CONV..	1	11	14*	-	0.1
443 UN C OF CHRIST	3	74	92*	0.3	0.4
449 UN METHODIST..	5	1,099	1,417	3.9	5.5
453 UN PRES CH USA	1	593	735*	2.0	2.9
469 WISC EVAN LUTH	4	599	805	2.2	3.2
DICKINSON	31	4,251	15,255*	64.2	100.0
081 CATHOLIC......	11	0	9,593	40.4	62.9
097 CR C AND C CR.	1	60	72*	0.3	0.5
193 EPISCOPAL.....	1	189	419	1.8	2.7
201 EVAN COV CH AM	3	428	512*	2.2	3.4
211 EV MENN BRETH.	1	19	23*	0.1	0.2
281 LUTH CH AMER..	5	1,935	2,618	11.0	17.2
283 LUTH--MO SYNOD	1	313	447	1.9	2.9
413 S-D ADVENTISTS	1	28	34*	0.1	0.2
449 UN METHODIST..	4	491	583	2.5	3.8
453 UN PRES CH USA	2	703	842*	3.5	5.5
469 WISC EVAN LUTH	1	85	112	0.5	0.7
EATON	57	8,651	21,120*	30.7	100.0
019 AMER BAPT CONV	2	590	747*	1.1	3.5
029 AMER LUTH CH..	2	605	941	1.4	4.5
081 CATHOLIC......	5	0	9,005	13.1	42.6
097 CR C AND C CR.	1	85	108*	0.2	0.5
123 CH GOD (ANDER)	1	26	75	0.1	0.4
127 CH GOD (CLEVE)	1	105	133*	0.2	0.6
157 CH OF BRETHREN	1	68	86*	0.1	0.4
165 CH OF NAZARENE	5	292	780	1.1	3.7
175 CONG CR CH....	2	324	410*	0.6	1.9
193 EPISCOPAL.....	2	340	598	0.9	2.8
221 FREE METH C NA	3	96	132	0.2	0.6
281 LUTH CH AMER..	1	86	165	0.2	0.8
283 LUTH--MO SYNOD	2	328	515	0.7	2.4
413 S-D ADVENTISTS	4	496	628*	0.9	3.0
419 SO BAPT CONV..	2	127	161*	0.2	0.8
443 UN C OF CHRIST	3	1,157	1,465*	2.1	6.9
449 UN METHODIST..	18	3,657	4,801	7.0	22.7
453 UN PRES CH USA	1	154	195*	0.3	0.9
469 WISC EVAN LUTH	1	115	175	0.3	0.8
EMMET	32	3,276	9,885*	53.9	100.0
081 CATHOLIC......	9	0	5,315	29.0	53.8
093 CR CH (DISC)..	1	359	443*	2.4	4.5
123 CH GOD (ANDER)	1	39	99	0.5	1.0
165 CH OF NAZARENE	1	75	135	0.7	1.4
193 EPISCOPAL.....	1	233	314	1.7	3.2
221 FREE METH C NA	1	26	31	0.2	0.3
283 LUTH--MO SYNOD	1	396	593	3.2	6.0
285 MENNONITE CH..	3	102	126*	0.7	1.3
353 PLY BRETHREN..	1	10	15	0.1	0.2
403 SALVATION ARMY	1	49	200	1.1	2.0
413 S-D ADVENTISTS	2	121	149*	0.8	1.5
443 UN C OF CHRIST	2	97	120*	0.7	1.2
449 UN METHODIST..	6	1,134	1,561	8.5	15.8
453 UN PRES CH USA	2	635	784*	4.3	7.9
GENESEE	226	60,765	155,148*	34.9	100.0
019 AMER BAPT CONV	10	3,473	4,434*	1.0	2.9
029 AMER LUTH CH..	2	314	563	0.1	0.4
059 BAPT MISS ASSN	5	981	1,252*	0.3	0.8
075 BRETHREN IN CR	1	35	45*	-	-
081 CATHOLIC......	28	0	70,381	15.8	45.4
093 CR CH (DISC)..	3	898	1,146*	0.3	0.7
097 CR C AND C CR.	3	415	530*	0.1	0.3
105 CHRISTIAN REF.	1	78	143	-	0.1
123 CH GOD (ANDER)	8	1,030	2,451	0.6	1.6
127 CH GOD (CLEVE)	3	631	806*	0.2	0.5
157 CH OF BRETHREN	1	151	193*	-	0.1
165 CH OF NAZARENE	15	1,989	4,069	0.9	2.6
193 EPISCOPAL.....	10	3,588	4,850	1.1	3.1
221 FREE METH C NA	14	832	1,194	0.3	0.8
281 LUTH CH AMER..	5	1,535	2,240	0.5	1.4
283 LUTH--MO SYNOD	17	8,271	12,058	2.7	7.8
285 MENNONITE CH..	2	64	82*	-	0.1
349 PENT HOLINESS.	1	39	50*	-	-
353 PLY BRETHREN..	2	178	290	0.1	0.2
371 REF CH IN AM..	2	265	446	0.1	0.3
403 SALVATION ARMY	3	400	1,394	0.3	0.9
413 S-D ADVENTISTS	4	829	1,058*	0.2	0.7
419 SO BAPT CONV..	18	4,694	5,993*	1.3	3.9
435 UNITARIAN-UNIV	1	180	240	0.1	0.2
443 UN C OF CHRIST	4	2,172	2,773*	0.6	1.8
449 UN METHODIST..	42	17,082	22,589	5.1	14.6
453 UN PRES CH USA	15	9,286	11,855*	2.7	7.6
469 WISC EVAN LUTH	6	1,355	2,023	0.5	1.3
GLADWIN	19	2,432	4,524*	33.6	100.0
029 AMER LUTH CH..	1	255	357	2.7	7.9
075 BRETHREN IN CR	1	12	15*	0.1	0.3
081 CATHOLIC......	1	0	1,200	8.9	26.5
123 CH GOD (ANDER)	1	50	116	0.9	2.6
157 CH OF BRETHREN	1	158	194*	1.4	4.3
165 CH OF NAZARENE	2	144	349	2.6	7.7
193 EPISCOPAL.....	1	98	248	1.8	5.5
221 FREE METH C NA	2	88	106	0.8	2.3
283 LUTH--MO SYNOD	1	481	633	4.7	14.0
313 NO AM BAPT GC.	1	164	201*	1.5	4.4
413 S-D ADVENTISTS	2	97	119*	0.9	2.6
449 UN METHODIST..	3	671	699	5.2	15.5
453 UN PRES CH USA	1	116	142*	1.1	3.1
469 WISC EVAN LUTH	1	98	145	1.1	3.2
GOGEBIC	32	5,836	15,144*	73.2	100.0
081 CATHOLIC......	8	0	7,453	36.0	49.2
165 CH OF NAZARENE	1	32	84	0.4	0.6
193 EPISCOPAL.....	1	157	195	0.9	1.3
201 EVAN COV CH AM	1	93	109*	0.5	0.7
281 LUTH CH AMER..	8	3,056	4,023	19.5	26.6
283 LUTH--MO SYNOD	6	1,247	1,779	8.6	11.7
413 S-D ADVENTISTS	1	67	79*	0.4	0.5
443 UN C OF CHRIST	1	61	72*	0.3	0.5
449 UN METHODIST..	2	772	938	4.5	6.2
453 UN PRES CH USA	3	351	412*	2.0	2.7
GRAND TRAVERSE	36	6,303	20,443*	52.2	100.0
019 AMER BAPT CONV	1	130	159*	0.4	0.8
081 CATHOLIC......	5	0	11,987	30.6	58.6
093 CR CH (DISC)..	1	167	204*	0.5	1.0
123 CH GOD (ANDER)	1	40	144	0.4	0.7
127 CH GOD (CLEVE)	1	52	63*	0.2	0.3
165 CH OF NAZARENE	1	116	215	0.5	1.1
175 CONG CR CH....	1	125	153*	0.4	0.7
193 EPISCOPAL.....	1	393	500	1.3	2.4
201 EVAN COV CH AM	1	67	82*	0.2	0.4
221 FREE METH C NA	3	46	48	0.1	0.2
226 FRIENDS-USA...	2	99	121*	0.3	0.6
281 LUTH CH AMER..	1	755	1,186	3.0	5.8
285 MENNONITE CH..	1	7	9*	-	-
371 REF CH IN AM..	1	181	270	0.7	1.3
403 SALVATION ARMY	1	66	253	0.6	1.2
413 S-D ADVENTISTS	1	99	121*	0.3	0.6
435 UNITARIAN-UNIV	1	40	83	0.2	0.4
443 UN C OF CHRIST	1	1,512	1,846*	4.7	9.0
449 UN METHODIST..	10	2,019	2,524	6.4	12.3
453 UN PRES CH USA	1	389	475*	1.2	2.3
GRATIOT	60	8,912	17,809*	45.4	100.0
019 AMER BAPT CONV	1	185	233*	0.6	1.3
081 CATHOLIC......	6	0	4,580	11.7	25.7
093 CR CH (DISC)..	1	125	158*	0.4	0.9
097 CR C AND C CR.	5	1,126	1,420*	3.6	8.0
123 CH GOD (ANDER)	4	574	1,492	3.8	8.4
157 CH OF BRETHREN	1	106	134*	0.3	0.8
165 CH OF NAZARENE	4	299	720	1.8	4.0
193 EPISCOPAL.....	1	265	417	1.1	2.3
221 FREE METH C NA	6	156	187	0.5	1.1
283 LUTH--MO SYNOD	2	757	1,126	2.9	6.3
285 MENNONITE CH..	1	154	194*	0.5	1.1
403 SALVATION ARMY	1	52	259	0.7	1.5
413 S-D ADVENTISTS	4	326	411*	1.0	2.3
443 UN C OF CHRIST	1	113	142*	0.4	0.8
449 UN METHODIST..	15	2,956	4,099	10.4	23.0
453 UN PRES CH USA	5	1,433	1,807*	4.6	10.1
469 WISC EVAN LUTH	2	285	430	1.1	2.4
HILLSDALE	46	6,202	9,629*	25.9	100.0
019 AMER BAPT CONV	5	862	1,063*	2.9	11.0
081 CATHOLIC......	1	0	1,100	3.0	11.4
097 CR C AND C CR.	2	315	388*	1.0	4.0
123 CH GOD (ANDER)	1	40	100	0.3	1.0
165 CH OF NAZARENE	2	172	416	1.1	4.3
175 CONG CR CH....	3	263	324*	0.9	3.4
193 EPISCOPAL.....	2	292	494	1.3	5.1
221 FREE METH C NA	1	135	179	0.5	1.9
281 LUTH CH AMER..	1	282	398	1.1	4.1
283 LUTH--MO SYNOD	1	320	481	1.3	5.0
285 MENNONITE CH..	3	137	169*	0.5	1.8
403 SALVATION ARMY	1	63	168	0.5	1.7
413 S-D ADVENTISTS	2	98	121*	0.3	1.3
419 SO BAPT CONV..	2	91	112*	0.3	1.2
443 UN C OF CHRIST	2	247	305*	0.8	3.2
449 UN METHODIST..	14	2,043	2,773	7.5	28.8
453 UN PRES CH USA	3	842	1,038*	2.8	10.8
HOUGHTON	39	5,654	18,474*	53.3	100.0
081 CATHOLIC......	9	0	10,937	31.6	59.2
193 EPISCOPAL.....	3	250	431	1.2	2.3
281 LUTH CH AMER..	9	2,745	3,703	10.7	20.0
283 LUTH--MO SYNOD	3	626	848	2.4	4.6
403 SALVATION ARMY	1	31	188	0.5	1.0
413 S-D ADVENTISTS	1	44	52*	0.2	0.3
443 UN C OF CHRIST	3	279	328*	0.9	1.8
449 UN METHODIST..	8	1,444	1,711	4.9	9.3
453 UN PRES CH USA	2	235	276*	0.8	1.5

*Total adherents estimated from known number of communicant, confirmed, full members.

—Represents a percent less than 0.1.

Percentages may not total due to rounding.

Table 3. Churches and Church Membership by State, County and Denomination: 1971

County and Denomination	Number of churches	Communicant, confirmed, full members	Total adherents: Number	Total adherents: Percent of total population	Total adherents: Percent of total adherents
HURON	63	10,069	25,547*	75.0	100.0
019 AMER BAPT CONV	2	356	440*	1.3	1.7
029 AMER LUTH CH..	1	382	523	1.5	2.0
081 CATHOLIC......	17	0	12,528	36.8	49.0
165 CH OF NAZARENE	2	102	202	0.6	0.8
193 EPISCOPAL.....	1	68	111	0.3	0.4
221 FREE METH C NA	2	34	49	0.1	0.2
283 LUTH--MO SYNOD	9	3,994	5,293	15.5	20.7
285 MENNONITE CH..	2	437	540*	1.6	2.1
353 PLY BRETHREN..	1	20	30	0.1	0.1
413 S-D ADVENTISTS	1	20	25*	0.1	0.1
443 UN C OF CHRIST	1	47	58*	0.2	0.2
449 UN METHODIST..	16	2,944	3,541	10.4	13.9
453 UN PRES CH USA	5	881	1,089*	3.2	4.3
469 WISC EVAN LUTH	3	784	1,118	3.3	4.4
INGHAM	150	48,814	102,804*	39.4	100.0
019 AMER BAPT CONV	13	5,786	7,085*	2.7	6.9
029 AMER LUTH CH..	4	1,988	2,786	1.1	2.7
059 BAPT MISS ASSN	1	143	175*	0.1	0.2
081 CATHOLIC......	13	0	38,732	14.8	37.7
093 CR CH (DISC)..	1	400	490*	0.2	0.5
097 CR C AND C CR.	4	961	1,177*	0.5	1.1
105 CHRISTIAN REF.	1	342	596	0.2	0.6
123 CH GOD (ANDER)	3	560	1,011	0.4	1.0
127 CH GOD (CLEVE)	5	320	392*	0.2	0.4
157 CH OF BRETHREN	1	142	174*	0.1	0.2
165 CH OF NAZARENE	15	1,445	3,110	1.2	3.0
175 CONG CR CH....	1	1,148	1,406*	0.5	1.4
193 EPISCOPAL.....	5	2,530	3,462	1.3	3.4
201 EVAN COV CH AM	1	149	182*	0.1	0.2
221 FREE METH C NA	7	446	596	0.2	0.6
226 FRIENDS-USA...	1	18	22*	-	-
281 LUTH CH AMER..	4	1,279	1,907	0.7	1.9
283 LUTH--MO SYNOD	6	2,941	4,287	1.6	4.2
313 NO AM BAPT GC.	1	460	563*	0.2	0.5
353 PLY BRETHREN..	1	10	15	-	-
371 REF CH IN AM..	2	316	516	0.2	0.5
403 SALVATION ARMY	1	168	364	0.1	0.4
413 S-D ADVENTISTS	6	802	982*	0.4	1.0
419 SO BAPT CONV..	5	1,324	1,621*	0.6	1.6
435 UNITARIAN-UNIV	1	192	282	0.1	0.3
443 UN C OF CHRIST	8	5,621	6,883*	2.6	6.7
449 UN METHODIST..	27	11,676	14,363	5.5	14.0
453 UN PRES CH USA	9	5,503	6,739*	2.6	6.6
469 WISC EVAN LUTH	3	2,144	2,886	1.1	2.8
IONIA	56	6,599	19,086*	41.6	100.0
019 AMER BAPT CONV	3	418	525*	1.1	2.8
081 CATHOLIC......	9	0	9,769	21.3	51.2
093 CR CH (DISC)..	4	375	471*	1.0	2.5
097 CR C AND C CR.	2	45	57*	0.1	0.3
105 CHRISTIAN REF.	1	65	106	0.2	0.6
123 CH GOD (ANDER)	1	72	207	0.5	1.1
127 CH GOD (CLEVE)	1	64	80*	0.2	0.4
165 CH OF NAZARENE	4	154	359	0.8	1.9
175 CONG CR CH....	1	125	157*	0.3	0.8
193 EPISCOPAL.....	2	360	676	1.5	3.5
221 FREE METH C NA	3	75	89	0.2	0.5
283 LUTH--MO SYNOD	2	601	993	2.2	5.2
413 S-D ADVENTISTS	3	168	211*	0.5	1.1
443 UN C OF CHRIST	3	697	876*	1.9	4.6
449 UN METHODIST..	14	2,941	3,939	8.6	20.6
453 UN PRES CH USA	2	412	518*	1.1	2.7
469 WISC EVAN LUTH	1	27	53	0.1	0.3
IOSCO	30	3,926	8,131*	32.6	100.0
019 AMER BAPT CONV	2	133	166*	0.7	2.0
081 CATHOLIC......	6	0	3,240	13.0	39.8
127 CH GOD (CLEVE)	1	22	27*	0.1	0.3
165 CH OF NAZARENE	2	77	174	0.7	2.1
193 EPISCOPAL.....	2	418	434	1.7	5.3
221 FREE METH C NA	1	13	17	0.1	0.2
281 LUTH CH AMER..	2	439	576	2.3	7.1
283 LUTH--MO SYNOD	3	788	1,027	4.1	12.6
413 S-D ADVENTISTS	2	60	75*	0.3	0.9
419 SO BAPT CONV..	2	260	325*	1.3	4.0
449 UN METHODIST..	6	1,276	1,468	5.9	18.1
469 WISC EVAN LUTH	1	440	602	2.4	7.4
IRON	27	2,833	7,527*	54.5	100.0
081 CATHOLIC......	8	0	3,996	28.9	53.1
193 EPISCOPAL.....	3	98	129	0.9	1.7
201 EVAN COV CH AM	3	187	214*	1.5	2.8
281 LUTH CH AMER..	4	1,378	1,799	13.0	23.9
283 LUTH--MO SYNOD	2	126	157	1.1	2.1
413 S-D ADVENTISTS	1	42	48*	0.3	0.6
449 UN METHODIST..	4	491	594	4.3	7.9
453 UN PRES CH USA	1	453	520*	3.8	6.9
469 WISC EVAN LUTH	1	58	70	0.5	0.9
ISABELLA	41	5,276	20,277*	45.5	100.0
019 AMER BAPT CONV	2	104	125*	0.3	0.6
081 CATHOLIC......	7	0	13,031	29.2	64.3
097 CR C AND C CR.	3	408	492*	1.1	2.4
121 CH GOD (ABR)..	1	90	109*	0.2	0.5
123 CH GOD (ANDER)	1	117	283	0.6	1.4
157 CH OF BRETHREN	1	126	152*	0.3	0.7
165 CH OF NAZARENE	3	141	458	1.0	2.3
193 EPISCOPAL.....	1	392	541	1.2	2.7
221 FREE METH C NA	1	41	54	0.1	0.3
226 FRIENDS-USA...	1	3	4*	-	-
283 LUTH--MO SYNOD	2	662	998	2.2	4.9
413 S-D ADVENTISTS	1	59	71*	0.2	0.4
435 UNITARIAN-UNIV	1	18	18	-	0.1
449 UN METHODIST..	13	1,944	2,517	5.6	12.4
453 UN PRES CH USA	2	1,101	1,328*	3.0	6.5
469 WISC EVAN LUTH	1	70	96	0.2	0.5
JACKSON	82	19,605	44,903*	31.3	100.0
019 AMER BAPT CONV	5	1,007	1,245*	0.9	2.8
029 AMER LUTH CH..	1	476	742	0.5	1.7
081 CATHOLIC......	8	0	18,516	12.9	41.2
097 CR C AND C CR.	1	400	494*	0.3	1.1
105 CHRISTIAN REF.	1	94	173	0.1	0.4
123 CH GOD (ANDER)	3	192	484	0.3	1.1
127 CH GOD (CLEVE)	1	40	49*	-	0.1
165 CH OF NAZARENE	4	298	799	0.6	1.8
175 CONG CR CH....	1	341	421*	0.3	0.9
193 EPISCOPAL.....	6	2,226	3,198	2.2	7.1
221 FREE METH C NA	3	557	727	0.5	1.6
226 FRIENDS-USA...	1	53	66*	-	0.1
281 LUTH CH AMER..	2	863	1,372	1.0	3.1
283 LUTH--MO SYNOD	2	1,539	2,136	1.5	4.8
285 MENNONITE CH..	1	44	54*	-	0.1
353 PLY BRETHREN..	1	20	40	-	0.1
403 SALVATION ARMY	1	95	525	0.4	1.2
413 S-D ADVENTISTS	2	342	423*	0.3	0.9
419 SO BAPT CONV..	6	1,219	1,507*	1.1	3.4
435 UNITARIAN-UNIV	3	120	172	0.1	0.4
443 UN C OF CHRIST	5	1,110	1,372*	1.0	3.1
449 UN METHODIST..	18	5,818	6,959	4.9	15.5
453 UN PRES CH USA	4	2,566	3,172*	2.2	7.1
469 WISC EVAN LUTH	2	185	257	0.2	0.6
KALAMAZOO	129	33,685	72,072*	35.8	100.0
019 AMER BAPT CONV	5	482	589*	0.3	0.8
029 AMER LUTH CH..	2	537	903	0.4	1.3
059 BAPT MISS ASSN	1	110	134*	0.1	0.2
081 CATHOLIC......	16	0	23,220	11.5	32.2
093 CR CH (DISC)..	2	660	806*	0.4	1.1
097 CR C AND C CR.	1	200	244*	0.1	0.3
105 CHRISTIAN REF.	15	3,741	6,318	3.1	8.8
123 CH GOD (ANDER)	4	419	1,001	0.5	1.4
127 CH GOD (CLEVE)	1	69	84*	-	0.1
157 CH OF BRETHREN	1	43	53*	-	0.1
165 CH OF NAZARENE	4	458	773	0.4	1.1
175 CONG CR CH....	1	370	452*	0.2	0.6
193 EPISCOPAL.....	5	2,464	3,827	1.9	5.3
201 EVAN COV CH AM	2	213	260*	0.1	0.4
221 FREE METH C NA	2	178	245	0.1	0.3
226 FRIENDS-USA...	1	43	53*	-	0.1
281 LUTH CH AMER..	2	823	1,188	0.6	1.6
283 LUTH--MO SYNOD	4	1,558	2,847	1.4	4.0
285 MENNONITE CH..	1	17	21*	-	-
371 REF CH IN AM..	18	5,409	8,239	4.1	11.4
403 SALVATION ARMY	1	138	490	0.2	0.7
413 S-D ADVENTISTS	2	428	523*	0.3	0.7
419 SO BAPT CONV..	4	670	819*	0.4	1.1
435 UNITARIAN-UNIV	1	375	375	0.2	0.5
443 UN C OF CHRIST	5	1,557	1,902*	0.9	2.6
449 UN METHODIST..	21	9,509	12,734	6.3	17.7
453 UN PRES CH USA	5	3,108	3,797*	1.9	5.3
469 WISC EVAN LUTH	2	106	175	0.1	0.2
KALKASKA	13	1,011	1,893*	35.9	100.0
019 AMER BAPT CONV	1	111	138*	2.6	7.3
081 CATHOLIC......	2	0	625	11.9	33.0
093 CR CH (DISC)..	2	90	112*	2.1	5.9
097 CR C AND C CR.	3	478	594*	11.3	31.4
127 CH GOD (CLEVE)	1	22	27*	0.5	1.4
283 LUTH--MO SYNOD	1	188	264	5.0	13.9
413 S-D ADVENTISTS	1	46	57*	1.1	3.0
449 UN METHODIST..	2	76	76	1.4	4.0
KENT	299	88,040	211,291*	51.4	100.0
019 AMER BAPT CONV	3	540	673*	0.2	0.3
029 AMER LUTH CH..	2	200	335	0.1	0.2
081 CATHOLIC......	45	0	81,171	19.7	38.4
093 CR CH (DISC)..	2	1,019	1,270*	0.3	0.6
097 CR C AND C CR.	5	821	1,024*	0.2	0.5
105 CHRISTIAN REF.	66	25,015	41,646	10.1	19.7
121 CH GOD (ABR)..	3	344	429*	0.1	0.2
123 CH GOD (ANDER)	5	433	981	0.2	0.5
127 CH GOD (CLEVE)	3	143	178*	-	0.1
157 CH OF BRETHREN	1	110	137*	-	0.1
165 CH OF NAZARENE	6	788	1,493	0.4	0.7
175 CONG CR CH....	2	975	1,216*	0.3	0.6
193 EPISCOPAL.....	9	3,408	4,903	1.2	2.3
201 EVAN COV CH AM	1	458	571*	0.1	0.3
221 FREE METH C NA	4	255	357	0.1	0.2
226 FRIENDS-USA...	1	7	9*	-	-
281 LUTH CH AMER..	9	4,942	7,496	1.8	3.5
283 LUTH--MO SYNOD	15	5,576	8,079	2.0	3.8
285 MENNONITE CH..	2	93	116*	-	0.1
353 PLY BRETHREN..	4	370	653	0.2	0.3
371 REF CH IN AM..	37	14,465	21,659	5.3	10.3
381 REF PRES-EVAN.	1	100	100	-	-
403 SALVATION ARMY	3	277	1,393	0.3	0.7
413 S-D ADVENTISTS	5	1,026	1,279*	0.3	0.6

*Total adherents estimated from known number of communicant, confirmed, full members.

—Represents a percent less than 0.1.

Percentages may not total due to rounding.

Table 3. Churches and Church Membership by State, County and Denomination: 1971

County and Denomination	Number of churches	Communicant, confirmed, full members	Total adherents		
			Number	Percent of total population	Percent of total adherents
419 SO BAPT CONV..	4	529	660*	0.2	0.3
435 UNITARIAN-UNIV	1	10	10	-	-
443 UN C OF CHRIST	16	9,993	12,458*	3.0	5.9
449 UN METHODIST..	34	11,699	15,387	3.7	7.3
453 UN PRES CH USA	9	4,356	5,431*	1.3	2.6
469 WISC EVAN LUTH	1	88	177	-	0.1
KEWEENAW	7	449	1,037*	45.8	100.0
081 CATHOLIC......	3	0	450	19.9	43.4
281 LUTH CH AMER..	1	262	364	16.1	35.1
353 PLY BRETHREN..	1	20	30	1.3	2.9
443 UN C OF CHRIST	1	84	98*	4.3	9.5
449 UN METHODIST..	1	83	95	4.2	9.2
LAKE	9	347	668*	11.8	100.0
081 CATHOLIC......	2	0	231	4.1	34.6
093 CR CH (DISC)..	1	49	59*	1.0	8.8
123 CH GOD (ANDER)	1	6	22	0.4	3.3
413 S-D ADVENTISTS	3	56	67*	1.2	10.0
443 UN C OF CHRIST	1	212	253*	4.5	37.9
449 UN METHODIST..	1	24	36	0.6	5.4
LAPEER	47	6,730	16,461*	31.5	100.0
019 AMER BAPT CONV	2	223	285*	0.5	1.7
029 AMER LUTH CH..	1	518	756	1.4	4.6
081 CATHOLIC......	7	0	6,820	13.0	41.4
097 CR C AND C CR.	3	323	413*	0.8	2.5
105 CHRISTIAN REF.	1	245	381	0.7	2.3
127 CH GOD (CLEVE)	1	32	41*	0.1	0.2
165 CH OF NAZARENE	3	130	453	0.9	2.8
193 EPISCOPAL.....	2	416	663	1.3	4.0
221 FREE METH C NA	1	29	33	0.1	0.2
283 LUTH--MO SYNOD	3	1,318	2,103	4.0	12.8
285 MENNONITE CH..	1	44	56*	0.1	0.3
413 S-D ADVENTISTS	3	161	206*	0.4	1.3
443 UN C OF CHRIST	1	204	261*	0.5	1.6
449 UN METHODIST..	16	2,493	3,204	6.1	19.5
453 UN PRES CH USA	1	507	648*	1.2	3.9
469 WISC EVAN LUTH	1	87	138	0.3	0.8
LEELANAU	24	1,331	5,679*	52.2	100.0
029 AMER LUTH CH..	2	152	216	2.0	3.8
081 CATHOLIC......	8	0	4,046	37.2	71.2
175 CONG CR CH....	1	105	129*	1.2	2.3
193 EPISCOPAL.....	1	41	54	0.5	1.0
201 EVAN COV CH AM	1	53	65*	0.6	1.1
283 LUTH--MO SYNOD	3	381	456	4.2	8.0
371 REF CH IN AM..	1	114	160	1.5	2.8
419 SO BAPT CONV..	1	52	64*	0.6	1.1
443 UN C OF CHRIST	1	144	177*	1.6	3.1
449 UN METHODIST..	4	274	294	2.7	5.2
453 UN PRES CH USA	1	15	18*	0.2	0.3
LENAWEE	90	18,422	35,291*	43.2	100.0
019 AMER BAPT CONV	7	1,853	2,288*	2.8	6.5
029 AMER LUTH CH..	3	1,193	1,603	2.0	4.5
081 CATHOLIC......	8	0	10,949	13.4	31.0
093 CR CH (DISC)..	1	175	216*	0.3	0.6
123 CH GOD (ANDER)	2	89	182	0.2	0.5
127 CH GOD (CLEVE)	3	163	201*	0.2	0.6
157 CH OF BRETHREN	2	206	254*	0.3	0.7
165 CH OF NAZARENE	5	470	1,125	1.4	3.2
175 CONG CR CH....	2	333	411*	0.5	1.2
193 EPISCOPAL.....	3	676	1,114	1.4	3.2
221 FREE METH C NA	2	94	117	0.1	0.3
226 FRIENDS-USA...	5	579	715*	0.9	2.0
281 LUTH CH AMER..	2	593	852	1.0	2.4
283 LUTH--MO SYNOD	5	1,789	2,456	3.0	7.0
403 SALVATION ARMY	1	66	223	0.3	0.6
413 S-D ADVENTISTS	1	124	153*	0.2	0.4
419 SO BAPT CONV..	5	758	936*	1.1	2.7
443 UN C OF CHRIST	5	1,336	1,650*	2.0	4.7
449 UN METHODIST..	18	4,395	5,253	6.4	14.9
453 UN PRES CH USA	6	1,946	2,403*	2.9	6.8
469 WISC EVAN LUTH	4	1,584	2,190	2.7	6.2
LIVINGSTON	41	8,219	20,167*	34.2	100.0
019 AMER BAPT CONV	2	658	834*	1.4	4.1
029 AMER LUTH CH..	3	1,549	2,065	3.5	10.2
081 CATHOLIC......	4	0	8,530	14.5	42.3
105 CHRISTIAN REF.	1	155	285	0.5	1.4
123 CH GOD (ANDER)	1	110	275	0.5	1.4
127 CH GOD (CLEVE)	1	26	33*	0.1	0.2
165 CH OF NAZARENE	2	355	956	1.6	4.7
193 EPISCOPAL.....	3	415	795	1.3	3.9
221 FREE METH C NA	1	48	61	0.1	0.3
283 LUTH--MO SYNOD	2	345	497	0.8	2.5
285 MENNONITE CH..	1	17	22*	-	0.1
403 SALVATION ARMY	1	50	123	0.2	0.6
413 S-D ADVENTISTS	1	122	155*	0.3	0.8
419 SO BAPT CONV..	2	141	179*	0.3	0.9
443 UN C OF CHRIST	1	360	456*	0.8	2.3
449 UN METHODIST..	10	2,516	3,159	5.4	15.7
453 UN PRES CH USA	4	1,276	1,617*	2.7	8.0
469 WISC EVAN LUTH	1	76	125	0.2	0.6
LUCE	9	1,162	2,780*	40.9	100.0
081 CATHOLIC......	1	0	1,307	19.3	47.0
127 CH GOD (CLEVE)	1	13	15*	0.2	0.5
193 EPISCOPAL.....	1	163	180	2.7	6.5
281 LUTH CH AMER..	1	278	361	5.3	13.0
283 LUTH--MO SYNOD	1	153	210	3.1	7.6
413 S-D ADVENTISTS	1	17	20*	0.3	0.7
449 UN METHODIST..	2	306	413	6.1	14.9
453 UN PRES CH USA	1	232	274*	4.0	9.9
MACKINAC	24	1,661	4,731*	49.0	100.0
081 CATHOLIC......	6	0	2,366	24.5	50.0
175 CONG CR CH....	1	12	15*	0.2	0.3
193 EPISCOPAL.....	3	176	266	2.8	5.6
221 FREE METH C NA	1	10	17	0.2	0.4
281 LUTH CH AMER..	4	628	1,009	10.4	21.3
283 LUTH--MO SYNOD	1	209	263	2.7	5.6
285 MENNONITE CH..	3	83	103*	1.1	2.2
449 UN METHODIST..	2	423	538	5.6	11.4
453 UN PRES CH USA	2	97	120*	1.2	2.5
469 WISC EVAN LUTH	1	23	34	0.4	0.7
MACOMB	190	61,672	391,466*	62.6	100.0
019 AMER BAPT CONV	5	1,314	1,697*	0.3	0.4
029 AMER LUTH CH..	15	8,665	13,153	2.1	3.4
081 CATHOLIC......	48	0	302,775	48.4	77.3
097 CR C AND C CR.	1	29	37*	-	-
105 CHRISTIAN REF.	1	72	143	-	-
123 CH GOD (ANDER)	2	77	175	-	-
127 CH GOD (CLEVE)	2	561	724*	0.1	0.2
165 CH OF NAZARENE	6	547	1,227	0.2	0.3
185 CUMBER PRESB..	2	620	801*	0.1	0.2
193 EPISCOPAL.....	6	2,013	2,924	0.5	0.7
201 EVAN COV CH AM	1	80	103*	-	-
221 FREE METH C NA	1	25	27	-	-
281 LUTH CH AMER..	6	2,110	3,277	0.5	0.8
283 LUTH--MO SYNOD	23	19,850	29,734	4.8	7.6
313 NO AM BAPT GC.	6	1,786	2,306*	0.4	0.6
371 REF CH IN AM..	1	148	244	-	0.1
403 SALVATION ARMY	1	72	270	-	0.1
413 S-D ADVENTISTS	1	310	400*	0.1	0.1
419 SO BAPT CONV..	16	3,390	4,378*	0.7	1.1
435 UNITARIAN-UNIV	1	52	52	-	-
443 UN C OF CHRIST	11	5,256	6,787*	1.1	1.7
449 UN METHODIST..	21	9,277	13,072	2.1	3.3
453 UN PRES CH USA	10	4,802	6,201*	1.0	1.6
469 WISC EVAN LUTH	3	616	959	0.2	0.2
MANISTEE	29	4,573	13,111*	65.2	100.0
081 CATHOLIC......	5	0	7,250	36.1	55.3
127 CH GOD (CLEVE)	1	13	16*	0.1	0.1
157 CH OF BRETHREN	3	284	350*	1.7	2.7
165 CH OF NAZARENE	1	25	121	0.6	0.9
193 EPISCOPAL.....	1	147	216	1.1	1.6
201 EVAN COV CH AM	1	53	65*	0.3	0.5
221 FREE METH C NA	1	6	6	-	-
281 LUTH CH AMER..	2	1,172	1,556	7.7	11.9
283 LUTH--MO SYNOD	3	1,492	1,684	8.4	12.8
285 MENNONITE CH..	1	7	9*	-	0.1
403 SALVATION ARMY	1	52	271	1.3	2.1
413 S-D ADVENTISTS	1	50	62*	0.3	0.5
443 UN C OF CHRIST	2	371	457*	2.3	3.5
449 UN METHODIST..	5	747	848	4.2	6.5
469 WISC EVAN LUTH	1	154	200	1.0	1.5
MARQUETTE	66	13,150	33,848*	52.3	100.0
019 AMER BAPT CONV	1	122	148*	0.2	0.4
029 AMER LUTH CH..	1	285	349	0.5	1.0
081 CATHOLIC......	15	0	16,227	25.1	47.9
121 CH GOD (ABR)..	1	10	12*	-	-
127 CH GOD (CLEVE)	1	13	16*	-	-
193 EPISCOPAL.....	5	877	1,359	2.1	4.0
201 EVAN COV CH AM	3	147	178*	0.3	0.5
221 FREE METH C NA	1	7	7	-	-
281 LUTH CH AMER..	14	6,256	8,636	13.4	25.5
283 LUTH--MO SYNOD	1	637	880	1.4	2.6
285 MENNONITE CH..	1	7	8*	-	-
353 PLY BRETHREN..	1	30	50	0.1	0.1
403 SALVATION ARMY	2	84	358	0.6	1.1
413 S-D ADVENTISTS	1	14	17*	-	0.1
419 SO BAPT CONV..	3	504	612*	0.9	1.8
435 UNITARIAN-UNIV	1	12	12	-	-
449 UN METHODIST..	11	3,302	3,956	6.1	11.7
453 UN PRES CH USA	3	843	1,023*	1.6	3.0
MASON	32	4,461	12,231*	54.1	100.0
081 CATHOLIC......	8	0	5,950	26.3	48.6
157 CH OF BRETHREN	1	134	162*	0.7	1.3
165 CH OF NAZARENE	1	80	146	0.6	1.2
193 EPISCOPAL.....	1	126	240	1.1	2.0
201 EVAN COV CH AM	2	93	113*	0.5	0.9
221 FREE METH C NA	2	54	83	0.4	0.7
281 LUTH CH AMER..	3	783	1,128	5.0	9.2
283 LUTH--MO SYNOD	2	941	1,322	5.8	10.8
371 REF CH IN AM..	1	97	154	0.7	1.3
403 SALVATION ARMY	1	32	299	1.3	2.4
413 S-D ADVENTISTS	1	43	52*	0.2	0.4
435 UNITARIAN-UNIV	1	21	21	0.1	0.2
449 UN METHODIST..	5	1,205	1,525	6.7	12.5
453 UN PRES CH USA	1	656	795*	3.5	6.5
469 WISC EVAN LUTH	2	196	241	1.1	2.0

*Total adherents estimated from known number of communicant, confirmed, full members.

—Represents a percent less than 0.1.

Percentages may not total due to rounding.

Table 3. Churches and Church Membership by State, County and Denomination: 1971

County and Denomination	Number of churches	Communicant, confirmed, full members	Total adherents: Number	Total adherents: Percent of total population	Total adherents: Percent of total adherents
MECOSTA	38	4,158	11,348*	40.5	100.0
081 CATHOLIC......	4	0	5,665	20.2	49.9
097 CR C AND C CR.	3	295	349*	1.2	3.1
105 CHRISTIAN REF.	1	67	108	0.4	1.0
123 CH GOD (ANDER)	3	216	503	1.8	4.4
127 CH GOD (CLEVE)	2	89	105*	0.4	0.9
157 CH OF BRETHREN	1	58	69*	0.2	0.6
165 CH OF NAZARENE	1	22	79	0.3	0.7
193 EPISCOPAL.....	1	218	344	1.2	3.0
221 FREE METH C NA	5	136	172	0.6	1.5
281 LUTH CH AMER..	1	303	392	1.4	3.5
283 LUTH--MO SYNOD	1	752	1,011	3.6	8.9
413 S-D ADVENTISTS	1	46	54*	0.2	0.5
435 UNITARIAN-UNIV	1	20	33	0.1	0.3
443 UN C OF CHRIST	1	256	303*	1.1	2.7
449 UN METHODIST..	10	1,270	1,641	5.9	14.5
453 UN PRES CH USA	1	285	337*	1.2	3.0
469 WISC EVAN LUTH	1	125	183	0.7	1.6
MENOMINEE	40	4,630	17,278*	70.3	100.0
029 AMER LUTH CH..	1	114	174	0.7	1.0
081 CATHOLIC......	14	0	11,170	45.4	64.6
127 CH GOD (CLEVE)	1	5	6*	-	-
165 CH OF NAZARENE	1	18	61	0.2	0.4
193 EPISCOPAL.....	2	163	249	1.0	1.4
201 EVAN COV CH AM	4	276	338*	1.4	2.0
221 FREE METH C NA	1	10	20	0.1	0.1
281 LUTH CH AMER..	4	1,517	2,094	8.5	12.1
293 MORAV CH-NORTH	1	160	211	0.9	1.2
413 S-D ADVENTISTS	2	214	262*	1.1	1.5
449 UN METHODIST..	4	775	978	4.0	5.7
453 UN PRES CH USA	1	610	747*	3.0	4.3
469 WISC EVAN LUTH	4	768	968	3.9	5.6
MIDLAND	61	16,467	35,498*	55.7	100.0
019 AMER BAPT CONV	1	603	775*	1.2	2.2
029 AMER LUTH CH..	1	1,167	1,990	3.1	5.6
081 CATHOLIC......	7	0	12,421	19.5	35.0
097 CR C AND C CR.	1	60	77*	0.1	0.2
123 CH GOD (ANDER)	7	582	1,523	2.4	4.3
127 CH GOD (CLEVE)	1	186	239*	0.4	0.7
157 CH OF BRETHREN	1	152	195*	0.3	0.5
165 CH OF NAZARENE	3	497	971	1.5	2.7
193 EPISCOPAL.....	2	1,066	1,418	2.2	4.0
221 FREE METH C NA	3	123	175	0.3	0.5
281 LUTH CH AMER..	1	93	163	0.3	0.5
283 LUTH--MO SYNOD	4	2,393	3,347	5.2	9.4
285 MENNONITE CH..	1	158	203*	0.3	0.6
315 NO AM OLD RC..	1	37	48*	0.1	0.1
353 PLY BRETHREN..	1	30	50	0.1	0.1
371 REF CH IN AM..	1	180	318	0.5	0.9
403 SALVATION ARMY	1	78	326	0.5	0.9
413 S-D ADVENTISTS	2	235	302*	0.5	0.9
419 SO BAPT CONV..	2	174	224*	0.4	0.6
435 UNITARIAN-UNIV	1	84	84	0.1	0.2
443 UN C OF CHRIST	1	405	521*	0.8	1.5
449 UN METHODIST..	14	5,311	6,456	10.1	18.2
453 UN PRES CH USA	3	2,840	3,651*	5.7	10.3
469 WISC EVAN LUTH	1	13	21	-	0.1
MISSAUKEE	25	2,068	3,803*	53.4	100.0
081 CATHOLIC......	2	0	400	5.6	10.5
105 CHRISTIAN REF.	6	919	1,600	22.5	42.1
165 CH OF NAZARENE	2	32	94	1.3	2.5
221 FREE METH C NA	3	53	61	0.9	1.6
281 LUTH CH AMER..	1	73	90	1.3	2.4
371 REF CH IN AM..	3	395	691	9.7	18.2
413 S-D ADVENTISTS	1	73	90*	1.3	2.4
449 UN METHODIST..	5	320	528	7.4	13.9
453 UN PRES CH USA	2	203	249*	3.5	6.5
MONROE	85	20,089	62,824*	53.0	100.0
019 AMER BAPT CONV	2	690	881*	0.7	1.4
029 AMER LUTH CH..	8	2,602	3,703	3.1	5.9
081 CATHOLIC......	15	0	35,200	29.7	56.0
093 CR CH (DISC)..	1	49	63*	0.1	0.1
123 CH GOD (ANDER)	1	41	141	0.1	0.2
127 CH GOD (CLEVE)	3	650	830*	0.7	1.3
165 CH OF NAZARENE	2	211	558	0.5	0.9
193 EPISCOPAL.....	1	301	505	0.4	0.8
197 EVAN CH OF NA.	1	105	134*	0.1	0.2
221 FREE METH C NA	2	101	145	0.1	0.2
281 LUTH CH AMER..	2	1,214	1,676	1.4	2.7
283 LUTH--MO SYNOD	6	3,992	5,581	4.7	8.9
403 SALVATION ARMY	1	72	290	0.2	0.5
413 S-D ADVENTISTS	2	95	121*	0.1	0.2
419 SO BAPT CONV..	14	3,007	3,841*	3.2	6.1
449 UN METHODIST..	17	4,714	6,163	5.2	9.8
453 UN PRES CH USA	4	1,124	1,436*	1.2	2.3
469 WISC EVAN LUTH	3	1,121	1,556	1.3	2.5
MONTCALM	64	7,601	11,573*	29.2	100.0
019 AMER BAPT CONV	3	304	379*	1.0	3.3
029 AMER LUTH CH..	4	911	1,260	3.2	10.9
081 CATHOLIC......	7	0	1,598	4.0	13.8
093 CR CH (DISC)..	1	72	90*	0.2	0.8
097 CR C AND C CR.	4	445	555*	1.4	4.8
123 CH GOD (ANDER)	3	197	495	1.2	4.3
127 CH GOD (CLEVE)	1	32	40*	0.1	0.3
157 CH OF BRETHREN	1	50	62*	0.2	0.5
165 CH OF NAZARENE	1	21	65	0.2	0.6
175 CONG CR CH....	2	550	686*	1.7	5.9
193 EPISCOPAL.....	1	133	228	0.6	2.0
221 FREE METH C NA	4	102	124	0.3	1.1
281 LUTH CH AMER..	2	266	356	0.9	3.1
283 LUTH--MO SYNOD	5	982	1,475	3.7	12.7
335 ORTH PRESB CH.	1	43	57	0.1	0.5
353 PLY BRETHREN..	1	10	15	-	0.1
413 S-D ADVENTISTS	6	545	680*	1.7	5.9
443 UN C OF CHRIST	5	801	999*	2.5	8.6
449 UN METHODIST..	12	2,137	2,409	6.1	20.8
MONTMORENCY	13	1,272	2,277*	43.4	100.0
075 BRETHREN IN CR	1	11	13*	0.2	0.6
081 CATHOLIC......	2	0	700	13.3	30.7
193 EPISCOPAL.....	2	161	194	3.7	8.5
221 FREE METH C NA	2	36	46	0.9	2.0
283 LUTH--MO SYNOD	2	591	744	14.2	32.7
443 UN C OF CHRIST	3	360	427*	8.1	18.8
449 UN METHODIST..	1	113	153	2.9	6.7
MUSKEGON	107	26,330	61,082*	38.8	100.0
019 AMER BAPT CONV	2	860	1,079*	0.7	1.8
029 AMER LUTH CH..	4	1,953	2,780	1.8	4.6
081 CATHOLIC......	14	0	24,230	15.4	39.7
093 CR CH (DISC)..	2	214	268*	0.2	0.4
097 CR C AND C CR.	2	210	263*	0.2	0.4
105 CHRISTIAN REF.	10	2,318	3,669	2.3	6.0
123 CH GOD (ANDER)	3	197	582	0.4	1.0
127 CH GOD (CLEVE)	2	137	172*	0.1	0.3
157 CH OF BRETHREN	1	112	140*	0.1	0.2
165 CH OF NAZARENE	2	268	531	0.3	0.9
175 CONG CR CH....	1	136	171*	0.1	0.3
193 EPISCOPAL.....	4	1,320	1,815	1.2	3.0
201 EVAN COV CH AM	4	607	761*	0.5	1.2
221 FREE METH C NA	4	106	135	0.1	0.2
281 LUTH CH AMER..	5	1,962	2,659	1.7	4.4
283 LUTH--MO SYNOD	5	2,492	3,481	2.2	5.7
353 PLY BRETHREN..	1	95	165	0.1	0.3
371 REF CH IN AM..	17	4,129	6,061	3.9	9.9
403 SALVATION ARMY	1	167	592	0.4	1.0
413 S-D ADVENTISTS	2	320	401*	0.3	0.7
419 SO BAPT CONV..	2	63	79*	0.1	0.1
435 UNITARIAN-UNIV	1	50	66	-	0.1
443 UN C OF CHRIST	3	2,379	2,984*	1.9	4.9
449 UN METHODIST..	13	5,447	6,987	4.4	11.4
453 UN PRES CH USA	1	580	727*	0.5	1.2
469 WISC EVAN LUTH	1	208	284	0.2	0.5
NEWAYGO	36	5,724	11,232*	40.1	100.0
081 CATHOLIC......	7	0	3,118	11.1	27.8
093 CR CH (DISC)..	1	217	271*	1.0	2.4
097 CR C AND C CR.	1	100	125*	0.4	1.1
105 CHRISTIAN REF.	6	1,602	2,668	9.5	23.8
127 CH GOD (CLEVE)	1	122	152*	0.5	1.4
193 EPISCOPAL.....	2	223	319	1.1	2.8
283 LUTH--MO SYNOD	2	436	667	2.4	5.9
285 MENNONITE CH..	1	57	71*	0.3	0.6
353 PLY BRETHREN..	1	15	30	0.1	0.3
371 REF CH IN AM..	3	780	1,183	4.2	10.5
413 S-D ADVENTISTS	1	72	90*	0.3	0.8
443 UN C OF CHRIST	4	918	1,147*	4.1	10.2
449 UN METHODIST..	6	1,182	1,391	5.0	12.4
OAKLAND	316	113,221	393,617*	43.4	100.0
019 AMER BAPT CONV	13	5,628	6,993*	0.8	1.8
029 AMER LUTH CH..	9	4,865	6,948	0.8	1.8
075 BRETHREN IN CR	1	18	22*	-	-
081 CATHOLIC......	58	0	236,968	26.1	60.2
093 CR CH (DISC)..	3	346	430*	-	0.1
097 CR C AND C CR.	6	711	883*	0.1	0.2
105 CHRISTIAN REF.	3	314	556	0.1	0.1
123 CH GOD (ANDER)	6	738	1,689	0.2	0.4
127 CH GOD (CLEVE)	9	1,214	1,508*	0.2	0.4
157 CH OF BRETHREN	1	225	280*	-	0.1
165 CH OF NAZARENE	14	1,187	2,474	0.3	0.6
175 CONG CR CH....	7	4,064	5,050*	0.6	1.3
193 EPISCOPAL.....	20	12,937	17,795	2.0	4.5
221 FREE METH C NA	6	457	620	0.1	0.2
226 FRIENDS-USA...	1	22	27*	-	-
281 LUTH CH AMER..	18	5,710	8,710	1.0	2.2
283 LUTH--MO SYNOD	29	16,809	25,278	2.8	6.4
313 NO AM BAPT GC.	2	366	455*	0.1	0.1
353 PLY BRETHREN..	1	50	100	-	-
371 REF CH IN AM..	1	102	156	-	-
403 SALVATION ARMY	3	509	1,953	0.2	0.5
413 S-D ADVENTISTS	7	1,572	1,953*	0.2	0.5
419 SO BAPT CONV..	18	4,349	5,404*	0.6	1.4
435 UNITARIAN-UNIV	4	942	1,667	0.2	0.4
443 UN C OF CHRIST	8	3,337	4,146*	0.5	1.1
449 UN METHODIST..	38	22,104	30,881	3.4	7.8
453 UN PRES CH USA	29	24,459	30,392*	3.3	7.7
469 WISC EVAN LUTH	1	186	279	-	0.1
OCEANA	29	2,838	7,080*	39.4	100.0
029 AMER LUTH CH..	1	169	234	1.3	3.3
081 CATHOLIC......	7	0	3,029	16.8	42.8
105 CHRISTIAN REF.	1	206	337	1.9	4.8
123 CH GOD (ANDER)	1	33	60	0.3	0.8

*Total adherents estimated from known number of communicant, confirmed, full members.

—Represents a percent less than 0.1.

Percentages may not total due to rounding.

Table 3. Churches and Church Membership by State, County and Denomination: 1971

County and Denomination	Number of churches	Communicant, confirmed, full members	Total adherents: Number	Percent of total population	Percent of total adherents
165 CH OF NAZARENE	1	17	26	0.1	0.4
193 EPISCOPAL.....	1	122	125	0.7	1.8
201 EVAN COV CH AM	1	17	21*	0.1	0.3
283 LUTH--MO SYNOD	1	256	328	1.8	4.6
371 REF CH IN AM..	1	245	377	2.1	5.3
413 S-D ADVENTISTS	1	29	36*	0.2	0.5
443 UN C OF CHRIST	2	474	591*	3.3	8.3
449 UN METHODIST..	9	1,021	1,565	8.7	22.1
453 UN PRES CH USA	1	124	155*	0.9	2.2
469 WISC EVAN LUTH	1	125	196	1.1	2.8
OGEMAW	17	1,793	5,976*	50.2	100.0
081 CATHOLIC......	4	0	3,704	31.1	62.0
127 CH GOD (CLEVE)	1	22	27*	0.2	0.5
157 CH OF BRETHREN	1	39	48*	0.4	0.8
165 CH OF NAZARENE	1	29	79	0.7	1.3
193 EPISCOPAL.....	2	277	356	3.0	6.0
221 FREE METH C NA	1	58	81	0.7	1.4
226 FRIENDS-USA...	1	96	117*	1.0	2.0
283 LUTH--MO SYNOD	2	474	626	5.3	10.5
449 UN METHODIST..	4	798	938	7.9	15.7
ONTONAGON	25	2,244	5,898*	55.9	100.0
081 CATHOLIC......	6	0	2,615	24.8	44.3
193 EPISCOPAL.....	2	92	263	2.5	4.5
281 LUTH CH AMER..	7	1,066	1,470	13.9	24.9
283 LUTH--MO SYNOD	2	414	599	5.7	10.2
449 UN METHODIST..	6	547	722	6.8	12.2
453 UN PRES CH USA	1	51	63*	0.6	1.1
469 WISC EVAN LUTH	1	74	166	1.6	2.8
OSCEOLA	40	3,664	6,280*	42.3	100.0
019 AMER BAPT CONV	1	48	59*	0.4	0.9
029 AMER LUTH CH..	2	731	1,005	6.8	16.0
081 CATHOLIC......	4	0	1,157	7.8	18.4
123 CH GOD (ANDER)	1	43	173	1.2	2.8
127 CH GOD (CLEVE)	1	11	14*	0.1	0.2
165 CH OF NAZARENE	2	94	222	1.5	3.5
201 EVAN COV CH AM	2	34	42*	0.3	0.7
221 FREE METH C NA	5	101	112	0.8	1.8
281 LUTH CH AMER..	2	273	348	2.3	5.5
283 LUTH--MO SYNOD	1	366	539	3.6	8.6
413 S-D ADVENTISTS	3	82	101*	0.7	1.6
443 UN C OF CHRIST	2	150	185*	1.2	2.9
449 UN METHODIST..	13	1,689	2,271	15.3	36.2
453 UN PRES CH USA	1	42	52*	0.4	0.8
OSCODA	11	1,274	2,107*	44.6	100.0
081 CATHOLIC......	2	0	436	9.2	20.7
123 CH GOD (ANDER)	1	26	75	1.6	3.6
283 LUTH--MO SYNOD	1	253	371	7.9	17.6
285 MENNONITE CH..	2	414	497*	10.5	23.6
287 MENN GEN CONF.	1	147	177*	3.7	8.4
413 S-D ADVENTISTS	1	95	114*	2.4	5.4
443 UN C OF CHRIST	1	43	52*	1.1	2.5
449 UN METHODIST..	1	250	328	6.9	15.6
469 WISC EVAN LUTH	1	46	57	1.2	2.7
OTSEGO	10	1,244	4,996*	47.9	100.0
081 CATHOLIC......	4	0	3,344	32.1	66.9
165 CH OF NAZARENE	1	64	142	1.4	2.8
193 EPISCOPAL.....	1	145	172	1.7	3.4
283 LUTH--MO SYNOD	1	253	371	3.6	7.4
413 S-D ADVENTISTS	1	30	38*	0.4	0.8
443 UN C OF CHRIST	1	221	282*	2.7	5.6
449 UN METHODIST..	1	531	647	6.2	13.0
OTTAWA	140	46,419	86,328*	67.3	100.0
081 CATHOLIC......	8	0	11,718	9.1	13.6
105 CHRISTIAN REF.	50	16,873	29,286	22.8	33.9
127 CH GOD (CLEVE)	3	217	276*	0.2	0.3
165 CH OF NAZARENE	1	194	429	0.3	0.5
193 EPISCOPAL.....	2	775	1,398	1.1	1.6
221 FREE METH C NA	3	63	103	0.1	0.1
283 LUTH--MO SYNOD	10	3,310	5,043	3.9	5.8
353 PLY BRETHREN..	2	110	198	0.2	0.2
371 REF CH IN AM..	43	18,805	29,402	22.9	34.1
403 SALVATION ARMY	2	153	1,076	0.8	1.2
413 S-D ADVENTISTS	4	421	535*	0.4	0.6
419 SO BAPT CONV..	2	144	183*	0.1	0.2
443 UN C OF CHRIST	3	712	904*	0.7	1.0
449 UN METHODIST..	4	2,247	2,736	2.1	3.2
453 UN PRES CH USA	3	2,395	3,041*	2.4	3.5
PRESQUE ISLE	22	3,414	9,501*	74.0	100.0
029 AMER LUTH CH..	4	365	519	4.0	5.5
081 CATHOLIC......	4	0	4,830	37.6	50.8
193 EPISCOPAL.....	1	26	44	0.3	0.5
221 FREE METH C NA	1	9	11	0.1	0.1
283 LUTH--MO SYNOD	6	1,960	2,628	20.5	27.7
403 SALVATION ARMY	1	69	298	2.3	3.1
413 S-D ADVENTISTS	1	88	109*	0.8	1.1
443 UN C OF CHRIST	1	56	69*	0.5	0.7
449 UN METHODIST..	2	390	434	3.4	4.6
453 UN PRES CH USA	1	451	559*	4.4	5.9
ROSCOMMON	17	1,272	2,936*	29.7	100.0
019 AMER BAPT CONV	3	167	196*	2.0	6.7
081 CATHOLIC......	5	0	1,241	12.5	42.3
165 CH OF NAZARENE	1	13	57	0.6	1.9
175 CONG CR CH....	1	234	275*	2.8	9.4
193 EPISCOPAL.....	2	125	264	2.7	9.0
221 FREE METH C NA	1	16	20	0.2	0.7
281 LUTH CH AMER..	1	108	140	1.4	4.8
283 LUTH--MO SYNOD	1	339	410	4.1	14.0
413 S-D ADVENTISTS	1	52	61*	0.6	2.1
449 UN METHODIST..	1	218	272	2.7	9.3
SAGINAW	141	46,251	124,195*	56.5	100.0
019 AMER BAPT CONV	6	1,295	1,653*	0.8	1.3
029 AMER LUTH CH..	10	6,474	9,297	4.2	7.5
059 BAPT MISS ASSN	1	42	54*	-	-
075 BRETHREN IN CR	1	15	19*	-	-
081 CATHOLIC......	33	0	59,903	27.3	48.2
093 CR CH (DISC)..	2	1,167	1,490*	0.7	1.2
097 CR C AND C CR.	1	97	124*	0.1	0.1
105 CHRISTIAN REF.	1	78	152	0.1	0.1
123 CH GOD (ANDER)	1	143	273	0.1	0.2
127 CH GOD (CLEVE)	2	129	165*	0.1	0.1
165 CH OF NAZARENE	6	610	1,117	0.5	0.9
175 CONG CR CH....	1	198	253*	0.1	0.2
193 EPISCOPAL.....	6	1,851	2,869	1.3	2.3
221 FREE METH C NA	2	76	115	0.1	0.1
281 LUTH CH AMER..	1	294	436	0.2	0.4
283 LUTH--MO SYNOD	13	13,963	19,532	8.9	15.7
285 MENNONITE CH..	2	83	106*	-	0.1
353 PLY BRETHREN..	2	46	60	-	-
403 SALVATION ARMY	1	89	464	0.2	0.4
413 S-D ADVENTISTS	4	443	565*	0.3	0.5
419 SO BAPT CONV..	1	109	139*	0.1	0.1
435 UNITARIAN-UNIV	1	28	49	-	-
443 UN C OF CHRIST	4	1,833	2,340*	1.1	1.9
449 UN METHODIST..	20	7,763	10,321	4.7	8.3
453 UN PRES CH USA	7	4,623	5,901*	2.7	4.8
469 WISC EVAN LUTH	12	4,802	6,798	3.1	5.5
ST CLAIR	94	19,051	64,589*	53.7	100.0
019 AMER BAPT CONV	4	848	1,061*	0.9	1.6
029 AMER LUTH CH..	6	2,299	3,079	2.6	4.8
081 CATHOLIC......	18	0	36,300	30.2	56.2
097 CR C AND C CR.	4	446	558*	0.5	0.9
127 CH GOD (CLEVE)	1	127	159*	0.1	0.2
165 CH OF NAZARENE	3	360	1,059	0.9	1.6
175 CONG CR CH....	2	165	206*	0.2	0.3
193 EPISCOPAL.....	7	2,306	3,915	3.3	6.1
221 FREE METH C NA	4	170	221	0.2	0.3
283 LUTH--MO SYNOD	9	3,486	5,356	4.5	8.3
403 SALVATION ARMY	1	274	2,083	1.7	3.2
413 S-D ADVENTISTS	2	129	161*	0.1	0.2
419 SO BAPT CONV..	1	29	36*	-	0.1
443 UN C OF CHRIST	3	1,691	2,116*	1.8	3.3
449 UN METHODIST..	24	4,991	6,058	5.0	9.4
453 UN PRES CH USA	4	1,430	1,789*	1.5	2.8
469 WISC EVAN LUTH	1	300	432	0.4	0.7
ST JOSEPH	58	10,467	19,905*	42.0	100.0
019 AMER BAPT CONV	2	589	728*	1.5	3.7
081 CATHOLIC......	6	0	4,701	9.9	23.6
097 CR C AND C CR.	1	200	247*	0.5	1.2
123 CH GOD (ANDER)	3	186	412	0.9	2.1
127 CH GOD (CLEVE)	2	32	40*	0.1	0.2
157 CH OF BRETHREN	1	70	87*	0.2	0.4
165 CH OF NAZARENE	3	343	811	1.7	4.1
193 EPISCOPAL.....	2	489	890	1.9	4.5
281 LUTH CH AMER..	3	935	1,285	2.7	6.5
283 LUTH--MO SYNOD	6	1,589	2,430	5.1	12.2
285 MENNONITE CH..	5	573	709*	1.5	3.6
353 PLY BRETHREN..	1	100	200	0.4	1.0
403 SALVATION ARMY	1	54	291	0.6	1.5
413 S-D ADVENTISTS	3	139	172*	0.4	0.9
419 SO BAPT CONV..	1	31	38*	0.1	0.2
443 UN C OF CHRIST	1	80	99*	0.2	0.5
449 UN METHODIST..	13	3,232	4,482	9.5	22.5
453 UN PRES CH USA	3	1,660	2,053*	4.3	10.3
469 WISC EVAN LUTH	1	165	230	0.5	1.2
SANILAC	66	6,244	14,560*	41.7	100.0
019 AMER BAPT CONV	3	282	351*	1.0	2.4
075 BRETHREN IN CR	1	30	37*	0.1	0.3
081 CATHOLIC......	9	0	6,208	17.8	42.6
127 CH GOD (CLEVE)	1	60	75*	0.2	0.5
165 CH OF NAZARENE	1	27	69	0.2	0.5
193 EPISCOPAL.....	3	262	475	1.4	3.3
221 FREE METH C NA	6	132	183	0.5	1.3
281 LUTH CH AMER..	3	267	394	1.1	2.7
283 LUTH--MO SYNOD	5	1,299	1,789	5.1	12.3
353 PLY BRETHREN..	1	20	30	0.1	0.2
413 S-D ADVENTISTS	1	20	25*	0.1	0.2
443 UN C OF CHRIST	1	61	76*	0.2	0.5
449 UN METHODIST..	25	2,663	3,451	9.9	23.7
453 UN PRES CH USA	6	1,121	1,397*	4.0	9.6
SCHOOLCRAFT	16	1,514	4,795*	58.3	100.0
019 AMER BAPT CONV	1	332	406*	4.9	8.5
081 CATHOLIC......	2	0	2,800	34.0	58.4
193 EPISCOPAL.....	1	42	105	1.3	2.2
221 FREE METH C NA	1	10	13	0.2	0.3

*Total adherents estimated from known number of communicant, confirmed, full members.

—Represents a percent less than 0.1.

Percentages may not total due to rounding.

Table 3. Churches and Church Membership by State, County and Denomination: 1971

County and Denomination	Number of churches	Communicant, confirmed, full members	Total adherents: Number	Total adherents: Percent of total population	Total adherents: Percent of total adherents
281 LUTH CH AMER..	1	510	736	8.9	15.3
283 LUTH--MO SYNOD	1	74	100	1.2	2.1
285 MENNONITE CH..	4	85	104*	1.3	2.2
413 S-D ADVENTISTS	1	18	22*	0.3	0.5
443 UN C OF CHRIST	1	71	87*	1.1	1.8
449 UN METHODIST..	2	187	196	2.4	4.1
453 UN PRES CH USA	1	185	226*	2.7	4.7
SHIAWASSEE	65	11,865	27,257*	43.2	100.0
019 AMER BAPT CONV	2	630	805*	1.3	3.0
029 AMER LUTH CH..	1	192	324	0.5	1.2
075 BRETHREN IN CR	1	9	11*	-	-
081 CATHOLIC......	5	0	9,797	15.5	35.9
097 CR C AND C CR.	4	1,212	1,549*	2.5	5.7
123 CH GOD (ANDER)	2	154	319	0.5	1.2
127 CH GOD (CLEVE)	1	120	153*	0.2	0.6
165 CH OF NAZARENE	6	491	1,207	1.9	4.4
175 CONG CR CH....	2	426	544*	0.9	2.0
193 EPISCOPAL.....	3	559	1,123	1.8	4.1
221 FREE METH C NA	4	265	350	0.6	1.3
353 PLY BRETHREN..	1	26	115	0.2	0.4
403 SALVATION ARMY	1	86	916	1.5	3.4
413 S-D ADVENTISTS	3	205	262*	0.4	1.0
419 SO BAPT CONV..	1	150	192*	0.3	0.7
443 UN C OF CHRIST	3	1,212	1,549*	2.5	5.7
449 UN METHODIST..	23	4,752	6,070	9.6	22.3
469 WISC EVAN LUTH	2	1,376	1,971	3.1	7.2
TUSCOLA	70	11,751	23,605*	48.6	100.0
019 AMER BAPT CONV	2	270	342*	0.7	1.4
029 AMER LUTH CH..	2	256	387	0.8	1.6
081 CATHOLIC......	10	0	7,241	14.9	30.7
097 CR C AND C CR.	2	201	255*	0.5	1.1
123 CH GOD (ANDER)	1	27	64	0.1	0.3
127 CH GOD (CLEVE)	1	51	65*	0.1	0.3
165 CH OF NAZARENE	8	438	918	1.9	3.9
221 FREE METH C NA	2	61	97	0.2	0.4
283 LUTH--MO SYNOD	7	4,048	5,897	12.1	25.0
285 MENNONITE CH..	1	25	32*	0.1	0.1
293 MORAV CH-NORTH	1	371	471	1.0	2.0
353 PLY BRETHREN..	1	9	50	0.1	0.2
413 S-D ADVENTISTS	1	87	110*	0.2	0.5
449 UN METHODIST..	21	3,957	5,080	10.5	21.5
453 UN PRES CH USA	8	1,473	1,868*	3.8	7.9
469 WISC EVAN LUTH	2	477	728	1.5	3.1
VAN BUREN	61	8,247	17,541*	31.2	100.0
019 AMER BAPT CONV	3	229	285*	0.5	1.6
059 BAPT MISS ASSN	1	52	65*	0.1	0.4
081 CATHOLIC......	7	0	6,533	11.6	37.2
093 CR CH (DISC)..	1	85	106*	0.2	0.6
097 CR C AND C CR.	2	425	529*	0.9	3.0
105 CHRISTIAN REF.	1	62	120	0.2	0.7
123 CH GOD (ANDER)	2	92	233	0.4	1.3
127 CH GOD (CLEVE)	3	95	118*	0.2	0.7
175 CONG CR CH....	1	100	124*	0.2	0.7
193 EPISCOPAL.....	2	394	668	1.2	3.8
221 FREE METH C NA	2	53	65	0.1	0.4
281 LUTH CH AMER..	1	436	613	1.1	3.5
283 LUTH--MO SYNOD	1	431	558	1.0	3.2
371 REF CH IN AM..	2	311	488	0.9	2.8
413 S-D ADVENTISTS	9	714	888*	1.6	5.1
419 SO BAPT CONV..	1	123	153*	0.3	0.9
443 UN C OF CHRIST	2	639	795*	1.4	4.5
449 UN METHODIST..	14	2,529	3,287	5.9	18.7
453 UN PRES CH USA	3	820	1,020*	1.8	5.8
469 WISC EVAN LUTH	3	657	893	1.6	5.1
WASHTENAW	125	39,459	79,841*	34.1	100.0
019 AMER BAPT CONV	7	2,357	2,842*	1.2	3.6
029 AMER LUTH CH..	6	3,900	5,489	2.3	6.9
081 CATHOLIC......	13	0	26,970	11.5	33.8
093 CR CH (DISC)..	1	182	219*	0.1	0.3
097 CR C AND C CR.	1	194	234*	0.1	0.3
105 CHRISTIAN REF.	1	175	347	0.1	0.4
123 CH GOD (ANDER)	3	191	513	0.2	0.6
127 CH GOD (CLEVE)	3	184	222*	0.1	0.3
165 CH OF NAZARENE	4	246	502	0.2	0.6
175 CONG CR CH....	1	855	1,031*	0.4	1.3
193 EPISCOPAL.....	7	3,032	4,722	2.0	5.9
221 FREE METH C NA	3	248	334	0.1	0.4
226 FRIENDS-USA...	2	332	400*	0.2	0.5
281 LUTH CH AMER..	4	1,167	1,880	0.8	2.4
283 LUTH--MO SYNOD	9	2,658	3,921	1.7	4.9
285 MENNONITE CH..	1	10	12*	-	-
287 MENN GEN CONF.	1	13	16*	-	-
353 PLY BRETHREN..	1	80	150	0.1	0.2
371 REF CH IN AM..	1	168	216	0.1	0.3
403 SALVATION ARMY	2	104	478	0.2	0.6
413 S-D ADVENTISTS	2	230	277*	0.1	0.3
419 SO BAPT CONV..	8	1,941	2,340*	1.0	2.9
435 UNITARIAN-UNIV	2	545	855	0.4	1.1
443 UN C OF CHRIST	11	5,610	6,764*	2.9	8.5
449 UN METHODIST..	18	9,469	12,111	5.2	15.2
453 UN PRES CH USA	7	4,023	4,850*	2.1	6.1
469 WISC EVAN LUTH	6	1,545	2,146	0.9	2.7
WAYNE	800	245,654	1,189,163*	44.6	100.0
019 AMER BAPT CONV	35	12,260	15,016*	0.6	1.3
029 AMER LUTH CH..	30	13,905	19,378	0.7	1.6

County and Denomination	Number of churches	Communicant, confirmed, full members	Total adherents: Number	Total adherents: Percent of total population	Total adherents: Percent of total adherents
081 CATHOLIC......	224	0	854,619	32.0	71.9
093 CR CH (DISC)..	7	2,208	2,704*	0.1	0.2
097 CR C AND C CR.	10	1,258	1,541*	0.1	0.1
105 CHRISTIAN REF.	3	590	1,000	-	0.1
123 CH GOD (ANDER)	16	2,077	3,856	0.1	0.3
127 CH GOD (CLEVE)	22	2,754	3,373*	0.1	0.3
157 CH OF BRETHREN	2	380	465*	-	-
165 CH OF NAZARENE	15	2,054	3,900	0.1	0.3
175 CONG CR CH....	4	2,101	2,573*	0.1	0.2
185 CUMBER PRESB..	1	109	134*	-	-
193 EPISCOPAL.....	47	21,523	29,060	1.1	2.4
201 EVAN COV CH AM	2	695	851*	-	0.1
221 FREE METH C NA	8	1,191	1,603	0.1	0.1
226 FRIENDS-USA...	2	132	162*	-	-
281 LUTH CH AMER..	37	13,599	19,145	0.7	1.6
283 LUTH--MO SYNOD	74	49,443	72,887	2.7	6.1
285 MENNONITE CH..	1	23	28*	-	-
293 MORAV CH-NORTH	1	133	224	-	-
313 NO AM BAPT GC.	2	1,513	1,853*	0.1	0.2
315 NO AM OLD RC..	2	194	238*	-	-
349 PENT HOLINESS.	2	90	110*	-	-
353 PLY BRETHREN..	16	1,219	1,876	0.1	0.2
371 REF CH IN AM..	12	2,147	3,021	0.1	0.3
403 SALVATION ARMY	11	1,249	6,009	0.2	0.5
413 S-D ADVENTISTS	14	4,190	5,132*	0.2	0.4
419 SO BAPT CONV..	33	9,371	11,477*	0.4	1.0
435 UNITARIAN-UNIV	3	1,077	1,243	-	0.1
443 UN C OF CHRIST	32	14,553	17,824*	0.7	1.5
449 UN METHODIST..	58	33,048	44,865	1.7	3.8
453 UN PRES CH USA	61	46,175	56,554*	2.1	4.8
469 WISC EVAN LUTH	13	4,393	6,442	0.2	0.5
WEXFORD	38	4,444	8,002*	40.6	100.0
019 AMER BAPT CONV	2	441	550*	2.8	6.9
081 CATHOLIC......	2	0	1,879	9.5	23.5
093 CR CH (DISC)..	4	230	287*	1.5	3.6
097 CR C AND C CR.	3	12	15*	0.1	0.2
105 CHRISTIAN REF.	1	141	245	1.2	3.1
123 CH GOD (ANDER)	2	77	202	1.0	2.5
127 CH GOD (CLEVE)	1	49	61*	0.3	0.8
165 CH OF NAZARENE	2	111	250	1.3	3.1
175 CONG CR CH....	1	50	62*	0.3	0.8
193 EPISCOPAL.....	1	119	133	0.7	1.7
201 EVAN COV CH AM	1	160	199*	1.0	2.5
221 FREE METH C NA	5	89	101	0.5	1.3
281 LUTH CH AMER..	2	662	859	4.4	10.7
283 LUTH--MO SYNOD	1	253	331	1.7	4.1
403 SALVATION ARMY	1	65	306	1.6	3.8
413 S-D ADVENTISTS	3	164	204*	1.0	2.5
443 UN C OF CHRIST	1	350	436*	2.2	5.4
449 UN METHODIST..	4	855	1,114	5.6	13.9
453 UN PRES CH USA	1	616	768*	3.9	9.6
CO DATA NOT AVAIL	648	18,247	34,938*	N/A	N/A
151 L-D SAINTS....	0	0	13,434	N/A	N/A
193 EPISCOPAL.....	2	217	304	N/A	N/A
223 FREE WILL BAPT	453	5,641	7,005*	N/A	N/A
231 GENERAL BAPT..	44	3,410	4,235*	N/A	N/A
467 WESLEYAN......	149	8,979	9,960	N/A	N/A

MINNESOTA

County and Denomination	Number of churches	Communicant, confirmed, full members	Total adherents: Number	Total adherents: Percent of total population	Total adherents: Percent of total adherents
THE STATE.....	4,038	1,095,566	2,522,913*	66.3	100.0
AITKIN	32	3,123	5,289*	46.4	100.0
029 AMER LUTH CH..	2	210	140	1.2	2.6
081 CATHOLIC......	5	0	1,265	11.1	23.9
097 CR C AND C CR.	1	25	30*	0.3	0.6
193 EPISCOPAL.....	1	44	57	0.5	1.1
281 LUTH CH AMER..	7	1,018	1,421	12.5	26.9
283 LUTH--MO SYNOD	4	581	824	7.2	15.6
413 S-D ADVENTISTS	1	54	64*	0.6	1.2
443 UN C OF CHRIST	1	148	175*	1.5	3.3
449 UN METHODIST..	7	884	1,125	9.9	21.3
453 UN PRES CH USA	3	159	188*	1.6	3.6
ANOKA	51	26,702	72,286*	46.8	100.0
029 AMER LUTH CH..	7	8,269	13,819	8.9	19.1
081 CATHOLIC......	8	0	29,399	19.0	40.7
093 CR CH (DISC)..	1	185	252*	0.2	0.3
097 CR C AND C CR.	2	122	166*	0.1	0.2
193 EPISCOPAL.....	1	214	392	0.3	0.5
201 EVAN COV CH AM	2	193	263*	0.2	0.4
281 LUTH CH AMER..	7	7,717	12,255	7.9	17.0
283 LUTH--MO SYNOD	8	4,852	7,965	5.2	11.0
413 S-D ADVENTISTS	1	97	132*	0.1	0.2
419 SO BAPT CONV..	2	161	219*	0.1	0.3
435 UNITARIAN-UNIV	1	61	61	-	0.1
443 UN C OF CHRIST	1	608	829*	0.5	1.1
449 UN METHODIST..	9	4,063	6,236	4.0	8.6
469 WISC EVAN LUTH	1	160	298	0.2	0.4

*Total adherents estimated from known number of communicant, confirmed, full members.

—Represents a percent less than 0.1.

Percentages may not total due to rounding.

Table 3. Churches and Church Membership by State, County and Denomination: 1971

County and Denomination	Number of churches	Communicant, confirmed, full members	Total adherents		
			Number	Percent of total population	Percent of total adherents
BECKER	47	8,771	17,486*	71.7	100.0
029 AMER LUTH CH..	11	3,936	5,525	22.7	31.6
081 CATHOLIC......	10	0	5,140	21.1	29.4
165 CH OF NAZARENE	1	34	90	0.4	0.5
193 EPISCOPAL.....	3	292	597	2.4	3.4
281 LUTH CH AMER..	6	1,150	1,505	6.2	8.6
283 LUTH--MO SYNOD	10	2,558	3,575	14.7	20.4
285 MENNONITE CH..	2	71	88*	0.4	0.5
413 S-D ADVENTISTS	1	136	168*	0.7	1.0
443 UN C OF CHRIST	1	58	72*	0.3	0.4
449 UN METHODIST..	2	536	726	3.0	4.2
BELTRAMI	33	6,174	13,166*	49.9	100.0
029 AMER LUTH CH..	11	3,323	5,144	19.5	39.1
081 CATHOLIC......	7	0	4,299	16.3	32.7
193 EPISCOPAL.....	1	133	177	0.7	1.3
201 EVAN COV CH AM	1	121	147*	0.6	1.1
221 FREE METH C NA	1	37	41	0.2	0.3
281 LUTH CH AMER..	3	374	486	1.8	3.7
283 LUTH--MO SYNOD	3	583	880	3.3	6.7
285 MENNONITE CH..	1	22	27*	0.1	0.2
413 S-D ADVENTISTS	1	103	125*	0.5	0.9
449 UN METHODIST..	1	811	1,028	3.9	7.8
453 UN PRES CH USA	3	667	812*	3.1	6.2
BENTON	23	3,502	18,168*	87.2	100.0
029 AMER LUTH CH..	1	246	322	1.5	1.8
081 CATHOLIC......	9	0	13,205	63.4	72.7
093 CR CH (DISC)..	1	38	49*	0.2	0.3
193 EPISCOPAL.....	1	74	292	1.4	1.6
201 EVAN COV CH AM	1	68	88*	0.4	0.5
281 LUTH CH AMER..	3	1,078	1,534	7.4	8.4
283 LUTH--MO SYNOD	3	1,635	2,213	10.6	12.2
443 UN C OF CHRIST	1	30	39*	0.2	0.2
449 UN METHODIST..	1	118	147	0.7	0.8
453 UN PRES CH USA	2	215	279*	1.3	1.5
BIG STONE	25	4,482	8,070*	101.6#	100.0
029 AMER LUTH CH..	4	1,295	1,719	21.6	21.3
081 CATHOLIC......	4	0	2,157	27.2	26.7
281 LUTH CH AMER..	2	632	813	10.2	10.1
283 LUTH--MO SYNOD	4	1,089	1,527	19.2	18.9
413 S-D ADVENTISTS	1	29	35*	0.4	0.4
443 UN C OF CHRIST	2	267	324*	4.1	4.0
449 UN METHODIST..	5	780	959	12.1	11.9
469 WISC EVAN LUTH	3	390	536	6.7	6.6
BLUE EARTH	64	17,939	36,342*	69.5	100.0
019 AMER BAPT CONV	2	731	870*	1.7	2.4
029 AMER LUTH CH..	10	5,201	7,329	14.0	20.2
081 CATHOLIC......	9	0	12,179	23.3	33.5
093 CR CH (DISC)..	2	314	374*	0.7	1.0
097 CR C AND C CR.	1	130	155*	0.3	0.4
123 CH GOD (ANDER)	1	35	85	0.2	0.2
193 EPISCOPAL.....	1	365	427	0.8	1.2
201 EVAN COV CH AM	1	192	228*	0.4	0.6
281 LUTH CH AMER..	2	1,118	1,616	3.1	4.4
283 LUTH--MO SYNOD	12	3,895	5,253	10.0	14.5
403 SALVATION ARMY	1	55	293	0.6	0.8
413 S-D ADVENTISTS	1	110	131*	0.3	0.4
435 UNITARIAN-UNIV	1	24	26	-	0.1
443 UN C OF CHRIST	2	644	766*	1.5	2.1
449 UN METHODIST..	9	2,422	3,207	6.1	8.8
453 UN PRES CH USA	6	1,916	2,280*	4.4	6.3
469 WISC EVAN LUTH	3	787	1,123	2.1	3.1
BROWN	35	9,937	26,829*	92.9	100.0
029 AMER LUTH CH..	11	3,867	5,388	18.7	20.1
081 CATHOLIC......	7	0	13,384	46.3	49.9
193 EPISCOPAL.....	1	67	92	0.3	0.3
197 EVAN CH OF NA.	1	25	31*	0.1	0.1
281 LUTH CH AMER..	1	282	364	1.3	1.4
283 LUTH--MO SYNOD	2	649	934	3.2	3.5
435 UNITARIAN-UNIV	1	219	254	0.9	0.9
443 UN C OF CHRIST	3	823	1,017*	3.5	3.8
449 UN METHODIST..	5	1,404	1,769	6.1	6.6
469 WISC EVAN LUTH	3	2,601	3,596	12.4	13.4
CARLTON	41	6,590	16,737*	59.6	100.0
029 AMER LUTH CH..	5	2,051	2,911	10.4	17.4
081 CATHOLIC......	10	0	7,297	26.0	43.6
193 EPISCOPAL.....	1	159	283	1.0	1.7
201 EVAN COV CH AM	3	183	227*	0.8	1.4
281 LUTH CH AMER..	6	1,664	2,453	8.7	14.7
283 LUTH--MO SYNOD	7	1,344	2,097	7.5	12.5
413 S-D ADVENTISTS	2	16	20*	0.1	0.1
449 UN METHODIST..	3	308	376	1.3	2.2
453 UN PRES CH USA	4	865	1,073*	3.8	6.4
CARVER	39	10,594	22,711*	80.2	100.0
029 AMER LUTH CH..	1	209	374	1.3	1.6
081 CATHOLIC......	9	0	8,314	29.4	36.6
281 LUTH CH AMER..	4	1,203	1,687	6.0	7.4
283 LUTH--MO SYNOD	12	6,678	9,124	32.2	40.2
293 MORAV CH-NORTH	3	700	888	3.1	3.9
443 UN C OF CHRIST	5	1,121	1,433*	5.1	6.3
449 UN METHODIST..	2	175	242	0.9	1.1
453 UN PRES CH USA	3	508	649*	2.3	2.9
CASS	36	3,247	6,903*	39.8	100.0
029 AMER LUTH CH..	11	1,254	1,766	10.2	25.6
081 CATHOLIC......	8	0	2,398	13.8	34.7
165 CH OF NAZARENE	1	76	165	1.0	2.4
193 EPISCOPAL.....	1	297	470	2.7	6.8
281 LUTH CH AMER..	1	154	241	1.4	3.5
283 LUTH--MO SYNOD	5	477	648	3.7	9.4
285 MENNONITE CH..	2	38	45*	0.3	0.7
413 S-D ADVENTISTS	1	32	38*	0.2	0.6
443 UN C OF CHRIST	4	574	686*	4.0	9.9
449 UN METHODIST..	2	345	446	2.6	6.5
CHIPPEWA	30	8,622	12,741*	84.3	100.0
029 AMER LUTH CH..	13	5,262	6,635	43.9	52.1
081 CATHOLIC......	2	0	1,315	8.7	10.3
105 CHRISTIAN REF.	1	246	466	3.1	3.7
197 EVAN CH OF NA.	2	28	34*	0.2	0.3
281 LUTH CH AMER..	1	305	431	2.9	3.4
283 LUTH--MO SYNOD	4	877	1,135	7.5	8.9
371 REF CH IN AM..	2	814	1,281	8.5	10.1
443 UN C OF CHRIST	1	249	302*	2.0	2.4
449 UN METHODIST..	3	750	1,032	6.8	8.1
453 UN PRES CH USA	1	91	110*	0.7	0.9
CHISAGO	26	7,064	12,167*	69.6	100.0
081 CATHOLIC......	5	0	2,270	13.0	18.7
123 CH GOD (ANDER)	1	28	28	0.2	0.2
201 EVAN COV CH AM	2	58	72*	0.4	0.6
281 LUTH CH AMER..	12	5,610	7,865	45.0	64.6
283 LUTH--MO SYNOD	2	429	633	3.6	5.2
449 UN METHODIST..	4	939	1,299	7.4	10.7
CLAY	51	17,346	30,446*	65.4	100.0
029 AMER LUTH CH..	24	12,363	17,368	37.3	57.0
081 CATHOLIC......	7	0	6,619	14.2	21.7
097 CR C AND C CR.	1	25	30*	0.1	0.1
165 CH OF NAZARENE	1	29	71	0.2	0.2
193 EPISCOPAL.....	1	176	200	0.4	0.7
201 EVAN COV CH AM	1	15	18*	-	0.1
281 LUTH CH AMER..	1	642	801	1.7	2.6
283 LUTH--MO SYNOD	4	1,452	2,020	4.3	6.6
443 UN C OF CHRIST	4	1,227	1,492*	3.2	4.9
449 UN METHODIST..	2	707	935	2.0	3.1
453 UN PRES CH USA	4	647	787*	1.7	2.6
469 WISC EVAN LUTH	1	63	105	0.2	0.3
CLEARWATER	14	2,204	3,278	40.9	100.0
029 AMER LUTH CH..	10	2,039	2,903	36.2	88.6
081 CATHOLIC......	3	0	140	1.7	4.3
283 LUTH--MO SYNOD	1	165	235	2.9	7.2
COOK	10	943	2,057*	60.1	100.0
029 AMER LUTH CH..	4	643	919	26.8	44.7
081 CATHOLIC......	4	0	774	22.6	37.6
413 S-D ADVENTISTS	1	9	11*	0.3	0.5
443 UN C OF CHRIST	1	291	353*	10.3	17.2
COTTONWOOD	30	8,533	12,677*	85.2	100.0
029 AMER LUTH CH..	10	3,688	5,137	34.5	40.5
081 CATHOLIC......	3	0	1,307	8.8	10.3
105 CHRISTIAN REF.	1	52	71	0.5	0.6
193 EPISCOPAL.....	1	89	122	0.8	1.0
211 EV MENN BRETH.	1	273	331*	2.2	2.6
283 LUTH--MO SYNOD	2	1,234	1,768	11.9	13.9
287 MENN GEN CONF.	4	1,330	1,614*	10.8	12.7
449 UN METHODIST..	5	1,241	1,567	10.5	12.4
453 UN PRES CH USA	3	626	760*	5.1	6.0
CROW WING	41	9,715	20,849*	59.9	100.0
029 AMER LUTH CH..	4	2,766	4,038	11.6	19.4
081 CATHOLIC......	8	0	6,811	19.6	32.7
097 CR C AND C CR.	1	70	85*	0.2	0.4
127 CH GOD (CLEVE)	1	11	13*	-	0.1
165 CH OF NAZARENE	2	135	426	1.2	2.0
193 EPISCOPAL.....	1	238	304	0.9	1.5
201 EVAN COV CH AM	1	49	60*	0.2	0.3
281 LUTH CH AMER..	6	2,196	3,214	9.2	15.4
283 LUTH--MO SYNOD	4	1,401	2,131	6.1	10.2
403 SALVATION ARMY	1	105	344	1.0	1.6
413 S-D ADVENTISTS	1	163	198*	0.6	0.9
443 UN C OF CHRIST	1	339	412*	1.2	2.0
449 UN METHODIST..	6	1,255	1,597	4.6	7.7
453 UN PRES CH USA	3	956	1,162*	3.3	5.6
469 WISC EVAN LUTH	1	31	54	0.2	0.3
DAKOTA	83	29,725	90,985*	65.1	100.0
019 AMER BAPT CONV	2	270	360*	0.3	0.4
029 AMER LUTH CH..	13	9,373	15,144	10.8	16.6
081 CATHOLIC......	20	0	44,582	31.9	49.0
105 CHRISTIAN REF.	1	71	137	0.1	0.2
193 EPISCOPAL.....	5	727	1,176	0.8	1.3
281 LUTH CH AMER..	7	5,337	8,652	6.2	9.5
283 LUTH--MO SYNOD	9	4,119	6,531	4.7	7.2
313 NO AM BAPT GC.	2	394	525*	0.4	0.6

*Total adherents estimated from known number of communicant, confirmed, full members.

—Represents a percent less than 0.1.

Percentages may not total due to rounding.

#See Introduction for explanation of why total adherents reported by churches exceed the 1970 population figure.

Table 3. Churches and Church Membership by State, County and Denomination: 1971

County and Denomination	Number of churches	Communicant, confirmed, full members	Total adherents: Number	Total adherents: Percent of total population	Total adherents: Percent of total adherents
419 SO BAPT CONV..	2	248	331*	0.2	0.4
443 UN C OF CHRIST	2	661	881*	0.6	1.0
449 UN METHODIST..	11	3,778	5,847	4.2	6.4
453 UN PRES CH USA	4	1,758	2,343*	1.7	2.6
469 WISC EVAN LUTH	5	2,989	4,476	3.2	4.9
DODGE	28	5,460	9,028*	69.2	100.0
029 AMER LUTH CH..	6	2,687	3,758	28.8	41.6
081 CATHOLIC......	6	0	1,563	12.0	17.3
097 CR C AND C CR.	2	183	229*	1.8	2.5
283 LUTH--MO SYNOD	3	565	790	6.1	8.8
413 S-D ADVENTISTS	1	55	69*	0.5	0.8
415 S-D BAPTIST GC	1	134	167*	1.3	1.8
443 UN C OF CHRIST	2	351	438*	3.4	4.9
449 UN METHODIST..	4	848	1,219	9.4	13.5
453 UN PRES CH USA	3	637	795*	6.1	8.8
DOUGLAS	48	10,118	19,166*	83.7	100.0
029 AMER LUTH CH..	12	4,155	5,662	24.7	29.5
081 CATHOLIC......	6	0	5,544	24.2	28.9
097 CR C AND C CR.	1	50	60*	0.3	0.3
193 EPISCOPAL.....	1	117	192	0.8	1.0
201 EVAN COV CH AM	4	307	370*	1.6	1.9
221 FREE METH C NA	2	51	70	0.3	0.4
281 LUTH CH AMER..	7	2,063	2,761	12.1	14.4
283 LUTH--MO SYNOD	8	1,911	2,679	11.7	14.0
353 PLY BRETHREN..	1	30	40	0.2	0.2
443 UN C OF CHRIST	1	516	622*	2.7	3.2
449 UN METHODIST..	2	554	690	3.0	3.6
453 UN PRES CH USA	2	297	358*	1.6	1.9
469 WISC EVAN LUTH	1	67	118	0.5	0.6
FARIBAULT	46	11,086	20,171*	96.5	100.0
019 AMER BAPT CONV	1	299	360*	1.7	1.8
029 AMER LUTH CH..	13	4,343	5,945	28.5	29.5
081 CATHOLIC......	7	0	5,606	26.8	27.8
193 EPISCOPAL.....	1	18	22	0.1	0.1
281 LUTH CH AMER..	2	327	441	2.1	2.2
283 LUTH--MO SYNOD	7	2,163	2,871	13.7	14.2
443 UN C OF CHRIST	2	508	611*	2.9	3.0
449 UN METHODIST..	11	2,921	3,705	17.7	18.4
453 UN PRES CH USA	2	507	610*	2.9	3.0
FILLMORE	58	12,649	20,366*	92.9	100.0
029 AMER LUTH CH..	25	8,069	11,083	50.6	54.4
081 CATHOLIC......	10	0	3,256	14.9	16.0
157 CH OF BRETHREN	1	152	184*	0.8	0.9
193 EPISCOPAL.....	2	115	141	0.6	0.7
221 FREE METH C NA	1	26	32	0.1	0.2
283 LUTH--MO SYNOD	4	1,260	1,791	8.2	8.8
371 REF CH IN AM..	1	393	505	2.3	2.5
449 UN METHODIST..	11	2,285	2,951	13.5	14.5
453 UN PRES CH USA	3	349	423*	1.9	2.1
FREEBORN	50	19,333	30,995*	81.4	100.0
019 AMER BAPT CONV	3	1,320	1,614*	4.2	5.2
029 AMER LUTH CH..	24	12,015	16,465	43.3	53.1
081 CATHOLIC......	4	0	4,434	11.6	14.3
097 CR C AND C CR.	1	137	168*	0.4	0.5
105 CHRISTIAN REF.	1	131	256	0.7	0.8
193 EPISCOPAL.....	1	202	294	0.8	0.9
221 FREE METH C NA	1	13	13	-	-
281 LUTH CH AMER..	2	1,548	2,241	5.9	7.2
283 LUTH--MO SYNOD	2	528	852	2.2	2.7
285 MENNONITE CH..	1	6	7*	-	-
371 REF CH IN AM..	1	298	455	1.2	1.5
403 SALVATION ARMY	1	78	260	0.7	0.8
413 S-D ADVENTISTS	1	67	82*	0.2	0.3
443 UN C OF CHRIST	1	310	379*	1.0	1.2
449 UN METHODIST..	5	1,454	1,976	5.2	6.4
453 UN PRES CH USA	1	1,226	1,499*	3.9	4.8
GOODHUE	58	18,825	30,977*	89.1	100.0
029 AMER LUTH CH..	16	6,824	9,303	26.8	30.0
081 CATHOLIC......	8	0	5,775	16.6	18.6
097 CR C AND C CR.	2	59	72*	0.2	0.2
193 EPISCOPAL.....	2	668	887	2.6	2.9
201 EVAN COV CH AM	1	140	171*	0.5	0.6
281 LUTH CH AMER..	9	5,221	7,179	20.7	23.2
283 LUTH--MO SYNOD	3	891	1,288	3.7	4.2
413 S-D ADVENTISTS	1	38	46*	0.1	0.1
443 UN C OF CHRIST	2	432	528*	1.5	1.7
449 UN METHODIST..	4	1,662	1,981	5.7	6.4
453 UN PRES CH USA	1	322	393*	1.1	1.3
469 WISC EVAN LUTH	9	2,568	3,354	9.6	10.8
GRANT	28	4,740	6,873*	92.1	100.0
029 AMER LUTH CH..	10	2,121	2,827	37.9	41.1
081 CATHOLIC......	2	0	654	8.8	9.5
127 CH GOD (CLEVE)	1	9	11*	0.1	0.2
201 EVAN COV CH AM	1	15	18*	0.2	0.3
281 LUTH CH AMER..	5	1,158	1,505	20.2	21.9
283 LUTH--MO SYNOD	3	548	720	9.6	10.5
371 REF CH IN AM..	1	89	117	1.6	1.7
449 UN METHODIST..	2	398	545	7.3	7.9
453 UN PRES CH USA	3	402	476*	6.4	6.9
HENNEPIN	438	234,563	516,631*	53.8	100.0
019 AMER BAPT CONV	13	3,730	4,562*	0.5	0.9
029 AMER LUTH CH..	58	54,470	75,981	7.9	14.7
081 CATHOLIC......	74	0	190,686	19.9	36.9
093 CR CH (DISC)..	2	1,570	1,920*	0.2	0.4
097 CR C AND C CR.	5	578	707*	0.1	0.1
105 CHRISTIAN REF.	2	281	528	0.1	0.1
121 CH GOD (ABR)..	1	50	61*	-	-
123 CH GOD (ANDER)	1	75	175	-	-
127 CH GOD (CLEVE)	2	152	186*	-	-
157 CH OF BRETHREN	1	55	67*	-	-
165 CH OF NAZARENE	6	764	1,475	0.2	0.3
175 CONG CR CH....	1	2,368	2,896*	0.3	0.6
193 EPISCOPAL.....	21	11,269	16,886	1.8	3.3
197 EVAN CH OF NA.	2	121	148*	-	-
201 EVAN COV CH AM	15	4,109	5,025*	0.5	1.0
221 FREE METH C NA	2	79	111	-	-
226 FRIENDS-USA...	1	222	272*	-	0.1
281 LUTH CH AMER..	65	64,623	94,416	9.8	18.3
283 LUTH--MO SYNOD	34	22,039	31,427	3.3	6.1
287 MENN GEN CONF.	1	51	62*	-	-
313 NO AM BAPT GC.	3	499	610*	0.1	0.1
353 PLY BRETHREN..	6	355	578	0.1	0.1
371 REF CH IN AM..	2	274	508	0.1	0.1
403 SALVATION ARMY	5	508	1,818	0.2	0.4
413 S-D ADVENTISTS	6	1,595	1,951*	0.2	0.4
419 SO BAPT CONV..	4	779	953*	0.1	0.2
435 UNITARIAN-UNIV	5	1,523	2,028	0.2	0.4
443 UN C OF CHRIST	22	11,540	14,114*	1.5	2.7
449 UN METHODIST..	44	29,241	39,383	4.1	7.6
453 UN PRES CH USA	26	18,052	22,078*	2.3	4.3
469 WISC EVAN LUTH	8	3,591	5,019	0.5	1.0
HOUSTON	34	6,967	15,125*	86.2	100.0
029 AMER LUTH CH..	8	3,982	5,559	31.7	36.8
081 CATHOLIC......	7	0	5,510	31.4	36.4
313 NO AM BAPT GC.	1	12	15*	0.1	0.1
443 UN C OF CHRIST	4	646	805*	4.6	5.3
449 UN METHODIST..	5	854	1,216	6.9	8.0
453 UN PRES CH USA	3	252	314*	1.8	2.1
469 WISC EVAN LUTH	6	1,221	1,706	9.7	11.3
HUBBARD	21	2,870	5,390*	50.9	100.0
029 AMER LUTH CH..	5	903	1,315	12.4	24.4
081 CATHOLIC......	5	0	1,404	13.3	26.0
097 CR C AND C CR.	1	85	102*	1.0	1.9
193 EPISCOPAL.....	1	46	56	0.5	1.0
221 FREE METH C NA	2	53	63	0.6	1.2
283 LUTH--MO SYNOD	4	1,179	1,658	15.7	30.8
449 UN METHODIST..	3	604	792	7.5	14.7
ISANTI	18	4,819	8,139*	49.1	100.0
081 CATHOLIC......	1	0	1,149	6.9	14.1
127 CH GOD (CLEVE)	1	5	6*	-	0.1
201 EVAN COV CH AM	1	103	128*	0.8	1.6
281 LUTH CH AMER..	8	3,121	4,584	27.7	56.3
283 LUTH--MO SYNOD	4	1,229	1,752	10.6	21.5
413 S-D ADVENTISTS	1	63	78*	0.5	1.0
449 UN METHODIST..	2	298	442	2.7	5.4
ITASCA	55	7,263	18,193*	51.2	100.0
029 AMER LUTH CH..	5	764	1,162	3.3	6.4
081 CATHOLIC......	18	0	8,845	24.9	48.6
097 CR C AND C CR.	1	120	147*	0.4	0.8
123 CH GOD (ANDER)	1	83	223	0.6	1.2
165 CH OF NAZARENE	1	120	265	0.7	1.5
201 EVAN COV CH AM	1	23	28*	0.1	0.2
281 LUTH CH AMER..	6	1,215	1,938	5.5	10.7
283 LUTH--MO SYNOD	5	1,706	1,893	5.3	10.4
285 MENNONITE CH..	2	29	35*	0.1	0.2
413 S-D ADVENTISTS	1	57	70*	0.2	0.4
435 UNITARIAN-UNIV	1	17	26	0.1	0.1
449 UN METHODIST..	5	1,173	1,173	3.3	6.4
453 UN PRES CH USA	8	1,956	2,388*	6.7	13.1
JACKSON	32	7,649	12,630*	88.0	100.0
029 AMER LUTH CH..	8	2,172	2,796	19.5	22.1
081 CATHOLIC......	4	0	2,580	18.0	20.4
281 LUTH CH AMER..	3	920	1,312	9.1	10.4
283 LUTH--MO SYNOD	9	2,742	3,696	25.8	29.3
285 MENNONITE CH..	1	51	61*	0.4	0.5
413 S-D ADVENTISTS	1	18	22*	0.2	0.2
449 UN METHODIST..	4	1,080	1,362	9.5	10.8
453 UN PRES CH USA	2	666	801*	5.6	6.3
KANABEC	17	3,065	5,665*	58.0	100.0
029 AMER LUTH CH..	1	357	509	5.2	9.0
081 CATHOLIC......	2	0	1,383	14.1	24.4
105 CHRISTIAN REF.	1	127	250	2.6	4.4
165 CH OF NAZARENE	1	38	71	0.7	1.3
201 EVAN COV CH AM	1	57	71*	0.7	1.3
221 FREE METH C NA	1	17	21	0.2	0.4
281 LUTH CH AMER..	3	920	1,312	13.4	23.2
283 LUTH--MO SYNOD	3	875	1,199	12.3	21.2
413 S-D ADVENTISTS	1	8	10*	0.1	0.2
449 UN METHODIST..	2	389	496	5.1	8.8
453 UN PRES CH USA	1	277	343*	3.5	6.1
KANDIYOHI	56	15,188	24,124*	79.0	100.0

*Total adherents estimated from known number of communicant, confirmed, full members.

—Represents a percent less than 0.1.

Percentages may not total due to rounding.

Table 3. Churches and Church Membership by State, County and Denomination: 1971

County and Denomination	Number of churches	Communicant, confirmed, full members	Total adherents: Number	Total adherents: Percent of total population	Total adherents: Percent of total adherents
029 AMER LUTH CH..	15	6,558	8,891	29.1	36.9
081 CATHOLIC......	6	0	3,228	10.6	13.4
105 CHRISTIAN REF.	3	857	1,497	4.9	6.2
123 CH GOD (ANDER)	1	97	205	0.7	0.8
165 CH OF NAZARENE	1	62	103	0.3	0.4
193 EPISCOPAL.....	1	125	212	0.7	0.9
201 EVAN COV CH AM	3	722	873*	2.9	3.6
281 LUTH CH AMER..	7	2,755	3,705	12.1	15.4
283 LUTH--MO SYNOD	3	931	1,245	4.1	5.2
353 PLY BRETHREN..	1	30	40	0.1	0.2
371 REF CH IN AM..	2	455	670	2.2	2.8
403 SALVATION ARMY	1	33	193	0.6	0.8
413 S-D ADVENTISTS	1	51	62*	0.2	0.3
435 UNITARIAN-UNIV	1	27	27	0.1	0.1
449 UN METHODIST..	6	1,293	1,714	5.6	7.1
453 UN PRES CH USA	3	1,107	1,339*	4.4	5.6
469 WISC EVAN LUTH	1	85	120	0.4	0.5
KITTSON	20	3,033	4,525*	66.0	100.0
029 AMER LUTH CH..	3	567	816	11.9	18.0
081 CATHOLIC......	2	0	509	7.4	11.2
193 EPISCOPAL.....	1	85	118	1.7	2.6
201 EVAN COV CH AM	4	153	182*	2.7	4.0
281 LUTH CH AMER..	6	1,763	2,342	34.2	51.8
419 SO BAPT CONV..	1	20	24*	0.4	0.5
449 UN METHODIST..	1	114	140	2.0	3.1
453 UN PRES CH USA	2	331	394*	5.7	8.7
KOOCHICHING	29	3,637	9,386*	54.8	100.0
029 AMER LUTH CH..	5	1,475	2,189	12.8	23.3
081 CATHOLIC......	4	0	3,998	23.3	42.6
165 CH OF NAZARENE	2	79	202	1.2	2.2
193 EPISCOPAL.....	1	220	359	2.1	3.8
201 EVAN COV CH AM	3	135	166*	1.0	1.8
281 LUTH CH AMER..	2	660	965	5.6	10.3
283 LUTH--MO SYNOD	1	326	444	2.6	4.7
285 MENNONITE CH..	4	60	74*	0.4	0.8
403 SALVATION ARMY	1	61	221	1.3	2.4
413 S-D ADVENTISTS	2	81	100*	0.6	1.1
443 UN C OF CHRIST	2	395	486*	2.8	5.2
449 UN METHODIST..	2	145	182	1.1	1.9
LAC QUI PARLE	31	6,689	10,156*	91.0	100.0
029 AMER LUTH CH..	13	4,667	5,969	53.5	58.8
081 CATHOLIC......	4	0	1,675	15.0	16.5
165 CH OF NAZARENE	1	20	34	0.3	0.3
201 EVAN COV CH AM	1	81	96*	0.9	0.9
281 LUTH CH AMER..	1	279	352	3.2	3.5
283 LUTH--MO SYNOD	4	751	977	8.8	9.6
371 REF CH IN AM..	1	48	60	0.5	0.6
443 UN C OF CHRIST	2	275	327*	2.9	3.2
449 UN METHODIST..	2	201	240	2.1	2.4
453 UN PRES CH USA	1	251	299*	2.7	2.9
469 WISC EVAN LUTH	1	116	127	1.1	1.3
LAKE	12	3,106	6,686*	50.1	100.0
029 AMER LUTH CH..	5	1,536	2,173	16.3	32.5
081 CATHOLIC......	2	0	2,230	16.7	33.4
281 LUTH CH AMER..	1	790	1,137	8.5	17.0
283 LUTH--MO SYNOD	2	252	459	3.4	6.9
449 UN METHODIST..	1	214	296	2.2	4.4
453 UN PRES CH USA	1	314	391*	2.9	5.8
LAKE OF THE WOODS	17	1,143	2,273*	57.0	100.0
029 AMER LUTH CH..	4	518	738	18.5	32.5
081 CATHOLIC......	3	0	698	17.5	30.7
201 EVAN COV CH AM	1	41	50*	1.3	2.2
281 LUTH CH AMER..	3	208	303	7.6	13.3
283 LUTH--MO SYNOD	1	103	153	3.8	6.7
285 MENNONITE CH..	2	23	28*	0.7	1.2
413 S-D ADVENTISTS	1	22	27*	0.7	1.2
443 UN C OF CHRIST	2	228	276*	6.9	12.1
LE SUEUR	34	5,753	17,581*	82.4	100.0
029 AMER LUTH CH..	4	1,446	1,992	9.3	11.3
081 CATHOLIC......	13	0	9,832	46.1	55.9
097 CR C AND C CR.	1	135	170*	0.8	1.0
281 LUTH CH AMER..	1	395	601	2.8	3.4
283 LUTH--MO SYNOD	4	934	1,282	6.0	7.3
443 UN C OF CHRIST	1	798	1,004*	4.7	5.7
449 UN METHODIST..	6	1,220	1,594	7.5	9.1
453 UN PRES CH USA	2	433	545*	2.6	3.1
469 WISC EVAN LUTH	2	392	561	2.6	3.2
LINCOLN	23	4,063	7,369	90.5	100.0
029 AMER LUTH CH..	7	1,841	2,448	30.1	33.2
081 CATHOLIC......	4	0	2,049	25.2	27.8
193 EPISCOPAL.....	1	25	33	0.4	0.4
281 LUTH CH AMER..	3	1,041	1,304	16.0	17.7
449 UN METHODIST..	4	480	634	7.8	8.6
469 WISC EVAN LUTH	4	676	901	11.1	12.2
LYON	38	8,331	19,083*	78.6	100.0
029 AMER LUTH CH..	10	4,074	5,569	22.9	29.2
081 CATHOLIC......	7	0	7,961	32.8	41.7
093 CR CH (DISC)..	1	96	117*	0.5	0.6
097 CR C AND C CR.	2	25	31*	0.1	0.2
193 EPISCOPAL.....	1	82	113	0.5	0.6
281 LUTH CH AMER..	2	368	452	1.9	2.4
283 LUTH--MO SYNOD	2	222	362	1.5	1.9
443 UN C OF CHRIST	1	108	132*	0.5	0.7
449 UN METHODIST..	5	1,603	2,120	8.7	11.1
453 UN PRES CH USA	5	1,051	1,286*	5.3	6.7
469 WISC EVAN LUTH	2	702	940	3.9	4.9
MC LEOD	45	14,426	26,826*	97.0	100.0
029 AMER LUTH CH..	8	3,316	4,678	16.9	17.4
081 CATHOLIC......	7	0	8,090	29.2	30.2
193 EPISCOPAL.....	1	76	101	0.4	0.4
283 LUTH--MO SYNOD	9	6,227	8,266	29.9	30.8
313 NO AM BAPT GC.	1	116	143*	0.5	0.5
413 S-D ADVENTISTS	1	373	461*	1.7	1.7
443 UN C OF CHRIST	8	1,764	2,179*	7.9	8.1
449 UN METHODIST..	4	1,143	1,155	4.2	4.3
453 UN PRES CH USA	2	449	555*	2.0	2.1
469 WISC EVAN LUTH	4	962	1,198	4.3	4.5
MAHNOMEN	17	1,735	5,217*	92.5	100.0
029 AMER LUTH CH..	6	1,283	1,754	31.1	33.6
081 CATHOLIC......	5	0	2,515	44.6	48.2
105 CHRISTIAN REF.	1	33	40	0.7	0.8
193 EPISCOPAL.....	1	70	470	8.3	9.0
283 LUTH--MO SYNOD	1	187	243	4.3	4.7
443 UN C OF CHRIST	2	121	154*	2.7	3.0
449 UN METHODIST..	1	41	41	0.7	0.8
MARSHALL	42	4,847	9,196*	70.4	100.0
029 AMER LUTH CH..	16	3,041	4,261	32.6	46.3
081 CATHOLIC......	11	0	2,577	19.7	28.0
201 EVAN COV CH AM	3	195	241*	1.8	2.6
281 LUTH CH AMER..	6	815	1,067	8.2	11.6
283 LUTH--MO SYNOD	2	254	389	3.0	4.2
413 S-D ADVENTISTS	1	84	104*	0.8	1.1
449 UN METHODIST..	1	269	323	2.5	3.5
453 UN PRES CH USA	2	189	234*	1.8	2.5
MARTIN	49	13,278	21,411*	88.1	100.0
019 AMER BAPT CONV	1	216	261*	1.1	1.2
029 AMER LUTH CH..	6	2,176	3,153	13.0	14.7
081 CATHOLIC......	5	0	3,851	15.8	18.0
097 CR C AND C CR.	3	345	417*	1.7	1.9
193 EPISCOPAL.....	1	117	182	0.7	0.9
201 EVAN COV CH AM	1	198	239*	1.0	1.1
281 LUTH CH AMER..	3	557	694	2.9	3.2
283 LUTH--MO SYNOD	12	5,542	7,319	30.1	34.2
403 SALVATION ARMY	1	49	184	0.8	0.9
413 S-D ADVENTISTS	1	9	11*	-	0.1
443 UN C OF CHRIST	7	2,007	2,424*	10.0	11.3
449 UN METHODIST..	8	2,062	2,676	11.0	12.5
MEEKER	43	8,769	16,062*	85.4	100.0
029 AMER LUTH CH..	5	1,960	2,784	14.8	17.3
081 CATHOLIC......	6	0	4,334	23.0	27.0
093 CR CH (DISC)..	1	125	153*	0.8	1.0
097 CR C AND C CR.	2	195	238*	1.3	1.5
121 CH GOD (ABR)..	1	45	55*	0.3	0.3
165 CH OF NAZARENE	2	138	223	1.2	1.4
193 EPISCOPAL.....	1	175	255	1.4	1.6
201 EVAN COV CH AM	3	434	530*	2.8	3.3
281 LUTH CH AMER..	10	2,890	3,816	20.3	23.8
283 LUTH--MO SYNOD	3	782	1,090	5.8	6.8
413 S-D ADVENTISTS	1	20	24*	0.1	0.1
443 UN C OF CHRIST	2	192	235*	1.2	1.5
449 UN METHODIST..	3	738	887	4.7	5.5
453 UN PRES CH USA	1	278	340*	1.8	2.1
469 WISC EVAN LUTH	2	797	1,098	5.8	6.8
MILLE LACS	27	5,249	10,992*	70.0	100.0
029 AMER LUTH CH..	3	1,038	1,547	9.9	14.1
081 CATHOLIC......	6	0	3,395	21.6	30.9
105 CHRISTIAN REF.	1	535	872	5.6	7.9
193 EPISCOPAL.....	1	70	132	0.8	1.2
201 EVAN COV CH AM	1	55	68*	0.4	0.6
281 LUTH CH AMER..	5	1,857	2,642	16.8	24.0
283 LUTH--MO SYNOD	3	601	838	5.3	7.6
413 S-D ADVENTISTS	2	10	12*	0.1	0.1
443 UN C OF CHRIST	1	154	190*	1.2	1.7
449 UN METHODIST..	3	842	1,189	7.6	10.8
453 UN PRES CH USA	1	87	107*	0.7	1.0
MORRISON	46	4,498	24,250*	90.0	100.0
029 AMER LUTH CH..	1	457	667	2.5	2.8
081 CATHOLIC......	20	0	18,124	67.3	74.7
097 CR C AND C CR.	1	60	76*	0.3	0.3
193 EPISCOPAL.....	2	92	129	0.5	0.5
201 EVAN COV CH AM	3	187	237*	0.9	1.0
221 FREE METH C NA	2	42	45	0.2	0.2
281 LUTH CH AMER..	4	863	1,195	4.4	4.9
283 LUTH--MO SYNOD	8	1,874	2,597	9.6	10.7
413 S-D ADVENTISTS	1	35	44*	0.2	0.2
443 UN C OF CHRIST	1	255	324*	1.2	1.3
449 UN METHODIST..	2	462	595	2.2	2.5
453 UN PRES CH USA	1	171	217*	0.8	0.9
MOWER	54	19,214	37,153*	84.9	100.0

*Total adherents estimated from known number of communicant, confirmed, full members.

—Represents a percent less than 0.1.

Percentages may not total due to rounding.

Table 3. Churches and Church Membership by State, County and Denomination: 1971

County and Denomination	Number of churches	Communicant, confirmed, full members	Total adherents		
			Number	Percent of total population	Percent of total adherents
029 AMER LUTH CH..	15	10,254	13,771	31.5	37.1
081 CATHOLIC......	10	0	11,498	26.3	30.9
093 CR CH (DISC)..	1	121	147*	0.3	0.4
097 CR C AND C CR.	1	550	670*	1.5	1.8
193 EPISCOPAL.....	1	399	468	1.1	1.3
201 EVAN COV CH AM	1	37	45*	0.1	0.1
221 FREE METH C NA	1	26	30	0.1	0.1
283 LUTH--MO SYNOD	7	2,109	2,981	6.8	8.0
403 SALVATION ARMY	1	122	525	1.2	1.4
435 UNITARIAN-UNIV	1	17	17	-	-
443 UN C OF CHRIST	3	706	860*	2.0	2.3
449 UN METHODIST..	9	3,400	4,340	9.9	11.7
453 UN PRES CH USA	2	1,317	1,605*	3.7	4.3
469 WISC EVAN LUTH	1	156	196	0.4	0.5
MURRAY	29	4,909	10,744*	85.9	100.0
029 AMER LUTH CH..	8	1,668	2,305	18.4	21.5
081 CATHOLIC......	7	0	3,978	31.8	37.0
105 CHRISTIAN REF.	1	208	356	2.8	3.3
281 LUTH CH AMER..	2	501	644	5.1	6.0
283 LUTH--MO SYNOD	2	746	1,016	8.1	9.5
353 PLY BRETHREN..	1	30	50	0.4	0.5
371 REF CH IN AM..	2	379	647	5.2	6.0
449 UN METHODIST..	2	595	791	6.3	7.4
453 UN PRES CH USA	4	782	957*	7.7	8.9
NICOLLET	27	6,974	15,880*	64.8	100.0
081 CATHOLIC......	9	0	6,749	27.5	42.5
093 CR CH (DISC)..	1	34	42*	0.2	0.3
193 EPISCOPAL.....	1	115	152	0.6	1.0
281 LUTH CH AMER..	6	2,731	3,693	15.1	23.3
283 LUTH--MO SYNOD	1	376	508	2.1	3.2
449 UN METHODIST..	3	864	1,039	4.2	6.5
453 UN PRES CH USA	1	318	389*	1.6	2.4
469 WISC EVAN LUTH	5	2,536	3,308	13.5	20.8
NOBLES	44	9,916	20,320*	87.6	100.0
029 AMER LUTH CH..	4	1,155	1,774	7.6	8.7
081 CATHOLIC......	8	0	6,590	28.4	32.4
097 CR C AND C CR.	1	425	523*	2.3	2.6
105 CHRISTIAN REF.	3	593	1,034	4.5	5.1
157 CH OF BRETHREN	1	127	156*	0.7	0.8
193 EPISCOPAL.....	1	39	83	0.4	0.4
201 EVAN COV CH AM	1	159	196*	0.8	1.0
281 LUTH CH AMER..	2	1,023	1,353	5.8	6.7
283 LUTH--MO SYNOD	4	1,878	2,669	11.5	13.1
371 REF CH IN AM..	3	586	1,026	4.4	5.0
435 UNITARIAN-UNIV	1	12	12	0.1	0.1
443 UN C OF CHRIST	1	39	48*	0.2	0.2
449 UN METHODIST..	4	1,316	1,700	7.3	8.4
453 UN PRES CH USA	10	2,564	3,156*	13.6	15.5
NORMAN	35	7,084	9,644*	96.4	100.0
029 AMER LUTH CH..	25	6,090	7,935	79.3	82.3
081 CATHOLIC......	2	0	391	3.9	4.1
281 LUTH CH AMER..	1	110	140	1.4	1.5
283 LUTH--MO SYNOD	3	504	707	7.1	7.3
443 UN C OF CHRIST	1	70	84*	0.8	0.9
449 UN METHODIST..	1	212	270	2.7	2.8
453 UN PRES CH USA	2	98	117*	1.2	1.2
OLMSTED	57	27,387	56,753*	67.5	100.0
029 AMER LUTH CH..	8	8,989	13,940	16.6	24.6
081 CATHOLIC......	8	0	16,811	20.0	29.6
093 CR CH (DISC)..	1	138	177*	0.2	0.3
097 CR C AND C CR.	3	405	518*	0.6	0.9
165 CH OF NAZARENE	1	76	211	0.3	0.4
193 EPISCOPAL.....	2	1,155	1,613	1.9	2.8
201 EVAN COV CH AM	1	123	157*	0.2	0.3
281 LUTH CH AMER..	2	481	846	1.0	1.5
283 LUTH--MO SYNOD	8	4,803	6,794	8.1	12.0
371 REF CH IN AM..	1	118	228	0.3	0.4
403 SALVATION ARMY	1	121	536	0.6	0.9
413 S-D ADVENTISTS	1	115	147*	0.2	0.3
419 SO BAPT CONV..	1	121	155*	0.2	0.3
435 UNITARIAN-UNIV	1	220	325	0.4	0.6
443 UN C OF CHRIST	4	1,712	2,190*	2.6	3.9
449 UN METHODIST..	10	6,447	8,984	10.7	15.8
453 UN PRES CH USA	2	1,859	2,378*	2.8	4.2
469 WISC EVAN LUTH	2	504	743	0.9	1.3
OTTER TAIL	104	21,567	35,528*	77.1	100.0
019 AMER BAPT CONV	1	62	74*	0.2	0.2
029 AMER LUTH CH..	33	9,674	12,975	28.1	36.5
081 CATHOLIC......	14	0	6,870	14.9	19.3
165 CH OF NAZARENE	1	47	135	0.3	0.4
193 EPISCOPAL.....	1	122	159	0.3	0.4
281 LUTH CH AMER..	10	2,678	3,653	7.9	10.3
283 LUTH--MO SYNOD	21	5,734	7,515	16.3	21.2
403 SALVATION ARMY	1	52	212	0.5	0.6
413 S-D ADVENTISTS	2	36	43*	0.1	0.1
435 UNITARIAN-UNIV	1	32	32	0.1	0.1
443 UN C OF CHRIST	6	805	964*	2.1	2.7
449 UN METHODIST..	10	1,663	2,103	4.6	5.9
453 UN PRES CH USA	3	662	793*	1.7	2.2
PENNINGTON	18	5,312	9,096*	68.6	100.0
029 AMER LUTH CH..	10	3,564	4,955	37.4	54.5

County and Denomination	Number of churches	Communicant, confirmed, full members	Total adherents		
			Number	Percent of total population	Percent of total adherents
081 CATHOLIC......	2	0	1,680	12.7	18.5
201 EVAN COV CH AM	1	130	158*	1.2	1.7
281 LUTH CH AMER..	2	684	1,079	8.1	11.9
283 LUTH--MO SYNOD	1	340	487	3.7	5.4
413 S-D ADVENTISTS	1	122	148*	1.1	1.6
449 UN METHODIST..	1	472	589	4.4	6.5
PINE	39	4,232	8,663*	51.5	100.0
081 CATHOLIC......	8	0	3,140	18.7	36.2
165 CH OF NAZARENE	1	31	49	0.3	0.6
193 EPISCOPAL.....	1	22	22	0.1	0.3
281 LUTH CH AMER..	10	2,057	2,706	16.1	31.2
283 LUTH--MO SYNOD	4	1,028	1,426	8.5	16.5
413 S-D ADVENTISTS	2	54	65*	0.4	0.8
443 UN C OF CHRIST	1	190	230*	1.4	2.7
449 UN METHODIST..	3	360	431	2.6	5.0
453 UN PRES CH USA	9	490	594*	3.5	6.9
PIPESTONE	29	6,929	11,745*	91.8	100.0
029 AMER LUTH CH..	3	1,511	2,026	15.8	17.2
081 CATHOLIC......	3	0	1,991	15.6	17.0
097 CR C AND C CR.	1	15	18*	0.1	0.2
105 CHRISTIAN REF.	4	973	1,831	14.3	15.6
193 EPISCOPAL.....	1	38	93	0.7	0.8
283 LUTH--MO SYNOD	6	1,719	2,277	17.8	19.4
371 REF CH IN AM..	2	551	872	6.8	7.4
413 S-D ADVENTISTS	1	29	35*	0.3	0.3
449 UN METHODIST..	5	1,253	1,575	12.3	13.4
453 UN PRES CH USA	3	840	1,027*	8.0	8.7
POLK	71	13,279	26,560*	77.1	100.0
029 AMER LUTH CH..	32	8,672	12,017	34.9	45.2
081 CATHOLIC......	14	0	8,494	24.7	32.0
097 CR C AND C CR.	1	100	122*	0.4	0.5
105 CHRISTIAN REF.	2	75	127	0.4	0.5
193 EPISCOPAL.....	1	25	29	0.1	0.1
201 EVAN COV CH AM	1	64	78*	0.2	0.3
281 LUTH CH AMER..	5	660	844	2.5	3.2
283 LUTH--MO SYNOD	7	1,867	2,629	7.6	9.9
449 UN METHODIST..	4	750	922	2.7	3.5
453 UN PRES CH USA	4	1,066	1,298*	3.8	4.9
POPE	29	5,937	9,367*	84.3	100.0
029 AMER LUTH CH..	15	4,702	6,058	54.5	64.7
081 CATHOLIC......	4	0	1,676	15.1	17.9
201 EVAN COV CH AM	1	66	79*	0.7	0.8
281 LUTH CH AMER..	2	108	147	1.3	1.6
283 LUTH--MO SYNOD	2	340	477	4.3	5.1
413 S-D ADVENTISTS	1	26	31*	0.3	0.3
443 UN C OF CHRIST	1	180	214*	1.9	2.3
449 UN METHODIST..	2	448	591	5.3	6.3
469 WISC EVAN LUTH	1	67	94	0.8	1.0
RAMSEY	215	95,429	311,466*	65.4	100.0
029 AMER LUTH CH..	26	18,844	26,878	5.6	8.6
081 CATHOLIC......	49	0	176,599	37.1	56.7
093 CR CH (DISC)..	1	25	321*	0.1	0.1
097 CR C AND C CR.	2	192	238*	-	0.1
105 CHRISTIAN REF.	1	142	300	0.1	0.1
123 CH GOD (ANDER)	1	62	120	-	-
127 CH GOD (CLEVE)	1	5	6*	-	-
165 CH OF NAZARENE	3	232	618	0.1	0.2
193 EPISCOPAL.....	15	5,833	7,885	1.7	2.5
201 EVAN COV CH AM	5	1,918	2,375*	0.5	0.8
226 FRIENDS-USA...	1	93	115*	-	-
281 LUTH CH AMER..	25	22,712	35,674	7.5	11.5
283 LUTH--MO SYNOD	20	13,549	18,930	4.0	6.1
313 NO AM BAPT GC.	1	173	214*	-	0.1
371 REF CH IN AM..	1	167	300	0.1	0.1
403 SALVATION ARMY	2	380	1,263	0.3	0.4
413 S-D ADVENTISTS	3	407	504*	0.1	0.2
419 SO BAPT CONV..	1	105	130*	-	-
435 UNITARIAN-UNIV	2	792	1,012	0.2	0.3
443 UN C OF CHRIST	11	6,078	7,527*	1.6	2.4
449 UN METHODIST..	22	9,585	12,994	2.7	4.2
453 UN PRES CH USA	15	9,986	12,367*	2.6	4.0
469 WISC EVAN LUTH	7	3,915	5,096	1.1	1.6
RED LAKE	16	1,373	4,685*	87.0	100.0
029 AMER LUTH CH..	6	862	1,264	23.5	27.0
081 CATHOLIC......	6	0	2,741	50.9	58.5
283 LUTH--MO SYNOD	2	333	453	8.4	9.7
453 UN PRES CH USA	2	178	227*	4.2	4.8
REDWOOD	54	9,065	18,535*	92.6	100.0
029 AMER LUTH CH..	12	3,585	4,890	24.4	26.4
081 CATHOLIC......	12	0	6,694	33.4	36.1
093 CR CH (DISC)..	1	60	74*	0.4	0.4
097 CR C AND C CR.	2	314	388*	1.9	2.1
165 CH OF NAZARENE	1	39	62	0.3	0.3
281 LUTH CH AMER..	1	269	334	1.7	1.8
283 LUTH--MO SYNOD	2	220	290	1.4	1.6
413 S-D ADVENTISTS	1	35	43*	0.2	0.2
449 UN METHODIST..	11	1,945	2,385	11.9	12.9
453 UN PRES CH USA	5	850	1,051*	5.2	5.7
469 WISC EVAN LUTH	6	1,748	2,324	11.6	12.5
RENVILLE	52	10,311	19,306*	91.3	100.0

*Total adherents estimated from known number of communicant, confirmed, full members.

—Represents a percent less than 0.1.

Percentages may not total due to rounding.

Table 3. Churches and Church Membership by State, County and Denomination: 1971

County and Denomination	Number of churches	Communicant, confirmed, full members	Total adherents: Number	Total adherents: Percent of total population	Total adherents: Percent of total adherents
029 AMER LUTH CH..	12	4,108	5,357	25.3	27.7
081 CATHOLIC......	8	0	5,819	27.5	30.1
105 CHRISTIAN REF.	1	158	254	1.2	1.3
121 CH GOD (ABR)..	1	30	37*	0.2	0.2
165 CH OF NAZARENE	2	61	83	0.4	0.4
193 EPISCOPAL.....	2	144	148	0.7	0.8
201 EVAN COV CH AM	1	61	74*	0.4	0.4
281 LUTH CH AMER..	4	1,296	1,745	8.3	9.0
449 UN METHODIST..	12	2,135	2,800	13.2	14.5
453 UN PRES CH USA	1	237	289*	1.4	1.5
469 WISC EVAN LUTH	8	2,081	2,700	12.8	14.0
RICE	44	13,030	28,289*	68.0	100.0
029 AMER LUTH CH..	12	5,136	7,210	17.3	25.5
081 CATHOLIC......	8	0	10,576	25.4	37.4
193 EPISCOPAL.....	3	764	997	2.4	3.5
283 LUTH--MO SYNOD	6	3,117	4,267	10.3	15.1
293 MORAV CH-NORTH	1	143	180	0.4	0.6
403 SALVATION ARMY	1	37	177	0.4	0.6
413 S-D ADVENTISTS	1	71	86*	0.2	0.3
435 UNITARIAN-UNIV	1	24	34	0.1	0.1
443 UN C OF CHRIST	4	1,577	1,913*	4.6	6.8
449 UN METHODIST..	7	2,161	2,849	6.9	10.1
ROCK	17	5,319	8,648*	76.2	100.0
029 AMER LUTH CH..	4	1,538	2,061	18.2	23.8
081 CATHOLIC......	1	0	1,240	10.9	14.3
105 CHRISTIAN REF.	2	291	556	4.9	6.4
193 EPISCOPAL.....	1	16	16	0.1	0.2
283 LUTH--MO SYNOD	2	1,118	1,545	13.6	17.9
371 REF CH IN AM..	2	612	1,124	9.9	13.0
449 UN METHODIST..	2	814	969	8.5	11.2
453 UN PRES CH USA	3	930	1,137*	10.0	13.1
ROSEAU	30	3,461	6,749*	58.3	100.0
029 AMER LUTH CH..	12	2,270	3,255	28.1	48.2
081 CATHOLIC......	6	0	1,786	15.4	26.5
123 CH GOD (ANDER)	1	13	48	0.4	0.7
175 CONG CR CH....	1	100	124*	1.1	1.8
193 EPISCOPAL.....	1	69	69	0.6	1.0
201 EVAN COV CH AM	3	69	86*	0.7	1.3
281 LUTH CH AMER..	4	744	1,125	9.7	16.7
287 MENN GEN CONF.	1	115	143*	1.2	2.1
449 UN METHODIST..	1	81	113	1.0	1.7
ST LOUIS	204	49,130	127,213*	57.6	100.0
019 AMER BAPT CONV	3	235	284*	0.1	0.2
029 AMER LUTH CH..	19	10,382	14,829	6.7	11.7
081 CATHOLIC......	50	0	59,358	26.9	46.7
093 CR CH (DISC)..	1	193	233*	0.1	0.2
097 CR C AND C CR.	1	35	42*	-	-
123 CH GOD (ANDER)	1	32	82	-	0.1
127 CH GOD (CLEVE)	1	16	19*	-	-
165 CH OF NAZARENE	2	67	159	0.1	0.1
175 CONG CR CH....	1	285	345*	0.2	0.3
193 EPISCOPAL.....	9	1,693	2,636	1.2	2.1
197 EVAN CH OF NA.	1	47	57*	-	-
201 EVAN COV CH AM	10	1,000	1,209*	0.5	1.0
281 LUTH CH AMER..	36	14,687	20,337	9.2	16.0
283 LUTH--MO SYNOD	13	3,530	5,165	2.3	4.1
353 PLY BRETHREN..	1	30	40	-	-
403 SALVATION ARMY	4	375	1,299	0.6	1.0
413 S-D ADVENTISTS	3	225	272*	0.1	0.2
419 SO BAPT CONV..	1	198	239*	0.1	0.2
435 UNITARIAN-UNIV	3	196	249	0.1	0.2
443 UN C OF CHRIST	4	1,796	2,172*	1.0	1.7
449 UN METHODIST..	23	8,281	11,111	5.0	8.7
453 UN PRES CH USA	16	5,798	7,012*	3.2	5.5
469 WISC EVAN LUTH	1	29	64	-	0.1
SCOTT	30	5,783	28,747*	88.7	100.0
029 AMER LUTH CH..	4	1,893	2,819	8.7	9.8
081 CATHOLIC......	13	0	20,274	62.5	70.5
281 LUTH CH AMER..	2	629	1,108	3.4	3.9
283 LUTH--MO SYNOD	3	1,139	1,686	5.2	5.9
449 UN METHODIST..	3	506	632	1.9	2.2
453 UN PRES CH USA	1	434	575*	1.8	2.0
469 WISC EVAN LUTH	4	1,182	1,653	5.1	5.8
SHERBURNE	21	3,536	9,178*	50.0	100.0
029 AMER LUTH CH..	5	1,125	1,758	9.6	19.2
081 CATHOLIC......	5	0	3,942	21.5	43.0
193 EPISCOPAL.....	1	45	68	0.4	0.7
281 LUTH CH AMER..	1	507	801	4.4	8.7
283 LUTH--MO SYNOD	3	811	1,242	6.8	13.5
443 UN C OF CHRIST	1	350	443*	2.4	4.8
449 UN METHODIST..	4	646	858	4.7	9.3
453 UN PRES CH USA	1	52	66*	0.4	0.7
SIBLEY	34	8,111	13,117*	82.8	100.0
029 AMER LUTH CH..	7	1,667	2,306	14.6	17.6
081 CATHOLIC......	8	0	2,522	15.9	19.2
201 EVAN COV CH AM	1	82	100*	0.6	0.8
281 LUTH CH AMER..	3	897	1,124	7.1	8.6
283 LUTH--MO SYNOD	7	2,276	3,050	19.2	23.3
443 UN C OF CHRIST	3	710	867*	5.5	6.6
449 UN METHODIST..	2	277	362	2.3	2.8
469 WISC EVAN LUTH	3	2,202	2,786	17.6	21.2
STEARNS	95	10,990	80,202*	84.1	100.0
029 AMER LUTH CH..	8	3,609	5,226	5.5	6.5
081 CATHOLIC......	53	0	64,852	68.0	80.9
097 CR C AND C CR.	1	115	146*	0.2	0.2
105 CHRISTIAN REF.	1	93	193	0.2	0.2
121 CH GOD (ABR)..	2	138	176*	0.2	0.2
193 EPISCOPAL.....	3	343	480	0.5	0.6
197 EVAN CH OF NA.	1	8	10*	-	-
201 EVAN COV CH AM	1	50	64*	0.1	0.1
283 LUTH--MO SYNOD	8	2,603	3,615	3.8	4.5
403 SALVATION ARMY	1	36	189	0.2	0.2
413 S-D ADVENTISTS	2	40	51*	0.1	0.1
435 UNITARIAN-UNIV	1	52	74	0.1	0.1
443 UN C OF CHRIST	2	469	597*	0.6	0.7
449 UN METHODIST..	7	2,411	3,211	3.4	4.0
453 UN PRES CH USA	3	991	1,261*	1.3	1.6
469 WISC EVAN LUTH	1	32	57	0.1	0.1
STEELE	33	11,115	21,154*	78.5	100.0
019 AMER BAPT CONV	1	292	362*	1.3	1.7
029 AMER LUTH CH..	12	6,413	8,992	33.4	42.5
081 CATHOLIC......	5	0	5,603	20.8	26.5
123 CH GOD (ANDER)	1	76	195	0.7	0.9
193 EPISCOPAL.....	1	125	178	0.7	0.8
201 EVAN COV CH AM	1	46	57*	0.2	0.3
283 LUTH--MO SYNOD	4	1,423	2,072	7.7	9.8
403 SALVATION ARMY	1	44	186	0.7	0.9
413 S-D ADVENTISTS	1	8	10*	-	-
443 UN C OF CHRIST	2	850	1,053*	3.9	5.0
449 UN METHODIST..	3	1,205	1,662	6.2	7.9
453 UN PRES CH USA	1	633	784*	2.9	3.7
STEVENS	21	4,289	8,806*	78.5	100.0
029 AMER LUTH CH..	7	2,759	3,880	34.6	44.1
081 CATHOLIC......	3	0	2,798	24.9	31.8
105 CHRISTIAN REF.	1	78	151	1.3	1.7
165 CH OF NAZARENE	1	82	132	1.2	1.5
281 LUTH CH AMER..	1	73	93	0.8	1.1
283 LUTH--MO SYNOD	1	222	311	2.8	3.5
443 UN C OF CHRIST	2	273	327*	2.9	3.7
449 UN METHODIST..	3	347	492	4.4	5.6
469 WISC EVAN LUTH	2	455	622	5.5	7.1
SWIFT	32	6,152	11,173*	84.8	100.0
029 AMER LUTH CH..	8	3,368	4,458	33.8	39.9
081 CATHOLIC......	8	0	3,099	23.5	27.7
193 EPISCOPAL.....	1	35	35	0.3	0.3
201 EVAN COV CH AM	2	46	56*	0.4	0.5
281 LUTH CH AMER..	3	511	660	5.0	5.9
283 LUTH--MO SYNOD	5	1,305	1,789	13.6	16.0
313 NO AM BAPT GC.	1	85	103*	0.8	0.9
443 UN C OF CHRIST	2	459	559*	4.2	5.0
449 UN METHODIST..	1	248	298	2.3	2.7
453 UN PRES CH USA	1	95	116*	0.9	1.0
TODD	51	6,430	15,816*	71.5	100.0
029 AMER LUTH CH..	8	1,863	2,617	11.8	16.5
081 CATHOLIC......	12	0	7,111	32.2	45.0
123 CH GOD (ANDER)	1	95	185	0.8	1.2
165 CH OF NAZARENE	2	79	198	0.9	1.3
201 EVAN COV CH AM	1	45	55*	0.2	0.3
221 FREE METH C NA	3	48	59	0.3	0.4
281 LUTH CH AMER..	3	322	405	1.8	2.6
283 LUTH--MO SYNOD	8	2,355	3,145	14.2	19.9
413 S-D ADVENTISTS	2	76	93*	0.4	0.6
443 UN C OF CHRIST	3	478	588*	2.7	3.7
449 UN METHODIST..	8	1,069	1,360	6.1	8.6
TRAVERSE	19	2,807	6,023*	96.3	100.0
081 CATHOLIC......	5	0	2,457	39.3	40.8
127 CH GOD (CLEVE)	1	3	4*	0.1	0.1
193 EPISCOPAL.....	1	53	131	2.1	2.2
201 EVAN COV CH AM	1	109	132*	2.1	2.2
281 LUTH CH AMER..	2	633	810	13.0	13.4
283 LUTH--MO SYNOD	4	1,319	1,670	26.7	27.7
443 UN C OF CHRIST	1	81	98*	1.6	1.6
449 UN METHODIST..	2	195	218	3.5	3.6
453 UN PRES CH USA	2	414	503*	8.0	8.4
WABASHA	38	6,759	15,899*	92.3	100.0
029 AMER LUTH CH..	1	79	155	0.9	1.0
081 CATHOLIC......	10	0	6,781	39.4	42.7
097 CR C AND C CR.	1	80	99*	0.6	0.6
193 EPISCOPAL.....	1	151	152	0.9	1.0
281 LUTH CH AMER..	1	376	523	3.0	3.3
283 LUTH--MO SYNOD	4	1,855	2,556	14.8	16.1
443 UN C OF CHRIST	4	602	746*	4.3	4.7
449 UN METHODIST..	8	1,030	1,358	7.9	8.5
453 UN PRES CH USA	1	194	240*	1.4	1.5
469 WISC EVAN LUTH	7	2,392	3,289	19.1	20.7
WADENA	29	3,990	8,761*	70.6	100.0
029 AMER LUTH CH..	3	1,015	1,448	11.7	16.5
081 CATHOLIC......	5	0	3,299	26.6	37.7
193 EPISCOPAL.....	1	55	81	0.7	0.9
197 EVAN CH OF NA.	2	48	59*	0.5	0.7
221 FREE METH C NA	1	6	6	-	0.1

*Total adherents estimated from known number of communicant, confirmed, full members.

—Represents a percent less than 0.1.

Percentages may not total due to rounding.

Table 3. Churches and Church Membership by State, County and Denomination: 1971

County and Denomination	Number of churches	Communicant, confirmed, full members	Total adherents		
			Number	Percent of total population	Percent of total adherents
281 LUTH CH AMER..	2	307	404	3.3	4.6
283 LUTH--MO SYNOD	6	1,400	1,960	15.8	22.4
285 MENNONITE CH..	1	15	19*	0.2	0.2
413 S-D ADVENTISTS	1	71	88*	0.7	1.0
443 UN C OF CHRIST	2	303	374*	3.0	4.3
449 UN METHODIST..	5	770	1,023	8.2	11.7
WASECA	30	8,105	15,040*	90.3	100.0
029 AMER LUTH CH..	8	3,162	4,289	25.7	28.5
081 CATHOLIC......	5	0	4,262	25.6	28.3
175 CONG CR CH....	1	396	490*	2.9	3.3
193 EPISCOPAL.....	2	118	143	0.9	1.0
201 EVAN COV CH AM	1	90	111*	0.7	0.7
281 LUTH CH AMER..	1	78	114	0.7	0.8
283 LUTH--MO SYNOD	5	2,526	3,353	20.1	22.3
443 UN C OF CHRIST	2	326	403*	2.4	2.7
449 UN METHODIST..	4	1,195	1,584	9.5	10.5
469 WISC EVAN LUTH	1	214	291	1.7	1.9
WASHINGTON	58	16,855	48,045*	57.9	100.0
029 AMER LUTH CH..	6	3,448	5,654	6.8	11.8
081 CATHOLIC......	10	0	22,164	26.7	46.1
097 CR C AND C CR.	2	312	417*	0.5	0.9
123 CH GOD (ANDER)	1	73	193	0.2	0.4
175 CONG CR CH....	2	265	354*	0.4	0.7
193 EPISCOPAL.....	3	180	519	0.6	1.1
201 EVAN COV CH AM	2	159	213*	0.3	0.4
281 LUTH CH AMER..	8	5,952	9,076	10.9	18.9
283 LUTH--MO SYNOD	5	1,452	2,403	2.9	5.0
353 PLY BRETHREN..	1	15	30	-	0.1
413 S-D ADVENTISTS	1	41	55*	0.1	0.1
443 UN C OF CHRIST	4	916	1,225*	1.5	2.5
449 UN METHODIST..	7	2,159	3,139	3.8	6.5
453 UN PRES CH USA	1	610	815*	1.0	1.7
469 WISC EVAN LUTH	5	1,273	1,788	2.2	3.7
WATONWAN	30	7,239	11,244*	84.6	100.0
029 AMER LUTH CH..	8	2,689	3,591	27.0	31.9
081 CATHOLIC......	2	0	1,841	13.8	16.4
097 CR C AND C CR.	1	90	108*	0.8	1.0
193 EPISCOPAL.....	1	30	30	0.2	0.3
281 LUTH CH AMER..	5	1,270	1,653	12.4	14.7
283 LUTH--MO SYNOD	4	913	1,204	9.1	10.7
287 MENN GEN CONF.	2	161	193*	1.5	1.7
449 UN METHODIST..	2	453	592	4.5	5.3
453 UN PRES CH USA	2	732	878*	6.6	7.8
469 WISC EVAN LUTH	3	901	1,154	8.7	10.3
WILKIN	19	3,202	6,895*	73.4	100.0
019 AMER BAPT CONV	1	58	71*	0.8	1.0
029 AMER LUTH CH..	5	1,738	2,527	26.9	36.6
081 CATHOLIC......	4	0	2,452	26.1	35.6
283 LUTH--MO SYNOD	4	705	960	10.2	13.9
443 UN C OF CHRIST	1	71	87*	0.9	1.3
449 UN METHODIST..	3	531	676	7.2	9.8
453 UN PRES CH USA	1	99	122*	1.3	1.8
WINONA	65	12,925	34,386*	77.4	100.0
019 AMER BAPT CONV	1	161	194*	0.4	0.6
029 AMER LUTH CH..	3	2,082	2,928	6.6	8.5
081 CATHOLIC......	16	0	16,489	37.1	48.0
097 CR C AND C CR.	1	75	91*	0.2	0.3
157 CH OF BRETHREN	1	112	135*	0.3	0.4
165 CH OF NAZARENE	1	94	252	0.6	0.7
193 EPISCOPAL.....	2	382	654	1.5	1.9
281 LUTH CH AMER..	1	215	385	0.9	1.1
283 LUTH--MO SYNOD	7	3,154	4,474	10.1	13.0
293 MORAV CH-NORTH	3	266	337	0.8	1.0
403 SALVATION ARMY	1	27	200	0.5	0.6
413 S-D ADVENTISTS	1	34	41*	0.1	0.1
435 UNITARIAN-UNIV	1	12	12	-	-
443 UN C OF CHRIST	3	739	892*	2.0	2.6
449 UN METHODIST..	10	1,949	2,511	5.7	7.3
453 UN PRES CH USA	3	404	488*	1.1	1.4
469 WISC EVAN LUTH	10	3,219	4,303	9.7	12.5
WRIGHT	59	11,195	28,334*	72.8	100.0
029 AMER LUTH CH..	3	598	889	2.3	3.1
081 CATHOLIC......	11	0	12,739	32.7	45.0
093 CR CH (DISC)..	1	90	116*	0.3	0.4
097 CR C AND C CR.	1	50	64*	0.2	0.2
193 EPISCOPAL.....	1	24	30	0.1	0.1
201 EVAN COV CH AM	4	420	541*	1.4	1.9
281 LUTH CH AMER..	10	3,330	4,837	12.4	17.1
283 LUTH--MO SYNOD	5	2,525	3,567	9.2	12.6
371 REF CH IN AM..	1	131	192	0.5	0.7
419 SO BAPT CONV..	1	38	49*	0.1	0.2
443 UN C OF CHRIST	2	294	379*	1.0	1.3
449 UN METHODIST..	9	1,548	1,937	5.0	6.8
453 UN PRES CH USA	4	566	730*	1.9	2.6
469 WISC EVAN LUTH	6	1,581	2,264	5.8	8.0
YELLOW MEDICINE	33	7,786	12,670*	87.9	100.0
029 AMER LUTH CH..	11	4,775	6,600	45.8	52.1
081 CATHOLIC......	4	0	2,047	14.2	16.2
097 CR C AND C CR.	1	100	120*	0.8	0.9
211 EV MENN BRETH.	1	21	25*	0.2	0.2
281 LUTH CH AMER..	2	271	347	2.4	2.7

County and Denomination	Number of churches	Communicant, confirmed, full members	Total adherents		
			Number	Percent of total population	Percent of total adherents
283 LUTH--MO SYNOD	4	930	1,310	9.1	10.3
413 S-D ADVENTISTS	1	10	12*	0.1	0.1
443 UN C OF CHRIST	1	182	219*	1.5	1.7
449 UN METHODIST..	3	232	290	2.0	2.3
453 UN PRES CH USA	2	454	546*	3.8	4.3
469 WISC EVAN LUTH	3	811	1,154	8.0	9.1
CO DATA NOT AVAIL	2	74	7,406*	N/A	N/A
151 L-D SAINTS....	0	0	7,277	N/A	N/A
193 EPISCOPAL.....	1	48	97	N/A	N/A
223 FREE WILL BAPT	1	26	32*	N/A	N/A

MISSISSIPPI

County and Denomination	Number of churches	Communicant, confirmed, full members	Number	Percent of total population	Percent of total adherents
THE STATE.....	4,382	856,746	1,132,375*	51.1	100.0
ADAMS	39	10,614	16,408*	44.0	100.0
059 BAPT MISS ASSN	2	129	162*	0.4	1.0
081 CATHOLIC......	4	0	3,299	8.8	20.1
127 CH GOD (CLEVE)	2	356	448*	1.2	2.7
165 CH OF NAZARENE	1	37	37	0.1	0.2
193 EPISCOPAL.....	1	625	713	1.9	4.3
283 LUTH--MO SYNOD	1	58	83	0.2	0.5
357 PRESB CH US...	5	1,081	1,359*	3.6	8.3
403 SALVATION ARMY	1	102	306	0.8	1.9
413 S-D ADVENTISTS	1	41	52*	0.1	0.3
419 SO BAPT CONV..	14	5,996	7,539*	20.2	45.9
449 UN METHODIST..	7	2,189	2,410	6.5	14.7
ALCORN	61	12,200	14,653*	53.9	100.0
059 BAPT MISS ASSN	2	532	644*	2.4	4.4
081 CATHOLIC......	1	0	260	1.0	1.8
097 CR C AND C CR.	4	585	708*	2.6	4.8
127 CH GOD (CLEVE)	1	25	30*	0.1	0.2
185 CUMBER PRESB..	1	50	61*	0.2	0.4
193 EPISCOPAL.....	1	66	77	0.3	0.5
283 LUTH--MO SYNOD	1	37	45	0.2	0.3
357 PRESB CH US...	3	477	577*	2.1	3.9
419 SO BAPT CONV..	30	7,915	9,578*	35.2	65.4
449 UN METHODIST..	15	2,484	2,638	9.7	18.0
453 UN PRES CH USA	2	29	35*	0.1	0.2
AMITE	40	5,394	6,665*	48.4	100.0
127 CH GOD (CLEVE)	2	89	111*	0.8	1.7
165 CH OF NAZARENE	2	63	121	0.9	1.8
357 PRESB CH US...	4	138	173*	1.3	2.6
419 SO BAPT CONV..	23	4,337	5,431*	39.5	81.5
449 UN METHODIST..	9	767	829	6.0	12.4
ATTALA	52	7,419	9,341*	47.7	100.0
081 CATHOLIC......	1	0	69	0.4	0.7
123 CH GOD (ANDER)	3	54	160	0.8	1.7
127 CH GOD (CLEVE)	2	70	86*	0.4	0.9
165 CH OF NAZARENE	1	23	49	0.3	0.5
185 CUMBER PRESB..	1	45	55*	0.3	0.6
193 EPISCOPAL.....	1	46	54	0.3	0.6
281 LUTH CH AMER..	1	54	66	0.3	0.7
357 PRESB CH US...	3	378	465*	2.4	5.0
419 SO BAPT CONV..	30	6,059	7,450*	38.1	79.8
449 UN METHODIST..	7	677	871	4.5	9.3
453 UN PRES CH USA	2	13	16*	0.1	0.2
BENTON	23	2,743	3,390*	45.2	100.0
097 CR C AND C CR.	1	47	60*	0.8	1.8
193 EPISCOPAL.....	1	16	26	0.3	0.8
357 PRESB CH US...	1	21	27*	0.4	0.8
419 SO BAPT CONV..	11	2,069	2,648*	35.3	78.1
449 UN METHODIST..	9	590	629	8.4	18.6
BOLIVAR	66	11,750	16,466*	33.3	100.0
081 CATHOLIC......	6	0	1,704	3.4	10.3
093 CR CH (DISC)..	3	128	168*	0.3	1.0
127 CH GOD (CLEVE)	1	112	147*	0.3	0.9
165 CH OF NAZARENE	3	246	341	0.7	2.1
193 EPISCOPAL.....	2	213	268	0.5	1.6
357 PRESB CH US...	5	1,114	1,463*	3.0	8.9
413 S-D ADVENTISTS	1	26	34*	0.1	0.2
419 SO BAPT CONV..	27	7,256	9,531*	19.3	57.9
449 UN METHODIST..	18	2,655	2,810	5.7	17.1
CALHOUN	64	9,624	11,561*	79.1	100.0
127 CH GOD (CLEVE)	1	27	33*	0.2	0.3
165 CH OF NAZARENE	1	39	44	0.3	0.4
419 SO BAPT CONV..	51	8,646	10,539*	72.1	91.2
449 UN METHODIST..	11	912	945	6.5	8.2
CARROLL	43	4,146	4,928*	52.4	100.0

*Total adherents estimated from known number of communicant, confirmed, full members.

—Represents a percent less than 0.1.

Percentages may not total due to rounding.

Table 3. Churches and Church Membership by State, County and Denomination: 1971

County and Denomination	Number of churches	Communicant, confirmed, full members	Total adherents		
			Number	Percent of total population	Percent of total adherents
093 CR CH (DISC)..	2	159	199*	2.1	4.0
193 EPISCOPAL.....	1	19	19	0.2	0.4
357 PRESB CH US...	4	196	245*	2.6	5.0
419 SO BAPT CONV..	19	2,501	3,131*	33.3	63.5
449 UN METHODIST..	17	1,271	1,334	14.2	27.1
CHICKASAW	63	7,464	9,019*	53.7	100.0
081 CATHOLIC......	2	0	85	0.5	0.9
097 CR C AND C CR.	1	123	154*	0.9	1.7
127 CH GOD (CLEVE)	2	173	216*	1.3	2.4
165 CH OF NAZARENE	3	172	284	1.7	3.1
193 EPISCOPAL.....	2	45	54	0.3	0.6
357 PRESB CH US...	5	309	386*	2.3	4.3
419 SO BAPT CONV..	21	4,197	5,249*	31.2	58.2
449 UN METHODIST..	27	2,445	2,591	15.4	28.7
CHOCTAW	36	4,101	5,025*	59.5	100.0
127 CH GOD (CLEVE)	1	45	55*	0.7	1.1
185 CUMBER PRESB..	1	77	94*	1.1	1.9
357 PRESB CH US...	7	423	519*	6.1	10.3
419 SO BAPT CONV..	25	3,380	4,146*	49.1	82.5
449 UN METHODIST..	2	176	211	2.5	4.2
CLAIBORNE	25	2,850	3,501*	34.7	100.0
081 CATHOLIC......	1	0	105	1.0	3.0
093 CR CH (DISC)..	11	895	1,100*	10.9	31.4
193 EPISCOPAL.....	1	79	90	0.9	2.6
357 PRESB CH US...	2	246	302*	3.0	8.6
413 S-D ADVENTISTS	1	70	86*	0.9	2.5
419 SO BAPT CONV..	5	1,024	1,258*	12.5	35.9
449 UN METHODIST..	4	536	560	5.6	16.0
CLARKE	77	8,466	10,190*	67.7	100.0
081 CATHOLIC......	1	0	39	0.3	0.4
123 CH GOD (ANDER)	5	54	225	1.5	2.2
127 CH GOD (CLEVE)	2	42	51*	0.3	0.5
193 EPISCOPAL.....	1	18	19*	0.1	0.2
349 PENT HOLINESS.	4	205	251*	1.7	2.5
413 S-D ADVENTISTS	1	22	27*	0.2	0.3
419 SO BAPT CONV..	29	5,116	6,258*	41.6	61.4
449 UN METHODIST..	34	3,009	3,320	22.1	32.6
CLAY	31	6,659	8,129*	43.1	100.0
081 CATHOLIC......	1	0	156	0.8	1.9
093 CR CH (DISC)..	4	488	609*	3.2	7.5
127 CH GOD (CLEVE)	2	125	156*	0.8	1.9
185 CUMBER PRESB..	2	78	97*	0.5	1.2
193 EPISCOPAL.....	1	98	126	0.7	1.6
357 PRESB CH US...	1	234	292*	1.5	3.6
419 SO BAPT CONV..	10	3,961	4,945*	26.2	60.8
449 UN METHODIST..	9	1,654	1,722	9.1	21.2
453 UN PRES CH USA	1	21	26*	0.1	0.3
COAHOMA	35	9,119	12,655*	31.3	100.0
059 BAPT MISS ASSN	1	157	205*	0.5	1.6
081 CATHOLIC......	3	0	1,418	3.5	11.2
093 CR CH (DISC)..	2	110	144*	0.4	1.1
097 CR C AND C CR.	1	150	196*	0.5	1.5
127 CH GOD (CLEVE)	1	109	142*	0.4	1.1
165 CH OF NAZARENE	1	97	99	0.2	0.8
193 EPISCOPAL.....	1	505	576	1.4	4.6
357 PRESB CH US...	1	429	561*	1.4	4.4
413 S-D ADVENTISTS	1	36	47*	0.1	0.4
419 SO BAPT CONV..	11	5,142	6,722*	16.6	53.1
449 UN METHODIST..	12	2,384	2,545	6.3	20.1
COPIAH	70	11,843	14,359*	58.0	100.0
081 CATHOLIC......	2	0	136	0.5	0.9
093 CR CH (DISC)..	1	28	35*	0.1	0.2
127 CH GOD (CLEVE)	2	104	129*	0.5	0.9
165 CH OF NAZARENE	1	30	49	0.2	0.3
193 EPISCOPAL.....	2	55	88	0.4	0.6
283 LUTH--MO SYNOD	1	23	29	0.1	0.2
349 PENT HOLINESS.	1	48	59*	0.2	0.4
357 PRESB CH US...	3	362	448*	1.8	3.1
419 SO BAPT CONV..	30	8,418	10,408*	42.1	72.5
449 UN METHODIST..	27	2,775	2,978	12.0	20.7
COVINGTON	39	6,600	8,062*	57.6	100.0
059 BAPT MISS ASSN	2	292	368*	2.6	4.6
127 CH GOD (CLEVE)	1	20	25*	0.2	0.3
193 EPISCOPAL.....	1	17	24	0.2	0.3
357 PRESB CH US...	4	338	426*	3.0	5.3
419 SO BAPT CONV..	17	4,527	5,707*	40.8	70.8
449 UN METHODIST..	14	1,406	1,512	10.8	18.8
DE SOTO	57	10,265	14,240*	39.7	100.0
081 CATHOLIC......	4	0	1,036	2.9	7.3
097 CR C AND C CR.	1	77	102*	0.3	0.7
127 CH GOD (CLEVE)	1	113	150*	0.4	1.1
165 CH OF NAZARENE	1	10	40	0.1	0.3
193 EPISCOPAL.....	2	120	202	0.6	1.4
283 LUTH--MO SYNOD	1	70	109	0.3	0.8
357 PRESB CH US...	2	174	231*	0.6	1.6
413 S-D ADVENTISTS	1	48	64*	0.2	0.4
419 SO BAPT CONV..	23	6,851	9,089*	25.3	63.8
449 UN METHODIST..	16	2,507	2,826	7.9	19.8
453 UN PRES CH USA	5	295	391*	1.1	2.7
FORREST	88	29,901	38,107*	65.9	100.0
059 BAPT MISS ASSN	7	906	1,103*	1.9	2.9
081 CATHOLIC......	3	0	2,323	4.0	6.1
093 CR CH (DISC)..	1	233	284*	0.5	0.7
123 CH GOD (ANDER)	2	146	326	0.6	0.9
127 CH GOD (CLEVE)	5	467	569*	1.0	1.5
165 CH OF NAZARENE	1	122	181	0.3	0.5
193 EPISCOPAL.....	2	519	629	1.1	1.7
283 LUTH--MO SYNOD	1	140	209	0.4	0.5
357 PRESB CH US...	5	1,354	1,649*	2.9	4.3
403 SALVATION ARMY	1	39	160	0.3	0.4
413 S-D ADVENTISTS	2	194	236*	0.4	0.6
419 SO BAPT CONV..	34	19,921	24,258*	41.9	63.7
449 UN METHODIST..	24	5,860	6,180	10.7	16.2
FRANKLIN	41	4,503	5,355*	66.8	100.0
081 CATHOLIC......	1	0	35	0.4	0.7
127 CH GOD (CLEVE)	4	214	256*	3.2	4.8
357 PRESB CH US...	2	76	91*	1.1	1.7
419 SO BAPT CONV..	22	3,278	3,916*	48.9	73.1
449 UN METHODIST..	12	935	1,057	13.2	19.7
GEORGE	36	5,726	7,124*	57.2	100.0
059 BAPT MISS ASSN	10	1,030	1,310*	10.5	18.4
081 CATHOLIC......	1	0	49	0.4	0.7
127 CH GOD (CLEVE)	3	180	229*	1.8	3.2
165 CH OF NAZARENE	1	21	58	0.5	0.8
357 PRESB CH US...	1	54	69*	0.6	1.0
413 S-D ADVENTISTS	1	14	18*	0.1	0.3
419 SO BAPT CONV..	10	3,150	4,006*	32.2	56.2
449 UN METHODIST..	9	1,277	1,385	11.1	19.4
GREENE	39	3,668	4,530*	53.0	100.0
059 BAPT MISS ASSN	4	333	416*	4.9	9.2
123 CH GOD (ANDER)	1	15	35	0.4	0.8
127 CH GOD (CLEVE)	3	107	134*	1.6	3.0
357 PRESB CH US...	2	208	260*	3.0	5.7
419 SO BAPT CONV..	20	2,424	3,028*	35.4	66.8
449 UN METHODIST..	9	581	657	7.7	14.5
GRENADA	27	6,494	8,173*	41.2	100.0
081 CATHOLIC......	1	0	256	1.3	3.1
127 CH GOD (CLEVE)	2	260	328*	1.7	4.0
165 CH OF NAZARENE	1	98	142	0.7	1.7
193 EPISCOPAL.....	1	142	169	0.9	2.1
357 PRESB CH US...	2	338	426*	2.1	5.2
419 SO BAPT CONV..	12	4,125	5,198*	26.2	63.6
449 UN METHODIST..	8	1,531	1,654	8.3	20.2
HANCOCK	30	2,909	11,933*	68.6	100.0
059 BAPT MISS ASSN	3	128	161*	0.9	1.3
081 CATHOLIC......	11	0	8,299	47.7	69.5
127 CH GOD (CLEVE)	1	6	8*	-	0.1
193 EPISCOPAL.....	1	202	332	1.9	2.8
283 LUTH--MO SYNOD	1	36	58	0.3	0.5
357 PRESB CH US...	1	95	119*	0.7	1.0
419 SO BAPT CONV..	7	1,686	2,119*	12.2	17.8
449 UN METHODIST..	5	756	837	4.8	7.0
HARRISON	125	35,295	67,131*	49.9	100.0
029 AMER LUTH CH..	1	118	206	0.2	0.3
059 BAPT MISS ASSN	6	1,197	1,487*	1.1	2.2
081 CATHOLIC......	22	0	23,684	17.6	35.3
093 CR CH (DISC)..	1	163	202*	0.2	0.3
097 CR C AND C CR.	1	16	20*	-	-
127 CH GOD (CLEVE)	2	145	180*	0.1	0.3
165 CH OF NAZARENE	3	208	439	0.3	0.7
193 EPISCOPAL.....	5	1,270	1,996	1.5	3.0
283 LUTH--MO SYNOD	3	512	745	0.6	1.1
285 MENNONITE CH..	2	87	108*	0.1	0.2
357 PRESB CH US...	7	2,186	2,715*	2.0	4.0
403 SALVATION ARMY	2	110	428	0.3	0.6
413 S-D ADVENTISTS	1	164	204*	0.2	0.3
419 SO BAPT CONV..	37	19,189	23,834*	17.7	35.5
435 UNITARIAN-UNIV	1	18	18	-	-
443 UN C OF CHRIST	1	30	37*	-	0.1
449 UN METHODIST..	30	9,882	10,828	8.0	16.1
HINDS	177	87,611	116,395*	54.1	100.0
059 BAPT MISS ASSN	5	1,294	1,615*	0.8	1.4
081 CATHOLIC......	10	0	9,033	4.2	7.8
093 CR CH (DISC)..	5	969	1,209*	0.6	1.0
097 CR C AND C CR.	1	170	212*	0.1	0.2
123 CH GOD (ANDER)	1	160	413	0.2	0.4
127 CH GOD (CLEVE)	6	701	875*	0.4	0.8
165 CH OF NAZARENE	6	421	844	0.4	0.7
185 CUMBER PRESB..	1	84	105*	-	0.1
193 EPISCOPAL.....	10	3,125	4,022	1.9	3.5
281 LUTH CH AMER..	2	327	450	0.2	0.4
283 LUTH--MO SYNOD	5	523	766	0.4	0.7
349 PENT HOLINESS.	1	30	37*	-	-
353 PLY BRETHREN..	1	20	30	-	-
357 PRESB CH US...	20	7,001	8,736*	4.1	7.5
403 SALVATION ARMY	1	100	329	0.2	0.3

*Total adherents estimated from known number of communicant, confirmed, full members.

—Represents a percent less than 0.1.

Percentages may not total due to rounding.

Table 3. Churches and Church Membership by State, County and Denomination: 1971

County and Denomination	Number of churches	Communicant, confirmed, full members	Total adherents: Number	Total adherents: Percent of total population	Total adherents: Percent of total adherents
413 S-D ADVENTISTS	2	539	673*	0.3	0.6
419 SO BAPT CONV..	56	51,786	64,619*	30.1	55.5
435 UNITARIAN-UNIV	1	47	67	-	0.1
443 UN C OF CHRIST	1	43	54*	-	-
449 UN METHODIST..	42	20,271	22,306	10.4	19.2
HOLMES	58	6,552	7,916*	34.2	100.0
059 BAPT MISS ASSN	1	35	45*	0.2	0.6
081 CATHOLIC......	1	0	71	0.3	0.9
123 CH GOD (ANDER)	1	25	54	0.2	0.7
165 CH OF NAZARENE	1	35	66	0.3	0.8
193 EPISCOPAL.....	1	47	60	0.3	0.8
357 PRESB CH US...	7	317	404*	1.7	5.1
419 SO BAPT CONV..	19	3,354	4,272*	18.5	54.0
449 UN METHODIST..	27	2,739	2,944	12.7	37.2
HUMPHREYS	23	3,615	4,663*	31.9	100.0
059 BAPT MISS ASSN	2	186	244*	1.7	5.2
081 CATHOLIC......	1	0	102	0.7	2.2
123 CH GOD (ANDER)	1	10	25	0.2	0.5
127 CH GOD (CLEVE)	1	76	100*	0.7	2.1
193 EPISCOPAL.....	1	36	52	0.4	1.1
357 PRESB CH US...	2	158	207*	1.4	4.4
413 S-D ADVENTISTS	1	49	64*	0.4	1.4
419 SO BAPT CONV..	8	2,244	2,946*	20.2	63.2
449 UN METHODIST..	6	856	923	6.3	19.8
ISSAQUENA	9	553	877*	32.0	100.0
123 CH GOD (ANDER)	4	155	374	13.7	42.6
419 SO BAPT CONV..	2	312	414*	15.1	47.2
449 UN METHODIST..	3	86	89	3.3	10.1
ITAWAMBA	56	7,388	8,698*	51.6	100.0
059 BAPT MISS ASSN	16	2,613	3,173*	18.8	36.5
123 CH GOD (ANDER)	4	185	438	2.6	5.0
419 SO BAPT CONV..	15	2,057	2,498*	14.8	28.7
449 UN METHODIST..	20	2,511	2,562	15.2	29.5
453 UN PRES CH USA	1	22	27*	0.2	0.3
JACKSON	97	26,983	43,798*	49.8	100.0
059 BAPT MISS ASSN	6	681	894*	1.0	2.0
081 CATHOLIC......	7	0	9,150	10.4	20.9
093 CR CH (DISC)..	1	37	49*	0.1	0.1
127 CH GOD (CLEVE)	2	151	198*	0.2	0.5
165 CH OF NAZARENE	2	161	405	0.5	0.9
193 EPISCOPAL.....	2	712	1,043	1.2	2.4
281 LUTH CH AMER..	2	233	343	0.4	0.8
283 LUTH--MO SYNOD	1	214	310	0.4	0.7
349 PENT HOLINESS.	1	38	50*	0.1	0.1
357 PRESB CH US...	4	910	1,194*	1.4	2.7
403 SALVATION ARMY	1	19	159	0.2	0.4
413 S-D ADVENTISTS	1	20	26*	-	0.1
419 SO BAPT CONV..	37	16,660	21,868*	24.9	49.9
449 UN METHODIST..	30	7,147	8,109	9.2	18.5
JASPER	64	7,376	8,940*	55.9	100.0
059 BAPT MISS ASSN	5	854	1,063*	6.6	11.9
081 CATHOLIC......	1	0	112	0.7	1.3
357 PRESB CH US...	8	300	373*	2.3	4.2
419 SO BAPT CONV..	22	3,381	4,207*	26.3	47.1
449 UN METHODIST..	28	2,841	3,185	19.9	35.6
JEFFERSON	31	2,466	3,162*	34.0	100.0
081 CATHOLIC......	2	0	200	2.2	6.3
093 CR CH (DISC)..	4	324	410*	4.4	13.0
357 PRESB CH US...	3	161	204*	2.2	6.5
419 SO BAPT CONV..	8	786	995*	10.7	31.5
449 UN METHODIST..	14	1,195	1,353	14.6	42.8
JEFFERSON DAVIS	30	5,078	6,717*	51.9	100.0
059 BAPT MISS ASSN	2	294	367*	2.8	5.5
081 CATHOLIC......	3	0	411	3.2	6.1
127 CH GOD (CLEVE)	1	54	67*	0.5	1.0
165 CH OF NAZARENE	1	21	135	1.0	2.0
357 PRESB CH US...	2	196	244*	1.9	3.6
419 SO BAPT CONV..	15	3,898	4,861*	37.6	72.4
449 UN METHODIST..	6	615	632	4.9	9.4
JONES	109	28,952	35,398*	62.8	100.0
059 BAPT MISS ASSN	18	4,028	4,882*	8.7	13.8
081 CATHOLIC......	1	0	908	1.6	2.6
127 CH GOD (CLEVE)	2	180	218*	0.4	0.6
165 CH OF NAZARENE	2	128	221	0.4	0.6
193 EPISCOPAL.....	1	360	446	0.8	1.3
281 LUTH CH AMER..	1	94	121	0.2	0.3
357 PRESB CH US...	5	984	1,193*	2.1	3.4
403 SALVATION ARMY	1	86	226	0.4	0.6
413 S-D ADVENTISTS	3	203	246*	0.4	0.7
419 SO BAPT CONV..	45	17,586	21,314*	37.8	60.2
435 UNITARIAN-UNIV	2	70	70	0.1	0.2
449 UN METHODIST..	28	5,233	5,553	9.9	15.7
KEMPER	52	3,877	4,475*	43.7	100.0
123 CH GOD (ANDER)	1	16	44	0.4	1.0
285 MENNONITE CH..	1	24	30*	0.3	0.7
357 PRESB CH US...	5	251	310*	3.0	6.9
419 SO BAPT CONV..	17	1,543	1,908*	18.6	42.6
449 UN METHODIST..	28	2,043	2,183	21.3	48.8
LAFAYETTE	56	9,249	11,167*	46.2	100.0
081 CATHOLIC......	1	0	265	1.1	2.4
165 CH OF NAZARENE	1	6	20	0.1	0.2
283 LUTH--MO SYNOD	1	18	43	0.2	0.4
357 PRESB CH US...	6	631	758*	3.1	6.8
419 SO BAPT CONV..	22	5,843	7,015*	29.0	62.8
449 UN METHODIST..	25	2,751	3,066	12.7	27.5
LAMAR	37	6,681	8,320*	54.7	100.0
059 BAPT MISS ASSN	5	801	996*	6.5	12.0
081 CATHOLIC......	1	0	223	1.5	2.7
127 CH GOD (CLEVE)	2	38	47*	0.3	0.6
357 PRESB CH US...	1	16	20*	0.1	0.2
413 S-D ADVENTISTS	1	120	149*	1.0	1.8
419 SO BAPT CONV..	14	4,385	5,452*	35.8	65.5
449 UN METHODIST..	13	1,321	1,433	9.4	17.2
LAUDERDALE	131	32,261	40,782*	60.8	100.0
059 BAPT MISS ASSN	1	51	62*	0.1	0.2
081 CATHOLIC......	2	0	1,561	2.3	3.8
093 CR CH (DISC)..	1	304	369*	0.6	0.9
097 CR C AND C CR.	1	20	24*	-	0.1
123 CH GOD (ANDER)	10	422	1,168	1.7	2.9
127 CH GOD (CLEVE)	2	120	146*	0.2	0.4
165 CH OF NAZARENE	3	249	627	0.9	1.5
193 EPISCOPAL.....	3	926	1,235	1.8	3.0
283 LUTH--MO SYNOD	2	122	194	0.3	0.5
285 MENNONITE CH..	1	10	12*	-	-
349 PENT HOLINESS.	4	119	145*	0.2	0.4
357 PRESB CH US...	9	1,604	1,949*	2.9	4.8
403 SALVATION ARMY	1	83	334	0.5	0.8
413 S-D ADVENTISTS	2	330	401*	0.6	1.0
419 SO BAPT CONV..	46	18,641	22,654*	33.8	55.5
449 UN METHODIST..	42	9,155	9,773	14.6	24.0
453 UN PRES CH USA	1	105	128*	0.2	0.3
LAWRENCE	29	5,334	6,568*	59.0	100.0
059 BAPT MISS ASSN	1	50	62*	0.6	0.9
123 CH GOD (ANDER)	1	36	76	0.7	1.2
127 CH GOD (CLEVE)	1	18	22*	0.2	0.3
165 CH OF NAZARENE	1	38	52	0.5	0.8
357 PRESB CH US...	1	28	35*	0.3	0.5
419 SO BAPT CONV..	20	4,673	5,814*	52.2	88.5
449 UN METHODIST..	4	491	507	4.6	7.7
LEAKE	63	7,115	8,650*	50.6	100.0
059 BAPT MISS ASSN	1	25	30*	0.2	0.3
081 CATHOLIC......	1	0	224	1.3	2.6
093 CR CH (DISC)..	1	65	78*	0.5	0.9
123 CH GOD (ANDER)	2	45	117	0.7	1.4
185 CUMBER PRESB..	3	201	243*	1.4	2.8
357 PRESB CH US...	2	159	192*	1.1	2.2
419 SO BAPT CONV..	37	5,150	6,213*	36.4	71.8
449 UN METHODIST..	15	1,442	1,519	8.9	17.6
453 UN PRES CH USA	1	28	34*	0.2	0.4
LEE	102	23,290	28,752*	62.3	100.0
055 AS REF PRES CH	1	117	145*	0.3	0.5
059 BAPT MISS ASSN	10	1,309	1,621*	3.5	5.6
081 CATHOLIC......	2	0	594	1.3	2.1
093 CR CH (DISC)..	1	212	262*	0.6	0.9
097 CR C AND C CR.	7	635	786*	1.7	2.7
127 CH GOD (CLEVE)	2	85	105*	0.2	0.4
165 CH OF NAZARENE	1	24	78	0.2	0.3
193 EPISCOPAL.....	1	211	325	0.7	1.1
283 LUTH--MO SYNOD	1	96	140	0.3	0.5
357 PRESB CH US...	5	878	1,087*	2.4	3.8
403 SALVATION ARMY	1	3	63	0.1	0.2
413 S-D ADVENTISTS	1	35	43*	0.1	0.1
419 SO BAPT CONV..	41	14,253	17,645*	38.2	61.4
449 UN METHODIST..	27	5,414	5,836	12.6	20.3
453 UN PRES CH USA	1	18	22*	-	0.1
LEFLORE	44	11,766	15,634*	37.1	100.0
081 CATHOLIC......	3	0	1,005	2.4	6.4
093 CR CH (DISC)..	3	386	495*	1.2	3.2
127 CH GOD (CLEVE)	2	203	260*	0.6	1.7
165 CH OF NAZARENE	1	46	46	0.1	0.3
193 EPISCOPAL.....	1	442	492	1.2	3.1
283 LUTH--MO SYNOD	1	46	66	0.2	0.4
357 PRESB CH US...	3	783	1,003*	2.4	6.4
403 SALVATION ARMY	1	83	255	0.6	1.6
413 S-D ADVENTISTS	1	75	96*	0.2	0.6
419 SO BAPT CONV..	12	6,559	8,403*	20.0	53.7
449 UN METHODIST..	16	3,143	3,513	8.3	22.5
LINCOLN	59	15,214	18,986*	72.5	100.0
029 AMER LUTH CH..	1	25	38	0.1	0.2
081 CATHOLIC......	1	0	388	1.5	2.0
123 CH GOD (ANDER)	1	24	55	0.2	0.3
127 CH GOD (CLEVE)	1	54	67*	0.3	0.4
165 CH OF NAZARENE	1	49	109	0.4	0.6
193 EPISCOPAL.....	1	58	101	0.4	0.5

*Total adherents estimated from known number of communicant, confirmed, full members.

—Represents a percent less than 0.1.

Percentages may not total due to rounding.

Table 3. Churches and Church Membership by State, County and Denomination: 1971

County and Denomination	Number of churches	Communicant, confirmed, full members	Total adherents: Number	Total adherents: Percent of total population	Total adherents: Percent of total adherents
357 PRESB CH US...	1	441	544*	2.1	2.9
413 S-D ADVENTISTS	2	47	58*	0.2	0.3
419 SO BAPT CONV..	39	12,413	15,309*	58.4	80.6
449 UN METHODIST..	11	2,103	2,317	8.8	12.2
LOWNDES	61	15,029	19,152*	38.5	100.0
059 BAPT MISS ASSN	1	118	148*	0.3	0.8
081 CATHOLIC......	1	0	650	1.3	3.4
097 CR C AND C CR.	1	190	238*	0.5	1.2
127 CH GOD (CLEVE)	1	61	76*	0.2	0.4
165 CH OF NAZARENE	2	93	179	0.4	0.9
185 CUMBER PRESB..	4	566	710*	1.4	3.7
193 EPISCOPAL.....	2	474	646	1.3	3.4
283 LUTH--MO SYNOD	1	134	189	0.4	1.0
357 PRESB CH US...	4	796	998*	2.0	5.2
403 SALVATION ARMY	1	65	245	0.5	1.3
413 S-D ADVENTISTS	2	142	178*	0.4	0.9
419 SO BAPT CONV..	23	8,974	11,252*	22.6	58.8
449 UN METHODIST..	18	3,416	3,643	7.3	19.0
MADISON	39	6,496	8,947*	30.1	100.0
081 CATHOLIC......	4	0	930	3.1	10.4
123 CH GOD (ANDER)	1	49	83	0.3	0.9
165 CH OF NAZARENE	1	24	32	0.1	0.4
193 EPISCOPAL.....	2	125	173	0.6	1.9
357 PRESB CH US...	6	579	748*	2.5	8.4
413 S-D ADVENTISTS	1	71	92*	0.3	1.0
419 SO BAPT CONV..	11	3,527	4,556*	15.3	50.9
449 UN METHODIST..	13	2,121	2,333	7.8	26.1
MARION	52	11,510	14,195*	62.1	100.0
059 BAPT MISS ASSN	2	381	471*	2.1	3.3
081 CATHOLIC......	2	0	260	1.1	1.8
127 CH GOD (CLEVE)	6	421	520*	2.3	3.7
165 CH OF NAZARENE	1	43	83	0.4	0.6
193 EPISCOPAL.....	1	37	47	0.2	0.3
285 MENNONITE CH..	1	13	16*	0.1	0.1
357 PRESB CH US...	1	184	227*	1.0	1.6
413 S-D ADVENTISTS	1	18	22*	0.1	0.2
419 SO BAPT CONV..	23	8,352	10,315*	45.1	72.7
449 UN METHODIST..	14	2,061	2,234	9.8	15.7
MARSHALL	43	6,439	8,013*	33.3	100.0
081 CATHOLIC......	1	0	187	0.8	2.3
193 EPISCOPAL.....	1	103	105	0.4	1.3
283 LUTH--MO SYNOD	1	27	40	0.2	0.5
357 PRESB CH US...	5	266	345*	1.4	4.3
419 SO BAPT CONV..	16	3,836	4,977*	20.7	62.1
449 UN METHODIST..	19	2,207	2,359	9.8	29.4
MONROE	68	12,345	14,765*	43.4	100.0
059 BAPT MISS ASSN	1	266	333*	1.0	2.3
081 CATHOLIC......	2	0	165	0.5	1.1
093 CR CH (DISC)..	1	36	45*	0.1	0.3
097 CR C AND C CR.	2	525	657*	1.9	4.4
127 CH GOD (CLEVE)	2	63	79*	0.2	0.5
193 EPISCOPAL.....	1	60	72	0.2	0.5
357 PRESB CH US...	3	293	367*	1.1	2.5
413 S-D ADVENTISTS	2	37	46*	0.1	0.3
419 SO BAPT CONV..	30	6,437	8,055*	23.7	54.6
449 UN METHODIST..	23	4,553	4,852	14.3	32.9
453 UN PRES CH USA	1	75	94*	0.3	0.6
MONTGOMERY	43	6,166	7,386*	57.2	100.0
081 CATHOLIC......	1	0	85	0.7	1.2
127 CH GOD (CLEVE)	2	98	121*	0.9	1.6
193 EPISCOPAL.....	1	22	22	0.2	0.3
357 PRESB CH US...	3	180	223*	1.7	3.0
419 SO BAPT CONV..	21	4,023	4,981*	38.6	67.4
449 UN METHODIST..	15	1,843	1,954	15.1	26.5
NESHOBA	72	8,824	11,432*	55.0	100.0
081 CATHOLIC......	4	0	886	4.3	7.8
123 CH GOD (ANDER)	2	92	216	1.0	1.9
127 CH GOD (CLEVE)	1	56	69*	0.3	0.6
185 CUMBER PRESB..	3	205	251*	1.2	2.2
193 EPISCOPAL.....	1	19	35	0.2	0.3
357 PRESB CH US...	3	288	353*	1.7	3.1
419 SO BAPT CONV..	37	5,814	7,124*	34.2	62.3
449 UN METHODIST..	20	2,314	2,454	11.8	21.5
453 UN PRES CH USA	1	36	44*	0.2	0.4
NEWTON	65	9,377	11,320*	59.6	100.0
059 BAPT MISS ASSN	1	157	188*	1.0	1.7
081 CATHOLIC......	2	0	280	1.5	2.5
097 CR C AND C CR.	2	200	239*	1.3	2.1
123 CH GOD (ANDER)	3	78	217	1.1	1.9
127 CH GOD (CLEVE)	5	203	243*	1.3	2.1
185 CUMBER PRESB..	1	7	8*	-	0.1
193 EPISCOPAL.....	1	18	31	0.2	0.3
357 PRESB CH US...	3	184	220*	1.2	1.9
413 S-D ADVENTISTS	1	84	101*	0.5	0.9
419 SO BAPT CONV..	30	6,066	7,259*	38.2	64.1
449 UN METHODIST..	16	2,380	2,534	13.3	22.4
NOXUBEE	43	4,011	4,853*	34.0	100.0

County and Denomination	Number of churches	Communicant, confirmed, full members	Total adherents: Number	Total adherents: Percent of total population	Total adherents: Percent of total adherents
081 CATHOLIC......	1	0	27	0.2	0.6
123 CH GOD (ANDER)	2	45	123	0.9	2.5
185 CUMBER PRESB..	2	149	191*	1.3	3.9
193 EPISCOPAL.....	2	49	65	0.5	1.3
285 MENNONITE CH..	1	50	64*	0.4	1.3
357 PRESB CH US...	3	137	176*	1.2	3.6
419 SO BAPT CONV..	11	1,731	2,221*	15.5	45.8
449 UN METHODIST..	21	1,850	1,986	13.9	40.9
OKTIBBEHA	56	12,425	16,217*	56.4	100.0
081 CATHOLIC......	1	0	1,400	4.9	8.6
093 CR CH (DISC)..	1	12	15*	0.1	0.1
097 CR C AND C CR.	1	30	37*	0.1	0.2
123 CH GOD (ANDER)	1	8	19	0.1	0.1
127 CH GOD (CLEVE)	2	129	157*	0.5	1.0
193 EPISCOPAL.....	1	169	331	1.2	2.0
281 LUTH CH AMER..	1	9	9	-	0.1
283 LUTH--MO SYNOD	1	33	50	0.2	0.3
357 PRESB CH US...	2	844	1,029*	3.6	6.3
419 SO BAPT CONV..	18	6,985	8,520*	29.6	52.5
449 UN METHODIST..	26	4,187	4,627	16.1	28.5
453 UN PRES CH USA	1	19	23*	0.1	0.1
PANOLA	58	9,041	11,154*	41.6	100.0
081 CATHOLIC......	2	0	141	0.5	1.3
123 CH GOD (ANDER)	1	50	150	0.6	1.3
127 CH GOD (CLEVE)	3	68	87*	0.3	0.8
165 CH OF NAZARENE	1	23	27	0.1	0.2
193 EPISCOPAL.....	1	56	71	0.3	0.6
357 PRESB CH US...	2	565	721*	2.7	6.5
419 SO BAPT CONV..	24	5,397	6,887*	25.7	61.7
449 UN METHODIST..	21	2,651	2,775	10.3	24.9
453 UN PRES CH USA	3	231	295*	1.1	2.6
PEARL RIVER	58	14,210	18,111*	65.1	100.0
059 BAPT MISS ASSN	17	2,427	3,038*	10.9	16.8
081 CATHOLIC......	2	0	540	1.9	3.0
127 CH GOD (CLEVE)	1	72	90*	0.3	0.5
165 CH OF NAZARENE	1	11	27	0.1	0.1
193 EPISCOPAL.....	1	95	126	0.5	0.7
283 LUTH--MO SYNOD	1	67	102	0.4	0.6
357 PRESB CH US...	2	128	160*	0.6	0.9
419 SO BAPT CONV..	29	10,154	12,712*	45.7	70.2
449 UN METHODIST..	4	1,256	1,316	4.7	7.3
PERRY	35	4,413	5,513*	60.8	100.0
059 BAPT MISS ASSN	6	609	768*	8.5	13.9
123 CH GOD (ANDER)	1	28	78	0.9	1.4
127 CH GOD (CLEVE)	4	108	136*	1.5	2.5
357 PRESB CH US...	1	24	30*	0.3	0.5
419 SO BAPT CONV..	17	3,087	3,895*	43.0	70.7
449 UN METHODIST..	6	557	606	6.7	11.0
PIKE	61	15,129	19,383*	61.0	100.0
059 BAPT MISS ASSN	1	94	115*	0.4	0.6
081 CATHOLIC......	3	0	897	2.8	4.6
093 CR CH (DISC)..	1	115	141*	0.4	0.7
127 CH GOD (CLEVE)	1	59	72*	0.2	0.4
165 CH OF NAZARENE	2	383	571	1.8	2.9
193 EPISCOPAL.....	2	114	140	0.4	0.7
283 LUTH--MO SYNOD	1	44	66	0.2	0.3
353 PLY BRETHREN..	1	15	20	0.1	0.1
357 PRESB CH US...	4	714	875*	2.8	4.5
403 SALVATION ARMY	1	12	159	0.5	0.8
413 S-D ADVENTISTS	2	39	48*	0.2	0.2
419 SO BAPT CONV..	28	10,735	13,158*	41.4	67.9
449 UN METHODIST..	14	2,805	3,121	9.8	16.1
PONTOTOC	52	9,662	11,885*	68.5	100.0
081 CATHOLIC......	1	0	70	0.4	0.6
127 CH GOD (CLEVE)	1	43	52*	0.3	0.4
165 CH OF NAZARENE	2	56	100	0.6	0.8
357 PRESB CH US...	5	228	278*	1.6	2.3
419 SO BAPT CONV..	43	9,335	11,385*	65.6	95.8
PRENTISS	46	8,000	9,372*	46.6	100.0
059 BAPT MISS ASSN	3	341	415*	2.1	4.4
081 CATHOLIC......	1	0	62	0.3	0.7
127 CH GOD (CLEVE)	2	172	209*	1.0	2.2
357 PRESB CH US...	1	50	61*	0.3	0.7
419 SO BAPT CONV..	21	4,932	6,003*	29.8	64.1
449 UN METHODIST..	18	2,505	2,622	13.0	28.0
QUITMAN	24	4,862	6,156*	38.7	100.0
093 CR CH (DISC)..	1	39	52*	0.3	0.8
127 CH GOD (CLEVE)	2	156	206*	1.3	3.3
165 CH OF NAZARENE	1	24	36	0.2	0.6
357 PRESB CH US...	1	218	288*	1.8	4.7
419 SO BAPT CONV..	11	3,323	4,389*	27.6	71.3
449 UN METHODIST..	8	1,102	1,185	7.5	19.2
RANKIN	80	17,847	21,861*	49.8	100.0
059 BAPT MISS ASSN	1	242	302*	0.7	1.4
081 CATHOLIC......	1	0	98	0.2	0.4
127 CH GOD (CLEVE)	1	23	29*	0.1	0.1
193 EPISCOPAL.....	1	37	71	0.2	0.3

*Total adherents estimated from known number of communicant, confirmed, full members.

—Represents a percent less than 0.1.

Percentages may not total due to rounding.

Table 3. Churches and Church Membership by State, County and Denomination: 1971

County and Denomination	Number of churches	Communicant, confirmed, full members	Total adherents: Number	Total adherents: Percent of total population	Total adherents: Percent of total adherents
357 PRESB CH US...	2	99	123*	0.3	0.6
413 S-D ADVENTISTS	1	96	120*	0.3	0.5
419 SO BAPT CONV..	45	13,387	16,698*	38.0	76.4
449 UN METHODIST..	28	3,963	4,420	10.1	20.2
SCOTT	63	7,448	9,514*	44.5	100.0
081 CATHOLIC......	1	0	94	0.4	1.0
097 CR C AND C CR.	1	32	40*	0.2	0.4
127 CH GOD (CLEVE)	2	112	139*	0.7	1.5
185 CUMBER PRESB..	1	33	41*	0.2	0.4
281 LUTH CH AMER..	1	19	20	0.1	0.2
357 PRESB CH US...	2	137	170*	0.8	1.8
419 SO BAPT CONV..	36	6,861	8,513*	39.8	89.5
449 UN METHODIST..	19	254	497	2.3	5.2
SHARKEY	15	2,376	3,053*	34.2	100.0
059 BAPT MISS ASSN	1	59	78*	0.9	2.6
081 CATHOLIC......	1	0	79	0.9	2.6
193 EPISCOPAL.....	1	80	94	1.1	3.1
357 PRESB CH US...	1	64	85*	1.0	2.8
419 SO BAPT CONV..	6	1,509	2,004*	22.4	65.6
449 UN METHODIST..	5	664	713	8.0	23.4
SIMPSON	59	11,840	14,557*	73.0	100.0
059 BAPT MISS ASSN	1	130	161*	0.8	1.1
081 CATHOLIC......	1	0	125	0.6	0.9
127 CH GOD (CLEVE)	4	242	300*	1.5	2.1
357 PRESB CH US...	2	192	238*	1.2	1.6
419 SO BAPT CONV..	43	10,013	12,401*	62.2	85.2
449 UN METHODIST..	8	1,263	1,332	6.7	9.2
SMITH	66	9,087	10,842*	79.9	100.0
059 BAPT MISS ASSN	5	451	554*	4.1	5.1
081 CATHOLIC......	1	0	42	0.3	0.4
281 LUTH CH AMER..	2	73	88	0.6	0.8
357 PRESB CH US...	2	86	106*	0.8	1.0
419 SO BAPT CONV..	40	6,770	8,311*	61.3	76.7
449 UN METHODIST..	16	1,707	1,741	12.8	16.1
STONE	21	3,357	4,048*	50.0	100.0
059 BAPT MISS ASSN	8	1,150	1,409*	17.4	34.8
081 CATHOLIC......	1	0	54	0.7	1.3
127 CH GOD (CLEVE)	1	11	13*	0.2	0.3
357 PRESB CH US...	1	101	124*	1.5	3.1
419 SO BAPT CONV..	5	1,391	1,704*	21.0	42.1
449 UN METHODIST..	5	704	744	9.2	18.4
SUNFLOWER	51	10,100	12,980*	35.0	100.0
059 BAPT MISS ASSN	1	50	65*	0.2	0.5
081 CATHOLIC......	3	0	470	1.3	3.6
093 CR CH (DISC)..	4	132	171*	0.5	1.3
097 CR C AND C CR.	1	50	65*	0.2	0.5
123 CH GOD (ANDER)	1	27	62	0.2	0.5
127 CH GOD (CLEVE)	6	335	435*	1.2	3.4
193 EPISCOPAL.....	2	203	249	0.7	1.9
353 PLY BRETHREN..	1	15	20	0.1	0.2
357 PRESB CH US...	1	165	214*	0.6	1.6
413 S-D ADVENTISTS	1	68	88*	0.2	0.7
419 SO BAPT CONV..	16	6,526	8,476*	22.9	65.3
449 UN METHODIST..	14	2,529	2,665	7.2	20.5
TALLAHATCHIE	37	5,203	6,591*	34.1	100.0
081 CATHOLIC......	1	0	8	-	0.1
127 CH GOD (CLEVE)	3	238	312*	1.6	4.7
193 EPISCOPAL.....	1	69	83	0.4	1.3
357 PRESB CH US...	5	287	376*	1.9	5.7
419 SO BAPT CONV..	17	3,660	4,800*	24.8	72.8
449 UN METHODIST..	8	919	973	5.0	14.8
453 UN PRES CH USA	2	30	39*	0.2	0.6
TATE	37	6,342	7,651*	41.3	100.0
281 LUTH CH AMER..	1	53	56	0.3	0.7
349 PENT HOLINESS.	1	8	10*	0.1	0.1
357 PRESB CH US...	1	105	134*	0.7	1.8
419 SO BAPT CONV..	18	4,390	5,619*	30.3	73.4
449 UN METHODIST..	16	1,786	1,832	9.9	23.9
TIPPAH	62	9,092	10,725*	67.7	100.0
055 AS REF PRES CH	1	153	186*	1.2	1.7
081 CATHOLIC......	1	0	43	0.3	0.4
127 CH GOD (CLEVE)	2	54	66*	0.4	0.6
185 CUMBER PRESB..	1	90	110*	0.7	1.0
357 PRESB CH US...	6	447	544*	3.4	5.1
419 SO BAPT CONV..	29	6,068	7,389*	46.6	68.9
449 UN METHODIST..	22	2,280	2,387	15.1	22.3
TISHOMINGO	57	6,459	7,423*	49.7	100.0
059 BAPT MISS ASSN	8	513	614*	4.1	8.3
127 CH GOD (CLEVE)	2	77	92*	0.6	1.2
193 EPISCOPAL.....	1	6	9	0.1	0.1
357 PRESB CH US...	2	2	2*	-	-
419 SO BAPT CONV..	24	4,034	4,832*	32.3	65.1
449 UN METHODIST..	20	1,827	1,874	12.5	25.2
TUNICA	11	2,098	2,624*	22.1	100.0

County and Denomination	Number of churches	Communicant, confirmed, full members	Total adherents: Number	Total adherents: Percent of total population	Total adherents: Percent of total adherents
193 EPISCOPAL.....	1	59	92	0.8	3.5
357 PRESB CH US...	1	185	249*	2.1	9.5
419 SO BAPT CONV..	5	1,111	1,494*	12.6	56.9
449 UN METHODIST..	4	743	789	6.7	30.1
UNION	55	13,051	15,571*	81.5	100.0
055 AS REF PRES CH	2	413	501*	2.6	3.2
081 CATHOLIC......	1	0	58	0.3	0.4
127 CH GOD (CLEVE)	2	106	128*	0.7	0.8
165 CH OF NAZARENE	1	19	36	0.2	0.2
419 SO BAPT CONV..	37	10,387	12,588*	65.9	80.8
449 UN METHODIST..	11	1,992	2,098	11.0	13.5
453 UN PRES CH USA	1	134	162*	0.8	1.0
WALTHALL	21	5,246	6,401*	51.2	100.0
419 SO BAPT CONV..	13	4,395	5,433*	43.5	84.9
449 UN METHODIST..	8	851	968	7.7	15.1
WARREN	48	14,424	21,374*	47.5	100.0
059 BAPT MISS ASSN	2	167	209*	0.5	1.0
081 CATHOLIC......	3	0	3,896	8.7	18.2
093 CR CH (DISC)..	2	174	218*	0.5	1.0
123 CH GOD (ANDER)	1	5	16	-	0.1
127 CH GOD (CLEVE)	2	87	109*	0.2	0.5
165 CH OF NAZARENE	1	126	200	0.4	0.9
193 EPISCOPAL.....	4	688	822	1.8	3.8
283 LUTH--MO SYNOD	1	83	130	0.3	0.6
357 PRESB CH US...	3	966	1,209*	2.7	5.7
403 SALVATION ARMY	1	58	201	0.4	0.9
413 S-D ADVENTISTS	2	113	141*	0.3	0.7
419 SO BAPT CONV..	13	7,978	9,989*	22.2	46.7
449 UN METHODIST..	13	3,979	4,234	9.4	19.8
WASHINGTON	56	18,829	26,916*	38.1	100.0
059 BAPT MISS ASSN	1	88	114*	0.2	0.4
081 CATHOLIC......	4	0	3,063	4.3	11.4
093 CR CH (DISC)..	1	161	209*	0.3	0.8
127 CH GOD (CLEVE)	4	372	484*	0.7	1.8
165 CH OF NAZARENE	1	46	118	0.2	0.4
193 EPISCOPAL.....	4	700	914	1.3	3.4
283 LUTH--MO SYNOD	1	64	99	0.1	0.4
357 PRESB CH US...	4	997	1,296*	1.8	4.8
403 SALVATION ARMY	1	57	230	0.3	0.9
413 S-D ADVENTISTS	5	302	393*	0.6	1.5
419 SO BAPT CONV..	20	11,969	15,560*	22.0	57.8
449 UN METHODIST..	10	4,073	4,436	6.3	16.5
WAYNE	46	5,755	7,067*	42.4	100.0
059 BAPT MISS ASSN	1	37	47*	0.3	0.7
081 CATHOLIC......	1	0	51	0.3	0.7
127 CH GOD (CLEVE)	1	127	160*	1.0	2.3
357 PRESB CH US...	3	219	275*	1.7	3.9
419 SO BAPT CONV..	23	4,079	5,128*	30.8	72.6
449 UN METHODIST..	17	1,293	1,406	8.4	19.9
WEBSTER	54	5,843	6,982*	69.5	100.0
127 CH GOD (CLEVE)	4	139	168*	1.7	2.4
419 SO BAPT CONV..	31	4,720	5,709*	56.8	81.8
449 UN METHODIST..	18	981	1,101	11.0	15.8
453 UN PRES CH USA	1	3	4*	-	0.1
WILKINSON	21	2,819	3,586*	32.3	100.0
081 CATHOLIC......	2	0	257	2.3	7.2
093 CR CH (DISC)..	1	92	116*	1.0	3.2
193 EPISCOPAL.....	1	108	143	1.3	4.0
357 PRESB CH US...	2	247	310*	2.8	8.6
419 SO BAPT CONV..	5	1,231	1,546*	13.9	43.1
449 UN METHODIST..	10	1,141	1,214	10.9	33.9
WINSTON	61	9,077	10,886*	59.1	100.0
081 CATHOLIC......	1	0	95	0.5	0.9
123 CH GOD (ANDER)	1	28	50	0.3	0.5
281 LUTH CH AMER..	2	84	96	0.5	0.9
357 PRESB CH US...	1	229	282*	1.5	2.6
419 SO BAPT CONV..	29	5,790	7,121*	38.7	65.4
435 UNITARIAN-UNIV	1	42	42	0.2	0.4
449 UN METHODIST..	22	2,653	2,891	15.7	26.6
453 UN PRES CH USA	4	251	309*	1.7	2.8
YALOBUSHA	41	5,971	7,098*	59.6	100.0
097 CR C AND C CR.	1	200	245*	2.1	3.5
127 CH GOD (CLEVE)	2	104	127*	1.1	1.8
165 CH OF NAZARENE	1	66	96	0.8	1.4
193 EPISCOPAL.....	1	16	16	0.1	0.2
357 PRESB CH US...	2	157	192*	1.6	2.7
419 SO BAPT CONV..	23	4,086	5,002*	42.0	70.5
449 UN METHODIST..	9	1,226	1,278	10.7	18.0
453 UN PRES CH USA	2	116	142*	1.2	2.0
YAZOO	49	9,851	12,913*	47.3	100.0
059 BAPT MISS ASSN	2	204	258*	0.9	2.0
081 CATHOLIC......	2	0	830	3.0	6.4
123 CH GOD (ANDER)	1	85	250	0.9	1.9
127 CH GOD (CLEVE)	1	96	122*	0.4	0.9
165 CH OF NAZARENE	1	17	42	0.2	0.3

*Total adherents estimated from known number of communicant, confirmed, full members.

—Represents a percent less than 0.1.

Percentages may not total due to rounding.

Table 3. Churches and Church Membership by State, County and Denomination: 1971

County and Denomination	Number of churches	Communicant, confirmed, full members	Total adherents		
			Number	Percent of total population	Percent of total adherents
193 EPISCOPAL.....	1	241	263	1.0	2.0
357 PRESB CH US...	1	477	604*	2.2	4.7
413 S-D ADVENTISTS	1	74	94*	0.3	0.7
419 SO BAPT CONV..	23	5,667	7,173*	26.3	55.5
449 UN METHODIST..	16	2,990	3,277	12.0	25.4
CO DATA NOT AVAIL	61	5,578	13,015*	N/A	N/A
127 CH GOD (CLEVE)	2	140	175*	N/A	N/A
151 L-D SAINTS....	0	0	6,079	N/A	N/A
223 FREE WILL BAPT	49	5,048	6,324*	N/A	N/A
349 PENT HOLINESS.	2	104	130*	N/A	N/A
467 WESLEYAN......	8	286	307	N/A	N/A

MISSOURI

County and Denomination	Number of churches	Communicant, confirmed, full members	Total adherents		
			Number	Percent of total population	Percent of total adherents
THE STATE.....	6,627	1,313,154	2,391,454*	51.1	100.0
ADAIR	33	6,184	8,871*	39.5	100.0
081 CATHOLIC......	2	0	885	3.9	10.0
093 CR CH (DISC)..	3	751	871*	3.9	9.8
097 CR C AND C CR.	1	28	32*	0.1	0.4
123 CH GOD (ANDER)	2	90	210	0.9	2.4
165 CH OF NAZARENE	1	113	201	0.9	2.3
193 EPISCOPAL.....	1	140	200	0.9	2.3
197 EVAN CH OF NA.	1	101	117*	0.5	1.3
283 LUTH--MO SYNOD	1	219	294	1.3	3.3
357 PRESB CH US...	2	262	304*	1.4	3.4
403 SALVATION ARMY	1	43	753	3.4	8.5
413 S-D ADVENTISTS	1	44	51*	0.2	0.6
419 SO BAPT CONV..	5	2,412	2,798*	12.5	31.5
449 UN METHODIST..	10	1,729	1,863	8.3	21.0
453 UN PRES CH USA	2	252	292*	1.3	3.3
ANDREW	34	4,051	5,234*	43.9	100.0
081 CATHOLIC......	1	0	405	3.4	7.7
093 CR CH (DISC)..	6	957	1,151*	9.7	22.0
097 CR C AND C CR.	5	30	36*	0.3	0.7
123 CH GOD (ANDER)	1	40	115	1.0	2.2
357 PRESB CH US...	2	45	54*	0.5	1.0
419 SO BAPT CONV..	7	1,213	1,459*	12.2	27.9
443 UN C OF CHRIST	2	392	471*	4.0	9.0
449 UN METHODIST..	7	1,287	1,438	12.1	27.5
453 UN PRES CH USA	3	87	105*	0.9	2.0
ATCHISON	25	4,507	5,563*	60.2	100.0
081 CATHOLIC......	1	0	242	2.6	4.4
093 CR CH (DISC)..	3	323	380*	4.1	6.8
097 CR C AND C CR.	1	100	118*	1.3	2.1
127 CH GOD (CLEVE)	1	48	57*	0.6	1.0
185 CUMBER PRESB..	1	33	39*	0.4	0.7
281 LUTH CH AMER..	2	840	1,029	11.1	18.5
357 PRESB CH US...	3	256	301*	3.3	5.4
419 SO BAPT CONV..	5	1,015	1,195*	12.9	21.5
449 UN METHODIST..	5	1,659	1,928	20.9	34.7
453 UN PRES CH USA	3	233	274*	3.0	4.9
AUDRAIN	64	12,165	16,770*	66.1	100.0
081 CATHOLIC......	4	0	2,074	8.2	12.4
093 CR CH (DISC)..	8	1,618	1,962*	7.7	11.7
097 CR C AND C CR.	9	1,525	1,849*	7.3	11.0
165 CH OF NAZARENE	2	124	239	0.9	1.4
193 EPISCOPAL.....	1	84	94	0.4	0.6
283 LUTH--MO SYNOD	2	258	313	1.2	1.9
357 PRESB CH US...	7	753	913*	3.6	5.4
419 SO BAPT CONV..	17	5,111	6,197*	24.4	37.0
443 UN C OF CHRIST	1	112	136*	0.5	0.8
449 UN METHODIST..	7	1,871	2,133	8.4	12.7
453 UN PRES CH USA	6	709	860*	3.4	5.1
BARRY	53	9,345	1[illegible],965	61.1	100.0
059 BAPT MISS ASSN	3	173	204*	1.0	1.7
081 CATHOLIC......	3	0	1,081	5.5	9.0
093 CR CH (DISC)..	1	172	203*	1.0	1.7
097 CR C AND C CR.	2	459	541*	2.8	4.5
165 CH OF NAZARENE	1	53	[illegible]9	0.7	1.1
193 EPISCOPAL.....	1	80	1[illegible]5	0.5	0.9
283 LUTH--MO SYNOD	2	252	313	1.6	2.6
413 S-D ADVENTISTS	1	31	37*	0.2	0.3
419 SO BAPT CONV..	29	6,261	7,374*	37.6	61.6
449 UN METHODIST..	8	1,677	1,758	9.0	14.7
453 UN PRES CH USA	2	187	220*	1.1	1.8
BARTON	36	4,390	5,261*	50.4	100.0
081 CATHOLIC......	2	0	218	2.1	4.1
093 CR CH (DISC)..	3	251	291*	2.8	5.5
097 CR C AND C CR.	4	1,070	1,239*	11.9	2[illegible].6
165 CH OF NAZARENE	1	77	112	1.1	2.1
185 CUMBER PRESB..	1	80	93*	0.9	1.8
283 LUTH--MO SYNOD	1	117	173	1.7	3.3
357 PRESB CH US...	2	46	53*	0.5	1.0
419 SO BAPT CONV..	11	1,511	1,750*	16.8	33.3
449 UN METHODIST..	10	1,211	1,301	12.5	24.7
453 UN PRES CH USA	1	27	31*	0.3	0.6
BATES	60	6,783	8,096*	52.3	100.0
029 AMER LUTH CH..	3	78	115	0.7	1.4
081 CATHOLIC......	2	0	236	1.5	2.9
093 CR CH (DISC)..	3	743	876*	5.7	10.8
097 CR C AND C CR.	10	988	1,165*	7.5	14.4
165 CH OF NAZARENE	2	38	95	0.6	1.2
283 LUTH--MO SYNOD	1	213	261	1.7	3.2
353 PLY BRETHREN..	1	10	10	0.1	0.1
357 PRESB CH US...	2	144	170*	1.1	2.1
419 SO BAPT CONV..	14	2,330	2,747*	17.8	33.9
443 UN C OF CHRIST	1	58	68*	0.4	0.8
449 UN METHODIST..	16	1,943	2,072	13.4	25.6
453 UN PRES CH USA	5	238	281*	1.8	3.5
BENTON	37	4,958	6,115*	63.1	100.0
029 AMER LUTH CH..	2	413	539	5.6	8.8
081 CATHOLIC......	2	0	275	2.8	4.5
093 CR CH (DISC)..	2	84	97*	1.0	1.6
157 CH OF BRETHREN	2	39	45*	0.5	0.7
165 CH OF NAZARENE	1	27	57	0.6	0.9
281 LUTH CH AMER..	1	128	159	1.6	2.6
283 LUTH--MO SYNOD	7	1,480	1,798	18.5	29.4
285 MENNONITE CH..	1	23	27*	0.3	0.4
419 SO BAPT CONV..	11	1,670	1,924*	19.8	31.5
449 UN METHODIST..	8	1,094	1,194	12.3	19.5
BOLLINGER	34	2,466	3,872*	43.9	100.0
059 BAPT MISS ASSN	1	16	19*	0.2	0.5
081 CATHOLIC......	2	0	842	9.5	21.7
123 CH GOD (ANDER)	1	40	138	1.6	3.6
127 CH GOD (CLEVE)	1	33	39*	0.4	1.0
281 LUTH CH AMER..	2	121	174	2.0	4.5
353 PLY BRETHREN..	1	32	101	1.1	2.6
419 SO BAPT CONV..	12	1,184	1,404*	15.9	36.3
449 UN METHODIST..	11	838	916	10.4	23.7
453 UN PRES CH USA	3	202	239*	2.7	6.2
BOONE	73	22,257	30,402*	37.6	100.0
019 AMER BAPT CONV	2	1,501	1,790*	2.2	5.9
081 CATHOLIC......	4	0	2,942	3.6	9.7
093 CR CH (DISC)..	12	3,263	3,891*	4.8	12.8
097 CR C AND C CR.	5	482	575*	0.7	1.9
123 CH GOD (ANDER)	1	70	220	0.3	0.7
165 CH OF NAZARENE	1	126	272	0.3	0.9
193 EPISCOPAL.....	1	700	1,158	1.4	3.8
226 FRIENDS-USA...	1	23	27*	-	0.1
281 LUTH CH AMER..	1	311	484	0.6	1.6
283 LUTH--MO SYNOD	3	737	981	1.2	3.2
357 PRESB CH US...	2	636	758*	0.9	2.5
403 SALVATION ARMY	1	35	175	0.2	0.6
413 S-D ADVENTISTS	2	406	484*	0.6	1.6
419 SO BAPT CONV..	22	8,409	10,027*	12.4	33.0
435 UNITARIAN-UNIV	1	92	133	0.2	0.4
443 UN C OF CHRIST	2	452	539*	0.7	1.8
449 UN METHODIST..	10	4,388	5,200	6.4	17.1
453 UN PRES CH USA	2	626	746*	0.9	2.5
BUCHANAN	102	28,975	49,300*	56.7	100.0
081 CATHOLIC......	11	0	13,926	16.0	28.2
093 CR CH (DISC)..	5	3,367	4,076*	4.7	8.3
097 CR C AND C CR.	8	1,469	1,778*	2.0	3.6
123 CH GOD (ANDER)	1	14	39	-	0.1
127 CH GOD (CLEVE)	2	130	157*	0.2	0.3
157 CH OF BRETHREN	1	61	74*	0.1	0.2
165 CH OF NAZARENE	3	225	494	0.6	1.0
185 CUMBER PRESB..	2	192	232*	0.3	0.5
193 EPISCOPAL.....	1	601	647	0.7	1.3
221 FREE METH C NA	1	14	27	-	0.1
281 LUTH CH AMER..	1	664	817	0.9	1.7
283 LUTH--MO SYNOD	2	943	1,294	1.5	2.6
357 PRESB CH US...	9	1,363	1,650*	1.9	3.3
403 SALVATION ARMY	1	107	393	0.5	0.8
413 S-D ADVENTISTS	2	233	282*	0.3	0.6
419 SO BAPT CONV..	20	9,733	11,781*	13.6	23.9
443 UN C OF CHRIST	2	794	961*	1.1	1.9
449 UN METHODIST..	21	7,724	9,049	10.4	18.4
453 UN PRES CH USA	9	1,341	1,623*	1.9	3.3
BUTLER	54	8,865	12,142*	36.2	100.0
059 BAPT MISS ASSN	8	563	671*	2.0	5.5
081 CATHOLIC......	2	0	1,164	3.5	9.6
093 CR CH (DISC)..	1	759	905*	2.7	7.5
123 CH GOD (ANDER)	3	235	625	1.9	5.1
127 CH GOD (CLEVE)	1	38	45*	0.1	0.4
165 CH OF NAZARENE	2	172	352	1.0	2.9
193 EPISCOPAL.....	1	107	182	0.5	1.5
283 LUTH--MO SYNOD	1	261	343	1.0	2.8
349 PENT HOLINESS.	1	24	29*	0.1	0.2
353 PLY BRETHREN..	1	10	15	-	0.1
413 S-D ADVENTISTS	1	122	145*	0.4	1.2
419 SO BAPT CONV..	22	4,821	5,747*	17.1	47.3
449 UN METHODIST..	8	1,478	1,591	4.7	13.1
453 UN PRES CH USA	2	275	328*	1.0	2.7

*Total adherents estimated from known number of communicant, confirmed, full members.

—Represents a percent less than 0.1.

Percentages may not total due to rounding.

Table 3. Churches and Church Membership by State, County and Denomination: 1971

County and Denomination	Number of churches	Communicant, confirmed, full members	Total adherents: Number	Total adherents: Percent of total population	Total adherents: Percent of total adherents
CALDWELL	32	4,574	5,673*	67.9	100.0
081 CATHOLIC......	2	0	339	4.1	6.0
093 CR CH (DISC)..	5	396	459*	5.5	8.1
097 CR C AND C CR.	1	47	55*	0.7	1.0
107 CHRISTIAN UN..	2	216	251*	3.0	4.4
165 CH OF NAZARENE	1	92	267	3.2	4.7
419 SO BAPT CONV..	9	1,815	2,106*	25.2	37.1
443 UN C OF CHRIST	1	121	140*	1.7	2.5
449 UN METHODIST..	11	1,887	2,056	24.6	36.2
CALLAWAY	69	9,243	11,944*	46.2	100.0
081 CATHOLIC......	2	0	1,113	4.3	9.3
093 CR CH (DISC)..	12	1,441	1,713*	6.6	14.3
097 CR C AND C CR.	2	60	71*	0.3	0.6
193 EPISCOPAL.....	2	73	87	0.3	0.7
283 LUTH--MO SYNOD	1	136	184	0.7	1.5
357 PRESB CH US...	6	426	506*	2.0	4.2
419 SO BAPT CONV..	19	4,539	5,396*	20.9	45.2
443 UN C OF CHRIST	1	129	153*	0.6	1.3
449 UN METHODIST..	18	2,041	2,248	8.7	18.8
453 UN PRES CH USA	6	398	473*	1.8	4.0
CAMDEN	26	4,933	6,049*	45.4	100.0
019 AMER BAPT CONV	1	73	85*	0.6	1.4
081 CATHOLIC......	1	0	300	2.3	5.0
093 CR CH (DISC)..	3	563	653*	4.9	10.8
193 EPISCOPAL.....	1	40	56	0.4	0.9
281 LUTH CH AMER..	2	447	539	4.0	8.9
283 LUTH--MO SYNOD	1	33	41	0.3	0.7
357 PRESB CH US...	1	25	29*	0.2	0.5
413 S-D ADVENTISTS	1	23	27*	0.2	0.4
419 SO BAPT CONV..	11	3,049	3,537*	26.6	58.5
449 UN METHODIST..	4	680	782	5.9	12.9
CAPE GIRARDEAU	70	22,665	33,966*	68.8	100.0
029 AMER LUTH CH..	1	189	247	0.5	0.7
059 BAPT MISS ASSN	1	29	34*	0.1	0.1
081 CATHOLIC......	3	0	5,955	12.1	17.5
093 CR CH (DISC)..	1	366	433*	0.9	1.3
097 CR C AND C CR.	1	76	90*	0.2	0.3
123 CH GOD (ANDER)	2	164	425	0.9	1.3
127 CH GOD (CLEVE)	1	17	20*	-	0.1
165 CH OF NAZARENE	1	212	347	0.7	1.0
193 EPISCOPAL.....	1	154	271	0.5	0.8
281 LUTH CH AMER..	1	111	160	0.3	0.5
283 LUTH--MO SYNOD	14	5,568	7,342	14.9	21.6
353 PLY BRETHREN..	2	115	230	0.5	0.7
357 PRESB CH US...	4	1,126	1,331*	2.7	3.9
419 SO BAPT CONV..	17	8,237	9,739*	19.7	28.7
443 UN C OF CHRIST	4	999	1,181*	2.4	3.5
449 UN METHODIST..	16	5,302	6,161	12.5	18.1
CARROLL	41	6,569	8,814*	70.1	100.0
081 CATHOLIC......	2	0	1,003	8.0	11.4
093 CR CH (DISC)..	8	670	790*	6.3	9.0
165 CH OF NAZARENE	1	52	132	1.1	1.5
193 EPISCOPAL.....	1	17	37	0.3	0.4
283 LUTH--MO SYNOD	2	740	959	7.6	10.9
357 PRESB CH US...	1	72	85*	0.7	1.0
419 SO BAPT CONV..	19	3,553	4,187*	33.3	47.5
449 UN METHODIST..	6	1,393	1,536	12.2	17.4
453 UN PRES CH USA	1	72	85*	0.7	1.0
CARTER	17	1,158	1,454*	37.5	100.0
059 BAPT MISS ASSN	2	125	151*	3.9	10.4
081 CATHOLIC......	2	0	66	1.7	4.5
285 MENNONITE CH..	1	38	46*	1.2	3.2
419 SO BAPT CONV..	6	752	908*	23.4	62.4
443 UN C OF CHRIST	1	16	19*	0.5	1.3
449 UN METHODIST..	5	227	264	6.8	18.2
CASS	68	12,760	16,871*	42.8	100.0
029 AMER LUTH CH..	1	133	185	0.5	1.1
081 CATHOLIC......	3	0	1,015	2.6	6.0
093 CR CH (DISC)..	10	1,580	1,988*	5.0	11.8
097 CR C AND C CR.	2	150	189*	0.5	1.1
165 CH OF NAZARENE	3	97	258	0.7	1.5
193 EPISCOPAL.....	1	212	264	0.7	1.6
221 FREE METH C NA	1	12	13	-	0.1
283 LUTH--MO SYNOD	1	79	107	0.3	0.6
285 MENNONITE CH..	2	230	289*	0.7	1.7
357 PRESB CH US...	4	214	269*	0.7	1.6
419 SO BAPT CONV..	23	6,798	8,553*	21.7	50.7
449 UN METHODIST..	12	2,930	3,305	8.4	19.6
453 UN PRES CH USA	4	207	260*	0.7	1.5
469 WISC EVAN LUTH	1	118	176	0.4	1.0
CEDAR	29	2,521	2,975*	31.6	100.0
081 CATHOLIC......	2	0	79	0.8	2.7
093 CR CH (DISC)..	1	246	286*	3.0	9.6
097 CR C AND C CR.	8	330	384*	4.1	12.9
165 CH OF NAZARENE	1	25	37	0.4	1.2
185 CUMBER PRESB..	1	75	87*	0.9	2.9
221 FREE METH C NA	1	14	14	0.1	0.5
283 LUTH--MO SYNOD	1	23	32	0.3	1.1
357 PRESB CH US...	3	94	109*	1.2	3.7
413 S-D ADVENTISTS	1	32	37*	0.4	1.2
419 SO BAPT CONV..	4	1,020	1,187*	12.6	39.9
449 UN METHODIST..	3	563	608	6.5	20.4
453 UN PRES CH USA	3	99	115*	1.2	3.9
CHARITON	45	5,297	9,194*	82.9	100.0
081 CATHOLIC......	7	0	3,094	27.9	33.7
093 CR CH (DISC)..	7	495	581*	5.2	6.3
097 CR C AND C CR.	2	70	82*	0.7	0.9
165 CH OF NAZARENE	1	8	16	0.1	0.2
283 LUTH--MO SYNOD	3	1,000	1,235	11.1	13.4
419 SO BAPT CONV..	11	1,716	2,014*	18.2	21.9
449 UN METHODIST..	14	2,008	2,172	19.6	23.6
CHRISTIAN	45	5,894	7,589*	50.2	100.0
081 CATHOLIC......	2	0	521	3.4	6.9
093 CR CH (DISC)..	5	539	653*	4.3	8.6
165 CH OF NAZARENE	2	58	89	0.6	1.2
357 PRESB CH US...	1	44	53*	0.4	0.7
419 SO BAPT CONV..	27	4,531	5,491*	36.3	72.4
443 UN C OF CHRIST	1	142	172*	1.1	2.3
449 UN METHODIST..	6	537	558	3.7	7.4
453 UN PRES CH USA	1	43	52*	0.3	0.7
CLARK	31	3,579	5,115*	61.9	100.0
081 CATHOLIC......	3	0	844	10.2	16.5
093 CR CH (DISC)..	3	318	390*	4.7	7.6
357 PRESB CH US...	2	78	96*	1.2	1.9
413 S-D ADVENTISTS	1	52	64*	0.8	1.3
419 SO BAPT CONV..	11	1,605	1,968*	23.8	38.5
443 UN C OF CHRIST	1	450	552*	6.7	10.8
449 UN METHODIST..	8	995	1,102	13.3	21.5
453 UN PRES CH USA	2	81	99*	1.2	1.9
CLAY	101	35,063	58,095*	47.1	100.0
029 AMER LUTH CH..	1	192	282	0.2	0.5
059 BAPT MISS ASSN	1	59	74*	0.1	0.1
081 CATHOLIC......	7	0	13,744	11.1	23.7
093 CR CH (DISC)..	14	4,823	6,025*	4.9	10.4
097 CR C AND C CR.	2	471	588*	0.5	1.0
107 CHRISTIAN UN..	1	130	162*	0.1	0.3
165 CH OF NAZARENE	3	132	346	0.3	0.6
193 EPISCOPAL.....	2	258	306	0.2	0.5
281 LUTH CH AMER..	3	931	1,429	1.2	2.5
283 LUTH--MO SYNOD	5	1,649	2,479	2.0	4.3
353 PLY BRETHREN..	1	30	40	-	0.1
357 PRESB CH US...	10	2,411	3,012*	2.4	5.2
413 S-D ADVENTISTS	1	79	99*	0.1	0.2
415 S-D BAPTIST GC	1	17	21*	-	-
419 SO BAPT CONV..	29	14,766	18,447*	15.0	31.8
449 UN METHODIST..	15	8,076	9,743	7.9	16.8
453 UN PRES CH USA	5	1,039	1,298*	1.1	2.2
CLINTON	28	4,887	6,688*	53.7	100.0
081 CATHOLIC......	3	0	919	7.4	13.7
093 CR CH (DISC)..	5	934	1,114*	8.9	16.7
157 CH OF BRETHREN	1	79	94*	0.8	1.4
165 CH OF NAZARENE	1	83	121	1.0	1.8
185 CUMBER PRESB..	1	10	12*	0.1	0.2
357 PRESB CH US...	2	82	98*	0.8	1.5
419 SO BAPT CONV..	7	2,250	2,683*	21.5	40.1
449 UN METHODIST..	5	1,336	1,512	12.1	22.6
453 UN PRES CH USA	3	113	135*	1.1	2.0
COLE	50	15,361	34,506*	74.6	100.0
029 AMER LUTH CH..	3	641	806	1.7	2.3
081 CATHOLIC......	7	0	15,387	33.3	44.6
093 CR CH (DISC)..	3	1,543	1,873*	4.1	5.4
097 CR C AND C CR.	3	376	456*	1.0	1.3
123 CH GOD (ANDER)	1	81	185	0.4	0.5
165 CH OF NAZARENE	1	43	90	0.2	0.3
193 EPISCOPAL.....	1	324	467	1.0	1.4
221 FREE METH C NA	1	32	38	0.1	0.1
283 LUTH--MO SYNOD	6	2,502	3,369	7.3	9.8
357 PRESB CH US...	2	506	614*	1.3	1.8
413 S-D ADVENTISTS	1	49	59*	0.1	0.2
419 SO BAPT CONV..	14	5,653	6,861*	14.8	19.9
443 UN C OF CHRIST	2	926	1,124*	2.4	3.3
449 UN METHODIST..	4	2,204	2,593	5.6	7.5
453 UN PRES CH USA	1	481	584*	1.3	1.7
COOPER	48	5,727	8,787*	59.6	100.0
081 CATHOLIC......	2	0	2,028	13.8	23.1
093 CR CH (DISC)..	4	410	485*	3.3	5.5
185 CUMBER PRESB..	1	10	12*	0.1	0.1
193 EPISCOPAL.....	1	62	62	0.4	0.7
283 LUTH--MO SYNOD	4	793	1,012	6.9	11.5
357 PRESB CH US...	5	18	21*	0.1	0.2
419 SO BAPT CONV..	14	2,553	3,018*	20.5	34.3
443 UN C OF CHRIST	4	706	835*	5.7	9.5
449 UN METHODIST..	8	997	1,104	7.5	12.6
453 UN PRES CH USA	5	178	210*	1.4	2.4
CRAWFORD	37	4,921	6,980*	47.1	100.0
059 BAPT MISS ASSN	3	495	603*	4.1	8.6
081 CATHOLIC......	4	0	813	5.5	11.6
127 CH GOD (CLEVE)	3	102	124*	0.8	1.8
165 CH OF NAZARENE	1	42	116	0.8	1.7

*Total adherents estimated from known number of communicant, confirmed, full members.

—Represents a percent less than 0.1.

Percentages may not total due to rounding.

Table 3. Churches and Church Membership by State, County and Denomination: 1971

County and Denomination	Number of churches	Communicant, confirmed, full members	Total adherents: Number	Total adherents: Percent of total population	Total adherents: Percent of total adherents
185 CUMBER PRESB..	1	23	28*	0.2	0.4
193 EPISCOPAL.....	1	29	70	0.5	1.0
283 LUTH--MO SYNOD	2	328	527	3.6	7.6
413 S-D ADVENTISTS	1	132	161*	1.1	2.3
419 SO BAPT CONV..	15	2,954	3,598*	24.3	51.5
449 UN METHODIST..	3	354	377	2.5	5.4
453 UN PRES CH USA	3	462	563*	3.8	8.1
DADE	47	3,694	4,326*	63.2	100.0
081 CATHOLIC......	1	0	35	0.5	0.8
093 CR CH (DISC)..	7	507	583*	8.5	13.5
097 CR C AND C CR.	7	251	289*	4.2	6.7
121 CH GOD (ABR)..	1	25	29*	0.4	0.7
165 CH OF NAZARENE	1	2	2	-	-
185 CUMBER PRESB..	2	34	39*	0.6	0.9
283 LUTH--MO SYNOD	1	457	573	8.4	13.2
357 PRESB CH US...	5	124	143*	2.1	3.3
419 SO BAPT CONV..	13	1,861	2,140*	31.2	49.5
449 UN METHODIST..	4	306	347	5.1	8.0
453 UN PRES CH USA	5	127	146*	2.1	3.4
DALLAS	30	3,366	4,036*	40.1	100.0
029 AMER LUTH CH..	1	57	63	0.6	1.6
081 CATHOLIC......	1	0	151	1.5	3.7
093 CR CH (DISC)..	5	543	633*	6.3	15.7
097 CR C AND C CR.	4	125	146*	1.5	3.6
285 MENNONITE CH..	1	150	175*	1.7	4.3
419 SO BAPT CONV..	16	2,098	2,446*	24.3	60.6
449 UN METHODIST..	2	393	422	4.2	10.5
DAVIESS	31	3,563	4,257*	50.6	100.0
081 CATHOLIC......	1	0	125	1.5	2.9
093 CR CH (DISC)..	6	608	715*	8.5	16.8
097 CR C AND C CR.	2	65	76*	0.9	1.8
357 PRESB CH US...	2	61	72*	0.9	1.7
413 S-D ADVENTISTS	1	30	35*	0.4	0.8
419 SO BAPT CONV..	11	1,798	2,114*	25.1	49.7
449 UN METHODIST..	6	939	1,047	12.4	24.6
453 UN PRES CH USA	2	62	73*	0.9	1.7
DE KALB	37	3,704	4,368*	59.8	100.0
081 CATHOLIC......	1	0	118	1.6	2.7
093 CR CH (DISC)..	3	246	292*	4.0	6.7
097 CR C AND C CR.	5	250	297*	4.1	6.8
127 CH GOD (CLEVE)	1	10	12*	0.2	0.3
357 PRESB CH US...	4	164	195*	2.7	4.5
419 SO BAPT CONV..	9	1,596	1,895*	25.9	43.4
449 UN METHODIST..	12	1,373	1,482	20.3	33.9
453 UN PRES CH USA	2	65	77*	1.1	1.8
DENT	31	5,081	6,357*	55.5	100.0
059 BAPT MISS ASSN	2	103	123*	1.1	1.9
081 CATHOLIC......	3	0	251	2.2	3.9
097 CR C AND C CR.	1	500	596*	5.2	9.4
165 CH OF NAZARENE	1	22	43	0.4	0.7
185 CUMBER PRESB..	2	60	72*	0.6	1.1
283 LUTH--MO SYNOD	1	180	267	2.3	4.2
413 S-D ADVENTISTS	1	50	60*	0.5	0.9
419 SO BAPT CONV..	16	3,612	4,306*	37.6	67.7
443 UN C OF CHRIST	1	41	49*	0.4	0.8
449 UN METHODIST..	3	513	590	5.1	9.3
DOUGLAS	10	1,103	1,610*	17.4	100.0
081 CATHOLIC......	2	0	121	1.3	7.5
123 CH GOD (ANDER)	1	20	70	0.8	4.3
165 CH OF NAZARENE	2	194	381	4.1	23.7
413 S-D ADVENTISTS	1	50	59*	0.6	3.7
419 SO BAPT CONV..	3	600	714*	7.7	44.3
449 UN METHODIST..	1	239	265	2.9	16.5
DUNKLIN	68	12,900	16,494*	48.9	100.0
081 CATHOLIC......	5	0	665	2.0	4.0
093 CR CH (DISC)..	1	135	163*	0.5	1.0
097 CR C AND C CR.	1	300	363*	1.1	2.2
123 CH GOD (ANDER)	1	80	240	0.7	1.5
127 CH GOD (CLEVE)	1	18	22*	0.1	0.1
165 CH OF NAZARENE	2	189	456	1.4	2.8
185 CUMBER PRESB..	1	12	15*	-	0.1
193 EPISCOPAL.....	1	18	20	0.1	0.1
283 LUTH--MO SYNOD	2	84	117	0.3	0.7
349 PENT HOLINESS.	3	206	249*	0.7	1.5
357 PRESB CH US...	3	382	462*	1.4	2.8
413 S-D ADVENTISTS	1	34	41*	0.1	0.2
419 SO BAPT CONV..	34	9,394	11,353*	33.6	68.8
449 UN METHODIST..	12	2,048	2,328	6.9	14.1
FRANKLIN	110	16,718	36,938*	67.0	100.0
059 BAPT MISS ASSN	6	533	669*	1.2	1.8
081 CATHOLIC......	19	0	15,742	28.6	42.6
093 CR CH (DISC)..	2	45	56*	0.1	0.2
097 CR C AND C CR.	7	416	522*	0.9	1.4
127 CH GOD (CLEVE)	1	15	19*	-	0.1
165 CH OF NAZARENE	2	188	500	0.9	1.4
193 EPISCOPAL.....	1	48	94	0.2	0.3
283 LUTH--MO SYNOD	8	2,305	3,005	5.5	8.1
357 PRESB CH US...	2	235	295*	0.5	0.8
413 S-D ADVENTISTS	1	45	56*	0.1	0.2
419 SO BAPT CONV..	28	6,294	7,897*	14.3	21.4
443 UN C OF CHRIST	13	3,217	4,037*	7.3	10.9
449 UN METHODIST..	15	2,181	2,545	4.6	6.9
453 UN PRES CH USA	5	1,196	1,501*	2.7	4.1
GASCONADE	40	5,308	7,906*	66.6	100.0
081 CATHOLIC......	3	0	1,674	14.1	21.2
097 CR C AND C CR.	3	287	335*	2.8	4.2
283 LUTH--MO SYNOD	3	475	626	5.3	7.9
357 PRESB CH US...	1	53	62*	0.5	0.8
413 S-D ADVENTISTS	1	19	22*	0.2	0.3
419 SO BAPT CONV..	6	1,283	1,495*	12.6	18.9
443 UN C OF CHRIST	11	2,003	2,335*	19.7	29.5
449 UN METHODIST..	9	993	1,125	9.5	14.2
453 UN PRES CH USA	2	168	196*	1.7	2.5
469 WISC EVAN LUTH	1	27	36	0.3	0.5
GENTRY	35	5,601	7,147*	88.7	100.0
081 CATHOLIC......	2	0	484	6.0	6.8
093 CR CH (DISC)..	5	621	725*	9.0	10.1
097 CR C AND C CR.	3	100	117*	1.5	1.6
185 CUMBER PRESB..	1	55	64*	0.8	0.9
283 LUTH--MO SYNOD	2	1,311	1,726	21.4	24.1
357 PRESB CH US...	1	97	113*	1.4	1.6
419 SO BAPT CONV..	12	2,308	2,694*	33.4	37.7
449 UN METHODIST..	6	940	1,027	12.7	14.4
453 UN PRES CH USA	3	169	197*	2.4	2.8
GREENE	147	52,469	70,197*	45.9	100.0
019 AMER BAPT CONV	1	1,285	1,543*	1.0	2.2
029 AMER LUTH CH..	1	106	148	0.1	0.2
059 BAPT MISS ASSN	2	119	143*	0.1	0.2
081 CATHOLIC......	5	0	6,995	4.6	10.0
093 CR CH (DISC)..	9	3,807	4,571*	3.0	6.5
097 CR C AND C CR.	7	1,428	1,715*	1.1	2.4
123 CH GOD (ANDER)	3	282	682	0.4	1.0
127 CH GOD (CLEVE)	2	168	202*	0.1	0.3
157 CH OF BRETHREN	1	56	67*	-	0.1
165 CH OF NAZARENE	5	633	1,026	0.7	1.5
185 CUMBER PRESB..	2	271	325*	0.2	0.5
193 EPISCOPAL.....	4	1,882	2,432	1.6	3.5
221 FREE METH C NA	1	3	3	-	-
281 LUTH CH AMER..	1	313	462	0.3	0.7
349 PENT HOLINESS.	1	17	20*	-	-
357 PRESB CH US...	8	1,233	1,480*	1.0	2.1
403 SALVATION ARMY	1	62	326	0.2	0.5
413 S-D ADVENTISTS	1	209	251*	0.2	0.4
419 SO BAPT CONV..	55	27,526	33,050*	21.6	47.1
435 UNITARIAN-UNIV	1	130	180	0.1	0.3
443 UN C OF CHRIST	2	612	735*	0.5	1.0
449 UN METHODIST..	25	9,975	11,017	7.2	15.7
453 UN PRES CH USA	9	2,352	2,824*	1.8	4.0
GRUNDY	42	6,708	8,138*	68.9	100.0
081 CATHOLIC......	1	0	240	2.0	2.9
093 CR CH (DISC)..	6	882	1,036*	8.8	12.7
097 CR C AND C CR.	4	165	194*	1.6	2.4
165 CH OF NAZARENE	1	74	195	1.6	2.4
185 CUMBER PRESB..	1	12	14*	0.1	0.2
193 EPISCOPAL.....	1	21	40	0.3	0.5
283 LUTH--MO SYNOD	1	106	169	1.4	2.1
357 PRESB CH US...	1	83	97*	0.8	1.2
419 SO BAPT CONV..	15	3,854	4,526*	38.3	55.6
449 UN METHODIST..	10	1,431	1,533	13.0	18.8
453 UN PRES CH USA	1	80	94*	0.8	1.2
HARRISON	43	4,939	5,777*	56.3	100.0
081 CATHOLIC......	3	0	221	2.2	3.8
093 CR CH (DISC)..	11	1,062	1,233*	12.0	21.3
107 CHRISTIAN UN..	2	153	178*	1.7	3.1
357 PRESB CH US...	1	21	24*	0.2	0.4
419 SO BAPT CONV..	12	2,036	2,363*	23.0	40.9
449 UN METHODIST..	13	1,646	1,734	16.9	30.0
453 UN PRES CH USA	1	21	24*	0.2	0.4
HENRY	64	9,820	12,553*	68.0	100.0
081 CATHOLIC......	4	0	1,038	5.6	8.3
093 CR CH (DISC)..	4	1,036	1,224*	6.6	9.8
097 CR C AND C CR.	4	189	223*	1.2	1.8
123 CH GOD (ANDER)	1	20	44	0.2	0.4
157 CH OF BRETHREN	1	58	68*	0.4	0.5
165 CH OF NAZARENE	2	34	66	0.4	0.5
185 CUMBER PRESB..	2	160	189*	1.0	1.5
193 EPISCOPAL.....	1	12	16	0.1	0.1
283 LUTH--MO SYNOD	1	126	171	0.9	1.4
357 PRESB CH US...	4	285	337*	1.8	2.7
413 S-D ADVENTISTS	1	68	80*	0.4	0.6
419 SO BAPT CONV..	23	5,600	6,614*	35.8	52.7
443 UN C OF CHRIST	1	73	86*	0.5	0.7
449 UN METHODIST..	11	1,888	2,077	11.3	16.5
453 UN PRES CH USA	4	271	320*	1.7	2.5
HICKORY	18	1,486	1,652*	36.9	100.0
093 CR CH (DISC)..	6	358	406*	9.1	24.6
121 CH GOD (ABR)..	1	35	40*	0.9	2.4
419 SO BAPT CONV..	5	784	888*	19.8	53.8
443 UN C OF CHRIST	1	16	18*	0.4	1.1
449 UN METHODIST..	5	293	300	6.7	18.2

*Total adherents estimated from known number of communicant, confirmed, full members.

—Represents a percent less than 0.1.

Percentages may not total due to rounding.

Table 3. Churches and Church Membership by State, County and Denomination: 1971

County and Denomination	Number of churches	Communicant, confirmed, full members	Total adherents: Number	Total adherents: Percent of total population	Total adherents: Percent of total adherents
HOLT	43	3,283	4,061*	61.0	100.0
081 CATHOLIC......	1	0	122	1.8	3.0
093 CR CH (DISC)..	4	353	408*	6.1	10.0
097 CR C AND C CR.	5	476	550*	8.3	13.5
123 CH GOD (ANDER)	1	36	108	1.6	2.7
157 CH OF BRETHREN	1	32	37*	0.6	0.9
165 CH OF NAZARENE	3	133	294	4.4	7.2
283 LUTH--MO SYNOD	3	336	448	6.7	11.0
357 PRESB CH US...	7	259	299*	4.5	7.4
419 SO BAPT CONV..	3	190	220*	3.3	5.4
449 UN METHODIST..	8	1,216	1,284	19.3	31.6
453 UN PRES CH USA	7	252	291*	4.4	7.2
HOWARD	36	3,961	6,040*	57.2	100.0
081 CATHOLIC......	2	0	1,451	13.7	24.0
093 CR CH (DISC)..	8	845	994*	9.4	16.5
193 EPISCOPAL.....	1	20	28	0.3	0.5
357 PRESB CH US...	2	30	35*	0.3	0.6
419 SO BAPT CONV..	13	1,394	1,640*	15.5	27.2
443 UN C OF CHRIST	1	302	355*	3.4	5.9
449 UN METHODIST..	8	1,365	1,531	14.5	25.3
453 UN PRES CH USA	1	5	6*	0.1	0.1
HOWELL	61	8,046	10,828*	46.0	100.0
059 BAPT MISS ASSN	2	56	67*	0.3	0.6
081 CATHOLIC......	4	0	697	3.0	6.4
093 CR CH (DISC)..	1	450	536*	2.3	5.0
097 CR C AND C CR.	4	480	571*	2.4	5.3
123 CH GOD (ANDER)	6	510	1,078	4.6	10.0
157 CH OF BRETHREN	1	54	64*	0.3	0.6
165 CH OF NAZARENE	3	113	228	1.0	2.1
185 CUMBER PRESB..	1	83	99*	0.4	0.9
193 EPISCOPAL.....	1	84	165	0.7	1.5
283 LUTH--MO SYNOD	2	232	286	1.2	2.6
349 PENT HOLINESS.	1	14	17*	0.1	0.2
357 PRESB CH US...	3	140	167*	0.7	1.5
413 S-D ADVENTISTS	2	138	164*	0.7	1.5
419 SO BAPT CONV..	21	4,567	5,435*	23.1	50.2
449 UN METHODIST..	6	1,000	1,105	4.7	10.2
453 UN PRES CH USA	3	125	149*	0.6	1.4
IRON	28	2,845	4,045*	42.4	100.0
081 CATHOLIC......	2	0	452	4.7	11.2
097 CR C AND C CR.	1	48	59*	0.6	1.5
123 CH GOD (ANDER)	1	17	44	0.5	1.1
165 CH OF NAZARENE	3	145	314	3.3	7.8
193 EPISCOPAL.....	1	73	94	1.0	2.3
283 LUTH--MO SYNOD	2	143	171	1.8	4.2
413 S-D ADVENTISTS	1	22	27*	0.3	0.7
419 SO BAPT CONV..	10	1,779	2,179*	22.9	53.9
449 UN METHODIST..	5	501	562	5.9	13.9
453 UN PRES CH USA	2	117	143*	1.5	3.5
JACKSON	422	149,927	278,579*	42.6	100.0
019 AMER BAPT CONV	5	3,161	3,847*	0.6	1.4
029 AMER LUTH CH..	5	1,455	2,196	0.3	0.8
059 BAPT MISS ASSN	4	669	814*	0.1	0.3
081 CATHOLIC......	48	0	90,584	13.8	32.5
093 CR CH (DISC)..	32	17,640	21,469*	3.3	7.7
097 CR C AND C CR.	17	2,274	2,768*	0.4	1.0
105 CHRISTIAN REF.	1	44	82	-	-
107 CHRISTIAN UN..	2	78	95*	-	-
121 CH GOD (ABR)..	1	37	45*	-	-
123 CH GOD (ANDER)	7	621	1,586	0.2	0.6
127 CH GOD (CLEVE)	6	250	304*	-	0.1
157 CH OF BRETHREN	1	220	268*	-	0.1
165 CH OF NAZARENE	15	2,045	3,862	0.6	1.4
175 CONG CR CH....	1	318	387*	0.1	0.1
185 CUMBER PRESB..	4	375	456*	0.1	0.2
193 EPISCOPAL.....	16	9,649	13,207	2.0	4.7
201 EVAN COV CH AM	1	214	260*	-	0.1
221 FREE METH C NA	1	37	48	-	-
226 FRIENDS-USA...	2	47	57*	-	-
281 LUTH CH AMER..	9	2,375	3,208	0.5	1.2
283 LUTH--MO SYNOD	15	6,163	8,599	1.3	3.1
285 MENNONITE CH..	1	37	45*	-	-
349 PENT HOLINESS.	1	7	9*	-	-
357 PRESB CH US...	31	6,519	7,934*	1.2	2.8
403 SALVATION ARMY	5	470	2,315	0.4	0.8
413 S-D ADVENTISTS	4	1,620	1,972*	0.3	0.7
419 SO BAPT CONV..	83	53,017	64,526*	9.9	23.2
435 UNITARIAN-UNIV	1	570	800	0.1	0.3
443 UN C OF CHRIST	11	3,296	4,011*	0.6	1.4
449 UN METHODIST..	59	29,790	34,392	5.3	12.3
453 UN PRES CH USA	33	6,929	8,433*	1.3	3.0
JASPER	143	33,030	44,702*	56.0	100.0
029 AMER LUTH CH..	1	133	187	0.2	0.4
059 BAPT MISS ASSN	1	108	129*	0.2	0.3
081 CATHOLIC......	4	0	3,937	4.9	8.8
093 CR CH (DISC)..	5	1,132	1,354*	1.7	3.0
097 CR C AND C CR.	28	5,426	6,489*	8.1	14.5
123 CH GOD (ANDER)	3	160	376	0.5	0.8
127 CH GOD (CLEVE)	2	178	213*	0.3	0.5
157 CH OF BRETHREN	2	63	75*	0.1	0.2
165 CH OF NAZARENE	6	793	1,663	2.1	3.7
193 EPISCOPAL.....	2	1,204	1,399	1.8	3.1
221 FREE METH C NA	2	26	39	-	0.1
226 FRIENDS-USA...	2	60	72*	0.1	0.2
283 LUTH--MO SYNOD	3	875	1,137	1.4	2.5
357 PRESB CH US...	10	2,348	2,808*	3.5	6.3
403 SALVATION ARMY	2	110	833	1.0	1.9
413 S-D ADVENTISTS	1	20	24*	-	0.1
419 SO BAPT CONV..	34	13,174	15,755*	19.7	35.2
443 UN C OF CHRIST	1	14	17*	-	-
449 UN METHODIST..	24	5,995	6,747	8.4	15.1
453 UN PRES CH USA	10	1,211	1,448*	1.8	3.2
JEFFERSON	98	23,717	52,347*	49.7	100.0
059 BAPT MISS ASSN	6	421	541*	0.5	1.0
081 CATHOLIC......	11	0	21,353	20.3	40.8
093 CR CH (DISC)..	3	368	473*	0.4	0.9
097 CR C AND C CR.	5	471	606*	0.6	1.2
121 CH GOD (ABR)..	1	20	26*	-	-
123 CH GOD (ANDER)	1	100	250	0.2	0.5
127 CH GOD (CLEVE)	4	227	292*	0.3	0.6
165 CH OF NAZARENE	4	272	547	0.5	1.0
193 EPISCOPAL.....	1	88	91	0.1	0.2
283 LUTH--MO SYNOD	9	3,165	4,747	4.5	9.1
357 PRESB CH US...	2	642	825*	0.8	1.6
419 SO BAPT CONV..	29	12,319	15,838*	15.0	30.3
443 UN C OF CHRIST	5	1,802	2,317*	2.2	4.4
449 UN METHODIST..	14	3,422	3,927	3.7	7.5
453 UN PRES CH USA	3	400	514*	0.5	1.0
JOHNSON	73	10,342	13,116*	38.4	100.0
081 CATHOLIC......	3	0	767	2.2	5.8
093 CR CH (DISC)..	7	986	1,169*	3.4	8.9
097 CR C AND C CR.	5	375	445*	1.3	3.4
157 CH OF BRETHREN	2	151	179*	0.5	1.4
165 CH OF NAZARENE	2	71	144	0.4	1.1
185 CUMBER PRESB..	4	390	462*	1.4	3.5
221 FREE METH C NA	1	12	15	-	0.1
283 LUTH--MO SYNOD	2	230	384	1.1	2.9
357 PRESB CH US...	6	418	496*	1.5	3.8
413 S-D ADVENTISTS	1	68	81*	0.2	0.6
419 SO BAPT CONV..	19	5,134	6,086*	17.8	46.4
435 UNITARIAN-UNIV	1	16	16	-	0.1
449 UN METHODIST..	13	2,092	2,399	7.0	18.3
453 UN PRES CH USA	7	399	473*	1.4	3.6
KNOX	26	1,797	2,926*	51.4	100.0
081 CATHOLIC......	2	0	904	15.9	30.9
093 CR CH (DISC)..	2	240	284*	5.0	9.7
097 CR C AND C CR.	7	250	295*	5.2	10.1
165 CH OF NAZARENE	1	15	27	0.5	0.9
419 SO BAPT CONV..	8	645	762*	13.4	26.0
449 UN METHODIST..	6	647	654	11.5	22.4
LACLEDE	55	8,093	10,558*	52.9	100.0
081 CATHOLIC......	2	0	628	3.1	5.9
093 CR CH (DISC)..	3	512	623*	3.1	5.9
097 CR C AND C CR.	6	585	711*	3.6	6.7
123 CH GOD (ANDER)	2	103	290	1.5	2.7
165 CH OF NAZARENE	1	74	132	0.7	1.3
185 CUMBER PRESB..	3	358	435*	2.2	4.1
193 EPISCOPAL.....	1	76	119	0.6	1.1
221 FREE METH C NA	1	9	9	-	0.1
283 LUTH--MO SYNOD	2	205	302	1.5	2.9
413 S-D ADVENTISTS	1	44	54*	0.3	0.5
419 SO BAPT CONV..	22	4,493	5,464*	27.4	51.8
443 UN C OF CHRIST	1	192	233*	1.2	2.2
449 UN METHODIST..	10	1,442	1,558	7.8	14.8
LAFAYETTE	65	14,217	18,350*	68.9	100.0
081 CATHOLIC......	5	0	1,299	4.9	7.1
093 CR CH (DISC)..	7	968	1,152*	4.3	6.3
193 EPISCOPAL.....	1	121	174	0.7	0.9
283 LUTH--MO SYNOD	8	3,691	4,721	17.7	25.7
353 PLY BRETHREN..	1	10	15	0.1	0.1
357 PRESB CH US...	6	305	363*	1.4	2.0
419 SO BAPT CONV..	14	4,289	5,104*	19.2	27.8
443 UN C OF CHRIST	6	2,157	2,567*	9.6	14.0
449 UN METHODIST..	13	2,377	2,599	9.8	14.2
453 UN PRES CH USA	4	299	356*	1.3	1.9
LAWRENCE	73	10,349	13,735*	55.9	100.0
081 CATHOLIC......	4	0	1,573	6.4	11.5
093 CR CH (DISC)..	4	380	448*	1.8	3.3
097 CR C AND C CR.	6	529	623*	2.5	4.5
165 CH OF NAZARENE	2	58	156	0.6	1.1
185 CUMBER PRESB..	3	246	290*	1.2	2.1
221 FREE METH C NA	2	25	34	0.1	0.2
283 LUTH--MO SYNOD	3	924	1,128	4.6	8.2
357 PRESB CH US...	7	547	644*	2.6	4.7
419 SO BAPT CONV..	22	5,583	6,578*	26.8	47.9
443 UN C OF CHRIST	3	230	271*	1.1	2.0
449 UN METHODIST..	11	1,500	1,605	6.5	11.7
453 UN PRES CH USA	6	327	385*	1.6	2.8
LEWIS	40	5,201	6,840*	62.2	100.0
081 CATHOLIC......	3	0	580	5.3	8.5
093 CR CH (DISC)..	6	827	1,002*	9.1	14.6
097 CR C AND C CR.	2	190	230*	2.1	3.4
283 LUTH--MO SYNOD	1	281	370	3.4	5.4
357 PRESB CH US...	4	49	59*	0.5	0.9
419 SO BAPT CONV..	13	2,928	3,548*	32.3	51.9

*Total adherents estimated from known number of communicant, confirmed, full members.

—Represents a percent less than 0.1.

Percentages may not total due to rounding.

Table 3. Churches and Church Membership by State, County and Denomination: 1971

County and Denomination	Number of churches	Communicant, confirmed, full members	Total adherents: Number	Total adherents: Percent of total population	Total adherents: Percent of total adherents
449 UN METHODIST..	8	882	998	9.1	14.6
453 UN PRES CH USA	3	44	53*	0.5	0.8
LINCOLN	52	6,531	11,510*	63.8	100.0
055 AS REF PRES CH	2	166	204*	1.1	1.8
081 CATHOLIC......	5	0	3,593	19.9	31.2
093 CR CH (DISC)..	5	507	624*	3.5	5.4
097 CR C AND C CR.	2	200	246*	1.4	2.1
283 LUTH--MO SYNOD	1	152	245	1.4	2.1
357 PRESB CH US...	4	184	226*	1.3	2.0
419 SO BAPT CONV..	15	2,942	3,620*	20.1	31.5
443 UN C OF CHRIST	3	461	567*	3.1	4.9
449 UN METHODIST..	12	1,830	2,075	11.5	18.0
453 UN PRES CH USA	3	89	110*	0.6	1.0
LINN	42	7,163	9,480*	62.7	100.0
081 CATHOLIC......	2	0	1,318	8.7	13.9
093 CR CH (DISC)..	4	943	1,087*	7.2	11.5
097 CR C AND C CR.	3	50	58*	0.4	0.6
165 CH OF NAZARENE	1	48	91	0.6	1.0
193 EPISCOPAL.....	1	30	48	0.3	0.5
357 PRESB CH US...	1	81	93*	0.6	1.0
413 S-D ADVENTISTS	1	16	18*	0.1	0.2
419 SO BAPT CONV..	15	3,488	4,019*	26.6	42.4
449 UN METHODIST..	13	2,423	2,651	17.5	28.0
453 UN PRES CH USA	1	84	97*	0.6	1.0
LIVINGSTON	44	7,360	10,389*	67.6	100.0
081 CATHOLIC......	3	0	1,480	9.6	14.2
093 CR CH (DISC)..	7	733	874*	5.7	8.4
127 CH GOD (CLEVE)	1	48	57*	0.4	0.5
193 EPISCOPAL.....	1	92	136	0.9	1.3
221 FREE METH C NA	2	56	68	0.4	0.7
283 LUTH--MO SYNOD	1	209	303	2.0	2.9
357 PRESB CH US...	3	182	217*	1.4	2.1
403 SALVATION ARMY	1	47	217	1.4	2.1
413 S-D ADVENTISTS	1	35	42*	0.3	0.4
419 SO BAPT CONV..	14	3,713	4,428*	28.8	42.6
443 UN C OF CHRIST	1	23	27*	0.2	0.3
449 UN METHODIST..	6	2,036	2,318	15.1	22.3
453 UN PRES CH USA	3	186	222*	1.4	2.1
MC DONALD	31	3,788	4,534*	36.7	100.0
081 CATHOLIC......	1	0	82	0.7	1.8
093 CR CH (DISC)..	1	28	33*	0.3	0.7
097 CR C AND C CR.	3	265	317*	2.6	7.0
165 CH OF NAZARENE	1	61	115	0.9	2.5
193 EPISCOPAL.....	1	75	78	0.6	1.7
419 SO BAPT CONV..	15	2,566	3,068*	24.8	67.7
449 UN METHODIST..	8	782	828	6.7	18.3
453 UN PRES CH USA	1	11	13*	0.1	0.3
MACON	58	7,201	9,330*	60.5	100.0
081 CATHOLIC......	2	0	920	6.0	9.9
093 CR CH (DISC)..	5	822	960*	6.2	10.3
097 CR C AND C CR.	10	470	549*	3.6	5.9
165 CH OF NAZARENE	1	52	135	0.9	1.4
193 EPISCOPAL.....	1	49	64	0.4	0.7
283 LUTH--MO SYNOD	1	171	228	1.5	2.4
357 PRESB CH US...	5	358	418*	2.7	4.5
413 S-D ADVENTISTS	2	87	102*	0.7	1.1
419 SO BAPT CONV..	17	3,399	3,968*	25.7	42.5
443 UN C OF CHRIST	2	119	139*	0.9	1.5
449 UN METHODIST..	7	1,327	1,442	9.3	15.5
453 UN PRES CH USA	5	347	405*	2.6	4.3
MADISON	26	3,614	4,778*	55.3	100.0
081 CATHOLIC......	1	0	475	5.5	9.9
093 CR CH (DISC)..	1	239	281*	3.3	5.9
121 CH GOD (ABR)..	1	59	69*	0.8	1.4
165 CH OF NAZARENE	1	94	218	2.5	4.6
283 LUTH--MO SYNOD	1	159	210	2.4	4.4
413 S-D ADVENTISTS	1	50	59*	0.7	1.2
419 SO BAPT CONV..	12	2,113	2,485*	28.8	52.0
449 UN METHODIST..	6	766	823	9.5	17.2
453 UN PRES CH USA	2	134	158*	1.8	3.3
MARIES	17	2,183	3,672*	53.6	100.0
081 CATHOLIC......	3	0	1,031	15.0	28.1
097 CR C AND C CR.	1	150	180*	2.6	4.9
123 CH GOD (ANDER)	1	31	67	1.0	1.8
283 LUTH--MO SYNOD	1	80	105	1.5	2.9
419 SO BAPT CONV..	8	1,591	1,910*	27.9	52.0
449 UN METHODIST..	3	331	379	5.5	10.3
MARION	56	12,410	18,763*	66.7	100.0
081 CATHOLIC......	2	0	3,010	10.7	16.0
093 CR CH (DISC)..	8	1,296	1,556*	5.5	8.3
097 CR C AND C CR.	3	780	937*	3.3	5.0
165 CH OF NAZARENE	2	233	689	2.5	3.7
193 EPISCOPAL.....	2	221	360	1.3	1.9
221 FREE METH C NA	1	9	14	-	0.1
283 LUTH--MO SYNOD	3	1,728	2,340	8.3	12.5
285 MENNONITE CH..	2	94	113*	0.4	0.6
357 PRESB CH US...	2	296	355*	1.3	1.9
403 SALVATION ARMY	1	54	339	1.2	1.8
413 S-D ADVENTISTS	1	15	18*	0.1	0.1
419 SO BAPT CONV..	17	5,054	6,070*	21.6	32.4
449 UN METHODIST..	9	2,301	2,567	9.1	13.7
453 UN PRES CH USA	3	329	395*	1.4	2.1
MERCER	25	2,616	2,976*	60.6	100.0
081 CATHOLIC......	1	0	54	1.1	1.8
093 CR CH (DISC)..	6	334	379*	7.7	12.7
097 CR C AND C CR.	3	90	102*	2.1	3.4
419 SO BAPT CONV..	10	1,504	1,707*	34.8	57.4
449 UN METHODIST..	5	688	734	14.9	24.7
MILLER	46	6,006	9,331*	62.1	100.0
081 CATHOLIC......	5	0	2,100	14.0	22.5
093 CR CH (DISC)..	4	484	580*	3.9	6.2
097 CR C AND C CR.	8	765	917*	6.1	9.8
165 CH OF NAZARENE	2	205	323	2.1	3.5
283 LUTH--MO SYNOD	1	114	148	1.0	1.6
357 PRESB CH US...	1	11	13*	0.1	0.1
419 SO BAPT CONV..	21	3,914	4,693*	31.2	50.3
443 UN C OF CHRIST	1	55	66*	0.4	0.7
449 UN METHODIST..	2	447	478	3.2	5.1
453 UN PRES CH USA	1	11	13*	0.1	0.1
MISSISSIPPI	35	6,080	8,795*	52.8	100.0
081 CATHOLIC......	2	0	896	5.4	10.2
093 CR CH (DISC)..	1	92	115*	0.7	1.3
097 CR C AND C CR.	3	400	499*	3.0	5.7
123 CH GOD (ANDER)	2	198	601	3.6	6.8
127 CH GOD (CLEVE)	1	40	50*	0.3	0.6
165 CH OF NAZARENE	2	52	161	1.0	1.8
349 PENT HOLINESS.	1	25	31*	0.2	0.4
413 S-D ADVENTISTS	3	85	106*	0.6	1.2
419 SO BAPT CONV..	13	3,930	4,901*	29.4	55.7
449 UN METHODIST..	7	1,258	1,435	8.6	16.3
MONITEAU	41	6,322	9,782*	91.1	100.0
081 CATHOLIC......	3	0	2,280	21.2	23.3
093 CR CH (DISC)..	4	478	570*	5.3	5.8
283 LUTH--MO SYNOD	2	384	520	4.8	5.3
287 MENN GEN CONF.	1	137	163*	1.5	1.7
357 PRESB CH US...	1	4	5*	-	0.1
419 SO BAPT CONV..	18	3,714	4,431*	41.2	45.3
443 UN C OF CHRIST	4	777	927*	8.6	9.5
449 UN METHODIST..	6	806	860	8.0	8.8
453 UN PRES CH USA	2	22	26*	0.2	0.3
MONROE	40	3,923	6,142*	64.4	100.0
081 CATHOLIC......	4	0	1,554	16.3	25.3
093 CR CH (DISC)..	10	1,200	1,428*	15.0	23.2
123 CH GOD (ANDER)	1	20	52	0.5	0.8
357 PRESB CH US...	3	106	126*	1.3	2.1
419 SO BAPT CONV..	12	1,572	1,871*	19.6	30.5
449 UN METHODIST..	8	939	1,009	10.6	16.4
453 UN PRES CH USA	2	86	102*	1.1	1.7
MONTGOMERY	49	4,716	7,088*	64.4	100.0
081 CATHOLIC......	5	0	1,401	12.7	19.8
093 CR CH (DISC)..	3	302	363*	3.3	5.1
097 CR C AND C CR.	3	245	295*	2.7	4.2
165 CH OF NAZARENE	1	13	36	0.3	0.5
283 LUTH--MO SYNOD	3	422	599	5.4	8.5
357 PRESB CH US...	6	152	183*	1.7	2.6
419 SO BAPT CONV..	11	1,678	2,017*	18.3	28.5
443 UN C OF CHRIST	2	200	240*	2.2	3.4
449 UN METHODIST..	12	1,611	1,842	16.7	26.0
453 UN PRES CH USA	3	93	112*	1.0	1.6
MORGAN	33	4,303	5,487*	54.5	100.0
029 AMER LUTH CH..	2	349	441	4.4	8.0
081 CATHOLIC......	2	0	465	4.6	8.5
093 CR CH (DISC)..	1	26	30*	0.3	0.5
097 CR C AND C CR.	4	225	263*	2.6	4.8
283 LUTH--MO SYNOD	2	402	516	5.1	9.4
285 MENNONITE CH..	1	53	62*	0.6	1.1
357 PRESB CH US...	2	111	130*	1.3	2.4
419 SO BAPT CONV..	10	1,998	2,332*	23.2	42.5
443 UN C OF CHRIST	1	109	127*	1.3	2.3
449 UN METHODIST..	5	895	963	9.6	17.6
453 UN PRES CH USA	3	135	158*	1.6	2.9
NEW MADRID	39	6,993	10,001*	42.7	100.0
059 BAPT MISS ASSN	2	254	315*	1.3	3.1
081 CATHOLIC......	2	0	1,025	4.4	10.2
093 CR CH (DISC)..	1	84	104*	0.4	1.0
123 CH GOD (ANDER)	3	216	462	2.0	4.6
127 CH GOD (CLEVE)	1	24	30*	0.1	0.3
157 CH OF BRETHREN	1	26	32*	0.1	0.3
165 CH OF NAZARENE	4	296	645	2.8	6.4
193 EPISCOPAL.....	1	98	119	0.5	1.2
283 LUTH--MO SYNOD	1	28	34	0.1	0.3
357 PRESB CH US...	1	96	119*	0.5	1.2
419 SO BAPT CONV..	14	4,605	5,719*	24.4	57.2
449 UN METHODIST..	8	1,266	1,397	6.0	14.0
NEWTON	69	11,716	15,103*	45.9	100.0
081 CATHOLIC......	3	0	853	2.6	5.6

*Total adherents estimated from known number of communicant, confirmed, full members.

—Represents a percent less than 0.1.

Percentages may not total due to rounding.

Table 3. Churches and Church Membership by State, County and Denomination: 1971

County and Denomination	Number of churches	Communicant, confirmed, full members	Total adherents: Number	Total adherents: Percent of total population	Total adherents: Percent of total adherents
093 CR CH (DISC)..	2	527	634*	1.9	4.2
097 CR C AND C CR.	8	977	1,175*	3.6	7.8
123 CH GOD (ANDER)	2	82	217	0.7	1.4
157 CH OF BRETHREN	1	31	37*	0.1	0.2
165 CH OF NAZARENE	2	125	309	0.9	2.0
175 CONG CR CH....	1	152	183*	0.6	1.2
185 CUMBER PRESB..	1	36	43*	0.1	0.3
193 EPISCOPAL.....	1	68	88	0.3	0.6
283 LUTH--MO SYNOD	1	207	287	0.9	1.9
357 PRESB CH US...	2	212	255*	0.8	1.7
413 S-D ADVENTISTS	2	178	214*	0.7	1.4
419 SO BAPT CONV..	33	7,170	8,621*	26.2	57.1
449 UN METHODIST..	9	1,758	1,955	5.9	12.9
453 UN PRES CH USA	1	193	232*	0.7	1.5
NODAWAY	49	7,468	11,903*	53.0	100.0
081 CATHOLIC......	5	0	3,411	15.2	28.7
093 CR CH (DISC)..	7	1,370	1,586*	7.1	13.3
097 CR C AND C CR.	12	660	764*	3.4	6.4
165 CH OF NAZARENE	1	17	45	0.2	0.4
193 EPISCOPAL.....	2	82	95	0.4	0.8
283 LUTH--MO SYNOD	1	121	152	0.7	1.3
357 PRESB CH US...	1	107	124*	0.6	1.0
419 SO BAPT CONV..	4	1,397	1,618*	7.2	13.6
449 UN METHODIST..	15	3,608	3,985	17.7	33.5
453 UN PRES CH USA	1	106	123*	0.5	1.0
OREGON	22	2,273	2,791*	30.4	100.0
059 BAPT MISS ASSN	1	40	47*	0.5	1.7
081 CATHOLIC......	1	0	75	0.8	2.7
093 CR CH (DISC)..	1	38	45*	0.5	1.6
123 CH GOD (ANDER)	1	38	123	1.3	4.4
185 CUMBER PRESB..	1	23	27*	0.3	1.0
419 SO BAPT CONV..	12	1,617	1,903*	20.7	68.2
449 UN METHODIST..	5	517	571	6.2	20.5
OSAGE	37	2,102	9,638*	87.7	100.0
081 CATHOLIC......	13	0	6,892	62.7	71.5
097 CR C AND C CR.	4	200	248*	2.3	2.6
165 CH OF NAZARENE	1	32	64	0.6	0.7
283 LUTH--MO SYNOD	2	98	116	1.1	1.2
353 PLY BRETHREN..	1	20	30	0.3	0.3
403 SALVATION ARMY	1	72	270	2.5	2.8
419 SO BAPT CONV..	6	885	1,100*	10.0	11.4
443 UN C OF CHRIST	3	227	282*	2.6	2.9
449 UN METHODIST..	5	510	564	5.1	5.9
453 UN PRES CH USA	1	58	72*	0.7	0.7
OZARK	9	696	945*	15.2	100.0
081 CATHOLIC......	1	0	55	0.9	5.8
097 CR C AND C CR.	1	143	166*	2.7	17.6
123 CH GOD (ANDER)	2	43	128	2.1	13.5
419 SO BAPT CONV..	4	414	481*	7.7	50.9
449 UN METHODIST..	1	96	115	1.8	12.2
PEMISCOT	51	9,624	12,182*	46.2	100.0
059 BAPT MISS ASSN	1	43	53*	0.2	0.4
081 CATHOLIC......	2	0	320	1.2	2.6
097 CR C AND C CR.	2	230	285*	1.1	2.3
127 CH GOD (CLEVE)	5	250	310*	1.2	2.5
165 CH OF NAZARENE	3	185	394	1.5	3.2
193 EPISCOPAL.....	1	48	49	0.2	0.4
349 PENT HOLINESS.	2	108	134*	0.5	1.1
357 PRESB CH US...	2	515	639*	2.4	5.2
419 SO BAPT CONV..	22	6,672	8,281*	31.4	68.0
449 UN METHODIST..	11	1,573	1,717	6.5	14.1
PERRY	31	4,625	13,824*	96.0	100.0
029 AMER LUTH CH..	1	187	236	1.6	1.7
081 CATHOLIC......	11	0	7,958	55.3	57.6
093 CR CH (DISC)..	1	151	184*	1.3	1.3
281 LUTH CH AMER..	1	22	31	0.2	0.2
283 LUTH--MO SYNOD	9	3,238	4,185	29.1	30.3
357 PRESB CH US...	2	145	177*	1.2	1.3
419 SO BAPT CONV..	5	646	787*	5.5	5.7
449 UN METHODIST..	1	236	266	1.8	1.9
PETTIS	72	15,385	21,911*	64.2	100.0
029 AMER LUTH CH..	1	119	185	0.5	0.8
081 CATHOLIC......	4	0	3,226	9.5	14.7
093 CR CH (DISC)..	1	906	1,080*	3.2	4.9
097 CR C AND C CR.	5	570	680*	2.0	3.1
127 CH GOD (CLEVE)	1	40	48*	0.1	0.2
165 CH OF NAZARENE	1	52	127	0.4	0.6
185 CUMBER PRESB..	1	48	57*	0.2	0.3
193 EPISCOPAL.....	1	248	423	1.2	1.9
221 FREE METH C NA	1	18	22	0.1	0.1
281 LUTH CH AMER..	1	186	223	0.7	1.0
283 LUTH--MO SYNOD	2	932	1,244	3.6	5.7
357 PRESB CH US...	5	510	608*	1.8	2.8
403 SALVATION ARMY	1	44	257	0.8	1.2
413 S-D ADVENTISTS	2	144	172*	0.5	0.8
419 SO BAPT CONV..	26	7,175	8,557*	25.1	39.1
443 UN C OF CHRIST	1	351	419*	1.2	1.9
449 UN METHODIST..	15	3,552	3,999	11.7	18.3
453 UN PRES CH USA	3	490	584*	1.7	2.7
PHELPS	40	10,098	14,346*	48.7	100.0

County and Denomination	Number of churches	Communicant, confirmed, full members	Total adherents: Number	Total adherents: Percent of total population	Total adherents: Percent of total adherents
059 BAPT MISS ASSN	1	38	45*	0.2	0.3
081 CATHOLIC......	3	0	1,554	5.3	10.8
097 CR C AND C CR.	4	1,800	2,151*	7.3	15.0
123 CH GOD (ANDER)	3	289	725	2.5	5.1
127 CH GOD (CLEVE)	1	28	33*	0.1	0.2
165 CH OF NAZARENE	1	44	74	0.3	0.5
193 EPISCOPAL.....	2	397	525	1.8	3.7
283 LUTH--MO SYNOD	3	816	1,223	4.1	8.5
357 PRESB CH US...	1	353	422*	1.4	2.9
413 S-D ADVENTISTS	1	86	103*	0.3	0.7
419 SO BAPT CONV..	15	4,722	5,641*	19.1	39.3
435 UNITARIAN-UNIV	1	34	51	0.2	0.4
449 UN METHODIST..	3	1,140	1,380	4.7	9.6
453 UN PRES CH USA	1	351	419*	1.4	2.9
PIKE	70	6,247	9,146*	54.0	100.0
081 CATHOLIC......	3	0	1,646	9.7	18.0
093 CR CH (DISC)..	10	703	852*	5.0	9.3
193 EPISCOPAL.....	3	105	118	0.7	1.3
221 FREE METH C NA	1	9	9	0.1	0.1
283 LUTH--MO SYNOD	1	79	130	0.8	1.4
357 PRESB CH US...	12	534	647*	3.8	7.1
419 SO BAPT CONV..	19	3,472	4,210*	24.9	46.0
449 UN METHODIST..	8	785	855	5.1	9.3
453 UN PRES CH USA	13	560	679*	4.0	7.4
PLATTE	40	8,110	14,012*	43.7	100.0
081 CATHOLIC......	2	0	3,671	11.4	26.2
093 CR CH (DISC)..	13	1,566	1,953*	6.1	13.9
165 CH OF NAZARENE	1	40	78	0.2	0.6
281 LUTH CH AMER..	1	183	266	0.8	1.9
283 LUTH--MO SYNOD	2	531	755	2.4	5.4
357 PRESB CH US...	1	229	286*	0.9	2.0
419 SO BAPT CONV..	12	3,370	4,203*	13.1	30.0
449 UN METHODIST..	6	1,878	2,410	7.5	17.2
453 UN PRES CH USA	2	313	390*	1.2	2.8
POLK	38	5,041	6,373*	41.3	100.0
081 CATHOLIC......	2	0	453	2.9	7.1
093 CR CH (DISC)..	3	376	441*	2.9	6.9
097 CR C AND C CR.	2	40	47*	0.3	0.7
123 CH GOD (ANDER)	1	6	14	0.1	0.2
165 CH OF NAZARENE	2	51	193	1.3	3.0
185 CUMBER PRESB..	1	38	45*	0.3	0.7
357 PRESB CH US...	1	17	20*	0.1	0.3
419 SO BAPT CONV..	13	3,397	3,985*	25.9	62.5
449 UN METHODIST..	12	1,099	1,155	7.5	18.1
453 UN PRES CH USA	1	17	20*	0.1	0.3
PULASKI	49	8,483	10,812*	20.1	100.0
059 BAPT MISS ASSN	1	59	68*	0.1	0.6
081 CATHOLIC......	4	0	824	1.5	7.6
093 CR CH (DISC)..	1	130	150*	0.3	1.4
097 CR C AND C CR.	7	951	1,096*	2.0	10.1
123 CH GOD (ANDER)	3	160	352	0.7	3.3
283 LUTH--MO SYNOD	1	164	252	0.5	2.3
357 PRESB CH US...	1	55	63*	0.1	0.6
413 S-D ADVENTISTS	1	31	36*	0.1	0.3
419 SO BAPT CONV..	25	6,209	7,157*	13.3	66.2
443 UN C OF CHRIST	1	18	21*	-	0.2
449 UN METHODIST..	3	650	728	1.4	6.7
453 UN PRES CH USA	1	56	65*	0.1	0.6
PUTNAM	19	1,938	2,315*	39.1	100.0
081 CATHOLIC......	1	0	72	1.2	3.1
093 CR CH (DISC)..	3	175	205*	3.5	8.9
097 CR C AND C CR.	4	600	702*	11.9	30.3
413 S-D ADVENTISTS	1	28	33*	0.6	1.4
419 SO BAPT CONV..	6	780	913*	15.4	39.4
449 UN METHODIST..	4	355	390	6.6	16.8
RALLS	33	2,848	3,682*	47.4	100.0
081 CATHOLIC......	2	0	304	3.9	8.3
093 CR CH (DISC)..	9	797	961*	12.4	26.1
097 CR C AND C CR.	3	125	151*	1.9	4.1
357 PRESB CH US...	2	107	129*	1.7	3.5
419 SO BAPT CONV..	10	1,274	1,537*	19.8	41.7
449 UN METHODIST..	5	472	512	6.6	13.9
453 UN PRES CH USA	2	73	88*	1.1	2.4
RANDOLPH	52	10,759	15,054*	67.1	100.0
081 CATHOLIC......	2	0	2,200	9.8	14.6
093 CR CH (DISC)..	8	1,727	2,038*	9.1	13.5
097 CR C AND C CR.	2	755	891*	4.0	5.9
123 CH GOD (ANDER)	1	17	47	0.2	0.3
127 CH GOD (CLEVE)	1	15	18*	0.1	0.1
165 CH OF NAZARENE	1	88	311	1.4	2.1
185 CUMBER PRESB..	2	141	166*	0.7	1.1
193 EPISCOPAL.....	1	58	78	0.3	0.5
283 LUTH--MO SYNOD	1	212	289	1.3	1.9
357 PRESB CH US...	2	177	209*	0.9	1.4
413 S-D ADVENTISTS	1	62	73*	0.3	0.5
419 SO BAPT CONV..	16	5,104	6,023*	26.8	40.0
449 UN METHODIST..	11	2,200	2,471	11.0	16.4
453 UN PRES CH USA	3	203	240*	1.1	1.6
RAY	51	8,643	10,705*	60.8	100.0

*Total adherents estimated from known number of communicant, confirmed, full members.

—Represents a percent less than 0.1.

Percentages may not total due to rounding.

Table 3. Churches and Church Membership by State, County and Denomination: 1971

County and Denomination	Number of churches	Communicant, confirmed, full members	Total adherents: Number	Total adherents: Percent of total population	Total adherents: Percent of total adherents
081 CATHOLIC......	1	0	196	1.1	1.8
093 CR CH (DISC)..	5	629	763*	4.3	7.1
097 CR C AND C CR.	1	36	44*	0.3	0.4
107 CHRISTIAN UN..	9	718	871*	4.9	8.1
157 CH OF BRETHREN	2	203	246*	1.4	2.3
165 CH OF NAZARENE	2	129	314	1.8	2.9
357 PRESB CH US...	3	205	249*	1.4	2.3
413 S-D ADVENTISTS	1	33	40*	0.2	0.4
419 SO BAPT CONV..	16	4,792	5,814*	33.0	54.3
449 UN METHODIST..	9	1,756	1,996	11.3	18.6
453 UN PRES CH USA	2	142	172*	1.0	1.6
REYNOLDS	21	1,892	2,513*	41.2	100.0
059 BAPT MISS ASSN	4	150	183*	3.0	7.3
081 CATHOLIC......	2	0	73	1.2	2.9
165 CH OF NAZARENE	2	37	198	3.2	7.9
413 S-D ADVENTISTS	1	50	61*	1.0	2.4
419 SO BAPT CONV..	11	1,501	1,833*	30.0	72.9
449 UN METHODIST..	1	154	165	2.7	6.6
RIPLEY	34	2,764	3,837*	39.1	100.0
059 BAPT MISS ASSN	9	812	955*	9.7	24.9
081 CATHOLIC......	1	0	265	2.7	6.9
093 CR CH (DISC)..	1	42	49*	0.5	1.3
097 CR C AND C CR.	1	60	71*	0.7	1.9
121 CH GOD (ABR)..	1	30	35*	0.4	0.9
123 CH GOD (ANDER)	4	213	586	6.0	15.3
127 CH GOD (CLEVE)	1	24	28*	0.3	0.7
413 S-D ADVENTISTS	1	33	39*	0.4	1.0
419 SO BAPT CONV..	8	1,168	1,373*	14.0	35.8
449 UN METHODIST..	6	312	354	3.6	9.2
453 UN PRES CH USA	1	70	82*	0.8	2.1
ST CHARLES	83	21,238	57,764*	62.1	100.0
059 BAPT MISS ASSN	2	139	182*	0.2	0.3
081 CATHOLIC......	17	0	25,048	26.9	43.4
093 CR CH (DISC)..	1	508	665*	0.7	1.2
097 CR C AND C CR.	4	515	675*	0.7	1.2
123 CH GOD (ANDER)	3	145	411	0.4	0.7
127 CH GOD (CLEVE)	1	115	151*	0.2	0.3
165 CH OF NAZARENE	2	147	354	0.4	0.6
193 EPISCOPAL.....	1	252	342	0.4	0.6
281 LUTH CH AMER..	1	136	230	0.2	0.4
283 LUTH--MO SYNOD	9	5,836	8,313	8.9	14.4
403 SALVATION ARMY	8	940	4,889	5.3	8.5
413 S-D ADVENTISTS	1	50	65*	0.1	0.1
419 SO BAPT CONV..	10	5,081	6,656*	7.2	11.5
443 UN C OF CHRIST	14	3,331	4,364*	4.7	7.6
449 UN METHODIST..	7	3,284	4,425	4.8	7.7
453 UN PRES CH USA	2	759	994*	1.1	1.7
ST CLAIR	26	3,192	3,629*	47.3	100.0
093 CR CH (DISC)..	4	265	306*	4.0	8.4
097 CR C AND C CR.	4	125	144*	1.9	4.0
157 CH OF BRETHREN	1	62	72*	0.9	2.0
185 CUMBER PRESB..	1	18	21*	0.3	0.6
283 LUTH--MO SYNOD	1	130	171	2.2	4.7
353 PLY BRETHREN..	1	10	10	0.1	0.3
357 PRESB CH US...	1	30	35*	0.5	1.0
419 SO BAPT CONV..	9	1,887	2,181*	28.4	60.1
449 UN METHODIST..	4	665	689	9.0	19.0
ST FRANCOIS	59	14,967	21,576*	58.6	100.0
059 BAPT MISS ASSN	2	101	122*	0.3	0.6
081 CATHOLIC......	5	0	3,175	8.6	14.7
093 CR CH (DISC)..	3	418	503*	1.4	2.3
123 CH GOD (ANDER)	3	179	497	1.3	2.3
127 CH GOD (CLEVE)	5	571	687*	1.9	3.2
165 CH OF NAZARENE	3	283	647	1.8	3.0
193 EPISCOPAL.....	1	16	18	-	0.1
283 LUTH--MO SYNOD	4	844	1,117	3.0	5.2
357 PRESB CH US...	1	294	354*	1.0	1.6
413 S-D ADVENTISTS	1	96	116*	0.3	0.5
419 SO BAPT CONV..	17	8,324	10,016*	27.2	46.4
443 UN C OF CHRIST	1	107	129*	0.4	0.6
449 UN METHODIST..	12	3,615	4,052	11.0	18.8
453 UN PRES CH USA	1	119	143*	0.4	0.7
ST LOUIS	393	157,962	499,947*	52.6	100.0
019 AMER BAPT CONV	3	129	159*	-	-
029 AMER LUTH CH..	3	917	1,470	0.2	0.3
059 BAPT MISS ASSN	9	731	900*	0.1	0.2
081 CATHOLIC......	99	0	295,280	31.0	59.1
093 CR CH (DISC)..	3	872	1,074*	0.1	0.2
097 CR C AND C CR.	8	1,006	1,239*	0.1	0.2
121 CH GOD (ABR)..	1	41	50*	-	-
123 CH GOD (ANDER)	1	34	84	-	-
127 CH GOD (CLEVE)	4	646	795*	0.1	0.2
193 EPISCOPAL.....	16	7,635	11,810	1.2	2.4
226 FRIENDS-USA...	1	125	154*	-	-
281 LUTH CH AMER..	4	1,252	1,879	0.2	0.4
283 LUTH--MO SYNOD	53	36,730	51,764	5.4	10.4
285 MENNONITE CH..	1	95	117*	-	-
353 PLY BRETHREN..	3	166	315	-	0.1
357 PRESB CH US...	11	5,683	6,997*	0.7	1.4
381 REF PRES-EVAN.	4	266	419	-	0.1
413 S-D ADVENTISTS	6	1,783	2,195*	0.2	0.4
419 SO BAPT CONV..	67	41,312	50,863*	5.3	10.2
435 UNITARIAN-UNIV	2	399	629	0.1	0.1
443 UN C OF CHRIST	27	18,630	22,937*	2.4	4.6
449 UN METHODIST..	43	31,682	39,126	4.1	7.8
453 UN PRES CH USA	22	7,702	9,483*	1.0	1.9
469 WISC EVAN LUTH	2	126	208	-	-
ST LOUIS CITY	305	113,839	270,287*	43.4	100.0
019 AMER BAPT CONV	8	7,124	8,569*	1.4	3.2
059 BAPT MISS ASSN	5	379	456*	0.1	0.2
081 CATHOLIC......	75	0	128,097	20.6	47.4
093 CR CH (DISC)..	13	5,336	6,418*	1.0	2.4
097 CR C AND C CR.	10	1,441	1,733*	0.3	0.6
105 CHRISTIAN REF.	1	45	99	-	-
123 CH GOD (ANDER)	12	1,243	3,168	0.5	1.2
127 CH GOD (CLEVE)	1	21	25*	-	-
165 CH OF NAZARENE	19	2,576	5,365	0.9	2.0
193 EPISCOPAL.....	12	2,849	3,925	0.6	1.5
201 EVAN COV CH AM	1	30	36*	-	-
221 FREE METH C NA	3	156	229	-	0.1
281 LUTH CH AMER..	7	2,575	3,309	0.5	1.2
283 LUTH--MO SYNOD	36	16,262	22,336	3.6	8.3
349 PENT HOLINESS.	2	55	66*	-	-
353 PLY BRETHREN..	5	456	590	0.1	0.2
381 REF PRES-EVAN.	4	571	821	0.1	0.3
419 SO BAPT CONV..	21	17,619	21,193*	3.4	7.8
435 UNITARIAN-UNIV	1	476	626	0.1	0.2
443 UN C OF CHRIST	34	16,806	20,215*	3.2	7.5
449 UN METHODIST..	4	16,170	16,971	2.7	6.3
453 UN PRES CH USA	31	21,649	26,040*	4.2	9.6
STE GENEVIEVE	27	2,331	11,578*	90.0	100.0
081 CATHOLIC......	9	0	8,626	67.0	74.5
123 CH GOD (ANDER)	1	20	50	0.4	0.4
127 CH GOD (CLEVE)	1	45	56*	0.4	0.5
193 EPISCOPAL.....	1	10	14	0.1	0.1
283 LUTH--MO SYNOD	1	122	153	1.2	1.3
357 PRESB CH US...	1	185	232*	1.8	2.0
419 SO BAPT CONV..	11	1,895	2,372*	18.4	20.5
449 UN METHODIST..	2	54	75	0.6	0.6
SALINE	84	12,020	16,462*	66.8	100.0
081 CATHOLIC......	4	0	2,244	9.1	13.6
093 CR CH (DISC)..	12	1,526	1,793*	7.3	10.9
165 CH OF NAZARENE	1	103	219	0.9	1.3
185 CUMBER PRESB..	3	236	277*	1.1	1.7
193 EPISCOPAL.....	1	87	161	0.7	1.0
283 LUTH--MO SYNOD	7	1,358	1,757	7.1	10.7
357 PRESB CH US...	6	392	461*	1.9	2.8
419 SO BAPT CONV..	19	4,929	5,791*	23.5	35.2
443 UN C OF CHRIST	5	569	668*	2.7	4.1
449 UN METHODIST..	19	2,405	2,603	10.6	15.8
453 UN PRES CH USA	7	415	488*	2.0	3.0
SCHUYLER	21	1,865	2,150*	46.1	100.0
093 CR CH (DISC)..	2	77	90*	1.9	4.2
097 CR C AND C CR.	6	673	783*	16.8	36.4
281 LUTH CH AMER..	1	107	148	3.2	6.9
419 SO BAPT CONV..	6	628	730*	15.6	34.0
449 UN METHODIST..	6	380	399	8.6	18.6
SCOTLAND	27	2,790	3,318*	60.3	100.0
081 CATHOLIC......	1	0	125	2.3	3.8
093 CR CH (DISC)..	1	43	50*	0.9	1.5
097 CR C AND C CR.	4	500	584*	10.6	17.6
283 LUTH--MO SYNOD	1	38	65	1.2	2.0
357 PRESB CH US...	2	116	136*	2.5	4.1
419 SO BAPT CONV..	9	892	1,042*	18.9	31.4
449 UN METHODIST..	7	1,100	1,198	21.8	36.1
453 UN PRES CH USA	2	101	118*	2.1	3.6
SCOTT	57	10,602	17,377*	52.3	100.0
059 BAPT MISS ASSN	2	186	231*	0.7	1.3
081 CATHOLIC......	7	0	4,222	12.7	24.3
093 CR CH (DISC)..	2	321	399*	1.2	2.3
123 CH GOD (ANDER)	5	259	669	2.0	3.8
127 CH GOD (CLEVE)	1	127	158*	0.5	0.9
283 LUTH--MO SYNOD	3	658	818	2.5	4.7
349 PENT HOLINESS.	1	20	25*	0.1	0.1
357 PRESB CH US...	1	158	196*	0.6	1.1
413 S-D ADVENTISTS	1	42	52*	0.2	0.3
419 SO BAPT CONV..	22	6,107	7,585*	22.8	43.6
449 UN METHODIST..	11	2,696	2,987	9.0	17.2
453 UN PRES CH USA	1	28	35*	0.1	0.2
SHANNON	15	1,960	2,387*	33.2	100.0
081 CATHOLIC......	1	0	16	0.2	0.7
097 CR C AND C CR.	2	287	347*	4.8	14.5
165 CH OF NAZARENE	1	18	60	0.8	2.5
285 MENNONITE CH..	1	10	12*	0.2	0.5
419 SO BAPT CONV..	6	1,293	1,564*	21.7	65.5
449 UN METHODIST..	4	352	388	5.4	16.3
SHELBY	43	4,337	6,290*	79.6	100.0
081 CATHOLIC......	4	0	1,242	15.7	19.7
093 CR CH (DISC)..	4	127	149*	1.9	2.4
097 CR C AND C CR.	11	1,415	1,661*	21.0	26.4
157 CH OF BRETHREN	1	50	59*	0.7	0.9
165 CH OF NAZARENE	1	44	70	0.9	1.1

*Total adherents estimated from known number of communicant, confirmed, full members.

—Represents a percent less than 0.1.

Percentages may not total due to rounding.

Table 3. Churches and Church Membership by State, County and Denomination: 1971

County and Denomination	Number of churches	Communicant, confirmed, full members	Total adherents: Number	Total adherents: Percent of total population	Total adherents: Percent of total adherents
221 FREE METH C NA	1	8	8	0.1	0.1
283 LUTH--MO SYNOD	1	97	135	1.7	2.1
285 MENNONITE CH..	1	44	52*	0.7	0.8
419 SO BAPT CONV..	11	1,369	1,607*	20.3	25.5
449 UN METHODIST..	8	1,183	1,307	16.5	20.8
STODDARD	49	6,327	8,462*	32.8	100.0
059 BAPT MISS ASSN	1	94	112*	0.4	1.3
081 CATHOLIC......	2	0	496	1.9	5.9
093 CR CH (DISC)..	1	296	353*	1.4	4.2
097 CR C AND C CR.	6	185	221*	0.9	2.6
123 CH GOD (ANDER)	1	38	98	0.4	1.2
127 CH GOD (CLEVE)	1	32	38*	0.1	0.4
157 CH OF BRETHREN	1	80	95*	0.4	1.1
165 CH OF NAZARENE	4	290	640	2.5	7.6
283 LUTH--MO SYNOD	1	60	85	0.3	1.0
419 SO BAPT CONV..	18	3,444	4,111*	16.0	48.6
449 UN METHODIST..	12	1,731	2,121	8.2	25.1
453 UN PRES CH USA	1	77	92*	0.4	1.1
STONE	25	2,420	2,881*	29.0	100.0
081 CATHOLIC......	1	0	95	1.0	3.3
097 CR C AND C CR.	3	125	146*	1.5	5.1
127 CH GOD (CLEVE)	1	54	63*	0.6	2.2
165 CH OF NAZARENE	1	39	55	0.6	1.9
357 PRESB CH US...	2	104	122*	1.2	4.2
419 SO BAPT CONV..	12	1,477	1,730*	17.4	60.0
449 UN METHODIST..	2	508	538	5.4	18.7
453 UN PRES CH USA	3	113	132*	1.3	4.6
SULLIVAN	38	3,349	3,980*	52.6	100.0
081 CATHOLIC......	1	0	191	2.5	4.8
093 CR CH (DISC)..	6	214	245*	3.2	6.2
097 CR C AND C CR.	6	659	756*	10.0	19.0
123 CH GOD (ANDER)	1	29	71	0.9	1.8
357 PRESB CH US...	2	71	81*	1.1	2.0
419 SO BAPT CONV..	13	1,561	1,790*	23.6	45.0
449 UN METHODIST..	7	745	766	10.1	19.2
453 UN PRES CH USA	2	70	80*	1.1	2.0
TANEY	20	2,751	3,615*	27.8	100.0
081 CATHOLIC......	2	0	396	3.0	11.0
093 CR CH (DISC)..	1	227	259*	2.0	7.2
165 CH OF NAZARENE	1	18	45	0.3	1.2
193 EPISCOPAL.....	1	160	199	1.5	5.5
283 LUTH--MO SYNOD	1	238	333	2.6	9.2
357 PRESB CH US...	4	472	538*	4.1	14.9
413 S-D ADVENTISTS	1	42	48*	0.4	1.3
419 SO BAPT CONV..	4	721	822*	6.3	22.7
449 UN METHODIST..	1	392	427	3.3	11.8
453 UN PRES CH USA	4	481	548*	4.2	15.2
TEXAS	48	7,152	8,896*	48.6	100.0
081 CATHOLIC......	3	0	231	1.3	2.6
093 CR CH (DISC)..	2	68	82*	0.4	0.9
097 CR C AND C CR.	6	853	1,022*	5.6	11.5
123 CH GOD (ANDER)	2	117	334	1.8	3.8
157 CH OF BRETHREN	2	144	173*	0.9	1.9
283 LUTH--MO SYNOD	1	56	77	0.4	0.9
349 PENT HOLINESS.	2	103	123*	0.7	1.4
419 SO BAPT CONV..	25	4,885	5,855*	32.0	65.8
449 UN METHODIST..	5	926	999	5.5	11.2
VERNON	55	7,003	9,015*	47.3	100.0
029 AMER LUTH CH..	1	130	180	0.9	2.0
081 CATHOLIC......	1	0	732	3.8	8.1
093 CR CH (DISC)..	3	779	907*	4.8	10.1
097 CR C AND C CR.	12	657	765*	4.0	8.5
165 CH OF NAZARENE	1	102	200	1.0	2.2
193 EPISCOPAL.....	1	184	190	1.0	2.1
283 LUTH--MO SYNOD	1	56	89	0.5	1.0
357 PRESB CH US...	1	111	129*	0.7	1.4
403 SALVATION ARMY	1	39	149	0.8	1.7
413 S-D ADVENTISTS	1	75	87*	0.5	1.0
419 SO BAPT CONV..	19	3,421	3,985*	20.9	44.2
449 UN METHODIST..	12	1,336	1,470	7.7	16.3
453 UN PRES CH USA	1	113	132*	0.7	1.5
WARREN	21	3,175	5,776*	59.6	100.0
081 CATHOLIC......	4	0	1,824	18.8	31.6
165 CH OF NAZARENE	1	33	51	0.5	0.9
193 EPISCOPAL.....	1	107	225	2.3	3.9
283 LUTH--MO SYNOD	1	133	200	2.1	3.5
419 SO BAPT CONV..	3	524	633*	6.5	11.0
443 UN C OF CHRIST	5	1,689	2,039*	21.0	35.3
449 UN METHODIST..	6	689	804	8.3	13.9
WASHINGTON	39	3,542	7,313*	48.5	100.0
059 BAPT MISS ASSN	13	1,092	1,377*	9.1	18.8
081 CATHOLIC......	4	0	2,865	19.0	39.2
127 CH GOD (CLEVE)	4	227	286*	1.9	3.9
165 CH OF NAZARENE	2	66	171	1.1	2.3
283 LUTH--MO SYNOD	1	29	46	0.3	0.6
357 PRESB CH US...	2	243	306*	2.0	4.2
419 SO BAPT CONV..	5	1,073	1,353*	9.0	18.5
449 UN METHODIST..	8	812	909	6.0	12.4
WAYNE	31	2,580	3,421*	40.0	100.0
081 CATHOLIC......	2	0	79	0.9	2.3
097 CR C AND C CR.	3	100	119*	1.4	3.5
165 CH OF NAZARENE	2	158	287	3.4	8.4
283 LUTH--MO SYNOD	1	52	55	0.6	1.6
403 SALVATION ARMY	1	79	335	3.9	9.8
419 SO BAPT CONV..	16	1,665	1,983*	23.2	58.0
449 UN METHODIST..	6	526	563	6.6	16.5
WEBSTER	48	6,220	8,007*	51.5	100.0
081 CATHOLIC......	1	0	375	2.4	4.7
093 CR CH (DISC)..	4	399	487*	3.1	6.1
127 CH GOD (CLEVE)	1	39	48*	0.3	0.6
165 CH OF NAZARENE	3	113	272	1.7	3.4
185 CUMBER PRESB..	1	81	99*	0.6	1.2
197 EVAN CH OF NA.	1	7	9*	0.1	0.1
283 LUTH--MO SYNOD	3	338	533	3.4	6.7
285 MENNONITE CH..	1	59	72*	0.5	0.9
413 S-D ADVENTISTS	2	201	245*	1.6	3.1
419 SO BAPT CONV..	20	3,411	4,164*	26.8	52.0
449 UN METHODIST..	11	1,572	1,703	10.9	21.3
WORTH	16	1,920	2,232*	66.4	100.0
093 CR CH (DISC)..	2	199	237*	7.1	10.6
097 CR C AND C CR.	3	350	416*	12.4	18.6
185 CUMBER PRESB..	1	46	55*	1.6	2.5
357 PRESB CH US...	1	17	20*	0.6	0.9
419 SO BAPT CONV..	5	725	863*	25.7	38.7
449 UN METHODIST..	4	583	641	19.1	28.7
WRIGHT	41	6,042	7,585*	55.5	100.0
081 CATHOLIC......	2	0	138	1.0	1.8
093 CR CH (DISC)..	3	169	200*	1.5	2.6
097 CR C AND C CR.	3	356	421*	3.1	5.6
123 CH GOD (ANDER)	2	102	250	1.8	3.3
157 CH OF BRETHREN	1	65	77*	0.6	1.0
165 CH OF NAZARENE	2	126	399	2.9	5.3
185 CUMBER PRESB..	1	122	144*	1.1	1.9
193 EPISCOPAL.....	1	37	40	0.3	0.5
413 S-D ADVENTISTS	1	75	89*	0.7	1.2
419 SO BAPT CONV..	19	3,709	4,388*	32.1	57.9
443 UN C OF CHRIST	2	664	786*	5.8	10.4
449 UN METHODIST..	4	617	653	4.8	8.6
CO DATA NOT AVAIL	377	30,283	48,182*	N/A	N/A
151 L-D SAINTS....	0	0	11,454	N/A	N/A
223 FREE WILL BAPT	140	14,409	17,471*	N/A	N/A
231 GENERAL BAPT..	220	15,224	18,459*	N/A	N/A
313 NO AM BAPT GC.	1	23	28*	N/A	N/A
349 PENT HOLINESS.	1	19	23*	N/A	N/A
467 WESLEYAN......	15	608	747	N/A	N/A

MONTANA

County and Denomination	Number of churches	Communicant, confirmed, full members	Total adherents: Number	Total adherents: Percent of total population	Total adherents: Percent of total adherents
THE STATE.....	995	122,411	323,738*	46.6	100.0
BEAVERHEAD	9	981	2,522*	30.8	100.0
029 AMER LUTH CH..	1	153	195	2.4	7.7
081 CATHOLIC......	3	0	1,250	15.3	49.6
193 EPISCOPAL.....	1	161	225	2.7	8.9
413 S-D ADVENTISTS	1	15	18*	0.2	0.7
449 UN METHODIST..	1	170	247	3.0	9.8
453 UN PRES CH USA	2	482	587*	7.2	23.3
BIG HORN	28	2,339	5,113*	50.8	100.0
019 AMER BAPT CONV	6	852	1,116*	11.1	21.8
029 AMER LUTH CH..	1	113	191	1.9	3.7
081 CATHOLIC......	9	0	2,030	20.2	39.7
123 CH GOD (ANDER)	1	40	90	0.9	1.8
193 EPISCOPAL.....	1	32	54	0.5	1.1
283 LUTH--MO SYNOD	2	155	259	2.6	5.1
287 MENN GEN CONF.	1	55	72*	0.7	1.4
443 UN C OF CHRIST	2	431	564*	5.6	11.0
449 UN METHODIST..	5	661	737	7.3	14.4
BLAINE	19	1,265	5,305*	78.9	100.0
029 AMER LUTH CH..	4	585	822	12.2	15.5
081 CATHOLIC......	7	0	3,676	54.6	69.3
097 CR C AND C CR.	1	86	107*	1.6	2.0
165 CH OF NAZARENE	1	12	19	0.3	0.4
197 EVAN CH OF NA.	1	22	27*	0.4	0.5
283 LUTH--MO SYNOD	1	55	96	1.4	1.8
449 UN METHODIST..	2	290	290	4.3	5.5
453 UN PRES CH USA	2	215	268*	4.0	5.1
BROADWATER	7	315	942*	37.3	100.0
029 AMER LUTH CH..	1	79	114	4.5	12.1
081 CATHOLIC......	2	0	507	20.1	53.8

*Total adherents estimated from known number of communicant, confirmed, full members.

—Represents a percent less than 0.1.

Percentages may not total due to rounding.

Table 3. Churches and Church Membership by State, County and Denomination: 1971

County and Denomination	Number of churches	Communicant, confirmed, full members	Total adherents: Number	Total adherents: Percent of total population	Total adherents: Percent of total adherents
193 EPISCOPAL.....	1	64	94	3.7	10.0
419 SO BAPT CONV..	1	55	67*	2.7	7.1
449 UN METHODIST..	2	117	160	6.3	17.0
CARBON	21	1,195	2,698*	38.1	100.0
029 AMER LUTH CH..	2	156	211	3.0	7.8
081 CATHOLIC......	5	0	1,200	16.9	44.5
093 CR CH (DISC)..	1	64	74*	1.0	2.7
193 EPISCOPAL.....	3	83	139	2.0	5.2
283 LUTH--MO SYNOD	2	243	339	4.8	12.6
413 S-D ADVENTISTS	1	49	57*	0.8	2.1
443 UN C OF CHRIST	1	206	239*	3.4	8.9
449 UN METHODIST..	6	394	439	6.2	16.3
CARTER	5	126	900*	46.0	100.0
029 AMER LUTH CH..	1	55	97	5.0	10.8
081 CATHOLIC......	2	0	700	35.8	77.8
175 CONG CR CH....	1	50	61*	3.1	6.8
469 WISC EVAN LUTH	1	21	42	2.1	4.7
CASCADE	62	12,370	29,667*	36.3	100.0
019 AMER BAPT CONV	2	331	415*	0.5	1.4
029 AMER LUTH CH..	3	2,764	4,139	5.1	14.0
081 CATHOLIC......	21	0	12,570	15.4	42.4
093 CR CH (DISC)..	1	375	470*	0.6	1.6
097 CR C AND C CR.	1	200	251*	0.3	0.8
123 CH GOD (ANDER)	1	37	99	0.1	0.3
127 CH GOD (CLEVE)	2	48	60*	0.1	0.2
165 CH OF NAZARENE	1	113	250	0.3	0.8
193 EPISCOPAL.....	2	1,319	1,478	1.8	5.0
197 EVAN CH OF NA.	1	150	188*	0.2	0.6
281 LUTH CH AMER..	3	871	1,400	1.7	4.7
283 LUTH--MO SYNOD	3	841	1,199	1.5	4.0
371 REF CH IN AM..	1	99	165	0.2	0.6
403 SALVATION ARMY	1	41	279	0.3	0.9
413 S-D ADVENTISTS	1	241	302*	0.4	1.0
419 SO BAPT CONV..	3	917	1,149*	1.4	3.9
435 UNITARIAN-UNIV	1	21	21	-	0.1
443 UN C OF CHRIST	1	399	500*	0.6	1.7
449 UN METHODIST..	10	1,984	2,690	3.3	9.1
453 UN PRES CH USA	2	1,572	1,971*	2.4	6.6
469 WISC EVAN LUTH	1	47	71	0.1	0.2
CHOUTEAU	21	1,912	4,701*	72.6	100.0
029 AMER LUTH CH..	1	256	375	5.8	8.0
081 CATHOLIC......	7	0	2,176	33.6	46.3
093 CR CH (DISC)..	1	275	333*	5.1	7.1
097 CR C AND C CR.	3	285	345*	5.3	7.3
123 CH GOD (ANDER)	1	26	59	0.9	1.3
193 EPISCOPAL.....	1	52	100	1.5	2.1
283 LUTH--MO SYNOD	1	120	151	2.3	3.2
419 SO BAPT CONV..	1	12	15*	0.2	0.3
449 UN METHODIST..	5	886	1,147	17.7	24.4
CUSTER	16	2,599	6,457*	53.0	100.0
019 AMER BAPT CONV	1	211	256*	2.1	4.0
029 AMER LUTH CH..	2	439	645	5.3	10.0
081 CATHOLIC......	4	0	3,210	26.4	49.7
093 CR CH (DISC)..	1	35	43*	0.4	0.7
127 CH GOD (CLEVE)	1	31	38*	0.3	0.6
193 EPISCOPAL.....	1	139	237	1.9	3.7
283 LUTH--MO SYNOD	1	294	395	3.2	6.1
413 S-D ADVENTISTS	1	87	106*	0.9	1.6
419 SO BAPT CONV..	1	97	118*	1.0	1.8
443 UN C OF CHRIST	1	97	118*	1.0	1.8
449 UN METHODIST..	1	599	599	4.9	9.3
453 UN PRES CH USA	1	570	692*	5.7	10.7
DANIELS	9	1,109	1,985	64.4	100.0
029 AMER LUTH CH..	4	941	1,279	41.5	64.4
081 CATHOLIC......	3	0	530	17.2	26.7
193 EPISCOPAL.....	1	15	23	0.7	1.2
449 UN METHODIST..	1	153	153	5.0	7.7
DAWSON	19	2,893	7,926*	70.3	100.0
029 AMER LUTH CH..	3	1,061	1,534	13.6	19.4
081 CATHOLIC......	3	0	4,000	35.5	50.5
193 EPISCOPAL.....	1	53	148	1.3	1.9
197 EVAN CH OF NA.	1	85	107*	0.9	1.3
283 LUTH--MO SYNOD	1	367	612	5.4	7.7
285 MENNONITE CH..	2	87	109*	1.0	1.4
287 MENN GEN CONF.	2	168	211*	1.9	2.7
413 S-D ADVENTISTS	1	19	24*	0.2	0.3
419 SO BAPT CONV..	1	163	204*	1.8	2.6
443 UN C OF CHRIST	1	224	281*	2.5	3.5
449 UN METHODIST..	2	625	625	5.5	7.9
469 WISC EVAN LUTH	1	41	71	0.6	0.9
DEER LODGE	14	1,132	6,993*	44.7	100.0
029 AMER LUTH CH..	1	199	300	1.9	4.3
081 CATHOLIC......	5	0	5,528	35.3	79.1
093 CR CH (DISC)..	1	25	30*	0.2	0.4
193 EPISCOPAL.....	1	74	74	0.5	1.1
281 LUTH CH AMER..	1	262	376	2.4	5.4
283 LUTH--MO SYNOD	1	57	73	0.5	1.0
413 S-D ADVENTISTS	1	8	10*	0.1	0.1
419 SO BAPT CONV..	1	60	72*	0.5	1.0
449 UN METHODIST..	1	191	224	1.4	3.2
453 UN PRES CH USA	1	256	306*	2.0	4.4
FALLON	7	726	1,431*	35.3	100.0
029 AMER LUTH CH..	2	353	515	12.7	36.0
081 CATHOLIC......	2	0	450	11.1	31.4
313 NO AM BAPT GC.	1	111	139*	3.4	9.7
419 SO BAPT CONV..	1	125	156*	3.9	10.9
443 UN C OF CHRIST	1	137	171*	4.2	11.9
FERGUS	25	2,741	5,566*	44.1	100.0
019 AMER BAPT CONV	1	163	197*	1.6	3.5
029 AMER LUTH CH..	3	602	878	7.0	15.8
081 CATHOLIC......	6	0	1,980	15.7	35.6
097 CR C AND C CR.	1	125	151*	1.2	2.7
165 CH OF NAZARENE	1	5	30	0.2	0.5
193 EPISCOPAL.....	1	112	291	2.3	5.2
283 LUTH--MO SYNOD	2	219	310	2.5	5.6
413 S-D ADVENTISTS	1	78	94*	0.7	1.7
419 SO BAPT CONV..	1	48	58*	0.5	1.0
449 UN METHODIST..	5	938	1,031	8.2	18.5
453 UN PRES CH USA	3	451	546*	4.3	9.8
FLATHEAD	39	6,652	13,446*	34.1	100.0
019 AMER BAPT CONV	1	89	110*	0.3	0.8
029 AMER LUTH CH..	6	2,168	3,270	8.3	24.3
081 CATHOLIC......	6	0	4,081	10.3	30.4
093 CR CH (DISC)..	3	469	580*	1.5	4.3
123 CH GOD (ANDER)	1	45	135	0.3	1.0
165 CH OF NAZARENE	2	192	399	1.0	3.0
193 EPISCOPAL.....	3	279	467	1.2	3.5
197 EVAN CH OF NA.	1	7	9*	-	0.1
283 LUTH--MO SYNOD	3	697	1,034	2.6	7.7
285 MENNONITE CH..	1	125	155*	0.4	1.2
403 SALVATION ARMY	1	51	247	0.6	1.8
413 S-D ADVENTISTS	1	160	198*	0.5	1.5
419 SO BAPT CONV..	1	151	187*	0.5	1.4
435 UNITARIAN-UNIV	1	17	17	-	0.1
449 UN METHODIST..	6	1,387	1,549	3.9	11.5
453 UN PRES CH USA	2	815	1,008*	2.6	7.5
GALLATIN	40	6,287	12,043*	37.0	100.0
019 AMER BAPT CONV	2	289	344*	1.1	2.9
029 AMER LUTH CH..	1	912	1,340	4.1	11.1
081 CATHOLIC......	4	0	2,972	9.1	24.7
093 CR CH (DISC)..	1	316	376*	1.2	3.1
105 CHRISTIAN REF.	4	810	1,529	4.7	12.7
123 CH GOD (ANDER)	1	15	50	0.2	0.4
127 CH GOD (CLEVE)	2	25	30*	0.1	0.2
165 CH OF NAZARENE	1	28	86	0.3	0.7
193 EPISCOPAL.....	2	352	701	2.2	5.8
197 EVAN CH OF NA.	1	20	24*	0.1	0.2
281 LUTH CH AMER..	1	197	351	1.1	2.9
283 LUTH--MO SYNOD	2	458	662	2.0	5.5
413 S-D ADVENTISTS	3	428	509*	1.6	4.2
419 SO BAPT CONV..	3	243	289*	0.9	2.4
435 UNITARIAN-UNIV	1	20	20	0.1	0.2
443 UN C OF CHRIST	1	115	137*	0.4	1.1
449 UN METHODIST..	4	1,105	1,487	4.6	12.3
453 UN PRES CH USA	5	940	1,118*	3.4	9.3
469 WISC EVAN LUTH	1	14	18	0.1	0.1
GARFIELD	5	200	556*	31.0	100.0
029 AMER LUTH CH..	1	67	146	8.1	26.3
081 CATHOLIC......	1	0	240	13.4	43.2
353 PLY BRETHREN..	1	20	30	1.7	5.4
413 S-D ADVENTISTS	1	43	53*	3.0	9.5
453 UN PRES CH USA	1	70	87*	4.8	15.6
GLACIER	13	1,319	4,742*	44.0	100.0
019 AMER BAPT CONV	1	83	108*	1.0	2.3
029 AMER LUTH CH..	1	583	749	6.9	15.8
059 BAPT MISS ASSN	1	50	65*	0.6	1.4
081 CATHOLIC......	5	0	2,975	27.6	62.7
097 CR C AND C CR.	1	40	52*	0.5	1.1
449 UN METHODIST..	3	155	262	2.4	5.5
453 UN PRES CH USA	1	408	531*	4.9	11.2
GOLDEN VALLEY	8	228	397	42.6	100.0
029 AMER LUTH CH..	2	69	86	9.2	21.7
081 CATHOLIC......	3	0	140	15.0	35.3
449 UN METHODIST..	2	133	137	14.7	34.5
469 WISC EVAN LUTH	1	26	34	3.7	8.6
GRANITE	5	182	473*	17.3	100.0
081 CATHOLIC......	2	0	274	10.0	57.9
449 UN METHODIST..	2	101	101	3.7	21.4
453 UN PRES CH USA	1	81	98*	3.6	20.7
HILL	35	3,682	7,024*	40.5	100.0
019 AMER BAPT CONV	2	142	174*	1.0	2.5
029 AMER LUTH CH..	7	1,463	2,050	11.8	29.2
081 CATHOLIC......	10	0	2,032	11.7	28.9
097 CR C AND C CR.	1	300	369*	2.1	5.3
157 CH OF BRETHREN	1	27	33*	0.2	0.5
165 CH OF NAZARENE	1	9	27	0.2	0.4

*Total adherents estimated from known number of communicant, confirmed, full members.

—Represents a percent less than 0.1.

Percentages may not total due to rounding.

Table 3. Churches and Church Membership by State, County and Denomination: 1971

County and Denomination	Number of churches	Communicant, confirmed, full members	Total adherents: Number	Total adherents: Percent of total population	Total adherents: Percent of total adherents
193 EPISCOPAL.....	1	69	219	1.3	3.1
197 EVAN CH OF NA.	2	51	63*	0.4	0.9
281 LUTH CH AMER..	1	132	282	1.6	4.0
283 LUTH--MO SYNOD	2	206	297	1.7	4.2
403 SALVATION ARMY	1	18	84	0.5	1.2
413 S-D ADVENTISTS	1	52	64*	0.4	0.9
419 SO BAPT CONV..	1	44	54*	0.3	0.8
449 UN METHODIST..	3	760	773	4.5	11.0
453 UN PRES CH USA	1	409	503*	2.9	7.2
JEFFERSON	14	944	1,864*	35.6	100.0
029 AMER LUTH CH..	1	57	71	1.4	3.8
081 CATHOLIC......	3	0	720	13.7	38.6
093 CR CH (DISC)..	1	38	46*	0.9	2.5
283 LUTH--MO SYNOD	2	79	108	2.1	5.8
353 PLY BRETHREN..	1	10	10	0.2	0.5
413 S-D ADVENTISTS	1	8	10*	0.2	0.5
419 SO BAPT CONV..	1	35	42*	0.8	2.3
449 UN METHODIST..	3	151	171	3.3	9.2
453 UN PRES CH USA	1	566	686*	13.1	36.8
JUDITH BASIN	10	383	925*	34.7	100.0
081 CATHOLIC......	4	0	500	18.7	54.1
449 UN METHODIST..	4	182	186	7.0	20.1
453 UN PRES CH USA	2	201	239*	9.0	25.8
LAKE	25	1,973	5,184*	35.9	100.0
029 AMER LUTH CH..	2	488	676	4.7	13.0
081 CATHOLIC......	7	0	2,592	17.9	50.0
093 CR CH (DISC)..	1	110	135*	0.9	2.6
097 CR C AND C CR.	2	70	86*	0.6	1.7
165 CH OF NAZARENE	1	30	50	0.3	1.0
193 EPISCOPAL.....	1	71	82	0.6	1.6
283 LUTH--MO SYNOD	3	354	505	3.5	9.7
413 S-D ADVENTISTS	1	76	93*	0.6	1.8
449 UN METHODIST..	5	463	584	4.0	11.3
453 UN PRES CH USA	2	311	381*	2.6	7.3
LEWIS AND CLARK	25	5,331	18,435*	55.4	100.0
019 AMER BAPT CONV	1	310	382*	1.1	2.1
029 AMER LUTH CH..	1	480	776	2.3	4.2
081 CATHOLIC......	7	0	10,677	32.1	57.9
093 CR CH (DISC)..	1	194	239*	0.7	1.3
165 CH OF NAZARENE	1	42	103	0.3	0.6
193 EPISCOPAL.....	1	493	1,023	3.1	5.5
201 EVAN COV CH AM	1	60	74*	0.2	0.4
281 LUTH CH AMER..	1	818	1,260	3.8	6.8
283 LUTH--MO SYNOD	1	418	608	1.8	3.3
403 SALVATION ARMY	1	35	246	0.7	1.3
413 S-D ADVENTISTS	1	70	86*	0.3	0.5
419 SO BAPT CONV..	2	196	241*	0.7	1.3
443 UN C OF CHRIST	1	309	380*	1.1	2.1
449 UN METHODIST..	4	1,238	1,517	4.6	8.2
453 UN PRES CH USA	1	668	823*	2.5	4.5
LIBERTY	10	851	1,404*	59.5	100.0
029 AMER LUTH CH..	4	576	810	34.3	57.7
081 CATHOLIC......	1	0	250	10.6	17.8
413 S-D ADVENTISTS	3	79	97*	4.1	6.9
449 UN METHODIST..	1	143	182	7.7	13.0
453 UN PRES CH USA	1	53	65*	2.8	4.6
LINCOLN	18	2,401	5,552*	30.7	100.0
019 AMER BAPT CONV	1	230	294*	1.6	5.3
029 AMER LUTH CH..	1	474	805	4.5	14.5
081 CATHOLIC......	4	0	1,818	10.1	32.7
097 CR C AND C CR.	1	120	153*	0.8	2.8
123 CH GOD (ANDER)	2	85	240	1.3	4.3
165 CH OF NAZARENE	1	61	168	0.9	3.0
193 EPISCOPAL.....	2	56	243	1.3	4.4
283 LUTH--MO SYNOD	2	617	870	4.8	15.7
419 SO BAPT CONV..	1	135	173*	1.0	3.1
449 UN METHODIST..	2	461	581	3.2	10.5
453 UN PRES CH USA	1	162	207*	1.1	3.7
MC CONE	9	628	1,656*	57.6	100.0
019 AMER BAPT CONV	1	68	84*	2.9	5.1
029 AMER LUTH CH..	1	336	475	16.5	28.7
081 CATHOLIC......	3	0	800	27.8	48.3
197 EVAN CH OF NA.	1	68	84*	2.9	5.1
443 UN C OF CHRIST	2	86	106*	3.7	6.4
469 WISC EVAN LUTH	1	70	107	3.7	6.5
MADISON	10	323	1,115*	22.2	100.0
081 CATHOLIC......	4	0	530	10.6	47.5
193 EPISCOPAL.....	3	42	257	5.1	23.0
449 UN METHODIST..	2	252	294	5.9	26.4
453 UN PRES CH USA	1	29	34*	0.7	3.0
MEAGHER	6	263	591*	27.9	100.0
029 AMER LUTH CH..	2	170	251	11.8	42.5
081 CATHOLIC......	2	0	212	10.0	35.9
193 EPISCOPAL.....	1	12	29	1.4	4.9
453 UN PRES CH USA	1	81	99*	4.7	16.8
MINERAL	6	248	784	26.5	100.0
081 CATHOLIC......	2	0	503	17.0	64.2
283 LUTH--MO SYNOD	1	76	109	3.7	13.9
449 UN METHODIST..	3	172	172	5.8	21.9
MISSOULA	40	8,670	23,664*	40.6	100.0
019 AMER BAPT CONV	1	405	497*	0.9	2.1
029 AMER LUTH CH..	3	1,584	3,054	5.2	12.9
081 CATHOLIC......	8	0	10,735	18.4	45.4
093 CR CH (DISC)..	1	246	302*	0.5	1.3
097 CR C AND C CR.	1	60	74*	0.1	0.3
123 CH GOD (ANDER)	1	20	52	0.1	0.2
127 CH GOD (CLEVE)	1	31	38*	0.1	0.2
165 CH OF NAZARENE	1	99	225	0.4	1.0
193 EPISCOPAL.....	1	581	822	1.4	3.5
197 EVAN CH OF NA.	1	101	124*	0.2	0.5
201 EVAN COV CH AM	1	89	109*	0.2	0.5
281 LUTH CH AMER..	2	747	1,534	2.6	6.5
283 LUTH--MO SYNOD	5	913	1,376	2.4	5.8
313 NO AM BAPT GC.	1	317	389*	0.7	1.6
353 PLY BRETHREN..	1	40	80	0.1	0.3
403 SALVATION ARMY	1	44	144	0.2	0.6
413 S-D ADVENTISTS	1	312	383*	0.7	1.6
419 SO BAPT CONV..	1	131	161*	0.3	0.7
435 UNITARIAN-UNIV	1	40	40	0.1	0.2
443 UN C OF CHRIST	1	494	606*	1.0	2.6
449 UN METHODIST..	3	1,569	1,880	3.2	7.9
453 UN PRES CH USA	3	847	1,039*	1.8	4.4
MUSSELSHELL	11	679	1,486*	39.8	100.0
019 AMER BAPT CONV	1	57	67*	1.8	4.5
029 AMER LUTH CH..	1	158	220	5.9	14.8
081 CATHOLIC......	3	0	600	16.1	40.4
175 CONG CR CH....	2	70	82*	2.2	5.5
193 EPISCOPAL.....	1	58	82	2.2	5.5
283 LUTH--MO SYNOD	1	87	116	3.1	7.8
449 UN METHODIST..	1	203	239	6.4	16.1
469 WISC EVAN LUTH	1	46	80	2.1	5.4
PARK	20	2,105	4,775*	42.6	100.0
019 AMER BAPT CONV	1	396	466*	4.2	9.8
029 AMER LUTH CH..	2	502	683	6.1	14.3
081 CATHOLIC......	4	0	1,959	17.5	41.0
127 CH GOD (CLEVE)	1	31	37*	0.3	0.8
165 CH OF NAZARENE	1	42	195	1.7	4.1
175 CONG CR CH....	1	34	40*	0.4	0.8
193 EPISCOPAL.....	2	154	253	2.3	5.3
281 LUTH CH AMER..	1	114	147	1.3	3.1
413 S-D ADVENTISTS	1	31	37*	0.3	0.8
419 SO BAPT CONV..	1	53	62*	0.6	1.3
449 UN METHODIST..	4	660	756	6.8	15.8
469 WISC EVAN LUTH	1	88	140	1.3	2.9
PETROLEUM	3	107	230	34.1	100.0
081 CATHOLIC......	1	0	80	11.9	34.8
449 UN METHODIST..	1	62	62	9.2	27.0
469 WISC EVAN LUTH	1	45	88	13.0	38.3
PHILLIPS	14	967	2,116*	39.3	100.0
029 AMER LUTH CH..	6	730	985	18.3	46.6
081 CATHOLIC......	5	0	830	15.4	39.2
097 CR C AND C CR.	1	60	74*	1.4	3.5
193 EPISCOPAL.....	1	34	51	0.9	2.4
443 UN C OF CHRIST	1	143	176*	3.3	8.3
PONDERA	13	1,807	5,278*	79.8	100.0
029 AMER LUTH CH..	3	850	1,161	17.6	22.0
081 CATHOLIC......	4	0	2,892	43.7	54.8
093 CR CH (DISC)..	1	152	188*	2.8	3.6
105 CHRISTIAN REF.	1	48	83	1.3	1.6
371 REF CH IN AM..	1	60	82	1.2	1.6
449 UN METHODIST..	2	330	417	6.3	7.9
453 UN PRES CH USA	1	367	455*	6.9	8.6
POWDER RIVER	16	288	862*	30.1	100.0
029 AMER LUTH CH..	1	68	103	3.6	11.9
081 CATHOLIC......	14	0	480	16.8	55.7
443 UN C OF CHRIST	1	220	279*	9.7	32.4
POWELL	10	620	1,086*	16.3	100.0
081 CATHOLIC......	4	0	141	2.1	13.0
093 CR CH (DISC)..	1	105	127*	1.9	11.7
193 EPISCOPAL.....	1	69	239	3.6	22.0
283 LUTH--MO SYNOD	1	159	210	3.2	19.3
419 SO BAPT CONV..	1	47	57*	0.9	5.2
449 UN METHODIST..	1	75	112	1.7	10.3
453 UN PRES CH USA	1	165	200*	3.0	18.4
PRAIRIE	8	538	821*	46.9	100.0
029 AMER LUTH CH..	1	96	100	5.7	12.2
081 CATHOLIC......	2	0	150	8.6	18.3
197 EVAN CH OF NA.	1	94	109*	6.2	13.3
283 LUTH--MO SYNOD	1	137	196	11.2	23.9
413 S-D ADVENTISTS	1	10	12*	0.7	1.5
453 UN PRES CH USA	1	140	163*	9.3	19.9
469 WISC EVAN LUTH	1	61	91	5.2	11.1

*Total adherents estimated from known number of communicant, confirmed, full members.

—Represents a percent less than 0.1.

Percentages may not total due to rounding.

Table 3. Churches and Church Membership by State, County and Denomination: 1971

County and Denomination	Number of churches	Communicant, confirmed, full members	Total adherents		
			Number	Percent of total population	Percent of total adherents
RAVALLI	20	2,168	3,308*	23.0	100.0
019 AMER BAPT CONV	3	355	429*	3.0	13.0
029 AMER LUTH CH..	1	241	337	2.3	10.2
081 CATHOLIC......	4	0	635	4.4	19.2
093 CR CH (DISC)..	1	79	95*	0.7	2.9
193 EPISCOPAL.....	1	55	120	0.8	3.6
283 LUTH--MO SYNOD	2	284	401	2.8	12.1
413 S-D ADVENTISTS	2	174	210*	1.5	6.3
419 SO BAPT CONV..	1	149	180*	1.2	5.4
449 UN METHODIST..	3	540	549	3.8	16.6
453 UN PRES CH USA	2	291	352*	2.4	10.6
RICHLAND	20	3,236	6,380*	64.9	100.0
029 AMER LUTH CH..	5	1,615	2,382	24.2	37.3
081 CATHOLIC......	4	0	1,840	18.7	28.8
165 CH OF NAZARENE	2	61	110	1.1	1.7
197 EVAN CH OF NA.	1	17	21*	0.2	0.3
283 LUTH--MO SYNOD	2	549	802	8.2	12.6
313 NO AM BAPT GC.	1	70	87*	0.9	1.4
413 S-D ADVENTISTS	1	27	33*	0.3	0.5
443 UN C OF CHRIST	2	284	351*	3.6	5.5
449 UN METHODIST..	1	432	530	5.4	8.3
453 UN PRES CH USA	1	181	224*	2.3	3.5
ROOSEVELT	31	2,925	5,453*	52.6	100.0
019 AMER BAPT CONV	1	44	55*	0.5	1.0
029 AMER LUTH CH..	8	1,554	2,139	20.6	39.2
081 CATHOLIC......	7	0	1,536	14.8	28.2
157 CH OF BRETHREN	1	38	48*	0.5	0.9
165 CH OF NAZARENE	1	28	54	0.5	1.0
283 LUTH--MO SYNOD	1	166	234	2.3	4.3
287 MENN GEN CONF.	1	53	67*	0.6	1.2
419 SO BAPT CONV..	2	185	233*	2.2	4.3
443 UN C OF CHRIST	1	46	58*	0.6	1.1
449 UN METHODIST..	2	105	130	1.3	2.4
453 UN PRES CH USA	5	668	842*	8.1	15.4
469 WISC EVAN LUTH	1	38	57	0.5	1.0
ROSEBUD	17	828	4,455*	73.9	100.0
029 AMER LUTH CH..	1	38	61	1.0	1.4
081 CATHOLIC......	7	0	3,200	53.1	71.8
193 EPISCOPAL.....	1	36	46	0.8	1.0
283 LUTH--MO SYNOD	3	239	495	8.2	11.1
287 MENN GEN CONF.	2	153	195*	3.2	4.4
419 SO BAPT CONV..	1	68	87*	1.4	2.0
449 UN METHODIST..	1	15	15	0.2	0.3
453 UN PRES CH USA	1	279	356*	5.9	8.0
SANDERS	18	808	1,987*	28.0	100.0
029 AMER LUTH CH..	3	236	385	5.4	19.4
081 CATHOLIC......	5	0	792	11.2	39.9
123 CH GOD (ANDER)	1	48	95	1.3	4.8
193 EPISCOPAL.....	1	7	7	0.1	0.4
413 S-D ADVENTISTS	1	44	54*	0.8	2.7
443 UN C OF CHRIST	2	197	241*	3.4	12.1
449 UN METHODIST..	4	187	304	4.3	15.3
453 UN PRES CH USA	1	89	109*	1.5	5.5
SHERIDAN	24	1,981	3,157*	54.6	100.0
029 AMER LUTH CH..	9	1,163	1,531	26.5	48.5
081 CATHOLIC......	5	0	599	10.4	19.0
197 EVAN CH OF NA.	1	14	17*	0.3	0.5
281 LUTH CH AMER..	2	390	490	8.5	15.5
283 LUTH--MO SYNOD	1	72	122	2.1	3.9
285 MENNONITE CH..	1	18	22*	0.4	0.7
413 S-D ADVENTISTS	1	44	53*	0.9	1.7
443 UN C OF CHRIST	2	203	246*	4.3	7.8
449 UN METHODIST..	2	77	77	1.3	2.4
SILVER BOW	22	2,114	17,773*	42.3	100.0
019 AMER BAPT CONV	2	172	211*	0.5	1.2
029 AMER LUTH CH..	1	408	578	1.4	3.3
081 CATHOLIC......	9	0	14,184	33.8	79.8
093 CR CH (DISC)..	1	79	97*	0.2	0.5
165 CH OF NAZARENE	1	27	57	0.1	0.3
193 EPISCOPAL.....	1	329	725	1.7	4.1
201 EVAN COV CH AM	1	32	39*	0.1	0.2
281 LUTH CH AMER..	1	377	768	1.8	4.3
283 LUTH--MO SYNOD	1	224	348	0.8	2.0
403 SALVATION ARMY	1	18	216	0.5	1.2
413 S-D ADVENTISTS	1	44	54*	0.1	0.3
419 SO BAPT CONV..	1	205	252*	0.6	1.4
443 UN C OF CHRIST	1	199	244*	0.6	1.4
STILLWATER	15	958	1,492*	32.2	100.0
029 AMER LUTH CH..	1	156	189	4.1	12.7
081 CATHOLIC......	3	0	250	5.4	16.8
193 EPISCOPAL.....	1	25	48	1.0	3.2
197 EVAN CH OF NA.	4	158	186*	4.0	12.5
281 LUTH CH AMER..	1	109	157	3.4	10.5
283 LUTH--MO SYNOD	2	206	303	6.5	20.3
443 UN C OF CHRIST	3	304	359*	7.8	24.1
SWEET GRASS	8	1,017	1,472*	49.4	100.0
029 AMER LUTH CH..	2	735	909	30.5	61.8
081 CATHOLIC......	1	0	208	7.0	14.1

County and Denomination	Number of churches	Communicant, confirmed, full members	Total adherents		
			Number	Percent of total population	Percent of total adherents
127 CH GOD (CLEVE)	1	36	42*	1.4	2.9
193 EPISCOPAL.....	1	41	72	2.4	4.9
197 EVAN CH OF NA.	1	59	69*	2.3	4.7
413 S-D ADVENTISTS	1	21	25*	0.8	1.7
443 UN C OF CHRIST	1	125	147*	4.9	10.0
TETON	17	2,127	3,804*	62.2	100.0
029 AMER LUTH CH..	4	901	1,215	[illegible]	31.9
081 CATHOLIC......	5	0	1,072	17.5	28.2
283 LUTH--MO SYNOD	2	223	293	4.8	7.7
413 S-D ADVENTISTS	1	58	70*	1.1	1.8
443 UN C OF CHRIST	2	245	[illegible]	4.8	7.8
449 UN METHODIST..	3	700	[illegible]	14.0	22.6
TOOLE	17	1,648	3,514*	60.2	100.0
029 AMER LUTH CH..	5	1,005	1,586	[illegible]	45.2
081 CATHOLIC......	5	0	1,082	[illegible]	30.8
283 LUTH--MO SYNOD	1	36	[illegible]	[illegible]	2.2
413 S-D ADVENTISTS	1	47	[illegible]	[illegible]	1.6
419 SO BAPT CONV..	1	138	[illegible]	2.9	4.8
449 UN METHODIST..	4	422	[illegible]	9.3	15.4
TREASURE	2	155	[illegible]	31.8	100.0
081 CATHOLIC......	1	0	[illegible]	14.0	44.1
453 UN PRES CH USA	1	155	190*	17.8	55.9
VALLEY	30	2,594	[illegible]	[illegible]	100.0
029 AMER LUTH CH..	9	1,585	2,321	20.2	36.4
081 CATHOLIC......	8	0	[illegible]	23.4	42.0
165 CH OF NAZARENE	1	18	39	0.3	0.6
193 EPISCOPAL.....	1	38	79	0.7	1.2
211 EV MENN BRETH.	1	110	138*	1.2	2.2
283 LUTH--MO SYNOD	1	72	120	1.0	1.9
287 MENN GEN CONF.	1	71	89*	0.8	1.4
413 S-D ADVENTISTS	1	27	34*	0.3	0.5
419 SO BAPT CONV..	2	107	134*	1.2	2.1
443 UN C OF CHRIST	1	137	172*	1.5	2.7
449 UN METHODIST..	3	354	478	4.2	7.5
453 UN PRES CH USA	1	75	94*	0.8	1.5
WHEATLAND	9	606	1,156*	45.7	100.0
029 AMER LUTH CH..	1	140	[illegible]	7.5	16.4
081 CATHOLIC......	3	0	396	15.7	34.4
193 EPISCOPAL.....	1	52	71	2.8	6.1
283 LUTH--MO SYNOD	1	119	177	7.0	15.3
449 UN METHODIST..	2	194	200	7.9	17.3
453 UN PRES CH USA	1	101	120*	4.7	10.4
WIBAUX	4	178	623	42.5	100.0
029 AMER LUTH CH..	1	127	182	12.4	29.2
081 CATHOLIC......	2	0	390	26.6	62.6
449 UN METHODIST..	1	51	51	3.5	8.2
YELLOWSTONE	66	19,689	40,882*	46.8	100.0
019 AMER BAPT CONV	1	632	774*	0.9	1.9
029 AMER LUTH CH..	7	3,561	5,391	6.2	13.2
081 CATHOLIC......	11	0	13,869	15.9	33.9
093 CR CH (DISC)..	2	[illegible]	895*	1.0	2.2
123 CH GOD (ANDER)	1	35	155	0.2	0.4
127 CH GOD (CLEVE)	1	32	39*	-	0.1
165 CH OF NAZARENE	4	228	530	0.6	1.3
193 EPISCOPAL.....	3	[illegible]	[illegible]	1.6	3.4
197 EVAN CH OF NA.	4	[illegible]	[illegible]	0.5	1.1
201 EVAN COV CH AM	1	51	62*	0.1	0.2
281 LUTH CH AMER..	3	[illegible]	1,209	1.4	3.0
283 LUTH--MO SYNOD	5	[illegible]	2,317	2.7	5.7
313 NO AM BAPT GC.	1	153	187*	0.2	0.5
403 SALVATION ARMY	1	59	[illegible]	0.5	1.0
413 S-D ADVENTISTS	1	292	358*	0.4	0.9
419 SO BAPT CONV..	3	[illegible]	1,099*	1.3	2.7
435 UNITARIAN-UNIV	1	44	44	0.1	0.1
443 UN C OF CHRIST	7	3,847	4,712*	5.4	11.5
449 UN METHODIST..	6	[illegible]	5,252	6.0	12.8
453 UN PRES CH USA	2	[illegible]	1,555*	1.8	3.8
469 WISC EVAN LUTH	1	[illegible]	228	0.3	0.6
YELLOWSTONE NAT PARK	0	0	0	-	-
CO DATA NOT AVAIL	0	0	22,847	N/A	N/A
151 L-D SAINTS....	0	0	22,847	N/A	N/A

NEBRASKA

County and Denomination	Number of churches	Communicant, confirmed, full members	Number	Percent of total population	Percent of total adherents
THE STATE.....	2,242	460,539	896,127*	60.4	100.0
ADAMS	41	14,317	23,641*	77.4	100.0
019 AMER BAPT CONV	2	605	[illegible]	2.4	3.0

*Total adherents estimated from known number of communicant, confirmed, full members.

—Represents a percent less than 0.1.

Percentages may not total due to rounding.

NEBRASKA

Table 3. Churches and Church Membership by State, County and Denomination: 1971

County and Denomination	Number of churches	Communicant, confirmed, full members	Total adherents: Number	Percent of total population	Percent of total adherents
029 AMER LUTH CH..	1	259	386	1.3	1.6
081 CATHOLIC......	5	0	5,132	16.8	21.7
093 CR CH (DISC)..	1	317	378*	1.2	1.6
097 CR C AND C CR.	1	21	25*	0.1	0.1
123 CH GOD (ANDER)	1	60	131	0.4	0.6
165 CH OF NAZARENE	2	175	458	1.5	1.9
193 EPISCOPAL.....	1	443	503	1.6	2.1
201 EVAN COV CH AM	1	28	33*	0.1	0.1
281 LUTH CH AMER..	3	2,202	2,862	9.4	12.1
283 LUTH--MO SYNOD	7	2,341	3,202	10.5	13.5
403 SALVATION ARMY	1	63	303	1.0	1.3
413 S-D ADVENTISTS	1	59	70*	0.2	0.3
443 UN C OF CHRIST	2	498	593*	1.9	2.5
449 UN METHODIST..	7	3,728	4,614	15.1	19.5
453 UN PRES CH USA	4	3,387	4,036*	13.2	17.1
469 WISC EVAN LUTH	1	131	194	0.6	0.8
ANTELOPE	24	3,443	6,309*	69.7	100.0
081 CATHOLIC......	4	0	1,911	21.1	30.3
097 CR C AND C CR.	3	151	182*	2.0	2.9
283 LUTH--MO SYNOD	5	1,362	1,819	20.1	28.8
413 S-D ADVENTISTS	1	72	87*	1.0	1.4
443 UN C OF CHRIST	4	563	678*	7.5	10.7
449 UN METHODIST..	7	1,295	1,632	18.0	25.9
ARTHUR	1	185	222*	36.6	100.0
019 AMER BAPT CONV	1	185	222*	36.6	100.0
BANNER	2	136	177	17.1	100.0
193 EPISCOPAL.....	1	48	67	6.5	37.9
449 UN METHODIST..	1	88	110	10.6	62.1
BLAINE	4	196	256*	30.2	100.0
443 UN C OF CHRIST	3	141	170*	20.1	66.4
469 WISC EVAN LUTH	1	55	86	10.2	33.6
BOONE	18	2,857	5,565*	67.9	100.0
019 AMER BAPT CONV	1	147	179*	2.2	3.2
029 AMER LUTH CH..	2	1,142	1,446	17.7	26.0
081 CATHOLIC......	3	0	1,975	24.1	35.5
123 CH GOD (ANDER)	1	31	51	0.6	0.9
165 CH OF NAZARENE	1	8	14	0.2	0.3
193 EPISCOPAL.....	1	23	33	0.4	0.6
413 S-D ADVENTISTS	1	34	41*	0.5	0.7
443 UN C OF CHRIST	1	128	156*	1.9	2.8
449 UN METHODIST..	4	1,032	1,290	15.8	23.2
453 UN PRES CH USA	3	312	380*	4.6	6.8
BOX BUTTE	17	3,923	6,882*	68.2	100.0
019 AMER BAPT CONV	1	253	303*	3.0	4.4
081 CATHOLIC......	2	0	1,949	19.3	28.3
093 CR CH (DISC)..	1	259	310*	3.1	4.5
123 CH GOD (ANDER)	2	27	142	1.4	2.1
165 CH OF NAZARENE	2	45	105	1.0	1.5
193 EPISCOPAL.....	1	348	378	3.7	5.5
281 LUTH CH AMER..	1	377	504	5.0	7.3
283 LUTH--MO SYNOD	1	461	649	6.4	9.4
413 S-D ADVENTISTS	2	112	134*	1.3	1.9
443 UN C OF CHRIST	1	100	120*	1.2	1.7
449 UN METHODIST..	2	1,326	1,551	15.4	22.5
453 UN PRES CH USA	1	615	737*	7.3	10.7
BOYD	17	1,174	2,120*	56.5	100.0
081 CATHOLIC......	4	0	661	17.6	31.2
201 EVAN COV CH AM	2	43	51*	1.4	2.4
281 LUTH CH AMER..	2	318	398	10.6	18.8
283 LUTH--MO SYNOD	3	238	325	8.7	15.3
413 S-D ADVENTISTS	1	33	39*	1.0	1.8
443 UN C OF CHRIST	1	113	134*	3.6	6.3
449 UN METHODIST..	3	258	295	7.9	13.9
469 WISC EVAN LUTH	1	171	217	5.8	10.2
BROWN	9	1,300	2,217*	55.1	100.0
081 CATHOLIC......	2	0	502	12.5	22.6
165 CH OF NAZARENE	1	80	164	4.1	7.4
283 LUTH--MO SYNOD	1	257	349	8.7	15.7
443 UN C OF CHRIST	1	234	284*	7.1	12.8
449 UN METHODIST..	3	677	855	21.3	38.6
453 UN PRES CH USA	1	52	63*	1.6	2.8
BUFFALO	48	10,377	17,818*	57.1	100.0
019 AMER BAPT CONV	2	511	607*	1.9	3.4
081 CATHOLIC......	8	0	4,314	13.8	24.2
093 CR CH (DISC)..	3	615	731*	2.3	4.1
097 CR C AND C CR.	2	25	30*	0.1	0.2
123 CH GOD (ANDER)	1	50	115	0.4	0.6
165 CH OF NAZARENE	1	70	214	0.7	1.2
193 EPISCOPAL.....	1	350	440	1.4	2.5
221 FREE METH C NA	1	21	30	0.1	0.2
281 LUTH CH AMER..	1	925	1,282	4.1	7.2
283 LUTH--MO SYNOD	8	2,126	3,123	10.0	17.5
381 REF PRES-EVAN.	1	76	90	0.3	0.5
403 SALVATION ARMY	1	85	273	0.9	1.5
413 S-D ADVENTISTS	3	196	233*	0.7	1.3
443 UN C OF CHRIST	1	161	191*	0.6	1.1
449 UN METHODIST..	13	4,520	5,378	17.2	30.2

County and Denomination	Number of churches	Communicant, confirmed, full members	Total adherents: Number	Percent of total population	Percent of total adherents
453 UN PRES CH USA	1	646	767*	2.5	4.3
BURT	18	3,321	4,959*	53.6	100.0
019 AMER BAPT CONV	2	541	638*	6.9	12.9
081 CATHOLIC......	3	0	704	7.6	14.2
201 EVAN COV CH AM	2	156	184*	2.0	3.7
281 LUTH CH AMER..	3	1,379	1,891	20.4	38.1
283 LUTH--MO SYNOD	2	310	438	4.7	8.8
413 S-D ADVENTISTS	2	25	30*	0.3	0.6
453 UN PRES CH USA	4	910	1,074*	11.6	21.7
BUTLER	26	1,757	7,605*	80.4	100.0
019 AMER BAPT CONV	2	134	161*	1.7	2.1
081 CATHOLIC......	11	0	5,258	55.6	69.1
093 CR CH (DISC)..	1	37	45*	0.5	0.6
281 LUTH CH AMER..	1	162	218	2.3	2.9
283 LUTH--MO SYNOD	2	296	391	4.1	5.1
443 UN C OF CHRIST	1	63	76*	0.8	1.0
449 UN METHODIST..	6	919	1,254	13.3	16.5
469 WISC EVAN LUTH	2	146	202	2.1	2.7
CASS	32	4,802	7,991*	44.2	100.0
019 AMER BAPT CONV	1	124	153*	0.8	1.9
081 CATHOLIC......	4	0	1,941	10.7	24.3
093 CR CH (DISC)..	5	512	631*	3.5	7.9
097 CR C AND C CR.	1	100	123*	0.7	1.5
193 EPISCOPAL.....	1	90	141	0.8	1.8
281 LUTH CH AMER..	1	207	285	1.6	3.6
283 LUTH--MO SYNOD	5	844	1,192	6.6	14.9
419 SO BAPT CONV..	1	316	390*	2.2	4.9
443 UN C OF CHRIST	3	492	607*	3.4	7.6
449 UN METHODIST..	8	1,639	1,939	10.7	24.3
453 UN PRES CH USA	2	478	589*	3.3	7.4
CEDAR	30	3,575	10,181*	83.5	100.0
019 AMER BAPT CONV	1	54	68*	0.6	0.7
029 AMER LUTH CH..	6	1,724	2,298	18.8	22.6
081 CATHOLIC......	12	0	5,489	45.0	53.9
097 CR C AND C CR.	1	40	50*	0.4	0.5
283 LUTH--MO SYNOD	1	170	375	3.1	3.7
443 UN C OF CHRIST	2	416	522*	4.3	5.1
449 UN METHODIST..	5	823	942	7.7	9.3
453 UN PRES CH USA	2	348	437*	3.6	4.3
CHASE	11	1,560	2,236*	54.2	100.0
081 CATHOLIC......	2	0	323	7.8	14.4
097 CR C AND C CR.	1	50	60*	1.5	2.7
157 CH OF BRETHREN	1	73	87*	2.1	3.9
165 CH OF NAZARENE	1	26	39	0.9	1.7
193 EPISCOPAL.....	1	29	32	0.8	1.4
283 LUTH--MO SYNOD	2	469	65[illegible]	15.9	29.4
449 UN METHODIST..	3	913	1,038	25.1	46.4
CHERRY	23	1,969	4,174*	61.0	100.0
019 AMER BAPT CONV	1	63	76*	1.1	1.8
081 CATHOLIC......	5	0	1,426	20.8	34.2
105 CHRISTIAN REF.	1	50	93	1.4	2.2
165 CH OF NAZARENE	1	32	72	1.1	1.7
193 EPISCOPAL.....	3	143	275	4.0	6.6
283 LUTH--MO SYNOD	3	156	253	3.7	6.1
413 S-D ADVENTISTS	1	44	53*	0.8	1.3
419 SO BAPT CONV..	1	67	81*	1.2	1.9
449 UN METHODIST..	5	782	1,048	15.3	25.1
453 UN PRES CH USA	1	458	556*	8.1	13.3
469 WISC EVAN LUTH	1	174	241	3.5	5.8
CHEYENNE	19	3,354	6,651*	61.7	100.0
029 AMER LUTH CH..	1	169	215	2.0	3.2
081 CATHOLIC......	3	0	2,420	22.5	36.4
093 CR CH (DISC)..	1	184	222*	2.1	3.3
165 CH OF NAZARENE	1	29	101	0.9	1.5
193 EPISCOPAL.....	1	144	249	2.3	3.7
283 LUTH--MO SYNOD	4	748	992	9.2	14.9
413 S-D ADVENTISTS	2	45	54*	0.5	0.8
419 SO BAPT CONV..	1	39	47*	0.4	0.7
449 UN METHODIST..	3	1,530	1,789	16.6	26.9
453 UN PRES CH USA	2	466	562*	5.2	8.4
CLAY	32	3,425	5,020*	60.7	100.0
019 AMER BAPT CONV	1	46	56*	0.7	1.1
029 AMER LUTH CH..	2	513	697	8.4	13.9
081 CATHOLIC......	4	0	753	9.1	15.0
093 CR CH (DISC)..	2	119	144*	1.7	2.9
097 CR C AND C CR.	4	100	121*	1.5	2.4
123 CH GOD (ANDER)	1	18	53	0.6	1.1
193 EPISCOPAL.....	1	10	10	0.1	0.2
281 LUTH CH AMER..	3	310	389	4.7	7.7
443 UN C OF CHRIST	3	822	992*	12.0	19.8
449 UN METHODIST..	9	1,202	1,458	17.6	29.0
453 UN PRES CH USA	1	238	287*	3.5	5.7
469 WISC EVAN LUTH	1	47	60	0.7	1.2
COLFAX	23	2,872	7,732*	81.4	100.0
081 CATHOLIC......	9	0	4,118	43.4	53.3
193 EPISCOPAL.....	1	22	31	0.3	0.4
281 LUTH CH AMER..	2	524	686	7.2	8.9

*Total adherents estimated from known number of communicant, confirmed, full members.

—Represents a percent less than 0.1.

Percentages may not total due to rounding.

Table 3. Churches and Church Membership by State, County and Denomination: 1971

County and Denomination	Number of churches	Communicant, confirmed, full members	Total adherents: Number	Total adherents: Percent of total population	Total adherents: Percent of total adherents
283 LUTH--MO SYNOD	4	680	900	9.5	11.6
443 UN C OF CHRIST	1	96	116*	1.2	1.5
449 UN METHODIST..	2	339	423	4.5	5.5
453 UN PRES CH USA	4	1,211	1,458*	15.4	18.9
CUMING	25	5,160	8,903*	74.0	100.0
081 CATHOLIC......	7	0	2,041	17.0	22.9
281 LUTH CH AMER..	2	980	1,478	12.3	16.6
283 LUTH--MO SYNOD	9	3,178	4,208	35.0	47.3
285 MENNONITE CH..	1	176	217*	1.8	2.4
443 UN C OF CHRIST	2	247	305*	2.5	3.4
449 UN METHODIST..	3	416	453	3.8	5.1
453 UN PRES CH USA	1	163	201*	1.7	2.3
CUSTER	46	4,820	7,955*	56.5	100.0
019 AMER BAPT CONV	4	696	824*	5.8	10.4
081 CATHOLIC......	9	0	1,870	13.3	23.5
093 CR CH (DISC)..	1	146	173*	1.2	2.2
097 CR C AND C CR.	5	316	374*	2.7	4.7
123 CH GOD (ANDER)	1	35	112	0.8	1.4
165 CH OF NAZARENE	2	37	97	0.7	1.2
193 EPISCOPAL.....	2	157	194	1.4	2.4
221 FREE METH C NA	2	44	47	0.3	0.6
281 LUTH CH AMER..	1	129	182	1.3	2.3
283 LUTH--MO SYNOD	3	138	199	1.4	2.5
285 MENNONITE CH..	1	28	33*	0.2	0.4
413 S-D ADVENTISTS	1	67	79*	0.6	1.0
449 UN METHODIST..	12	2,647	3,289	23.3	41.3
453 UN PRES CH USA	1	277	328*	2.3	4.1
469 WISC EVAN LUTH	1	103	154	1.1	1.9
DAKOTA	19	3,381	7,182*	54.7	100.0
081 CATHOLIC......	6	0	2,375	18.1	33.1
193 EPISCOPAL.....	1	14	94	0.7	1.3
197 EVAN CH OF NA.	1	32	41*	0.3	0.6
281 LUTH CH AMER..	4	1,548	2,130	16.2	29.7
283 LUTH--MO SYNOD	1	346	520	4.0	7.2
413 S-D ADVENTISTS	1	54	69*	0.5	1.0
449 UN METHODIST..	3	903	1,334	10.2	18.6
453 UN PRES CH USA	2	484	619*	4.7	8.6
DAWES	19	2,770	4,348*	44.9	100.0
019 AMER BAPT CONV	2	478	552*	5.7	12.7
029 AMER LUTH CH..	1	266	362	3.7	8.3
081 CATHOLIC......	2	0	803	8.3	18.5
097 CR C AND C CR.	1	80	92*	0.9	2.1
165 CH OF NAZARENE	2	71	163	1.7	3.7
175 CONG CR CH....	1	93	107*	1.1	2.5
193 EPISCOPAL.....	1	175	220	2.3	5.1
283 LUTH--MO SYNOD	2	353	493	5.1	11.3
413 S-D ADVENTISTS	2	77	89*	0.9	2.0
443 UN C OF CHRIST	2	220	254*	2.6	5.8
449 UN METHODIST..	3	957	1,213	12.5	27.9
DAWSON	39	9,045	14,200*	72.9	100.0
019 AMER BAPT CONV	2	201	243*	1.2	1.7
029 AMER LUTH CH..	3	1,432	2,106	10.8	14.8
081 CATHOLIC......	6	0	2,447	12.6	17.2
093 CR CH (DISC)..	1	42	51*	0.3	0.4
097 CR C AND C CR.	3	700	846*	4.3	6.0
123 CH GOD (ANDER)	1	63	141	0.7	1.0
165 CH OF NAZARENE	3	123	329	1.7	2.3
193 EPISCOPAL.....	2	76	116	0.6	0.8
281 LUTH CH AMER..	2	314	437	2.2	3.1
283 LUTH--MO SYNOD	3	662	972	5.0	6.8
413 S-D ADVENTISTS	1	63	76*	0.4	0.5
419 SO BAPT CONV..	1	106	128*	0.7	0.9
449 UN METHODIST..	7	3,848	4,598	23.6	32.4
453 UN PRES CH USA	4	1,415	1,710*	8.8	12.0
DEUEL	9	1,565	2,153*	79.2	100.0
081 CATHOLIC......	1	0	223	8.2	10.4
281 LUTH CH AMER..	2	226	298	11.0	13.8
283 LUTH--MO SYNOD	2	338	429	15.8	19.9
285 MENNONITE CH..	1	15	18*	0.7	0.8
413 S-D ADVENTISTS	1	7	8*	0.3	0.4
449 UN METHODIST..	2	979	1,177	43.3	54.7
DIXON	24	4,125	6,630*	89.0	100.0
029 AMER LUTH CH..	1	112	150	2.0	2.3
081 CATHOLIC......	5	0	1,349	18.1	20.3
097 CR C AND C CR.	1	225	269*	3.6	4.1
226 FRIENDS-USA...	1	106	127*	1.7	1.9
281 LUTH CH AMER..	6	2,212	2,832	38.0	42.7
283 LUTH--MO SYNOD	5	756	1,052	14.1	15.9
449 UN METHODIST..	4	623	742	10.0	11.2
453 UN PRES CH USA	1	91	109*	1.5	1.6
DODGE	44	12,458	19,525*	56.1	100.0
019 AMER BAPT CONV	1	651	796*	2.3	4.1
029 AMER LUTH CH..	2	1,278	1,799	5.2	9.2
081 CATHOLIC......	7	0	2,996	8.6	15.3
093 CR CH (DISC)..	1	348	426*	1.2	2.2
127 CH GOD (CLEVE)	1	11	13*	-	0.1
175 CONG CR CH....	1	35	43*	0.1	0.2
193 EPISCOPAL.....	1	415	478	1.4	2.4
221 FREE METH C NA	1	16	28	0.1	0.1
281 LUTH CH AMER..	13	3,917	5,151	14.8	26.4
283 LUTH--MO SYNOD	8	2,912	4,074	11.7	20.9
403 SALVATION ARMY	1	92	331	1.0	1.7
413 S-D ADVENTISTS	1	46	56*	0.2	0.3
443 UN C OF CHRIST	3	945	1,156*	3.3	5.9
449 UN METHODIST..	1	85	90	0.3	0.5
453 UN PRES CH USA	2	1,707	2,088*	6.0	10.7
DOUGLAS	194	60,818	205,654*	52.8	100.0
019 AMER BAPT CONV	10	3,369	4,201*	1.1	2.0
029 AMER LUTH CH..	10	5,272	7,473	1.9	3.6
081 CATHOLIC......	50	0	121,636	31.2	59.1
093 CR CH (DISC)..	4	1,356	1,691*	0.4	0.8
097 CR C AND C CR.	6	1,230	1,534*	0.4	0.7
105 CHRISTIAN REF.	1	71	141	-	0.1
121 CH GOD (ABR)..	1	84	105*	-	0.1
123 CH GOD (ANDER)	2	78	195	0.1	0.1
127 CH GOD (CLEVE)	4	267	333*	0.1	0.2
165 CH OF NAZARENE	3	334	671	0.2	0.3
193 EPISCOPAL.....	8	3,435	4,627	1.2	2.2
201 EVAN COV CH AM	2	715	892*	0.2	0.4
211 EV MENN BRETH.	2	161	201*	0.1	0.1
221 FREE METH C NA	1	36	60	-	-
226 FRIENDS-USA...	1	78	97*	-	-
281 LUTH CH AMER..	19	13,052	19,304	5.0	9.4
283 LUTH--MO SYNOD	18	9,471	13,446	3.5	6.5
285 MENNONITE CH..	1	35	44*	-	-
335 ORTH PRESB CH.	1	49	62	-	-
353 PLY BRETHREN..	2	110	180	-	0.1
371 REF CH IN AM..	1	193	345	0.1	0.2
403 SALVATION ARMY	3	382	2,030	0.5	1.0
413 S-D ADVENTISTS	2	967	1,206*	0.3	0.6
419 SO BAPT CONV..	4	923	1,151*	0.3	0.6
435 UNITARIAN-UNIV	1	411	511	0.1	0.2
443 UN C OF CHRIST	5	3,971	4,951*	1.3	2.4
453 UN PRES CH USA	29	14,331	17,869*	4.6	8.7
469 WISC EVAN LUTH	3	437	698	0.2	0.3
DUNDY	16	1,471	1,948*	66.6	100.0
019 AMER BAPT CONV	1	62	72*	2.5	3.7
029 AMER LUTH CH..	2	297	387	13.2	19.9
081 CATHOLIC......	1	0	148	5.1	7.6
226 FRIENDS-USA...	2	79	91*	3.1	4.7
283 LUTH--MO SYNOD	1	135	156	5.3	8.0
413 S-D ADVENTISTS	2	46	53*	1.8	2.7
419 SO BAPT CONV..	1	73	84*	2.9	4.3
449 UN METHODIST..	5	698	863	29.5	44.3
453 UN PRES CH USA	1	81	94*	3.2	4.8
FILLMORE	23	3,200	5,092*	62.6	100.0
029 AMER LUTH CH..	1	190	263	3.2	5.2
081 CATHOLIC......	5	0	1,215	14.9	23.9
281 LUTH CH AMER..	3	364	439	5.4	8.6
283 LUTH--MO SYNOD	1	125	154	1.9	3.0
285 MENNONITE CH..	1	230	271*	3.3	5.3
287 MENN GEN CONF.	1	42	49*	0.6	1.0
443 UN C OF CHRIST	4	687	809*	9.9	15.9
449 UN METHODIST..	5	1,384	1,660	20.4	32.6
469 WISC EVAN LUTH	2	178	232	2.9	4.6
FRANKLIN	23	2,678	3,906*	85.5	100.0
019 AMER BAPT CONV	1	30	34*	0.7	0.9
029 AMER LUTH CH..	3	527	671	14.7	17.2
081 CATHOLIC......	5	0	587	12.9	15.0
093 CR CH (DISC)..	1	52	60*	1.3	1.5
281 LUTH CH AMER..	1	292	367	8.0	9.4
283 LUTH--MO SYNOD	3	470	614	13.4	15.7
443 UN C OF CHRIST	3	287	329*	7.2	8.4
449 UN METHODIST..	5	812	1,006	22.0	25.8
453 UN PRES CH USA	1	208	238*	5.2	6.1
FRONTIER	15	1,681	2,319*	58.2	100.0
029 AMER LUTH CH..	1	394	501	12.6	21.6
081 CATHOLIC......	2	0	156	3.9	6.7
097 CR C AND C CR.	1	75	89*	2.2	3.8
121 CH GOD (ABR)..	1	25	30*	0.8	1.3
165 CH OF NAZARENE	1	10	63	1.6	2.7
283 LUTH--MO SYNOD	1	216	288	7.2	12.4
413 S-D ADVENTISTS	1	11	13*	0.3	0.6
443 UN C OF CHRIST	2	95	112*	2.8	4.8
449 UN METHODIST..	5	855	1,067	26.8	46.0
FURNAS	28	3,863	5,189*	75.2	100.0
019 AMER BAPT CONV	3	371	426*	6.2	8.2
029 AMER LUTH CH..	1	95	125	1.8	2.4
081 CATHOLIC......	3	0	478	6.9	9.2
093 CR CH (DISC)..	1	81	93*	1.3	1.8
097 CR C AND C CR.	3	365	419*	6.1	8.1
121 CH GOD (ABR)..	1	38	44*	0.6	0.8
193 EPISCOPAL.....	1	66	97	1.4	1.9
221 FREE METH C NA	1	15	22	0.3	0.4
283 LUTH--MO SYNOD	2	773	1,032	15.0	19.9
413 S-D ADVENTISTS	2	46	53*	0.8	1.0
443 UN C OF CHRIST	1	222	255*	3.7	4.9
449 UN METHODIST..	8	1,616	1,944	28.2	37.5
453 UN PRES CH USA	1	175	201*	2.9	3.9
GAGE	60	13,582	18,898*	73.5	100.0

*Total adherents estimated from known number of communicant, confirmed, full members.

—Represents a percent less than 0.1.

Percentages may not total due to rounding.

Table 3. Churches and Church Membership by State, County and Denomination: 1971

County and Denomination	Number of churches	Communicant, confirmed, full members	Total adherents: Number	Total adherents: Percent of total population	Total adherents: Percent of total adherents
019 AMER BAPT CONV	2	297	350*	1.4	1.9
029 AMER LUTH CH..	10	4,011	5,397	21.0	28.6
081 CATHOLIC......	5	0	1,603	6.2	8.5
093 CR CH (DISC)..	5	1,236	1,456*	5.7	7.7
097 CR C AND C CR.	3	430	507*	2.0	2.7
123 CH GOD (ANDER)	1	24	55	0.2	0.3
157 CH OF BRETHREN	2	206	243*	0.9	1.3
165 CH OF NAZARENE	1	60	155	0.6	0.8
193 EPISCOPAL.....	2	211	340	1.3	1.8
281 LUTH CH AMER..	1	206	277	1.1	1.5
283 LUTH--MO SYNOD	4	1,371	1,870	7.3	9.9
287 MENN GEN CONF.	2	452	533*	2.1	2.8
313 NO AM BAPT GC.	1	140	165*	0.6	0.9
371 REF CH IN AM..	1	160	227	0.9	1.2
403 SALVATION ARMY	1	64	199	0.8	1.1
413 S-D ADVENTISTS	1	29	34*	0.1	0.2
419 SO BAPT CONV..	1	128	151*	0.6	0.8
443 UN C OF CHRIST	1	122	144*	0.6	0.8
449 UN METHODIST..	10	3,119	3,587	13.9	19.0
453 UN PRES CH USA	4	980	1,155*	4.5	6.1
469 WISC EVAN LUTH	2	336	450	1.7	2.4
GARDEN	11	1,004	1,492*	50.9	100.0
081 CATHOLIC......	3	0	305	10.4	20.4
193 EPISCOPAL.....	1	22	25	0.9	1.7
281 LUTH CH AMER..	2	340	499	17.0	33.4
413 S-D ADVENTISTS	1	23	27*	0.9	1.8
449 UN METHODIST..	3	523	523	17.9	35.1
453 UN PRES CH USA	1	96	113*	3.9	7.6
GARFIELD	5	729	1,202*	49.9	100.0
081 CATHOLIC......	1	0	312	12.9	26.0
097 CR C AND C CR.	1	120	141*	5.8	11.7
283 LUTH--MO SYNOD	1	121	175	7.3	14.6
443 UN C OF CHRIST	1	185	217*	9.0	18.1
449 UN METHODIST..	1	303	357	14.8	29.7
GOSPER	5	977	1,317*	60.5	100.0
029 AMER LUTH CH..	1	296	393	18.0	29.8
081 CATHOLIC......	1	0	58	2.7	4.4
093 CR CH (DISC)..	1	121	143*	6.6	10.9
283 LUTH--MO SYNOD	1	272	365	16.8	27.7
449 UN METHODIST..	1	288	358	16.4	27.2
GRANT	5	364	616*	60.5	100.0
081 CATHOLIC......	1	0	70	6.9	11.4
193 EPISCOPAL.....	1	121	223	21.9	36.2
283 LUTH--MO SYNOD	1	21	44	4.3	7.1
443 UN C OF CHRIST	2	222	279*	27.4	45.3
GREELEY	13	1,329	4,101*	102.5 #	100.0
081 CATHOLIC......	5	0	2,341	58.5	57.1
281 LUTH CH AMER..	1	209	343	8.6	8.4
283 LUTH--MO SYNOD	1	215	282	7.1	6.9
449 UN METHODIST..	4	576	734	18.4	17.9
453 UN PRES CH USA	2	329	401*	10.0	9.8
HALL	36	17,488	33,055*	77.1	100.0
019 AMER BAPT CONV	1	528	654*	1.5	2.0
029 AMER LUTH CH..	1	298	487	1.1	1.5
081 CATHOLIC......	4	0	10,549	24.6	31.9
093 CR CH (DISC)..	1	352	436*	1.0	1.3
097 CR C AND C CR.	1	59	73*	0.2	0.2
127 CH GOD (CLEVE)	1	21	26*	0.1	0.1
165 CH OF NAZARENE	2	125	286	0.7	0.9
193 EPISCOPAL.....	1	417	608	1.4	1.8
281 LUTH CH AMER..	2	2,784	3,634	8.5	11.0
283 LUTH--MO SYNOD	5	2,817	3,946	9.2	11.9
285 MENNONITE CH..	2	86	106*	0.2	0.3
403 SALVATION ARMY	1	60	435	1.0	1.3
413 S-D ADVENTISTS	1	142	176*	0.4	0.5
419 SO BAPT CONV..	1	86	106*	0.2	0.3
443 UN C OF CHRIST	1	233	289*	0.7	0.9
449 UN METHODIST..	8	7,656	8,941	20.9	27.0
453 UN PRES CH USA	2	1,664	2,061*	4.8	6.2
469 WISC EVAN LUTH	1	160	242	0.6	0.7
HAMILTON	19	3,793	5,285*	59.6	100.0
029 AMER LUTH CH..	2	259	350	3.9	6.6
081 CATHOLIC......	2	0	480	5.4	9.1
093 CR CH (DISC)..	1	257	315*	3.6	6.0
201 EVAN COV CH AM	1	105	129*	1.5	2.4
281 LUTH CH AMER..	2	404	491	5.5	9.3
283 LUTH--MO SYNOD	3	757	1,019	11.5	19.3
443 UN C OF CHRIST	1	83	102*	1.2	1.9
449 UN METHODIST..	5	1,629	2,024	22.8	38.3
453 UN PRES CH USA	1	195	239*	2.7	4.5
469 WISC EVAN LUTH	1	104	136	1.5	2.6
HARLAN	16	2,009	2,864*	65.7	100.0
029 AMER LUTH CH..	2	235	290	6.7	10.1
081 CATHOLIC......	2	0	365	8.4	12.7
093 CR CH (DISC)..	2	253	295*	6.8	10.3
221 FREE METH C NA	1	24	25	0.6	0.9
281 LUTH CH AMER..	1	175	235	5.4	8.2
283 LUTH--MO SYNOD	1	282	372	8.5	13.0
449 UN METHODIST..	5	761	956	21.9	33.4
453 UN PRES CH USA	2	279	326*	7.5	11.4
HAYES	3	185	303*	19.8	100.0
081 CATHOLIC......	1	0	92	6.0	30.4
283 LUTH--MO SYNOD	1	60	63	4.1	20.8
443 UN C OF CHRIST	1	125	148*	9.7	48.8
HITCHCOCK	15	1,485	2,256*	55.7	100.0
081 CATHOLIC......	3	0	329	8.1	14.6
123 CH GOD (ANDER)	2	69	185	4.6	8.2
283 LUTH--MO SYNOD	3	253	304	7.5	13.5
353 PLY BRETHREN..	1	20	30	0.7	1.3
413 S-D ADVENTISTS	1	19	22*	0.5	1.0
443 UN C OF CHRIST	1	85	100*	2.5	4.4
449 UN METHODIST..	4	1,039	1,286	31.7	57.0
HOLT	28	3,221	8,166*	63.1	100.0
029 AMER LUTH CH..	1	140	191	1.5	2.3
081 CATHOLIC......	7	0	4,118	31.8	50.4
097 CR C AND C CR.	3	132	164*	1.3	2.0
221 FREE METH C NA	2	23	24	0.2	0.3
283 LUTH--MO SYNOD	3	539	730	5.6	8.9
449 UN METHODIST..	6	1,553	1,905	14.7	23.3
453 UN PRES CH USA	6	834	1,034*	8.0	12.7
HOOKER	4	556	756	80.5	100.0
081 CATHOLIC......	1	0	102	10.9	13.5
193 EPISCOPAL.....	1	224	251	26.7	33.2
449 UN METHODIST..	2	332	403	42.9	53.3
HOWARD	14	1,767	4,126*	60.6	100.0
029 AMER LUTH CH..	2	490	666	9.8	16.1
081 CATHOLIC......	5	0	1,844	27.1	44.7
283 LUTH--MO SYNOD	1	215	290	4.3	7.0
449 UN METHODIST..	5	681	853	12.5	20.7
453 UN PRES CH USA	1	381	473*	6.9	11.5
JEFFERSON	32	6,228	8,457*	81.0	100.0
019 AMER BAPT CONV	1	509	589*	5.6	7.0
029 AMER LUTH CH..	3	848	1,084	10.4	12.8
081 CATHOLIC......	1	0	597	5.7	7.1
093 CR CH (DISC)..	1	338	391*	3.7	4.6
123 CH GOD (ANDER)	1	45	125	1.2	1.5
165 CH OF NAZARENE	1	63	140	1.3	1.7
193 EPISCOPAL.....	1	103	109	1.0	1.3
211 EV MENN BRETH.	1	67	78*	0.7	0.9
281 LUTH CH AMER..	2	269	366	3.5	4.3
283 LUTH--MO SYNOD	5	1,290	1,653	15.8	19.5
413 S-D ADVENTISTS	1	38	44*	0.4	0.5
443 UN C OF CHRIST	5	519	601*	5.8	7.1
449 UN METHODIST..	6	1,280	1,627	15.6	19.2
453 UN PRES CH USA	2	590	683*	6.5	8.1
469 WISC EVAN LUTH	1	269	370	3.5	4.4
JOHNSON	18	2,994	4,486*	78.1	100.0
019 AMER BAPT CONV	1	264	314*	5.5	7.0
029 AMER LUTH CH..	2	787	1,007	17.5	22.4
081 CATHOLIC......	2	0	748	13.0	16.7
193 EPISCOPAL.....	1	10	16	0.3	0.4
281 LUTH CH AMER..	1	66	77	1.3	1.7
283 LUTH--MO SYNOD	2	471	640	11.1	14.3
443 UN C OF CHRIST	2	392	466*	8.1	10.4
449 UN METHODIST..	6	798	973	16.9	21.7
453 UN PRES CH USA	1	206	245*	4.3	5.5
KEARNEY	19	3,198	4,738*	70.6	100.0
029 AMER LUTH CH..	2	527	698	10.4	14.7
081 CATHOLIC......	2	0	470	7.0	9.9
093 CR CH (DISC)..	1	161	194*	2.9	4.1
281 LUTH CH AMER..	3	487	628	9.4	13.3
283 LUTH--MO SYNOD	3	592	854	12.7	18.0
413 S-D ADVENTISTS	2	20	24*	0.4	0.5
449 UN METHODIST..	5	943	1,307	19.5	27.6
453 UN PRES CH USA	1	468	563*	8.4	11.9
KEITH	17	3,289	6,089*	71.7	100.0
019 AMER BAPT CONV	1	29	35*	0.4	0.6
081 CATHOLIC......	2	0	1,760	20.7	28.9
123 CH GOD (ANDER)	1	18	58	0.7	1.0
193 EPISCOPAL.....	1	97	117	1.4	1.9
281 LUTH CH AMER..	1	261	391	4.6	6.4
283 LUTH--MO SYNOD	3	812	1,151	13.6	18.9
413 S-D ADVENTISTS	1	19	23*	0.3	0.4
443 UN C OF CHRIST	2	621	757*	8.9	12.4
449 UN METHODIST..	2	1,211	1,528	18.0	25.1
453 UN PRES CH USA	3	221	269*	3.2	4.4
KEYA PAHA	5	510	635*	47.4	100.0
283 LUTH--MO SYNOD	2	163	217	16.2	34.2
413 S-D ADVENTISTS	1	42	51*	3.8	8.0
449 UN METHODIST..	2	305	367	27.4	57.8
KIMBALL	11	2,031	3,426*	57.0	100.0
029 AMER LUTH CH..	1	355	482	8.0	14.1

*Total adherents estimated from known number of communicant, confirmed, full members.

—Represents a percent less than 0.1.

Percentages may not total due to rounding.

#See Introduction for explanation of why total adherents reported by churches exceed the 1970 population figure.

Table 3. Churches and Church Membership by State, County and Denomination: 1971

County and Denomination	Number of churches	Communicant, confirmed, full members	Total adherents		
			Number	Percent of total population	Percent of total adherents
081 CATHOLIC......	1	0	720	12.0	21.0
165 CH OF NAZARENE	1	36	125	2.1	3.6
193 EPISCOPAL.....	1	131	180	3.0	5.3
283 LUTH--MO SYNOD	1	202	300	5.0	8.8
419 SO BAPT CONV..	2	268	338*	5.6	9.9
449 UN METHODIST..	2	746	911	15.2	26.6
453 UN PRES CH USA	2	293	370*	6.2	10.8
KNOX	28	4,988	8,362*	71.3	100.0
029 AMER LUTH CH..	2	534	751	6.4	9.0
081 CATHOLIC......	3	0	1,706	14.6	20.4
193 EPISCOPAL.....	1	184	301	2.6	3.6
201 EVAN COV CH AM	1	202	243*	2.1	2.9
281 LUTH CH AMER..	4	1,580	2,110	18.0	25.2
283 LUTH--MO SYNOD	5	1,109	1,524	13.0	18.2
353 PLY BRETHREN..	1	10	10	0.1	0.1
443 UN C OF CHRIST	3	200	241*	2.1	2.9
449 UN METHODIST..	6	1,020	1,296	11.1	15.5
453 UN PRES CH USA	2	149	180*	1.5	2.2
LANCASTER	139	56,922	95,041*	56.6	100.0
019 AMER BAPT CONV	4	1,432	1,717*	1.0	1.8
029 AMER LUTH CH..	6	3,015	4,664	2.8	4.9
081 CATHOLIC......	13	0	20,327	12.1	21.4
093 CR CH (DISC)..	6	2,156	2,585*	1.5	2.7
097 CR C AND C CR.	3	460	552*	0.3	0.6
123 CH GOD (ANDER)	2	54	137	0.1	0.1
127 CH GOD (CLEVE)	1	61	73*	-	0.1
157 CH OF BRETHREN	1	145	174*	0.1	0.2
165 CH OF NAZARENE	3	214	496	0.3	0.5
175 CONG CR CH....	1	127	152*	0.1	0.2
193 EPISCOPAL.....	4	1,845	2,314	1.4	2.4
201 EVAN COV CH AM	2	454	544*	0.3	0.6
211 EV MENN BRETH.	1	74	89*	0.1	0.1
221 FREE METH C NA	1	11	19	-	-
226 FRIENDS-USA...	1	34	41*	-	-
281 LUTH CH AMER..	8	3,839	5,283	3.1	5.6
283 LUTH--MO SYNOD	12	7,257	10,342	6.2	10.9
285 MENNONITE CH..	1	25	30*	-	-
335 ORTH PRESB CH.	1	69	97	0.1	0.1
353 PLY BRETHREN..	1	38	100	0.1	0.1
371 REF CH IN AM..	2	445	640	0.4	0.7
403 SALVATION ARMY	1	156	668	0.4	0.7
413 S-D ADVENTISTS	6	2,489	2,984*	1.8	3.1
419 SO BAPT CONV..	2	534	640*	0.4	0.7
435 UNITARIAN-UNIV	1	356	531	0.3	0.6
443 UN C OF CHRIST	10	4,357	5,224*	3.1	5.5
449 UN METHODIST..	32	18,803	24,376	14.5	25.6
453 UN PRES CH USA	10	8,151	9,773*	5.8	10.3
469 WISC EVAN LUTH	3	321	469	0.3	0.5
LINCOLN	38	9,141	17,387*	58.9	100.0
019 AMER BAPT CONV	3	745	914*	3.1	5.3
029 AMER LUTH CH..	1	50	62	0.2	0.4
081 CATHOLIC......	6	0	4,989	16.9	28.7
093 CR CH (DISC)..	1	744	913*	3.1	5.3
097 CR C AND C CR.	2	60	74*	0.3	0.4
123 CH GOD (ANDER)	1	26	61	0.2	0.4
127 CH GOD (CLEVE)	1	77	95*	0.3	0.5
157 CH OF BRETHREN	1	105	129*	0.4	0.7
165 CH OF NAZARENE	1	202	434	1.5	2.5
193 EPISCOPAL.....	1	409	614	2.1	3.5
201 EVAN COV CH AM	1	24	29*	0.1	0.2
281 LUTH CH AMER..	4	1,475	2,427	8.2	14.0
283 LUTH--MO SYNOD	1	728	1,010	3.4	5.8
403 SALVATION ARMY	1	126	402	1.4	2.3
413 S-D ADVENTISTS	1	156	191*	0.6	1.1
419 SO BAPT CONV..	1	89	109*	0.4	0.6
449 UN METHODIST..	8	2,800	3,263	11.0	18.8
453 UN PRES CH USA	2	1,223	1,501*	5.1	8.6
469 WISC EVAN LUTH	1	102	170	0.6	1.0
LOGAN	2	153	419*	42.3	100.0
081 CATHOLIC......	1	0	240	24.2	57.3
453 UN PRES CH USA	1	153	179*	18.1	42.7
LOUP	1	72	72	8.4	100.0
449 UN METHODIST..	1	72	72	8.4	100.0
MC PHERSON	2	83	95*	15.2	100.0
019 AMER BAPT CONV	1	58	69*	11.1	72.6
221 FREE METH C NA	1	25	26	4.2	27.4
MADISON	41	13,623	19,202*	70.1	100.0
019 AMER BAPT CONV	1	234	282*	1.0	1.5
029 AMER LUTH CH..	2	569	712	2.6	3.7
081 CATHOLIC......	5	0	1,410	5.1	7.3
093 CR CH (DISC)..	1	41	49*	0.2	0.3
097 CR C AND C CR.	2	584	704*	2.6	3.7
127 CH GOD (CLEVE)	1	18	22*	0.1	0.1
165 CH OF NAZARENE	1	12	31	0.1	0.2
193 EPISCOPAL.....	1	228	330	1.2	1.7
281 LUTH CH AMER..	3	1,081	1,530	5.6	8.0
283 LUTH--MO SYNOD	9	5,445	7,301	26.6	38.0
413 S-D ADVENTISTS	1	46	55*	0.2	0.3
443 UN C OF CHRIST	3	707	853*	3.1	4.4
449 UN METHODIST..	8	3,130	3,987	14.6	20.8
453 UN PRES CH USA	2	710	856*	3.1	4.5
469 WISC EVAN LUTH	1	818	1,080	3.9	5.6
MERRICK	23	3,655	6,023*	68.8	100.0
081 CATHOLIC......	3	0	1,229	14.0	20.4
097 CR C AND C CR.	2	200	249*	2.8	4.1
165 CH OF NAZARENE	1	8	22	0.3	0.4
193 EPISCOPAL.....	1	95	134	1.5	2.2
226 FRIENDS-USA...	1	212	264*	3.0	4.4
281 LUTH CH AMER..	1	150	219	2.5	3.6
283 LUTH--MO SYNOD	3	733	1,081	12.4	17.9
449 UN METHODIST..	10	2,009	2,516	28.8	41.8
453 UN PRES CH USA	1	248	309*	3.5	5.1
MORRILL	18	2,382	3,419*	58.8	100.0
019 AMER BAPT CONV	1	328	387*	6.7	11.3
081 CATHOLIC......	3	0	415	7.1	12.1
097 CR C AND C CR.	2	192	226*	3.9	6.6
165 CH OF NAZARENE	1	14	15	0.3	0.4
193 EPISCOPAL.....	2	97	154	2.6	4.5
281 LUTH CH AMER..	1	175	258	4.4	7.5
283 LUTH--MO SYNOD	2	319	474	8.2	13.9
413 S-D ADVENTISTS	1	26	31*	0.5	0.9
443 UN C OF CHRIST	1	347	409*	7.0	12.0
449 UN METHODIST..	1	164	201	3.5	5.9
453 UN PRES CH USA	3	720	849*	14.6	24.8
NANCE	12	1,739	4,714*	91.7	100.0
019 AMER BAPT CONV	1	67	81*	1.6	1.7
081 CATHOLIC......	3	0	2,466	48.0	52.3
175 CONG CR CH....	1	125	151*	2.9	3.2
281 LUTH CH AMER..	1	324	393	7.6	8.3
283 LUTH--MO SYNOD	1	142	220	4.3	4.7
449 UN METHODIST..	4	805	1,071	20.8	22.7
453 UN PRES CH USA	1	276	332*	6.5	7.0
NEMAHA	28	4,610	6,162*	68.6	100.0
019 AMER BAPT CONV	2	60	70*	0.8	1.1
029 AMER LUTH CH..	4	950	1,168	13.0	19.0
081 CATHOLIC......	3	0	447	5.0	7.3
093 CR CH (DISC)..	5	680	795*	8.9	12.9
097 CR C AND C CR.	1	585	684*	7.6	11.1
281 LUTH CH AMER..	3	909	1,146	12.8	18.6
283 LUTH--MO SYNOD	1	73	226	2.5	3.7
449 UN METHODIST..	8	1,227	1,479	16.5	24.0
453 UN PRES CH USA	1	126	147*	1.6	2.4
NUCKOLLS	23	3,030	5,281*	71.3	100.0
019 AMER BAPT CONV	1	244	291*	3.9	5.5
029 AMER LUTH CH..	2	487	644	8.7	12.2
081 CATHOLIC......	4	0	1,386	18.7	26.2
093 CR CH (DISC)..	1	113	135*	1.8	2.6
097 CR C AND C CR.	2	70	84*	1.1	1.6
165 CH OF NAZARENE	1	29	115	1.6	2.2
281 LUTH CH AMER..	2	243	320	4.3	6.1
283 LUTH--MO SYNOD	2	395	539	7.3	10.2
413 S-D ADVENTISTS	1	44	52*	0.7	1.0
449 UN METHODIST..	4	893	1,104	14.9	20.9
453 UN PRES CH USA	3	512	611*	8.3	11.6
OTOE	36	7,062	11,045*	70.9	100.0
019 AMER BAPT CONV	1	99	117*	0.8	1.1
029 AMER LUTH CH..	5	1,972	2,528	16.2	22.9
081 CATHOLIC......	8	0	2,241	14.4	20.3
093 CR CH (DISC)..	3	930	1,102*	7.1	10.0
193 EPISCOPAL.....	1	138	188	1.2	1.7
281 LUTH CH AMER..	3	748	1,020	6.5	9.2
283 LUTH--MO SYNOD	1	83	130	0.8	1.2
443 UN C OF CHRIST	4	961	1,139*	7.3	10.3
449 UN METHODIST..	6	1,383	1,693	10.9	15.3
453 UN PRES CH USA	4	748	887*	5.7	8.0
PAWNEE	15	2,014	3,034*	67.8	100.0
019 AMER BAPT CONV	1	154	177*	4.0	5.8
029 AMER LUTH CH..	1	69	87	1.9	2.9
081 CATHOLIC......	2	0	616	13.8	20.3
093 CR CH (DISC)..	1	125	144*	3.2	4.7
097 CR C AND C CR.	1	70	81*	1.8	2.7
283 LUTH--MO SYNOD	2	372	495	11.1	16.3
443 UN C OF CHRIST	1	242	279*	6.2	9.2
449 UN METHODIST..	5	695	824	18.4	27.2
453 UN PRES CH USA	1	287	331*	7.4	10.9
PERKINS	10	1,566	2,318*	67.7	100.0
081 CATHOLIC......	2	0	418	12.2	18.0
283 LUTH--MO SYNOD	3	387	504	14.7	21.7
443 UN C OF CHRIST	1	305	358*	10.5	15.4
449 UN METHODIST..	4	874	1,038	30.3	44.8
PHELPS	17	4,594	6,516*	68.2	100.0
019 AMER BAPT CONV	1	374	448*	4.7	6.9
081 CATHOLIC......	1	0	479	5.0	7.4
193 EPISCOPAL.....	1	82	173	1.8	2.7
201 EVAN COV CH AM	1	50	60*	0.6	0.9
281 LUTH CH AMER..	4	1,244	1,660	17.4	25.5
283 LUTH--MO SYNOD	2	557	856	9.0	13.1
413 S-D ADVENTISTS	1	54	65*	0.7	1.0

*Total adherents estimated from known number of communicant, confirmed, full members.

—Represents a percent less than 0.1.

Percentages may not total due to rounding.

Table 3. Churches and Church Membership by State, County and Denomination: 1971

County and Denomination	Number of churches	Communicant, confirmed, full members	Total adherents: Number	Total adherents: Percent of total population	Total adherents: Percent of total adherents
449 UN METHODIST..	5	1,687	2,121	22.2	32.6
453 UN PRES CH USA	1	546	654*	6.8	10.0
PIERCE	18	4,437	7,035*	82.8	100.0
029 AMER LUTH CH..	1	377	484	5.7	6.9
081 CATHOLIC......	3	0	1,233	14.5	17.5
226 FRIENDS-USA...	1	33	40*	0.5	0.6
281 LUTH CH AMER..	1	245	332	3.9	4.7
283 LUTH--MO SYNOD	5	2,113	2,830	33.3	40.2
443 UN C OF CHRIST	2	626	762*	9.0	10.8
449 UN METHODIST..	4	780	989	11.6	14.1
469 WISC EVAN LUTH	1	263	365	4.3	5.2
PLATTE	37	8,365	22,708*	85.7	100.0
019 AMER BAPT CONV	2	247	308*	1.2	1.4
081 CATHOLIC......	8	0	11,717	44.2	51.6
193 EPISCOPAL.....	1	165	259	1.0	1.1
281 LUTH CH AMER..	7	2,190	3,017	11.4	13.3
283 LUTH--MO SYNOD	6	2,675	3,519	13.3	15.5
313 NO AM BAPT GC.	3	209	261*	1.0	1.1
413 S-D ADVENTISTS	1	21	26*	0.1	0.1
443 UN C OF CHRIST	3	856	1,067*	4.0	4.7
449 UN METHODIST..	4	1,572	1,995	7.5	8.8
453 UN PRES CH USA	1	415	517*	2.0	2.3
469 WISC EVAN LUTH	1	15	22	0.1	0.1
POLK	17	2,821	4,572*	70.7	100.0
019 AMER BAPT CONV	1	243	287*	4.4	6.3
081 CATHOLIC......	4	0	1,140	17.6	24.9
201 EVAN COV CH AM	1	127	150*	2.3	3.3
281 LUTH CH AMER..	4	952	1,229	19.0	26.9
283 LUTH--MO SYNOD	1	17	18	0.3	0.4
449 UN METHODIST..	6	1,482	1,748	27.0	38.2
RED WILLOW	22	3,950	7,182*	58.9	100.0
019 AMER BAPT CONV	1	231	279*	2.3	3.9
029 AMER LUTH CH..	1	158	277	2.3	3.9
081 CATHOLIC......	2	0	2,152	17.7	30.0
093 CR CH (DISC)..	1	237	287*	2.4	4.0
097 CR C AND C CR.	3	275	333*	2.7	4.6
123 CH GOD (ANDER)	1	42	104	0.9	1.4
127 CH GOD (CLEVE)	1	32	39*	0.3	0.5
165 CH OF NAZARENE	1	20	59	0.5	0.8
193 EPISCOPAL.....	1	409	512	4.2	7.1
283 LUTH--MO SYNOD	2	738	1,029	8.4	14.3
413 S-D ADVENTISTS	1	48	58*	0.5	0.8
419 SO BAPT CONV..	1	109	132*	1.1	1.8
449 UN METHODIST..	3	1,525	1,756	14.4	24.5
453 UN PRES CH USA	2	112	135*	1.1	1.9
469 WISC EVAN LUTH	1	14	30	0.2	0.4
RICHARDSON	33	3,729	5,900*	48.1	100.0
019 AMER BAPT CONV	1	130	154*	1.3	2.6
081 CATHOLIC......	5	0	897	7.3	15.2
093 CR CH (DISC)..	4	632	746*	6.1	12.6
127 CH GOD (CLEVE)	1	21	25*	0.2	0.4
165 CH OF NAZARENE	1	76	154	1.3	2.6
175 CONG CR CH....	1	64	76*	0.6	1.3
193 EPISCOPAL.....	1	93	140	1.1	2.4
281 LUTH CH AMER..	3	748	1,111	9.0	18.8
283 LUTH--MO SYNOD	3	630	866	7.1	14.7
413 S-D ADVENTISTS	1	32	38*	0.3	0.6
443 UN C OF CHRIST	3	249	294*	2.4	5.0
449 UN METHODIST..	7	744	1,033	8.4	17.5
453 UN PRES CH USA	2	310	366*	3.0	6.2
ROCK	7	537	880	39.4	100.0
029 AMER LUTH CH..	1	98	187	8.4	21.3
081 CATHOLIC......	1	0	200	9.0	22.7
193 EPISCOPAL.....	1	63	104	4.7	11.8
449 UN METHODIST..	4	376	389	17.4	44.2
SALINE	23	4,412	6,724*	52.5	100.0
019 AMER BAPT CONV	1	24	28*	0.2	0.4
029 AMER LUTH CH..	1	360	486	3.8	7.2
081 CATHOLIC......	4	0	1,109	8.7	16.5
193 EPISCOPAL.....	2	40	50	0.4	0.7
281 LUTH CH AMER..	1	301	406	3.2	6.0
283 LUTH--MO SYNOD	2	915	1,243	9.7	18.5
443 UN C OF CHRIST	4	855	992*	7.7	14.8
449 UN METHODIST..	8	1,917	2,410	18.8	35.8
SARPY	24	7,235	19,379*	30.4	100.0
029 AMER LUTH CH..	2	466	75	0.1	0.4
081 CATHOLIC......	4	0	10,018	15.7	51.7
093 CR CH (DISC)..	1	240	320*	0.5	1.7
097 CR C AND C CR.	1	64	85*	0.1	0.4
193 EPISCOPAL.....	2	347	516	0.8	2.7
221 FREE METH C NA	1	22	28	-	0.1
281 LUTH CH AMER..	3	1,289	1,907	3.0	9.8
283 LUTH--MO SYNOD	3	1,031	1,394	2.2	7.2
419 SO BAPT CONV..	4	2,200	2,934*	4.6	15.1
453 UN PRES CH USA	3	1,576	2,102*	3.3	10.8
SAUNDERS	44	5,396	11,399*	67.0	100.0
019 AMER BAPT CONV	2	149	179*	1.1	1.6
029 AMER LUTH CH..	2	284	390	2.3	3.4
081 CATHOLIC......	12	0	4,579	26.9	40.2
093 CR CH (DISC)..	2	260	312*	1.8	2.7
097 CR C AND C CR.	1	40	48*	0.3	0.4
175 CONG CR CH....	1	162	195*	1.1	1.7
193 EPISCOPAL.....	1	12	18	0.1	0.2
201 EVAN COV CH AM	4	342	411*	2.4	3.6
281 LUTH CH AMER..	6	1,546	2,151	12.6	18.9
283 LUTH--MO SYNOD	2	394	508	3.0	4.5
443 UN C OF CHRIST	2	183	220*	1.3	1.9
449 UN METHODIST..	5	1,180	1,374	8.1	12.1
453 UN PRES CH USA	4	844	1,014*	6.0	8.9
SCOTTS BLUFF	46	11,385	19,489*	53.5	100.0
019 AMER BAPT CONV	1	416	508*	1.4	2.6
029 AMER LUTH CH..	1	531	779	2.1	4.0
081 CATHOLIC......	6	0	5,039	13.8	25.9
093 CR CH (DISC)..	2	454	554*	1.5	2.8
097 CR C AND C CR.	6	805	982*	2.7	5.0
123 CH GOD (ANDER)	2	82	172	0.5	0.9
165 CH OF NAZARENE	1	107	183	0.5	0.9
193 EPISCOPAL.....	3	825	1,014	2.8	5.2
283 LUTH--MO SYNOD	4	1,247	1,786	4.9	9.2
413 S-D ADVENTISTS	3	262	320*	0.9	1.6
419 SO BAPT CONV..	1	174	212*	0.6	1.1
443 UN C OF CHRIST	5	1,140	1,391*	3.8	7.1
449 UN METHODIST..	8	3,922	4,816	13.2	24.7
453 UN PRES CH USA	3	1,420	1,733*	4.8	8.9
SEWARD	36	7,520	10,647*	73.6	100.0
029 AMER LUTH CH..	1	183	242	1.7	2.3
081 CATHOLIC......	4	0	1,001	6.9	9.4
093 CR CH (DISC)..	1	31	36*	0.2	0.3
193 EPISCOPAL.....	1	37	42	0.3	0.4
281 LUTH CH AMER..	1	251	360	2.5	3.4
283 LUTH--MO SYNOD	9	3,552	4,685	32.4	44.0
285 MENNONITE CH..	5	832	975*	6.7	9.2
413 S-D ADVENTISTS	1	26	30*	0.2	0.3
443 UN C OF CHRIST	3	410	481*	3.3	4.5
449 UN METHODIST..	6	1,875	2,417	16.7	22.7
453 UN PRES CH USA	3	281	329*	2.3	3.1
469 WISC EVAN LUTH	1	42	49	0.3	0.5
SHERIDAN	24	2,817	4,795*	65.8	100.0
029 AMER LUTH CH..	1	101	137	1.9	2.9
081 CATHOLIC......	4	0	962	13.2	20.1
123 CH GOD (ANDER)	2	103	275	3.8	5.7
193 EPISCOPAL.....	2	177	220	3.0	4.6
226 FRIENDS-USA...	1	58	69*	0.9	1.4
281 LUTH CH AMER..	1	216	314	4.3	6.5
283 LUTH--MO SYNOD	3	486	744	10.2	15.5
413 S-D ADVENTISTS	3	77	92*	1.3	1.9
443 UN C OF CHRIST	1	29	35*	0.5	0.7
449 UN METHODIST..	5	1,154	1,450	19.9	30.2
453 UN PRES CH USA	1	416	497*	6.8	10.4
SHERMAN	14	937	3,573*	75.6	100.0
029 AMER LUTH CH..	1	108	174	3.7	4.9
081 CATHOLIC......	4	0	2,340	49.5	65.5
097 CR C AND C CR.	1	80	98*	2.1	2.7
165 CH OF NAZARENE	1	7	7	0.1	0.2
283 LUTH--MO SYNOD	1	124	194	4.1	5.4
413 S-D ADVENTISTS	1	21	26*	0.6	0.7
443 UN C OF CHRIST	1	54	66*	1.4	1.8
449 UN METHODIST..	3	411	507	10.7	14.2
453 UN PRES CH USA	1	132	161*	3.4	4.5
SIOUX	4	257	529	26.0	100.0
081 CATHOLIC......	2	0	202	9.9	38.2
283 LUTH--MO SYNOD	1	44	62	3.0	11.7
449 UN METHODIST..	1	213	265	13.0	50.1
STANTON	9	1,798	2,681*	46.6	100.0
081 CATHOLIC......	1	0	417	7.2	15.6
281 LUTH CH AMER..	2	248	305	5.3	11.4
283 LUTH--MO SYNOD	2	517	702	12.2	26.2
443 UN C OF CHRIST	1	400	495*	8.6	18.5
449 UN METHODIST..	2	321	387	6.7	14.4
469 WISC EVAN LUTH	1	312	375	6.5	14.0
THAYER	30	5,390	7,331*	94.2	100.0
029 AMER LUTH CH..	8	2,313	2,967	38.1	40.5
081 CATHOLIC......	3	0	631	8.1	8.6
093 CR CH (DISC)..	1	215	252*	3.2	3.4
097 CR C AND C CR.	2	100	117*	1.5	1.6
281 LUTH CH AMER..	1	258	336	4.3	4.6
283 LUTH--MO SYNOD	5	1,120	1,401	18.0	19.1
443 UN C OF CHRIST	1	79	93*	1.2	1.3
449 UN METHODIST..	6	963	1,134	14.6	15.5
453 UN PRES CH USA	3	342	400*	5.1	5.5
THOMAS	5	210	320*	33.5	100.0
081 CATHOLIC......	2	0	70	7.3	21.9
443 UN C OF CHRIST	3	210	250*	26.2	78.1
THURSTON	21	2,853	4,583*	66.0	100.0

*Total adherents estimated from known number of communicant, confirmed, full members.

—Represents a percent less than 0.1.

Percentages may not total due to rounding.

Table 3. Churches and Church Membership by State, County and Denomination: 1971

County and Denomination	Number of churches	Communicant, confirmed, full members	Total adherents: Number	Percent of total population	Percent of total adherents
081 CATHOLIC......	4	0	722	10.4	15.8
193 EPISCOPAL.....	1	11	65	0.9	1.4
201 EVAN COV CH AM	1	29	36*	0.5	0.8
281 LUTH CH AMER..	3	1,006	1,310	18.9	28.6
283 LUTH--MO SYNOD	1	265	432	6.2	9.4
371 REF CH IN AM..	2	239	375	5.4	8.2
449 UN METHODIST..	4	624	798	11.5	17.4
453 UN PRES CH USA	5	679	845*	12.2	18.4
VALLEY	15	2,111	3,965*	68.6	100.0
029 AMER LUTH CH..	1	150	217	3.8	5.5
081 CATHOLIC......	5	0	1,333	23.1	33.6
097 CR C AND C CR.	1	217	257*	4.4	6.5
283 LUTH--MO SYNOD	1	184	236	4.1	6.0
415 S-D BAPTIST GC	1	229	272*	4.7	6.9
443 UN C OF CHRIST	1	24	28*	0.5	0.7
449 UN METHODIST..	4	1,113	1,392	24.1	35.1
453 UN PRES CH USA	1	194	230*	4.0	5.8
WASHINGTON	20	4,474	6,799*	51.1	100.0
019 AMER BAPT CONV	2	291	349*	2.6	5.1
029 AMER LUTH CH..	4	1,455	1,891	14.2	27.8
081 CATHOLIC......	2	0	1,041	7.8	15.3
093 CR CH (DISC)..	1	166	199*	1.5	2.9
097 CR C AND C CR.	1	200	240*	1.8	3.5
121 CH GOD (ABR)..	1	20	24*	0.2	0.4
193 EPISCOPAL.....	1	161	253	1.9	3.7
281 LUTH CH AMER..	1	297	387	2.9	5.7
283 LUTH--MO SYNOD	3	1,076	1,446	10.9	21.3
413 S-D ADVENTISTS	1	12	14*	0.1	0.2
443 UN C OF CHRIST	2	570	684*	5.1	10.1
453 UN PRES CH USA	1	226	271*	2.0	4.0
WAYNE	23	4,845	7,065*	67.9	100.0
019 AMER BAPT CONV	1	103	120*	1.2	1.7
081 CATHOLIC......	2	0	685	6.6	9.7
193 EPISCOPAL.....	1	16	25	0.2	0.4
201 EVAN COV CH AM	1	199	232*	2.2	3.3
281 LUTH CH AMER..	3	1,358	1,863	17.9	26.4
283 LUTH--MO SYNOD	6	1,363	1,852	17.8	26.2
443 UN C OF CHRIST	2	99	115*	1.1	1.6
449 UN METHODIST..	4	1,051	1,370	13.2	19.4
453 UN PRES CH USA	2	403	469*	4.5	6.6
469 WISC EVAN LUTH	1	253	334	3.2	4.7
WEBSTER	16	2,403	3,214*	49.6	100.0
019 AMER BAPT CONV	1	61	71*	1.1	2.2
081 CATHOLIC......	1	0	203	3.1	6.3
097 CR C AND C CR.	2	20	23*	0.4	0.7
281 LUTH CH AMER..	1	252	336	5.2	10.5
283 LUTH--MO SYNOD	3	684	897	13.8	27.9
443 UN C OF CHRIST	1	154	180*	2.8	5.6
449 UN METHODIST..	7	1,232	1,504	23.2	46.8
WHEELER	3	191	371	35.2	100.0
081 CATHOLIC......	1	0	132	12.5	35.6
449 UN METHODIST..	2	191	239	22.7	64.4
YORK	32	7,870	11,052*	80.8	100.0
019 AMER BAPT CONV	1	78	93*	0.7	0.8
081 CATHOLIC......	2	0	1,188	8.7	10.7
165 CH OF NAZARENE	1	88	173	1.3	1.6
193 EPISCOPAL.....	1	34	73	0.5	0.7
211 EV MENN BRETH.	1	129	154*	1.1	1.4
281 LUTH CH AMER..	3	590	788	5.8	7.1
283 LUTH--MO SYNOD	6	2,167	2,910	21.3	26.3
287 MENN GEN CONF.	1	1,777	2,127*	15.5	19.2
413 S-D ADVENTISTS	1	19	23*	0.2	0.2
419 SO BAPT CONV..	1	29	35*	0.3	0.3
443 UN C OF CHRIST	2	109	130*	0.9	1.2
449 UN METHODIST..	9	2,087	2,442	17.8	22.1
453 UN PRES CH USA	2	706	845*	6.2	7.6
469 WISC EVAN LUTH	1	57	71	0.5	0.6
CO DATA NOT AVAIL	31	645	5,816*	N/A	N/A
151 L-D SAINTS....	0	0	5,067	N/A	N/A
231 GENERAL BAPT..	3	47	57*	N/A	N/A
467 WESLEYAN......	28	598	692	N/A	N/A

NEVADA

County and Denomination	Number of churches	Communicant, confirmed, full members	Total adherents: Number	Percent of total population	Percent of total adherents
THE STATE.....	231	32,975	184,561*	37.8	100.0
CARSON CITY CITY	10	1,698	4,877*	31.5	100.0
019 AMER BAPT CONV	1	46	57*	0.4	1.2
081 CATHOLIC......	1	0	2,600	16.8	53.3
097 CR C AND C CR.	1	30	37*	0.2	0.8
127 CH GOD (CLEVE)	1	13	16*	0.1	0.3
193 EPISCOPAL.....	1	225	400	2.6	8.2
283 LUTH--MO SYNOD	1	216	346	2.2	7.1
413 S-D ADVENTISTS	1	86	106*	0.7	2.2
419 SO BAPT CONV..	1	291	359*	2.3	7.4
449 UN METHODIST..	1	345	405	2.6	8.3
453 UN PRES CH USA	1	446	551*	3.6	11.3
CHURCHILL	7	780	2,074*	19.7	100.0
081 CATHOLIC......	1	0	1,040	9.9	50.1
165 CH OF NAZARENE	1	58	152	1.4	7.3
193 EPISCOPAL.....	1	98	164	1.6	7.9
283 LUTH--MO SYNOD	1	52	87	0.8	4.2
413 S-D ADVENTISTS	1	102	125*	1.2	6.0
419 SO BAPT CONV..	1	162	198*	1.9	9.5
449 UN METHODIST..	1	308	308	2.9	14.9
CLARK	81	17,512	77,469*	28.3	100.0
019 AMER BAPT CONV	9	1,323	1,662*	0.6	2.1
029 AMER LUTH CH..	2	1,059	1,627	0.6	2.1
059 BAPT MISS ASSN	1	50	63*	-	0.1
081 CATHOLIC......	10	0	53,736	19.7	69.4
093 CR CH (DISC)..	1	316	397*	0.1	0.5
097 CR C AND C CR.	2	285	358*	0.1	0.5
123 CH GOD (ANDER)	2	35	125	-	0.2
127 CH GOD (CLEVE)	4	150	188*	0.1	0.2
165 CH OF NAZARENE	3	246	875	0.3	1.1
193 EPISCOPAL.....	7	1,820	2,372	0.9	3.1
226 FRIENDS-USA...	1	13	16*	-	-
281 LUTH CH AMER..	1	458	776	0.3	1.0
283 LUTH--MO SYNOD	5	1,403	2,417	0.9	3.1
353 PLY BRETHREN..	1	10	10	-	-
403 SALVATION ARMY	2	68	323	0.1	0.4
413 S-D ADVENTISTS	3	296	372*	0.1	0.5
419 SO BAPT CONV..	14	4,947	6,216*	2.3	8.0
435 UNITARIAN-UNIV	1	32	32	-	-
443 UN C OF CHRIST	2	351	441*	0.2	0.6
449 UN METHODIST..	6	3,303	3,757	1.4	4.8
453 UN PRES CH USA	3	1,326	1,666*	0.6	2.2
469 WISC EVAN LUTH	1	21	40	-	0.1
DOUGLAS	6	451	1,523	22.1	100.0
081 CATHOLIC......	2	0	820	11.9	53.8
193 EPISCOPAL.....	2	91	216	3.1	14.2
283 LUTH--MO SYNOD	1	273	397	5.8	26.1
449 UN METHODIST..	1	87	90	1.3	5.9
ELKO	15	1,341	3,940*	28.2	100.0
019 AMER BAPT CONV	1	141	175*	1.3	4.4
081 CATHOLIC......	3	0	2,100	15.0	53.3
165 CH OF NAZARENE	1	33	53	0.4	1.3
193 EPISCOPAL.....	2	234	431	3.1	10.9
283 LUTH--MO SYNOD	1	50	92	0.7	2.3
413 S-D ADVENTISTS	1	20	25*	0.2	0.6
419 SO BAPT CONV..	1	72	89*	0.6	2.3
449 UN METHODIST..	1	68	78	0.6	2.0
453 UN PRES CH USA	4	723	897*	6.4	22.8
ESMERALDA	0	0	0	-	-
EUREKA	5	83	473*	49.9	100.0
081 CATHOLIC......	1	0	348	36.7	73.6
165 CH OF NAZARENE	1	18	28	3.0	5.9
193 EPISCOPAL.....	1	17	39	4.1	8.2
419 SO BAPT CONV..	1	24	29*	3.1	6.1
453 UN PRES CH USA	1	24	29*	3.1	6.1
HUMBOLDT	6	398	1,798*	28.2	100.0
081 CATHOLIC......	1	0	1,248	19.6	69.4
193 EPISCOPAL.....	1	39	47	0.7	2.6
283 LUTH--MO SYNOD	1	65	124	1.9	6.9
413 S-D ADVENTISTS	1	16	20*	0.3	1.1
419 SO BAPT CONV..	1	70	87*	1.4	4.8
449 UN METHODIST..	1	208	272	4.3	15.1
LANDER	5	109	653*	24.5	100.0
081 CATHOLIC......	1	0	480	18.0	73.5
193 EPISCOPAL.....	1	11	41	1.5	6.3
283 LUTH--MO SYNOD	1	22	30	1.1	4.6
419 SO BAPT CONV..	1	41	53*	2.0	8.1
449 UN METHODIST..	1	35	49	1.8	7.5
LINCOLN	4	55	390	15.3	100.0
081 CATHOLIC......	1	0	248	9.7	63.6
193 EPISCOPAL.....	2	34	107	4.2	27.4
449 UN METHODIST..	1	21	35	1.4	9.0
LYON	12	541	2,147*	26.1	100.0
081 CATHOLIC......	2	0	1,316	16.0	61.3
165 CH OF NAZARENE	3	54	200	2.4	9.3
193 EPISCOPAL.....	1	29	91	1.1	4.2
221 FREE METH C NA	1	5	6	0.1	0.3
283 LUTH--MO SYNOD	1	25	25	0.3	1.2
413 S-D ADVENTISTS	1	37	46*	0.6	2.1
419 SO BAPT CONV..	1	236	294*	3.6	13.7
449 UN METHODIST..	2	155	169	2.1	7.9
MINERAL	8	579	2,355*	33.4	100.0

*Total adherents estimated from known number of communicant, confirmed, full members.

—Represents a percent less than 0.1.

Percentages may not total due to rounding.

Table 3. Churches and Church Membership by State, County and Denomination: 1971

County and Denomination	Number of churches	Communicant, confirmed, full members	Total adherents		
			Number	Percent of total population	Percent of total adherents
081 CATHOLIC......	1	0	1,540	21.8	65.4
165 CH OF NAZARENE	1	32	88	1.2	3.7
193 EPISCOPAL.....	1	53	74	1.0	3.1
283 LUTH--MO SYNOD	1	60	110	1.6	4.7
413 S-D ADVENTISTS	1	22	27*	0.4	1.1
419 SO BAPT CONV..	1	305	377*	5.3	16.0
449 UN METHODIST..	1	26	39	0.6	1.7
453 UN PRES CH USA	1	81	100*	1.4	4.2
NYE	7	167	488*	8.7	100.0
019 AMER BAPT CONV	1	46	56*	1.0	11.5
081 CATHOLIC......	1	0	280	5.0	57.4
097 CR C AND C CR.	1	10	12*	0.2	2.5
193 EPISCOPAL.....	2	40	54	1.0	11.1
419 SO BAPT CONV..	1	11	13*	0.2	2.7
453 UN PRES CH USA	1	60	73*	1.3	15.0
PERSHING	4	212	605*	22.7	100.0
081 CATHOLIC......	1	0	360	13.5	59.5
283 LUTH--MO SYNOD	1	33	45	1.7	7.4
419 SO BAPT CONV..	1	97	118*	4.4	19.5
449 UN METHODIST..	1	82	82	3.1	13.6
STOREY	1	0	200	28.8	100.0
081 CATHOLIC......	1	0	200	28.8	100.0
WASHOE	51	8,419	36,068*	29.8	100.0
019 AMER BAPT CONV	3	901	1,088*	0.9	3.0
029 AMER LUTH CH..	1	397	646	0.5	1.8
081 CATHOLIC......	11	0	24,384	20.1	67.6
097 CR C AND C CR.	3	105	127*	0.1	0.4
123 CH GOD (ANDER)	2	222	385	0.3	1.1
127 CH GOD (CLEVE)	1	25	30*	-	0.1
165 CH OF NAZARENE	5	180	517	0.4	1.4
193 EPISCOPAL.....	6	1,440	2,258	1.9	6.3
226 FRIENDS-USA...	1	14	17*	-	-
281 LUTH CH AMER..	2	594	936	0.8	2.6
283 LUTH--MO SYNOD	2	684	892	0.7	2.5
403 SALVATION ARMY	1	48	179	0.1	0.5
413 S-D ADVENTISTS	1	215	260*	0.2	0.7
419 SO BAPT CONV..	4	853	1,030*	0.9	2.9
435 UNITARIAN-UNIV	1	65	75	0.1	0.2
443 UN C OF CHRIST	1	258	312*	0.3	0.9
449 UN METHODIST..	3	1,641	1,994	1.6	5.5
453 UN PRES CH USA	3	777	938*	0.8	2.6
WHITE PINE	9	630	2,232*	22.0	100.0
081 CATHOLIC......	1	0	1,400	13.8	62.7
127 CH GOD (CLEVE)	1	5	6*	0.1	0.3
165 CH OF NAZARENE	1	12	73	0.7	3.3
193 EPISCOPAL.....	1	88	120	1.2	5.4
283 LUTH--MO SYNOD	1	28	33	0.3	1.5
413 S-D ADVENTISTS	1	12	15*	0.1	0.7
419 SO BAPT CONV..	1	220	278*	2.7	12.5
449 UN METHODIST..	2	265	307	3.0	13.8
CO DATA NOT AVAIL	0	0	47,269	N/A	N/A
151 L-D SAINTS....	0	0	47,269	N/A	N/A

NEW HAMPSHIRE

County and Denomination	Number of churches	Communicant, confirmed, full members	Total adherents		
			Number	Percent of total population	Percent of total adherents
THE STATE.....	650	79,511	370,751*	50.3	100.0
BELKNAP	39	2,557	14,464*	44.7	100.0
019 AMER BAPT CONV	11	0	0*	-	-
081 CATHOLIC......	11	0	10,967	33.9	75.8
175 CONG CR CH....	3	170	206*	0.6	1.4
193 EPISCOPAL.....	3	427	892	2.8	6.2
403 SALVATION ARMY	1	38	211	0.7	1.5
413 S-D ADVENTISTS	1	39	47*	0.1	0.3
435 UNITARIAN-UNIV	1	79	93	0.3	0.6
443 UN C OF CHRIST	6	1,142	1,385*	4.3	9.6
449 UN METHODIST..	2	662	663	2.0	4.6
CARROLL	37	2,628	5,967*	32.2	100.0
019 AMER BAPT CONV	6	591	707*	3.8	11.8
081 CATHOLIC......	7	0	2,600	14.0	43.6
165 CH OF NAZARENE	1	24	74	0.4	1.2
175 CONG CR CH....	1	240	287*	1.5	4.8
193 EPISCOPAL.....	4	593	905	4.9	15.2
226 FRIENDS-USA...	1	9	11*	0.1	0.2
443 UN C OF CHRIST	9	971	1,161*	6.3	19.5
449 UN METHODIST..	8	200	222	1.2	3.7
CHESHIRE	66	7,409	20,776*	39.7	100.0
019 AMER BAPT CONV	6	1,247	1,526*	2.9	7.3
081 CATHOLIC......	16	0	11,273	21.5	54.3
165 CH OF NAZARENE	1	56	123	0.2	0.6
175 CONG CR CH....	1	159	195*	0.4	0.9
193 EPISCOPAL.....	1	555	857	1.6	4.1
226 FRIENDS-USA...	1	52	64*	0.1	0.3
283 LUTH--MO SYNOD	2	595	722	1.4	3.5
403 SALVATION ARMY	1	36	270	0.5	1.3
435 UNITARIAN-UNIV	6	496	733	1.4	3.5
443 UN C OF CHRIST	21	3,474	4,250*	8.1	20.5
449 UN METHODIST..	10	739	763	1.5	3.7
COOS	46	3,611	21,649*	63.1	100.0
019 AMER BAPT CONV	3	375	454*	1.3	2.1
029 AMER LUTH CH..	2	253	417	1.2	1.9
081 CATHOLIC......	15	0	17,053	49.7	78.8
193 EPISCOPAL.....	4	388	805	2.3	3.7
403 SALVATION ARMY	1	26	127	0.4	0.6
413 S-D ADVENTISTS	1	75	91*	0.3	0.4
443 UN C OF CHRIST	7	709	859*	2.5	4.0
449 UN METHODIST..	13	1,785	1,843	5.4	8.5
GRAFTON	82	9,049	23,260*	42.4	100.0
019 AMER BAPT CONV	10	1,232	1,462*	2.7	6.3
081 CATHOLIC......	19	0	11,989	21.8	51.5
165 CH OF NAZARENE	1	10	54	0.1	0.2
175 CONG CR CH....	1	159	189*	0.3	0.8
193 EPISCOPAL.....	8	1,120	2,165	3.9	9.3
226 FRIENDS-USA...	1	90	107*	0.2	0.5
283 LUTH--MO SYNOD	2	179	319	0.6	1.4
413 S-D ADVENTISTS	1	165	196*	0.4	0.8
443 UN C OF CHRIST	19	3,170	3,762*	6.9	16.2
449 UN METHODIST..	20	2,924	3,017	5.5	13.0
HILLSBOROUGH	120	19,320	142,602*	63.7	100.0
019 AMER BAPT CONV	8	2,118	2,652*	1.2	1.9
081 CATHOLIC......	43	0	116,764	52.1	81.9
097 CR C AND C CR.	3	101	126*	0.1	0.1
165 CH OF NAZARENE	1	81	310	0.1	0.2
175 CONG CR CH....	2	188	235*	0.1	0.2
193 EPISCOPAL.....	7	2,547	4,627	2.1	3.2
201 EVAN COV CH AM	1	125	157*	0.1	0.1
226 FRIENDS-USA...	1	64	80*	-	0.1
281 LUTH CH AMER..	1	230	260	0.1	0.2
283 LUTH--MO SYNOD	3	534	892	0.4	0.6
403 SALVATION ARMY	2	102	622	0.3	0.4
413 S-D ADVENTISTS	2	149	187*	0.1	0.1
435 UNITARIAN-UNIV	5	759	1,070	0.5	0.8
443 UN C OF CHRIST	24	7,772	9,733*	4.3	6.8
449 UN METHODIST..	11	3,414	3,464	1.5	2.4
453 UN PRES CH USA	6	1,136	1,423*	0.6	1.0
MERRIMACK	75	11,222	35,718*	44.1	100.0
019 AMER BAPT CONV	15	2,644	3,209*	4.0	9.0
081 CATHOLIC......	14	0	21,575	26.7	60.4
165 CH OF NAZARENE	2	122	247	0.3	0.7
175 CONG CR CH....	2	168	204*	0.3	0.6
193 EPISCOPAL.....	6	1,486	2,465	3.0	6.9
226 FRIENDS-USA...	1	9	11*	-	-
281 LUTH CH AMER..	1	253	347	0.4	1.0
353 PLY BRETHREN..	1	10	20	-	0.1
403 SALVATION ARMY	1	58	236	0.3	0.7
413 S-D ADVENTISTS	1	59	72*	0.1	0.2
435 UNITARIAN-UNIV	3	430	497	0.6	1.4
443 UN C OF CHRIST	18	3,782	4,590*	5.7	12.9
449 UN METHODIST..	10	2,201	2,245	2.8	6.3
ROCKINGHAM	99	13,924	60,871*	43.8	100.0
019 AMER BAPT CONV	21	3,559	4,517*	3.3	7.4
081 CATHOLIC......	23	0	42,398	30.5	69.7
127 CH GOD (CLEVE)	1	23	29*	-	-
165 CH OF NAZARENE	1	46	107	0.1	0.2
175 CONG CR CH....	2	532	675*	0.5	1.1
193 EPISCOPAL.....	7	1,767	3,278	2.4	5.4
281 LUTH CH AMER..	2	373	651	0.5	1.1
403 SALVATION ARMY	1	48	175	0.1	0.3
413 S-D ADVENTISTS	1	38	48*	-	0.1
419 SO BAPT CONV..	1	342	434*	0.3	0.7
435 UNITARIAN-UNIV	4	372	556	0.4	0.9
443 UN C OF CHRIST	19	3,951	5,015*	3.6	8.2
449 UN METHODIST..	14	2,544	2,570	1.8	4.2
453 UN PRES CH USA	2	329	418*	0.3	0.7
STRAFFORD	46	5,384	29,672*	42.1	100.0
019 AMER BAPT CONV	8	558	682*	1.0	2.3
029 AMER LUTH CH..	1	93	170	0.2	0.6
081 CATHOLIC......	14	0	22,610	32.1	76.2
123 CH GOD (ANDER)	1	28	58	0.1	0.2
193 EPISCOPAL.....	2	685	1,310	1.9	4.4
226 FRIENDS-USA...	2	117	143*	0.2	0.5
403 SALVATION ARMY	1	64	275	0.4	0.9
413 S-D ADVENTISTS	1	119	145*	0.2	0.5
435 UNITARIAN-UNIV	1	54	74	0.1	0.2
443 UN C OF CHRIST	9	2,343	2,864*	4.1	9.7
449 UN METHODIST..	6	1,323	1,341	1.9	4.5
SULLIVAN	36	4,249	13,545*	43.8	100.0
019 AMER BAPT CONV	7	1,038	1,273*	4.1	9.4
081 CATHOLIC......	4	0	8,004	25.9	59.1

*Total adherents estimated from known number of communicant, confirmed, full members.

—Represents a percent less than 0.1.

Percentages may not total due to rounding.

Table 3. Churches and Church Membership by State, County and Denomination: 1971

County and Denomination	Number of churches	Communicant, confirmed, full members	Total adherents: Number	Total adherents: Percent of total population	Total adherents: Percent of total adherents
165 CH OF NAZARENE	1	35	130	0.4	1.0
175 CONG CR CH....	1	128	157*	0.5	1.2
193 EPISCOPAL.....	4	390	967	3.1	7.1
283 LUTH--MO SYNOD	1	108	151	C.5	1.1
413 S-D ADVENTISTS	2	40	49*	0.2	0.4
435 UNITARIAN-UNIV	2	187	225	0.7	1.7
443 UN C OF CHRIST	5	1,044	1,280*	4.1	9.4
449 UN METHODIST..	9	1,279	1,309	4.2	9.7
CO DATA NOT AVAIL	4	158	2,227*	N/A	N/A
151 L-D SAINTS....	0	0	2,019	N/A	N/A
193 EPISCOPAL.....	1	26	45	N/A	N/A
223 FREE WILL BAPT	3	132	163*	N/A	N/A

NEW JERSEY

County and Denomination	Number of churches	Communicant, confirmed, full members	Total adherents: Number	Total adherents: Percent of total population	Total adherents: Percent of total adherents
THE STATE.....	3,093	726,408	3,655,469*	51.0	100.0
ATLANTIC	108	16,585	69,022*	39.4	100.0
019 AMER BAPT CONV	6	1,113	1,334*	0.8	1.9
081 CATHOLIC......	21	C	48,854	27.9	70.8
123 CH GOD (ANDER)	2	59	112	0.1	0.2
127 CH GOD (CLEVE)	2	45	54*	-	0.1
165 CH OF NAZARENE	4	155	300	0.2	0.4
175 CONG CR CH....	1	50	60*	-	0.1
193 EPISCOPAL.....	9	2,608	3,394	1.9	4.9
226 FRIENDS-USA...	1	30	36*	-	0.1
281 LUTH CH AMER..	7	2,170	3,353	1.9	4.9
293 MORAV CH-NORTH	1	279	419	0.2	0.6
353 PLY BRETHREN..	2	80	140	0.1	0.2
381 REF PRES-EVAN.	1	38	53	-	0.1
403 SALVATION ARMY	1	45	224	0.1	0.3
413 S-D ADVENTISTS	5	238	285*	0.2	0.4
419 SO BAPT CONV..	1	159	191*	0.1	0.3
435 UNITARIAN-UNIV	1	10	10	-	-
443 UN C OF CHRIST	3	547	656*	0.4	1.0
449 UN METHODIST..	29	6,513	6,615	3.8	9.6
453 UN PRES CH USA	11	2,446	2,932*	1.7	4.2
BERGEN	321	94,664	514,333*	57.3	100.0
019 AMER BAPT CONV	17	3,392	4,042*	0.5	0.8
029 AMER LUTH CH..	4	1,348	1,859	0.2	0.4
081 CATHOLIC......	80	0	390,470	43.5	75.9
097 CR C AND C CR.	1	32	38*	-	-
105 CHRISTIAN REF.	7	1,674	2,740	0.3	0.5
165 CH OF NAZARENE	1	175	489	0.1	0.1
193 EPISCOPAL.....	42	15,406	24,884	2.8	4.8
226 FRIENDS-USA...	1	204	243*	-	-
281 LUTH CH AMER..	24	10,258	14,605	1.6	2.8
283 LUTH--MO SYNOD	17	7,654	11,456	1.3	2.2
335 ORTH PRESB CH.	2	166	229	-	-
353 PLY BRETHREN..	4	160	260	-	0.1
371 REF CH IN AM..	39	16,222	20,075	2.2	3.9
403 SALVATION ARMY	1	20	121	-	-
413 S-D ADVENTISTS	4	377	449*	-	0.1
419 SO BAPT CONV..	3	389	463*	0.1	0.1
435 UNITARIAN-UNIV	3	639	879	0.1	0.2
443 UN C OF CHRIST	12	4,190	4,992*	0.6	1.0
449 UN METHODIST..	28	13,616	13,708	1.5	2.7
453 UN PRES CH USA	31	18,742	22,331*	2.5	4.3
BURLINGTON	143	22,625	114,196*	35.3	100.0
019 AMER BAPT CONV	16	3,177	3,953*	1.2	3.5
081 CATHOLIC......	22	0	83,377	25.8	73.0
127 CH GOD (CLEVE)	2	104	129*	-	0.1
165 CH OF NAZARENE	2	194	475	0.1	0.4
193 EPISCOPAL.....	18	6,446	9,484	2.9	8.3
226 FRIENDS-USA...	10	1,136	1,414*	0.4	1.2
281 LUTH CH AMER..	9	4,808	7,020	2.2	6.1
283 LUTH--MO SYNOD	2	391	527	0.2	0.5
293 MORAV CH-NORTH	2	603	799	0.2	0.7
371 REF CH IN AM..	1	205	289	C.1	0.3
413 S-D ADVENTISTS	2	113	141	-	0.1
419 SO BAPT CONV..	2	1,683	2,094*	0.6	1.8
435 UNITARIAN-UNIV	1	20	35	-	-
443 UN C OF CHRIST	2	490	610*	0.2	0.5
449 UN METHODIST..	43	1,285	1,398	0.4	1.2
453 UN PRES CH USA	9	1,970	2,451*	0.8	2.1
CAMDEN	224	54,947	248,[illegible]7*	54.4	100.0
019 AMER BAPT CONV	22	6,037	7,440*	1.6	3.0
059 BAPT MISS ASSN	1	53	65*	-	-
081 CATHOLIC......	56	0	176,990	38.8	71.2
123 CH GOD (ANDER)	2	113	268	0.1	0.1
127 CH GOD (CLEVE)	1	28	35*	-	-
193 EPISCOPAL.....	22	7,346	13,216	2.9	5.3
226 FRIENDS-USA...	2	281	346*	0.1	0.1
281 LUTH CH AMER..	21	8,634	12,856	2.8	5.2
283 LUTH--MO SYNOD	2	749	1,080	0.2	0.4
335 ORTH PRESB CH.	3	331	527	C.1	0.2
353 PLY BRETHREN..	4	110	180	-	0.1

*Total adherents estimated from known number of communicant, confirmed, full members.

County and Denomination	Number of churches	Communicant, confirmed, full members	Total adherents: Number	Total adherents: Percent of total population	Total adherents: Percent of total adherents
381 REF PRES-EVAN.	2	339	373	0.1	0.2
403 SALVATION ARMY	1	75	574	0.1	0.2
413 S-D ADVENTISTS	3	336	414*	0.1	0.2
419 SO BAPT CONV..	1	250	308*	0.1	0.1
435 UNITARIAN-UNIV	1	415	527	0.1	0.2
449 UN METHODIST..	55	16,352	16,583	3.6	6.7
453 UN PRES CH USA	25	13,498	16,635*	3.6	6.7
CAPE MAY	68	11,067	26,807*	45.0	100.0
019 AMER BAPT CONV	6	1,147	1,345*	2.3	5.0
081 CATHOLIC......	14	0	13,386	22.5	49.9
123 CH GOD (ANDER)	1	8	31	0.1	0.1
165 CH OF NAZARENE	3	106	306	0.5	1.1
193 EPISCOPAL.....	6	1,912	2,993	5.0	11.2
226 FRIENDS-USA...	1	42	49*	0.1	0.2
281 LUTH CH AMER..	5	1,398	1,858	3.1	6.9
335 ORTH PRESB CH.	1	57	89	C.1	0.3
353 PLY BRETHREN..	1	40	60	0.1	0.2
413 S-D ADVENTISTS	2	86	101*	0.2	0.4
419 SO BAPT CONV..	1	74	87*	0.1	0.3
449 UN METHODIST..	23	4,891	4,971	8.3	18.5
453 UN PRES CH USA	4	1,306	1,531*	2.6	5.7
CUMBERLAND	105	20,511	57,662*	47.5	100.0
019 AMER BAPT CONV	8	2,358	2,923*	2.4	5.1
081 CATHOLIC......	19	0	33,252	27.4	57.7
127 CH GOD (CLEVE)	7	357	442*	C.4	0.8
165 CH OF NAZARENE	3	459	1,163	1.0	2.0
193 EPISCOPAL.....	3	1,376	1,930	1.6	3.3
226 FRIENDS-USA...	1	63	78*	0.1	0.1
281 LUTH CH AMER..	3	858	1,243	1.0	2.2
283 LUTH--MO SYNOD	1	336	438	0.4	0.8
285 MENNONITE CH..	2	28	35*	-	0.1
335 ORTH PRESB CH.	2	402	526	0.4	0.9
403 SALVATION ARMY	1	32	257	0.2	0.4
413 S-D ADVENTISTS	4	394	488*	0.4	0.8
415 S-D BAPTIST GC	2	490	607*	C.5	1.1
443 UN C OF CHRIST	1	99	123*	C.1	0.2
449 UN METHODIST..	38	10,079	10,216	8.4	17.7
453 UN PRES CH USA	10	3,180	3,941*	3.2	6.8
ESSEX	288	68,954	417,004*	44.8	100.0
019 AMER BAPT CONV	20	6,729	8,169*	0.9	2.0
081 CATHOLIC......	82	0	331,371	35.6	79.5
093 CR CH (DISC)..	1	154	187*	-	-
097 CR C AND C CR.	2	79	96*	-	-
123 CH GOD (ANDER)	1	58	126	-	-
127 CH GOD (CLEVE)	3	172	209*	-	0.1
175 CONG CR CH....	1	135	164*	-	-
193 EPISCOPAL.....	30	11,038	15,717	1.7	3.8
201 EVAN COV CH AM	2	389	472*	0.1	0.1
226 FRIENDS-USA...	1	220	267*	-	0.1
281 LUTH CH AMER..	10	2,746	3,956	0.4	0.9
283 LUTH--MO SYNOD	7	1,829	2,528	0.3	0.6
313 NO AM BAPT GC.	1	74	90*	-	-
315 NO AM OLD RC..	1	31	38*	-	-
353 PLY BRETHREN..	7	353	520	0.1	0.1
371 REF CH IN AM..	12	2,907	3,426	0.4	0.8
403 SALVATION ARMY	5	205	989	0.1	0.2
413 S-D ADVENTISTS	6	1,007	1,222*	0.1	0.3
415 S-D BAPTIST GC	1	14	17*	-	-
435 UNITARIAN-UNIV	2	660	876	0.1	0.2
443 UN C OF CHRIST	17	8,172	9,920*	1.1	2.4
449 UN METHODIST..	26	10,607	10,696	1.2	2.6
453 UN PRES CH USA	50	21,375	25,948*	2.8	6.2
GLOUCESTER	82	16,474	62,261*	36.1	100.0
019 AMER BAPT CONV	7	2,551	3,199*	1.9	5.1
081 CATHOLIC......	19	C	40,143	23.2	64.5
127 CH GOD (CLEVE)	2	64	80*	-	0.1
165 CH OF NAZARENE	2	149	285	0.2	0.5
193 EPISCOPAL.....	10	2,053	3,539	2.0	5.7
226 FRIENDS-USA...	3	417	523*	0.3	0.8
281 LUTH CH AMER..	6	2,754	4,536	2.6	7.3
381 REF PRES-EVAN.	1	30	45	-	0.1
413 S-D ADVENTISTS	2	322	404*	0.2	0.6
443 UN C OF CHRIST	1	113	142*	0.1	0.2
449 UN METHODIST..	17	3,381	3,546	2.1	5.7
453 UN PRES CH USA	12	4,640	5,819*	3.4	9.3
HUDSON	206	24,809	369,962*	60.7	100.0
019 AMER BAPT CONV	11	2,294	2,728*	0.4	0.7
029 AMER LUTH CH..	2	259	385	0.1	0.1
081 CATHOLIC......	69	0	335,891	55.1	90.8
123 CH GOD (ANDER'	3	161	408	0.1	0.1
127 CH GOD (CLEV	2	58	69*	-	-
165 CH OF NAZAREN	1	9	67	-	-
193 EPISCOPAL.....	19	3,666	6,404	1.1	1.7
281 LUTH CH AMER..	17	5,191	6,944	1.1	1.9
283 LUTH--MO SYNOD	9	1,760	2,436	0.4	0.7
313 NO AM BAPT GC.	3	175	208*	-	0.1
315 NO AM OLD RC..	2	87	103*	-	-
353 PLY BRETHREN..	8	376	695	0.1	0.2
371 REF CH IN AM..	16	3,926	4,909	0.8	1.3
403 SALVATION ARMY	5	256	1,550	0.3	0.4
413 S-D ADVENTISTS	6	433	515*	0.1	0.1
419 SO BAPT CONV..	2	67	80*	-	-
443 UN C OF CHRIST	1	55	65*	-	-
449 UN METHODIST..	18	3,828	3,879	0.6	1.0
453 UN PRES CH USA	12	2,208	2,626*	0.4	0.7

—Represents a percent less than 0.1.

Percentages may not total due to rounding.

Table 3. Churches and Church Membership by State, County and Denomination: 1971

County and Denomination	Number of churches	Communicant, confirmed, full members	Total adherents: Number	Total adherents: Percent of total population	Total adherents: Percent of total adherents
HUNTERDON	77	13,342	29,809*	42.8	100.0
019 AMER BAPT CONV	7	918	1,129*	1.6	3.8
081 CATHOLIC......	10	0	13,031	18.7	43.7
157 CH OF BRETHREN	1	134	165*	0.2	0.6
165 CH OF NAZARENE	1	32	98	0.1	0.3
193 EPISCOPAL.....	3	741	1,186	1.7	4.0
226 FRIENDS-USA...	1	53	65*	0.1	0.2
281 LUTH CH AMER..	2	287	504	0.7	1.7
283 LUTH--MO SYNOD	1	429	1,044	1.5	3.5
285 MENNONITE CH..	1	33	41*	0.1	0.1
335 ORTH PRESB CH.	1	67	98	0.1	0.3
371 REF CH IN AM..	8	1,959	2,644	3.8	8.9
449 UN METHODIST..	25	4,167	4,241	6.1	14.2
453 UN PRES CH USA	16	4,522	5,563*	8.0	18.7
MERCER	149	40,155	160,002*	52.6	100.0
019 AMER BAPT CONV	24	6,236	7,500*	2.5	4.7
081 CATHOLIC......	35	0	108,416	35.7	67.8
123 CH GOD (ANDER)	2	71	279	0.1	0.2
127 CH GOD (CLEVE)	1	38	46*	-	-
165 CH OF NAZARENE	1	175	244	0.1	0.2
193 EPISCOPAL.....	11	6,006	9,634	3.2	6.0
226 FRIENDS-USA...	2	224	269*	0.1	0.2
281 LUTH CH AMER..	11	3,645	5,000	1.6	3.1
283 LUTH--MO SYNOD	4	821	1,405	0.5	0.9
335 ORTH PRESB CH.	1	69	87	-	0.1
353 PLY BRETHREN..	1	100	150	-	0.1
371 REF CH IN AM..	1	233	281	0.1	0.2
381 REF PRES-EVAN.	1	67	86	-	0.1
403 SALVATION ARMY	1	46	717	0.2	0.4
413 S-D ADVENTISTS	3	689	829*	0.3	0.5
419 SO BAPT CONV..	1	113	136*	-	0.1
435 UNITARIAN-UNIV	2	560	919	0.3	0.6
443 UN C OF CHRIST	2	166	200*	0.1	0.1
449 UN METHODIST..	23	7,089	7,199	2.4	4.5
453 UN PRES CH USA	22	13,807	16,605*	5.5	10.4
MIDDLESEX	193	45,948	335,581*	57.5	100.0
019 AMER BAPT CONV	11	2,439	3,024*	0.5	0.9
029 AMER LUTH CH..	1	407	598	0.1	0.2
081 CATHOLIC......	69	0	277,513	47.5	82.7
093 CR CH (DISC)..	2	114	141*	-	-
097 CR C AND C CR.	1	62	77*	-	-
127 CH GOD (CLEVE)	1	99	123*	-	-
165 CH OF NAZARENE	1	82	167	-	-
193 EPISCOPAL.....	17	6,554	8,790	1.5	2.6
201 EVAN COV CH AM	1	195	242*	-	0.1
226 FRIENDS-USA...	1	58	72*	-	-
281 LUTH CH AMER..	13	4,350	6,504	1.1	1.9
283 LUTH--MO SYNOD	3	1,919	2,762	0.5	0.8
313 NO AM BAPT GC.	1	175	217*	-	0.1
353 PLY BRETHREN..	2	68	215	-	0.1
371 REF CH IN AM..	10	4,003	5,055	0.9	1.5
403 SALVATION ARMY	2	64	401	0.1	0.1
413 S-D ADVENTISTS	5	359	445*	0.1	0.1
419 SO BAPT CONV..	3	459	569*	0.1	0.2
435 UNITARIAN-UNIV	1	243	336	0.1	0.1
443 UN C OF CHRIST	6	2,479	3,073*	0.5	0.9
449 UN METHODIST..	18	8,031	8,107	1.4	2.4
453 UN PRES CH USA	23	13,719	17,007*	2.9	5.1
469 WISC EVAN LUTH	1	69	143	-	-
MONMOUTH	187	50,597	210,517*	45.8	100.0
019 AMER BAPT CONV	11	1,560	1,942*	0.4	0.9
029 AMER LUTH CH..	2	558	885	0.2	0.4
081 CATHOLIC......	45	0	147,518	32.1	70.1
097 CR C AND C CR.	1	73	91*	-	-
127 CH GOD (CLEVE)	4	162	202*	-	0.1
193 EPISCOPAL.....	20	8,481	12,312	2.7	5.8
226 FRIENDS-USA...	2	132	164*	-	0.1
281 LUTH CH AMER..	9	3,820	5,885	1.3	2.8
283 LUTH--MO SYNOD	3	613	1,010	0.2	0.5
335 ORTH PRESB CH.	1	33	66	-	-
353 PLY BRETHREN..	3	175	380	0.1	0.2
371 REF CH IN AM..	9	2,953	4,031	0.9	1.9
403 SALVATION ARMY	2	397	1,236	0.3	0.6
413 S-D ADVENTISTS	2	182	227*	-	0.1
419 SO BAPT CONV..	2	516	642*	0.1	0.3
435 UNITARIAN-UNIV	1	272	472	0.1	0.2
443 UN C OF CHRIST	2	327	407*	0.1	0.2
449 UN METHODIST..	49	20,143	20,350	4.4	9.7
453 UN PRES CH USA	19	10,200	12,697*	2.8	6.0
MORRIS	164	47,848	171,547*	44.7	100.0
019 AMER BAPT CONV	4	773	971*	0.3	0.6
029 AMER LUTH CH..	5	1,337	2,081	0.5	1.2
081 CATHOLIC......	38	0	108,426	28.3	63.2
097 CR C AND C CR.	1	48	60*	-	-
105 CHRISTIAN REF.	2	209	419	0.1	0.2
123 CH GOD (ANDER)	1	50	169	-	0.1
127 CH GOD (CLEVE)	1	75	94*	-	0.1
165 CH OF NAZARENE	4	302	596	0.2	0.3
193 EPISCOPAL.....	17	8,233	14,081	3.7	8.2
221 FREE METH C NA	1	29	36	-	-
226 FRIENDS-USA...	2	216	271*	0.1	0.2
281 LUTH CH AMER..	7	1,802	2,885	0.8	1.7
283 LUTH--MO SYNOD	3	1,165	1,694	0.4	1.0
285 MENNONITE CH..	1	11	14*	-	-
313 NO AM BAPT GC.	1	35	44*	-	-
335 ORTH PRESB CH.	1	95	138	-	0.1
353 PLY BRETHREN..	1	100	150	-	0.1
371 REF CH IN AM..	6	2,797	3,729	1.0	2.2
403 SALVATION ARMY	2	94	625	0.2	0.4
413 S-D ADVENTISTS	3	213	267*	0.1	0.2
419 SO BAPT CONV..	2	524	658*	0.2	0.4
435 UNITARIAN-UNIV	2	348	479	0.1	0.3
443 UN C OF CHRIST	3	1,965	2,467*	0.6	1.4
449 UN METHODIST..	31	13,117	13,210	3.4	7.7
453 UN PRES CH USA	24	14,125	17,736*	4.6	10.3
469 WISC EVAN LUTH	1	185	247	0.1	0.1
OCEAN	94	20,889	101,448*	48.7	100.0
019 AMER BAPT CONV	4	1,058	1,300*	0.6	1.3
081 CATHOLIC......	19	0	75,402	36.2	74.3
127 CH GOD (CLEVE)	2	81	100*	-	0.1
165 CH OF NAZARENE	2	79	261	0.1	0.3
193 EPISCOPAL.....	7	3,116	4,718	2.3	4.7
199 EVAN CONG CH..	1	103	127*	0.1	0.1
281 LUTH CH AMER..	9	3,479	4,898	2.3	4.8
283 LUTH--MO SYNOD	1	485	677	0.3	0.7
315 NO AM OLD RC..	1	31	38*	-	-
353 PLY BRETHREN..	2	145	250	0.1	0.2
381 REF PRES-EVAN.	2	68	91	-	0.1
413 S-D ADVENTISTS	2	66	81*	-	0.1
419 SO BAPT CONV..	2	298	366*	0.2	0.4
435 UNITARIAN-UNIV	2	60	70	-	0.1
449 UN METHODIST..	29	6,595	6,647	3.2	6.6
453 UN PRES CH USA	9	5,225	6,422*	3.1	6.3
PASSAIC	186	38,026	223,289*	48.5	100.0
019 AMER BAPT CONV	12	3,497	4,249*	0.9	1.9
029 AMER LUTH CH..	1	122	211	-	0.1
081 CATHOLIC......	58	0	171,892	37.3	77.0
097 CR C AND C CR.	1	45	55*	-	-
105 CHRISTIAN REF.	12	3,206	4,562	1.0	2.0
123 CH GOD (ANDER)	2	95	160	-	0.1
127 CH GOD (CLEVE)	3	206	250*	0.1	0.1
165 CH OF NAZARENE	1	141	310	0.1	0.1
193 EPISCOPAL.....	16	5,693	9,838	2.1	4.4
281 LUTH CH AMER..	3	1,828	2,723	0.6	1.2
283 LUTH--MO SYNOD	7	1,852	2,885	0.6	1.3
315 NO AM OLD RC..	1	71	86*	-	-
371 REF CH IN AM..	20	7,005	9,431	2.0	4.2
403 SALVATION ARMY	2	63	633	0.1	0.3
413 S-D ADVENTISTS	4	282	343*	0.1	0.2
419 SO BAPT CONV..	2	101	123*	-	0.1
435 UNITARIAN-UNIV	1	81	111	-	-
443 UN C OF CHRIST	4	1,678	2,039*	0.4	0.9
449 UN METHODIST..	18	6,157	6,216	1.3	2.8
453 UN PRES CH USA	18	5,903	7,172*	1.6	3.2
SALEM	59	11,576	21,532*	35.7	100.0
019 AMER BAPT CONV	5	1,543	1,894*	3.1	8.8
081 CATHOLIC......	6	0	7,788	12.9	36.2
127 CH GOD (CLEVE)	1	18	22*	-	0.1
165 CH OF NAZARENE	3	269	568	0.9	2.6
193 EPISCOPAL.....	4	976	1,516	2.5	7.0
226 FRIENDS-USA...	2	269	330*	0.5	1.5
281 LUTH CH AMER..	1	217	285	0.5	1.3
283 LUTH--MO SYNOD	2	405	647	1.1	3.0
285 MENNONITE CH..	1	3	4*	-	-
335 ORTH PRESB CH.	1	57	81	0.1	0.4
413 S-D ADVENTISTS	3	187	230*	0.4	1.1
449 UN METHODIST..	25	5,684	5,776	9.6	26.8
453 UN PRES CH USA	5	1,948	2,391*	4.0	11.1
SOMERSET	96	27,634	106,558*	53.7	100.0
019 AMER BAPT CONV	2	689	852*	0.4	0.8
081 CATHOLIC......	22	0	71,888	36.2	67.5
175 CONG CR CH....	1	583	721*	0.4	0.7
193 EPISCOPAL.....	9	5,291	6,658	3.4	6.2
221 FREE METH C NA	1	15	15	-	-
226 FRIENDS-USA...	1	27	33*	-	-
281 LUTH CH AMER..	4	1,149	1,763	0.9	1.7
283 LUTH--MO SYNOD	4	1,436	2,042	1.0	1.9
371 REF CH IN AM..	21	5,713	7,976	4.0	7.5
413 S-D ADVENTISTS	1	179	221*	0.1	0.2
419 SO BAPT CONV..	1	68	84*	-	0.1
435 UNITARIAN-UNIV	1	73	113	0.1	0.1
443 UN C OF CHRIST	2	132	163*	0.1	0.2
449 UN METHODIST..	15	5,453	5,591	2.8	5.2
453 UN PRES CH USA	11	6,826	8,438*	4.3	7.9
SUSSEX	63	11,770	51,439*	66.3	100.0
019 AMER BAPT CONV	3	555	703*	0.9	1.4
029 AMER LUTH CH..	1	22	27	-	0.1
081 CATHOLIC......	12	0	36,000	46.4	70.0
105 CHRISTIAN REF.	2	350	753	1.0	1.5
165 CH OF NAZARENE	1	71	223	0.3	0.4
193 EPISCOPAL.....	4	1,276	2,038	2.6	4.0
281 LUTH CH AMER..	2	293	522	0.7	1.0
283 LUTH--MO SYNOD	3	708	1,253	1.6	2.4
413 S-D ADVENTISTS	2	275	348*	0.4	0.7
435 UNITARIAN-UNIV	1	29	38	-	0.1
449 UN METHODIST..	17	3,377	3,439	4.4	6.7
453 UN PRES CH USA	15	4,814	6,095*	7.9	11.8
UNION	183	68,422	308,524*	56.8	100.0
019 AMER BAPT CONV	15	5,144	6,117*	1.1	2.0

*Total adherents estimated from known number of communicant, confirmed, full members.

—Represents a percent less than 0.1.

Percentages may not total due to rounding.

Table 3. Churches and Church Membership by State, County and Denomination: 1971

County and Denomination	Number of churches	Communicant, confirmed, full members	Total adherents		
			Number	Percent of total population	Percent of total adherents
081 CATHOLIC......	46	0	226,692	41.7	73.5
097 CR C AND C CR.	1	100	119*	-	-
123 CH GOD (ANDER)	2	130	249	-	0.1
127 CH GOD (CLEVE)	1	50	59*	-	-
193 EPISCOPAL.....	20	10,469	13,029	2.4	4.2
201 EVAN COV CH AM	1	73	87*	-	-
226 FRIENDS-USA...	2	543	646*	0.1	0.2
281 LUTH CH AMER..	12	5,267	7,160	1.3	2.3
283 LUTH--MO SYNOD	6	1,893	2,819	0.5	0.9
293 MORAV CH-NORTH	1	177	224	-	0.1
313 NO AM BAPT GC.	1	284	338*	0.1	0.1
315 NO AM OLD RC..	1	120	143*	-	-
335 ORTH PRESB CH.	1	181	266	-	0.1
349 PENT HOLINESS.	1	67	80*	-	-
353 PLY BRETHREN..	4	368	640	0.1	0.2
371 REF CH IN AM..	2	730	889	0.2	0.3
403 SALVATION ARMY	2	98	389	0.1	0.1
413 S-D ADVENTISTS	3	256	304*	0.1	0.1
415 S-D BAPTIST GC	1	102	121*	-	-
419 SO BAPT CONV..	2	293	348*	0.1	0.1
435 UNITARIAN-UNIV	3	942	1,221	0.2	0.4
443 UN C OF CHRIST	3	2,951	3,509*	0.6	1.1
449 UN METHODIST..	22	12,757	12,840	2.4	4.2
453 UN PRES CH USA	30	25,427	30,235*	5.6	9.8
WARREN	82	18,893	47,627*	64.5	100.0
081 CATHOLIC......	12	0	24,113	32.6	50.6
127 CH GOD (CLEVE)	1	13	16*	-	-
165 CH OF NAZARENE	1	40	61	0.1	0.1
193 EPISCOPAL.....	5	1,027	1,894	2.6	4.0
281 LUTH CH AMER..	5	2,851	4,129	5.6	8.7
283 LUTH--MO SYNOD	1	212	371	0.5	0.8
285 MENNONITE CH..	1	55	67*	0.1	0.1
335 ORTH PRESB CH.	1	240	390	0.5	0.8
413 S-D ADVENTISTS	2	151	184*	0.2	0.4
443 UN C OF CHRIST	1	50	61*	0.1	0.1
449 UN METHODIST..	26	5,185	5,281	7.1	11.1
453 UN PRES CH USA	26	9,069	11,060*	15.0	23.2
CO DATA NOT AVAIL	15	672	7,932	N/A	N/A
151 L-D SAINTS....	0	0	6,192	N/A	N/A
193 EPISCOPAL.....	2	152	1,102	N/A	N/A
467 WESLEYAN......	13	520	638	N/A	N/A

NEW MEXICO

County and Denomination	Number of churches	Communicant, confirmed, full members	Number	Percent of total population	Percent of total adherents
THE STATE.....	1,142	204,049	643,408*	63.3	100.0
BERNALILLO	141	56,656	190,050*	60.2	100.0
019 AMER BAPT CONV	1	341	428*	0.1	0.2
029 AMER LUTH CH..	2	788	1,168	0.4	0.6
059 BAPT MISS ASSN	1	80	101*	-	0.1
075 BRETHREN IN CR	1	32	40*	-	-
081 CATHOLIC......	27	0	117,615	37.2	61.9
083 CR CATH CH DOB	1	22	23	-	-
093 CR CH (DISC)..	3	1,280	1,608*	0.5	0.8
097 CR C AND C CR.	5	1,520	1,910*	0.6	1.0
105 CHRISTIAN REF.	1	96	168	0.1	0.1
123 CH GOD (ANDER)	2	146	373	0.1	0.2
127 CH GOD (CLEVE)	4	122	153*	-	0.1
165 CH OF NAZARENE	5	878	1,839	0.6	1.0
185 CUMBER PRESB..	1	489	614*	0.2	0.3
193 EPISCOPAL.....	6	4,944	6,389	2.0	3.4
201 EVAN COV CH AM	1	73	92*	-	-
221 FREE METH C NA	1	12	15	-	-
226 FRIENDS-USA...	2	98	123*	-	0.1
281 LUTH CH AMER..	5	2,891	4,466	1.4	2.3
283 LUTH--MO SYNOD	5	2,200	3,091	1.0	1.6
285 MENNONITE CH..	1	31	39*	-	-
349 PENT HOLINESS.	1	27	34*	-	-
353 PLY BRETHREN..	2	100	150	-	0.1
403 SALVATION ARMY	1	51	249	0.1	0.1
413 S-D ADVENTISTS	5	857	1,077*	0.3	0.6
419 SO BAPT CONV..	27	16,810	21,123*	6.7	11.1
435 UNITARIAN-UNIV	1	572	764	0.2	0.4
443 UN C OF CHRIST	3	791	994*	0.3	0.5
449 UN METHODIST..	15	14,866	17,175	5.4	9.0
453 UN PRES CH USA	10	6,491	8,156*	2.6	4.3
469 WISC EVAN LUTH	1	48	73	-	-
CATRON	11	396	854*	38.9	100.0
081 CATHOLIC......	1	0	367	16.7	43.0
413 S-D ADVENTISTS	1	10	12*	0.5	1.4
419 SO BAPT CONV..	4	256	317*	14.4	37.1
449 UN METHODIST..	1	12	12	0.5	1.4
453 UN PRES CH USA	4	118	146*	6.6	17.1
CHAVES	49	13,583	22,961*	53.0	100.0
059 BAPT MISS ASSN	1	116	145*	0.3	0.6
081 CATHOLIC......	5	0	6,150	14.2	26.8
093 CR CH (DISC)..	1	547	683*	1.6	3.0

County and Denomination	Number of churches	Communicant, confirmed, full members	Total adherents		
			Number	Percent of total population	Percent of total adherents
097 CR C AND C CR.	1	61	76*	0.2	0.3
123 CH GOD (ANDER)	1	10	37	0.1	0.2
127 CH GOD (CLEVE)	1	47	59*	0.1	0.3
165 CH OF NAZARENE	3	239	471	1.1	2.1
193 EPISCOPAL.....	2	457	633	1.5	2.8
281 LUTH CH AMER..	1	113	150	0.3	0.7
283 LUTH--MO SYNOD	1	203	262	0.6	1.1
403 SALVATION ARMY	1	59	270	0.6	1.2
413 S-D ADVENTISTS	2	97	121*	0.3	0.5
419 SO BAPT CONV..	17	6,873	8,582*	19.8	37.4
435 UNITARIAN-UNIV	1	11	11	-	-
449 UN METHODIST..	7	3,872	4,215	9.7	18.4
453 UN PRES CH USA	4	878	1,096*	2.5	4.8
COLFAX	21	2,284	10,209*	83.9	100.0
081 CATHOLIC......	5	0	7,513	61.7	73.6
093 CR CH (DISC)..	1	78	96*	0.8	0.9
165 CH OF NAZARENE	1	25	29	0.2	0.3
193 EPISCOPAL.....	1	55	57	0.5	0.6
283 LUTH--MO SYNOD	1	16	37	0.3	0.4
413 S-D ADVENTISTS	1	16	20*	0.2	0.2
419 SO BAPT CONV..	5	941	1,160*	9.5	11.4
449 UN METHODIST..	4	939	1,033	8.5	10.1
453 UN PRES CH USA	2	214	264*	2.2	2.6
CURRY	44	13,735	23,584*	59.7	100.0
029 AMER LUTH CH..	1	97	133	0.3	0.6
059 BAPT MISS ASSN	1	94	119*	0.3	0.5
081 CATHOLIC......	6	0	6,000	15.2	25.4
097 CR C AND C CR.	2	1,230	1,559*	3.9	6.6
123 CH GOD (ANDER)	1	100	266	0.7	1.1
127 CH GOD (CLEVE)	1	41	52*	0.1	0.2
157 CH OF BRETHREN	1	119	151*	0.4	0.6
165 CH OF NAZARENE	4	356	680	1.7	2.9
193 EPISCOPAL.....	1	296	431	1.1	1.8
283 LUTH--MO SYNOD	1	174	225	0.6	1.0
353 PLY BRETHREN..	1	43	110	0.3	0.5
403 SALVATION ARMY	1	46	322	0.8	1.4
413 S-D ADVENTISTS	1	47	60*	0.2	0.3
419 SO BAPT CONV..	15	7,602	9,635*	24.4	40.9
449 UN METHODIST..	5	3,094	3,339	8.4	14.2
453 UN PRES CH USA	2	396	502*	1.3	2.1
DE BACA	9	880	1,738*	68.2	100.0
081 CATHOLIC......	4	0	700	27.5	40.3
165 CH OF NAZARENE	1	23	27	1.1	1.6
193 EPISCOPAL.....	1	34	53	2.1	3.0
419 SO BAPT CONV..	2	599	708*	27.8	40.7
449 UN METHODIST..	1	224	250	9.8	14.4
DONA ANA	62	10,793	42,189*	60.5	100.0
029 AMER LUTH CH..	1	80	124	0.2	0.3
081 CATHOLIC......	19	0	28,348	40.6	67.2
093 CR CH (DISC)..	1	160	205*	0.3	0.5
097 CR C AND C CR.	1	53	68*	0.1	0.2
123 CH GOD (ANDER)	1	50	104	0.1	0.2
127 CH GOD (CLEVE)	1	34	43*	0.1	0.1
165 CH OF NAZARENE	1	92	120	0.2	0.3
193 EPISCOPAL.....	5	967	1,453	2.1	3.4
221 FREE METH C NA	1	14	17	-	-
281 LUTH CH AMER..	1	100	155	0.2	0.4
283 LUTH--MO SYNOD	1	172	248	0.4	0.6
349 PENT HOLINESS.	2	22	28*	-	0.1
381 REF PRES-EVAN.	1	168	220	0.3	0.5
403 SALVATION ARMY	1	8	58	0.1	0.1
413 S-D ADVENTISTS	3	108	138*	0.2	0.3
419 SO BAPT CONV..	14	4,909	6,[illegible]78*	9.0	14.9
435 UNITARIAN-UNIV	1	60	68	0.1	0.2
449 UN METHODIST..	6	2,874	3,335	4.8	7.9
453 UN PRES CH USA	1	922	1,179*	1.7	2.8
EDDY	53	14,117	21,601*	52.5	100.0
059 BAPT MISS ASSN	2	294	362*	0.9	1.7
081 CATHOLIC......	4	0	4,492	10.9	20.8
093 CR CH (DISC)..	2	410	505*	1.2	2.3
097 CR C AND C CR.	1	120	148*	0.4	0.7
127 CH GOD (CLEVE)	4	326	401*	1.0	1.9
165 CH OF NAZARENE	3	216	611	1.5	2.8
193 EPISCOPAL.....	2	358	444	1.1	2.1
281 LUTH CH AMER..	1	76	104	0.3	0.5
283 LUTH--MO SYNOD	2	188	247	0.6	1.1
285 MENNONITE CH..	1	22	27*	0.1	0.1
413 S-D ADVENTISTS	1	38	47*	0.1	0.2
419 SO BAPT CONV..	18	7,470	9,193*	22.4	42.6
449 UN METHODIST..	10	3,724	3,943	9.6	18.3
453 UN PRES CH USA	2	875	1,077*	2.6	5.0
GRANT	27	2,881	13,889*	63.0	100.0
059 BAPT MISS ASSN	1	12	15*	0.1	0.1
081 CATHOLIC......	12	0	10,107	45.9	72.8
127 CH GOD (CLEVE)	1	69	87*	0.4	0.6
193 EPISCOPAL.....	1	132	367	1.7	2.6
283 LUTH--MO SYNOD	1	96	147	0.7	1.1
419 SO BAPT CONV..	4	1,335	1,686*	7.7	12.1
443 UN C OF CHRIST	3	143	181*	0.8	1.3
449 UN METHODIST..	2	885	1,035	4.7	7.5
453 UN PRES CH USA	2	209	264*	1.2	1.9
GUADALUPE	13	588	5,176*	104.2 #	100.0

*Total adherents estimated from known number of communicant, confirmed, full members.

—Represents a percent less than 0.1.

Percentages may not total due to rounding.

#See Introduction for explanation of why total adherents reported by churches exceed the 1970 population figure.

Table 3. Churches and Church Membership by State, County and Denomination: 1971

County and Denomination	Number of churches	Communicant, confirmed, full members	Total adherents: Number	Total adherents: Percent of total population	Total adherents: Percent of total adherents
081 CATHOLIC......	9	0	4,500	90.6	86.9
419 SO BAPT CONV..	3	211	275*	5.5	5.3
449 UN METHODIST..	1	377	401	8.1	7.7
HARDING	8	323	1,083*	80.3	100.0
081 CATHOLIC......	4	0	700	51.9	64.6
093 CR CH (DISC)..	1	31	37*	2.7	3.4
419 SO BAPT CONV..	2	216	259*	19.2	23.9
449 UN METHODIST..	1	76	87	6.5	8.0
HIDALGO	10	837	4,057*	85.7	100.0
081 CATHOLIC......	3	0	3,000	63.4	73.9
097 CR C AND C CR.	1	60	78*	1.6	1.9
419 SO BAPT CONV..	4	488	638*	13.5	15.7
449 UN METHODIST..	1	251	291	6.1	7.2
453 UN PRES CH USA	1	38	50*	1.1	1.2
LEA	68	21,352	30,899*	62.4	100.0
059 BAPT MISS ASSN	3	113	141*	0.3	0.5
081 CATHOLIC......	4	0	4,565	9.2	14.8
093 CR CH (DISC)..	1	123	153*	0.3	0.5
097 CR C AND C CR.	3	640	797*	1.6	2.6
123 CH GOD (ANDER)	1	25	50	0.1	0.2
127 CH GOD (CLEVE)	4	130	162*	0.3	0.5
165 CH OF NAZARENE	3	321	714	1.4	2.3
193 EPISCOPAL.....	3	396	476	1.0	1.5
281 LUTH CH AMER..	1	82	115	0.2	0.4
283 LUTH--MO SYNOD	2	183	233	0.5	0.8
315 NO AM OLD RC..	1	27	34*	0.1	0.1
349 PENT HOLINESS.	2	53	66*	0.1	0.2
357 PRESB CH US...	1	66	82*	0.2	0.3
403 SALVATION ARMY	1	19	118	0.2	0.4
413 S-D ADVENTISTS	1	23	29*	0.1	0.1
419 SO BAPT CONV..	28	14,323	17,834*	36.0	57.7
449 UN METHODIST..	6	4,226	4,580	9.2	14.8
453 UN PRES CH USA	3	602	750*	1.5	2.4
LINCOLN	25	1,899	5,289*	70.0	100.0
081 CATHOLIC......	9	0	3,000	39.7	56.7
093 CR CH (DISC)..	1	67	81*	1.1	1.5
165 CH OF NAZARENE	1	21	21	0.3	0.4
193 EPISCOPAL.....	1	154	243	3.2	4.6
419 SO BAPT CONV..	6	958	1,153*	15.3	21.8
449 UN METHODIST..	3	548	609	8.1	11.5
453 UN PRES CH USA	4	151	182*	2.4	3.4
LOS ALAMOS	15	6,234	11,202*	73.7	100.0
019 AMER BAPT CONV	1	1,309	1,664*	10.9	14.9
081 CATHOLIC......	1	0	3,000	19.7	26.8
093 CR CH (DISC)..	1	75	95*	0.6	0.8
097 CR C AND C CR.	1	240	305*	2.0	2.7
165 CH OF NAZARENE	1	12	32	0.2	0.3
193 EPISCOPAL.....	1	555	727	4.8	6.5
281 LUTH CH AMER..	1	586	911	6.0	8.1
419 SO BAPT CONV..	3	1,069	1,359*	8.9	12.1
435 UNITARIAN-UNIV	1	176	293	1.9	2.6
443 UN C OF CHRIST	1	1,028	1,307*	8.6	11.7
449 UN METHODIST..	1	748	955	6.3	8.5
453 UN PRES CH USA	2	436	554*	3.6	4.9
LUNA	17	2,492	4,646*	39.7	100.0
059 BAPT MISS ASSN	1	40	50*	0.4	1.1
081 CATHOLIC......	4	0	1,525	13.0	32.8
097 CR C AND C CR.	1	150	189*	1.6	4.1
165 CH OF NAZARENE	1	32	50	0.4	1.1
193 EPISCOPAL.....	1	69	139	1.2	3.0
283 LUTH--MO SYNOD	1	64	109	0.9	2.3
413 S-D ADVENTISTS	1	51	64*	0.5	1.4
419 SO BAPT CONV..	4	1,039	1,307*	11.2	28.1
449 UN METHODIST..	2	891	1,017	8.7	21.9
453 UN PRES CH USA	1	156	196*	1.7	4.2
MC KINLEY	36	3,246	13,666*	31.6	100.0
081 CATHOLIC......	12	0	9,025	20.9	66.0
083 CR CATH CH DOB	1	49	58	0.1	0.4
097 CR C AND C CR.	2	106	147*	0.3	1.1
105 CHRISTIAN REF.	3	236	477	1.1	3.5
127 CH GOD (CLEVE)	5	344	476*	1.1	3.5
165 CH OF NAZARENE	1	69	159	0.4	1.2
193 EPISCOPAL.....	1	99	173	0.4	1.3
283 LUTH--MO SYNOD	2	89	199	0.5	1.5
419 SO BAPT CONV..	6	1,387	1,918*	4.4	14.0
443 UN C OF CHRIST	1	59	82*	0.2	0.6
449 UN METHODIST..	1	699	801	1.9	5.9
453 UN PRES CH USA	1	109	151*	0.3	1.1
MORA	35	158	4,701*	100.6#	100.0
081 CATHOLIC......	33	0	4,500	96.3	95.7
419 SO BAPT CONV..	1	55	70*	1.5	1.5
453 UN PRES CH USA	1	103	131*	2.8	2.8
OTERO	43	8,434	18,688*	45.5	100.0
059 BAPT MISS ASSN	1	54	70*	0.2	0.4
081 CATHOLIC......	9	0	7,767	18.9	41.6
093 CR CH (DISC)..	1	105	136*	0.3	0.7
097 CR C AND C CR.	1	125	162*	0.4	0.9
127 CH GOD (CLEVE)	1	50	65*	0.2	0.3
165 CH OF NAZARENE	2	88	198	0.5	1.1
193 EPISCOPAL.....	2	172	255	0.6	1.4
281 LUTH CH AMER..	1	130	173	0.4	0.9
283 LUTH--MO SYNOD	1	155	225	0.5	1.2
371 REF CH IN AM..	1	107	173	0.4	0.9
381 REF PRES-EVAN.	1	104	135	0.3	0.7
413 S-D ADVENTISTS	1	63	82*	0.2	0.4
419 SO BAPT CONV..	14	4,219	5,474*	13.3	29.3
435 UNITARIAN-UNIV	1	20	20	-	0.1
449 UN METHODIST..	5	2,711	3,324	8.1	17.8
453 UN PRES CH USA	1	331	429*	1.0	2.3
QUAY	26	4,287	8,321*	76.3	100.0
059 BAPT MISS ASSN	1	28	34*	0.3	0.4
081 CATHOLIC......	5	0	3,200	29.3	38.5
097 CR C AND C CR.	1	120	146*	1.3	1.8
127 CH GOD (CLEVE)	1	16	20*	0.2	0.2
165 CH OF NAZARENE	1	37	56	0.5	0.7
193 EPISCOPAL.....	1	38	44	0.4	0.5
413 S-D ADVENTISTS	1	38	46*	0.4	0.6
419 SO BAPT CONV..	8	2,945	3,594*	33.0	43.2
449 UN METHODIST..	6	948	1,038	9.5	12.5
453 UN PRES CH USA	1	117	143*	1.3	1.7
RIO ARRIBA	65	1,185	20,025*	79.6	100.0
081 CATHOLIC......	48	0	18,548	73.7	92.6
193 EPISCOPAL.....	1	74	91	0.4	0.5
371 REF CH IN AM..	1	81	123	0.5	0.6
413 S-D ADVENTISTS	2	71	94*	0.4	0.5
419 SO BAPT CONV..	3	247	326*	1.3	1.6
449 UN METHODIST..	6	411	446	1.8	2.2
453 UN PRES CH USA	4	301	397*	1.6	2.0
ROOSEVELT	27	7,012	12,020*	72.9	100.0
081 CATHOLIC......	3	0	3,800	23.1	31.6
097 CR C AND C CR.	1	190	226*	1.4	1.9
127 CH GOD (CLEVE)	1	39	46*	0.3	0.4
165 CH OF NAZARENE	1	109	145	0.9	1.2
193 EPISCOPAL.....	1	30	92	0.6	0.8
413 S-D ADVENTISTS	1	80	95*	0.6	0.8
419 SO BAPT CONV..	15	4,942	5,883*	35.7	48.9
449 UN METHODIST..	3	1,517	1,608	9.8	13.4
453 UN PRES CH USA	1	105	125*	0.8	1.0
SANDOVAL	21	590	14,779*	84.5	100.0
081 CATHOLIC......	11	0	14,011	80.1	94.8
157 CH OF BRETHREN	1	58	77*	0.4	0.5
413 S-D ADVENTISTS	1	170	224*	1.3	1.5
419 SO BAPT CONV..	3	185	244*	1.4	1.7
449 UN METHODIST..	1	35	35	0.2	0.2
453 UN PRES CH USA	4	142	188*	1.1	1.3
SAN JUAN	47	10,997	19,507*	37.1	100.0
075 BRETHREN IN CR	1	29	38*	0.1	0.2
081 CATHOLIC......	6	0	4,804	9.1	24.6
093 CR CH (DISC)..	1	188	249*	0.5	1.3
097 CR C AND C CR.	2	185	245*	0.5	1.3
105 CHRISTIAN REF.	1	41	67	0.1	0.3
127 CH GOD (CLEVE)	2	56	74*	0.1	0.4
165 CH OF NAZARENE	2	170	344	0.7	1.8
193 EPISCOPAL.....	5	426	892	1.7	4.6
221 FREE METH C NA	2	29	48	0.1	0.2
281 LUTH CH AMER..	1	235	373	0.7	1.9
283 LUTH--MO SYNOD	1	128	176	0.3	0.9
403 SALVATION ARMY	1	17	109	0.2	0.6
413 S-D ADVENTISTS	3	315	418*	0.8	2.1
419 SO BAPT CONV..	12	6,021	7,987*	15.2	40.9
449 UN METHODIST..	5	2,519	2,837	5.4	14.5
453 UN PRES CH USA	2	638	846*	1.6	4.3
SAN MIGUEL	42	1,494	14,020*	63.9	100.0
081 CATHOLIC......	35	0	12,200	55.6	87.0
093 CR CH (DISC)..	1	99	122*	0.6	0.9
193 EPISCOPAL.....	1	25	48	0.2	0.3
283 LUTH--MO SYNOD	1	108	150	0.7	1.1
419 SO BAPT CONV..	2	614	760*	3.5	5.4
449 UN METHODIST..	1	453	499	2.3	3.6
453 UN PRES CH USA	1	195	241*	1.1	1.7
SANTA FE	52	6,291	38,709*	72.0	100.0
081 CATHOLIC......	31	0	30,746	57.2	79.4
093 CR CH (DISC)..	1	83	105*	0.2	0.3
165 CH OF NAZARENE	1	25	55	0.1	0.1
193 EPISCOPAL.....	2	808	1,041	1.9	2.7
226 FRIENDS-USA...	1	24	30*	0.1	0.1
281 LUTH CH AMER..	1	135	205	0.4	0.5
283 LUTH--MO SYNOD	1	170	255	0.5	0.7
413 S-D ADVENTISTS	1	69	88*	0.2	0.2
419 SO BAPT CONV..	6	1,682	2,135*	4.0	5.5
435 UNITARIAN-UNIV	1	105	117	0.2	0.3
449 UN METHODIST..	3	2,096	2,544	4.7	6.6
453 UN PRES CH USA	3	1,094	1,388*	2.6	3.6
SIERRA	16	1,457	3,831*	53.3	100.0
081 CATHOLIC......	8	0	2,159	30.0	56.4
093 CR CH (DISC)..	1	41	48*	0.7	1.3

*Total adherents estimated from known number of communicant, confirmed, full members. —Represents a percent less than 0.1. Percentages may not total due to rounding.

#See Introduction for explanation of why total adherents reported by churches exceed the 1970 population figure.

Table 3. Churches and Church Membership by State, County and Denomination: 1971

County and Denomination	Number of churches	Communicant, confirmed, full members	Total adherents: Number	Total adherents: Percent of total population	Total adherents: Percent of total adherents
097 CR C AND C CR.	1	70	82*	1.1	2.1
127 CH GOD (CLEVE)	1	6	7*	0.1	0.2
165 CH OF NAZARENE	1	15	25	0.3	0.7
283 LUTH--MO SYNOD	1	59	74	1.0	1.9
413 S-D ADVENTISTS	1	22	26*	0.4	0.7
419 SO BAPT CONV..	1	772	909*	12.6	23.7
449 UN METHODIST..	1	472	501	7.0	13.1
SOCORRO	20	1,467	9,015*	92.3	100.0
081 CATHOLIC......	10	0	7,135	73.1	79.1
127 CH GOD (CLEVE)	1	14	18*	0.2	0.2
193 EPISCOPAL.....	1	68	97	1.0	1.1
413 S-D ADVENTISTS	1	46	58*	0.6	0.6
419 SO BAPT CONV..	3	788	997*	10.2	11.1
449 UN METHODIST..	2	307	401	4.1	4.4
453 UN PRES CH USA	2	244	309*	3.2	3.4
TAOS	36	849	16,518*	94.3	100.0
081 CATHOLIC......	26	0	15,400	87.9	93.2
193 EPISCOPAL.....	1	114	190	1.1	1.2
413 S-D ADVENTISTS	1	33	43*	0.2	0.3
419 SO BAPT CONV..	3	236	305*	1.7	1.8
449 UN METHODIST..	2	125	139	0.8	0.8
453 UN PRES CH USA	3	341	441*	2.5	2.7
TORRANCE	24	1,192	4,399*	83.2	100.0
081 CATHOLIC......	15	0	2,921	55.2	66.4
165 CH OF NAZARENE	2	67	125	2.4	2.8
419 SO BAPT CONV..	4	750	913*	17.3	20.8
449 UN METHODIST..	3	375	440	8.3	10.0
UNION	15	1,579	3,636*	73.8	100.0
081 CATHOLIC......	3	0	1,800	36.5	49.5
127 CH GOD (CLEVE)	2	46	56*	1.1	1.5
349 PENT HOLINESS.	1	18	22*	0.4	0.6
413 S-D ADVENTISTS	1	21	26*	0.5	0.7
419 SO BAPT CONV..	4	786	959*	19.5	26.4
449 UN METHODIST..	4	708	773	15.7	21.3
VALENCIA	53	4,021	29,205*	72.0	100.0
081 CATHOLIC......	26	0	23,920	59.0	81.9
097 CR C AND C CR.	3	76	100*	0.2	0.3
123 CH GOD (ANDER)	1	25	74	0.2	0.3
127 CH GOD (CLEVE)	1	63	83*	0.2	0.3
165 CH OF NAZARENE	1	62	137	0.3	0.5
193 EPISCOPAL.....	2	95	153	0.4	0.5
283 LUTH--MO SYNOD	1	71	110	0.3	0.4
413 S-D ADVENTISTS	2	134	177*	0.4	0.6
419 SO BAPT CONV..	9	2,189	2,888*	7.1	9.9
449 UN METHODIST..	4	907	1,037	2.6	3.6
453 UN PRES CH USA	3	399	526*	1.3	1.8
CO DATA NOT AVAIL	11	740	22,941*	N/A	N/A
151 L-D SAINTS....	0	0	21,843	N/A	N/A
193 EPISCOPAL.....	1	66	243	N/A	N/A
223 FREE WILL BAPT	9	641	814*	N/A	N/A
467 WESLEYAN......	1	33	41	N/A	N/A

NEW YORK

County and Denomination	Number of churches	Communicant, confirmed, full members	Total adherents: Number	Total adherents: Percent of total population	Total adherents: Percent of total adherents
THE STATE.....	7,880	1,592,333	8,567,413*	47.0	100.0
ALBANY	169	33,951	153,749*	53.6	100.0
019 AMER BAPT CONV	9	1,494	1,790*	0.6	1.2
081 CATHOLIC......	62	0	112,500	39.2	73.2
127 CH GOD (CLEVE)	3	60	72*	-	-
165 CH OF NAZARENE	1	52	75	-	-
193 EPISCOPAL.....	13	4,434	5,743	2.0	3.7
226 FRIENDS-USA...	1	100	120*	-	0.1
281 LUTH CH AMER..	8	3,247	4,468	1.6	2.9
283 LUTH--MO SYNOD	6	2,080	3,298	1.2	2.1
371 REF CH IN AM..	20	4,733	5,838	2.0	3.8
403 SALVATION ARMY	2	74	544	0.2	0.4
413 S-D ADVENTISTS	2	323	387*	0.1	0.3
415 S-D BAPTIST GC	1	11	13*	-	-
435 UNITARIAN-UNIV	1	395	640	0.2	0.4
443 UN C OF CHRIST	5	1,221	1,463*	0.5	1.0
449 UN METHODIST..	20	10,525	10,566	3.7	6.9
453 UN PRES CH USA	15	5,202	6,232*	2.2	4.1
ALLEGANY	81	8,237	18,429*	39.7	100.0
019 AMER BAPT CONV	7	1,119	1,360*	2.9	7.4
081 CATHOLIC......	14	0	7,374	15.9	40.0
093 CR CH (DISC)..	1	457	555*	1.2	3.0
097 CR C AND C CR.	2	145	176*	0.4	1.0
165 CH OF NAZARENE	1	21	40	0.1	0.2
193 EPISCOPAL.....	7	549	940	2.0	5.1
221 FREE METH C NA	2	51	65	0.1	0.4
226 FRIENDS-USA...	1	33	40*	0.1	0.2
283 LUTH--MO SYNOD	2	701	1,032	2.2	5.6
285 MENNONITE CH..	2	56	68*	0.1	0.4
403 SALVATION ARMY	1	48	219	0.5	1.2
413 S-D ADVENTISTS	2	63	77*	0.2	0.4
415 S-D BAPTIST GC	5	580	705*	1.5	3.8
435 UNITARIAN-UNIV	1	22	43	0.1	0.2
443 UN C OF CHRIST	1	245	298*	0.6	1.6
449 UN METHODIST..	27	3,586	4,755	10.2	25.8
453 UN PRES CH USA	5	561	682*	1.5	3.7
BRONX	238	29,868	621,659*	42.2	100.0
019 AMER BAPT CONV	17	1,303	1,595*	0.1	0.3
029 AMER LUTH CH..	8	1,601	2,184	0.1	0.4
075 BRETHREN IN CR	1	30	37*	-	-
081 CATHOLIC......	70	0	581,800	39.5	93.6
083 CR CATH CH OOB	1	36	36	-	-
093 CR CH (DISC)..	2	220	269*	-	-
127 CH GOD (CLEVE)	12	429	525*	-	0.1
193 EPISCOPAL.....	20	4,276	7,770	0.5	1.2
201 EVAN COV CH AM	3	163	199*	-	-
281 LUTH CH AMER..	13	2,801	3,987	0.3	0.6
283 LUTH--MO SYNOD	6	1,559	2,256	0.2	0.4
285 MENNONITE CH..	6	262	321*	-	0.1
293 MORAV CH-NORTH	1	151	179	-	-
315 NO AM OLD RC..	10	3,231	3,954*	0.3	0.6
353 PLY BRETHREN..	5	329	495	-	0.1
371 REF CH IN AM..	4	355	435	-	0.1
403 SALVATION ARMY	2	82	571	-	0.1
413 S-D ADVENTISTS	9	1,791	2,192*	0.1	0.4
419 SO BAPT CONV..	2	286	350*	-	0.1
443 UN C OF CHRIST	9	1,507	1,844*	0.1	0.3
449 UN METHODIST..	16	4,188	4,213	0.3	0.7
453 UN PRES CH USA	21	5,268	6,447*	0.4	1.0
BROOME	143	40,480	115,846*	52.2	100.0
019 AMER BAPT CONV	9	3,336	4,081*	1.8	3.5
081 CATHOLIC......	31	0	63,664	28.7	55.0
093 CR CH (DISC)..	1	209	256*	0.1	0.2
097 CR C AND C CR.	3	180	220*	0.1	0.2
105 CHRISTIAN REF.	1	79	14[illegible]	0.1	0.1
165 CH OF NAZARENE	2	341	614	0.3	0.5
193 EPISCOPAL.....	9	4,022	6,083	2.7	5.3
221 FREE METH C NA	3	92	121	0.1	0.1
281 LUTH CH AMER..	6	1,855	2,791	1.3	2.4
283 LUTH--MO SYNOD	2	523	757	0.3	0.7
403 SALVATION ARMY	1	73	594	0.3	0.5
413 S-D ADVENTISTS	1	180	220*	0.1	0.2
419 SO BAPT CONV..	2	237	290*	0.1	0.3
435 UNITARIAN-UNIV	1	275	325	0.1	0.3
443 UN C OF CHRIST	6	1,554	1,901*	0.9	1.6
449 UN METHODIST..	48	20,995	25,795	11.6	22.3
453 UN PRES CH USA	17	6,529	7,986*	3.6	6.9
CATTARAUGUS	88	10,197	38,409*	47.0	100.0
019 AMER BAPT CONV	5	1,364	1,678*	2.1	4.4
081 CATHOLIC......	26	0	24,109	29.5	62.8
165 CH OF NAZARENE	2	28	74	0.1	0.2
193 EPISCOPAL.....	6	1,607	1,899	2.3	4.9
221 FREE METH C NA	10	438	536	0.7	1.4
281 LUTH CH AMER..	1	179	228	0.3	0.6
283 LUTH--MO SYNOD	7	1,681	2,662	3.3	6.9
403 SALVATION ARMY	2	92	341	0.4	0.9
413 S-D ADVENTISTS	4	216	266*	0.3	0.7
443 UN C OF CHRIST	4	743	914*	1.1	2.4
449 UN METHODIST..	13	1,535	2,855	3.5	7.4
453 UN PRES CH USA	8	2,314	2,847*	3.5	7.4
CAYUGA	88	12,806	44,760*	57.8	100.0
019 AMER BAPT CONV	10	1,776	2,182*	2.8	4.9
081 CATHOLIC......	20	0	28,233	36.5	63.1
093 CR CH (DISC)..	2	196	241*	0.3	0.5
157 CH OF BRETHREN	1	101	124*	0.2	0.3
165 CH OF NAZARENE	1	129	234	0.3	0.5
193 EPISCOPAL.....	4	1,230	1,412	1.8	3.2
221 FREE METH C NA	1	18	20	-	-
226 FRIENDS-USA...	1	129	158*	0.2	0.4
283 LUTH--MO SYNOD	1	139	207	0.3	0.5
371 REF CH IN AM..	2	265	384	0.5	0.9
403 SALVATION ARMY	1	56	565	0.7	1.3
413 S-D ADVENTISTS	2	281	345*	0.4	0.8
435 UNITARIAN-UNIV	1	28	31	-	0.1
443 UN C OF CHRIST	4	440	541*	0.7	1.2
449 UN METHODIST..	22	4,920	6,277	8.1	14.0
453 UN PRES CH USA	15	3,098	3,806*	4.9	8.5
CHAUTAUQUA	161	31,292	73,171*	49.7	100.0
019 AMER BAPT CONV	10	2,362	2,863*	1.9	3.9
081 CATHOLIC......	26	0	31,618	21.5	43.2
093 CR CH (DISC)..	1	52	63*	-	0.1
123 CH GOD (ANDER)	4	266	635	0.4	0.9
127 CH GOD (CLEVE)	2	52	63*	-	0.1
165 CH OF NAZARENE	2	135	269	0.2	0.4
193 EPISCOPAL.....	8	1,975	2,954	2.0	4.0
201 EVAN COV CH AM	2	1,289	1,562*	1.1	2.1
221 FREE METH C NA	4	[illegible]58	366	0.2	0.5
226 FRIENDS-USA...	1	22	27*	-	-
281 LUTH CH AMER..	13	5,100	7,575	5.1	10.4
283 LUTH--MO SYNOD	3	537	754	0.5	1.0
349 PENT HOLINESS.	1	9	11*	-	-

*Total adherents estimated from known number of communicant, confirmed, full members.

—Represents a percent less than 0.1.

Percentages may not total due to rounding.

Table 3. Churches and Church Membership by State, County and Denomination: 1971

County and Denomination	Number of churches	Communicant, confirmed, full members	Total adherents		
			Number	Percent of total population	Percent of total adherents
353 PLY BRETHREN..	1	20	115	0.1	0.2
371 REF CH IN AM..	2	486	670	0.5	0.9
403 SALVATION ARMY	2	249	1,593	1.1	2.2
413 S-D ADVENTISTS	2	214	259*	0.2	0.4
419 SO BAPT CONV..	1	75	91*	0.1	0.1
435 UNITARIAN-UNIV	2	205	222	0.2	0.3
443 UN C OF CHRIST	5	1,559	1,890*	1.3	2.6
449 UN METHODIST..	61	13,120	15,563	10.6	21.3
453 UN PRES CH USA	8	3,307	4,008*	2.7	5.5
CHEMUNG	77	19,653	54,622*	53.8	100.0
019 AMER BAPT CONV	8	1,889	2,320*	2.3	4.2
029 AMER LUTH CH..	1	31	39	-	0.1
081 CATHOLIC......	11	0	28,192	27.8	51.6
093 CR CH (DISC)..	1	284	349*	0.3	0.6
097 CR C AND C CR.	3	36	44*	-	0.1
165 CH OF NAZARENE	4	343	856	0.8	1.6
193 EPISCOPAL.....	8	1,718	3,949	3.9	7.2
221 FREE METH C NA	1	23	25	-	-
226 FRIENDS-USA...	1	27	33*	-	0.1
281 LUTH CH AMER..	3	996	1,382	1.4	2.5
403 SALVATION ARMY	1	108	405	0.4	0.7
413 S-D ADVENTISTS	1	361	443*	0.4	0.8
419 SO BAPT CONV..	2	236	290*	0.3	0.5
435 UNITARIAN-UNIV	1	35	50	-	0.1
443 UN C OF CHRIST	2	552	678*	0.7	1.2
449 UN METHODIST..	23	8,845	10,448	10.3	19.1
453 UN PRES CH USA	6	4,169	5,119*	5.0	9.4
CHENANGO	60	10,395	19,622*	42.3	100.0
019 AMER BAPT CONV	9	1,799	2,253*	4.9	11.5
081 CATHOLIC......	7	0	5,308	11.4	27.1
193 EPISCOPAL.....	8	2,041	3,334	7.2	17.0
221 FREE METH C NA	2	62	86	0.2	0.4
281 LUTH CH AMER..	1	255	363	0.8	1.8
413 S-D ADVENTISTS	1	88	110*	0.2	0.6
443 UN C OF CHRIST	6	1,201	1,504*	3.2	7.7
449 UN METHODIST..	21	4,258	5,799	12.5	29.6
453 UN PRES CH USA	5	691	865*	1.9	4.4
CLINTON	65	5,748	53,082*	72.8	100.0
019 AMER BAPT CONV	2	158	198*	0.3	0.4
081 CATHOLIC......	29	0	45,973	63.0	86.6
127 CH GOD (CLEVE)	1	26	33*	-	0.1
165 CH OF NAZARENE	2	146	300	0.4	0.6
193 EPISCOPAL.....	5	994	1,579	2.2	3.0
283 LUTH--MO SYNOD	1	74	182	0.2	0.3
403 SALVATION ARMY	1	71	257	0.4	0.5
413 S-D ADVENTISTS	1	13	16*	-	-
435 UNITARIAN-UNIV	1	45	60	0.1	0.1
449 UN METHODIST..	16	3,376	3,423	4.7	6.4
453 UN PRES CH USA	6	845	1,061*	1.5	2.0
COLUMBIA	77	11,989	28,276*	54.9	100.0
019 AMER BAPT CONV	2	265	321*	0.6	1.1
029 AMER LUTH CH..	2	157	234	0.5	0.8
081 CATHOLIC......	12	0	12,789	24.8	45.2
193 EPISCOPAL.....	5	1,336	2,295	4.5	8.1
226 FRIENDS-USA...	2	38	46*	0.1	0.2
281 LUTH CH AMER..	13	2,888	3,833	7.4	13.6
283 LUTH--MO SYNOD	2	332	556	1.1	2.0
371 REF CH IN AM..	13	3,004	3,938	7.6	13.9
413 S-D ADVENTISTS	1	111	135*	0.3	0.5
443 UN C OF CHRIST	2	284	344*	0.7	1.2
449 UN METHODIST..	19	2,926	2,999	5.8	10.6
453 UN PRES CH USA	4	648	786*	1.5	2.8
CORTLAND	47	9,220	20,143*	43.9	100.0
019 AMER BAPT CONV	5	1,552	1,905*	4.2	9.5
081 CATHOLIC......	5	0	7,693	16.8	38.2
165 CH OF NAZARENE	1	33	170	0.4	0.8
193 EPISCOPAL.....	3	580	1,694	3.7	8.4
221 FREE METH C NA	1	61	78	0.2	0.4
281 LUTH CH AMER..	1	107	191	0.4	0.9
283 LUTH--MO SYNOD	1	83	121	0.3	0.6
353 PLY BRETHREN..	1	6	10	-	-
403 SALVATION ARMY	1	41	140	0.3	0.7
413 S-D ADVENTISTS	1	148	182*	0.4	0.9
415 S-D BAPTIST GC	1	54	66*	0.1	0.3
435 UNITARIAN-UNIV	1	70	95	0.2	0.5
443 UN C OF CHRIST	4	1,059	1,300*	2.8	6.5
449 UN METHODIST..	17	3,870	4,588	10.0	22.8
453 UN PRES CH USA	4	1,556	1,910*	4.2	9.5
DELAWARE	88	12,132	19,828*	44.3	100.0
019 AMER BAPT CONV	7	645	780*	1.7	3.9
081 CATHOLIC......	13	0	4,955	11.1	25.0
193 EPISCOPAL.....	11	818	1,636	3.7	8.3
221 FREE METH C NA	3	36	48	0.1	0.2
281 LUTH CH AMER..	1	193	296	0.7	1.5
283 LUTH--MO SYNOD	2	160	209	0.5	1.1
371 REF CH IN AM..	1	281	376	0.8	1.9
443 UN C OF CHRIST	2	667	807*	1.8	4.1
449 UN METHODIST..	26	5,979	6,664	14.9	33.6
453 UN PRES CH USA	22	3,353	4,057*	9.1	20.5
DUTCHESS	135	27,055	98,081*	44.1	100.0
019 AMER BAPT CONV	13	1,643	2,029*	0.9	2.1
081 CATHOLIC......	29	0	63,900	28.7	65.2
097 CR C AND C CR.	1	17	21*	-	-
105 CHRISTIAN REF.	1	40	105	-	0.1
165 CH OF NAZARENE	2	142	305	0.1	0.3
193 EPISCOPAL.....	21	4,725	8,646	3.9	8.8
226 FRIENDS-USA...	3	345	426*	0.2	0.4
281 LUTH CH AMER..	6	2,273	3,202	1.4	3.3
283 LUTH--MO SYNOD	3	762	1,169	0.5	1.2
371 REF CH IN AM..	8	5,111	4,531	2.0	4.6
403 SALVATION ARMY	2	100	474	0.2	0.5
413 S-D ADVENTISTS	2	190	235*	0.1	0.2
419 SO BAPT CONV..	1	321	396*	0.2	0.4
435 UNITARIAN-UNIV	1	175	295	0.1	0.3
443 UN C OF CHRIST	2	634	783*	0.4	0.8
449 UN METHODIST..	26	6,638	6,700	3.0	6.8
453 UN PRES CH USA	14	3,939	4,864*	2.2	5.0
ERIE	498	124,906	686,561*	61.7	100.0
019 AMER BAPT CONV	32	6,170	7,523*	0.7	1.1
029 AMER LUTH CH..	12	3,250	4,577	0.4	0.7
075 BRETHREN IN CR	1	122	149*	-	-
081 CATHOLIC......	158	0	524,556	47.1	76.4
093 CR CH (DISC)..	9	1,353	1,650*	0.1	0.2
097 CR C AND C CR.	4	430	524*	-	0.1
123 CH GOD (ANDER)	2	187	307	-	-
127 CH GOD (CLEVE)	2	62	76*	-	-
165 CH OF NAZARENE	3	235	576	0.1	0.1
193 EPISCOPAL.....	34	16,025	22,298	2.0	3.2
201 EVAN COV CH AM	1	139	169*	-	-
221 FREE METH C NA	7	335	482	-	0.1
226 FRIENDS-USA...	3	234	285*	-	-
281 LUTH CH AMER..	29	14,460	20,138	1.8	2.9
283 LUTH--MO SYNOD	30	11,290	15,982	1.4	2.3
285 MENNONITE CH..	3	391	477*	-	0.1
313 NO AM BAPT GC.	3	557	679*	0.1	0.1
353 PLY BRETHREN..	2	85	195	-	-
371 REF CH IN AM..	2	225	284	-	-
403 SALVATION ARMY	4	238	1,861	0.2	0.3
413 S-D ADVENTISTS	2	773	942*	0.1	0.1
415 S-D BAPTIST GC	1	14	17*	-	-
419 SO BAPT CONV..	6	525	640*	0.1	0.1
435 UNITARIAN-UNIV	4	871	1,030	0.1	0.2
443 UN C OF CHRIST	47	17,545	21,391*	1.9	3.1
449 UN METHODIST..	53	24,882	29,873	2.7	4.4
453 UN PRES CH USA	44	24,508	29,880*	2.7	4.4
ESSEX	66	7,118	20,607*	59.5	100.0
019 AMER BAPT CONV	5	870	1,074*	3.1	5.2
081 CATHOLIC......	18	0	12,297	35.5	59.7
165 CH OF NAZARENE	3	194	368	1.1	1.8
193 EPISCOPAL.....	8	625	1,099	3.2	5.3
413 S-D ADVENTISTS	1	8	10*	-	-
443 UN C OF CHRIST	9	958	1,183*	3.4	5.7
449 UN METHODIST..	19	4,189	4,238	12.2	20.6
453 UN PRES CH USA	3	274	338*	1.0	1.6
FRANKLIN	71	5,311	34,139*	77.7	100.0
019 AMER BAPT CONV	2	150	188*	0.4	0.6
081 CATHOLIC......	26	0	27,082	61.6	79.3
165 CH OF NAZARENE	2	64	175	0.4	0.5
193 EPISCOPAL.....	4	514	800	1.8	2.3
221 FREE METH C NA	2	18	21	-	0.1
413 S-D ADVENTISTS	3	74	93*	0.2	0.3
419 SO BAPT CONV..	1	158	198*	0.5	0.6
435 UNITARIAN-UNIV	1	24	24	0.1	0.1
443 UN C OF CHRIST	2	332	415*	0.9	1.2
449 UN METHODIST..	20	2,983	3,900	8.9	11.4
453 UN PRES CH USA	8	994	1,243*	2.8	3.6
FULTON	46	11,167	29,121*	55.3	100.0
019 AMER BAPT CONV	3	792	958*	1.8	3.3
081 CATHOLIC......	11	0	15,652	29.7	53.7
093 CR CH (DISC)..	1	38	46*	0.1	0.2
193 EPISCOPAL.....	2	583	1,047	2.0	3.6
221 FREE METH C NA	1	35	62	0.1	0.2
226 FRIENDS-USA...	1	5	6*	-	-
281 LUTH CH AMER..	3	1,309	2,013	3.8	6.9
371 REF CH IN AM..	1	428	550	1.0	1.9
381 REF PRES-EVAN.	1	85	100	0.2	0.3
403 SALVATION ARMY	1	95	378	0.7	1.3
413 S-D ADVENTISTS	1	14	17*	-	0.1
443 UN C OF CHRIST	1	132	160*	0.3	0.5
449 UN METHODIST..	13	5,892	6,005	11.4	20.6
453 UN PRES CH USA	6	1,759	2,127*	4.0	7.3
GENESEE	65	11,874	34,012*	57.9	100.0
019 AMER BAPT CONV	12	2,376	2,966*	5.1	8.7
081 CATHOLIC......	16	0	18,590	31.7	54.7
093 CR CH (DISC)..	1	127	159*	0.3	0.5
193 EPISCOPAL.....	4	1,327	1,709	2.9	5.0
221 FREE METH C NA	1	80	100	0.2	0.3
283 LUTH--MO SYNOD	1	551	767	1.3	2.3
403 SALVATION ARMY	1	50	334	0.6	1.0
413 S-D ADVENTISTS	1	35	44*	0.1	0.1
435 UNITARIAN-UNIV	1	23	37	0.1	0.1
443 UN C OF CHRIST	2	246	307*	0.5	0.9
449 UN METHODIST..	13	3,311	4,321	7.4	12.7
453 UN PRES CH USA	12	3,748	4,678*	8.0	13.8
GREENE	71	6,954	16,927*	51.1	100.0

*Total adherents estimated from known number of communicant, confirmed, full members.

—Represents a percent less than 0.1.

Percentages may not total due to rounding.

Table 3. Churches and Church Membership by State, County and Denomination: 1971

County and Denomination	Number of churches	Communicant, confirmed, full members	Total adherents		
			Number	Percent of total population	Percent of total adherents
019 AMER BAPT CONV	4	382	457*	1.4	2.7
081 CATHOLIC......	15	0	8,555	25.8	50.5
193 EPISCOPAL.....	6	558	1,030	3.1	6.1
221 FREE METH C NA	1	50	77	0.2	0.5
281 LUTH CH AMER..	1	468	602	1.8	3.6
283 LUTH--MO SYNOD	2	358	571	1.7	3.4
371 REF CH IN AM..	7	1,174	1,479	4.5	8.7
443 UN C OF CHRIST	2	244	292*	0.9	1.7
449 UN METHODIST..	30	3,509	3,612	10.9	21.3
453 UN PRES CH USA	3	211	252*	0.8	1.5
HAMILTON	16	758	2,795*	59.3	100.0
081 CATHOLIC......	7	0	1,972	41.8	70.6
193 EPISCOPAL.....	1	62	103	2.2	3.7
449 UN METHODIST..	7	659	675	14.3	24.2
453 UN PRES CH USA	1	37	45*	1.0	1.6
HERKIMER	76	12,991	40,842*	60.4	100.0
019 AMER BAPT CONV	11	2,128	2,601*	3.8	6.4
081 CATHOLIC......	17	0	23,644	35.0	57.9
175 CONG CR CH....	1	55	67*	0.1	0.2
193 EPISCOPAL.....	4	1,036	1,826	2.7	4.5
221 FREE METH C NA	1	45	64	0.1	0.2
281 LUTH CH AMER..	5	1,349	1,778	2.6	4.4
371 REF CH IN AM..	2	828	1,059	1.6	2.6
403 SALVATION ARMY	1	40	252	0.4	0.6
413 S-D ADVENTISTS	1	25	31*	-	0.1
435 UNITARIAN-UNIV	4	385	445	0.7	1.1
443 UN C OF CHRIST	1	152	186*	0.3	0.5
449 UN METHODIST..	23	5,220	6,777	10.0	16.6
453 UN PRES CH USA	5	1,728	2,112*	3.1	5.2
JEFFERSON	121	15,780	49,804*	56.3	100.0
019 AMER BAPT CONV	8	1,318	1,636*	1.8	3.3
081 CATHOLIC......	23	0	27,611	31.2	55.4
093 CR CH (DISC)..	3	180	223*	0.3	0.4
097 CR C AND C CR.	2	35	43*	-	0.1
165 CH OF NAZARENE	2	184	425	0.5	0.9
193 EPISCOPAL.....	16	2,601	4,374	4.9	8.8
221 FREE METH C NA	2	75	92	0.1	0.2
281 LUTH CH AMER..	3	356	510	0.6	1.0
285 MENNONITE CH..	2	63	78*	0.1	0.2
371 REF CH IN AM..	1	282	347	0.4	0.7
403 SALVATION ARMY	1	77	372	0.4	0.7
413 S-D ADVENTISTS	2	77	96*	0.1	0.2
415 S-D BAPTIST GC	1	59	73*	0.1	0.1
419 SO BAPT CONV..	1	86	107*	0.1	0.2
435 UNITARIAN-UNIV	3	294	349	0.4	0.7
443 UN C OF CHRIST	5	1,038	1,288*	1.5	2.6
449 UN METHODIST..	36	6,986	9,612	10.9	19.3
453 UN PRES CH USA	10	2,069	2,568*	2.9	5.2
KINGS	429	87,328	979,652*	37.6	100.0
019 AMER BAPT CONV	38	17,439	21,168*	0.8	2.2
029 AMER LUTH CH..	5	2,021	3,039	0.1	0.3
075 BRETHREN IN CR	1	7	8*	-	-
081 CATHOLIC......	137	0	871,098	33.5	88.9
093 CR CH (DISC)..	11	2,770	3,362*	0.1	0.3
097 CR C AND C CR.	1	32	39*	-	-
123 CH GOD (ANDER)	7	473	1,060	-	0.1
127 CH GOD (CLEVE)	6	193	234*	-	-
157 CH OF BRETHREN	1	70	85*	-	-
175 CONG CR CH....	5	3,583	4,349*	0.2	0.4
193 EPISCOPAL.....	36	13,634	16,911	0.6	1.7
201 EVAN COV CH AM	1	141	171*	-	-
221 FREE METH C NA	2	63	65	-	-
281 LUTH CH AMER..	32	7,559	10,555	0.4	1.1
283 LUTH--MO SYNOD	11	2,767	3,920	0.2	0.4
285 MENNONITE CH..	1	30	36*	-	-
293 MORAV CH-NORTH	1	219	357	-	-
315 NO AM OLD RC..	6	3,951	4,796*	0.2	0.5
353 PLY BRETHREN..	6	370	555	-	0.1
371 REF CH IN AM..	16	4,528	5,280	0.2	0.5
403 SALVATION ARMY	5	392	2,225	0.1	0.2
413 S-D ADVENTISTS	14	4,944	6,001*	0.2	0.6
419 SO BAPT CONV..	8	899	1,091*	-	0.1
435 UNITARIAN-UNIV	3	828	978	-	0.1
443 UN C OF CHRIST	8	1,264	1,534*	0.1	0.2
449 UN METHODIST..	28	12,141	12,226	0.5	1.2
453 UN PRES CH USA	39	7,010	8,509*	0.3	0.9
LEWIS	48	4,192	14,957*	63.3	100.0
019 AMER BAPT CONV	2	68	86*	0.4	0.6
081 CATHOLIC......	17	0	9,452	40.0	63.2
093 CR CH (DISC)..	2	118	150*	0.6	1.0
165 CH OF NAZARENE	1	88	219	0.9	1.5
193 EPISCOPAL.....	4	410	603	2.6	4.0
285 MENNONITE CH..	5	999	1,266*	5.4	8.5
413 S-D ADVENTISTS	1	20	25*	0.1	0.2
443 UN C OF CHRIST	3	176	223*	0.9	1.5
449 UN METHODIST..	11	1,681	2,132	9.0	14.3
453 UN PRES CH USA	2	632	801*	3.4	5.4
LIVINGSTON	69	7,367	22,372*	41.4	100.0
019 AMER BAPT CONV	3	175	215*	0.4	1.0
081 CATHOLIC......	15	0	12,300	22.8	55.0
123 CH GOD (ANDER)	1	25	60	0.1	0.3
127 CH GOD (CLEVE)	2	31	38*	0.1	0.2
193 EPISCOPAL.....	5	729	1,663	3.1	7.4
221 FREE METH C NA	1	50	62	0.1	0.3
281 LUTH CH AMER..	1	344	538	1.0	2.4
283 LUTH--MO SYNOD	1	181	283	0.5	1.3
353 PLY BRETHREN..	1	20	30	0.1	0.1
435 UNITARIAN-UNIV	1	20	20	-	0.1
443 UN C OF CHRIST	2	102	126*	0.2	0.6
449 UN METHODIST..	18	2,149	2,680	5.0	12.0
453 UN PRES CH USA	18	3,541	4,357*	8.1	19.5
MADISON	72	12,460	27,386*	43.6	100.0
019 AMER BAPT CONV	16	2,397	2,992*	4.8	10.9
081 CATHOLIC......	7	0	10,575	16.8	38.6
165 CH OF NAZARENE	1	48	145	0.2	0.5
193 EPISCOPAL.....	5	1,236	2,420	3.8	8.8
221 FREE METH C NA	2	72	118	0.2	0.4
226 FRIENDS-USA...	1	30	37*	0.1	0.1
283 LUTH--MO SYNOD	1	136	257	0.4	0.9
403 SALVATION ARMY	1	26	172	0.3	0.6
413 S-D ADVENTISTS	1	35	44*	0.1	0.2
415 S-D BAPTIST GC	2	79	99*	0.2	0.4
443 UN C OF CHRIST	4	363	453*	0.7	1.7
449 UN METHODIST..	25	5,848	7,340	11.7	26.8
453 UN PRES CH USA	6	2,190	2,734*	4.3	10.0
MONROE	301	94,286	350,311*	49.2	100.0
019 AMER BAPT CONV	35	13,039	16,099*	2.3	4.6
029 AMER LUTH CH..	4	1,065	1,565	0.2	0.4
081 CATHOLIC......	75	0	225,767	31.7	64.4
093 CR CH (DISC)..	2	171	211*	-	0.1
097 CR C AND C CR.	2	56	69*	-	-
105 CHRISTIAN REF.	2	330	598	0.1	0.2
123 CH GOD (ANDER)	1	70	230	-	0.1
127 CH GOD (CLEVE)	6	264	326*	-	0.1
165 CH OF NAZARENE	4	622	1,301	0.2	0.4
193 EPISCOPAL.....	24	10,269	15,141	2.1	4.3
201 EVAN COV CH AM	1	192	237*	-	0.1
221 FREE METH C NA	7	957	1,264	0.2	0.4
226 FRIENDS-USA...	1	151	186*	-	0.1
281 LUTH CH AMER..	19	9,635	13,434	1.9	3.8
283 LUTH--MO SYNOD	13	5,553	8,799	1.2	2.5
313 NO AM BAPT GC.	2	214	264*	-	0.1
335 ORTH PRESB CH.	2	251	355	-	0.1
353 PLY BRETHREN..	2	180	350	-	0.1
371 REF CH IN AM..	4	1,318	1,754	0.2	0.5
403 SALVATION ARMY	1	120	543	0.1	0.2
413 S-D ADVENTISTS	3	959	1,184*	0.2	0.3
419 SO BAPT CONV..	3	257	317*	-	0.1
435 UNITARIAN-UNIV	2	1,047	1,379	0.2	0.4
443 UN C OF CHRIST	16	6,948	8,578*	1.2	2.4
449 UN METHODIST..	34	15,561	19,423	2.7	5.5
453 UN PRES CH USA	36	25,057	30,937*	4.3	8.8
MONTGOMERY	64	10,905	36,242*	64.9	100.0
019 AMER BAPT CONV	1	226	268*	0.5	0.7
081 CATHOLIC......	13	0	22,575	40.4	62.3
193 EPISCOPAL.....	4	898	1,290	2.3	3.6
221 FREE METH C NA	1	23	44	0.1	0.1
281 LUTH CH AMER..	8	2,208	3,220	5.8	8.9
371 REF CH IN AM..	17	3,039	3,937	7.0	10.9
413 S-D ADVENTISTS	1	15	18*	-	-
435 UNITARIAN-UNIV	1	160	180	0.3	0.5
443 UN C OF CHRIST	1	90	107*	0.2	0.3
449 UN METHODIST..	13	2,915	3,025	5.4	8.3
453 UN PRES CH USA	4	1,331	1,578*	2.8	4.4
NASSAU	288	105,690	664,679*	46.5	100.0
019 AMER BAPT CONV	10	1,878	2,249*	0.2	0.3
029 AMER LUTH CH..	11	4,231	6,762	0.5	1.0
081 CATHOLIC......	66	0	528,898	37.0	79.6
097 CR C AND C CR.	4	160	192*	-	-
123 CH GOD (ANDER)	2	65	165	-	-
165 CH OF NAZARENE	5	378	659	-	0.1
193 EPISCOPAL.....	39	19,231	28,367	2.0	4.3
201 EVAN COV CH AM	1	129	154*	-	-
226 FRIENDS-USA...	4	1,129	1,352*	0.1	0.2
281 LUTH CH AMER..	23	14,615	20,537	1.4	3.1
283 LUTH--MO SYNOD	16	10,268	14,179	1.0	2.1
313 NO AM BAPT GC.	2	131	157*	-	-
335 ORTH PRESB CH.	1	96	161	-	-
353 PLY BRETHREN..	5	353	520	-	0.1
371 REF CH IN AM..	12	4,496	6,027	0.4	0.9
403 SALVATION ARMY	2	235	1,543	0.1	0.2
413 S-D ADVENTISTS	6	677	811*	0.1	0.1
419 SO BAPT CONV..	2	550	659*	-	0.1
435 UNITARIAN-UNIV	5	1,024	1,469	0.1	0.2
443 UN C OF CHRIST	9	7,047	8,439*	0.6	1.3
449 UN METHODIST..	40	27,285	27,353	1.9	4.1
453 UN PRES CH USA	23	11,712	14,026*	1.0	2.1
NEW YORK	390	88,968	598,460*	38.9	100.0
019 AMER BAPT CONV	35	1,055	1,198*	0.1	0.2
029 AMER LUTH CH..	1	69	97	-	-
081 CATHOLIC......	118	0	485,472	31.5	81.1
093 CR CH (DISC)..	5	924	1,049*	0.1	0.2
097 CR C AND C CR.	2	52	59*	-	-
105 CHRISTIAN REF.	1	40	85	-	-
123 CH GOD (ANDER)	5	517	869	0.1	0.1
127 CH GOD (CLEVE)	19	808	917*	0.1	0.2
165 CH OF NAZARENE	9	640	1,576	0.1	0.3
193 EPISCOPAL.....	42	20,828	31,928	2.1	5.3

*Total adherents estimated from known number of communicant, confirmed, full members.

—Represents a percent less than 0.1.

Percentages may not total due to rounding.

Table 3. Churches and Church Membership by State, County and Denomination: 1971

County and Denomination	Number of churches	Communicant, confirmed, full members	Total adherents: Number	Total adherents: Percent of total population	Total adherents: Percent of total adherents
221 FREE METH C NA	1	12	12	-	-
226 FRIENDS-USA...	5	1,113	1,264*	0.1	0.2
281 LUTH CH AMER..	14	3,871	5,401	0.4	0.9
283 LUTH--MO SYNOD	7	2,156	4,493	0.3	0.8
285 MENNONITE CH..	1	24	27*	-	-
293 MORAV CH-NORTH	2	684	846	0.1	0.1
315 NO AM OLD RC..	15	9,765	11,087*	0.7	1.9
353 PLY BRETHREN..	5	240	430	-	0.1
371 REF CH IN AM..	5	7,305	7,867	0.5	1.3
403 SALVATION ARMY	7	555	2,375	0.2	0.4
413 S-D ADVENTISTS	13	4,305	4,888*	0.3	0.8
419 SO BAPT CONV..	5	661	750*	-	0.1
435 UNITARIAN-UNIV	4	2,040	2,216	0.1	0.4
443 UN C OF CHRIST	11	3,504	3,978*	0.3	0.7
449 UN METHODIST..	24	15,092	15,148	1.0	2.5
453 UN PRES CH USA	34	12,708	14,428*	0.9	2.4
NIAGARA	170	43,113	145,369*	61.7	100.0
019 AMER BAPT CONV	11	2,229	2,736*	1.2	1.9
029 AMER LUTH CH..	8	2,450	3,376	1.4	2.3
081 CATHOLIC......	36	0	86,748	36.8	59.7
093 CR CH (DISC)..	2	811	995*	0.4	0.7
123 CH GOD (ANDER)	1	125	285	0.1	0.2
127 CH GOD (CLEVE)	1	57	70*	-	-
165 CH OF NAZARENE	1	113	367	0.2	0.3
193 EPISCOPAL.....	13	4,923	7,252	3.1	5.0
221 FREE METH C NA	7	326	438	0.2	0.3
226 FRIENDS-USA...	1	55	68*	-	-
281 LUTH CH AMER..	5	2,674	3,716	1.6	2.6
283 LUTH--MO SYNOD	20	8,863	12,243	5.2	8.4
315 NO AM OLD RC..	1	216	265*	0.1	0.2
353 PLY BRETHREN..	5	270	480	0.2	0.3
403 SALVATION ARMY	2	179	1,321	0.6	0.9
413 S-D ADVENTISTS	3	165	203*	0.1	0.1
419 SO BAPT CONV..	3	359	441*	0.2	0.3
435 UNITARIAN-UNIV	2	188	188	0.1	0.1
443 UN C OF CHRIST	11	2,982	3,660*	1.6	2.5
449 UN METHODIST..	23	9,049	11,829	5.0	8.1
453 UN PRES CH USA	14	7,079	8,688*	3.7	6.0
ONEIDA	203	36,414	147,799*	54.1	100.0
019 AMER BAPT CONV	17	3,309	4,063*	1.5	2.7
081 CATHOLIC......	49	0	95,645	35.0	64.7
123 CH GOD (ANDER)	5	316	642	0.2	0.4
127 CH GOD (CLEVE)	1	8	10*	-	-
165 CH OF NAZARENE	2	84	191	0.1	0.1
193 EPISCOPAL.....	20	5,569	9,577	3.5	6.5
221 FREE METH C NA	1	19	22	-	-
226 FRIENDS-USA...	2	32	39*	-	-
281 LUTH CH AMER..	4	1,960	2,753	1.0	1.9
283 LUTH--MO SYNOD	4	1,319	3,565	1.3	2.4
293 MORAV CH-NORTH	1	203	253	0.1	0.2
371 REF CH IN AM..	2	402	575	0.2	0.4
403 SALVATION ARMY	2	127	1,022	0.4	0.7
413 S-D ADVENTISTS	4	295	362*	0.1	0.2
415 S-D BAPTIST GC	1	103	126*	-	0.1
435 UNITARIAN-UNIV	2	195	249	0.1	0.2
443 UN C OF CHRIST	9	1,594	1,957*	0.7	1.3
449 UN METHODIST..	47	12,739	16,754	6.1	11.3
453 UN PRES CH USA	30	8,140	9,994*	3.7	6.8
ONONDAGA	233	68,295	341,930*	72.3	100.0
019 AMER BAPT CONV	20	6,172	7,635*	1.6	2.2
081 CATHOLIC......	55	0	253,645	53.7	74.2
093 CR CH (DISC)..	3	276	341*	0.1	0.1
097 CR C AND C CR.	4	175	216*	-	0.1
127 CH GOD (CLEVE)	1	6	7*	-	-
165 CH OF NAZARENE	3	294	598	0.1	0.2
193 EPISCOPAL.....	22	8,936	14,353	3.0	4.2
201 EVAN COV CH AM	1	62	77*	-	-
221 FREE METH C NA	2	96	113	-	-
226 FRIENDS-USA...	1	138	171*	-	0.1
281 LUTH CH AMER..	14	6,194	8,584	1.8	2.5
283 LUTH--MO SYNOD	2	388	669	0.1	0.2
315 NO AM OLD RC..	1	71	88*	-	-
371 REF CH IN AM..	2	693	931	0.2	0.3
403 SALVATION ARMY	1	136	1,303	0.3	0.4
413 S-D ADVENTISTS	4	635	785*	0.2	0.2
415 S-D BAPTIST GC	1	18	22*	-	-
419 SO BAPT CONV..	6	1,025	1,268*	0.3	0.4
435 UNITARIAN-UNIV	2	763	1,077	0.2	0.3
443 UN C OF CHRIST	9	2,293	2,836*	0.6	0.8
449 UN METHODIST..	54	30,109	35,070	7.4	10.3
453 UN PRES CH USA	25	9,815	12,141*	2.6	3.6
ONTARIO	69	15,908	42,507*	53.9	100.0
019 AMER BAPT CONV	9	2,120	2,633*	3.3	6.2
081 CATHOLIC......	12	0	21,300	27.0	50.1
097 CR C AND C CR.	2	60	75*	0.1	0.2
165 CH OF NAZARENE	1	70	103	0.1	0.2
193 EPISCOPAL.....	5	1,105	1,539	2.0	3.6
281 LUTH CH AMER..	1	191	316	0.4	0.7
283 LUTH--MO SYNOD	3	544	928	1.2	2.2
403 SALVATION ARMY	2	85	563	0.7	1.3
419 SO BAPT CONV..	1	63	78*	0.1	0.2
443 UN C OF CHRIST	7	1,805	2,242*	2.8	5.3
449 UN METHODIST..	17	5,983	7,908	10.0	18.6
453 UN PRES CH USA	9	3,882	4,822*	6.1	11.3
ORANGE	165	29,411	112,883*	50.9	100.0
019 AMER BAPT CONV	4	1,073	1,325*	0.6	1.2
081 CATHOLIC......	37	0	75,400	34.0	66.8
105 CHRISTIAN REF.	1	288	572	0.3	0.5
127 CH GOD (CLEVE)	2	52	64*	-	0.1
165 CH OF NAZARENE	2	73	322	0.1	0.3
193 EPISCOPAL.....	16	3,075	4,865	2.2	4.3
221 FREE METH C NA	1	12	16	-	-
226 FRIENDS-USA...	1	81	100*	-	0.1
281 LUTH CH AMER..	5	1,723	2,536	1.1	2.2
283 LUTH--MO SYNOD	5	1,018	1,636	0.7	1.4
371 REF CH IN AM..	12	3,567	4,619	2.1	4.1
381 REF PRES-EVAN.	1	94	107	-	0.1
403 SALVATION ARMY	3	124	886	0.4	0.8
413 S-D ADVENTISTS	4	376	464*	0.2	0.4
419 SO BAPT CONV..	1	272	336*	0.2	0.3
435 UNITARIAN-UNIV	2	162	207	0.1	0.2
443 UN C OF CHRIST	4	951	1,175*	0.5	1.0
449 UN METHODIST..	33	9,295	9,391	4.2	8.3
453 UN PRES CH USA	31	7,175	8,862*	4.0	7.9
ORLEANS	42	7,418	17,155*	46.0	100.0
019 AMER BAPT CONV	7	1,567	1,966*	5.3	11.5
029 AMER LUTH CH..	3	507	731	2.0	4.3
081 CATHOLIC......	6	0	7,430	19.9	43.3
193 EPISCOPAL.....	2	315	491	1.3	2.9
221 FREE METH C NA	1	42	53	0.1	0.3
281 LUTH CH AMER..	1	284	382	1.0	2.2
283 LUTH--MO SYNOD	1	287	384	1.0	2.2
435 UNITARIAN-UNIV	1	55	65	0.2	0.4
443 UN C OF CHRIST	1	100	125*	0.3	0.7
449 UN METHODIST..	14	2,595	3,438	9.2	20.0
453 UN PRES CH USA	5	1,666	2,090*	5.6	12.2
OSWEGO	102	15,873	39,922*	39.6	100.0
019 AMER BAPT CONV	10	1,361	1,707*	1.7	4.3
081 CATHOLIC......	19	0	18,043	17.9	45.2
097 CR C AND C CR.	1	95	119*	0.1	0.3
165 CH OF NAZARENE	2	120	358	0.4	0.9
193 EPISCOPAL.....	9	1,527	2,855	2.8	7.2
221 FREE METH C NA	1	29	45	-	0.1
226 FRIENDS-USA...	1	113	142*	0.1	0.4
281 LUTH CH AMER..	1	674	919	0.9	2.3
283 LUTH--MO SYNOD	1	89	143	0.1	0.4
403 SALVATION ARMY	2	115	573	0.6	1.4
413 S-D ADVENTISTS	3	195	245*	0.2	0.6
419 SO BAPT CONV..	1	184	231*	0.2	0.6
435 UNITARIAN-UNIV	1	91	136	0.1	0.3
443 UN C OF CHRIST	7	1,275	1,599*	1.6	4.0
449 UN METHODIST..	36	8,704	11,175	11.1	28.0
453 UN PRES CH USA	7	1,301	1,632*	1.6	4.1
OTSEGO	85	12,911	26,767*	47.6	100.0
019 AMER BAPT CONV	11	1,972	2,338*	4.2	8.7
081 CATHOLIC......	11	0	10,320	18.4	38.6
193 EPISCOPAL.....	9	1,561	2,217	3.9	8.3
226 FRIENDS-USA...	1	67	79	0.1	0.3
281 LUTH CH AMER..	4	710	997	1.8	3.7
403 SALVATION ARMY	1	43	234	0.4	0.9
435 UNITARIAN-UNIV	2	134	189	0.3	0.7
449 UN METHODIST..	33	5,[illegible]40	7,448	13.3	27.8
453 UN PRES CH USA	13	2,4[illegible]	2,945*	5.2	11.0
PUTNAM	28	4,813	23,970*	42.3	100.0
019 AMER BAPT CONV	3	552	714*	1.3	3.0
081 CATHOLIC......	6	0	17,300	30.5	72.2
193 EPISCOPAL.....	4	664	1,332	2.3	5.6
281 LUTH CH AMER..	1	564	943	1.7	3.9
283 LUTH--MO SYNOD	1	246	571	1.0	2.4
449 UN METHODIST..	8	1,749	1,767	3.1	7.4
453 UN PRES CH USA	5	1,038	1,343*	2.4	5.6
QUEENS	327	67,323	764,735*	38.5	100.0
019 AMER BAPT CONV	10	2,515	2,926*	0.1	0.4
029 AMER LUTH CH..	3	1,492	1,863	0.1	0.2
081 CATHOLIC......	101	0	674,528	34.0	88.2
093 CR CH (DISC)..	1	73	85*	-	-
097 CR C AND C CR.	1	40	47*	-	-
105 CHRISTIAN REF.	1	84	123	-	-
127 CH GOD (CLEVE)	4	134	156*	-	-
175 CONG CR CH....	2	650	756*	-	0.1
193 EPISCOPAL.....	35	12,722	19,702	1.0	2.6
281 LUTH CH AMER..	36	11,937	17,253	0.9	2.3
283 LUTH--MO SYNOD	27	9,114	14,173	0.7	1.9
313 NO AM BAPT GC.	2	541	629*	-	0.1
315 NO AM OLD RC..	3	561	653*	-	0.1
353 PLY BRETHREN..	1	30	50	-	-
371 REF CH IN AM..	19	3,531	4,333	0.2	0.6
403 SALVATION ARMY	3	132	1,250	0.1	0.2
413 S-D ADVENTISTS	7	1,773	2,063*	0.1	0.3
419 SO BAPT CONV..	3	677	788*	-	0.1
435 UNITARIAN-UNIV	2	366	434	-	0.1
443 UN C OF CHRIST	14	4,858	5,652*	0.3	0.7
449 UN METHODIST..	26	9,453	9,546	0.5	1.2
453 UN PRES CH USA	26	6,640	7,725*	0.4	1.0
RENSSELAER	122	21,477	86,594*	56.8	100.0
019 AMER BAPT CONV	10	1,942	2,365*	1.6	2.7
081 CATHOLIC......	29	0	60,096	39.4	69.4
093 CR CH (DISC)..	3	283	345*	0.2	0.4

*Total adherents estimated from known number of communicant, confirmed, full members.

—Represents a percent less than 0.1.

Percentages may not total due to rounding.

Table 3. Churches and Church Membership by State, County and Denomination: 1971

County and Denomination	Number of churches	Communicant, confirmed, full members	Total adherents: Number	Percent of total population	Percent of total adherents
123 CH GOD (ANDER)	1	25	47	-	0.1
193 EPISCOPAL.....	11	2,834	4,470	2.9	5.2
201 EVAN COV CH AM	1	41	50*	-	0.1
281 LUTH CH AMER..	9	1,694	2,478	1.6	2.9
283 LUTH--MO SYNOD	2	415	583	0.4	0.7
371 REF CH IN AM..	9	2,423	3,134	2.1	3.6
403 SALVATION ARMY	1	61	294	0.2	0.3
413 S-D ADVENTISTS	1	75	91*	0.1	0.1
415 S-D BAPTIST GC	1	59	72*	-	0.1
443 UN C OF CHRIST	6	746	908*	0.6	1.0
449 UN METHODIST..	27	7,708	7,800	5.1	9.0
453 UN PRES CH USA	11	3,171	3,861*	2.5	4.5
RICHMOND	97	17,587	158,788*	53.7	100.0
019 AMER BAPT CONV	2	360	447*	0.2	0.3
029 AMER LUTH CH..	3	1,335	2,031	0.7	1.3
081 CATHOLIC......	35	0	135,500	45.9	85.3
127 CH GOD (CLEVE)	1	13	16*	-	-
165 CH OF NAZARENE	2	72	113	-	0.1
193 EPISCOPAL.....	10	2,947	4,388	1.5	2.8
281 LUTH CH AMER..	5	2,939	3,890	1.3	2.4
283 LUTH--MO SYNOD	2	1,207	1,679	0.6	1.1
293 MORAV CH-NORTH	6	1,852	2,469	0.8	1.6
315 NO AM OLD RC..	1	171	212*	0.1	0.1
353 PLY BRETHREN..	1	25	65	-	-
371 REF CH IN AM..	5	968	1,270	0.4	0.8
403 SALVATION ARMY	2	67	384	0.1	0.2
413 S-D ADVENTISTS	2	177	220*	0.1	0.1
419 SO BAPT CONV..	1	76	94*	-	0.1
435 UNITARIAN-UNIV	1	134	234	0.1	0.1
443 UN C OF CHRIST	4	1,051	1,305*	0.4	0.8
449 UN METHODIST..	10	3,147	3,172	1.1	2.0
453 UN PRES CH USA	4	1,046	1,299*	0.4	0.8
ROCKLAND	76	15,612	83,507*	36.3	100.0
019 AMER BAPT CONV	1	214	273*	0.1	0.3
081 CATHOLIC......	19	0	63,300	27.5	75.8
105 CHRISTIAN REF.	1	64	123	0.1	0.1
165 CH OF NAZARENE	1	46	134	0.1	0.2
193 EPISCOPAL.....	11	3,224	4,721	2.1	5.7
226 FRIENDS-USA...	1	110	140*	0.1	0.2
281 LUTH CH AMER..	3	2,373	3,558	1.5	4.3
283 LUTH--MO SYNOD	2	417	632	0.3	0.8
371 REF CH IN AM..	6	1,684	2,098	0.9	2.5
413 S-D ADVENTISTS	3	371	473*	0.2	0.6
419 SO BAPT CONV..	1	51	65*	-	0.1
435 UNITARIAN-UNIV	1	182	232	0.1	0.3
443 UN C OF CHRIST	1	92	117*	0.1	0.1
449 UN METHODIST..	13	3,811	3,854	1.7	4.6
453 UN PRES CH USA	12	2,973	3,787*	1.6	4.5
ST LAWRENCE	129	14,830	64,227*	57.4	100.0
019 AMER BAPT CONV	5	669	822*	0.7	1.3
081 CATHOLIC......	31	0	43,128	38.5	67.1
165 CH OF NAZARENE	3	141	335	0.3	0.5
193 EPISCOPAL.....	10	1,747	3,224	2.9	5.0
221 FREE METH C NA	2	27	38	-	0.1
283 LUTH--MO SYNOD	2	148	222	0.2	0.3
335 ORTH PRESB CH.	1	50	74	0.1	0.1
403 SALVATION ARMY	2	42	804	0.7	1.3
413 S-D ADVENTISTS	2	89	109*	0.1	0.2
419 SO BAPT CONV..	1	243	298*	0.3	0.5
435 UNITARIAN-UNIV	1	160	205	0.2	0.3
443 UN C OF CHRIST	8	1,486	1,825*	1.6	2.8
449 UN METHODIST..	40	6,843	9,231	8.2	14.4
453 UN PRES CH USA	21	3,185	3,912*	3.5	6.1
SARATOGA	84	17,617	57,684*	47.4	100.0
019 AMER BAPT CONV	6	1,900	2,409*	2.0	4.2
059 BAPT MISS ASSN	1	26	33*	-	0.1
081 CATHOLIC......	17	0	36,676	30.1	63.6
165 CH OF NAZARENE	1	50	159	0.1	0.3
193 EPISCOPAL.....	8	2,890	4,149	3.4	7.2
221 FREE METH C NA	2	60	87	0.1	0.2
226 FRIENDS-USA...	2	120	152*	0.1	0.3
283 LUTH--MO SYNOD	1	368	535	0.4	0.9
371 REF CH IN AM..	4	775	1,154	0.9	2.0
381 REF PRES-EVAN.	1	23	41	-	0.1
403 SALVATION ARMY	2	41	235	0.2	0.4
413 S-D ADVENTISTS	1	58	74*	0.1	0.1
443 UN C OF CHRIST	1	35	44*	-	0.1
449 UN METHODIST..	27	9,137	9,230	7.6	16.0
453 UN PRES CH USA	10	2,134	2,706*	2.2	4.7
SCHENECTADY	94	28,006	115,232*	71.6	100.0
019 AMER BAPT CONV	8	2,087	2,515*	1.6	2.2
081 CATHOLIC......	23	0	79,800	49.6	69.3
093 CR CH (DISC)..	1	71	86*	0.1	0.1
165 CH OF NAZARENE	1	71	250	0.2	0.2
193 EPISCOPAL.....	6	3,325	5,114	3.2	4.4
226 FRIENDS-USA...	2	100	121*	0.1	0.1
281 LUTH CH AMER..	5	1,761	2,712	1.7	2.4
283 LUTH--MO SYNOD	4	1,729	2,413	1.5	2.1
335 ORTH PRESB CH.	1	137	195	0.1	0.2
353 PLY BRETHREN..	1	60	100	0.1	0.1
371 REF CH IN AM..	13	7,092	9,313	5.8	8.1
381 REF PRES-EVAN.	1	92	149	0.1	0.1
403 SALVATION ARMY	1	72	244	0.2	0.2
413 S-D ADVENTISTS	1	83	100*	0.1	0.1
419 SO BAPT CONV..	1	123	148*	0.1	0.1
435 UNITARIAN-UNIV	1	705	857	0.5	0.7
443 UN C OF CHRIST	2	273	329*	0.2	0.3
449 UN METHODIST..	15	7,697	7,740	4.8	6.7
453 UN PRES CH USA	7	2,528	3,046*	1.9	2.6
SCHOHARIE	57	6,517	10,565*	42.7	100.0
019 AMER BAPT CONV	2	210	254*	1.0	2.4
081 CATHOLIC......	6	0	2,970	12.0	28.1
193 EPISCOPAL.....	2	72	176	0.7	1.7
221 FREE METH C NA	1	10	12	-	0.1
281 LUTH CH AMER..	8	1,364	1,901	7.7	18.0
371 REF CH IN AM..	6	514	732	3.0	6.9
443 UN C OF CHRIST	2	46	56*	0.2	0.5
449 UN METHODIST..	25	3,841	3,908	15.8	37.0
453 UN PRES CH USA	5	460	556*	2.2	5.3
SCHUYLER	26	3,581	9,471*	56.6	100.0
019 AMER BAPT CONV	5	621	773*	4.6	8.2
081 CATHOLIC......	1	0	4,980	29.8	52.6
165 CH OF NAZARENE	1	24	77	0.5	0.8
193 EPISCOPAL.....	3	424	622	3.7	6.6
443 UN C OF CHRIST	1	59	73*	0.4	0.8
449 UN METHODIST..	11	1,752	2,073	12.4	21.9
453 UN PRES CH USA	4	701	873*	5.2	9.2
SENECA	32	5,064	14,835*	42.3	100.0
019 AMER BAPT CONV	3	130	157*	0.4	1.1
081 CATHOLIC......	4	0	7,803	22.2	52.6
127 CH GOD (CLEVE)	1	32	39*	0.1	0.3
165 CH OF NAZARENE	1	37	37	0.1	0.2
193 EPISCOPAL.....	4	861	1,858	5.3	12.5
281 LUTH CH AMER..	1	66	87	0.2	0.6
283 LUTH--MO SYNOD	2	230	377	1.1	2.5
371 REF CH IN AM..	2	467	555	1.6	3.7
443 UN C OF CHRIST	1	11	13*	-	0.1
449 UN METHODIST..	5	1,377	1,667	4.8	11.2
453 UN PRES CH USA	8	1,853	2,242*	6.4	15.1
STEUBEN	114	19,097	42,028*	42.2	100.0
019 AMER BAPT CONV	16	2,360	2,911*	2.9	6.9
081 CATHOLIC......	18	0	16,640	16.7	39.6
165 CH OF NAZARENE	2	134	311	0.3	0.7
193 EPISCOPAL.....	5	1,775	2,649	2.7	6.3
221 FREE METH C NA	2	52	56	0.1	0.1
281 LUTH CH AMER..	2	341	483	0.5	1.1
283 LUTH--MO SYNOD	2	253	330	0.3	0.8
285 MENNONITE CH..	2	106	131*	0.1	0.3
403 SALVATION ARMY	2	124	715	0.7	1.7
413 S-D ADVENTISTS	2	170	210*	0.2	0.5
435 UNITARIAN-UNIV	1	18	18	-	-
443 UN C OF CHRIST	5	858	1,058*	1.1	2.5
449 UN METHODIST..	38	8,537	11,128	11.2	26.5
453 UN PRES CH USA	17	4,369	5,388*	5.4	12.8
SUFFOLK	299	86,941	564,785*	50.2	100.0
019 AMER BAPT CONV	6	699	899*	0.1	0.2
029 AMER LUTH CH..	8	2,538	4,489	0.4	0.8
081 CATHOLIC......	72	0	441,223	39.2	78.1
097 CR C AND C CR.	5	331	426*	-	0.1
105 CHRISTIAN REF.	2	198	341	-	0.1
165 CH OF NAZARENE	5	316	969	0.1	0.2
193 EPISCOPAL.....	43	18,878	31,350	2.8	5.6
201 EVAN COV CH AM	1	82	106*	-	-
226 FRIENDS-USA...	2	98	126*	-	-
281 LUTH CH AMER..	15	8,226	13,968	1.2	2.5
283 LUTH--MO SYNOD	18	9,763	18,154	1.6	3.2
353 PLY BRETHREN..	4	180	280	-	-
371 REF CH IN AM..	3	753	1,051	0.1	0.2
403 SALVATION ARMY	1	50	203	-	-
413 S-D ADVENTISTS	6	734	944*	0.1	0.2
419 SO BAPT CONV..	4	831	1,069*	0.1	0.2
435 UNITARIAN-UNIV	6	658	923	0.1	0.2
443 UN C OF CHRIST	14	3,237	4,165*	0.4	0.7
449 UN METHODIST..	45	23,436	23,597	2.1	4.2
453 UN PRES CH USA	39	15,933	20,502*	1.8	3.6
SULLIVAN	85	6,501	13,407*	25.5	100.0
019 AMER BAPT CONV	1	51	61*	0.1	0.5
081 CATHOLIC......	24	0	5,800	11.0	43.3
123 CH GOD (ANDER)	1	35	63	0.1	0.5
193 EPISCOPAL.....	4	265	470	0.9	3.5
221 FREE METH C NA	3	48	55	0.1	0.4
226 FRIENDS-USA...	1	29	35*	0.1	0.3
281 LUTH CH AMER..	4	483	736	1.4	5.5
353 PLY BRETHREN..	1	20	40	0.1	0.3
371 REF CH IN AM..	6	449	536	1.0	4.0
443 UN C OF CHRIST	1	144	172*	0.3	1.3
449 UN METHODIST..	30	3,425	3,582	6.8	26.7
453 UN PRES CH USA	9	1,552	1,857*	3.5	13.9
TIOGA	46	9,846	16,641*	35.8	100.0
019 AMER BAPT CONV	3	1,095	1,414*	3.0	8.5
081 CATHOLIC......	4	0	3,408	7.3	20.5
165 CH OF NAZARENE	2	151	487	1.0	2.9
193 EPISCOPAL.....	3	745	1,142	2.5	6.9
281 LUTH CH AMER..	1	142	214	0.5	1.3
283 LUTH--MO SYNOD	1	309	473	1.0	2.8
413 S-D ADVENTISTS	1	38	49*	0.1	0.3

*Total adherents estimated from known number of communicant, confirmed, full members.

—Represents a percent less than 0.1.

Percentages may not total due to rounding.

Table 3. Churches and Church Membership by State, County and Denomination: 1971

County and Denomination	Number of churches	Communicant, confirmed, full members	Total adherents: Number	Percent of total population	Percent of total adherents
443 UN C OF CHRIST	4	498	643*	1.4	3.9
449 UN METHODIST..	23	5,713	7,319	15.7	44.0
453 UN PRES CH USA	4	1,155	1,492*	3.2	9.0
TOMPKINS	57	10,675	26,081*	33.9	100.0
019 AMER BAPT CONV	7	877	1,040*	1.4	4.0
081 CATHOLIC......	6	0	12,268	16.0	47.0
165 CH OF NAZARENE	2	62	170	0.2	0.7
193 EPISCOPAL.....	5	823	1,871	2.4	7.2
226 FRIENDS-USA...	2	150	178*	0.2	0.7
281 LUTH CH AMER..	1	455	647	0.8	2.5
283 LUTH--MO SYNOD	1	162	245	0.3	0.9
403 SALVATION ARMY	1	45	376	0.5	1.4
413 S-D ADVENTISTS	7	56	66*	0.1	0.3
435 UNITARIAN-UNIV	1	250	352	0.5	1.3
443 UN C OF CHRIST	6	1,180	1,399*	1.8	5.4
449 UN METHODIST..	15	4,380	4,819	6.3	18.5
453 UN PRES CH USA	3	2,235	2,650*	3.4	10.2
ULSTER	137	19,622	58,406*	41.4	100.0
019 AMER BAPT CONV	2	396	484*	0.3	0.8
081 CATHOLIC......	36	0	34,100	24.1	58.4
165 CH OF NAZARENE	2	171	305	0.2	0.5
175 CONG CR CH....	2	216	264*	0.2	0.5
193 EPISCOPAL.....	9	1,233	2,054	1.5	3.5
221 FREE METH C NA	2	18	21	-	-
226 FRIENDS-USA...	3	190	232*	0.2	0.4
281 LUTH CH AMER..	9	2,683	3,920	2.8	6.7
283 LUTH--MO SYNOD	1	430	570	0.4	1.0
353 PLY BRETHREN..	1	10	10	-	-
371 REF CH IN AM..	22	5,849	7,411	5.2	12.7
403 SALVATION ARMY	1	42	180	0.1	0.3
413 S-D ADVENTISTS	3	192	235*	0.2	0.4
419 SO BAPT CONV..	1	76	93*	0.1	0.2
435 UNITARIAN-UNIV	1	54	96	0.1	0.2
443 UN C OF CHRIST	1	70	86*	0.1	0.1
449 UN METHODIST..	37	7,079	7,229	5.1	12.4
453 UN PRES CH USA	4	913	1,116*	0.8	1.9
WARREN	67	8,723	21,720*	44.0	100.0
019 AMER BAPT CONV	7	829	1,035*	2.1	4.8
081 CATHOLIC......	22	0	10,685	21.6	49.2
127 CH GOD (CLEVE)	1	62	77*	0.2	0.4
193 EPISCOPAL.....	10	1,378	2,448	5.0	11.3
221 FREE METH C NA	2	46	67	0.1	0.3
226 FRIENDS-USA...	1	53	66*	0.1	0.3
283 LUTH--MO SYNOD	1	237	325	0.7	1.5
403 SALVATION ARMY	1	65	277	0.6	1.3
413 S-D ADVENTISTS	1	11	14*	-	0.1
435 UNITARIAN-UNIV	1	32	48	0.1	0.2
449 UN METHODIST..	14	3,567	3,629	7.3	16.7
453 UN PRES CH USA	6	2,443	3,049*	6.2	14.0
WASHINGTON	77	10,341	26,366*	50.0	100.0
019 AMER BAPT CONV	13	1,854	2,325*	4.4	8.8
081 CATHOLIC......	14	0	14,238	27.0	54.0
193 EPISCOPAL.....	8	920	1,429	2.7	5.4
226 FRIENDS-USA...	1	41	51*	0.1	0.2
285 MENNONITE CH..	1	4	5*	-	-
371 REF CH IN AM..	1	109	144	0.3	0.5
413 S-D ADVENTISTS	2	189	237*	0.4	0.9
443 UN C OF CHRIST	1	47	59*	0.1	0.2
449 UN METHODIST..	20	4,763	4,850	9.2	18.4
453 UN PRES CH USA	16	2,414	3,028*	5.7	11.5
WAYNE	94	18,141	30,558*	38.5	100.0
019 AMER BAPT CONV	14	2,527	3,172*	4.0	10.4
081 CATHOLIC......	10	0	6,914	8.7	22.6
093 CR CH (DISC)..	1	86	108*	0.1	0.4
105 CHRISTIAN REF.	1	160	286	0.4	0.9
123 CH GOD (ANDER)	2	28	68	0.1	0.2
127 CH GOD (CLEVE)	1	20	25*	-	0.1
193 EPISCOPAL.....	7	1,039	1,698	2.1	5.6
221 FREE METH C NA	4	133	153	0.2	0.5
226 FRIENDS-USA...	1	251	315*	0.4	1.0
281 LUTH CH AMER..	2	722	1,151	1.4	3.8
283 LUTH--MO SYNOD	2	257	381	0.5	1.2
353 PLY BRETHREN..	1	30	50	0.1	0.2
371 REF CH IN AM..	8	1,700	2,398	3.0	7.8
413 S-D ADVENTISTS	1	85	107*	0.1	0.4
443 UN C OF CHRIST	2	289	363*	0.5	1.2
449 UN METHODIST..	24	7,276	8,927	11.2	29.2
453 UN PRES CH USA	13	3,538	4,442*	5.6	14.5
WESTCHESTER	325	82,977	485,283*	54.3	100.0
019 AMER BAPT CONV	17	5,246	6,275*	0.7	1.3
029 AMER LUTH CH..	4	993	1,730	0.2	0.4
081 CATHOLIC......	99	0	377,330	42.2	77.8
123 CH GOD (ANDER)	1	40	95	-	-
165 CH OF NAZARENE	1	59	190	-	-
193 EPISCOPAL.....	55	16,976	28,194	3.2	5.8
201 EVAN COV CH AM	1	107	128*	-	-
226 FRIENDS-USA...	4	675	807*	0.1	0.2
281 LUTH CH AMER..	18	7,102	9,645	1.1	2.0
283 LUTH--MO SYNOD	13	3,599	5,464	0.6	1.1
353 PLY BRETHREN..	3	242	342	-	0.1
371 REF CH IN AM..	11	6,474	7,369	0.8	1.5
403 SALVATION ARMY	7	131	1,124	0.1	0.2
413 S-D ADVENTISTS	7	972	1,163*	0.1	0.2

County and Denomination	Number of churches	Communicant, confirmed, full members	Total adherents: Number	Percent of total population	Percent of total adherents
419 SO BAPT CONV..	1	98	117*	-	-
435 UNITARIAN-UNIV	5	1,046	1,461	0.2	0.3
443 UN C OF CHRIST	11	5,203	6,223*	0.7	1.3
449 UN METHODIST..	36	16,304	16,444	1.8	3.4
453 UN PRES CH USA	31	17,710	21,182*	2.4	4.4
WYOMING	58	5,720	18,311*	48.6	100.0
019 AMER BAPT CONV	6	456	563*	1.5	3.1
081 CATHOLIC......	16	0	11,100	29.5	60.6
127 CH GOD (CLEVE)	1	19	23*	0.1	0.1
193 EPISCOPAL.....	3	418	528	1.4	2.9
221 FREE METH C NA	2	46	63	0.2	0.3
283 LUTH--MO SYNOD	2	170	252	0.7	1.4
313 NO AM BAPT GC.	1	48	59*	0.2	0.3
413 S-D ADVENTISTS	1	21	26*	0.1	0.1
443 UN C OF CHRIST	8	1,489	1,840*	4.9	10.0
449 UN METHODIST..	13	2,008	2,566	6.8	14.0
453 UN PRES CH USA	5	1,045	1,291*	3.4	7.1
YATES	38	5,740	8,994*	45.4	100.0
019 AMER BAPT CONV	8	1,156	1,405*	7.1	15.6
029 AMER LUTH CH..	1	257	369	1.9	4.1
081 CATHOLIC......	3	0	1,943	9.8	21.6
165 CH OF NAZARENE	1	21	70	0.4	0.8
193 EPISCOPAL.....	2	198	392	2.0	4.4
281 LUTH CH AMER..	1	192	259	1.3	2.9
403 SALVATION ARMY	1	39	133	0.7	1.5
413 S-D ADVENTISTS	1	72	87*	0.4	1.0
443 UN C OF CHRIST	2	105	128*	0.6	1.4
449 UN METHODIST..	13	2,947	3,293	16.6	36.6
453 UN PRES CH USA	5	753	915*	4.6	10.2
CO DATA NOT AVAIL	134	5,161	22,349	N/A	N/A
151 L-D SAINTS....	0	0	15,972	N/A	N/A
193 EPISCOPAL.....	3	84	124	N/A	N/A
467 WESLEYAN......	131	5,077	6,253	N/A	N/A

NORTH CAROLINA

County and Denomination	Number of churches	Communicant, confirmed, full members	Total adherents: Number	Percent of total population	Percent of total adherents
THE STATE.....	8,985	2,053,652	2,578,641*	50.7	100.0
ALAMANCE	146	44,999	54,902*	57.0	100.0
055 AS REF PRES CH	8	3,207	3,894*	4.0	7.1
059 BAPT MISS ASSN	1	165	200*	0.2	0.4
081 CATHOLIC......	1	0	1,320	1.4	2.4
093 CR CH (DISC)..	1	116	141*	0.1	0.3
097 CR C AND C CR.	1	18	22*	-	-
127 CH GOD (CLEVE)	6	333	404*	0.4	0.7
165 CH OF NAZARENE	3	406	803	0.8	1.5
193 EPISCOPAL.....	3	459	563	0.6	1.0
226 FRIENDS-USA...	6	659	800*	0.8	1.5
281 LUTH CH AMER..	6	1,558	2,078	2.2	3.8
283 LUTH--MO SYNOD	1	62	91	0.1	0.2
349 PENT HOLINESS.	3	341	414*	0.4	0.8
357 PRESB CH US...	13	5,374	6,525*	6.8	11.9
403 SALVATION ARMY	1	84	394	0.4	0.7
413 S-D ADVENTISTS	2	135	164*	0.2	0.3
419 SO BAPT CONV..	28	12,748	15,479*	16.1	28.2
443 UN C OF CHRIST	32	6,874	8,347*	8.7	15.2
449 UN METHODIST..	29	12,388	13,176	13.7	24.0
453 UN PRES CH USA	1	72	87*	0.1	0.2
ALEXANDER	56	12,704	15,583*	80.1	100.0
029 AMER LUTH CH..	1	146	191	1.0	1.2
055 AS REF PRES CH	2	369	456*	2.3	2.9
127 CH GOD (CLEVE)	1	66	82*	0.4	0.5
281 LUTH CH AMER..	3	908	1,278	6.6	8.2
283 LUTH--MO SYNOD	2	262	333	1.7	2.1
357 PRESB CH US...	2	203	251*	1.3	1.6
419 SO BAPT CONV..	34	8,902	11,012*	56.6	70.7
449 UN METHODIST..	11	1,848	1,980	10.2	12.7
ALLEGHANY	24	2,376	2,769*	34.0	100.0
081 CATHOLIC......	1	0	14	0.2	0.5
157 CH OF BRETHREN	3	306	365*	4.5	13.2
349 PENT HOLINESS.	1	8	10*	0.1	0.4
357 PRESB CH US...	2	132	157*	1.9	5.7
419 SO BAPT CONV..	11	1,334	1,590*	19.5	57.4
449 UN METHODIST..	6	596	633	7.8	22.9
ANSON	64	9,836	11,608*	49.4	100.0
081 CATHOLIC......	1	0	30	0.1	0.3
127 CH GOD (CLEVE)	1	85	105*	0.4	0.9
193 EPISCOPAL.....	2	195	282	1.2	2.4
349 PENT HOLINESS.	1	22	27*	0.1	0.2
357 PRESB CH US...	4	373	460*	2.0	4.0
419 SO BAPT CONV..	27	5,708	7,040*	30.0	60.6
449 UN METHODIST..	26	3,374	3,567	15.2	30.7
453 UN PRES CH USA	2	79	97*	0.4	0.8

*Total adherents estimated from known number of communicant, confirmed, full members.

—Represents a percent less than 0.1.

Percentages may not total due to rounding.

Table 3. Churches and Church Membership by State, County and Denomination: 1971

County and Denomination	Number of churches	Communicant, confirmed, full members	Total adherents: Number	Total adherents: Percent of total population	Total adherents: Percent of total adherents
ASHE	105	10,098	11,900*	60.8	100.0
081 CATHOLIC......	1	0	106	0.5	0.9
093 CR CH (DISC)..	2	119	144*	0.7	1.2
097 CR C AND C CR.	2	120	145*	0.7	1.2
127 CH GOD (CLEVE)	1	9	11*	0.1	0.1
157 CH OF BRETHREN	3	102	123*	0.6	1.0
193 EPISCOPAL.....	1	139	171	0.9	1.4
285 MENNONITE CH..	2	42	51*	0.3	0.4
357 PRESB CH US...	7	419	506*	2.6	4.3
413 S-D ADVENTISTS	1	22	27*	0.1	0.2
419 SO BAPT CONV..	58	6,913	8,340*	42.6	70.1
449 UN METHODIST..	27	2,213	2,276	11.6	19.1
AVERY	61	7,221	8,682*	68.6	100.0
093 CR CH (DISC)..	4	537	650*	5.1	7.5
097 CR C AND C CR.	3	445	539*	4.3	6.2
127 CH GOD (CLEVE)	1	44	53*	0.4	0.6
357 PRESB CH US...	8	671	813*	6.4	9.4
413 S-D ADVENTISTS	1	150	182*	1.4	2.1
419 SO BAPT CONV..	35	4,930	5,970*	47.2	68.8
449 UN METHODIST..	9	444	475	3.8	5.5
BEAUFORT	98	12,376	15,291*	42.5	100.0
081 CATHOLIC......	1	0	317	0.9	2.1
093 CR CH (DISC)..	32	3,286	4,001*	11.1	26.2
097 CR C AND C CR.	20	3,558	4,332*	12.0	28.3
105 CHRISTIAN REF.	1	86	170	0.5	1.1
127 CH GOD (CLEVE)	7	319	388*	1.1	2.5
285 MENNONITE CH..	1	28	34*	0.1	0.2
349 PENT HOLINESS.	10	314	382*	1.1	2.5
357 PRESB CH US...	3	428	521*	1.4	3.4
403 SALVATION ARMY	1	66	278	0.8	1.8
413 S-D ADVENTISTS	1	23	28*	0.1	0.2
419 SO BAPT CONV..	9	1,600	1,948*	5.4	12.7
449 UN METHODIST..	12	2,668	2,892	8.0	18.9
BERTIE	35	7,533	9,249*	45.1	100.0
093 CR CH (DISC)..	2	137	170*	0.8	1.8
349 PENT HOLINESS.	3	205	254*	1.2	2.7
419 SO BAPT CONV..	24	6,700	8,296*	40.4	89.7
449 UN METHODIST..	6	491	529	2.6	5.7
BLADEN	68	10,454	12,636*	47.7	100.0
081 CATHOLIC......	1	0	45	0.2	0.4
123 CH GOD (ANDER)	1	20	48	0.2	0.4
127 CH GOD (CLEVE)	2	73	90*	0.3	0.7
349 PENT HOLINESS.	3	104	128*	0.5	1.0
357 PRESB CH US...	8	972	1,196*	4.5	9.5
413 S-D ADVENTISTS	1	69	85*	0.3	0.7
419 SO BAPT CONV..	36	7,288	8,971*	33.9	71.0
449 UN METHODIST..	15	1,882	2,016	7.6	16.0
453 UN PRES CH USA	1	46	57*	0.2	0.5
BRUNSWICK	64	9,629	11,949*	49.3	100.0
081 CATHOLIC......	1	0	174	0.7	1.5
127 CH GOD (CLEVE)	3	268	336*	1.4	2.8
353 PLY BRETHREN..	1	40	80	0.3	0.7
357 PRESB CH US...	4	1,296	1,624*	6.7	13.6
413 S-D ADVENTISTS	1	137	172*	0.7	1.4
419 SO BAPT CONV..	43	6,043	7,573*	31.3	63.4
449 UN METHODIST..	11	1,845	1,990	8.2	16.7
BUNCOMBE	253	64,638	81,311*	56.1	100.0
019 AMER BAPT CONV	1	788	948*	0.7	1.2
081 CATHOLIC......	6	0	3,192	2.2	3.9
093 CR CH (DISC)..	10	662	796*	0.5	1.0
097 CR C AND C CR.	3	140	168*	0.1	0.2
123 CH GOD (ANDER)	3	57	167	0.1	0.2
127 CH GOD (CLEVE)	9	769	925*	0.6	1.1
165 CH OF NAZARENE	2	212	387	0.3	0.5
193 EPISCOPAL.....	12	2,456	3,512	2.4	4.3
221 FREE METH C NA	1	17	34	-	-
226 FRIENDS-USA...	1	15	18*	-	-
281 LUTH CH AMER..	2	474	600	0.4	0.7
283 LUTH--MO SYNOD	1	300	400	0.3	0.5
349 PENT HOLINESS.	4	63	76*	0.1	0.1
353 PLY BRETHREN..	1	40	70	-	0.1
357 PRESB CH US...	18	5,495	6,610*	4.6	8.1
403 SALVATION ARMY	1	123	641	0.4	0.8
413 S-D ADVENTISTS	4	698	840*	0.6	1.0
419 SO BAPT CONV..	111	37,869	45,550*	31.4	56.0
435 UNITARIAN-UNIV	1	225	300	0.2	0.4
443 UN C OF CHRIST	1	192	231*	0.2	0.3
449 UN METHODIST..	57	13,610	15,325	10.6	18.8
453 UN PRES CH USA	4	433	521*	0.4	0.6
BURKE	134	31,809	38,953*	64.5	100.0
081 CATHOLIC......	1	0	248	0.4	0.6
097 CR C AND C CR.	2	101	123*	0.2	0.3
123 CH GOD (ANDER)	2	279	819	1.4	2.1
127 CH GOD (CLEVE)	3	452	552*	0.9	1.4
193 EPISCOPAL.....	4	594	690	1.1	1.8
281 LUTH CH AMER..	2	522	668	1.1	1.7
349 PENT HOLINESS.	1	19	23*	-	0.1
357 PRESB CH US...	6	1,380	1,686*	2.8	4.3
413 S-D ADVENTISTS	3	232	283*	0.5	0.7
419 SO BAPT CONV..	78	22,145	27,056*	44.8	69.5
449 UN METHODIST..	31	6,054	6,767	11.2	17.4
453 UN PRES CH USA	1	31	38*	0.1	0.1
CABARRUS	156	40,024	49,613*	66.5	100.0
055 AS REF PRES CH	1	118	143*	0.2	0.3
081 CATHOLIC......	2	0	620	0.8	1.2
093 CR CH (DISC)..	4	403	488*	0.7	1.0
097 CR C AND C CR.	1	200	242*	0.3	0.5
123 CH GOD (ANDER)	2	185	388	0.5	0.8
127 CH GOD (CLEVE)	8	1,053	1,275*	1.7	2.6
165 CH OF NAZARENE	4	279	691	0.9	1.4
193 EPISCOPAL.....	1	243	400	0.5	0.8
281 LUTH CH AMER..	16	4,243	5,517	7.4	11.1
283 LUTH--MO SYNOD	2	324	585	0.8	1.2
349 PENT HOLINESS.	3	168	203*	0.3	0.4
357 PRESB CH US...	15	4,183	5,064*	6.8	10.2
381 REF PRES-EVAN.	1	62	62	0.1	0.1
403 SALVATION ARMY	1	53	220	0.3	0.4
419 SO BAPT CONV..	51	16,170	19,575*	26.2	39.5
443 UN C OF CHRIST	9	1,428	1,729*	2.3	3.5
449 UN METHODIST..	31	10,310	11,682	15.7	23.5
453 UN PRES CH USA	4	602	729*	1.0	1.5
CALDWELL	120	28,555	35,487*	62.6	100.0
081 CATHOLIC......	1	0	298	0.5	0.8
097 CR C AND C CR.	1	45	56*	0.1	0.2
121 CH GOD (ABR)..	1	75	94*	0.2	0.3
123 CH GOD (ANDER)	1	50	95	0.2	0.3
127 CH GOD (CLEVE)	5	417	523*	0.9	1.5
193 EPISCOPAL.....	2	282	311	0.5	0.9
281 LUTH CH AMER..	3	431	568	1.0	1.6
349 PENT HOLINESS.	3	139	174*	0.3	0.5
357 PRESB CH US...	4	835	1,048*	1.8	3.0
413 S-D ADVENTISTS	1	38	48*	0.1	0.1
419 SO BAPT CONV..	72	21,270	26,698*	47.1	75.2
443 UN C OF CHRIST	1	156	196*	0.3	0.6
449 UN METHODIST..	24	4,708	5,241	9.2	14.8
453 UN PRES CH USA	1	109	137*	0.2	0.4
CAMDEN	11	1,799	2,055*	37.7	100.0
093 CR CH (DISC)..	1	34	42*	0.8	2.0
097 CR C AND C CR.	1	20	25*	0.5	1.2
349 PENT HOLINESS.	1	25	31*	0.6	1.5
419 SO BAPT CONV..	3	978	1,215*	22.3	59.1
449 UN METHODIST..	5	742	742	13.6	36.1
CARTERET	54	10,873	13,171*	41.7	100.0
081 CATHOLIC......	2	0	393	1.2	3.0
093 CR CH (DISC)..	3	214	261*	0.8	2.0
127 CH GOD (CLEVE)	3	167	203*	0.6	1.5
193 EPISCOPAL.....	2	529	709	2.2	5.4
349 PENT HOLINESS.	5	387	471*	1.5	3.6
357 PRESB CH US...	2	384	468*	1.5	3.6
419 SO BAPT CONV..	12	3,920	4,774*	15.1	36.2
443 UN C OF CHRIST	2	68	83*	0.3	0.6
449 UN METHODIST..	23	5,204	5,809	18.4	44.1
CASWELL	41	4,726	5,513*	28.9	100.0
093 CR CH (DISC)..	1	90	112*	0.6	2.0
127 CH GOD (CLEVE)	1	108	134*	0.7	2.4
193 EPISCOPAL.....	2	14	14	0.1	0.3
349 PENT HOLINESS.	2	38	47*	0.2	0.9
357 PRESB CH US...	7	485	602*	3.2	10.9
413 S-D ADVENTISTS	1	189	234*	1.2	4.2
419 SO BAPT CONV..	11	1,682	2,087*	11.0	37.9
443 UN C OF CHRIST	1	120	149*	0.8	2.7
449 UN METHODIST..	15	2,000	2,134	11.2	38.7
CATAWBA	163	51,169	65,329*	71.9	100.0
029 AMER LUTH CH..	6	2,662	3,625	4.0	5.5
081 CATHOLIC......	1	0	741	0.8	1.1
123 CH GOD (ANDER)	2	120	363	0.4	0.6
127 CH GOD (CLEVE)	6	470	580*	0.6	0.9
193 EPISCOPAL.....	2	484	741	0.8	1.1
281 LUTH CH AMER..	23	8,276	10,844	11.9	16.6
283 LUTH--MO SYNOD	13	5,289	7,441	8.2	11.4
285 MENNONITE CH..	2	48	59*	0.1	0.1
349 PENT HOLINESS.	4	348	429*	0.5	0.7
353 PLY BRETHREN..	1	20	40	-	0.1
357 PRESB CH US...	6	1,755	2,164*	2.4	3.3
403 SALVATION ARMY	1	110	407	0.4	0.6
419 SO BAPT CONV..	48	18,465	22,772*	25.1	34.9
435 UNITARIAN-UNIV	1	13	13	-	-
443 UN C OF CHRIST	12	2,761	3,405*	3.7	5.2
449 UN METHODIST..	34	10,343	11,699	12.9	17.9
453 UN PRES CH USA	1	5	6*	-	-
CHATHAM	86	13,669	16,196*	54.8	100.0
081 CATHOLIC......	1	0	72	0.2	0.4
123 CH GOD (ANDER)	1	30	85	0.3	0.5
127 CH GOD (CLEVE)	2	61	74*	0.3	0.5
193 EPISCOPAL.....	1	46	89	0.3	0.5
226 FRIENDS-USA...	4	654	798*	2.7	4.9
349 PENT HOLINESS.	1	97	118*	0.4	0.7
353 PLY BRETHREN..	2	90	160	0.5	1.0
357 PRESB CH US...	7	361	441*	1.5	2.7
413 S-D ADVENTISTS	1	68	83*	0.3	0.5
419 SO BAPT CONV..	32	7,314	8,929*	30.2	55.1

*Total adherents estimated from known number of communicant, confirmed, full members.

—Represents a percent less than 0.1.

Percentages may not total due to rounding.

Table 3. Churches and Church Membership by State, County and Denomination: 1971

County and Denomination	Number of churches	Communicant, confirmed, full members	Total adherents		
			Number	Percent of total population	Percent of total adherents
443 UN C OF CHRIST	5	687	839*	2.8	5.2
449 UN METHODIST..	29	4,261	4,508	15.3	27.8
CHEROKEE	77	11,113	13,440*	82.3	100.0
081 CATHOLIC......	3	0	169	1.0	1.3
127 CH GOD (CLEVE)	4	109	131*	0.8	1.0
193 EPISCOPAL.....	1	69	96	0.6	0.7
221 FREE METH C NA	2	30	37	0.2	0.3
281 LUTH CH AMER..	1	108	140	0.9	1.0
357 PRESB CH US...	3	131	158*	1.0	1.2
413 S-D ADVENTISTS	1	28	34*	0.2	0.3
419 SO BAPT CONV..	50	9,387	11,309*	69.3	84.1
449 UN METHODIST..	10	1,195	1,299	8.0	9.7
453 UN PRES CH USA	2	56	67*	0.4	0.5
CHOWAN	20	4,432	5,432*	50.5	100.0
081 CATHOLIC......	1	0	99	0.9	1.8
093 CR CH (DISC)..	2	295	356*	3.3	6.6
097 CR C AND C CR.	2	45	54*	0.5	1.0
127 CH GOD (CLEVE)	1	25	30*	0.3	0.6
193 EPISCOPAL.....	2	294	382	3.5	7.0
349 PENT HOLINESS.	2	118	142*	1.3	2.6
357 PRESB CH US...	1	42	51*	0.5	0.9
419 SO BAPT CONV..	6	3,228	3,897*	36.2	71.7
449 UN METHODIST..	3	385	421	3.9	7.8
CLAY	36	3,446	4,066*	78.5	100.0
081 CATHOLIC......	1	0	45	0.9	1.1
127 CH GOD (CLEVE)	3	227	269*	5.2	6.6
193 EPISCOPAL.....	1	22	45	0.9	1.1
357 PRESB CH US...	1	16	19*	0.4	0.5
419 SO BAPT CONV..	21	2,525	2,990*	57.7	73.5
449 UN METHODIST..	9	656	698	13.5	17.2
CLEVELAND	148	41,391	50,633*	69.8	100.0
055 AS REF PRES CH	1	267	331*	0.5	0.7
081 CATHOLIC......	2	0	208	0.3	0.4
127 CH GOD (CLEVE)	4	366	454*	0.6	0.9
165 CH OF NAZARENE	2	105	182	0.3	0.4
193 EPISCOPAL.....	2	194	218	0.3	0.4
281 LUTH CH AMER..	3	884	1,101	1.5	2.2
349 PENT HOLINESS.	1	28	35*	-	0.1
357 PRESB CH US...	5	1,197	1,484*	2.0	2.9
403 SALVATION ARMY	1	61	256	0.4	0.5
413 S-D ADVENTISTS	1	32	40*	0.1	0.1
419 SO BAPT CONV..	84	30,171	37,411*	51.6	73.9
443 UN C OF CHRIST	1	59	73*	0.1	0.1
449 UN METHODIST..	39	7,926	8,715	12.0	17.2
453 UN PRES CH USA	2	101	125*	0.2	0.2
COLUMBUS	106	20,293	24,560*	52.3	100.0
081 CATHOLIC......	2	0	216	0.5	0.9
127 CH GOD (CLEVE)	8	275	339*	0.7	1.4
193 EPISCOPAL.....	1	121	134	0.3	0.5
349 PENT HOLINESS.	4	329	406*	0.9	1.7
357 PRESB CH US...	6	1,175	1,450*	3.1	5.9
413 S-D ADVENTISTS	1	40	49*	0.1	0.2
419 SO BAPT CONV..	62	14,462	17,848*	38.0	72.7
449 UN METHODIST..	20	3,824	4,035	8.6	16.4
453 UN PRES CH USA	2	67	83*	0.2	0.3
CRAVEN	75	14,687	20,980*	33.5	100.0
081 CATHOLIC......	3	0	3,167	5.1	15.1
093 CR CH (DISC)..	15	1,608	1,997*	3.2	9.5
127 CH GOD (CLEVE)	3	167	207*	0.3	1.0
165 CH OF NAZARENE	1	12	29	-	0.1
193 EPISCOPAL.....	3	906	1,085	1.7	5.2
281 LUTH CH AMER..	2	120	156	0.2	0.7
283 LUTH--MO SYNOD	1	186	292	0.5	1.4
349 PENT HOLINESS.	6	350	435*	0.7	2.1
357 PRESB CH US...	5	1,216	1,510*	2.4	7.2
403 SALVATION ARMY	1	88	225	0.4	1.1
413 S-D ADVENTISTS	3	205	255*	0.4	1.2
419 SO BAPT CONV..	11	4,591	5,700*	9.1	27.2
443 UN C OF CHRIST	2	255	317*	0.5	1.5
449 UN METHODIST..	18	4,892	5,492	8.8	26.2
453 UN PRES CH USA	1	91	113*	0.2	0.5
CUMBERLAND	148	40,704	53,253*	25.1	100.0
081 CATHOLIC......	2	0	2,410	1.1	4.5
093 CR CH (DISC)..	8	497	621*	0.3	1.2
097 CR C AND C CR.	1	25	31*	-	0.1
127 CH GOD (CLEVE)	7	886	1,110*	0.5	2.1
165 CH OF NAZARENE	1	42	112	0.1	0.2
193 EPISCOPAL.....	5	1,285	2,015	1.0	3.8
281 LUTH CH AMER..	2	698	1,120	0.5	2.1
283 LUTH--MO SYNOD	1	174	302	0.1	0.6
349 PENT HOLINESS.	9	1,226	1,533*	0.7	2.9
357 PRESB CH US...	24	5,769	7,213*	3.4	13.5
403 SALVATION ARMY	1	107	495	0.2	0.9
413 S-D ADVENTISTS	2	187	234*	0.1	0.4
419 SO BAPT CONV..	50	20,868	26,092*	12.3	49.0
435 UNITARIAN-UNIV	1	25	37	-	0.1
443 UN C OF CHRIST	3	255	319*	0.2	0.6
449 UN METHODIST..	29	8,440	9,336	4.4	17.5
453 UN PRES CH USA	2	218	273*	0.1	0.5
CURRITUCK	20	4,485	5,119*	73.4	100.0

County and Denomination	Number of churches	Communicant, confirmed, full members	Total adherents		
			Number	Percent of total population	Percent of total adherents
093 CR CH (DISC)..	3	75	91*	1.3	1.8
097 CR C AND C CR.	2	371	450*	6.5	8.8
349 PENT HOLINESS.	1	46	56*	0.8	1.1
419 SO BAPT CONV..	6	1,444	1,750*	25.1	34.2
449 UN METHODIST..	8	2,549	2,772	39.7	54.2
DARE	22	2,939	3,510*	50.2	100.0
081 CATHOLIC......	3	0	125	1.8	3.6
093 CR CH (DISC)..	1	50	59*	0.8	1.7
193 EPISCOPAL.....	1	108	195	2.8	5.6
419 SO BAPT CONV..	3	402	477*	6.8	13.6
449 UN METHODIST..	14	2,379	2,654	37.9	75.6
DAVIDSON	153	40,899	49,261*	51.5	100.0
081 CATHOLIC......	2	0	431	0.5	0.9
127 CH GOD (CLEVE)	4	317	390*	0.4	0.8
157 CH OF BRETHREN	1	79	97*	0.1	0.2
165 CH OF NAZARENE	1	36	66	0.1	0.1
193 EPISCOPAL.....	2	201	314	0.3	0.6
226 FRIENDS-USA...	2	466	573*	0.6	1.2
281 LUTH CH AMER..	9	1,906	2,510	2.6	5.1
295 MORAV CH-SOUTH	2	174	234	0.2	0.5
349 PENT HOLINESS.	2	170	209*	0.2	0.4
357 PRESB CH US...	4	1,125	1,384*	1.4	2.8
381 REF PRES-EVAN.	1	175	175	0.2	0.4
403 SALVATION ARMY	2	77	419	0.4	0.9
413 S-D ADVENTISTS	2	183	225*	0.2	0.5
419 SO BAPT CONV..	43	13,927	17,133*	17.9	34.8
443 UN C OF CHRIST	17	5,470	6,729*	7.0	13.7
449 UN METHODIST..	58	16,500	18,258	19.1	37.1
453 UN PRES CH USA	1	93	114*	0.1	0.2
DAVIE	55	9,522	10,783*	57.2	100.0
081 CATHOLIC......	1	0	56	0.3	0.5
127 CH GOD (CLEVE)	2	80	98*	0.5	0.9
193 EPISCOPAL.....	2	121	128	0.7	1.2
281 LUTH CH AMER..	1	88	134	0.7	1.2
295 MORAV CH-SOUTH	1	304	436	2.3	4.0
349 PENT HOLINESS.	2	119	145*	0.8	1.3
357 PRESB CH US...	3	472	576*	3.1	5.3
413 S-D ADVENTISTS	1	31	38*	0.2	0.4
419 SO BAPT CONV..	14	3,754	4,579*	24.3	42.5
449 UN METHODIST..	27	4,503	4,532	24.0	42.0
453 UN PRES CH USA	1	50	61*	0.3	0.6
DUPLIN	78	12,050	14,330*	37.7	100.0
081 CATHOLIC......	1	0	65	0.2	0.5
093 CR CH (DISC)..	9	444	546*	1.4	3.8
127 CH GOD (CLEVE)	1	61	75*	0.2	0.5
349 PENT HOLINESS.	5	421	518*	1.4	3.6
357 PRESB CH US...	17	2,116	2,601*	6.8	18.2
419 SO BAPT CONV..	26	6,035	7,419*	19.5	51.8
435 UNITARIAN-UNIV	1	95	110	0.3	0.8
449 UN METHODIST..	18	2,878	2,996	7.9	20.9
DURHAM	119	44,138	56,875*	42.9	100.0
019 AMER BAPT CONV	4	1,233	1,489*	1.1	2.6
029 AMER LUTH CH..	1	75	122	0.1	0.2
081 CATHOLIC......	3	0	2,914	2.2	5.1
093 CR CH (DISC)..	2	213	257*	0.2	0.5
097 CR C AND C CR.	1	71	86*	0.1	0.2
123 CH GOD (ANDER)	1	12	28	-	-
127 CH GOD (CLEVE)	2	198	239*	0.2	0.4
165 CH OF NAZARENE	1	61	106	0.1	0.2
193 EPISCOPAL.....	7	1,550	2,320	1.7	4.1
226 FRIENDS-USA...	2	117	141*	0.1	0.2
281 LUTH CH AMER..	3	476	696	0.5	1.2
283 LUTH--MO SYNOD	1	180	238	0.2	0.4
285 MENNONITE CH..	1	5	6*	-	-
349 PENT HOLINESS.	2	301	364*	0.3	0.6
353 PLY BRETHREN..	3	340	899	0.7	1.6
357 PRESB CH US...	8	2,877	3,475*	2.6	6.1
381 REF PRES-EVAN.	1	41	45	-	0.1
403 SALVATION ARMY	1	122	902	0.7	1.6
413 S-D ADVENTISTS	2	357	431*	0.3	0.8
419 SO BAPT CONV..	37	22,408	27,063*	20.4	47.6
443 UN C OF CHRIST	5	628	758*	0.6	1.3
449 UN METHODIST..	30	12,685	14,069	10.6	24.7
453 UN PRES CH USA	1	188	227*	0.2	0.4
EDGECOMBE	63	12,047	15,342*	29.3	100.0
081 CATHOLIC......	2	0	241	0.5	1.6
093 CR CH (DISC)..	5	680	850*	1.6	5.5
097 CR C AND C CR.	2	95	119*	0.2	0.8
127 CH GOD (CLEVE)	6	910	1,137*	2.2	7.4
193 EPISCOPAL.....	3	489	659	1.3	4.3
281 LUTH CH AMER..	1	254	324	0.6	2.1
349 PENT HOLINESS.	4	511	639*	1.2	4.2
357 PRESB CH US...	9	1,552	1,940*	3.7	12.6
403 SALVATION ARMY	1	59	307	0.6	2.0
413 S-D ADVENTISTS	1	112	140*	0.3	0.9
419 SO BAPT CONV..	20	6,017	7,520*	14.4	49.0
443 UN C OF CHRIST	1	33	41*	0.1	0.3
449 UN METHODIST..	8	1,335	1,425	2.7	9.3
FORSYTH	243	84,761	108,989*	50.8	100.0
029 AMER LUTH CH..	1	67	94	-	0.1
055 AS REF PRES CH	1	60	73*	-	0.1

*Total adherents estimated from known number of communicant, confirmed, full members.

—Represents a percent less than 0.1.

Percentages may not total due to rounding.

Table 3. Churches and Church Membership by State, County and Denomination: 1971

County and Denomination	Number of churches	Communicant, confirmed, full members	Total adherents: Number	Total adherents: Percent of total population	Total adherents: Percent of total adherents
081 CATHOLIC......	4	0	4,272	2.0	3.9
093 CR CH (DISC)..	10	2,736	3,338*	1.6	3.1
097 CR C AND C CR.	11	1,874	2,286*	1.1	2.1
123 CH GOD (ANDER)	3	68	177	0.1	0.2
127 CH GOD (CLEVE)	3	215	262*	0.1	0.2
157 CH OF BRETHREN	1	215	262*	0.1	0.2
165 CH OF NAZARENE	1	73	98	-	0.1
193 EPISCOPAL.....	3	2,127	2,927	1.4	2.7
226 FRIENDS-USA...	6	1,359	1,658*	0.8	1.5
281 LUTH CH AMER..	4	1,399	1,824	0.9	1.7
283 LUTH--MO SYNOD	3	395	607	0.3	0.6
285 MENNONITE CH..	1	4	5*	-	-
295 MORAV CH-SOUTH	31	13,303	17,891	8.3	16.4
349 PENT HOLINESS.	5	389	475*	0.2	0.4
353 PLY BRETHREN..	3	250	430	0.2	0.4
357 PRESB CH US...	12	4,832	5,895*	2.8	5.4
403 SALVATION ARMY	1	70	1,266	0.6	1.2
413 S-D ADVENTISTS	2	607	741*	0.3	0.7
419 SO BAPT CONV..	61	30,651	37,397*	17.4	34.3
435 UNITARIAN-UNIV	1	88	113	0.1	0.1
443 UN C OF CHRIST	10	1,485	1,812*	0.8	1.7
449 UN METHODIST..	63	21,907	24,370	11.4	22.4
453 UN PRES CH USA	2	587	716*	0.3	0.7
FRANKLIN	62	12,857	15,270*	56.9	100.0
093 CR CH (DISC)..	3	345	417*	1.6	2.7
127 CH GOD (CLEVE)	1	47	57*	0.2	0.4
193 EPISCOPAL.....	2	142	215	0.8	1.4
349 PENT HOLINESS.	1	54	65*	0.2	0.4
419 SO BAPT CONV..	31	9,241	11,178*	41.7	73.2
443 UN C OF CHRIST	11	1,029	1,245*	4.6	8.2
449 UN METHODIST..	11	1,841	1,902	7.1	12.5
453 UN PRES CH USA	2	158	191*	0.7	1.3
GASTON	218	66,581	85,236*	57.4	100.0
055 AS REF PRES CH	6	1,621	2,006*	1.4	2.4
081 CATHOLIC......	4	0	2,122	1.4	2.5
093 CR CH (DISC)..	1	44	54*	-	0.1
127 CH GOD (CLEVE)	22	3,165	3,916*	2.6	4.6
165 CH OF NAZARENE	3	155	285	0.2	0.3
193 EPISCOPAL.....	4	581	872	0.6	1.0
281 LUTH CH AMER..	15	4,303	5,750	3.9	6.7
283 LUTH--MO SYNOD	1	81	127	0.1	0.1
349 PENT HOLINESS.	5	423	523*	0.4	0.6
353 PLY BRETHREN..	1	20	40	-	-
357 PRESB CH US...	22	5,648	6,989*	4.7	8.2
403 SALVATION ARMY	1	179	1,478	1.0	1.7
419 SO BAPT CONV..	92	38,595	47,757*	32.2	56.0
449 UN METHODIST..	39	11,512	13,003	8.8	15.3
453 UN PRES CH USA	2	254	314*	0.2	0.4
GATES	19	4,165	4,980*	58.4	100.0
193 EPISCOPAL.....	1	36	48	0.6	1.0
419 SO BAPT CONV..	10	2,941	3,593*	42.2	72.1
443 UN C OF CHRIST	2	373	456*	5.3	9.2
449 UN METHODIST..	6	815	883	10.4	17.7
GRAHAM	22	3,985	4,902*	74.7	100.0
127 CH GOD (CLEVE)	1	22	27*	0.4	0.6
419 SO BAPT CONV..	20	3,797	4,698*	71.6	95.8
449 UN METHODIST..	1	166	177	2.7	3.6
GRANVILLE	59	14,545	17,435*	53.2	100.0
081 CATHOLIC......	1	0	70	0.2	0.4
093 CR CH (DISC)..	1	392	476*	1.5	2.7
127 CH GOD (CLEVE)	1	45	55*	0.2	0.3
193 EPISCOPAL.....	2	272	406	1.2	2.3
357 PRESB CH US...	7	545	662*	2.0	3.8
419 SO BAPT CONV..	29	10,404	12,634*	38.6	72.5
443 UN C OF CHRIST	2	118	143*	0.4	0.8
449 UN METHODIST..	15	2,615	2,802	8.6	16.1
453 UN PRES CH USA	1	154	187*	0.6	1.1
GREENE	20	2,742	3,117*	20.8	100.0
093 CR CH (DISC)..	5	316	393*	2.6	12.6
349 PENT HOLINESS.	1	78	97*	0.6	3.1
357 PRESB CH US...	2	133	165*	1.1	5.3
419 SO BAPT CONV..	2	448	557*	3.7	17.9
449 UN METHODIST..	9	1,697	1,818	12.1	58.3
453 UN PRES CH USA	1	70	87*	0.6	2.8
GUILFORD	289	110,178	141,521*	49.0	100.0
029 AMER LUTH CH..	1	175	273	0.1	0.2
081 CATHOLIC......	6	0	5,924	2.1	4.2
093 CR CH (DISC)..	6	933	1,139*	0.4	0.8
097 CR C AND C CR.	6	771	942*	0.3	0.7
123 CH GOD (ANDER)	3	173	427	0.1	0.3
127 CH GOD (CLEVE)	8	850	1,038*	0.4	0.7
165 CH OF NAZARENE	7	656	1,092	0.4	0.8
193 EPISCOPAL.....	8	3,546	5,126	1.8	3.6
281 LUTH CH AMER..	12	3,384	4,505	1.6	3.2
283 LUTH--MO SYNOD	5	881	1,216	0.4	0.9
295 MORAV CH-SOUTH	2	537	722	0.3	0.5
349 PENT HOLINESS.	8	580	708*	0.2	0.5
353 PLY BRETHREN..	3	525	970	0.3	0.7
357 PRESB CH US...	25	13,124	16,027*	5.6	11.3
403 SALVATION ARMY	3	229	2,252	0.8	1.6
413 S-D ADVENTISTS	3	837	1,022*	0.4	0.7
419 SO BAPT CONV..	82	42,570	51,988*	18.0	36.7
435 UNITARIAN-UNIV	1	108	168	0.1	0.1
443 UN C OF CHRIST	19	4,707	5,748*	2.0	4.1
449 UN METHODIST..	78	35,015	39,529	13.7	27.9
453 UN PRES CH USA	3	577	705*	0.2	0.5
HALIFAX	76	17,821	21,482*	39.9	100.0
081 CATHOLIC......	2	0	212	0.4	1.0
097 CR C AND C CR.	6	1,227	1,530*	2.8	7.1
127 CH GOD (CLEVE)	3	290	362*	0.7	1.7
193 EPISCOPAL.....	7	665	877	1.6	4.1
349 PENT HOLINESS.	6	630	786*	1.5	3.7
357 PRESB CH US...	2	445	555*	1.0	2.6
413 S-D ADVENTISTS	1	27	34*	0.1	0.2
419 SO BAPT CONV..	24	9,039	11,271*	20.9	52.5
443 UN C OF CHRIST	1	79	99*	0.2	0.5
449 UN METHODIST..	23	5,371	5,696	10.6	26.5
453 UN PRES CH USA	1	48	60*	0.1	0.3
HARNETT	83	18,956	22,835*	46.0	100.0
081 CATHOLIC......	2	0	249	0.5	1.1
093 CR CH (DISC)..	3	266	324*	0.7	1.4
127 CH GOD (CLEVE)	5	587	715*	1.4	3.1
193 EPISCOPAL.....	1	133	249	0.5	1.1
226 FRIENDS-USA...	1	144	175*	0.4	0.8
349 PENT HOLINESS.	3	276	336*	0.7	1.5
357 PRESB CH US...	17	2,645	3,222*	6.5	14.1
413 S-D ADVENTISTS	1	51	62*	0.1	0.3
419 SO BAPT CONV..	30	10,969	13,361*	26.9	58.5
443 UN C OF CHRIST	1	139	169*	0.3	0.7
449 UN METHODIST..	16	3,558	3,744	7.5	16.4
453 UN PRES CH USA	3	188	229*	0.5	1.0
HAYWOOD	107	24,295	29,317*	70.3	100.0
081 CATHOLIC......	3	0	258	0.6	0.9
127 CH GOD (CLEVE)	4	345	417*	1.0	1.4
165 CH OF NAZARENE	1	29	69	0.2	0.2
193 EPISCOPAL.....	2	287	351	0.8	1.2
221 FREE METH C NA	1	26	43	0.1	0.1
283 LUTH--MO SYNOD	1	53	102	0.2	0.3
353 PLY BRETHREN..	1	40	80	0.2	0.3
357 PRESB CH US...	4	799	966*	2.3	3.3
403 SALVATION ARMY	2	69	277	0.7	0.9
413 S-D ADVENTISTS	1	45	54*	0.1	0.2
419 SO BAPT CONV..	59	16,878	20,412*	48.9	69.6
449 UN METHODIST..	28	5,724	6,288	15.1	21.4
HENDERSON	88	22,205	27,382*	64.0	100.0
081 CATHOLIC......	1	0	845	2.0	3.1
121 CH GOD (ABR)..	1	25	30*	0.1	0.1
123 CH GOD (ANDER)	1	28	56	0.1	0.2
127 CH GOD (CLEVE)	2	105	127*	0.3	0.5
165 CH OF NAZARENE	1	306	504	1.2	1.8
193 EPISCOPAL.....	5	1,302	1,490	3.5	5.4
283 LUTH--MO SYNOD	1	49	63	0.1	0.2
349 PENT HOLINESS.	2	67	81*	0.2	0.3
357 PRESB CH US...	4	1,515	1,826*	4.3	6.7
403 SALVATION ARMY	1	16	139	0.3	0.5
413 S-D ADVENTISTS	2	921	1,110*	2.6	4.1
419 SO BAPT CONV..	53	14,629	17,631*	41.2	64.4
443 UN C OF CHRIST	1	248	299*	0.7	1.1
449 UN METHODIST..	13	2,994	3,181	7.4	11.6
HERTFORD	32	7,210	8,894*	37.8	100.0
081 CATHOLIC......	1	0	110	0.5	1.2
097 CR C AND C CR.	1	34	42*	0.2	0.5
127 CH GOD (CLEVE)	1	26	32*	0.1	0.4
193 EPISCOPAL.....	2	119	179	0.8	2.0
349 PENT HOLINESS.	1	26	32*	0.1	0.4
357 PRESB CH US...	1	144	178*	0.8	2.0
419 SO BAPT CONV..	19	5,766	7,136*	30.3	80.2
449 UN METHODIST..	6	1,095	1,185	5.0	13.3
HOKE	26	4,427	5,520*	33.6	100.0
081 CATHOLIC......	1	0	53	0.3	1.0
127 CH GOD (CLEVE)	1	57	73*	0.4	1.3
349 PENT HOLINESS.	1	46	59*	0.4	1.1
353 PLY BRETHREN..	1	35	78	0.5	1.4
357 PRESB CH US...	5	1,111	1,418*	8.6	25.7
419 SO BAPT CONV..	11	2,121	2,708*	16.5	49.1
449 UN METHODIST..	5	1,026	1,091	6.6	19.8
453 UN PRES CH USA	1	31	40*	0.2	0.7
HYDE	36	2,093	2,419*	43.4	100.0
093 CR CH (DISC)..	13	450	550*	9.9	22.7
097 CR C AND C CR.	7	433	529*	9.5	21.9
193 EPISCOPAL.....	1	13	21	0.4	0.9
349 PENT HOLINESS.	1	29	35*	0.6	1.4
357 PRESB CH US...	1	34	42*	0.8	1.7
419 SO BAPT CONV..	4	187	228*	4.1	9.4
449 UN METHODIST..	9	947	1,014	18.2	41.9
IREDELL	150	35,629	43,463*	60.2	100.0
055 AS REF PRES CH	7	2,182	2,672*	3.7	6.1
081 CATHOLIC......	2	0	567	0.8	1.3
127 CH GOD (CLEVE)	5	421	516*	0.7	1.2
165 CH OF NAZARENE	2	119	247	0.3	0.6

*Total adherents estimated from known number of communicant, confirmed, full members.

—Represents a percent less than 0.1.

Percentages may not total due to rounding.

Table 3. Churches and Church Membership by State, County and Denomination: 1971

County and Denomination	Number of churches	Communicant, confirmed, full members	Total adherents		
			Number	Percent of total population	Percent of total adherents
193 EPISCOPAL.....	2	329	471	0.7	1.1
226 FRIENDS-USA...	2	200	245*	0.3	0.6
281 LUTH CH AMER..	7	2,228	2,792	3.9	6.4
283 LUTH--MO SYNOD	1	79	119	0.2	0.3
349 PENT HOLINESS.	1	6	7*	-	-
357 PRESB CH US...	18	3,509	4,297*	6.0	9.9
403 SALVATION ARMY	1	41	165	0.2	0.4
413 S-D ADVENTISTS	1	48	59*	0.1	0.1
419 SO BAPT CONV..	49	15,328	18,772*	26.0	43.2
443 UN C OF CHRIST	4	261	320*	0.4	0.7
449 UN METHODIST..	43	10,265	11,463	15.9	26.4
453 UN PRES CH USA	5	613	751*	1.0	1.7
JACKSON	77	11,977	14,165*	65.6	100.0
081 CATHOLIC......	2	0	173	0.8	1.2
127 CH GOD (CLEVE)	4	163	193*	0.9	1.4
193 EPISCOPAL.....	3	189	252	1.2	1.8
357 PRESB CH US...	2	188	222*	1.0	1.6
419 SO BAPT CONV..	53	9,888	11,699*	54.2	82.6
449 UN METHODIST..	13	1,549	1,626	7.5	11.5
JOHNSTON	125	23,273	28,248*	45.8	100.0
081 CATHOLIC......	1	0	247	0.4	0.9
093 CR CH (DISC)..	16	1,157	1,407*	2.3	5.0
123 CH GOD (ANDER)	1	70	175	0.3	0.6
127 CH GOD (CLEVE)	9	534	649*	1.1	2.3
226 FRIENDS-USA...	1	159	193*	0.3	0.7
349 PENT HOLINESS.	10	663	806*	1.3	2.9
357 PRESB CH US...	16	3,599	4,377*	7.1	15.5
403 SALVATION ARMY	1	72	264	0.4	0.9
419 SO BAPT CONV..	45	12,466	15,162*	24.6	53.7
443 UN C OF CHRIST	4	575	699*	1.1	2.5
449 UN METHODIST..	20	3,945	4,229	6.9	15.0
453 UN PRES CH USA	1	33	40*	0.1	0.1
JONES	28	3,132	3,799*	38.8	100.0
081 CATHOLIC......	1	0	20	0.2	0.5
093 CR CH (DISC)..	6	443	549*	5.6	14.5
193 EPISCOPAL.....	1	37	46	0.5	1.2
349 PENT HOLINESS.	1	60	74*	0.8	1.9
357 PRESB CH US...	1	94	116*	1.2	3.1
419 SO BAPT CONV..	6	1,265	1,567*	16.0	41.2
443 UN C OF CHRIST	3	142	176*	1.8	4.6
449 UN METHODIST..	9	1,091	1,251	12.8	32.9
LEE	54	12,144	14,953*	49.1	100.0
081 CATHOLIC......	1	0	239	0.8	1.6
093 CR CH (DISC)..	2	180	222*	0.7	1.5
127 CH GOD (CLEVE)	1	198	244*	0.8	1.6
165 CH OF NAZARENE	1	14	78	0.3	0.5
175 CONG CR CH....	1	50	62*	0.2	0.4
193 EPISCOPAL.....	1	203	287	0.9	1.9
281 LUTH CH AMER..	1	136	206	0.7	1.4
349 PENT HOLINESS.	2	141	174*	0.6	1.2
353 PLY BRETHREN..	1	135	220	0.7	1.5
357 PRESB CH US...	13	1,834	2,258*	7.4	15.1
419 SO BAPT CONV..	13	4,846	5,967*	19.6	39.9
443 UN C OF CHRIST	7	996	1,226*	4.0	8.2
449 UN METHODIST..	9	3,097	3,383	11.1	22.6
453 UN PRES CH USA	1	314	387*	1.3	2.6
LENOIR	86	16,866	21,147*	38.3	100.0
081 CATHOLIC......	1	0	636	1.2	3.0
093 CR CH (DISC)..	24	3,631	4,435*	8.0	21.0
097 CR C AND C CR.	1	19	23*	-	0.1
127 CH GOD (CLEVE)	3	162	198*	0.4	0.9
165 CH OF NAZARENE	1	48	98	0.2	0.5
193 EPISCOPAL.....	5	1,139	1,508	2.7	7.1
281 LUTH CH AMER..	4	467	590	1.1	2.8
283 LUTH--MO SYNOD	1	110	146	0.3	0.7
349 PENT HOLINESS.	3	308	376*	0.7	1.8
357 PRESB CH US...	7	1,253	1,530*	2.8	7.2
403 SALVATION ARMY	1	161	607	1.1	2.9
413 S-D ADVENTISTS	2	253	309*	0.6	1.5
419 SO BAPT CONV..	14	4,733	5,781*	10.5	27.3
435 UNITARIAN-UNIV	1	77	97	0.2	0.5
443 UN C OF CHRIST	1	75	92*	0.2	0.4
449 UN METHODIST..	16	4,380	4,660	8.4	22.0
453 UN PRES CH USA	1	50	61*	0.1	0.3
LINCOLN	89	17,780	21,372*	65.4	100.0
081 CATHOLIC......	1	0	175	0.5	0.8
093 CR CH (DISC)..	1	67	82*	0.3	0.4
127 CH GOD (CLEVE)	3	255	312*	1.0	1.5
193 EPISCOPAL.....	2	164	211	0.6	1.0
281 LUTH CH AMER..	9	2,259	2,843	8.7	13.3
349 PENT HOLINESS.	1	59	72*	0.2	0.3
357 PRESB CH US...	4	708	866*	2.6	4.1
413 S-D ADVENTISTS	1	14	17*	0.1	0.1
419 SO BAPT CONV..	36	8,275	10,125*	31.0	47.4
443 UN C OF CHRIST	1	142	174*	0.5	0.8
449 UN METHODIST..	29	5,806	6,457	19.8	30.2
453 UN PRES CH USA	1	31	38*	0.1	0.2
MC DOWELL	77	13,907	16,723*	54.6	100.0
081 CATHOLIC......	1	C	103	0.3	0.6
097 CR C AND C CR.	1	70	85*	0.3	0.5
127 CH GOD (CLEVE)	3	224	273*	0.9	1.6
193 EPISCOPAL.....	1	61	99	0.3	0.6
283 LUTH--MO SYNOD	1	82	98	0.3	0.6
349 PENT HOLINESS.	4	247	301*	1.0	1.8
357 PRESB CH US...	7	671	819*	2.7	4.9
413 S-D ADVENTISTS	1	90	110*	0.4	0.7
419 SO BAPT CONV..	39	9,673	11,802*	38.5	70.6
449 UN METHODIST..	19	2,789	3,033	9.9	18.1
MACON	77	11,110	13,352*	84.6	100.0
081 CATHOLIC......	2	0	186	1.2	1.4
127 CH GOD (CLEVE)	3	116	138*	0.9	1.0
193 EPISCOPAL.....	1	73	111	0.7	0.8
357 PRESB CH US...	3	313	374*	2.4	2.8
403 SALVATION ARMY	1	28	171	1.1	1.3
413 S-D ADVENTISTS	1	64	76*	0.5	0.6
419 SO BAPT CONV..	50	8,586	10,248*	64.9	76.8
449 UN METHODIST..	16	1,930	2,048	13.0	15.3
MADISON	72	10,133	12,150*	75.9	100.0
081 CATHOLIC......	2	0	48	0.3	0.4
097 CR C AND C CR.	2	53	62*	0.4	0.5
127 CH GOD (CLEVE)	1	18	21*	0.1	0.2
403 SALVATION ARMY	1	78	348	2.2	2.9
419 SO BAPT CONV..	53	9,228	10,855*	67.8	89.3
449 UN METHODIST..	9	537	558	3.5	4.6
453 UN PRES CH USA	4	219	258*	1.6	2.1
MARTIN	62	10,020	12,197*	49.3	100.0
081 CATHOLIC......	1	0	65	0.3	0.5
093 CR CH (DISC)..	17	2,171	2,674*	10.8	21.9
097 CR C AND C CR.	12	2,355	2,900*	11.7	23.8
127 CH GOD (CLEVE)	2	140	172*	0.7	1.4
193 EPISCOPAL.....	1	150	179	0.7	1.5
226 FRIENDS-USA...	1	35	43*	0.2	0.4
349 PENT HOLINESS.	6	375	462*	1.9	3.8
357 PRESB CH US...	3	277	341*	1.4	2.8
419 SO BAPT CONV..	10	3,329	4,100*	16.6	33.6
449 UN METHODIST..	9	1,188	1,261	5.1	10.3
MECKLENBURG	286	130,471	173,838*	49.0	100.0
019 AMER BAPT CONV	4	1,615	2,005*	0.6	1.2
029 AMER LUTH CH..	1	158	230	0.1	0.1
055 AS REF PRES CH	5	1,145	1,421*	0.4	0.8
081 CATHOLIC......	7	0	10,793	3.0	6.2
093 CR CH (DISC)..	3	563	699*	0.2	0.4
097 CR C AND C CR.	2	190	236*	0.1	0.1
123 CH GOD (ANDER)	3	225	493	0.1	0.3
127 CH GOD (CLEVE)	12	1,161	1,441*	0.4	0.8
165 CH OF NAZARENE	5	552	1,250	0.4	0.7
193 EPISCOPAL.....	12	6,051	8,701	2.5	5.0
226 FRIENDS-USA...	1	45	56*	-	-
281 LUTH CH AMER..	10	4,367	6,103	1.7	3.5
283 LUTH--MO SYNOD	4	1,257	1,855	0.5	1.1
295 MORAV CH-SOUTH	2	527	681	0.2	0.4
349 PENT HOLINESS.	1	66	82*	-	-
353 PLY BRETHREN..	1	81	120	-	0.1
357 PRESB CH US...	58	30,217	37,510*	10.6	21.6
381 REF PRES-EVAN.	1	130	140	-	0.1
403 SALVATION ARMY	2	239	1,508	0.4	0.9
413 S-D ADVENTISTS	3	1,140	1,415*	0.4	0.8
419 SO BAPT CONV..	71	42,266	52,467*	14.8	30.2
435 UNITARIAN-UNIV	1	430	653	0.2	0.4
443 UN C OF CHRIST	4	674	837*	0.2	0.5
449 UN METHODIST..	53	33,514	38,353	10.8	22.1
453 UN PRES CH USA	20	3,858	4,789*	1.4	2.8
MITCHELL	60	9,445	11,218*	83.4	100.0
081 CATHOLIC......	1	0	55	0.4	0.5
093 CR CH (DISC)..	2	185	220*	1.6	2.0
127 CH GOD (CLEVE)	2	53	63*	0.5	0.6
157 CH OF BRETHREN	3	124	148*	1.1	1.3
193 EPISCOPAL.....	1	77	112	0.8	1.0
357 PRESB CH US...	6	380	452*	3.4	4.0
419 SO BAPT CONV..	37	7,839	9,329*	69.4	83.2
449 UN METHODIST..	8	787	839	6.2	7.5
MONTGOMERY	59	7,763	9,036*	46.9	100.0
127 CH GOD (CLEVE)	3	92	113*	0.6	1.3
349 PENT HOLINESS.	4	90	110*	0.6	1.2
419 SO BAPT CONV..	28	4,470	5,467*	28.4	60.5
443 UN C OF CHRIST	4	255	312*	1.6	3.5
449 UN METHODIST..	20	2,856	3,034	15.7	33.6
MOORE	50	5,831	8,219*	21.0	100.0
081 CATHOLIC......	2	0	813	2.1	9.9
127 CH GOD (CLEVE)	3	83	101*	0.3	1.2
175 CONG CR CH....	2	110	134*	0.3	1.6
193 EPISCOPAL.....	1	520	721	1.8	8.8
226 FRIENDS-USA...	5	274	333*	0.9	4.1
281 LUTH CH AMER..	1	150	201	0.5	2.4
283 LUTH--MO SYNOD	1	34	74	0.2	0.9
349 PENT HOLINESS.	1	34	41*	0.1	0.5
357 PRESB CH US...	18	3,129	3,806*	9.7	46.3
419 SO BAPT CONV..	3	547	665*	1.7	8.1
443 UN C OF CHRIST	5	529	643*	1.6	7.8
449 UN METHODIST..	3	211	432	1.1	5.3
453 UN PRES CH USA	5	210	255*	0.7	3.1

*Total adherents estimated from known number of communicant, confirmed, full members.

—Represents a percent less than 0.1.

Percentages may not total due to rounding.

Table 3. Churches and Church Membership by State, County and Denomination: 1971

County and Denomination	Number of churches	Communicant, confirmed, full members	Total adherents		
			Number	Percent of total population	Percent of total adherents
NASH	88	22,924	27,931*	47.2	100.0
081 CATHOLIC......	1	0	320	0.5	1.1
093 CR CH (DISC)..	4	778	955*	1.6	3.4
097 CR C AND C CR.	1	336	413*	0.7	1.5
127 CH GOD (CLEVE)	5	351	431*	0.7	1.5
193 EPISCOPAL.....	5	1,336	1,776	3.0	6.4
349 PENT HOLINESS.	6	215	264*	0.4	0.9
357 PRESB CH US...	5	1,216	1,493*	2.5	5.3
413 S-D ADVENTISTS	1	43	53*	0.1	0.2
419 SO BAPT CONV..	40	13,627	16,735*	28.3	59.9
449 UN METHODIST..	19	4,853	5,283	8.9	18.9
453 UN PRES CH USA	1	169	208*	0.4	0.7
NEW HANOVER	86	31,317	40,110*	48.3	100.0
081 CATHOLIC......	5	0	1,514	1.8	3.8
093 CR CH (DISC)..	1	393	482*	0.6	1.2
097 CR C AND C CR.	1	65	80*	0.1	0.2
127 CH GOD (CLEVE)	2	630	773*	0.9	1.9
165 CH OF NAZARENE	1	56	127	0.2	0.3
193 EPISCOPAL.....	6	2,282	3,246	3.9	8.1
281 LUTH CH AMER..	3	1,291	1,656	2.0	4.1
283 LUTH--MO SYNOD	1	103	146	0.2	0.4
349 PENT HOLINESS.	2	300	368*	0.4	0.9
357 PRESB CH US...	14	4,649	5,702*	6.9	14.2
381 REF PRES-EVAN.	1	56	65	0.1	0.2
403 SALVATION ARMY	1	95	287	0.3	0.7
413 S-D ADVENTISTS	2	341	418*	0.5	1.0
419 SO BAPT CONV..	29	14,677	18,002*	21.7	44.9
435 UNITARIAN-UNIV	1	52	92	0.1	0.2
443 UN C OF CHRIST	1	131	161*	0.2	0.4
449 UN METHODIST..	14	6,055	6,818	8.2	17.0
453 UN PRES CH USA	1	141	173*	0.2	0.4
NORTHAMPTON	40	7,376	8,553*	35.6	100.0
193 EPISCOPAL.....	2	48	65	0.3	0.8
226 FRIENDS-USA...	1	88	108*	0.4	1.3
419 SO BAPT CONV..	18	4,438	5,452*	22.7	63.7
449 UN METHODIST..	19	2,802	2,928	12.2	34.2
ONSLOW	64	15,656	23,108*	22.4	100.0
081 CATHOLIC......	3	0	3,773	3.7	16.3
093 CR CH (DISC)..	4	687	842*	0.8	3.6
097 CR C AND C CR.	1	50	61*	0.1	0.3
123 CH GOD (ANDER)	4	104	280	0.3	1.2
127 CH GOD (CLEVE)	2	83	102*	0.1	0.4
165 CH OF NAZARENE	1	43	80	0.1	0.3
193 EPISCOPAL.....	2	330	628	0.6	2.7
281 LUTH CH AMER..	1	170	248	0.2	1.1
283 LUTH--MO SYNOD	1	137	218	0.2	0.9
349 PENT HOLINESS.	5	176	216*	0.2	0.9
357 PRESB CH US...	2	569	697*	0.7	3.0
413 S-D ADVENTISTS	1	26	32*	-	0.1
419 SO BAPT CONV..	22	9,094	11,144*	10.8	48.2
443 UN C OF CHRIST	1	17	21*	-	0.1
449 UN METHODIST..	14	4,170	4,766	4.6	20.6
ORANGE	84	20,923	27,045*	46.9	100.0
019 AMER BAPT CONV	1	620	732*	1.3	2.7
081 CATHOLIC......	2	0	2,181	3.8	8.1
123 CH GOD (ANDER)	1	45	110	0.2	0.4
127 CH GOD (CLEVE)	2	138	163*	0.3	0.6
193 EPISCOPAL.....	3	1,333	1,973	3.4	7.3
281 LUTH CH AMER..	1	321	458	0.8	1.7
349 PENT HOLINESS.	1	22	26*	-	0.1
353 PLY BRETHREN..	1	30	50	0.1	0.2
357 PRESB CH US...	10	1,711	2,020*	3.5	7.5
419 SO BAPT CONV..	40	11,371	13,423*	23.3	49.6
435 UNITARIAN-UNIV	1	85	132	0.2	0.5
443 UN C OF CHRIST	4	319	377*	0.7	1.4
449 UN METHODIST..	17	4,928	5,400	9.4	20.0
PAMLICO	34	2,802	3,273*	34.6	100.0
093 CR CH (DISC)..	7	691	842*	8.9	25.7
097 CR C AND C CR.	1	50	61*	0.6	1.9
127 CH GOD (CLEVE)	1	33	40*	0.4	1.2
349 PENT HOLINESS.	5	126	153*	1.6	4.7
419 SO BAPT CONV..	3	267	325*	3.4	9.9
443 UN C OF CHRIST	4	541	659*	7.0	20.1
449 UN METHODIST..	13	1,094	1,19[illegible]	12.6	36.4
PASQUOTANK	32	8,528	11,045*	41.2	100.0
081 CATHOLIC......	3	0	569	2.1	5.2
093 CR CH (DISC)..	4	462	565*	2.1	5.1
097 CR C AND C CR.	1	200	244*	0.9	2.2
127 CH GOD (CLEVE)	1	32	39*	0.1	0.4
193 EPISCOPAL.....	1	320	[illegible]25	2.0	4.8
349 PENT HOLINESS.	1	132	161*	0.6	1.5
357 PRESB CH US...	1	270	330*	1.2	3.0
403 SALVATION ARMY	1	72	267	1.0	2.4
413 S-D ADVENTISTS	1	40	49*	0.2	0.4
419 SO BAPT CONV..	8	4,241	5,184*	19.3	46.9
449 UN METHODIST..	9	2,741	3,090	11.5	28.0
453 UN PRES CH USA	1	18	22*	0.1	0.2
PENDER	40	6,132	7,574*	41.7	100.0
081 CATHOLIC......	1	0	119	0.7	1.6
093 CR CH (DISC)..	1	25	31*	0.2	0.4

County and Denomination	Number of churches	Communicant, confirmed, full members	Total adherents		
			Number	Percent of total population	Percent of total adherents
193 EPISCOPAL.....	1	0	53	0.3	0.7
349 PENT HOLINESS.	1	42	52*	0.3	0.7
357 PRESB CH US...	10	859	1,058*	5.8	14.0
419 SO BAPT CONV..	19	4,285	5,275*	29.1	69.6
449 UN METHODIST..	7	921	986	5.4	13.0
PERQUIMANS	21	3,291	3,782*	45.3	100.0
093 CR CH (DISC)..	1	48	57*	0.7	1.5
097 CR C AND C CR.	2	221	264*	3.2	7.0
193 EPISCOPAL.....	1	114	138	1.7	3.6
226 FRIENDS-USA...	2	261	312*	3.7	8.2
419 SO BAPT CONV..	8	1,451	1,735*	20.8	45.9
449 UN METHODIST..	7	1,196	1,276	15.3	33.7
PERSON	42	11,044	12,933*	49.9	100.0
081 CATHOLIC......	2	0	143	0.6	1.1
127 CH GOD (CLEVE)	1	112	137*	0.5	1.1
193 EPISCOPAL.....	1	57	96	0.4	0.7
349 PENT HOLINESS.	1	22	27*	0.1	0.2
357 PRESB CH US...	1	171	209*	0.8	1.6
419 SO BAPT CONV..	21	6,674	8,149*	31.4	63.0
449 UN METHODIST..	15	4,008	4,172	16.1	32.3
PITT	97	16,443	21,005*	28.4	100.0
081 CATHOLIC......	4	0	795	1.1	3.8
093 CR CH (DISC)..	23	3,508	4,230*	5.7	20.1
097 CR C AND C CR.	4	310	374*	0.5	1.8
127 CH GOD (CLEVE)	5	309	373*	0.5	1.8
193 EPISCOPAL.....	2	68	707	1.0	3.4
281 LUTH CH AMER..	1	141	204	0.3	1.0
349 PENT HOLINESS.	13	861	1,038*	1.4	4.9
357 PRESB CH US...	13	1,528	1,842*	2.5	8.8
403 SALVATION ARMY	1	84	392	0.5	1.9
413 S-D ADVENTISTS	1	66	80*	0.1	0.4
419 SO BAPT CONV..	14	4,156	5,011*	6.8	23.9
435 UNITARIAN-UNIV	1	28	38	0.1	0.2
449 UN METHODIST..	15	5,384	5,921	8.0	28.2
POLK	46	8,217	9,750*	83.1	100.0
055 AS REF PRES CH	1	92	109*	0.9	1.1
081 CATHOLIC......	1	0	65	0.6	0.7
127 CH GOD (CLEVE)	1	29	34*	0.3	0.3
157 CH OF BRETHREN	2	256	304*	2.6	3.1
193 EPISCOPAL.....	3	565	686	5.8	7.0
349 PENT HOLINESS.	1	77	91*	0.8	0.9
357 PRESB CH US...	3	856	1,015*	8.6	10.4
413 S-D ADVENTISTS	1	90	107*	0.9	1.1
419 SO BAPT CONV..	25	5,269	6,247*	53.2	64.1
443 UN C OF CHRIST	1	309	366*	3.1	3.8
449 UN METHODIST..	7	674	726	6.2	7.4
RANDOLPH	182	31,104	37,128*	48.6	100.0
081 CATHOLIC......	1	0	202	0.3	0.5
097 CR C AND C CR.	1	20	24*	-	0.1
127 CH GOD (CLEVE)	5	542	663*	0.9	1.8
165 CH OF NAZARENE	2	119	303	0.4	0.8
193 EPISCOPAL.....	1	241	366	0.5	1.0
226 FRIENDS-USA...	13	2,469	3,022*	4.0	8.1
281 LUTH CH AMER..	3	461	608	0.8	1.6
349 PENT HOLINESS.	4	188	230*	0.3	0.6
353 PLY BRETHREN..	1	80	120	0.2	0.3
357 PRESB CH US...	4	680	832*	1.1	2.2
403 SALVATION ARMY	1	4	46	0.1	0.1
413 S-D ADVENTISTS	1	62	76*	0.1	0.2
419 SO BAPT CONV..	50	12,144	14,863*	19.5	40.0
443 UN C OF CHRIST	20	2,350	2,876*	3.8	7.7
449 UN METHODIST..	75	11,744	12,897	16.9	34.7
RICHMOND	69	14,533	17,147*	43.0	100.0
081 CATHOLIC......	1	0	156	0.4	0.9
097 CR C AND C CR.	2	50	61*	0.2	0.4
127 CH GOD (CLEVE)	4	209	257*	0.6	1.5
193 EPISCOPAL.....	1	71	85	0.2	0.5
281 LUTH CH AMER..	1	190	270	0.7	1.6
349 PENT HOLINESS.	7	459	564*	1.4	3.3
419 SO BAPT CONV..	28	7,348	9,035*	22.7	52.7
443 UN C OF CHRIST	1	191	235*	0.6	1.4
449 UN METHODIST..	24	6,015	6,484	16.3	37.8
ROBESON	172	33,653	42,737*	50.4	100.0
081 CATHOLIC......	2	0	421	0.5	1.0
093 CR CH (DISC)..	1	60	77*	0.1	0.2
127 CH GOD (CLEVE	13	1,044	1,336*	1.6	3.1
193 EPISCOPAL...	1	215	344	0.4	0.8
281 LUTH CH AMER.	1	103	150	0.2	0.4
349 PENT HOLINESS.	5	531	679*	0.8	1.6
353 PLY BRETHREN..	1	75	150	0.2	0.4
357 PRESB CH US...	18	3,037	3,885*	4.6	9.1
413 S-D ADVENTISTS	2	54	69*	0.1	0.2
419 SO BAPT CONV..	88	21,253	27,190*	32.0	63.6
449 UN METHODIST..	35	6,728	7,729	9.1	18.1
453 UN PRES CH USA	5	553	707*	0.8	1.7
ROCKINGHAM	135	25,862	31,340*	43.3	100.0
081 CATHOLIC......	2	0	419	0.6	1.3
093 CR CH (DISC)..	10	994	1,211*	1.7	3.9
097 CR C AND C CR.	11	1,326	1,616*	2.2	5.2

*Total adherents estimated from known number of communicant, confirmed, full members.

—Represents a percent less than 0.1.

Percentages may not total due to rounding.

Table 3. Churches and Church Membership by State, County and Denomination: 1971

County and Denomination	Number of churches	Communicant, confirmed, full members	Total adherents: Number	Total adherents: Percent of total population	Total adherents: Percent of total adherents
127 CH GOD (CLEVE)	4	248	302*	0.4	1.0
157 CH OF BRETHREN	1	523	637*	0.9	2.0
193 EPISCOPAL.....	5	793	906	1.3	2.9
226 FRIENDS-USA...	2	131	160*	0.2	0.5
281 LUTH CH AMER..	1	78	108	0.1	0.3
295 MORAV CH-SOUTH	2	483	604	0.8	1.9
349 PENT HOLINESS.	7	627	764*	1.1	2.4
357 PRESB CH US...	11	1,723	2,099*	2.9	6.7
381 REF PRES-EVAN.	1	27	38	0.1	0.1
403 SALVATION ARMY	1	101	404	0.6	1.3
419 SO BAPT CONV..	35	10,516	12,813*	17.7	40.9
443 UN C OF CHRIST	2	767	935*	1.3	3.0
449 UN METHODIST..	40	7,525	8,324	11.5	26.6
ROWAN	161	46,192	56,548*	62.8	100.0
055 AS REF PRES CH	1	126	150*	0.2	0.3
081 CATHOLIC......	1	0	812	0.9	1.4
097 CR C AND C CR.	1	85	101*	0.1	0.2
123 CH GOD (ANDER)	1	10	35	-	0.1
127 CH GOD (CLEVE)	8	489	584*	0.6	1.0
165 CH OF NAZARENE	1	65	163	0.2	0.3
193 EPISCOPAL.....	8	1,151	1,360	1.5	2.4
281 LUTH CH AMER..	33	12,856	16,357	18.2	28.9
283 LUTH--MO SYNOD	1	103	157	0.2	0.3
357 PRESB CH US...	13	3,393	4,050*	4.5	7.2
413 S-D ADVENTISTS	1	133	159*	0.2	0.3
419 SO BAPT CONV..	46	14,829	17,702*	19.7	31.3
443 UN C OF CHRIST	11	2,554	3,049*	3.4	5.4
449 UN METHODIST..	31	9,833	11,195	12.4	19.8
453 UN PRES CH USA	4	565	674*	0.7	1.2
RUTHERFORD	125	30,987	37,187*	78.6	100.0
081 CATHOLIC......	1	0	150	0.3	0.4
127 CH GOD (CLEVE)	3	137	167*	0.4	0.4
157 CH OF BRETHREN	1	110	134*	0.3	0.4
193 EPISCOPAL.....	1	206	248	0.5	0.7
281 LUTH CH AMER..	1	97	119	0.3	0.3
283 LUTH--MO SYNOD	1	14	18	-	-
357 PRESB CH US...	8	841	1,022*	2.2	2.7
413 S-D ADVENTISTS	1	50	61*	0.1	0.2
419 SO BAPT CONV..	80	24,843	30,202*	63.8	81.2
449 UN METHODIST..	28	4,689	5,066	10.7	13.6
SAMPSON	113	19,014	23,173*	51.5	100.0
081 CATHOLIC......	3	0	473	1.1	2.0
093 CR CH (DISC)..	19	1,764	2,147*	4.8	9.3
127 CH GOD (CLEVE)	5	242	294*	0.7	1.3
193 EPISCOPAL.....	1	36	187	0.4	0.8
349 PENT HOLINESS.	7	626	762*	1.7	3.3
357 PRESB CH US...	5	742	903*	2.0	3.9
413 S-D ADVENTISTS	1	11	13*	-	0.1
419 SO BAPT CONV..	43	11,312	13,765*	30.6	59.4
435 UNITARIAN-UNIV	2	65	65	0.1	0.3
449 UN METHODIST..	26	4,162	4,498	10.0	19.4
453 UN PRES CH USA	1	54	66*	0.1	0.3
SCOTLAND	51	8,155	10,157*	37.7	100.0
081 CATHOLIC......	1	0	254	0.9	2.5
127 CH GOD (CLEVE)	2	269	334*	1.2	3.3
193 EPISCOPAL.....	1	63	63	0.2	0.6
281 LUTH CH AMER..	1	107	166	0.6	1.6
349 PENT HOLINESS.	7	400	497*	1.8	4.9
353 PLY BRETHREN..	1	50	90	0.3	0.9
357 PRESB CH US...	9	1,922	2,387*	8.9	23.5
413 S-D ADVENTISTS	1	67	83*	0.3	0.8
419 SO BAPT CONV..	11	2,132	2,648*	9.8	26.1
449 UN METHODIST..	14	2,973	3,421	12.7	33.7
453 UN PRES CH USA	3	172	214*	0.8	2.1
STANLY	108	24,971	29,627*	69.2	100.0
081 CATHOLIC......	1	0	306	0.7	1.0
127 CH GOD (CLEVE)	4	233	281*	0.7	0.9
165 CH OF NAZARENE	2	74	163	0.4	0.6
193 EPISCOPAL.....	1	161	225	0.5	0.8
281 LUTH CH AMER..	4	910	1,120	2.6	3.8
349 PENT HOLINESS.	1	22	27*	0.1	0.1
357 PRESB CH US...	7	1,498	1,808*	4.2	6.1
381 REF PRES-EVAN.	1	242	276	0.6	0.9
413 S-D ADVENTISTS	1	85	103*	0.2	0.3
419 SO BAPT CONV..	52	14,765	17,825*	41.6	60.2
443 UN C OF CHRIST	1	247	298*	0.7	1.0
449 UN METHODIST..	33	6,734	7,195	16.8	24.3
STOKES	62	9,280	11,085*	46.6	100.0
097 CR C AND C CR.	7	1,425	1,744*	7.3	15.7
127 CH GOD (CLEVE)	3	91	111*	0.5	1.0
193 EPISCOPAL.....	2	66	84	0.4	0.8
226 FRIENDS-USA...	2	121	148*	0.6	1.3
295 MORAV CH-SOUTH	2	256	371	1.6	3.3
349 PENT HOLINESS.	1	48	59*	0.2	0.5
357 PRESB CH US...	6	395	483*	2.0	4.4
419 SO BAPT CONV..	19	4,809	5,885*	24.7	53.1
443 UN C OF CHRIST	1	88	108*	0.5	1.0
449 UN METHODIST..	19	1,981	2,092	8.8	18.9
SURRY	133	23,995	29,237*	56.9	100.0
081 CATHOLIC......	2	0	175	0.3	0.6
097 CR C AND C CR.	2	226	274*	0.5	0.9
127 CH GOD (CLEVE)	2	186	226*	0.4	0.8
157 CH OF BRETHREN	2	217	264*	0.5	0.9
193 EPISCOPAL.....	2	151	278	0.5	1.0
226 FRIENDS-USA...	8	1,103	1,340*	2.6	4.6
281 LUTH CH AMER..	1	63	93	0.2	0.3
295 MORAV CH-SOUTH	1	433	549	1.1	1.9
349 PENT HOLINESS.	7	379	460*	0.9	1.6
357 PRESB CH US...	6	797	968*	1.9	3.3
403 SALVATION ARMY	1	56	294	0.6	1.0
419 SO BAPT CONV..	72	16,670	20,244*	39.4	69.2
449 UN METHODIST..	26	3,696	4,050	7.9	13.9
453 UN PRES CH USA	1	18	22*	-	0.1
SWAIN	41	4,726	5,724*	72.8	100.0
081 CATHOLIC......	1	0	80	1.0	1.4
127 CH GOD (CLEVE)	4	134	161*	2.0	2.8
193 EPISCOPAL.....	1	12	12	0.2	0.2
349 PENT HOLINESS.	2	33	40*	0.5	0.7
357 PRESB CH US...	1	96	115*	1.5	2.0
419 SO BAPT CONV..	31	4,234	5,082*	64.6	88.8
449 UN METHODIST..	1	217	234	3.0	4.1
TRANSYLVANIA	49	9,639	12,199*	61.9	100.0
081 CATHOLIC......	1	0	351	1.8	2.9
127 CH GOD (CLEVE)	4	189	232*	1.2	1.9
165 CH OF NAZARENE	1	22	77	0.4	0.6
193 EPISCOPAL.....	1	257	405	2.1	3.3
281 LUTH CH AMER..	1	95	129	0.7	1.1
357 PRESB CH US...	1	643	790*	4.0	6.5
413 S-D ADVENTISTS	1	58	71*	0.4	0.6
419 SO BAPT CONV..	32	7,115	8,747*	44.4	71.7
449 UN METHODIST..	7	1,260	1,397	7.1	11.5
TYRRELL	11	1,248	1,465*	38.5	100.0
097 CR C AND C CR.	3	400	482*	12.7	32.9
127 CH GOD (CLEVE)	1	15	18*	0.5	1.2
193 EPISCOPAL.....	1	29	40	1.1	2.7
419 SO BAPT CONV..	2	429	517*	13.6	35.3
449 UN METHODIST..	4	375	408	10.7	27.8
UNION	124	24,216	29,928*	54.7	100.0
081 CATHOLIC......	1	0	285	0.5	1.0
123 CH GOD (ANDER)	3	80	189	0.3	0.6
127 CH GOD (CLEVE)	2	78	97*	0.2	0.3
165 CH OF NAZARENE	1	93	194	0.4	0.6
193 EPISCOPAL.....	1	236	306	0.6	1.0
281 LUTH CH AMER..	1	164	220	0.4	0.7
349 PENT HOLINESS.	1	45	56*	0.1	0.2
357 PRESB CH US...	17	2,037	2,537*	4.6	8.5
419 SO BAPT CONV..	56	15,574	19,400*	35.5	64.8
449 UN METHODIST..	36	5,530	6,172	11.3	20.6
453 UN PRES CH USA	5	379	472*	0.9	1.6
VANCE	62	14,307	17,325*	53.0	100.0
081 CATHOLIC......	1	0	79	0.2	0.5
127 CH GOD (CLEVE)	2	343	423*	1.3	2.4
165 CH OF NAZARENE	1	26	66	0.2	0.4
193 EPISCOPAL.....	4	492	635	1.9	3.7
349 PENT HOLINESS.	3	328	405*	1.2	2.3
357 PRESB CH US...	5	650	802*	2.5	4.6
403 SALVATION ARMY	1	59	385	1.2	2.2
419 SO BAPT CONV..	18	6,021	7,425*	22.7	42.9
443 UN C OF CHRIST	9	1,693	2,088*	6.4	12.1
449 UN METHODIST..	17	4,441	4,704	14.4	27.2
453 UN PRES CH USA	1	254	313*	1.0	1.8
WAKE	216	82,116	109,150*	47.8	100.0
029 AMER LUTH CH..	1	182	289	0.1	0.3
081 CATHOLIC......	10	0	7,998	3.5	7.3
097 CR C AND C CR.	2	185	226*	0.1	0.2
123 CH GOD (ANDER)	3	178	419	0.2	0.4
127 CH GOD (CLEVE)	9	676	825*	0.4	0.8
165 CH OF NAZARENE	1	212	257	0.1	0.2
193 EPISCOPAL.....	12	4,984	6,632	2.9	6.1
226 FRIENDS-USA...	1	41	50*	-	-
281 LUTH CH AMER..	3	1,174	1,702	0.7	1.6
283 LUTH--MO SYNOD	1	372	516	0.2	0.5
335 ORTH PRESB CH.	1	7	8	-	-
349 PENT HOLINESS.	5	406	496*	0.2	0.5
353 PLY BRETHREN..	3	320	505	0.2	0.5
357 PRESB CH US...	17	6,989	8,532*	3.7	7.8
403 SALVATION ARMY	1	134	1,362	0.6	1.2
413 S-D ADVENTISTS	2	345	421*	0.2	0.4
419 SO BAPT CONV..	87	42,619	52,027*	22.8	47.7
435 UNITARIAN-UNIV	1	98	158	0.1	0.1
443 UN C OF CHRIST	22	3,179	3,881*	1.7	3.6
449 UN METHODIST..	32	19,772	22,549	9.9	20.7
453 UN PRES CH USA	2	243	297*	0.1	0.3
WARREN	43	7,659	8,960*	56.7	100.0
081 CATHOLIC......	1	0	42	0.3	0.5
127 CH GOD (CLEVE)	1	73	89*	0.6	1.0
193 EPISCOPAL.....	3	164	196	1.2	2.2
283 LUTH--MO SYNOD	1	193	262	1.7	2.9
349 PENT HOLINESS.	1	48	58*	0.4	0.6
357 PRESB CH US...	3	152	185*	1.2	2.1
419 SO BAPT CONV..	16	3,901	4,740*	30.0	52.9
443 UN C OF CHRIST	3	808	982*	6.2	11.0

*Total adherents estimated from known number of communicant, confirmed, full members.

—Represents a percent less than 0.1.

Percentages may not total due to rounding.

Table 3. Churches and Church Membership by State, County and Denomination: 1971

County and Denomination	Number of churches	Communicant, confirmed, full members	Total adherents: Number	Percent of total population	Percent of total adherents
449 UN METHODIST..	14	2,320	2,406	15.2	26.9
WASHINGTON	40	5,195	6,539*	46.6	100.0
081 CATHOLIC......	1	0	70	0.5	1.1
093 CR CH (DISC)..	8	1,219	1,540*	11.0	23.6
097 CR C AND C CR.	9	1,285	1,623*	11.6	24.8
127 CH GOD (CLEVE)	2	134	169*	1.2	2.6
165 CH OF NAZARENE	1	73	183	1.3	2.8
193 EPISCOPAL.....	4	185	248	1.8	3.8
349 PENT HOLINESS.	2	129	163*	1.2	2.5
357 PRESB CH US...	1	80	101*	0.7	1.5
413 S-D ADVENTISTS	1	25	32*	0.2	0.5
419 SO BAPT CONV..	5	1,062	1,341*	9.6	20.5
449 UN METHODIST..	6	1,003	1,069	7.6	16.3
WATAUGA	76	11,971	14,143*	60.4	100.0
081 CATHOLIC......	1	0	218	0.9	1.5
097 CR C AND C CR.	1	50	58*	0.2	0.4
127 CH GOD (CLEVE)	2	63	73*	0.3	0.5
193 EPISCOPAL.....	2	222	265	1.1	1.9
281 LUTH CH AMER..	3	600	787	3.4	5.6
357 PRESB CH US...	3	556	646*	2.8	4.6
413 S-D ADVENTISTS	1	21	24*	0.1	0.2
419 SO BAPT CONV..	50	8,962	10,420*	44.5	73.7
435 UNITARIAN-UNIV	1	13	24	0.1	0.2
449 UN METHODIST..	12	1,484	1,628	7.0	11.5
WAYNE	106	20,556	25,705*	30.1	100.0
081 CATHOLIC......	2	0	615	0.7	2.4
093 CR CH (DISC)..	20	1,927	2,399*	2.8	9.3
127 CH GOD (CLEVE)	4	486	605*	0.7	2.4
165 CH OF NAZARENE	1	48	85	0.1	0.3
193 EPISCOPAL.....	3	629	783	0.9	3.0
226 FRIENDS-USA...	6	933	1,161*	1.4	4.5
281 LUTH CH AMER..	1	173	222	0.3	0.9
283 LUTH--MO SYNOD	1	96	164	0.2	0.6
349 PENT HOLINESS.	11	892	1,110*	1.3	4.3
353 PLY BRETHREN..	1	50	80	0.1	0.3
357 PRESB CH US...	5	1,355	1,687*	2.0	6.6
403 SALVATION ARMY	1	209	818	1.0	3.2
413 S-D ADVENTISTS	1	50	62*	0.1	0.2
419 SO BAPT CONV..	17	6,001	7,470*	8.7	29.1
443 UN C OF CHRIST	1	85	106*	0.1	0.4
449 UN METHODIST..	28	7,528	8,221	9.6	32.0
453 UN PRES CH USA	3	94	117	0.1	0.5
WILKES	125	27,312	33,415*	67.5	100.0
081 CATHOLIC......	1	0	106	0.2	0.3
093 CR CH (DISC)..	1	74	91*	0.2	0.3
127 CH GOD (CLEVE)	3	236	290*	0.6	0.9
157 CH OF BRETHREN	2	110	135*	0.3	0.4
193 EPISCOPAL.....	1	95	182	0.4	0.5
281 LUTH CH AMER..	1	133	182	0.4	0.5
349 PENT HOLINESS.	3	136	167*	0.3	0.5
357 PRESB CH US...	3	586	720*	1.5	2.2
413 S-D ADVENTISTS	1	17	21*	-	0.1
419 SO BAPT CONV..	93	23,585	28,982*	58.5	86.7
449 UN METHODIST..	16	2,340	2,539	5.1	7.6
WILSON	69	13,879	17,855*	31.1	100.0
081 CATHOLIC......	2	0	457	0.8	2.6
093 CR CH (DISC)..	12	1,847	2,280*	4.0	12.8
123 CH GOD (ANDER)	2	36	96	0.2	0.5
127 CH GOD (CLEVE)	4	435	537*	0.9	3.0
193 EPISCOPAL.....	2	407	717	1.2	4.0
281 LUTH CH AMER..	1	129	203	0.4	1.1
283 LUTH--MO SYNOD	1	110	134	0.2	0.8
349 PENT HOLINESS.	10	702	867*	1.5	4.9
353 PLY BRETHREN..	1	30	50	0.1	0.3
357 PRESB CH US...	6	1,141	1,409*	2.5	7.9
403 SALVATION ARMY	1	154	703	1.2	3.9
413 S-D ADVENTISTS	2	122	151*	0.3	0.8
419 SO BAPT CONV..	10	4,527	5,589*	9.7	31.3
449 UN METHODIST..	13	4,098	4,488	7.8	25.1
453 UN PRES CH USA	2	141	174*	0.3	1.0
YADKIN	69	13,627	15,998*	65.0	100.0
127 CH GOD (CLEVE)	2	40	48*	0.2	0.3
226 FRIENDS-USA...	5	962	1,157*	4.7	7.2
281 LUTH CH AMER..	1	66	106	0.4	0.7
349 PENT HOLINESS.	4	446	537*	2.2	3.4
357 PRESB CH US...	1	43	52*	0.2	0.3
419 SO BAPT CONV..	32	9,224	11,097*	45.1	69.4
443 UN C OF CHRIST	1	26	31*	0.1	0.2
449 UN METHODIST..	22	2,776	2,917	11.9	18.2
453 UN PRES CH USA	1	44	53*	0.2	0.3
YANCEY	51	6,882	8,215*	65.0	100.0
081 CATHOLIC......	1	0	34	0.3	0.4
123 CH GOD (ANDER)	1	25	65	0.5	0.8
127 CH GOD (CLEVE)	1	73	88*	0.7	1.1
226 FRIENDS-USA...	1	17	20*	0.2	0.2
357 PRESB CH US...	6	316	380*	3.0	4.6
419 SO BAPT CONV..	31	5,497	6,610*	52.3	80.5
449 UN METHODIST..	9	866	912	7.2	11.1
453 UN PRES CH USA	1	88	106*	0.8	1.3
CO DATA NOT AVAIL	327	34,984	57,585*	N/A	N/A
127 CH GOD (CLEVE)	2	89	109*	N/A	N/A
151 L-D SAINTS....	0	0	15,047	N/A	N/A
193 EPISCOPAL.....	6	561	673	N/A	N/A
223 FREE WILL BAPT	162	24,254	29,714*	N/A	N/A
349 PENT HOLINESS.	2	21	26*	N/A	N/A
467 WESLEYAN......	155	10,059	12,016	N/A	N/A

NORTH DAKOTA

County and Denomination	Number of churches	Communicant, confirmed, full members	Total adherents: Number	Percent of total population	Percent of total adherents
THE STATE.....	1,562	220,835	473,332*	76.6	100.0
ADAMS	13	1,588	2,670*	69.7	100.0
029 AMER LUTH CH..	5	1,242	1,804	47.1	67.6
081 CATHOLIC......	2	0	426	11.1	16.0
313 NO AM BAPT GC.	1	38	46*	1.2	1.7
443 UN C OF CHRIST	2	167	202*	5.3	7.6
449 UN METHODIST..	1	86	124	3.2	4.6
469 WISC EVAN LUTH	2	55	68	1.8	2.5
BARNES	42	6,078	11,860*	80.9	100.0
019 AMER BAPT CONV	1	90	107*	0.7	0.9
029 AMER LUTH CH..	17	3,684	5,174	35.3	43.6
081 CATHOLIC......	6	0	3,323	22.7	28.0
165 CH OF NAZARENE	1	24	38	0.3	0.3
193 EPISCOPAL.....	2	80	131	0.9	1.1
221 FREE METH C NA	1	9	10	0.1	0.1
281 LUTH CH AMER..	1	321	528	3.6	4.5
283 LUTH--MO SYNOD	1	196	271	1.8	2.3
353 PLY BRETHREN..	1	31	50	0.3	0.4
371 REF CH IN AM..	1	42	66	0.4	0.6
403 SALVATION ARMY	1	35	167	1.1	1.4
413 S-D ADVENTISTS	1	20	24*	0.2	0.2
443 UN C OF CHRIST	1	408	485*	3.3	4.1
449 UN METHODIST..	5	1,024	1,333	9.1	11.2
453 UN PRES CH USA	1	43	51*	0.3	0.4
469 WISC EVAN LUTH	1	71	102	0.7	0.9
BENSON	33	2,856	6,499*	78.8	100.0
029 AMER LUTH CH..	18	2,479	3,327	40.4	51.2
081 CATHOLIC......	8	0	2,712	32.9	41.7
157 CH OF BRETHREN	1	57	72*	0.9	1.1
193 EPISCOPAL.....	1	32	45	0.5	0.7
281 LUTH CH AMER..	2	191	223	2.7	3.4
449 UN METHODIST..	1	27	32	0.4	0.5
453 UN PRES CH USA	2	70	88*	1.1	1.4
BILLINGS	5	55	458*	38.2	100.0
029 AMER LUTH CH..	1	43	53	4.4	11.6
081 CATHOLIC......	3	0	390	32.6	85.2
443 UN C OF CHRIST	1	12	15*	1.3	3.3
BOTTINEAU	36	4,906	7,690*	81.0	100.0
019 AMER BAPT CONV	1	128	153*	1.6	2.0
029 AMER LUTH CH..	15	2,767	3,758	39.6	48.9
081 CATHOLIC......	5	0	1,189	12.5	15.5
127 CH GOD (CLEVE)	1	30	36*	0.4	0.5
281 LUTH CH AMER..	1	164	222	2.3	2.9
283 LUTH--MO SYNOD	5	852	1,126	11.9	14.6
413 S-D ADVENTISTS	1	35	42*	0.4	0.5
449 UN METHODIST..	4	371	496	5.2	6.4
453 UN PRES CH USA	3	559	668*	7.0	8.7
BOWMAN	15	1,633	3,439*	88.2	100.0
029 AMER LUTH CH..	7	1,279	1,761	45.1	51.2
081 CATHOLIC......	3	0	1,200	30.8	34.9
127 CH GOD (CLEVE)	1	5	6*	0.2	0.2
413 S-D ADVENTISTS	1	62	76*	1.9	2.2
443 UN C OF CHRIST	1	77	94*	2.4	2.7
449 UN METHODIST..	1	195	284	7.3	8.3
453 UN PRES CH USA	1	15	18*	0.5	0.5
BURKE	21	2,048	3,216*	67.9	100.0
019 AMER BAPT CONV	1	261	316*	6.7	9.8
029 AMER LUTH CH..	7	1,294	1,843	38.9	57.3
081 CATHOLIC......	5	0	417	8.8	13.0
127 CH GOD (CLEVE)	1	24	29*	0.6	0.9
283 LUTH--MO SYNOD	2	117	180	3.8	5.6
449 UN METHODIST..	3	255	314	6.6	9.8
453 UN PRES CH USA	2	97	117*	2.5	3.6
BURLEIGH	43	12,940	31,312*	76.9	100.0
019 AMER BAPT CONV	1	328	413*	1.0	1.3
029 AMER LUTH CH..	7	5,375	7,781	19.1	24.8
081 CATHOLIC......	8	0	13,174	32.4	42.1
127 CH GOD (CLEVE)	1	37	47*	0.1	0.2
165 CH OF NAZARENE	1	82	102	0.3	0.3
193 EPISCOPAL.....	1	294	356	0.9	1.1
281 LUTH CH AMER..	3	1,117	1,629	4.0	5.2

*Total adherents estimated from known number of communicant, confirmed, full members.

—Represents a percent less than 0.1.

Percentages may not total due to rounding.

Table 3. Churches and Church Membership by State, County and Denomination: 1971

County and Denomination	Number of churches	Communicant, confirmed, full members	Total adherents: Number	Total adherents: Percent of total population	Total adherents: Percent of total adherents
283 LUTH--MO SYNOD	3	1,025	1,602	3.9	5.1
287 MENN GEN CONF.	1	30	38*	0.1	0.1
313 NO AM BAPT GC.	1	403	508*	1.2	1.6
371 REF CH IN AM..	1	101	170	0.4	0.5
403 SALVATION ARMY	1	121	362	0.9	1.2
419 SO BAPT CONV..	1	65	82*	0.2	0.3
435 UNITARIAN-UNIV	1	30	38	0.1	0.1
443 UN C OF CHRIST	2	331	417*	1.0	1.3
449 UN METHODIST..	7	2,205	2,808	6.9	9.0
453 UN PRES CH USA	2	1,307	1,647*	4.0	5.3
469 WISC EVAN LUTH	1	89	138	0.3	0.4
CASS	103	28,605	55,105*	74.8	100.0
019 AMER BAPT CONV	1	349	424*	0.6	0.8
029 AMER LUTH CH..	30	14,394	19,935	27.1	36.2
081 CATHOLIC......	14	0	16,317	22.2	29.6
093 CR CH (DISC)..	1	68	83*	0.1	0.2
097 CR C AND C CR.	1	56	68*	0.1	0.1
123 CH GOD (ANDER)	2	41	80	0.1	0.1
127 CH GOD (CLEVE)	1	21	26*	-	-
165 CH OF NAZARENE	1	30	81	0.1	0.1
201 EVAN COV CH AM	1	75	91*	0.1	0.2
221 FREE METH C NA	1	28	38	0.1	0.1
281 LUTH CH AMER..	7	4,053	5,539	7.5	10.1
283 LUTH--MO SYNOD	4	1,833	2,712	3.7	4.9
285 MENNONITE CH..	1	66	80*	0.1	0.1
293 MORAV CH-NORTH	6	659	821	1.1	1.5
313 NO AM BAPT GC.	1	134	163*	0.2	0.3
353 PLY BRETHREN..	1	15	30	-	0.1
403 SALVATION ARMY	1	67	313	0.4	0.6
413 S-D ADVENTISTS	1	107	130*	0.2	0.2
419 SO BAPT CONV..	1	88	107*	0.1	0.2
435 UNITARIAN-UNIV	1	42	57	0.1	0.1
443 UN C OF CHRIST	4	780	948*	1.3	1.7
449 UN METHODIST..	13	3,474	4,357	5.9	7.9
453 UN PRES CH USA	9	2,225	2,705*	3.7	4.9
CAVALIER	40	2,762	6,965*	84.8	100.0
029 AMER LUTH CH..	12	1,237	1,701	20.7	24.4
081 CATHOLIC......	9	0	3,317	40.4	47.6
193 EPISCOPAL.....	1	40	68	0.8	1.0
197 EVAN CH OF NA.	1	68	84*	1.0	1.2
281 LUTH CH AMER..	1	39	62	0.8	0.9
283 LUTH--MO SYNOD	2	198	264	3.2	3.8
287 MENN GEN CONF.	3	252	311*	3.8	4.5
449 UN METHODIST..	4	370	469	5.7	6.7
453 UN PRES CH USA	7	558	689*	8.4	9.9
DICKEY	24	3,033	5,049*	72.4	100.0
019 AMER BAPT CONV	1	134	159*	2.3	3.1
029 AMER LUTH CH..	3	631	858	12.3	17.0
081 CATHOLIC......	3	0	1,110	15.9	22.0
165 CH OF NAZARENE	2	110	171	2.5	3.4
193 EPISCOPAL.....	2	83	120	1.7	2.4
283 LUTH--MO SYNOD	5	1,113	1,497	21.5	29.6
413 S-D ADVENTISTS	1	108	128*	1.8	2.5
443 UN C OF CHRIST	1	50	59*	0.8	1.2
449 UN METHODIST..	4	604	709	10.2	14.0
453 UN PRES CH USA	2	200	238*	3.4	4.7
DIVIDE	19	1,786	2,903*	63.6	100.0
029 AMER LUTH CH..	12	1,610	2,102	46.1	72.4
081 CATHOLIC......	4	0	583	12.8	20.1
283 LUTH--MO SYNOD	1	12	20	0.4	0.7
449 UN METHODIST..	1	36	46	1.0	1.6
453 UN PRES CH USA	1	128	152*	3.3	5.2
DUNN	20	1,535	4,158*	84.9	100.0
019 AMER BAPT CONV	1	41	51*	1.0	1.2
029 AMER LUTH CH..	7	886	1,175	24.0	28.3
081 CATHOLIC......	8	0	2,121	43.3	51.0
281 LUTH CH AMER..	1	405	546	11.2	13.1
283 LUTH--MO SYNOD	1	135	180	3.7	4.3
413 S-D ADVENTISTS	1	11	14*	0.3	0.3
443 UN C OF CHRIST	1	57	71*	1.5	1.7
EDDY	14	2,014	3,563*	86.8	100.0
029 AMER LUTH CH..	5	1,192	1,657	40.4	46.5
081 CATHOLIC......	1	0	839	20.4	23.5
165 CH OF NAZARENE	1	25	40	1.0	1.1
281 LUTH CH AMER..	2	166	219	5.3	6.1
283 LUTH--MO SYNOD	1	111	168	4.1	4.7
443 UN C OF CHRIST	1	136	165*	4.0	4.6
449 UN METHODIST..	2	283	352	8.6	9.9
453 UN PRES CH USA	1	101	123*	3.0	3.5
EMMONS	17	1,163	5,466*	75.9	100.0
029 AMER LUTH CH..	1	147	204	2.8	3.7
081 CATHOLIC......	8	0	3,826	53.1	70.0
105 CHRISTIAN REF.	1	105	188	2.6	3.4
313 NO AM BAPT GC.	1	142	181*	2.5	3.3
371 REF CH IN AM..	2	204	346	4.8	6.3
413 S-D ADVENTISTS	1	20	25*	0.3	0.5
449 UN METHODIST..	2	306	373	5.2	6.8
469 WISC EVAN LUTH	1	239	323	4.5	5.9
FOSTER	16	2,409	4,336*	89.7	100.0
029 AMER LUTH CH..	5	1,370	1,877	38.8	43.3
081 CATHOLIC......	3	0	991	20.5	22.9
165 CH OF NAZARENE	1	34	106	2.2	2.4
283 LUTH--MO SYNOD	1	203	313	6.5	7.2
313 NO AM BAPT GC.	1	133	166*	3.4	3.8
413 S-D ADVENTISTS	1	71	89*	1.8	2.1
443 UN C OF CHRIST	1	238	297*	6.1	6.8
449 UN METHODIST..	3	360	497	10.3	11.5
GOLDEN VALLEY	12	784	2,033*	77.9	100.0
029 AMER LUTH CH..	2	333	449	17.2	22.1
081 CATHOLIC......	3	0	1,033	39.6	50.8
197 EVAN CH OF NA.	2	61	74*	2.8	3.6
283 LUTH--MO SYNOD	1	168	206	7.9	10.1
413 S-D ADVENTISTS	1	59	72*	2.8	3.5
443 UN C OF CHRIST	2	130	158*	6.1	7.8
449 UN METHODIST..	1	33	41	1.6	2.0
GRAND FORKS	67	17,128	37,666*	61.6	100.0
019 AMER BAPT CONV	1	441	546*	0.9	1.4
029 AMER LUTH CH..	27	9,806	13,834	22.6	36.7
081 CATHOLIC......	8	0	13,776	22.5	36.6
127 CH GOD (CLEVE)	1	31	38*	0.1	0.1
165 CH OF NAZARENE	2	73	170	0.3	0.5
193 EPISCOPAL.....	1	409	512	0.8	1.4
221 FREE METH C NA	1	14	27	-	0.1
281 LUTH CH AMER..	2	1,019	1,527	2.5	4.1
283 LUTH--MO SYNOD	5	1,056	1,533	2.5	4.1
313 NO AM BAPT GC.	1	237	293*	0.5	0.8
353 PLY BRETHREN..	1	10	10	-	-
403 SALVATION ARMY	1	56	286	0.5	0.8
413 S-D ADVENTISTS	1	80	99*	0.2	0.3
419 SO BAPT CONV..	3	809	1,001*	1.6	2.7
435 UNITARIAN-UNIV	1	25	34	0.1	0.1
443 UN C OF CHRIST	2	273	338*	0.6	0.9
449 UN METHODIST..	4	1,524	2,076	3.4	5.5
453 UN PRES CH USA	5	1,265	1,566*	2.6	4.2
GRANT	22	1,878	3,873*	77.3	100.0
029 AMER LUTH CH..	3	1,036	1,378	27.5	35.6
081 CATHOLIC......	5	0	1,393	27.8	36.0
313 NO AM BAPT GC.	1	99	121*	2.4	3.1
335 ORTH PRESB CH.	3	69	114	2.3	2.9
443 UN C OF CHRIST	4	204	250*	5.0	6.5
449 UN METHODIST..	1	120	151	3.0	3.9
453 UN PRES CH USA	1	92	113*	2.3	2.9
469 WISC EVAN LUTH	4	258	353	7.0	9.1
GRIGGS	16	1,879	2,907*	69.5	100.0
029 AMER LUTH CH..	9	1,569	2,074	49.6	71.3
081 CATHOLIC......	2	0	436	10.4	15.0
283 LUTH--MO SYNOD	2	135	188	4.5	6.5
449 UN METHODIST..	1	39	50	1.2	1.7
453 UN PRES CH USA	2	136	159*	3.8	5.5
HETTINGER	17	1,612	4,474*	88.2	100.0
029 AMER LUTH CH..	5	934	1,181	23.3	26.4
081 CATHOLIC......	3	0	2,403	47.3	53.7
165 CH OF NAZARENE	1	19	51	1.0	1.1
413 S-D ADVENTISTS	1	12	15*	0.3	0.3
443 UN C OF CHRIST	4	396	495*	9.8	11.1
449 UN METHODIST..	2	213	279	5.5	6.2
469 WISC EVAN LUTH	1	38	50	1.0	1.1
KIDDER	24	2,042	3,299*	75.6	100.0
029 AMER LUTH CH..	6	910	1,244	28.5	37.7
081 CATHOLIC......	3	0	514	11.8	15.6
165 CH OF NAZARENE	1	23	62	1.4	1.9
197 EVAN CH OF NA.	1	35	43*	1.0	1.3
283 LUTH--MO SYNOD	1	161	218	5.0	6.6
413 S-D ADVENTISTS	1	22	27*	0.6	0.8
443 UN C OF CHRIST	4	119	145*	3.3	4.4
449 UN METHODIST..	5	438	584	13.4	17.7
453 UN PRES CH USA	1	84	103*	2.4	3.1
469 WISC EVAN LUTH	1	250	359	8.2	10.9
LA MOURE	35	3,765	6,488*	91.2	100.0
029 AMER LUTH CH..	10	1,224	1,616	22.7	24.9
081 CATHOLIC......	6	0	1,650	23.2	25.4
165 CH OF NAZARENE	1	47	83	1.2	1.3
283 LUTH--MO SYNOD	4	810	1,020	14.3	15.7
371 REF CH IN AM..	1	78	133	1.9	2.0
413 S-D ADVENTISTS	2	101	121*	1.7	1.9
443 UN C OF CHRIST	3	431	518*	7.3	8.0
449 UN METHODIST..	6	803	1,021	14.3	15.7
453 UN PRES CH USA	2	271	326*	4.6	5.0
LOGAN	17	1,618	3,604*	84.9	100.0
029 AMER LUTH CH..	3	680	930	21.9	25.8
081 CATHOLIC......	4	0	1,511	35.6	41.9
283 LUTH--MO SYNOD	1	116	154	3.6	4.3
313 NO AM BAPT GC.	4	342	423*	10.0	11.7
413 S-D ADVENTISTS	2	79	98*	2.3	2.7
443 UN C OF CHRIST	2	224	277*	6.5	7.7
449 UN METHODIST..	1	177	211	5.0	5.9
MC HENRY	39	3,835	8,050*	89.7	100.0

*Total adherents estimated from known number of communicant, confirmed, full members.

—Represents a percent less than 0.1.

Percentages may not total due to rounding.

Table 3. Churches and Church Membership by State, County and Denomination: 1971

County and Denomination	Number of churches	Communicant, confirmed, full members	Total adherents: Number	Total adherents: Percent of total population	Total adherents: Percent of total adherents
019 AMER BAPT CONV	2	71	87*	1.0	1.1
029 AMER LUTH CH..	14	2,494	3,449	38.4	42.8
081 CATHOLIC......	8	0	2,874	32.0	35.7
127 CH GOD (CLEVE)	1	12	15*	0.2	0.2
165 CH OF NAZARENE	1	27	35	0.4	0.4
197 EVAN CH OF NA.	1	7	9*	0.1	0.1
283 LUTH--MO SYNOD	4	573	772	8.6	9.6
313 NO AM BAPT GC.	2	105	128*	1.4	1.6
443 UN C OF CHRIST	2	99	121*	1.3	1.5
449 UN METHODIST..	3	285	362	4.0	4.5
453 UN PRES CH USA	1	162	198*	2.2	2.5
MC INTOSH	19	3,489	5,513*	99.4	100.0
029 AMER LUTH CH..	5	1,841	2,382	43.0	43.2
081 CATHOLIC......	3	0	1,138	20.5	20.6
283 LUTH--MO SYNOD	1	126	165	3.0	3.0
313 NO AM BAPT GC.	3	611	732*	13.2	13.3
443 UN C OF CHRIST	3	285	342*	6.2	6.2
449 UN METHODIST..	3	476	556	10.0	10.1
469 WISC EVAN LUTH	1	150	198	3.6	3.6
MC KENZIE	24	1,987	3,345*	54.6	100.0
029 AMER LUTH CH..	13	1,641	2,367	38.6	70.8
081 CATHOLIC......	3	0	533	8.7	15.9
165 CH OF NAZARENE	1	20	28	0.5	0.8
283 LUTH--MO SYNOD	2	115	158	2.6	4.7
413 S-D ADVENTISTS	2	68	84*	1.4	2.5
443 UN C OF CHRIST	1	23	29*	0.5	0.9
449 UN METHODIST..	1	20	22	0.4	0.7
453 UN PRES CH USA	1	100	124*	2.0	3.7
MC LEAN	56	5,166	8,450*	75.1	100.0
029 AMER LUTH CH..	17	2,517	3,313	29.4	39.2
081 CATHOLIC......	10	0	1,821	16.2	21.6
127 CH GOD (CLEVE)	2	25	30*	0.3	0.4
165 CH OF NAZARENE	1	39	47	0.4	0.6
281 LUTH CH AMER..	4	545	754	6.7	8.9
283 LUTH--MO SYNOD	3	488	667	5.9	7.9
313 NO AM BAPT GC.	4	423	515*	4.6	6.1
381 REF PRES-EVAN.	1	59	62	0.6	0.7
413 S-D ADVENTISTS	3	176	214*	1.9	2.5
443 UN C OF CHRIST	4	415	505*	4.5	6.0
449 UN METHODIST..	6	321	330	2.9	3.9
453 UN PRES CH USA	1	158	192*	1.7	2.3
MERCER	18	3,678	5,406*	87.5	100.0
029 AMER LUTH CH..	7	2,337	3,083	49.9	57.0
081 CATHOLIC......	2	0	629	10.2	11.6
127 CH GOD (CLEVE)	1	100	123*	2.0	2.3
283 LUTH--MO SYNOD	5	895	1,166	18.9	21.6
313 NO AM BAPT GC.	1	68	83*	1.3	1.5
443 UN C OF CHRIST	1	166	203*	3.3	3.8
449 UN METHODIST..	1	112	119	1.9	2.2
MORTON	40	5,491	18,296*	90.1	100.0
029 AMER LUTH CH..	5	1,647	2,260	11.1	12.4
081 CATHOLIC......	13	0	11,033	54.3	60.3
165 CH OF NAZARENE	1	29	35	0.2	0.2
193 EPISCOPAL.....	1	49	93	0.5	0.5
283 LUTH--MO SYNOD	3	422	647	3.2	3.5
313 NO AM BAPT GC.	1	203	258*	1.3	1.4
413 S-D ADVENTISTS	1	13	16*	0.1	0.1
419 SO BAPT CONV..	1	57	72*	0.4	0.4
443 UN C OF CHRIST	6	1,759	2,232*	11.0	12.2
449 UN METHODIST..	4	607	712	3.5	3.9
453 UN PRES CH USA	2	464	589*	2.9	3.2
469 WISC EVAN LUTH	2	241	349	1.7	1.9
MOUNTRAIL	36	3,307	5,660*	67.1	100.0
019 AMER BAPT CONV	3	133	163*	1.9	2.9
029 AMER LUTH CH..	21	2,829	4,001	47.4	70.7
081 CATHOLIC......	4	0	1,072	12.7	18.9
127 CH GOD (CLEVE)	1	18	22*	0.3	0.4
193 EPISCOPAL.....	1	9	12	0.1	0.2
197 EVAN CH OF NA.	1	4	5*	0.1	0.1
443 UN C OF CHRIST	4	212	260*	3.1	4.6
453 UN PRES CH USA	1	102	125*	1.5	2.2
NELSON	28	3,516	5,505*	95.3	100.0
029 AMER LUTH CH..	19	3,236	4,197	72.7	76.2
081 CATHOLIC......	4	0	954	16.5	17.3
193 EPISCOPAL.....	1	30	52	0.9	0.9
283 LUTH--MO SYNOD	2	109	136	2.4	2.5
443 UN C OF CHRIST	2	141	166*	2.9	3.0
OLIVER	6	741	1,533	66.0	100.0
029 AMER LUTH CH..	2	401	533	23.0	34.8
081 CATHOLIC......	1	0	550	23.7	35.9
165 CH OF NAZARENE	1	15	30	1.3	2.0
283 LUTH--MO SYNOD	1	266	361	15.5	23.5
449 UN METHODIST..	1	59	59	2.5	3.8
PEMBINA	47	4,782	9,339*	87.1	100.0
029 AMER LUTH CH..	7	1,026	1,432	13.3	15.3
081 CATHOLIC......	9	0	3,233	30.1	34.6
193 EPISCOPAL.....	1	49	58	0.5	0.6
201 EVAN COV CH AM	1	59	71*	0.7	0.8
281 LUTH CH AMER..	7	964	1,232	11.5	13.2
283 LUTH--MO SYNOD	4	615	818	7.6	8.8
413 S-D ADVENTISTS	1	3	4*	-	-
449 UN METHODIST..	12	1,331	1,607	15.0	17.2
453 UN PRES CH USA	5	735	884*	8.2	9.5
PIERCE	18	2,234	6,046*	95.6	100.0
029 AMER LUTH CH..	8	1,741	2,294	36.3	37.9
081 CATHOLIC......	4	0	3,045	48.2	50.4
193 EPISCOPAL.....	1	39	119	1.9	2.0
283 LUTH--MO SYNOD	1	95	155	2.5	2.6
285 MENNONITE CH..	1	142	178*	2.8	2.9
449 UN METHODIST..	1	99	107	1.7	1.8
453 UN PRES CH USA	2	118	148*	2.3	2.4
RAMSEY	34	4,622	10,712*	82.9	100.0
029 AMER LUTH CH..	14	3,238	4,264	33.0	39.8
081 CATHOLIC......	8	0	4,633	35.9	43.3
193 EPISCOPAL.....	1	62	103	0.8	1.0
283 LUTH--MO SYNOD	2	301	439	3.4	4.1
413 S-D ADVENTISTS	1	22	27*	0.2	0.3
419 SO BAPT CONV..	1	35	43*	0.3	0.4
449 UN METHODIST..	5	678	852	6.6	8.0
453 UN PRES CH USA	2	286	351*	2.7	3.3
RANSOM	20	3,936	6,251*	88.0	100.0
019 AMER BAPT CONV	1	70	83*	1.2	1.3
029 AMER LUTH CH..	8	2,891	3,861	54.4	61.8
081 CATHOLIC......	3	0	1,075	15.1	17.2
165 CH OF NAZARENE	1	5	9	0.1	0.1
193 EPISCOPAL.....	1	37	44	0.6	0.7
283 LUTH--MO SYNOD	1	221	296	4.2	4.7
413 S-D ADVENTISTS	1	44	52*	0.7	0.8
449 UN METHODIST..	3	514	648	9.1	10.4
453 UN PRES CH USA	1	154	183*	2.6	2.9
RENVILLE	20	2,013	3,195*	83.5	100.0
019 AMER BAPT CONV	1	115	141*	3.7	4.4
029 AMER LUTH CH..	7	1,157	1,462	38.2	45.8
081 CATHOLIC......	4	0	588	15.4	18.4
165 CH OF NAZARENE	1	36	60	1.6	1.9
281 LUTH CH AMER..	3	344	469	12.3	14.7
283 LUTH--MO SYNOD	1	125	179	4.7	5.6
449 UN METHODIST..	3	236	296	7.7	9.3
RICHLAND	47	6,342	15,029*	83.1	100.0
029 AMER LUTH CH..	15	2,957	3,950	21.8	26.3
081 CATHOLIC......	9	0	6,615	36.6	44.0
127 CH GOD (CLEVE)	1	40	47*	0.3	0.3
193 EPISCOPAL.....	1	53	135	0.7	0.9
283 LUTH--MO SYNOD	9	2,424	3,104	17.2	20.7
413 S-D ADVENTISTS	1	130	154*	0.9	1.0
443 UN C OF CHRIST	3	627	741*	4.1	4.9
449 UN METHODIST..	8	111	283	1.6	1.9
ROLETTE	21	1,597	12,504*	108.3#	100.0
029 AMER LUTH CH..	6	959	1,441	12.5	11.5
081 CATHOLIC......	8	0	10,081	87.3	80.6
127 CH GOD (CLEVE)	1	7	10*	0.1	0.1
193 EPISCOPAL.....	1	27	180	1.6	1.4
283 LUTH--MO SYNOD	1	192	266	2.3	2.1
285 MENNONITE CH..	1	31	42*	0.4	0.3
449 UN METHODIST..	1	102	102	0.9	0.8
453 UN PRES CH USA	2	279	382*	3.3	3.1
SARGENT	23	2,566	4,911*	82.7	100.0
019 AMER BAPT CONV	1	72	88*	1.5	1.8
029 AMER LUTH CH..	9	1,557	2,178	36.7	44.3
081 CATHOLIC......	6	0	1,347	22.7	27.4
097 CR C AND C CR.	1	40	49*	0.8	1.0
281 LUTH CH AMER..	1	293	424	7.1	8.6
283 LUTH--MO SYNOD	2	354	532	9.0	10.8
443 UN C OF CHRIST	1	27	33*	0.6	0.7
449 UN METHODIST..	2	223	260	4.4	5.3
SHERIDAN	16	1,536	2,104*	65.1	100.0
029 AMER LUTH CH..	4	439	627	19.4	29.8
081 CATHOLIC......	1	0	125	3.9	5.9
165 CH OF NAZARENE	1	16	22	0.7	1.0
283 LUTH--MO SYNOD	1	261	360	11.1	17.1
313 NO AM BAPT GC.	4	437	525*	16.2	25.0
413 S-D ADVENTISTS	2	154	185*	5.7	8.8
449 UN METHODIST..	3	229	260	8.0	12.4
SIOUX	9	177	2,541*	70.0	100.0
081 CATHOLIC......	5	0	2,078	57.2	81.8
193 EPISCOPAL.....	2	134	404	11.1	15.9
443 UN C OF CHRIST	2	43	59*	1.6	2.3
SLOPE	3	78	397	26.8	100.0
029 AMER LUTH CH..	1	78	106	7.1	26.7
081 CATHOLIC......	2	0	291	19.6	73.3
STARK	28	2,192	17,018*	86.8	100.0

*Total adherents estimated from known number of communicant, confirmed, full members.

—Represents a percent less than 0.1.

Percentages may not total due to rounding.

#See Introduction for explanation of why total adherents reported by churches exceed the 1970 population figure.

Table 3. Churches and Church Membership by State, County and Denomination: 1971

County and Denomination	Number of churches	Communicant, confirmed, full members	Total adherents: Number	Total adherents: Percent of total population	Total adherents: Percent of total adherents
029 AMER LUTH CH..	4	1,096	1,558	7.9	9.2
081 CATHOLIC......	13	0	13,874	70.7	81.5
165 CH OF NAZARENE	1	60	196	1.0	1.2
193 EPISCOPAL.....	1	66	78	0.4	0.5
283 LUTH--MO SYNOD	2	185	291	1.5	1.7
313 NO AM BAPT GC.	1	51	64*	0.3	0.4
413 S-D ADVENTISTS	1	61	77*	0.4	0.5
419 SO BAPT CONV..	1	31	39*	0.2	0.2
443 UN C OF CHRIST	2	288	362*	1.8	2.1
449 UN METHODIST..	1	275	380	1.9	2.2
453 UN PRES CH USA	1	79	99*	0.5	0.6
STEELE	21	2,175	3,208*	85.6	100.0
029 AMER LUTH CH..	12	1,733	2,229	59.5	69.5
081 CATHOLIC......	2	C	419	11.2	13.1
283 LUTH--MO SYNOD	1	75	100	2.7	3.1
419 SO BAPT CONV..	1	48	58*	1.5	1.8
443 UN C OF CHRIST	1	58	70*	1.9	2.2
449 UN METHODIST..	2	165	216	5.8	6.7
453 UN PRES CH USA	2	96	116*	3.1	3.6
STUTSMAN	46	8,920	16,695*	70.9	100.0
029 AMER LUTH CH..	9	3,855	5,265	22.4	31.5
081 CATHOLIC......	8	0	4,691	19.9	28.1
165 CH OF NAZARENE	2	116	205	0.9	1.2
193 EPISCOPAL.....	1	149	207	0.9	1.2
197 EVAN CH OF NA.	1	93	112*	C.5	0.7
221 FREE METH C NA	1	27	34	0.1	0.2
281 LUTH CH AMER..	1	151	211	0.9	1.3
283 LUTH--MO SYNOD	3	679	975	4.1	5.8
313 NO AM BAPT GC.	3	189	227*	1.0	1.4
403 SALVATION ARMY	1	40	204	0.9	1.2
413 S-D ADVENTISTS	4	416	500*	2.1	3.0
443 UN C OF CHRIST	3	719	865*	3.7	5.2
449 UN METHODIST..	7	1,773	2,341	9.9	14.0
453 UN PRES CH USA	2	713	858*	3.6	5.1
TOWNER	16	1,815	3,471*	74.7	100.0
029 AMER LUTH CH..	3	837	1,071	23.1	30.9
081 CATHOLIC......	4	0	1,153	24.8	33.2
157 CH OF BRETHREN	2	151	182*	3.9	5.2
283 LUTH--MO SYNOD	2	380	509	11.0	14.7
449 UN METHCDIST..	3	346	434	9.3	12.5
453 UN PRES CH USA	2	101	122*	2.6	3.5
TRAILL	30	5,338	7,892*	82.5	100.0
029 AMER LUTH CH..	21	4,529	5,956	62.2	75.5
081 CATHOLIC......	2	0	895	9.4	11.3
165 CH OF NAZARENE	1	8	50	0.5	0.6
283 LUTH--MO SYNOD	1	238	309	3.2	3.9
443 UN C OF CHRIST	2	262	306*	3.2	3.9
449 UN METHODIST..	2	161	213	2.2	2.7
453 UN PRES CH USA	1	140	163*	1.7	2.1
WALSH	45	5,344	13,766*	84.7	100.0
029 AMER LUTH CH..	20	4,310	5,815	35.8	42.2
081 CATHOLIC......	12	0	6,654	40.9	48.3
165 CH OF NAZARENE	1	4	4	-	-
193 EPISCOPAL.....	2	39	66	0.4	0.5
281 LUTH CH AMER..	1	38	51	0.3	0.4
283 LUTH--MO SYNOD	1	168	250	1.5	1.8
449 UN METHODIST..	3	243	272	1.7	2.0
453 UN PRES CH USA	5	542	654*	4.0	4.8
WARD	68	15,513	32,161*	54.9	100.0
019 AMER BAPT CONV	4	354	446*	0.8	1.4
029 AMER LUTH CH..	17	7,819	10,767	18.4	33.5
081 CATHOLIC......	14	C	10,206	17.4	31.7
123 CH GOD (ANDER)	1	13	58	0.1	0.2
127 CH GOD (CLEVE)	3	199	251*	0.4	0.8
157 CH OF BRETHREN	1	76	96*	0.2	0.3
165 CH OF NAZARENE	4	179	375	0.6	1.2
193 EPISCOPAL.....	1	187	399	0.7	1.2
281 LUTH CH AMER..	3	716	1,109	1.9	3.4
283 LUTH--MO SYNOD	4	1,858	2,775	4.7	8.6
285 MENNONITE CH..	1	54	68*	0.1	0.2
313 NO AM BAPT GC.	1	210	265*	0.5	0.8
403 SALVATION ARMY	1	72	471	0.8	1.5
413 S-D ADVENTISTS	2	175	220*	0.4	0.7
419 SO BAPT CONV..	1	505	636*	1.1	2.0
443 UN C OF CHRIST	1	274	345*	0.6	1.1
449 UN METHODIST..	7	1,145	1,561	2.7	4.9
453 UN PRES CH USA	2	1,677	2,113*	3.6	6.6
WELLS	38	3,240	6,689*	85.2	100.0
029 AMER LUTH CH..	12	1,946	2,619	33.4	39.2
081 CATHOLIC......	5	0	2,337	29.8	34.9
123 CH GOD (ANDER)	1	34	78	1.0	1.2
165 CH OF NAZARENE	2	94	163	2.1	2.4
283 LUTH--MO SYNOD	2	136	183	2.3	2.7
313 NO AM BAPT GC.	4	371	453*	5.8	6.8
353 PLY BRETHREN..	2	18	38	0.5	0.6
413 S-D ADVENTISTS	5	324	395*	5.0	5.9
443 UN C OF CHRIST	2	60	73*	0.9	1.1
449 UN METHODIST..	3	257	350	4.5	5.2
WILLIAMS	51	8,293	15,635*	81.0	100.0

*Total adherents estimated from known number of communicant, confirmed, full members.

County and Denomination	Number of churches	Communicant, confirmed, full members	Total adherents: Number	Total adherents: Percent of total population	Total adherents: Percent of total adherents
019 AMER BAPT CONV	2	184	227*	1.2	1.5
029 AMER LUTH CH..	30	6,377	9,012	46.7	57.6
081 CATHOLIC......	6	0	3,832	19.9	24.5
165 CH OF NAZARENE	2	35	77	0.4	0.5
193 EPISCOPAL.....	1	127	232	1.2	1.5
197 EVAN CH OF NA.	1	22	27*	0.1	0.2
283 LUTH--MO SYNOD	1	273	382	2.0	2.4
403 SALVATION ARMY	1	49	263	1.4	1.7
413 S-D ADVENTISTS	1	62	77*	0.4	0.5
443 UN C OF CHRIST	1	157	194*	1.0	1.2
449 UN METHODIST..	4	850	1,118	5.8	7.2
453 UN PRES CH USA	1	157	194*	1.0	1.2
CO DATA NOT AVAIL	24	795	2,977	N/A	N/A
151 L-D SAINTS....	0	0	2,026	N/A	N/A
467 WESLEYAN......	24	795	951	N/A	N/A

OHIO

County and Denomination	Number of churches	Communicant, confirmed, full members	Total adherents: Number	Total adherents: Percent of total population	Total adherents: Percent of total adherents
THE STATE.....	8,932	2,127,682	5,043,970*	47.4	100.0
ADAMS	56	4,987	6,408*	33.8	100.0
019 AMER BAPT CONV	2	177	216*	1.1	3.4
081 CATHOLIC......	4	0	300	1.6	4.7
097 CR C AND C CR.	7	790	964*	5.1	15.0
107 CHRISTIAN UN..	9	385	470*	2.5	7.3
123 CH GOD (ANDER)	1	57	137	0.7	2.1
127 CH GOD (CLEVE)	1	21	26*	0.1	0.4
157 CH OF BRETHREN	2	30	37*	0.2	0.6
165 CH OF NAZARENE	2	116	445	2.3	6.9
413 S-D ADVENTISTS	1	23	28*	0.1	0.4
443 UN C OF CHRIST	2	468	571*	3.0	8.9
449 UN METHODIST..	18	2,149	2,273	12.0	35.5
453 UN PRES CH USA	7	771	941*	5.0	14.7
ALLEN	107	28,639	58,336*	52.5	100.0
019 AMER BAPT CONV	4	1,194	1,483*	1.3	2.5
029 AMER LUTH CH..	3	1,343	2,013	1.8	3.5
081 CATHOLIC......	8	0	20,916	18.8	35.9
093 CR CH (DISC)..	2	2,020	2,509*	2.3	4.3
097 CR C AND C CR.	4	310	385*	0.3	0.7
107 CHRISTIAN UN..	4	126	157*	0.1	0.3
123 CH GOD (ANDER)	2	375	1,060	1.0	1.8
127 CH GOD (CLEVE)	1	70	87*	0.1	0.1
157 CH OF BRETHREN	4	893	1,109*	1.0	1.9
165 CH OF NAZARENE	4	478	1,267	1.1	2.2
193 EPISCOPAL.....	1	415	759	0.7	1.3
221 FREE METH C NA	2	52	80	0.1	0.1
226 FRIENDS-USA...	1	39	48*	-	0.1
281 LUTH CH AMER..	4	1,515	2,224	2.0	3.8
283 LUTH--MO SYNOD	1	454	674	0.6	1.2
285 MENNONITE CH..	6	534	663*	0.6	1.1
287 MENN GEN CONF.	3	1,217	1,512*	1.4	2.6
413 S-D ADVENTISTS	1	141	175*	0.2	0.3
419 SO BAPT CONV..	3	563	699*	0.6	1.2
435 UNITARIAN-UNIV	1	29	29	-	-
443 UN C OF CHRIST	7	2,819	3,502*	3.2	6.0
449 UN METHODIST..	35	12,141	14,611	13.1	25.0
453 UN PRES CH USA	6	1,911	2,374*	2.1	4.1
ASHLAND	62	14,695	19,614*	45.3	100.0
019 AMER BAPT CONV	2	521	633*	1.5	3.2
029 AMER LUTH CH..	2	1,061	1,408	3.3	7.2
075 BRETHREN IN CR	1	47	57*	0.1	0.3
081 CATHOLIC......	2	0	1,699	3.9	8.7
093 CR CH (DISC)..	1	884	1,074*	2.5	5.5
097 CR C AND C CR.	5	648	787*	1.8	4.0
123 CH GOD (ANDER)	2	52	132	0.3	0.7
127 CH GOD (CLEVE)	2	149	181*	0.4	0.9
157 CH OF BRETHREN	3	813	988*	2.3	5.0
165 CH OF NAZARENE	3	223	391	0.9	2.0
193 EPISCOPAL.....	1	139	191	0.4	1.0
281 LUTH CH AMER..	7	2,207	2,986	6.9	15.2
419 SO BAPT CONV..	3	95	115*	0.3	0.6
443 UN C OF CHRIST	4	492	598*	1.4	3.0
449 UN METHODIST..	19	6,060	6,790	15.7	34.6
453 UN PRES CH USA	5	1,304	1,584*	3.7	8.1
ASHTABULA	106	22,096	49,299*	50.2	100.0
019 AMER BAPT CONV	6	1,865	2,309*	2.4	4.7
029 AMER LUTH CH..	2	148	213	0.2	0.4
081 CATHOLIC......	13	0	20,848	21.2	42.3
093 CR CH (DISC)..	3	622	770*	0.8	1.6
097 CR C AND C CR.	2	334	413*	0.4	0.8
123 CH GOD (ANDER)	1	55	180	0.2	0.4
127 CH GOD (CLEVE)	2	48	59*	C.1	0.1
165 CH OF NAZARENE	8	744	1,618	1.6	3.3
175 CONG CR CH....	1	35	43*	-	0.1
193 EPISCOPAL.....	4	1,651	2,228	2.3	4.5
201 EVAN COV CH AM	1	113	140*	0.1	0.3
221 FREE METH C NA	3	60	91	0.1	0.2
281 LUTH CH AMER..	5	2,626	3,554	3.6	7.2

—Represents a percent less than 0.1.

Percentages may not total due to rounding.

Table 3. Churches and Church Membership by State, County and Denomination: 1971

County and Denomination	Number of churches	Communicant, confirmed, full members	Total adherents: Number	Total adherents: Percent of total population	Total adherents: Percent of total adherents
283 LUTH--MO SYNOD	2	568	738	0.8	1.5
349 PENT HOLINESS.	2	83	103*	0.1	0.2
413 S-D ADVENTISTS	3	152	188*	0.2	0.4
419 SO BAPT CONV..	2	283	350*	0.4	0.7
443 UN C OF CHRIST	10	2,765	3,423*	3.5	6.9
449 UN METHODIST..	26	6,916	8,283	8.4	16.8
453 UN PRES CH USA	10	3,028	3,748*	3.8	7.6
ATHENS	93	9,891	18,770*	34.2	100.0
019 AMER BAPT CONV	2	123	143*	0.3	0.8
081 CATHOLIC......	7	0	6,308	11.5	33.6
093 CR CH (DISC)..	8	1,215	1,410*	2.6	7.5
097 CR C AND C CR.	11	1,267	1,470*	2.7	7.8
123 CH GOD (ANDER)	3	117	402	0.7	2.1
165 CH OF NAZARENE	7	374	831	1.5	4.4
193 EPISCOPAL.....	2	315	498	0.9	2.7
221 FREE METH C NA	2	10	21	-	0.1
281 LUTH CH AMER..	1	187	297	0.5	1.6
403 SALVATION ARMY	1	34	152	0.3	0.8
413 S-D ADVENTISTS	2	57	66*	0.1	0.4
419 SO BAPT CONV..	2	206	239*	0.4	1.3
435 UNITARIAN-UNIV	1	22	52	0.1	0.3
443 UN C OF CHRIST	3	35	41*	0.1	0.2
449 UN METHODIST..	35	4,901	5,647	10.3	30.1
453 UN PRES CH USA	6	1,028	1,193*	2.2	6.4
AUGLAIZE	50	13,602	30,345*	78.6	100.0
019 AMER BAPT CONV	2	388	482*	1.2	1.6
029 AMER LUTH CH..	4	2,057	2,893	7.5	9.5
081 CATHOLIC......	7	0	12,333	31.9	40.6
097 CR C AND C CR.	2	233	289*	0.7	1.0
107 CHRISTIAN UN..	2	250	310*	0.8	1.0
123 CH GOD (ANDER)	1	18	73	0.2	0.2
165 CH OF NAZARENE	4	416	1,212	3.1	4.0
226 FRIENDS-USA...	1	35	43*	0.1	0.1
281 LUTH CH AMER..	1	534	712	1.8	2.3
283 LUTH--MO SYNOD	1	118	150	0.4	0.5
419 SO BAPT CONV..	2	147	183*	0.5	0.6
443 UN C OF CHRIST	7	5,004	6,214*	16.1	20.5
449 UN METHODIST..	15	4,285	5,306	13.7	17.5
453 UN PRES CH USA	1	117	145*	0.4	0.5
BELMONT	121	18,959	37,982*	46.9	100.0
019 AMER BAPT CONV	2	672	802*	1.0	2.1
029 AMER LUTH CH..	1	383	498	0.6	1.3
081 CATHOLIC......	19	0	13,717	17.0	36.1
093 CR CH (DISC)..	4	835	996*	1.2	2.6
097 CR C AND C CR.	9	2,187	2,610*	3.2	6.9
123 CH GOD (ANDER)	1	116	314	0.4	0.8
165 CH OF NAZARENE	6	428	908	1.1	2.4
193 EPISCOPAL.....	2	283	424	0.5	1.1
221 FREE METH C NA	1	14	23	-	0.1
226 FRIENDS-USA...	3	480	573*	0.7	1.5
281 LUTH CH AMER..	3	821	1,249	1.5	3.3
285 MENNONITE CH..	1	34	41*	0.1	0.1
403 SALVATION ARMY	1	49	228	0.3	0.6
419 SO BAPT CONV..	1	73	87*	0.1	0.2
443 UN C OF CHRIST	3	491	586*	0.7	1.5
449 UN METHODIST..	41	6,413	8,148	10.1	21.5
453 UN PRES CH USA	23	5,680	6,778*	8.4	17.8
BROWN	57	6,426	12,124*	45.5	100.0
029 AMER LUTH CH..	1	345	518	1.9	4.3
081 CATHOLIC......	8	0	3,707	13.9	30.6
093 CR CH (DISC)..	1	60	75*	0.3	0.6
097 CR C AND C CR.	9	2,200	2,734*	10.3	22.6
107 CHRISTIAN UN..	1	30	37*	0.1	0.3
165 CH OF NAZARENE	5	265	765	2.9	6.3
419 SO BAPT CONV..	5	562	698*	2.6	5.8
443 UN C OF CHRIST	6	315	391*	1.5	3.2
449 UN METHODIST..	15	1,935	2,312	8.7	19.1
453 UN PRES CH USA	6	714	887*	3.3	7.3
BUTLER	174	51,699	102,099*	45.1	100.0
019 AMER BAPT CONV	4	3,955	4,856*	2.1	4.8
029 AMER LUTH CH..	4	2,261	3,042	1.3	3.0
081 CATHOLIC......	17	0	31,547	13.9	30.9
093 CR CH (DISC)..	5	1,235	1,516*	0.7	1.5
097 CR C AND C CR.	7	2,435	2,990*	1.3	2.9
123 CH GOD (ANDER)	16	3,753	9,084	4.0	8.9
127 CH GOD (CLEVE)	11	2,350	2,885*	1.3	2.8
157 CH OF BRETHREN	2	133	163*	0.1	0.2
165 CH OF NAZARENE	10	1,671	3,279	1.4	3.2
193 EPISCOPAL.....	3	1,574	2,088	0.9	2.0
281 LUTH CH AMER..	3	628	888	0.4	0.9
283 LUTH--MO SYNOD	2	600	856	0.4	0.8
287 MENN GEN CONF.	1	143	176*	0.1	0.2
403 SALVATION ARMY	2	285	1,468	0.6	1.4
413 S-D ADVENTISTS	2	288	354*	0.2	0.3
419 SO BAPT CONV..	36	9,043	11,103*	4.9	10.9
435 UNITARIAN-UNIV	1	26	41	-	-
443 UN C OF CHRIST	8	2,984	3,664*	1.6	3.6
449 UN METHODIST..	27	10,712	12,739	5.6	12.5
453 UN PRES CH USA	13	7,623	9,360*	4.1	9.2
CARROLL	44	5,775	8,750*	40.5	100.0
029 AMER LUTH CH..	3	565	886	4.1	10.1
081 CATHOLIC......	4	0	1,532	7.1	17.5
093 CR CH (DISC)..	1	268	329*	1.5	3.8

County and Denomination	Number of churches	Communicant, confirmed, full members	Total adherents: Number	Total adherents: Percent of total population	Total adherents: Percent of total adherents
097 CR C AND C CR.	2	312	382*	1.8	4.4
165 CH OF NAZARENE	3	110	283	1.3	3.2
281 LUTH CH AMER..	2	506	651	3.0	7.4
413 S-D ADVENTISTS	1	22	27*	0.1	0.3
443 UN C OF CHRIST	1	22	27*	0.1	0.3
449 UN METHODIST..	19	2,890	3,309	15.3	37.8
453 UN PRES CH USA	8	1,080	1,324*	6.1	15.1
CHAMPAIGN	45	7,991	12,630*	41.4	100.0
019 AMER BAPT CONV	6	1,100	1,344*	4.4	10.6
081 CATHOLIC......	4	0	2,031	6.7	16.1
097 CR C AND C CR.	1	33	40*	0.1	0.3
123 CH GOD (ANDER)	4	250	792	2.6	6.3
127 CH GOD (CLEVE)	1	17	21*	0.1	0.2
165 CH OF NAZARENE	3	237	675	2.2	5.3
193 EPISCOPAL.....	2	275	417	1.4	3.3
221 FREE METH C NA	1	18	32	0.1	0.3
226 FRIENDS-USA...	2	74	90*	0.3	0.7
281 LUTH CH AMER..	3	479	624	2.0	4.9
449 UN METHODIST..	16	4,808	5,708	18.7	45.2
453 UN PRES CH USA	2	700	856*	2.8	6.8
CLARK	124	35,570	61,523*	39.2	100.0
019 AMER BAPT CONV	6	1,445	1,790*	1.1	2.9
029 AMER LUTH CH..	2	521	717	0.5	1.2
075 BRETHREN IN CR	1	48	59*	-	0.1
081 CATHOLIC......	7	0	13,730	8.7	22.3
093 CR CH (DISC)..	3	438	543*	0.3	0.9
097 CR C AND C CR.	5	1,887	2,337*	1.5	3.8
121 CH GOD (ABR)..	2	158	196*	0.1	0.3
123 CH GOD (ANDER)	6	1,645	3,416	2.2	5.6
127 CH GOD (CLEVE)	5	292	362*	0.2	0.6
157 CH OF BRETHREN	3	1,022	1,266*	0.8	2.1
165 CH OF NAZARENE	7	801	2,125	1.4	3.5
193 EPISCOPAL.....	1	535	965	0.6	1.6
226 FRIENDS-USA...	1	76	94*	0.1	0.2
281 LUTH CH AMER..	17	8,326	11,716	7.5	19.0
285 MENNONITE CH..	2	101	125*	0.1	0.2
403 SALVATION ARMY	1	40	190	0.1	0.3
413 S-D ADVENTISTS	3	375	465*	0.3	0.8
419 SO BAPT CONV..	7	1,455	1,802*	1.1	2.9
443 UN C OF CHRIST	10	1,944	2,408*	1.5	3.9
449 UN METHODIST..	28	11,192	13,130	8.4	21.3
453 UN PRES CH USA	6	3,198	3,961*	2.5	6.4
469 WISC EVAN LUTH	1	71	126	0.1	0.2
CLERMONT	114	18,518	38,183*	39.9	100.0
019 AMER BAPT CONV	1	326	415*	0.4	1.1
081 CATHOLIC......	12	0	14,231	14.9	37.3
097 CR C AND C CR.	17	4,730	6,016*	6.3	15.8
107 CHRISTIAN UN..	2	19	24*	-	0.1
123 CH GOD (ANDER)	1	85	167	0.2	0.4
127 CH GOD (CLEVE)	5	275	350*	0.4	0.9
157 CH OF BRETHREN	1	50	64*	0.1	0.2
165 CH OF NAZARENE	10	880	2,019	2.1	5.3
281 LUTH CH AMER..	1	167	247	0.3	0.6
283 LUTH--MO SYNOD	1	204	294	0.3	0.8
349 PENT HOLINESS.	1	33	42*	-	0.1
353 PLY BRETHREN..	1	50	90	0.1	0.2
413 S-D ADVENTISTS	1	180	229*	0.2	0.6
419 SO BAPT CONV..	15	2,438	3,101*	3.2	8.1
443 UN C OF CHRIST	3	141	179*	0.2	0.5
449 UN METHODIST..	35	7,439	8,806	9.2	23.1
453 UN PRES CH USA	7	1,501	1,909*	2.0	5.0
CLINTON	58	10,413	15,191*	48.3	100.0
019 AMER BAPT CONV	2	501	617*	2.0	4.1
081 CATHOLIC......	3	0	2,094	6.7	13.8
093 CR CH (DISC)..	1	519	639*	2.0	4.2
097 CR C AND C CR.	8	2,150	2,647*	8.4	17.4
107 CHRISTIAN UN..	1	60	74*	0.2	0.5
123 CH GOD (ANDER)	2	138	371	1.2	2.4
127 CH GOD (CLEVE)	2	113	139*	0.4	0.9
165 CH OF NAZARENE	2	105	445	1.4	2.9
193 EPISCOPAL.....	1	29	39	0.1	0.3
226 FRIENDS-USA...	10	1,679	2,067*	6.6	13.6
281 LUTH CH AMER..	1	181	234	0.7	1.5
413 S-D ADVENTISTS	1	36	44*	0.1	0.3
419 SO BAPT CONV..	4	479	590*	1.9	3.9
443 UN C OF CHRIST	2	230	283*	0.9	1.9
449 UN METHODIST..	17	3,943	4,600	14.6	30.3
453 UN PRES CH USA	1	250	308*	1.0	2.0
COLUMBIANA	143	34,907	59,079*	54.5	100.0
019 AMER BAPT CONV	6	1,563	1,900*	1.8	3.2
029 AMER LUTH CH..	4	1,685	2,328	2.1	3.9
081 CATHOLIC......	12	0	13,720	12.7	23.2
093 CR CH (DISC)..	4	1,799	2,187*	2.0	3.7
097 CR C AND C CR.	14	3,274	3,980*	3.7	6.7
123 CH GOD (ANDER)	1	71	197	0.2	0.3
127 CH GOD (CLEVE)	1	8	10*	-	-
157 CH OF BRETHREN	1	58	71*	0.1	0.1
165 CH OF NAZARENE	9	1,666	3,477	3.2	5.9
193 EPISCOPAL.....	4	725	917	0.8	1.6
221 FREE METH C NA	5	251	340	0.3	0.6
226 FRIENDS-USA...	7	1,382	1,680*	1.6	2.8
281 LUTH CH AMER..	4	1,998	2,863	2.6	4.8
285 MENNONITE CH..	3	353	429*	0.4	0.7
287 MENN GEN CONF.	1	11	13*	-	-
403 SALVATION ARMY	2	166	798	0.7	1.4

*Total adherents estimated from known number of communicant, confirmed, full members.

—Represents a percent less than 0.1.

Percentages may not total due to rounding.

Table 3. Churches and Church Membership by State, County and Denomination: 1971

County and Denomination	Number of churches	Communicant, confirmed, full members	Total adherents		
			Number	Percent of total population	Percent of total adherents
413 S-D ADVENTISTS	2	89	108*	0.1	0.2
443 UN C OF CHRIST	3	1,071	1,302*	1.2	2.2
449 UN METHODIST..	32	10,183	12,361	11.4	20.9
453 UN PRES CH USA	28	8,554	10,398*	9.6	17.6
COSHOCTON	66	11,470	16,900*	50.5	100.0
019 AMER BAPT CONV	6	662	811*	2.4	4.8
029 AMER LUTH CH..	1	106	124	0.4	0.7
081 CATHOLIC......	3	0	2,082	6.2	12.3
093 CR CH (DISC)..	2	207	253*	0.8	1.5
097 CR C AND C CR.	1	55	67*	0.2	0.4
123 CH GOD (ANDER)	2	93	321	1.0	1.9
127 CH GOD (CLEVE)	1	28	34*	0.1	0.2
165 CH OF NAZARENE	3	432	830	2.5	4.9
193 EPISCOPAL.....	1	219	335	1.0	2.0
221 FREE METH C NA	1	12	15	-	0.1
281 LUTH CH AMER..	1	584	752	2.2	4.4
285 MENNONITE CH..	2	88	108*	0.3	0.6
403 SALVATION ARMY	1	125	831	2.5	4.9
413 S-D ADVENTISTS	1	24	29*	0.1	0.2
419 SO BAPT CONV..	1	120	147*	0.4	0.9
443 UN C OF CHRIST	6	1,479	1,811*	5.4	10.7
449 UN METHODIST..	27	5,940	6,763	20.2	40.0
453 UN PRES CH USA	6	1,296	1,587*	4.7	9.4
CRAWFORD	65	16,812	27,957*	55.5	100.0
019 AMER BAPT CONV	1	153	190*	0.4	0.7
029 AMER LUTH CH..	8	3,999	5,385	10.7	19.3
081 CATHOLIC......	5	0	6,178	12.3	22.1
093 CR CH (DISC)..	1	144	179*	0.4	0.6
097 CR C AND C CR.	2	220	273*	0.5	1.0
127 CH GOD (CLEVE)	2	51	63*	0.1	0.2
165 CH OF NAZARENE	2	441	1,007	2.0	3.6
193 EPISCOPAL.....	2	310	321	0.6	1.1
221 FREE METH C NA	1	58	93	0.2	0.3
281 LUTH CH AMER..	8	2,678	3,757	7.5	13.4
403 SALVATION ARMY	1	70	286	0.6	1.0
413 S-D ADVENTISTS	2	213	265*	0.5	0.9
419 SO BAPT CONV..	1	259	322*	0.6	1.2
443 UN C OF CHRIST	3	1,131	1,406*	2.8	5.0
449 UN METHODIST..	23	5,993	6,875	13.7	24.6
453 UN PRES CH USA	3	1,092	1,357*	2.7	4.9
CUYAHOGA	606	190,879	867,143*	50.4	100.0
019 AMER BAPT CONV	30	7,407	8,969*	0.5	1.0
029 AMER LUTH CH..	19	10,992	15,417	0.9	1.8
081 CATHOLIC......	159	0	611,958	35.6	70.6
093 CR CH (DISC)..	22	8,203	9,933*	0.6	1.1
097 CR C AND C CR.	6	286	346*	-	-
105 CHRISTIAN REF.	3	468	748	-	0.1
121 CH GOD (ABR)..	3	147	178*	-	-
123 CH GOD (ANDER)	9	686	1,797	0.1	0.2
127 CH GOD (CLEVE)	11	1,039	1,258*	0.1	0.1
157 CH OF BRETHREN	2	357	432*	-	-
165 CH OF NAZARENE	9	963	2,256	0.1	0.3
175 CONG CR CH....	4	488	591*	-	0.1
193 EPISCOPAL.....	27	14,033	20,500	1.2	2.4
201 EVAN COV CH AM	2	404	489*	-	0.1
221 FREE METH C NA	3	118	182	-	-
226 FRIENDS-USA...	5	374	453*	-	0.1
281 LUTH CH AMER..	23	8,029	10,897	0.6	1.3
283 LUTH--MO SYNOD	50	26,772	36,888	2.1	4.3
285 MENNONITE CH..	4	340	412*	-	-
313 NO AM BAPT GC.	5	1,184	1,434*	0.1	0.2
353 PLY BRETHREN..	6	350	640	-	0.1
371 REF CH IN AM..	5	1,199	1,660	0.1	0.2
403 SALVATION ARMY	8	465	10,791	0.6	1.2
413 S-D ADVENTISTS	7	2,323	2,813*	0.2	0.3
419 SO BAPT CONV..	15	2,858	3,461*	0.2	0.4
435 UNITARIAN-UNIV	6	2,045	2,750	0.2	0.3
443 UN C OF CHRIST	51	25,528	30,911*	1.8	3.6
449 UN METHODIST..	67	44,658	53,666	3.1	6.2
453 UN PRES CH USA	45	29,163	35,313*	2.1	4.1
DARKE	73	14,116	24,803*	50.5	100.0
029 AMER LUTH CH..	7	1,651	2,237	4.6	9.0
081 CATHOLIC......	5	0	7,045	14.3	28.4
097 CR C AND C CR.	2	280	348*	0.7	1.4
123 CH GOD (ANDER)	1	185	456	0.9	1.8
127 CH GOD (CLEVE)	1	47	58*	0.1	0.2
157 CH OF BRETHREN	11	2,237	2,784*	5.7	11.2
165 CH OF NAZARENE	1	113	362	0.7	1.5
193 EPISCOPAL.....	1	150	252	0.5	1.0
281 LUTH CH AMER..	2	904	1,167	2.4	4.7
419 SO BAPT CONV..	3	312	388*	0.8	1.6
435 UNITARIAN-UNIV	1	75	75	0.2	0.3
443 UN C OF CHRIST	8	2,015	2,508*	5.1	10.1
449 UN METHODIST..	27	5,184	5,924	12.1	23.9
453 UN PRES CH USA	3	963	1,199*	2.4	4.8
DEFIANCE	51	12,111	24,499*	66.3	100.0
019 AMER BAPT CONV	1	322	407*	1.1	1.7
029 AMER LUTH CH..	3	1,055	1,427	3.9	5.8
081 CATHOLIC......	6	0	8,179	22.1	33.4
093 CR CH (DISC)..	1	60	76*	0.2	0.3
097 CR C AND C CR.	4	740	934*	2.5	3.8
123 CH GOD (ANDER)	1	170	548	1.5	2.2
157 CH OF BRETHREN	2	259	327*	0.9	1.3
165 CH OF NAZARENE	2	168	546	1.5	2.2
193 EPISCOPAL.....	1	221	289	0.8	1.2
281 LUTH CH AMER..	2	877	1,253	3.4	5.1
283 LUTH--MO SYNOD	4	2,227	3,209	8.7	13.1
285 MENNONITE CH..	2	57	72*	0.2	0.3
413 S-D ADVENTISTS	2	60	76*	0.2	0.3
419 SO BAPT CONV..	2	400	505*	1.4	2.1
443 UN C OF CHRIST	2	434	548*	1.5	2.2
449 UN METHODIST..	17	4,173	4,982	13.5	20.3
453 UN PRES CH USA	2	888	1,121*	3.0	4.6
DELAWARE	48	9,061	12,697*	29.6	100.0
019 AMER BAPT CONV	4	809	981*	2.3	7.7
029 AMER LUTH CH..	1	443	574	1.3	4.5
081 CATHOLIC......	1	0	1,442	3.4	11.4
097 CR C AND C CR.	2	285	345*	0.8	2.7
107 CHRISTIAN UN..	1	66	80*	0.2	0.6
123 CH GOD (ANDER)	1	63	161	0.4	1.3
127 CH GOD (CLEVE)	1	34	41*	0.1	0.3
165 CH OF NAZARENE	3	210	394	0.9	3.1
193 EPISCOPAL.....	1	104	218	0.5	1.7
226 FRIENDS-USA...	1	57	69*	0.2	0.5
285 MENNONITE CH..	1	20	24*	0.1	0.2
413 S-D ADVENTISTS	1	76	92*	0.2	0.7
419 SO BAPT CONV..	1	134	162*	0.4	1.3
443 UN C OF CHRIST	2	473	573*	1.3	4.5
449 UN METHODIST..	20	4,612	5,511	12.8	43.4
453 UN PRES CH USA	7	1,675	2,030*	4.7	16.0
ERIE	58	16,986	42,401*	55.9	100.0
019 AMER BAPT CONV	1	278	347*	0.5	0.8
029 AMER LUTH CH..	8	5,459	7,613	10.0	18.0
081 CATHOLIC......	7	0	19,989	26.3	47.1
097 CR C AND C CR.	3	118	147*	0.2	0.3
127 CH GOD (CLEVE)	2	98	122*	0.2	0.3
165 CH OF NAZARENE	2	179	506	0.7	1.2
193 EPISCOPAL.....	3	1,311	1,610	2.1	3.8
226 FRIENDS-USA...	1	79	99*	0.1	0.2
315 NO AM OLD RC..	1	54	67*	0.1	0.2
403 SALVATION ARMY	1	35	205	0.3	0.5
413 S-D ADVENTISTS	2	76	95*	0.1	0.2
419 SO BAPT CONV..	3	952	1,188*	1.6	2.8
435 UNITARIAN-UNIV	1	70	86	0.1	0.2
443 UN C OF CHRIST	10	4,219	5,266*	6.9	12.4
449 UN METHODIST..	10	2,777	3,462	4.6	8.2
453 UN PRES CH USA	3	1,281	1,599*	2.1	3.8
FAIRFIELD	91	20,483	31,941*	43.6	100.0
029 AMER LUTH CH..	7	1,636	2,226	3.0	7.0
081 CATHOLIC......	5	0	6,051	8.3	18.9
097 CR C AND C CR.	3	1,317	1,625*	2.2	5.1
107 CHRISTIAN UN..	1	85	105*	0.1	0.3
123 CH GOD (ANDER)	1	80	245	0.3	0.8
127 CH GOD (CLEVE)	1	167	206*	0.3	0.6
165 CH OF NAZARENE	3	258	630	0.9	2.0
193 EPISCOPAL.....	1	334	440	0.6	1.4
281 LUTH CH AMER..	8	1,519	2,255	3.1	7.1
283 LUTH--MO SYNOD	3	949	1,266	1.7	4.0
285 MENNONITE CH..	1	35	43*	0.1	0.1
403 SALVATION ARMY	1	77	285	0.4	0.9
413 S-D ADVENTISTS	1	43	53*	0.1	0.2
419 SO BAPT CONV..	2	342	422*	0.6	1.3
443 UN C OF CHRIST	8	1,208	1,490*	2.0	4.7
449 UN METHODIST..	40	10,602	12,340	16.8	38.6
453 UN PRES CH USA	5	1,831	2,259*	3.1	7.1
FAYETTE	33	6,912	9,211*	36.2	100.0
019 AMER BAPT CONV	1	633	770*	3.0	8.4
081 CATHOLIC......	1	0	657	2.6	7.1
093 CR CH (DISC)..	1	76	92*	0.4	1.0
097 CR C AND C CR.	5	1,395	1,697*	6.7	18.4
123 CH GOD (ANDER)	2	64	149	0.6	1.6
127 CH GOD (CLEVE)	1	17	21*	0.1	0.2
165 CH OF NAZARENE	1	56	144	0.6	1.6
193 EPISCOPAL.....	1	161	313	1.2	3.4
281 LUTH CH AMER..	1	235	325	1.3	3.5
413 S-D ADVENTISTS	1	15	18*	0.1	0.2
419 SO BAPT CONV..	1	174	212*	0.8	2.3
449 UN METHODIST..	14	3,175	3,705	14.6	40.2
453 UN PRES CH USA	3	911	1,108*	4.4	12.0
FRANKLIN	415	157,155	299,991*	36.0	100.0
019 AMER BAPT CONV	18	7,083	8,719*	1.0	2.9
029 AMER LUTH CH..	38	19,654	27,893	3.3	9.3
081 CATHOLIC......	47	0	95,943	11.5	32.0
093 CR CH (DISC)..	12	5,375	6,617*	0.8	2.2
097 CR C AND C CR.	24	8,755	10,778*	1.3	3.6
105 CHRISTIAN REF.	1	132	236	-	0.1
107 CHRISTIAN UN..	1	19	23*	-	-
121 CH GOD (ABR)..	1	26	32*	-	-
123 CH GOD (ANDER)	9	948	2,228	0.3	0.7
127 CH GOD (CLEVE)	10	1,378	1,696*	0.2	0.6
157 CH OF BRETHREN	1	60	74*	-	-
165 CH OF NAZARENE	19	3,387	6,687	0.8	2.2
175 CONG CR CH....	1	89	110*	-	-
193 EPISCOPAL.....	11	5,684	8,726	1.0	2.9
199 EVAN CONG CH..	1	169	208*	-	0.1
221 FREE METH C NA	2	121	159	-	0.1
226 FRIENDS-USA...	3	478	588*	0.1	0.2
281 LUTH CH AMER..	9	3,934	5,463	0.7	1.8
283 LUTH--MO SYNOD	9	2,118	2,982	0.4	1.0
285 MENNONITE CH..	2	89	110*	-	-

*Total adherents estimated from known number of communicant, confirmed, full members.

—Represents a percent less than 0.1.

Percentages may not total due to rounding.

Table 3. Churches and Church Membership by State, County and Denomination: 1971

County and Denomination	Number of churches	Communicant, confirmed, full members	Total adherents: Number	Total adherents: Percent of total population	Total adherents: Percent of total adherents
287 MENN GEN CONF.	1	76	94*	-	-
315 NO AM OLD RC..	1	30	37*	-	-
371 REF CH IN AM..	1	119	175	-	0.1
381 REF PRES-EVAN.	1	62	81	-	-
403 SALVATION ARMY	3	284	922	0.1	0.3
413 S-D ADVENTISTS	5	1,574	1,938*	0.2	0.6
419 SO BAPT CONV..	35	9,279	11,423*	1.4	3.8
435 UNITARIAN-UNIV	2	534	768	0.1	0.3
443 UN C OF CHRIST	12	6,956	8,563*	1.0	2.9
449 UN METHODIST..	98	55,242	67,684	8.1	22.6
453 UN PRES CH USA	34	22,595	27,815*	3.3	9.3
469 WISC EVAN LUTH	3	905	1,219	0.1	0.4
FULTON	65	12,112	22,478*	68.0	100.0
029 AMER LUTH CH..	4	1,416	1,970	6.0	8.8
081 CATHOLIC......	6	0	6,756	20.4	30.1
093 CR CH (DISC)..	5	1,207	1,520*	4.6	6.8
097 CR C AND C CR.	3	533	671*	2.0	3.0
107 CHRISTIAN UN..	3	103	130*	0.4	0.6
121 CH GOD (ABR)..	1	50	63*	0.2	0.3
123 CH GOD (ANDER)	1	120	320	1.0	1.4
127 CH GOD (CLEVE)	2	49	62*	0.2	0.3
157 CH OF BRETHREN	1	104	131*	0.4	0.6
165 CH OF NAZARENE	4	244	449	1.4	2.0
283 LUTH--MO SYNOD	4	997	1,568	4.7	7.0
285 MENNONITE CH..	8	1,855	2,336*	7.1	10.4
419 SO BAPT CONV..	1	75	94*	0.3	0.4
435 UNITARIAN-UNIV	1	86	121	0.4	0.5
443 UN C OF CHRIST	3	817	1,029*	3.1	4.6
449 UN METHODIST..	18	4,456	5,258	15.9	23.4
GALLIA	37	4,141	5,697*	22.6	100.0
019 AMER BAPT CONV	6	575	685*	2.7	12.0
081 CATHOLIC......	1	0	380	1.5	6.7
097 CR C AND C CR.	1	60	71*	0.3	1.2
123 CH GOD (ANDER)	1	145	405	1.6	7.1
127 CH GOD (CLEVE)	1	44	52*	0.2	0.9
165 CH OF NAZARENE	1	191	688	2.7	12.1
175 CONG CR CH....	1	50	60*	0.2	1.1
193 EPISCOPAL.....	1	208	292	1.2	5.1
285 MENNONITE CH..	1	48	57*	0.2	1.0
419 SO BAPT CONV..	1	143	170*	0.7	3.0
449 UN METHODIST..	21	2,334	2,429	9.6	42.6
453 UN PRES CH USA	1	343	408*	1.6	7.2
GEAUGA	38	7,171	21,911*	34.8	100.0
019 AMER BAPT CONV	1	289	366*	0.6	1.7
081 CATHOLIC......	6	0	12,570	20.0	57.4
093 CR CH (DISC)..	2	531	673*	1.1	3.1
097 CR C AND C CR.	1	125	158*	0.3	0.7
127 CH GOD (CLEVE)	1	49	62*	0.1	0.3
165 CH OF NAZARENE	1	20	32	0.1	0.1
193 EPISCOPAL.....	1	177	280	0.4	1.3
221 FREE METH C NA	1	10	22	-	0.1
281 LUTH CH AMER..	1	64	85	0.1	0.4
283 LUTH--MO SYNOD	3	676	959	1.5	4.4
285 MENNONITE CH..	3	223	283*	0.4	1.3
419 SO BAPT CONV..	1	134	170*	0.3	0.8
443 UN C OF CHRIST	8	2,314	2,933*	4.7	13.4
449 UN METHODIST..	6	1,783	2,334	3.7	10.7
453 UN PRES CH USA	2	776	984*	1.6	4.5
GREENE	90	23,920	43,106*	34.5	100.0
019 AMER BAPT CONV	2	318	393*	0.3	0.9
029 AMER LUTH CH..	1	237	331	0.3	0.8
081 CATHOLIC......	5	0	10,945	8.8	25.4
093 CR CH (DISC)..	1	79	98*	0.1	0.2
097 CR C AND C CR.	9	2,370	2,933*	2.3	6.8
123 CH GOD (ANDER)	5	430	1,221	1.0	2.8
127 CH GOD (CLEVE)	3	364	450*	0.4	1.0
157 CH OF BRETHREN	1	277	343*	0.3	0.8
165 CH OF NAZARENE	6	1,065	3,032	2.4	7.0
193 EPISCOPAL.....	2	612	680	0.5	1.6
226 FRIENDS-USA...	4	812	1,005*	0.8	2.3
281 LUTH CH AMER..	3	1,089	1,710	1.4	4.0
283 LUTH--MO SYNOD	1	336	573	0.5	1.3
313 NO AM BAPT GC.	1	145	179*	0.1	0.4
413 S-D ADVENTISTS	1	20	25*	-	0.1
419 SO BAPT CONV..	8	3,192	3,950*	3.2	9.2
435 UNITARIAN-UNIV	1	45	65	0.1	0.2
443 UN C OF CHRIST	4	912	1,128*	0.9	2.6
449 UN METHODIST..	21	7,067	8,415	6.7	19.5
453 UN PRES CH USA	11	4,550	5,630*	4.5	13.1
GUERNSEY	71	10,116	15,722*	41.7	100.0
019 AMER BAPT CONV	5	858	1,037*	2.8	6.6
081 CATHOLIC......	5	0	3,190	8.5	20.3
093 CR CH (DISC)..	2	288	348*	0.9	2.2
097 CR C AND C CR.	2	70	85*	0.2	0.5
123 CH GOD (ANDER)	1	55	135	0.4	0.9
165 CH OF NAZARENE	2	175	544	1.4	3.5
193 EPISCOPAL.....	1	285	347	0.9	2.2
221 FREE METH C NA	2	66	68	0.2	0.4
281 LUTH CH AMER..	3	452	558	1.5	3.5
283 LUTH--MO SYNOD	1	96	131	0.3	0.8
403 SALVATION ARMY	1	42	282	0.7	1.8
419 SO BAPT CONV..	1	48	58*	0.2	0.4
449 UN METHODIST..	33	5,507	6,311	16.8	40.1
453 UN PRES CH USA	12	2,174	2,628*	7.0	16.7

County and Denomination	Number of churches	Communicant, confirmed, full members	Total adherents: Number	Total adherents: Percent of total population	Total adherents: Percent of total adherents
HAMILTON	496	138,801	456,428*	49.4	100.0
019 AMER BAPT CONV	18	7,784	9,574*	1.0	2.1
029 AMER LUTH CH..	9	3,375	4,741	0.5	1.0
075 BRETHREN IN CR	1	13	16*	-	-
081 CATHOLIC......	107	0	277,708	30.1	60.8
093 CR CH (DISC)..	16	3,793	4,665*	0.5	1.0
097 CR C AND C CR.	26	9,895	12,170*	1.3	2.7
105 CHRISTIAN REF.	1	125	204	-	-
123 CH GOD (ANDER)	11	1,076	2,845	0.3	0.6
127 CH GOD (CLEVE)	20	1,823	2,242*	0.2	0.5
165 CH OF NAZARENE	18	2,018	4,291	0.5	0.9
193 EPISCOPAL.....	25	10,356	15,972	1.7	3.5
221 FREE METH C NA	1	22	39	-	-
226 FRIENDS-USA...	4	361	444*	-	0.1
281 LUTH CH AMER..	6	1,658	2,225	0.2	0.5
283 LUTH--MO SYNOD	14	4,177	6,028	0.7	1.3
285 MENNONITE CH..	3	74	91*	-	-
313 NO AM BAPT GC.	1	37	46*	-	-
353 PLY BRETHREN..	1	150	175	-	-
403 SALVATION ARMY	3	240	1,055	0.1	0.2
413 S-D ADVENTISTS	4	1,172	1,441*	0.2	0.3
419 SO BAPT CONV..	39	10,759	13,233*	1.4	2.9
435 UNITARIAN-UNIV	5	788	1,101	0.1	0.2
443 UN C OF CHRIST	33	13,204	16,240*	1.8	3.6
449 UN METHODIST..	75	37,095	44,443	4.8	9.7
453 UN PRES CH USA	54	28,773	35,389*	3.8	7.8
469 WISC EVAN LUTH	1	33	50	-	-
HANCOCK	69	20,685	33,599*	54.9	100.0
029 AMER LUTH CH..	2	835	1,131	1.8	3.4
081 CATHOLIC......	1	0	6,373	10.4	19.0
093 CR CH (DISC)..	1	292	362*	0.6	1.1
097 CR C AND C CR.	4	1,217	1,508*	2.5	4.5
123 CH GOD (ANDER)	1	300	650	1.1	1.9
127 CH GOD (CLEVE)	1	132	164*	0.3	0.5
157 CH OF BRETHREN	2	114	141*	0.2	0.4
165 CH OF NAZARENE	3	204	435	0.7	1.3
193 EPISCOPAL.....	1	396	680	1.1	2.0
199 EVAN CONG CH..	1	84	104*	0.2	0.3
281 LUTH CH AMER..	5	2,518	3,635	5.9	10.8
283 LUTH--MO SYNOD	1	207	324	0.5	1.0
403 SALVATION ARMY	1	68	382	0.6	1.1
413 S-D ADVENTISTS	1	71	88*	0.1	0.3
419 SO BAPT CONV..	1	124	154*	0.3	0.5
443 UN C OF CHRIST	1	71	88*	0.1	0.3
449 UN METHODIST..	35	11,244	13,802	22.5	41.1
453 UN PRES CH USA	5	2,157	2,672*	4.4	8.0
469 WISC EVAN LUTH	2	651	906	1.5	2.7
HARDIN	54	8,963	12,318*	40.0	100.0
019 AMER BAPT CONV	2	264	321*	1.0	2.6
029 AMER LUTH CH..	1	300	390	1.3	3.2
081 CATHOLIC......	1	0	1,149	3.7	9.3
093 CR CH (DISC)..	2	372	452*	1.5	3.7
097 CR C AND C CR.	8	560	681*	2.2	5.5
123 CH GOD (ANDER)	2	32	107	0.3	0.9
127 CH GOD (CLEVE)	1	20	24*	0.1	0.2
165 CH OF NAZARENE	1	125	360	1.2	2.9
193 EPISCOPAL.....	1	21	29	0.1	0.2
281 LUTH CH AMER..	1	136	222	0.7	1.8
443 UN C OF CHRIST	4	1,055	1,283*	4.2	10.4
449 UN METHODIST..	25	5,395	6,425	20.9	52.2
453 UN PRES CH USA	4	613	745*	2.4	6.0
469 WISC EVAN LUTH	1	70	130	0.4	1.1
HARRISON	51	5,621	7,553*	44.4	100.0
081 CATHOLIC......	6	0	556	3.3	7.4
093 CR CH (DISC)..	1	204	245*	1.4	3.2
097 CR C AND C CR.	4	445	535*	3.1	7.1
123 CH GOD (ANDER)	1	50	175	1.0	2.3
165 CH OF NAZARENE	4	116	326	1.9	4.3
226 FRIENDS-USA...	2	100	120*	0.7	1.6
281 LUTH CH AMER..	1	117	139	0.8	1.8
449 UN METHODIST..	21	2,845	3,359	19.7	44.5
453 UN PRES CH USA	11	1,744	2,098*	12.3	27.8
HENRY	50	13,012	21,108*	78.0	100.0
029 AMER LUTH CH..	8	3,130	4,139	15.3	19.6
081 CATHOLIC......	5	0	4,088	15.1	19.4
107 CHRISTIAN UN..	1	45	56*	0.2	0.3
165 CH OF NAZARENE	2	32	163	0.6	0.8
193 EPISCOPAL.....	1	104	177	0.7	0.8
281 LUTH CH AMER..	3	697	1,005	3.7	4.8
283 LUTH--MO SYNOD	9	3,739	5,028	18.6	23.8
413 S-D ADVENTISTS	1	38	47*	0.2	0.2
419 SO BAPT CONV..	1	148	184*	0.7	0.9
443 UN C OF CHRIST	2	816	1,015*	3.8	4.8
449 UN METHODIST..	15	3,638	4,429	16.4	21.0
453 UN PRES CH USA	2	625	777*	2.9	3.7
HIGHLAND	71	9,554	12,588*	43.4	100.0
019 AMER BAPT CONV	3	776	946*	3.3	7.5
081 CATHOLIC......	2	0	896	3.1	7.1
097 CR C AND C CR.	17	2,738	3,339*	11.5	26.5
107 CHRISTIAN UN..	3	82	100*	0.3	0.8
123 CH GOD (ANDER)	1	29	58	0.2	0.5
127 CH GOD (CLEVE)	1	47	57*	0.2	0.5
157 CH OF BRETHREN	1	20	24*	0.1	0.2
165 CH OF NAZARENE	2	193	529	1.8	4.2

*Total adherents estimated from known number of communicant, confirmed, full members.

—Represents a percent less than 0.1.

Percentages may not total due to rounding.

Table 3. Churches and Church Membership by State, County and Denomination: 1971

County and Denomination	Number of churches	Communicant, confirmed, full members	Total adherents: Number	Total adherents: Percent of total population	Total adherents: Percent of total adherents
193 EPISCOPAL.....	1	84	118	0.4	0.9
226 FRIENDS-USA...	6	605	738*	2.5	5.9
281 LUTH CH AMER..	1	200	270	0.9	2.1
413 S-D ADVENTISTS	1	30	37*	0.1	0.3
449 UN METHODIST..	25	3,759	4,268	14.7	33.9
453 UN PRES CH USA	7	991	1,208*	4.2	9.6
HOCKING	55	5,579	7,938*	39.1	100.0
019 AMER BAPT CONV	1	139	172*	0.8	2.2
029 AMER LUTH CH..	3	543	710	3.5	8.9
081 CATHOLIC......	2	0	890	4.4	11.2
093 CR CH (DISC)..	1	62	77*	0.4	1.0
097 CR C AND C CR.	1	250	309*	1.5	3.9
123 CH GOD (ANDER)	2	115	326	1.6	4.1
127 CH GOD (CLEVE)	1	13	16*	0.1	0.2
165 CH OF NAZARENE	1	143	524	2.6	6.6
193 EPISCOPAL.....	1	53	76	0.4	1.0
283 LUTH--MO SYNOD	1	104	155	0.8	2.0
285 MENNONITE CH..	3	65	80*	0.4	1.0
419 SO BAPT CONV..	2	371	459*	2.3	5.8
449 UN METHODIST..	34	3,150	3,437	16.9	43.3
453 UN PRES CH USA	2	571	707*	3.5	8.9
HOLMES	44	6,786	9,126*	39.6	100.0
019 AMER BAPT CONV	1	103	134*	0.6	1.5
081 CATHOLIC......	3	0	517	2.2	5.7
097 CR C AND C CR.	8	2,026	2,629*	11.4	28.8
165 CH OF NAZARENE	1	28	73	0.3	0.8
221 FREE METH C NA	1	10	10	-	0.1
281 LUTH CH AMER..	1	303	376	1.6	4.1
283 LUTH--MO SYNOD	1	65	80	0.3	0.9
285 MENNONITE CH..	11	1,763	2,287*	9.9	25.1
413 S-D ADVENTISTS	1	39	51*	0.2	0.6
443 UN C OF CHRIST	5	745	967*	4.2	10.6
449 UN METHODIST..	8	1,286	1,460	6.3	16.0
453 UN PRES CH USA	3	418	542*	2.4	5.9
HURON	69	13,591	31,486*	63.5	100.0
019 AMER BAPT CONV	3	625	783*	1.6	2.5
029 AMER LUTH CH..	6	2,946	4,201	8.5	13.3
081 CATHOLIC......	10	0	14,341	28.9	45.5
093 CR CH (DISC)..	1	50	63*	0.1	0.2
097 CR C AND C CR.	2	185	232*	0.5	0.7
105 CHRISTIAN REF.	1	226	390	0.8	1.2
127 CH GOD (CLEVE)	3	195	244*	0.5	0.8
165 CH OF NAZARENE	3	196	315	0.6	1.0
193 EPISCOPAL.....	3	619	832	1.7	2.6
226 FRIENDS-USA...	1	30	38*	0.1	0.1
403 SALVATION ARMY	1	38	142	0.3	0.5
413 S-D ADVENTISTS	2	132	165*	0.3	0.5
419 SO BAPT CONV..	4	255	319*	0.6	1.0
435 UNITARIAN-UNIV	1	40	44	0.1	0.1
443 UN C OF CHRIST	9	1,868	2,340*	4.7	7.4
449 UN METHODIST..	16	5,122	5,704	11.5	18.1
453 UN PRES CH USA	3	1,064	1,333*	2.7	4.2
JACKSON	42	5,891	7,466*	27.5	100.0
019 AMER BAPT CONV	4	474	574*	2.1	7.7
081 CATHOLIC......	2	0	554	2.0	7.4
093 CR CH (DISC)..	2	456	552*	2.0	7.4
127 CH GOD (CLEVE)	2	82	99*	0.4	1.3
165 CH OF NAZARENE	2	212	455	1.7	6.1
281 LUTH CH AMER..	1	107	142	0.5	1.9
285 MENNONITE CH..	1	30	36*	0.1	0.5
349 PENT HOLINESS.	1	32	39*	0.1	0.5
413 S-D ADVENTISTS	1	41	50*	0.2	0.7
419 SO BAPT CONV..	1	157	190*	0.7	2.5
449 UN METHODIST..	18	3,207	3,452	12.7	46.2
453 UN PRES CH USA	7	1,093	1,323*	4.9	17.7
JEFFERSON	134	22,365	46,816*	48.7	100.0
019 AMER BAPT CONV	2	334	402*	0.4	0.9
029 AMER LUTH CH..	1	97	143	0.1	0.3
081 CATHOLIC......	28	0	18,496	19.2	39.5
093 CR CH (DISC)..	2	336	404*	0.4	0.9
097 CR C AND C CR.	8	2,123	2,556*	2.7	5.5
123 CH GOD (ANDER)	3	260	778	0.8	1.7
165 CH OF NAZARENE	8	544	1,223	1.3	2.6
193 EPISCOPAL.....	2	639	1,167	1.2	2.5
226 FRIENDS-USA...	3	257	309*	0.3	0.7
281 LUTH CH AMER..	1	487	659	0.7	1.4
283 LUTH--MO SYNOD	1	193	255	0.3	0.5
353 PLY BRETHREN..	3	60	90	0.1	0.2
403 SALVATION ARMY	1	38	341	0.4	0.7
413 S-D ADVENTISTS	1	25	30*	-	0.1
419 SO BAPT CONV..	1	77	93*	0.1	0.2
443 UN C OF CHRIST	2	638	768*	0.8	1.6
449 UN METHODIST..	45	9,902	11,452	11.9	24.5
453 UN PRES CH USA	22	6,355	7,650*	8.0	16.3
KNOX	70	13,596	21,078*	50.4	100.0
019 AMER BAPT CONV	4	909	1,097*	2.6	5.2
029 AMER LUTH CH..	3	648	986	2.4	4.7
081 CATHOLIC......	2	0	3,600	8.6	17.1
093 CR CH (DISC)..	1	709	856*	2.0	4.1
097 CR C AND C CR.	13	1,521	1,836*	4.4	8.7
123 CH GOD (ANDER)	2	157	457	1.1	2.2
127 CH GOD (CLEVE)	1	158	191*	0.5	0.9
157 CH OF BRETHREN	2	247	298*	0.7	1.4
165 CH OF NAZARENE	3	552	805	1.9	3.8
193 EPISCOPAL.....	2	600	883	2.1	4.2
285 MENNONITE CH..	1	71	86*	0.2	0.4
403 SALVATION ARMY	1	74	327	0.8	1.6
413 S-D ADVENTISTS	2	781	943*	2.3	4.5
419 SO BAPT CONV..	1	59	71*	0.2	0.3
443 UN C OF CHRIST	3	569	687*	1.6	3.3
449 UN METHODIST..	25	5,340	6,505	15.6	30.9
453 UN PRES CH USA	4	1,201	1,450*	3.5	6.9
LAKE	82	26,190	101,888*	51.7	100.0
019 AMER BAPT CONV	6	1,701	2,156*	1.1	2.1
029 AMER LUTH CH..	2	376	631	0.3	0.6
081 CATHOLIC......	13	0	66,327	33.6	65.1
093 CR CH (DISC)..	4	883	1,119*	0.6	1.1
097 CR C AND C CR.	2	1,351	1,712*	0.9	1.7
123 CH GOD (ANDER)	1	25	70	-	0.1
127 CH GOD (CLEVE)	4	247	313*	0.2	0.3
157 CH OF BRETHREN	1	219	278*	0.1	0.3
165 CH OF NAZARENE	2	240	517	0.3	0.5
193 EPISCOPAL.....	5	1,760	2,997	1.5	2.9
281 LUTH CH AMER..	4	1,732	2,586	1.3	2.5
283 LUTH--MO SYNOD	8	3,048	4,402	2.2	4.3
353 PLY BRETHREN..	1	50	100	0.1	0.1
403 SALVATION ARMY	1	97	369	0.2	0.4
413 S-D ADVENTISTS	2	188	238*	0.1	0.2
419 SO BAPT CONV..	4	1,122	1,422*	0.7	1.4
435 UNITARIAN-UNIV	1	172	277	0.1	0.3
443 UN C OF CHRIST	8	3,033	3,843*	1.9	3.8
449 UN METHODIST..	11	9,687	12,162	6.2	11.9
453 UN PRES CH USA	1	199	252*	0.1	0.2
469 WISC EVAN LUTH	1	60	117	0.1	0.1
LAWRENCE	68	9,655	15,613*	27.5	100.0
019 AMER BAPT CONV	7	1,935	2,388*	4.2	15.3
029 AMER LUTH CH..	1	230	281	0.5	1.8
081 CATHOLIC......	4	0	3,255	5.7	20.8
097 CR C AND C CR.	3	1,761	2,173*	3.8	13.9
123 CH GOD (ANDER)	1	3	13	-	0.1
127 CH GOD (CLEVE)	2	183	226*	0.4	1.4
165 CH OF NAZARENE	11	848	1,935	3.4	12.4
193 EPISCOPAL.....	1	87	277	0.5	1.8
285 MENNONITE CH..	1	37	46*	0.1	0.3
349 PENT HOLINESS.	1	24	30*	0.1	0.2
357 PRESB CH US...	1	119	147*	0.3	0.9
413 S-D ADVENTISTS	1	13	16*	-	0.1
419 SO BAPT CONV..	1	150	185*	0.3	1.2
449 UN METHODIST..	32	4,027	4,347	7.6	27.8
453 UN PRES CH USA	1	238	294*	0.5	1.9
LICKING	129	27,740	45,163*	41.9	100.0
019 AMER BAPT CONV	13	2,662	3,282*	3.0	7.3
081 CATHOLIC......	6	0	10,365	9.6	23.0
093 CR CH (DISC)..	3	1,390	1,714*	1.6	3.8
097 CR C AND C CR.	13	1,979	2,440*	2.3	5.4
107 CHRISTIAN UN..	8	405	499*	0.5	1.1
123 CH GOD (ANDER)	1	60	160	0.1	0.4
127 CH GOD (CLEVE)	2	156	192*	0.2	0.4
165 CH OF NAZARENE	7	584	1,226	1.1	2.7
193 EPISCOPAL.....	2	754	1,020	0.9	2.3
221 FREE METH C NA	1	27	33	-	0.1
281 LUTH CH AMER..	6	1,837	2,672	2.5	5.9
283 LUTH--MO SYNOD	2	295	433	0.4	1.0
403 SALVATION ARMY	1	41	267	0.2	0.6
413 S-D ADVENTISTS	1	218	269*	0.2	0.6
419 SO BAPT CONV..	6	871	1,074*	1.0	2.4
435 UNITARIAN-UNIV	1	72	102	0.1	0.2
443 UN C OF CHRIST	4	1,197	1,476*	1.4	3.3
449 UN METHODIST..	40	11,073	12,861	11.9	28.5
453 UN PRES CH USA	12	4,119	5,078*	4.7	11.2
LOGAN	67	12,620	19,183*	54.7	100.0
019 AMER BAPT CONV	2	68	83*	0.2	0.4
081 CATHOLIC......	2	0	2,176	6.2	11.3
093 CR CH (DISC)..	1	743	902*	2.6	4.7
097 CR C AND C CR.	7	739	897*	2.6	4.7
123 CH GOD (ANDER)	4	643	2,015	5.7	10.5
157 CH OF BRETHREN	2	325	395*	1.1	2.1
165 CH OF NAZARENE	4	184	621	1.8	3.2
193 EPISCOPAL.....	1	195	280	0.8	1.5
226 FRIENDS-USA...	5	279	339*	1.0	1.8
281 LUTH CH AMER..	4	968	1,414	4.0	7.4
285 MENNONITE CH..	5	630	765*	2.2	4.0
413 S-D ADVENTISTS	1	45	55*	0.2	0.3
443 UN C OF CHRIST	1	253	307*	0.9	1.6
449 UN METHODIST..	22	6,043	7,107	20.3	37.0
453 UN PRES CH USA	6	1,505	1,827*	5.2	9.5
LORAIN	161	38,830	132,424*	51.6	100.0
019 AMER BAPT CONV	6	1,023	1,296*	0.5	1.0
029 AMER LUTH CH..	2	601	906	0.4	0.7
081 CATHOLIC......	37	0	81,079	31.6	61.2
093 CR CH (DISC)..	4	1,380	1,748*	0.7	1.3
097 CR C AND C CR.	2	130	165*	0.1	0.1
123 CH GOD (ANDER)	1	85	310	0.1	0.2
127 CH GOD (CLEVE)	6	520	659*	0.3	0.5
157 CH OF BRETHREN	1	88	111*	-	0.1
165 CH OF NAZARENE	7	520	1,233	0.5	0.9
193 EPISCOPAL.....	4	1,652	2,406	0.9	1.8
226 FRIENDS-USA...	1	13	16*	-	-

*Total adherents estimated from known number of communicant, confirmed, full members.

—Represents a percent less than 0.1.

Percentages may not total due to rounding.

Table 3. Churches and Church Membership by State, County and Denomination: 1971

County and Denomination	Number of churches	Communicant, confirmed, full members	Total adherents: Number	Total adherents: Percent of total population	Total adherents: Percent of total adherents
281 LUTH CH AMER..	7	1,934	2,648	1.0	2.0
283 LUTH--MO SYNOD	11	3,771	5,339	2.1	4.0
349 PENT HOLINESS.	1	33	42*	-	-
353 PLY BRETHREN..	2	40	70	-	0.1
403 SALVATION ARMY	2	169	887	0.3	0.7
413 S-D ADVENTISTS	3	19	24*	-	-
419 SO BAPT CONV..	10	3,155	3,995*	1.6	3.0
435 UNITARIAN-UNIV	1	22	47	-	-
443 UN C OF CHRIST	23	11,670	14,779*	5.8	11.2
449 UN METHODIST..	28	11,331	13,810	5.4	10.4
453 UN PRES CH USA	2	674	854*	0.3	0.6
LUCAS	259	94,027	264,793*	54.7	100.0
019 AMER BAPT CONV	12	4,590	5,637*	1.2	2.1
029 AMER LUTH CH..	17	15,455	22,909	4.7	8.7
059 BAPT MISS ASSN	1	125	154*	-	0.1
081 CATHOLIC......	48	0	135,130	27.9	51.0
093 CR CH (DISC)..	5	1,329	1,632*	0.3	0.6
097 CR C AND C CR.	6	1,831	2,249*	0.5	0.8
105 CHRISTIAN REF.	1	41	116	-	-
123 CH GOD (ANDER)	8	787	2,005	0.4	0.8
127 CH GOD (CLEVE)	6	360	442*	0.1	0.2
157 CH OF BRETHREN	1	206	253*	0.1	0.1
165 CH OF NAZARENE	5	663	1,573	0.3	0.6
175 CONG CR CH....	3	1,325	1,627*	0.3	0.6
193 EPISCOPAL.....	9	5,601	8,634	1.8	3.3
221 FREE METH C NA	4	144	216	-	0.1
226 FRIENDS-USA...	1	26	32*	-	-
281 LUTH CH AMER..	23	17,642	25,305	5.2	9.6
283 LUTH--MO SYNOD	11	3,919	5,602	1.2	2.1
285 MENNONITE CH..	2	91	112*	-	-
349 PENT HOLINESS.	5	223	274*	0.1	0.1
353 PLY BRETHREN..	1	150	300	0.1	0.1
403 SALVATION ARMY	2	133	1,717	0.4	0.6
413 S-D ADVENTISTS	3	497	610*	0.1	0.2
419 SO BAPT CONV..	10	2,845	3,494*	0.7	1.3
435 UNITARIAN-UNIV	1	875	1,000	0.2	0.4
443 UN C OF CHRIST	13	5,892	7,236*	1.5	2.7
449 UN METHODIST..	45	21,319	26,606	5.5	10.0
453 UN PRES CH USA	11	6,797	8,347*	1.7	3.2
469 WISC EVAN LUTH	5	1,161	1,581	0.3	0.6
MADISON	37	7,086	10,123*	35.7	100.0
019 AMER BAPT CONV	1	176	217*	0.8	2.1
029 AMER LUTH CH..	1	302	444	1.6	4.4
081 CATHOLIC......	4	0	780	2.8	7.7
123 CH GOD (ANDER)	1	25	70	0.2	0.7
127 CH GOD (CLEVE)	1	20	25*	0.1	0.2
165 CH OF NAZARENE	2	220	769	2.7	7.6
193 EPISCOPAL.....	1	90	179	0.6	1.8
281 LUTH CH AMER..	1	474	671	2.4	6.6
285 MENNONITE CH..	4	423	521*	1.8	5.1
415 S-D BAPTIST GC	1	17	21*	0.1	0.2
419 SO BAPT CONV..	2	482	593*	2.1	5.9
443 UN C OF CHRIST	3	380	468*	1.7	4.6
449 UN METHODIST..	11	3,285	3,898	13.8	38.5
453 UN PRES CH USA	4	1,192	1,467*	5.2	14.5
MAHONING	201	54,223	198,285*	65.3	100.0
019 AMER BAPT CONV	6	2,145	2,577*	0.8	1.3
029 AMER LUTH CH..	8	3,663	5,179	1.7	2.6
081 CATHOLIC......	48	0	128,548	42.4	64.8
093 CR CH (DISC)..	7	2,189	2,630*	0.9	1.3
097 CR C AND C CR.	6	1,759	2,113*	0.7	1.1
123 CH GOD (ANDER)	3	205	514	0.2	0.3
127 CH GOD (CLEVE)	3	209	251*	0.1	0.1
157 CH OF BRETHREN	3	580	697*	0.2	0.4
165 CH OF NAZARENE	5	605	1,163	0.4	0.6
193 EPISCOPAL.....	4	1,810	2,645	0.9	1.3
199 EVAN CONG CH..	1	146	175*	0.1	0.1
201 EVAN COV CH AM	1	609	732*	0.2	0.4
221 FREE METH C NA	3	126	214	0.1	0.1
226 FRIENDS-USA...	6	860	1,033*	0.3	0.5
281 LUTH CH AMER..	16	5,559	7,545	2.5	3.8
283 LUTH--MO SYNOD	6	1,449	2,149	0.7	1.1
285 MENNONITE CH..	4	217	261*	0.1	0.1
353 PLY BRETHREN..	1	50	100	-	0.1
403 SALVATION ARMY	2	216	1,276	0.4	0.6
413 S-D ADVENTISTS	3	498	598*	0.2	0.3
419 SO BAPT CONV..	3	477	573*	0.2	0.3
435 UNITARIAN-UNIV	1	195	240	0.1	0.1
443 UN C OF CHRIST	10	3,970	4,769*	1.6	2.4
449 UN METHODIST..	26	12,900	15,741	5.2	7.9
453 UN PRES CH USA	25	13,786	16,562*	5.5	8.4
MARION	63	19,186	39,542*	61.1	100.0
019 AMER BAPT CONV	7	2,174	2,699*	4.2	6.8
029 AMER LUTH CH..	5	3,418	5,031	7.8	12.7
081 CATHOLIC......	4	0	14,880	23.0	37.6
093 CR CH (DISC)..	1	515	639*	1.0	1.6
097 CR C AND C CR.	3	595	739*	1.1	1.9
123 CH GOD (ANDER)	1	75	195	0.3	0.5
127 CH GOD (CLEVE)	2	97	120*	0.2	0.3
157 CH OF BRETHREN	2	265	329*	0.5	0.8
165 CH OF NAZARENE	3	584	796	1.2	2.0
193 EPISCOPAL.....	1	265	370	0.6	0.9
197 EVAN CH OF NA.	1	10	12*	-	-
201 EVAN COV CH AM	1	41	51*	0.1	0.1
281 LUTH CH AMER..	1	300	427	0.7	1.1
403 SALVATION ARMY	1	84	432	0.7	1.1
413 S-D ADVENTISTS	1	113	140*	0.2	0.4
443 UN C OF CHRIST	5	1,031	1,280*	2.0	3.2
449 UN METHODIST..	21	8,173	9,607	14.8	24.3
453 UN PRES CH USA	3	1,446	1,795*	2.8	4.5
MEDINA	71	17,325	36,841*	44.5	100.0
019 AMER BAPT CONV	2	221	280*	0.3	0.8
029 AMER LUTH CH..	4	961	1,333	1.6	3.6
081 CATHOLIC......	5	0	13,797	16.7	37.5
093 CR CH (DISC)..	4	1,179	1,492*	1.8	4.0
127 CH GOD (CLEVE)	3	101	128*	0.2	0.3
157 CH OF BRETHREN	1	101	128*	0.2	0.3
165 CH OF NAZARENE	3	347	741	0.9	2.0
175 CONG CR CH....	1	75	95*	0.1	0.3
193 EPISCOPAL.....	2	577	821	1.0	2.2
226 FRIENDS-USA...	1	43	54*	0.1	0.1
281 LUTH CH AMER..	5	2,371	3,400	4.1	9.2
283 LUTH--MO SYNOD	3	1,071	1,602	1.9	4.3
285 MENNONITE CH..	1	115	146*	0.2	0.4
287 MENN GEN CONF.	1	197	249*	0.3	0.7
371 REF CH IN AM..	1	84	145	0.2	0.4
403 SALVATION ARMY	1	41	195	0.2	0.5
413 S-D ADVENTISTS	1	62	78*	0.1	0.2
419 SO BAPT CONV..	5	559	708*	0.9	1.9
435 UNITARIAN-UNIV	1	36	36	-	0.1
443 UN C OF CHRIST	9	3,205	4,056*	4.9	11.0
449 UN METHODIST..	16	5,825	7,162	8.7	19.4
453 UN PRES CH USA	1	154	195*	0.2	0.5
MEIGS	70	5,080	6,584*	33.3	100.0
019 AMER BAPT CONV	4	745	900*	4.5	13.7
029 AMER LUTH CH..	2	219	284	1.4	4.3
081 CATHOLIC......	2	0	256	1.3	3.9
093 CR CH (DISC)..	2	118	143*	0.7	2.2
097 CR C AND C CR.	13	782	945*	4.8	14.4
127 CH GOD (CLEVE)	3	70	85*	0.4	1.3
165 CH OF NAZARENE	6	255	686	3.5	10.4
175 CONG CR CH....	1	358	433*	2.2	6.6
193 EPISCOPAL.....	1	45	120	0.6	1.8
221 FREE METH C NA	2	66	94	0.5	1.4
413 S-D ADVENTISTS	1	33	40*	0.2	0.6
449 UN METHODIST..	30	2,175	2,339	11.8	35.5
453 UN PRES CH USA	3	214	259*	1.3	3.9
MERCER	58	6,902	31,788*	90.1	100.0
019 AMER BAPT CONV	1	32	41*	0.1	0.1
029 AMER LUTH CH..	6	1,613	2,160	6.1	6.8
081 CATHOLIC......	20	0	23,001	65.2	72.4
097 CR C AND C CR.	3	443	562*	1.6	1.8
165 CH OF NAZARENE	4	330	748	2.1	2.4
226 FRIENDS-USA...	3	54	69*	0.2	0.2
419 SO BAPT CONV..	1	112	142*	0.4	0.4
443 UN C OF CHRIST	3	552	701*	2.0	2.2
449 UN METHODIST..	15	3,395	3,893	11.0	12.2
453 UN PRES CH USA	2	371	471*	1.3	1.5
MIAMI	97	23,891	39,978*	47.4	100.0
019 AMER BAPT CONV	6	2,121	2,635*	3.1	6.6
029 AMER LUTH CH..	1	417	532	0.6	1.3
075 BRETHREN IN CR	3	167	207*	0.2	0.5
081 CATHOLIC......	7	0	9,148	10.8	22.9
093 CR CH (DISC)..	1	76	94*	0.1	0.2
097 CR C AND C CR.	3	485	602*	0.7	1.5
121 CH GOD (ABR)..	3	237	294*	0.3	0.7
123 CH GOD (ANDER)	2	285	640	0.8	1.6
127 CH GOD (CLEVE)	2	75	93*	0.1	0.2
157 CH OF BRETHREN	9	2,378	2,954*	3.5	7.4
165 CH OF NAZARENE	5	424	1,374	1.6	3.4
193 EPISCOPAL.....	2	436	652	0.8	1.6
226 FRIENDS-USA...	2	434	539*	0.6	1.3
281 LUTH CH AMER..	7	2,153	2,915	3.5	7.3
403 SALVATION ARMY	1	58	310	0.4	0.8
413 S-D ADVENTISTS	1	45	56*	0.1	0.1
419 SO BAPT CONV..	6	834	1,036*	1.2	2.6
443 UN C OF CHRIST	16	5,361	6,659*	7.9	16.7
449 UN METHODIST..	15	5,982	6,849	8.1	17.1
453 UN PRES CH USA	5	1,923	2,389*	2.8	6.0
MONROE	49	4,088	6,007*	38.2	100.0
019 AMER BAPT CONV	4	292	365*	2.3	6.1
081 CATHOLIC......	5	0	1,103	7.0	18.4
097 CR C AND C CR.	3	310	388*	2.5	6.5
107 CHRISTIAN UN..	1	7	9*	0.1	0.1
123 CH GOD (ANDER)	1	32	87	0.6	1.4
165 CH OF NAZARENE	1	42	143	0.9	2.4
221 FREE METH C NA	1	29	39	0.2	0.6
419 SO BAPT CONV..	1	313	391*	2.5	6.5
443 UN C OF CHRIST	5	800	1,000*	6.4	16.6
449 UN METHODIST..	24	2,041	2,204	14.0	36.7
453 UN PRES CH USA	3	222	278*	1.8	4.6
MONTGOMERY	333	115,062	249,389*	41.1	100.0
019 AMER BAPT CONV	15	5,908	7,269*	1.2	2.9
029 AMER LUTH CH..	18	8,262	11,192	1.8	4.5
075 BRETHREN IN CR	3	154	189*	-	0.1
081 CATHOLIC......	33	0	100,677	16.6	40.4
093 CR CH (DISC)..	6	1,999	2,460*	0.4	1.0
097 CR C AND C CR.	6	1,381	1,699*	0.3	0.7
105 CHRISTIAN REF.	1	22	42	-	-
107 CHRISTIAN UN..	1	30	37*	-	-

*Total adherents estimated from known number of communicant, confirmed, full members.

—Represents a percent less than 0.1.

Percentages may not total due to rounding.

Table 3. Churches and Church Membership by State, County and Denomination: 1971

County and Denomination	Number of churches	Communicant, confirmed, full members	Total adherents		
			Number	Percent of total population	Percent of total adherents
121 CH GOD (ABR)..	1	75	92*	-	-
123 CH GOD (ANDER)	13	2,010	5,117	0.8	2.1
127 CH GOD (CLEVE)	18	2,184	2,687*	0.4	1.1
157 CH OF BRETHREN	12	3,559	4,379*	0.7	1.8
165 CH OF NAZARENE	20	2,569	5,793	1.0	2.3
193 EPISCOPAL.....	5	1,351	2,656	0.4	1.1
221 FREE METH C NA	1	20	22	-	-
226 FRIENDS-USA...	1	79	97*	-	-
281 LUTH CH AMER..	21	9,077	12,401	2.0	5.0
283 LUTH--MO SYNOD	3	1,031	1,560	0.3	0.6
285 MENNONITE CH..	2	60	74*	-	-
313 NO AM BAPT GC.	1	389	479*	0.1	0.2
335 ORTH PRESB CH.	1	21	30	-	-
349 PENT HOLINESS.	2	52	64*	-	-
403 SALVATION ARMY	2	186	952	0.2	0.4
413 S-D ADVENTISTS	5	1,878	2,311*	0.4	0.9
419 SO BAPT CONV..	42	16,934	20,836*	3.4	8.4
435 UNITARIAN-UNIV	3	266	361	0.1	0.1
443 UN C OF CHRIST	27	9,746	11,991*	2.0	4.8
449 UN METHODIST..	54	35,233	40,897	6.7	16.4
453 UN PRES CH USA	16	10,586	13,025*	2.1	5.2
MORGAN	38	3,733	4,711*	38.1	100.0
029 AMER LUTH CH..	1	63	88	0.7	1.9
081 CATHOLIC......	1	0	200	1.6	4.2
093 CR CH (DISC)..	2	125	153*	1.2	3.2
097 CR C AND C CR.	6	757	926*	7.5	19.7
165 CH OF NAZARENE	2	119	284	2.3	6.0
221 FREE METH C NA	1	3	3	-	0.1
226 FRIENDS-USA...	1	33	40*	0.3	0.8
281 LUTH CH AMER..	1	71	86	0.7	1.8
449 UN METHODIST..	20	2,183	2,468	19.9	52.4
453 UN PRES CH USA	3	379	463*	3.7	9.8
MORROW	40	6,886	9,197*	43.1	100.0
019 AMER BAPT CONV	3	669	829*	3.9	9.0
029 AMER LUTH CH..	2	604	789	3.7	8.6
081 CATHOLIC......	2	0	643	3.0	7.0
097 CR C AND C CR.	2	574	711*	3.3	7.7
127 CH GOD (CLEVE)	1	20	25*	0.1	0.3
165 CH OF NAZARENE	3	310	553	2.6	6.0
226 FRIENDS-USA...	2	215	266*	1.2	2.9
281 LUTH CH AMER..	2	445	638	3.0	6.9
413 S-D ADVENTISTS	1	33	41*	0.2	0.4
449 UN METHODIST..	20	3,575	4,156	19.5	45.2
453 UN PRES CH USA	2	441	546*	2.6	5.9
MUSKINGUM	116	24,528	35,694*	45.9	100.0
019 AMER BAPT CONV	11	1,866	2,294*	2.9	6.4
029 AMER LUTH CH..	1	426	566	0.7	1.6
081 CATHOLIC......	5	0	5,000	6.4	14.0
093 CR CH (DISC)..	1	716	880*	1.1	2.5
097 CR C AND C CR.	4	350	430*	0.6	1.2
123 CH GOD (ANDER)	2	132	339	0.4	0.9
157 CH OF BRETHREN	1	129	159*	0.2	0.4
165 CH OF NAZARENE	5	436	753	1.0	2.1
193 EPISCOPAL.....	2	537	584	0.8	1.6
221 FREE METH C NA	3	156	212	0.3	0.6
281 LUTH CH AMER..	7	1,883	2,659	3.4	7.4
283 LUTH--MO SYNOD	1	910	1,225	1.6	3.4
403 SALVATION ARMY	1	77	379	0.5	1.1
413 S-D ADVENTISTS	2	125	154*	0.2	0.4
419 SO BAPT CONV..	2	232	285*	0.4	0.8
443 UN C OF CHRIST	1	693	852*	1.1	2.4
449 UN METHODIST..	48	11,709	13,819	17.8	38.7
453 UN PRES CH USA	19	4,151	5,104*	6.6	14.3
NOBLE	34	2,383	4,815*	46.2	100.0
081 CATHOLIC......	5	0	1,934	18.5	40.2
097 CR C AND C CR.	2	450	550*	5.3	11.4
165 CH OF NAZARENE	1	18	48	0.5	1.0
221 FREE METH C NA	3	68	100	1.0	2.1
281 LUTH CH AMER..	1	99	118	1.1	2.5
443 UN C OF CHRIST	1	38	46*	0.4	1.0
449 UN METHODIST..	19	1,476	1,733	16.6	36.0
453 UN PRES CH USA	2	234	286*	2.7	5.9
OTTAWA	45	12,808	24,933*	67.2	100.0
029 AMER LUTH CH..	12	5,875	8,323	22.4	33.4
081 CATHOLIC......	6	0	7,653	20.6	30.7
093 CR CH (DISC)..	2	166	205*	0.6	0.8
123 CH GOD (ANDER)	2	79	289	0.8	1.2
127 CH GOD (CLEVE)	2	13	16*	-	0.1
165 CH OF NAZARENE	1	32	106	0.3	0.4
193 EPISCOPAL.....	2	273	437	1.2	1.8
283 LUTH--MO SYNOD	1	323	446	1.2	1.8
413 S-D ADVENTISTS	1	170	210*	0.6	0.8
419 SO BAPT CONV..	2	362	447*	1.2	1.8
443 UN C OF CHRIST	5	2,205	2,721*	7.3	10.9
449 UN METHODIST..	8	3,204	3,949	10.6	15.8
453 UN PRES CH USA	1	106	131*	0.4	0.5
PAULDING	43	5,658	11,593*	60.0	100.0
029 AMER LUTH CH..	2	313	422	2.2	3.6
081 CATHOLIC......	5	0	3,100	16.0	26.7
093 CR CH (DISC)..	1	273	348*	1.8	3.0
097 CR C AND C CR.	3	110	140*	0.7	1.2
107 CHRISTIAN UN..	2	83	106*	0.5	0.9
123 CH GOD (ANDER)	4	220	623	3.2	5.4
165 CH OF NAZARENE	3	261	871	4.5	7.5
193 EPISCOPAL.....	1	1,172	1,907	9.9	16.4
281 LUTH CH AMER..	1	287	454	2.3	3.9
283 LUTH--MO SYNOD	1	126	201	1.0	1.7
449 UN METHODIST..	17	2,379	2,867	14.8	24.7
453 UN PRES CH USA	3	434	554*	2.9	4.8
PERRY	59	5,972	12,078*	44.0	100.0
019 AMER BAPT CONV	2	205	254*	0.9	2.1
029 AMER LUTH CH..	6	1,228	1,676	6.1	13.9
081 CATHOLIC......	9	0	3,717	13.5	30.8
093 CR CH (DISC)..	4	388	481*	1.8	4.0
107 CHRISTIAN UN..	3	76	94*	0.3	0.8
123 CH GOD (ANDER)	2	73	213	0.8	1.8
157 CH OF BRETHREN	1	161	200*	0.7	1.7
165 CH OF NAZARENE	2	206	530	1.9	4.4
221 FREE METH C NA	2	45	73	0.3	0.6
419 SO BAPT CONV..	1	45	56*	0.2	0.5
443 UN C OF CHRIST	4	334	414*	1.5	3.4
449 UN METHODIST..	21	3,032	4,148	15.1	34.3
453 UN PRES CH USA	2	179	222*	0.8	1.8
PICKAWAY	42	9,013	12,470*	31.1	100.0
029 AMER LUTH CH..	4	1,548	2,107	5.3	16.9
081 CATHOLIC......	1	0	1,025	2.6	8.2
097 CR C AND C CR.	2	322	397*	1.0	3.2
127 CH GOD (CLEVE)	1	95	117*	0.3	0.9
157 CH OF BRETHREN	1	79	98*	0.2	0.8
165 CH OF NAZARENE	2	261	726	1.8	5.8
193 EPISCOPAL.....	1	123	235	0.6	1.9
281 LUTH CH AMER..	1	63	90	0.2	0.7
419 SO BAPT CONV..	3	653	806*	2.0	6.5
449 UN METHODIST..	25	5,374	6,258	15.6	50.2
453 UN PRES CH USA	1	495	611*	1.5	4.9
PIKE	29	2,779	3,780*	19.8	100.0
019 AMER BAPT CONV	2	71	88*	0.5	2.3
081 CATHOLIC......	1	0	462	2.4	12.2
097 CR C AND C CR.	2	150	187*	1.0	4.9
107 CHRISTIAN UN..	6	81	101*	0.5	2.7
165 CH OF NAZARENE	1	45	79	0.4	2.1
283 LUTH--MO SYNOD	1	75	111	0.6	2.9
285 MENNONITE CH..	1	29	36*	0.2	1.0
419 SO BAPT CONV..	2	402	501*	2.6	13.3
443 UN C OF CHRIST	1	53	66*	0.3	1.7
449 UN METHODIST..	11	1,358	1,507	7.9	39.9
453 UN PRES CH USA	1	515	642*	3.4	17.0
PORTAGE	77	16,171	48,562*	38.6	100.0
029 AMER LUTH CH..	2	604	925	0.7	1.9
081 CATHOLIC......	10	0	26,712	21.2	55.0
093 CR CH (DISC)..	6	1,842	2,266*	1.8	4.7
123 CH GOD (ANDER)	4	197	626	0.5	1.3
127 CH GOD (CLEVE)	2	134	165*	0.1	0.3
157 CH OF BRETHREN	1	187	230	0.2	0.5
165 CH OF NAZARENE	5	410	1,037	0.8	2.1
193 EPISCOPAL.....	1	347	508	0.4	1.0
221 FREE METH C NA	1	30	45	-	0.1
226 FRIENDS-USA...	2	80	98*	0.1	0.2
281 LUTH CH AMER..	2	5[illegible]	864	0.7	1.8
283 LUTH--MO SYNOD	3	768	1,124	0.9	2.3
285 MENNONITE CH..	1	114	140*	0.1	0.3
353 PLY BRETHREN..	1	20	30	-	0.1
413 S-D ADVENTISTS	1	79	97*	0.1	0.2
419 SO BAPT CONV..	6	599	737*	0.6	1.5
435 UNITARIAN-UNIV	1	83	123	0.1	0.3
443 UN C OF CHRIST	8	3,155	3,881*	3.1	8.0
449 UN METHODIST..	19	6,662	8,575	6.8	17.7
453 UN PRES CH USA	1	308	379*	0.3	0.8
PREBLE	57	9,929	14,708*	42.4	100.0
029 AMER LUTH CH..	2	1,072	1,444	4.2	9.8
081 CATHOLIC......	3	0	1,566	4.5	10.6
097 CR C AND C CR.	3	353	435*	1.3	3.0
123 CH GOD (ANDER)	4	265	896	2.6	6.1
127 CH GOD (CLEVE)	2	165	203*	0.6	1.4
157 CH OF BRETHREN	4	787	970*	2.8	6.6
165 CH OF NAZARENE	1	89	258	0.7	1.8
226 FRIENDS-USA...	1	135	166*	0.5	1.1
281 LUTH CH AMER..	3	980	1,322	3.8	9.0
419 SO BAPT CONV..	8	1,317	1,624*	4.7	11.0
435 UNITARIAN-UNIV	1	90	125	0.4	0.8
443 UN C OF CHRIST	5	910	1,122*	3.2	7.6
449 UN METHODIST..	14	2,981	3,609	10.4	24.5
453 UN PRES CH USA	6	785	968*	2.8	6.6
PUTNAM	49	5,377	25,242*	81.1	100.0
029 AMER LUTH CH..	1	87	105	0.3	0.4
081 CATHOLIC......	13	0	18,569	59.6	73.6
093 CR CH (DISC)..	1	268	347*	1.1	1.4
097 CR C AND C CR.	1	50	65*	0.2	0.3
107 CHRISTIAN UN..	2	28	36*	0.1	0.1
123 CH GOD (ANDER)	1	58	128	0.4	0.5
127 CH GOD (CLEVE)	1	24	31*	0.1	0.1
157 CH OF BRETHREN	1	106	137*	0.4	0.5
165 CH OF NAZARENE	1	44	182	0.6	0.7
221 FREE METH C NA	1	12	19	0.1	0.1
281 LUTH CH AMER..	3	386	496	1.6	2.0
285 MENNONITE CH..	1	48	62*	0.2	0.2

*Total adherents estimated from known number of communicant, confirmed, full members.

—Represents a percent less than 0.1.

Percentages may not total due to rounding.

Table 3. Churches and Church Membership by State, County and Denomination: 1971

County and Denomination	Number of churches	Communicant, confirmed, full members	Total adherents: Number	Total adherents: Percent of total population	Total adherents: Percent of total adherents
287 MENN GEN CONF.	2	632	818*	2.6	3.2
449 UN METHODIST..	18	3,351	3,881	12.5	15.4
453 UN PRES CH USA	2	283	366*	1.2	1.4
RICHLAND	98	30,090	55,119*	42.4	100.0
019 AMER BAPT CONV	5	1,274	1,575*	1.2	2.9
081 CATHOLIC......	5	0	15,249	11.7	27.7
093 CR CH (DISC)..	4	1,700	2,102*	1.6	3.8
097 CR C AND C CR.	7	600	742*	0.6	1.3
123 CH GOD (ANDER)	2	338	920	0.7	1.7
127 CH GOD (CLEVE)	5	244	302*	0.2	0.5
157 CH OF BRETHREN	2	221	273*	0.2	0.5
165 CH OF NAZARENE	5	420	867	0.7	1.6
175 CONG CR CH....	1	1,148	1,420*	1.1	2.6
193 EPISCOPAL.....	2	673	1,368	1.1	2.5
199 EVAN CONG CH..	1	33	41*	-	0.1
221 FREE METH C NA	1	98	122	0.1	0.2
226 FRIENDS-USA...	1	33	41*	-	0.1
281 LUTH CH AMER..	18	9,676	13,045	10.0	23.7
283 LUTH--MO SYNOD	1	166	267	0.2	0.5
353 PLY BRETHREN..	2	85	195	0.2	0.4
403 SALVATION ARMY	1	89	923	0.7	1.7
413 S-D ADVENTISTS	2	195	241*	0.2	0.4
419 SO BAPT CONV..	3	593	733*	0.6	1.3
435 UNITARIAN-UNIV	1	20	30	-	0.1
443 UN C OF CHRIST	4	1,614	1,996*	1.5	3.6
449 UN METHODIST..	18	7,885	8,976	6.9	16.3
453 UN PRES CH USA	7	2,985	3,691*	2.8	6.7
ROSS	79	12,692	19,961*	32.6	100.0
019 AMER BAPT CONV	3	1,269	1,554*	2.5	7.8
081 CATHOLIC......	2	0	3,919	6.4	19.6
093 CR CH (DISC)..	1	165	202*	0.3	1.0
097 CR C AND C CR.	3	675	827*	1.4	4.1
107 CHRISTIAN UN..	7	120	147*	0.2	0.7
123 CH GOD (ANDER)	2	108	378	0.6	1.9
127 CH GOD (CLEVE)	3	144	176*	0.3	0.9
157 CH OF BRETHREN	1	66	81*	0.1	0.4
165 CH OF NAZARENE	3	262	656	1.1	3.3
193 EPISCOPAL.....	1	369	576	0.9	2.9
226 FRIENDS-USA...	2	30	37*	0.1	0.2
281 LUTH CH AMER..	1	344	476	0.8	2.4
283 LUTH--MO SYNOD	1	70	112	0.2	0.6
403 SALVATION ARMY	1	85	436	0.7	2.2
419 SO BAPT CONV..	1	264	323*	0.5	1.6
443 UN C OF CHRIST	3	701	859*	1.4	4.3
449 UN METHODIST..	34	6,054	6,794	11.1	34.0
453 UN PRES CH USA	10	1,966	2,408*	3.9	12.1
SANDUSKY	57	17,651	37,009*	60.7	100.0
029 AMER LUTH CH..	10	6,810	9,205	15.1	24.9
081 CATHOLIC......	7	0	14,702	24.1	39.7
093 CR CH (DISC)..	2	216	270*	0.4	0.7
097 CR C AND C CR.	2	83	104*	0.2	0.3
123 CH GOD (ANDER)	1	61	140	0.2	0.4
127 CH GOD (CLEVE)	3	59	74*	0.1	0.2
165 CH OF NAZARENE	3	121	281	0.5	0.8
193 EPISCOPAL.....	1	340	579	0.9	1.6
281 LUTH CH AMER..	1	396	547	0.9	1.5
353 PLY BRETHREN..	1	20	30	-	0.1
413 S-D ADVENTISTS	2	59	74*	0.1	0.2
419 SO BAPT CONV..	4	568	710*	1.2	1.9
443 UN C OF CHRIST	1	332	415*	0.7	1.1
449 UN METHODIST..	16	7,273	8,238	13.5	22.3
453 UN PRES CH USA	3	1,313	1,640*	2.7	4.4
SCIOTO	89	15,489	23,602*	30.7	100.0
019 AMER BAPT CONV	1	419	510*	0.7	2.2
029 AMER LUTH CH..	2	359	469	0.6	2.0
081 CATHOLIC......	7	0	4,406	5.7	18.7
093 CR CH (DISC)..	1	500	609*	0.8	2.6
097 CR C AND C CR.	11	2,689	3,273*	4.3	13.9
107 CHRISTIAN UN..	3	86	105*	0.1	0.4
123 CH GOD (ANDER)	2	148	425	0.6	1.8
127 CH GOD (CLEVE)	4	289	352*	0.5	1.5
165 CH OF NAZARENE	10	949	2,107	2.7	8.9
193 EPISCOPAL.....	1	404	552	0.7	2.3
285 MENNONITE CH..	1	30	37*	-	0.2
413 S-D ADVENTISTS	1	139	169*	0.2	0.7
419 SO BAPT CONV..	2	222	270*	0.4	1.1
443 UN C OF CHRIST	1	540	657*	0.9	2.8
449 UN METHODIST..	39	7,336	7,982	10.4	33.8
453 UN PRES CH USA	3	1,379	1,679*	2.2	7.1
SENECA	69	14,193	41,038*	67.6	100.0
019 AMER BAPT CONV	2	400	495*	0.8	1.2
029 AMER LUTH CH..	3	1,244	1,662	2.7	4.0
081 CATHOLIC......	14	0	22,560	37.2	55.0
093 CR CH (DISC)..	2	319	395*	0.7	1.0
097 CR C AND C CR.	1	212	263*	0.4	0.6
127 CH GOD (CLEVE)	1	14	17*	-	-
157 CH OF BRETHREN	1	124	154*	0.3	0.4
165 CH OF NAZARENE	2	496	913	1.5	2.2
193 EPISCOPAL.....	2	319	584	1.0	1.4
281 LUTH CH AMER..	1	976	1,349	2.2	3.3
283 LUTH--MO SYNOD	1	65	106	0.2	0.3
403 SALVATION ARMY	1	70	230	0.4	0.6
413 S-D ADVENTISTS	1	28	35*	0.1	0.1
443 UN C OF CHRIST	13	3,603	4,462*	7.4	10.9
449 UN METHODIST..	21	5,379	6,644	10.9	16.2
453 UN PRES CH USA	3	944	1,169*	1.9	2.8
SHELBY	51	10,557	26,077*	69.1	100.0
019 AMER BAPT CONV	1	388	494*	1.3	1.9
029 AMER LUTH CH..	7	3,199	4,240	11.2	16.3
081 CATHOLIC......	8	0	12,349	32.7	47.4
093 CR CH (DISC)..	1	380	484*	1.3	1.9
097 CR C AND C CR.	2	145	185*	0.5	0.7
123 CH GOD (ANDER)	1	71	227	0.6	0.9
127 CH GOD (CLEVE)	3	146	186*	0.5	0.7
157 CH OF BRETHREN	1	100	127*	0.3	0.5
165 CH OF NAZARENE	1	88	301	0.8	1.2
193 EPISCOPAL.....	1	42	50	0.1	0.2
283 LUTH--MO SYNOD	1	63	90	0.2	0.3
403 SALVATION ARMY	1	39	189	0.5	0.7
413 S-D ADVENTISTS	1	8	10*	-	-
415 S-D BAPTIST GC	1	10	13*	-	-
419 SO BAPT CONV..	4	502	639*	1.7	2.5
443 UN C OF CHRIST	4	1,141	1,453*	3.8	5.6
449 UN METHODIST..	12	3,668	4,318	11.4	16.6
453 UN PRES CH USA	1	567	722*	1.9	2.8
STARK	255	88,853	151,726*	40.8	100.0
019 AMER BAPT CONV	5	2,507	3,066*	0.8	2.0
029 AMER LUTH CH..	14	6,304	8,757	2.4	5.8
075 BRETHREN IN CR	4	175	214*	0.1	0.1
081 CATHOLIC......	29	0	37,010	9.9	24.4
093 CR CH (DISC)..	6	2,826	3,456*	0.9	2.3
097 CR C AND C CR.	13	8,151	9,969*	2.7	6.6
123 CH GOD (ANDER)	8	1,133	3,108	0.8	2.0
127 CH GOD (CLEVE)	9	1,189	1,454*	0.4	1.0
157 CH OF BRETHREN	9	1,398	1,710*	0.5	1.1
165 CH OF NAZARENE	9	1,429	3,137	0.8	2.1
193 EPISCOPAL.....	4	2,394	3,077	0.8	2.0
199 EVAN CONG CH..	1	103	126*	-	0.1
221 FREE METH C NA	1	127	156	-	0.1
226 FRIENDS-USA...	3	686	839*	0.2	0.6
281 LUTH CH AMER..	13	5,006	6,827	1.8	4.5
283 LUTH--MO SYNOD	3	998	1,458	0.4	1.0
285 MENNONITE CH..	12	1,728	2,113*	0.6	1.4
353 PLY BRETHREN..	1	20	30	-	-
403 SALVATION ARMY	3	261	1,169	0.3	0.8
413 S-D ADVENTISTS	2	184	225*	0.1	0.1
419 SO BAPT CONV..	3	199	243*	0.1	0.2
435 UNITARIAN-UNIV	1	35	61	-	-
443 UN C OF CHRIST	28	14,347	17,546*	4.7	11.6
449 UN METHODIST..	59	27,717	33,823	9.1	22.3
453 UN PRES CH USA	15	9,936	12,152*	3.3	8.0
SUMMIT	285	100,221	239,316*	43.2	100.0
019 AMER BAPT CONV	14	6,875	8,415*	1.5	3.5
029 AMER LUTH CH..	4	1,595	2,384	0.4	1.0
081 CATHOLIC......	43	0	109,295	19.8	45.7
093 CR CH (DISC)..	17	5,484	6,713*	1.2	2.8
097 CR C AND C CR.	16	5,247	6,422*	1.2	2.7
105 CHRISTIAN REF.	1	89	193	-	0.1
123 CH GOD (ANDER)	9	1,321	3,076	0.6	1.3
127 CH GOD (CLEVE)	4	627	767*	0.1	0.3
157 CH OF BRETHREN	3	722	884*	0.2	0.4
165 CH OF NAZARENE	16	2,216	5,147	0.9	2.2
193 EPISCOPAL.....	10	5,443	5,842	1.1	2.4
199 EVAN CONG CH..	5	709	868*	0.2	0.4
201 EVAN COV CH AM	2	243	297*	0.1	0.1
221 FREE METH C NA	1	57	65	-	-
226 FRIENDS-USA...	2	191	234*	-	0.1
281 LUTH CH AMER..	13	6,938	9,453	1.7	4.0
283 LUTH--MO SYNOD	12	5,729	8,029	1.5	3.4
285 MENNONITE CH..	1	29	35*	-	-
353 PLY BRETHREN..	3	120	190	-	0.1
403 SALVATION ARMY	3	218	1,027	0.2	0.4
413 S-D ADVENTISTS	4	857	1,049*	0.2	0.4
419 SO BAPT CONV..	12	1,406	1,721*	0.3	0.7
435 UNITARIAN-UNIV	1	555	720	0.1	0.3
443 UN C OF CHRIST	24	14,432	17,665*	3.2	7.4
449 UN METHODIST..	49	28,715	36,073	6.5	15.1
453 UN PRES CH USA	15	10,366	12,688*	2.3	5.3
469 WISC EVAN LUTH	1	37	64	-	-
TRUMBULL	152	43,442	99,002*	42.6	100.0
019 AMER BAPT CONV	7	2,611	3,222*	1.4	3.3
029 AMER LUTH CH..	4	2,393	3,434	1.5	3.5
081 CATHOLIC......	22	0	40,484	17.4	40.9
093 CR CH (DISC)..	18	6,422	7,924*	3.4	8.0
097 CR C AND C CR.	6	1,335	1,647*	0.7	1.7
123 CH GOD (ANDER)	5	557	1,849	0.8	1.9
127 CH GOD (CLEVE)	4	239	295*	0.1	0.3
157 CH OF BRETHREN	1	91	112*	-	0.1
165 CH OF NAZARENE	9	1,119	3,095	1.3	3.1
193 EPISCOPAL.....	2	1,114	1,944	0.8	2.0
199 EVAN CONG CH..	3	292	360*	0.2	0.4
221 FREE METH C NA	1	64	82	-	0.1
226 FRIENDS-USA...	1	22	27*	-	-
281 LUTH CH AMER..	7	2,237	3,174	1.4	3.2
283 LUTH--MO SYNOD	1	184	248	0.1	0.3
285 MENNONITE CH..	1	24	30*	-	-
403 SALVATION ARMY	1	93	359	0.2	0.4
413 S-D ADVENTISTS	3	200	247*	C.1	0.2
419 SO BAPT CONV..	4	1,212	1,495*	0.6	1.5
435 UNITARIAN-UNIV	1	16	16	-	-
443 UN C OF CHRIST	3	730	901*	0.4	0.9
449 UN METHODIST..	36	16,166	20,258	8.7	20.5

*Total adherents estimated from known number of communicant, confirmed, full members.

—Represents a percent less than 0.1.

Percentages may not total due to rounding.

Table 3. Churches and Church Membership by State, County and Denomination: 1971

County and Denomination	Number of churches	Communicant, confirmed, full members	Total adherents: Number	Total adherents: Percent of total population	Total adherents: Percent of total adherents
453 UN PRES CH USA	12	6,321	7,799*	3.4	7.9
TUSCARAWAS	128	28,733	46,301*	60.0	100.0
019 AMER BAPT CONV	2	219	267*	0.3	0.6
081 CATHOLIC......	10	0	8,968	11.6	19.4
093 CR CH (DISC)..	3	938	1,143*	1.5	2.5
097 CR C AND C CR.	2	662	807*	1.0	1.7
123 CH GOD (ANDER)	3	264	691	0.9	1.5
127 CH GOD (CLEVE)	6	242	295*	0.4	0.6
157 CH OF BRETHREN	3	373	455*	0.6	1.0
165 CH OF NAZARENE	7	1,052	2,126	2.8	4.6
193 EPISCOPAL.....	1	148	242	0.3	0.5
221 FREE METH C NA	1	31	36	-	0.1
281 LUTH CH AMER..	17	5,295	7,161	9.3	15.5
285 MENNONITE CH..	4	279	340*	0.4	0.7
287 MENN GEN CONF.	1	268	327*	0.4	0.7
293 MORAV CH-NORTH	8	2,195	2,906	3.8	6.3
403 SALVATION ARMY	1	104	419	0.5	0.9
413 S-D ADVENTISTS	1	42	51*	0.1	0.1
419 SO BAPT CONV..	1	143	174*	0.2	0.4
443 UN C OF CHRIST	14	6,102	7,436*	9.6	16.1
449 UN METHODIST..	38	9,137	10,947	14.2	23.6
453 UN PRES CH USA	5	1,239	1,510*	2.0	3.3
UNION	43	9,186	12,636*	53.1	100.0
019 AMER BAPT CONV	2	254	310*	1.3	2.5
029 AMER LUTH CH..	1	921	1,327	5.6	10.5
081 CATHOLIC......	1	0	901	3.8	7.1
097 CR C AND C CR.	3	267	326*	1.4	2.6
123 CH GOD (ANDER)	1	53	131	0.6	1.0
127 CH GOD (CLEVE)	1	24	29*	0.1	0.2
165 CH OF NAZARENE	1	53	229	1.0	1.8
226 FRIENDS-USA...	3	114	139*	0.6	1.1
281 LUTH CH AMER..	1	183	255	1.1	2.0
283 LUTH--MO SYNOD	2	1,187	1,614	6.8	12.8
413 S-D ADVENTISTS	1	17	21*	0.1	0.2
419 SO BAPT CONV..	1	84	103*	0.4	0.8
443 UN C OF CHRIST	2	252	308*	1.3	2.4
449 UN METHODIST..	22	5,097	6,112	25.7	48.4
453 UN PRES CH USA	1	680	831*	3.5	6.6
VAN WERT	50	9,786	14,252*	48.8	100.0
081 CATHOLIC......	1	0	1,821	6.2	12.8
097 CR C AND C CR.	1	167	203*	0.7	1.4
123 CH GOD (ANDER)	2	86	294	1.0	2.1
165 CH OF NAZARENE	2	145	359	1.2	2.5
193 EPISCOPAL.....	1	30	35	0.1	0.2
226 FRIENDS-USA...	3	192	233*	0.8	1.6
281 LUTH CH AMER..	4	1,343	1,755	6.0	12.3
283 LUTH--MO SYNOD	4	961	1,355	4.6	9.5
403 SALVATION ARMY	1	27	156	0.5	1.1
413 S-D ADVENTISTS	1	14	17*	0.1	0.1
419 SO BAPT CONV..	1	73	89*	0.3	0.6
443 UN C OF CHRIST	2	498	605*	2.1	4.2
449 UN METHODIST..	22	4,697	5,443	18.6	38.2
453 UN PRES CH USA	5	1,553	1,887*	6.5	13.2
VINTON	30	1,603	2,111*	22.4	100.0
019 AMER BAPT CONV	2	14	17*	0.2	0.8
081 CATHOLIC......	3	0	200	2.1	9.5
093 CR CH (DISC)..	3	199	243*	2.6	11.5
165 CH OF NAZARENE	2	94	154	1.6	7.3
193 EPISCOPAL.....	1	18	19	0.2	0.9
449 UN METHODIST..	17	1,148	1,319	14.0	62.5
453 UN PRES CH USA	2	130	159*	1.7	7.5
WARREN	92	17,677	28,501*	33.6	100.0
019 AMER BAPT CONV	5	1,782	2,265*	2.7	7.9
081 CATHOLIC......	5	0	4,936	5.8	17.3
097 CR C AND C CR.	8	886	1,126*	1.3	4.0
123 CH GOD (ANDER)	9	942	2,257	2.7	7.9
127 CH GOD (CLEVE)	5	454	577*	0.7	2.0
165 CH OF NAZARENE	4	405	862	1.0	3.0
193 EPISCOPAL.....	1	195	229	0.3	0.8
226 FRIENDS-USA...	1	161	205*	0.2	0.7
281 LUTH CH AMER..	3	445	623	0.7	2.2
419 SO BAPT CONV..	15	4,092	5,202*	6.1	18.3
443 UN C OF CHRIST	7	776	986*	1.2	3.5
449 UN METHODIST..	19	4,412	5,258	6.2	18.4
453 UN PRES CH USA	10	3,127	3,975*	4.7	13.9
WASHINGTON	108	14,397	22,789*	39.9	100.0
019 AMER BAPT CONV	10	2,385	2,925*	5.1	12.8
081 CATHOLIC......	8	0	4,764	8.3	20.9
093 CR CH (DISC)..	1	111	136*	0.2	0.6
097 CR C AND C CR.	7	433	531*	0.9	2.3
107 CHRISTIAN UN..	5	37	45*	0.1	0.2
127 CH GOD (CLEVE)	2	146	179*	0.3	0.8
165 CH OF NAZARENE	3	370	806	1.4	3.5
175 CONG CR CH....	1	128	157*	0.3	0.7
193 EPISCOPAL.....	1	313	358	0.6	1.6
281 LUTH CH AMER..	1	504	636	1.1	2.8
335 ORTH PRESB CH.	1	10	25	-	0.1
403 SALVATION ARMY	1	58	464	0.8	2.0
413 S-D ADVENTISTS	2	50	61*	0.1	0.3
419 SO BAPT CONV..	1	147	180*	0.3	0.8
435 UNITARIAN-UNIV	2	112	162	0.3	0.7
443 UN C OF CHRIST	9	1,460	1,791*	3.1	7.9
449 UN METHODIST..	45	6,821	7,960	13.9	34.9
453 UN PRES CH USA	8	1,312	1,609*	2.8	7.1
WAYNE	113	26,926	40,738*	46.8	100.0
019 AMER BAPT CONV	2	47	58*	0.1	0.1
029 AMER LUTH CH..	2	321	505	0.6	1.2
081 CATHOLIC......	5	0	6,875	7.9	16.9
093 CR CH (DISC)..	2	1,105	1,367*	1.6	3.4
097 CR C AND C CR.	5	1,360	1,683*	1.9	4.1
123 CH GOD (ANDER)	3	143	658	0.8	1.6
127 CH GOD (CLEVE)	1	74	92*	0.1	0.2
157 CH OF BRETHREN	5	772	955*	1.1	2.3
165 CH OF NAZARENE	4	326	650	0.7	1.6
193 EPISCOPAL.....	1	279	279	0.3	0.7
226 FRIENDS-USA...	1	16	20*	-	-
281 LUTH CH AMER..	10	2,969	4,001	4.6	9.8
283 LUTH--MO SYNOD	1	85	131	0.2	0.3
285 MENNONITE CH..	16	2,835	3,508*	4.0	8.6
287 MENN GEN CONF.	2	592	732*	0.8	1.8
413 S-D ADVENTISTS	1	76	94*	0.1	0.2
419 SO BAPT CONV..	4	736	911*	1.0	2.2
435 UNITARIAN-UNIV	1	32	50	0.1	0.1
443 UN C OF CHRIST	8	3,296	4,078*	4.7	10.0
449 UN METHODIST..	28	7,732	8,981	10.3	22.0
453 UN PRES CH USA	11	4,130	5,110*	5.9	12.5
WILLIAMS	55	11,271	18,520*	55.0	100.0
029 AMER LUTH CH..	3	1,181	1,704	5.1	9.2
081 CATHOLIC......	5	0	3,904	11.6	21.1
097 CR C AND C CR.	6	1,512	1,880*	5.6	10.2
107 CHRISTIAN UN..	3	144	179*	0.5	1.0
157 CH OF BRETHREN	2	399	496*	1.5	2.7
165 CH OF NAZARENE	3	244	678	2.0	3.7
193 EPISCOPAL.....	1	113	140	0.4	0.8
221 FREE METH C NA	1	12	15	-	0.1
281 LUTH CH AMER..	3	699	937	2.8	5.1
285 MENNONITE CH..	2	506	629*	1.9	3.4
413 S-D ADVENTISTS	1	31	39*	0.1	0.2
419 SO BAPT CONV..	1	68	85*	0.3	0.5
449 UN METHODIST..	18	4,972	6,106	18.1	33.0
453 UN PRES CH USA	6	1,390	1,728*	5.1	9.3
WOOD	101	22,840	45,083*	50.2	100.0
019 AMER BAPT CONV	2	407	489*	0.5	1.1
029 AMER LUTH CH..	13	5,349	7,261	8.1	16.1
081 CATHOLIC......	10	0	15,537	17.3	34.5
093 CR CH (DISC)..	3	789	949*	1.1	2.1
097 CR C AND C CR.	6	867	1,042*	1.2	2.3
123 CH GOD (ANDER)	1	55	143	0.2	0.3
157 CH OF BRETHREN	2	278	334*	0.4	0.7
165 CH OF NAZARENE	6	316	787	0.9	1.7
175 CONG CR CH....	2	321	386*	0.4	0.9
193 EPISCOPAL.....	2	614	855	1.0	1.9
281 LUTH CH AMER..	3	2,273	3,066	3.4	6.8
283 LUTH--MO SYNOD	1	90	139	0.2	0.3
413 S-D ADVENTISTS	1	31	37*	-	0.1
419 SO BAPT CONV..	2	250	301*	0.3	0.7
435 UNITARIAN-UNIV	1	50	65	0.1	0.1
443 UN C OF CHRIST	3	480	577*	0.6	1.3
449 UN METHODIST..	34	8,510	10,518	11.7	23.3
453 UN PRES CH USA	9	2,160	2,597*	2.9	5.8
WYANDOT	42	8,541	15,506*	71.0	100.0
019 AMER BAPT CONV	1	51	63*	0.3	0.4
029 AMER LUTH CH..	3	1,096	1,562	7.2	10.1
081 CATHOLIC......	5	0	4,181	19.2	27.0
107 CHRISTIAN UN..	2	92	114*	0.5	0.7
123 CH GOD (ANDER)	1	55	161	0.7	1.0
165 CH OF NAZARENE	2	156	491	2.2	3.2
281 LUTH CH AMER..	3	1,483	2,165	9.9	14.0
443 UN C OF CHRIST	4	1,271	1,575*	7.2	10.2
449 UN METHODIST..	19	4,038	4,824	22.1	31.1
453 UN PRES CH USA	2	299	370*	1.7	2.4
CO DATA NOT AVAIL	295	14,335	35,005*	N/A	N/A
151 L-D SAINTS....	0	0	17,700	N/A	N/A
193 EPISCOPAL.....	3	320	463	N/A	N/A
223 FREE WILL BAPT	129	9,278	11,397*	N/A	N/A
467 WESLEYAN......	163	4,737	5,445	N/A	N/A

OKLAHOMA

County and Denomination	Number of churches	Communicant, confirmed, full members	Total adherents: Number	Total adherents: Percent of total population	Total adherents: Percent of total adherents
THE STATE.....	4,085	1,073,997	1,410,323*	55.1	100.0
ADAIR	39	5,499	6,610*	43.7	100.0
093 CR CH (DISC)..	1	41	50*	0.3	0.8
097 CR C AND C CR.	2	298	365*	2.4	5.5
123 CH GOD (ANDER)	1	17	87	0.6	1.3
349 PENT HOLINESS.	2	134	164*	1.1	2.5
381 REF PRES-EVAN.	1	21	23	0.2	0.3
413 S-D ADVENTISTS	2	102	125*	0.8	1.9

*Total adherents estimated from known number of communicant, confirmed, full members.

—Represents a percent less than 0.1.

Percentages may not total due to rounding.

Table 3. Churches and Church Membership by State, County and Denomination: 1971

County and Denomination	Number of churches	Communicant, confirmed, full members	Total adherents		
			Number	Percent of total population	Percent of total adherents
419 SO BAPT CONV..	23	3,862	4,731*	31.2	71.6
449 UN METHODIST..	6	1,020	1,060	7.0	16.0
453 UN PRES CH USA	1	4	5*	-	0.1
ALFALFA	32	3,839	4,666*	64.6	100.0
081 CATHOLIC......	3	0	368	5.1	7.9
093 CR CH (DISC)..	5	920	1,043*	14.4	22.4
097 CR C AND C CR.	3	175	198*	2.7	4.2
107 CHRISTIAN UN..	1	47	53*	0.7	1.1
157 CH OF BRETHREN	1	41	46*	0.6	1.0
165 CH OF NAZARENE	3	109	167	2.3	3.6
221 FREE METH C NA	1	47	65	0.9	1.4
226 FRIENDS-USA...	1	190	215*	3.0	4.6
283 LUTH--MO SYNOD	1	25	35	0.5	0.8
313 NO AM BAPT GC.	1	36	41*	0.6	0.9
419 SO BAPT CONV..	3	682	773*	10.7	16.6
443 UN C OF CHRIST	1	55	62*	0.9	1.3
449 UN METHODIST..	8	1,512	1,600	22.1	34.3
ATOKA	36	4,813	5,802*	52.9	100.0
059 BAPT MISS ASSN	1	34	40*	0.4	0.7
081 CATHOLIC......	1	0	85	0.8	1.5
093 CR CH (DISC)..	1	36	43*	0.4	0.7
165 CH OF NAZARENE	1	25	55	0.5	0.9
185 CUMBER PRESB..	3	110	131*	1.2	2.3
349 PENT HOLINESS.	3	108	128*	1.2	2.2
419 SO BAPT CONV..	19	3,823	4,541*	41.4	78.3
449 UN METHODIST..	5	636	730	6.7	12.6
453 UN PRES CH USA	2	41	49*	0.4	0.8
BEAVER	22	2,926	3,598*	57.3	100.0
081 CATHOLIC......	1	0	58	0.9	1.6
097 CR C AND C CR.	2	247	293*	4.7	8.1
123 CH GOD (ANDER)	1	58	143	2.3	4.0
165 CH OF NAZARENE	2	63	133	2.1	3.7
226 FRIENDS-USA...	1	116	138*	2.2	3.8
283 LUTH--MO SYNOD	1	37	60	1.0	1.7
287 MENN GEN CONF.	1	97	115*	1.8	3.2
419 SO BAPT CONV..	7	1,228	1,459*	23.2	40.6
449 UN METHODIST..	5	1,030	1,140	18.1	31.7
453 UN PRES CH USA	1	50	59*	0.9	1.6
BECKHAM	38	8,572	11,509*	73.1	100.0
059 BAPT MISS ASSN	1	72	83*	0.5	0.7
081 CATHOLIC......	2	0	1,537	9.8	13.4
093 CR CH (DISC)..	2	430	498*	3.2	4.3
097 CR C AND C CR.	1	90	104*	0.7	0.9
123 CH GOD (ANDER)	1	101	223	1.4	1.9
165 CH OF NAZARENE	3	167	277	1.8	2.4
283 LUTH--MO SYNOD	1	21	30	0.2	0.3
349 PENT HOLINESS.	2	64	74*	0.5	0.6
413 S-D ADVENTISTS	1	39	45*	0.3	0.4
419 SO BAPT CONV..	17	5,375	6,224*	39.5	54.1
449 UN METHODIST..	5	1,999	2,166	13.7	18.8
453 UN PRES CH USA	2	214	248*	1.6	2.2
BLAINE	43	6,017	7,628*	64.7	100.0
019 AMER BAPT CONV	2	154	183*	1.6	2.4
059 BAPT MISS ASSN	1	25	30*	0.3	0.4
081 CATHOLIC......	4	0	457	3.9	6.0
093 CR CH (DISC)..	3	429	510*	4.3	6.7
097 CR C AND C CR.	3	480	571*	4.8	7.5
123 CH GOD (ANDER)	2	45	110	0.9	1.4
165 CH OF NAZARENE	1	92	209	1.8	2.7
193 EPISCOPAL.....	1	21	44	0.4	0.6
221 FREE METH C NA	1	17	25	0.2	0.3
283 LUTH--MO SYNOD	1	132	181	1.5	2.4
287 MENN GEN CONF.	2	198	235*	2.0	3.1
313 NO AM BAPT GC.	1	135	161*	1.4	2.1
349 PENT HOLINESS.	2	38	45*	0.4	0.6
413 S-D ADVENTISTS	3	226	269*	2.3	3.5
419 SO BAPT CONV..	7	1,918	2,280*	19.3	29.9
443 UN C OF CHRIST	1	65	77*	0.7	1.0
449 UN METHODIST..	8	2,042	2,241	19.0	29.4
BRYAN	75	12,728	15,175*	59.4	100.0
081 CATHOLIC......	1	0	255	1.0	1.7
093 CR CH (DISC)..	4	485	568*	2.2	3.7
097 CR C AND C CR.	2	18	21*	0.1	0.1
123 CH GOD (ANDER)	1	9	18	0.1	0.1
165 CH OF NAZARENE	3	307	479	1.9	3.2
193 EPISCOPAL.....	1	68	123	0.5	0.8
281 LUTH CH AMER..	1	84	118	0.5	0.8
349 PENT HOLINESS.	2	316	370*	1.4	2.4
357 PRESB CH US...	7	496	581*	2.3	3.8
413 S-D ADVENTISTS	1	62	73*	0.3	0.5
419 SO BAPT CONV..	39	8,862	10,380*	40.6	68.4
449 UN METHODIST..	13	2,021	2,189	8.6	14.4
CADDO	96	16,633	20,779*	71.8	100.0
019 AMER BAPT CONV	3	103	125*	0.4	0.6
081 CATHOLIC......	5	0	886	3.1	4.3
093 CR CH (DISC)..	8	1,598	1,945*	6.7	9.4
097 CR C AND C CR.	9	270	329*	1.1	1.6
127 CH GOD (CLEVE)	2	126	153*	0.5	0.7
165 CH OF NAZARENE	3	243	599	2.1	2.9
283 LUTH--MO SYNOD	2	142	208	0.7	1.0
285 MENNONITE CH..	1	167	203*	0.7	1.0
287 MENN GEN CONF.	2	104	127*	0.4	0.6
349 PENT HOLINESS.	9	391	476*	1.6	2.3
371 REF CH IN AM..	1	73	141	0.5	0.7
419 SO BAPT CONV..	24	8,389	10,212*	35.3	49.1
443 UN C OF CHRIST	1	78	95*	0.3	0.5
449 UN METHODIST..	25	4,833	5,139	17.8	24.7
453 UN PRES CH USA	1	116	141*	0.5	0.7
CANADIAN	47	11,087	17,295*	53.6	100.0
029 AMER LUTH CH..	1	190	265	0.8	1.5
081 CATHOLIC......	5	0	3,613	11.2	20.9
097 CR C AND C CR.	1	60	73*	0.2	0.4
165 CH OF NAZARENE	6	370	813	2.5	4.7
193 EPISCOPAL.....	2	137	207	0.6	1.2
226 FRIENDS-USA...	1	49	60*	0.2	0.3
283 LUTH--MO SYNOD	2	550	822	2.5	4.8
349 PENT HOLINESS.	3	110	134*	0.4	0.8
353 PLY BRETHREN..	2	130	190	0.6	1.1
413 S-D ADVENTISTS	1	33	40*	0.1	0.2
419 SO BAPT CONV..	11	5,131	6,241*	19.4	36.1
449 UN METHODIST..	10	3,935	4,360	13.5	25.2
453 UN PRES CH USA	2	392	477*	1.5	2.8
CARTER	59	18,295	22,757*	60.9	100.0
059 BAPT MISS ASSN	1	151	180*	0.5	0.8
081 CATHOLIC......	2	0	563	1.5	2.5
097 CR C AND C CR.	2	320	382*	1.0	1.7
123 CH GOD (ANDER)	1	39	81	0.2	0.4
127 CH GOD (CLEVE)	2	50	60*	0.2	0.3
165 CH OF NAZARENE	2	118	216	0.6	0.9
193 EPISCOPAL.....	1	370	486	1.3	2.1
283 LUTH--MO SYNOD	1	115	183	0.5	0.8
349 PENT HOLINESS.	6	217	259*	0.7	1.1
403 SALVATION ARMY	1	58	908	2.4	4.0
413 S-D ADVENTISTS	2	270	322*	0.9	1.4
419 SO BAPT CONV..	26	10,824	12,925*	34.6	56.8
449 UN METHODIST..	10	5,295	5,633	15.1	24.8
453 UN PRES CH USA	2	468	559*	1.5	2.5
CHEROKEE	42	6,582	8,036*	34.7	100.0
081 CATHOLIC......	2	0	228	1.0	2.8
097 CR C AND C CR.	2	75	89*	0.4	1.1
123 CH GOD (ANDER)	1	85	235	1.0	2.9
127 CH GOD (CLEVE)	1	16	19*	0.1	0.2
165 CH OF NAZARENE	1	37	120	0.5	1.5
185 CUMBER PRESB..	1	142	169*	0.7	2.1
193 EPISCOPAL.....	1	103	119	0.5	1.5
283 LUTH--MO SYNOD	1	20	32	0.1	0.4
349 PENT HOLINESS.	2	50	60*	0.3	0.7
419 SO BAPT CONV..	21	3,760	4,479*	19.3	55.7
449 UN METHODIST..	7	1,887	2,001	8.6	24.9
453 UN PRES CH USA	2	407	485*	2.1	6.0
CHOCTAW	63	7,631	9,097*	60.1	100.0
081 CATHOLIC......	1	0	125	0.8	1.4
127 CH GOD (CLEVE)	1	59	71*	0.5	0.8
165 CH OF NAZARENE	1	8	12	0.1	0.1
185 CUMBER PRESB..	1	14	17*	0.1	0.2
193 EPISCOPAL.....	1	36	63	0.4	0.7
357 PRESB CH US...	1	149	179*	1.2	2.0
419 SO BAPT CONV..	44	5,884	7,071*	46.7	77.7
449 UN METHODIST..	11	1,467	1,542	10.2	17.0
453 UN PRES CH USA	2	14	17*	0.1	0.2
CIMARRON	14	2,445	2,951*	71.2	100.0
081 CATHOLIC......	1	0	100	2.4	3.4
097 CR C AND C CR.	1	163	196*	4.7	6.6
123 CH GOD (ANDER)	1	25	46	1.1	1.6
165 CH OF NAZARENE	1	22	73	1.8	2.5
283 LUTH--MO SYNOD	1	36	60	1.4	2.0
349 PENT HOLINESS.	1	19	23*	0.6	0.8
419 SO BAPT CONV..	4	1,070	1,286*	31.0	43.6
449 UN METHODIST..	4	1,110	1,167	28.2	39.5
CLEVELAND	69	24,959	35,951*	43.9	100.0
059 BAPT MISS ASSN	2	348	423*	0.5	1.2
081 CATHOLIC......	4	0	4,992	6.1	13.9
097 CR C AND C CR.	3	265	322*	0.4	0.9
123 CH GOD (ANDER)	1	47	127	0.2	0.4
127 CH GOD (CLEVE)	3	153	186*	0.2	0.5
165 CH OF NAZARENE	8	1,035	2,331	2.8	6.5
193 EPISCOPAL.....	4	763	921	1.1	2.6
221 FREE METH C NA	1	15	19	-	0.1
283 LUTH--MO SYNOD	3	814	1,127	1.4	3.1
349 PENT HOLINESS.	3	156	190*	0.2	0.5
357 PRESB CH US...	1	115	140*	0.2	0.4
419 SO BAPT CONV..	24	13,718	16,684*	20.4	46.4
435 UNITARIAN-UNIV	1	60	100	0.1	0.3
449 UN METHODIST..	9	6,451	7,150	8.7	19.9
453 UN PRES CH USA	2	1,019	1,239*	1.5	3.4
COAL	20	2,068	2,951*	53.4	100.0
081 CATHOLIC......	2	0	525	9.5	17.8
165 CH OF NAZARENE	1	32	110	2.0	3.7
185 CUMBER PRESB..	1	20	24*	0.4	0.8
193 EPISCOPAL.....	1	42	73	1.3	2.5
349 PENT HOLINESS.	2	61	72*	1.3	2.4
357 PRESB CH US...	1	43	51*	0.9	1.7

*Total adherents estimated from known number of communicant, confirmed, full members.

—Represents a percent less than 0.1.

Percentages may not total due to rounding.

Table 3. Churches and Church Membership by State, County and Denomination: 1971

County and Denomination	Number of churches	Communicant, confirmed, full members	Total adherents: Number	Total adherents: Percent of total population	Total adherents: Percent of total adherents
419 SO BAPT CONV..	6	1,120	1,317*	23.8	44.6
449 UN METHODIST..	6	750	779	14.1	26.4
COMANCHE	79	33,096	43,460*	40.2	100.0
059 BAPT MISS ASSN	1	112	137*	0.1	0.3
081 CATHOLIC......	5	0	2,769	2.6	6.4
097 CR C AND C CR.	4	503	617*	0.6	1.4
123 CH GOD (ANDER)	1	80	200	0.2	0.5
127 CH GOD (CLEVE)	4	437	536*	0.5	1.2
165 CH OF NAZARENE	2	135	440	0.4	1.0
193 EPISCOPAL.....	2	631	683	0.6	1.6
281 LUTH CH AMER..	1	179	303	0.3	0.7
283 LUTH--MO SYNOD	2	361	507	0.5	1.2
349 PENT HOLINESS.	2	89	109*	0.1	0.3
357 PRESB CH US...	2	302	370*	0.3	0.9
371 REF CH IN AM..	1	103	147	0.1	0.3
403 SALVATION ARMY	1	109	560	0.5	1.3
413 S-D ADVENTISTS	1	134	164*	0.2	0.4
419 SO BAPT CONV..	27	20,484	25,127*	23.2	57.8
443 UN C OF CHRIST	1	337	413*	0.4	1.0
449 UN METHODIST..	19	8,126	9,183	8.5	21.1
453 UN PRES CH USA	3	974	1,195*	1.1	2.7
COTTON	23	4,413	5,329*	78.0	100.0
019 AMER BAPT CONV	2	110	129*	1.9	2.4
081 CATHOLIC......	1	0	130	1.9	2.4
123 CH GOD (ANDER)	1	119	258	3.8	4.8
127 CH GOD (CLEVE)	1	19	22*	0.3	0.4
165 CH OF NAZARENE	1	62	80	1.2	1.5
419 SO BAPT CONV..	11	3,073	3,610*	52.8	67.7
449 UN METHODIST..	4	956	1,013	14.8	19.0
453 UN PRES CH USA	2	74	87*	1.3	1.6
CRAIG	30	6,088	7,446*	50.6	100.0
081 CATHOLIC......	2	0	448	3.0	6.0
097 CR C AND C CR.	2	820	954*	6.5	12.8
165 CH OF NAZARENE	1	30	124	0.8	1.7
193 EPISCOPAL.....	1	72	85	0.6	1.1
413 S-D ADVENTISTS	2	148	172*	1.2	2.3
419 SO BAPT CONV..	15	3,333	3,880*	26.4	52.1
449 UN METHODIST..	6	1,444	1,502	10.2	20.2
453 UN PRES CH USA	1	241	281*	1.9	3.8
CREEK	68	20,301	26,969*	59.2	100.0
059 BAPT MISS ASSN	2	187	228*	0.5	0.8
081 CATHOLIC......	3	0	872	1.9	3.2
097 CR C AND C CR.	4	843	1,026*	2.3	3.8
123 CH GOD (ANDER)	8	758	1,911	4.2	7.1
165 CH OF NAZARENE	3	525	1,464	3.2	5.4
193 EPISCOPAL.....	1	136	157	0.3	0.6
349 PENT HOLINESS.	2	75	91*	0.2	0.3
413 S-D ADVENTISTS	3	219	267*	0.6	1.0
419 SO BAPT CONV..	29	13,398	16,314*	35.8	60.5
449 UN METHODIST..	11	3,457	3,783	8.3	14.0
453 UN PRES CH USA	2	703	856*	1.9	3.2
CUSTER	44	10,468	12,834*	56.6	100.0
029 AMER LUTH CH..	1	234	300	1.3	2.3
075 BRETHREN IN CR	1	84	98*	0.4	0.8
081 CATHOLIC......	3	0	465	2.1	3.6
097 CR C AND C CR.	4	628	735*	3.2	5.7
123 CH GOD (ANDER)	1	104	256	1.1	2.0
157 CH OF BRETHREN	1	75	88*	0.4	0.7
165 CH OF NAZARENE	3	82	222	1.0	1.7
185 CUMBER PRESB..	1	108	126*	0.6	1.0
193 EPISCOPAL.....	1	103	131	0.6	1.0
221 FREE METH C NA	1	7	7	-	0.1
283 LUTH--MO SYNOD	1	78	112	0.5	0.9
287 MENN GEN CONF.	3	236	276*	1.2	2.2
349 PENT HOLINESS.	3	89	104*	0.5	0.8
403 SALVATION ARMY	1	34	157	0.7	1.2
419 SO BAPT CONV..	7	5,176	6,061*	26.7	47.2
443 UN C OF CHRIST	1	23	27*	0.1	0.2
449 UN METHODIST..	9	3,247	3,482	15.4	27.1
453 UN PRES CH USA	2	160	187*	0.8	1.5
DELAWARE	44	5,810	7,054*	39.7	100.0
029 AMER LUTH CH..	1	113	197	1.1	2.8
059 BAPT MISS ASSN	2	138	165*	0.9	2.3
081 CATHOLIC......	1	0	130	0.7	1.8
097 CR C AND C CR.	3	450	537*	3.0	7.6
127 CH GOD (CLEVE)	1	55	66*	0.4	0.9
165 CH OF NAZARENE	1	12	25	0.1	0.4
193 EPISCOPAL.....	1	30	32	0.2	0.5
349 PENT HOLINESS.	1	13	16*	0.1	0.2
413 S-D ADVENTISTS	1	93	111*	0.6	1.6
419 SO BAPT CONV..	28	4,116	4,916*	27.7	69.7
449 UN METHODIST..	4	790	859	4.8	12.2
DEWEY	23	2,426	2,927*	51.8	100.0
059 BAPT MISS ASSN	1	155	181*	3.2	6.2
075 BRETHREN IN CR	1	28	33*	0.6	1.1
081 CATHOLIC......	1	0	32	0.6	1.1
097 CR C AND C CR.	4	251	293*	5.2	10.0
165 CH OF NAZARENE	2	70	171	3.0	5.8
226 FRIENDS-USA...	1	83	97*	1.7	3.3
287 MENN GEN CONF.	1	66	77*	1.4	2.6
419 SO BAPT CONV..	5	875	1,023*	18.1	35.0
449 UN METHODIST..	7	898	1,020	18.0	34.8
ELLIS	19	2,457	3,033*	59.1	100.0
081 CATHOLIC......	1	0	105	2.0	3.5
097 CR C AND C CR.	1	150	175*	3.4	5.8
123 CH GOD (ANDER)	2	63	169	3.3	5.6
165 CH OF NAZARENE	3	89	174	3.4	5.7
283 LUTH--MO SYNOD	1	77	96	1.9	3.2
313 NO AM BAPT GC.	1	69	80*	1.6	2.6
413 S-D ADVENTISTS	1	187	218*	4.3	7.2
419 SO BAPT CONV..	4	793	924*	18.0	30.5
449 UN METHODIST..	5	1,029	1,092	21.3	36.0
GARFIELD	66	22,105	28,271*	51.1	100.0
029 AMER LUTH CH..	1	158	224	0.4	0.8
081 CATHOLIC......	3	0	1,927	3.5	6.8
097 CR C AND C CR.	3	1,419	1,693*	3.1	6.0
107 CHRISTIAN UN..	3	264	315*	0.6	1.1
123 CH GOD (ANDER)	1	65	160	0.3	0.6
127 CH GOD (CLEVE)	1	38	45*	0.1	0.2
157 CH OF BRETHREN	1	78	93*	0.2	0.3
165 CH OF NAZARENE	5	377	605	1.1	2.1
193 EPISCOPAL.....	1	383	709	1.3	2.5
221 FREE METH C NA	2	102	134	0.2	0.5
226 FRIENDS-USA...	1	90	107*	0.2	0.4
283 LUTH--MO SYNOD	8	2,397	3,118	5.6	11.0
287 MENN GEN CONF.	1	191	228*	0.4	0.8
313 NO AM BAPT GC.	1	30	36*	0.1	0.1
349 PENT HOLINESS.	2	279	333*	0.6	1.2
403 SALVATION ARMY	1	75	292	0.5	1.0
413 S-D ADVENTISTS	2	168	200*	0.4	0.7
419 SO BAPT CONV..	13	7,482	8,926*	16.1	31.6
443 UN C OF CHRIST	2	182	217*	0.4	0.8
449 UN METHODIST..	13	7,137	7,489	13.5	26.5
453 UN PRES CH USA	1	1,190	1,420*	2.6	5.0
GARVIN	54	14,282	16,954*	68.2	100.0
059 BAPT MISS ASSN	5	544	636*	2.6	3.8
081 CATHOLIC......	2	0	322	1.3	1.9
093 CR CH (DISC)..	2	399	467*	1.9	2.8
097 CR C AND C CR.	1	100	117*	0.5	0.7
123 CH GOD (ANDER)	1	43	168	0.7	1.0
127 CH GOD (CLEVE)	1	75	88*	0.4	0.5
165 CH OF NAZARENE	2	77	129	0.5	0.8
193 EPISCOPAL.....	2	85	137	0.6	0.8
349 PENT HOLINESS.	2	233	273*	1.1	1.6
419 SO BAPT CONV..	24	9,163	10,718*	43.1	63.2
449 UN METHODIST..	9	3,262	3,547	14.3	20.9
453 UN PRES CH USA	3	301	352*	1.4	2.1
GRADY	53	15,468	19,073*	65.0	100.0
059 BAPT MISS ASSN	3	545	651*	2.2	3.4
081 CATHOLIC......	2	0	610	2.1	3.2
093 CR CH (DISC)..	5	1,490	1,779*	6.1	9.3
097 CR C AND C CR.	1	105	125*	0.4	0.7
127 CH GOD (CLEVE)	1	68	81*	0.3	0.4
165 CH OF NAZARENE	2	96	263	0.9	1.4
193 EPISCOPAL.....	1	133	139	0.5	0.7
283 LUTH--MO SYNOD	1	93	127	0.4	0.7
349 PENT HOLINESS.	3	126	150*	0.5	0.8
381 REF PRES-EVAN.	1	84	98	0.3	0.5
403 SALVATION ARMY	1	81	290	1.0	1.5
413 S-D ADVENTISTS	1	17	20*	0.1	0.1
419 SO BAPT CONV..	20	9,168	10,947*	37.3	57.4
449 UN METHODIST..	10	3,239	3,527	12.0	18.5
453 UN PRES CH USA	1	223	266*	0.9	1.4
GRANT	33	4,114	5,069*	71.2	100.0
081 CATHOLIC......	3	0	395	5.6	7.8
093 CR CH (DISC)..	7	832	970*	13.6	19.1
097 CR C AND C CR.	3	160	186*	2.6	3.7
165 CH OF NAZARENE	2	67	119	1.7	2.3
287 MENN GEN CONF.	2	139	162*	2.3	3.2
419 SO BAPT CONV..	6	1,058	1,233*	17.3	24.3
443 UN C OF CHRIST	1	65	76*	1.1	1.5
449 UN METHODIST..	9	1,793	1,928	27.1	38.0
GREER	18	4,526	5,135*	64.4	100.0
081 CATHOLIC......	1	0	100	1.3	1.9
093 CR CH (DISC)..	1	93	105*	1.3	2.0
127 CH GOD (CLEVE)	1	35	39*	0.5	0.8
165 CH OF NAZARENE	1	41	69	0.9	1.3
283 LUTH--MO SYNOD	1	138	173	2.2	3.4
357 PRESB CH US...	1	111	125*	1.6	2.4
419 SO BAPT CONV..	7	2,935	3,301*	41.4	64.3
449 UN METHODIST..	5	1,173	1,223	15.3	23.8
HARMON	14	2,645	3,145*	61.2	100.0
081 CATHOLIC......	1	0	37	0.7	1.2
165 CH OF NAZARENE	4	98	158	3.1	5.0
419 SO BAPT CONV..	7	2,032	2,417*	47.1	76.9
449 UN METHODIST..	2	515	533	10.4	16.9
HARPER	15	2,746	3,479*	67.5	100.0
081 CATHOLIC......	1	0	225	4.4	6.5
093 CR CH (DISC)..	3	281	334*	6.5	9.6
097 CR C AND C CR.	1	150	178*	3.5	5.1

*Total adherents estimated from known number of communicant, confirmed, full members.

—Represents a percent less than 0.1.

Percentages may not total due to rounding.

Table 3. Churches and Church Membership by State, County and Denomination: 1971

County and Denomination	Number of churches	Communicant, confirmed, full members	Total adherents		
			Number	Percent of total population	Percent of total adherents
165 CH OF NAZARENE	1	14	51	1.0	1.5
193 EPISCOPAL.....	1	9	11	0.2	0.3
283 LUTH--MO SYNOD	1	124	169	3.3	4.9
419 SO BAPT CONV..	3	1,225	1,454*	28.2	41.8
449 UN METHODIST..	4	943	1,057	20.5	30.4
HASKELL	27	3,472	4,150*	43.3	100.0
081 CATHOLIC......	2	0	46	0.5	1.1
093 CR CH (DISC)..	2	121	144*	1.5	3.5
165 CH OF NAZARENE	1	17	59	0.6	1.4
349 PENT HOLINESS.	2	38	45*	0.5	1.1
419 SO BAPT CONV..	16	2,627	3,128*	32.7	75.4
449 UN METHODIST..	4	669	728	7.6	17.5
HUGHES	48	6,728	8,195*	62.0	100.0
059 BAPT MISS ASSN	2	150	174*	1.3	2.1
081 CATHOLIC......	1	0	213	1.6	2.6
093 CR CH (DISC)..	2	145	168*	1.3	2.1
123 CH GOD (ANDER)	2	125	275	2.1	3.4
165 CH OF NAZARENE	3	209	334	2.5	4.1
193 EPISCOPAL.....	1	53	69	0.5	0.8
349 PENT HOLINESS.	3	73	85*	0.6	1.0
357 PRESB CH US...	1	33	38*	0.3	0.5
419 SO BAPT CONV..	22	4,458	5,161*	39.0	63.0
449 UN METHODIST..	11	1,482	1,678	12.7	20.5
JACKSON	38	11,786	16,090*	52.1	100.0
081 CATHOLIC......	1	0	300	1.0	1.9
093 CR CH (DISC)..	1	265	330*	1.1	2.1
127 CH GOD (CLEVE)	1	43	54*	0.2	0.3
165 CH OF NAZARENE	2	86	183	0.6	1.1
193 EPISCOPAL.....	1	143	238	0.8	1.5
283 LUTH--MO SYNOD	1	157	268	0.9	1.7
349 PENT HOLINESS.	3	69	86*	0.3	0.5
403 SALVATION ARMY	1	69	1,586	5.1	9.9
413 S-D ADVENTISTS	1	35	44*	0.1	0.3
419 SO BAPT CONV..	14	7,379	9,188*	29.7	57.1
449 UN METHODIST..	11	3,368	3,599	11.6	22.4
453 UN PRES CH USA	1	172	214*	0.7	1.3
JEFFERSON	14	3,648	4,245*	59.6	100.0
081 CATHOLIC......	1	0	70	1.0	1.6
093 CR CH (DISC)..	1	54	62*	0.9	1.5
165 CH OF NAZARENE	2	69	144	2.0	3.4
413 S-D ADVENTISTS	1	28	32*	0.4	0.8
419 SO BAPT CONV..	2	2,376	2,750*	38.6	64.8
449 UN METHODIST..	6	1,097	1,159	16.3	27.3
453 UN PRES CH USA	1	24	28*	0.4	0.7
JOHNSTON	33	3,926	4,718*	59.9	100.0
081 CATHOLIC......	1	0	90	1.1	1.9
093 CR CH (DISC)..	1	73	85*	1.1	1.8
127 CH GOD (CLEVE)	3	107	124*	1.6	2.6
165 CH OF NAZARENE	2	163	294	3.7	6.2
349 PENT HOLINESS.	1	40	46*	0.6	1.0
357 PRESB CH US...	1	33	38*	0.5	0.8
419 SO BAPT CONV..	16	2,712	3,151*	40.0	66.8
449 UN METHODIST..	7	722	802	10.2	17.0
453 UN PRES CH USA	1	76	88*	1.1	1.9
KAY	77	26,012	35,277*	72.3	100.0
081 CATHOLIC......	4	0	4,109	8.4	11.6
093 CR CH (DISC)..	9	3,269	3,861*	7.9	10.9
097 CR C AND C CR.	3	428	505*	1.0	1.4
123 CH GOD (ANDER)	3	376	785	1.6	2.2
127 CH GOD (CLEVE)	1	9	11*	-	-
165 CH OF NAZARENE	7	558	1,016	2.1	2.9
193 EPISCOPAL.....	2	513	621	1.3	1.8
221 FREE METH C NA	2	15	15	-	-
283 LUTH--MO SYNOD	4	1,130	1,469	3.0	4.2
349 PENT HOLINESS.	2	124	146*	0.3	0.4
413 S-D ADVENTISTS	1	35	41*	0.1	0.1
419 SO BAPT CONV..	19	9,688	11,441*	23.4	32.4
449 UN METHODIST..	16	7,603	8,583	17.6	24.3
453 UN PRES CH USA	4	2,264	2,674*	5.5	7.6
KINGFISHER	40	7,634	10,072*	78.3	100.0
081 CATHOLIC......	3	0	917	7.1	9.1
093 CR CH (DISC)..	6	1,052	1,278*	9.9	12.7
097 CR C AND C CR.	4	212	258*	2.0	2.6
107 CHRISTIAN UN..	1	110	134*	1.0	1.3
165 CH OF NAZARENE	4	145	295	2.3	2.9
283 LUTH--MO SYNOD	1	201	268	2.1	2.7
313 NO AM BAPT GC.	1	44	53*	0.4	0.5
349 PENT HOLINESS.	2	85	103*	0.8	1.0
419 SO BAPT CONV..	8	3,466	4,210*	32.7	41.8
443 UN C OF CHRIST	4	377	458*	3.6	4.5
449 UN METHODIST..	5	1,849	1,985	15.4	19.7
453 UN PRES CH USA	1	93	113*	0.9	1.1
KIOWA	37	7,807	9,238*	73.7	100.0
019 AMER BAPT CONV	2	193	225*	1.8	2.4
029 AMER LUTH CH..	1	114	139	1.1	1.5
081 CATHOLIC......	1	0	250	2.0	2.7
093 CR CH (DISC)..	4	270	315*	2.5	3.4
097 CR C AND C CR.	2	146	170*	1.4	1.8
165 CH OF NAZARENE	2	40	149	1.2	1.6

County and Denomination	Number of churches	Communicant, confirmed, full members	Total adherents		
			Number	Percent of total population	Percent of total adherents
226 FRIENDS-USA...	2	69	81*	0.6	0.9
283 LUTH--MO SYNOD	1	152	193	1.5	2.1
349 PENT HOLINESS.	3	81	95*	0.8	1.0
419 SO BAPT CONV..	10	4,601	5,369*	42.8	58.1
449 UN METHODIST..	8	1,984	2,069	16.5	22.4
453 UN PRES CH USA	1	157	183*	1.5	2.0
LATIMER	26	3,184	3,915*	45.5	100.0
081 CATHOLIC......	1	0	182	2.1	4.6
097 CR C AND C CR.	1	50	59*	0.7	1.5
185 CUMBER PRESB..	1	19	23*	0.3	0.6
283 LUTH--MO SYNOD	1	84	109	1.3	2.8
349 PENT HOLINESS.	1	8	9*	0.1	0.2
419 SO BAPT CONV..	17	2,547	3,020*	35.1	77.1
449 UN METHODIST..	3	432	461	5.4	11.8
453 UN PRES CH USA	1	44	52*	0.6	1.3
LE FLORE	83	13,138	15,970*	49.7	100.0
081 CATHOLIC......	2	0	277	0.9	1.7
093 CR CH (DISC)..	2	284	342*	1.1	2.1
097 CR C AND C CR.	5	283	341*	1.1	2.1
165 CH OF NAZARENE	5	261	541	1.7	3.4
185 CUMBER PRESB..	1	65	78*	0.2	0.5
357 PRESB CH US...	1	25	30*	0.1	0.2
419 SO BAPT CONV..	48	9,457	11,402*	35.5	71.4
449 UN METHODIST..	16	2,665	2,841	8.8	17.8
453 UN PRES CH USA	3	98	118*	0.4	0.7
LINCOLN	56	7,949	10,048*	51.6	100.0
081 CATHOLIC......	5	0	592	3.0	5.9
093 CR CH (DISC)..	8	542	644*	3.3	6.4
097 CR C AND C CR.	7	491	584*	3.0	5.8
107 CHRISTIAN UN..	1	74	88*	0.5	0.9
165 CH OF NAZARENE	5	244	490	2.5	4.9
221 FREE METH C NA	1	9	9	-	0.1
226 FRIENDS-USA...	2	107	127*	0.7	1.3
413 S-D ADVENTISTS	1	10	12*	0.1	0.1
419 SO BAPT CONV..	17	4,712	5,602*	28.8	55.8
449 UN METHODIST..	6	1,634	1,750	9.0	17.4
453 UN PRES CH USA	3	126	150*	0.8	1.5
LOGAN	37	4,261	5,840*	29.7	100.0
081 CATHOLIC......	5	0	821	4.2	14.1
093 CR CH (DISC)..	5	987	1,161*	5.9	19.9
097 CR C AND C CR.	3	274	322*	1.6	5.5
127 CH GOD (CLEVE)	1	65	76*	0.4	1.3
165 CH OF NAZARENE	3	131	275	1.4	4.7
193 EPISCOPAL.....	2	170	222	1.1	3.8
221 FREE METH C NA	1	29	38	0.2	0.7
283 LUTH--MO SYNOD	1	180	223	1.1	3.8
353 PLY BRETHREN..	1	30	50	0.3	0.9
413 S-D ADVENTISTS	2	45	53*	0.3	0.9
419 SO BAPT CONV..	1	75	88*	0.4	1.5
443 UN C OF CHRIST	1	82	96*	0.5	1.6
449 UN METHODIST..	10	1,883	2,050	10.4	35.1
453 UN PRES CH USA	1	310	365*	1.9	6.3
LOVE	19	3,080	3,592*	63.7	100.0
093 CR CH (DISC)..	1	60	71*	1.3	2.0
349 PENT HOLINESS.	4	111	131*	2.3	3.6
357 PRESB CH US...	1	46	54*	1.0	1.5
419 SO BAPT CONV..	10	2,362	2,793*	49.5	77.8
449 UN METHODIST..	3	501	543	9.6	15.1
MC CLAIN	45	9,140	10,994*	77.7	100.0
059 BAPT MISS ASSN	3	649	782*	5.5	7.1
081 CATHOLIC......	1	0	325	2.3	3.0
093 CR CH (DISC)..	1	60	72*	0.5	0.7
123 CH GOD (ANDER)	1	37	104	0.7	0.9
127 CH GOD (CLEVE)	1	26	31*	0.2	0.3
165 CH OF NAZARENE	4	62	196	1.4	1.8
349 PENT HOLINESS.	4	108	130*	0.9	1.2
419 SO BAPT CONV..	14	5,226	6,296*	44.5	57.3
449 UN METHODIST..	14	2,912	2,986	21.1	27.2
453 UN PRES CH USA	2	60	72*	0.5	0.7
MC CURTAIN	68	6,589	8,455*	29.5	100.0
059 BAPT MISS ASSN	2	267	330*	1.2	3.9
081 CATHOLIC......	1	0	213	0.7	2.5
093 CR CH (DISC)..	2	145	179*	0.6	2.1
097 CR C AND C CR.	4	120	149*	0.5	1.8
127 CH GOD (CLEVE)	5	164	203*	0.7	2.4
165 CH OF NAZARENE	1	41	85	0.3	1.0
185 CUMBER PRESB..	6	199	246*	0.9	2.9
193 EPISCOPAL.....	1	82	116	0.4	1.4
357 PRESB CH US...	4	321	397*	1.4	4.7
419 SO BAPT CONV..	18	3,928	4,862*	17.0	57.5
449 UN METHODIST..	11	927	1,186	4.1	14.0
453 UN PRES CH USA	13	395	489*	1.7	5.8
MC INTOSH	30	4,812	5,684*	45.6	100.0
081 CATHOLIC......	1	0	87	0.7	1.5
093 CR CH (DISC)..	1	24	28*	0.2	0.5
097 CR C AND C CR.	2	151	178*	1.4	3.1
193 EPISCOPAL.....	1	18	22	0.2	0.4
349 PENT HOLINESS.	1	49	58*	0.5	1.0
419 SO BAPT CONV..	20	3,730	4,385*	35.2	77.1

*Total adherents estimated from known number of communicant, confirmed, full members.

—Represents a percent less than 0.1.

Percentages may not total due to rounding.

Table 3. Churches and Church Membership by State, County and Denomination: 1971

County and Denomination	Number of churches	Communicant, confirmed, full members	Total adherents: Number	Total adherents: Percent of total population	Total adherents: Percent of total adherents
449 UN METHODIST..	3	815	897	7.2	15.8
453 UN PRES CH USA	1	25	29*	0.2	0.5
MAJOR	30	3,932	4,659*	61.9	100.0
081 CATHOLIC......	1	0	125	1.7	2.7
093 CR CH (DISC)..	4	324	382*	5.1	8.2
097 CR C AND C CR.	2	50	59*	0.8	1.3
107 CHRISTIAN UN..	1	21	25*	0.3	0.5
165 CH OF NAZARENE	4	193	404	5.4	8.7
221 FREE METH C NA	1	16	16	0.2	0.3
287 MENN GEN CONF.	3	358	422*	5.6	9.1
419 SO BAPT CONV..	5	944	1,112*	14.8	23.9
449 UN METHODIST..	8	1,938	2,010	26.7	43.1
453 UN PRES CH USA	1	88	104*	1.4	2.2
MARSHALL	21	3,127	3,710*	48.3	100.0
081 CATHOLIC......	1	0	160	2.1	4.3
165 CH OF NAZARENE	2	79	148	1.9	4.0
349 PENT HOLINESS.	2	67	78*	1.0	2.1
357 PRESB CH US...	1	37	43*	0.6	1.2
413 S-D ADVENTISTS	1	29	34*	0.4	0.9
419 SO BAPT CONV..	10	1,885	2,182*	28.4	58.8
449 UN METHODIST..	4	1,030	1,065	13.9	28.7
MAYES	56	9,612	12,070*	51.8	100.0
081 CATHOLIC......	2	0	353	1.5	2.9
093 CR CH (DISC)..	3	548	654*	2.8	5.4
097 CR C AND C CR.	4	202	241*	1.0	2.0
123 CH GOD (ANDER)	2	205	645	2.8	5.3
127 CH GOD (CLEVE)	3	137	164*	0.7	1.4
165 CH OF NAZARENE	1	40	70	0.3	0.6
185 CUMBER PRESB..	1	94	112*	0.5	0.9
193 EPISCOPAL.....	1	100	115	0.5	1.0
283 LUTH--MO SYNOD	2	138	189	0.8	1.6
285 MENNONITE CH..	2	186	222*	1.0	1.8
349 PENT HOLINESS.	1	50	60*	0.3	0.5
413 S-D ADVENTISTS	1	70	84*	0.4	0.7
419 SO BAPT CONV..	24	5,566	6,646*	28.5	55.1
449 UN METHODIST..	7	2,014	2,202	9.4	18.2
453 UN PRES CH USA	2	262	313*	1.3	2.6
MURRAY	23	5,060	5,942*	55.7	100.0
081 CATHOLIC......	1	0	123	1.2	2.1
093 CR CH (DISC)..	1	96	113*	1.1	1.9
097 CR C AND C CR.	1	146	171*	1.6	2.9
165 CH OF NAZARENE	1	10	37	0.3	0.6
283 LUTH--MO SYNOD	1	12	15	0.1	0.3
349 PENT HOLINESS.	2	149	175*	1.6	2.9
357 PRESB CH US...	1	70	82*	0.8	1.4
413 S-D ADVENTISTS	2	56	66*	0.6	1.1
419 SO BAPT CONV..	8	3,339	3,919*	36.7	66.0
449 UN METHODIST..	3	1,108	1,154	10.8	19.4
453 UN PRES CH USA	2	74	87*	0.8	1.5
MUSKOGEE	91	27,433	34,642*	58.2	100.0
059 BAPT MISS ASSN	1	47	56*	0.1	0.2
081 CATHOLIC......	4	0	1,957	3.3	5.6
093 CR CH (DISC)..	5	278	334*	0.6	1.0
097 CR C AND C CR.	8	1,738	2,086*	3.5	6.0
123 CH GOD (ANDER)	2	133	339	0.6	1.0
127 CH GOD (CLEVE)	2	99	119*	0.2	0.3
165 CH OF NAZARENE	2	229	399	0.7	1.2
185 CUMBER PRESB..	1	101	121*	0.2	0.3
193 EPISCOPAL.....	2	532	652	1.1	1.9
283 LUTH--MO SYNOD	2	316	469	0.8	1.4
349 PENT HOLINESS.	3	215	258*	0.4	0.7
403 SALVATION ARMY	1	73	300	0.5	0.9
413 S-D ADVENTISTS	2	257	308*	0.5	0.9
419 SO BAPT CONV..	38	14,994	17,995*	30.2	51.9
449 UN METHODIST..	14	7,233	7,823	13.1	22.6
453 UN PRES CH USA	4	1,188	1,426*	2.4	4.1
NOBLE	28	4,686	5,799*	57.7	100.0
081 CATHOLIC......	2	0	202	2.0	3.5
093 CR CH (DISC)..	6	744	884*	8.8	15.2
097 CR C AND C CR.	1	50	59*	0.6	1.0
157 CH OF BRETHREN	1	55	65*	0.6	1.1
165 CH OF NAZARENE	1	57	143	1.4	2.5
193 EPISCOPAL.....	1	23	39	0.4	0.7
281 LUTH CH AMER..	1	186	224	2.2	3.9
283 LUTH--MO SYNOD	1	489	638	6.4	11.0
413 S-D ADVENTISTS	1	37	44*	0.4	0.8
419 SO BAPT CONV..	8	1,450	1,722*	17.1	29.7
449 UN METHODIST..	4	1,271	1,394	13.9	24.0
453 UN PRES CH USA	1	324	385*	3.8	6.6
NOWATA	24	4,171	5,296*	54.2	100.0
081 CATHOLIC......	1	0	87	0.9	1.6
093 CR CH (DISC)..	1	230	269*	2.8	5.1
097 CR C AND C CR.	2	374	438*	4.5	8.3
123 CH GOD (ANDER)	3	199	491	5.0	9.3
165 CH OF NAZARENE	1	51	163	1.7	3.1
193 EPISCOPAL.....	1	15	25	0.3	0.5
349 PENT HOLINESS.	1	131	153*	1.6	2.9
413 S-D ADVENTISTS	1	64	75*	0.8	1.4
419 SO BAPT CONV..	6	1,592	1,865*	19.1	35.2
449 UN METHODIST..	6	1,379	1,571	16.1	29.7
453 UN PRES CH USA	1	136	159*	1.6	3.0
OKFUSKEE	22	3,518	4,448*	41.6	100.0
081 CATHOLIC......	1	0	182	1.7	4.1
093 CR CH (DISC)..	3	145	174*	1.6	3.9
123 CH GOD (ANDER)	2	45	155	1.5	3.5
165 CH OF NAZARENE	1	36	53	0.5	1.2
349 PENT HOLINESS.	1	62	74*	0.7	1.7
419 SO BAPT CONV..	10	2,584	3,098*	29.0	69.6
449 UN METHODIST..	3	610	669	6.3	15.0
453 UN PRES CH USA	1	36	43*	0.4	1.0
OKLAHOMA	367	201,512	273,559*	51.9	100.0
029 AMER LUTH CH..	4	788	1,107	0.2	0.4
059 BAPT MISS ASSN	5	978	1,199*	0.2	0.4
081 CATHOLIC......	16	0	23,284	4.4	8.5
093 CR CH (DISC)..	26	12,938	15,857*	3.0	5.8
097 CR C AND C CR.	14	2,051	2,514*	0.5	0.9
107 CHRISTIAN UN..	1	21	26*	-	-
123 CH GOD (ANDER)	6	1,199	2,635	0.5	1.0
127 CH GOD (CLEVE)	7	422	517*	0.1	0.2
157 CH OF BRETHREN	1	61	75*	-	-
165 CH OF NAZARENE	29	4,082	9,867	1.9	3.6
175 CONG CR CH....	3	604	740*	0.1	0.3
185 CUMBER PRESB..	1	152	186*	-	0.1
193 EPISCOPAL.....	13	5,152	6,842	1.3	2.5
221 FREE METH C NA	3	239	359	0.1	0.1
226 FRIENDS-USA...	2	85	104*	-	-
281 LUTH CH AMER..	4	1,142	1,720	0.3	0.6
283 LUTH--MO SYNOD	9	3,193	4,470	0.8	1.6
285 MENNONITE CH..	1	23	28*	-	-
335 ORTH PRESB CH.	1	37	60	-	-
349 PENT HOLINESS.	25	1,753	2,148*	0.4	0.8
357 PRESB CH US...	6	2,567	3,146*	0.6	1.2
403 SALVATION ARMY	1	158	369	0.1	0.1
413 S-D ADVENTISTS	6	1,307	1,602*	0.3	0.6
419 SO BAPT CONV..	113	102,371	125,465*	23.8	45.9
435 UNITARIAN-UNIV	1	346	531	0.1	0.2
443 UN C OF CHRIST	2	220	270*	0.1	0.1
449 UN METHODIST..	54	51,973	59,036	11.2	21.6
453 UN PRES CH USA	12	7,548	9,251*	1.8	3.4
469 WISC EVAN LUTH	1	102	151	-	0.1
OKMULGEE	49	13,322	17,645*	49.9	100.0
081 CATHOLIC......	4	0	1,796	5.1	10.2
093 CR CH (DISC)..	5	986	1,173*	3.3	6.6
097 CR C AND C CR.	1	125	149*	0.4	0.8
123 CH GOD (ANDER)	2	39	107	0.3	0.6
165 CH OF NAZARENE	2	379	535	1.5	3.0
193 EPISCOPAL.....	2	196	279	0.8	1.6
283 LUTH--MO SYNOD	1	82	119	0.3	0.7
349 PENT HOLINESS.	3	225	268*	0.8	1.5
403 SALVATION ARMY	1	49	161	0.5	0.9
413 S-D ADVENTISTS	1	9	11*	-	0.1
419 SO BAPT CONV..	15	7,871	9,362*	26.5	53.1
443 UN C OF CHRIST	1	9	11*	-	0.1
449 UN METHODIST..	9	2,964	3,213	9.1	18.2
453 UN PRES CH USA	2	388	461*	1.3	2.6
OSAGE	52	10,809	14,584*	49.0	100.0
081 CATHOLIC......	4	0	1,254	4.2	8.6
093 CR CH (DISC)..	3	400	474*	1.6	3.3
097 CR C AND C CR.	3	575	681*	2.3	4.7
127 CH GOD (CLEVE)	1	33	39*	0.1	0.3
165 CH OF NAZARENE	6	378	922	3.1	6.3
193 EPISCOPAL.....	1	550	872	2.9	6.0
226 FRIENDS-USA...	1	46	55*	0.2	0.4
349 PENT HOLINESS.	2	21	25*	0.1	0.2
353 PLY BRETHREN..	1	10	10	-	0.1
413 S-D ADVENTISTS	1	10	12*	-	0.1
419 SO BAPT CONV..	17	6,076	7,200*	24.2	49.4
449 UN METHODIST..	8	2,228	2,469	8.3	16.9
453 UN PRES CH USA	4	482	571*	1.9	3.9
OTTAWA	64	18,623	22,491*	75.5	100.0
081 CATHOLIC......	1	0	560	1.9	2.5
093 CR CH (DISC)..	4	1,573	1,858*	6.2	8.3
097 CR C AND C CR.	10	2,920	3,449*	11.6	15.3
123 CH GOD (ANDER)	1	37	112	0.4	0.5
127 CH GOD (CLEVE)	1	22	26*	0.1	0.1
165 CH OF NAZARENE	2	148	366	1.2	1.6
193 EPISCOPAL.....	2	437	459	1.5	2.0
226 FRIENDS-USA...	3	175	207*	0.7	0.9
283 LUTH--MO SYNOD	2	296	410	1.4	1.8
349 PENT HOLINESS.	1	20	24*	0.1	0.1
413 S-D ADVENTISTS	1	19	22*	0.1	0.1
419 SO BAPT CONV..	27	9,712	11,472*	38.5	51.0
449 UN METHODIST..	8	2,925	3,126	10.5	13.9
453 UN PRES CH USA	1	339	400*	1.3	1.8
PAWNEE	31	5,727	7,426*	65.5	100.0
081 CATHOLIC......	3	0	359	3.2	4.8
093 CR CH (DISC)..	3	418	488*	4.3	6.6
097 CR C AND C CR.	2	552	644*	5.7	8.7
123 CH GOD (ANDER)	1	12	36	0.3	0.5
165 CH OF NAZARENE	1	22	202	1.8	2.7
193 EPISCOPAL.....	1	37	54	0.5	0.7
349 PENT HOLINESS.	1	16	19*	0.2	0.3
403 SALVATION ARMY	1	108	439	3.9	5.9
419 SO BAPT CONV..	12	3,554	4,149*	36.6	55.9
449 UN METHODIST..	6	1,008	1,036	9.1	14.0

*Total adherents estimated from known number of communicant, confirmed, full members.

—Represents a percent less than 0.1.

Percentages may not total due to rounding.

Table 3. Churches and Church Membership by State, County and Denomination: 1971

County and Denomination	Number of churches	Communicant, confirmed, full members	Total adherents		
			Number	Percent of total population	Percent of total adherents
PAYNE	64	17,697	22,820*	45.1	100.0
029 AMER LUTH CH..	1	96	121	0.2	0.5
081 CATHOLIC......	3	0	1,563	3.1	6.8
093 CR CH (DISC)..	5	1,655	1,913*	3.8	8.4
097 CR C AND C CR.	6	505	584*	1.2	2.6
123 CH GOD (ANDER)	4	248	654	1.3	2.9
127 CH GOD (CLEVE)	1	27	31*	0.1	0.1
157 CH OF BRETHREN	1	164	190*	0.4	0.8
165 CH OF NAZARENE	3	370	597	1.2	2.6
193 EPISCOPAL.....	2	359	576	1.1	2.5
221 FREE METH C NA	1	30	46	0.1	0.2
226 FRIENDS-USA...	2	61	71*	0.1	0.3
281 LUTH CH AMER..	1	168	222	0.4	1.0
283 LUTH--MO SYNOD	3	330	446	0.9	2.0
349 PENT HOLINESS.	1	35	40*	0.1	0.2
403 SALVATION ARMY	1	40	141	0.3	0.6
413 S-D ADVENTISTS	2	91	105*	0.2	0.5
419 SO BAPT CONV..	13	6,589	7,617*	15.0	33.4
435 UNITARIAN-UNIV	1	40	40	0.1	0.2
449 UN METHODIST..	11	5,555	6,321	12.5	27.7
453 UN PRES CH USA	2	1,334	1,542*	3.0	6.8
PITTSBURG	72	16,394	20,971*	55.9	100.0
059 BAPT MISS ASSN	1	120	142*	0.4	0.7
081 CATHOLIC......	4	0	1,674	4.5	8.0
093 CR CH (DISC)..	2	452	536*	1.4	2.6
097 CR C AND C CR.	4	626	743*	2.0	3.5
123 CH GOD (ANDER)	1	15	75	0.2	0.4
165 CH OF NAZARENE	2	197	387	1.0	1.8
193 EPISCOPAL.....	1	136	163	0.4	0.8
283 LUTH--MO SYNOD	1	13	20	0.1	0.1
349 PENT HOLINESS.	2	55	65*	0.2	0.3
413 S-D ADVENTISTS	1	75	89*	0.2	0.4
419 SO BAPT CONV..	37	10,889	12,922*	34.4	61.6
449 UN METHODIST..	14	3,253	3,487	9.3	16.6
453 UN PRES CH USA	2	563	668*	1.8	3.2
PONTOTOC	56	14,081	16,875*	60.6	100.0
059 BAPT MISS ASSN	4	305	355*	1.3	2.1
081 CATHOLIC......	1	0	240	0.9	1.4
093 CR CH (DISC)..	1	436	507*	1.8	3.0
127 CH GOD (CLEVE)	2	147	171*	0.6	1.0
165 CH OF NAZARENE	3	298	546	2.0	3.2
185 CUMBER PRESB..	1	140	163*	0.6	1.0
193 EPISCOPAL.....	1	216	278	1.0	1.6
283 LUTH--MO SYNOD	1	93	147	0.5	0.9
349 PENT HOLINESS.	4	292	340*	1.2	2.0
403 SALVATION ARMY	1	85	309	1.1	1.8
413 S-D ADVENTISTS	1	34	40*	0.1	0.2
419 SO BAPT CONV..	25	9,089	10,573*	37.9	62.7
449 UN METHODIST..	10	2,664	2,878	10.3	17.1
453 UN PRES CH USA	1	282	328*	1.2	1.9
POTTAWATOMIE	72	21,410	26,402*	61.2	100.0
081 CATHOLIC......	4	0	1,192	2.8	4.5
093 CR CH (DISC)..	2	587	694*	1.6	2.6
123 CH GOD (ANDER)	1	113	245	0.6	0.9
127 CH GOD (CLEVE)	3	99	117*	0.3	0.4
165 CH OF NAZARENE	2	179	350	0.8	1.3
193 EPISCOPAL.....	1	203	298	0.7	1.1
283 LUTH--MO SYNOD	1	209	292	0.7	1.1
349 PENT HOLINESS.	4	295	349*	0.8	1.3
357 PRESB CH US...	1	73	86*	0.2	0.3
413 S-D ADVENTISTS	1	91	108*	0.3	0.4
419 SO BAPT CONV..	36	14,936	17,656*	40.9	66.9
449 UN METHODIST..	14	4,050	4,335	10.1	16.4
453 UN PRES CH USA	2	575	680*	1.6	2.6
PUSHMATAHA	39	3,536	4,266*	45.5	100.0
081 CATHOLIC......	1	0	45	0.5	1.1
093 CR CH (DISC)..	1	73	88*	0.9	2.1
097 CR C AND C CR.	9	211	254*	2.7	6.0
165 CH OF NAZARENE	1	35	94	1.0	2.2
193 EPISCOPAL.....	1	9	14	0.1	0.3
357 PRESB CH US...	1	46	55*	0.6	1.3
419 SO BAPT CONV..	16	2,194	2,638*	28.1	61.8
449 UN METHODIST..	8	915	1,014	10.8	23.8
453 UN PRES CH USA	1	53	64*	0.7	1.5
ROGER MILLS	15	2,206	2,57[illegible]	57.9	100.0
081 CATHOLIC......	1	0	35	0.8	1.4
165 CH OF NAZARENE	2	26	36	0.8	1.4
349 PENT HOLINESS.	2	52	61*	1.4	2.4
419 SO BAPT CONV..	6	1,524	1,788*	40.2	69.4
449 UN METHODIST..	4	604	58	14.8	25.5
ROGERS	43	10,689	13,4[illegible]3*	47.3	100.0
081 CATHOLIC......	1	0	392	1.4	2.9
093 CR CH (DISC)..	1	396	486*	1.7	3.6
097 CR C AND C CR.	3	350	430*	1.5	3.2
123 CH GOD (ANDER)	1	75	190	0.7	1.4
165 CH OF NAZARENE	2	143	285	1.0	2.1
193 EPISCOPAL.....	1	74	104	0.4	0.8
283 LUTH--MO SYNOD	2	232	322	1.1	2.4
287 MENN GEN CONF.	1	167	205*	0.7	1.5
413 S-D ADVENTISTS	1	60	74*	0.3	.6
419 SO BAPT CONV..	20	6,620	8,133*	28.6	60.5
449 UN METHODIST..	8	2,305	2,494	8.8	18.6
453 UN PRES CH USA	2	267	328*	1.2	2.4
SEMINOLE	59	13,005	17,579*	69.9	100.0
081 CATHOLIC......	2	0	2,228	8.9	12.7
093 CR CH (DISC)..	2	376	446*	1.8	2.5
123 CH GOD (ANDER)	3	139	448	1.8	2.5
127 CH GOD (CLEVE)	2	73	87*	0.3	0.5
165 CH OF NAZARENE	3	131	179	0.7	1.0
193 EPISCOPAL.....	1	41	66	0.3	0.4
349 PENT HOLINESS.	5	271	321*	1.3	1.8
357 PRESB CH US...	1	59	70*	0.3	0.4
413 S-D ADVENTISTS	1	45	53*	0.2	0.3
419 SO BAPT CONV..	23	8,879	10,529*	41.9	59.9
449 UN METHODIST..	11	2,707	2,815	11.2	16.0
453 UN PRES CH USA	5	284	337*	1.3	1.9
SEQUOYAH	29	5,895	7,392*	31.6	100.0
059 BAPT MISS ASSN	1	124	155*	0.7	2.1
081 CATHOLIC......	1	0	109	0.5	1.5
097 CR C AND C CR.	1	125	157*	0.7	2.1
165 CH OF NAZARENE	2	140	333	1.4	4.5
221 FREE METH C NA	1	13	35	0.1	0.5
413 S-D ADVENTISTS	1	42	53*	0.2	0.7
419 SO BAPT CONV..	16	3,793	4,755*	20.3	64.3
449 UN METHODIST..	5	1,531	1,636	7.0	22.1
453 UN PRES CH USA	1	127	159*	0.7	2.2
STEPHENS	52	19,393	23,477*	65.4	100.0
081 CATHOLIC......	2	0	735	2.0	3.1
093 CR CH (DISC)..	3	928	1,089*	3.0	4.6
097 CR C AND C CR.	2	148	174*	0.5	0.7
123 CH GOD (ANDER)	1	18	46	0.1	0.2
127 CH GOD (CLEVE)	2	76	89*	0.2	0.4
165 CH OF NAZARENE	4	386	680	1.9	2.9
185 CUMBER PRESB..	3	203	238*	0.7	1.0
193 EPISCOPAL.....	1	201	294	0.8	1.3
283 LUTH--MO SYNOD	1	110	148	0.4	0.6
357 PRESB CH US...	1	440	516*	1.4	2.2
413 S-D ADVENTISTS	1	31	36*	0.1	0.2
419 SO BAPT CONV..	23	12,698	14,903*	41.5	63.5
449 UN METHODIST..	8	4,154	4,529	12.6	19.3
TEXAS	42	8,607	10,971*	67.1	100.0
081 CATHOLIC......	2	0	560	3.4	5.1
093 CR CH (DISC)..	4	547	666*	4.1	6.1
097 CR C AND C CR.	1	300	365*	2.2	3.3
123 CH GOD (ANDER)	3	106	271	1.7	2.5
165 CH OF NAZARENE	3	233	437	2.7	4.0
193 EPISCOPAL.....	1	8	74	0.5	0.7
211 EV MENN BRETH.	1	72	88*	0.5	0.8
283 LUTH--MO SYNOD	3	432	572	3.5	5.2
349 PENT HOLINESS.	2	63	77*	0.5	0.7
413 S-D ADVENTISTS	2	65	79*	0.5	0.7
419 SO BAPT CONV..	10	3,053	3,714*	22.7	33.9
449 UN METHODIST..	9	3,432	3,708	22.7	33.8
453 UN PRES CH USA	1	296	360*	2.2	3.3
TILLMAN	29	7,589	9,190*	71.2	100.0
081 CATHOLIC......	3	0	247	1.9	2.7
093 CR CH (DISC)..	3	292	354*	2.7	3.9
165 CH OF NAZARENE	1	46	79	0.6	0.9
349 PENT HOLINESS.	1	10	12*	0.1	0.1
419 SO BAPT CONV..	13	5,362	6,495*	50.3	70.7
449 UN METHODIST..	6	1,707	1,795	13.9	19.5
453 UN PRES CH USA	2	172	208*	1.6	2.3
TULSA	277	147,217	208,156*	51.8	100.0
019 AMER BAPT CONV	2	496	608*	0.2	0.3
029 AMER LUTH CH..	2	476	728	0.2	0.3
059 BAPT MISS ASSN	3	409	501*	0.1	0.2
081 CATHOLIC......	20	0	26,781	6.7	12.9
093 CR CH (DISC)..	22	9,196	11,266*	2.8	5.4
097 CR C AND C CR.	21	5,015	6,144*	1.5	3.0
123 CH GOD (ANDER)	5	920	2,315	0.6	1.1
127 CH GOD (CLEVE)	5	294	360*	0.1	0.2
165 CH OF NAZARENE	13	1,419	2,725	0.7	1.3
185 CUMBER PRESB..	2	156	191*	-	0.1
193 EPISCOPAL.....	9	4,923	6,499	1.6	3.1
221 FREE METH C NA	1	90	122	-	0.1
226 FRIENDS-USA...	2	96	118*	-	0.1
281 LUTH CH AMER..	3	1,000	1,405	0.3	0.7
283 LUTH--MO SYNOD	6	2,529	3,636	0.9	1.7
335 ORTH PRESB CH.	1	37	52	-	-
349 PENT HOLINESS	5	841	1,030*	0.3	0.5
381 REF PRES-EVAN.	1	47	55	-	-
403 SALVATION ARMY	3	251	883	0.2	0.4
413 S-D ADVENTISTS	3	717	878*	0.2	0.4
419 SO BAPT CONV..	86	65,277	79,969*	19.9	38.4
435 UNITARIAN-UNIV	2	920	1,456	0.4	0.7
443 UN C OF CHRIST	1	271	332*	0.1	0.2
449 UN METHODIST..	44	39,976	45,567	11.3	21.9
453 UN PRES CH USA	14	11,849	14,516*	3.6	7.0
469 WISC EVAN LUTH	1	12	19	-	-
WAGONER	26	4,608	5,921*	26.7	100.0
081 CATHOLIC......	1	0	157	0.7	2.7
093 CR CH (DISC)..	2	244	302*	1.4	5.1
097 CR C AND C CR.	2	282	348*	1.6	5.9

*Total adherents estimated from known number of communicant, confirmed, full members.

—Represents a percent less than 0.1.

Percentages may not total due to rounding.

Table 3. Churches and Church Membership by State, County and Denomination: 1971

County and Denomination	Number of churches	Communicant, confirmed, full members	Total adherents: Number	Total adherents: Percent of total population	Total adherents: Percent of total adherents
127 CH GOD (CLEVE)	1	75	93*	0.4	1.6
165 CH OF NAZARENE	2	97	411	1.9	6.9
193 EPISCOPAL.....	1	25	30	0.1	0.5
349 PENT HOLINESS.	1	120	148*	0.7	2.5
413 S-D ADVENTISTS	1	43	53*	0.2	0.9
419 SO BAPT CONV..	9	2,516	3,109*	14.0	52.5
449 UN METHODIST..	5	1,129	1,175	5.3	19.8
453 UN PRES CH USA	1	77	95*	0.4	1.6
WASHINGTON	53	22,008	29,036*	68.7	100.0
081 CATHOLIC......	3	0	2,480	5.9	8.5
093 CR CH (DISC)..	4	1,343	1,603*	3.8	5.5
097 CR C AND C CR.	4	1,155	1,379*	3.3	4.7
123 CH GOD (ANDER)	1	92	292	0.7	1.0
127 CH GOD (CLEVE)	1	17	20*	-	0.1
157 CH OF BRETHREN	1	52	62*	0.1	0.2
165 CH OF NAZARENE	3	423	732	1.7	2.5
226 FRIENDS-USA...	3	143	171*	0.4	0.6
283 LUTH--MO SYNOD	1	500	700	1.7	2.4
335 ORTH PRESB CH.	1	33	43	0.1	0.1
349 PENT HOLINESS.	2	121	144*	0.3	0.5
403 SALVATION ARMY	1	139	498	1.2	1.7
413 S-D ADVENTISTS	1	98	117*	0.3	0.4
419 SO BAPT CONV..	15	8,803	10,509*	24.9	36.2
435 UNITARIAN-UNIV	1	19	19	-	0.1
449 UN METHODIST..	9	6,311	6,973	16.5	24.0
453 UN PRES CH USA	2	2,759	3,294*	7.8	11.3
WASHITA	29	6,007	6,896*	56.8	100.0
029 AMER LUTH CH..	1	271	312	2.6	4.5
081 CATHOLIC......	1	0	50	0.4	0.7
093 CR CH (DISC)..	1	12	14*	0.1	0.2
097 CR C AND C CR.	1	12	14*	0.1	0.2
123 CH GOD (ANDER)	1	15	40	0.3	0.6
157 CH OF BRETHREN	1	25	29*	0.2	0.4
165 CH OF NAZARENE	1	36	39	0.3	0.6
185 CUMBER PRESB..	2	115	135*	1.1	2.0
287 MENN GEN CONF.	1	176	206*	1.7	3.0
313 NO AM BAPT GC.	1	137	160*	1.3	2.3
349 PENT HOLINESS.	1	27	32*	0.3	0.5
419 SO BAPT CONV..	7	3,239	3,790*	31.2	55.0
449 UN METHODIST..	8	1,743	1,842	15.2	26.7
453 UN PRES CH USA	2	199	233*	1.9	3.4
WOODS	28	5,388	6,777*	56.9	100.0
081 CATHOLIC......	2	0	316	2.7	4.7
093 CR CH (DISC)..	4	720	823*	6.9	12.1
123 CH GOD (ANDER)	3	194	513	4.3	7.6
165 CH OF NAZARENE	3	141	324	2.7	4.8
193 EPISCOPAL.....	1	20	25	0.2	0.4
226 FRIENDS-USA...	1	192	220*	1.8	3.2
283 LUTH--MO SYNOD	1	358	444	3.7	6.6
349 PENT HOLINESS.	1	4	5*	-	0.1
413 S-D ADVENTISTS	1	30	34*	0.3	0.5
419 SO BAPT CONV..	3	1,172	1,340*	11.2	19.8
443 UN C OF CHRIST	1	44	50*	0.4	0.7
449 UN METHODIST..	6	2,254	2,387	20.0	35.2
453 UN PRES CH USA	1	259	296*	2.5	4.4
WOODWARD	28	6,999	9,079*	58.4	100.0
081 CATHOLIC......	2	0	566	3.6	6.2
093 CR CH (DISC)..	4	728	877*	5.6	9.7
097 CR C AND C CR.	2	35	42*	0.3	0.5
165 CH OF NAZARENE	2	172	470	3.0	5.2
193 EPISCOPAL.....	1	107	174	1.1	1.9
221 FREE METH C NA	1	25	29	0.2	0.3
283 LUTH--MO SYNOD	1	135	183	1.2	2.0
413 S-D ADVENTISTS	1	55	66*	0.4	0.7
419 SO BAPT CONV..	6	2,782	3,353*	21.6	36.9
449 UN METHODIST..	7	2,672	2,972	19.1	32.7
453 UN PRES CH USA	1	288	347*	2.2	3.8
CO DATA NOT AVAIL	258	21,531	34,757*	N/A	N/A
151 L-D SAINTS....	0	0	8,788	N/A	N/A
223 FREE WILL BAPT	231	19,842	23,919*	N/A	N/A
231 GENERAL BAPT..	12	1,081	1,303*	N/A	N/A
467 WESLEYAN......	15	608	747	N/A	N/A

OREGON

County and Denomination	Number of churches	Communicant, confirmed, full members	Total adherents: Number	Total adherents: Percent of total population	Total adherents: Percent of total adherents
THE STATE.....	1,721	317,405	691,085*	33.0	100.0
BAKER	21	2,102	4,820*	32.3	100.0
029 AMER LUTH CH..	1	228	355	2.4	7.4
081 CATHOLIC......	5	0	1,647	11.0	34.2
097 CR C AND C CR.	2	460	556*	3.7	11.5
123 CH GOD (ANDER)	1	51	133	0.9	2.8
165 CH OF NAZARENE	2	112	382	2.6	7.9
193 EPISCOPAL.....	1	189	365	2.4	7.6
403 SALVATION ARMY	1	42	172	1.2	3.6
413 S-D ADVENTISTS	2	165	199*	1.3	4.1
449 UN METHODIST..	4	399	460	3.1	9.5
453 UN PRES CH USA	2	456	551*	3.7	11.4
BENTON	28	8,365	13,595*	25.3	100.0
081 CATHOLIC......	3	0	3,251	6.0	23.9
093 CR CH (DISC)..	1	673	791*	1.5	5.8
097 CR C AND C CR.	1	123	145*	0.3	1.1
123 CH GOD (ANDER)	1	55	102	0.2	0.8
127 CH GOD (CLEVE)	1	12	14*	-	0.1
165 CH OF NAZARENE	2	170	439	0.8	3.2
193 EPISCOPAL.....	1	1,674	1,978	3.7	14.5
197 EVAN CH OF NA.	1	189	222*	0.4	1.6
221 FREE METH C NA	1	32	42	0.1	0.3
226 FRIENDS-USA...	1	25	29*	0.1	0.2
281 LUTH CH AMER..	1	880	1,313	2.4	9.7
283 LUTH--MO SYNOD	3	668	918	1.7	6.8
285 MENNONITE CH..	1	65	76*	0.1	0.6
413 S-D ADVENTISTS	1	266	313*	0.6	2.3
419 SO BAPT CONV..	1	399	469*	0.9	3.4
435 UNITARIAN-UNIV	1	116	182	0.3	1.3
443 UN C OF CHRIST	1	702	825*	1.5	6.1
449 UN METHODIST..	4	1,355	1,356	2.5	10.0
453 UN PRES CH USA	2	961	1,130*	2.1	8.3
CLACKAMAS	129	31,743	59,290*	35.7	100.0
019 AMER BAPT CONV	2	430	527*	0.3	0.9
029 AMER LUTH CH..	8	3,759	5,353	3.2	9.0
081 CATHOLIC......	11	0	17,456	10.5	29.4
093 CR CH (DISC)..	1	234	287*	0.2	0.5
097 CR C AND C CR.	9	2,322	2,847*	1.7	4.8
123 CH GOD (ANDER)	2	85	214	0.1	0.4
165 CH OF NAZARENE	7	759	1,268	0.8	2.1
175 CONG CR CH....	1	250	306*	0.2	0.5
193 EPISCOPAL.....	22	10,936	14,579	8.8	24.6
197 EVAN CH OF NA.	9	758	929*	0.6	1.6
201 EVAN COV CH AM	1	81	99*	0.1	0.2
221 FREE METH C NA	1	17	24	-	-
281 LUTH CH AMER..	2	462	695	0.4	1.2
283 LUTH--MO SYNOD	7	1,478	2,149	1.3	3.6
285 MENNONITE CH..	2	73	89*	0.1	0.2
287 MENN GEN CONF.	1	245	300*	0.2	0.5
313 NO AM BAPT GC.	1	96	118*	0.1	0.2
335 ORTH PRESB CH.	1	21	31	-	0.1
353 PLY BRETHREN..	1	20	30	-	0.1
413 S-D ADVENTISTS	5	1,313	1,610*	1.0	2.7
419 SO BAPT CONV..	4	380	466*	0.3	0.8
435 UNITARIAN-UNIV	2	285	338	0.2	0.6
443 UN C OF CHRIST	8	1,086	1,331*	0.8	2.2
449 UN METHODIST..	13	3,387	4,240	2.6	7.2
453 UN PRES CH USA	8	3,266	4,004*	2.4	6.8
CLATSOP	32	4,279	7,935*	27.9	100.0
019 AMER BAPT CONV	1	205	241*	0.8	3.0
029 AMER LUTH CH..	1	466	612	2.1	7.7
081 CATHOLIC......	6	0	2,487	8.7	31.3
097 CR C AND C CR.	3	310	364*	1.3	4.6
165 CH OF NAZARENE	2	76	192	0.7	2.4
193 EPISCOPAL.....	2	468	598	2.1	7.5
226 FRIENDS-USA...	1	80	94*	0.3	1.2
281 LUTH CH AMER..	4	1,047	1,492	5.2	18.8
283 LUTH--MO SYNOD	1	102	125	0.4	1.6
353 PLY BRETHREN..	1	20	40	0.1	0.5
413 S-D ADVENTISTS	2	117	137*	0.5	1.7
435 UNITARIAN-UNIV	1	6	6	-	0.1
443 UN C OF CHRIST	1	65	76*	0.3	1.0
449 UN METHODIST..	3	936	1,023	3.6	12.9
453 UN PRES CH USA	3	381	448*	1.6	5.6
COLUMBIA	33	4,314	8,554*	29.7	100.0
081 CATHOLIC......	6	0	2,750	9.6	32.1
093 CR CH (DISC)..	1	192	237*	0.8	2.8
097 CR C AND C CR.	2	141	174*	0.6	2.0
123 CH GOD (ANDER)	2	240	850	3.0	9.9
165 CH OF NAZARENE	2	110	222	0.8	2.6
193 EPISCOPAL.....	3	1,475	1,508	5.2	17.6
197 EVAN CH OF NA.	1	82	101*	0.4	1.2
221 FREE METH C NA	1	33	34	0.1	0.4
281 LUTH CH AMER..	3	603	850	3.0	9.9
283 LUTH--MO SYNOD	2	193	270	0.9	3.2
413 S-D ADVENTISTS	4	251	310*	1.1	3.6
419 SO BAPT CONV..	1	36	44*	0.2	0.5
449 UN METHODIST..	3	655	830	2.9	9.7
453 UN PRES CH USA	2	303	374*	1.3	4.4
COOS	53	7,419	12,797*	22.6	100.0
019 AMER BAPT CONV	2	409	502*	0.9	3.9
029 AMER LUTH CH..	2	431	601	1.1	4.7
081 CATHOLIC......	5	0	2,573	4.6	20.1
093 CR CH (DISC)..	3	577	708*	1.3	5.5
097 CR C AND C CR.	5	715	878*	1.6	6.9
123 CH GOD (ANDER)	4	272	706	1.2	5.5
127 CH GOD (CLEVE)	3	117	144*	0.3	1.1
157 CH OF BRETHREN	1	47	58*	0.1	0.5
165 CH OF NAZARENE	3	345	891	1.6	7.0
193 EPISCOPAL.....	5	913	1,179	2.1	9.2
221 FREE METH C NA	1	24	46	0.1	0.4
281 LUTH CH AMER..	1	296	362	0.6	2.8
283 LUTH--MO SYNOD	2	272	394	0.7	3.1
403 SALVATION ARMY	1	39	182	0.3	1.4

*Total adherents estimated from known number of communicant, confirmed, full members.

—Represents a percent less than 0.1.

Percentages may not total due to rounding.

Table 3. Churches and Church Membership by State, County and Denomination: 1971

County and Denomination	Number of churches	Communicant, confirmed, full members	Total adherents		
			Number	Percent of total population	Percent of total adherents
413 S-D ADVENTISTS	4	523	642*	1.1	5.0
419 SO BAPT CONV..	2	439	539*	1.0	4.2
449 UN METHODIST..	4	1,131	1,325	2.3	10.4
453 UN PRES CH USA	5	869	1,067*	1.9	8.3
CROOK	9	747	1,820*	18.2	100.0
029 AMER LUTH CH..	1	282	411	4.1	22.6
081 CATHOLIC......	1	0	590	5.9	32.4
097 CR C AND C CR.	2	90	109*	1.1	6.0
123 CH GOD (ANDER)	1	20	50	0.5	2.7
127 CH GOD (CLEVE)	1	19	23*	0.2	1.3
165 CH OF NAZARENE	1	77	235	2.4	12.9
193 EPISCOPAL.....	1	210	343	3.4	18.8
419 SO BAPT CONV..	1	49	59*	0.6	3.2
CURRY	18	1,129	2,728*	21.0	100.0
019 AMER BAPT CONV	1	161	195*	1.5	7.1
029 AMER LUTH CH..	3	262	355	2.7	13.0
081 CATHOLIC......	4	0	1,250	9.6	45.8
097 CR C AND C CR.	1	25	30*	0.2	1.1
165 CH OF NAZARENE	1	61	116	0.9	4.3
193 EPISCOPAL.....	3	139	199	1.5	7.3
413 S-D ADVENTISTS	2	116	141*	1.1	5.2
419 SO BAPT CONV..	1	52	63*	0.5	2.3
453 UN PRES CH USA	2	313	379*	2.9	13.9
DESCHUTES	34	4,773	9,116*	29.9	100.0
029 AMER LUTH CH..	2	607	845	2.8	9.3
081 CATHOLIC......	4	0	2,592	8.5	28.4
093 CR CH (DISC)..	1	204	247*	0.8	2.7
097 CR C AND C CR.	4	561	679*	2.2	7.4
123 CH GOD (ANDER)	1	20	55	0.2	0.6
127 CH GOD (CLEVE)	1	21	25*	0.1	0.3
165 CH OF NAZARENE	2	105	328	1.1	3.6
193 EPISCOPAL.....	2	368	547	1.8	6.0
221 FREE METH C NA	2	75	111	0.4	1.2
283 LUTH--MO SYNOD	2	451	705	2.3	7.7
335 ORTH PRESB CH.	1	95	131	0.4	1.4
413 S-D ADVENTISTS	3	307	372*	1.2	4.1
419 SO BAPT CONV..	3	417	505*	1.7	5.5
435 UNITARIAN-UNIV	1	40	55	0.2	0.6
449 UN METHODIST..	1	629	857	2.8	9.4
453 UN PRES CH USA	3	851	1,030*	3.4	11.3
469 WISC EVAN LUTH	1	22	32	0.1	0.4
DOUGLAS	78	10,181	18,040*	25.1	100.0
019 AMER BAPT CONV	3	1,055	1,296*	1.8	7.2
081 CATHOLIC......	6	0	4,176	5.8	23.1
093 CR CH (DISC)..	2	95	117*	0.2	0.6
097 CR C AND C CR.	14	1,218	1,497*	2.1	8.3
123 CH GOD (ANDER)	3	142	411	0.6	2.3
127 CH GOD (CLEVE)	3	176	216*	0.3	1.2
165 CH OF NAZARENE	3	383	919	1.3	5.1
193 EPISCOPAL.....	5	889	1,192	1.7	6.6
221 FREE METH C NA	2	76	103	0.1	0.6
281 LUTH CH AMER..	1	485	763	1.1	4.2
283 LUTH--MO SYNOD	3	435	724	1.0	4.0
285 MENNONITE CH..	1	30	37*	0.1	0.2
403 SALVATION ARMY	1	34	246	0.3	1.4
413 S-D ADVENTISTS	7	1,186	1,457*	2.0	8.1
419 SO BAPT CONV..	6	729	896*	1.2	5.0
435 UNITARIAN-UNIV	1	40	40	0.1	0.2
449 UN METHODIST..	12	1,916	2,362	3.3	13.1
453 UN PRES CH USA	5	1,292	1,588*	2.2	8.8
GILLIAM	6	291	563*	24.0	100.0
081 CATHOLIC......	2	0	165	7.0	29.3
165 CH OF NAZARENE	1	19	59	2.5	10.5
413 S-D ADVENTISTS	1	16	19*	0.8	3.4
443 UN C OF CHRIST	1	173	207*	8.8	36.8
449 UN METHODIST..	1	83	113	4.8	20.1
GRANT	14	627	1,348*	19.3	100.0
081 CATHOLIC......	3	0	410	5.9	30.4
093 CR CH (DISC)..	1	98	118*	1.7	8.8
165 CH OF NAZARENE	1	42	110	1.6	8.2
193 EPISCOPAL.....	1	66	144	2.1	10.7
283 LUTH--MO SYNOD	1	90	170	2.4	12.6
413 S-D ADVENTISTS	2	76	92*	1.3	6.8
449 UN METHODIST..	2	187	222	3.2	16.5
453 UN PRES CH USA	3	68	82*	1.2	6.1
HARNEY	9	686	1,635*	22.7	100.0
081 CATHOLIC......	3	0	556	7.7	34.0
093 CR CH (DISC)..	1	172	210*	2.9	12.8
165 CH OF NAZARENE	1	55	181	2.5	11.1
193 EPISCOPAL.....	1	107	214	3.0	13.1
283 LUTH--MO SYNOD	1	135	210	2.9	12.8
413 S-D ADVENTISTS	1	52	63*	0.9	3.9
453 UN PRES CH USA	1	165	201*	2.8	12.3
HOOD RIVER	18	2,668	4,280*	32.5	100.0
081 CATHOLIC......	1	0	627	4.8	14.6
093 CR CH (DISC)..	1	300	358*	2.7	8.4
123 CH GOD (ANDER)	1	20	55	0.4	1.3
165 CH OF NAZARENE	2	200	385	2.9	9.0
193 EPISCOPAL.....	1	213	451	3.4	10.5
281 LUTH CH AMER..	1	128	171	1.3	4.0
283 LUTH--MO SYNOD	1	135	190	1.4	4.4
413 S-D ADVENTISTS	1	190	226*	1.7	5.3
419 SO BAPT CONV..	3	448	534*	4.0	12.5
443 UN C OF CHRIST	2	394	470*	3.6	11.0
449 UN METHODIST..	3	475	616	4.7	14.4
453 UN PRES CH USA	1	165	197*	1.5	4.6
JACKSON	63	11,998	21,621*	22.9	100.0
019 AMER BAPT CONV	1	352	421*	0.4	1.9
029 AMER LUTH CH..	1	262	401	0.4	1.9
081 CATHOLIC......	5	0	5,734	6.1	26.5
093 CR CH (DISC)..	1	311	372*	0.4	1.7
097 CR C AND C CR.	7	756	904*	1.0	4.2
123 CH GOD (ANDER)	2	142	324	0.3	1.5
127 CH GOD (CLEVE)	2	51	61*	0.1	0.3
165 CH OF NAZARENE	8	1,630	2,712	2.9	12.5
193 EPISCOPAL.....	3	331	575	0.6	2.7
221 FREE METH C NA	2	95	103	0.1	0.5
226 FRIENDS-USA...	2	426	509*	0.5	2.4
281 LUTH CH AMER..	1	401	508	0.5	2.3
283 LUTH--MO SYNOD	3	715	937	1.0	4.3
403 SALVATION ARMY	1	112	450	0.5	2.1
413 S-D ADVENTISTS	4	1,263	1,510*	1.6	7.0
419 SO BAPT CONV..	5	783	936*	1.0	4.3
435 UNITARIAN-UNIV	1	66	66	0.1	0.3
443 UN C OF CHRIST	2	410	490*	0.5	2.3
449 UN METHODIST..	5	1,533	1,788	1.9	8.3
453 UN PRES CH USA	7	2,359	2,820*	3.0	13.0
JEFFERSON	15	2,043	3,182*	37.2	100.0
029 AMER LUTH CH..	1	105	158	1.8	5.0
081 CATHOLIC......	2	0	545	6.4	17.1
093 CR CH (DISC)..	1	293	371*	4.3	11.7
097 CR C AND C CR.	1	75	95*	1.1	3.0
127 CH GOD (CLEVE)	1	17	22*	0.3	0.7
165 CH OF NAZARENE	1	26	82	1.0	2.6
193 EPISCOPAL.....	1	81	120	1.4	3.8
221 FREE METH C NA	1	59	76	0.9	2.4
226 FRIENDS-USA...	1	103	130*	1.5	4.1
413 S-D ADVENTISTS	1	89	113*	1.3	3.6
419 SO BAPT CONV..	2	823	1,043*	12.2	32.8
449 UN METHODIST..	1	312	351	4.1	11.0
453 UN PRES CH USA	1	60	76*	0.9	2.4
JOSEPHINE	27	4,548	8,100*	22.7	100.0
019 AMER BAPT CONV	3	882	1,046*	2.9	12.9
029 AMER LUTH CH..	1	194	259	0.7	3.2
075 BRETHREN IN CR	1	74	88*	0.2	1.1
081 CATHOLIC......	2	0	2,280	6.4	28.1
093 CR CH (DISC)..	1	233	276*	0.8	3.4
123 CH GOD (ANDER)	1	41	78	0.2	1.0
127 CH GOD (CLEVE)	1	31	37*	0.1	0.5
157 CH OF BRETHREN	1	118	140*	0.4	1.7
165 CH OF NAZARENE	1	89	159	0.4	2.0
193 EPISCOPAL.....	2	524	561	1.6	6.9
221 FREE METH C NA	1	29	61	0.2	0.8
283 LUTH--MO SYNOD	2	286	641	1.8	7.9
285 MENNONITE CH..	1	34	40*	0.1	0.5
353 PLY BRETHREN..	1	17	41	0.1	0.5
413 S-D ADVENTISTS	3	662	785*	2.2	9.7
419 SO BAPT CONV..	1	143	170*	0.5	2.1
449 UN METHODIST..	3	721	881	2.5	10.9
453 UN PRES CH USA	1	470	557*	1.6	6.9
KLAMATH	37	6,125	13,030*	26.0	100.0
029 AMER LUTH CH..	1	504	747	1.5	5.7
081 CATHOLIC......	6	0	4,693	9.4	36.0
097 CR C AND C CR.	3	829	1,019*	2.0	7.8
123 CH GOD (ANDER)	1	150	429	0.9	3.3
127 CH GOD (CLEVE)	1	47	58*	0.1	0.4
157 CH OF BRETHREN	1	90	111*	0.2	0.9
165 CH OF NAZARENE	1	126	180	0.4	1.4
193 EPISCOPAL.....	1	79	114	0.2	0.9
226 FRIENDS-USA...	2	64	79*	0.2	0.6
283 LUTH--MO SYNOD	1	354	540	1.1	4.1
403 SALVATION ARMY	1	31	314	0.6	2.4
413 S-D ADVENTISTS	1	220	270*	0.5	2.1
419 SO BAPT CONV..	4	1,604	1,971*	3.9	15.1
435 UNITARIAN-UNIV	1	15	15	-	0.1
443 UN C OF CHRIST	1	63	77*	0.2	0.6
449 UN METHODIST..	6	889	1,111	2.2	8.5
453 UN PRES CH USA	5	1,060	1,302*	2.6	10.0
LAKE	12	524	1,366*	21.5	100.0
081 CATHOLIC......	4	0	678	10.7	49.6
127 CH GOD (CLEVE)	1	32	39*	0.6	2.9
193 EPISCOPAL.....	1	50	75	1.2	5.5
283 LUTH--MO SYNOD	1	79	108	1.7	7.9
413 S-D ADVENTISTS	1	24	29*	0.5	2.1
419 SO BAPT CONV..	1	78	94*	1.5	6.9
449 UN METHODIST..	2	111	162	2.6	11.9
453 UN PRES CH USA	1	150	181*	2.9	13.3
LANE	150	30,776	55,725*	26.1	100.0
019 AMER BAPT CONV	4	1,114	1,354*	0.6	2.4
029 AMER LUTH CH..	8	3,031	4,225	2.0	7.6
059 BAPT MISS ASSN	1	34	41*	-	0.1
081 CATHOLIC......	14	0	15,459	7.2	27.7

*Total adherents estimated from known number of communicant, confirmed, full members.

—Represents a percent less than 0.1.

Percentages may not total due to rounding.

Table 3. Churches and Church Membership by State, County and Denomination: 1971

County and Denomination	Number of churches	Communicant, confirmed, full members	Total adherents		
			Number	Percent of total population	Percent of total adherents
093 CR CH (DISC)..	11	2,464	2,995*	1.4	5.4
097 CR C AND C CR.	29	4,225	5,135*	2.4	9.2
123 CH GOD (ANDER)	5	537	1,233	0.6	2.2
127 CH GOD (CLEVE)	2	105	128*	0.1	0.2
157 CH OF BRETHREN	1	141	171*	0.1	0.3
165 CH OF NAZARENE	3	312	757	0.4	1.4
193 EPISCOPAL.....	7	2,159	2,787	1.3	5.0
197 EVAN CH OF NA.	6	608	739*	0.3	1.3
221 FREE METH C NA	3	169	254	0.1	0.5
226 FRIENDS-USA...	2	177	215*	0.1	0.4
281 LUTH CH AMER..	3	942	1,414	0.7	2.5
283 LUTH--MO SYNOD	8	2,047	3,066	1.4	5.5
285 MENNONITE CH..	1	26	32*	-	0.1
349 PENT HOLINESS.	2	94	114*	0.1	0.2
353 PLY BRETHREN..	1	100	150	0.1	0.3
403 SALVATION ARMY	1	66	306	0.1	0.5
413 S-D ADVENTISTS	8	1,786	2,171*	1.0	3.9
419 SO BAPT CONV..	9	1,934	2,350*	1.1	4.2
435 UNITARIAN-UNIV	1	206	251	0.1	0.5
443 UN C OF CHRIST	1	1,120	1,361*	0.6	2.4
449 UN METHODIST..	11	4,976	6,049	2.8	10.9
453 UN PRES CH USA	7	2,319	2,818*	1.3	5.1
469 WISC EVAN LUTH	1	84	150	0.1	0.3
LINCOLN	37	3,640	6,387*	24.8	100.0
019 AMER BAPT CONV	1	55	64*	0.2	1.0
081 CATHOLIC......	5	0	1,479	5.7	23.2
097 CR C AND C CR.	5	445	522*	2.0	8.2
165 CH OF NAZARENE	3	238	446	1.7	7.0
193 EPISCOPAL.....	4	486	963	3.7	15.1
197 EVAN CH OF NA.	1	30	35*	0.1	0.5
221 FREE METH C NA	1	31	43	0.2	0.7
281 LUTH CH AMER..	1	117	168	0.7	2.6
283 LUTH--MO SYNOD	3	185	259	1.0	4.1
285 MENNONITE CH..	1	74	87*	0.3	1.4
413 S-D ADVENTISTS	3	224	263*	1.0	4.1
419 SO BAPT CONV..	3	478	560*	2.2	8.8
443 UN C OF CHRIST	1	284	333*	1.3	5.2
449 UN METHODIST..	1	255	300	1.2	4.7
453 UN PRES CH USA	4	738	865*	3.4	13.5
LINN	84	12,594	21,417*	29.8	100.0
029 AMER LUTH CH..	3	755	1,055	1.5	4.9
059 BAPT MISS ASSN	3	191	236*	0.3	1.1
081 CATHOLIC......	8	0	4,860	6.8	22.7
093 CR CH (DISC)..	4	1,149	1,419*	2.0	6.6
097 CR C AND C CR.	11	1,300	1,605*	2.2	7.5
123 CH GOD (ANDER)	3	191	454	0.6	2.1
127 CH GOD (CLEVE)	2	106	131*	0.2	0.6
165 CH OF NAZARENE	3	275	687	1.0	3.2
193 EPISCOPAL.....	2	154	223	0.3	1.0
197 EVAN CH OF NA.	7	894	1,104*	1.5	5.2
221 FREE METH C NA	3	152	234	0.3	1.1
283 LUTH--MO SYNOD	4	1,068	1,557	2.2	7.3
285 MENNONITE CH..	11	1,217	1,503*	2.1	7.0
287 MENN GEN CONF.	1	114	141*	0.2	0.7
413 S-D ADVENTISTS	3	470	580*	0.8	2.7
419 SO BAPT CONV..	3	724	894*	1.2	4.2
443 UN C OF CHRIST	1	62	77*	0.1	0.4
449 UN METHODIST..	7	2,434	3,005	4.2	14.0
453 UN PRES CH USA	5	1,338	1,652*	2.3	7.7
MALHEUR	32	3,598	8,406*	36.3	100.0
019 AMER BAPT CONV	1	364	448*	1.9	5.3
029 AMER LUTH CH..	2	219	299	1.3	3.6
081 CATHOLIC......	7	0	3,394	14.6	40.4
093 CR CH (DISC)..	2	307	378*	1.6	4.5
097 CR C AND C CR.	2	325	400*	1.7	4.8
165 CH OF NAZARENE	4	367	779	3.4	9.3
193 EPISCOPAL.....	3	379	616	2.7	7.3
226 FRIENDS-USA...	1	45	55*	0.2	0.7
281 LUTH CH AMER..	1	123	204	0.9	2.4
283 LUTH--MO SYNOD	1	220	340	1.5	4.0
413 S-D ADVENTISTS	1	51	63*	0.3	0.7
419 SO BAPT CONV..	1	29	36*	0.2	0.4
449 UN METHODIST..	4	839	988	4.3	11.8
453 UN PRES CH USA	2	330	406*	1.8	4.8
MARION	138	25,667	57,286*	37.9	100.0
019 AMER BAPT CONV	3	1,029	1,243*	0.8	2.2
029 AMER LUTH CH..	9	2,694	3,669	2.4	6.4
075 BRETHREN IN CR	2	13	16*	-	-
081 CATHOLIC......	18	0	22,102	14.6	38.6
093 CR CH (DISC)..	8	2,229	2,693*	1.8	4.7
097 CR C AND C CR.	14	2,222	2,684*	1.8	4.7
105 CHRISTIAN REF.	1	91	187	0.1	0.3
123 CH GOD (ANDER)	2	295	620	0.4	1.1
127 CH GOD (CLEVE)	5	227	274*	0.2	0.5
165 CH OF NAZARENE	5	992	1,846	1.2	3.2
193 EPISCOPAL.....	4	553	2,645	1.7	4.6
197 EVAN CH OF NA.	4	556	672*	0.4	1.2
201 EVAN COV CH AM	1	81	98*	0.1	0.2
211 EV MENN BRETH.	1	52	63*	-	0.1
221 FREE METH C NA	3	168	210	0.1	0.4
226 FRIENDS-USA...	8	655	791*	0.5	1.4
281 LUTH CH AMER..	3	1,492	2,048	1.4	3.6
283 LUTH--MO SYNOD	6	1,289	1,827	1.2	3.2
285 MENNONITE CH..	4	547	661*	0.4	1.2
287 MENN GEN CONF.	1	252	304*	0.2	0.5
313 NO AM BAPT GC.	1	220	266*	0.2	0.5
349 PENT HOLINESS.	2	50	60*	-	0.1

County and Denomination	Number of churches	Communicant, confirmed, full members	Total adherents		
			Number	Percent of total population	Percent of total adherents
353 PLY BRETHREN..	1	80	120	0.1	0.2
413 S-D ADVENTISTS	7	1,393	1,683*	1.1	2.9
419 SO BAPT CONV..	2	588	710*	0.5	1.2
435 UNITARIAN-UNIV	1	116	161	0.1	0.3
443 UN C OF CHRIST	4	858	1,037*	0.7	1.8
449 UN METHODIST..	11	4,041	5,097	3.4	8.9
453 UN PRES CH USA	6	2,832	3,421*	2.3	6.0
469 WISC EVAN LUTH	1	52	78	0.1	0.1
MORROW	21	1,457	2,423*	54.3	100.0
019 AMER BAPT CONV	1	31	37*	0.8	1.5
029 AMER LUTH CH..	2	172	217	4.9	9.0
081 CATHOLIC......	2	0	406	9.1	16.8
093 CR CH (DISC)..	2	160	193*	4.3	8.0
097 CR C AND C CR.	2	170	205*	4.6	8.5
165 CH OF NAZARENE	1	10	62	1.4	2.6
193 EPISCOPAL.....	1	92	175	3.9	7.2
353 PLY BRETHREN..	6	495	745	16.7	30.7
413 S-D ADVENTISTS	2	43	52*	1.2	2.1
443 UN C OF CHRIST	1	133	160*	3.6	6.6
449 UN METHODIST..	1	151	171	3.8	7.1
MULTNOMAH	274	79,940	179,257*	32.2	100.0
019 AMER BAPT CONV	18	5,881	6,983*	1.3	3.9
029 AMER LUTH CH..	11	5,495	7,243	1.3	4.0
081 CATHOLIC......	39	0	77,005	13.8	43.0
093 CR CH (DISC)..	4	2,017	2,395*	0.4	1.3
097 CR C AND C CR.	15	3,594	4,267*	0.8	2.4
105 CHRISTIAN REF.	2	181	323	0.1	0.2
123 CH GOD (ANDER)	9	1,142	2,683	0.5	1.5
127 CH GOD (CLEVE)	3	291	346*	0.1	0.2
157 CH OF BRETHREN	1	108	128*	-	0.1
165 CH OF NAZARENE	10	2,009	3,447	0.6	1.9
193 EPISCOPAL.....	1	472	651	0.1	0.4
197 EVAN CH OF NA.	7	1,422	1,688*	0.3	0.9
201 EVAN COV CH AM	6	763	906*	0.2	0.5
221 FREE METH C NA	7	361	527	0.1	0.3
226 FRIENDS-USA...	7	1,228	1,458*	0.3	0.8
281 LUTH CH AMER..	12	5,107	7,828	1.4	4.4
283 LUTH--MO SYNOD	15	5,987	8,832	1.6	4.9
285 MENNONITE CH..	1	147	175*	-	0.1
287 MENN GEN CONF.	1	89	106*	-	0.1
313 NO AM BAPT GC.	4	1,316	1,563*	0.3	0.9
335 ORTH PRESB CH.	1	172	287	0.1	0.2
349 PENT HOLINESS.	1	72	85*	-	-
403 SALVATION ARMY	3	288	767	0.1	0.4
413 S-D ADVENTISTS	13	5,937	7,049*	1.3	3.9
419 SO BAPT CONV..	13	3,641	4,323*	0.8	2.4
435 UNITARIAN-UNIV	2	839	1,061	0.2	0.6
443 UN C OF CHRIST	12	3,151	3,741*	0.7	2.1
449 UN METHODIST..	26	10,900	12,708	2.3	7.1
453 UN PRES CH USA	28	16,996	20,181*	3.6	11.3
469 WISC EVAN LUTH	2	334	501	0.1	0.3
POLK	36	4,717	6,900*	19.5	100.0
029 AMER LUTH CH..	1	219	309	0.9	4.5
081 CATHOLIC......	3	0	1,000	2.8	14.5
093 CR CH (DISC)..	2	270	322*	0.9	4.7
097 CR C AND C CR.	2	253	302*	0.9	4.4
123 CH GOD (ANDER)	1	28	39	0.1	0.6
127 CH GOD (CLEVE)	1	48	57*	0.2	0.8
165 CH OF NAZARENE	2	152	340	1.0	4.9
193 EPISCOPAL.....	2	134	161	0.5	2.3
197 EVAN CH OF NA.	3	199	237*	0.7	3.4
211 EV MENN BRETH.	1	527	629*	1.8	9.1
221 FREE METH C NA	1	27	36	0.1	0.5
283 LUTH--MO SYNOD	2	534	765	2.2	11.1
285 MENNONITE CH..	1	28	33*	0.1	0.5
287 MENN GEN CONF.	1	303	361*	1.0	5.2
313 NO AM BAPT GC.	1	352	420*	1.2	6.1
413 S-D ADVENTISTS	2	145	173*	0.5	2.5
419 SO BAPT CONV..	1	169	202*	0.6	2.9
435 UNITARIAN-UNIV	1	52	52	0.1	0.8
449 UN METHODIST..	6	840	941	2.7	13.6
453 UN PRES CH USA	2	437	521*	1.5	7.6
SHERMAN	7	314	684*	32.0	100.0
081 CATHOLIC......	3	0	240	11.2	35.1
097 CR C AND C CR.	1	40	47*	2.2	6.9
165 CH OF NAZARENE	1	13	60	2.8	8.8
449 UN METHODIST..	1	132	184	8.6	26.9
453 UN PRES CH USA	1	129	153*	7.2	22.4
TILLAMOOK	24	2,612	4,894*	27.3	100.0
081 CATHOLIC......	3	0	1,393	7.8	28.5
097 CR C AND C CR.	3	493	591*	3.3	12.1
165 CH OF NAZARENE	2	282	597	3.3	12.2
193 EPISCOPAL.....	1	184	226	1.3	4.6
226 FRIENDS-USA...	2	54	65*	0.4	1.3
281 LUTH CH AMER..	1	83	133	0.7	2.7
283 LUTH--MO SYNOD	1	165	264	1.5	5.4
285 MENNONITE CH..	1	23	28*	0.2	0.6
413 S-D ADVENTISTS	2	149	179*	1.0	3.7
419 SO BAPT CONV..	1	155	186*	1.0	3.8
443 UN C OF CHRIST	1	220	264*	1.5	5.4
449 UN METHODIST..	4	705	849	4.7	17.3
453 UN PRES CH USA	2	99	119*	0.7	2.4
UMATILLA	61	10,682	18,157*	40.4	100.0

*Total adherents estimated from known number of communicant, confirmed, full members.

—Represents a percent less than 0.1.

Percentages may not total due to rounding.

Table 3. Churches and Church Membership by State, County and Denomination: 1971

County and Denomination	Number of churches	Communicant, confirmed, full members	Total adherents: Number	Percent of total population	Percent of total adherents
019 AMER BAPT CONV	5	944	1,133*	2.5	6.2
029 AMER LUTH CH..	3	1,088	1,542	3.4	8.5
081 CATHOLIC......	8	0	3,867	8.6	21.3
093 CR CH (DISC)..	3	984	1,181*	2.6	6.5
097 CR C AND C CR.	2	844	1,013*	2.3	5.6
123 CH GOD (ANDER)	2	89	297	0.7	1.6
127 CH GOD (CLEVE)	3	122	146*	0.3	0.8
157 CH OF BRETHREN	1	108	130*	0.3	0.7
165 CH OF NAZARENE	4	250	574	1.3	3.2
193 EPISCOPAL.....	3	735	1,276	2.8	7.0
221 FREE METH C NA	1	19	42	0.1	0.2
283 LUTH--MO SYNOD	2	176	271	0.6	1.5
403 SALVATION ARMY	1	19	278	0.6	1.5
413 S-D ADVENTISTS	6	2,252	2,703*	6.0	14.9
419 SO BAPT CONV..	2	265	318*	0.7	1.8
443 UN C OF CHRIST	2	212	254*	0.6	1.4
449 UN METHODIST..	5	1,298	1,599	3.6	8.8
453 UN PRES CH USA	8	1,277	1,533*	3.4	8.4
UNION	24	2,886	5,649*	29.2	100.0
029 AMER LUTH CH..	1	271	409	2.1	7.2
081 CATHOLIC......	4	0	1,141	5.9	20.2
093 CR CH (DISC)..	1	527	631*	3.3	11.2
097 CR C AND C CR.	2	100	120*	0.6	2.1
123 CH GOD (ANDER)	1	49	145	0.7	2.6
165 CH OF NAZARENE	3	203	603	3.1	10.7
193 EPISCOPAL.....	1	181	585	3.0	10.4
283 LUTH--MO SYNOD	1	80	122	0.6	2.2
403 SALVATION ARMY	1	20	148	0.8	2.6
413 S-D ADVENTISTS	3	240	288*	1.5	5.1
449 UN METHODIST..	5	827	992	5.1	17.6
453 UN PRES CH USA	1	388	465*	2.4	8.2
WALLOWA	12	908	1,543*	24.7	100.0
081 CATHOLIC......	2	0	397	6.4	25.7
097 CR C AND C CR.	2	240	284*	4.5	18.4
165 CH OF NAZARENE	1	27	71	1.1	4.6
193 EPISCOPAL.....	1	62	78	1.2	5.1
283 LUTH--MO SYNOD	1	52	81	1.3	5.2
413 S-D ADVENTISTS	1	64	76*	1.2	4.9
443 UN C OF CHRIST	1	213	252*	4.0	16.3
449 UN METHODIST..	2	199	244	3.9	15.8
453 UN PRES CH USA	1	51	60*	1.0	3.9
WASCO	22	3,248	6,412*	31.8	100.0
081 CATHOLIC......	3	0	2,130	10.6	33.2
093 CR CH (DISC)..	2	244	293*	1.5	4.6
097 CR C AND C CR.	1	400	480*	2.4	7.5
123 CH GOD (ANDER)	1	18	65	0.3	1.0
165 CH OF NAZARENE	1	70	137	0.7	2.1
193 EPISCOPAL.....	1	308	382	1.9	6.0
197 EVAN CH OF NA.	2	183	220*	1.1	3.4
281 LUTH CH AMER..	1	452	642	3.2	10.0
283 LUTH--MO SYNOD	1	142	191	0.9	3.0
403 SALVATION ARMY	1	23	144	0.7	2.2
413 S-D ADVENTISTS	2	231	277*	1.4	4.3
419 SO BAPT CONV..	1	310	372*	1.8	5.8
443 UN C OF CHRIST	1	234	281*	1.4	4.4
449 UN METHODIST..	3	424	547	2.7	8.5
453 UN PRES CH USA	1	209	251*	1.2	3.9
WASHINGTON	93	20,809	47,423*	30.0	100.0
019 AMER BAPT CONV	1	543	674*	0.4	1.4
029 AMER LUTH CH..	3	1,563	2,520	1.6	5.3
081 CATHOLIC......	13	0	19,263	12.2	40.6
093 CR CH (DISC)..	3	1,139	1,414*	0.9	3.0
097 CR C AND C CR.	5	1,256	1,559*	1.0	3.3
123 CH GOD (ANDER)	3	224	483	0.3	1.0
127 CH GOD (CLEVE)	1	24	30*	-	0.1
165 CH OF NAZARENE	2	454	812	0.5	1.7
193 EPISCOPAL.....	4	1,707	2,436	1.5	5.1
197 EVAN CH OF NA.	1	102	127*	0.1	0.3
221 FREE METH C NA	2	35	47	-	0.1
226 FRIENDS-USA...	4	444	551*	0.3	1.2
281 LUTH CH AMER..	3	1,046	1,537	1.0	3.2
283 LUTH--MO SYNOD	8	2,836	4,128	2.6	8.7
313 NO AM BAPT GC.	2	95	118*	0.1	0.2
349 PENT HOLINESS.	2	29	36*	-	0.1
413 S-D ADVENTISTS	6	1,431	1,777*	1.1	3.7
419 SO BAPT CONV..	4	535	664*	0.4	1.4
435 UNITARIAN-UNIV	1	160	230	0.1	0.5
443 UN C OF CHRIST	4	1,234	1,532*	1.0	3.2
449 UN METHODIST..	13	4,388	5,446	3.4	11.5
453 UN PRES CH USA	7	1,421	1,764*	1.1	3.7
469 WISC EVAN LUTH	1	143	275	0.2	0.6
WHEELER	2	87	141	7.6	100.0
081 CATHOLIC......	1	0	54	2.9	38.3
449 UN METHODIST..	1	87	87	4.7	61.7
YAMHILL	54	8,549	14,969*	37.2	100.0
019 AMER BAPT CONV	3	1,054	1,264*	3.1	8.4
029 AMER LUTH CH..	1	446	646	1.6	4.3
081 CATHOLIC......	5	0	3,933	9.8	26.3
093 CR CH (DISC)..	1	129	155*	0.4	1.0
097 CR C AND C CR.	7	1,237	1,484*	3.7	9.9
123 CH GOD (ANDER)	1	84	209	0.5	1.4
165 CH OF NAZARENE	3	362	680	1.7	4.5
193 EPISCOPAL.....	2	373	612	1.5	4.1
197 EVAN CH OF NA.	3	223	268*	0.7	1.8
221 FREE METH C NA	3	166	219	0.5	1.5
226 FRIENDS-USA...	3	738	885*	2.2	5.9
281 LUTH CH AMER..	2	359	533	1.3	3.6
283 LUTH--MO SYNOD	2	344	474	1.2	3.2
285 MENNONITE CH..	3	241	289*	0.7	1.9
335 ORTH PRESB CH.	1	32	48	0.1	0.3
413 S-D ADVENTISTS	4	582	698*	1.7	4.7
449 UN METHODIST..	8	1,558	1,827	4.5	12.2
453 UN PRES CH USA	2	621	745*	1.9	5.0
CO DATA NOT AVAIL	14	359	59,592	N/A	N/A
151 L-D SAINTS....	0	0	59,178	N/A	N/A
467 WESLEYAN......	14	359	414	N/A	N/A

PENNSYLVANIA

County and Denomination	Number of churches	Communicant, confirmed, full members	Total adherents: Number	Percent of total population	Percent of total adherents
THE STATE.....	10,927	2,506,350	6,981,986*	59.2	100.0
ADAMS	97	19,115	37,639*	66.1	100.0
019 AMER BAPT CONV	3	164	202*	0.4	0.5
075 BRETHREN IN CR	2	74	91*	0.2	0.2
081 CATHOLIC......	9	0	13,669	24.0	36.3
123 CH GOD (ANDER)	1	95	235	0.4	0.6
127 CH GOD (CLEVE)	2	59	73*	0.1	0.2
157 CH OF BRETHREN	4	794	980*	1.7	2.6
165 CH OF NAZARENE	1	53	88	0.2	0.2
193 EPISCOPAL.....	1	186	275	0.5	0.7
226 FRIENDS-USA...	1	87	107*	0.2	0.3
281 LUTH CH AMER..	26	9,503	12,654	22.2	33.6
285 MENNONITE CH..	3	144	178*	0.3	0.5
287 MENN GEN CONF.	1	113	139*	0.2	0.4
413 S-D ADVENTISTS	3	160	197*	0.3	0.5
419 SO BAPT CONV..	1	121	149*	0.3	0.4
443 UN C OF CHRIST	17	3,545	4,375*	7.7	11.6
449 UN METHODIST..	19	3,357	3,412	6.0	9.1
453 UN PRES CH USA	3	660	815*	1.4	2.2
ALLEGHENY	867	238,250	1,077,083*	67.1	100.0
019 AMER BAPT CONV	40	10,131	12,069*	0.8	1.1
029 AMER LUTH CH..	31	12,209	16,236	1.0	1.5
081 CATHOLIC......	254	0	774,478	48.3	71.9
093 CR CH (DISC)..	6	1,224	1,458*	0.1	0.1
097 CR C AND C CR.	25	5,369	6,396*	0.4	0.6
123 CH GOD (ANDER)	4	423	862	0.1	0.1
127 CH GOD (CLEVE)	6	403	480*	-	-
157 CH OF BRETHREN	4	604	720*	-	0.1
165 CH OF NAZARENE	13	1,013	2,099	0.1	0.2
175 CONG CR CH....	6	1,204	1,434*	0.1	0.1
193 EPISCOPAL.....	39	17,679	23,133	1.4	2.1
201 EVAN COV CH AM	1	88	105*	-	-
221 FREE METH C NA	6	244	386	-	-
226 FRIENDS-USA...	1	164	195*	-	-
281 LUTH CH AMER..	75	28,171	37,520	2.3	3.5
283 LUTH--MO SYNOD	33	8,476	11,137	0.7	1.0
285 MENNONITE CH..	1	25	30*	-	-
313 NO AM BAPT GC.	3	501	597*	-	0.1
315 NO AM OLD RC..	1	120	143*	-	-
335 ORTH PRESB CH.	2	181	283	-	-
353 PLY BRETHREN..	9	452	655	-	0.1
381 REF PRES-EVAN.	1	353	479	-	-
403 SALVATION ARMY	12	664	7,962	0.5	0.7
413 S-D ADVENTISTS	2	350	417*	-	-
419 SO BAPT CONV..	8	1,222	1,456*	0.1	0.1
435 UNITARIAN-UNIV	5	799	1,122	0.1	0.1
443 UN C OF CHRIST	25	5,443	6,484*	0.4	0.6
449 UN METHODIST..	58	32,899	40,278	2.5	3.7
453 UN PRES CH USA	195	107,805	128,425*	8.0	11.9
469 WISC EVAN LUTH	1	34	44	-	-
ARMSTRONG	148	28,559	56,488*	74.7	100.0
019 AMER BAPT CONV	8	1,864	2,239*	3.0	4.0
081 CATHOLIC......	21	0	18,844	24.9	33.4
123 CH GOD (ANDER)	6	820	2,233	3.0	4.0
127 CH GOD (CLEVE)	2	40	48*	0.1	0.1
157 CH OF BRETHREN	3	403	484*	0.6	0.9
165 CH OF NAZARENE	1	116	274	0.4	0.5
193 EPISCOPAL.....	6	585	927	1.2	1.6
221 FREE METH C NA	4	210	287	0.4	0.5
281 LUTH CH AMER..	27	7,806	10,559	14.0	18.7
349 PENT HOLINESS.	1	74	89*	0.1	0.2
381 REF PRES-EVAN.	1	77	119	0.2	0.2
403 SALVATION ARMY	1	86	290	0.4	0.5
413 S-D ADVENTISTS	2	93	112*	0.1	0.2
443 UN C OF CHRIST	8	1,411	1,695*	2.2	3.0
449 UN METHODIST..	30	5,308	6,680	8.8	11.8
453 UN PRES CH USA	27	9,666	11,608*	15.4	20.5
BEAVER	172	41,928	124,631*	59.8	100.0
019 AMER BAPT CONV	7	1,484	1,792*	0.9	1.4
029 AMER LUTH CH..	4	1,037	1,368	0.7	1.1

*Total adherents estimated from known number of communicant, confirmed, full members.

—Represents a percent less than 0.1.

Percentages may not total due to rounding.

Table 3. Churches and Church Membership by State, County and Denomination: 1971

County and Denomination	Number of churches	Communicant, confirmed, full members	Total adherents: Number	Total adherents: Percent of total population	Total adherents: Percent of total adherents
081 CATHOLIC......	32	0	71,610	34.4	57.5
093 CR CH (DISC)..	1	172	208*	0.1	0.2
097 CR C AND C CR.	1	327	395*	0.2	0.3
123 CH GOD (ANDER)	1	87	177	0.1	0.1
127 CH GOD (CLEVE)	2	104	126*	0.1	0.1
165 CH OF NAZARENE	7	621	1,631	0.8	1.3
175 CONG CR CH....	1	67	81*	-	0.1
193 EPISCOPAL.....	4	939	1,546	0.7	1.2
221 FREE METH C NA	6	276	409	0.2	0.3
281 LUTH CH AMER..	20	6,924	9,150	4.4	7.3
283 LUTH--MO SYNOD	3	359	546	0.3	0.4
381 REF PRES-EVAN.	4	362	478	0.2	0.4
413 S-D ADVENTISTS	1	42	51*	-	-
419 SO BAPT CONV..	1	58	70*	-	0.1
449 UN METHODIST..	32	12,467	14,965	7.2	12.0
453 UN PRES CH USA	45	16,582	20,028*	9.6	16.1
BEDFORD	124	16,829	22,095*	52.2	100.0
075 BRETHREN IN CR	6	181	223*	0.5	1.0
081 CATHOLIC......	3	0	1,609	3.8	7.3
127 CH GOD (CLEVE)	3	497	612*	1.4	2.8
157 CH OF BRETHREN	17	3,843	4,729*	11.2	21.4
165 CH OF NAZARENE	4	178	397	0.9	1.8
193 EPISCOPAL.....	1	103	156	0.4	0.7
226 FRIENDS-USA...	2	91	112*	0.3	0.5
281 LUTH CH AMER..	19	3,070	3,950	9.3	17.9
285 MENNONITE CH..	1	52	64*	0.2	0.3
287 MENN GEN CONF.	1	69	85*	0.2	0.4
353 PLY BRETHREN..	1	30	40	0.1	0.2
413 S-D ADVENTISTS	2	90	111*	0.3	0.5
415 S-D BAPTIST GC	1	50	62*	0.1	0.3
419 SO BAPT CONV..	1	59	73*	0.2	0.3
443 UN C OF CHRIST	26	3,491	4,296*	10.1	19.4
449 UN METHODIST..	35	4,585	5,035	11.9	22.8
453 UN PRES CH USA	1	440	541*	1.3	2.4
BERKS	298	106,956	183,206*	61.8	100.0
019 AMER BAPT CONV	3	689	822*	0.3	0.4
081 CATHOLIC......	22	0	48,177	16.3	26.3
097 CR C AND C CR.	1	26	31*	-	-
123 CH GOD (ANDER)	3	165	366	0.1	0.2
127 CH GOD (CLEVE)	2	142	169*	0.1	0.1
157 CH OF BRETHREN	3	990	1,181*	0.4	0.6
165 CH OF NAZARENE	4	443	891	0.3	0.5
193 EPISCOPAL.....	9	2,423	3,682	1.2	2.0
199 EVAN CONG CH..	21	3,767	4,495*	1.5	2.5
226 FRIENDS-USA...	2	120	143*	-	0.1
281 LUTH CH AMER..	86	48,099	67,024	22.6	36.6
285 MENNONITE CH..	19	1,258	1,501*	0.5	0.8
287 MENN GEN CONF.	2	235	280*	0.1	0.2
293 MORAV CH-NORTH	1	208	321	0.1	0.2
353 PLY BRETHREN..	3	144	215	0.1	0.1
403 SALVATION ARMY	1	90	967	0.3	0.5
413 S-D ADVENTISTS	5	1,019	1,216*	0.4	0.7
435 UNITARIAN-UNIV	1	85	100	-	0.1
443 UN C OF CHRIST	80	37,203	44,388*	15.0	24.2
449 UN METHODIST..	26	8,386	5,490	1.9	3.0
453 UN PRES CH USA	4	1,464	1,747*	0.6	1.0
BLAIR	165	39,964	78,539*	58.0	100.0
019 AMER BAPT CONV	3	455	548*	0.4	0.7
075 BRETHREN IN CR	4	129	155*	0.1	0.2
081 CATHOLIC......	23	0	31,967	23.6	40.7
097 CR C AND C CR.	1	500	602*	0.4	0.8
127 CH GOD (CLEVE)	3	404	486*	0.4	0.6
157 CH OF BRETHREN	18	5,104	6,144*	4.5	7.8
193 EPISCOPAL.....	3	817	1,018	0.8	1.3
221 FREE METH C NA	1	59	69	0.1	0.1
281 LUTH CH AMER..	27	10,617	13,836	10.2	17.6
285 MENNONITE CH..	3	202	243*	0.2	0.3
287 MENN GEN CONF.	2	93	112*	0.1	0.1
353 PLY BRETHREN..	1	31	70	0.1	0.1
403 SALVATION ARMY	2	137	572	0.4	0.7
413 S-D ADVENTISTS	1	51	61*	-	0.1
419 SO BAPT CONV..	1	130	156*	0.1	0.2
443 UN C OF CHRIST	12	1,930	2,323*	1.7	3.0
449 UN METHODIST..	49	15,976	16,170	11.9	20.6
453 UN PRES CH USA	11	3,329	4,007*	3.0	5.1
BRADFORD	114	15,989	25,419*	43.9	100.0
019 AMER BAPT CONV	10	1,640	2,069*	3.6	8.1
081 CATHOLIC......	12	0	6,191	10.7	24.4
093 CR CH (DISC)..	5	893	1,127*	1.9	4.4
097 CR C AND C CR.	5	355	448*	0.8	1.8
123 CH GOD (ANDER)	1	88	185	0.3	0.7
175 CONG CR CH....	2	357	450*	0.8	1.8
193 EPISCOPAL.....	4	1,191	1,823	3.1	7.2
221 FREE METH C NA	1	17	25	-	0.1
281 LUTH CH AMER..	3	805	1,157	2.0	4.6
285 MENNONITE CH..	2	45	57*	0.1	0.2
403 SALVATION ARMY	1	35	195	0.3	0.8
413 S-D ADVENTISTS	2	110	139*	0.2	0.5
435 UNITARIAN-UNIV	3	115	132	0.2	0.5
443 UN C OF CHRIST	4	241	304*	0.5	1.2
449 UN METHODIST..	46	7,339	7,637	13.2	30.0
453 UN PRES CH USA	13	2,758	3,480*	6.0	13.7
BUCKS	236	72,804	223,398*	53.8	100.0
019 AMER BAPT CONV	6	1,259	1,582*	0.4	0.7
075 BRETHREN IN CR	1	46	58*	-	-
081 CATHOLIC......	35	0	128,213	30.9	57.4
093 CR CH (DISC)..	1	78	98*	-	-
097 CR C AND C CR.	2	164	206*	-	0.1
127 CH GOD (CLEVE)	1	28	35*	-	-
157 CH OF BRETHREN	2	279	350*	0.1	0.2
165 CH OF NAZARENE	1	45	72	-	-
193 EPISCOPAL.....	17	5,659	8,919	2.1	4.0
221 FREE METH C NA	1	31	36	-	-
226 FRIENDS-USA...	11	1,669	2,097*	0.5	0.9
281 LUTH CH AMER..	37	20,345	29,293	7.1	13.1
283 LUTH--MO SYNOD	5	1,462	2,443	0.6	1.1
285 MENNONITE CH..	12	1,738	2,183*	0.5	1.0
287 MENN GEN CONF.	7	1,253	1,574*	0.4	0.7
293 MORAV CH-NORTH	1	60	78	-	-
335 ORTH PRESB CH.	1	111	200	-	0.1
353 PLY BRETHREN..	2	200	400	0.1	0.2
371 REF CH IN AM..	8	3,621	4,946	1.2	2.2
381 REF PRES-EVAN.	2	233	317	0.1	0.1
413 S-D ADVENTISTS	1	161	202*	-	0.1
419 SO BAPT CONV..	1	262	329*	0.1	0.1
435 UNITARIAN-UNIV	3	252	378	0.1	0.2
443 UN C OF CHRIST	26	8,905	11,187*	2.7	5.0
449 UN METHODIST..	33	12,709	12,833	3.1	5.7
453 UN PRES CH USA	19	12,234	15,369*	3.7	6.9
BUTLER	157	37,616	86,559*	67.7	100.0
019 AMER BAPT CONV	2	232	286*	0.2	0.3
029 AMER LUTH CH..	5	3,376	4,629	3.6	5.3
081 CATHOLIC......	26	0	37,329	29.2	43.1
093 CR CH (DISC)..	1	98	121*	0.1	0.1
097 CR C AND C CR.	3	667	821*	0.6	0.9
123 CH GOD (ANDER)	2	498	1,083	0.8	1.3
165 CH OF NAZARENE	4	210	413	0.3	0.5
193 EPISCOPAL.....	1	388	506	0.4	0.6
221 FREE METH C NA	3	119	203	0.2	0.2
281 LUTH CH AMER..	17	5,563	7,646	6.0	8.8
283 LUTH--MO SYNOD	1	510	748	0.6	0.9
335 ORTH PRESB CH.	1	150	224	0.2	0.3
353 PLY BRETHREN..	1	125	200	0.2	0.2
381 REF PRES-EVAN.	1	39	70	0.1	0.1
403 SALVATION ARMY	1	90	333	0.3	0.4
413 S-D ADVENTISTS	2	84	103*	0.1	0.1
443 UN C OF CHRIST	7	2,555	3,145*	2.5	3.6
449 UN METHODIST..	31	7,589	9,837	7.7	11.4
453 UN PRES CH USA	48	15,323	18,862*	14.7	21.8
CAMBRIA	229	39,205	150,324*	80.5	100.0
019 AMER BAPT CONV	5	994	1,188*	0.6	0.8
075 BRETHREN IN CR	1	10	12*	-	-
081 CATHOLIC......	89	0	100,740	53.9	67.0
093 CR CH (DISC)..	3	631	754*	0.4	0.5
097 CR C AND C CR.	2	225	269*	0.1	0.2
123 CH GOD (ANDER)	3	124	343	0.2	0.2
127 CH GOD (CLEVE)	1	129	154*	0.1	0.1
157 CH OF BRETHREN	11	3,619	4,326*	2.3	2.9
165 CH OF NAZARENE	5	342	536	0.3	0.4
175 CONG CR CH....	1	35	42*	-	-
193 EPISCOPAL.....	6	1,670	2,272	1.2	1.5
199 EVAN CONG CH..	1	190	227*	0.1	0.2
281 LUTH CH AMER..	18	7,781	10,861	5.8	7.2
283 LUTH--MO SYNOD	1	147	167	0.1	0.1
285 MENNONITE CH..	4	252	301*	0.2	0.2
403 SALVATION ARMY	1	55	247	0.1	0.2
413 S-D ADVENTISTS	1	71	85*	-	0.1
443 UN C OF CHRIST	7	1,325	1,584*	0.8	1.1
449 UN METHODIST..	57	17,668	21,509	11.5	14.3
453 UN PRES CH USA	12	3,937	4,707*	2.5	3.1
CAMERON	10	1,620	3,613*	50.9	100.0
019 AMER BAPT CONV	1	257	315*	4.4	8.7
081 CATHOLIC......	2	0	1,559	22.0	43.1
193 EPISCOPAL.....	1	81	169	2.4	4.7
221 FREE METH C NA	1	29	43	0.6	1.2
283 LUTH--MO SYNOD	1	126	174	2.5	4.8
449 UN METHODIST..	3	855	1,019	14.4	28.2
453 UN PRES CH USA	1	272	334*	4.7	9.2
CARBON	100	18,111	42,927*	84.9	100.0
019 AMER BAPT CONV	2	312	370*	0.7	0.9
081 CATHOLIC......	21	0	19,405	38.4	45.2
123 CH GOD (ANDER)	1	20	62	0.1	0.1
157 CH OF BRETHREN	1	73	87*	0.2	0.2
165 CH OF NAZARENE	1	32	70	0.1	0.2
193 EPISCOPAL.....	6	694	1,627	3.2	3.8
199 EVAN CONG CH..	5	907	1,077*	2.1	2.5
281 LUTH CH AMER..	26	9,055	12,133	24.0	28.3
443 UN C OF CHRIST	18	4,688	5,567*	11.0	13.0
449 UN METHODIST..	15	1,724	1,809	3.6	4.2
453 UN PRES CH USA	4	606	720*	1.4	1.7
CENTRE	135	27,607	42,381*	42.7	100.0
019 AMER BAPT CONV	4	871	1,040*	1.0	2.5
075 BRETHREN IN CR	4	141	168*	0.2	0.4
081 CATHOLIC......	6	0	10,230	10.3	24.1
093 CR CH (DISC)..	2	220	263*	0.3	0.6
097 CR C AND C CR.	3	512	611*	0.6	1.4
123 CH GOD (ANDER)	1	22	72	0.1	0.2
127 CH GOD (CLEVE)	1	39	47*	-	0.1
157 CH OF BRETHREN	1	404	482*	0.5	1.1
165 CH OF NAZARENE	1	92	167	0.2	0.4

*Total adherents estimated from known number of communicant, confirmed, full members.

—Represents a percent less than 0.1.

Percentages may not total due to rounding.

Table 3. Churches and Church Membership by State, County and Denomination: 1971

County and Denomination	Number of churches	Communicant, confirmed, full members	Total adherents: Number	Percent of total population	Percent of total adherents
193 EPISCOPAL.....	3	1,437	1,718	1.7	4.1
221 FREE METH C NA	4	107	166	0.2	0.4
226 FRIENDS-USA...	1	176	210*	0.2	0.5
281 LUTH CH AMER..	19	5,192	7,308	7.4	17.2
285 MENNONITE CH..	2	48	57*	0.1	0.1
413 S-D ADVENTISTS	1	18	21*	-	-
419 SO BAPT CONV..	1	115	137*	0.1	0.3
435 UNITARIAN-UNIV	1	130	250	0.3	0.6
443 UN C OF CHRIST	17	2,814	3,360*	3.4	7.9
449 UN METHODIST..	54	12,293	12,520	12.6	29.5
453 UN PRES CH USA	9	2,976	3,554*	3.6	8.4
CHESTER	230	61,909	138,490*	49.8	100.0
019 AMER BAPT CONV	21	6,398	7,819*	2.8	5.6
081 CATHOLIC......	28	0	60,370	21.7	43.6
121 CH GOD (ABR)..	1	12	15*	-	-
127 CH GOD (CLEVE)	2	208	254*	0.1	0.2
157 CH OF BRETHREN	5	848	1,036*	0.4	0.7
165 CH OF NAZARENE	5	690	1,449	0.5	1.0
193 EPISCOPAL.....	14	6,764	9,350	3.4	6.8
226 FRIENDS-USA...	17	2,881	3,521*	1.3	2.5
281 LUTH CH AMER..	13	6,292	9,113	3.3	6.6
283 LUTH--MO SYNOD	1	291	425	0.2	0.3
285 MENNONITE CH..	20	1,488	1,818*	0.7	1.3
335 ORTH PRESB CH.	1	164	242	0.1	0.2
349 PENT HOLINESS.	1	8	10*	-	-
353 PLY BRETHREN..	1	84	100	-	0.1
403 SALVATION ARMY	1	24	129	-	0.1
413 S-D ADVENTISTS	2	157	192*	0.1	0.1
419 SO BAPT CONV..	1	297	363*	0.1	0.3
435 UNITARIAN-UNIV	2	453	672	0.2	0.5
443 UN C OF CHRIST	12	2,723	3,328*	1.2	2.4
449 UN METHODIST..	42	14,562	16,819	6.0	12.1
453 UN PRES CH USA	40	17,565	21,465*	7.7	15.5
CLARION	92	11,522	21,611*	56.3	100.0
019 AMER BAPT CONV	4	588	711*	1.9	3.3
029 AMER LUTH CH..	1	279	474	1.2	2.2
081 CATHOLIC......	9	0	6,228	16.2	28.8
123 CH GOD (ANDER)	6	355	1,367	3.6	6.3
165 CH OF NAZARENE	3	168	465	1.2	2.2
193 EPISCOPAL.....	1	17	22	0.1	0.1
199 EVAN CONG CH..	3	327	395*	1.0	1.8
221 FREE METH C NA	2	38	50	0.1	0.2
281 LUTH CH AMER..	7	1,173	1,505	3.9	7.0
443 UN C OF CHRIST	8	944	1,142*	3.0	5.3
449 UN METHODIST..	34	4,780	5,801	15.1	26.8
453 UN PRES CH USA	14	2,853	3,451*	9.0	16.0
CLEARFIELD	163	19,970	38,980*	52.2	100.0
019 AMER BAPT CONV	3	618	755*	1.0	1.9
081 CATHOLIC......	21	0	15,207	20.4	39.0
093 CR CH (DISC)..	1	24	29*	-	0.1
123 CH GOD (ANDER)	1	76	246	0.3	0.6
127 CH GOD (CLEVE)	1	26	32*	-	0.1
157 CH OF BRETHREN	3	127	155*	0.2	0.4
165 CH OF NAZARENE	3	124	306	0.4	0.8
193 EPISCOPAL.....	5	378	639	0.9	1.6
197 EVAN CH OF NA.	2	87	106*	0.1	0.3
201 EVAN COV CH AM	1	77	94*	0.1	0.2
221 FREE METH C NA	6	76	86	0.1	0.2
226 FRIENDS-USA...	1	85	104*	0.1	0.3
281 LUTH CH AMER..	13	3,388	4,347	5.8	11.2
283 LUTH--MO SYNOD	2	186	266	0.4	0.7
313 NO AM BAPT GC.	1	91	111*	0.1	0.3
403 SALVATION ARMY	2	94	404	0.5	1.0
413 S-D ADVENTISTS	1	19	23*	-	0.1
443 UN C OF CHRIST	4	429	524*	0.7	1.3
449 UN METHODIST..	78	11,746	12,711	17.0	32.6
453 UN PRES CH USA	14	2,319	2,835*	3.8	7.3
CLINTON	68	12,628	19,789*	52.5	100.0
075 BRETHREN IN CR	1	71	85*	0.2	0.4
081 CATHOLIC......	3	0	4,997	13.2	25.3
097 CR C AND C CR.	6	2,590	3,111*	8.2	15.7
157 CH OF BRETHREN	1	95	114*	0.3	0.6
193 EPISCOPAL.....	2	321	386	1.0	2.0
201 EVAN COV CH AM	1	33	40*	0.1	0.2
221 FREE METH C NA	2	63	88	0.2	0.4
281 LUTH CH AMER..	10	1,358	2,043	5.4	10.3
403 SALVATION ARMY	1	112	505	1.3	2.6
413 S-D ADVENTISTS	1	21	25*	0.1	0.1
443 UN C OF CHRIST	4	879	1,056*	2.8	5.3
449 UN METHODIST..	33	6,421	6,541	17.3	33.1
453 UN PRES CH USA	3	664	798*	2.1	4.0
COLUMBIA	109	13,186	25,668*	46.6	100.0
019 AMER BAPT CONV	2	404	481*	0.9	1.9
081 CATHOLIC......	8	0	8,149	14.8	31.7
093 CR CH (DISC)..	3	370	441*	0.8	1.7
097 CR C AND C CR.	7	1,065	1,269*	2.3	4.9
165 CH OF NAZARENE	1	120	322	0.6	1.3
193 EPISCOPAL.....	2	408	630	1.1	2.5
226 FRIENDS-USA...	1	43	51*	0.1	0.2
281 LUTH CH AMER..	16	6,035	8,374	15.2	32.6
403 SALVATION ARMY	1	45	236	0.4	0.9
413 S-D ADVENTISTS	1	69	82*	0.1	0.3
435 UNITARIAN-UNIV	1	23	23	-	0.1
443 UN C OF CHRIST	10	2,210	2,633*	4.8	10.3
449 UN METHODIST..	51	1,255	1,620	2.9	6.3

*Total adherents estimated from known number of communicant, confirmed, full members.

County and Denomination	Number of churches	Communicant, confirmed, full members	Total adherents: Number	Percent of total population	Percent of total adherents
453 UN PRES CH USA	5	1,139	1,357*	2.5	5.3
CRAWFORD	118	18,619	37,286*	45.8	100.0
019 AMER BAPT CONV	8	1,547	1,886*	2.3	5.1
081 CATHOLIC......	13	0	12,356	15.2	33.1
097 CR C AND C CR.	3	711	867*	1.1	2.3
123 CH GOD (ANDER)	4	302	699	0.9	1.9
165 CH OF NAZARENE	4	192	506	0.6	1.4
193 EPISCOPAL.....	2	394	650	0.8	1.7
221 FREE METH C NA	4	116	160	0.2	0.4
281 LUTH CH AMER..	6	1,486	2,124	2.6	5.7
285 MENNONITE CH..	4	293	357*	0.4	1.0
349 PENT HOLINESS.	2	45	55*	0.1	0.1
403 SALVATION ARMY	2	80	378	0.5	1.0
413 S-D ADVENTISTS	1	15	18*	-	-
435 UNITARIAN-UNIV	2	215	265	0.3	0.7
443 UN C OF CHRIST	9	1,580	1,926*	2.4	5.2
449 UN METHODIST..	40	7,213	9,638	11.8	25.8
453 UN PRES CH USA	14	4,430	5,401*	6.6	14.5
CUMBERLAND	155	53,468	85,290*	53.9	100.0
019 AMER BAPT CONV	1	323	391*	0.2	0.5
075 BRETHREN IN CR	10	1,151	1,392*	0.9	1.6
081 CATHOLIC......	6	0	21,823	13.8	25.6
093 CR CH (DISC)..	1	290	351*	0.2	0.4
123 CH GOD (ANDER)	1	40	135	0.1	0.2
127 CH GOD (CLEVE)	5	234	283*	0.2	0.3
157 CH OF BRETHREN	8	1,392	1,683*	1.1	2.0
165 CH OF NAZARENE	3	264	547	0.3	0.6
193 EPISCOPAL.....	4	1,312	1,578	1.0	1.9
221 FREE METH C NA	1	15	29	-	-
281 LUTH CH AMER..	29	15,517	21,648	13.7	25.4
285 MENNONITE CH..	4	294	356*	0.2	0.4
353 PLY BRETHREN..	2	120	200	0.1	0.2
403 SALVATION ARMY	1	47	289	0.2	0.3
413 S-D ADVENTISTS	1	103	125*	0.1	0.1
419 SO BAPT CONV..	2	541	654*	0.4	0.8
435 UNITARIAN-UNIV	1	23	23	-	-
443 UN C OF CHRIST	10	2,701	3,266*	2.1	3.8
449 UN METHODIST..	54	22,651	22,718	14.4	26.6
453 UN PRES CH USA	11	6,450	7,799*	4.9	9.1
DAUPHIN	225	68,978	117,111*	52.3	100.0
019 AMER BAPT CONV	8	835	999*	0.4	0.9
075 BRETHREN IN CR	5	442	529*	0.2	0.5
081 CATHOLIC......	22	0	34,918	15.6	29.8
097 CR C AND C CR.	1	80	96*	-	0.1
123 CH GOD (ANDER)	2	125	267	0.1	0.2
127 CH GOD (CLEVE)	3	111	133*	0.1	0.1
157 CH OF BRETHREN	6	2,041	2,442*	1.1	2.1
165 CH OF NAZARENE	2	122	354	0.2	0.3
193 EPISCOPAL.....	6	1,711	2,171	1.0	1.9
199 EVAN CONG CH..	14	1,548	1,852*	0.8	1.6
226 FRIENDS-USA...	1	105	126*	0.1	0.1
281 LUTH CH AMER..	41	20,802	28,070	12.5	24.0
283 LUTH--MO SYNOD	1	189	362	0.2	0.3
285 MENNONITE CH..	6	355	425*	0.2	0.4
335 ORTH PRESB CH.	1	199	319	0.1	0.3
403 SALVATION ARMY	1	76	618	0.3	0.5
413 S-D ADVENTISTS	4	497	595*	0.3	0.5
419 SO BAPT CONV..	3	365	437*	0.2	0.4
435 UNITARIAN-UNIV	1	150	225	0.1	0.2
443 UN C OF CHRIST	17	6,228	7,453*	3.3	6.4
449 UN METHODIST..	68	25,363	25,585	11.4	21.8
453 UN PRES CH USA	12	7,634	9,135*	4.1	7.8
DELAWARE	249	87,617	372,421*	62.1	100.0
019 AMER BAPT CONV	20	5,546	6,694*	1.1	1.8
081 CATHOLIC......	52	0	263,778	44.0	70.8
093 CR CH (DISC)..	1	106	128*	-	-
097 CR C AND C CR.	1	91	110*	-	-
127 CH GOD (CLEVE)	1	35	42*	-	-
157 CH OF BRETHREN	1	157	190*	-	0.1
165 CH OF NAZARENE	3	388	957	0.2	0.3
193 EPISCOPAL.....	34	15,240	22,486	3.7	6.0
226 FRIENDS-USA...	10	2,229	2,690*	0.4	0.7
281 LUTH CH AMER..	22	11,653	15,814	2.6	4.2
283 LUTH--MO SYNOD	4	802	1,325	0.2	0.4
285 MENNONITE CH..	1	15	18*	-	-
335 ORTH PRESB CH.	1	15	33	-	-
353 PLY BRETHREN..	1	80	100	-	-
381 REF PRES-EVAN.	3	236	278	-	0.1
403 SALVATION ARMY	2	113	444	0.1	0.1
413 S-D ADVENTISTS	4	348	420*	0.1	0.1
419 SO BAPT CONV..	1	134	162*	-	-
435 UNITARIAN-UNIV	1	289	394	0.1	0.1
443 UN C OF CHRIST	4	1,157	1,397*	0.2	0.4
449 UN METHODIST..	52	27,077	28,520	4.8	7.7
453 UN PRES CH USA	30	21,906	26,441*	4.4	7.1
ELK	45	6,186	28,087*	74.4	100.0
019 AMER BAPT CONV	1	221	278*	0.7	1.0
081 CATHOLIC......	13	0	20,043	53.1	71.4
097 CR C AND C CR.	1	243	306*	0.8	1.1
165 CH OF NAZARENE	1	55	123	0.3	0.4
193 EPISCOPAL.....	2	309	361	1.0	1.3
201 EVAN COV CH AM	3	144	181*	0.5	0.6
221 FREE METH C NA	1	11	16	-	0.1
281 LUTH CH AMER..	5	1,788	2,399	6.4	8.5
403 SALVATION ARMY	1	53	183	0.5	0.7

—Represents a percent less than 0.1.

Percentages may not total due to rounding.

Table 3. Churches and Church Membership by State, County and Denomination: 1971

County and Denomination	Number of churches	Communicant, confirmed, full members	Total adherents: Number	Total adherents: Percent of total population	Total adherents: Percent of total adherents
443 UN C OF CHRIST	1	373	469*	1.2	1.7
449 UN METHODIST..	12	2,158	2,683	7.1	9.6
453 UN PRES CH USA	4	831	1,045*	2.8	3.7
ERIE	201	45,646	157,395*	59.7	100.0
019 AMER BAPT CONV	12	3,165	3,901*	1.5	2.5
081 CATHOLIC......	48	0	93,752	35.6	59.6
093 CR CH (DISC)..	1	226	279*	0.1	0.2
123 CH GOD (ANDER)	4	200	510	0.2	0.3
127 CH GOD (CLEVE)	3	276	340*	0.1	0.2
157 CH OF BRETHREN	1	178	219*	0.1	0.1
165 CH OF NAZARENE	6	517	1,252	0.5	0.8
193 EPISCOPAL.....	9	1,870	2,813	1.1	1.8
201 EVAN COV CH AM	1	110	136*	0.1	0.1
221 FREE METH C NA	5	159	209	0.1	0.1
281 LUTH CH AMER..	28	11,134	15,944	6.0	10.1
283 LUTH--MO SYNOD	4	982	1,404	0.5	0.9
285 MENNONITE CH..	1	123	152*	0.1	0.1
313 NO AM BAPT GC.	2	156	192*	0.1	0.1
315 NO AM OLD RC..	1	81	100*	-	0.1
349 PENT HOLINESS.	2	254	313*	0.1	0.2
353 PLY BRETHREN..	1	35	63	-	-
403 SALVATION ARMY	3	255	3,138	1.2	2.0
413 S-D ADVENTISTS	4	314	387*	0.1	0.2
419 SO BAPT CONV..	1	111	137*	0.1	0.1
435 UNITARIAN-UNIV	2	145	186	0.1	0.1
443 UN C OF CHRIST	3	644	794*	0.3	0.5
449 UN METHODIST..	35	13,859	17,798	6.8	11.3
453 UN PRES CH USA	24	10,852	13,376*	5.1	8.5
FAYETTE	234	34,061	99,730*	64.5	100.0
019 AMER BAPT CONV	14	2,304	2,777*	1.8	2.8
075 BRETHREN IN CR	2	15	18*	-	-
081 CATHOLIC......	47	0	57,133	36.9	57.3
093 CR CH (DISC)..	8	2,800	3,375*	2.2	3.4
097 CR C AND C CR.	9	1,193	1,438*	0.9	1.4
123 CH GOD (ANDER)	5	230	486	0.3	0.5
127 CH GOD (CLEVE)	3	213	257*	0.2	0.3
157 CH OF BRETHREN	12	1,427	1,720*	1.1	1.7
165 CH OF NAZARENE	6	473	1,025	0.7	1.0
193 EPISCOPAL.....	3	374	574	0.4	0.6
197 EVAN CH OF NA.	2	541	652*	0.4	0.7
221 FREE METH C NA	13	380	565	0.4	0.6
226 FRIENDS-USA...	1	17	20*	-	-
281 LUTH CH AMER..	7	3,223	4,438	2.9	4.5
285 MENNONITE CH..	4	196	236*	0.2	0.2
403 SALVATION ARMY	2	132	508	0.3	0.5
413 S-D ADVENTISTS	1	83	100*	0.1	0.1
443 UN C OF CHRIST	1	12	14*	-	-
449 UN METHODIST..	63	13,068	15,498	10.0	15.5
453 UN PRES CH USA	31	7,380	8,896*	5.8	8.9
FOREST	18	1,146	1,700*	34.5	100.0
029 AMER LUTH CH..	1	61	104	2.1	6.1
081 CATHOLIC......	1	0	115	2.3	6.8
123 CH GOD (ANDER)	2	140	323	6.6	19.0
221 FREE METH C NA	4	47	55	1.1	3.2
449 UN METHODIST..	7	568	704	14.3	41.4
453 UN PRES CH USA	3	330	399*	8.1	23.5
FRANKLIN	139	32,033	43,862*	43.5	100.0
019 AMER BAPT CONV	1	100	123*	0.1	0.3
075 BRETHREN IN CR	9	1,360	1,667*	1.7	3.8
081 CATHOLIC......	7	0	5,734	5.7	13.1
097 CR C AND C CR.	1	175	214*	0.2	0.5
127 CH GOD (CLEVE)	4	359	440*	0.4	1.0
157 CH OF BRETHREN	9	2,517	3,085*	3.1	7.0
193 EPISCOPAL.....	4	574	734	0.7	1.7
281 LUTH CH AMER..	21	7,010	9,581	9.5	21.8
285 MENNONITE CH..	14	1,080	1,324*	1.3	3.0
353 PLY BRETHREN..	3	185	275	0.3	0.6
403 SALVATION ARMY	1	69	233	0.2	0.5
413 S-D ADVENTISTS	2	183	224*	0.2	0.5
419 SO BAPT CONV..	1	182	223*	0.2	0.5
443 UN C OF CHRIST	16	4,184	5,127*	5.1	11.7
449 UN METHODIST..	37	11,110	11,269	11.2	25.7
453 UN PRES CH USA	9	2,945	3,609*	3.6	8.2
FULTON	43	3,658	4,414*	41.0	100.0
081 CATHOLIC......	2	0	100	0.9	2.3
127 CH GOD (CLEVE)	1	35	43*	0.4	1.0
157 CH OF BRETHREN	3	433	536*	5.0	12.1
165 CH OF NAZARENE	3	149	252	2.3	5.7
281 LUTH CH AMER..	3	495	641	5.9	14.5
285 MENNONITE CH..	2	60	74*	0.7	1.7
357 PRESB CH US...	1	91	113*	1.0	2.6
443 UN C OF CHRIST	5	415	514*	4.8	11.6
449 UN METHODIST..	20	1,693	1,786	16.6	40.5
453 UN PRES CH USA	3	287	355*	3.3	8.0
GREENE	82	10,609	17,352*	48.1	100.0
019 AMER BAPT CONV	9	1,538	1,831*	5.1	10.6
081 CATHOLIC......	8	0	4,745	13.1	27.3
093 CR CH (DISC)..	3	248	295*	0.8	1.7
097 CR C AND C CR.	4	915	1,089*	3.0	6.3
127 CH GOD (CLEVE)	2	262	312*	0.9	1.8
165 CH OF NAZARENE	2	321	682	1.9	3.9
193 EPISCOPAL.....	1	46	86	0.2	0.5
221 FREE METH C NA	1	50	62	0.2	0.4
281 LUTH CH AMER..	1	176	201	0.6	1.2
419 SO BAPT CONV..	1	88	105*	0.3	0.6
449 UN METHODIST..	41	4,498	5,007	13.9	28.9
453 UN PRES CH USA	9	2,467	2,937*	8.1	16.9
HUNTINGDON	117	14,087	19,189*	49.1	100.0
019 AMER BAPT CONV	6	521	631*	1.6	3.3
075 BRETHREN IN CR	4	47	57*	0.1	0.3
081 CATHOLIC......	5	0	2,333	6.0	12.2
123 CH GOD (ANDER)	1	92	337	0.9	1.8
127 CH GOD (CLEVE)	3	118	143*	0.4	0.7
157 CH OF BRETHREN	8	1,247	1,510*	3.9	7.9
165 CH OF NAZARENE	4	293	591	1.5	3.1
193 EPISCOPAL.....	2	1,009	1,361	3.5	7.1
197 EVAN CH OF NA.	1	62	75*	0.2	0.4
221 FREE METH C NA	1	27	36	0.1	0.2
281 LUTH CH AMER..	8	1,223	1,614	4.1	8.4
349 PENT HOLINESS.	1	32	39*	0.1	0.2
403 SALVATION ARMY	1	44	268	0.7	1.4
443 UN C OF CHRIST	9	1,019	1,234*	3.2	6.4
449 UN METHODIST..	49	6,283	6,453	16.5	33.6
453 UN PRES CH USA	14	2,070	2,507*	6.4	13.1
INDIANA	143	20,093	45,885*	57.8	100.0
019 AMER BAPT CONV	7	587	706*	0.9	1.5
081 CATHOLIC......	23	0	20,490	25.8	44.7
093 CR CH (DISC)..	2	232	279*	0.4	0.6
097 CR C AND C CR.	5	80	96*	0.1	0.2
123 CH GOD (ANDER)	4	129	308	0.4	0.7
157 CH OF BRETHREN	5	473	569*	0.7	1.2
165 CH OF NAZARENE	2	244	466	0.6	1.0
193 EPISCOPAL.....	2	596	885	1.1	1.9
221 FREE METH C NA	4	121	168	0.2	0.4
281 LUTH CH AMER..	14	2,847	3,767	4.7	8.2
349 PENT HOLINESS.	1	20	24*	-	0.1
353 PLY BRETHREN..	1	30	50	0.1	0.1
403 SALVATION ARMY	1	84	314	0.4	0.7
413 S-D ADVENTISTS	1	83	100*	0.1	0.2
435 UNITARIAN-UNIV	1	26	41	0.1	0.1
449 UN METHODIST..	41	6,756	8,253	10.4	18.0
453 UN PRES CH USA	29	7,785	9,369*	11.8	20.4
JEFFERSON	116	14,050	32,485*	74.3	100.0
019 AMER BAPT CONV	4	940	1,125*	2.6	3.5
081 CATHOLIC......	15	0	14,440	33.0	44.5
097 CR C AND C CR.	1	75	90*	0.2	0.3
123 CH GOD (ANDER)	2	261	632	1.4	1.9
165 CH OF NAZARENE	3	123	311	0.7	1.0
193 EPISCOPAL.....	2	117	181	0.4	0.6
221 FREE METH C NA	3	55	65	0.1	0.2
281 LUTH CH AMER..	9	1,057	1,459	3.3	4.5
283 LUTH--MO SYNOD	1	75	106	0.2	0.3
285 MENNONITE CH..	1	6	7*	-	-
353 PLY BRETHREN..	1	30	[illegible]	0.1	0.2
403 SALVATION ARMY	1	53	20[illegible]	0.5	0.6
413 S-D ADVENTISTS	1	31	3[illegible]	0.1	0.1
443 UN C OF CHRIST	3	527	631*	1.4	1.9
449 UN METHODIST..	51	7,[illegible]08	9,209	21.1	28.3
453 UN PRES CH USA	18	3,[illegible]92	3,939*	9.0	12.1
JUNIATA	57	8,[illegible]	10,088*	60.4	100.0
075 BRETHREN IN CR	1	69	85*	0.5	0.8
081 CATHOLIC......	1	0	120	0.7	1.2
157 CH OF BRETHREN	3	342	419*	2.5	4.2
281 LUTH CH AMER..	10	2,709	3,710	22.2	36.8
285 MENNONITE CH..	5	344	422*	2.5	4.2
413 S-D ADVENTISTS	1	50	61*	0.4	0.6
443 UN C OF CHRIST	2	147	180*	1.1	1.8
449 UN METHODIST..	27	3,684	3,749	22.4	37.2
453 UN PRES CH USA	7	1,095	1,342*	8.0	13.3
LACKAWANNA	194	31,198	167,689*	71.6	100.0
019 AMER BAPT CONV	21	4,232	4,980*	2.1	3.0
081 CATHOLIC......	83	0	130,220	55.6	77.7
093 CR CH (DISC)..	2	230	271*	0.1	0.2
123 CH GOD (ANDER)	1	41	131	0.1	0.1
193 EPISCOPAL.....	7	2,132	2,802	1.2	1.7
221 FREE METH C NA	1	36	51	-	-
281 LUTH CH AMER..	7	1,889	2,456	1.0	1.5
283 LUTH--MO SYNOD	3	858	1,138	0.5	0.7
403 SALVATION ARMY	1	99	358	0.2	0.2
413 S-D ADVENTISTS	1	72	85*	-	0.1
435 UNITARIAN-UNIV	2	40	40	-	-
443 UN C OF CHRIST	9	2,191	2,578*	1.1	1.5
449 UN METHODIST..	39	12,495	14,480	6.2	8.6
453 UN PRES CH USA	17	6,883	8,099*	3.5	4.8
LANCASTER	391	112,991	171,841*	53.8	100.0
019 AMER BAPT CONV	2	729	893*	0.3	0.5
075 BRETHREN IN CR	15	1,605	1,967*	0.6	1.1
081 CATHOLIC......	20	0	33,775	10.6	19.7
097 CR C AND C CR.	1	550	674*	0.2	0.4
127 CH GOD (CLEVE)	4	171	210*	0.1	0.1
157 CH OF BRETHREN	20	8,061	9,879*	3.1	5.7
165 CH OF NAZARENE	2	329	884	0.3	0.5
193 EPISCOPAL.....	10	3,184	4,629	1.4	2.7
199 EVAN CONG CH..	25	5,879	7,205*	2.3	4.2
226 FRIENDS-USA...	2	227	278*	0.1	0.2
281 LUTH CH AMER..	47	24,139	33,400	10.4	19.4

*Total adherents estimated from known number of communicant, confirmed, full members.

—Represents a percent less than 0.1.

Percentages may not total due to rounding.

Table 3. Churches and Church Membership by State, County and Denomination: 1971

County and Denomination	Number of churches	Communicant, confirmed, full members	Total adherents: Number	Total adherents: Percent of total population	Total adherents: Percent of total adherents
283 LUTH--MO SYNOD	2	450	597	0.2	0.3
285 MENNONITE CH..	94	14,002	17,159*	5.4	10.0
287 MENN GEN CONF.	3	425	521*	0.2	0.3
293 MORAV CH-NORTH	2	1,372	1,776	0.6	1.0
335 ORTH PRESB CH.	1	67	85	-	-
353 PLY BRETHREN..	1	50	80	-	-
381 REF PRES-EVAN.	2	345	440	0.1	0.3
403 SALVATION ARMY	1	78	344	0.1	0.2
413 S-D ADVENTISTS	2	133	163*	0.1	0.1
419 SO BAPT CONV..	6	909	1,114*	0.3	0.6
435 UNITARIAN-UNIV	1	413	533	0.2	0.3
443 UN C OF CHRIST	36	14,083	17,259*	5.4	10.0
449 UN METHODIST..	76	27,191	27,438	8.6	16.0
453 UN PRES CH USA	16	8,599	10,538*	3.3	6.1
LAWRENCE	116	27,867	71,357*	66.5	100.0
019 AMER BAPT CONV	6	927	1,105*	1.0	1.5
081 CATHOLIC......	18	0	37,214	34.7	52.2
093 CR CH (DISC)..	2	338	403*	0.4	0.6
097 CR C AND C CR.	7	1,362	1,623*	1.5	2.3
123 CH GOD (ANDER)	2	182	517	0.5	0.7
127 CH GOD (CLEVE)	1	63	75*	0.1	0.1
165 CH OF NAZARENE	2	82	278	0.3	0.4
175 CONG CR CH....	1	50	60*	0.1	0.1
193 EPISCOPAL.....	1	1,127	1,233	1.1	1.7
201 EVAN COV CH AM	1	76	91*	0.1	0.1
221 FREE METH C NA	5	189	233	0.2	0.3
281 LUTH CH AMER..	4	1,583	2,068	1.9	2.9
283 LUTH--MO SYNOD	1	219	276	0.3	0.4
285 MENNONITE CH..	1	55	66*	0.1	0.1
335 ORTH PRESB CH.	1	75	129	0.1	0.2
349 PENT HOLINESS.	1	12	14*	-	-
381 REF PRES-EVAN.	2	175	197	0.2	0.3
403 SALVATION ARMY	1	50	182	0.2	0.3
413 S-D ADVENTISTS	1	37	44*	-	0.1
443 UN C OF CHRIST	1	125	149*	0.1	0.2
449 UN METHODIST..	19	5,623	6,909	6.4	9.7
453 UN PRES CH USA	38	15,517	18,491*	17.2	25.9
LEBANON	134	38,113	60,524*	60.7	100.0
075 BRETHREN IN CR	2	396	481*	0.5	0.8
081 CATHOLIC......	9	0	13,839	13.9	22.9
127 CH GOD (CLEVE)	1	180	219*	0.2	0.4
157 CH OF BRETHREN	8	3,373	4,101*	4.1	6.8
193 EPISCOPAL.....	1	490	684	0.7	1.1
199 EVAN CONG CH..	12	2,341	2,846*	2.9	4.7
281 LUTH CH AMER..	21	9,141	13,518	13.6	22.3
285 MENNONITE CH..	12	584	710*	0.7	1.2
293 MORAV CH-NORTH	1	276	373	0.4	0.6
353 PLY BRETHREN..	1	50	60	0.1	0.1
403 SALVATION ARMY	1	28	180	0.2	0.3
413 S-D ADVENTISTS	1	73	89*	0.1	0.1
443 UN C OF CHRIST	24	9,031	10,979*	11.0	18.1
449 UN METHODIST..	38	11,357	11,481	11.5	19.0
453 UN PRES CH USA	2	793	964*	1.0	1.6
LEHIGH	201	79,806	165,985*	65.0	100.0
019 AMER BAPT CONV	2	519	619*	0.2	0.4
081 CATHOLIC......	26	0	62,800	24.6	37.8
097 CR C AND C CR.	1	155	185*	0.1	0.1
123 CH GOD (ANDER)	1	57	112	-	0.1
165 CH OF NAZARENE	3	435	714	0.3	0.4
193 EPISCOPAL.....	7	1,963	3,078	1.2	1.9
199 EVAN CONG CH..	13	3,546	4,231*	1.7	2.5
221 FREE METH C NA	2	20	32	-	-
281 LUTH CH AMER..	59	34,769	48,284	18.9	29.1
285 MENNONITE CH..	1	53	63*	-	-
287 MENN GEN CONF.	3	312	372*	0.1	0.2
293 MORAV CH-NORTH	7	2,396	3,098	1.2	1.9
353 PLY BRETHREN..	1	80	100	-	0.1
403 SALVATION ARMY	1	49	613	0.2	0.4
413 S-D ADVENTISTS	5	411	490*	0.2	0.3
443 UN C OF CHRIST	52	25,176	30,043*	11.8	18.1
449 UN METHODIST..	11	3,438	3,482	1.4	2.1
453 UN PRES CH USA	6	6,427	7,669*	3.0	4.6
LUZERNE	334	50,993	256,327*	74.9	100.0
019 AMER BAPT CONV	16	2,467	2,897*	0.8	1.1
075 BRETHREN IN CR	1	4	5*	-	-
081 CATHOLIC......	134	0	193,597	56.6	75.5
093 CR CH (DISC)..	2	385	452*	0.1	0.2
097 CR C AND C CR.	4	1,180	1,386*	0.4	0.5
193 EPISCOPAL.....	13	3,153	4,316	1.3	1.7
199 EVAN CONG CH..	1	89	105*	-	-
221 FREE METH C NA	5	131	177	0.1	0.1
281 LUTH CH AMER..	26	9,654	12,595	3.7	4.9
283 LUTH--MO SYNOD	4	1,023	1,302	0.4	0.5
403 SALVATION ARMY	3	216	1,221	0.4	0.5
413 S-D ADVENTISTS	2	64	75*	-	-
419 SO BAPT CONV..	2	115	135*	-	0.1
443 UN C OF CHRIST	22	4,253	4,994*	1.5	1.9
449 UN METHODIST..	77	20,613	24,092	7.0	9.4
453 UN PRES CH USA	22	7,646	8,978*	2.6	3.5
LYCOMING	174	38,022	64,282*	56.7	100.0
019 AMER BAPT CONV	13	2,891	3,520*	3.1	5.5
075 BRETHREN IN CR	1	17	21*	-	-
081 CATHOLIC......	13	0	17,913	15.8	27.9
093 CR CH (DISC)..	1	225	274*	0.2	0.4
097 CR C AND C CR.	4	657	800*	0.7	1.2
123 CH GOD (ANDER)	1	150	300	0.3	0.5
127 CH GOD (CLEVE)	1	32	39*	-	0.1
165 CH OF NAZARENE	4	184	477	0.4	0.7
193 EPISCOPAL.....	8	1,786	2,531	2.2	3.9
221 FREE METH C NA	2	77	84	0.1	0.1
226 FRIENDS-USA...	3	192	234*	0.2	0.4
281 LUTH CH AMER..	25	10,390	15,022	13.3	23.4
285 MENNONITE CH..	1	15	18*	-	-
403 SALVATION ARMY	1	75	516	0.5	0.8
413 S-D ADVENTISTS	2	180	219*	0.2	0.3
443 UN C OF CHRIST	2	737	897*	0.8	1.4
449 UN METHODIST..	81	17,361	17,700	15.6	27.5
453 UN PRES CH USA	11	3,053	3,717*	3.3	5.8
MC KEAN	78	12,696	29,414*	56.7	100.0
019 AMER BAPT CONV	3	927	1,131*	2.2	3.8
081 CATHOLIC......	13	0	12,597	24.3	42.8
123 CH GOD (ANDER)	2	101	284	0.5	1.0
165 CH OF NAZARENE	4	250	798	1.5	2.7
193 EPISCOPAL.....	6	772	1,132	2.2	3.8
197 EVAN CH OF NA.	5	285	348*	0.7	1.2
201 EVAN COV CH AM	4	159	194*	0.4	0.7
221 FREE METH C NA	7	202	292	0.6	1.0
281 LUTH CH AMER..	8	2,384	3,234	6.2	11.0
283 LUTH--MO SYNOD	1	161	203	0.4	0.7
285 MENNONITE CH..	1	35	43*	0.1	0.1
403 SALVATION ARMY	1	65	179	0.3	0.6
413 S-D ADVENTISTS	4	179	218*	0.4	0.7
419 SO BAPT CONV..	1	440	537*	1.0	1.8
449 UN METHODIST..	14	4,797	5,858	11.3	19.9
453 UN PRES CH USA	4	1,939	2,366*	4.6	8.0
MERCER	139	39,418	81,190*	63.8	100.0
019 AMER BAPT CONV	8	2,181	2,628*	2.1	3.2
029 AMER LUTH CH..	1	368	533	0.4	0.7
081 CATHOLIC......	20	0	30,100	23.7	37.1
093 CR CH (DISC)..	3	843	1,016*	0.8	1.3
097 CR C AND C CR.	3	355	428*	0.3	0.5
123 CH GOD (ANDER)	6	494	1,261	1.0	1.6
165 CH OF NAZARENE	5	406	949	0.7	1.2
193 EPISCOPAL.....	4	1,599	2,766	2.2	3.4
221 FREE METH C NA	2	104	147	0.1	0.2
281 LUTH CH AMER..	5	2,910	3,743	2.9	4.6
283 LUTH--MO SYNOD	1	358	425	0.3	0.5
335 ORTH PRESB CH.	1	83	129	0.1	0.2
349 PENT HOLINESS.	4	277	334*	0.3	0.4
403 SALVATION ARMY	2	127	843	0.7	1.0
413 S-D ADVENTISTS	1	0	0*	-	-
443 UN C OF CHRIST	6	2,837	3,418*	2.7	4.2
449 UN METHODIST..	33	12,016	15,049	11.8	18.5
453 UN PRES CH USA	34	14,460	17,421*	13.7	21.5
MIFFLIN	76	17,791	23,604*	52.1	100.0
019 AMER BAPT CONV	2	510	629*	1.4	2.7
075 BRETHREN IN CR	1	33	41*	0.1	0.2
081 CATHOLIC......	3	0	2,135	4.7	9.0
157 CH OF BRETHREN	6	1,169	1,442*	3.2	6.1
165 CH OF NAZARENE	1	29	171	0.4	0.7
175 CONG CR CH....	1	135	167*	0.4	0.7
193 EPISCOPAL.....	2	490	602	1.3	2.6
281 LUTH CH AMER..	10	3,507	5,238	11.6	22.2
285 MENNONITE CH..	7	1,308	1,614*	3.6	6.8
353 PLY BRETHREN..	1	20	40	0.1	0.2
403 SALVATION ARMY	1	74	295	0.7	1.2
413 S-D ADVENTISTS	1	40	49*	0.1	0.2
419 SO BAPT CONV..	1	41	51*	0.1	0.2
443 UN C OF CHRIST	2	665	820*	1.8	3.5
449 UN METHODIST..	29	8,081	8,226	18.2	34.9
453 UN PRES CH USA	8	1,689	2,084*	4.6	8.8
MONROE	74	14,432	24,952*	54.9	100.0
081 CATHOLIC......	14	0	7,718	17.0	30.9
193 EPISCOPAL.....	2	461	586	1.3	2.3
281 LUTH CH AMER..	12	3,777	5,214	11.5	20.9
283 LUTH--MO SYNOD	1	125	171	0.4	0.7
293 MORAV CH-NORTH	1	160	245	0.5	1.0
403 SALVATION ARMY	1	90	551	1.2	2.2
413 S-D ADVENTISTS	1	137	163*	0.4	0.7
435 UNITARIAN-UNIV	1	16	30	0.1	0.1
443 UN C OF CHRIST	9	1,443	1,719*	3.8	6.9
449 UN METHODIST..	27	6,922	7,006	15.4	28.1
453 UN PRES CH USA	5	1,301	1,549*	3.4	6.2
MONTGOMERY	376	141,659	386,937*	62.0	100.0
019 AMER BAPT CONV	30	9,343	11,290*	1.8	2.9
029 AMER LUTH CH..	1	189	280	-	0.1
075 BRETHREN IN CR	3	236	285*	-	0.1
081 CATHOLIC......	60	0	207,461	33.3	53.6
123 CH GOD (ANDER)	2	142	374	0.1	0.1
127 CH GOD (CLEVE)	1	49	59*	-	-
157 CH OF BRETHREN	10	1,695	2,048*	0.3	0.5
165 CH OF NAZARENE	6	637	1,563	0.3	0.4
193 EPISCOPAL.....	31	16,696	22,200	3.6	5.7
199 EVAN CONG CH..	8	1,253	1,514*	0.2	0.4
221 FREE METH C NA	3	110	161	-	-
226 FRIENDS-USA...	11	2,510	3,033*	0.5	0.8
281 LUTH CH AMER..	50	37,744	52,928	8.5	13.7
283 LUTH--MO SYNOD	2	448	600	0.1	0.2
285 MENNONITE CH..	21	3,161	3,820*	0.6	1.0
287 MENN GEN CONF.	6	1,611	1,947*	0.3	0.5

*Total adherents estimated from known number of communicant, confirmed, full members.

—Represents a percent less than 0.1.

Percentages may not total due to rounding.

Table 3. Churches and Church Membership by State, County and Denomination: 1971

County and Denomination	Number of churches	Communicant, confirmed, full members	Total adherents: Number	Percent of total population	Percent of total adherents
335 ORTH PRESB CH.	2	188	243	-	0.1
353 PLY BRETHREN..	1	80	100	-	-
381 REF PRES-EVAN.	4	788	1,292	C.2	0.3
403 SALVATION ARMY	2	121	578	0.1	0.1
413 S-D ADVENTISTS	11	2,397	2,896*	0.5	0.7
419 SO BAPT CONV..	2	315	381*	0.1	0.1
435 UNITARIAN-UNIV	2	84	134	-	-
443 UN C OF CHRIST	39	16,989	20,529*	3.3	5.3
449 UN METHODIST..	34	17,724	18,414	3.0	4.8
453 UN PRES CH USA	33	27,138	32,793*	5.3	8.5
469 WISC EVAN LUTH	1	11	14	-	-
MONTOUR	31	6,297	11,445*	69.3	100.0
019 AMER BAPT CONV	2	120	142*	0.9	1.2
081 CATHOLIC......	5	0	3,645	22.1	31.8
193 EPISCOPAL.....	1	178	230	1.4	2.0
281 LUTH CH AMER..	9	2,512	3,507	21.2	30.6
285 MENNONITE CH..	2	67	79*	0.5	0.7
413 S-D ADVENTISTS	1	81	96*	0.6	0.8
443 UN C OF CHRIST	4	1,507	1,783*	10.8	15.6
449 UN METHODIST..	4	1,115	1,115	6.8	9.7
453 UN PRES CH USA	3	717	848*	5.1	7.4
NORTHAMPTON	188	65,728	151,073*	70.5	100.0
019 AMER BAPT CONV	4	959	1,143*	0.5	0.8
081 CATHOLIC......	32	0	67,469	31.5	44.7
165 CH OF NAZARENE	3	181	512	0.2	0.3
193 EPISCOPAL.....	5	2,792	3,997	1.9	2.6
199 EVAN CONG CH..	6	1,673	1,994*	0.9	1.3
226 FRIENDS-USA...	1	144	172*	0.1	0.1
281 LUTH CH AMER..	46	25,734	34,841	16.3	23.1
283 LUTH--MO SYNOD	2	574	896	0.4	0.6
285 MENNONITE CH..	3	95	113*	0.1	0.1
293 MORAV CH-NORTH	9	4,323	5,511	2.6	3.6
313 NO AM BAPT GC.	1	238	284*	0.1	0.2
403 SALVATION ARMY	3	127	1,039	0.5	0.7
413 S-D ADVENTISTS	1	80	95*	-	0.1
419 SO BAPT CONV..	1	117	139*	0.1	0.1
435 UNITARIAN-UNIV	1	210	290	0.1	0.2
443 UN C OF CHRIST	37	17,669	21,056*	9.8	13.9
449 UN METHODIST..	24	7,579	7,669	3.6	5.1
453 UN PRES CH USA	9	3,233	3,853*	1.8	2.6
NORTHUMBERLAND	158	32,462	69,894*	70.5	100.0
019 AMER BAPT CONV	7	698	831*	0.8	1.2
081 CATHOLIC......	27	0	30,131	30.4	43.1
193 EPISCOPAL.....	6	563	797	0.8	1.1
199 EVAN CONG CH..	5	1,042	1,240*	1.3	1.8
281 LUTH CH AMER..	35	12,347	16,875	17.0	24.1
285 MENNONITE CH..	2	95	113*	0.1	0.2
353 PLY BRETHREN..	1	34	60	0.1	0.1
403 SALVATION ARMY	3	147	736	0.7	1.1
413 S-D ADVENTISTS	1	31	37*	-	0.1
443 UN C OF CHRIST	26	5,349	6,367*	6.4	9.1
449 UN METHODIST..	36	9,956	10,088	10.2	14.4
453 UN PRES CH USA	9	2,200	2,619*	2.6	3.7
PERRY	72	10,997	14,280*	49.9	100.0
075 BRETHREN IN CR	3	62	75*	0.3	0.5
081 CATHOLIC......	3	0	1,178	4.1	8.2
127 CH GOD (CLEVE)	1	45	55*	0.2	0.4
157 CH OF BRETHREN	2	227	276*	1.0	1.9
193 EPISCOPAL.....	1	76	96	0.3	0.7
281 LUTH CH AMER..	15	3,402	4,784	16.7	33.5
413 S-D ADVENTISTS	1	52	63*	0.2	0.4
443 UN C OF CHRIST	11	1,356	1,648*	5.8	11.5
449 UN METHODIST..	30	4,863	4,994	17.5	35.0
453 UN PRES CH USA	5	914	1,111*	3.9	7.8
PHILADELPHIA	642	132,746	855,142*	43.9	100.0
019 AMER BAPT CONV	65	9,553	11,511*	0.6	1.3
029 AMER LUTH CH..	2	710	1,121	0.1	0.1
081 CATHOLIC......	163	0	689,628	35.4	80.6
093 CR CH (DISC)..	3	453	546*	-	0.1
105 CHRISTIAN REF.	1	94	165	-	-
123 CH GOD (ANDER)	6	465	817	-	0.1
127 CH GOD (CLEVE)	3	120	145*	-	-
157 CH OF BRETHREN	2	160	193*	-	-
165 CH OF NAZARENE	3	237	343	-	-
175 CONG CR CH....	1	50	60*	-	-
193 EPISCOPAL.....	76	26,325	36,620	1.9	4.3
226 FRIENDS-USA...	7	1,807	2,177*	0.1	0.3
281 LUTH CH AMER..	62	25,592	35,611	1.8	4.2
283 LUTH--MO SYNOD	8	1,862	3,031	0.2	0.4
285 MENNONITE CH..	3	91	110*	-	-
287 MENN GEN CONF.	2	60	72*	-	-
293 MORAV CH-NORTH	2	288	341	-	-
313 NO AM BAPT GC.	2	402	484*	-	0.1
315 NO AM OLD RC..	2	97	117*	-	-
335 ORTH PRESB CH.	2	22	30	-	-
353 PLY BRETHREN..	11	723	1,007	0.1	0.1
371 REF CH IN AM..	1	300	338	-	-
381 REF PRES-EVAN.	2	228	330	-	-
413 S-D ADVENTISTS	4	592	713*	-	0.1
419 SO BAPT CONV..	2	67	81*	-	-
435 UNITARIAN-UNIV	3	996	1,219	0.1	0.1
443 UN C OF CHRIST	24	5,159	6,216*	0.3	0.7
449 UN METHODIST..	97	29,563	29,907	1.5	3.5
453 UN PRES CH USA	83	26,730	32,209*	1.7	3.8

County and Denomination	Number of churches	Communicant, confirmed, full members	Total adherents: Number	Percent of total population	Percent of total adherents
PIKE	19	1,980	4,128*	34.9	100.0
029 AMER LUTH CH..	1	44	44	0.4	1.1
081 CATHOLIC......	5	0	1,719	14.5	41.6
193 EPISCOPAL.....	1	175	225	1.9	5.5
281 LUTH CH AMER..	3	246	327	2.8	7.9
371 REF CH IN AM..	1	110	174	1.5	4.2
443 UN C OF CHRIST	1	217	257*	2.2	6.2
449 UN METHODIST..	6	998	1,157	9.8	28.0
453 UN PRES CH USA	1	190	225*	1.9	5.5
POTTER	39	3,216	5,360*	32.7	100.0
019 AMER BAPT CONV	4	390	482*	2.9	9.0
081 CATHOLIC......	6	0	1,609	9.8	30.0
193 EPISCOPAL.....	2	145	199	1.2	3.7
221 FREE METH C NA	4	89	116	0.7	2.2
281 LUTH CH AMER..	3	311	456	2.8	8.5
285 MENNONITE CH..	1	27	33*	0.2	0.6
413 S-D ADVENTISTS	3	111	137*	0.8	2.6
415 S-D BAPTIST GC	1	58	72*	0.4	1.3
449 UN METHODIST..	13	1,713	1,796	11.0	33.5
453 UN PRES CH USA	2	372	460*	2.8	8.6
SCHUYLKILL	280	46,020	131,262*	82.0	100.0
019 AMER BAPT CONV	7	584	688*	0.4	0.5
075 BRETHREN IN CR	2	65	77*	-	0.1
081 CATHOLIC......	80	0	74,237	46.4	56.6
157 CH OF BRETHREN	1	358	422*	0.3	0.3
165 CH OF NAZARENE	3	142	307	0.2	0.2
175 CONG CR CH....	1	50	59*	-	-
193 EPISCOPAL.....	4	939	1,320	0.8	1.0
199 EVAN CONG CH..	16	2,974	3,502*	2.2	2.7
281 LUTH CH AMER..	49	17,467	24,028	15.0	18.3
285 MENNONITE CH..	6	156	184*	0.1	0.1
353 PLY BRETHREN..	1	50	70	-	0.1
403 SALVATION ARMY	2	202	567	0.4	0.4
413 S-D ADVENTISTS	2	59	69*	-	0.1
443 UN C OF CHRIST	51	13,416	15,800*	9.9	12.0
449 UN METHODIST..	49	8,505	8,692	5.4	6.6
453 UN PRES CH USA	6	1,053	1,240*	0.8	0.9
SNYDER	75	11,957	16,191*	55.3	100.0
081 CATHOLIC......	1	0	1,251	4.3	7.7
157 CH OF BRETHREN	1	118	143*	0.5	0.9
165 CH OF NAZARENE	1	70	265	0.9	1.6
193 EPISCOPAL.....	1	60	80	0.3	0.5
281 LUTH CH AMER..	19	4,894	7,043	24.1	43.5
285 MENNONITE CH..	10	339	410*	1.4	2.5
443 UN C OF CHRIST	13	2,510	3,033*	10.4	18.7
449 UN METHODIST..	29	3,966	3,966	13.6	24.5
SOMERSET	182	28,742	50,783*	66.8	100.0
019 AMER BAPT CONV	2	187	225*	0.3	0.4
081 CATHOLIC......	23	0	14,571	19.2	28.7
093 CR CH (DISC)..	2	152	183*	0.2	0.4
097 CR C AND C CR.	5	1,017	1,224*	1.6	2.4
123 CH GOD (ANDER)	1	17	51	0.1	0.1
127 CH GOD (CLEVE)	7	637	767*	1.0	1.5
157 CH OF BRETHREN	23	4,829	5,812*	7.6	11.4
165 CH OF NAZARENE	5	330	722	0.9	1.4
193 EPISCOPAL.....	1	146	197	0.3	0.4
281 LUTH CH AMER..	42	10,535	14,070	18.5	27.7
283 LUTH--MO SYNOD	2	112	140	0.2	0.3
285 MENNONITE CH..	8	934	1,124*	1.5	2.2
413 S-D ADVENTISTS	1	31	37*	-	0.1
443 UN C OF CHRIST	19	3,546	4,267*	5.6	8.4
449 UN METHODIST..	38	5,566	6,547	8.6	12.9
453 UN PRES CH USA	3	703	846*	1.1	1.7
SULLIVAN	21	1,238	3,073*	51.6	100.0
081 CATHOLIC......	6	0	1,648	27.6	53.6
281 LUTH CH AMER..	2	301	392	6.6	12.8
285 MENNONITE CH..	2	47	57*	1.0	1.9
443 UN C OF CHRIST	2	185	224*	3.8	7.3
449 UN METHODIST..	9	705	752	12.6	24.5
SUSQUEHANNA	73	6,902	16,875*	49.1	100.0
019 AMER BAPT CONV	5	554	685*	2.0	4.1
081 CATHOLIC......	18	C	8,207	23.9	48.6
193 EPISCOPAL.....	3	294	434	1.3	2.6
283 LUTH--MO SYNOD	1	182	235	0.7	1.4
285 MENNONITE CH..	1	44	54*	0.2	0.3
413 S-D ADVENTISTS	1	58	72*	0.2	0.4
435 UNITARIAN-UNIV	1	95	125	0.4	0.7
443 UN C OF CHRIST	1	222	274*	0.8	1.6
449 UN METHODIST..	33	4,486	5,594	16.3	33.1
453 UN PRES CH USA	9	967	1,195*	3.5	7.1
TIOGA	92	9,301	13,815*	34.8	100.0
019 AMER BAPT CONV	10	1,321	1,624*	4.1	11.8
075 BRETHREN IN CR	1	22	27*	C.1	0.2
081 CATHOLIC......	10	0	2,943	7.4	21.3
093 CR CH (DISC)..	5	520	639*	1.6	4.6
193 EPISCOPAL.....	7	696	1,067	2.7	7.7
221 FREE METH C NA	2	29	48	0.1	0.3
281 LUTH CH AMER..	5	399	577	1.5	4.2
283 LUTH--MO SYNOD	1	189	270	0.7	2.0
285 MENNONITE CH..	2	58	71*	0.2	0.5

*Total adherents estimated from known number of communicant, confirmed, full members.

—Represents a percent less than 0.1.

Percentages may not total due to rounding.

Table 3. Churches and Church Membership by State, County and Denomination: 1971

County and Denomination	Number of churches	Communicant, confirmed, full members	Total adherents: Number	Total adherents: Percent of total population	Total adherents: Percent of total adherents
413 S-D ADVENTISTS	3	170	209*	0.5	1.5
443 UN C OF CHRIST	1	155	191*	0.5	1.4
449 UN METHODIST..	37	4,583	4,724	11.9	34.2
453 UN PRES CH USA	8	1,159	1,425*	3.6	10.3
UNION	58	10,625	14,929*	52.2	100.0
019 AMER BAPT CONV	3	378	448*	1.6	3.0
081 CATHOLIC......	1	0	1,896	6.6	12.7
157 CH OF BRETHREN	1	172	204*	0.7	1.4
165 CH OF NAZARENE	3	397	905	3.2	6.1
193 EPISCOPAL.....	1	202	290	1.0	1.9
226 FRIENDS-USA...	1	28	33*	0.1	0.2
281 LUTH CH AMER..	10	3,634	4,785	16.7	32.1
285 MENNONITE CH..	2	110	130*	0.5	0.9
335 ORTH PRESB CH.	1	14	14	-	0.1
353 PLY BRETHREN..	1	30	40	0.1	0.3
435 UNITARIAN-UNIV	1	14	26	0.1	0.2
443 UN C OF CHRIST	9	1,787	2,117*	7.4	14.2
449 UN METHODIST..	20	3,225	3,290	11.5	22.0
453 UN PRES CH USA	4	634	751*	2.6	5.0
VENANGO	104	17,774	34,658*	55.6	100.0
019 AMER BAPT CONV	3	501	605*	1.0	1.7
029 AMER LUTH CH..	2	971	1,543	2.5	4.5
081 CATHOLIC......	8	0	10,519	16.9	30.4
093 CR CH (DISC)..	1	51	62*	0.1	0.2
123 CH GOD (ANDER)	4	324	856	1.4	2.5
165 CH OF NAZARENE	3	369	885	1.4	2.6
193 EPISCOPAL.....	1	312	415	0.7	1.2
199 EVAN CONG CH..	1	44	53*	0.1	0.2
221 FREE METH C NA	9	315	372	0.6	1.1
281 LUTH CH AMER..	4	561	824	1.3	2.4
283 LUTH--MO SYNOD	1	388	495	0.8	1.4
381 REF PRES-EVAN.	1	86	120	0.2	0.3
403 SALVATION ARMY	2	171	599	1.0	1.7
413 S-D ADVENTISTS	2	83	100*	0.2	0.3
435 UNITARIAN-UNIV	1	14	14	-	-
443 UN C OF CHRIST	1	37	45*	0.1	0.1
449 UN METHODIST..	42	9,527	12,299	19.7	35.5
453 UN PRES CH USA	18	4,020	4,852*	7.8	14.0
WARREN	61	11,386	23,955*	50.2	100.0
019 AMER BAPT CONV	1	381	462*	1.0	1.9
081 CATHOLIC......	8	0	8,896	18.7	37.1
123 CH GOD (ANDER)	1	116	299	0.6	1.2
127 CH GOD (CLEVE)	1	26	32*	0.1	0.1
165 CH OF NAZARENE	1	317	682	1.4	2.8
175 CONG CR CH....	1	125	152*	0.3	0.6
193 EPISCOPAL.....	1	501	624	1.3	2.6
197 EVAN CH OF NA.	1	63	76*	0.2	0.3
201 EVAN COV CH AM	4	209	253*	0.5	1.1
221 FREE METH C NA	9	170	226	0.5	0.9
281 LUTH CH AMER..	6	2,169	2,847	6.0	11.9
403 SALVATION ARMY	1	56	201	0.4	0.8
413 S-D ADVENTISTS	1	69	84*	0.2	0.4
443 UN C OF CHRIST	2	456	553*	1.2	2.3
449 UN METHODIST..	17	4,626	6,020	12.6	25.1
453 UN PRES CH USA	6	2,102	2,548*	5.3	10.6
WASHINGTON	233	50,695	131,665*	62.4	100.0
019 AMER BAPT CONV	18	3,548	4,222*	2.0	3.2
029 AMER LUTH CH..	1	264	354	0.2	0.3
081 CATHOLIC......	41	0	69,717	33.1	53.0
093 CR CH (DISC)..	11	2,808	3,341*	1.6	2.5
097 CR C AND C CR.	5	579	689*	0.3	0.5
105 CHRISTIAN REF.	1	51	87	-	0.1
123 CH GOD (ANDER)	1	40	70	-	0.1
127 CH GOD (CLEVE)	2	205	244*	0.1	0.2
157 CH OF BRETHREN	1	56	67*	-	0.1
165 CH OF NAZARENE	7	753	1,432	0.7	1.1
193 EPISCOPAL.....	5	1,352	1,732	0.8	1.3
221 FREE METH C NA	4	110	147	0.1	0.1
281 LUTH CH AMER..	8	2,864	3,617	1.7	2.7
283 LUTH--MO SYNOD	3	505	663	0.3	0.5
353 PLY BRETHREN..	1	50	80	-	0.1
381 REF PRES-EVAN.	1	88	123	0.1	0.1
403 SALVATION ARMY	1	44	193	0.1	0.1
413 S-D ADVENTISTS	3	692	823*	0.4	0.6
419 SO BAPT CONV..	3	443	527*	0.2	0.4
443 UN C OF CHRIST	1	24	29*	-	-
449 UN METHODIST..	53	13,935	16,993	8.1	12.9
453 UN PRES CH USA	62	22,284	26,515*	12.6	20.1
WAYNE	62	7,223	15,900*	53.8	100.0
019 AMER BAPT CONV	7	609	736*	2.5	4.6
081 CATHOLIC......	17	0	6,868	23.2	43.2
193 EPISCOPAL.....	2	342	470	1.6	3.0
221 FREE METH C NA	2	108	160	0.5	1.0
281 LUTH CH AMER..	3	1,375	1,765	6.0	11.1
293 MORAV CH-NORTH	1	221	277	0.9	1.7
413 S-D ADVENTISTS	2	52	63*	0.2	0.4
449 UN METHODIST..	23	3,680	4,551	15.4	28.6
453 UN PRES CH USA	5	836	1,010*	3.4	6.4
WESTMORELAND	359	93,208	267,024*	70.8	100.0
019 AMER BAPT CONV	12	3,375	4,081*	1.1	1.5
081 CATHOLIC......	80	0	147,687	39.2	55.3
093 CR CH (DISC)..	3	743	898*	0.2	0.3
097 CR C AND C CR.	7	1,570	1,898*	0.5	0.7
123 CH GOD (ANDER)	3	171	428	0.1	0.2
127 CH GOD (CLEVE)	2	73	88*	-	-
157 CH OF BRETHREN	4	1,472	1,780*	0.5	0.7
165 CH OF NAZARENE	5	414	973	0.3	0.4
193 EPISCOPAL.....	8	1,804	2,613	0.7	1.0
221 FREE METH C NA	6	216	349	0.1	0.1
281 LUTH CH AMER..	52	22,086	30,595	8.1	11.5
283 LUTH--MO SYNOD	4	881	1,156	0.3	0.4
285 MENNONITE CH..	1	218	264*	0.1	0.1
313 NO AM BAPT GC.	1	207	250*	0.1	0.1
349 PENT HOLINESS.	3	129	156*	-	0.1
403 SALVATION ARMY	6	328	1,522	0.4	0.6
413 S-D ADVENTISTS	1	70	85*	-	-
435 UNITARIAN-UNIV	1	58	88	-	-
443 UN C OF CHRIST	29	7,462	9,022*	2.4	3.4
449 UN METHODIST..	76	28,197	34,387	9.1	12.9
453 UN PRES CH USA	54	23,698	28,653*	7.6	10.7
469 WISC EVAN LUTH	1	36	51	-	-
WYOMING	37	4,317	8,515*	44.6	100.0
019 AMER BAPT CONV	2	39	48*	0.3	0.6
081 CATHOLIC......	6	0	2,775	14.5	32.6
193 EPISCOPAL.....	2	142	240	1.3	2.8
221 FREE METH C NA	2	37	39	0.2	0.5
281 LUTH CH AMER..	1	110	210	1.1	2.5
283 LUTH--MO SYNOD	1	99	130	0.7	1.5
413 S-D ADVENTISTS	2	100	124*	0.6	1.5
449 UN METHODIST..	19	3,386	4,448	23.3	52.2
453 UN PRES CH USA	2	404	501*	2.6	5.9
YORK	313	102,581	151,485*	55.6	100.0
019 AMER BAPT CONV	1	488	595*	0.2	0.4
075 BRETHREN IN CR	6	186	227*	0.1	0.1
081 CATHOLIC......	11	0	24,251	8.9	16.0
127 CH GOD (CLEVE)	1	53	65*	-	-
157 CH OF BRETHREN	12	4,117	5,016*	1.8	3.3
165 CH OF NAZARENE	5	442	1,015	0.4	0.7
193 EPISCOPAL.....	3	1,538	2,500	0.9	1.7
199 EVAN CONG CH..	3	896	1,092*	0.4	0.7
226 FRIENDS-USA...	2	39	48*	-	-
281 LUTH CH AMER..	80	37,966	52,004	19.1	34.3
283 LUTH--MO SYNOD	3	1,136	1,552	0.6	1.0
285 MENNONITE CH..	11	553	674*	0.2	0.4
293 MORAV CH-NORTH	2	481	677	0.2	0.4
335 ORTH PRESB CH.	1	92	134	-	0.1
353 PLY BRETHREN..	1	70	114	-	0.1
403 SALVATION ARMY	1	62	923	0.3	0.6
413 S-D ADVENTISTS	2	197	240*	0.1	0.2
419 SO BAPT CONV..	5	460	560*	0.2	0.4
435 UNITARIAN-UNIV	1	70	115	-	0.1
443 UN C OF CHRIST	47	19,474	23,726*	8.7	15.7
449 UN METHODIST..	98	27,923	28,235	10.4	18.6
453 UN PRES CH USA	17	6,338	7,722*	2.8	5.1
CO DATA NOT AVAIL	85	3,510	15,297*	N/A	N/A
127 CH GOD (CLEVE)	1	26	31*	N/A	N/A
151 L-D SAINTS....	0	0	11,080	N/A	N/A
193 EPISCOPAL.....	1	0	16	N/A	N/A
467 WESLEYAN......	83	3,484	4,170	N/A	N/A

RHODE ISLAND

County and Denomination	Number of churches	Communicant, confirmed, full members	Total adherents: Number	Total adherents: Percent of total population	Total adherents: Percent of total adherents
THE STATE.....	455	83,997	712,787*	75.3	100.0
BRISTOL	27	5,602	39,619*	86.2	100.0
019 AMER BAPT CONV	2	358	437*	1.0	1.1
081 CATHOLIC......	11	0	32,206	70.1	81.3
193 EPISCOPAL.....	4	2,323	3,382	7.4	8.5
281 LUTH CH AMER..	1	304	434	0.9	1.1
353 PLY BRETHREN..	3	165	293	0.6	0.7
443 UN C OF CHRIST	2	1,042	1,271*	2.8	3.2
449 UN METHODIST..	2	594	601	1.3	1.5
453 UN PRES CH USA	2	816	995*	2.2	2.5
KENT	65	13,487	112,104*	78.7	100.0
019 AMER BAPT CONV	13	3,782	4,639*	3.3	4.1
081 CATHOLIC......	25	0	93,059	65.4	83.0
123 CH GOD (ANDER)	1	16	29	-	-
127 CH GOD (CLEVE)	1	101	124*	0.1	0.1
175 CONG CR CH....	1	150	184*	0.1	0.2
193 EPISCOPAL.....	9	4,603	8,152	5.7	7.3
201 EVAN COV CH AM	2	81	99*	0.1	0.1
281 LUTH CH AMER..	4	1,889	2,683	1.9	2.4
435 UNITARIAN-UNIV	1	188	248	0.2	0.2
443 UN C OF CHRIST	2	105	129*	0.1	0.1
449 UN METHODIST..	5	1,837	1,856	1.3	1.7
453 UN PRES CH USA	1	735	902*	0.6	0.8
NEWPORT	50	6,677	51,596*	54.6	100.0
019 AMER BAPT CONV	8	1,354	1,638*	1.7	3.2

*Total adherents estimated from known number of communicant, confirmed, full members.

—Represents a percent less than 0.1.

Percentages may not total due to rounding.

Table 3. Churches and Church Membership by State, County and Denomination: 1971

County and Denomination	Number of churches	Communicant, confirmed, full members	Total adherents: Number	Total adherents: Percent of total population	Total adherents: Percent of total adherents
081 CATHOLIC......	16	0	42,246	44.7	81.9
127 CH GOD (CLEVE)	1	16	19*	-	-
165 CH OF NAZARENE	1	40	104	0.1	0.2
193 EPISCOPAL.....	11	2,685	4,262	4.5	8.3
226 FRIENDS-USA...	2	62	75*	0.1	0.1
281 LUTH CH AMER..	1	355	561	0.6	1.1
353 PLY BRETHREN..	1	20	40	-	0.1
403 SALVATION ARMY	1	35	222	0.2	0.4
419 SO BAPT CONV..	2	450	544*	0.6	1.1
435 UNITARIAN-UNIV	1	221	318	0.3	0.6
449 UN METHODIST..	4	873	882	0.9	1.7
453 UN PRES CH USA	1	566	685*	0.7	1.3
PROVIDENCE	250	46,979	465,773*	80.3	100.0
019 AMER BAPT CONV	43	12,796	15,314*	2.6	3.3
081 CATHOLIC......	102	0	407,863	70.3	87.6
097 CR C AND C CR.	1	21	25*	-	-
123 CH GOD (ANDER)	1	48	124	-	-
127 CH GOD (CLEVE)	3	98	117*	-	-
165 CH OF NAZARENE	4	243	492	0.1	0.1
175 CONG CR CH....	1	75	90*	-	-
193 EPISCOPAL.....	33	15,763	20,647	3.6	4.4
201 EVAN COV CH AM	4	374	448*	0.1	0.1
226 FRIENDS-USA...	2	256	306*	0.1	0.1
281 LUTH CH AMER..	4	1,753	2,400	0.4	0.5
283 LUTH--MO SYNOD	2	887	1,305	0.2	0.3
413 S-D ADVENTISTS	3	476	570*	0.1	0.1
419 SO BAPT CONV..	1	45	54*	-	-
435 UNITARIAN-UNIV	6	1,176	1,424	0.2	0.3
443 UN C OF CHRIST	21	6,889	8,244*	1.4	1.8
449 UN METHODIST..	14	4,978	5,032	0.9	1.1
453 UN PRES CH USA	5	1,101	1,318*	0.2	0.3
WASHINGTON	62	10,188	41,012*	49.1	100.0
019 AMER BAPT CONV	18	3,548	4,358*	5.2	10.6
081 CATHOLIC......	14	0	26,959	32.3	65.7
123 CH GOD (ANDER)	2	90	190	0.2	0.5
165 CH OF NAZARENE	1	31	38	-	0.1
193 EPISCOPAL.....	9	3,021	5,168	6.2	12.6
226 FRIENDS-USA...	1	51	63*	0.1	0.2
281 LUTH CH AMER..	1	155	248	0.3	0.6
283 LUTH--MO SYNOD	1	195	285	0.3	0.7
353 PLY BRETHREN..	1	30	50	0.1	0.1
413 S-D ADVENTISTS	1	50	61*	0.1	0.1
415 S-D BAPTIST GC	4	412	506*	0.6	1.2
419 SO BAPT CONV..	1	419	515*	0.6	1.3
443 UN C OF CHRIST	3	1,169	1,436*	1.7	3.5
449 UN METHODIST..	3	590	610	0.7	1.5
453 UN PRES CH USA	2	427	525*	0.6	1.3
CO DATA NOT AVAIL	1	1,064	2,683	N/A	N/A
151 L-D SAINTS....	0	0	904	N/A	N/A
193 EPISCOPAL.....	1	1,064	1,779	N/A	N/A

SOUTH CAROLINA

County and Denomination	Number of churches	Communicant, confirmed, full members	Total adherents: Number	Total adherents: Percent of total population	Total adherents: Percent of total adherents
THE STATE......	4,331	1,053,836	1,356,819*	52.4	100.0
ABBEVILLE	59	10,656	12,827*	60.8	100.0
055 AS REF PRES CH	3	466	567*	2.7	4.4
081 CATHOLIC......	1	0	65	0.3	0.5
127 CH GOD (CLEVE)	4	270	328*	1.6	2.6
193 EPISCOPAL.....	1	77	97	0.5	0.8
349 PENT HOLINESS.	4	515	626*	3.0	4.9
357 PRESB CH US...	12	1,424	1,732*	8.2	13.5
419 SO BAPT CONV..	20	5,902	7,178*	34.0	56.0
449 UN METHODIST..	12	1,865	2,067	9.8	16.1
453 UN PRES CH USA	2	137	167*	0.8	1.3
AIKEN	147	38,947	51,247*	56.3	100.0
081 CATHOLIC......	4	0	2,998	3.3	5.9
093 CR CH (DISC)..	5	334	417*	0.5	0.8
123 CH GOD (ANDER)	3	83	188	0.2	0.4
127 CH GOD (CLEVE)	10	802	1,001*	1.1	2.0
165 CH OF NAZARENE	3	257	501	0.6	1.0
193 EPISCOPAL.....	6	1,299	1,711	1.9	3.3
281 LUTH CH AMER..	3	1,001	1,377	1.5	2.7
283 LUTH--MO SYNOD	1	100	124	0.1	0.2
349 PENT HOLINESS.	9	602	752*	0.8	1.5
353 PLY BRETHREN..	1	40	60	0.1	0.1
357 PRESB CH US...	4	2,470	3,084*	3.4	6.0
403 SALVATION ARMY	1	66	245	0.3	0.5
413 S-D ADVENTISTS	1	30	37*	-	0.1
419 SO BAPT CONV..	76	25,239	31,512*	34.6	61.5
435 UNITARIAN-UNIV	1	16	16	-	-
449 UN METHODIST..	19	6,608	7,224	7.9	14.1
ALLENDALE	25	3,624	5,088*	52.5	100.0
081 CATHOLIC......	1	0	32	0.3	0.6
093 CR CH (DISC)..	2	76	95*	1.0	1.9
127 CH GOD (CLEVE)	1	28	35*	0.4	0.7
193 EPISCOPAL.....	1	104	124	1.3	2.4
281 LUTH CH AMER..	2	147	177	1.8	3.5
285 MENNONITE CH..	1	22	27*	0.3	0.5
357 PRESB CH US...	1	80	100*	1.0	2.0
419 SO BAPT CONV..	10	2,257	2,812*	29.0	55.3
449 UN METHODIST..	6	910	1,686	17.4	33.1
ANDERSON	174	53,524	66,170*	62.7	100.0
055 AS REF PRES CH	3	435	531*	0.5	0.8
081 CATHOLIC......	2	0	677	0.6	1.0
121 CH GOD (ABR)..	1	236	288*	0.3	0.4
127 CH GOD (CLEVE)	13	2,373	2,897*	2.7	4.4
193 EPISCOPAL.....	1	366	526	0.5	0.8
281 LUTH CH AMER..	1	270	349	0.3	0.5
285 MENNONITE CH..	1	10	12*	-	-
349 PENT HOLINESS.	9	995	1,215*	1.2	1.8
353 PLY BRETHREN..	1	6	50	-	0.1
357 PRESB CH US...	19	3,447	4,207*	4.0	6.4
381 REF PRES-EVAN.	1	142	170	0.2	0.3
403 SALVATION ARMY	1	89	809	0.8	1.2
413 S-D ADVENTISTS	1	48	59*	0.1	0.1
419 SO BAPT CONV..	83	38,504	46,998*	44.6	71.0
449 UN METHODIST..	36	6,521	7,282	6.9	11.0
453 UN PRES CH USA	1	82	100*	0.1	0.2
BAMBERG	53	7,255	9,102*	57.1	100.0
081 CATHOLIC......	0	0	12	0.1	0.1
093 CR CH (DISC)..	3	208	261*	1.6	2.9
127 CH GOD (CLEVE)	4	87	109*	0.7	1.2
165 CH OF NAZARENE	1	107	260	1.6	2.9
193 EPISCOPAL.....	2	104	111	0.7	1.2
281 LUTH CH AMER..	2	137	163	1.0	1.8
349 PENT HOLINESS.	1	82	103*	0.6	1.1
357 PRESB CH US...	2	98	123*	0.8	1.4
419 SO BAPT CONV..	14	3,432	4,313*	27.0	47.4
449 UN METHODIST..	24	3,000	3,647	22.9	40.1
BARNWELL	40	7,567	9,522*	55.4	100.0
081 CATHOLIC......	2	0	104	0.6	1.1
097 CR C AND C CR.	1	150	188*	1.1	2.0
123 CH GOD (ANDER)	1	14	14	0.1	0.1
127 CH GOD (CLEVE)	3	124	155*	0.9	1.6
193 EPISCOPAL.....	2	110	194	1.1	2.0
349 PENT HOLINESS.	1	45	56*	0.3	0.6
357 PRESB CH US...	3	287	360*	2.1	3.8
419 SO BAPT CONV..	22	6,005	7,525*	43.8	79.0
449 UN METHODIST..	5	832	926	5.4	9.7
BEAUFORT	37	8,012	10,966*	21.4	100.0
081 CATHOLIC......	4	0	813	1.6	7.4
093 CR CH (DISC)..	3	181	224*	0.4	2.0
097 CR C AND C CR.	1	50	62*	0.1	0.6
127 CH GOD (CLEVE)	1	102	126*	0.2	1.1
165 CH OF NAZARENE	1	37	103	0.2	0.9
193 EPISCOPAL.....	3	1,164	1,675	3.3	15.3
281 LUTH CH AMER..	1	170	265	0.5	2.4
349 PENT HOLINESS.	1	23	28*	0.1	0.3
353 PLY BRETHREN..	2	35	90	0.2	0.8
357 PRESB CH US...	2	743	920*	1.8	8.4
419 SO BAPT CONV..	8	3,925	4,862*	9.5	44.3
449 UN METHODIST..	9	1,575	1,789	3.5	16.3
453 UN PRES CH USA	1	7	9*	-	0.1
BERKELEY	106	13,912	20,406*	36.3	100.0
081 CATHOLIC......	3	0	1,902	3.4	9.3
093 CR CH (DISC)..	7	489	659*	1.2	3.2
097 CR C AND C CR.	3	414	558*	1.0	2.7
123 CH GOD (ANDER)	1	32	122	0.2	0.6
127 CH GOD (CLEVE)	4	289	389*	0.7	1.9
165 CH OF NAZARENE	1	45	86	0.2	0.4
193 EPISCOPAL.....	6	348	475	0.8	2.3
281 LUTH CH AMER..	3	384	659	1.2	3.2
349 PENT HOLINESS.	13	489	659*	1.2	3.2
357 PRESB CH US...	4	1,565	2,109*	3.8	10.3
413 S-D ADVENTISTS	2	22	30*	0.1	0.1
419 SO BAPT CONV..	20	6,155	8,293*	14.8	40.6
449 UN METHODIST..	39	3,680	4,465	7.9	21.9
CALHOUN	26	3,702	4,450*	41.3	100.0
081 CATHOLIC......	0	0	21	0.2	0.5
123 CH GOD (ANDER)	1	37	74	0.7	1.7
193 EPISCOPAL.....	1	97	138	1.3	3.1
281 LUTH CH AMER..	5	444	536	5.0	12.0
357 PRESB CH US...	1	111	140*	1.3	3.1
419 SO BAPT CONV..	6	1,339	1,689*	15.7	38.0
449 UN METHODIST..	12	1,674	1,852	17.2	41.6
CHARLESTON	207	75,665	108,337*	43.7	100.0
081 CATHOLIC......	15	0	13,425	5.4	12.4
093 CR CH (DISC)..	3	702	877*	0.4	0.8
097 CR C AND C CR.	2	140	175*	0.1	0.2
123 CH GOD (ANDER)	2	57	112	-	0.1
127 CH GOD (CLEVE)	5	535	668*	0.3	0.6
165 CH OF NAZARENE	5	517	901	0.4	0.8
193 EPISCOPAL.....	22	9,216	11,913	4.8	11.0
281 LUTH CH AMER..	13	5,298	7,014	2.8	6.5
283 LUTH--MO SYNOD	1	170	300	0.1	0.3

*Total adherents estimated from known number of communicant, confirmed, full members.

—Represents a percent less than 0.1.

Percentages may not total due to rounding.

Table 3. Churches and Church Membership by State, County and Denomination: 1971

County and Denomination	Number of churches	Communicant, confirmed, full members	Total adherents: Number	Total adherents: Percent of total population	Total adherents: Percent of total adherents
349 PENT HOLINESS.	11	594	742*	0.3	0.7
353 PLY BRETHREN..	4	192	296	0.1	0.3
357 PRESB CH US...	14	4,761	5,945*	2.4	5.5
381 REF PRES-EVAN.	2	38	47	-	-
403 SALVATION ARMY	1	58	278	0.1	0.3
413 S-D ADVENTISTS	3	450	562*	0.2	0.5
419 SO BAPT CONV..	50	35,274	44,047*	17.8	40.7
435 UNITARIAN-UNIV	1	87	130	0.1	0.1
443 UN C OF CHRIST	1	69	86*	-	0.1
449 UN METHODIST..	41	15,397	18,184	7.3	16.8
453 UN PRES CH USA	11	2,110	2,635*	1.1	2.4
CHEROKEE	76	20,350	25,482*	69.3	100.0
055 AS REF PRES CH	1	125	155*	0.4	0.6
081 CATHOLIC......	1	0	123	0.3	0.5
127 CH GOD (CLEVE)	4	481	597*	1.6	2.3
193 EPISCOPAL.....	1	84	100	0.3	0.4
281 LUTH CH AMER..	1	64	98	0.3	0.4
357 PRESB CH US...	3	567	703*	1.9	2.8
403 SALVATION ARMY	1	123	465	1.3	1.8
419 SO BAPT CONV..	55	17,319	21,486*	58.4	84.3
449 UN METHODIST..	7	1,527	1,681	4.6	6.6
453 UN PRES CH USA	2	60	74*	0.2	0.3
CHESTER	70	12,050	14,849*	49.8	100.0
055 AS REF PRES CH	4	604	748*	2.5	5.0
081 CATHOLIC......	2	0	122	0.4	0.8
127 CH GOD (CLEVE)	4	439	544*	1.8	3.7
165 CH OF NAZARENE	2	330	591	2.0	4.0
193 EPISCOPAL.....	2	89	138	0.5	0.9
281 LUTH CH AMER..	1	60	76	0.3	0.5
349 PENT HOLINESS.	1	113	140*	0.5	0.9
357 PRESB CH US...	16	1,630	2,019*	6.8	13.6
419 SO BAPT CONV..	17	5,968	7,394*	24.8	49.8
449 UN METHODIST..	18	2,657	2,879	9.7	19.4
453 UN PRES CH USA	3	160	198*	0.7	1.3
CHESTERFIELD	109	17,499	21,193*	62.9	100.0
081 CATHOLIC......	1	0	82	0.2	0.4
127 CH GOD (CLEVE)	6	292	369*	1.1	1.7
193 EPISCOPAL.....	1	200	276	0.8	1.3
349 PENT HOLINESS.	1	47	59*	0.2	0.3
357 PRESB CH US...	10	1,194	1,508*	4.5	7.1
419 SO BAPT CONV..	53	10,598	13,386*	39.8	63.2
449 UN METHODIST..	34	4,901	5,176	15.4	24.4
453 UN PRES CH USA	3	267	337*	1.0	1.6
CLARENDON	44	7,634	9,524*	37.2	100.0
081 CATHOLIC......	1	0	26	0.1	0.3
123 CH GOD (ANDER)	1	6	41	0.2	0.4
127 CH GOD (CLEVE)	3	84	108*	0.4	1.1
193 EPISCOPAL.....	3	808	1,053	4.1	11.1
349 PENT HOLINESS.	2	186	239*	0.9	2.5
357 PRESB CH US...	5	827	1,063*	4.2	11.2
419 SO BAPT CONV..	12	3,023	3,885*	15.2	40.8
449 UN METHODIST..	13	1,970	2,171	8.5	22.8
453 UN PRES CH USA	4	730	938*	3.7	9.8
COLLETON	91	11,996	14,900*	53.9	100.0
081 CATHOLIC......	2	0	260	0.9	1.7
093 CR CH (DISC)..	4	405	511*	1.8	3.4
097 CR C AND C CR.	1	150	189*	0.7	1.3
123 CH GOD (ANDER)	1	45	81	0.3	0.5
127 CH GOD (CLEVE)	3	201	254*	0.9	1.7
165 CH OF NAZARENE	1	19	44	0.2	0.3
193 EPISCOPAL.....	2	213	286	1.0	1.9
281 LUTH CH AMER..	1	109	142	0.5	1.0
349 PENT HOLINESS.	3	66	83*	0.3	0.6
357 PRESB CH US...	1	244	308*	1.1	2.1
419 SO BAPT CONV..	26	6,163	7,773*	28.1	52.2
449 UN METHODIST..	43	4,152	4,680	16.9	31.4
453 UN PRES CH USA	3	229	289*	1.0	1.9
DARLINGTON	62	10,442	13,639*	25.5	100.0
081 CATHOLIC......	3	0	345	0.6	2.5
123 CH GOD (ANDER)	6	507	1,386	2.6	10.2
127 CH GOD (CLEVE)	6	337	423*	0.8	3.1
165 CH OF NAZARENE	2	138	391	0.7	2.9
193 EPISCOPAL.....	2	413	439	0.8	3.2
281 LUTH CH AMER..	1	84	142	0.3	1.0
349 PENT HOLINESS.	4	284	357*	0.7	2.6
357 PRESB CH US...	5	1,188	1,492*	2.8	10.9
413 S-D ADVENTISTS	1	25	31*	0.1	0.2
419 SO BAPT CONV..	6	1,683	2,114*	4.0	15.5
449 UN METHODIST..	25	5,765	6,496	12.2	47.6
453 UN PRES CH USA	1	18	23*		0.2
DILLON	55	10,572	13,217*	45.8	100.0
081 CATHOLIC......	1	0	94	0.3	0.7
127 CH GOD (CLEVE)	5	657	844*	2.9	6.4
193 EPISCOPAL.....	2	71	76	0.3	0.6
349 PENT HOLINESS.	3	162	208*	0.7	1.6
357 PRESB CH US...	9	978	1,257*	4.4	9.5
419 SO BAPT CONV..	21	6,146	7,897*	27.4	59.7
449 UN METHODIST..	14	2,558	2,841	9.9	21.5
DORCHESTER	61	13,864	18,152*	56.2	100.0
081 CATHOLIC......	1	0	777	2.4	4.3
093 CR CH (DISC)..	7	506	649*	2.0	3.6
097 CR C AND C CR.	1	51	65*	0.2	0.4
123 CH GOD (ANDER)	2	230	494	1.5	2.7
127 CH GOD (CLEVE)	1	108	139*	0.4	0.8
165 CH OF NAZARENE	1	80	190	0.6	1.0
193 EPISCOPAL.....	1	105	111	0.3	0.6
281 LUTH CH AMER..	1	402	572	1.8	3.2
349 PENT HOLINESS.	2	45	58*	0.2	0.3
357 PRESB CH US...	1	416	534*	1.7	2.9
419 SO BAPT CONV..	14	5,130	6,584*	20.4	36.3
449 UN METHODIST..	29	6,791	7,979	24.7	44.0
EDGEFIELD	33	5,526	8,068*	51.4	100.0
081 CATHOLIC......	2	0	1,232	7.9	15.3
127 CH GOD (CLEVE)	2	122	154*	1.0	1.9
193 EPISCOPAL.....	1	38	39	0.2	0.5
281 LUTH CH AMER..	2	405	482	3.1	6.0
349 PENT HOLINESS.	1	39	49*	0.3	0.6
357 PRESB CH US...	3	136	172*	1.1	2.1
413 S-D ADVENTISTS	1	39	49*	0.3	0.6
419 SO BAPT CONV..	16	3,883	4,906*	31.3	60.8
449 UN METHODIST..	5	864	985	6.3	12.2
FAIRFIELD	43	5,917	7,474*	37.4	100.0
055 AS REF PRES CH	4	386	489*	2.4	6.5
081 CATHOLIC......	1	0	44	0.2	0.6
123 CH GOD (ANDER)	1	10	25	0.1	0.3
127 CH GOD (CLEVE)	1	132	167*	0.8	2.2
165 CH OF NAZARENE	1	120	270	1.4	3.6
193 EPISCOPAL.....	3	211	267	1.3	3.6
349 PENT HOLINESS.	1	60	76*	0.4	1.0
357 PRESB CH US...	8	946	1,199*	6.0	16.0
419 SO BAPT CONV..	12	2,666	3,378*	16.9	45.2
449 UN METHODIST..	8	1,095	1,190	6.0	15.9
453 UN PRES CH USA	3	291	369*	1.8	4.9
FLORENCE	142	34,954	44,185*	49.3	100.0
081 CATHOLIC......	3	0	1,396	1.6	3.2
097 CR C AND C CR.	1	26	33*	-	0.1
123 CH GOD (ANDER)	3	88	253	0.3	0.6
127 CH GOD (CLEVE)	7	543	680*	0.8	1.5
165 CH OF NAZARENE	1	39	160	0.2	0.4
193 EPISCOPAL.....	3	985	1,434	1.6	3.2
281 LUTH CH AMER..	1	322	442	0.5	1.0
283 LUTH--MO SYNOD	1	55	85	0.1	0.2
349 PENT HOLINESS.	21	1,620	2,027*	2.3	4.6
353 PLY BRETHREN..	2	90	130	0.1	0.3
357 PRESB CH US...	11	2,667	3,338*	3.7	7.6
403 SALVATION ARMY	1	86	336	0.4	0.8
413 S-D ADVENTISTS	2	183	229*	0.3	0.5
419 SO BAPT CONV..	39	16,324	20,429*	22.8	46.2
449 UN METHODIST..	46	11,926	13,213	14.7	29.9
GEORGETOWN	64	9,198	11,982*	35.8	100.0
081 CATHOLIC......	3	0	462	1.4	3.9
123 CH GOD (ANDER)	1	6	12	-	0.1
127 CH GOD (CLEVE)	3	273	347*	1.0	2.9
193 EPISCOPAL.....	6	796	1,024	3.1	8.5
281 LUTH CH AMER..	1	105	148	0.4	1.2
349 PENT HOLINESS.	14	936	1,189*	3.5	9.9
357 PRESB CH US...	5	732	930*	2.8	7.8
413 S-D ADVENTISTS	1	106	135*	0.4	1.1
419 SO BAPT CONV..	15	4,375	5,556*	16.6	46.4
449 UN METHODIST..	15	1,869	2,179	6.5	18.2
GREENVILLE	310	116,267	148,494*	61.7	100.0
055 AS REF PRES CH	1	515	632*	0.3	0.4
081 CATHOLIC......	3	0	5,610	2.3	3.8
093 CR CH (DISC)..	1	134	164*	0.1	0.1
097 CR C AND C CR.	3	225	276*	0.1	0.2
121 CH GOD (ABR)..	1	25	31*	-	-
123 CH GOD (ANDER)	2	76	185	0.1	0.1
127 CH GOD (CLEVE)	27	3,511	4,309*	1.8	2.9
157 CH OF BRETHREN	1	48	59*	-	-
165 CH OF NAZARENE	1	106	250	0.1	0.2
193 EPISCOPAL.....	9	4,160	5,708	2.4	3.8
281 LUTH CH AMER..	5	1,535	2,164	0.9	1.5
283 LUTH--MO SYNOD	1	162	247	0.1	0.2
315 NO AM OLD RC..	1	128	157*	0.1	0.1
349 PENT HOLINESS.	12	1,343	1,648*	0.7	1.1
353 PLY BRETHREN..	2	130	190	0.1	0.1
357 PRESB CH US...	19	7,323	8,987*	3.7	6.1
381 REF PRES-EVAN.	3	1,075	1,260	0.5	0.8
403 SALVATION ARMY	1	152	1,232	0.5	0.8
413 S-D ADVENTISTS	2	430	528*	0.2	0.4
419 SO BAPT CONV..	146	77,378	94,963*	39.5	64.0
435 UNITARIAN-UNIV	1	39	54	-	-
449 UN METHODIST..	66	17,718	19,774	8.2	13.3
453 UN PRES CH USA	2	54	66*	-	-
GREENWOOD	86	22,673	27,857*	56.1	100.0
055 AS REF PRES CH	4	498	612*	1.2	2.2
081 CATHOLIC......	1	0	483	1.0	1.7
097 CR C AND C CR.	1	66	81*	0.2	0.3
123 CH GOD (ANDER)	1	7	27	0.1	0.1
127 CH GOD (CLEVE)	6	841	1,034*	2.1	3.7
193 EPISCOPAL.....	1	376	433	0.9	1.6
281 LUTH CH AMER..	1	263	345	0.7	1.2

*Total adherents estimated from known number of communicant, confirmed, full members.

—Represents a percent less than 0.1.

Percentages may not total due to rounding.

Table 3. Churches and Church Membership by State, County and Denomination: 1971

County and Denomination	Number of churches	Communicant, confirmed, full members	Total adherents: Number	Total adherents: Percent of total population	Total adherents: Percent of total adherents
349 PENT HOLINESS.	9	772	949*	1.9	3.4
357 PRESB CH US...	7	1,702	2,093*	4.2	7.5
403 SALVATION ARMY	1	52	274	0.6	1.0
413 S-D ADVENTISTS	2	39	48*	0.1	0.2
419 SO BAPT CONV..	28	11,584	14,243*	28.7	51.1
449 UN METHODIST..	24	6,473	7,235	14.6	26.0
HAMPTON	48	6,125	7,662*	48.3	100.0
081 CATHOLIC......	1	0	78	0.5	1.0
093 CR CH (DISC)..	5	333	417*	2.6	5.4
097 CR C AND C CR.	1	71	89*	0.6	1.2
123 CH GOD (ANDER)	1	25	75	0.5	1.0
127 CH GOD (CLEVE)	3	97	121*	0.8	1.6
165 CH OF NAZARENE	1	38	53	0.3	0.7
193 EPISCOPAL.....	3	77	97	0.6	1.3
349 PENT HOLINESS.	1	10	13*	0.1	0.2
357 PRESB CH US...	3	228	285*	1.8	3.7
419 SO BAPT CONV..	19	4,369	5,470*	34.5	71.4
449 UN METHODIST..	10	877	964	6.1	12.6
HORRY	145	29,488	37,140*	53.1	100.0
081 CATHOLIC......	3	0	797	1.1	2.1
127 CH GOD (CLEVE)	5	423	527*	0.8	1.4
165 CH OF NAZARENE	1	69	150	0.2	0.4
193 EPISCOPAL.....	3	612	922	1.3	2.5
281 LUTH CH AMER..	1	223	316	0.5	0.9
349 PENT HOLINESS.	8	619	772*	1.1	2.1
353 PLY BRETHREN..	2	108	175	0.3	0.5
357 PRESB CH US...	5	1,251	1,560*	2.2	4.2
381 REF PRES-EVAN.	1	58	76	0.1	0.2
403 SALVATION ARMY	1	32	153	0.2	0.4
413 S-D ADVENTISTS	1	16	20*	-	0.1
419 SO BAPT CONV..	85	19,968	24,897*	35.6	67.0
449 UN METHODIST..	29	6,109	6,775	9.7	18.2
JASPER	19	2,964	3,728*	31.4	100.0
081 CATHOLIC......	2	0	80	0.7	2.1
127 CH GOD (CLEVE)	1	42	53*	0.4	1.4
419 SO BAPT CONV..	11	2,380	3,019*	25.4	81.0
449 UN METHODIST..	5	542	576	4.8	15.5
KERSHAW	79	16,735	21,778*	62.7	100.0
081 CATHOLIC......	1	0	514	1.5	2.4
123 CH GOD (ANDER)	2	166	531	1.5	2.4
127 CH GOD (CLEVE)	3	288	358*	1.0	1.6
165 CH OF NAZARENE	2	102	244	0.7	1.1
193 EPISCOPAL.....	1	289	799	2.3	3.7
281 LUTH CH AMER..	1	174	240	0.7	1.1
349 PENT HOLINESS.	2	94	117*	0.3	0.5
357 PRESB CH US...	6	1,195	1,484*	4.3	6.8
413 S-D ADVENTISTS	1	35	43*	0.1	0.2
419 SO BAPT CONV..	38	10,958	13,606*	39.2	62.5
449 UN METHODIST..	20	3,339	3,724	10.7	17.1
453 UN PRES CH USA	2	95	118*	0.3	0.5
LANCASTER	88	23,620	29,277*	67.6	100.0
055 AS REF PRES CH	6	1,138	1,425*	3.3	4.9
081 CATHOLIC......	1	0	227	0.5	0.8
127 CH GOD (CLEVE)	1	178	223*	0.5	0.8
165 CH OF NAZARENE	1	42	95	0.2	0.3
193 EPISCOPAL.....	1	213	302	0.7	1.0
281 LUTH CH AMER..	1	91	125	0.3	0.4
349 PENT HOLINESS.	2	211	264*	0.6	0.9
357 PRESB CH US...	11	1,426	1,786*	4.1	6.1
419 SO BAPT CONV..	46	16,003	20,040*	46.3	68.4
449 UN METHODIST..	17	4,276	4,737	10.9	16.2
453 UN PRES CH USA	1	42	53*	0.1	0.2
LAURENS	107	21,694	26,234*	52.8	100.0
055 AS REF PRES CH	2	224	273*	0.5	1.0
081 CATHOLIC......	2	0	151	0.3	0.6
123 CH GOD (ANDER)	1	22	57	0.1	0.2
127 CH GOD (CLEVE)	8	802	977*	2.0	3.7
165 CH OF NAZARENE	1	25	70	0.1	0.3
193 EPISCOPAL.....	2	126	216	0.4	0.8
281 LUTH CH AMER..	2	263	326	0.7	1.2
349 PENT HOLINESS.	5	386	470*	0.9	1.8
357 PRESB CH US...	17	2,513	3,063*	6.2	11.7
413 S-D ADVENTISTS	1	44	54*	0.1	0.2
419 SO BAPT CONV..	44	13,242	16,138*	32.5	61.5
449 UN METHODIST..	21	3,992	4,372	8.8	16.7
453 UN PRES CH USA	1	55	67*	0.1	0.3
LEE	64	15,574	19,682*	107.4#	100.0
081 CATHOLIC......	0	0	9	-	-
123 CH GOD (ANDER)	1	20	60	0.3	0.3
127 CH GOD (CLEVE)	1	41	52*	0.3	0.3
165 CH OF NAZARENE	2	108	217	1.2	1.1
193 EPISCOPAL.....	1	15	15	0.1	0.1
357 PRESB CH US...	5	543	695*	3.8	3.5
419 SO BAPT CONV..	33	11,569	14,812*	80.8	75.3
449 UN METHODIST..	18	3,016	3,487	19.0	17.7
453 UN PRES CH USA	3	262	335*	1.8	1.7
LEXINGTON	136	39,509	49,851*	56.0	100.0
055 AS REF PRES CH	1	134	169*	0.2	0.3
081 CATHOLIC......	1	0	64	0.1	0.1
097 CR C AND C CR.	1	50	63*	0.1	0.1
127 CH GOD (CLEVE)	2	101	127*	0.1	0.3
165 CH OF NAZARENE	2	201	271	0.3	0.5
193 EPISCOPAL.....	2	300	418	0.5	0.8
281 LUTH CH AMER..	36	10,140	13,663	15.3	27.4
283 LUTH--MO SYNOD	1	178	280	0.3	0.6
349 PENT HOLINESS.	7	317	400*	0.4	0.8
357 PRESB CH US...	3	741	934*	1.0	1.9
419 SO BAPT CONV..	55	19,472	24,549*	27.6	49.2
449 UN METHODIST..	25	7,875	8,913	10.0	17.9
MC CORMICK	18	2,473	3,032*	38.1	100.0
055 AS REF PRES CH	2	43	55*	0.7	1.8
081 CATHOLIC......	1	0	27	0.3	0.9
127 CH GOD (CLEVE)	1	46	59*	0.7	1.9
349 PENT HOLINESS.	1	7	9*	0.1	0.3
357 PRESB CH US...	1	20	26*	0.3	0.9
419 SO BAPT CONV..	7	1,307	1,675*	21.1	55.2
449 UN METHODIST..	5	1,050	1,181	14.8	39.0
MARION	43	9,829	11,835*	39.1	100.0
081 CATHOLIC......	1	0	132	0.4	1.1
127 CH GOD (CLEVE)	3	319	395*	1.3	3.3
193 EPISCOPAL.....	2	96	109	0.4	0.9
349 PENT HOLINESS.	3	100	124*	0.4	1.0
357 PRESB CH US...	2	590	731*	2.4	6.2
413 S-D ADVENTISTS	1	70	87*	0.3	0.7
419 SO BAPT CONV..	14	5,698	7,064*	23.3	59.7
449 UN METHODIST..	17	2,956	3,193	10.5	27.0
MARLBORO	59	8,948	10,907*	40.2	100.0
081 CATHOLIC......	1	0	91	0.3	0.8
123 CH GOD (ANDER)	1	25	81	0.3	0.7
127 CH GOD (CLEVE)	2	233	298*	1.1	2.7
165 CH OF NAZARENE	2	171	396	1.5	3.6
193 EPISCOPAL.....	1	201	254	0.9	2.3
349 PENT HOLINESS.	3	226	289*	1.1	2.6
357 PRESB CH US...	6	681	871*	3.2	8.0
419 SO BAPT CONV..	11	2,932	3,751*	13.8	34.4
449 UN METHODIST..	32	4,479	4,876	18.0	44.7
NEWBERRY	68	12,252	15,565*	53.2	100.0
055 AS REF PRES CH	2	339	409*	1.4	2.6
081 CATHOLIC......	1	0	63	0.2	0.4
123 CH GOD (ANDER)	1	28	74	0.3	0.5
127 CH GOD (CLEVE)	3	177	214*	0.7	1.4
193 EPISCOPAL.....	2	129	194	0.7	1.2
281 LUTH CH AMER..	26	5,940	7,523	25.7	48.3
349 PENT HOLINESS.	4	277	334*	1.1	2.1
357 PRESB CH US...	7	914	1,104*	3.8	7.1
419 SO BAPT CONV..	14	3,375	4,075*	13.9	26.2
435 UNITARIAN-UNIV	1	38	58	0.2	0.4
449 UN METHODIST..	5	887	1,338	4.6	8.6
453 UN PRES CH USA	2	148	179*	0.6	1.2
OCONEE	105	19,761	24,382*	59.9	100.0
081 CATHOLIC......	1	0	149	0.4	0.6
127 CH GOD (CLEVE)	13	1,228	1,510*	3.7	6.2
165 CH OF NAZARENE	1	22	80	0.2	0.3
193 EPISCOPAL.....	1	68	102	0.3	0.4
281 LUTH CH AMER..	1	311	372	0.9	1.5
349 PENT HOLINESS.	1	13	16*	-	0.1
357 PRESB CH US...	6	883	1,086*	2.7	4.5
413 S-D ADVENTISTS	1	63	77*	0.2	0.3
419 SO BAPT CONV..	62	15,524	19,092*	46.9	78.3
449 UN METHODIST..	18	1,649	1,898	4.7	7.8
ORANGEBURG	134	26,995	33,735*	48.3	100.0
081 CATHOLIC......	3	0	757	1.1	2.2
093 CR CH (DISC)..	2	252	317*	0.5	0.9
097 CR C AND C CR.	1	125	157*	0.2	0.5
123 CH GOD (ANDER)	2	19	69	0.1	0.2
127 CH GOD (CLEVE)	8	467	588*	0.8	1.7
165 CH OF NAZARENE	3	176	466	0.7	1.4
193 EPISCOPAL.....	4	779	886	1.3	2.6
281 LUTH CH AMER..	2	728	975	1.4	2.9
349 PENT HOLINESS.	7	286	360*	0.5	1.1
357 PRESB CH US...	1	634	798*	1.1	2.4
403 SALVATION ARMY	1	72	274	0.4	0.8
413 S-D ADVENTISTS	2	117	147*	0.2	0.4
419 SO BAPT CONV..	39	11,020	13,874*	19.9	41.1
449 UN METHODIST..	58	12,230	13,954	20.0	41.4
453 UN PRES CH USA	1	90	113*	0.2	0.3
PICKENS	110	27,399	34,138*	57.9	100.0
081 CATHOLIC......	2	0	1,422	2.4	4.2
127 CH GOD (CLEVE)	13	978	1,181*	2.0	3.5
193 EPISCOPAL.....	2	564	703	1.2	2.1
281 LUTH CH AMER..	1	144	240	0.4	0.7
349 PENT HOLINESS.	1	68	82*	0.1	0.2
357 PRESB CH US...	5	1,201	1,451*	2.5	4.3
419 SO BAPT CONV..	60	19,794	23,907*	40.6	70.0
435 UNITARIAN-UNIV	1	40	70	0.1	0.2
449 UN METHODIST..	25	4,610	5,082	8.6	14.9
RICHLAND	165	74,869	98,399*	42.1	100.0
055 AS REF PRES CH	2	773	927*	0.4	0.9

*Total adherents estimated from known number of communicant, confirmed, full members.

—Represents a percent less than 0.1.

Percentages may not total due to rounding.

#See Introduction for explanation of why total adherents reported by churches exceed the 1970 population figure.

Table 3. Churches and Church Membership by State, County and Denomination: 1971

County and Denomination	Number of churches	Communicant, confirmed, full members	Total adherents		
			Number	Percent of total population	Percent of total adherents
081 CATHOLIC......	3	0	6,796	2.9	6.9
093 CR CH (DISC)..	1	258	309*	0.1	0.3
097 CR C AND C CR.	1	133	159*	0.1	0.2
123 CH GOD (ANDER)	6	561	1,253	0.5	1.3
127 CH GOD (CLEVE)	8	679	814*	0.3	0.8
165 CH OF NAZARENE	5	659	1,061	0.5	1.1
193 EPISCOPAL.....	12	6,760	9,283	4.0	9.4
226 FRIENDS-USA...	1	14	17*	-	-
281 LUTH CH AMER..	19	7,982	10,318	4.4	10.5
283 LUTH--MO SYNOD	2	300	440	0.2	0.4
349 PENT HOLINESS.	9	636	763*	0.3	0.8
353 PLY BRETHREN..	1	75	100	-	0.1
357 PRESB CH US...	13	8,923	10,699*	4.6	10.9
403 SALVATION ARMY	1	107	336	0.1	0.3
413 S-D ADVENTISTS	3	482	578*	0.2	0.6
419 SO BAPT CONV..	43	30,429	36,484*	15.6	37.1
435 UNITARIAN-UNIV	1	60	84	-	0.1
449 UN METHODIST..	31	15,826	17,710	7.6	18.0
453 UN PRES CH USA	2	199	239*	0.1	0.2
469 WISC EVAN LUTH	1	13	29	-	-
SALUDA	43	7,065	8,548*	58.8	100.0
081 CATHOLIC......	1	0	153	1.1	1.8
127 CH GOD (CLEVE)	1	28	35*	0.2	0.4
193 EPISCOPAL.....	1	40	46	0.3	0.5
281 LUTH CH AMER..	7	827	998	6.9	11.7
349 PENT HOLINESS.	4	168	209*	1.4	2.4
357 PRESB CH US...	1	83	103*	0.7	1.2
419 SO BAPT CONV..	15	3,487	4,335*	29.8	50.7
449 UN METHODIST..	13	2,432	2,669	18.4	31.2
SPARTANBURG	253	85,690	105,620*	60.8	100.0
055 AS REF PRES CH	3	181	222*	0.1	0.2
081 CATHOLIC......	2	0	1,793	1.0	1.7
123 CH GOD (ANDER)	1	216	439	0.3	0.4
127 CH GOD (CLEVE)	13	1,344	1,647*	0.9	1.6
165 CH OF NAZARENE	2	57	109	0.1	0.1
193 EPISCOPAL.....	6	1,715	2,401	1.4	2.3
281 LUTH CH AMER..	3	725	1,013	0.6	1.0
283 LUTH--MO SYNOD	1	74	132	0.1	0.1
315 NO AM OLD RC..	1	97	119*	0.1	0.1
349 PENT HOLINESS.	5	148	181*	0.1	0.2
357 PRESB CH US...	21	5,430	6,655*	3.8	6.3
381 REF PRES-EVAN.	1	38	46	-	-
413 S-D ADVENTISTS	2	266	326*	0.2	0.3
419 SO BAPT CONV..	123	60,817	74,533*	42.9	70.6
435 UNITARIAN-UNIV	1	31	41	-	-
449 UN METHODIST..	66	14,455	15,845	9.1	15.0
453 UN PRES CH USA	2	96	118*	0.1	0.1
SUMTER	94	23,949	31,604*	39.8	100.0
055 AS REF PRES CH	1	92	118*	0.1	0.4
081 CATHOLIC......	2	0	1,011	1.3	3.2
097 CR C AND C CR.	1	53	68*	0.1	0.2
123 CH GOD (ANDER)	2	170	378	0.5	1.2
127 CH GOD (CLEVE)	1	123	157*	0.2	0.5
165 CH OF NAZARENE	3	403	887	1.1	2.8
193 EPISCOPAL.....	6	876	1,199	1.5	3.8
281 LUTH CH AMER..	1	323	448	0.6	1.4
349 PENT HOLINESS.	4	285	365*	0.5	1.2
357 PRESB CH US...	13	2,325	2,977*	3.7	9.4
403 SALVATION ARMY	1	49	384	0.5	1.2
413 S-D ADVENTISTS	2	154	197*	0.2	0.6
419 SO BAPT CONV..	26	10,905	13,963*	17.6	44.2
449 UN METHODIST..	26	6,449	7,222	9.1	22.9
453 UN PRES CH USA	5	1,742	2,230*	2.8	7.1
UNION	58	15,352	18,423*	63.0	100.0
081 CATHOLIC......	1	0	59	0.2	0.3
127 CH GOD (CLEVE)	3	217	267*	0.9	1.4
193 EPISCOPAL.....	1	123	144	0.5	0.8
281 LUTH CH AMER..	1	59	83	0.3	0.5
357 PRESB CH US...	8	896	1,102*	3.8	6.0
403 SALVATION ARMY	1	47	222	0.8	1.2
413 S-D ADVENTISTS	1	51	63*	0.2	0.3
419 SO BAPT CONV..	26	10,177	12,518*	42.8	67.9
449 UN METHODIST..	16	3,782	3,965	13.6	21.5
WILLIAMSBURG	76	11,541	13,827*	40.4	100.0
081 CATHOLIC......	2	0	91	0.3	0.7
127 CH GOD (CLEVE)	4	301	386*	1.1	2.8
165 CH OF NAZARENE	1	21	29	0.1	0.2
193 EPISCOPAL.....	1	63	91	0.3	0.7
349 PENT HOLINESS.	9	493	632*	1.8	4.6
357 PRESB CH US...	9	1,647	2,111*	6.2	15.3
413 S-D ADVENTISTS	2	33	42*	0.1	0.3
419 SO BAPT CONV..	14	2,850	3,[illegible]52*	10.7	26.4
449 UN METHODIST..	34	6,133	6,793	19.8	49.1
YORK	144	37,981	48,205*	56.6	100.0
055 AS REF PRES CH	10	2,528	3,126*	3.7	6.5
081 CATHOLIC......	3	0	1,073	1.3	2.2
097 CR C AND C CR.	1	36	45*	0.1	0.1
127 CH GOD (CLEVE)	11	1,578	1,951*	2.3	4.0
165 CH OF NAZARENE	6	579	1,256	1.5	2.6
193 EPISCOPAL.....	3	604	1,057	1.2	2.2
281 LUTH CH AMER..	2	279	395	0.5	0.8
349 PENT HOLINESS.	2	101	125*	0.1	0.3
357 PRESB CH US...	25	6,955	8,599*	10.1	17.8

*Total adherents estimated from known number of communicant, confirmed, full members.

County and Denomination	Number of churches	Communicant, confirmed, full members	Total adherents		
			Number	Percent of total population	Percent of total adherents
403 SALVATION ARMY	1	76	351	0.4	0.7
419 SO BAPT CONV..	43	16,202	20,032*	23.5	41.6
449 UN METHODIST..	35	8,396	10,013	11.8	20.8
453 UN PRES CH USA	2	147	182*	0.2	0.4
CO DATA NOT AVAIL	155	12,217	26,116*	N/A	N/A
127 CH GOD (CLEVE)	1	17	21*	N/A	N/A
151 L-D SAINTS....	0	0	11,153	N/A	N/A
223 FREE WILL BAPT	77	9,228	11,463*	N/A	N/A
349 PENT HOLINESS.	6	200	248*	N/A	N/A
467 WESLEYAN......	71	2,772	3,231	N/A	N/A

SOUTH DAKOTA

County and Denomination	Number of churches	Communicant, confirmed, full members	Total adherents		
			Number	Percent of total population	Percent of total adherents
THE STATE.....	1,479	235,535	460,456*	69.2	100.0
AURORA	14	1,521	3,394*	81.1	100.0
029 AMER LUTH CH..	2	446	632	15.1	18.6
081 CATHOLIC......	3	0	1,280	30.6	37.7
283 LUTH--MO SYNOD	2	375	492	11.8	14.5
371 REF CH IN AM..	1	200	382	9.1	11.3
449 UN METHODIST..	5	463	563	13.5	16.6
453 UN PRES CH USA	1	37	45*	1.1	1.3
BEADLE	31	8,158	14,161*	67.8	100.0
019 AMER BAPT CONV	1	320	385*	1.8	2.7
029 AMER LUTH CH..	4	1,826	2,810	13.5	19.8
081 CATHOLIC......	4	0	3,090	14.8	21.8
097 CR C AND C CR.	1	170	205*	1.0	1.4
165 CH OF NAZARENE	1	45	100	0.5	0.7
193 EPISCOPAL.....	1	165	364	1.7	2.6
221 FREE METH C NA	1	10	10	-	0.1
283 LUTH--MO SYNOD	4	1,333	1,758	8.4	12.4
287 MENN GEN CONF.	1	162	195*	0.9	1.4
335 ORTH PRESB CH.	1	11	15	0.1	0.1
413 S-D ADVENTISTS	1	36	43*	0.2	0.3
419 SO BAPT CONV..	1	79	95*	0.5	0.7
443 UN C OF CHRIST	1	524	631*	3.0	4.5
449 UN METHODIST..	5	2,145	2,857	13.7	20.2
453 UN PRES CH USA	4	1,332	1,603*	7.7	11.3
BENNETT	12	821	1,692*	54.8	100.0
081 CATHOLIC......	2	0	358	11.6	21.2
193 EPISCOPAL.....	5	289	625	20.2	36.9
413 S-D ADVENTISTS	1	18	23*	0.7	1.4
419 SO BAPT CONV..	1	134	174*	5.6	10.3
453 UN PRES CH USA	2	304	395*	12.8	23.3
469 WISC EVAN LUTH	1	76	117	3.8	6.9
BON HOMME	26	3,734	7,944*	92.6	100.0
029 AMER LUTH CH..	2	286	377	4.4	4.7
081 CATHOLIC......	5	0	3,151	36.7	39.7
193 EPISCOPAL.....	2	18	23	0.3	0.3
283 LUTH--MO SYNOD	4	566	752	8.8	9.5
287 MENN GEN CONF.	1	77	91*	1.1	1.1
313 NO AM BAPT GC.	3	491	580*	6.8	7.3
371 REF CH IN AM..	1	334	584	6.8	7.4
443 UN C OF CHRIST	2	724	856*	10.0	10.8
449 UN METHODIST..	2	477	630	7.3	7.9
453 UN PRES CH USA	4	761	900*	10.5	11.3
BROOKINGS	36	8,439	13,569*	61.2	100.0
019 AMER BAPT CONV	1	194	227*	1.0	1.7
029 AMER LUTH CH..	6	3,618	4,902	22.1	36.1
081 CATHOLIC......	4	0	2,035	9.2	15.0
097 CR C AND C CR.	2	61	71*	0.3	0.5
105 CHRISTIAN REF.	1	236	393	1.8	2.9
123 CH GOD (ANDER)	1	170	360	1.6	2.7
127 CH GOD (CLEVE)	1	4	5*	-	-
193 EPISCOPAL.....	1	128	172	0.8	1.3
281 LUTH CH AMER..	1	65	79	0.4	0.6
283 LUTH--MO SYNOD	3	723	1,020	4.6	7.5
335 ORTH PRESB CH.	1	80	130	0.6	1.0
371 REF CH IN AM..	2	146	215	1.0	1.6
435 UNITARIAN-UNIV	1	16	16	0.1	0.1
443 UN C OF CHRIST	1	144	169*	0.8	1.2
449 UN METHODIST..	6	1,998	2,717	12.3	20.0
453 UN PRES CH USA	2	638	747*	3.4	5.5
469 WISC EVAN LUTH	2	218	311	1.4	2.3
BROWN	48	13,082	26,406*	71.5	100.0
019 AMER BAPT CONV	1	578	707*	1.9	2.7
029 AMER LUTH CH..	10	4,331	6,291	17.0	23.8
081 CATHOLIC......	5	0	8,329	22.6	31.5
093 CR CH (DISC)..	1	29	35*	0.1	0.1
127 CH GOD (CLEVE)	1	35	43*	0.1	0.2
165 CH OF NAZARENE	2	27	68	0.2	0.3
193 EPISCOPAL.....	1	208	482	1.3	1.8
281 LUTH CH AMER..	1	70	91	0.2	0.3

—Represents a percent less than 0.1.

Percentages may not total due to rounding.

Table 3. Churches and Church Membership by State, County and Denomination: 1971

County and Denomination	Number of churches	Communicant, confirmed, full members	Total adherents: Number	Total adherents: Percent of total population	Total adherents: Percent of total adherents
283 LUTH--MO SYNOD	8	2,692	3,706	10.0	14.0
313 NO AM BAPT GC.	1	191	234*	0.6	0.9
403 SALVATION ARMY	1	74	207	0.6	0.8
413 S-D ADVENTISTS	1	64	78*	0.2	0.3
443 UN C OF CHRIST	4	873	1,068*	2.9	4.0
449 UN METHODIST..	7	2,598	3,395	9.2	12.9
453 UN PRES CH USA	3	1,083	1,325*	3.6	5.0
469 WISC EVAN LUTH	1	229	347	0.9	1.3
BRULE	10	1,382	3,876*	66.0	100.0
029 AMER LUTH CH..	1	140	185	3.2	4.8
081 CATHOLIC......	3	0	2,036	34.7	52.5
193 EPISCOPAL.....	2	114	126	2.1	3.3
283 LUTH--MO SYNOD	1	484	683	11.6	17.6
443 UN C OF CHRIST	1	532	661*	11.3	17.1
449 UN METHODIST..	1	81	146	2.5	3.8
453 UN PRES CH USA	1	31	39*	0.7	1.0
BUFFALO	4	265	805*	46.3	100.0
081 CATHOLIC......	1	0	500	28.8	62.1
193 EPISCOPAL.....	2	209	227	13.1	28.2
453 UN PRES CH USA	1	56	78*	4.5	9.7
BUTTE	12	1,833	3,393*	43.4	100.0
019 AMER BAPT CONV	1	374	451*	5.8	13.3
029 AMER LUTH CH..	3	620	912	11.7	26.9
081 CATHOLIC......	2	0	892	11.4	26.3
193 EPISCOPAL.....	1	95	110	1.4	3.2
226 FRIENDS-USA...	1	34	41*	0.5	1.2
283 LUTH--MO SYNOD	1	69	109	1.4	3.2
443 UN C OF CHRIST	2	358	432*	5.5	12.7
449 UN METHODIST..	1	283	446	5.7	13.1
CAMPBELL	11	1,182	1,982*	69.2	100.0
029 AMER LUTH CH..	3	471	634	22.1	32.0
081 CATHOLIC......	1	0	449	15.7	22.7
127 CH GOD (CLEVE)	1	14	17*	0.6	0.9
313 NO AM BAPT GC.	1	240	298*	10.4	15.0
443 UN C OF CHRIST	1	36	45*	1.6	2.3
449 UN METHODIST..	2	57	80	2.8	4.0
453 UN PRES CH USA	1	244	303*	10.6	15.3
469 WISC EVAN LUTH	1	120	156	5.4	7.9
CHARLES MIX	30	3,123	7,553*	75.6	100.0
029 AMER LUTH CH..	3	551	778	7.8	10.3
081 CATHOLIC......	7	0	3,107	31.1	41.1
105 CHRISTIAN REF.	1	362	680	6.8	9.0
193 EPISCOPAL.....	4	259	402	4.0	5.3
283 LUTH--MO SYNOD	2	317	443	4.4	5.9
371 REF CH IN AM..	1	150	258	2.6	3.4
413 S-D ADVENTISTS	1	31	39*	0.4	0.5
419 SO BAPT CONV..	1	41	51*	0.5	0.7
443 UN C OF CHRIST	1	69	86*	0.9	1.1
449 UN METHODIST..	2	615	804	8.0	10.6
453 UN PRES CH USA	6	708	880*	8.8	11.7
469 WISC EVAN LUTH	1	20	25	0.3	0.3
CLARK	24	3,289	4,707*	85.3	100.0
019 AMER BAPT CONV	1	41	48*	0.9	1.0
029 AMER LUTH CH..	8	1,376	1,830	33.2	38.9
081 CATHOLIC......	2	0	503	9.1	10.7
287 MENN GEN CONF.	1	237	278*	5.0	5.9
371 REF CH IN AM..	1	118	155	2.8	3.3
443 UN C OF CHRIST	2	268	315*	5.7	6.7
449 UN METHODIST..	3	631	781	14.2	16.6
453 UN PRES CH USA	2	236	277*	5.0	5.9
469 WISC EVAN LUTH	4	382	520	9.4	11.0
CLAY	21	3,470	6,464*	50.0	100.0
019 AMER BAPT CONV	2	52	61*	0.5	0.9
029 AMER LUTH CH..	7	1,745	2,328	18.0	36.0
081 CATHOLIC......	2	0	1,914	14.8	29.6
193 EPISCOPAL.....	1	90	141	1.1	2.2
281 LUTH CH AMER..	2	363	463	3.6	7.2
283 LUTH--MO SYNOD	1	159	241	1.9	3.7
435 UNITARIAN-UNIV	1	13	13	0.1	0.2
443 UN C OF CHRIST	2	463	540*	4.2	8.4
449 UN METHODIST..	3	585	763	5.9	11.8
CODINGTON	32	7,452	15,551*	81.2	100.0
019 AMER BAPT CONV	2	236	288*	1.5	1.9
029 AMER LUTH CH..	6	2,865	3,906	20.4	25.1
081 CATHOLIC......	7	0	5,543	29.0	35.6
097 CR C AND C CR.	1	20	24*	0.1	0.2
193 EPISCOPAL.....	1	180	258	1.3	1.7
283 LUTH--MO SYNOD	1	200	303	1.6	1.9
403 SALVATION ARMY	1	88	345	1.8	2.2
413 S-D ADVENTISTS	1	63	77*	0.4	0.5
443 UN C OF CHRIST	2	717	876*	4.6	5.6
449 UN METHODIST..	4	1,426	1,701	8.9	10.9
469 WISC EVAN LUTH	6	1,657	2,230	11.7	14.3
CORSON	26	1,864	3,574*	71.6	100.0
029 AMER LUTH CH..	3	520	728	14.6	20.4
081 CATHOLIC......	4	0	944	18.9	26.4
127 CH GOD (CLEVE)	1	5	7*	0.1	0.2
193 EPISCOPAL.....	6	492	788	15.8	22.0
313 NO AM BAPT GC.	2	156	206*	4.1	5.8
413 S-D ADVENTISTS	1	15	20*	0.4	0.6
443 UN C OF CHRIST	3	303	401*	8.0	11.2
449 UN METHODIST..	1	65	86	1.7	2.4
453 UN PRES CH USA	2	156	206*	4.1	5.8
469 WISC EVAN LUTH	3	152	188	3.8	5.3
CUSTER	12	1,008	1,707*	36.3	100.0
019 AMER BAPT CONV	1	28	34*	0.7	2.0
029 AMER LUTH CH..	2	153	222	4.7	13.0
081 CATHOLIC......	2	0	422	9.0	24.7
283 LUTH--MO SYNOD	1	227	286	6.1	16.8
413 S-D ADVENTISTS	1	34	41*	0.9	2.4
443 UN C OF CHRIST	2	438	531*	11.3	31.1
449 UN METHODIST..	3	128	171	3.6	10.0
DAVISON	26	6,266	14,109*	81.5	100.0
019 AMER BAPT CONV	1	165	200*	1.2	1.4
029 AMER LUTH CH..	6	1,828	2,478	14.3	17.6
081 CATHOLIC......	4	0	5,477	31.6	38.8
165 CH OF NAZARENE	1	84	260	1.5	1.8
193 EPISCOPAL.....	1	239	367	2.1	2.6
281 LUTH CH AMER..	1	149	217	1.3	1.5
283 LUTH--MO SYNOD	2	965	1,305	7.5	9.2
371 REF CH IN AM..	1	146	242	1.4	1.7
403 SALVATION ARMY	1	54	221	1.3	1.6
413 S-D ADVENTISTS	1	18	22*	0.1	0.2
419 SO BAPT CONV..	1	6	7*	-	-
443 UN C OF CHRIST	2	412	500*	2.9	3.5
449 UN METHODIST..	3	1,922	2,476	14.3	17.5
453 UN PRES CH USA	1	278	337*	1.9	2.4
DAY	27	3,559	7,359*	84.5	100.0
019 AMER BAPT CONV	1	34	41*	0.5	0.6
029 AMER LUTH CH..	9	1,856	2,472	28.4	33.6
081 CATHOLIC......	6	0	2,510	28.8	34.1
193 EPISCOPAL.....	2	202	447	5.1	6.1
281 LUTH CH AMER..	1	395	528	6.1	7.2
283 LUTH--MO SYNOD	2	347	456	5.2	6.2
419 SO BAPT CONV..	1	15	18*	0.2	0.2
443 UN C OF CHRIST	1	114	137*	1.6	1.9
449 UN METHODIST..	3	541	684	7.9	9.3
453 UN PRES CH USA	1	55	66*	0.8	0.9
DEUEL	21	3,122	4,693*	82.5	100.0
019 AMER BAPT CONV	2	93	112*	2.0	2.4
029 AMER LUTH CH..	8	1,676	2,236	39.3	47.6
081 CATHOLIC......	2	0	535	9.4	11.4
105 CHRISTIAN REF.	1	104	184	3.2	3.9
201 EVAN COV CH AM	1	8	10*	0.2	0.2
443 UN C OF CHRIST	1	105	127*	2.2	2.7
449 UN METHODIST..	2	439	562	9.9	12.0
453 UN PRES CH USA	1	84	101*	1.8	2.2
469 WISC EVAN LUTH	3	613	826	14.5	17.6
DEWEY	19	1,338	3,067*	59.3	100.0
019 AMER BAPT CONV	1	201	273*	5.3	8.9
029 AMER LUTH CH..	2	208	281	5.4	9.2
081 CATHOLIC......	3	0	1,259	24.4	41.0
127 CH GOD (CLEVE)	1	22	30*	0.6	1.0
193 EPISCOPAL.....	4	332	448	8.7	14.6
313 NO AM BAPT GC.	1	64	87*	1.7	2.8
419 SO BAPT CONV..	1	28	38*	0.7	1.2
443 UN C OF CHRIST	3	214	291*	5.6	9.5
449 UN METHODIST..	1	123	168	3.2	5.5
469 WISC EVAN LUTH	2	146	192	3.7	6.3
DOUGLAS	19	3,002	4,749*	103.9 #	100.0
029 AMER LUTH CH..	6	748	1,003	22.0	21.1
081 CATHOLIC......	1	0	470	10.3	9.9
105 CHRISTIAN REF.	3	676	1,071	23.4	22.6
283 LUTH--MO SYNOD	3	592	802	17.6	16.9
371 REF CH IN AM..	3	504	811	17.8	17.1
443 UN C OF CHRIST	2	415	512*	11.2	10.8
449 UN METHODIST..	1	67	80	1.8	1.7
EDMUNDS	18	2,063	4,584*	82.6	100.0
019 AMER BAPT CONV	1	155	192*	3.5	4.2
029 AMER LUTH CH..	2	592	777	14.0	17.0
081 CATHOLIC......	4	0	1,950	35.1	42.5
283 LUTH--MO SYNOD	1	82	125	2.3	2.7
413 S-D ADVENTISTS	1	88	109*	2.0	2.4
443 UN C OF CHRIST	4	350	435*	7.8	9.5
449 UN METHODIST..	1	74	92	1.7	2.0
453 UN PRES CH USA	2	136	169*	3.0	3.7
469 WISC EVAN LUTH	2	586	735	13.2	16.0
FALL RIVER	18	2,286	4,091*	54.5	100.0
019 AMER BAPT CONV	1	715	826*	11.0	20.2
029 AMER LUTH CH..	1	162	225	3.0	5.5
081 CATHOLIC......	3	0	1,021	13.6	25.0
097 CR C AND C CR.	2	75	87*	1.2	2.1
193 EPISCOPAL.....	1	64	83	1.1	2.0
283 LUTH--MO SYNOD	2	439	626	8.3	15.3
413 S-D ADVENTISTS	1	36	42*	0.6	1.0
443 UN C OF CHRIST	1	82	95*	1.3	2.3

*Total adherents estimated from known number of communicant, confirmed, full members.

—Represents a percent less than 0.1.

Percentages may not total due to rounding.

#See Introduction for explanation of why total adherents reported by churches exceed the 1970 population figure.

Table 3. Churches and Church Membership by State, County and Denomination: 1971

County and Denomination	Number of churches	Communicant, confirmed, full members	Total adherents: Number	Total adherents: Percent of total population	Total adherents: Percent of total adherents
449 UN METHODIST..	5	545	892	11.9	21.8
453 UN PRES CH USA	1	168	194*	2.6	4.7
FAULK	17	1,442	3,102*	79.7	100.0
029 AMER LUTH CH..	1	93	125	3.2	4.0
081 CATHOLIC......	4	0	1,219	31.3	39.3
283 LUTH--MO SYNOD	5	358	476	12.2	15.3
443 UN C OF CHRIST	2	116	143*	3.7	4.6
449 UN METHODIST..	5	875	1,139	29.3	36.7
GRANT	20	3,876	7,431*	82.5	100.0
029 AMER LUTH CH..	3	875	1,286	14.3	17.3
081 CATHOLIC......	3	0	2,194	24.4	29.5
193 EPISCOPAL.....	1	51	56	0.6	0.8
201 EVAN COV CH AM	2	129	159*	1.8	2.1
281 LUTH CH AMER..	2	324	414	4.6	5.6
283 LUTH--MO SYNOD	3	1,226	1,730	19.2	23.3
443 UN C OF CHRIST	1	118	145*	1.6	2.0
449 UN METHODIST..	4	1,095	1,376	15.3	18.5
453 UN PRES CH USA	1	58	71*	0.8	1.0
GREGORY	27	2,434	4,438*	66.1	100.0
019 AMER BAPT CONV	5	414	501*	7.5	11.3
081 CATHOLIC......	5	0	1,160	17.3	26.1
193 EPISCOPAL.....	3	120	240	3.6	5.4
283 LUTH--MO SYNOD	3	562	759	11.3	17.1
443 UN C OF CHRIST	3	324	392*	5.8	8.8
449 UN METHODIST..	3	490	714	10.6	16.1
453 UN PRES CH USA	1	38	46*	0.7	1.0
469 WISC EVAN LUTH	4	486	626	9.3	14.1
HAAKON	14	885	1,871*	66.8	100.0
019 AMER BAPT CONV	1	12	15*	0.5	0.8
029 AMER LUTH CH..	4	459	647	23.1	34.6
081 CATHOLIC......	4	0	676	24.1	36.1
283 LUTH--MO SYNOD	2	183	258	9.2	13.8
449 UN METHODIST..	1	73	79	2.8	4.2
453 UN PRES CH USA	2	158	196*	7.0	10.5
HAMLIN	20	2,857	4,479*	86.6	100.0
029 AMER LUTH CH..	7	1,548	2,122	41.0	47.4
081 CATHOLIC......	3	0	708	13.7	15.8
201 EVAN COV CH AM	1	83	99*	1.9	2.2
281 LUTH CH AMER..	1	299	385	7.4	8.6
371 REF CH IN AM..	1	108	173	3.3	3.9
443 UN C OF CHRIST	2	206	247*	4.8	5.5
449 UN METHODIST..	2	146	182	3.5	4.1
453 UN PRES CH USA	1	310	371*	7.2	8.3
469 WISC EVAN LUTH	2	157	192	3.7	4.3
HAND	13	1,602	3,846*	65.4	100.0
029 AMER LUTH CH..	1	419	561	9.5	14.6
081 CATHOLIC......	4	0	1,685	28.6	43.8
165 CH OF NAZARENE	1	28	129	2.2	3.4
285 MENNONITE CH..	1	20	25*	0.4	0.7
443 UN C OF CHRIST	2	172	212*	3.6	5.5
449 UN METHODIST..	2	492	654	11.1	17.0
453 UN PRES CH USA	2	471	580*	9.9	15.1
HANSON	10	1,140	2,308*	61.0	100.0
081 CATHOLIC......	3	0	922	24.4	39.9
283 LUTH--MO SYNOD	2	265	330	8.7	14.3
313 NO AM BAPT GC.	2	459	572*	15.1	24.8
449 UN METHODIST..	2	298	337	8.9	14.6
453 UN PRES CH USA	1	118	147*	3.9	6.4
HARDING	13	432	1,073*	57.8	100.0
029 AMER LUTH CH..	4	316	428	23.1	39.9
081 CATHOLIC......	5	0	505	27.2	47.1
281 LUTH CH AMER..	1	16	20	1.1	1.9
443 UN C OF CHRIST	1	48	58*	3.1	5.4
449 UN METHODIST..	2	52	62	3.3	5.8
HUGHES	23	4,201	7,983*	68.6	100.0
019 AMER BAPT CONV	1	245	306*	2.6	3.8
029 AMER LUTH CH..	1	900	1,263	10.9	15.8
081 CATHOLIC......	3	0	1,870	16.1	23.4
093 CR CH (DISC)..	1	22	27*	0.2	0.3
097 CR C AND C CR.	1	97	121*	1.0	1.5
127 CH GOD (CLEVE)	1	5	6*	0.1	0.1
165 CH OF NAZARENE	2	59	76	0.7	1.0
193 EPISCOPAL.....	2	221	398	3.4	5.0
281 LUTH CH AMER..	1	96	153	1.3	1.9
283 LUTH--MO SYNOD	3	540	826	7.1	10.3
419 SO BAPT CONV..	1	162	202*	1.7	2.5
443 UN C OF CHRIST	1	404	504*	4.3	6.3
449 UN METHODIST..	3	1,233	1,944	16.7	24.4
453 UN PRES CH USA	1	186	232*	2.0	2.9
469 WISC EVAN LUTH	1	31	55	0.5	0.7
HUTCHINSON	27	6,027	9,609*	92.6	100.0
029 AMER LUTH CH..	5	1,167	1,444	13.9	15.0
081 CATHOLIC......	3	0	2,165	20.9	22.5
105 CHRISTIAN REF.	1	80	101	1.0	1.1
283 LUTH--MO SYNOD	6	1,176	1,585	15.3	16.5
287 MENN GEN CONF.	4	1,632	1,958*	18.9	20.4
313 NO AM BAPT GC.	1	129	155*	1.5	1.6
443 UN C OF CHRIST	5	1,569	1,882*	18.1	19.6
449 UN METHODIST..	2	274	319	3.1	3.3
HYDE	6	787	1,694*	67.4	100.0
029 AMER LUTH CH..	1	430	588	23.4	34.7
081 CATHOLIC......	2	0	650	25.8	38.4
093 CR CH (DISC)..	1	17	21*	0.8	1.2
097 CR C AND C CR.	1	20	25*	1.0	1.5
449 UN METHODIST..	1	320	410	16.3	24.2
JACKSON	9	577	884*	57.7	100.0
029 AMER LUTH CH..	1	125	190	12.4	21.5
081 CATHOLIC......	1	0	135	8.8	15.3
193 EPISCOPAL.....	2	21	37	2.4	4.2
283 LUTH--MO SYNOD	1	56	67	4.4	7.6
453 UN PRES CH USA	4	375	455*	29.7	51.5
JERAULD	15	1,670	2,412*	72.9	100.0
029 AMER LUTH CH..	1	410	526	15.9	21.8
081 CATHOLIC......	2	0	330	10.0	13.7
165 CH OF NAZARENE	1	3	3	0.1	0.1
221 FREE METH C NA	1	61	81	2.4	3.4
226 FRIENDS-USA...	1	7	8*	0.2	0.3
283 LUTH--MO SYNOD	1	119	167	5.0	6.9
313 NO AM BAPT GC.	2	124	147*	4.4	6.1
443 UN C OF CHRIST	3	426	505*	15.3	20.9
449 UN METHODIST..	3	520	645	19.5	26.7
JONES	7	581	963	51.2	100.0
081 CATHOLIC......	2	0	207	11.0	21.5
283 LUTH--MO SYNOD	2	208	294	15.6	30.5
371 REF CH IN AM..	1	33	56	3.0	5.8
449 UN METHODIST..	2	340	406	21.6	42.2
KINGSBURY	31	4,266	6,660*	87.0	100.0
029 AMER LUTH CH..	8	2,505	3,336	43.6	50.1
081 CATHOLIC......	4	0	1,140	14.9	17.1
097 CR C AND C CR.	1	35	41*	0.5	0.6
165 CH OF NAZARENE	1	3	3	-	-
193 EPISCOPAL.....	1	20	20	0.3	0.3
201 EVAN COV CH AM	1	13	15*	0.2	0.2
281 LUTH CH AMER..	1	73	91	1.2	1.4
283 LUTH--MO SYNOD	1	72	82	1.1	1.2
335 ORTH PRESB CH.	2	59	83	1.1	1.2
371 REF CH IN AM..	1	51	81	1.1	1.2
443 UN C OF CHRIST	3	501	588*	7.7	8.8
449 UN METHODIST..	6	837	1,066	13.9	16.0
453 UN PRES CH USA	1	97	114*	1.5	1.7
LAKE	23	4,738	8,337*	72.8	100.0
019 AMER BAPT CONV	1	109	129*	1.1	1.5
029 AMER LUTH CH..	7	2,341	3,228	28.2	38.7
081 CATHOLIC......	2	0	1,975	17.2	23.7
165 CH OF NAZARENE	1	65	105	0.9	1.3
193 EPISCOPAL.....	1	69	78	0.7	0.9
283 LUTH--MO SYNOD	3	544	762	6.7	9.1
313 NO AM BAPT GC.	1	248	294*	2.6	3.5
413 S-D ADVENTISTS	1	44	52*	0.5	0.6
443 UN C OF CHRIST	1	113	134*	1.2	1.6
449 UN METHODIST..	3	909	1,229	10.7	14.7
453 UN PRES CH USA	2	296	351*	3.1	4.2
LAWRENCE	27	4,793	8,713*	49.9	100.0
019 AMER BAPT CONV	2	309	373*	2.1	4.3
029 AMER LUTH CH..	2	905	1,228	7.0	14.1
081 CATHOLIC......	5	0	2,465	14.1	28.3
193 EPISCOPAL.....	3	458	641	3.7	7.4
221 FREE METH C NA	1	19	19	0.1	0.2
281 LUTH CH AMER..	2	317	466	2.7	5.3
283 LUTH--MO SYNOD	2	400	556	3.2	6.4
413 S-D ADVENTISTS	1	133	160*	0.9	1.8
443 UN C OF CHRIST	2	335	404*	2.3	4.6
449 UN METHODIST..	4	1,486	1,884	10.8	21.6
453 UN PRES CH USA	2	414	500*	2.9	5.7
469 WISC EVAN LUTH	1	17	17	0.1	0.2
LINCOLN	23	4,896	8,130*	69.1	100.0
029 AMER LUTH CH..	12	3,392	5,080	43.2	62.5
081 CATHOLIC......	4	0	1,043	8.9	12.8
371 REF CH IN AM..	1	105	199	1.7	2.4
443 UN C OF CHRIST	1	106	127*	1.1	1.6
449 UN METHODIST..	3	758	1,041	8.9	12.8
453 UN PRES CH USA	2	535	640*	5.4	7.9
LYMAN	17	1,141	2,207	54.4	100.0
029 AMER LUTH CH..	3	365	482	11.9	21.8
081 CATHOLIC......	5	0	564	13.9	25.6
193 EPISCOPAL.....	3	110	335	8.3	15.2
283 LUTH--MO SYNOD	1	184	222	5.5	10.1
449 UN METHODIST..	5	482	604	14.9	27.4
MC COOK	21	2,322	5,422*	74.8	100.0
029 AMER LUTH CH..	3	573	765	10.6	14.1

*Total adherents estimated from known number of communicant, confirmed, full members.

—Represents a percent less than 0.1.

Percentages may not total due to rounding.

Table 3. Churches and Church Membership by State, County and Denomination: 1971

County and Denomination	Number of churches	Communicant, confirmed, full members	Total adherents		
			Number	Percent of total population	Percent of total adherents
081 CATHOLIC......	4	0	2,335	32.2	43.1
097 CR C AND C CR.	1	50	61*	0.8	1.1
165 CH OF NAZARENE	1	24	50	0.7	0.9
201 EVAN COV CH AM	1	35	43*	0.6	0.8
281 LUTH CH AMER..	1	225	298	4.1	5.5
283 LUTH--MO SYNOD	3	612	849	11.7	15.7
335 ORTH PRESB CH.	1	46	63	0.9	1.2
449 UN METHODIST..	3	401	522	7.2	9.6
453 UN PRES CH USA	3	356	436*	6.0	8.0
MC PHERSON	13	2,760	4,097*	81.6	100.0
029 AMER LUTH CH..	3	1,600	2,086	41.5	50.9
081 CATHOLIC......	2	0	559	11.1	13.6
283 LUTH--MO SYNOD	1	189	256	5.1	6.2
313 NO AM BAPT GC.	2	261	311*	6.2	7.6
413 S-D ADVENTISTS	1	38	45*	0.9	1.1
443 UN C OF CHRIST	1	287	342*	6.8	8.3
449 UN METHODIST..	2	370	480	9.6	11.7
453 UN PRES CH USA	1	15	18*	0.4	0.4
MARSHALL	23	3,340	5,498*	92.2	100.0
029 AMER LUTH CH..	8	1,852	2,569	43.1	46.7
081 CATHOLIC......	4	0	1,024	17.2	18.6
193 EPISCOPAL.....	1	19	60	1.0	1.1
281 LUTH CH AMER..	1	118	133	2.2	2.4
283 LUTH--MO SYNOD	1	195	244	4.1	4.4
371 REF CH IN AM..	1	90	143	2.4	2.6
449 UN METHODIST..	2	330	425	7.1	7.7
453 UN PRES CH USA	5	736	900*	15.1	16.4
MEADE	20	2,009	6,161*	37.1	100.0
019 AMER BAPT CONV	1	51	63*	0.4	1.0
029 AMER LUTH CH..	1	524	708	4.3	11.5
081 CATHOLIC......	6	0	3,568	21.5	57.9
193 EPISCOPAL.....	1	80	123	0.7	2.0
419 SO BAPT CONV..	1	145	180*	1.1	2.9
443 UN C OF CHRIST	2	69	86*	0.5	1.4
449 UN METHODIST..	3	573	699	4.2	11.3
453 UN PRES CH USA	3	443	551*	3.3	8.9
469 WISC EVAN LUTH	2	124	183	1.1	3.0
MELLETTE	17	629	1,286*	53.1	100.0
019 AMER BAPT CONV	1	13	17*	0.7	1.3
081 CATHOLIC......	3	0	346	14.3	26.9
165 CH OF NAZARENE	2	57	64	2.6	5.0
193 EPISCOPAL.....	6	202	361	14.9	28.1
283 LUTH--MO SYNOD	1	118	172	7.1	13.4
413 S-D ADVENTISTS	1	18	23*	1.0	1.8
443 UN C OF CHRIST	1	62	80*	3.3	6.2
449 UN METHODIST..	1	132	185	7.6	14.4
469 WISC EVAN LUTH	1	27	38	1.6	3.0
MINER	18	2,023	3,955*	88.8	100.0
029 AMER LUTH CH..	3	710	914	20.5	23.1
081 CATHOLIC......	3	0	1,308	29.4	33.1
097 CR C AND C CR.	1	15	18*	0.4	0.5
165 CH OF NAZARENE	1	27	47	1.1	1.2
193 EPISCOPAL.....	1	29	29	0.7	0.7
281 LUTH CH AMER..	1	225	297	6.7	7.5
283 LUTH--MO SYNOD	1	356	480	10.8	12.1
443 UN C OF CHRIST	3	213	252*	5.7	6.4
449 UN METHODIST..	2	350	494	11.1	12.5
453 UN PRES CH USA	2	98	116*	2.6	2.9
MINNEHAHA	108	37,883	73,050*	76.7	100.0
019 AMER BAPT CONV	6	2,419	3,002*	3.2	4.1
029 AMER LUTH CH..	26	17,584	24,873	26.1	34.0
081 CATHOLIC......	11	0	19,935	20.9	27.3
093 CR CH (DISC)..	1	593	736*	0.8	1.0
097 CR C AND C CR.	1	35	43*	-	0.1
105 CHRISTIAN REF.	2	519	993	1.0	1.4
123 CH GOD (ANDER)	1	55	131	0.1	0.2
127 CH GOD (CLEVE)	1	10	12*	-	-
165 CH OF NAZARENE	1	55	128	0.1	0.2
193 EPISCOPAL.....	4	853	1,077	1.1	1.5
201 EVAN COV CH AM	2	143	177*	0.2	0.2
221 FREE METH C NA	2	47	57	0.1	0.1
281 LUTH CH AMER..	4	1,323	1,782	1.9	2.4
283 LUTH--MO SYNOD	7	2,843	3,997	4.2	5.5
287 MENN GEN CONF.	1	69	86*	0.1	0.1
313 NO AM BAPT GC.	2	255	316*	0.3	0.4
371 REF CH IN AM..	7	1,300	2,022	2.1	2.8
403 SALVATION ARMY	1	77	351	0.4	0.5
413 S-D ADVENTISTS	1	168	208*	0.2	0.3
419 SO BAPT CONV..	2	220	273*	0.3	0.4
435 UNITARIAN-UNIV	1	31	33	-	-
443 UN C OF CHRIST	5	1,620	2,010*	2.1	2.8
449 UN METHODIST..	12	5,634	8,249	8.7	11.3
453 UN PRES CH USA	5	1,852	2,298*	2.4	3.1
469 WISC EVAN LUTH	2	178	261	0.3	0.4
MOODY	17	2,838	4,881*	64.0	100.0
019 AMER BAPT CONV	2	183	219*	2.9	4.5
029 AMER LUTH CH..	4	1,435	1,900	24.9	38.9
081 CATHOLIC......	2	0	1,170	15.4	24.0
193 EPISCOPAL.....	1	32	57	0.7	1.2
283 LUTH--MO SYNOD	1	68	85	1.1	1.7
413 S-D ADVENTISTS	1	9	11*	0.1	0.2
449 UN METHODIST..	3	538	750	9.8	15.4
453 UN PRES CH USA	2	473	567*	7.4	11.6
469 WISC EVAN LUTH	1	100	122	1.6	2.5
PENNINGTON	58	15,693	29,074*	49.0	100.0
019 AMER BAPT CONV	2	465	583*	1.0	2.0
029 AMER LUTH CH..	5	3,819	5,572	9.4	19.2
081 CATHOLIC......	9	0	7,500	12.6	25.8
097 CR C AND C CR.	1	350	439*	0.7	1.5
105 CHRISTIAN REF.	1	57	123	0.2	0.4
123 CH GOD (ANDER)	1	66	127	0.2	0.4
127 CH GOD (CLEVE)	1	22	28*	-	0.1
165 CH OF NAZARENE	1	65	122	0.2	0.4
193 EPISCOPAL.....	3	1,007	1,362	2.3	4.7
221 FREE METH C NA	1	40	59	0.1	0.2
283 LUTH--MO SYNOD	6	1,911	2,718	4.6	9.3
313 NO AM BAPT GC.	2	130	163*	0.3	0.6
403 SALVATION ARMY	1	98	399	0.7	1.4
413 S-D ADVENTISTS	1	183	230*	0.4	0.8
419 SO BAPT CONV..	4	1,536	1,927*	3.2	6.6
443 UN C OF CHRIST	5	1,088	1,365*	2.3	4.7
449 UN METHODIST..	9	2,968	3,910	6.6	13.4
453 UN PRES CH USA	4	1,628	2,043*	3.4	7.0
469 WISC EVAN LUTH	1	260	404	0.7	1.4
PERKINS	24	1,815	3,368*	70.6	100.0
029 AMER LUTH CH..	8	958	1,326	27.8	39.4
081 CATHOLIC......	4	0	969	20.3	28.8
127 CH GOD (CLEVE)	1	157	190*	4.0	5.6
193 EPISCOPAL.....	1	15	18	0.4	0.5
313 NO AM BAPT GC.	2	54	65*	1.4	1.9
381 REF PRES-EVAN.	1	59	74	1.6	2.2
413 S-D ADVENTISTS	2	37	45*	0.9	1.3
449 UN METHODIST..	1	30	52	1.1	1.5
453 UN PRES CH USA	3	441	535*	11.2	15.9
469 WISC EVAN LUTH	1	64	94	2.0	2.8
POTTER	12	1,216	3,724*	83.7	100.0
081 CATHOLIC......	3	0	2,068	46.5	55.5
127 CH GOD (CLEVE)	2	39	49*	1.1	1.3
193 EPISCOPAL.....	1	76	125	2.8	3.4
283 LUTH--MO SYNOD	2	484	689	15.5	18.5
413 S-D ADVENTISTS	1	28	35*	0.8	0.9
449 UN METHODIST..	2	568	733	16.5	19.7
469 WISC EVAN LUTH	1	21	25	0.6	0.7
ROBERTS	36	4,927	8,722*	74.7	100.0
029 AMER LUTH CH..	9	2,634	3,529	30.2	40.5
081 CATHOLIC......	4	0	2,085	17.9	23.9
165 CH OF NAZARENE	1	8	13	0.1	0.1
193 EPISCOPAL.....	2	224	403	3.5	4.6
221 FREE METH C NA	1	7	7	0.1	0.1
281 LUTH CH AMER..	3	293	397	3.4	4.6
283 LUTH--MO SYNOD	5	699	951	8.1	10.9
313 NO AM BAPT GC.	1	96	120*	1.0	1.4
449 UN METHODIST..	4	175	215	1.8	2.5
453 UN PRES CH USA	5	700	875*	7.5	10.0
469 WISC EVAN LUTH	1	91	127	1.1	1.5
SANBORN	16	1,235	2,891*	78.2	100.0
029 AMER LUTH CH..	4	668	881	23.8	30.5
081 CATHOLIC......	3	0	1,239	33.5	42.9
165 CH OF NAZARENE	2	46	102	2.8	3.5
283 LUTH--MO SYNOD	1	94	137	3.7	4.7
443 UN C OF CHRIST	1	106	126*	3.4	4.4
449 UN METHODIST..	4	273	349	9.4	12.1
453 UN PRES CH USA	1	48	57*	1.5	2.0
SHANNON	30	1,321	6,488*	79.1	100.0
081 CATHOLIC......	6	0	4,150	50.6	64.0
123 CH GOD (ANDER)	1	10	69	0.8	1.1
193 EPISCOPAL.....	17	1,002	1,822	22.2	28.1
413 S-D ADVENTISTS	1	42	60*	0.7	0.9
453 UN PRES CH USA	4	147	211*	2.6	3.3
469 WISC EVAN LUTH	1	120	176	2.1	2.7
SPINK	27	3,375	6,422*	60.6	100.0
029 AMER LUTH CH..	2	567	767	7.2	11.9
081 CATHOLIC......	7	0	2,134	20.1	33.2
283 LUTH--MO SYNOD	3	522	703	6.6	10.9
413 S-D ADVENTISTS	1	44	52*	0.5	0.8
443 UN C OF CHRIST	5	713	848*	8.0	13.2
449 UN METHODIST..	8	1,467	1,844	17.4	28.7
453 UN PRES CH USA	1	62	74*	0.7	1.2
STANLEY	6	304	793*	32.3	100.0
029 AMER LUTH CH..	1	57	75	3.1	9.5
081 CATHOLIC......	1	0	375	15.3	47.3
193 EPISCOPAL.....	2	63	110	4.5	13.9
413 S-D ADVENTISTS	1	102	129*	5.3	16.3
443 UN C OF CHRIST	1	82	104*	4.2	13.1
SULLY	7	649	1,245*	52.7	100.0
081 CATHOLIC......	2	0	350	14.8	28.1
283 LUTH--MO SYNOD	2	200	278	11.8	22.3
449 UN METHODIST..	2	279	402	17.0	32.3

*Total adherents estimated from known number of communicant, confirmed, full members.

—Represents a percent less than 0.1.

Percentages may not total due to rounding.

Table 3. Churches and Church Membership by State, County and Denomination: 1971

County and Denomination	Number of churches	Communicant, confirmed, full members	Total adherents: Number	Percent of total population	Percent of total adherents
453 UN PRES CH USA	1	170	215*	9.1	17.3
TODD	12	631	1,786	27.0	100.0
081 CATHOLIC......	3	0	708	10.7	39.6
193 EPISCOPAL......	7	395	761	11.5	42.6
449 UN METHODIST..	1	87	111	1.7	6.2
469 WISC EVAN LUTH	1	149	206	3.1	11.5
TRIPP	26	2,235	4,472*	54.7	100.0
019 AMER BAPT CONV	3	197	241*	2.9	5.4
029 AMER LUTH CH..	1	63	59	0.7	1.3
081 CATHOLIC......	6	0	1,248	15.3	27.9
093 CR CH (DISC)..	1	114	140*	1.7	3.1
193 EPISCOPAL.....	1	146	382	4.7	8.5
283 LUTH--MO SYNOD	2	173	235	2.9	5.3
335 ORTH PRESB CH.	2	106	193	2.4	4.3
443 UN C OF CHRIST	2	36	44*	0.5	1.0
449 UN METHODIST..	3	719	978	12.0	21.9
453 UN PRES CH USA	1	71	87*	1.1	1.9
469 WISC EVAN LUTH	4	610	865	10.6	19.3
TURNER	42	6,049	8,941*	90.6	100.0
019 AMER BAPT CONV	4	438	514*	5.2	5.7
029 AMER LUTH CH..	7	1,901	2,476	25.1	27.7
081 CATHOLIC......	4	0	1,238	12.5	13.8
123 CH GOD (ANDER)	1	124	259	2.6	2.9
165 CH OF NAZARENE	1	27	41	0.4	0.5
211 EV MENN BRETH.	1	143	168*	1.7	1.9
281 LUTH CH AMER..	1	249	290	2.9	3.2
283 LUTH--MO SYNOD	4	506	666	6.7	7.4
287 MENN GEN CONF.	2	288	338*	3.4	3.8
313 NO AM BAPT GC.	1	222	260*	2.6	2.9
371 REF CH IN AM..	4	539	784	7.9	8.8
413 S-D ADVENTISTS	1	69	81*	0.8	0.9
443 UN C OF CHRIST	1	99	116*	1.2	1.3
449 UN METHODIST..	5	580	697	7.1	7.8
453 UN PRES CH USA	5	864	1,013*	10.3	11.3
UNION	22	3,530	6,837*	70.9	100.0
029 AMER LUTH CH..	7	1,771	2,314	24.0	33.8
081 CATHOLIC......	5	0	2,400	24.9	35.1
201 EVAN COV CH AM	1	68	83*	0.9	1.2
281 LUTH CH AMER..	3	582	716	7.4	10.5
283 LUTH--MO SYNOD	1	245	286	3.0	4.2
443 UN C OF CHRIST	3	460	558*	5.8	8.2
449 UN METHODIST..	2	404	480	5.0	7.0
WALWORTH	21	3,825	6,418*	81.8	100.0
019 AMER BAPT CONV	1	236	295*	3.8	4.6
029 AMER LUTH CH..	4	1,730	2,361	30.1	36.8
081 CATHOLIC......	2	0	1,320	16.8	20.6
127 CH GOD (CLEVE)	1	50	62*	0.8	1.0
193 EPISCOPAL.....	1	85	126	1.6	2.0
313 NO AM BAPT GC.	1	48	60*	0.8	0.9
413 S-D ADVENTISTS	1	46	57*	0.7	0.9
443 UN C OF CHRIST	5	803	1,003*	12.8	15.6
449 UN METHODIST..	2	281	406	5.2	6.3
469 WISC EVAN LUTH	3	546	728	9.3	11.3
WASHABAUGH	6	227	1,248	89.8	100.0
029 AMER LUTH CH..	1	41	69	5.0	5.5
081 CATHOLIC......	2	0	847	61.0	67.9
193 EPISCOPAL.....	3	186	332	23.9	26.6
YANKTON	24	2,938	12,546*	65.9	100.0
029 AMER LUTH CH..	8	224	3,046	16.0	24.3
081 CATHOLIC......	4	0	5,680	29.8	45.3
165 CH OF NAZARENE	1	51	167	0.9	1.3
193 EPISCOPAL.....	1	230	355	1.9	2.8
221 FREE METH C NA	1	19	27	0.1	0.2
283 LUTH--MO SYNOD	2	779	1,104	5.8	8.8
371 REF CH IN AM..	1	72	119	0.6	0.9
413 S-D ADVENTISTS	1	17	21*	0.1	0.2
443 UN C OF CHRIST	3	805	973*	5.1	7.8
449 UN METHODIST..	2	741	1,054	5.5	8.4
ZIEBACH	10	344	1,305*	58.8	100.0
081 CATHOLIC......	3	0	839	37.8	64.3
193 EPISCOPAL.....	4	125	170	7.7	13.0
443 UN C OF CHRIST	2	159	215*	9.7	16.5
469 WISC EVAN LUTH	1	60	81	3.6	6.2
CO DATA NOT AVAIL	24	813	4,256*	N/A	N/A
127 CH GOD (CLEVE)	1	17	21*	N/A	N/A
151 L-D SAINTS....	0	0	3,282	N/A	N/A
467 WESLEYAN......	23	796	953	N/A	N/A

TENNESSEE

County and Denomination	Number of churches	Communicant, confirmed, full members	Total adherents: Number	Percent of total population	Percent of total adherents
THE STATE.....	6,608	1,556,836	1,965,320*	50.1	100.0
ANDERSON	111	35,250	45,310*	75.1	100.0
081 CATHOLIC......	3	0	2,679	4.4	5.9
093 CR CH (DISC)..	1	234	284*	0.5	0.6
097 CR C AND C CR.	2	179	218*	0.4	0.5
123 CH GOD (ANDER)	1	37	86	0.1	0.2
127 CH GOD (CLEVE)	4	366	445*	0.7	1.0
165 CH OF NAZARENE	1	89	153	0.3	0.3
185 CUMBER PRESB..	1	234	284*	0.5	0.6
193 EPISCOPAL.....	2	809	1,149	1.9	2.5
281 LUTH CH AMER..	1	427	548	0.9	1.2
283 LUTH--MO SYNOD	1	279	385	0.6	0.8
357 PRESB CH US...	1	280	340*	0.6	0.8
419 SO BAPT CONV..	72	25,533	31,042*	51.5	68.5
435 UNITARIAN-UNIV	1	239	359	0.6	0.8
449 UN METHODIST..	19	5,998	6,674	11.1	14.7
453 UN PRES CH USA	1	546	664*	1.1	1.5
BEDFORD	62	10,012	11,841*	47.3	100.0
081 CATHOLIC......	1	0	168	0.7	1.4
093 CR CH (DISC)..	1	371	449*	1.8	3.8
123 CH GOD (ANDER)	1	21	51	0.2	0.4
127 CH GOD (CLEVE)	1	69	84*	0.3	0.7
165 CH OF NAZARENE	4	246	409	1.6	3.5
185 CUMBER PRESB..	3	86	104*	0.4	0.9
193 EPISCOPAL.....	1	53	91	0.4	0.8
281 LUTH CH AMER..	4	192	231	0.9	2.0
353 PLY BRETHREN..	1	40	75	0.3	0.6
357 PRESB CH US...	2	499	604*	2.4	5.1
419 SO BAPT CONV..	16	4,547	5,507*	22.0	46.5
449 UN METHODIST..	26	3,854	4,027	16.1	34.0
453 UN PRES CH USA	1	34	41*	0.2	0.3
BENTON	35	5,152	6,059*	50.0	100.0
081 CATHOLIC......	1	0	123	1.0	2.0
165 CH OF NAZARENE	1	61	124	1.0	2.0
185 CUMBER PRESB..	2	233	281*	2.3	4.6
419 SO BAPT CONV..	11	3,003	3,624*	29.9	59.8
449 UN METHODIST..	19	1,830	1,877	15.5	31.0
453 UN PRES CH USA	1	25	30*	0.2	0.5
BLEDSOE	17	1,354	1,555*	20.3	100.0
127 CH GOD (CLEVE)	7	303	363*	4.7	23.3
413 S-D ADVENTISTS	1	30	36*	0.5	2.3
419 SO BAPT CONV..	4	551	660*	8.6	42.4
449 UN METHODIST..	5	470	496	6.5	31.9
BLOUNT	130	35,189	42,388*	66.5	100.0
081 CATHOLIC......	2	0	500	0.8	1.2
097 CR C AND C CR.	4	555	670*	1.1	1.6
123 CH GOD (ANDER)	1	15	41	0.1	0.1
127 CH GOD (CLEVE)	4	466	562*	0.9	1.3
165 CH OF NAZARENE	2	128	244	0.4	0.6
185 CUMBER PRESB..	2	332	401*	0.6	0.9
193 EPISCOPAL.....	1	353	451	0.7	1.1
226 FRIENDS-USA...	2	209	252*	0.4	0.6
281 LUTH CH AMER..	1	138	213	0.3	0.5
357 PRESB CH US...	1	97	117*	0.2	0.3
413 S-D ADVENTISTS	1	52	63*	0.1	0.1
419 SO BAPT CONV..	77	24,586	29,672*	46.5	70.0
449 UN METHODIST..	23	6,556	7,148	11.2	16.9
453 UN PRES CH USA	9	1,702	2,054*	3.2	4.8
BRADLEY	103	22,388	28,191*	55.6	100.0
059 BAPT MISS ASSN	3	236	294*	0.6	1.0
081 CATHOLIC......	1	0	846	1.7	3.0
093 CR CH (DISC)..	2	110	137*	0.3	0.5
097 CR C AND C CR.	2	95	118*	0.2	0.4
127 CH GOD (CLEVE)	12	2,720	3,385*	6.7	12.0
165 CH OF NAZARENE	1	62	126	0.2	0.4
185 CUMBER PRESB..	7	784	976*	1.9	3.5
193 EPISCOPAL.....	1	456	460	0.9	1.6
283 LUTH--MO SYNOD	1	179	273	0.5	1.0
357 PRESB CH US...	2	370	460*	0.9	1.6
413 S-D ADVENTISTS	1	346	431*	0.9	1.5
419 SO BAPT CONV..	49	13,367	16,634*	32.8	59.0
449 UN METHODIST..	21	3,663	4,051	8.0	14.4
CAMPBELL	60	11,504	13,824*	53.1	100.0
081 CATHOLIC......	1	0	46	0.2	0.3
093 CR CH (DISC)..	1	22	27*	0.1	0.2
097 CR C AND C CR.	1	50	61*	0.2	0.4
127 CH GOD (CLEVE)	5	509	620*	2.4	4.5
357 PRESB CH US...	2	125	152*	0.6	1.1
419 SO BAPT CONV..	41	9,260	11,273*	43.3	81.5
449 UN METHODIST..	9	1,538	1,645	6.3	11.9
CANNON	23	2,604	3,009*	35.5	100.0
127 CH GOD (CLEVE)	1	64	77*	0.9	2.6
165 CH OF NAZARENE	1	25	48	0.6	1.6
221 FREE METH C NA	1	28	37	0.4	1.2
357 PRESB CH US...	1	12	14*	0.2	0.5
413 S-D ADVENTISTS	1	79	94*	1.1	3.1
419 SO BAPT CONV..	9	1,673	2,000*	23.6	66.5
449 UN METHODIST..	9	723	739	8.7	24.6

*Total adherents estimated from known number of communicant, confirmed, full members.

—Represents a percent less than 0.1.

Percentages may not total due to rounding.

Table 3. Churches and Church Membership by State, County and Denomination: 1971

County and Denomination	Number of churches	Communicant, confirmed, full members	Total adherents: Number	Total adherents: Percent of total population	Total adherents: Percent of total adherents
CARROLL	61	9,706	11,030*	42.8	100.0
081 CATHOLIC......	1	0	35	0.1	0.3
185 CUMBER PRESB..	10	807	958*	3.7	8.7
357 PRESB CH US...	1	15	18*	0.1	0.2
413 S-D ADVENTISTS	2	105	125*	0.5	1.1
419 SO BAPT CONV..	19	5,518	6,552*	25.5	59.4
449 UN METHODIST..	25	3,086	3,134	12.2	28.4
453 UN PRES CH USA	3	175	208*	0.8	1.9
CARTER	94	20,457	24,822*	58.3	100 0
081 CATHOLIC......	1	0	127	0.3	0.5
093 CR CH (DISC)..	5	531	640*	1.5	2.6
097 CR C AND C CR.	23	3,895	4,697*	11.0	18.9
123 CH GOD (ANDER)	2	86	283	0.7	1.1
127 CH GOD (CLEVE)	2	195	235*	0.6	0.9
165 CH OF NAZARENE	1	57	106	0.2	0.4
193 EPISCOPAL.....	1	65	65	0.2	0.3
283 LUTH--MO SYNOD	1	86	108	0.3	0.4
357 PRESB CH US...	4	310	374*	0.9	1.5
413 S-D ADVENTISTS	1	38	46*	0.1	0.2
419 SO BAPT CONV..	42	13,287	16,021*	37.6	64.5
449 UN METHODIST..	10	1,745	1,925	4.5	7.8
453 UN PRES CH USA	1	162	195*	0.5	0.8
CHEATHAM	15	2,104	2,500*	18.9	100.0
165 CH OF NAZARENE	3	89	236	1.8	9.4
413 S-D ADVENTISTS	1	39	49*	0.4	2.0
419 SO BAPT CONV..	2	562	702*	5.3	28.1
449 UN METHODIST..	9	1,414	1,513	11.5	60.5
CHESTER	18	2,909	3,392*	34.2	100.0
081 CATHOLIC......	0	0	25	0.3	0.7
093 CR CH (DISC)..	1	49	59*	0.6	1.7
127 CH GOD (CLEVE)	1	35	42*	0.4	1.2
185 CUMBER PRESB..	1	114	136*	1.4	4.0
419 SO BAPT CONV..	11	2,065	2,469*	24.9	72.8
449 UN METHODIST..	4	646	661	6.7	19.5
CLAIBORNE	96	13,686	16,310*	84.0	100.0
097 CR C AND C CR.	2	107	129*	0.7	0.8
413 S-D ADVENTISTS	1	20	24*	0.1	0.1
419 SO BAPT CONV..	82	12,284	14,845*	76.4	91.0
449 UN METHODIST..	11	1,275	1,312	6.8	8.0
CLAY	7	819	956*	14.4	100.0
123 CH GOD (ANDER)	1	50	141	2.1	14.7
413 S-D ADVENTISTS	1	20	24*	0.4	2.5
419 SO BAPT CONV..	1	187	225*	3.4	23.5
449 UN METHODIST..	4	562	566	8.5	59.2
COCKE	65	10,309	12,747*	50.4	100.0
081 CATHOLIC......	1	0	57	0.2	0.4
093 CR CH (DISC)..	1	140	173*	0.7	1.4
097 CR C AND C CR.	4	462	571*	2.3	4.5
123 CH GOD (ANDER)	2	98	231	0.9	1.8
127 CH GOD (CLEVE)	3	410	507*	2.0	4.0
165 CH OF NAZARENE	1	25	168	0.7	1.3
193 EPISCOPAL.....	1	36	43	0.2	0.3
281 LUTH CH AMER..	3	529	616	2.4	4.8
357 PRESB CH US...	1	137	169*	0.7	1.3
419 SO BAPT CONV..	37	7,041	8,707*	34.4	68.3
449 UN METHODIST..	10	1,423	1,495	5.9	11.7
453 UN PRES CH USA	1	8	10*	-	0.1
COFFEE	57	11,634	14,973*	46.0	100.0
081 CATHOLIC......	2	0	880	2.7	5.9
093 CR CH (DISC)..	1	421	520*	1.6	3.5
097 CR C AND C CR.	1	34	42*	0.1	0.3
123 CH GOD (ANDER)	1	49	124	0.4	0.8
127 CH GOD (CLEVE)	2	111	137*	0.4	0.9
165 CH OF NAZARENE	6	273	555	1.7	3.7
185 CUMBER PRESB..	4	293	362*	1.1	2.4
193 EPISCOPAL.....	2	303	343	1.1	2.3
281 LUTH CH AMER..	1	398	558	1.7	3.7
283 LUTH--MO SYNOD	1	139	193	0.6	1.3
357 PRESB CH US...	1	97	120*	0.4	0.8
419 SO BAPT CONV..	13	5,241	6,468*	19.9	43.2
435 UNITARIAN-UNIV	1	25	45	0.1	0.3
449 UN METHODIST..	20	3,976	4,288	13.2	28.6
453 UN PRES CH USA	1	274	338*	1.0	2.3
CROCKETT	30	5,767	6,738*	46.8	100.0
081 CATHOLIC......	0	0	84	0.6	1.2
093 CR CH (DISC)..	2	141	170*	1.2	2.5
127 CH GOD (CLEVE)	1	32	39*	0.3	0.6
185 CUMBER PRESB..	2	214	258*	1.8	3.8
419 SO BAPT CONV..	13	3,684	4,445*	30.9	66.0
449 UN METHODIST..	12	1,696	1,742	12.1	25.9
CUMBERLAND	47	5,999	7,261*	35.0	100.0
081 CATHOLIC......	1	0	127	0.6	1.7
093 CR CH (DISC)..	1	305	376*	1.8	5.2
127 CH GOD (CLEVE)	2	175	216*	1.0	3.0
165 CH OF NAZARENE	2	111	171	0.8	2.4
413 S-D ADVENTISTS	1	90	111*	0.5	1.5
419 SO BAPT CONV..	25	3,502	4,315*	20.8	59.4
443 UN C OF CHRIST	2	294	362*	1.7	5.0
449 UN METHODIST..	11	1,393	1,424	6.9	19.6
453 UN PRES CH USA	2	129	159*	0.8	2.2
DAVIDSON	313	141,032	191,838*	42.8	100.0
029 AMER LUTH CH..	1	174	246	0.1	0.1
081 CATHOLIC......	15	0	22,201	5.0	11.6
093 CR CH (DISC)..	11	3,523	4,253*	0.9	2.2
097 CR C AND C CR.	2	400	483*	0.1	0.3
123 CH GOD (ANDER)	3	250	599	0.1	0.3
127 CH GOD (CLEVE)	6	782	944*	0.2	0.5
165 CH OF NAZARENE	31	3,099	5,720	1.3	3.0
185 CUMBER PRESB..	13	4,006	4,836*	1.1	2.5
193 EPISCOPAL.....	10	5,205	6,571	1.5	3.4
221 FREE METH C NA	1	13	19	-	-
226 FRIENDS-USA...	1	24	29*	-	-
281 LUTH CH AMER..	5	1,474	2,011	0.4	1.0
283 LUTH--MO SYNOD	4	604	822	0.2	0.4
315 NO AM OLD RC..	1	73	88*	-	-
353 PLY BRETHREN..	1	85	140	-	0.1
357 PRESB CH US...	19	9,047	10,922*	2.4	5.7
381 REF PRES-EVAN.	1	23	42	-	-
403 SALVATION ARMY	2	95	399	0.1	0.2
413 S-D ADVENTISTS	7	2,445	2,952*	0.7	1.5
419 SO BAPT CONV..	94	68,960	83,253*	18.6	43.4
435 UNITARIAN-UNIV	1	236	371	0.1	0.2
443 UN C OF CHRIST	2	275	332*	0.1	0.2
449 UN METHODIST..	76	39,329	43,504	9.7	22.7
453 UN PRES CH USA	5	903	1,090*	0.2	0.6
469 WISC EVAN LUTH	1	7	11	-	-
DECATUR	33	3,601	4,095*	43.3	100.0
081 CATHOLIC......	1	0	20	0.2	0.5
185 CUMBER PRESB..	3	166	198*	2.1	4.8
413 S-D ADVENTISTS	1	10	12*	0.1	0.3
419 SO BAPT CONV..	18	2,158	2,569*	27.2	62.7
449 UN METHODIST..	10	1,267	1,296	13.7	31.6
DE KALB	41	5,733	6,541*	58.7	100.0
075 BRETHREN IN CR	1	52	63*	0.6	1.0
127 CH GOD (CLEVE)	1	120	145*	1.3	2.2
165 CH OF NAZARENE	1	14	32	0.3	0.5
185 CUMBER PRESB..	2	250	302*	2.7	4.6
419 SO BAPT CONV..	18	3,261	3,941*	35.3	60.3
449 UN METHODIST..	17	1,989	2,001	17.9	30.6
453 UN PRES CH USA	1	47	57*	0.5	0.9
DICKSON	47	5,505	6,495*	29.6	100.0
081 CATHOLIC......	1	0	324	1.5	5.0
165 CH OF NAZARENE	2	143	221	1.0	3.4
185 CUMBER PRESB..	4	279	343*	1.6	5.3
193 EPISCOPAL.....	1	21	25	0.1	0.4
349 PENT HOLINESS.	1	5	6*	-	0.1
413 S-D ADVENTISTS	1	57	70*	0.3	1.1
419 SO BAPT CONV..	10	1,941	2,389*	10.9	36.8
449 UN METHODIST..	23	2,871	2,886	13.1	44.4
453 UN PRES CH USA	4	188	231*	1.1	3.6
DYER	68	13,735	16,306*	53.6	100.0
081 CATHOLIC......	1	0	281	0.9	1.7
097 CR C AND C CR.	2	295	358*	1.2	2.2
127 CH GOD (CLEVE)	2	234	284*	0.9	1.7
185 CUMBER PRESB..	6	777	942*	3.1	5.8
193 EPISCOPAL.....	1	103	108	0.4	0.7
357 PRESB CH US...	1	163	198*	0.7	1.2
413 S-D ADVENTISTS	2	64	78*	0.3	0.5
419 SO BAPT CONV..	29	8,255	10,007*	32.9	61.4
449 UN METHODIST..	22	3,747	3,932	12.9	24.1
453 UN PRES CH USA	2	97	118*	0.4	0.7
FAYETTE	37	5,174	6,512*	28.7	100.0
081 CATHOLIC......	0	0	35	0.2	0.5
093 CR CH (DISC)..	2	124	162*	0.7	2.5
127 CH GOD (CLEVE)	1	62	81*	0.4	1.2
185 CUMBER PRESB..	3	150	196*	0.9	3.0
193 EPISCOPAL.....	2	28	32	0.1	0.5
357 PRESB CH US...	3	314	411*	1.8	6.3
419 SO BAPT CONV..	15	3,192	4,181*	18.4	64.2
449 UN METHODIST..	11	1,304	1,414	6.2	21.7
FENTRESS	23	2,971	3,575*	28.4	100.0
127 CH GOD (CLEVE)	2	66	83*	0.7	2.3
165 CH OF NAZARENE	2	79	257	2.0	7.2
419 SO BAPT CONV..	8	1,385	1,748*	13.9	48.9
449 UN METHODIST..	10	1,338	1,357	10.8	38.0
453 UN PRES CH USA	1	103	130*	1.0	3.6
FRANKLIN	67	9,791	12,348*	45.3	100.0
081 CATHOLIC......	2	0	436	1.6	3.5
127 CH GOD (CLEVE)	5	159	193*	0.7	1.6
165 CH OF NAZARENE	6	317	851	3.1	6.9
185 CUMBER PRESB..	12	1,358	1,644*	6.0	13.3
193 EPISCOPAL.....	5	798	931	3.4	7.5
357 PRESB CH US...	1	89	108*	0.4	0.9
413 S-D ADVENTISTS	1	61	74*	0.3	0.6
419 SO BAPT CONV..	19	4,356	5,275*	19.4	42.7

*Total adherents estimated from known number of communicant, confirmed, full members.

—Represents a percent less than 0.1.

Percentages may not total due to rounding.

Table 3. Churches and Church Membership by State, County and Denomination: 1971

County and Denomination	Number of churches	Communicant, confirmed, full members	Total adherents: Number	Total adherents: Percent of total population	Total adherents: Percent of total adherents
443 UN C OF CHRIST	1	153	185*	0.7	1.5
449 UN METHODIST..	13	2,421	2,555	9.4	20.7
453 UN PRES CH USA	2	79	96*	0.4	0.8
GIBSON	102	23,550	27,942*	58.4	100.0
081 CATHOLIC......	1	0	410	0.9	1.5
093 CR CH (DISC)..	1	233	281*	0.6	1.0
127 CH GOD (CLEVE)	1	104	125*	0.3	0.4
185 CUMBER PRESB..	13	1,822	2,198*	4.6	7.9
193 EPISCOPAL.....	2	62	94	0.2	0.3
349 PENT HOLINESS.	1	60	72*	0.2	0.3
357 PRESB CH US...	4	432	521*	1.1	1.9
419 SO BAPT CONV..	46	14,876	17,944*	37.5	64.2
449 UN METHODIST..	30	5,604	5,866	12.3	21.0
453 UN PRES CH USA	3	357	431*	0.9	1.5
GILES	59	9,105	10,478*	47.3	100.0
081 CATHOLIC......	1	0	114	0.5	1.1
123 CH GOD (ANDER)	2	54	136	0.6	1.3
127 CH GOD (CLEVE)	1	49	59*	0.3	0.6
185 CUMBER PRESB..	2	60	72*	0.3	0.7
193 EPISCOPAL.....	1	84	167	0.8	1.6
357 PRESB CH US...	5	415	496*	2.2	4.7
419 SO BAPT CONV..	21	4,481	5,357*	24.2	51.1
449 UN METHODIST..	26	3,962	4,077	18.4	38.9
GRAINGER	62	10,342	12,560*	90.0	100.0
157 CH OF BRETHREN	1	32	40*	0.3	0.3
357 PRESB CH US...	2	21	26*	0.2	0.2
419 SO BAPT CONV..	47	9,225	11,409*	81.8	90.8
449 UN METHODIST..	12	1,064	1,085	7.8	8.6
GREENE	129	18,062	22,527*	47.3	100.0
081 CATHOLIC......	1	0	396	0.8	1.8
093 CR CH (DISC)..	1	156	189*	0.4	0.8
097 CR C AND C CR.	2	430	520*	1.1	2.3
123 CH GOD (ANDER)	6	850	2,226	4.7	9.9
127 CH GOD (CLEVE)	3	192	232*	0.5	1.0
157 CH OF BRETHREN	1	208	252*	0.5	1.1
165 CH OF NAZARENE	2	100	242	0.5	1.1
185 CUMBER PRESB..	11	1,565	1,894*	4.0	8.4
193 EPISCOPAL.....	1	140	262	0.6	1.2
281 LUTH CH AMER..	4	1,038	1,238	2.6	5.5
283 LUTH--MO SYNOD	1	48	64	0.1	0.3
335 ORTH PRESB CH.	1	12	12	-	0.1
349 PENT HOLINESS.	2	53	64*	0.1	0.3
357 PRESB CH US...	3	163	197*	0.4	0.9
413 S-D ADVENTISTS	2	236	286*	0.6	1.3
419 SO BAPT CONV..	21	4,671	5,653*	11.9	25.1
449 UN METHODIST..	58	7,263	7,666	16.1	34.0
453 UN PRES CH USA	9	937	1,134*	2.4	5.0
GRUNDY	29	2,032	2,430*	22.9	100.0
127 CH GOD (CLEVE)	4	170	207*	1.9	8.5
165 CH OF NAZARENE	2	87	153	1.4	6.3
185 CUMBER PRESB..	1	30	37*	0.3	1.5
193 EPISCOPAL.....	2	121	156	1.5	6.4
353 PLY BRETHREN..	1	10	15	0.1	0.6
413 S-D ADVENTISTS	3	200	244*	2.3	10.0
419 SO BAPT CONV..	7	532	648*	6.1	26.7
449 UN METHODIST..	9	882	970	9.1	39.9
HAMBLEN	68	19,018	23,873*	61.7	100.0
081 CATHOLIC......	1	0	378	1.0	1.6
097 CR C AND C CR.	1	250	311*	0.8	1.3
123 CH GOD (ANDER)	1	52	128	0.3	0.5
127 CH GOD (CLEVE)	2	189	235*	0.6	1.0
165 CH OF NAZARENE	1	30	82	0.2	0.3
185 CUMBER PRESB..	1	127	158*	0.4	0.7
193 EPISCOPAL.....	1	123	339	0.9	1.4
281 LUTH CH AMER..	1	120	178	0.5	0.7
283 LUTH--MO SYNOD	1	47	76	0.2	0.3
357 PRESB CH US...	2	766	952*	2.5	4.0
413 S-D ADVENTISTS	1	91	113*	0.3	0.5
419 SO BAPT CONV..	39	13,856	17,225*	44.5	72.2
449 UN METHODIST..	14	3,190	3,478	9.0	14.6
453 UN PRES CH USA	2	177	220*	0.6	0.9
HAMILTON	275	101,449	129,474*	50.9	100.0
081 CATHOLIC......	6	0	6,113	2.4	4.7
093 CR CH (DISC)..	3	1,105	1,341*	0.5	1.0
097 CR C AND C CR.	3	709	860*	0.3	0.7
123 CH GOD (ANDER)	5	278	716	0.3	0.6
127 CH GOD (CLEVE)	36	4,351	5,281*	2.1	4.1
165 CH OF NAZARENE	9	1,231	2,032	0.8	1.6
185 CUMBER PRESB..	7	2,712	3,291*	1.3	2.5
193 EPISCOPAL.....	9	4,335	5,192	2.0	4.0
226 FRIENDS-USA...	1	7	8*	-	-
281 LUTH CH AMER..	2	533	749	0.3	0.6
283 LUTH--MO SYNOD	4	1,022	1,414	0.6	1.1
357 PRESB CH US...	17	8,247	10,009*	3.9	7.7
403 SALVATION ARMY	2	174	1,528	0.6	1.2
413 S-D ADVENTISTS	7	3,764	4,568*	1.8	3.5
419 SO BAPT CONV..	105	50,256	60,993*	24.0	47.1
435 UNITARIAN-UNIV	1	167	217	0.1	0.2
443 UN C OF CHRIST	2	420	510*	0.2	0.4
449 UN METHODIST..	51	20,832	23,067	9.1	17.8
453 UN PRES CH USA	5	1,306	1,585*	0.6	1.2
HANCOCK	41	6,833	8,162*	121.5#	100.0
201 EVAN COV CH AM	1	36	43*	0.6	0.5
419 SO BAPT CONV..	36	6,543	7,855*	116.9	96.2
449 UN METHODIST..	2	214	216	3.2	2.6
453 UN PRES CH USA	2	40	48*	0.7	0.6
HARDEMAN	52	8,682	10,495*	46.8	100.0
081 CATHOLIC......	1	0	28	0.1	0.3
127 CH GOD (CLEVE)	1	25	31*	0.1	0.3
185 CUMBER PRESB..	4	219	271*	1.2	2.6
193 EPISCOPAL.....	1	42	50	0.2	0.5
357 PRESB CH US...	1	24	30*	0.1	0.3
419 SO BAPT CONV..	31	6,965	8,615*	38.4	82.1
449 UN METHODIST..	12	1,390	1,449	6.5	13.8
453 UN PRES CH USA	1	17	21*	0.1	0.2
HARDIN	52	6,280	7,349*	40.4	100.0
081 CATHOLIC......	1	0	150	0.8	2.0
093 CR CH (DISC)..	3	133	161*	0.9	2.2
123 CH GOD (ANDER)	1	30	70	0.4	1.0
127 CH GOD (CLEVE)	1	25	30*	0.2	0.4
185 CUMBER PRESB..	5	556	672*	3.7	9.1
413 S-D ADVENTISTS	1	99	120*	0.7	1.6
419 SO BAPT CONV..	16	2,784	3,367*	18.5	45.8
449 UN METHODIST..	23	2,627	2,748	15.1	37.4
453 UN PRES CH USA	1	26	31*	0.2	0.4
HAWKINS	111	18,170	22,000*	65.2	100.0
081 CATHOLIC......	1	0	101	0.3	0.5
097 CR C AND C CR.	4	271	334*	1.0	1.5
123 CH GOD (ANDER)	1	25	83	0.2	0.4
127 CH GOD (CLEVE)	1	64	79*	0.2	0.4
157 CH OF BRETHREN	3	101	124*	0.4	0.6
165 CH OF NAZARENE	1	29	105	0.3	0.5
185 CUMBER PRESB..	2	60	74*	0.2	0.3
357 PRESB CH US...	3	494	609*	1.8	2.8
419 SO BAPT CONV..	64	13,749	16,936*	50.2	77.0
449 UN METHODIST..	29	3,344	3,514	10.4	16.0
453 UN PRES CH USA	2	33	41*	0.1	0.2
HAYWOOD	41	6,800	8,159*	41.6	100.0
081 CATHOLIC......	1	0	75	0.4	0.9
127 CH GOD (CLEVE)	1	46	58*	0.3	0.7
193 EPISCOPAL.....	1	22	33	0.2	0.4
357 PRESB CH US...	3	314	395*	2.0	4.8
413 S-D ADVENTISTS	1	14	18*	0.1	0.2
419 SO BAPT CONV..	15	3,966	4,995*	25.5	61.2
449 UN METHODIST..	19	2,438	2,585	13.2	31.7
HENDERSON	43	5,951	6,975*	40.3	100.0
081 CATHOLIC......	0	0	65	0.4	0.9
127 CH GOD (CLEVE)	1	61	73*	0.4	1.0
185 CUMBER PRESB..	3	186	223*	1.3	3.2
357 PRESB CH US...	1	14	17*	0.1	0.2
419 SO BAPT CONV..	22	4,248	5,097*	29.5	73.1
449 UN METHODIST..	16	1,442	1,500	8.7	21.5
HENRY	59	10,909	12,894*	54.3	100.0
081 CATHOLIC......	1	0	288	1.2	2.2
093 CR CH (DISC)..	1	259	306*	1.3	2.4
165 CH OF NAZARENE	1	88	164	0.7	1.3
185 CUMBER PRESB..	4	142	168*	0.7	1.3
193 EPISCOPAL.....	1	89	124	0.5	1.0
413 S-D ADVENTISTS	1	60	71*	0.3	0.6
419 SO BAPT CONV..	27	7,297	8,627*	36.3	66.9
449 UN METHODIST..	22	2,781	2,918	12.3	22.6
453 UN PRES CH USA	1	193	228*	1.0	1.8
HICKMAN	23	2,194	2,472*	20.4	100.0
165 CH OF NAZARENE	1	20	20	0.2	0.8
185 CUMBER PRESB..	2	58	70*	0.6	2.8
413 S-D ADVENTISTS	1	5	6*	-	0.2
419 SO BAPT CONV..	9	1,041	1,254*	10.4	50.7
449 UN METHODIST..	10	1,070	1,122	9.3	45.4
HOUSTON	19	1,475	1,684*	28.8	100.0
165 CH OF NAZARENE	3	154	173	3.0	10.3
185 CUMBER PRESB..	5	384	465*	8.0	27.6
349 PENT HOLINESS.	1	64	78*	1.3	4.6
419 SO BAPT CONV..	3	315	382*	6.5	22.7
449 UN METHODIST..	7	558	586	10.0	34.8
HUMPHREYS	38	4,311	5,707*	42.1	100.0
081 CATHOLIC......	1	0	560	4.1	9.8
165 CH OF NAZARENE	3	135	301	2.2	5.3
185 CUMBER PRESB..	5	381	467*	3.4	8.2
193 EPISCOPAL.....	1	78	99	0.7	1.7
349 PENT HOLINESS.	4	233	286*	2.1	5.0
419 SO BAPT CONV..	8	1,573	1,928*	14.2	33.8
449 UN METHODIST..	15	1,872	2,018	14.9	35.4
453 UN PRES CH USA	1	39	48*	0.4	0.8
JACKSON	5	289	342*	4.2	100.0
221 FREE METH C NA	1	12	15	0.2	4.4

*Total adherents estimated from known number of communicant, confirmed, full members.

—Represents a percent less than 0.1.

Percentages may not total due to rounding.

#See Introduction for explanation of why total adherents reported by churches exceed the 1970 population figure.

Table 3. Churches and Church Membership by State, County and Denomination: 1971

County and Denomination	Number of churches	Communicant, confirmed, full members	Total adherents Number	Percent of total population	Percent of total adherents
419 SO BAPT CONV..	3	270	319*	3.9	93.3
453 UN PRES CH USA	1	7	8*	0.1	2.3
JEFFERSON	81	15,101	17,869*	71.6	100.0
097 CR C AND C CR.	1	135	164*	0.7	0.9
123 CH GOD (ANDER)	2	47	139	0.6	0.8
127 CH GOD (CLEVE)	4	201	244*	1.0	1.4
157 CH OF BRETHREN	1	86	104*	0.4	0.6
185 CUMBER PRESB..	2	127	154*	0.6	0.9
226 FRIENDS-USA...	1	14	17*	0.1	0.1
357 PRESB CH US...	2	305	371*	1.5	2.1
419 SO BAPT CONV..	35	10,433	12,676*	50.8	70.9
449 UN METHODIST..	26	3,460	3,644	14.6	20.4
453 UN PRES CH USA	7	293	356*	1.4	2.0
JOHNSON	48	6,542	7,756*	67.0	100.0
093 CR CH (DISC)..	1	47	57*	0.5	0.7
097 CR C AND C CR.	10	821	996*	8.6	12.8
127 CH GOD (CLEVE)	1	12	15*	0.1	0.2
285 MENNONITE CH..	1	12	15*	0.1	0.2
349 PENT HOLINESS.	1	24	29*	0.3	0.4
357 PRESB CH US...	3	143	173*	1.5	2.2
419 SO BAPT CONV..	24	4,603	5,582*	48.2	72.0
449 UN METHODIST..	7	880	889	7.7	11.5
KNOX	362	143,619	175,121*	63.4	100.0
029 AMER LUTH CH..	1	25	40	-	-
059 BAPT MISS ASSN	4	652	780*	0.3	0.4
081 CATHOLIC......	3	0	6,913	2.5	3.9
093 CR CH (DISC)..	4	907	1,085*	0.4	0.6
097 CR C AND C CR.	12	1,401	1,676*	0.6	1.0
123 CH GOD (ANDER)	1	84	166	0.1	0.1
127 CH GOD (CLEVE)	20	1,837	2,198*	0.8	1.3
157 CH OF BRETHREN	1	63	75*	-	-
165 CH OF NAZARENE	4	166	303	0.1	0.2
185 CUMBER PRESB..	5	1,380	1,651*	0.6	0.9
193 EPISCOPAL.....	7	2,853	3,486	1.3	2.0
226 FRIENDS-USA...	2	66	79*	-	-
281 LUTH CH AMER..	5	976	1,303	0.5	0.7
283 LUTH--MO SYNOD	3	587	856	0.3	0.5
285 MENNONITE CH..	2	63	75*	-	-
315 NO AM OLD RC..	1	92	110*	-	0.1
349 PENT HOLINESS.	1	16	19*	-	-
357 PRESB CH US...	19	7,015	8,392*	3.0	4.8
403 SALVATION ARMY	1	93	474	0.2	0.3
413 S-D ADVENTISTS	3	573	685*	0.2	0.4
419 SO BAPT CONV..	174	93,977	112,427*	40.7	64.2
435 UNITARIAN-UNIV	1	519	791	0.3	0.5
443 UN C OF CHRIST	1	145	173*	0.1	0.1
449 UN METHODIST..	70	25,853	26,249	9.5	15.0
453 UN PRES CH USA	17	4,276	5,115*	1.9	2.9
LAKE	18	3,133	3,799*	48.1	100.0
081 CATHOLIC......	0	0	50	0.6	1.3
127 CH GOD (CLEVE)	2	38	47*	0.6	1.2
357 PRESB CH US...	1	44	55*	0.7	1.4
419 SO BAPT CONV..	10	2,097	2,612*	33.1	68.8
435 UNITARIAN-UNIV	1	20	20	0.3	0.5
449 UN METHODIST..	4	934	1,015	12.9	26.7
LAUDERDALE	55	9,362	10,895*	53.7	100.0
081 CATHOLIC......	1	0	46	0.2	0.4
093 CR CH (DISC)..	1	88	108*	0.5	1.0
127 CH GOD (CLEVE)	3	121	149*	0.7	1.4
185 CUMBER PRESB..	3	105	129*	0.6	1.2
193 EPISCOPAL.....	1	67	86	0.4	0.8
357 PRESB CH US...	1	66	81*	0.4	0.7
419 SO BAPT CONV..	23	5,585	6,868*	33.9	63.0
449 UN METHODIST..	22	3,330	3,428	16.9	31.5
LAWRENCE	84	12,039	15,537*	53.4	100.0
081 CATHOLIC......	3	0	1,575	5.4	10.1
127 CH GOD (CLEVE)	4	240	296*	1.0	1.9
165 CH OF NAZARENE	4	260	292	1.0	1.9
185 CUMBER PRESB..	3	331	408*	1.4	2.6
283 LUTH--MO SYNOD	1	28	37	0.1	0.2
357 PRESB CH US...	1	74	91*	0.3	0.6
413 S-D ADVENTISTS	1	128	158*	0.5	1.0
419 SO BAPT CONV..	34	6,691	8,240*	28.3	53.0
449 UN METHODIST..	33	4,287	4,440	15.3	28.6
LEWIS	13	1,357	1,584*	23.4	100.0
127 CH GOD (CLEVE)	1	14	17*	0.3	1.1
165 CH OF NAZARENE	1	66	137	2.0	8.6
185 CUMBER PRESB..	1	88	108*	1.6	6.8
419 SO BAPT CONV..	3	471	576*	8.5	36.4
449 UN METHODIST..	7	718	746	11.0	47.1
LINCOLN	63	10,174	12,233*	50.3	100.0
055 AS REF PRES CH	3	500	603*	2.5	4.9
081 CATHOLIC......	1	0	73	0.3	0.6
123 CH GOD (ANDER)	2	147	307	1.3	2.5
165 CH OF NAZARENE	1	77	133	0.5	1.1
185 CUMBER PRESB..	9	1,122	1,353*	5.6	11.1
193 EPISCOPAL.....	1	79	91	0.4	0.7
357 PRESB CH US...	5	379	457*	1.9	3.7
413 S-D ADVENTISTS	1	33	40*	0.2	0.3
419 SO BAPT CONV..	25	5,955	7,183*	29.5	58.7
449 UN METHODIST..	15	1,882	1,993	8.2	16.3
LOUDON	64	14,801	17,715*	73.0	100.0
081 CATHOLIC......	1	0	84	0.3	0.5
123 CH GOD (ANDER)	1	30	77	0.3	0.4
127 CH GOD (CLEVE)	8	812	970*	4.0	5.5
165 CH OF NAZARENE	3	149	364	1.5	2.1
185 CUMBER PRESB..	4	423	506*	2.1	2.9
357 PRESB CH US...	1	100	120*	0.5	0.7
413 S-D ADVENTISTS	1	45	54*	0.2	0.3
419 SO BAPT CONV..	34	11,005	13,152*	54.2	74.2
449 UN METHODIST..	9	2,028	2,138	8.8	12.1
453 UN PRES CH USA	2	209	250*	1.0	1.4
MC MINN	102	21,710	26,628*	75.1	100.0
081 CATHOLIC......	1	0	201	0.6	0.8
097 CR C AND C CR.	3	335	407*	1.1	1.5
123 CH GOD (ANDER)	6	435	1,005	2.8	3.8
127 CH GOD (CLEVE)	4	296	360*	1.0	1.4
165 CH OF NAZARENE	2	71	158	0.4	0.6
193 EPISCOPAL.....	1	211	228	0.6	0.9
357 PRESB CH US...	2	307	373*	1.1	1.4
413 S-D ADVENTISTS	1	66	80*	0.2	0.3
419 SO BAPT CONV..	61	16,301	19,811*	55.9	74.4
449 UN METHODIST..	20	3,635	3,941	11.1	14.8
453 UN PRES CH USA	1	53	64*	0.2	0.2
MC NAIRY	55	7,510	8,767*	47.7	100.0
081 CATHOLIC......	1	0	35	0.2	0.4
097 CR C AND C CR.	4	350	419*	2.3	4.8
127 CH GOD (CLEVE)	1	24	29*	0.2	0.3
185 CUMBER PRESB..	5	483	578*	3.1	6.6
357 PRESB CH US...	3	153	183*	1.0	2.1
419 SO BAPT CONV..	20	4,569	5,470*	29.8	62.4
449 UN METHODIST..	18	1,724	1,805	9.8	20.6
453 UN PRES CH USA	3	207	248*	1.4	2.8
MACON	13	782	860*	7.0	100.0
127 CH GOD (CLEVE)	3	97	115*	0.9	13.4
419 SO BAPT CONV..	3	294	348*	2.8	40.5
449 UN METHODIST..	7	391	397	3.2	46.2
MADISON	91	28,124	34,409*	52.4	100.0
081 CATHOLIC......	1	0	705	1.1	2.0
093 CR CH (DISC)..	1	59	72*	0.1	0.2
097 CR C AND C CR.	1	400	488*	0.7	1.4
127 CH GOD (CLEVE)	2	233	284*	0.4	0.8
165 CH OF NAZARENE	1	88	146	0.2	0.4
185 CUMBER PRESB..	6	778	948*	1.4	2.8
193 EPISCOPAL.....	1	417	549	0.8	1.6
283 LUTH--MO SYNOD	1	189	295	0.4	0.9
357 PRESB CH US...	4	939	1,145*	1.7	3.3
403 SALVATION ARMY	1	63	202	0.3	0.6
413 S-D ADVENTISTS	2	136	166*	0.3	0.5
419 SO BAPT CONV..	40	17,525	21,361*	32.5	62.1
449 UN METHODIST..	30	7,297	8,048	12.2	23.4
MARION	50	6,283	7,585*	36.9	100.0
081 CATHOLIC......	1	0	37	0.2	0.5
127 CH GOD (CLEVE)	11	763	950*	4.6	12.5
165 CH OF NAZARENE	2	81	115	0.6	1.5
185 CUMBER PRESB..	7	611	760*	3.7	10.0
193 EPISCOPAL.....	1	35	69	0.3	0.9
413 S-D ADVENTISTS	1	80	100*	0.5	1.3
419 SO BAPT CONV..	15	3,177	3,954*	19.2	52.1
449 UN METHODIST..	12	1,536	1,600	7.8	21.1
MARSHALL	34	5,615	6,437*	37.2	100.0
081 CATHOLIC......	1	0	79	0.5	1.2
123 CH GOD (ANDER)	1	37	102	0.6	1.6
127 CH GOD (CLEVE)	3	111	132*	0.8	2.1
185 CUMBER PRESB..	5	479	570*	3.3	8.9
349 PENT HOLINESS.	1	12	14*	0.1	0.2
357 PRESB CH US...	4	424	504*	2.9	7.8
419 SO BAPT CONV..	6	2,454	2,919*	16.9	45.3
449 UN METHODIST..	13	2,098	2,117	12.2	32.9
MAURY	87	13,591	16,225*	37.4	100.0
055 AS REF PRES CH	1	29	35*	0.1	0.2
081 CATHOLIC......	1	0	402	0.9	2.5
093 CR CH (DISC)..	1	229	279*	0.6	1.7
127 CH GOD (CLEVE)	3	143	174*	0.4	1.1
165 CH OF NAZARENE	8	499	750	1.7	4.6
185 CUMBER PRESB..	12	1,332	1,621*	3.7	10.0
193 EPISCOPAL.....	1	408	456	1.1	2.8
283 LUTH--MO SYNOD	1	63	96	0.2	0.6
357 PRESB CH US...	5	804	979*	2.3	6.0
419 SO BAPT CONV..	22	4,872	5,930*	13.7	36.5
449 UN METHODIST..	29	4,975	5,215	12.0	32.1
453 UN PRES CH USA	3	237	288*	0.7	1.8
MEIGS	25	2,817	3,385*	64.9	100.0
127 CH GOD (CLEVE)	3	131	162*	3.1	4.8
413 S-D ADVENTISTS	1	47	58*	1.1	1.7
419 SO BAPT CONV..	14	2,108	2,607*	50.0	77.0

*Total adherents estimated from known number of communicant, confirmed, full members.

—Represents a percent less than 0.1.

Percentages may not total due to rounding.

Table 3. Churches and Church Membership by State, County and Denomination: 1971

County and Denomination	Number of churches	Communicant, confirmed, full members	Total adherents: Number	Total adherents: Percent of total population	Total adherents: Percent of total adherents
449 UN METHODIST..	7	531	558	10.7	16.5
MONROE	102	17,162	20,886*	89.0	100.0
097 CR C AND C CR.	1	45	55*	0.2	0.3
123 CH GOD (ANDER)	1	60	168	0.7	0.8
127 CH GOD (CLEVE)	5	492	601*	2.6	2.9
165 CH OF NAZARENE	2	82	281	1.2	1.3
185 CUMBER PRESB..	2	50	61*	0.3	0.3
226 FRIENDS-USA...	3	148	181*	0.8	0.9
281 LUTH CH AMER..	1	25	26	0.1	0.1
357 PRESB CH US...	9	963	1,176*	5.0	5.6
419 SO BAPT CONV..	63	13,367	16,322*	69.5	78.1
449 UN METHODIST..	14	1,896	1,973	8.4	9.4
453 UN PRES CH USA	1	34	42*	0.2	0.2
MONTGOMERY	81	21,118	25,844*	41.2	100.0
081 CATHOLIC......	1	0	1,300	2.1	5.0
093 CR CH (DISC)..	1	445	539*	0.9	2.1
123 CH GOD (ANDER)	1	40	105	0.2	0.4
127 CH GOD (CLEVE)	3	136	165*	0.3	0.6
165 CH OF NAZARENE	4	612	1,145	1.8	4.4
185 CUMBER PRESB..	7	1,192	1,445*	2.3	5.6
193 EPISCOPAL.....	3	388	517	0.8	2.0
283 LUTH--MO SYNOD	1	174	259	0.4	1.0
357 PRESB CH US...	2	675	818*	1.3	3.2
413 S-D ADVENTISTS	1	32	39*	0.1	0.2
419 SO BAPT CONV..	26	9,850	11,938*	19.0	46.2
449 UN METHODIST..	31	7,574	7,574	12.1	29.3
MOORE	9	860	909*	25.5	100.0
127 CH GOD (CLEVE)	1	33	39*	1.1	4.3
419 SO BAPT CONV..	1	165	197*	5.5	21.7
449 UN METHODIST..	7	662	673	18.9	74.0
MORGAN	33	5,581	6,964*	51.1	100.0
081 CATHOLIC......	1	0	31	0.2	0.4
127 CH GOD (CLEVE)	1	38	46*	0.3	0.7
165 CH OF NAZARENE	3	58	182	1.3	2.6
283 LUTH--MO SYNOD	2	379	525	3.9	7.5
413 S-D ADVENTISTS	2	116	141*	1.0	2.0
419 SO BAPT CONV..	17	4,602	5,610*	41.2	80.6
443 UN C OF CHRIST	1	31	38*	0.3	0.5
449 UN METHODIST..	4	309	332	2.4	4.8
453 UN PRES CH USA	2	48	59*	0.4	0.8
OBION	83	14,503	17,428*	58.2	100.0
055 AS REF PRES CH	2	115	138*	0.5	0.8
081 CATHOLIC......	1	0	430	1.4	2.5
093 CR CH (DISC)..	1	228	274*	0.9	1.6
127 CH GOD (CLEVE)	6	224	269*	0.9	1.5
165 CH OF NAZARENE	2	89	164	0.5	0.9
185 CUMBER PRESB..	18	1,666	1,999*	6.7	11.5
193 EPISCOPAL.....	1	127	147	0.5	0.8
283 LUTH--MO SYNOD	1	81	123	0.4	0.7
357 PRESB CH US...	1	113	136*	0.5	0.8
419 SO BAPT CONV..	25	8,188	9,824*	32.8	56.4
449 UN METHODIST..	25	3,672	3,924	13.1	22.5
OVERTON	42	5,553	6,295*	42.3	100.0
093 CR CH (DISC)..	6	309	374*	2.5	5.9
123 CH GOD (ANDER)	1	52	122	0.8	1.9
127 CH GOD (CLEVE)	2	50	60*	0.4	1.0
185 CUMBER PRESB..	1	22	27*	0.2	0.4
419 SO BAPT CONV..	14	2,660	3,218*	21.6	51.1
449 UN METHODIST..	17	2,416	2,441	16.4	38.8
453 UN PRES CH USA	1	44	53*	0.4	0.8
PERRY	16	1,687	1,788*	34.1	100.0
081 CATHOLIC......	1	0	10	0.2	0.6
097 CR C AND C CR.	1	200	234*	4.5	13.1
413 S-D ADVENTISTS	1	17	20*	0.4	1.1
419 SO BAPT CONV..	2	261	306*	5.8	17.1
449 UN METHODIST..	11	1,209	1,218	23.3	68.1
PICKETT	9	1,129	1,313*	34.8	100.0
093 CR CH (DISC)..	2	123	146*	3.9	11.1
097 CR C AND C CR.	2	260	310*	8.2	23.6
419 SO BAPT CONV..	3	581	692*	18.3	52.7
449 UN METHODIST..	2	165	165	4.4	12.6
POLK	57	9,902	12,046*	103.2#	100.0
081 CATHOLIC......	1	0	97	0.8	0.8
127 CH GOD (CLEVE)	3	135	164*	1.4	1.4
193 EPISCOPAL.....	1	79	96	0.8	0.8
357 PRESB CH US...	1	115	140*	1.2	1.2
419 SO BAPT CONV..	45	8,621	10,502*	90.0	87.2
449 UN METHODIST..	6	952	1,047	9.0	8.7
PUTNAM	67	11,702	14,228*	40.1	100.0
081 CATHOLIC......	1	0	377	1.1	2.6
123 CH GOD (ANDER)	3	205	459	1.3	3.2
127 CH GOD (CLEVE)	5	254	300*	0.8	2.1
165 CH OF NAZARENE	2	219	488	1.4	3.4
185 CUMBER PRESB..	3	392	463*	1.3	3.3
193 EPISCOPAL.....	1	96	150	0.4	1.1
283 LUTH--MO SYNOD	1	68	99	0.3	0.7
285 MENNONITE CH..	1	18	21*	0.1	0.1
357 PRESB CH US...	2	77	91*	0.3	0.6
413 S-D ADVENTISTS	1	30	35*	0.1	0.2
419 SO BAPT CONV..	27	6,792	8,017*	22.6	56.3
449 UN METHODIST..	15	3,154	3,259	9.2	22.9
453 UN PRES CH USA	5	397	469*	1.3	3.3
RHEA	50	7,126	8,523*	49.5	100.0
081 CATHOLIC......	1	0	60	0.3	0.7
127 CH GOD (CLEVE)	6	519	641*	3.7	7.5
349 PENT HOLINESS.	1	22	27*	0.2	0.3
413 S-D ADVENTISTS	5	410	507*	2.9	5.9
419 SO BAPT CONV..	22	4,311	5,327*	31.0	62.5
449 UN METHODIST..	14	1,759	1,831	10.6	21.5
453 UN PRES CH USA	1	105	130*	0.8	1.5
ROANE	78	19,067	23,064*	59.3	100.0
081 CATHOLIC......	1	0	290	0.7	1.3
093 CR CH (DISC)..	1	374	455*	1.2	2.0
097 CR C AND C CR.	5	644	784*	2.0	3.4
127 CH GOD (CLEVE)	3	117	142*	0.4	0.6
165 CH OF NAZARENE	1	22	29	0.1	0.1
185 CUMBER PRESB..	3	221	269*	0.7	1.2
193 EPISCOPAL.....	1	135	164	0.4	0.7
283 LUTH--MO SYNOD	1	93	126	0.3	0.5
335 ORTH PRESB CH.	1	93	123	0.3	0.5
413 S-D ADVENTISTS	2	50	61*	0.2	0.3
419 SO BAPT CONV..	40	13,791	16,782*	43.2	72.8
449 UN METHODIST..	16	2,886	3,059	7.9	13.3
453 UN PRES CH USA	3	641	780*	2.0	3.4
ROBERTSON	64	14,607	17,696*	60.8	100.0
081 CATHOLIC......	2	0	325	1.1	1.8
093 CR CH (DISC)..	1	45	55*	0.2	0.3
127 CH GOD (CLEVE)	1	90	110*	0.4	0.6
165 CH OF NAZARENE	2	212	346	1.2	2.0
185 CUMBER PRESB..	3	335	410*	1.4	2.3
413 S-D ADVENTISTS	3	222	271*	0.9	1.5
419 SO BAPT CONV..	25	10,147	12,407*	42.6	70.1
449 UN METHODIST..	25	3,316	3,479	12.0	19.7
453 UN PRES CH USA	2	240	293*	1.0	1.7
RUTHERFORD	88	17,916	22,439*	37.8	100.0
081 CATHOLIC......	1	0	842	1.4	3.8
093 CR CH (DISC)..	1	308	374*	0.6	1.7
123 CH GOD (ANDER)	2	145	355	0.6	1.6
127 CH GOD (CLEVE)	2	61	74*	0.1	0.3
165 CH OF NAZARENE	2	145	293	0.5	1.3
185 CUMBER PRESB..	7	866	1,050*	1.8	4.7
193 EPISCOPAL.....	1	173	253	0.4	1.1
221 FREE METH C NA	1	16	22	-	0.1
281 LUTH CH AMER..	1	91	122	0.2	0.5
283 LUTH--MO SYNOD	1	82	123	0.2	0.5
357 PRESB CH US...	6	930	1,128*	1.9	5.0
413 S-D ADVENTISTS	2	69	84*	0.1	0.4
419 SO BAPT CONV..	35	9,977	12,102*	20.4	53.9
449 UN METHODIST..	24	4,940	5,480	9.2	24.4
453 UN PRES CH USA	2	113	137*	0.2	0.6
SCOTT	38	5,810	7,208*	48.8	100.0
081 CATHOLIC......	1	0	27	0.2	0.4
127 CH GOD (CLEVE)	2	88	110*	0.7	1.5
419 SO BAPT CONV..	30	5,356	6,677*	45.2	92.6
443 UN C OF CHRIST	2	36	45*	0.3	0.6
449 UN METHODIST..	2	276	282	1.9	3.9
453 UN PRES CH USA	1	54	67*	0.5	0.9
SEQUATCHIE	13	1,489	1,795*	28.4	100.0
127 CH GOD (CLEVE)	4	238	297*	4.7	16.5
413 S-D ADVENTISTS	1	96	120*	1.9	6.7
419 SO BAPT CONV..	6	802	1,002*	15.8	55.8
449 UN METHODIST..	2	353	376	5.9	20.9
SEVIER	96	18,745	22,488*	79.6	100.0
081 CATHOLIC......	1	0	104	0.4	0.5
127 CH GOD (CLEVE)	5	501	611*	2.2	2.7
193 EPISCOPAL.....	1	119	179	0.6	0.8
281 LUTH CH AMER..	1	51	56	0.2	0.2
357 PRESB CH US...	2	94	115*	0.4	0.5
419 SO BAPT CONV..	62	14,805	18,052*	63.9	80.3
449 UN METHODIST..	23	3,039	3,205	11.3	14.3
453 UN PRES CH USA	1	136	166*	0.6	0.7
SHELBY	383	214,621	299,559*	41.5	100.0
029 AMER LUTH CH..	4	571	769	0.1	0.3
055 AS REF PRES CH	3	464	574*	0.1	0.2
059 BAPT MISS ASSN	3	595	737*	0.1	0.2
081 CATHOLIC......	21	0	35,981	5.0	12.0
093 CR CH (DISC)..	16	5,512	6,824*	0.9	2.3
097 CR C AND C CR.	7	1,107	1,370*	0.2	0.5
123 CH GOD (ANDER)	4	110	397	0.1	0.1
127 CH GOD (CLEVE)	9	1,079	1,336*	0.2	0.4
165 CH OF NAZARENE	12	857	1,726	0.2	0.6
185 CUMBER PRESB..	14	4,360	5,398*	0.7	1.8
193 EPISCOPAL.....	18	10,232	13,147	1.8	4.4
281 LUTH CH AMER..	4	985	1,399	0.2	0.5

*Total adherents estimated from known number of communicant, confirmed, full members.

—Represents a percent less than 0.1.

Percentages may not total due to rounding.

#See Introduction for explanation of why total adherents reported by churches exceed the 1970 population figure.

Table 3. Churches and Church Membership by State, County and Denomination: 1971

County and Denomination	Number of churches	Communicant, confirmed, full members	Total adherents		
			Number	Percent of total population	Percent of total adherents
283 LUTH--MO SYNOD	10	2,560	3,657	0.5	1.2
349 PENT HOLINESS.	6	361	447*	0.1	0.1
353 PLY BRETHREN..	1	20	40	-	-
357 PRESB CH US...	29	15,743	19,490*	2.7	6.5
381 REF PRES-EVAN.	1	79	89	-	-
403 SALVATION ARMY	2	217	782	0.1	0.3
413 S-D ADVENTISTS	4	1,167	1,445*	0.2	0.5
419 SO BAPT CONV..	128	121,042	149,853*	20.8	50.0
435 UNITARIAN-UNIV	2	379	593	0.1	0.2
443 UN C OF CHRIST	2	387	479*	0.1	0.2
449 UN METHODIST..	77	46,156	52,236	7.2	17.4
453 UN PRES CH USA	6	638	790*	0.1	0.3
SMITH	37	4,407	5,082*	40.6	100.0
093 CR CH (DISC)..	1	36	43*	0.3	0.8
127 CH GOD (CLEVE)	2	138	166*	1.3	3.3
165 CH OF NAZARENE	2	97	218	1.7	4.3
185 CUMBER PRESB..	2	131	157*	1.3	3.1
419 SO BAPT CONV..	13	2,247	2,697*	21.6	53.1
449 UN METHODIST..	17	1,758	1,801	14.4	35.4
STEWART	43	3,975	4,634*	63.3	100.0
093 CR CH (DISC)..	1	69	81*	1.1	1.7
123 CH GOD (ANDER)	2	144	384	5.2	8.3
165 CH OF NAZARENE	4	111	208	2.8	4.5
185 CUMBER PRESB..	1	39	46*	0.6	1.0
419 SO BAPT CONV..	13	1,516	1,775*	24.3	38.3
449 UN METHODIST..	22	2,096	2,140	29.2	46.2
SULLIVAN	181	53,971	66,438*	52.2	100.0
081 CATHOLIC......	1	0	994	0.8	1.5
093 CR CH (DISC)..	1	39	48*	-	0.1
097 CR C AND C CR.	19	3,919	4,787*	3.8	7.2
123 CH GOD (ANDER)	2	423	1,000	0.8	1.5
127 CH GOD (CLEVE)	3	509	622*	0.5	0.9
157 CH OF BRETHREN	3	227	277*	0.2	0.4
165 CH OF NAZARENE	3	147	381	0.3	0.6
185 CUMBER PRESB..	1	66	81*	0.1	0.1
193 EPISCOPAL.....	4	817	1,226	1.0	1.8
281 LUTH CH AMER..	5	1,022	1,290	1.0	1.9
283 LUTH--MO SYNOD	2	172	278	0.2	0.4
349 PENT HOLINESS.	1	32	39*	-	0.1
357 PRESB CH US...	27	6,698	8,182*	6.4	12.3
381 REF PRES-EVAN.	1	34	39	-	0.1
403 SALVATION ARMY	2	210	716	0.6	1.1
413 S-D ADVENTISTS	2	153	187*	0.1	0.3
419 SO BAPT CONV..	50	23,360	28,536*	22.4	43.0
435 UNITARIAN-UNIV	1	73	124	0.1	0.2
449 UN METHODIST..	50	15,685	17,161	13.5	25.8
453 UN PRES CH USA	3	385	470*	0.4	0.7
SUMNER	73	15,719	21,074*	37.6	100.0
081 CATHOLIC......	2	0	1,441	2.6	6.8
093 CR CH (DISC)..	1	70	88*	0.2	0.4
127 CH GOD (CLEVE)	2	49	61*	0.1	0.3
165 CH OF NAZARENE	5	296	839	1.5	4.0
185 CUMBER PRESB..	3	403	504*	0.9	2.4
193 EPISCOPAL.....	3	216	347	0.6	1.6
221 FREE METH C NA	2	32	52	0.1	0.2
281 LUTH CH AMER..	1	152	240	0.4	1.1
357 PRESB CH US...	3	725	907*	1.6	4.3
413 S-D ADVENTISTS	5	417	522*	0.9	2.5
419 SO BAPT CONV..	22	8,478	10,607*	18.9	50.3
449 UN METHODIST..	22	4,781	5,341	9.5	25.3
453 UN PRES CH USA	2	100	125*	0.2	0.6
TIPTON	58	10,561	13,290*	47.5	100.0
055 AS REF PRES CH	4	764	970*	3.5	7.3
059 BAPT MISS ASSN	1	64	81*	0.3	0.6
081 CATHOLIC......	1	0	91	0.3	0.7
097 CR C AND C CR.	2	72	91*	0.3	0.7
127 CH GOD (CLEVE)	2	161	204*	0.7	1.5
165 CH OF NAZARENE	2	91	283	1.0	2.1
185 CUMBER PRESB..	4	508	645*	2.3	4.9
193 EPISCOPAL.....	4	158	245	0.9	1.8
357 PRESB CH US...	4	480	609*	2.2	4.6
419 SO BAPT CONV..	16	5,325	6,758*	24.1	50.9
449 UN METHODIST..	16	2,807	3,147	11.2	23.7
453 UN PRES CH USA	2	131	166*	0.6	1.2
TROUSDALE	9	1,061	1,213*	23.5	100.0
185 CUMBER PRESB..	1	70	84*	1.6	6.9
419 SO BAPT CONV..	3	542	648*	12.6	53.4
449 UN METHODIST..	5	449	481	9.3	39.7
UNICOI	36	7,654	9,137*	59.9	100.0
081 CATHOLIC......	1	0	40	0.3	0.4
093 CR CH (DISC)..	2	403	485*	3.2	5.3
097 CR C AND C CR.	5	800	962*	6.3	10.5
123 CH GOD (ANDER)	1	25	115	0.8	1.3
127 CH GOD (CLEVE)	2	155	186*	1.2	2.0
157 CH OF BRETHREN	1	42	51*	0.3	0.6
165 CH OF NAZARENE	1	15	43	0.3	0.5
283 LUTH--MO SYNOD	1	12	12	0.1	0.1
349 PENT HOLINESS.	1	102	123*	0.8	1.3
419 SO BAPT CONV..	14	4,335	5,214*	34.2	57.1
449 UN METHODIST..	4	1,242	1,277	8.4	14.0
453 UN PRES CH USA	3	523	629*	4.1	6.9

County and Denomination	Number of churches	Communicant, confirmed, full members	Total adherents		
			Number	Percent of total population	Percent of total adherents
UNION	22	3,630	4,468*	49.3	100.0
419 SO BAPT CONV..	17	3,402	4,235*	46.7	94.8
449 UN METHODIST..	5	228	233	2.6	5.2
VAN BUREN	8	665	803*	21.4	100.0
127 CH GOD (CLEVE)	3	87	105*	2.8	13.1
413 S-D ADVENTISTS	1	16	19*	0.5	2.4
419 SO BAPT CONV..	4	562	679*	18.1	84.6
WARREN	52	7,013	8,606*	31.9	100.0
075 BRETHREN IN CR	1	18	22*	0.1	0.3
081 CATHOLIC......	1	0	211	0.8	2.5
123 CH GOD (ANDER)	1	47	111	0.4	1.3
127 CH GOD (CLEVE)	3	338	413*	1.5	4.8
165 CH OF NAZARENE	1	12	43	0.2	0.5
185 CUMBER PRESB..	8	426	521*	1.9	6.1
193 EPISCOPAL.....	1	75	134	0.5	1.6
221 FREE METH C NA	1	23	24	0.1	0.3
285 MENNONITE CH..	1	9	11*	-	0.1
357 PRESB CH US...	1	73	89*	0.3	1.0
413 S-D ADVENTISTS	1	76	93*	0.3	1.1
419 SO BAPT CONV..	12	3,442	4,208*	15.6	48.9
449 UN METHODIST..	18	2,216	2,411	8.9	28.0
453 UN PRES CH USA	2	258	315*	1.2	3.7
WASHINGTON	147	35,873	43,657*	59.1	100.0
081 CATHOLIC......	1	0	861	1.2	2.0
093 CR CH (DISC)..	4	453	543*	0.7	1.2
097 CR C AND C CR.	21	4,098	4,915*	6.6	11.3
123 CH GOD (ANDER)	2	328	732	1.0	1.7
127 CH GOD (CLEVE)	2	293	351*	0.5	0.8
157 CH OF BRETHREN	9	816	979*	1.3	2.2
165 CH OF NAZARENE	1	75	119	0.2	0.3
185 CUMBER PRESB..	3	243	291*	0.4	0.7
193 EPISCOPAL.....	1	485	490	0.7	1.1
221 FREE METH C NA	1	6	12	-	-
281 LUTH CH AMER..	2	173	289	0.4	0.7
283 LUTH--MO SYNOD	1	260	333	0.5	0.8
349 PENT HOLINESS.	1	11	13*	-	-
357 PRESB CH US...	9	2,471	2,964*	4.0	6.8
403 SALVATION ARMY	2	148	470	0.6	1.1
419 SO BAPT CONV..	49	16,745	20,085*	27.2	46.0
449 UN METHODIST..	33	8,567	9,369	12.7	21.5
453 UN PRES CH USA	5	701	841*	1.1	1.9
WAYNE	41	4,089	4,761*	38.5	100.0
081 CATHOLIC......	1	0	20	0.2	0.4
093 CR CH (DISC)..	1	55	68*	0.5	1.4
127 CH GOD (CLEVE)	2	59	72*	0.6	1.5
165 CH OF NAZARENE	1	23	40	0.3	0.8
185 CUMBER PRESB..	1	126	155*	1.3	3.3
349 PENT HOLINESS.	1	22	27*	0.2	0.6
413 S-D ADVENTISTS	1	123	151*	1.2	3.2
419 SO BAPT CONV..	18	2,181	2,679*	21.7	56.3
449 UN METHODIST..	14	1,460	1,500	12.1	31.5
453 UN PRES CH USA	1	40	49*	0.4	1.0
WEAKLEY	92	14,423	16,497*	57.2	100.0
081 CATHOLIC......	1	0	49	0.2	0.3
093 CR CH (DISC)..	1	73	85*	0.3	0.5
185 CUMBER PRESB..	11	692	805*	2.8	4.9
193 EPISCOPAL.....	1	41	88	0.3	0.5
349 PENT HOLINESS.	1	22	26*	0.1	0.2
419 SO BAPT CONV..	43	9,956	11,580*	40.2	70.2
449 UN METHODIST..	31	3,477	3,676	12.8	22.3
453 UN PRES CH USA	3	162	188*	0.7	1.1
WHITE	43	5,069	5,920*	34.6	100.0
075 BRETHREN IN CR	1	24	29*	0.2	0.5
093 CR CH (DISC)..	1	120	145*	0.8	2.4
127 CH GOD (CLEVE)	6	510	616*	3.6	10.4
165 CH OF NAZARENE	2	124	341	2.0	5.8
185 CUMBER PRESB..	1	45	54*	0.3	0.9
419 SO BAPT CONV..	12	2,028	2,448*	14.3	41.4
449 UN METHODIST..	17	2,010	2,036	11.9	34.4
453 UN PRES CH USA	3	208	251*	1.5	4.2
WILLIAMSON	48	8,213	10,691*	31.1	100.0
081 CATHOLIC......	1	0	801	2.3	7.5
165 CH OF NAZARENE	4	166	364	1.1	3.4
185 CUMBER PRESB..	3	215	265*	0.8	2.5
193 EPISCOPAL.....	1	88	297	0.9	2.8
357 PRESB CH US...	4	803	988*	2.9	9.2
413 S-D ADVENTISTS	1	47	58*	0.2	0.5
419 SO BAPT CONV..	12	2,688	3,308*	9.6	30.9
449 UN METHODIST..	22	4,206	4,610	13.4	43.1
WILSON	74	14,750	18,170*	49.1	100.0
081 CATHOLIC......	1	0	323	0.9	1.8
097 CR C AND C CR.	1	60	74*	0.2	0.4
123 CH GOD (ANDER)	1	33	109	0.3	0.6
127 CH GOD (CLEVE)	2	213	261*	0.7	1.4
165 CH OF NAZARENE	3	165	322	0.9	1.8
185 CUMBER PRESB..	8	534	655*	1.8	3.6
193 EPISCOPAL.....	1	54	54	0.1	0.3
357 PRESB CH US...	3	101	124*	0.3	0.7

*Total adherents estimated from known number of communicant, confirmed, full members.

—Represents a percent less than 0.1.

Percentages may not total due to rounding.

Table 3. Churches and Church Membership by State, County and Denomination: 1971

County and Denomination	Number of churches	Communicant, confirmed, full members	Total adherents		
			Number	Percent of total population	Percent of total adherents
419 SO BAPT CONV..	30	10,454	12,827*	34.7	70.6
449 UN METHODIST..	23	2,827	3,042	8.2	16.7
453 UN PRES CH USA	1	309	379*	1.0	2.1
CO DATA NOT AVAIL	222	24,788	37,462*	N/A	N/A
127 CH GOD (CLEVE)	4	142	173*	N/A	N/A
151 L-D SAINTS....	0	0	7,325	N/A	N/A
223 FREE WILL BAPT	172	20,801	25,340*	N/A	N/A
231 GENERAL BAPT..	24	3,311	4,034*	N/A	N/A
467 WESLEYAN......	22	534	590	N/A	N/A

TEXAS

County and Denomination	Number of churches	Communicant, confirmed, full members	Total adherents		
			Number	Percent of total population	Percent of total adherents
THE STATE.....	11,223	3,462,852	6,294,555*	56.2	100.0
ANDERSON	60	11,928	14,347*	51.6	100.0
059 BAPT MISS ASSN	7	9	11*	-	0.1
081 CATHOLIC......	1	0	483	1.7	3.4
093 CR CH (DISC)..	6	555	657*	2.4	4.6
097 CR C AND C CR.	3	150	178*	0.6	1.2
127 CH GOD (CLEVE)	1	16	19*	0.1	0.1
193 EPISCOPAL.....	1	372	486	1.7	3.4
283 LUTH--MO SYNOD	1	115	163	0.6	1.1
357 PRESB CH US...	2	443	524*	1.9	3.7
413 S-D ADVENTISTS	1	69	82*	0.3	0.6
419 SO BAPT CONV..	22	7,521	8,901*	32.0	62.0
449 UN METHODIST..	15	2,678	2,843	10.2	19.8
ANDREWS	13	5,092	6,810*	65.7	100.0
081 CATHOLIC......	1	0	537	5.2	7.9
093 CR CH (DISC)..	1	112	137*	1.3	2.0
127 CH GOD (CLEVE)	1	57	70*	0.7	1.0
165 CH OF NAZARENE	1	24	139	1.3	2.0
193 EPISCOPAL.....	1	18	30	0.3	0.4
283 LUTH--MO SYNOD	1	97	148	1.4	2.2
357 PRESB CH US...	1	163	199*	1.9	2.9
419 SO BAPT CONV..	4	3,736	4,563*	44.0	67.0
449 UN METHODIST..	2	885	987	9.5	14.5
ANGELINA	55	20,151	26,297*	53.3	100.0
059 BAPT MISS ASSN	2	2,899	3,599*	7.3	13.7
081 CATHOLIC......	2	0	1,400	2.8	5.3
093 CR CH (DISC)..	1	508	631*	1.3	2.4
123 CH GOD (ANDER)	1	28	63	0.1	0.2
127 CH GOD (CLEVE)	1	58	72*	0.1	0.3
165 CH OF NAZARENE	2	230	423	0.9	1.6
193 EPISCOPAL.....	1	591	702	1.4	2.7
283 LUTH--MO SYNOD	1	157	224	0.5	0.9
357 PRESB CH US...	1	308	382*	0.8	1.5
403 SALVATION ARMY	1	65	190	0.4	0.7
413 S-D ADVENTISTS	1	53	66*	0.1	0.3
419 SO BAPT CONV..	32	12,403	15,398*	31.2	58.6
449 UN METHODIST..	9	2,851	3,147	6.4	12.0
ARANSAS	11	2,041	4,420*	49.7	100.0
081 CATHOLIC......	1	0	1,929	21.7	43.6
123 CH GOD (ANDER)	1	12	50	0.6	1.1
165 CH OF NAZARENE	1	20	58	0.7	1.3
193 EPISCOPAL.....	1	116	142	1.6	3.2
283 LUTH--MO SYNOD	1	62	74	0.8	1.7
357 PRESB CH US...	1	313	381*	4.3	8.6
419 SO BAPT CONV..	4	1,119	1,363*	15.3	30.8
449 UN METHODIST..	1	399	423	4.8	9.6
ARCHER	14	2,541	4,319*	75.0	100.0
081 CATHOLIC......	3	0	1,349	23.4	31.2
093 CR CH (DISC)..	1	36	43*	0.7	1.0
419 SO BAPT CONV..	6	1,917	2,296*	39.9	53.2
449 UN METHODIST..	4	588	631	11.0	14.6
ARMSTRONG	6	1,222	1,607*	84.8	100.0
081 CATHOLIC......	0	0	200	10.6	12.4
093 CR CH (DISC)..	1	51	59*	3.1	3.7
419 SO BAPT CONV..	4	790	911*	48.1	56.7
449 UN METHODIST..	1	381	437	23.1	27.2
ATASCOSA	29	4,797	14,728*	78.8	100.0
029 AMER LUTH CH..	1	256	358	1.9	2.4
081 CATHOLIC......	9	0	8,876	47.5	60.3
193 EPISCOPAL.....	1	67	87	0.5	0.6
357 PRESB CH US...	1	72	90*	0.5	0.6
419 SO BAPT CONV..	11	3,218	4,028*	21.5	27.3
449 UN METHODIST..	6	1,184	1,289	6.9	8.8
AUSTIN	28	4,823	7,858*	56.8	100.0
029 AMER LUTH CH..	4	1,479	1,843	13.3	23.5
081 CATHOLIC......	4	C	2,041	14.8	26.0

*Total adherents estimated from known number of communicant, confirmed, full members.

County and Denomination	Number of churches	Communicant, confirmed, full members	Total adherents		
			Number	Percent of total population	Percent of total adherents
193 EPISCOPAL.....	2	179	336	2.4	4.3
283 LUTH--MO SYNOD	2	660	797	5.8	10.1
419 SO BAPT CONV..	3	809	953*	6.9	12.1
449 UN METHODIST..	10	1,346	1,496	10.8	19.0
461 UNITY OF BRETH	3	350	392	2.8	5.0
BAILEY	21	3,680	6,508*	76.7	100.0
059 BAPT MISS ASSN	2	192	242*	2.9	3.7
081 CATHOLIC......	1	0	2,000	[illegible]	30.7
093 CR CH (DISC)..	1	58	73*	0.9	1.1
165 CH OF NAZARENE	1	17	42	0.5	0.6
419 SO BAPT CONV..	10	2,566	3,235*	38.1	49.7
449 UN METHODIST..	5	830	895	10.5	13.8
453 UN PRES CH USA	1	17	21*	0.2	0.3
BANDERA	11	1,358	2,312*	48.7	100.0
029 AMER LUTH CH..	1	55	75	1.6	3.2
081 CATHOLIC......	2	0	794	16.7	34.3
193 EPISCOPAL.....	1	43	64	1.3	2.8
419 SO BAPT CONV..	4	724	829*	17.5	35.9
449 UN METHODIST..	3	536	550	11.6	23.8
BASTROP	33	5,181	6,773*	39.2	100.0
029 AMER LUTH CH..	4	576	766	4.4	11.3
081 CATHOLIC......	4	0	589	3.4	8.7
093 CR CH (DISC)..	3	154	186*	1.1	2.7
097 CR C AND C CR.	1	50	60*	0.3	0.9
283 LUTH--MO SYNOD	2	349	457	2.6	6.7
357 PRESB CH US...	1	68	82*	0.5	1.2
413 S-D ADVENTISTS	2	143	172*	1.0	2.5
419 SO BAPT CONV..	7	2,380	2,868*	16.6	42.3
449 UN METHODIST..	7	1,309	1,412	8.2	20.8
453 UN PRES CH USA	1	128	154*	0.9	2.3
461 UNITY OF BRETH	1	24	28	0.2	0.4
BAYLOR	12	3,046	4,380*	83.9	100.0
081 CATHOLIC......	2	0	892	17.1	20.4
093 CR CH (DISC)..	1	92	107*	2.0	2.4
127 CH GOD (CLEVE)	1	16	19*	0.4	0.4
283 LUTH--MO SYNOD	1	36	50	1.0	1.1
357 PRESB CH US...	1	57	66*	1.3	1.5
419 SO BAPT CONV..	4	2,123	2,464*	47.2	56.3
449 UN METHODIST..	1	665	716	13.7	16.3
453 UN PRES CH USA	1	57	66	1.3	1.5
BEE	32	4,968	9,616*	42.3	100.0
029 AMER LUTH CH..	1	161	249	1.1	2.6
081 CATHOLIC......	5	0	3,463	15.2	36.0
093 CR CH (DISC)..	2	105	131*	0.6	1.4
165 CH OF NAZARENE	1	18	68	0.3	0.7
193 EPISCOPAL.....	1	125	178	0.8	1.9
283 LUTH--MO SYNOD	1	87	127	0.6	1.3
357 PRESB CH US...	1	371	463*	2.0	4.8
413 S-D ADVENTISTS	1	97	121*	0.5	1.3
419 SO BAPT CONV..	12	2,673	3,333*	14.7	34.7
443 UN C OF CHRIST	1	56	70*	0.3	0.7
449 UN METHODIST..	6	1,275	1,413	6.2	14.7
BELL	112	34,129	49,987*	40.2	100.0
029 AMER LUTH CH..	3	1,406	1,759	1.4	3.5
059 BAPT MISS ASSN	1	54	65*	0.1	0.1
081 CATHOLIC......	3	0	8,742	7.0	17.5
093 CR CH (DISC)..	9	1,057	1,282*	1.0	2.6
123 CH GOD (ANDER)	1	25	45	-	0.1
127 CH GOD (CLEVE)	2	59	72*	0.1	0.1
165 CH OF NAZARENE	5	464	744	0.6	1.5
193 EPISCOPAL.....	4	1,097	1,433	1.2	2.9
283 LUTH--MO SYNOD	3	918	1,223	1.0	2.4
357 PRESB CH US...	4	402	487*	0.4	1.0
413 S-D ADVENTISTS	2	90	109*	0.1	0.2
419 SO BAPT CONV..	46	21,442	25,998*	20.9	52.0
449 UN METHODIST..	19	5,685	6,301	5.1	12.6
453 UN PRES CH USA	5	724	878*	0.7	1.8
461 UNITY OF BRETH	5	706	849	0.7	1.7
BEXAR	350	140,033	537,535*	64.7	100.0
029 AMER LUTH CH..	16	10,162	12,789	1.5	2.4
059 BAPT MISS ASSN	3	403	506*	0.1	0.1
081 CATHOLIC......	86	0	361,623	43.5	67.3
093 CR CH (DISC)..	9	3,798	4,768*	0.6	0.9
097 CR C AND C CR.	13	1,568	1,968*	0.2	0.4
123 CH GOD (ANDER)	6	304	698	0.1	0.1
127 CH GOD (CLEVE)	1	140	176*	-	-
165 CUMBER PRESB..	2	467	586*	0.1	0.1
193 EPISCOPAL.....	17	10,938	15,234	1.8	2.8
221 FREE METH C NA	3	64	112	-	-
281 LUTH CH AMER..	8	2,036	2,856	0.3	0.5
283 LUTH--MO SYNOD	12	5,628	8,145	1.0	1.5
353 PLY BRETHREN..	3	60	120	-	-
357 PRESB CH US...	22	8,002	10,045*	1.2	1.9
403 SALVATION ARMY	1	100	356	-	0.1
413 S-D ADVENTISTS	4	864	1,085*	0.1	0.2
419 SO BAPT CONV..	81	59,892	75,186*	9.1	14.0
435 UNITARIAN-UNIV	1	318	458	0.1	0.1
443 UN C OF CHRIST	3	974	1,223*	0.1	0.2
449 UN METHODIST..	49	31,654	36,259	4.4	6.7
453 UN PRES CH USA	9	2,627	3,298*	0.4	0.6
469 WISC EVAN LUTH	1	34	44	-	-

—Represents a percent less than 0.1.

Percentages may not total due to rounding.

Table 3. Churches and Church Membership by State, County and Denomination: 1971

County and Denomination	Number of churches	Communicant, confirmed, full members	Total adherents		
			Number	Percent of total population	Percent of total adherents
BLANCO	12	3,135	4,206*	117.9#	100.0
C29 AMER LUTH CH..	3	690	816	22.9	19.4
081 CATHOLIC......	1	C	601	16.8	14.3
093 CR CH (DISC)..	1	34	39*	1.1	0.9
193 EPISCOPAL.....	1	35	40	1.1	1.0
419 SO BAPT CONV..	3	1,748	2,021*	56.7	48.1
449 UN METHODIST..	3	628	689	19.3	16.4
BORDEN	4	1,486	2,066*	232.7#	100.0
081 CATHOLIC......	0	0	250	28.2	12.1
419 SO BAPT CONV..	3	1,425	1,741*	196.1	84.3
449 UN METHODIST..	1	61	75	8.4	3.6
BOSQUE	42	7,196	8,203*	74.8	100.0
029 AMER LUTH CH..	4	1,271	1,512	13.8	18.4
C81 CATHOLIC......	1	0	65	0.6	0.8
093 CR CH (DISC)..	1	8	9*	0.1	0.1
193 EPISCOPAL.....	1	22	22	0.2	0.3
283 LUTH--MO SYNOD	1	155	195	1.8	2.4
357 PRESB CH US...	2	70	79*	0.7	1.0
419 SO BAPT CONV..	18	3,818	4,322*	39.4	52.7
443 UN C OF CHRIST	1	207	234*	2.1	2.9
449 UN METHODIST..	11	1,572	1,682	15.3	20.5
453 UN PRES CH USA	2	73	83*	0.8	1.0
BOWIE	97	28,678	35,943*	53.0	100.0
029 AMER LUTH CH..	1	104	143	0.2	0.4
059 BAPT MISS ASSN	4	633	772*	1.1	2.1
081 CATHOLIC......	2	0	1,295	1.9	3.6
093 CR CH (DISC)..	2	640	780*	1.2	2.2
097 CR C AND C CR.	6	897	1,093*	1.6	3.0
123 CH GOD (ANDER)	1	5	12	-	-
127 CH GOD (CLEVE)	2	102	124*	0.2	0.3
165 CH OF NAZARENE	2	411	507	0.7	1.4
175 CONG CR CH....	1	107	130*	0.2	0.4
193 EPISCOPAL.....	3	732	1,282	1.9	3.6
283 LUTH--MO SYNOD	1	257	345	0.5	1.0
357 PRESB CH US...	6	1,328	1,619*	2.4	4.5
403 SALVATION ARMY	1	95	275	0.4	0.8
413 S-D ADVENTISTS	1	72	88*	0.1	0.2
419 SO BAPT CONV..	44	16,875	20,570*	30.3	57.2
435 UNITARIAN-UNIV	1	21	21	-	0.1
449 UN METHODIST..	18	6,176	6,615	9.8	18.4
453 UN PRES CH USA	1	223	272*	0.4	0.8
BRAZORIA	115	37,469	63,542*	58.7	100.0
029 AMER LUTH CH..	6	1,122	1,561	1.4	2.5
059 BAPT MISS ASSN	1	42	53*	-	0.1
081 CATHOLIC......	14	0	16,979	15.7	26.7
093 CR CH (DISC)..	5	691	864*	0.8	1.4
123 CH GOD (ANDER)	1	34	73	0.1	0.1
127 CH GOD (CLEVE)	1	56	70*	0.1	0.1
165 CH OF NAZARENE	6	312	598	0.6	0.9
193 EPISCOPAL.....	6	1,261	1,936	1.8	3.0
281 LUTH CH AMER..	1	292	435	0.4	0.7
283 LUTH--MO SYNOD	3	376	525	0.5	0.8
349 PENT HOLINESS.	1	52	65*	0.1	0.1
353 PLY BRETHREN..	1	20	40	-	0.1
357 PRESB CH US...	10	2,238	2,799*	2.6	4.4
413 S-D ADVENTISTS	1	44	55*	0.1	0.1
419 SO BAPT CONV..	37	22,919	28,666*	26.5	45.1
435 UNITARIAN-UNIV	1	15	23	-	-
449 UN METHODIST..	19	7,951	8,737	8.1	13.7
469 WISC EVAN LUTH	1	44	63	0.1	0.1
BRAZOS	46	19,037	28,915*	49.9	100.0
029 AMER LUTH CH..	1	528	736	1.3	2.5
059 BAPT MISS ASSN	1	267	327*	0.6	1.1
081 CATHOLIC......	2	0	5,742	9.9	19.9
093 CR CH (DISC)..	1	278	340*	0.6	1.2
097 CR C AND C CR.	1	100	122*	0.2	0.4
165 CH OF NAZARENE	1	65	104	0.2	0.4
193 EPISCOPAL.....	2	583	793	1.4	2.7
283 LUTH--MO SYNOD	2	553	764	1.3	2.6
349 PENT HOLINESS.	1	30	37*	0.1	0.1
357 PRESB CH US...	2	1,335	1,633*	2.8	5.6
403 SALVATION ARMY	1	17	164	0.3	0.6
413 S-D ADVENTISTS	1	25	31*	0.1	0.1
419 SO BAPT CONV..	18	10,928	13,368*	23.1	46.2
435 UNITARIAN-UNIV	1	54	96	0.2	0.3
443 UN C OF CHRIST	2	413	505*	0.9	1.7
449 UN METHODIST..	9	3,861	4,153	7.2	14.4
BREWSTER	13	2,049	5,661*	72.8	100.0
081 CATHOLIC......	3	0	3,000	38.6	53.0
093 CR CH (DISC)..	1	84	101*	1.3	1.8
165 CH OF NAZARENE	1	17	59	0.8	1.0
193 EPISCOPAL.....	1	49	67	0.9	1.2
419 SO BAPT CONV..	3	995	1,201*	15.4	21.2
449 UN METHODIST..	3	726	1,018	13.1	18.0
453 UN PRES CH USA	1	178	215*	2.8	3.8
BRISCOE	6	1,575	3,883*	139.0#	100.0
081 CATHOLIC......	2	0	2,000	71.6	51.5
419 SO BAPT CONV..	2	1,246	1,515*	54.2	39.0
449 UN METHODIST..	2	329	368	13.2	9.5
BROOKS	14	1,308	6,333*	79.1	100.0
081 CATHOLIC......	4	0	4,590	57.3	72.5
123 CH GOD (ANDER)	1	58	139	1.7	2.2
157 CH OF BRETHREN	1	114	146*	1.8	2.3
193 EPISCOPAL.....	1	16	25	0.3	0.4
349 PENT HOLINESS.	1	15	19*	0.2	0.3
357 PRESB CH US...	2	169	216*	2.7	3.4
413 S-D ADVENTISTS	1	20	26*	0.3	0.4
419 SO BAPT CONV..	1	646	825*	10.3	13.0
449 UN METHODIST..	2	270	347	4.3	5.5
BROWN	50	14,402	17,769*	68.7	100.0
081 CATHOLIC......	1	0	965	3.7	5.4
093 CR CH (DISC)..	1	318	370*	1.4	2.1
165 CH OF NAZARENE	2	124	321	1.2	1.8
193 EPISCOPAL.....	2	317	438	1.7	2.5
283 LUTH--MO SYNOD	1	142	219	0.8	1.2
357 PRESB CH US...	1	203	236*	0.9	1.3
413 S-D ADVENTISTS	1	41	48*	0.2	0.3
419 SO BAPT CONV..	30	10,323	12,026*	46.5	67.7
449 UN METHODIST..	10	2,717	2,893	11.2	16.3
453 UN PRES CH USA	1	217	253*	1.0	1.4
BURLESON	32	3,580	5,304*	53.0	100.0
029 AMER LUTH CH..	4	521	675	6.8	12.7
081 CATHOLIC......	3	0	1,035	10.4	19.5
093 CR CH (DISC)..	2	69	82*	0.8	1.5
123 CH GOD (ANDER)	1	32	72	0.7	1.4
283 LUTH--MO SYNOD	1	30	36	0.4	0.7
357 PRESB CH US...	2	71	84*	0.8	1.6
419 SO BAPT CONV..	11	1,640	1,944*	19.4	36.7
443 UN C OF CHRIST	1	145	172*	1.7	3.2
449 UN METHODIST..	5	686	744	7.4	14.0
461 UNITY OF BRETH	2	386	460	4.6	8.7
BURNET	31	4,910	6,392*	56.0	100.0
029 AMER LUTH CH..	2	151	199	1.7	3.1
081 CATHOLIC......	3	0	597	5.2	9.3
093 CR CH (DISC)..	4	216	250*	2.2	3.9
185 CUMBER PRESB..	1	152	176*	1.5	2.8
193 EPISCOPAL.....	3	168	350	3.1	5.5
357 PRESB CH US...	2	211	244*	2.1	3.8
419 SO BAPT CONV..	11	3,140	3,634*	31.8	56.9
449 UN METHODIST..	5	872	942	8.2	14.7
CALDWELL	49	6,318	9,749*	46.0	100.0
029 AMER LUTH CH..	2	159	191	0.9	2.0
081 CATHOLIC......	4	0	2,389	11.3	24.5
093 CR CH (DISC)..	3	306	363*	1.7	3.7
165 CH OF NAZARENE	2	2	2	-	-
193 EPISCOPAL.....	2	201	294	1.4	3.0
357 PRESB CH US...	3	194	230*	1.1	2.4
413 S-D ADVENTISTS	2	14	17*	0.1	0.2
419 SO BAPT CONV..	13	3,480	4,125*	19.5	42.3
443 UN C OF CHRIST	3	359	426*	2.0	4.4
449 UN METHODIST..	14	1,581	1,686	8.0	17.3
453 UN PRES CH USA	1	22	26*	0.1	0.3
CALHOUN	18	4,446	10,929*	61.3	100.0
081 CATHOLIC......	4	0	5,112	28.7	46.8
093 CR CH (DISC)..	1	25	32*	0.2	0.3
193 EPISCOPAL.....	1	208	378	2.1	3.5
281 LUTH CH AMER..	2	558	[illegible]	4.4	7.1
357 PRESB CH US...	1	296	381*	2.1	3.5
419 SO BAPT CONV..	5	2,488	3,202*	18.0	29.3
449 UN METHODIST..	3	808	965	5.4	8.8
453 UN PRES CH USA	1	63	81*	0.5	0.7
CALLAHAN	22	4,409	4,977*	60.7	100.0
059 BAPT MISS ASSN	1	114	130*	1.6	2.6
081 CATHOLIC......	1	C	60	0.7	1.2
127 CH GOD (CLEVE)	2	49	56*	0.7	1.1
357 PRESB CH US...	2	40	46*	0.6	0.9
419 SO BAPT CONV..	9	3,045	3,478*	42.4	69.9
449 UN METHODIST..	5	1,119	1,159	14.1	23.3
453 UN PRES CH USA	2	42	48*	0.6	1.0
CAMERON	110	20,362	115,626*	82.4	100.0
081 CATHOLIC......	35	0	89,292	63.6	77.2
093 CR CH (DISC)..	3	337	438*	0.3	0.4
097 CR C AND C CR.	2	330	429*	0.3	0.4
121 CH GOD (ABR)..	1	19	25*	-	-
123 CH GOD (ANDER)	1	32	75	0.1	0.1
165 CH OF NAZARENE	2	207	311	0.2	0.3
193 EPISCOPAL.....	5	1,279	1,984	1.4	1.7
281 LUTH CH AMER..	1	191	223	0.2	0.2
283 LUTH--MO SYNOD	5	733	1,027	0.7	0.9
285 MENNONITE CH..	1	6	8*	-	-
349 PENT HOLINESS.	5	209	272*	0.2	0.2
357 PRESB CH US...	8	1,826	2,372*	1.7	2.1
403 SALVATION ARMY	1	59	253	0.2	0.2
413 S-D ADVENTISTS	2	92	120*	0.1	0.1
419 SO BAPT CONV..	24	10,306	13,389*	9.5	11.6
435 UNITARIAN-UNIV	1	30	37	-	-
449 UN METHODIST..	13	4,706	5,371	3.8	4.6
CAMP	24	3,833	4,549*	56.8	100.0

*Total adherents estimated from known number of communicant, confirmed, full members.

—Represents a percent less than 0.1.

Percentages may not total due to rounding.

#See Introduction for explanation of why total adherents reported by churches exceed the 1970 population figure.

Table 3. Churches and Church Membership by State, County and Denomination: 1971

County and Denomination	Number of churches	Communicant, confirmed, full members	Total adherents: Number	Total adherents: Percent of total population	Total adherents: Percent of total adherents
059 BAPT MISS ASSN	8	944	1,139*	14.2	25.0
127 CH GOD (CLEVE)	1	22	27*	0.3	0.6
165 CH OF NAZARENE	1	31	59	0.7	1.3
185 CUMBER PRESB..	1	30	36*	0.4	0.8
193 EPISCOPAL.....	1	105	132	1.6	2.9
357 PRESB CH US...	1	24	29*	0.4	0.6
413 S-D ADVENTISTS	1	30	36*	0.4	0.8
419 SO BAPT CONV..	8	2,028	2,447*	30.6	53.8
449 UN METHODIST..	2	619	644	8.0	14.2
CARSON	11	3,530	7,144*	112.4#	100.0
081 CATHOLIC......	3	0	3,000	47.2	42.0
093 CR CH (DISC)..	1	214	256*	4.0	3.6
419 SO BAPT CONV..	4	2,325	2,785*	43.8	39.0
449 UN METHODIST..	3	991	1,103	17.3	15.4
CASS	58	12,202	14,525*	60.2	100.0
081 CATHOLIC......	1	0	64	0.3	0.4
123 CH GOD (ANDER)	1	34	85	0.4	0.6
165 CH OF NAZARENE	1	125	161	0.7	1.1
193 EPISCOPAL.....	1	29	54	0.2	0.4
413 S-D ADVENTISTS	2	123	149*	0.6	1.0
419 SO BAPT CONV..	38	9,398	11,357*	47.1	78.2
449 UN METHODIST..	13	2,446	2,598	10.8	17.9
453 UN PRES CH USA	1	47	57*	0.2	0.4
CASTRO	16	3,385	8,366*	80.5	100.0
081 CATHOLIC......	3	0	4,000	38.5	47.8
097 CR C AND C CR.	1	38	51*	0.5	0.6
419 SO BAPT CONV..	8	2,536	3,399*	32.7	40.6
449 UN METHODIST..	3	777	870	8.4	10.4
453 UN PRES CH USA	1	34	46*	0.4	0.5
CHAMBERS	20	4,443	6,199*	50.9	100.0
081 CATHOLIC......	2	0	841	6.9	13.6
193 EPISCOPAL.....	1	30	42	0.3	0.7
419 SO BAPT CONV..	10	2,961	3,657*	30.0	59.0
449 UN METHODIST..	7	1,452	1,659	13.6	26.8
CHEROKEE	69	13,468	15,980*	49.9	100.0
059 BAPT MISS ASSN	16	3,743	4,379*	13.7	27.4
081 CATHOLIC......	2	0	350	1.1	2.2
093 CR CH (DISC)..	4	288	337*	1.1	2.1
127 CH GOD (CLEVE)	1	20	23*	0.1	0.1
165 CH OF NAZARENE	2	104	181	0.6	1.1
185 CUMBER PRESB..	2	91	106*	0.3	0.7
193 EPISCOPAL.....	2	133	176	0.5	1.1
357 PRESB CH US...	1	88	103*	0.3	0.6
413 S-D ADVENTISTS	1	77	90*	0.3	0.6
419 SO BAPT CONV..	21	5,698	6,667*	20.8	41.7
449 UN METHODIST..	16	2,970	3,268	10.2	20.5
453 UN PRES CH USA	1	256	300*	0.9	1.9
CHILDRESS	16	3,267	5,166*	78.2	100.0
059 BAPT MISS ASSN	1	50	57*	0.9	1.1
081 CATHOLIC......	1	0	1,500	22.7	29.0
093 CR CH (DISC)..	1	110	126*	1.9	2.4
127 CH GOD (CLEVE)	1	17	20*	0.3	0.4
165 CH OF NAZARENE	1	17	44	0.7	0.9
193 EPISCOPAL.....	1	5	10	0.2	0.2
419 SO BAPT CONV..	6	2,112	2,423*	36.7	46.9
449 UN METHODIST..	3	888	908	13.7	17.6
453 UN PRES CH USA	1	68	78*	1.2	1.5
CLAY	23	4,347	5,273*	65.3	100.0
081 CATHOLIC......	1	0	301	3.7	5.7
093 CR CH (DISC)..	1	59	69*	0.9	1.3
127 CH GOD (CLEVE)	1	118	137*	1.7	2.6
193 EPISCOPAL.....	1	70	107	1.3	2.0
419 SO BAPT CONV..	12	3,257	3,791*	46.9	71.9
449 UN METHODIST..	7	843	868	10.7	16.5
COCHRAN	7	2,477	4,517*	84.8	100.0
059 BAPT MISS ASSN	1	462	583*	10.9	12.9
081 CATHOLIC......	1	0	1,500	28.2	33.2
419 SO BAPT CONV..	3	1,479	1,868*	35.1	41.4
449 UN METHODIST..	2	536	566	10.6	12.5
COKE	10	1,787	2,327*	75.4	100.0
059 BAPT MISS ASSN	2	205	238*	7.7	10.2
081 CATHOLIC......	2	0	300	9.7	12.9
419 SO BAPT CONV..	4	1,099	1,274*	41.3	54.7
449 UN METHODIST..	2	483	515	16.7	22.1
COLEMAN	43	5,709	6,961*	67.7	100.0
059 BAPT MISS ASSN	2	203	232*	2.3	3.3
081 CATHOLIC......	1	0	550	5.3	7.9
093 CR CH (DISC)..	2	358	410*	4.0	5.9
123 CH GOD (ANDER)	1	10	20	0.2	0.3
165 CH OF NAZARENE	1	30	30	0.3	0.4
193 EPISCOPAL.....	1	73	87	0.8	1.2
357 PRESB CH US...	2	89	102*	1.0	1.5
413 S-D ADVENTISTS	1	78	89*	0.9	1.3
419 SO BAPT CONV..	18	3,469	3,972*	38.6	57.1
449 UN METHODIST..	12	1,308	1,365	13.3	19.6

County and Denomination	Number of churches	Communicant, confirmed, full members	Total adherents: Number	Total adherents: Percent of total population	Total adherents: Percent of total adherents
453 UN PRES CH USA	2	91	104*	1.0	1.5
COLLIN	115	27,041	38,272*	57.2	100.0
059 BAPT MISS ASSN	1	97	123*	0.2	0.3
081 CATHOLIC......	4	0	4,331	6.5	11.3
093 CR CH (DISC)..	13	1,552	1,974*	2.9	5.2
097 CR C AND C CR.	3	410	521*	0.8	1.4
127 CH GOD (CLEVE)	3	130	165*	0.2	0.4
165 CH OF NAZARENE	2	92	170	0.3	0.4
193 EPISCOPAL.....	3	563	879	1.3	2.3
283 LUTH--MO SYNOD	1	164	261	0.4	0.7
349 PENT HOLINESS.	1	15	19*	-	-
357 PRESB CH US...	1	249	317*	0.5	0.8
419 SO BAPT CONV..	51	18,352	23,339*	34.9	61.0
449 UN METHODIST..	24	4,750	5,325	8.0	13.9
453 UN PRES CH USA	8	667	848*	1.3	2.2
COLLINGSWORTH	12	2,639	4,003*	84.2	100.0
081 CATHOLIC......	1	0	1,000	21.0	25.0
097 CR C AND C CR.	1	108	126*	2.6	3.1
165 CH OF NAZARENE	2	144	173	3.6	4.3
419 SO BAPT CONV..	5	1,678	1,955*	41.1	48.8
449 UN METHODIST..	3	709	749	15.8	18.7
COLORADO	36	4,878	11,671*	66.2	100.0
029 AMER LUTH CH..	5	1,213	1,510	8.6	12.9
081 CATHOLIC......	6	0	5,772	32.7	49.5
123 CH GOD (ANDER)	1	13	31	0.2	0.3
165 CH OF NAZARENE	1	11	38	0.2	0.3
193 EPISCOPAL.....	2	200	319	1.8	2.7
419 SO BAPT CONV..	8	1,728	2,051*	11.6	17.6
443 UN C OF CHRIST	2	445	528*	3.0	4.5
449 UN METHODIST..	11	1,268	1,422	8.1	12.2
COMAL	20	5,950	15,958*	66.0	100.0
029 AMER LUTH CH..	2	1,152	1,501	6.2	9.4
081 CATHOLIC......	5	0	8,662	35.8	54.3
097 CR C AND C CR.	1	23	28*	0.1	0.2
193 EPISCOPAL.....	1	300	395	1.6	2.5
283 LUTH--MO SYNOD	1	337	472	2.0	3.0
349 PENT HOLINESS.	1	34	41*	0.2	0.3
357 PRESB CH US...	2	215	258*	1.1	1.6
419 SO BAPT CONV..	3	468	562*	2.3	3.5
443 UN C OF CHRIST	2	2,310	2,774*	11.5	17.4
449 UN METHODIST..	2	1,111	1,265	5.2	7.9
COMANCHE	40	5,712	6,985*	58.7	100.0
081 CATHOLIC......	1	0	500	4.2	7.2
093 CR CH (DISC)..	1	43	50*	0.4	0.7
097 CR C AND C CR.	1	35	40*	0.3	0.6
193 EPISCOPAL.....	1	56	96	0.8	1.4
357 PRESB CH US...	1	25	29*	0.2	0.4
419 SO BAPT CONV..	26	4,275	4,930*	41.4	70.6
449 UN METHODIST..	8	1,254	1,312	11.0	18.8
453 UN PRES CH USA	1	24	28*	0.2	0.4
CONCHO	15	1,242	1,598*	54.4	100.0
081 CATHOLIC......	2	0	200	6.8	12.5
093 CR CH (DISC)..	1	3	4*	0.1	0.3
193 EPISCOPAL.....	1	18	21	0.7	1.3
283 LUTH--MO SYNOD	2	194	219	7.5	13.7
357 PRESB CH US...	1	8	9*	0.3	0.6
419 SO BAPT CONV..	4	694	814*	27.7	50.9
449 UN METHODIST..	4	325	331	11.3	20.7
COOKE	45	9,327	15,315*	65.3	100.0
081 CATHOLIC......	4	0	4,420	18.8	28.9
093 CR CH (DISC)..	1	261	312*	1.3	2.0
127 CH GOD (CLEVE)	1	17	20*	0.1	0.1
165 CH OF NAZARENE	1	68	89	0.4	0.6
193 EPISCOPAL.....	1	104	120	0.5	0.8
349 PENT HOLINESS.	1	14	17*	0.1	0.1
381 REF PRES-EVAN.	2	205	228	1.0	1.5
413 S-D ADVENTISTS	2	85	102*	0.4	0.7
419 SO BAPT CONV..	21	6,321	7,557*	32.2	49.3
449 UN METHODIST..	10	2,105	2,274	9.7	14.8
453 UN PRES CH USA	1	147	176*	0.7	1.1
CORYELL	53	10,158	12,144*	34.4	100.0
029 AMER LUTH CH..	1	169	211	0.6	1.7
081 CATHOLIC......	2	0	421	1.2	3.5
093 CR CH (DISC)..	2	42	49*	0.1	0.4
121 CH GOD (ABR)..	1	45	52*	0.1	0.4
283 LUTH--MO SYNOD	4	567	796	2.3	6.6
313 NO AM BAPT GC.	1	59	68*	0.2	0.6
357 PRESB CH US...	2	79	91*	0.3	0.7
419 SO BAPT CONV..	27	6,985	8,080*	22.9	66.5
449 UN METHODIST..	10	2,017	2,150	6.1	17.7
453 UN PRES CH USA	3	195	226*	0.6	1.9
COTTLE	8	1,851	2,950*	92.1	100.0
059 BAPT MISS ASSN	1	331	391*	12.2	13.3
081 CATHOLIC......	1	0	800	25.0	27.1
093 CR CH (DISC)..	1	89	105*	3.3	3.6
419 SO BAPT CONV..	3	1,089	1,288*	40.2	43.7
449 UN METHODIST..	2	342	366	11.4	12.4

*Total adherents estimated from known number of communicant, confirmed, full members.

—Represents a percent less than 0.1.

Percentages may not total due to rounding.

#See Introduction for explanation of why total adherents reported by churches exceed the 1970 population figure.

Table 3. Churches and Church Membership by State, County and Denomination: 1971

County and Denomination	Number of churches	Communicant, confirmed, full members	Total adherents: Number	Total adherents: Percent of total population	Total adherents: Percent of total adherents
CRANE	5	1,032	1,690*	40.5	100.0
081 CATHOLIC......	1	0	500	12.0	29.6
097 CR C AND C CR.	1	125	154*	3.7	9.1
357 PRESB CH US...	1	37	46*	1.1	2.7
419 SO BAPT CONV..	1	408	503*	12.1	29.8
449 UN METHODIST..	1	462	487	11.7	28.8
CROCKETT	6	935	1,600*	41.2	100.0
081 CATHOLIC......	1	0	500	12.9	31.3
283 LUTH--MO SYNOD	1	20	22	0.6	1.4
419 SO BAPT CONV..	3	453	566*	14.6	35.4
449 UN METHODIST..	1	462	512	13.2	32.0
CROSBY	13	4,048	7,961*	87.6	100.0
059 BAPT MISS ASSN	1	35	45*	0.5	0.6
081 CATHOLIC......	3	0	3,000	33.0	37.7
419 SO BAPT CONV..	6	2,967	3,783*	41.6	47.5
449 UN METHODIST..	3	1,046	1,133	12.5	14.2
CULBERSON	6	767	2,116*	61.7	100.0
081 CATHOLIC......	1	0	1,147	33.4	54.2
165 CH OF NAZARENE	1	11	30	0.9	1.4
357 PRESB CH US...	1	41	55*	1.6	2.6
419 SO BAPT CONV..	1	375	502*	14.6	23.7
449 UN METHODIST..	2	340	382	11.1	18.1
DALLAM	12	3,674	5,872*	97.7	100.0
081 CATHOLIC......	2	0	1,500	25.0	25.5
097 CR C AND C CR.	1	350	433*	7.2	7.4
165 CH OF NAZARENE	1	51	51	0.8	0.9
193 EPISCOPAL.....	1	86	106	1.8	1.8
413 S-D ADVENTISTS	1	40	49*	0.8	0.8
419 SO BAPT CONV..	3	2,313	2,860*	47.6	48.7
449 UN METHODIST..	2	779	805	13.4	13.7
453 UN PRES CH USA	1	55	68*	1.1	1.2
DALLAS	606	406,194	597,913*	45.0	100.0
019 AMER BAPT CONV	4	1,006	1,261*	0.1	0.2
029 AMER LUTH CH..	8	2,900	4,069	0.3	0.7
059 BAPT MISS ASSN	50	14,832	18,589*	1.4	3.1
081 CATHOLIC......	32	0	89,085	6.7	14.9
093 CR CH (DISC)..	42	18,444	23,116*	1.7	3.9
097 CR C AND C CR.	11	2,081	2,608*	0.2	0.4
123 CH GOD (ANDER)	1	173	453	-	0.1
127 CH GOD (CLEVE)	9	999	1,252*	0.1	0.2
165 CH OF NAZARENE	15	2,382	3,893	0.3	0.7
185 CUMBER PRESB..	1	335	420*	-	0.1
193 EPISCOPAL.....	36	19,307	26,027	2.0	4.4
221 FREE METH C NA	4	219	407	-	0.1
226 FRIENDS-USA...	1	65	81*	-	-
281 LUTH CH AMER..	11	3,433	4,973	0.4	0.8
283 LUTH--MO SYNOD	16	6,457	9,421	0.7	1.6
313 NO AM BAPT GC.	1	82	103*	-	-
349 PENT HOLINESS.	2	170	213*	-	-
353 PLY BRETHREN..	2	285	639	-	0.1
357 PRESB CH US...	30	20,720	25,969*	2.0	4.3
381 REF PRES-EVAN.	1	32	42	-	-
403 SALVATION ARMY	4	397	4,983	0.4	0.8
413 S-D ADVENTISTS	7	2,072	2,597*	0.2	0.4
419 SO BAPT CONV..	193	203,360	254,872*	19.2	42.6
435 UNITARIAN-UNIV	3	706	1,061	0.1	0.2
443 UN C OF CHRIST	4	1,764	2,211*	0.2	0.4
449 UN METHODIST..	95	96,177	109,712	8.3	18.3
453 UN PRES CH USA	20	7,450	9,337*	0.7	1.6
461 UNITY OF BRETH	1	76	100	-	-
469 WISC EVAN LUTH	2	270	419	-	0.1
DAWSON	26	8,047	13,031*	78.5	100.0
059 BAPT MISS ASSN	2	870	1,098*	6.6	8.4
081 CATHOLIC......	2	0	3,000	18.1	23.0
093 CR CH (DISC)..	1	82	103*	0.6	0.8
127 CH GOD (CLEVE)	1	28	35*	0.2	0.3
165 CH OF NAZARENE	1	82	245	1.5	1.9
193 EPISCOPAL.....	1	23	29	0.2	0.2
283 LUTH--MO SYNOD	1	140	179	1.1	1.4
419 SO BAPT CONV..	11	5,126	6,467*	38.9	49.6
449 UN METHODIST..	5	1,426	1,534	9.2	11.8
453 UN PRES CH USA	1	270	341*	2.1	2.6
DEAF SMITH	16	5,880	10,543*	55.5	100.0
081 CATHOLIC......	1	0	3,000	15.8	28.5
093 CR CH (DISC)..	1	374	494*	2.6	4.7
165 CH OF NAZARENE	1	89	170	0.9	1.6
193 EPISCOPAL.....	1	99	135	0.7	1.3
283 LUTH--MO SYNOD	1	116	171	0.9	1.6
413 S-D ADVENTISTS	1	41	54*	0.3	0.5
419 SO BAPT CONV..	6	3,512	4,642*	24.4	44.0
449 UN METHODIST..	3	1,470	1,640	8.6	15.6
453 UN PRES CH USA	1	179	237*	1.2	2.2
DELTA	21	3,266	3,664*	74.4	100.0
059 BAPT MISS ASSN	1	71	82*	1.7	2.2
093 CR CH (DISC)..	1	25	29*	0.6	0.8
165 CH OF NAZARENE	1	13	18	0.4	0.5
419 SO BAPT CONV..	10	2,085	2,415*	49.0	65.9
449 UN METHODIST..	6	1,018	1,057	21.5	28.8
453 UN PRES CH USA	2	54	63*	1.3	1.7
DENTON	95	19,069	27,592*	36.5	100.0
059 BAPT MISS ASSN	2	358	430*	0.6	1.6
081 CATHOLIC......	5	0	3,700	4.9	13.4
093 CR CH (DISC)..	4	660	792*	1.0	2.9
097 CR C AND C CR.	1	65	78*	0.1	0.3
127 CH GOD (CLEVE)	2	54	65*	0.1	0.2
165 CH OF NAZARENE	4	191	365	0.5	1.3
185 CUMBER PRESB..	1	132	158*	0.2	0.6
193 EPISCOPAL.....	3	691	918	1.2	3.3
281 LUTH CH AMER..	1	101	158	0.2	0.6
283 LUTH--MO SYNOD	2	339	503	0.7	1.8
357 PRESB CH US...	6	1,105	1,326*	1.8	4.8
413 S-D ADVENTISTS	1	40	48*	0.1	0.2
419 SO BAPT CONV..	41	14,360	17,232*	22.8	62.5
435 UNITARIAN-UNIV	1	40	75	0.1	0.3
443 UN C OF CHRIST	1	93	112*	0.1	0.4
449 UN METHODIST..	15	231	901	1.2	3.3
453 UN PRES CH USA	5	609	731*	1.0	2.6
DE WITT	28	5,763	11,115*	59.6	100.0
029 AMER LUTH CH..	4	1,507	1,830	9.8	16.5
081 CATHOLIC......	6	0	4,247	22.8	38.2
193 EPISCOPAL.....	1	161	168	0.9	1.5
281 LUTH CH AMER..	2	1,643	2,016	10.8	18.1
357 PRESB CH US...	2	368	435*	2.3	3.9
419 SO BAPT CONV..	9	1,504	1,778*	9.5	16.0
449 UN METHODIST..	4	580	641	3.4	5.8
DICKENS	13	2,237	4,060*	108.6#	100.0
059 BAPT MISS ASSN	1	121	142*	3.8	3.5
081 CATHOLIC......	1	0	1,500	40.1	36.9
093 CR CH (DISC)..	1	26	31*	0.8	0.8
165 CH OF NAZARENE	1	11	19	0.5	0.5
419 SO BAPT CONV..	5	1,590	1,868*	50.0	46.0
449 UN METHODIST..	4	489	500	13.4	12.3
DIMMIT	12	1,536	8,397*	92.9	100.0
081 CATHOLIC......	4	0	6,461	71.5	76.9
193 EPISCOPAL.....	1	66	85	0.9	1.0
357 PRESB CH US...	1	13	17*	0.2	0.2
413 S-D ADVENTISTS	1	24	31*	0.3	0.4
419 SO BAPT CONV..	2	989	1,296*	14.3	15.4
449 UN METHODIST..	3	444	507	5.6	6.0
DONLEY	10	2,141	3,213*	88.2	100.0
081 CATHOLIC......	1	0	800	22.0	24.9
097 CR C AND C CR.	1	75	84*	2.3	2.6
165 CH OF NAZARENE	1	18	31	0.9	1.0
193 EPISCOPAL.....	1	39	84	2.3	2.6
419 SO BAPT CONV..	3	1,371	1,539*	42.3	47.9
449 UN METHODIST..	2	589	620	17.0	19.3
453 UN PRES CH USA	1	49	55*	1.5	1.7
DUVAL	12	1,227	8,535*	72.8	100.0
081 CATHOLIC......	6	0	6,980	59.5	81.8
419 SO BAPT CONV..	4	1,056	1,324*	11.3	15.5
449 UN METHODIST..	2	171	231	2.0	2.7
EASTLAND	49	10,244	11,932*	66.0	100.0
081 CATHOLIC......	3	0	400	2.2	3.4
093 CR CH (DISC)..	3	286	323*	1.8	2.7
123 CH GOD (ANDER)	2	41	89	0.5	0.7
127 CH GOD (CLEVE)	2	73	82*	0.5	0.7
165 CH OF NAZARENE	2	87	149	0.8	1.2
193 EPISCOPAL.....	1	19	27	0.1	0.2
283 LUTH--MO SYNOD	1	162	189	1.0	1.6
357 PRESB CH US...	2	68	77*	0.4	0.6
419 SO BAPT CONV..	24	7,628	8,609*	47.6	72.2
449 UN METHODIST..	7	1,813	1,911	10.6	16.0
453 UN PRES CH USA	2	67	76*	0.4	0.6
ECTOR	62	35,052	54,761*	59.6	100.0
029 AMER LUTH CH..	2	692	1,034	1.1	1.9
059 BAPT MISS ASSN	1	695	871*	0.9	1.6
081 CATHOLIC......	6	0	10,746	11.7	19.6
093 CR CH (DISC)..	2	694	870*	0.9	1.6
097 CR C AND C CR.	3	631	791*	0.9	1.4
123 CH GOD (ANDER)	1	85	215	0.2	0.4
127 CH GOD (CLEVE)	2	151	189*	0.2	0.3
165 CH OF NAZARENE	3	283	532	0.6	1.0
185 CUMBER PRESB..	1	356	446*	0.5	0.8
193 EPISCOPAL.....	1	663	884	1.0	1.6
283 LUTH--MO SYNOD	1	342	480	0.5	0.9
349 PENT HOLINESS.	1	34	43*	-	0.1
357 PRESB CH US...	3	1,517	1,901*	2.1	3.5
403 SALVATION ARMY	1	125	354	0.4	0.6
413 S-D ADVENTISTS	1	99	124*	0.1	0.2
419 SO BAPT CONV..	25	23,041	28,877*	31.5	52.7
435 UNITARIAN-UNIV	1	19	25	-	-
449 UN METHODIST..	7	5,625	6,379	6.9	11.6
EDWARDS	7	717	1,622*	77.0	100.0
081 CATHOLIC......	1	0	720	34.2	44.4
357 PRESB CH US...	1	69	88*	4.2	5.4

*Total adherents estimated from known number of communicant, confirmed, full members.

—Represents a percent less than 0.1.

Percentages may not total due to rounding.

#See Introduction for explanation of why total adherents reported by churches exceed the 1970 population figure.

Table 3. Churches and Church Membership by State, County and Denomination: 1971

County and Denomination	Number of churches	Communicant, confirmed, full members	Total adherents		
			Number	Percent of total population	Percent of total adherents
419 SO BAPT CONV..	2	463	592*	28.1	36.5
449 UN METHODIST..	3	185	222	10.5	13.7
ELLIS	82	19,737	27,497*	59.0	100.0
059 BAPT MISS ASSN	15	4,217	5,187*	11.1	18.9
081 CATHOLIC......	3	0	4,000	8.6	14.5
093 CR CH (DISC)..	7	588	723*	1.6	2.6
127 CH GOD (CLEVE)	1	64	79*	0.2	0.3
185 CUMBER PRESB..	1	108	133*	0.3	0.5
193 EPISCOPAL.....	3	284	393	0.8	1.4
283 LUTH--MO SYNOD	1	82	137	0.3	0.5
357 PRESB CH US...	8	609	749*	1.6	2.7
413 S-D ADVENTISTS	1	27	33*	0.1	0.1
419 SO BAPT CONV..	14	8,544	10,509*	22.5	38.2
449 UN METHODIST..	22	4,782	5,029	10.8	18.3
453 UN PRES CH USA	5	406	499*	1.1	1.8
461 UNITY OF BRETH	1	26	26	0.1	0.1
EL PASO	148	49,785	209,193*	58.2	100.0
029 AMER LUTH CH..	1	275	375	0.1	0.2
059 BAPT MISS ASSN	2	140	179*	-	0.1
081 CATHOLIC......	34	0	146,012	40.6	69.8
093 CR CH (DISC)..	7	1,509	1,934*	0.5	0.9
097 CR C AND C CR.	4	220	282*	0.1	0.1
123 CH GOD (ANDER)	1	15	45	-	-
127 CH GOD (CLEVE)	1	45	58*	-	-
165 CH OF NAZARENE	5	619	1,263	0.4	0.6
193 EPISCOPAL.....	6	3,946	5,710	1.6	2.7
226 FRIENDS-USA...	1	6	8*	-	-
281 LUTH CH AMER..	4	643	885	0.2	0.4
283 LUTH--MO SYNOD	5	1,124	1,841	0.5	0.9
349 PENT HOLINESS.	1	21	27*	-	-
353 PLY BRETHREN..	2	62	135	-	0.1
357 PRESB CH US...	5	1,093	1,400*	0.4	0.7
403 SALVATION ARMY	2	107	436	0.1	0.2
413 S-D ADVENTISTS	4	400	513*	0.1	0.2
419 SO BAPT CONV..	31	21,365	27,375*	7.6	13.1
435 UNITARIAN-UNIV	1	160	160	-	0.1
443 UN C OF CHRIST	3	402	515*	0.1	0.2
449 UN METHODIST..	20	14,921	16,530	4.6	7.9
453 UN PRES CH USA	6	2,638	3,380*	0.9	1.6
469 WISC EVAN LUTH	2	74	130	-	0.1
ERATH	47	8,484	10,697*	59.0	100.0
081 CATHOLIC......	2	0	1,100	6.1	10.3
093 CR CH (DISC)..	2	212	241*	1.3	2.3
127 CH GOD (CLEVE)	2	21	24*	0.1	0.2
165 CH OF NAZARENE	1	35	68	0.4	0.6
193 EPISCOPAL.....	2	148	188	1.0	1.8
283 LUTH--MO SYNOD	1	68	87	0.5	0.8
357 PRESB CH US...	1	52	59*	0.3	0.6
419 SO BAPT CONV..	25	6,312	7,169*	39.5	67.0
449 UN METHODIST..	10	1,587	1,705	9.4	15.9
453 UN PRES CH USA	1	49	56*	0.3	0.5
FALLS	51	7,869	11,029*	63.8	100.0
029 AMER LUTH CH..	1	300	347	2.0	3.1
081 CATHOLIC......	4	0	1,791	10.4	16.2
093 CR CH (DISC)..	2	52	61*	0.4	0.6
193 EPISCOPAL.....	1	84	184	1.1	1.7
283 LUTH--MO SYNOD	3	649	829	4.8	7.5
357 PRESB CH US...	2	162	191*	1.1	1.7
419 SO BAPT CONV..	20	4,406	5,202*	30.1	47.2
443 UN C OF CHRIST	3	338	399*	2.3	3.6
449 UN METHODIST..	13	1,721	1,840	10.6	16.7
453 UN PRES CH USA	2	157	185*	1.1	1.7
FANNIN	81	12,744	14,627*	64.4	100.0
081 CATHOLIC......	1	0	139	0.6	1.0
093 CR CH (DISC)..	6	456	529*	2.3	3.6
127 CH GOD (CLEVE)	3	193	224*	1.0	1.5
165 CH OF NAZARENE	3	127	181	0.8	1.2
193 EPISCOPAL.....	2	39	57	0.3	0.4
283 LUTH--MO SYNOD	1	73	89	0.4	0.6
357 PRESB CH US...	1	159	184*	0.8	1.3
419 SO BAPT CONV..	35	8,495	9,846*	43.4	67.3
449 UN METHODIST..	25	3,002	3,146	13.9	21.5
453 UN PRES CH USA	4	200	232*	1.0	1.6
FAYETTE	52	5,683	13,912*	78.8	100.0
029 AMER LUTH CH..	10	2,364	2,783	15.8	20.0
081 CATHOLIC......	18	0	7,290	41.3	52.4
193 EPISCOPAL.....	1	52	61	0.3	0.4
281 LUTH CH AMER..	1	250	306	1.7	2.2
283 LUTH--MO SYNOD	4	1,151	1,382	7.8	9.9
357 PRESB CH US...	1	145	165*	0.9	1.2
419 SO BAPT CONV..	5	747	848*	4.8	6.1
443 UN C OF CHRIST	1	140	159*	0.9	1.1
449 UN METHODIST..	10	765	849	4.8	6.1
461 UNITY OF BRETH	1	69	69	0.4	0.5
FISHER	21	3,876	4,822*	76.0	100.0
081 CATHOLIC......	2	0	312	4.9	6.5
165 CH OF NAZARENE	2	133	180	2.8	3.7
419 SO BAPT CONV..	12	2,985	3,535*	55.7	73.3
449 UN METHODIST..	5	758	795	12.5	16.5
FLOYD	18	5,120	8,021*	72.6	100.0
029 AMER LUTH CH..	1	131	158	1.4	2.0
081 CATHOLIC......	2	0	1,800	16.3	22.4
093 CR CH (DISC)..	1	87	110*	1.0	1.4
165 CH OF NAZARENE	1	43	87	0.8	1.1
185 CUMBER PRESB..	1	10	13*	0.1	0.2
419 SO BAPT CONV..	9	3,524	4,447*	40.3	55.4
449 UN METHODIST..	3	1,325	1,406	12.7	17.5
FOARD	8	1,324	1,524*	68.9	100.0
081 CATHOLIC......	1	0	50	2.3	3.3
097 CR C AND C CR.	1	85	98*	4.4	6.4
419 SO BAPT CONV..	3	733	844*	38.2	55.4
449 UN METHODIST..	3	506	532	24.1	34.9
FORT BEND	52	10,694	30,857*	59.0	100.0
029 AMER LUTH CH..	2	482	666	1.3	2.2
081 CATHOLIC......	8	0	17,254	33.0	55.9
093 CR CH (DISC)..	1	100	128*	0.2	0.4
097 CR C AND C CR.	1	90	116*	0.2	0.4
123 CH GOD (ANDER)	5	162	406	0.8	1.3
193 EPISCOPAL.....	3	423	545	1.0	1.8
283 LUTH--MO SYNOD	1	221	298	0.6	1.0
357 PRESB CH US...	1	281	361*	0.7	1.2
413 S-D ADVENTISTS	1	36	46*	0.1	0.1
419 SO BAPT CONV..	11	4,340	5,570*	10.6	18.1
443 UN C OF CHRIST	3	1,035	1,328*	2.5	4.3
449 UN METHODIST..	11	2,850	3,284	6.3	10.6
453 UN PRES CH USA	3	525	674*	1.3	2.2
461 UNITY OF BRETH	1	149	181	0.3	0.6
FRANKLIN	18	2,677	3,036*	57.4	100.0
059 BAPT MISS ASSN	1	82	95*	1.8	3.1
093 CR CH (DISC)..	1	28	32*	0.6	1.1
127 CH GOD (CLEVE)	1	34	39*	0.7	1.3
419 SO BAPT CONV..	12	2,073	2,394*	45.2	78.9
449 UN METHODIST..	3	460	476	9.0	15.7
FREESTONE	34	5,403	6,218*	55.9	100.0
059 BAPT MISS ASSN	12	1,392	1,625*	14.6	26.1
081 CATHOLIC......	1	0	75	0.7	1.2
357 PRESB CH US...	2	94	110*	1.0	1.8
419 SO BAPT CONV..	7	2,334	2,725*	24.5	43.8
449 UN METHODIST..	10	1,472	1,553	14.0	25.0
453 UN PRES CH USA	2	111	130*	1.2	2.1
FRIO	17	2,302	8,811*	79.0	100.0
081 CATHOLIC......	5	0	6,027	54.0	68.4
093 CR CH (DISC)..	1	25	33*	0.3	0.4
283 LUTH--MO SYNOD	1	71	95	0.9	1.1
419 SO BAPT CONV..	3	1,197	1,573*	14.1	17.9
449 UN METHODIST..	6	969	1,030	9.2	11.7
453 UN PRES CH USA	1	40	53*	0.5	0.6
GAINES	19	5,350	8,153*	70.3	100.0
059 BAPT MISS ASSN	1	66	84*	0.7	1.0
081 CATHOLIC......	2	0	1,500	12.9	18.4
093 CR CH (DISC)..	1	47	60*	0.5	0.7
127 CH GOD (CLEVE)	2	128	163*	1.4	2.0
165 CH OF NAZARENE	2	37	54	0.5	0.7
357 PRESB CH US...	2	207	264*	2.3	3.2
419 SO BAPT CONV..	7	4,025	5,126*	44.2	62.9
449 UN METHODIST..	2	840	902	7.8	11.1
GALVESTON	117	40,046	82,135*	48.4	100.0
029 AMER LUTH CH..	5	2,120	2,781	1.6	3.4
081 CATHOLIC......	15	0	31,974	18.8	38.9
093 CR CH (DISC)..	4	840	1,038*	0.6	1.3
097 CR C AND C CR.	2	475	587*	0.3	0.7
123 CH GOD (ANDER)	3	133	318	0.2	0.4
127 CH GOD (CLEVE)	1	11	14*	-	-
165 CH OF NAZARENE	3	246	383	0.2	0.5
193 EPISCOPAL.....	10	3,810	5,330	3.1	6.5
226 FRIENDS-USA...	4	838	1,036*	0.6	1.3
281 LUTH CH AMER..	1	135	178	0.1	0.2
283 LUTH--MO SYNOD	3	1,306	1,749	1.0	2.1
349 PENT HOLINESS.	1	36	45*	-	0.1
353 PLY BRETHREN..	4	321	507	0.3	0.6
357 PRESB CH US...	7	2,040	2,522*	1.5	3.1
403 SALVATION ARMY	1	64	284	0.2	0.3
413 S-D ADVENTISTS	2	63	78*	-	0.1
419 SO BAPT CONV..	28	18,697	23,113*	13.6	28.1
435 UNITARIAN-UNIV	1	40	73	-	0.1
449 UN METHODIST..	22	8,871	10,125	6.0	12.3
GARZA	16	2,416	3,834*	72.5	100.0
081 CATHOLIC......	1	0	900	17.0	23.5
093 CR CH (DISC)..	1	110	135*	2.6	3.5
165 CH OF NAZARENE	1	97	159	3.0	4.1
283 LUTH--MO SYNOD	1	23	24	0.5	0.6
419 SO BAPT CONV..	8	1,685	2,061*	39.0	53.8
449 UN METHODIST..	3	462	507	9.6	13.2
453 UN PRES CH USA	1	39	48*	0.9	1.3
GILLESPIE	18	4,860	8,980*	85.1	100.0
029 AMER LUTH CH..	7	3,230	3,929	37.2	43.8
081 CATHOLIC......	3	0	3,229	30.6	36.0

*Total adherents estimated from known number of communicant, confirmed, full members.

—Represents a percent less than 0.1.

Percentages may not total due to rounding.

Table 3. Churches and Church Membership by State, County and Denomination: 1971

County and Denomination	Number of churches	Communicant, confirmed, full members	Total adherents: Number	Total adherents: Percent of total population	Total adherents: Percent of total adherents
193 EPISCOPAL.....	1	45	50	0.5	0.6
357 PRESB CH US...	1	68	80*	0.8	0.9
419 SO BAPT CONV..	2	592	696*	6.6	7.8
449 UN METHODIST..	3	840	896	8.5	10.0
453 UN PRES CH USA	1	85	100*	0.9	1.1
GLASSCOCK	5	285	841*	72.8	100.0
081 CATHOLIC......	2	0	500	43.3	59.5
185 CUMBER PRESB..	1	32	41*	3.5	4.9
419 SO BAPT CONV..	1	153	197*	17.1	23.4
449 UN METHODIST..	1	100	103	8.9	12.2
GOLIAD	17	1,687	3,628*	74.5	100.0
029 AMER LUTH CH..	1	226	274	5.6	7.6
081 CATHOLIC......	5	0	1,611	33.1	44.4
193 EPISCOPAL.....	1	42	50	1.0	1.4
281 LUTH CH AMER..	4	746	899	18.5	24.8
357 PRESB CH US...	1	87	104*	2.1	2.9
419 SO BAPT CONV..	2	355	425*	8.7	11.7
449 UN METHODIST..	3	231	265	5.4	7.3
GONZALES	30	3,848	9,159*	55.9	100.0
029 AMER LUTH CH..	1	286	394	2.4	4.3
081 CATHOLIC......	6	0	4,443	27.1	48.5
193 EPISCOPAL.....	1	104	138	0.8	1.5
357 PRESB CH US...	1	207	250*	1.5	2.7
419 SO BAPT CONV..	14	2,539	3,065*	18.7	33.5
449 UN METHODIST..	5	671	819	5.0	8.9
453 UN PRES CH USA	2	41	50*	0.3	0.5
GRAY	29	13,337	17,631*	65.4	100.0
081 CATHOLIC......	1	0	1,500	5.6	8.5
093 CR CH (DISC)..	1	598	716*	2.7	4.1
097 CR C AND C CR.	1	125	150*	0.6	0.9
127 CH GOD (CLEVE)	1	121	145*	0.5	0.8
157 CH OF BRETHREN	1	98	117*	0.4	0.7
165 CH OF NAZARENE	2	113	170	0.6	1.0
193 EPISCOPAL.....	1	258	497	1.8	2.8
283 LUTH--MO SYNOD	1	185	253	0.9	1.4
349 PENT HOLINESS.	3	75	90*	0.3	0.5
403 SALVATION ARMY	1	74	196	0.7	1.1
413 S-D ADVENTISTS	1	27	32*	0.1	0.2
419 SO BAPT CONV..	9	8,962	10,737*	39.8	60.9
449 UN METHODIST..	5	2,465	2,745	10.2	15.6
453 UN PRES CH USA	1	236	283*	1.1	1.6
GRAYSON	106	36,359	45,733*	55.0	100.0
029 AMER LUTH CH..	1	136	213	0.3	0.5
081 CATHOLIC......	2	0	2,098	2.5	4.6
093 CR CH (DISC)..	6	1,072	1,291*	1.6	2.8
097 CR C AND C CR.	1	35	42*	0.1	0.1
127 CH GOD (CLEVE)	3	182	219*	0.3	0.5
165 CH OF NAZARENE	3	380	600	0.7	1.3
185 CUMBER PRESB..	1	48	58*	0.1	0.1
193 EPISCOPAL.....	2	777	901	1.1	2.0
226 FRIENDS-USA...	1	23	28*	-	0.1
283 LUTH--MO SYNOD	1	210	303	0.4	0.7
349 PENT HOLINESS.	1	10	12*	-	-
357 PRESB CH US...	3	798	961*	1.2	2.1
403 SALVATION ARMY	1	87	539	0.6	1.2
413 S-D ADVENTISTS	1	118	142*	0.2	0.3
419 SO BAPT CONV..	49	24,174	29,121*	35.0	63.7
449 UN METHODIST..	24	7,161	7,822	9.4	17.1
453 UN PRES CH USA	6	1,148	1,383*	1.7	3.0
GREGG	79	33,305	41,953*	55.3	100.0
029 AMER LUTH CH..	1	208	304	0.4	0.7
059 BAPT MISS ASSN	5	940	1,146*	1.5	2.7
081 CATHOLIC......	3	0	1,764	2.3	4.2
093 CR CH (DISC)..	7	1,734	2,113*	2.8	5.0
097 CR C AND C CR.	1	55	67*	0.1	0.2
123 CH GOD (ANDER)	3	165	309	0.4	0.7
127 CH GOD (CLEVE)	4	156	190*	0.3	0.5
165 CH OF NAZARENE	4	320	593	0.8	1.4
185 CUMBER PRESB..	3	884	1,077*	1.4	2.6
193 EPISCOPAL.....	4	1,094	1,415	1.9	3.4
283 LUTH--MO SYNOD	2	231	322	0.4	0.8
357 PRESB CH US...	6	1,844	2,247*	3.0	5.4
413 S-D ADVENTISTS	1	16	20*	-	-
419 SO BAPT CONV..	25	18,911	23,049*	30.4	54.9
449 UN METHODIST..	10	6,747	7,337	9.7	17.5
GRIMES	40	4,923	8,629*	72.8	100.0
059 BAPT MISS ASSN	6	351	417*	3.5	4.8
081 CATHOLIC......	5	0	2,927	24.7	33.9
193 EPISCOPAL.....	1	108	120	1.0	1.4
283 LUTH--MO SYNOD	3	806	952	8.0	11.0
357 PRESB CH US...	1	194	231*	1.9	2.7
413 S-D ADVENTISTS	1	44	52*	0.4	0.6
419 SO BAPT CONV..	11	2,315	2,753*	23.2	31.9
449 UN METHODIST..	11	1,067	1,132	9.5	13.1
453 UN PRES CH USA	1	38	45*	0.4	0.5
GUADALUPE	34	8,908	17,815*	53.1	100.0
029 AMER LUTH CH..	4	2,612	3,406	10.2	19.1
081 CATHOLIC......	5	0	6,858	20.4	38.5
127 CH GOD (CLEVE)	1	15	18*	0.1	0.1
193 EPISCOPAL.....	1	301	425	1.3	2.4
283 LUTH--MO SYNOD	2	223	284	0.8	1.6
313 NO AM BAPT GC.	1	15	18*	0.1	0.1
349 PENT HOLINESS.	1	25	31*	0.1	0.2
357 PRESB CH US...	1	215	263*	0.8	1.5
419 SO BAPT CONV..	7	1,738	2,125*	6.3	11.9
443 UN C OF CHRIST	4	1,702	2,081*	6.2	11.7
449 UN METHODIST..	7	2,062	2,306	6.9	12.9
HALE	47	17,670	24,509*	71.8	100.0
059 BAPT MISS ASSN	1	138	174*	0.5	0.7
081 CATHOLIC......	4	0	2,500	7.3	10.2
093 CR CH (DISC)..	1	266	336*	1.0	1.4
127 CH GOD (CLEVE)	1	76	96*	0.3	0.4
165 CH OF NAZARENE	3	290	417	1.2	1.7
193 EPISCOPAL.....	1	241	311	0.9	1.3
283 LUTH--MO SYNOD	1	275	404	1.2	1.6
349 PENT HOLINESS.	1	53	67*	0.2	0.3
357 PRESB CH US...	1	197	249*	0.7	1.0
403 SALVATION ARMY	1	88	325	1.0	1.3
413 S-D ADVENTISTS	1	53	67*	0.2	0.3
419 SO BAPT CONV..	17	11,826	14,934*	43.7	60.9
449 UN METHODIST..	12	3,930	4,330	12.7	17.7
453 UN PRES CH USA	2	237	299*	0.9	1.2
HALL	15	3,697	5,258*	87.4	100.0
081 CATHOLIC......	2	0	1,000	16.6	19.0
097 CR C AND C CR.	1	140	165*	2.7	3.1
127 CH GOD (CLEVE)	1	19	22*	0.4	0.4
419 SO BAPT CONV..	6	2,570	3,035*	50.5	57.7
449 UN METHODIST..	4	936	998	16.6	19.0
453 UN PRES CH USA	1	32	38*	0.6	0.7
HAMILTON	31	4,308	5,142*	71.4	100.0
029 AMER LUTH CH..	2	273	334	4.6	6.5
081 CATHOLIC......	1	0	341	4.7	6.6
093 CR CH (DISC)..	1	53	59*	0.8	1.1
193 EPISCOPAL.....	1	31	32	0.4	0.6
283 LUTH--MO SYNOD	3	574	686	9.5	13.3
357 PRESB CH US...	1	60	67*	0.9	1.3
419 SO BAPT CONV..	16	2,281	2,536*	35.2	49.3
449 UN METHODIST..	5	983	1,028	14.3	20.0
453 UN PRES CH USA	1	53	59*	0.8	1.1
HANSFORD	10	2,974	4,364*	68.7	100.0
029 AMER LUTH CH..	1	166	210	3.3	4.8
081 CATHOLIC......	1	0	800	12.6	18.3
093 CR CH (DISC)..	2	217	273*	4.3	6.3
419 SO BAPT CONV..	3	1,566	1,973*	31.1	45.2
449 UN METHODIST..	2	991	1,065	16.8	24.4
453 UN PRES CH USA	1	34	43*	0.7	1.0
HARDEMAN	13	3,275	3,977*	58.5	100.0
081 CATHOLIC......	1	0	150	2.2	3.8
093 CR CH (DISC)..	1	120	140*	2.1	3.5
165 CH OF NAZARENE	2	91	103	1.5	2.6
193 EPISCOPAL.....	1	35	40	0.6	1.0
357 PRESB CH US...	1	37	43*	0.6	1.1
419 SO BAPT CONV..	6	2,954	3,457*	50.9	86.9
453 UN PRES CH USA	1	38	44*	0.6	1.1
HARDIN	41	10,742	14,935*	49.8	100.0
059 BAPT MISS ASSN	1	110	137*	0.5	0.9
081 CATHOLIC......	3	0	1,786	6.0	12.0
093 CR CH (DISC)..	1	78	97*	0.3	0.6
097 CR C AND C CR.	1	100	124*	0.4	0.8
127 CH GOD (CLEVE)	2	84	104*	0.3	0.7
193 EPISCOPAL.....	1	113	134	0.4	0.9
353 PLY BRETHREN..	1	10	14	-	0.1
357 PRESB CH US...	1	63	78*	0.3	0.5
413 S-D ADVENTISTS	1	10	12*		0.1
419 SO BAPT CONV..	22	8,584	10,679*	35.6	71.5
449 UN METHODIST..	7	1,590	1,770	5.9	11.9
HARRIS	755	435,641	784,357*	45.0	100.0
019 AMER BAPT CONV	2	143	180*	-	-
029 AMER LUTH CH..	16	8,276	11,311	0.6	1.4
059 BAPT MISS ASSN	23	4,801	6,035*	0.3	0.8
081 CATHOLIC......	72	0	234,086	13.4	29.8
093 CR CH (DISC)..	23	7,088	8,910*	0.5	1.1
097 CR C AND C CR.	11	1,922	2,416*	0.1	0.3
123 CH GOD (ANDER)	10	1,044	2,528	0.1	0.3
127 CH GOD (CLEVE)	11	843	1,060*	0.1	0.1
165 CH OF NAZARENE	21	2,380	4,572	0.3	0.6
175 CONG CR CH....	1	555	698*	-	0.1
185 CUMBER PRESB..	1	228	287*	-	-
193 EPISCOPAL.....	43	31,010	41,438	2.4	5.3
221 FREE METH C NA	1	31	43	-	-
226 FRIENDS-USA...	3	130	163*	-	-
281 LUTH CH AMER..	13	3,399	4,810	0.3	0.6
283 LUTH--MO SYNOD	46	21,259	31,100	1.8	4.0
287 MENN GEN CONF.	1	45	57*	-	-
313 NO AM BAPT GC.	1	42	53*	-	-
349 PENT HOLINESS.	2	40	50*	-	-
357 PRESB CH US...	38	22,041	27,708*	1.6	3.5
413 S-D ADVENTISTS	7	1,750	2,200*	0.1	0.3
419 SO BAPT CONV..	245	217,119	272,942*	15.7	34.8
435 UNITARIAN-UNIV	4	1,071	1,625	0.1	0.2

*Total adherents estimated from known number of communicant, confirmed, full members.

—Represents a percent less than 0.1.

Percentages may not total due to rounding.

Table 3. Churches and Church Membership by State, County and Denomination: 1971

County and Denomination	Number of churches	Communicant, confirmed, full members	Total adherents: Number	Total adherents: Percent of total population	Total adherents: Percent of total adherents
443 UN C OF CHRIST	11	3,196	4,018*	0.2	0.5
449 UN METHODIST..	126	100,795	117,901	6.8	15.0
453 UN PRES CH USA	16	5,885	7,398*	0.4	0.9
461 UNITY OF BRETH	4	407	557	-	0.1
469 WISC EVAN LUTH	3	141	211	-	-
HARRISON	70	17,918	21,744*	48.5	100.0
059 BAPT MISS ASSN	1	99	120*	0.3	0.6
081 CATHOLIC......	1	0	483	1.1	2.2
093 CR CH (DISC)..	2	437	531*	1.2	2.4
165 CH OF NAZARENE	2	141	155	0.3	0.7
185 CUMBER PRESB..	2	423	514*	1.1	2.4
193 EPISCOPAL.....	2	537	618	1.4	2.8
281 LUTH CH AMER..	1	54	71	0.2	0.3
353 PLY BRETHREN..	1	25	50	0.1	0.2
357 PRESB CH US...	3	613	745*	1.7	3.4
403 SALVATION ARMY	1	86	236	0.5	1.1
413 S-D ADVENTISTS	3	192	233*	0.5	1.1
419 SO BAPT CONV..	35	11,340	13,787*	30.7	63.4
449 UN METHODIST..	16	3,971	4,201	9.4	19.3
HARTLEY	5	842	1,249*	44.9	100.0
081 CATHOLIC......	0	0	300	10.8	24.0
419 SO BAPT CONV..	2	387	468*	16.8	37.5
449 UN METHODIST..	3	455	481	17.3	38.5
HASKELL	30	6,323	7,644*	89.8	100.0
029 AMER LUTH CH..	2	337	405	4.8	5.3
059 BAPT MISS ASSN	2	212	250*	2.9	3.3
081 CATHOLIC......	1	0	300	3.5	3.9
093 CR CH (DISC)..	1	15	18*	0.2	0.2
097 CR C AND C CR.	1	115	136*	1.6	1.8
127 CH GOD (CLEVE)	2	62	73*	0.9	1.0
357 PRESB CH US...	2	64	76*	0.9	1.0
419 SO BAPT CONV..	11	4,506	5,317*	62.5	69.6
449 UN METHODIST..	6	947	992	11.7	13.0
453 UN PRES CH USA	2	65	77*	0.9	1.0
HAYS	35	8,880	13,405*	48.5	100.0
029 AMER LUTH CH..	1	292	405	1.5	3.0
081 CATHOLIC......	4	0	2,876	10.4	21.5
093 CR CH (DISC)..	1	185	220*	0.8	1.6
097 CR C AND C CR.	1	76	90*	0.3	0.7
165 CH OF NAZARENE	2	20	53	0.2	0.4
193 EPISCOPAL.....	1	245	327	1.2	2.4
283 LUTH--MO SYNOD	1	105	150	0.5	1.1
313 NO AM BAPT GC.	1	40	48*	0.2	0.4
349 PENT HOLINESS.	1	18	21*	0.1	0.2
357 PRESB CH US...	2	359	427*	1.5	3.2
413 S-D ADVENTISTS	1	79	94*	0.3	0.7
419 SO BAPT CONV..	12	5,736	6,819*	24.7	50.9
449 UN METHODIST..	7	1,725	1,875	6.8	14.0
HEMPHILL	9	1,286	2,145*	69.6	100.0
081 CATHOLIC......	1	0	600	19.5	28.0
097 CR C AND C CR.	1	244	296*	9.6	13.8
165 CH OF NAZARENE	1	8	44	1.4	2.1
419 SO BAPT CONV..	2	601	730*	23.7	34.0
449 UN METHODIST..	3	348	372	12.1	17.3
453 UN PRES CH USA	1	85	103*	3.3	4.8
HENDERSON	55	10,038	11,904*	45.0	100.0
059 BAPT MISS ASSN	10	1,429	1,700*	6.4	14.3
081 CATHOLIC......	1	0	175	0.7	1.5
093 CR CH (DISC)..	2	274	326*	1.2	2.7
123 CH GOD (ANDER)	1	27	54	0.2	0.5
193 EPISCOPAL.....	1	129	188	0.7	1.6
413 S-D ADVENTISTS	1	41	49*	0.2	0.4
419 SO BAPT CONV..	22	5,625	6,690*	25.3	56.2
449 UN METHODIST..	16	2,277	2,441	9.2	20.5
453 UN PRES CH USA	1	236	281*	1.1	2.4
HIDALGO	151	25,408	189,983*	104.7#	100.0
029 AMER LUTH CH..	5	610	893	0.5	0.5
059 BAPT MISS ASSN	2	154	201*	0.1	0.1
081 CATHOLIC......	50	0	157,655	86.8	83.0
093 CR CH (DISC)..	6	870	1,136*	0.6	0.6
097 CR C AND C CR.	2	300	392*	0.2	0.2
123 CH GOD (ANDER)	1	40	97	0.1	0.1
127 CH GOD (CLEVE)	1	33	43*	-	-
165 CH OF NAZARENE	3	171	247	0.1	0.1
193 EPISCOPAL.....	4	479	487	0.3	0.3
201 EVAN COV CH AM	1	57	74*	-	-
221 FREE METH C NA	1	11	12	-	-
281 LUTH CH AMER..	1	115	139	0.1	0.1
283 LUTH--MO SYNOD	4	1,088	1,504	0.8	0.8
313 NO AM BAPT GC.	2	56	73*	-	-
349 PENT HOLINESS.	7	326	426*	0.2	0.2
357 PRESB CH US...	10	1,780	2,325*	1.3	1.2
403 SALVATION ARMY	1	56	199	0.1	0.1
413 S-D ADVENTISTS	6	483	631*	0.3	0.3
419 SO BAPT CONV..	22	11,247	14,689*	8.1	7.7
435 UNITARIAN-UNIV	1	15	15	-	-
449 UN METHODIST..	21	7,517	8,745	4.8	4.6
HILL	70	9,146	11,964*	52.9	100.0
029 AMER LUTH CH..	1	117	150	0.7	1.3
059 BAPT MISS ASSN	2	320	371*	1.6	3.1
081 CATHOLIC......	3	0	1,529	6.8	12.8
093 CR CH (DISC)..	1	136	158*	0.7	1.3
123 CH GOD (ANDER)	1	25	51	0.2	0.4
165 CH OF NAZARENE	1	89	115	0.5	1.0
185 CUMBER PRESB..	4	139	161*	0.7	1.3
193 EPISCOPAL.....	2	84	99	0.4	0.8
283 LUTH--MO SYNOD	2	435	512	2.3	4.3
357 PRESB CH US...	3	214	248*	1.1	2.1
413 S-D ADVENTISTS	1	54	63*	0.3	0.5
419 SO BAPT CONV..	26	4,789	5,556*	24.6	46.4
449 UN METHODIST..	19	2,509	2,677	11.8	22.4
453 UN PRES CH USA	3	209	242*	1.1	2.0
469 WISC EVAN LUTH	1	26	32	0.1	0.3
HOCKLEY	32	10,426	13,776*	67.5	100.0
029 AMER LUTH CH..	1	63	89	0.4	0.6
059 BAPT MISS ASSN	3	997	1,247*	6.1	9.1
081 CATHOLIC......	2	0	1,000	4.9	7.3
093 CR CH (DISC)..	1	142	178*	0.9	1.3
127 CH GOD (CLEVE)	1	27	34*	0.2	0.2
165 CH OF NAZARENE	2	117	160	0.8	1.2
193 EPISCOPAL.....	2	593	742	3.6	5.4
357 PRESB CH US...	1	170	213*	1.0	1.5
419 SO BAPT CONV..	12	6,467	8,090*	39.7	58.7
449 UN METHODIST..	6	1,751	1,899	9.3	13.8
453 UN PRES CH USA	1	99	124*	0.6	0.9
HOOD	20	3,680	4,273*	67.1	100.0
081 CATHOLIC......	1	0	75	1.2	1.8
093 CR CH (DISC)..	1	25	29*	0.5	0.7
357 PRESB CH US...	1	11	13*	0.2	0.3
419 SO BAPT CONV..	10	2,756	3,220*	50.6	75.4
449 UN METHODIST..	6	876	922	14.5	21.6
453 UN PRES CH USA	1	12	14*	0.2	0.3
HOPKINS	67	10,718	12,640*	61.0	100.0
059 BAPT MISS ASSN	12	1,831	2,167*	10.5	17.1
081 CATHOLIC......	1	0	185	0.9	1.5
093 CR CH (DISC)..	1	358	424*	2.0	3.4
127 CH GOD (CLEVE)	1	93	110*	0.5	0.9
165 CH OF NAZARENE	1	126	185	0.9	1.5
185 CUMBER PRESB..	2	60	71*	0.3	0.6
193 EPISCOPAL.....	1	63	87	0.4	0.7
283 LUTH--MO SYNOD	1	70	100	0.5	0.8
357 PRESB CH US...	1	172	204*	1.0	1.6
413 S-D ADVENTISTS	1	21	25*	0.1	0.2
419 SO BAPT CONV..	25	5,234	6,195*	29.9	49.0
449 UN METHODIST..	17	2,606	2,788	13.5	22.1
453 UN PRES CH USA	3	84	99*	0.5	0.8
HOUSTON	43	6,288	7,453*	41.7	100.0
059 BAPT MISS ASSN	3	567	671*	3.8	9.0
081 CATHOLIC......	1	0	156	0.9	2.1
093 CR CH (DISC)..	4	189	224*	1.3	3.0
127 CH GOD (CLEVE)	1	93	110*	0.6	1.5
165 CH OF NAZARENE	1	20	20	0.1	0.3
193 EPISCOPAL.....	1	40	50	0.3	0.7
357 PRESB CH US...	2	159	188*	1.1	2.5
419 SO BAPT CONV..	19	3,807	4,508*	25.2	60.5
449 UN METHODIST..	11	1,413	1,526	8.5	20.5
HOWARD	50	15,878	23,543*	62.3	100.0
081 CATHOLIC......	4	0	3,902	10.3	16.6
093 CR CH (DISC)..	1	409	502*	1.3	2.1
097 CR C AND C CR.	1	40	49*	0.1	0.2
123 CH GOD (ANDER)	2	94	303	0.8	1.3
127 CH GOD (CLEVE)	1	136	167*	0.4	0.7
165 CH OF NAZARENE	1	145	196	0.5	0.8
193 EPISCOPAL.....	1	260	348	0.9	1.5
281 LUTH CH AMER..	1	61	82	0.2	0.3
283 LUTH--MO SYNOD	1	208	272	0.7	1.2
357 PRESB CH US...	3	810	994*	2.6	4.2
403 SALVATION ARMY	1	67	236	0.6	1.0
413 S-D ADVENTISTS	1	19	23*	0.1	0.1
419 SO BAPT CONV..	25	10,532	12,931*	34.2	54.9
449 UN METHODIST..	7	3,097	3,538	9.4	15.0
HUDSPETH	9	694	2,549*	106.6#	100.0
081 CATHOLIC......	3	0	1,700	71.1	66.7
419 SO BAPT CONV..	3	526	667*	27.9	26.2
449 UN METHODIST..	3	168	182	7.6	7.1
HUNT	88	21,691	26,012*	54.3	100.0
059 BAPT MISS ASSN	3	251	298*	0.6	1.1
081 CATHOLIC......	2	0	610	1.3	2.3
093 CR CH (DISC)..	7	963	1,143*	2.4	4.4
127 CH GOD (CLEVE)	1	53	63*	0.1	0.2
165 CH OF NAZARENE	2	176	295	0.6	1.1
193 EPISCOPAL.....	2	235	335	0.7	1.3
281 LUTH CH AMER..	1	56	95	0.2	0.4
283 LUTH--MO SYNOD	1	56	85	0.2	0.3
353 PLY BRETHREN..	1	20	40	0.1	0.2
357 PRESB CH US...	2	596	708*	1.5	2.7
403 SALVATION ARMY	1	32	94	0.2	0.4
413 S-D ADVENTISTS	1	47	56*	0.1	0.2
419 SO BAPT CONV..	43	13,836	16,425*	34.3	63.1
449 UN METHODIST..	20	5,057	5,393	11.2	20.7

*Total adherents estimated from known number of communicant, confirmed, full members. —Represents a percent less than 0.1. Percentages may not total due to rounding.

#See Introduction for explanation of why total adherents reported by churches exceed the 1970 population figure.

Table 3. Churches and Church Membership by State, County and Denomination: 1971

County and Denomination	Number of churches	Communicant, confirmed, full members	Total adherents		
			Number	Percent of total population	Percent of total adherents
453 UN PRES CH USA	1	313	372*	0.8	1.4
HUTCHINSON	32	11,586	14,956*	61.2	100.0
081 CATHOLIC......	2	0	1,500	6.1	10.0
093 CR CH (DISC)..	3	753	883*	3.6	5.9
127 CH GOD (CLEVE)	1	131	154*	0.6	1.0
165 CH OF NAZARENE	4	208	315	1.3	2.1
193 EPISCOPAL.....	1	120	134	0.5	0.9
283 LUTH--MO SYNOD	1	235	295	1.2	2.0
349 PENT HOLINESS.	2	45	53*	0.2	0.4
403 SALVATION ARMY	1	42	132	0.5	0.9
413 S-D ADVENTISTS	1	22	26*	0.1	0.2
419 SO BAPT CONV..	10	7,059	8,276*	33.9	55.3
449 UN METHODIST..	6	2,971	3,188	13.0	21.3
IRION	7	692	993*	92.8	100.0
081 CATHOLIC......	1	0	200	18.7	20.1
093 CR CH (DISC)..	1	26	31*	2.9	3.1
419 SO BAPT CONV..	2	254	300*	28.0	30.2
449 UN METHODIST..	2	238	256	23.9	25.8
453 UN PRES CH USA	1	174	206*	19.3	20.7
JACK	23	3,702	4,292*	64.0	100.0
059 BAPT MISS ASSN	1	44	51*	0.8	1.2
081 CATHOLIC......	1	0	50	0.7	1.2
093 CR CH (DISC)..	1	129	151*	2.3	3.5
357 PRESB CH US...	1	40	47*	0.7	1.1
419 SO BAPT CONV..	13	2,731	3,188*	47.5	74.3
449 UN METHODIST..	5	718	758	11.3	17.7
453 UN PRES CH USA	1	40	47*	0.7	1.1
JACKSON	27	4,841	9,599*	74.0	100.0
029 AMER LUTH CH..	1	317	414	3.2	4.3
081 CATHOLIC......	4	0	3,817	29.4	39.8
093 CR CH (DISC)..	1	37	45*	0.3	0.5
193 EPISCOPAL.....	1	34	34	0.3	0.4
283 LUTH--MO SYNOD	1	179	248	1.9	2.6
357 PRESB CH US...	2	245	301*	2.3	3.1
419 SO BAPT CONV..	9	2,784	3,416*	26.3	35.6
449 UN METHODIST..	7	1,164	1,214	9.4	12.6
469 WISC EVAN LUTH	1	81	110	0.8	1.1
JASPER	47	9,996	12,719*	51.5	100.0
059 BAPT MISS ASSN	9	886	1,095*	4.4	8.6
081 CATHOLIC......	5	0	533	2.2	4.2
165 CH OF NAZARENE	2	133	165	0.7	1.3
193 EPISCOPAL.....	2	84	117	0.5	0.9
283 LUTH--MO SYNOD	1	20	30	0.1	0.2
419 SO BAPT CONV..	18	7,173	8,868*	35.9	69.7
449 UN METHODIST..	9	1,652	1,852	7.5	14.6
453 UN PRES CH USA	1	48	59*	0.2	0.5
JEFF DAVIS	5	376	1,697*	111.1 #	100.0
081 CATHOLIC......	2	0	1,250	81.9	73.7
419 SO BAPT CONV..	1	166	202*	13.2	11.9
449 UN METHODIST..	1	99	110	7.2	6.5
453 UN PRES CH USA	1	111	135*	8.8	8.0
JEFFERSON	173	81,536	155,649*	63.6	100.0
029 AMER LUTH CH..	4	987	1,285	0.5	0.8
059 BAPT MISS ASSN	7	1,977	2,407*	1.0	1.5
081 CATHOLIC......	24	0	56,080	22.9	36.0
093 CR CH (DISC)..	6	1,544	1,880*	0.8	1.2
097 CR C AND C CR.	2	170	207*	0.1	0.1
121 CH GOD (ABR)..	1	15	18*	-	-
123 CH GOD (ANDER)	2	186	513	0.2	0.3
127 CH GOD (CLEVE)	1	62	75*	-	-
165 CH OF NAZARENE	8	576	1,059	0.4	0.7
193 EPISCOPAL.....	6	3,246	4,460	1.8	2.9
283 LUTH--MO SYNOD	7	1,925	2,708	1.1	1.7
357 PRESB CH US...	7	2,290	2,788*	1.1	1.8
403 SALVATION ARMY	2	237	949	0.4	0.6
413 S-D ADVENTISTS	4	206	251*	0.1	0.2
419 SO BAPT CONV..	59	46,465	56,579*	23.1	36.4
435 UNITARIAN-UNIV	1	114	154	0.1	0.1
443 UN C OF CHRIST	1	70	85*	-	0.1
449 UN METHODIST..	29	20,040	22,415	9.2	14.4
453 UN PRES CH USA	2	1,426	1,736*	0.7	1.1
JIM HOGG	9	416	2,507*	53.9	100.0
081 CATHOLIC......	5	0	2,000	43.0	79.8
193 EPISCOPAL.....	1	29	61	1.3	2.4
419 SO BAPT CONV..	1	219	278*	6.0	11.1
449 UN METHODIST..	2	168	168	3.6	6.7
JIM WELLS	37	7,944	21,991*	66.6	100.0
029 AMER LUTH CH..	3	786	1,020	3.1	4.6
081 CATHOLIC......	11	0	11,888	36.0	54.1
093 CR CH (DISC)..	1	133	170*	0.5	0.8
193 EPISCOPAL.....	1	216	437	1.3	2.0
283 LUTH--MO SYNOD	2	119	143	0.4	0.7
285 MENNONITE CH..	3	111	142*	0.4	0.6
357 PRESB CH US...	2	406	518*	1.6	2.4
413 S-D ADVENTISTS	2	55	70*	0.2	0.3
419 SO BAPT CONV..	7	4,617	5,886*	17.8	26.8
443 UN C OF CHRIST	1	152	194*	0.6	0.9
449 UN METHODIST..	4	1.349	1,523	4.6	6.9
JOHNSON	67	21,416	26,333*	57.5	100.0
059 BAPT MISS ASSN	1	76	93*	0.2	0.4
081 CATHOLIC......	2	0	625	1.4	2.4
093 CR CH (DISC)..	3	248	302*	0.7	1.1
127 CH GOD (CLEVE)	2	56	68*	0.1	0.3
165 CH OF NAZARENE	2	128	228	0.5	0.9
193 EPISCOPAL.....	2	174	253	0.6	1.0
283 LUTH--MO SYNOD	1	87	112	0.2	0.4
357 PRESB CH US...	2	280	341*	0.7	1.3
413 S-D ADVENTISTS	5	2,100	2,559*	5.6	9.7
419 SO BAPT CONV..	33	13,884	16,921*	37.0	64.3
449 UN METHODIST..	13	4,106	4,493	9.8	17.1
453 UN PRES CH USA	1	277	338*	0.7	1.3
JONES	45	10,007	13,802*	85.7	100.0
029 AMER LUTH CH..	1	117	138	0.9	1.0
059 BAPT MISS ASSN	3	452	535*	3.3	3.9
081 CATHOLIC......	3	0	2,260	14.0	16.4
093 CR CH (DISC)..	1	67	79*	0.5	0.6
193 EPISCOPAL.....	2	679	692	4.3	5.0
281 LUTH CH AMER..	1	299	351	2.2	2.5
357 PRESB CH US...	2	75	89*	0.6	0.6
419 SO BAPT CONV..	20	6,323	7,487*	46.5	54.2
449 UN METHODIST..	10	1,922	2,085	12.9	15.1
453 UN PRES CH USA	2	73	86*	0.5	0.6
KARNES	29	3,380	10,193*	75.7	100.0
029 AMER LUTH CH..	2	338	446	3.3	4.4
081 CATHOLIC......	9	0	6,042	44.9	59.3
193 EPISCOPAL.....	1	39	44	0.3	0.4
281 LUTH CH AMER..	2	316	402	3.0	3.9
357 PRESB CH US...	1	144	179*	1.3	1.8
419 SO BAPT CONV..	10	1,922	2,392*	17.8	23.5
449 UN METHODIST..	4	621	688	5.1	6.7
KAUFMAN	63	11,864	14,929*	46.1	100.0
059 BAPT MISS ASSN	14	2,007	2,402*	7.4	16.1
081 CATHOLIC......	3	0	936	2.9	6.3
093 CR CH (DISC)..	2	520	622*	1.9	4.2
165 CH OF NAZARENE	1	30	63	0.2	0.4
185 CUMBER PRESB..	1	51	61*	0.2	0.4
193 EPISCOPAL.....	2	169	237	0.7	1.6
413 S-D ADVENTISTS	1	49	59*	0.2	0.4
419 SO BAPT CONV..	17	6,280	7,516*	23.2	50.3
449 UN METHODIST..	16	2,430	2,640	8.2	17.7
453 UN PRES CH USA	6	328	393*	1.2	2.6
KENDALL	11	2,234	4,241*	60.9	100.0
029 AMER LUTH CH..	2	452	612	8.8	14.4
081 CATHOLIC......	2	0	1,528	21.9	36.0
193 EPISCOPAL.....	2	288	364	5.2	8.6
419 SO BAPT CONV..	2	660	778*	11.2	18.3
449 UN METHODIST..	2	708	810	11.6	19.1
453 UN PRES CH USA	1	126	149*	2.1	3.5
KENEDY	2	0	400	59.0	100.0
081 CATHOLIC......	2	0	400	59.0	100.0
KENT	4	550	1,121*	78.2	100.0
081 CATHOLIC......	1	0	500	34.9	44.6
419 SO BAPT CONV..	2	391	453*	31.6	40.4
449 UN METHODIST..	1	159	168	11.7	15.0
KERR	27	7,058	10,836*	55.7	100.0
029 AMER LUTH CH..	1	515	644	3.3	5.9
081 CATHOLIC......	1	0	2,506	12.9	23.1
093 CR CH (DISC)..	2	173	199*	1.0	1.8
123 CH GOD (ANDER)	1	39	85	0.4	0.8
165 CH OF NAZARENE	1	38	106	0.5	1.0
193 EPISCOPAL.....	1	438	615	3.2	5.7
283 LUTH--MO SYNOD	1	177	236	1.2	2.2
357 PRESB CH US...	1	855	986*	5.1	9.1
413 S-D ADVENTISTS	2	47	54*	0.3	0.5
419 SO BAPT CONV..	9	3,317	3,825*	19.7	35.3
449 UN METHODIST..	6	1,412	1,526	7.8	14.1
453 UN PRES CH USA	1	47	54*	0.3	0.5
KIMBLE	10	1,458	3,087*	79.1	100.0
029 AMER LUTH CH..	1	26	34	0.9	1.1
081 CATHOLIC......	2	0	1,338	34.3	43.3
193 EPISCOPAL.....	1	40	80	2.0	2.6
357 PRESB CH US...	1	159	194*	5.0	6.3
419 SO BAPT CONV..	2	910	1,110*	28.4	36.0
449 UN METHODIST..	3	323	331	8.5	10.7
KING	4	288	717*	154.5 #	100.0
029 AMER LUTH CH..	1	161	263	56.7	36.7
081 CATHOLIC......	0	0	300	64.7	41.8
419 SO BAPT CONV..	2	80	98*	21.1	13.7
449 UN METHODIST..	1	47	56	12.1	7.8
KINNEY	5	1,672	2,991*	149.1 #	100.0

*Total adherents estimated from known number of communicant, confirmed, full members.

—Represents a percent less than 0.1.

Percentages may not total due to rounding.

#See Introduction for explanation of why total adherents reported by churches exceed the 1970 population figure.

Table 3. Churches and Church Membership by State, County and Denomination: 1971

County and Denomination	Number of churches	Communicant, confirmed, full members	Total adherents		
			Number	Percent of total population	Percent of total adherents
081 CATHOLIC......	2	0	923	46.0	30.9
419 SO BAPT CONV..	2	1,623	2,011*	100.2	67.2
449 UN METHODIST..	1	49	57	2.8	1.9
KLEBERG	29	6,379	16,393*	49.4	100.0
029 AMER LUTH CH..	1	138	178	0.5	1.1
081 CATHOLIC......	8	0	8,462	25.5	51.6
093 CR CH (DISC)..	1	238	293*	0.9	1.8
165 CH OF NAZARENE	1	27	86	0.3	0.5
193 EPISCOPAL.....	1	257	358	1.1	2.2
283 LUTH--MO SYNOD	1	269	365	1.1	2.2
349 PENT HOLINESS.	1	14	17*	0.1	0.1
357 PRESB CH US...	2	430	529*	1.6	3.2
413 S-D ADVENTISTS	1	14	17*	0.1	0.1
419 SO BAPT CONV..	7	3,528	4,342*	13.1	26.5
449 UN METHODIST..	5	1,464	1,746	5.3	10.7
KNOX	18	3,347	4,412*	73.9	100.0
081 CATHOLIC......	2	0	576	9.6	13.1
093 CR CH (DISC)..	2	52	62*	1.0	1.4
097 CR C AND C CR.	1	45	53*	0.9	1.2
419 SO BAPT CONV..	7	2,330	2,766*	46.3	62.7
449 UN METHODIST..	6	920	955	16.0	21.6
LAMAR	74	15,216	18,387*	51.0	100.0
059 BAPT MISS ASSN	1	50	61*	0.2	0.3
081 CATHOLIC......	1	0	381	1.1	2.1
093 CR CH (DISC)..	7	582	706*	2.0	3.8
127 CH GOD (CLEVE)	3	364	441*	1.2	2.4
165 CH OF NAZARENE	2	107	185	0.5	1.0
193 EPISCOPAL.....	1	207	207	0.6	1.1
283 LUTH--MO SYNOD	1	99	151	0.4	0.8
357 PRESB CH US...	3	276	335*	0.9	1.8
403 SALVATION ARMY	1	91	216	0.6	1.2
413 S-D ADVENTISTS	1	40	49*	0.1	0.3
419 SO BAPT CONV..	30	9,383	11,380*	31.6	61.9
449 UN METHODIST..	21	3,467	3,608	10.0	19.6
453 UN PRES CH USA	2	550	667*	1.8	3.6
LAMB	30	8,901	12,228*	68.8	100.0
029 AMER LUTH CH..	1	81	103	0.6	0.8
059 BAPT MISS ASSN	2	187	231*	1.3	1.9
081 CATHOLIC......	2	0	1,500	8.4	12.3
093 CR CH (DISC)..	1	56	69*	0.4	0.6
165 CH OF NAZARENE	2	75	134	0.8	1.1
185 CUMBER PRESB..	1	12	15*	0.1	0.1
283 LUTH--MO SYNOD	1	116	143	0.8	1.2
413 S-D ADVENTISTS	1	15	19*	0.1	0.2
419 SO BAPT CONV..	12	6,425	7,945*	44.7	65.0
449 UN METHODIST..	6	1,874	1,995	11.2	16.3
453 UN PRES CH USA	1	60	74*	0.4	0.6
LAMPASAS	21	3,849	5,096*	54.7	100.0
081 CATHOLIC......	2	0	572	6.1	11.2
093 CR CH (DISC)..	1	167	197*	2.1	3.9
193 EPISCOPAL.....	1	102	170	1.8	3.3
283 LUTH--MO SYNOD	1	46	82	0.9	1.6
419 SO BAPT CONV..	10	2,573	3,033*	32.5	59.5
449 UN METHODIST..	4	712	748	8.0	14.7
453 UN PRES CH USA	2	249	294*	3.2	5.8
LA SALLE	11	1,019	3,840*	76.6	100.0
059 BAPT MISS ASSN	1	119	153*	3.1	4.0
081 CATHOLIC......	2	0	2,606	52.0	67.9
193 EPISCOPAL.....	1	25	25	0.5	0.7
357 PRESB CH US...	2	64	82*	1.6	2.1
419 SO BAPT CONV..	3	457	587*	11.7	15.3
449 UN METHODIST..	2	354	387	7.7	10.1
LAVACA	38	4,843	14,834*	82.9	100.0
029 AMER LUTH CH..	6	845	960	5.4	6.5
081 CATHOLIC......	9	0	9,246	51.6	62.3
093 CR CH (DISC)..	1	16	19*	0.1	0.1
123 CH GOD (ANDER)	1	19	36	0.2	0.2
193 EPISCOPAL.....	1	32	44	0.2	0.3
281 LUTH CH AMER..	1	550	660	3.7	4.4
357 PRESB CH US...	1	83	96*	0.5	0.6
419 SO BAPT CONV..	11	2,654	3,082*	17.2	20.8
449 UN METHODIST..	7	644	691	3.9	4.7
LEE	26	4,724	6,382*	79.3	100.0
029 AMER LUTH CH..	[illegible]	711	868	10.8	13.6
081 CATHOLIC......	3	0	694	8.6	10.9
093 CR CH (DISC)..	[illegible]	35	41*	0.5	0.6
123 CH GOD (ANDER)	1	8	17	0.2	0.3
283 LUTH--MO SYNOD	8	2,429	2,994	37.2	46.9
357 PRESB CH US...	1	58	67*	0.8	1.0
419 SO BAPT CONV..	6	922	1,070*	13.3	16.8
449 UN METHODIST..	3	492	551	6.8	8.6
461 UNITY OF BRETH	1	69	80	1.0	1.3
LEON	41	4,558	5,221*	59.8	100.0
029 AMER LUTH CH..	1	563	691	7.9	13.2
059 BAPT MISS ASSN	14	902	1,055*	12.1	[illegible].2
081 CATHOLIC......	1	0	23	0.3	0.4
093 CR CH (DISC)..	1	31	36*	0.4	0.7

County and Denomination	Number of churches	Communicant, confirmed, full members	Total adherents		
			Number	Percent of total population	Percent of total adherents
127 CH GOD (CLEVE)	1	31	36*	0.4	0.7
419 SO BAPT CONV..	7	1,724	2,016*	23.1	38.6
449 UN METHODIST..	16	1,307	1,364	15.6	26.1
LIBERTY	59	14,891	20,083*	60.8	100.0
059 BAPT MISS ASSN	5	476	581*	1.8	2.9
081 CATHOLIC......	5	0	2,239	6.8	11.1
093 CR CH (DISC)..	2	51	62*	0.2	0.3
127 CH GOD (CLEVE)	1	59	72*	0.2	0.4
193 EPISCOPAL.....	3	474	604	1.8	3.0
283 LUTH--MO SYNOD	1	66	94	0.3	0.5
357 PRESB CH US...	2	91	111*	0.3	0.6
419 SO BAPT CONV..	31	11,016	13,435*	40.7	66.9
449 UN METHODIST..	9	2,658	2,885	8.7	14.4
LIMESTONE	41	9,036	10,438*	57.7	100.0
059 BAPT MISS ASSN	3	392	444*	2.5	4.3
081 CATHOLIC......	1	0	357	2.0	3.4
093 CR CH (DISC)..	1	100	113*	0.6	1.1
193 EPISCOPAL.....	1	19	50	0.3	0.5
357 PRESB CH US...	1	189	214*	1.2	2.1
419 SO BAPT CONV..	18	5,997	6,800*	37.6	65.1
449 UN METHODIST..	14	2,304	2,420	13.4	23.2
453 UN PRES CH USA	2	35	40*	0.2	0.4
LIPSCOMB	15	1,925	3,045*	87.3	100.0
081 CATHOLIC......	1	0	800	22.9	26.3
097 CR C AND C CR.	1	150	177*	5.1	5.8
165 CH OF NAZARENE	1	43	58	1.7	1.9
226 FRIENDS-USA...	1	124	146*	4.2	4.8
281 LUTH CH AMER..	1	156	185	5.3	6.1
283 LUTH--MO SYNOD	1	40	48	1.4	1.6
419 SO BAPT CONV..	5	646	761*	21.8	25.0
449 UN METHODIST..	4	766	870	25.0	28.6
LIVE OAK	17	2,051	5,194*	77.6	100.0
081 CATHOLIC......	4	0	2,685	40.1	51.7
193 EPISCOPAL.....	1	45	68	1.0	1.3
281 LUTH CH AMER..	2	199	299	4.5	5.8
283 LUTH--MO SYNOD	1	41	46	0.7	0.9
419 SO BAPT CONV..	6	1,208	1,492*	22.3	28.7
449 UN METHODIST..	3	558	604	9.0	11.6
LLANO	16	2,628	3,701*	53.0	100.0
029 AMER LUTH CH..	2	232	296	4.2	8.0
081 CATHOLIC......	2	0	785	11.2	21.2
093 CR CH (DISC)..	1	120	134*	1.9	3.6
193 EPISCOPAL.....	1	48	57	0.8	1.5
357 PRESB CH US...	1	47	53*	0.8	1.4
419 SO BAPT CONV..	6	1,611	1,800*	25.8	48.6
449 UN METHODIST..	3	570	576	8.3	15.6
LOVING	0	0	0	-	-
LUBBOCK	134	67,623	92,259*	51.5	100.0
029 AMER LUTH CH..	3	493	628	0.4	0.7
059 BAPT MISS ASSN	8	2,768	3,444*	1.9	3.7
081 CATHOLIC......	9	0	10,000	5.6	10.8
093 CR CH (DISC)..	5	2,489	3,097*	1.7	3.4
097 CR C AND C CR.	3	92	114*	0.1	0.1
123 CH GOD (ANDER)	1	31	109	0.1	0.1
127 CH GOD (CLEVE)	4	246	306*	0.2	0.3
165 CH OF NAZARENE	7	700	1,032	0.6	1.1
185 CUMBER PRESB..	1	543	676*	0.4	0.7
193 EPISCOPAL.....	3	1,405	1,655	0.9	1.8
281 LUTH CH AMER..	1	165	228	0.1	0.2
283 LUTH--MO SYNOD	4	774	1,105	0.6	1.2
349 PENT HOLINESS.	3	71	88*	-	0.1
353 PLY BRETHREN..	1	35	70	-	0.1
357 PRESB CH US...	4	2,167	2,696*	1.5	2.9
413 S-D ADVENTISTS	3	193	240*	0.1	0.3
419 SO BAPT CONV..	46	37,893	47,150*	26.3	51.1
435 UNITARIAN-UNIV	1	74	121	0.1	0.1
443 UN C OF CHRIST	1	10	12*	-	-
449 UN METHODIST..	20	16,368	18,112	10.1	19.6
453 UN PRES CH USA	6	1,106	1,376*	0.8	1.5
LYNN	21	4,558	6,543*	71.8	100.0
029 AMER LUTH CH..	1	101	142	1.6	2.2
081 CATHOLIC......	2	0	1,000	11.0	15.3
165 CH OF NAZARENE	2	61	94	1.0	1.4
283 LUTH--MO SYNOD	1	141	162	1.8	2.5
419 SO BAPT CONV..	8	3,162	4,008*	44.0	61.3
449 UN METHODIST.	7	1,093	1,137	12.5	17.4
MC CULLOCH	27	3,382	5,097*	59.5	100.0
081 CATHOLIC......	2	0	1,143	13.3	22.4
093 CR CH (DISC)..	2	256	304*	3.5	6.0
165 CH OF NAZARENE	1	5	5	0.1	0.1
193 EPISCOPAL.....	1	76	107	1.2	2.1
283 LUTH--MO SYNOD	1	70	80	0.9	1.6
419 SO BAPT CONV..	11	2,006	2,384*	27.8	46.8
449 UN METHODIST..	6	823	900	10.5	17.7
453 UN PRES CH USA	3	146	174*	2.0	3.4
MC LENNAN	174	69,589	112,415*	76.2	100.0

*Total adherents estimated from known number of communicant, confirmed, full members.

—Represents a percent less than 0.1.

Percentages may not total due to rounding.

Table 3. Churches and Church Membership by State, County and Denomination: 1971

County and Denomination	Number of churches	Communicant, confirmed, full members	Total adherents: Number	Percent of total population	Percent of total adherents
029 AMER LUTH CH..	4	1,332	1,735	1.2	1.5
059 BAPT MISS ASSN	2	284	338*	0.2	0.3
081 CATHOLIC......	10	0	30,124	20.4	26.8
093 CR CH (DISC)..	7	1,214	1,443*	1.0	1.3
123 CH GOD (ANDER)	1	20	58	-	0.1
165 CH OF NAZARENE	4	383	519	0.4	0.5
193 EPISCOPAL.....	5	2,142	2,578	1.7	2.3
281 LUTH CH AMER..	1	193	274	0.2	0.2
283 LUTH--MO SYNOD	4	1,650	2,176	1.5	1.9
313 NO AM BAPT GC.	2	326	388*	0.3	0.3
353 PLY BRETHREN..	1	50	80	0.1	0.1
357 PRESB CH US...	7	823	978*	0.7	0.9
403 SALVATION ARMY	1	144	540	0.4	0.5
413 S-D ADVENTISTS	2	149	177*	0.1	0.2
419 SO BAPT CONV..	69	43,465	51,674*	35.0	46.0
435 UNITARIAN-UNIV	1	38	46	-	-
443 UN C OF CHRIST	5	964	1,146*	0.8	1.0
449 UN METHODIST..	40	15,467	17,024	11.5	15.1
453 UN PRES CH USA	7	789	938*	0.6	0.8
461 UNITY OF BRETH	1	156	179	0.1	0.2
MC MULLEN	3	222	325*	29.7	100.0
081 CATHOLIC......	1	0	59	5.4	18.2
419 SO BAPT CONV..	2	222	266*	24.3	81.8
MADISON	10	2,760	3,098*	40.3	100.0
059 BAPT MISS ASSN	1	78	91*	1.2	2.9
283 LUTH--MO SYNOD	1	30	39	0.5	1.3
419 SO BAPT CONV..	5	1,952	2,268*	29.5	73.2
449 UN METHODIST..	3	700	700	9.1	22.6
MARION	25	3,275	4,029*	47.3	100.0
081 CATHOLIC......	1	0	169	2.0	4.2
093 CR CH (DISC)..	1	40	48*	0.6	1.2
165 CH OF NAZARENE	1	34	37	0.4	0.9
185 CUMBER PRESB..	1	12	14*	0.2	0.3
193 EPISCOPAL.....	1	45	71	0.8	1.8
413 S-D ADVENTISTS	2	351	421*	4.9	10.4
419 SO BAPT CONV..	8	1,912	2,293*	26.9	56.9
449 UN METHODIST..	10	881	976	11.5	24.2
MARTIN	8	1,502	2,539*	53.2	100.0
081 CATHOLIC......	2	0	700	14.7	27.6
419 SO BAPT CONV..	5	1,111	1,415*	29.6	55.7
449 UN METHODIST..	1	391	424	8.9	16.7
MASON	11	1,822	2,492*	74.3	100.0
029 AMER LUTH CH..	1	448	565	16.8	22.7
081 CATHOLIC......	1	0	421	12.5	16.9
093 CR CH (DISC)..	1	62	72*	2.1	2.9
419 SO BAPT CONV..	3	481	558*	16.6	22.4
449 UN METHODIST..	5	831	876	26.1	35.2
MATAGORDA	48	9,815	18,823*	67.4	100.0
029 AMER LUTH CH..	1	259	351	1.3	1.9
081 CATHOLIC......	5	0	6,985	25.0	37.1
093 CR CH (DISC)..	4	797	987*	3.5	5.2
165 CH OF NAZARENE	2	79	155	0.6	0.8
193 EPISCOPAL.....	3	388	497	1.8	2.6
283 LUTH--MO SYNOD	1	17	29	0.1	0.2
357 PRESB CH US...	5	836	1,035*	3.7	5.5
419 SO BAPT CONV..	13	4,712	5,835*	20.9	31.0
449 UN METHODIST..	14	2,727	2,949	10.6	15.7
MAVERICK	15	1,080	16,403*	90.7	100.0
081 CATHOLIC......	6	0	15,089	83.4	92.0
097 CR C AND C CR.	2	72	96*	0.5	0.6
193 EPISCOPAL.....	1	185	214	1.2	1.3
419 SO BAPT CONV..	3	482	645*	3.6	3.9
449 UN METHODIST..	3	341	359	2.0	2.2
MEDINA	26	4,104	17,052*	84.2	100.0
029 AMER LUTH CH..	3	872	1,039	5.1	6.1
081 CATHOLIC......	10	0	12,129	59.9	71.1
093 CR CH (DISC)..	1	49	61*	0.3	0.4
283 LUTH--MO SYNOD	1	38	59	0.3	0.3
357 PRESB CH US...	1	26	32*	0.2	0.2
413 S-D ADVENTISTS	1	28	35*	0.2	0.2
419 SO BAPT CONV..	5	1,987	2,482*	12.3	14.6
449 UN METHODIST..	4	1,104	1,215	6.0	7.1
MENARD	10	993	2,115*	79.9	100.0
081 CATHOLIC......	2	0	866	32.7	40.9
093 CR CH (DISC)..	1	35	42*	1.6	2.0
193 EPISCOPAL.....	2	80	176	6.7	8.3
283 LUTH--MO SYNOD	1	40	50	1.9	2.4
413 S-D ADVENTISTS	1	51	61*	2.3	2.9
419 SO BAPT CONV..	1	549	654*	24.7	30.9
449 UN METHODIST..	1	182	199	7.5	9.4
453 UN PRES CH USA	1	56	67*	2.5	3.2
MIDLAND	47	27,980	41,073*	62.8	100.0
029 AMER LUTH CH..	1	368	527	0.8	1.3
059 BAPT MISS ASSN	1	251	312*	0.5	0.8
081 CATHOLIC......	2	0	6,487	9.9	15.8

County and Denomination	Number of churches	Communicant, confirmed, full members	Total adherents: Number	Percent of total population	Percent of total adherents
093 CR CH (DISC)..	2	1,140	1,416*	2.2	3.4
097 CR C AND C CR.	1	131	163*	0.2	0.4
127 CH GOD (CLEVE)	1	64	79*	0.1	0.2
165 CH OF NAZARENE	2	151	237	0.4	0.6
193 EPISCOPAL.....	2	1,565	2,216	3.4	5.4
221 FREE METH C NA	2	28	53	0.1	0.1
281 LUTH CH AMER..	1	124	184	0.3	0.4
283 LUTH--MO SYNOD	1	387	517	0.8	1.3
349 PENT HOLINESS.	1	12	15*	-	-
357 PRESB CH US...	3	2,250	2,794*	4.3	6.8
413 S-D ADVENTISTS	1	65	81*	0.1	0.2
419 SO BAPT CONV..	17	14,959	18,577*	28.4	45.2
435 UNITARIAN-UNIV	1	48	65	0.1	0.2
449 UN METHODIST..	7	6,154	6,999	10.7	17.0
453 UN PRES CH USA	1	283	351*	0.5	0.9
MILAM	52	7,525	10,737*	53.6	100.0
029 AMER LUTH CH..	4	884	1,132	5.7	10.5
081 CATHOLIC......	3	0	1,728	8.6	16.1
093 CR CH (DISC)..	5	340	404*	2.0	3.8
165 CH OF NAZARENE	1	30	49	0.2	0.5
193 EPISCOPAL.....	1	57	73	0.4	0.7
283 LUTH--MO SYNOD	2	555	749	3.7	7.0
357 PRESB CH US...	3	141	168*	0.8	1.6
419 SO BAPT CONV..	21	3,990	4,745*	23.7	44.2
443 UN C OF CHRIST	1	155	184*	0.9	1.7
449 UN METHODIST..	7	1,194	1,292	6.5	12.0
453 UN PRES CH USA	4	179	213*	1.1	2.0
MILLS	13	2,617	3,188*	75.7	100.0
029 AMER LUTH CH..	1	308	360	8.5	11.3
081 CATHOLIC......	1	0	271	6.4	8.5
419 SO BAPT CONV..	7	1,645	1,852*	44.0	58.1
449 UN METHODIST..	4	664	705	16.7	22.1
MITCHELL	21	4,131	6,009*	66.2	100.0
059 BAPT MISS ASSN	1	52	63*	0.7	1.0
081 CATHOLIC......	2	0	1,180	13.0	19.6
093 CR CH (DISC)..	1	87	105*	1.2	1.7
193 EPISCOPAL.....	1	67	74	0.8	1.2
357 PRESB CH US...	1	87	105*	1.2	1.7
419 SO BAPT CONV..	8	2,833	3,425*	37.7	57.0
449 UN METHODIST..	6	965	1,009	11.1	16.8
453 UN PRES CH USA	1	40	48*	0.5	0.8
MONTAGUE	44	6,996	8,248*	53.8	100.0
059 BAPT MISS ASSN	2	107	124*	0.8	1.5
081 CATHOLIC......	2	0	183	1.2	2.2
093 CR CH (DISC)..	3	204	237*	1.5	2.9
157 CH OF BRETHREN	1	97	113*	0.7	1.4
165 CH OF NAZARENE	3	142	245	1.6	3.0
185 CUMBER PRESB..	1	10	12*	0.1	0.1
193 EPISCOPAL.....	1	20	28	0.2	0.3
283 LUTH--MO SYNOD	1	116	150	1.0	1.8
357 PRESB CH US...	3	84	98*	0.6	1.2
419 SO BAPT CONV..	15	4,668	5,420*	35.4	65.7
449 UN METHODIST..	9	1,476	1,554	10.1	18.8
453 UN PRES CH USA	3	72	84*	0.5	1.0
MONTGOMERY	61	15,502	21,460*	43.4	100.0
059 BAPT MISS ASSN	9	1,369	1,686*	3.4	7.9
081 CATHOLIC......	1	0	2,430	4.9	11.3
093 CR CH (DISC)..	1	226	278*	0.6	1.3
123 CH GOD (ANDER)	1	24	60	0.1	0.3
127 CH GOD (CLEVE)	2	51	63*	0.1	0.3
165 CH OF NAZARENE	1	98	174	0.4	0.8
281 LUTH CH AMER..	1	119	192	0.4	0.9
283 LUTH--MO SYNOD	1	304	453	0.9	2.1
357 PRESB CH US...	1	510	628*	1.3	2.9
413 S-D ADVENTISTS	2	81	100*	0.2	0.5
419 SO BAPT CONV..	27	9,788	12,053*	24.4	56.2
449 UN METHODIST..	14	2,932	3,343	6.8	15.6
MOORE	18	5,620	7,921*	56.3	100.0
081 CATHOLIC......	2	0	1,000	7.1	12.6
093 CR CH (DISC)..	1	255	320*	2.3	4.0
097 CR C AND C CR.	1	75	94*	0.7	1.2
127 CH GOD (CLEVE)	1	11	14*	0.1	0.2
165 CH OF NAZARENE	1	67	104	0.7	1.3
193 EPISCOPAL.....	1	24	42	0.3	0.5
283 LUTH--MO SYNOD	1	127	188	1.3	2.4
349 PENT HOLINESS.	1	12	15*	0.1	0.2
419 SO BAPT CONV..	4	3,541	4,444*	31.6	56.1
449 UN METHODIST..	4	1,338	1,487	10.6	18.8
453 UN PRES CH USA	1	170	213*	1.5	2.7
MORRIS	21	4,693	5,665*	46.0	100.0
059 BAPT MISS ASSN	1	99	119*	1.0	2.1
081 CATHOLIC......	1	0	213	1.7	3.8
093 CR CH (DISC)..	3	225	271*	2.2	4.8
097 CR C AND C CR.	2	55	66*	0.5	1.2
185 CUMBER PRESB..	1	60	72*	0.6	1.3
193 EPISCOPAL.....	1	50	56	0.5	1.0
419 SO BAPT CONV..	7	2,828	3,408*	27.7	60.2
449 UN METHODIST..	5	1,376	1,460	11.9	25.8
MOTLEY	9	1,425	2,410*	110.7#	100.0

*Total adherents estimated from known number of communicant, confirmed, full members.

—Represents a percent less than 0.1.

Percentages may not total due to rounding.

#See Introduction for explanation of why total adherents reported by churches exceed the 1970 population figure.

Table 3. Churches and Church Membership by State, County and Denomination: 1971

County and Denomination	Number of churches	Communicant, confirmed, full members	Total adherents: Number	Total adherents: Percent of total population	Total adherents: Percent of total adherents
059 BAPT MISS ASSN	1	25	29*	1.3	1.2
081 CATHOLIC......	1	0	800	36.7	33.2
419 SO BAPT CONV..	4	988	1,151*	52.8	47.8
449 UN METHODIST..	3	412	430	19.7	17.8
NACOGDOCHES	71	13,067	16,042*	44.1	100.0
059 BAPT MISS ASSN	22	2,252	2,629*	7.2	16.4
081 CATHOLIC......	3	0	735	2.0	4.6
093 CR CH (DISC)..	1	175	204*	0.6	1.3
123 CH GOD (ANDER)	1	30	80	0.2	0.5
165 CH OF NAZARENE	1	172	267	0.7	1.7
193 EPISCOPAL.....	1	381	650	1.8	4.1
221 FREE METH C NA	1	10	10	-	0.1
283 LUTH--MO SYNOD	1	49	66	0.2	0.4
413 S-D ADVENTISTS	2	83	97*	0.3	0.6
419 SO BAPT CONV..	20	7,498	8,753*	24.1	54.6
435 UNITARIAN-UNIV	1	15	18	-	0.1
449 UN METHODIST..	13	2,090	2,169	6.0	13.5
453 UN PRES CH USA	4	312	364*	1.0	2.3
NAVARRO	63	17,074	20,739*	66.6	100.0
059 BAPT MISS ASSN	10	1,182	1,397*	4.5	6.7
081 CATHOLIC......	1	0	652	2.1	3.1
093 CR CH (DISC)..	3	251	297*	1.0	1.4
127 CH GOD (CLEVE)	1	39	46*	0.1	0.2
165 CH OF NAZARENE	1	39	107	0.3	0.5
185 CUMBER PRESB..	1	25	30*	0.1	0.1
193 EPISCOPAL.....	1	310	377	1.2	1.8
283 LUTH--MO SYNOD	1	44	71	0.2	0.3
357 PRESB CH US...	1	275	325*	1.0	1.6
403 SALVATION ARMY	1	62	296	1.0	1.4
413 S-D ADVENTISTS	2	42	50*	0.2	0.2
419 SO BAPT CONV..	21	10,592	12,515*	40.2	60.3
449 UN METHODIST..	17	3,880	4,183	13.4	20.2
453 UN PRES CH USA	2	333	393*	1.3	1.9
NEWTON	18	2,846	3,738*	32.1	100.0
059 BAPT MISS ASSN	2	105	133*	1.1	3.6
081 CATHOLIC......	1	0	12	0.1	0.3
123 CH GOD (ANDER)	3	235	478	4.1	12.8
419 SO BAPT CONV..	8	2,087	2,647*	22.7	70.8
449 UN METHODIST..	4	419	468	4.0	12.5
NOLAN	31	8,035	11,351*	70.0	100.0
029 AMER LUTH CH..	1	155	193	1.2	1.7
059 BAPT MISS ASSN	1	114	137*	0.8	1.2
081 CATHOLIC......	3	0	1,784	11.0	15.7
093 CR CH (DISC)..	1	224	270*	1.7	2.4
123 CH GOD (ANDER)	1	13	26	0.2	0.2
127 CH GOD (CLEVE)	1	82	99*	0.6	0.9
165 CH OF NAZARENE	1	19	44	0.3	0.4
193 EPISCOPAL.....	1	54	54	0.3	0.5
283 LUTH--MO SYNOD	1	96	140	0.9	1.2
357 PRESB CH US...	2	150	181*	1.1	1.6
419 SO BAPT CONV..	10	5,112	6,156*	38.0	54.2
449 UN METHODIST..	6	1,865	2,085	12.9	18.4
453 UN PRES CH USA	2	151	182*	1.1	1.6
NUECES	151	57,384	135,763*	57.2	100.0
029 AMER LUTH CH..	5	1,889	2,570	1.1	1.9
081 CATHOLIC......	31	0	63,297	26.6	46.6
093 CR CH (DISC)..	6	2,018	2,552*	1.1	1.9
097 CR C AND C CR.	1	16	20*	-	-
123 CH GOD (ANDER)	4	136	412	0.2	0.3
127 CH GOD (CLEVE)	2	42	53*	-	-
165 CH OF NAZARENE	3	346	639	0.3	0.5
193 EPISCOPAL.....	7	3,432	4,519	1.9	3.3
221 FREE METH C NA	1	57	78	-	0.1
281 LUTH CH AMER..	1	462	635	0.3	0.5
283 LUTH--MO SYNOD	5	1,539	2,148	0.9	1.6
285 MENNONITE CH..	1	26	33*	-	-
349 PENT HOLINESS.	3	94	119*	0.1	0.1
357 PRESB CH US...	12	3,702	4,682*	2.0	3.4
403 SALVATION ARMY	1	83	787	0.3	0.6
413 S-D ADVENTISTS	2	204	258*	0.1	0.2
419 SO BAPT CONV..	44	30,735	38,875*	16.4	28.6
435 UNITARIAN-UNIV	1	98	143	0.1	0.1
443 UN C OF CHRIST	2	208	263*	0.1	0.2
449 UN METHODIST..	18	12,260	13,637	5.7	10.0
461 UNITY OF BRETH	1	37	43	-	-
OCHILTREE	15	3,577	5,328*	54.9	100.0
081 CATHOLIC......	1	0	900	9.3	16.9
093 CR CH (DISC)..	1	362	459*	4.7	8.6
097 CR C AND C CR.	1	91	115*	1.2	2.2
127 CH GOD (CLEVE)	1	23	29*	0.3	0.5
157 CH OF BRETHREN	1	80	101*	1.0	1.9
165 CH OF NAZARENE	1	81	150	1.5	2.8
193 EPISCOPAL.....	1	14	24	0.2	0.5
283 LUTH--MO SYNOD	1	61	100	1.0	1.9
285 MENNONITE CH..	1	71	90*	0.9	1.7
349 PENT HOLINESS.	1	26	33*	0.3	0.6
419 SO BAPT CONV..	3	1,645	2,087*	21.5	39.2
449 UN METHODIST..	1	1,070	1,173	12.1	22.0
453 UN PRES CH USA	1	53	67*	0.7	1.3
OLDHAM	6	1,094	1,872*	82.9	100.0
081 CATHOLIC......	1	0	600	26.6	32.1
419 SO BAPT CONV..	2	616	737*	32.6	39.4
449 UN METHODIST..	3	478	535	23.7	28.6
ORANGE	56	26,218	43,514*	61.1	100.0
029 AMER LUTH CH..	1	161	237	0.3	0.5
059 BAPT MISS ASSN	4	831	1,050*	1.5	2.4
081 CATHOLIC......	6	0	10,806	15.2	24.8
093 CR CH (DISC)..	3	446	563*	0.8	1.3
097 CR C AND C CR.	4	273	345*	0.5	0.8
123 CH GOD (ANDER)	1	34	104	0.1	0.2
127 CH GOD (CLEVE)	1	49	62*	0.1	0.1
165 CH OF NAZARENE	2	213	322	0.5	0.7
193 EPISCOPAL.....	1	403	483	0.7	1.1
283 LUTH--MO SYNOD	1	123	187	0.3	0.4
357 PRESB CH US...	2	957	1,209*	1.7	2.8
413 S-D ADVENTISTS	1	35	44*	0.1	0.1
419 SO BAPT CONV..	23	18,648	23,560*	33.1	54.1
449 UN METHODIST..	6	4,045	4,542	6.4	10.4
PALO PINTO	222	9,642	13,520*	46.7	100.0
059 BAPT MISS ASSN	3	566	702*	2.4	5.2
081 CATHOLIC......	4	0	1,775	6.1	13.1
093 CR CH (DISC)..	2	193	239*	0.8	1.8
127 CH GOD (CLEVE)	1	172	213*	0.7	1.6
165 CH OF NAZARENE	1	48	109	0.4	0.8
193 EPISCOPAL.....	1	112	119	0.4	0.9
283 LUTH--MO SYNOD	1	126	182	0.6	1.3
357 PRESB CH US...	2	145	180*	0.6	1.3
413 S-D ADVENTISTS	1	61	76*	0.3	0.6
419 SO BAPT CONV..	196	6,387	7,924*	27.4	58.6
449 UN METHODIST..	8	1,686	1,820	6.3	13.5
453 UN PRES CH USA	2	146	181*	0.6	1.3
PANOLA	42	6,759	7,783*	49.0	100.0
059 BAPT MISS ASSN	9	1,366	1,612*	10.1	20.7
081 CATHOLIC......	1	0	105	0.7	1.3
097 CR C AND C CR.	1	150	177*	1.1	2.3
193 EPISCOPAL.....	1	47	72	0.5	0.9
419 SO BAPT CONV..	15	2,877	3,395*	21.4	43.6
449 UN METHODIST..	13	2,227	2,313	14.6	29.7
453 UN PRES CH USA	2	92	109*	0.7	1.4
PARKER	65	13,303	16,875*	49.8	100.0
059 BAPT MISS ASSN	4	265	316*	0.9	1.9
081 CATHOLIC......	1	0	1,200	3.5	7.1
093 CR CH (DISC)..	1	223	266*	0.8	1.6
127 CH GOD (CLEVE)	2	147	175*	0.5	1.0
165 CH OF NAZARENE	1	23	42	0.1	0.2
193 EPISCOPAL.....	1	116	217	0.6	1.3
283 LUTH--MO SYNOD	1	92	125	0.4	0.7
357 PRESB CH US...	1	182	217*	0.6	1.3
413 S-D ADVENTISTS	1	43	51*	0.2	0.3
419 SO BAPT CONV..	36	9,338	11,141*	32.9	66.0
449 UN METHODIST..	14	2,682	2,896	8.5	17.2
453 UN PRES CH USA	2	192	229*	0.7	1.4
PARMER	19	5,086	7,876*	74.9	100.0
059 BAPT MISS ASSN	1	52	68*	0.6	0.9
081 CATHOLIC......	2	0	1,500	14.3	19.0
283 LUTH--MO SYNOD	3	179	245	2.3	3.1
349 PENT HOLINESS.	1	13	17*	0.2	0.2
419 SO BAPT CONV..	6	3,388	4,416*	42.0	56.1
443 UN C OF CHRIST	1	83	108*	1.0	1.4
449 UN METHODIST..	5	1,371	1,522	14.5	19.3
PECOS	19	4,661	9,129*	66.4	100.0
019 AMER BAPT CONV	1	316	412*	3.0	4.5
081 CATHOLIC......	3	0	3,192	23.2	35.0
093 CR CH (DISC)..	1	134	175*	1.3	1.9
097 CR C AND C CR.	1	85	111*	0.8	1.2
165 CH OF NAZARENE	1	3	3	-	-
193 EPISCOPAL.....	1	10	11	0.1	0.1
283 LUTH--MO SYNOD	1	53	78	0.6	0.9
357 PRESB CH US...	1	238	311*	2.3	3.4
419 SO BAPT CONV..	6	2,859	3,731*	27.1	40.9
449 UN METHODIST..	3	963	1,105	8.0	12.1
POLK	45	6,335	7,629*	52.8	100.0
059 BAPT MISS ASSN	17	2,298	2,789*	19.3	36.6
081 CATHOLIC......	1	0	70	0.5	0.9
193 EPISCOPAL.....	1	55	59	0.4	0.8
283 LUTH--MO SYNOD	1	71	90	0.6	1.2
357 PRESB CH US...	3	231	280*	1.9	3.7
419 SO BAPT CONV..	14	2,831	3,436*	23.8	45.0
449 UN METHODIST..	8	849	905	6.3	11.9
POTTER	77	47,132	68,579*	75.8	100.0
029 AMER LUTH CH..	1	401	615	0.7	0.9
059 BAPT MISS ASSN	3	523	638*	0.7	0.9
081 CATHOLIC......	6	0	10,000	11.0	14.6
093 CR CH (DISC)..	4	1,845	2,251*	2.5	3.3
097 CR C AND C CR.	5	2,560	3,123*	3.5	4.6
123 CH GOD (ANDER)	1	72	151	0.2	0.2
127 CH GOD (CLEVE)	2	172	210*	0.2	0.3
165 CH OF NAZARENE	6	726	1,530	1.7	2.2
193 EPISCOPAL.....	2	1,306	2,122	2.3	3.1
283 LUTH--MO SYNOD	3	961	1,410	1.6	2.1

*Total adherents estimated from known number of communicant, confirmed, full members.

—Represents a percent less than 0.1.

Percentages may not total due to rounding.

Table 3. Churches and Church Membership by State, County and Denomination: 1971

County and Denomination	Number of churches	Communicant, confirmed, full members	Total adherents: Number	Total adherents: Percent of total population	Total adherents: Percent of total adherents
349 PENT HOLINESS.	3	203	248*	0.3	0.4
357 PRESB CH US...	1	258	315*	0.3	0.5
413 S-D ADVENTISTS	3	515	628*	0.7	0.9
419 SO BAPT CONV..	22	25,790	31,466*	34.8	45.9
449 UN METHODIST..	10	9,719	11,333	12.5	16.5
453 UN PRES CH USA	5	2,081	2,539*	2.8	3.7
PRESIDIO	14	1,238	4,079*	84.2	100.0
081 CATHOLIC......	6	0	2,550	52.7	62.5
093 CR CH (DISC)..	1	44	55*	1.1	1.3
193 EPISCOPAL.....	1	51	109	2.3	2.7
419 SO BAPT CONV..	3	635	796*	16.4	19.5
449 UN METHODIST..	2	426	466	9.6	11.4
453 UN PRES CH USA	1	82	103*	2.1	2.5
RAINS	13	1,626	1,848*	49.3	100.0
059 BAPT MISS ASSN	3	196	225*	6.0	12.2
127 CH GOD (CLEVE)	1	62	71*	1.9	3.8
419 SO BAPT CONV..	7	1,173	1,347*	35.9	72.9
449 UN METHODIST..	2	195	205	5.5	11.1
RANDALL	23	12,243	18,139*	33.7	100.0
059 BAPT MISS ASSN	1	131	162*	0.3	0.9
081 CATHOLIC......	3	0	3,000	5.6	16.5
093 CR CH (DISC)..	1	172	213*	0.4	1.2
165 CH OF NAZARENE	1	25	71	0.1	0.4
193 EPISCOPAL.....	1	50	61	0.1	0.3
283 LUTH--MO SYNOD	1	112	162	0.3	0.9
357 PRESB CH US...	1	71	88*	0.2	0.5
419 SO BAPT CONV..	9	8,225	10,163*	18.9	56.0
435 UNITARIAN-UNIV	1	67	113	0.2	0.6
449 UN METHODIST..	3	3,228	3,906	7.2	21.5
453 UN PRES CH USA	1	162	200*	0.4	1.1
REAGAN	8	1,365	1,782*	55.0	100.0
081 CATHOLIC......	1	0	200	6.2	11.2
093 CR CH (DISC)..	1	10	12*	0.4	0.7
419 SO BAPT CONV..	3	826	1,012*	31.2	56.8
449 UN METHODIST..	2	500	522	16.1	29.3
453 UN PRES CH USA	1	29	36*	1.1	2.0
REAL	6	776	1,355*	67.3	100.0
081 CATHOLIC......	2	0	421	20.9	31.1
419 SO BAPT CONV..	3	698	856*	42.5	63.2
449 UN METHODIST..	1	78	78	3.9	5.8
RED RIVER	40	6,147	7,122*	49.8	100.0
081 CATHOLIC......	1	0	102	0.7	1.4
093 CR CH (DISC)..	2	66	78*	0.5	1.1
127 CH GOD (CLEVE)	1	16	19*	0.1	0.3
185 CUMBER PRESB..	2	48	57*	0.4	0.8
193 EPISCOPAL.....	1	9	12	0.1	0.2
283 LUTH--MO SYNOD	1	56	77	0.5	1.1
419 SO BAPT CONV..	13	3,691	4,347*	30.4	61.0
449 UN METHODIST..	16	1,955	2,070	14.5	29.1
453 UN PRES CH USA	3	306	360*	2.5	5.1
REEVES	20	4,186	11,801*	71.4	100.0
059 BAPT MISS ASSN	1	98	129*	0.8	1.1
081 CATHOLIC......	5	0	6,425	38.9	54.4
093 CR CH (DISC)..	1	212	280*	1.7	2.4
283 LUTH--MO SYNOD	1	70	106	0.6	0.9
357 PRESB CH US...	1	220	291*	1.8	2.5
419 SO BAPT CONV..	7	2,508	3,314*	20.1	28.1
449 UN METHODIST..	4	1,078	1,256	7.6	10.6
REFUGIO	25	2,835	6,987*	73.6	100.0
029 AMER LUTH CH..	1	152	199	2.1	2.8
081 CATHOLIC......	8	0	3,495	36.8	50.0
123 CH GOD (ANDER)	1	13	33	0.3	0.5
193 EPISCOPAL.....	1	63	67	0.7	1.0
281 LUTH CH AMER..	1	55	77	0.8	1.1
283 LUTH--MO SYNOD	1	35	43	0.5	0.6
357 PRESB CH US...	3	194	239*	2.5	3.4
419 SO BAPT CONV..	5	1,686	2,077*	21.9	29.7
443 UN C OF CHRIST	1	89	110*	1.2	1.6
449 UN METHODIST..	3	548	647	6.8	9.3
ROBERTS	3	627	941*	97.3	100.0
081 CATHOLIC......	0	0	200	20.7	21.3
093 CR CH (DISC)..	1	107	128*	13.2	13.6
419 SO BAPT CONV..	1	292	349*	36.1	37.1
449 UN METHODIST..	1	228	264	27.3	28.1
ROBERTSON	29	6,579	8,634*	60.0	100.0
081 CATHOLIC......	2	0	756	5.3	8.8
193 EPISCOPAL.....	2	52	86	0.6	1.0
357 PRESB CH US...	1	44	53*	0.4	0.6
419 SO BAPT CONV..	18	5,633	6,829*	47.5	79.1
449 UN METHODIST..	6	850	910	6.3	10.5
ROCKWALL	15	3,225	3,872*	55.0	100.0
059 BAPT MISS ASSN	1	135	166*	2.4	4.3
093 CR CH (DISC)..	3	138	170*	2.4	4.4
193 EPISCOPAL.....	1	54	63	0.9	1.6
221 FREE METH C NA	1	49	83	1.2	2.1
419 SO BAPT CONV..	3	1,860	2,291*	32.5	59.2
449 UN METHODIST..	4	890	977	13.9	25.2
453 UN PRES CH USA	2	99	122*	1.7	3.2
RUNNELS	42	6,447	10,641*	87.9	100.0
029 AMER LUTH CH..	1	256	311	2.6	2.9
081 CATHOLIC......	7	0	3,180	26.3	29.9
093 CR CH (DISC)..	1	64	75*	0.6	0.7
123 CH GOD (ANDER)	1	10	45	0.4	0.4
165 CH OF NAZARENE	1	27	44	0.4	0.4
281 LUTH CH AMER..	1	158	177	1.5	1.7
283 LUTH--MO SYNOD	1	68	75	0.6	0.7
357 PRESB CH US...	4	242	284*	2.3	2.7
419 SO BAPT CONV..	16	4,166	4,896*	40.4	46.0
443 UN C OF CHRIST	1	90	106*	0.9	1.0
449 UN METHODIST..	8	1,366	1,448	12.0	13.6
RUSK	67	13,054	15,355*	45.0	100.0
059 BAPT MISS ASSN	6	599	706*	2.1	4.6
081 CATHOLIC......	1	0	203	0.6	1.3
093 CR CH (DISC)..	5	384	453*	1.3	3.0
165 CH OF NAZARENE	2	75	102	0.3	0.7
185 CUMBER PRESB..	2	97	114*	0.3	0.7
193 EPISCOPAL.....	1	51	101	0.3	0.7
357 PRESB CH US...	2	229	270*	0.8	1.8
419 SO BAPT CONV..	28	8,874	10,462*	30.7	68.1
449 UN METHODIST..	17	2,664	2,849	8.4	18.6
453 UN PRES CH USA	3	81	95*	0.3	0.6
SABINE	31	2,466	3,179*	44.2	100.0
059 BAPT MISS ASSN	6	549	668*	9.3	21.0
081 CATHOLIC......	2	0	24	0.3	0.8
123 CH GOD (ANDER)	4	125	371	5.2	11.7
221 FREE METH C NA	1	33	34	0.5	1.1
419 SO BAPT CONV..	5	1,099	1,338*	18.6	42.1
449 UN METHODIST..	13	660	744	10.4	23.4
SAN AUGUSTINE	13	1,874	2,286*	29.1	100.0
081 CATHOLIC......	1	0	20	0.3	0.9
123 CH GOD (ANDER)	1	12	33	0.4	1.4
193 EPISCOPAL.....	1	25	45	0.6	2.0
357 PRESB CH US...	1	86	105*	1.3	4.6
419 SO BAPT CONV..	6	1,351	1,648*	21.0	72.1
449 UN METHODIST..	3	400	435	5.5	19.0
SAN JACINTO	15	1,671	2,002*	29.9	100.0
059 BAPT MISS ASSN	2	186	226*	3.4	11.3
357 PRESB CH US...	1	47	57*	0.9	2.8
419 SO BAPT CONV..	8	1,214	1,474*	22.0	73.6
449 UN METHODIST..	4	224	245	3.7	12.2
SAN PATRICIO	52	10,616	34,141*	72.2	100.0
029 AMER LUTH CH..	3	425	582	1.2	1.7
059 BAPT MISS ASSN	1	196	252*	0.5	0.7
081 CATHOLIC......	14	0	20,761	43.9	60.8
093 CR CH (DISC)..	2	120	154*	0.3	0.5
097 CR C AND C CR.	2	100	129*	0.3	0.4
127 CH GOD (CLEVE)	1	11	14*	-	-
165 CH OF NAZARENE	1	58	81	0.2	0.2
193 EPISCOPAL.....	1	42	84	0.2	0.2
281 LUTH CH AMER..	1	150	224	0.5	0.7
283 LUTH--MO SYNOD	2	94	122	0.3	0.4
285 MENNONITE CH..	1	117	150*	0.3	0.4
349 PENT HOLINESS.	2	30	39*	0.1	0.1
357 PRESB CH US...	4	509	654*	1.4	1.9
419 SO BAPT CONV..	9	6,286	8,083*	17.1	23.7
449 UN METHODIST..	8	2,478	2,812	5.9	8.2
SAN SABA	23	2,711	3,301*	59.6	100.0
081 CATHOLIC......	1	0	238	4.3	7.2
093 CR CH (DISC)..	1	54	62*	1.1	1.9
193 EPISCOPAL.....	1	12	12	0.2	0.4
357 PRESB CH US...	2	141	163*	2.9	4.9
419 SO BAPT CONV..	11	1,823	2,109*	38.1	63.9
449 UN METHODIST..	5	541	555	10.0	16.8
453 UN PRES CH USA	2	140	162*	2.9	4.9
SCHLEICHER	7	1,511	2,210*	97.1	100.0
081 CATHOLIC......	1	0	400	17.6	18.1
093 CR CH (DISC)..	1	15	18*	0.8	0.8
193 EPISCOPAL.....	1	16	16	0.7	0.7
357 PRESB CH US...	1	110	131*	5.8	5.9
419 SO BAPT CONV..	2	1,076	1,281*	56.3	58.0
449 UN METHODIST..	1	294	364	16.0	16.5
SCURRY	31	7,362	10,905*	69.2	100.0
059 BAPT MISS ASSN	1	218	262*	1.7	2.4
081 CATHOLIC......	3	0	2,187	13.9	20.1
093 CR CH (DISC)..	1	172	207*	1.3	1.9
123 CH GOD (ANDER)	1	28	63	0.4	0.6
127 CH GOD (CLEVE)	1	49	59*	0.4	0.5
193 EPISCOPAL.....	1	53	72	0.5	0.7
281 LUTH CH AMER..	1	69	96	0.6	0.9
419 SO BAPT CONV..	12	5,096	6,134*	38.9	56.2

*Total adherents estimated from known number of communicant, confirmed, full members.

—Represents a percent less than 0.1.

Percentages may not total due to rounding.

Table 3. Churches and Church Membership by State, County and Denomination: 1971

County and Denomination	Number of churches	Communicant, confirmed, full members	Total adherents: Number	Total adherents: Percent of total population	Total adherents: Percent of total adherents
449 UN METHODIST..	8	1,601	1,734	11.0	15.9
453 UN PRES CH USA	2	76	91*	0.6	0.8
SHACKELFORD	12	2,148	2,424*	72.9	100.0
093 CR CH (DISC)..	2	108	123*	3.7	5.1
193 EPISCOPAL.....	1	8	9	0.3	0.4
283 LUTH--MO SYNOD	1	121	158	4.8	6.5
357 PRESB CH US...	1	55	62*	1.9	2.6
419 SO BAPT CONV..	4	1,336	1,517*	45.7	62.6
449 UN METHODIST..	2	463	490	14.7	20.2
453 UN PRES CH USA	1	57	65*	2.0	2.7
SHELBY	42	6,842	8,098*	41.2	100.0
059 BAPT MISS ASSN	11	1,551	1,855*	9.4	22.9
081 CATHOLIC......	1	0	79	0.4	1.0
093 CR CH (DISC)..	3	197	236*	1.2	2.9
097 CR C AND C CR.	2	125	149*	0.8	1.8
165 CH OF NAZARENE	1	25	25	0.1	0.3
193 EPISCOPAL.....	1	36	67	0.3	0.8
419 SO BAPT CONV..	11	3,486	4,169*	21.2	51.5
449 UN METHODIST..	10	1,311	1,385	7.0	17.1
453 UN PRES CH USA	2	111	133*	0.7	1.6
SHERMAN	5	1,366	2,036*	55.7	100.0
081 CATHOLIC......	1	0	350	9.6	17.2
093 CR CH (DISC)..	1	204	259*	7.1	12.7
419 SO BAPT CONV..	1	660	838*	22.9	41.2
449 UN METHODIST..	2	502	589	16.1	28.9
SMITH	114	42,207	55,577*	57.2	100.0
059 BAPT MISS ASSN	10	1,213	1,482*	1.5	2.7
081 CATHOLIC......	2	0	4,715	4.9	8.5
093 CR CH (DISC)..	3	1,316	1,608*	1.7	2.9
123 CH GOD (ANDER)	1	46	102	0.1	0.2
127 CH GOD (CLEVE)	4	211	258*	0.3	0.5
165 CH OF NAZARENE	5	429	678	0.7	1.2
185 CUMBER PRESB..	1	150	183*	0.2	0.3
193 EPISCOPAL.....	3	999	1,268	1.3	2.3
281 LUTH CH AMER..	1	137	180	0.2	0.3
283 LUTH--MO SYNOD	1	278	388	0.4	0.7
357 PRESB CH US...	5	1,893	2,313*	2.4	4.2
413 S-D ADVENTISTS	2	188	230*	0.2	0.4
419 SO BAPT CONV..	52	26,057	31,833*	32.8	57.3
435 UNITARIAN-UNIV	1	37	46	-	0.1
449 UN METHODIST..	23	9,253	10,293	10.6	18.5
SOMERVELL	7	1,408	1,676*	60.0	100.0
081 CATHOLIC......	1	0	50	1.8	3.0
419 SO BAPT CONV..	5	1,108	1,298*	46.5	77.4
449 UN METHODIST..	1	300	328	11.7	19.6
STARR	17	1,019	16,518*	93.3	100.0
081 CATHOLIC......	12	0	15,170	85.7	91.8
313 NO AM BAPT GC.	1	70	92*	0.5	0.6
419 SO BAPT CONV..	3	630	827*	4.7	5.0
449 UN METHODIST..	1	319	429	2.4	2.6
STEPHENS	20	3,647	4,649*	55.3	100.0
081 CATHOLIC......	1	0	370	4.4	8.0
093 CR CH (DISC)..	1	382	447*	5.3	9.6
127 CH GOD (CLEVE)	1	13	15*	0.2	0.3
165 CH OF NAZARENE	1	18	86	1.0	1.8
193 EPISCOPAL.....	1	135	175	2.1	3.8
357 PRESB CH US...	1	77	90*	1.1	1.9
413 S-D ADVENTISTS	1	20	23*	0.3	0.5
419 SO BAPT CONV..	7	2,181	2,554*	30.4	54.9
449 UN METHODIST..	5	749	805	9.6	17.3
453 UN PRES CH USA	1	72	84*	1.0	1.8
STERLING	4	607	877*	83.0	100.0
081 CATHOLIC......	1	0	150	14.2	17.1
357 PRESB CH US...	1	42	52*	4.9	5.9
419 SO BAPT CONV..	1	372	457*	43.3	52.1
449 UN METHODIST..	1	193	218	20.6	24.9
STONEWALL	6	1,380	1,674*	69.8	100.0
059 BAPT MISS ASSN	1	254	294*	12.3	17.6
081 CATHOLIC......	1	0	100	4.2	6.0
419 SO BAPT CONV..	3	947	1,094*	45.6	65.4
449 UN METHODIST..	1	179	186	7.8	11.1
SUTTON	6	870	2,271*	71.5	100.0
081 CATHOLIC......	1	0	1,250	39.4	55.0
283 LUTH--MO SYNOD	1	34	43	1.4	1.9
357 PRESB CH US...	1	72	89*	2.8	3.9
419 SO BAPT CONV..	2	386	476*	15.0	21.0
449 UN METHODIST..	1	378	413	13.0	18.2
SWISHER	19	4,900	6,939*	66.9	100.0
059 BAPT MISS ASSN	1	50	63*	0.6	0.9
081 CATHOLIC......	2	0	1,000	9.6	14.4
093 CR CH (DISC)..	1	45	57*	0.5	0.8
283 LUTH--MO SYNOD	1	62	76	0.7	1.1
419 SO BAPT CONV..	6	3,373	4,245*	40.9	61.2
449 UN METHODIST..	6	1,238	1,332	12.8	19.2
453 UN PRES CH USA	2	132	166*	1.6	2.4
TARRANT	432	232,929	329,165*	46.0	100.0
029 AMER LUTH CH..	5	2,127	2,954	0.4	0.9
059 BAPT MISS ASSN	16	2,146	2,660*	0.4	0.8
081 CATHOLIC......	24	0	42,428	5.9	12.9
093 CR CH (DISC)..	25	10,973	13,599*	1.9	4.1
097 CR C AND C CR.	6	992	1,229*	0.2	0.4
123 CH GOD (ANDER)	2	115	289	-	0.1
127 CH GOD (CLEVE)	10	1,066	1,321*	0.2	0.4
165 CH OF NAZARENE	13	1,444	2,287	0.3	0.7
185 CUMBER PRESB..	6	801	993*	0.1	0.3
193 EPISCOPAL.....	21	8,797	12,298	1.7	3.7
221 FREE METH C NA	1	42	78	-	-
281 LUTH CH AMER..	5	1,051	1,549	0.2	0.5
283 LUTH--MO SYNOD	9	3,427	5,014	0.7	1.5
349 PENT HOLINESS.	2	47	58*	-	-
353 PLY BRETHREN..	3	116	161	-	-
357 PRESB CH US...	24	5,459	6,765*	0.9	2.1
381 REF PRES-EVAN.	1	50	62	-	-
403 SALVATION ARMY	1	133	486	0.1	0.1
413 S-D ADVENTISTS	6	1,067	1,322*	0.2	0.4
419 SO BAPT CONV..	152	131,659	163,167*	22.8	49.6
435 UNITARIAN-UNIV	3	233	388	0.1	0.1
443 UN C OF CHRIST	2	665	824*	0.1	0.3
449 UN METHODIST..	69	54,389	61,629	8.6	18.7
453 UN PRES CH USA	25	6,107	7,569*	1.1	2.3
469 WISC EVAN LUTH	1	23	35	-	-
TAYLOR	100	37,968	50,017*	51.1	100.0
029 AMER LUTH CH..	1	286	443	0.5	0.9
059 BAPT MISS ASSN	2	971	1,180*	1.2	2.4
081 CATHOLIC......	4	0	3,957	4.0	7.9
093 CR CH (DISC)..	2	1,058	1,286*	1.3	2.6
097 CR C AND C CR.	2	101	123*	0.1	0.2
123 CH GOD (ANDER)	1	50	85	0.1	0.2
127 CH GOD (CLEVE)	1	103	125*	0.1	0.2
165 CH OF NAZARENE	4	350	471	0.5	0.9
193 EPISCOPAL.....	2	1,161	1,629	1.7	3.3
221 FREE METH C NA	2	41	48	-	0.1
283 LUTH--MO SYNOD	2	522	739	0.8	1.5
335 ORTH PRESB CH.	1	29	37	-	0.1
357 PRESB CH US...	3	682	829*	0.8	1.7
403 SALVATION ARMY	1	140	442	0.5	0.9
413 S-D ADVENTISTS	1	60	73*	0.1	0.1
419 SO BAPT CONV..	39	23,651	28,740*	29.4	57.5
435 UNITARIAN-UNIV	1	12	21	-	-
449 UN METHODIST..	28	8,077	8,970	9.2	17.9
453 UN PRES CH USA	3	674	819*	0.8	1.6
TERRELL	6	694	1,302*	67.1	100.0
081 CATHOLIC......	1	0	477	24.6	36.6
357 PRESB CH US...	1	110	135*	7.0	10.4
419 SO BAPT CONV..	1	239	293*	15.1	22.5
449 UN METHODIST..	3	345	397	20.5	30.5
TERRY	22	6,474	9,555*	67.7	100.0
059 BAPT MISS ASSN	1	165	211*	1.5	2.2
081 CATHOLIC......	1	0	1,500	10.6	15.7
093 CR CH (DISC)..	1	132	169*	1.2	1.8
127 CH GOD (CLEVE)	1	105	134*	0.9	1.4
165 CH OF NAZARENE	1	47	67	0.5	0.7
193 EPISCOPAL.....	1	45	46	0.3	0.5
419 SO BAPT CONV..	10	4,703	6,011*	42.6	62.9
449 UN METHODIST..	5	1,135	1,235	8.7	12.9
453 UN PRES CH USA	1	142	182*	1.3	1.9
THROCKMORTON	12	1,679	1,912*	86.7	100.0
081 CATHOLIC......	1	0	65	2.9	3.4
093 CR CH (DISC)..	2	75	84*	3.8	4.4
357 PRESB CH US...	1	17	19*	0.9	1.0
419 SO BAPT CONV..	4	1,206	1,353*	61.4	70.8
449 UN METHODIST..	3	365	373	16.9	19.5
453 UN PRES CH USA	1	16	18*	0.8	0.9
TITUS	31	6,982	8,472*	50.7	100.0
059 BAPT MISS ASSN	2	433	520*	3.1	6.1
081 CATHOLIC......	1	0	147	0.9	1.7
093 CR CH (DISC)..	2	101	121*	0.7	1.4
127 CH GOD (CLEVE)	1	20	24*	0.1	0.3
165 CH OF NAZARENE	2	71	147	0.9	1.7
193 EPISCOPAL.....	1	50	63	0.4	0.7
357 PRESB CH US...	2	325	391*	2.3	4.6
419 SO BAPT CONV..	13	4,798	5,766*	34.5	68.1
449 UN METHODIST..	7	1,184	1,293	7.7	15.3
TOM GREEN	71	24,439	40,538*	57.1	100.0
029 AMER LUTH CH..	1	247	360	0.5	0.9
059 BAPT MISS ASSN	1	89	108*	0.2	0.3
081 CATHOLIC......	11	0	10,522	14.8	26.0
093 CR CH (DISC)..	3	956	1,158*	1.6	2.9
123 CH GOD (ANDER)	1	27	59	0.1	0.1
165 CH OF NAZARENE	11	783	1,358	1.9	3.3
193 EPISCOPAL.....	2	728	1,018	1.4	2.5
281 LUTH CH AMER..	1	136	231	0.3	0.6
283 LUTH--MO SYNOD	1	511	700	1.0	1.7
357 PRESB CH US...	2	1,226	1,485*	2.1	3.7

*Total adherents estimated from known number of communicant, confirmed, full members.

—Represents a percent less than 0.1.

Percentages may not total due to rounding.

Table 3. Churches and Church Membership by State, County and Denomination: 1971

County and Denomination	Number of churches	Communicant, confirmed, full members	Total adherents: Number	Percent of total population	Percent of total adherents
413 S-D ADVENTISTS	1	15	18*	-	-
419 SO BAPT CONV..	18	14,595	17,677*	24.9	43.6
435 UNITARIAN-UNIV	1	24	36	0.1	0.1
449 UN METHODIST..	13	4,434	4,999	7.0	12.3
453 UN PRES CH USA	3	563	682*	1.0	1.7
461 UNITY OF BRETH	1	105	127	0.2	0.3
TRAVIS	171	80,984	166,176*	56.2	100.0
029 AMER LUTH CH..	8	4,813	6,409	2.2	3.9
059 BAPT MISS ASSN	3	159	193*	0.1	0.1
081 CATHOLIC......	17	0	65,848	22.3	39.6
093 CR CH (DISC)..	7	2,727	3,308*	1.1	2.0
097 CR C AND C CR.	2	225	273*	0.1	0.2
123 CH GOD (ANDER)	1	52	152	0.1	0.1
127 CH GOD (CLEVE)	1	51	62*	-	-
165 CH OF NAZARENE	3	403	705	0.2	0.4
185 CUMBER PRESB..	2	1,029	1,248*	0.4	0.8
193 EPISCOPAL.....	11	6,651	8,688	2.9	5.2
226 FRIENDS-USA...	1	78	95*	-	0.1
281 LUTH CH AMER..	7	2,189	2,836	1.0	1.7
283 LUTH--MO SYNOD	9	4,349	6,037	2.0	3.6
349 PENT HOLINESS.	3	84	102*	-	0.1
357 PRESB CH US...	10	4,241	5,145*	1.7	3.1
403 SALVATION ARMY	1	123	672	0.2	0.4
413 S-D ADVENTISTS	2	291	353*	0.1	0.2
419 SO BAPT CONV..	48	36,204	43,917*	14.9	26.4
435 UNITARIAN-UNIV	1	285	428	0.1	0.3
443 UN C OF CHRIST	3	454	551*	0.2	0.3
449 UN METHODIST..	25	15,501	17,813	6.0	10.7
453 UN PRES CH USA	4	947	1,149*	0.4	0.7
461 UNITY OF BRETH	1	90	140	-	0.1
469 WISC EVAN LUTH	1	38	52	-	-
TRINITY	23	3,301	3,871*	50.7	100.0
093 CR CH (DISC)..	3	65	77*	1.0	2.0
127 CH GOD (CLEVE)	1	42	50*	0.7	1.3
357 PRESB CH US...	1	18	21*	0.3	0.5
419 SO BAPT CONV..	14	2,702	3,206*	42.0	82.8
449 UN METHODIST..	4	474	517	6.8	13.4
TYLER	38	5,875	7,200*	58.0	100.0
059 BAPT MISS ASSN	1	24	29*	0.2	0.4
081 CATHOLIC......	1	0	210	1.7	2.9
093 CR CH (DISC)..	1	71	85*	0.7	1.2
193 EPISCOPAL.....	1	25	33	0.3	0.5
413 S-D ADVENTISTS	1	16	19*	0.2	0.3
419 SO BAPT CONV..	30	5,234	6,272*	50.5	87.1
449 UN METHODIST..	3	505	552	4.4	7.7
UPSHUR	46	8,968	10,513*	50.1	100.0
059 BAPT MISS ASSN	18	2,708	3,226*	15.4	30.7
093 CR CH (DISC)..	1	43	51*	0.2	0.5
127 CH GOD (CLEVE)	1	24	29*	0.1	0.3
165 CH OF NAZARENE	1	50	50	0.2	0.5
419 SO BAPT CONV..	18	4,975	5,926*	28.3	56.4
449 UN METHODIST..	7	1,168	1,231	5.9	11.7
UPTON	12	3,501	5,142*	109.5 #	100.0
081 CATHOLIC......	2	0	900	19.2	17.5
093 CR CH (DISC)..	1	81	100*	2.1	1.9
283 LUTH--MO SYNOD	1	47	66	1.4	1.3
419 SO BAPT CONV..	4	2,852	3,535*	75.3	68.7
449 UN METHODIST..	3	507	524	11.2	10.2
453 UN PRES CH USA	1	14	17*	0.4	0.3
UVALDE	26	4,842	12,486*	72.0	100.0
029 AMER LUTH CH..	1	176	208	1.2	1.7
081 CATHOLIC......	3	0	6,549	37.8	52.5
093 CR CH (DISC)..	1	176	222*	1.3	1.8
097 CR C AND C CR.	1	125	157*	0.9	1.3
165 CH OF NAZARENE	1	25	51	0.3	0.4
193 EPISCOPAL.....	1	196	260	1.5	2.1
221 FREE METH C NA	1	12	34	0.2	0.3
283 LUTH--MO SYNOD	1	98	126	0.7	1.0
357 PRESB CH US...	1	210	264*	1.5	2.1
413 S-D ADVENTISTS	1	10	13*	0.1	0.1
419 SO BAPT CONV..	8	2,612	3,290*	19.0	26.3
449 UN METHODIST..	6	1,202	1,312	7.6	10.5
VAL VERDE	19	4,595	14,021*	51.0	100.0
081 CATHOLIC......	4	0	8,223	29.9	58.6
093 CR CH (DISC)..	1	166	215*	0.8	1.5
193 EPISCOPAL.....	1	327	465	1.7	3.3
283 LUTH--MO SYNOD	1	127	193	0.7	1.4
357 PRESB CH US...	1	306	396*	1.4	2.8
413 S-D ADVENTISTS	1	28	36*	0.1	0.3
419 SO BAPT CONV..	7	2,480	3,212*	11.7	22.9
449 UN METHODIST..	3	1,161	1,281	4.7	9.1
VAN ZANDT	61	11,786	13,569*	61.2	100.0
029 AMER LUTH CH..	1	42	65	0.3	0.5
059 BAPT MISS ASSN	19	2,448	2,864*	12.9	21.1
093 CR CH (DISC)..	1	50	58*	0.3	0.4
127 CH GOD (CLEVE)	1	102	119*	0.5	0.9
165 CH OF NAZARENE	1	18	25	0.1	0.2
419 SO BAPT CONV..	22	6,542	7,654*	34.5	56.4
449 UN METHODIST..	13	2,444	2,620	11.8	19.3
453 UN PRES CH USA	3	140	164*	0.7	1.2
VICTORIA	44	14,503	37,128*	69.1	100.0
029 AMER LUTH CH..	2	1,372	1,855	3.5	5.0
081 CATHOLIC......	8	0	18,439	34.3	49.7
093 CR CH (DISC)..	1	215	271*	0.5	0.7
123 CH GOD (ANDER)	1	10	33	0.1	0.1
127 CH GOD (CLEVE)	1	36	45*	0.1	0.1
165 CH OF NAZARENE	1	67	134	0.2	0.4
193 EPISCOPAL.....	2	673	1,135	2.1	3.1
281 LUTH CH AMER..	4	2,054	2,811	5.2	7.6
283 LUTH--MO SYNOD	1	186	260	0.5	0.7
357 PRESB CH US...	3	1,178	1,486*	2.8	4.0
413 S-D ADVENTISTS	1	9	11*	-	-
419 SO BAPT CONV..	11	6,095	7,688*	14.3	20.7
435 UNITARIAN-UNIV	1	13	19	-	0.1
449 UN METHODIST..	7	2,595	2,941	5.5	7.9
WALKER	34	7,396	9,906*	35.8	100.0
059 BAPT MISS ASSN	3	120	135*	0.5	1.4
081 CATHOLIC......	2	0	1,497	5.4	15.1
093 CR CH (DISC)..	1	200	225*	0.8	2.3
123 CH GOD (ANDER)	1	8	22	0.1	0.2
193 EPISCOPAL.....	2	268	331	1.2	3.3
283 LUTH--MO SYNOD	1	120	167	0.6	1.7
357 PRESB CH US...	1	270	304*	1.1	3.1
419 SO BAPT CONV..	13	5,012	5,640*	20.4	56.9
449 UN METHODIST..	10	1,398	1,585	5.7	16.0
WALLER	24	3,327	5,002*	35.0	100.0
029 AMER LUTH CH..	2	283	377	2.6	7.5
081 CATHOLIC......	3	0	1,057	7.4	21.1
193 EPISCOPAL.....	1	65	99	0.7	2.0
283 LUTH--MO SYNOD	1	105	146	1.0	2.9
357 PRESB CH US...	1	15	18*	0.1	0.4
413 S-D ADVENTISTS	1	30	36*	0.3	0.7
419 SO BAPT CONV..	8	1,936	2,299*	16.1	46.0
449 UN METHODIST..	7	893	970	6.8	19.4
WARD	25	6,035	9,875*	75.9	100.0
081 CATHOLIC......	3	0	2,500	19.2	25.3
093 CR CH (DISC)..	2	96	121*	0.9	1.2
097 CR C AND C CR.	1	100	126*	1.0	1.3
127 CH GOD (CLEVE)	1	8	10*	0.1	0.1
165 CH OF NAZARENE	1	20	44	0.3	0.4
193 EPISCOPAL.....	1	43	66	0.5	0.7
283 LUTH--MO SYNOD	1	38	53	0.4	0.5
357 PRESB CH US...	1	63	79*	0.6	0.8
419 SO BAPT CONV..	9	4,032	5,072*	39.0	51.4
449 UN METHODIST..	4	1,408	1,518	11.7	15.4
453 UN PRES CH USA	1	227	286*	2.2	2.9
WASHINGTON	35	8,214	11,327*	60.1	100.0
029 AMER LUTH CH..	12	4,307	5,218	27.7	46.1
081 CATHOLIC......	2	0	1,372	7.3	12.1
093 CR CH (DISC)..	2	57	67*	0.4	0.6
123 CH GOD (ANDER)	1	22	93	0.5	0.8
193 EPISCOPAL.....	1	216	267	1.4	2.4
283 LUTH--MO SYNOD	2	917	1,159	6.2	10.2
313 NO AM BAPT GC.	1	82	96*	0.5	0.8
357 PRESB CH US...	1	88	103*	0.5	0.9
419 SO BAPT CONV..	4	887	1,041*	5.5	9.2
443 UN C OF CHRIST	3	788	925*	4.9	8.2
449 UN METHODIST..	5	751	860	4.6	7.6
461 UNITY OF BRETH	1	99	126	0.7	1.1
WEBB	27	2,922	52,726*	72.4	100.0
081 CATHOLIC......	11	0	49,030	67.3	93.0
093 CR CH (DISC)..	1	104	137*	0.2	0.3
193 EPISCOPAL.....	1	230	307	0.4	0.6
221 FREE METH C NA	1	10	20	-	-
283 LUTH--MO SYNOD	1	60	103	0.1	0.2
357 PRESB CH US...	2	187	246*	0.3	0.5
413 S-D ADVENTISTS	1	77	101*	0.1	0.2
419 SO BAPT CONV..	5	1,273	1,677*	2.3	3.2
449 UN METHODIST..	4	981	1,105	1.5	2.1
WHARTON	51	8,673	22,819*	62.1	100.0
029 AMER LUTH CH..	3	645	1,050	2.9	4.6
081 CATHOLIC......	12	0	12,125	33.0	53.1
093 CR CH (DISC)..	2	191	235*	0.6	1.0
123 CH GOD (ANDER)	2	66	148	0.4	0.6
193 EPISCOPAL.....	1	151	211	0.6	0.9
281 LUTH CH AMER..	2	454	536	1.5	2.3
283 LUTH--MO SYNOD	1	258	361	1.0	1.6
357 PRESB CH US...	4	536	658*	1.8	2.9
413 S-D ADVENTISTS	1	22	27*	0.1	0.1
419 SO BAPT CONV..	10	3,659	4,494*	12.2	19.7
449 UN METHODIST..	13	2,691	2,974	8.1	13.0
WHEELER	22	4,063	5,150*	80.0	100.0
081 CATHOLIC......	1	0	500	7.8	9.7
093 CR CH (DISC)..	1	19	22*	0.3	0.4
097 CR C AND C CR.	1	15	17*	0.3	0.3
127 CH GOD (CLEVE)	1	32	37*	0.6	0.7
165 CH OF NAZARENE	2	27	46	0.7	0.9
193 EPISCOPAL.....	1	9	12	0.2	0.2

*Total adherents estimated from known number of communicant, confirmed, full members.

—Represents a percent less than 0.1.

Percentages may not total due to rounding.

#See Introduction for explanation of why total adherents reported by churches exceed the 1970 population figure.

Table 3. Churches and Church Membership by State, County and Denomination: 1971

County and Denomination	Number of churches	Communicant, confirmed, full members	Total adherents: Number	Total adherents: Percent of total population	Total adherents: Percent of total adherents
283 LUTH--MO SYNOD	1	90	114	1.8	2.2
419 SO BAPT CONV..	7	2,746	3,203*	49.8	62.2
449 UN METHODIST..	7	1,125	1,199	18.6	23.3
WICHITA	101	49,148	67,204*	55.1	100.0
029 AMER LUTH CH..	1	298	413	0.3	0.6
059 BAPT MISS ASSN	1	177	213*	0.2	0.3
081 CATHOLIC......	6	0	7,590	6.2	11.3
093 CR CH (DISC)..	6	2,233	2,689*	2.2	4.0
097 CR C AND C CR.	1	190	229*	0.2	0.3
123 CH GOD (ANDER)	1	25	60	-	0.1
127 CH GOD (CLEVE)	5	520	626*	0.5	0.9
165 CH OF NAZARENE	4	364	568	0.5	0.8
193 EPISCOPAL.....	4	742	1,612	1.3	2.4
281 LUTH CH AMER..	1	116	198	0.2	0.3
283 LUTH--MO SYNOD	5	1,152	1,567	1.3	2.3
349 PENT HOLINESS.	1	44	53*	-	0.1
357 PRESB CH US...	6	1,364	1,642*	1.3	2.4
413 S-D ADVENTISTS	2	133	160*	0.1	0.2
419 SO BAPT CONV..	33	30,343	36,534*	30.0	54.4
435 UNITARIAN-UNIV	1	5	5	-	-
449 UN METHODIST..	17	10,168	11,511	9.4	17.1
453 UN PRES CH USA	6	1,274	1,534*	1.3	2.3
WILBARGER	26	9,426	12,939*	84.3	100.0
081 CATHOLIC......	1	0	2,000	13.0	15.5
093 CR CH (DISC)..	1	254	298*	1.9	2.3
127 CH GOD (CLEVE)	1	85	100*	0.7	0.8
165 CH OF NAZARENE	1	20	44	0.3	0.3
193 EPISCOPAL.....	1	67	99	0.6	0.8
281 LUTH CH AMER..	1	117	157	1.0	1.2
283 LUTH--MO SYNOD	3	706	911	5.9	7.0
357 PRESB CH US...	1	109	128*	0.8	1.0
413 S-D ADVENTISTS	1	13	15*	0.1	0.1
419 SO BAPT CONV..	11	6,169	7,229*	47.1	55.9
449 UN METHODIST..	3	1,767	1,819	11.8	14.1
453 UN PRES CH USA	1	119	139*	0.9	1.1
WILLACY	24	2,960	11,809*	75.8	100.0
081 CATHOLIC......	7	0	8,164	52.4	69.1
093 CR CH (DISC)..	1	50	65*	0.4	0.6
193 EPISCOPAL.....	1	34	37	0.2	0.3
201 EVAN COV CH AM	1	13	17*	0.1	0.1
281 LUTH CH AMER..	1	98	132	0.8	1.1
283 LUTH--MO SYNOD	1	154	186	1.2	1.6
349 PENT HOLINESS.	1	37	48*	0.3	0.4
357 PRESB CH US...	1	134	174*	1.1	1.5
413 S-D ADVENTISTS	1	28	36*	0.2	0.3
419 SO BAPT CONV..	5	1,445	1,876*	12.0	15.9
449 UN METHODIST..	4	967	1,074	6.9	9.1
WILLIAMSON	69	13,941	20,387*	54.6	100.0
029 AMER LUTH CH..	7	2,156	2,603	7.0	12.8
081 CATHOLIC......	5	0	3,742	10.0	18.4
093 CR CH (DISC)..	2	65	79*	0.2	0.4
097 CR C AND C CR.	1	122	147*	0.4	0.7
127 CH GOD (CLEVE)	1	10	12*	-	0.1
185 CUMBER PRESB..	1	30	36*	0.1	0.2
193 EPISCOPAL.....	2	170	219	0.6	1.1
281 LUTH CH AMER..	2	561	751	2.0	3.7
283 LUTH--MO SYNOD	3	773	998	2.7	4.9
357 PRESB CH US...	4	415	501*	1.3	2.5
413 S-D ADVENTISTS	1	34	41*	0.1	0.2
419 SO BAPT CONV..	18	5,692	6,877*	18.4	33.7
443 UN C OF CHRIST	1	320	387*	1.0	1.9
449 UN METHODIST..	19	3,093	3,406	9.1	16.7
461 UNITY OF BRETH	2	500	588	1.6	2.9
WILSON	23	3,002	9,503*	72.9	100.0
029 AMER LUTH CH..	5	1,155	1,438	11.0	15.1
081 CATHOLIC......	7	0	5,826	44.7	61.3
419 SO BAPT CONV..	6	1,026	1,274*	9.8	13.4
449 UN METHODIST..	5	821	965	7.4	10.2
WINKLER	15	4,510	6,282*	65.2	100.0
081 CATHOLIC......	2	0	900	9.3	14.3
093 CR CH (DISC)..	1	70	86*	0.9	1.4
097 CR C AND C CR.	1	110	135*	1.4	2.1
127 CH GOD (CLEVE)	1	34	42*	0.4	0.7
165 CH OF NAZARENE	1	37	62	0.6	1.0
193 EPISCOPAL.....	1	35	40	0.4	0.6
283 LUTH--MO SYNOD	1	58	88	0.9	1.4
419 SO BAPT CONV..	5	3,169	3,884*	40.3	61.8
449 UN METHODIST..	2	997	1,045	10.8	16.6
WISE	55	8,531	10,545*	53.6	100.0
081 CATHOLIC......	2	0	530	2.7	5.0
093 CR CH (DISC)..	3	60	72*	0.4	0.7
127 CH GOD (CLEVE)	1	25	30*	0.2	0.3
165 CH OF NAZARENE	1	16	42	0.2	0.4
185 CUMBER PRESB..	1	64	77*	0.4	0.7
193 EPISCOPAL.....	2	97	110	0.6	1.0
283 LUTH--MO SYNOD	1	31	41	0.2	0.4
357 PRESB CH US...	1	45	54*	0.3	0.5
419 SO BAPT CONV..	30	6,103	7,361*	37.4	69.8
449 UN METHODIST..	12	2,045	2,174	11.0	20.6
453 UN PRES CH USA	1	45	54*	0.3	0.5
WOOD	63	11,216	12,924*	69.5	100.0
059 BAPT MISS ASSN	25	3,410	3,929*	21.1	30.4
081 CATHOLIC......	1	0	132	0.7	1.0
093 CR CH (DISC)..	4	214	247*	1.3	1.9
165 CH OF NAZARENE	3	184	256	1.4	2.0
193 EPISCOPAL.....	1	89	114	0.6	0.9
357 PRESB CH US...	1	36	41*	0.2	0.3
419 SO BAPT CONV..	16	5,093	5,868*	31.6	45.4
449 UN METHODIST..	12	2,190	2,337	12.6	18.1
YOAKUM	12	3,448	5,062*	68.9	100.0
081 CATHOLIC......	2	0	800	10.9	15.8
093 CR CH (DISC)..	1	21	26*	0.4	0.5
097 CR C AND C CR.	1	49	62*	0.8	1.2
127 CH GOD (CLEVE)	1	37	46*	0.6	0.9
165 CH OF NAZARENE	1	45	108	1.5	2.1
357 PRESB CH US...	1	22	28*	0.4	0.6
419 SO BAPT CONV..	3	2,646	3,323*	45.2	65.6
449 UN METHODIST..	2	628	669	9.1	13.2
YOUNG	41	8,862	10,422*	67.7	100.0
029 AMER LUTH CH..	1	14	14	0.1	0.1
081 CATHOLIC......	2	0	282	1.8	2.7
093 CR CH (DISC)..	4	253	294*	1.9	2.8
127 CH GOD (CLEVE)	2	289	335*	2.2	3.2
165 CH OF NAZARENE	1	32	35	0.2	0.3
185 CUMBER PRESB..	1	125	145*	0.9	1.4
193 EPISCOPAL.....	1	19	25	0.2	0.2
283 LUTH--MO SYNOD	2	247	326	2.1	3.1
357 PRESB CH US...	1	164	190*	1.2	1.8
413 S-D ADVENTISTS	1	5	6*	-	0.1
419 SO BAPT CONV..	15	5,295	6,145*	39.9	59.0
449 UN METHODIST..	9	2,260	2,440	15.8	23.4
453 UN PRES CH USA	1	159	185*	1.2	1.8
ZAPATA	5	19	3,715	85.4	100.0
081 CATHOLIC......	4	0	3,696	84.9	99.5
449 UN METHODIST..	1	19	19	0.4	0.5
ZAVALA	15	1,462	8,546*	75.2	100.0
081 CATHOLIC......	3	0	6,693	58.9	78.3
165 CH OF NAZARENE	1	8	8	0.1	0.1
283 LUTH--MO SYNOD	1	21	27	0.2	0.3
357 PRESB CH US...	1	38	50*	0.4	0.6
413 S-D ADVENTISTS	1	5	7*	0.1	0.1
419 SO BAPT CONV..	4	869	1,147*	10.1	13.4
449 UN METHODIST..	4	521	614	5.4	7.2
CO DATA NOT AVAIL	79	4,444	48,004*	N/A	N/A
151 L-D SAINTS....	0	0	42,514	N/A	N/A
185 CUMBER PRESB..	2	52	64*	N/A	N/A
193 EPISCOPAL.....	3	137	156	N/A	N/A
223 FREE WILL BAPT	64	4,000	4,950*	N/A	N/A
467 WESLEYAN......	10	255	320	N/A	N/A

UTAH

County and Denomination	Number of churches	Communicant, confirmed, full members	Total adherents: Number	Total adherents: Percent of total population	Total adherents: Percent of total adherents
THE STATE.....	223	32,865	885,332*	83.6	100.0
BEAVER	3	35	3,368*	88.6	100.0
081 CATHOLIC......	1	0	54	1.4	1.6
151 L-D SAINTS....	0	0	3,272	86.1	97.1
413 S-D ADVENTISTS	1	20	24*	0.6	0.7
419 SO BAPT CONV..	1	15	18*	0.5	0.5
BOX ELDER	8	917	25,129*	89.3	100.0
081 CATHOLIC......	1	0	1,048	3.7	4.2
151 L-D SAINTS....	0	0	22,933	81.5	91.3
193 EPISCOPAL.....	1	105	112	0.4	0.4
281 LUTH CH AMER..	1	128	195	0.7	0.8
419 SO BAPT CONV..	2	240	313*	1.1	1.2
449 UN METHODIST..	2	166	166	0.6	0.7
453 UN PRES CH USA	1	278	362*	1.3	1.4
CACHE	8	774	40,557*	95.8	100.0
081 CATHOLIC......	1	0	725	1.7	1.8
151 L-D SAINTS....	0	0	38,849	91.8	95.8
193 EPISCOPAL.....	1	105	125	0.3	0.3
226 FRIENDS-USA...	1	11	14*	-	-
283 LUTH--MO SYNOD	1	72	114	0.3	0.3
419 SO BAPT CONV..	1	166	207*	0.5	0.5
453 UN PRES CH USA	3	420	523*	1.2	1.3
CARBON	10	479	10,981*	70.2	100.0
081 CATHOLIC......	3	0	3,018	19.3	27.5
151 L-D SAINTS....	0	0	7,340	46.9	66.8

*Total adherents estimated from known number of communicant, confirmed, full members.

—Represents a percent less than 0.1.

Percentages may not total due to rounding.

Table 3. Churches and Church Membership by State, County and Denomination: 1971

County and Denomination	Number of churches	Communicant, confirmed, full members	Total adherents		
			Number	Percent of total population	Percent of total adherents
193 EPISCOPAL.....	2	36	36	0.2	0.3
283 LUTH--MO SYNOD	1	23	34	0.2	0.3
413 S-D ADVENTISTS	1	19	23*	0.1	0.2
419 SO BAPT CONV..	2	255	305*	1.9	2.8
449 UN METHODIST..	1	146	225	1.4	2.0
DAGGETT	0	0	307	46.1	100.0
081 CATHOLIC......	0	0	16	2.4	5.2
151 L-D SAINTS....	0	0	291	43.7	94.8
DAVIS	14	2,402	81,929*	82.7	100.0
019 AMER BAPT CONV	3	726	970*	1.0	1.2
081 CATHOLIC......	2	0	5,250	5.3	6.4
151 L-D SAINTS....	0	0	73,184	73.9	89.3
165 CH OF NAZARENE	1	31	64	0.1	0.1
193 EPISCOPAL.....	2	127	227	0.2	0.3
283 LUTH--MO SYNOD	2	456	815	0.8	1.0
419 SO BAPT CONV..	3	597	798*	0.8	1.0
443 UN C OF CHRIST	1	465	621*	0.6	0.8
DUCHESNE	11	235	7,154*	98.0	100.0
081 CATHOLIC......	1	0	199	2.7	2.8
151 L-D SAINTS....	0	0	6,655	91.2	93.0
193 EPISCOPAL.....	1	13	14	0.2	0.2
419 SO BAPT CONV..	2	184	237*	3.2	3.3
453 UN PRES CH USA	7	38	49*	0.7	0.7
EMERY	1	0	4,121	80.2	100.0
081 CATHOLIC......	1	0	25	0.5	0.6
151 L-D SAINTS....	0	0	4,096	79.7	99.4
GARFIELD	1	0	2,812	89.1	100.0
081 CATHOLIC......	1	0	15	0.5	0.5
151 L-D SAINTS....	0	0	2,797	88.6	99.5
GRAND	6	714	3,270*	48.9	100.0
019 AMER BAPT CONV	1	399	521*	7.8	15.9
081 CATHOLIC......	1	0	340	5.1	10.4
151 L-D SAINTS....	0	0	1,991	29.8	60.9
283 LUTH--MO SYNOD	1	19	31	0.5	0.9
413 S-D ADVENTISTS	2	64	84*	1.3	2.6
419 SO BAPT CONV..	1	232	303*	4.5	9.3
IRON	3	196	10,977*	90.1	100.0
081 CATHOLIC......	1	0	90	0.7	0.8
151 L-D SAINTS....	0	0	10,642	87.4	96.9
419 SO BAPT CONV..	1	99	124*	1.0	1.1
453 UN PRES CH USA	1	97	121*	1.0	1.1
JUAB	3	91	3,768	82.4	100.0
081 CATHOLIC......	1	0	110	2.4	2.9
151 L-D SAINTS....	0	0	3,548	77.6	94.2
449 UN METHODIST..	2	91	110	2.4	2.9
KANE	1	0	2,805	115.9 #	100.0
081 CATHOLIC......	1	0	21	0.9	0.7
151 L-D SAINTS....	0	0	2,784	115.0	99.3
MILLARD	2	22	6,345*	90.8	100.0
081 CATHOLIC......	1	0	41	0.6	0.6
151 L-D SAINTS....	0	0	6,277	89.8	98.9
453 UN PRES CH USA	1	22	27*	0.4	0.4
MORGAN	1	151	4,031	101.2 #	100.0
081 CATHOLIC......	0	0	40	1.0	1.0
151 L-D SAINTS....	0	0	3,789	95.1	94.0
193 EPISCOPAL.....	1	151	202	5.1	5.0
PIUTE	0	0	936	80.4	100.0
081 CATHOLIC......	0	0	4	0.3	0.4
151 L-D SAINTS....	0	0	932	80.1	99.6
RICH	0	0	1,366	84.6	100.0
081 CATHOLIC......	0	0	5	0.3	0.4
151 L-D SAINTS....	0	0	1,361	84.3	99.6
SALT LAKE	79	16,853	365,878*	79.8	100.0
019 AMER BAPT CONV	4	1,118	1,429*	0.3	0.4
029 AMER LUTH CH..	3	731	1,214	0.3	0.3
081 CATHOLIC......	15	0	26,722	5.8	7.3
093 CR CH (DISC)..	2	330	422*	0.1	0.1
097 CR C AND C CR.	2	520	665*	0.1	0.2
105 CHRISTIAN REF.	2	155	330	0.1	0.1
151 L-D SAINTS....	0	0	315,813	68.9	86.3
165 CH OF NAZARENE	2	175	281	0.1	0.1
175 CONG CR CH....	1	497	635*	0.1	0.2
193 EPISCOPAL.....	5	2,225	3,411	0.7	0.9
226 FRIENDS-USA...	1	5	6*	-	-
281 LUTH CH AMER..	4	919	1,349	0.3	0.4
283 LUTH--MO SYNOD	3	1,131	1,661	0.4	0.5
353 PLY BRETHREN..	2	60	120	-	-
403 SALVATION ARMY	1	75	243	0.1	0.1
413 S-D ADVENTISTS	2	289	369*	0.1	0.1
419 SO BAPT CONV..	13	2,085	2,665*	0.6	0.7
435 UNITARIAN-UNIV	1	406	621	0.1	0.2
443 UN C OF CHRIST	3	530	677*	0.1	0.2
449 UN METHODIST..	7	2,836	3,710	0.8	1.0
453 UN PRES CH USA	6	2,766	3,535*	0.8	1.0
SAN JUAN	7	1,112	5,255*	54.7	100.0
081 CATHOLIC......	2	0	196	2.0	3.7
151 L-D SAINTS....	0	0	3,304	34.4	62.9
193 EPISCOPAL.....	1	735	1,223	12.7	23.3
413 S-D ADVENTISTS	1	185	261*	2.7	5.0
419 SO BAPT CONV..	3	192	271*	2.8	5.2
SANPETE	2	75	10,407*	94.8	100.0
081 CATHOLIC......	1	0	35	0.3	0.3
151 L-D SAINTS....	0	0	10,281	93.7	98.8
453 UN PRES CH USA	1	75	91*	0.8	0.9
SEVIER	2	27	9,220*	91.3	100.0
081 CATHOLIC......	1	0	51	0.5	0.6
151 L-D SAINTS....	0	0	9,136	90.4	99.1
453 UN PRES CH USA	1	27	33*	0.3	0.4
SUMMIT	2	36	5,395	91.8	100.0
081 CATHOLIC......	1	0	304	5.2	5.6
151 L-D SAINTS....	0	0	5,046	85.8	93.5
449 UN METHODIST..	1	36	45	0.8	0.8
TOOELE	6	563	15,441*	71.7	100.0
081 CATHOLIC......	1	0	1,657	7.7	10.7
151 L-D SAINTS....	0	0	13,035	60.5	84.4
193 EPISCOPAL.....	1	34	40	0.2	0.3
283 LUTH--MO SYNOD	1	89	129	0.6	0.8
419 SO BAPT CONV..	2	192	248*	1.2	1.6
449 UN METHODIST..	1	248	332	1.5	2.2
UINTAH	6	743	9,501*	74.9	100.0
081 CATHOLIC......	1	0	380	3.0	4.0
151 L-D SAINTS....	0	0	8,096	63.8	85.2
193 EPISCOPAL.....	2	85	125	1.0	1.3
283 LUTH--MO SYNOD	1	112	186	1.5	2.0
419 SO BAPT CONV..	1	416	544*	4.3	5.7
443 UN C OF CHRIST	1	130	170*	1.3	1.8
UTAH	14	1,064	133,105*	96.6	100.0
081 CATHOLIC......	3	0	1,180	0.9	0.9
127 CH GOD (CLEVE)	1	9	11*	-	-
151 L-D SAINTS....	0	0	130,552	94.8	98.1
165 CH OF NAZARENE	1	40	67	-	0.1
283 LUTH--MO SYNOD	1	141	193	0.1	0.1
413 S-D ADVENTISTS	1	80	101*	0.1	0.1
419 SO BAPT CONV..	3	242	305*	0.2	0.2
443 UN C OF CHRIST	2	[illegible]	502*	0.4	0.4
453 UN PRES CH USA	2	[illegible]	194*	0.1	0.1
WASATCH	1	0	5,570	95.0	100.0
081 CATHOLIC......	1	0	100	1.7	1.8
151 L-D SAINTS....	0	0	5,470	93.3	98.2
WASHINGTON	3	138	12,410*	90.8	100.0
019 AMER BAPT CONV	1	74	93*	0.7	0.7
081 CATHOLIC......	1	0	40	0.3	0.3
151 L-D SAINTS....	0	0	12,196	89.2	98.3
419 SO BAPT CONV..	1	64	81*	0.6	0.7
WAYNE	0	0	1,408	94.9	100.0
081 CATHOLIC......	0	0	5	0.3	0.4
151 L-D SAINTS....	0	0	1,403	94.6	99.6
WEBER	29	6,238	101,886*	80.7	100.0
019 AMER BAPT CONV	1	657	825*	0.7	0.8
029 AMER LUTH CH..	1	113	161	0.1	0.2
081 CATHOLIC......	4	0	8,910	7.1	8.7
093 CR CH (DISC)..	1	243	305*	0.2	0.3
097 CR C AND C CR.	2	64	80*	0.1	0.1
105 CHRISTIAN REF.	1	75	138	0.1	0.1
127 CH GOD (CLEVE)	1	33	41*	-	-
151 L-D SAINTS....	0	0	84,346	66.8	82.8
165 CH OF NAZARENE	1	66	147	0.1	0.1
193 EPISCOPAL.....	1	451	857	0.7	0.8
281 LUTH CH AMER..	2	646	966	0.8	0.9
283 LUTH--MO SYNOD	1	496	705	0.6	0.7
403 SALVATION ARMY	1	34	199	0.2	0.2
413 S-D ADVENTISTS	1	154	193*	0.2	0.2
419 SO BAPT CONV..	4	580	729*	0.6	0.7
443 UN C OF CHRIST	2	229	288*	0.2	0.3
449 UN METHODIST..	2	1,101	1,368	1.1	1.3
453 UN PRES CH USA	3	1,296	1,628*	1.3	1.6

*Total adherents estimated from known number of communicant, confirmed, full members.

—Represents a percent less than 0.1.

Percentages may not total due to rounding.

#See Introduction for explanation of why total adherents reported by churches exceed the 1970 population figure.

Table 3. Churches and Church Membership by State, County and Denomination: 1971

VERMONT

County and Denomination	Number of churches	Communicant, confirmed, full members	Total adherents: Number	Percent of total population	Percent of total adherents
THE STATE.....	638	68,084	231,449*	52.1	100.0
ADDISON	37	3,925	12,474*	51.4	100.0
019 AMER BAPT CONV	6	560	698*	2.9	5.6
081 CATHOLIC......	7	0	7,455	30.7	59.8
105 CHRISTIAN REF.	1	92	219	0.9	1.8
193 EPISCOPAL.....	2	213	646	2.7	5.2
413 S-D ADVENTISTS	1	23	29*	0.1	0.2
443 UN C OF CHRIST	9	1,478	1,843*	7.6	14.8
449 UN METHODIST..	11	1,559	1,584	6.5	12.7
BENNINGTON	36	4,630	14,594*	49.8	100.0
019 AMER BAPT CONV	5	1,177	1,453*	5.0	10.0
029 AMER LUTH CH..	1	45	49	0.2	0.3
081 CATHOLIC......	8	0	8,686	29.7	59.5
097 CR C AND C CR.	1	50	62*	0.2	0.4
123 CH GOD (ANDER)	1	29	106	0.4	0.7
175 CONG CR CH....	2	207	256*	0.9	1.8
193 EPISCOPAL.....	3	823	1,448	4.9	9.9
226 FRIENDS-USA...	1	29	36*	0.1	0.2
413 S-D ADVENTISTS	1	57	70*	0.2	0.5
435 UNITARIAN-UNIV	1	18	18	0.1	0.1
443 UN C OF CHRIST	5	808	997*	3.4	6.8
449 UN METHODIST..	7	1,387	1,413	4.8	9.7
CALEDONIA	46	5,281	10,578*	46.4	100.0
019 AMER BAPT CONV	6	797	967*	4.2	9.1
081 CATHOLIC......	5	0	4,300	18.9	40.7
165 CH OF NAZARENE	1	10	20	0.1	0.2
193 EPISCOPAL.....	3	227	518	2.3	4.9
353 PLY BRETHREN..	1	20	30	0.1	0.3
413 S-D ADVENTISTS	1	66	80*	0.4	0.8
435 UNITARIAN-UNIV	1	30	30	0.1	0.3
443 UN C OF CHRIST	13	1,818	2,206*	9.7	20.9
449 UN METHODIST..	10	1,919	1,949	8.6	18.4
453 UN PRES CH USA	5	394	478*	2.1	4.5
CHITTENDEN	70	10,577	58,750*	59.3	100.0
019 AMER BAPT CONV	5	864	1,090*	1.1	1.9
081 CATHOLIC......	20	0	45,125	45.5	76.8
165 CH OF NAZARENE	1	50	166	0.2	0.3
193 EPISCOPAL.....	9	1,676	2,849	2.9	4.8
221 FREE METH C NA	1	26	37	-	0.1
226 FRIENDS-USA...	2	82	103*	0.1	0.2
281 LUTH CH AMER..	1	145	278	0.3	0.5
283 LUTH--MO SYNOD	1	223	313	0.3	0.5
403 SALVATION ARMY	1	28	151	0.2	0.3
413 S-D ADVENTISTS	1	32	40*	-	0.1
419 SO BAPT CONV..	1	121	153*	0.2	0.3
435 UNITARIAN-UNIV	1	275	365	0.4	0.6
443 UN C OF CHRIST	13	3,695	4,662*	4.7	7.9
449 UN METHODIST..	12	3,278	3,315	3.3	5.6
453 UN PRES CH USA	1	82	103*	0.1	0.2
ESSEX	14	623	2,594*	47.9	100.0
081 CATHOLIC......	3	0	1,808	33.4	69.7
193 EPISCOPAL.....	2	95	158	2.9	6.1
435 UNITARIAN-UNIV	1	55	100	1.8	3.9
443 UN C OF CHRIST	3	171	209*	3.9	8.1
449 UN METHODIST..	5	302	319	5.9	12.3
FRANKLIN	53	4,235	20,329*	65.0	100.0
019 AMER BAPT CONV	5	448	565*	1.8	2.8
081 CATHOLIC......	16	0	15,319	49.0	75.4
165 CH OF NAZARENE	1	33	55	0.2	0.3
193 EPISCOPAL.....	7	593	1,019	3.3	5.0
413 S-D ADVENTISTS	1	17	21*	0.1	0.1
443 UN C OF CHRIST	6	511	645*	2.1	3.2
449 UN METHODIST..	17	2,633	2,705	8.6	13.3
GRAND ISLE	11	568	2,513*	70.3	100.0
081 CATHOLIC......	4	0	1,836	51.4	73.1
193 EPISCOPAL.....	1	5	25	0.7	1.0
443 UN C OF CHRIST	2	268	335*	9.4	13.3
449 UN METHODIST..	4	295	317	8.9	12.6
LAMOILLE	26	1,869	5,158*	38.8	100.0
081 CATHOLIC......	6	0	2,759	20.7	53.5
165 CH OF NAZARENE	3	109	308	2.3	6.0
193 EPISCOPAL.....	1	91	167	1.3	3.2
413 S-D ADVENTISTS	1	52	65*	0.5	1.3
443 UN C OF CHRIST	9	922	1,149*	8.6	22.3
449 UN METHODIST..	6	695	710	5.3	13.8
ORANGE	45	3,671	6,135*	34.7	100.0
019 AMER BAPT CONV	4	330	408*	2.3	6.7
081 CATHOLIC......	5	0	1,684	9.5	27.4
193 EPISCOPAL.....	3	98	203	1.1	3.3
315 NO AM OLD RC..	1	38	47*	0.3	0.8
413 S-D ADVENTISTS	2	59	73*	0.4	1.2
435 UNITARIAN-UNIV	1	25	25	0.1	0.4
443 UN C OF CHRIST	19	2,284	2,821*	16.0	46.0
449 UN METHODIST..	9	795	822	4.7	13.4
453 UN PRES CH USA	1	42	52*	0.3	0.8
ORLEANS	45	3,382	11,189*	55.5	100.0
019 AMER BAPT CONV	3	219	271*	1.3	2.4
081 CATHOLIC......	10	0	7,119	35.3	63.6
165 CH OF NAZARENE	2	86	212	1.1	1.9
193 EPISCOPAL.....	1	206	316	1.6	2.8
435 UNITARIAN-UNIV	1	50	80	0.4	0.7
443 UN C OF CHRIST	16	1,410	1,743*	8.6	15.6
449 UN METHODIST..	10	1,262	1,264	6.3	11.3
453 UN PRES CH USA	2	149	184*	0.9	1.6
RUTLAND	70	6,846	27,844*	52.9	100.0
019 AMER BAPT CONV	8	510	625*	1.2	2.2
081 CATHOLIC......	21	0	19,091	36.3	68.6
097 CR C AND C CR.	1	44	54*	0.1	0.2
165 CH OF NAZARENE	1	43	95	0.2	0.3
175 CONG CR CH....	1	86	105*	0.2	0.4
193 EPISCOPAL.....	7	906	1,803	3.4	6.5
201 EVAN COV CH AM	1	22	27*	0.1	0.1
281 LUTH CH AMER..	2	462	614	1.2	2.2
403 SALVATION ARMY	1	31	131	0.2	0.5
413 S-D ADVENTISTS	1	47	58*	0.1	0.2
435 UNITARIAN-UNIV	1	66	81	0.2	0.3
443 UN C OF CHRIST	12	2,096	2,569*	4.9	9.2
449 UN METHODIST..	12	2,435	2,471	4.7	8.9
453 UN PRES CH USA	1	98	120*	0.2	0.4
WASHINGTON	53	7,556	24,045*	50.5	100.0
019 AMER BAPT CONV	4	577	711*	1.5	3.0
081 CATHOLIC......	10	0	15,000	31.5	62.4
193 EPISCOPAL.....	3	615	1,072	2.2	4.5
226 FRIENDS-USA...	1	52	64*	0.1	0.3
403 SALVATION ARMY	1	32	164	0.3	0.7
413 S-D ADVENTISTS	1	64	79*	0.2	0.3
435 UNITARIAN-UNIV	4	461	647	1.4	2.7
443 UN C OF CHRIST	13	2,093	2,581*	5.4	10.7
449 UN METHODIST..	16	3,662	3,727	7.8	15.5
WINDHAM	65	6,575	14,984*	45.3	100.0
019 AMER BAPT CONV	17	1,888	2,303*	7.0	15.4
081 CATHOLIC......	9	0	6,657	20.1	44.4
097 CR C AND C CR.	1	13	16*	-	0.1
193 EPISCOPAL.....	3	771	1,349	4.1	9.0
201 EVAN COV CH AM	1	5	6*	-	-
226 FRIENDS-USA...	1	45	55*	0.2	0.4
281 LUTH CH AMER..	1	162	209	0.6	1.4
285 MENNONITE CH..	1	33	40*	0.1	0.3
413 S-D ADVENTISTS	2	138	168*	0.5	1.1
435 UNITARIAN-UNIV	2	286	301	0.9	2.0
443 UN C OF CHRIST	19	2,476	3,020*	9.1	20.2
449 UN METHODIST..	6	324	331	1.0	2.2
453 UN PRES CH USA	2	434	529*	1.6	3.5
WINDSOR	66	8,301	18,462*	41.9	100.0
019 AMER BAPT CONV	6	1,219	1,485*	3.4	8.0
081 CATHOLIC......	12	0	8,343	18.9	45.2
097 CR C AND C CR.	1	5	6*	-	-
193 EPISCOPAL.....	7	722	1,393	3.2	7.5
285 MENNONITE CH..	2	69	84*	0.2	0.5
435 UNITARIAN-UNIV	7	511	583	1.3	3.2
443 UN C OF CHRIST	21	3,523	4,293*	9.7	23.3
449 UN METHODIST..	10	2,252	2,275	5.2	12.3
CO DATA NOT AVAIL	1	45	1,800*	N/A	N/A
151 L-D SAINTS....	0	0	1,744	N/A	N/A
223 FREE WILL BAPT	1	45	56*	N/A	N/A

VIRGINIA

County and Denomination	Number of churches	Communicant, confirmed, full members	Total adherents: Number	Percent of total population	Percent of total adherents
THE STATE.....	5,952	1,429,205	2,011,887*	43.3	100.0
ACCOMACK	79	12,524	14,754*	50.9	100.0
081 CATHOLIC......	2	0	212	0.7	1.4
193 EPISCOPAL.....	3	296	360	1.2	2.4
357 PRESB CH US...	5	340	406*	1.4	2.8
419 SO BAPT CONV..	17	3,505	4,183*	14.4	28.4
449 UN METHODIST..	52	8,383	9,593	33.1	65.0
ALBEMARLE-CHARLOTTES #	89	26,307	36,222*	47.3	100.0
019 AMER BAPT CONV	2	761	915*	1.2	2.5
081 CATHOLIC......	2	0	4,425	5.8	12.2
093 CR CH (DISC)..	2	124	149*	0.2	0.4
097 CR C AND C CR.	4	1,198	1,440*	1.9	4.0
127 CH GOD (CLEVE)	3	224	269*	0.4	0.7
157 CH OF BRETHREN	3	458	551*	0.7	1.5

*Total adherents estimated from known number of communicant, confirmed, full members.

—Represents a percent less than 0.1.

Percentages may not total due to rounding.

#See Introduction for explanation of how church data was collected for Virginia's independent cities.

Table 3. Churches and Church Membership by State, County and Denomination: 1971

County and Denomination	Number of churches	Communicant, confirmed, full members	Total adherents: Number	Total adherents: Percent of total population	Total adherents: Percent of total adherents
165 CH OF NAZARENE	1	75	190	0.2	0.5
193 EPISCOPAL.....	12	3,189	4,573	6.0	12.6
226 FRIENDS-USA...	1	30	36*	-	0.1
281 LUTH CH AMER..	1	350	544	0.7	1.5
283 LUTH--MO SYNOD	1	155	204	0.3	0.6
285 MENNONITE CH..	1	35	42*	0.1	0.1
349 PENT HOLINESS.	1	14	17*	-	-
357 PRESB CH US...	8	2,943	3,538*	4.6	9.8
403 SALVATION ARMY	1	110	549	0.7	1.5
413 S-D ADVENTISTS	2	94	113*	0.1	0.3
419 SO BAPT CONV..	24	9,419	11,323*	14.8	31.3
435 UNITARIAN-UNIV	1	230	305	0.4	0.8
449 UN METHODIST..	19	6,898	7,039	9.2	19.4
ALLEGHANY-CLF FR-COV #	60	13,059	15,938*	56.9	100.0
055 AS REF PRES CH	2	474	578*	2.1	3.6
081 CATHOLIC......	2	0	548	2.0	3.4
093 CR CH (DISC)..	3	420	512*	1.8	3.2
097 CR C AND C CR.	5	965	1,177*	4.2	7.4
157 CH OF BRETHREN	1	30	37*	0.1	0.2
165 CH OF NAZARENE	1	81	122	0.4	0.8
193 EPISCOPAL.....	2	302	374	1.3	2.3
281 LUTH CH AMER..	1	27	38	0.1	0.2
349 PENT HOLINESS.	2	95	116*	0.4	0.7
357 PRESB CH US...	10	2,700	3,294*	11.8	20.7
403 SALVATION ARMY	1	55	272	1.0	1.7
413 S-D ADVENTISTS	1	18	22*	0.1	0.1
419 SO BAPT CONV..	9	2,658	3,242*	11.6	20.3
449 UN METHODIST..	20	5,234	5,606	20.0	35.2
AMELIA	27	2,153	2,524*	33.2	100.0
093 CR CH (DISC)..	1	53	65*	0.9	2.6
127 CH GOD (CLEVE)	1	68	83*	1.1	3.3
193 EPISCOPAL.....	2	82	101	1.3	4.0
283 LUTH--MO SYNOD	1	32	45	0.6	1.8
285 MENNONITE CH..	1	61	75*	1.0	3.0
357 PRESB CH US...	5	311	381*	5.0	15.1
419 SO BAPT CONV..	6	782	958*	12.6	38.0
449 UN METHODIST..	8	633	656	8.6	26.0
453 UN PRES CH USA	2	131	160*	2.1	6.3
AMHERST	50	8,859	10,441*	40.0	100.0
093 CR CH (DISC)..	3	548	663*	2.5	6.3
097 CR C AND C CR.	1	10	12*	-	0.1
127 CH GOD (CLEVE)	2	98	119*	0.5	1.1
157 CH OF BRETHREN	1	66	80*	0.3	0.8
193 EPISCOPAL.....	4	291	538	2.1	5.2
349 PENT HOLINESS.	2	43	52*	0.2	0.5
357 PRESB CH US...	4	448	542*	2.1	5.2
419 SO BAPT CONV..	14	3,629	4,389*	16.8	42.0
449 UN METHODIST..	19	3,726	4,046	15.5	38.8
APPOMATTOX	29	5,559	6,558*	67.0	100.0
193 EPISCOPAL.....	1	43	56	0.6	0.9
349 PENT HOLINESS.	2	86	105*	1.1	1.6
357 PRESB CH US...	3	210	257*	2.6	3.9
413 S-D ADVENTISTS	1	42	51*	0.5	0.8
419 SO BAPT CONV..	14	3,455	4,231*	43.2	64.5
449 UN METHODIST..	8	1,723	1,858	19.0	28.3
ARLINGTON-ALEXANDRIA #	120	69,339	121,353*	42.5	100.0
029 AMER LUTH CH..	4	2,066	3,108	1.1	2.6
081 CATHOLIC......	11	0	35,477	12.4	29.2
093 CR CH (DISC)..	3	664	776*	0.3	0.6
123 CH GOD (ANDER)	2	52	152	0.1	0.1
127 CH GOD (CLEVE)	1	230	269*	0.1	0.2
157 CH OF BRETHREN	1	380	444*	0.2	0.4
165 CH OF NAZARENE	2	116	278	0.1	0.2
193 EPISCOPAL.....	21	10,664	16,735	5.9	13.8
221 FREE METH C NA	1	48	59	-	-
281 LUTH CH AMER..	2	1,333	1,591	0.6	1.3
283 LUTH--MO SYNOD	2	942	1,284	0.5	1.1
349 PENT HOLINESS.	2	67	78*	-	0.1
357 PRESB CH US...	7	5,363	6,266*	2.2	5.2
403 SALVATION ARMY	2	191	808	0.3	0.7
413 S-D ADVENTISTS	2	404	472*	0.2	0.4
419 SO BAPT CONV..	16	12,738	14,883*	5.2	12.3
435 UNITARIAN-UNIV	1	687	971	0.3	0.8
443 UN C OF CHRIST	3	1,102	1,288*	0.5	1.1
449 UN METHODIST..	30	30,315	34,104	12.0	28.1
453 UN PRES CH USA	7	1,977	2,310*	0.8	1.9
AUGUSTA-STAUN-WAYNES #	161	38,665	49,335*	57.7	100.0
019 AMER BAPT CONV	2	61	74*	0.1	0.1
055 AS REF PRES CH	1	435	525*	0.6	1.1
081 CATHOLIC......	2	0	2,510	2.9	5.1
097 CR C AND C CR.	2	290	350*	0.4	0.7
123 CH GOD (ANDER)	1	84	208	0.2	0.4
127 CH GOD (CLEVE)	5	185	223*	0.3	0.5
157 CH OF BRETHREN	17	3,962	4,782*	5.6	9.7
165 CH OF NAZARENE	3	287	806	0.9	1.6
193 EPISCOPAL.....	2	711	957	1.1	1.9
221 FREE METH C NA	1	50	82	0.1	0.2
281 LUTH CH AMER..	13	2,623	3,421	4.0	6.9
283 LUTH--MO SYNOD	1	247	332	0.4	0.7
285 MENNONITE CH..	6	484	584*	0.7	1.2
349 PENT HOLINESS.	1	94	113*	0.1	0.2
353 PLY BRETHREN..	1	40	75	0.1	0.2
357 PRESB CH US...	25	8,850	10,682*	12.5	21.7
403 SALVATION ARMY	2	138	525	0.6	1.1
413 S-D ADVENTISTS	4	542	654*	0.8	1.3
419 SO BAPT CONV..	17	6,539	7,892*	9.2	16.0
435 UNITARIAN-UNIV	1	34	58	0.1	0.1
443 UN C OF CHRIST	2	306	369*	0.4	0.7
449 UN METHODIST..	52	12,703	14,113	16.5	28.6
BATH	25	2,355	2,921*	56.3	100.0
081 CATHOLIC......	1	0	90	1.7	3.1
157 CH OF BRETHREN	1	55	67*	1.3	2.3
193 EPISCOPAL.....	1	44	99	1.9	3.4
349 PENT HOLINESS.	1	53	64*	1.2	2.2
357 PRESB CH US...	6	690	835*	16.1	28.6
419 SO BAPT CONV..	4	446	540*	10.4	18.5
449 UN METHODIST..	11	1,067	1,226	23.6	42.0
BEDFORD-BEDFORD CITY #	97	15,354	18,185*	55.5	100.0
019 AMER BAPT CONV	3	159	192*	0.6	1.1
081 CATHOLIC......	1	0	221	0.7	1.2
093 CR CH (DISC)..	2	304	367*	1.1	2.0
123 CH GOD (ANDER)	2	22	72	0.2	0.4
127 CH GOD (CLEVE)	1	57	69*	0.2	0.4
157 CH OF BRETHREN	5	659	796*	2.4	4.4
193 EPISCOPAL.....	3	431	640	2.0	3.5
349 PENT HOLINESS.	2	122	147*	0.4	0.8
357 PRESB CH US...	7	655	791*	2.4	4.3
419 SO BAPT CONV..	34	7,868	9,507*	29.0	52.3
449 UN METHODIST..	37	5,077	5,383	16.4	29.6
BLAND	37	2,445	2,658*	49.0	100.0
093 CR CH (DISC)..	3	234	277*	5.1	10.4
097 CR C AND C CR.	2	85	101*	1.9	3.8
127 CH GOD (CLEVE)	3	133	157*	2.9	5.9
281 LUTH CH AMER..	3	78	99	1.8	3.7
349 PENT HOLINESS.	1	31	37*	0.7	1.4
357 PRESB CH US...	2	94	111*	2.0	4.2
413 S-D ADVENTISTS	1	16	19*	0.4	0.7
419 SO BAPT CONV..	4	310	367*	6.8	13.8
449 UN METHODIST..	18	1,464	1,490	27.5	56.1
BOTETOURT	50	8,014	9,571*	52.6	100.0
093 CR CH (DISC)..	1	69	84*	0.5	0.9
127 CH GOD (CLEVE)	1	18	22*	0.1	0.2
157 CH OF BRETHREN	8	1,580	1,918*	10.5	20.0
193 EPISCOPAL.....	2	134	194	1.1	2.0
281 LUTH CH AMER..	3	232	280	1.5	2.9
357 PRESB CH US...	6	667	810*	4.5	8.5
419 SO BAPT CONV..	17	3,957	4,803*	26.4	50.2
449 UN METHODIST..	12	1,357	1,460	8.0	15.3
BRUNSWICK	37	5,851	6,683*	41.3	100.0
093 CR CH (DISC)..	3	150	183*	1.1	2.7
097 CR C AND C CR.	1	375	458*	2.8	6.9
193 EPISCOPAL.....	4	226	324	2.0	4.8
357 PRESB CH US...	2	170	208*	1.3	3.1
419 SO BAPT CONV..	8	1,453	1,775*	11.0	26.6
443 UN C OF CHRIST	1	49	60*	0.4	0.9
449 UN METHODIST..	18	3,428	3,675	22.7	55.0
BUCHANAN	42	5,163	6,492*	20.2	100.0
081 CATHOLIC......	1	0	52	0.2	0.8
093 CR CH (DISC)..	4	284	365*	1.1	5.6
097 CR C AND C CR.	11	1,708	2,197*	6.9	33.8
127 CH GOD (CLEVE)	5	136	175*	0.5	2.7
281 LUTH CH AMER..	1	127	145	0.5	2.2
357 PRESB CH US...	6	450	579*	1.8	8.9
419 SO BAPT CONV..	6	1,692	2,177*	6.8	33.5
449 UN METHODIST..	8	766	802	2.5	12.4
BUCKINGHAM	39	5,049	6,033*	56.9	100.0
165 CH OF NAZARENE	1	0	20	0.2	0.3
193 EPISCOPAL.....	1	39	43	0.4	0.7
349 PENT HOLINESS.	1	45	57*	0.5	0.9
357 PRESB CH US...	4	186	234*	2.2	3.9
419 SO BAPT CONV..	18	3,153	3,964*	37.4	65.7
449 UN METHODIST..	14	1,626	1,715	16.2	28.4
CAMPBELL-LYNCHBURG #	128	41,300	52,532*	53.9	100.0
081 CATHOLIC......	1	0	3,207	3.3	6.1
093 CR CH (DISC)..	6	3,273	3,967*	4.1	7.6
097 CR C AND C CR.	2	240	291*	0.3	0.6
123 CH GOD (ANDER)	1	140	265	0.3	0.5
127 CH GOD (CLEVE)	1	101	122*	0.1	0.2
157 CH OF BRETHREN	1	116	141*	0.1	0.3
165 CH OF NAZARENE	1	55	114	0.1	0.2
193 EPISCOPAL.....	6	2,004	2,746	2.8	5.2
281 LUTH CH AMER..	2	588	823	0.8	1.6
283 LUTH--MO SYNOD	1	107	150	0.2	0.3
285 MENNONITE CH..	1	59	72*	0.1	0.1
349 PENT HOLINESS.	3	260	315*	0.3	0.6
357 PRESB CH US...	17	4,633	5,615*	5.8	10.7
403 SALVATION ARMY	1	90	561	0.6	1.1
413 S-D ADVENTISTS	3	309	375*	0.4	0.7
419 SO BAPT CONV..	34	14,838	17,984*	18.5	34.2
435 UNITARIAN-UNIV	1	51	75	0.1	0.1
443 UN C OF CHRIST	1	37	45*	-	0.1
449 UN METHODIST..	45	14,399	15,664	16.1	29.8

*Total adherents estimated from known number of communicant, confirmed, full members.

—Represents a percent less than 0.1.

Percentages may not total due to rounding.

#See Introduction for explanation of how church data was collected for Virginia's independent cities.

Table 3. Churches and Church Membership by State, County and Denomination: 1971

County and Denomination	Number of churches	Communicant, confirmed, full members	Total adherents		
			Number	Percent of total population	Percent of total adherents
CAROLINE	24	3,888	4,907*	35.2	100.0
093 CR CH (DISC)..	1	5	6*	-	0.1
097 CR C AND C CR.	1	54	68*	0.5	1.4
193 EPISCOPAL.....	3	91	218	1.6	4.4
357 PRESB CH US...	1	146	185*	1.3	3.8
419 SO BAPT CONV..	12	2,824	3,570*	25.6	72.8
449 UN METHODIST..	6	768	860	6.2	17.5
CARROLL-GALAX CITY #	86	9,136	10,549*	35.9	100.0
075 BRETHREN IN CR	1	27	32*	0.1	0.3
081 CATHOLIC......	1	0	62	0.2	0.6
093 CR CH (DISC)..	8	534	639*	2.2	6.1
097 CR C AND C CR.	5	395	473*	1.6	4.5
127 CH GOD (CLEVE)	9	494	591*	2.0	5.6
157 CH OF BRETHREN	3	373	446*	1.5	4.2
226 FRIENDS-USA...	5	211	253*	0.9	2.4
281 LUTH CH AMER..	1	177	195	0.7	1.8
295 MORAV CH-SOUTH	2	172	195	0.7	1.8
349 PENT HOLINESS.	3	105	126*	0.4	1.2
357 PRESB CH US...	7	644	771*	2.6	7.3
413 S-D ADVENTISTS	1	87	104*	0.4	1.0
419 SO BAPT CONV..	22	3,004	3,595*	12.2	34.1
443 UN C OF CHRIST	2	66	79*	0.3	0.7
449 UN METHODIST..	16	2,847	2,988	10.2	28.3
CHARLES CITY	6	1,030	1,300*	21.1	100.0
193 EPISCOPAL.....	1	143	202	3.3	15.5
357 PRESB CH US...	1	30	39*	0.6	3.0
419 SO BAPT CONV..	2	626	808*	13.1	62.2
449 UN METHODIST..	2	231	251	4.1	19.3
CHARLOTTE	42	6,066	7,699*	66.7	100.0
093 CR CH (DISC)..	1	71	88*	0.8	1.1
097 CR C AND C CR.	2	610	753*	6.5	9.8
193 EPISCOPAL.....	1	28	35	0.3	0.5
357 PRESB CH US...	14	683	844*	7.3	11.0
419 SO BAPT CONV..	12	2,723	3,363*	29.1	43.7
449 UN METHODIST..	11	1,758	2,378	20.6	30.9
453 UN PRES CH USA	1	193	238*	2.1	3.1
CHESTERFIELD	76	31,219	44,181*	57.5	100.0
029 AMER LUTH CH..	2	480	769	1.0	1.7
081 CATHOLIC......	4	0	4,242	5.5	9.6
193 EPISCOPAL.....	6	1,621	2,836	3.7	6.4
283 LUTH--MO SYNOD	2	414	629	0.8	1.4
349 PENT HOLINESS.	1	38	48*	0.1	0.1
353 PLY BRETHREN..	3	137	221	0.3	0.5
357 PRESB CH US...	7	2,191	2,757*	3.6	6.2
419 SO BAPT CONV..	37	22,079	27,784*	36.2	62.9
449 UN METHODIST..	13	4,122	4,723	6.1	10.7
453 UN PRES CH USA	1	137	172*	0.2	0.4
CLARKE	19	2,940	3,612*	44.6	100.0
019 AMER BAPT CONV	2	90	109*	1.3	3.0
193 EPISCOPAL.....	3	383	594	7.3	16.4
357 PRESB CH US...	2	218	263*	3.2	7.3
419 SO BAPT CONV..	4	843	1,017*	12.6	28.2
449 UN METHODIST..	8	1,406	1,629	20.1	45.1
CRAIG	23	1,844	2,102*	59.6	100.0
093 CR CH (DISC)..	11	617	727*	20.6	34.6
097 CR C AND C CR.	8	732	862*	24.5	41.0
449 UN METHODIST..	4	495	513	14.6	24.4
CULPEPER	31	5,738	7,508*	41.2	100.0
081 CATHOLIC......	0	0	402	2.2	5.4
097 CR C AND C CR.	1	11	14*	0.1	0.2
193 EPISCOPAL.....	3	428	674	3.7	9.0
221 FREE METH C NA	1	25	28	0.2	0.4
281 LUTH CH AMER..	1	205	275	1.5	3.7
353 PLY BRETHREN..	1	35	90	0.5	1.2
357 PRESB CH US...	2	397	493*	2.7	6.6
413 S-D ADVENTISTS	1	32	40*	0.2	0.5
419 SO BAPT CONV..	13	2,990	3,712*	20.4	49.4
449 UN METHODIST..	8	1,615	1,780	9.8	23.7
CUMBERLAND	17	1,687	1,958*	31.7	100.0
357 PRESB CH US...	3	301	373*	6.0	19.1
419 SO BAPT CONV..	7	755	936*	15.1	47.8
449 UN METHODIST..	7	631	649	10.5	33.1
DICKENSON	15	1,311	1,603*	10.0	100.0
081 CATHOLIC......	1	0	26	0.2	1.6
097 CR C AND C CR.	2	80	100*	0.6	6.2
127 CH GOD (CLEVE)	1	24	30*	0.2	1.9
157 CH OF BRETHREN	1	51	63*	0.4	3.9
357 PRESB CH US...	1	124	154*	1.0	9.6
419 SO BAPT CONV..	4	651	810*	5.0	50.5
449 UN METHODIST..	5	381	420	2.6	26.2
DINWIDDIE-COL HT-PET #	77	21,151	27,905*	36.6	100.0
019 AMER BAPT CONV	2	713	872*	1.1	3.1
029 AMER LUTH CH..	1	213	349	0.5	1.3
081 CATHOLIC......	2	0	2,233	2.9	8.0
093 CR CH (DISC)..	3	487	595*	0.8	2.1
127 CH GOD (CLEVE)	2	65	79*	0.1	0.3
165 CH OF NAZARENE	1	53	83	0.1	0.3
193 EPISCOPAL.....	10	1,729	2,530	3.3	9.1
281 LUTH CH AMER..	1	204	337	0.4	1.2
349 PENT HOLINESS.	1	60	73*	0.1	0.3
353 PLY BRETHREN..	1	30	40	0.1	0.1
357 PRESB CH US...	9	2,111	2,581*	3.4	9.2
403 SALVATION ARMY	1	59	233	0.3	0.8
413 S-D ADVENTISTS	3	402	491*	0.6	1.8
419 SO BAPT CONV..	16	6,442	7,876*	10.3	28.2
449 UN METHODIST..	24	8,583	9,533	12.5	34.2
ESSEX	15	2,616	3,429*	48.3	100.0
081 CATHOLIC......	1	0	187	2.6	5.5
093 CR CH (DISC)..	1	147	181*	2.5	5.3
127 CH GOD (CLEVE)	1	23	28*	0.4	0.8
193 EPISCOPAL.....	3	320	431	6.1	12.6
413 S-D ADVENTISTS	1	107	132*	1.9	3.8
419 SO BAPT CONV..	7	1,752	2,156*	30.4	62.9
449 UN METHODIST..	1	267	314	4.4	9.2
FAIRFAX-FAIRFX-FL CH #	204	90,643	206,042*	42.2	100.0
029 AMER LUTH CH..	6	3,179	4,878	1.0	2.4
059 BAPT MISS ASSN	1	51	64*	-	-
081 CATHOLIC......	18	0	83,845	17.2	40.7
093 CR CH (DISC)..	5	1,672	2,099*	0.4	1.0
097 CR C AND C CR.	4	270	339*	0.1	0.2
121 CH GOD (ABR)..	1	29	36*	-	-
123 CH GOD (ANDER)	2	86	230	-	0.1
127 CH GOD (CLEVE)	4	244	306*	0.1	0.1
157 CH OF BRETHREN	2	438	550*	0.1	0.3
165 CH OF NAZARENE	3	602	1,351	0.3	0.7
193 EPISCOPAL.....	18	11,815	19,695	4.0	9.6
226 FRIENDS-USA...	1	120	151*	-	0.1
281 LUTH CH AMER..	8	3,554	5,159	1.1	2.5
283 LUTH--MO SYNOD	5	2,321	3,257	0.7	1.6
335 ORTH PRESB CH.	1	85	147	-	0.1
349 PENT HOLINESS.	1	36	45*	-	-
353 PLY BRETHREN..	1	60	120	-	0.1
357 PRESB CH US...	7	4,180	5,248*	1.1	2.5
381 REF PRES-EVAN.	2	260	346	0.1	0.2
403 SALVATION ARMY	1	72	275	0.1	0.1
413 S-D ADVENTISTS	2	353	443*	0.1	0.2
419 SO BAPT CONV..	36	21,684	27,226*	5.6	13.2
435 UNITARIAN-UNIV	4	820	1,365	0.3	0.7
443 UN C OF CHRIST	2	1,026	1,288*	0.3	0.6
449 UN METHODIST..	43	29,568	37,313	7.6	18.1
453 UN PRES CH USA	25	7,961	9,996*	2.0	4.9
469 WISC EVAN LUTH	1	157	270	0.1	0.1
FAUQUIER	60	8,582	11,599*	44.0	100.0
081 CATHOLIC......	1	0	843	3.2	7.3
157 CH OF BRETHREN	1	105	130*	0.5	1.1
165 CH OF NAZARENE	1	46	109	0.4	0.9
193 EPISCOPAL.....	9	1,438	1,995	7.6	17.2
281 LUTH CH AMER..	1	117	167	0.6	1.4
353 PLY BRETHREN..	1	30	60	0.2	0.5
357 PRESB CH US...	4	364	450*	1.7	3.9
413 S-D ADVENTISTS	1	20	25*	0.1	0.2
419 SO BAPT CONV..	16	3,618	4,475*	17.0	38.6
449 UN METHODIST..	21	2,662	3,120	11.8	26.9
453 UN PRES CH USA	4	182	225*	0.9	1.9
FLOYD	38	3,663	4,245*	43.4	100.0
093 CR CH (DISC)..	2	114	136*	1.4	3.2
127 CH GOD (CLEVE)	1	48	57*	0.6	1.3
157 CH OF BRETHREN	10	1,420	1,695*	17.3	39.9
165 CH OF NAZARENE	1	56	98	1.0	2.3
281 LUTH CH AMER..	2	76	81	0.8	1.9
349 PENT HOLINESS.	2	99	118*	1.2	2.8
357 PRESB CH US...	4	324	387*	4.0	9.1
419 SO BAPT CONV..	5	652	778*	8.0	18.3
449 UN METHODIST..	11	874	895	9.2	21.1
FLUVANNA	26	2,736	3,504*	46.0	100.0
081 CATHOLIC......	1	0	229	3.0	6.5
093 CR CH (DISC)..	2	92	114*	1.5	3.3
193 EPISCOPAL.....	2	86	124	1.6	3.5
357 PRESB CH US...	1	60	74*	1.0	2.1
419 SO BAPT CONV..	12	1,684	2,085*	27.4	59.5
435 UNITARIAN-UNIV	1	13	20	0.3	0.6
449 UN METHODIST..	7	801	858	11.3	24.5
FRANKLIN	76	11,159	13,440*	50.0	100.0
019 AMER BAPT CONV	1	69	84*	0.3	0.6
075 BRETHREN IN CR	1	38	46*	0.2	0.3
093 CR CH (DISC)..	7	971	1,183*	4.4	8.8
097 CR C AND C CR.	2	200	244*	0.9	1.8
123 CH GOD (ANDER)	1	50	180	0.7	1.3
127 CH GOD (CLEVE)	3	200	244*	0.9	1.8
157 CH OF BRETHREN	13	2,332	2,840*	10.6	21.1
193 EPISCOPAL.....	2	131	198	0.7	1.5
349 PENT HOLINESS.	1	47	57*	0.2	0.4
353 PLY BRETHREN..	1	20	30	0.1	0.2
357 PRESB CH US...	2	225	274*	1.0	2.0
419 SO BAPT CONV..	19	2,790	3,398*	12.7	25.3
443 UN C OF CHRIST	3	1,110	1,352*	5.0	10.1
449 UN METHODIST..	20	2,976	3,310	12.3	24.6

*Total adherents estimated from known number of communicant, confirmed, full members. —Represents a percent less than 0.1. Percentages may not total due to rounding.

#See Introduction for explanation of how church data was collected for Virginia's independent cities.

Table 3. Churches and Church Membership by State, County and Denomination: 1971

County and Denomination	Number of churches	Communicant, confirmed, full members	Total adherents: Number	Total adherents: Percent of total population	Total adherents: Percent of total adherents
FREDERICK-WINCHESTER #	85	15,754	20,081*	46.1	100.0
019 AMER BAPT CONV	1	185	226*	0.5	1.1
081 CATHOLIC......	1	0	1,420	3.3	7.1
093 CR CH (DISC)..	4	324	396*	0.9	2.0
097 CR C AND C CR.	3	740	905*	2.1	4.5
127 CH GOD (CLEVE)	1	57	70*	0.2	0.3
157 CH OF BRETHREN	3	498	609*	1.4	3.0
165 CH OF NAZARENE	1	79	200	0.5	1.0
193 EPISCOPAL.....	1	756	1,066	2.4	5.3
226 FRIENDS-USA...	2	57	70*	0.2	0.3
281 LUTH CH AMER..	7	1,387	1,841	4.2	9.2
285 MENNONITE CH..	1	66	81*	0.2	0.4
357 PRESB CH US...	11	2,154	2,634*	6.1	13.1
403 SALVATION ARMY	1	45	244	0.6	1.2
413 S-D ADVENTISTS	1	153	187*	0.4	0.9
419 SO BAPT CONV..	3	1,157	1,415*	3.3	7.0
435 UNITARIAN-UNIV	1	24	24	0.1	0.1
443 UN C OF CHRIST	2	285	348*	0.8	1.7
449 UN METHODIST..	41	7,787	8,345	19.2	41.6
GILES	61	6,788	8,131*	48.6	100.0
081 CATHOLIC......	1	0	185	1.1	2.3
093 CR CH (DISC)..	11	1,093	1,330*	7.9	16.4
097 CR C AND C CR.	2	226	275*	1.6	3.4
123 CH GOD (ANDER)	2	125	376	2.2	4.6
127 CH GOD (CLEVE)	2	77	94*	0.6	1.2
157 CH OF BRETHREN	1	68	83*	0.5	1.0
193 EPISCOPAL.....	1	103	103	0.6	1.3
281 LUTH CH AMER..	3	104	137	0.8	1.7
349 PENT HOLINESS.	1	113	138*	0.8	1.7
357 PRESB CH US...	3	295	359*	2.1	4.4
413 S-D ADVENTISTS	1	27	33*	0.2	0.4
419 SO BAPT CONV..	7	1,070	1,302*	7.8	16.0
449 UN METHODIST..	26	3,487	3,716	22.2	45.7
GLOUCESTER	25	5,864	7,367*	52.4	100.0
081 CATHOLIC......	1	0	248	1.8	3.4
123 CH GOD (ANDER)	1	25	65	0.5	0.9
127 CH GOD (CLEVE)	1	75	91*	0.6	1.2
193 EPISCOPAL.....	2	558	886	6.3	12.0
349 PENT HOLINESS.	1	22	27*	0.2	0.4
357 PRESB CH US...	3	421	510*	3.6	6.9
419 SO BAPT CONV..	8	2,829	3,427*	24.4	46.5
449 UN METHODIST..	8	1,934	2,113	15.0	28.7
GOOCHLAND	18	2,916	3,583*	35.6	100.0
093 CR CH (DISC)..	3	307	381*	3.8	10.6
193 EPISCOPAL.....	1	85	158	1.6	4.4
349 PENT HOLINESS.	1	32	40*	0.4	1.1
357 PRESB CH US...	2	99	123*	1.2	3.4
419 SO BAPT CONV..	8	1,839	2,281*	22.7	63.7
449 UN METHODIST..	3	554	600	6.0	16.7
GRAYSON	71	8,659	9,734*	63.0	100.0
093 CR CH (DISC)..	1	315	373*	2.4	3.8
097 CR C AND C CR.	1	28	33*	0.2	0.3
281 LUTH CH AMER..	1	35	45	0.3	0.5
349 PENT HOLINESS.	2	108	128*	0.8	1.3
419 SO BAPT CONV..	32	5,080	6,010*	38.9	61.7
449 UN METHODIST..	34	3,093	3,145	20.4	32.3
GREENE	16	1,773	2,081*	39.7	100.0
157 CH OF BRETHREN	1	135	170*	3.2	8.2
193 EPISCOPAL.....	1	92	98	1.9	4.7
285 MENNONITE CH..	1	35	44*	0.8	2.1
413 S-D ADVENTISTS	2	60	75*	1.4	3.6
419 SO BAPT CONV..	4	774	973*	18.5	46.8
443 UN C OF CHRIST	1	68	85*	1.6	4.1
449 UN METHODIST..	6	609	636	12.1	30.6
GREENSVILLE-EMPORIA #	25	4,610	5,581*	37.4	100.0
081 CATHOLIC......	1	0	126	0.8	2.3
093 CR CH (DISC)..	1	25	31*	0.2	0.6
123 CH GOD (ANDER)	1	60	180	1.2	3.2
193 EPISCOPAL.....	3	306	405	2.7	7.3
283 LUTH--MO SYNOD	1	111	143	1.0	2.6
357 PRESB CH US...	2	284	350*	2.3	6.3
419 SO BAPT CONV..	7	1,622	1,997*	13.4	35.8
449 UN METHODIST..	9	2,202	2,349	15.8	42.1
HALIFAX-SOUTH BOSTON #	76	16,940	20,415*	55.2	100.0
081 CATHOLIC......	0	0	160	0.4	0.8
127 CH GOD (CLEVE)	1	156	191*	0.5	0.9
193 EPISCOPAL.....	5	471	583	1.6	2.9
285 MENNONITE CH..	1	40	49*	0.1	0.2
349 PENT HOLINESS.	1	30	37*	0.1	0.2
357 PRESB CH US...	11	1,114	1,364*	3.7	6.7
413 S-D ADVENTISTS	2	51	62*	0.2	0.3
419 SO BAPT CONV..	33	10,565	12,935*	35.0	63.4
443 UN C OF CHRIST	5	1,152	1,410*	3.8	6.9
449 UN METHODIST..	16	3,311	3,563	9.6	17.5
453 UN PRES CH USA	1	50	61*	0.2	0.3
HAMPTON CITY #	55	25,514	34,813*	28.8	100.0
059 BAPT MISS ASSN	2	515	647*	0.5	1.9
081 CATHOLIC......	3	0	2,187#	1.8	6.3
093 CR CH (DISC)..	2	603	757*	0.6	2.2
097 CR C AND C CR.	2	718	902*	0.7	2.6
127 CH GOD (CLEVE)	1	45	57*	-	0.2
165 CH OF NAZARENE	1	169	359	0.3	1.0
193 EPISCOPAL.....	4	1,492	2,717	2.2	7.8
281 LUTH CH AMER..	2	478	725	0.6	2.1
283 LUTH--MO SYNOD	1	285	401	0.3	1.2
349 PENT HOLINESS.	1	239	300*	0.2	0.9
357 PRESB CH US...	6	2,200	2,763*	2.3	7.9
381 REF PRES-EVAN.	1	75	96	0.1	0.3
403 SALVATION ARMY	1	57	203	0.2	0.6
413 S-D ADVENTISTS	1	225	283*	0.2	0.8
419 SO BAPT CONV..	12	10,360	13,013*	10.8	37.4
443 UN C OF CHRIST	2	670	842*	0.7	2.4
449 UN METHODIST..	13	7,383	8,561	7.1	24.6
HANOVER	58	13,675	16,784*	44.8	100.0
081 CATHOLIC......	1	0	302	0.8	1.8
093 CR CH (DISC)..	6	761	932*	2.5	5.6
097 CR C AND C CR.	6	1,065	1,304*	3.5	7.8
123 CH GOD (ANDER)	1	11	36	0.1	0.2
127 CH GOD (CLEVE)	1	138	169*	0.5	1.0
193 EPISCOPAL.....	7	942	1,403	3.7	8.4
226 FRIENDS-USA...	1	75	92*	0.2	0.5
281 LUTH CH AMER..	1	72	103	0.3	0.6
283 LUTH--MO SYNOD	1	61	92	0.2	0.5
349 PENT HOLINESS.	2	45	55*	0.1	0.3
357 PRESB CH US...	4	782	958*	2.6	5.7
419 SO BAPT CONV..	13	5,816	7,122*	19.0	42.4
449 UN METHODIST..	14	3,907	4,216	11.2	25.1
HENRICO-RICHMOND CTY #	252	133,021	184,559*	45.7	100.0
019 AMER BAPT CONV	15	2,673	3,218*	0.8	1.7
081 CATHOLIC......	13	0	22,040	5.5	11.9
093 CR CH (DISC)..	10	3,068	3,694*	0.9	2.0
097 CR C AND C CR.	10	1,518	1,828*	0.5	1.0
123 CH GOD (ANDER)	2	112	271	0.1	0.1
127 CH GOD (CLEVE)	3	396	477*	0.1	0.3
157 CH OF BRETHREN	1	116	140*	-	0.1
165 CH OF NAZARENE	4	461	1,322	0.3	0.7
193 EPISCOPAL.....	26	15,218	22,165	5.5	12.0
226 FRIENDS-USA...	1	56	67*	-	-
281 LUTH CH AMER..	5	2,285	2,988	0.7	1.6
283 LUTH--MO SYNOD	4	1,225	1,705	0.4	0.9
285 MENNONITE CH..	1	49	59*	-	-
349 PENT HOLINESS.	5	779	938*	0.2	0.5
357 PRESB CH US...	28	14,193	17,087*	4.2	9.3
381 REF PRES-EVAN.	1	37	55	-	-
413 S-D ADVENTISTS	3	1,091	1,313*	0.3	0.7
419 SO BAPT CONV..	65	52,540	63,264*	15.7	34.3
435 UNITARIAN-UNIV	1	476	662	0.2	0.4
443 UN C OF CHRIST	2	921	1,109*	0.3	0.6
449 UN METHODIST..	52	35,798	40,157	9.9	21.8
HENRY-MARTINSVILLE #	101	22,428	27,921*	39.6	100.0
081 CATHOLIC......	1	0	466	0.7	1.7
093 CR CH (DISC)..	19	2,373	2,967*	4.2	10.6
097 CR C AND C CR.	9	1,783	2,229*	3.2	8.0
123 CH GOD (ANDER)	1	58	148	0.2	0.5
127 CH GOD (CLEVE)	3	295	369*	0.5	1.3
157 CH OF BRETHREN	4	652	815*	1.2	2.9
165 CH OF NAZARENE	1	11	45	0.1	0.2
193 EPISCOPAL.....	2	483	634	0.9	2.3
226 FRIENDS-USA...	1	102	128*	0.2	0.5
281 LUTH CH AMER..	1	147	192	0.3	0.7
349 PENT HOLINESS.	8	555	694*	1.0	2.5
357 PRESB CH US...	3	1,027	1,284*	1.8	4.6
403 SALVATION ARMY	1	3	29	-	0.1
413 S-D ADVENTISTS	2	39	49*	0.1	0.2
419 SO BAPT CONV..	27	11,020	13,778*	19.5	49.3
449 UN METHODIST..	15	3,694	3,861	5.5	13.8
453 UN PRES CH USA	3	186	233*	0.3	0.8
HIGHLAND	20	1,476	1,661*	65.7	100.0
157 CH OF BRETHREN	2	50	58*	2.3	3.5
357 PRESB CH US...	5	319	369*	14.6	22.2
413 S-D ADVENTISTS	1	28	32*	1.3	1.9
449 UN METHODIST..	12	1,079	1,202	47.5	72.4
ISLE OF WIGHT	28	6,375	7,706*	42.1	100.0
097 CR C AND C CR.	1	75	93*	0.5	1.2
193 EPISCOPAL.....	1	206	208	1.1	2.7
226 FRIENDS-USA...	1	12	15*	0.1	0.2
353 PLY BRETHREN..	1	220	300	1.6	3.9
357 PRESB CH US...	2	182	227*	1.2	2.9
419 SO BAPT CONV..	8	3,207	3,994*	21.8	51.8
443 UN C OF CHRIST	6	906	1,128*	6.2	14.6
449 UN METHODIST..	8	1,567	1,741	9.5	22.6
JAMES CITY-WILLIAMS #	22	6,926	10,926*	40.6	100.0
081 CATHOLIC......	1	0	2,293	8.5	21.0
093 CR CH (DISC)..	1	219	259*	1.0	2.4
097 CR C AND C CR.	1	91	108*	0.4	1.0
165 CH OF NAZARENE	1	63	143	0.5	1.3
193 EPISCOPAL.....	3	1,058	1,574	5.8	14.4
281 LUTH CH AMER..	2	582	845	3.1	7.7
349 PENT HOLINESS.	1	30	36*	0.1	0.3
357 PRESB CH US...	3	800	948*	3.5	8.7
419 SO BAPT CONV..	5	2,146	2,543*	9.4	23.3

*Total adherents estimated from known number of communicant, confirmed, full members.

—Represents a percent less than 0.1.

Percentages may not total due to rounding.

#See Introduction for explanation of how church data was collected for Virginia's independent cities.

#The corrected Catholic population of Hampton City is 5,187

Table 3. Churches and Church Membership by State, County and Denomination: 1971

County and Denomination	Number of churches	Communicant, confirmed, full members	Total adherents: Number	Total adherents: Percent of total population	Total adherents: Percent of total adherents
435 UNITARIAN-UNIV	1	20	20	0.1	0.2
449 UN METHODIST..	3	1,917	2,157	8.0	19.7
KING AND QUEEN	15	2,323	2,737*	49.8	100.0
093 CR CH (DISC)..	1	138	169*	3.1	6.2
226 FRIENDS-USA...	1	36	44*	0.8	1.6
419 SO BAPT CONV..	8	1,540	1,883*	34.3	68.8
449 UN METHODIST..	5	609	641	11.7	23.4
KING GEORGE	16	3,032	4,065*	50.6	100.0
081 CATHOLIC......	1	0	217	2.7	5.3
193 EPISCOPAL.....	3	197	391	4.9	9.6
283 LUTH--MO SYNOD	1	35	47	0.6	1.2
419 SO BAPT CONV..	8	2,356	2,932*	36.5	72.1
449 UN METHODIST..	3	444	478	5.9	11.8
KING WILLIAM	21	3,373	4,670*	62.3	100.0
081 CATHOLIC......	1	0	460	6.1	9.9
093 CR CH (DISC)..	2	246	306*	4.1	6.6
097 CR C AND C CR.	1	60	75*	1.0	1.6
193 EPISCOPAL.....	3	219	391	5.2	8.4
357 PRESB CH US...	2	150	187*	2.5	4.0
419 SO BAPT CONV..	9	1,956	2,433*	32.5	52.1
449 UN METHODIST..	3	742	818	10.9	17.5
LANCASTER	23	4,175	5,266*	57.7	100.0
081 CATHOLIC......	1	0	253	2.8	4.8
193 EPISCOPAL.....	3	380	682	7.5	13.0
357 PRESB CH US...	2	281	328*	3.6	6.2
413 S-D ADVENTISTS	1	59	69*	0.8	1.3
419 SO BAPT CONV..	9	2,127	2,484*	27.2	47.2
449 UN METHODIST..	7	1,328	1,450	15.9	27.5
LEE	98	10,859	12,424*	61.1	100.0
081 CATHOLIC......	1	0	30	0.1	0.2
093 CR CH (DISC)..	8	466	550*	2.7	4.4
097 CR C AND C CR.	8	222	262*	1.3	2.1
127 CH GOD (CLEVE)	2	74	87*	0.4	0.7
157 CH OF BRETHREN	1	52	61*	0.3	0.5
165 CH OF NAZARENE	1	6	6	-	-
201 EVAN COV CH AM	2	97	114*	0.6	0.9
357 PRESB CH US...	1	75	88*	0.4	0.7
413 S-D ADVENTISTS	1	103	121*	0.6	1.0
419 SO BAPT CONV..	40	6,288	7,417*	36.5	59.7
449 UN METHODIST..	33	3,476	3,688	18.1	29.7
LOUDOUN	71	9,686	17,479*	47.0	100.0
029 AMER LUTH CH..	1	15	27	0.1	0.2
081 CATHOLIC......	4	0	4,323	11.6	24.7
097 CR C AND C CR.	1	44	57*	0.2	0.3
165 CH OF NAZARENE	2	126	282	0.8	1.6
193 EPISCOPAL.....	7	721	1,386	3.7	7.9
226 FRIENDS-USA...	1	145	188*	0.5	1.1
281 LUTH CH AMER..	3	698	1,100	3.0	6.3
335 ORTH PRESB CH.	1	19	34	0.1	0.2
357 PRESB CH US...	6	757	979*	2.6	5.6
413 S-D ADVENTISTS	1	26	34*	0.1	0.2
419 SO BAPT CONV..	13	2,700	3,492*	9.4	20.0
443 UN C OF CHRIST	1	64	83*	0.2	0.5
449 UN METHODIST..	24	3,981	4,990	13.4	28.5
453 UN PRES CH USA	6	390	504*	1.4	2.9
LOUISA	41	5,191	6,129*	43.8	100.0
093 CR CH (DISC)..	9	678	828*	5.9	13.5
097 CR C AND C CR.	2	300	366*	2.6	6.0
127 CH GOD (CLEVE)	1	25	31*	0.2	0.5
157 CH OF BRETHREN	1	25	31*	0.2	0.5
193 EPISCOPAL.....	1	128	172	1.2	2.8
357 PRESB CH US...	3	116	142*	1.0	2.3
419 SO BAPT CONV..	14	2,514	3,069*	21.9	50.1
435 UNITARIAN-UNIV	1	15	15	0.1	0.2
449 UN METHODIST..	9	1,390	1,475	10.5	24.1
LUNENBERG	38	6,307	7,504*	64.2	100.0
093 CR CH (DISC)..	8	1,399	1,711*	14.6	22.8
097 CR C AND C CR.	1	125	153*	1.3	2.0
127 CH GOD (CLEVE)	2	74	91*	0.8	1.2
165 CH OF NAZARENE	1	127	314	2.7	4.2
193 EPISCOPAL.....	3	73	88	0.8	1.2
283 LUTH--MO SYNOD	1	47	81	0.7	1.1
353 PLY BRETHREN..	1	20	30	0.3	0.4
357 PRESB CH US...	3	161	197*	1.7	2.6
419 SO BAPT CONV..	7	1,722	2,106*	18.0	28.1
449 UN METHODIST..	11	2,559	2,733	23.4	36.4
MADISON	26	3,363	3,820*	44.2	100.0
093 CR CH (DISC)..	2	126	153*	1.8	4.0
157 CH OF BRETHREN	1	39	47*	0.5	1.2
193 EPISCOPAL.....	1	46	56	0.6	1.5
221 FREE METH C NA	1	24	33	0.4	0.9
281 LUTH CH AMER..	2	281	380	4.4	9.9
357 PRESB CH US...	1	58	71*	0.8	1.9
419 SO BAPT CONV..	8	1,304	1,586*	18.4	41.5
449 UN METHODIST..	10	1,485	1,494	17.3	39.1
MATHEWS	21	3,500	4,078*	56.9	100.0
093 CR CH (DISC)..	2	94	109*	1.5	2.7
193 EPISCOPAL.....	1	111	277	3.9	6.8
226 FRIENDS-USA...	2	95	110*	1.5	2.7
419 SO BAPT CONV..	5	1,130	1,308*	18.2	32.1
449 UN METHODIST..	11	2,070	2,274	31.7	55.8
MECKLENBURG	69	12,567	14,688*	49.9	100.0
081 CATHOLIC......	1	0	121	0.4	0.8
093 CR CH (DISC)..	3	99	120*	0.4	0.8
097 CR C AND C CR.	1	35	43*	0.1	0.3
127 CH GOD (CLEVE)	2	93	113*	0.4	0.8
193 EPISCOPAL.....	8	437	586	2.0	4.0
357 PRESB CH US...	4	232	282*	1.0	1.9
419 SO BAPT CONV..	23	6,557	7,966*	27.1	54.2
443 UN C OF CHRIST	2	291	354*	1.2	2.4
449 UN METHODIST..	22	4,660	4,905	16.7	33.4
453 UN PRES CH USA	3	163	198*	0.7	1.3
MIDDLESEX	17	3,144	3,623*	57.6	100.0
093 CR CH (DISC)..	1	178	208*	3.3	5.7
165 CH OF NAZARENE	1	28	57	0.9	1.6
193 EPISCOPAL.....	1	189	240	3.8	6.6
349 PENT HOLINESS.	1	22	26*	0.4	0.7
419 SO BAPT CONV..	6	1,529	1,790*	28.4	49.4
449 UN METHODIST..	7	1,198	1,302	20.7	35.9
MONTGOMERY-RADFORD #	89	15,831	20,335*	34.6	100.0
081 CATHOLIC......	2	0	1,191	2.0	5.9
093 CR CH (DISC)..	6	875	1,038*	1.8	5.1
097 CR C AND C CR.	5	611	725*	1.2	3.6
123 CH GOD (ANDER)	4	246	770	1.3	3.8
127 CH GOD (CLEVE)	5	617	732*	1.2	3.6
157 CH OF BRETHREN	1	289	343*	0.6	1.7
193 EPISCOPAL.....	2	363	561	1.0	2.8
226 FRIENDS-USA...	1	16	19*	-	0.1
281 LUTH CH AMER..	5	706	983	1.7	4.8
349 PENT HOLINESS.	11	645	765*	1.3	3.8
357 PRESB CH US...	6	1,805	2,142*	3.6	10.5
413 S-D ADVENTISTS	1	63	75*	0.1	0.4
419 SO BAPT CONV..	8	3,570	4,236*	7.2	20.8
435 UNITARIAN-UNIV	1	40	90	0.2	0.4
449 UN METHODIST..	31	5,985	6,665	11.3	32.8
NANSEMOND-SUFFOLK #	50	14,245	17,765*	39.5	100.0
081 CATHOLIC......	1	0	338	0.8	1.9
093 CR CH (DISC)..	1	11	14*	-	0.1
127 CH GOD (CLEVE)	1	74	91*	0.2	0.5
165 CH OF NAZARENE	1	61	154	0.3	0.9
193 EPISCOPAL.....	4	509	678	1.5	3.8
226 FRIENDS-USA...	1	78	96*	0.2	0.5
349 PENT HOLINESS.	1	62	77*	0.2	0.4
357 PRESB CH US...	1	107	132*	0.3	0.7
381 REF PRES-EVAN.	1	68	78	0.2	0.4
403 SALVATION ARMY	1	45	291	0.6	1.6
419 SO BAPT CONV..	10	5,239	6,467*	14.4	36.4
443 UN C OF CHRIST	16	4,712	5,817*	12.9	32.7
449 UN METHODIST..	11	3,279	3,532	7.8	19.9
NELSON	43	7,229	8,506*	72.7	100.0
093 CR CH (DISC)..	5	223	270*	2.3	3.2
127 CH GOD (CLEVE)	1	8	10*	0.1	0.1
157 CH OF BRETHREN	1	93	112*	1.0	1.3
193 EPISCOPAL.....	2	138	191	1.6	2.2
285 MENNONITE CH..	1	25	30*	0.3	0.4
349 PENT HOLINESS.	2	30	36*	0.3	0.4
357 PRESB CH US...	2	175	212*	1.8	2.5
419 SO BAPT CONV..	19	4,604	5,567*	47.6	65.4
449 UN METHODIST..	10	1,933	2,078	17.8	24.4
NEW KENT	11	1,769	2,178*	41.1	100.0
193 EPISCOPAL.....	1	163	226	4.3	10.4
357 PRESB CH US...	1	171	213*	4.0	9.8
419 SO BAPT CONV..	6	962	1,200*	22.6	55.1
449 UN METHODIST..	3	473	539	10.2	24.7
NEWPORT NEWS CITY #	76	38,530	53,934*	39.0	100.0
059 BAPT MISS ASSN	1	25	31*	-	0.1
081 CATHOLIC......	3	0	6,287	4.5	11.7
093 CR CH (DISC)..	2	415	515*	0.4	1.0
097 CR C AND C CR.	3	2,065	2,561*	1.9	4.7
123 CH GOD (ANDER)	2	200	450	0.3	0.8
157 CH OF BRETHREN	1	364	451*	0.3	0.8
165 CH OF NAZARENE	1	93	142	0.1	0.3
193 EPISCOPAL.....	6	2,404	3,448	2.5	6.4
226 FRIENDS-USA...	2	183	227*	0.2	0.4
281 LUTH CH AMER..	2	940	1,262	0.9	2.3
283 LUTH--MO SYNOD	1	249	364	0.3	0.7
285 MENNONITE CH..	4	479	594*	0.4	1.1
349 PENT HOLINESS.	1	44	55*	-	0.1
357 PRESB CH US...	7	3,739	4,637*	3.4	8.6
403 SALVATION ARMY	1	54	238	0.2	0.4
413 S-D ADVENTISTS	1	33	41*	-	0.1
419 SO BAPT CONV..	18	17,498	21,700*	15.7	40.2
435 UNITARIAN-UNIV	1	44	74	0.1	0.1
443 UN C OF CHRIST	6	1,129	1,400*	1.0	2.6
449 UN METHODIST..	12	8,153	8,937	6.5	16.6
453 UN PRES CH USA	1	419	520*	0.4	1.0

*Total adherents estimated from known number of communicant, confirmed, full members.

—Represents a percent less than 0.1.

Percentages may not total due to rounding.

#See Introduction for explanation of how church data was collected for Virginia's independent cities.

Table 3. Churches and Church Membership by State, County and Denomination: 1971

County and Denomination	Number of churches	Communicant, confirmed, full members	Total adherents: Number	Percent of total population	Percent of total adherents
NORFOLK-CHESAP-PORTS #	263	109,158	155,573*	30.6	100.0
019 AMER BAPT CONV	10	628	767*	0.2	0.5
029 AMER LUTH CH..	1	119	215	-	0.1
081 CATHOLIC......	12	0	22,625	4.4	14.5
093 CR CH (DISC)..	18	2,081	2,542*	0.5	1.6
097 CR C AND C CR.	8	933	1,140*	0.2	0.7
123 CH GOD (ANDER)	2	207	467	0.1	0.3
127 CH GOD (CLEVE)	8	765	934*	0.2	0.6
165 CH OF NAZARENE	3	394	966	0.2	0.6
193 EPISCOPAL.....	16	6,893	10,197	2.0	6.6
226 FRIENDS-USA...	1	200	244*	-	0.2
281 LUTH CH AMER..	8	2,438	3,595	0.7	2.3
283 LUTH--MO SYNOD	5	1,385	1,978	0.4	1.3
285 MENNONITE CH..	2	58	71*	-	-
349 PENT HOLINESS.	5	599	732*	0.1	0.5
357 PRESB CH US...	26	10,044	12,269*	2.4	7.9
381 REF PRES-EVAN.	1	171	196	-	0.1
403 SALVATION ARMY	1	152	664	0.1	0.4
413 S-D ADVENTISTS	4	726	887*	0.2	0.6
419 SO BAPT CONV..	66	47,775	58,359*	11.5	37.5
435 UNITARIAN-UNIV	1	144	199	-	0.1
443 UN C OF CHRIST	15	2,949	3,602*	0.7	2.3
449 UN METHODIST..	44	30,027	32,325	6.4	20.8
453 UN PRES CH USA	5	440	537*	0.1	0.3
469 WISC EVAN LUTH	1	30	62	-	-
NORTHAMPTON	38	6,110	7,634*	52.9	100.0
081 CATHOLIC......	1	0	129	0.9	1.7
097 CR C AND C CR.	8	1,207	1,439*	10.0	18.8
123 CH GOD (ANDER)	1	30	79	0.5	1.0
193 EPISCOPAL.....	5	685	1,125	7.8	14.7
285 MENNONITE CH..	1	166	198*	1.4	2.6
349 PENT HOLINESS.	6	314	374*	2.6	4.9
357 PRESB CH US...	2	249	297*	2.1	3.9
419 SO BAPT CONV..	6	1,306	1,557*	10.8	20.4
449 UN METHODIST..	8	2,153	2,436	16.9	31.9
NORTHUMBERLAND	25	4,848	5,628*	60.9	100.0
123 CH GOD (ANDER)	1	75	175	1.9	3.1
193 EPISCOPAL.....	3	216	301	3.3	5.3
419 SO BAPT CONV..	9	2,356	2,764*	29.9	49.1
449 UN METHODIST..	12	2,201	2,388	25.8	42.4
NOTTOWAY	28	4,959	5,941*	41.7	100.0
081 CATHOLIC......	1	0	183	1.3	3.1
093 CR CH (DISC)..	2	233	281*	2.0	4.7
097 CR C AND C CR.	3	359	433*	3.0	7.3
127 CH GOD (CLEVE)	1	74	89*	0.6	1.5
165 CH OF NAZARENE	1	43	96	0.7	1.6
193 EPISCOPAL.....	2	144	190	1.3	3.2
357 PRESB CH US...	4	568	684*	4.8	11.5
413 S-D ADVENTISTS	1	36	43*	0.3	0.7
419 SO BAPT CONV..	3	1,524	1,837*	12.9	30.9
449 UN METHODIST..	9	1,920	2,035	14.3	34.3
453 UN PRES CH USA	1	58	70*	0.5	1.2
ORANGE	39	6,863	8,491*	61.6	100.0
081 CATHOLIC......	2	0	283	2.1	3.3
093 CR CH (DISC)..	3	149	182*	1.3	2.1
097 CR C AND C CR.	2	300	366*	2.7	4.3
127 CH GOD (CLEVE)	1	13	16*	0.1	0.2
165 CH OF NAZARENE	1	20	35	0.3	0.4
193 EPISCOPAL.....	2	399	531	3.9	6.3
349 PENT HOLINESS.	2	51	62*	0.4	0.7
357 PRESB CH US...	4	485	592*	4.3	7.0
413 S-D ADVENTISTS	1	31	38*	0.3	0.4
419 SO BAPT CONV..	13	3,848	4,695*	34.0	55.3
449 UN METHODIST..	8	1,567	1,691	12.3	19.9
PAGE	45	6,454	7,903*	47.7	100.0
019 AMER BAPT CONV	2	28	34*	0.2	0.4
081 CATHOLIC......	0	0	92	0.6	1.2
093 CR CH (DISC)..	3	609	739*	4.5	9.4
157 CH OF BRETHREN	5	859	1,043*	6.3	13.2
193 EPISCOPAL.....	3	160	344	2.1	4.4
281 LUTH CH AMER..	9	1,183	1,572	9.5	19.9
285 MENNONITE CH..	2	42	51*	0.3	0.6
349 PENT HOLINESS.	1	71	86*	0.5	1.1
413 S-D ADVENTISTS	3	255	310*	1.9	3.9
419 SO BAPT CONV..	4	1,025	1,244*	7.5	15.7
443 UN C OF CHRIST	3	432	524*	3.2	6.6
449 UN METHODIST..	10	1,790	1,864	11.2	23.6
PATRICK	44	3,848	4,501*	29.5	100.0
093 CR CH (DISC)..	5	150	182*	1.2	4.0
127 CH GOD (CLEVE)	2	67	81*	0.5	1.8
157 CH OF BRETHREN	2	198	240*	1.6	5.3
349 PENT HOLINESS.	6	305	370*	2.4	8.2
357 PRESB CH US...	6	293	356*	2.3	7.9
419 SO BAPT CONV..	11	1,673	2,032*	13.3	45.1
449 UN METHODIST..	12	1,162	1,240	8.1	27.5
PITTSYLVANIA-DANVILL #	174	38,568	46,485*	44.2	100.0
081 CATHOLIC......	2	0	829	0.8	1.8
093 CR CH (DISC)..	11	900	1,088*	1.0	2.3
097 CR C AND C CR.	10	1,070	1,294*	1.2	2.8
127 CH GOD (CLEVE)	4	503	608*	0.6	1.3
157 CH OF BRETHREN	3	342	414*	0.4	0.9
193 EPISCOPAL.....	6	809	1,037	1.0	2.2
226 FRIENDS-USA...	2	139	168*	0.2	0.4
281 LUTH CH AMER..	1	271	370	0.4	0.8
283 LUTH--MO SYNOD	1	116	173	0.2	0.4
349 PENT HOLINESS.	14	1,151	1,392*	1.3	3.0
353 PLY BRETHREN..	1	20	30	-	0.1
357 PRESB CH US...	10	2,106	2,546*	2.4	5.5
403 SALVATION ARMY	1	61	301	0.3	0.6
413 S-D ADVENTISTS	2	124	150*	0.1	0.3
419 SO BAPT CONV..	60	20,429	24,701*	23.5	53.1
449 UN METHODIST..	44	10,348	11,168	10.6	24.0
453 UN PRES CH USA	2	179	216*	0.2	0.5
POWHATAN	16	2,097	2,693*	35.0	100.0
081 CATHOLIC......	1	0	193	2.5	7.2
093 CR CH (DISC)..	1	32	38*	0.5	1.4
193 EPISCOPAL.....	2	143	210	2.7	7.8
285 MENNONITE CH..	1	34	41*	0.5	1.5
357 PRESB CH US...	2	167	200*	2.6	7.4
419 SO BAPT CONV..	6	1,407	1,685*	21.9	62.6
449 UN METHODIST..	3	314	326	4.2	12.1
PRINCE EDWARD	34	5,081	6,127*	42.6	100.0
081 CATHOLIC......	1	0	318	2.2	5.2
093 CR CH (DISC)..	2	287	336*	2.3	5.5
097 CR C AND C CR.	3	36	42*	0.3	0.7
127 CH GOD (CLEVE)	1	10	12*	0.1	0.2
193 EPISCOPAL.....	2	242	269	1.9	4.4
283 LUTH--MO SYNOD	2	104	150	1.0	2.4
357 PRESB CH US...	6	876	1,024*	7.1	16.7
413 S-D ADVENTISTS	1	20	23*	0.2	0.4
419 SO BAPT CONV..	9	2,140	2,503*	17.4	40.9
449 UN METHODIST..	7	1,366	1,450	10.1	23.7
PRINCE GEORGE-HOPEWE #	42	10,290	14,126*	26.9	100.0
081 CATHOLIC......	2	0	1,601	3.0	11.3
093 CR CH (DISC)..	1	314	383*	0.7	2.7
097 CR C AND C CR.	1	60	73*	0.1	0.5
127 CH GOD (CLEVE)	2	205	250*	0.5	1.8
157 CH OF BRETHREN	1	156	190*	0.4	1.3
165 CH OF NAZARENE	1	58	184	0.4	1.3
193 EPISCOPAL.....	2	286	462	0.9	3.3
283 LUTH--MO SYNOD	1	301	468	0.9	3.3
349 PENT HOLINESS.	1	128	156*	0.3	1.1
353 PLY BRETHREN..	1	20	30	0.1	0.2
357 PRESB CH US...	8	2,262	2,757*	5.2	19.5
413 S-D ADVENTISTS	1	54	66*	0.1	0.5
419 SO BAPT CONV..	6	2,922	3,562*	6.8	25.2
443 UN C OF CHRIST	3	159	194*	0.4	1.4
449 UN METHODIST..	10	3,252	3,612	6.9	25.6
453 UN PRES CH USA	1	113	138*	0.3	1.0
PRINCE WILLIAM	61	18,194	36,847*	33.2	100.0
029 AMER LUTH CH..	1	265	504	0.5	1.4
081 CATHOLIC......	4	0	10,004	9.0	27.2
093 CR CH (DISC)..	2	70	96*	0.1	0.3
097 CR C AND C CR.	2	143	196*	0.2	0.5
127 CH GOD (CLEVE)	3	303	415*	0.4	1.1
157 CH OF BRETHREN	3	639	874*	0.8	2.4
165 CH OF NAZARENE	2	135	483	0.4	1.3
193 EPISCOPAL.....	5	1,231	3,340	3.0	9.1
281 LUTH CH AMER..	2	815	1,303	1.2	3.5
283 LUTH--MO SYNOD	2	538	883	0.8	2.4
335 ORTH PRESB CH.	1	24	53	-	0.1
349 PENT HOLINESS.	1	30	41*	-	0.1
357 PRESB CH US...	3	653	893*	0.8	2.4
413 S-D ADVENTISTS	1	116	159*	0.1	0.4
419 SO BAPT CONV..	11	5,795	7,929*	7.1	21.5
449 UN METHODIST..	14	7,022	9,106	8.2	24.7
453 UN PRES CH USA	4	415	568*	0.5	1.5
PULASKI	73	10,607	13,074*	44.2	100.0
075 BRETHREN IN CR	1	20	24*	0.1	0.2
081 CATHOLIC......	1	0	103	0.3	0.8
093 CR CH (DISC)..	9	747	914*	3.1	7.0
097 CR C AND C CR.	4	227	278*	0.9	2.1
127 CH GOD (CLEVE)	5	776	950*	3.2	7.3
157 CH OF BRETHREN	1	209	256*	0.9	2.0
165 CH OF NAZARENE	1	60	81	0.3	0.6
193 EPISCOPAL.....	1	211	255	0.9	2.0
281 LUTH CH AMER..	1	215	260	0.9	2.0
349 PENT HOLINESS.	7	352	431*	1.5	3.3
357 PRESB CH US...	8	1,466	1,794*	6.1	13.7
403 SALVATION ARMY	2	111	692	2.3	5.3
413 S-D ADVENTISTS	1	66	81*	0.3	0.6
419 SO BAPT CONV..	6	1,820	2,227*	7.5	17.0
449 UN METHODIST..	25	4,327	4,728	16.0	36.2
RAPPAHANNOCK	15	1,983	2,435*	46.8	100.0
193 EPISCOPAL.....	1	120	197	3.8	8.1
353 PLY BRETHREN..	1	17	40	0.8	1.6
419 SO BAPT CONV..	8	1,266	1,543*	29.7	63.4
449 UN METHODIST..	5	580	655	12.6	26.9
RICHMOND	22	3,389	4,077*	69.8	100.0
093 CR CH (DISC)..	1	105	127*	2.2	3.1
097 CR C AND C CR.	2	85	103*	1.8	2.5

*Total adherents estimated from known number of communicant, confirmed, full members. —Represents a percent less than 0.1. Percentages may not total due to rounding.

#See Introduction for explanation of how church data was collected for Virginia's independent cities.

Table 3. Churches and Church Membership by State, County and Denomination: 1971

County and Denomination	Number of churches	Communicant, confirmed, full members	Total adherents: Number	Percent of total population	Percent of total adherents
127 CH GOD (CLEVE)	3	204	247*	4.2	6.1
193 EPISCOPAL.....	4	221	340	5.8	8.3
357 PRESB CH US...	1	118	143*	2.4	3.5
419 SO BAPT CONV..	7	1,983	2,404*	41.2	59.0
449 UN METHODIST..	4	673	713	12.2	17.5
ROANOKE-ROANOKE-SALM #	167	75,677	96,911*	53.4	100.0
055 AS REF PRES CH	1	126	151*	0.1	0.2
075 BRETHREN IN CR	1	84	101*	0.1	0.1
081 CATHOLIC......	5	0	5,411	3.0	5.6
093 CR CH (DISC)..	9	2,757	3,313*	1.8	3.4
097 CR C AND C CR.	8	1,658	1,992*	1.1	2.1
123 CH GOD (ANDER)	5	372	1,004	0.6	1.0
127 CH GOD (CLEVE)	5	415	499*	0.3	0.5
157 CH OF BRETHREN	13	4,028	4,840*	2.7	5.0
165 CH OF NAZARENE	5	802	1,604	0.9	1.7
193 EPISCOPAL.....	5	2,905	4,198	2.3	4.3
281 LUTH CH AMER..	9	3,075	3,835	2.1	4.0
349 PENT HOLINESS.	3	470	565*	0.3	0.6
353 PLY BRETHREN..	1	60	107	0.1	0.1
357 PRESB CH US...	14	7,106	8,539*	4.7	8.8
413 S-D ADVENTISTS	2	380	457*	0.3	0.5
419 SO BAPT CONV..	47	33,604	40,381*	22.3	41.7
435 UNITARIAN-UNIV	1	160	242	0.1	0.2
449 UN METHODIST..	32	17,549	19,521	10.8	20.1
453 UN PRES CH USA	1	126	151*	0.1	0.2
ROCKBRIDGE-BN VS-LEX #	71	21,014	23,901*	78.0	100.0
055 AS REF PRES CH	5	1,149	1,367*	4.5	5.7
081 CATHOLIC......	1	0	401	1.3	1.7
127 CH GOD (CLEVE)	1	16	19*	0.1	0.1
157 CH OF BRETHREN	2	367	437*	1.4	1.8
193 EPISCOPAL.....	3	559	860	2.8	3.6
281 LUTH CH AMER..	3	329	479	1.6	2.0
349 PENT HOLINESS.	6	483	574*	1.9	2.4
357 PRESB CH US...	18	3,667	4,362*	14.2	18.3
381 REF PRES-EVAN.	1	38	38	0.1	0.2
413 S-D ADVENTISTS	1	103	123*	0.4	0.5
419 SO BAPT CONV..	9	3,197	3,802*	12.4	15.9
449 UN METHODIST..	21	11,106	11,439	37.3	47.9
ROCKINGHAM-HARRISON #	145	25,629	31,138*	49.8	100.0
029 AMER LUTH CH..	1	173	209	0.3	0.7
081 CATHOLIC......	2	0	536	0.9	1.7
093 CR CH (DISC)..	1	105	126*	0.2	0.4
097 CR C AND C CR.	3	180	216*	0.3	0.7
127 CH GOD (CLEVE)	4	553	664*	1.1	2.1
157 CH OF BRETHREN	21	5,830	7,003*	11.2	22.5
165 CH OF NAZARENE	3	231	625	1.0	2.0
193 EPISCOPAL.....	2	525	794	1.3	2.5
281 LUTH CH AMER..	6	1,158	1,506	2.4	4.8
285 MENNONITE CH..	30	2,926	3,515*	5.6	11.3
349 PENT HOLINESS.	1	60	72*	0.1	0.2
357 PRESB CH US...	7	2,175	2,613*	4.2	8.4
403 SALVATION ARMY	1	72	357	0.6	1.1
413 S-D ADVENTISTS	2	94	113*	0.2	0.4
419 SO BAPT CONV..	7	1,257	1,510*	2.4	4.8
443 UN C OF CHRIST	16	1,713	2,058*	3.3	6.6
449 UN METHODIST..	38	8,577	9,221	14.8	29.6
RUSSELL	59	6,596	7,726*	31.5	100.0
081 CATHOLIC......	1	0	38	0.2	0.5
093 CR CH (DISC)..	2	162	198*	0.8	2.6
097 CR C AND C CR.	2	335	409*	1.7	5.3
127 CH GOD (CLEVE)	2	161	197*	0.8	2.5
357 PRESB CH US...	2	116	142*	0.6	1.8
419 SO BAPT CONV..	27	3,433	4,196*	17.1	54.3
449 UN METHODIST..	23	2,389	2,546	10.4	33.0
SCOTT	63	7,149	8,271*	33.9	100.0
055 AS REF PRES CH	1	117	141*	0.6	1.7
081 CATHOLIC......	2	0	67	0.3	0.8
093 CR CH (DISC)..	1	63	76*	0.3	0.9
097 CR C AND C CR.	5	1,015	1,223*	5.0	14.8
193 EPISCOPAL.....	1	348	513	2.1	6.2
285 MENNONITE CH..	2	224	270*	1.1	3.3
349 PENT HOLINESS.	1	31	37*	0.2	0.4
357 PRESB CH US...	2	117	141*	0.6	1.7
419 SO BAPT CONV..	15	2,272	2,737*	11.2	33.1
449 UN METHODIST..	33	2,962	3,066	12.6	37.1
SHENANDOAH	89	13,301	16,203*	70.9	100.0
029 AMER LUTH CH..	2	79	92	0.4	0.6
081 CATHOLIC......	1	0	166	0.7	1.0
093 CR CH (DISC)..	8	1,016	1,216*	5.3	7.5
121 CH GOD (ABR)..	2	68	81*	0.4	0.5
127 CH GOD (CLEVE)	1	35	42*	0.2	0.3
157 CH OF BRETHREN	7	1,460	1,748*	7.6	10.8
165 CH OF NAZARENE	1	22	50	0.2	0.3
193 EPISCOPAL.....	2	128	213	0.9	1.3
281 LUTH CH AMER..	25	4,609	6,012	26.3	37.1
285 MENNONITE CH..	1	33	40*	0.2	0.2
357 PRESB CH US...	2	519	621*	2.7	3.8
413 S-D ADVENTISTS	2	248	297*	1.3	1.8
419 SO BAPT CONV..	1	103	123*	0.5	0.8
443 UN C OF CHRIST	12	1,109	1,328*	5.8	8.2
449 UN METHODIST..	22	3,872	4,174	18.3	25.8
SMYTH	90	12,806	15,951*	50.9	100.0
081 CATHOLIC......	1	0	162	0.5	1.0
093 CR CH (DISC)..	3	276	331*	1.1	2.1
097 CR C AND C CR.	4	200	240*	0.8	1.5
123 CH GOD (ANDER)	7	476	1,197	3.8	7.5
127 CH GOD (CLEVE)	2	186	223*	0.7	1.4
157 CH OF BRETHREN	2	107	128*	0.4	0.8
165 CH OF NAZARENE	2	83	210	0.7	1.3
193 EPISCOPAL.....	2	122	156	0.5	1.0
281 LUTH CH AMER..	6	665	882	2.8	5.5
349 PENT HOLINESS.	2	48	58*	0.2	0.4
353 PLY BRETHREN..	1	40	50	0.2	0.3
357 PRESB CH US...	7	633	759*	2.4	4.8
413 S-D ADVENTISTS	1	48	58*	0.2	0.4
419 SO BAPT CONV..	22	6,110	7,325*	23.4	45.9
449 UN METHODIST..	28	3,812	4,172	13.3	26.2
SOUTHAMPTON-FRANKLIN #	42	8,707	10,678*	41.9	100.0
081 CATHOLIC......	1	0	180	0.7	1.7
123 CH GOD (ANDER)	1	26	61	0.2	0.6
193 EPISCOPAL.....	2	307	440	1.7	4.1
226 FRIENDS-USA...	2	184	227*	0.9	2.1
357 PRESB CH US...	1	154	190*	0.7	1.8
419 SO BAPT CONV..	18	5,518	6,821*	26.8	63.9
443 UN C OF CHRIST	3	348	430*	1.7	4.0
449 UN METHODIST..	14	2,170	2,329	9.1	21.8
SPOTSYLVANIA-FREDERI #	43	13,091	17,649*	57.2	100.0
081 CATHOLIC......	1	0	1,624	5.3	9.2
093 CR CH (DISC)..	3	510	614*	2.0	3.5
097 CR C AND C CR.	1	11	13*	-	0.1
127 CH GOD (CLEVE)	1	28	34*	0.1	0.2
165 CH OF NAZARENE	1	31	100	0.3	0.6
193 EPISCOPAL.....	3	1,051	1,647	5.3	9.3
281 LUTH CH AMER..	1	269	378	1.2	2.1
349 PENT HOLINESS.	1	14	17*	0.1	0.1
357 PRESB CH US...	1	583	702*	2.3	4.0
403 SALVATION ARMY	1	59	331	1.1	1.9
413 S-D ADVENTISTS	1	148	178*	0.6	1.0
419 SO BAPT CONV..	19	7,642	9,196*	29.8	52.1
435 UNITARIAN-UNIV	1	33	45	0.1	0.3
449 UN METHODIST..	8	2,712	2,770	9.0	15.7
STAFFORD	26	5,919	7,621*	31.0	100.0
081 CATHOLIC......	1	0	294	1.2	3.9
127 CH GOD (CLEVE)	1	53	67*	0.3	0.9
157 CH OF BRETHREN	1	56	70*	0.3	0.9
193 EPISCOPAL.....	1	293	345	1.4	4.5
349 PENT HOLINESS.	1	21	26*	0.1	0.3
357 PRESB CH US...	1	153	192*	0.8	2.5
419 SO BAPT CONV..	13	4,368	5,486*	22.3	72.0
449 UN METHODIST..	6	902	1,049	4.3	13.8
453 UN PRES CH USA	1	73	92*	0.4	1.2
SURRY	13	1,411	1,682*	28.6	100.0
081 CATHOLIC......	0	0	9	0.2	0.5
193 EPISCOPAL.....	1	23	28	0.5	1.7
419 SO BAPT CONV..	5	810	1,028*	17.5	61.1
443 UN C OF CHRIST	1	21	27*	0.5	1.6
449 UN METHODIST..	5	515	537	9.1	31.9
453 UN PRES CH USA	1	42	53*	0.9	3.2
SUSSEX	24	3,522	4,189*	36.5	100.0
081 CATHOLIC......	0	0	71	0.6	1.7
127 CH GOD (CLEVE)	1	16	20*	0.2	0.5
193 EPISCOPAL.....	1	35	45	0.4	1.1
413 S-D ADVENTISTS	1	91	115*	1.0	2.7
419 SO BAPT CONV..	7	1,460	1,846*	16.1	44.1
443 UN C OF CHRIST	6	349	441*	3.8	10.5
449 UN METHODIST..	8	1,571	1,651	14.4	39.4
TAZEWELL	108	13,278	15,797*	39.7	100.0
081 CATHOLIC......	3	0	287	0.7	1.8
093 CR CH (DISC)..	11	1,391	1,680*	4.2	10.6
097 CR C AND C CR.	7	714	862*	2.2	5.5
123 CH GOD (ANDER)	4	147	452	1.1	2.9
127 CH GOD (CLEVE)	10	605	731*	1.8	4.6
193 EPISCOPAL.....	4	275	325	0.8	2.1
281 LUTH CH AMER..	1	42	50	0.1	0.3
285 MENNONITE CH..	1	22	27*	0.1	0.2
349 PENT HOLINESS.	3	109	132*	0.3	0.8
357 PRESB CH US...	10	1,732	2,092*	5.3	13.2
413 S-D ADVENTISTS	2	62	75*	0.2	0.5
419 SO BAPT CONV..	11	2,650	3,201*	8.0	20.3
449 UN METHODIST..	41	5,529	5,883	14.8	37.2
VIRGINIA BEACH CITY #	78	32,529	57,384*	33.3	100.0
081 CATHOLIC......	5	0	14,657	8.5	25.5
093 CR CH (DISC)..	4	432	547*	0.3	1.0
097 CR C AND C CR.	5	1,100	1,392*	0.8	2.4
127 CH GOD (CLEVE)	2	179	227*	0.1	0.4
157 CH OF BRETHREN	1	145	184*	0.1	0.3
165 CH OF NAZARENE	1	338	1,030	0.6	1.8
193 EPISCOPAL.....	7	3,571	6,001	3.5	10.5
226 FRIENDS-USA...	2	190	240*	0.1	0.4
283 LUTH--MO SYNOD	1	235	394	0.2	0.7
285 MENNONITE CH..	2	136	172*	0.1	0.3
349 PENT HOLINESS.	2	29	37*	-	0.1
357 PRESB CH US...	10	4,514	5,714*	3.3	10.0

*Total adherents estimated from known number of communicant, confirmed, full members. —Represents a percent less than 0.1. Percentages may not total due to rounding.

#See Introduction for explanation of how church data was collected for Virginia's independent cities.

Table 3. Churches and Church Membership by State, County and Denomination: 1971

County and Denomination	Number of churches	Communicant, confirmed, full members	Total adherents: Number	Total adherents: Percent of total population	Total adherents: Percent of total adherents
419 SO BAPT CONV..	15	10,709	13,555*	7.9	23.6
443 UN C OF CHRIST	5	965	1,221*	0.7	2.1
449 UN METHODIST..	16	9,986	12,013	7.0	20.9
WARREN	26	5,557	6,813*	44.5	100.0
081 CATHOLIC......	1	0	331	2.2	4.9
121 CH GOD (ABR)..	2	74	90*	0.6	1.3
127 CH GOD (CLEVE)	1	39	47*	0.3	0.7
157 CH OF BRETHREN	1	172	208*	1.4	3.1
193 EPISCOPAL.....	1	345	360	2.4	5.3
281 LUTH CH AMER..	1	191	273	1.8	4.0
357 PRESB CH US...	3	448	543*	3.5	8.0
403 SALVATION ARMY	1	50	195	1.3	2.9
413 S-D ADVENTISTS	1	30	36*	0.2	0.5
419 SO BAPT CONV..	4	1,671	2,025*	13.2	29.7
449 UN METHODIST..	10	2,537	2,705	17.7	39.7
WASHINGTON-BRISTOL #	120	23,633	29,142*	52.3	100.0
081 CATHOLIC......	1	0	1,159	2.1	4.0
093 CR CH (DISC)..	5	420	505*	0.9	1.7
097 CR C AND C CR.	10	567	681*	1.2	2.3
123 CH GOD (ANDER)	2	98	317	0.6	1.1
127 CH GOD (CLEVE)	4	266	320*	0.6	1.1
157 CH OF BRETHREN	1	74	89*	0.2	0.3
165 CH OF NAZARENE	1	26	76	0.1	0.3
193 EPISCOPAL.....	4	974	1,543	2.8	5.3
281 LUTH CH AMER..	3	195	262	0.5	0.9
349 PENT HOLINESS.	4	280	336*	0.6	1.2
353 PLY BRETHREN..	1	20	30	0.1	0.1
357 PRESB CH US...	17	2,982	3,583*	6.4	12.3
413 S-D ADVENTISTS	1	62	74*	0.1	0.3
419 SO BAPT CONV..	30	9,524	11,442*	20.5	39.3
443 UN C OF CHRIST	1	250	300*	0.5	1.0
449 UN METHODIST..	35	7,895	8,425	15.1	28.9
WESTMORELAND	21	3,792	4,904*	40.4	100.0
081 CATHOLIC......	1	0	336	2.8	6.9
093 CR CH (DISC)..	1	81	99*	0.8	2.0
193 EPISCOPAL.....	3	449	694	5.7	14.2
419 SO BAPT CONV..	6	1,431	1,754*	14.4	35.8
449 UN METHODIST..	10	1,831	2,021	16.6	41.2
WISE-NORTON CITY #	58	9,365	11,527*	28.9	100.0
081 CATHOLIC......	4	0	382	1.0	3.3
097 CR C AND C CR.	3	377	456*	1.1	4.0
123 CH GOD (ANDER)	3	282	580	1.5	5.0
127 CH GOD (CLEVE)	3	163	197*	0.5	1.7
193 EPISCOPAL.....	3	168	392	1.0	3.4
357 PRESB CH US...	9	624	755*	1.9	6.5
419 SO BAPT CONV..	13	3,923	4,749*	11.9	41.2
449 UN METHODIST..	20	3,828	4,016	10.1	34.8
WYTHE	75	8,858	10,581*	47.8	100.0
081 CATHOLIC......	1	0	135	0.6	1.3
093 CR CH (DISC)..	5	459	554*	2.5	5.2
123 CH GOD (ANDER)	1	60	170	0.8	1.6
127 CH GOD (CLEVE)	2	84	101*	0.5	1.0
193 EPISCOPAL.....	1	217	352	1.6	3.3
281 LUTH CH AMER..	8	1,140	1,429	6.5	13.5
349 PENT HOLINESS.	12	818	987*	4.5	9.3
357 PRESB CH US...	4	694	837*	3.8	7.9
413 S-D ADVENTISTS	1	107	129*	0.6	1.2
419 SO BAPT CONV..	4	1,012	1,221*	5.5	11.5
449 UN METHODIST..	36	4,267	4,666	21.1	44.1
YORK	20	8,531	10,844*	32.7	100.0
081 CATHOLIC......	1	0	614	1.8	5.7
093 CR CH (DISC)..	1	180	225*	0.7	2.1
127 CH GOD (CLEVE)	1	68	85*	0.3	0.8
193 EPISCOPAL.....	1	304	350	1.1	3.2
281 LUTH CH AMER..	1	74	113	0.3	1.0
349 PENT HOLINESS.	1	11	14*	-	0.1
357 PRESB CH US...	1	550	689*	2.1	6.4
419 SO BAPT CONV..	7	3,188	3,993*	12.0	36.8
449 UN METHODIST..	6	4,156	4,761	14.3	43.9
CO DATA NOT AVAIL	152	11,143	33,113*	N/A	N/A
151 L-D SAINTS....	0	0	19,756	N/A	N/A
193 EPISCOPAL.....	2	37	56	N/A	N/A
223 FREE WILL BAPT	91	8,177	10,007*	N/A	N/A
349 PENT HOLINESS.	5	154	188*	N/A	N/A
467 WESLEYAN......	54	2,775	3,106	N/A	N/A

WASHINGTON

County and Denomination	Number of churches	Communicant, confirmed, full members	Total adherents: Number	Total adherents: Percent of total population	Total adherents: Percent of total adherents
THE STATE.....	2,372	494,859	1,108,916*	32.5	100.0
ADAMS	25	3,270	6,076*	50.6	100.0
029 AMER LUTH CH..	3	822	1,125	9.4	18.5
081 CATHOLIC......	4	0	1,765	14.7	29.0
093 CR CH (DISC)..	1	100	125*	1.0	2.1
165 CH OF NAZARENE	2	123	286	2.4	4.7
193 EPISCOPAL.....	1	52	70	0.6	1.2
283 LUTH--MO SYNOD	1	58	88	0.7	1.4
287 MENN GEN CONF.	1	171	215*	1.8	3.5
349 PENT HOLINESS.	1	12	15*	0.1	0.2
413 S-D ADVENTISTS	2	59	74*	0.6	1.2
419 SO BAPT CONV..	1	125	157*	1.3	2.6
443 UN C OF CHRIST	3	565	709*	5.9	11.7
449 UN METHODIST..	3	696	836	7.0	13.8
453 UN PRES CH USA	2	487	611*	5.1	10.1
ASOTIN	9	1,566	3,917*	28.4	100.0
029 AMER LUTH CH..	1	331	447	3.2	11.4
081 CATHOLIC......	1	0	1,900	13.8	48.5
093 CR CH (DISC)..	1	194	236*	1.7	6.0
123 CH GOD (ANDER)	1	185	361	2.6	9.2
221 FREE METH C NA	1	10	17	0.1	0.4
413 S-D ADVENTISTS	1	109	133*	1.0	3.4
419 SO BAPT CONV..	1	163	198*	1.4	5.1
449 UN METHODIST..	2	574	625	4.5	16.0
BENTON	62	14,386	29,050*	43.0	100.0
019 AMER BAPT CONV	3	329	410*	0.6	1.4
029 AMER LUTH CH..	3	1,531	2,137	3.2	7.4
059 BAPT MISS ASSN	1	16	20*	-	0.1
081 CATHOLIC......	4	0	9,935	14.7	34.2
093 CR CH (DISC)..	4	1,164	1,450*	2.1	5.0
097 CR C AND C CR.	1	80	100*	0.1	0.3
123 CH GOD (ANDER)	1	108	339	0.5	1.2
127 CH GOD (CLEVE)	2	116	144*	0.2	0.5
165 CH OF NAZARENE	4	505	1,003	1.5	3.5
193 EPISCOPAL.....	3	954	1,404	2.1	4.8
221 FREE METH C NA	1	13	18	-	0.1
281 LUTH CH AMER..	1	129	235	0.3	0.8
283 LUTH--MO SYNOD	4	1,032	1,500	2.2	5.2
353 PLY BRETHREN..	1	11	11	-	-
413 S-D ADVENTISTS	2	230	286*	0.4	1.0
419 SO BAPT CONV..	6	2,506	3,121*	4.6	10.7
435 UNITARIAN-UNIV	1	47	47	0.1	0.2
443 UN C OF CHRIST	1	92	115*	0.2	0.4
449 UN METHODIST..	10	3,805	4,619	6.8	15.9
453 UN PRES CH USA	8	1,695	2,111*	3.1	7.3
469 WISC EVAN LUTH	1	23	45	0.1	0.2
CHELAN	48	10,112	15,678*	37.9	100.0
019 AMER BAPT CONV	2	317	376*	0.9	2.4
029 AMER LUTH CH..	4	1,201	1,611	3.9	10.3
081 CATHOLIC......	4	0	2,840	6.9	18.1
093 CR CH (DISC)..	3	598	710*	1.7	4.5
121 CH GOD (ABR)..	2	140	166*	0.4	1.1
123 CH GOD (ANDER)	1	52	130	0.3	0.8
127 CH GOD (CLEVE)	2	75	89*	0.2	0.6
157 CH OF BRETHREN	2	587	697*	1.7	4.4
165 CH OF NAZARENE	3	232	490	1.2	3.1
193 EPISCOPAL.....	3	789	1,112	2.7	7.1
221 FREE METH C NA	1	192	273	0.7	1.7
283 LUTH--MO SYNOD	1	340	486	1.2	3.1
403 SALVATION ARMY	1	35	213	0.5	1.4
413 S-D ADVENTISTS	4	555	659*	1.6	4.2
419 SO BAPT CONV..	5	689	818*	2.0	5.2
443 UN C OF CHRIST	1	125	148*	0.4	0.9
449 UN METHODIST..	6	2,793	3,208	7.8	20.5
453 UN PRES CH USA	3	1,392	1,652*	4.0	10.5
CLALLAM	32	5,036	9,968*	28.7	100.0
019 AMER BAPT CONV	1	367	443*	1.3	4.4
029 AMER LUTH CH..	2	1,232	1,790	5.1	18.0
081 CATHOLIC......	4	0	3,010	8.7	30.2
093 CR CH (DISC)..	1	131	158*	0.5	1.6
123 CH GOD (ANDER)	1	45	112	0.3	1.1
127 CH GOD (CLEVE)	1	18	22*	0.1	0.2
165 CH OF NAZARENE	1	83	202	0.6	2.0
193 EPISCOPAL.....	2	569	722	2.1	7.2
221 FREE METH C NA	1	24	39	0.1	0.4
226 FRIENDS-USA...	1	33	40*	0.1	0.4
283 LUTH--MO SYNOD	2	403	605	1.7	6.1
403 SALVATION ARMY	1	23	149	0.4	1.5
413 S-D ADVENTISTS	3	230	278*	0.8	2.8
419 SO BAPT CONV..	2	233	281*	0.8	2.8
435 UNITARIAN-UNIV	1	12	12	-	0.1
443 UN C OF CHRIST	2	129	156*	0.4	1.6
449 UN METHODIST..	2	943	1,272	3.7	12.8
453 UN PRES CH USA	4	561	677*	1.9	6.8
CLARK	84	19,733	38,699*	30.1	100.0
019 AMER BAPT CONV	3	664	825*	0.6	2.1
029 AMER LUTH CH..	6	1,916	2,657	2.1	6.9
081 CATHOLIC......	8	0	10,529	8.2	27.2
093 CR CH (DISC)..	3	743	923*	0.7	2.4
105 CHRISTIAN REF.	1	60	126	0.1	0.3
121 CH GOD (ABR)..	1	20	25*	-	0.1
123 CH GOD (ANDER)	4	535	1,037	0.8	2.7
127 CH GOD (CLEVE)	1	66	82*	0.1	0.2
165 CH OF NAZARENE	10	1,363	3,110	2.4	8.0
193 EPISCOPAL.....	2	552	1,085	0.8	2.8
197 EVAN CH OF NA.	3	253	314*	0.2	0.8
201 EVAN COV CH AM	1	10	12*	-	-

*Total adherents estimated from known number of communicant, confirmed, full members.

—Represents a percent less than 0.1.

Percentages may not total due to rounding.

#See Introduction for explanation of how church data was collected for Virginia's independent cities.

Table 3. Churches and Church Membership by State, County and Denomination: 1971

County and Denomination	Number of churches	Communicant, confirmed, full members	Total adherents		
			Number	Percent of total population	Percent of total adherents
221 FREE METH C NA	1	21	26	-	0.1
226 FRIENDS-USA...	4	425	528*	0.4	1.4
281 LUTH CH AMER..	4	1,799	2,601	2.0	6.7
283 LUTH--MO SYNOD	4	1,697	2,610	2.0	6.7
403 SALVATION ARMY	1	68	305	0.2	0.8
413 S-D ADVENTISTS	6	1,676	2,083*	1.6	5.4
419 SO BAPT CONV..	6	997	1,239*	1.0	3.2
435 UNITARIAN-UNIV	1	23	39	-	0.1
443 UN C OF CHRIST	1	373	464*	0.4	1.2
449 UN METHODIST..	10	4,181	5,232	4.1	13.5
453 UN PRES CH USA	3	2,291	2,847*	2.2	7.4
COLUMBIA	10	763	1,556*	35.1	100.0
081 CATHOLIC......	2	0	595	13.4	38.2
093 CR CH (DISC)..	1	60	70*	1.6	4.5
097 CR C AND C CR.	1	60	70*	1.6	4.5
165 CH OF NAZARENE	1	31	58	1.3	3.7
193 EPISCOPAL.....	1	32	52	1.2	3.3
283 LUTH--MO SYNOD	1	88	142	3.2	9.1
413 S-D ADVENTISTS	1	37	43*	1.0	2.8
443 UN C OF CHRIST	1	205	239*	5.4	15.4
449 UN METHODIST..	1	250	287	6.5	18.4
COWLITZ	48	11,706	20,431*	29.8	100.0
019 AMER BAPT CONV	3	650	807*	1.2	3.9
029 AMER LUTH CH..	3	1,345	1,852	2.7	9.1
081 CATHOLIC......	5	0	4,831	7.0	23.6
093 CR CH (DISC)..	3	874	1,085*	1.6	5.3
097 CR C AND C CR.	1	230	286*	0.4	1.4
123 CH GOD (ANDER)	1	31	77	0.1	0.4
127 CH GOD (CLEVE)	3	236	293*	0.4	1.4
165 CH OF NAZARENE	4	515	1,011	1.5	4.9
193 EPISCOPAL.....	1	555	794	1.2	3.9
226 FRIENDS-USA...	1	232	288*	0.4	1.4
281 LUTH CH AMER..	2	1,437	1,881	2.7	9.2
283 LUTH--MO SYNOD	1	414	639	0.9	3.1
403 SALVATION ARMY	1	34	167	0.2	0.8
413 S-D ADVENTISTS	3	500	621*	0.9	3.0
419 SO BAPT CONV..	8	2,406	2,987*	4.4	14.6
435 UNITARIAN-UNIV	1	21	21	-	0.1
449 UN METHODIST..	4	1,413	1,782	2.6	8.7
453 UN PRES CH USA	3	813	1,009*	1.5	4.9
DOUGLAS	23	1,929	3,371*	20.1	100.0
019 AMER BAPT CONV	1	285	348*	2.1	10.3
029 AMER LUTH CH..	2	266	354	2.1	10.5
081 CATHOLIC......	4	0	862	5.1	25.6
093 CR CH (DISC)..	2	189	231*	1.4	6.9
123 CH GOD (ANDER)	1	44	144	0.9	4.3
193 EPISCOPAL.....	1	23	32	0.2	0.9
226 FRIENDS-USA...	2	85	104*	0.6	3.1
283 LUTH--MO SYNOD	1	135	218	1.3	6.5
419 SO BAPT CONV..	1	188	229*	1.4	6.8
449 UN METHODIST..	3	345	396	2.4	11.7
453 UN PRES CH USA	3	286	349*	2.1	10.4
469 WISC EVAN LUTH	2	83	104	0.6	3.1
FERRY	8	218	1,093*	29.9	100.0
081 CATHOLIC......	3	0	734	20.1	67.2
165 CH OF NAZARENE	1	10	66	1.8	6.0
193 EPISCOPAL.....	1	26	47	1.3	4.3
283 LUTH--MO SYNOD	1	35	66	1.8	6.0
453 UN PRES CH USA	2	147	180*	4.9	16.5
FRANKLIN	29	4,731	10,363*	40.1	100.0
019 AMER BAPT CONV	1	103	127*	0.5	1.2
029 AMER LUTH CH..	3	702	1,013	3.9	9.8
081 CATHOLIC......	3	0	4,100	15.9	39.6
097 CR C AND C CR.	1	465	574*	2.2	5.5
127 CH GOD (CLEVE)	3	180	222*	0.9	2.1
165 CH OF NAZARENE	2	227	398	1.5	3.8
193 EPISCOPAL.....	1	182	320	1.2	3.1
283 LUTH--MO SYNOD	2	208	309	1.2	3.0
285 MENNONITE CH..	1	15	19*	0.1	0.2
403 SALVATION ARMY	1	20	56	0.2	0.5
413 S-D ADVENTISTS	1	445	549*	2.1	5.3
419 SO BAPT CONV..	3	563	695*	2.7	6.7
443 UN C OF CHRIST	2	380	469*	1.8	4.5
449 UN METHODIST..	4	985	1,196	4.6	11.5
453 UN PRES CH USA	1	256	316*	1.2	3.0
GARFIELD	7	1,589	2,444*	84.0	100.0
081 CATHOLIC......	1	0	450	15.5	18.4
097 CR C AND C CR.	1	222	261*	9.0	10.7
165 CH OF NAZARENE	1	94	178	6.1	7.3
193 EPISCOPAL.....	1	101	200	6.9	8.2
283 LUTH--MO SYNOD	1	50	79	2.7	3.2
449 UN METHODIST..	1	515	562	19.3	23.0
453 UN PRES CH USA	1	607	714*	24.5	29.2
GRANT	59	6,187	12,727*	30.4	100.0
029 AMER LUTH CH..	5	1,242	1,714	4.1	13.5
081 CATHOLIC......	9	0	4,329	10.3	34.0
093 CR CH (DISC)..	2	178	223*	0.5	1.8
105 CHRISTIAN REF.	1	48	104	0.2	0.8
123 CH GOD (ANDER)	1	23	80	0.2	0.6
127 CH GOD (CLEVE)	1	24	30*	0.1	0.2
165 CH OF NAZARENE	5	243	661	1.6	5.2
193 EPISCOPAL.....	3	218	338	0.8	2.7
221 FREE METH C NA	2	107	158	0.4	1.2
226 FRIENDS-USA...	1	44	55*	0.1	0.4
283 LUTH--MO SYNOD	6	626	874	2.1	6.9
287 MENN GEN CONF.	1	51	64*	0.2	0.5
413 S-D ADVENTISTS	3	318	398*	1.0	3.1
419 SO BAPT CONV..	4	413	517*	1.2	4.1
443 UN C OF CHRIST	4	405	507*	1.2	4.0
449 UN METHODIST..	5	1,096	1,234	2.9	9.7
453 UN PRES CH USA	6	1,151	1,441*	3.4	11.3
GRAYS HARBOR	52	7,767	15,007*	25.2	100.0
019 AMER BAPT CONV	3	707	861*	1.4	5.7
029 AMER LUTH CH..	4	764	1,074	1.8	7.2
081 CATHOLIC......	6	0	4,500	7.6	30.0
093 CR CH (DISC)..	2	277	337*	0.6	2.2
097 CR C AND C CR.	1	60	73*	0.1	0.5
123 CH GOD (ANDER)	3	228	676	1.1	4.5
165 CH OF NAZARENE	1	50	99	0.2	0.7
193 EPISCOPAL.....	4	500	843	1.4	5.6
201 EVAN COV CH AM	1	70	85*	0.1	0.6
221 FREE METH C NA	1	59	69	0.1	0.5
281 LUTH CH AMER..	3	451	567	1.0	3.8
283 LUTH--MO SYNOD	1	320	480	0.8	3.2
353 PLY BRETHREN..	1	80	110	0.2	0.7
403 SALVATION ARMY	1	44	178	0.3	1.2
413 S-D ADVENTISTS	3	257	313*	0.5	2.1
419 SO BAPT CONV..	3	238	290*	0.5	1.9
443 UN C OF CHRIST	1	48	58*	0.1	0.4
449 UN METHODIST..	8	2,124	2,580	4.3	17.2
453 UN PRES CH USA	5	1,490	1,814*	3.0	12.1
ISLAND	23	4,262	9,366*	34.7	100.0
019 AMER BAPT CONV	1	333	410*	1.5	4.4
029 AMER LUTH CH..	4	807	1,132	4.2	12.1
081 CATHOLIC......	3	0	3,358	12.4	35.9
105 CHRISTIAN REF.	1	175	317	1.2	3.4
165 CH OF NAZARENE	1	100	337	1.2	3.6
193 EPISCOPAL.....	3	379	555	2.1	5.9
221 FREE METH C NA	1	31	55	0.2	0.6
283 LUTH--MO SYNOD	1	170	335	1.2	3.6
371 REF CH IN AM..	1	383	548	2.0	5.9
413 S-D ADVENTISTS	2	105	129*	0.5	1.4
419 SO BAPT CONV..	1	429	528*	2.0	5.6
449 UN METHODIST..	3	1,243	1,530	5.7	16.3
453 UN PRES CH USA	1	107	132*	0.5	1.4
JEFFERSON	8	1,059	1,869*	17.5	100.0
081 CATHOLIC......	1	0	572	5.4	30.6
193 EPISCOPAL.....	1	142	226	2.1	12.1
283 LUTH--MO SYNOD	1	165	224	2.1	12.0
419 SO BAPT CONV..	1	32	38*	0.4	2.0
449 UN METHODIST..	2	433	469	4.4	25.1
453 UN PRES CH USA	2	287	340*	3.2	18.2
KING	521	152,055	333,501*	28.8	100.0
019 AMER BAPT CONV	35	9,681	11,754*	1.0	3.5
029 AMER LUTH CH..	38	20,725	30,486	2.6	9.1
059 BAPT MISS ASSN	1	46	56*	-	-
081 CATHOLIC......	57	0	128,936	11.1	38.7
093 CR CH (DISC)..	14	3,453	4,192*	0.4	1.3
097 CR C AND C CR.	14	2,090	2,537*	0.2	0.8
105 CHRISTIAN REF.	3	453	855	0.1	0.3
123 CH GOD (ANDER)	10	725	1,726	0.1	0.5
127 CH GOD (CLEVE)	5	163	198*	-	0.1
157 CH OF BRETHREN	3	777	943*	0.1	0.3
165 CH OF NAZARENE	21	2,633	4,918	0.4	1.5
175 CONG CR CH....	1	75	91*	-	-
193 EPISCOPAL.....	32	16,073	24,050	2.1	7.2
197 EVAN CH OF NA.	4	480	583*	0.1	0.2
201 EVAN COV CH AM	9	1,554	1,887*	0.2	0.6
221 FREE METH C NA	13	2,077	2,738	0.2	0.8
226 FRIENDS-USA...	5	483	586*	0.1	0.2
281 LUTH CH AMER..	28	11,453	17,516	1.5	5.3
283 LUTH--MO SYNOD	26	9,561	14,315	1.2	4.3
287 MENN GEN CONF.	1	30	36*	-	-
313 NO AM BAPT GC.	3	217	263*	-	0.1
335 ORTH PRESB CH.	1	33	58	-	-
349 PENT HOLINESS.	1	18	22*	-	-
371 REF CH IN AM..	1	308	500	-	0.1
381 REF PRES-EVAN.	3	296	394	-	0.1
403 SALVATION ARMY	4	268	723	0.1	0.2
413 S-D ADVENTISTS	19	4,420	5,366*	0.5	1.6
415 S-D BAPTIST GC	1	49	59*	-	-
419 SO BAPT CONV..	27	5,408	6,566*	0.6	2.0
435 UNITARIAN-UNIV	8	1,382	2,013	0.2	0.6
443 UN C OF CHRIST	29	9,335	11,333*	1.0	3.4
449 UN METHODIST..	45	25,574	30,654	2.7	9.2
453 UN PRES CH USA	54	21,840	26,516*	2.3	8.0
469 WISC EVAN LUTH	5	375	631	0.1	0.2
KITSAP	62	13,260	27,817*	27.3	100.0
019 AMER BAPT CONV	6	1,370	1,653*	1.6	5.9
029 AMER LUTH CH..	7	3,209	4,513	4.4	16.2
081 CATHOLIC......	6	0	9,810	9.6	35.3
093 CR CH (DISC)..	3	643	776*	0.8	2.8
097 CR C AND C CR.	3	176	212*	0.2	0.8
123 CH GOD (ANDER)	1	55	130	0.1	0.5
127 CH GOD (CLEVE)	1	28	34*	-	0.1
165 CH OF NAZARENE	3	247	733	0.7	2.6

*Total adherents estimated from known number of communicant, confirmed, full members.

—Represents a percent less than 0.1.

Percentages may not total due to rounding.

Table 3. Churches and Church Membership by State, County and Denomination: 1971

County and Denomination	Number of churches	Communicant, confirmed, full members	Total adherents: Number	Total adherents: Percent of total population	Total adherents: Percent of total adherents
193 EPISCOPAL.....	3	1,173	1,533	1.5	5.5
201 EVAN COV CH AM	1	129	156*	0.2	0.6
221 FREE METH C NA	1	129	154	0.2	0.6
281 LUTH CH AMER..	3	731	1,145	1.1	4.1
283 LUTH--MO SYNOD	2	794	1,157	1.1	4.2
353 PLY BRETHREN..	2	160	330	0.3	1.2
403 SALVATION ARMY	1	52	182	0.2	0.7
413 S-D ADVENTISTS	4	516	623*	0.6	2.2
419 SO BAPT CONV..	2	526	635*	0.6	2.3
435 UNITARIAN-UNIV	1	48	48	-	0.2
443 UN C OF CHRIST	2	311	375*	0.4	1.3
449 UN METHODIST..	8	2,575	3,147	3.1	11.3
453 UN PRES CH USA	1	365	440*	0.4	1.6
469 WISC EVAN LUTH	1	23	31	-	0.1
KITTITAS	31	3,587	7,064*	28.2	100.0
019 AMER BAPT CONV	4	330	383*	1.5	5.4
029 AMER LUTH CH..	1	410	508	2.0	7.2
081 CATHOLIC......	3	0	2,497	10.0	35.3
093 CR CH (DISC)..	1	148	172*	0.7	2.4
097 CR C AND C CR.	2	127	147*	0.6	2.1
123 CH GOD (ANDER)	1	25	62	0.2	0.9
127 CH GOD (CLEVE)	1	28	33*	0.1	0.5
165 CH OF NAZARENE	2	84	352	1.4	5.0
193 EPISCOPAL.....	3	296	556	2.2	7.9
221 FREE METH C NA	1	44	54	0.2	0.8
413 S-D ADVENTISTS	2	86	100*	0.4	1.4
419 SO BAPT CONV..	1	232	269*	1.1	3.8
449 UN METHODIST..	4	1,158	1,203	4.8	17.0
453 UN PRES CH USA	3	537	623*	2.5	8.8
469 WISC EVAN LUTH	2	82	105	0.4	1.5
KLICKITAT	22	2,004	3,493*	28.8	100.0
019 AMER BAPT CONV	1	273	332*	2.7	9.5
081 CATHOLIC......	3	0	784	6.5	22.4
097 CR C AND C CR.	1	50	61*	0.5	1.7
123 CH GOD (ANDER)	1	30	68	0.6	1.9
165 CH OF NAZARENE	2	60	287	2.4	8.2
281 LUTH CH AMER..	1	124	165	1.4	4.7
283 LUTH--MO SYNOD	2	194	267	2.2	7.6
413 S-D ADVENTISTS	3	228	277*	2.3	7.9
419 SO BAPT CONV..	2	104	126*	1.0	3.6
443 UN C OF CHRIST	1	89	108*	0.9	3.1
449 UN METHODIST..	3	694	826	6.8	23.6
453 UN PRES CH USA	2	158	192*	1.6	5.5
LEWIS	55	6,931	13,882*	30.5	100.0
019 AMER BAPT CONV	3	318	383*	0.8	2.8
029 AMER LUTH CH..	1	292	433	1.0	3.1
081 CATHOLIC......	9	0	4,500	9.9	32.4
093 CR CH (DISC)..	2	541	652*	1.4	4.7
123 CH GOD (ANDER)	3	133	363	0.8	2.6
127 CH GOD (CLEVE)	1	37	45*	0.1	0.3
157 CH OF BRETHREN	2	183	220*	0.5	1.6
165 CH OF NAZARENE	2	184	430	0.9	3.1
193 EPISCOPAL.....	2	333	466	1.0	3.4
197 EVAN CH OF NA.	1	70	84*	0.2	0.6
201 EVAN COV CH AM	1	39	47*	0.1	0.3
221 FREE METH C NA	1	80	115	0.3	0.8
281 LUTH CH AMER..	4	847	1,293	2.8	9.3
283 LUTH--MO SYNOD	1	180	255	0.6	1.8
353 PLY BRETHREN..	1	40	100	0.2	0.7
403 SALVATION ARMY	1	29	170	0.4	1.2
413 S-D ADVENTISTS	5	496	598*	1.3	4.3
419 SO BAPT CONV..	2	201	242*	0.5	1.7
449 UN METHODIST..	7	1,996	2,363	5.2	17.0
453 UN PRES CH USA	6	932	1,123*	2.5	8.1
LINCOLN	30	3,962	5,686*	59.4	100.0
029 AMER LUTH CH..	7	1,295	1,690	17.7	29.7
081 CATHOLIC......	6	0	800	8.4	14.1
093 CR CH (DISC)..	1	97	115*	1.2	2.0
165 CH OF NAZARENE	1	48	90	0.9	1.6
283 LUTH--MO SYNOD	1	116	165	1.7	2.9
313 NO AM BAPT GC.	1	49	58*	0.6	1.0
443 UN C OF CHRIST	4	1,116	1,321*	13.8	23.2
449 UN METHODIST..	5	474	539	5.6	9.5
453 UN PRES CH USA	4	767	908*	9.5	16.0
MASON	11	2,207	4,553*	21.8	100.0
019 AMER BAPT CONV	1	264	316*	1.5	6.9
029 AMER LUTH CH..	2	376	558	2.7	12.3
081 CATHOLIC......	1	0	1,575	7.5	34.6
097 CR C AND C CR.	1	125	150*	0.7	3.3
165 CH OF NAZARENE	1	22	63	0.3	1.4
193 EPISCOPAL.....	1	288	378	1.8	8.3
283 LUTH--MO SYNOD	1	217	320	1.5	7.0
413 S-D ADVENTISTS	1	109	131*	0.6	2.9
419 SO BAPT CONV..	1	42	50*	0.2	1.1
449 UN METHODIST..	1	764	1,012	4.8	22.2
OKANOGAN	46	3,495	6,676*	25.8	100.0
019 AMER BAPT CONV	2	177	214*	0.8	3.2
081 CATHOLIC......	9	0	2,220	8.6	33.3
157 CH OF BRETHREN	2	275	332*	1.3	5.0
193 EPISCOPAL.....	5	363	592	2.3	8.9
221 FREE METH C NA	3	151	214	0.8	3.2
283 LUTH--MO SYNOD	4	303	415	1.6	6.2
353 PLY BRETHREN..	1	10	15	0.1	0.2
413 S-D ADVENTISTS	4	350	423*	1.6	6.3
419 SO BAPT CONV..	1	73	88*	0.3	1.3
443 UN C OF CHRIST	1	111	134*	0.5	2.0
449 UN METHODIST..	10	1,015	1,186	4.6	17.8
453 UN PRES CH USA	2	562	678*	2.6	10.2
469 WISC EVAN LUTH	2	105	165	0.6	2.5
PACIFIC	23	1,615	3,144*	19.9	100.0
019 AMER BAPT CONV	1	400	469*	3.0	14.9
029 AMER LUTH CH..	2	214	280	1.8	8.9
081 CATHOLIC......	4	0	1,221	7.7	38.8
165 CH OF NAZARENE	1	15	66	0.4	2.1
201 EVAN COV CH AM	1	30	35*	0.2	1.1
413 S-D ADVENTISTS	2	67	79*	0.5	2.5
443 UN C OF CHRIST	1	53	62*	0.4	2.0
449 UN METHODIST..	9	508	548	3.5	17.4
453 UN PRES CH USA	2	328	384*	2.4	12.2
PEND OREILLE	17	817	1,754*	29.1	100.0
019 AMER BAPT CONV	1	75	90*	1.5	5.1
029 AMER LUTH CH..	1	174	260	4.3	14.8
081 CATHOLIC......	5	0	641	10.6	36.5
165 CH OF NAZARENE	1	32	120	2.0	6.8
175 CONG CR CH....	1	50	60*	1.0	3.4
193 EPISCOPAL.....	1	13	13	0.2	0.7
287 MENN GEN CONF.	1	60	72*	1.2	4.1
413 S-D ADVENTISTS	2	103	124*	2.1	7.1
419 SO BAPT CONV..	1	91	110*	1.8	6.3
443 UN C OF CHRIST	3	219	264*	4.4	15.1
PIERCE	209	49,435	111,314*	27.1	100.0
019 AMER BAPT CONV	15	2,390	2,899*	0.7	2.6
029 AMER LUTH CH..	18	10,363	15,595	3.8	14.0
081 CATHOLIC......	23	0	43,865	10.7	39.4
093 CR CH (DISC)..	8	1,878	2,278*	0.6	2.0
097 CR C AND C CR.	9	971	1,178*	0.3	1.1
105 CHRISTIAN REF.	1	111	232	0.1	0.2
123 CH GOD (ANDER)	3	164	373	0.1	0.3
127 CH GOD (CLEVE)	1	54	66*	-	0.1
157 CH OF BRETHREN	1	84	102*	-	0.1
165 CH OF NAZARENE	6	709	1,930	0.5	1.7
175 CONG CR CH....	1	216	262*	0.1	0.2
193 EPISCOPAL.....	10	3,214	4,508	1.1	4.0
201 EVAN COV CH AM	3	416	505*	0.1	0.5
221 FREE METH C NA	4	207	267	0.1	0.2
226 FRIENDS-USA...	3	253	307*	0.1	0.3
281 LUTH CH AMER..	10	2,522	3,602	0.9	3.2
283 LUTH--MO SYNOD	7	3,884	6,167	1.5	5.5
313 NO AM BAPT GC.	2	588	713*	0.2	0.6
349 PENT HOLINESS.	1	48	58*	-	0.1
353 PLY BRETHREN..	6	320	540	0.1	0.5
381 REF PRES-EVAN.	1	335	382	0.1	0.3
403 SALVATION ARMY	1	78	213	0.1	0.2
413 S-D ADVENTISTS	5	1,296	1,572*	0.4	1.4
419 SO BAPT CONV..	8	2,408	2,921*	0.7	2.6
435 UNITARIAN-UNIV	1	175	235	0.1	0.2
443 UN C OF CHRIST	8	888	1,077*	0.3	1.0
449 UN METHODIST..	25	11,098	13,611	3.3	12.2
453 UN PRES CH USA	26	4,466	5,417*	1.3	4.9
469 WISC EVAN LUTH	2	299	439	0.1	0.4
SAN JUAN	5	199	414*	10.7	100.0
081 CATHOLIC......	1	0	186	4.8	44.9
413 S-D ADVENTISTS	1	25	29*	0.8	7.0
443 UN C OF CHRIST	1	55	63*	1.6	15.2
449 UN METHODIST..	1	15	17	0.4	4.1
453 UN PRES CH USA	1	104	119*	3.1	28.7
SKAGIT	67	10,599	18,167*	34.7	100.0
019 AMER BAPT CONV	4	1,049	1,259*	2.4	6.9
029 AMER LUTH CH..	6	1,880	2,668	5.1	14.7
081 CATHOLIC......	6	0	3,903	7.5	21.5
093 CR CH (DISC)..	2	197	236*	0.5	1.3
097 CR C AND C CR.	5	552	662*	1.3	3.6
105 CHRISTIAN REF.	1	340	656	1.3	3.6
127 CH GOD (CLEVE)	2	113	136*	0.3	0.7
165 CH OF NAZARENE	3	195	459	0.9	2.5
193 EPISCOPAL.....	3	527	761	1.5	4.2
201 EVAN COV CH AM	2	168	202*	0.4	1.1
221 FREE METH C NA	5	144	200	0.4	1.1
281 LUTH CH AMER..	3	1,027	1,363	2.6	7.5
283 LUTH--MO SYNOD	1	357	540	1.0	3.0
403 SALVATION ARMY	1	36	202	0.4	1.1
413 S-D ADVENTISTS	3	239	287*	0.5	1.6
419 SO BAPT CONV..	4	534	641*	1.2	3.5
443 UN C OF CHRIST	2	80	96*	0.2	0.5
449 UN METHODIST..	10	2,169	2,706	5.2	14.9
453 UN PRES CH USA	4	992	1,190*	2.3	6.6
SKAMANIA	7	390	730*	12.5	100.0
081 CATHOLIC......	1	0	110	1.9	15.1
165 CH OF NAZARENE	2	72	248	4.2	34.0
281 LUTH CH AMER..	1	82	122	2.1	16.7
413 S-D ADVENTISTS	1	48	59*	1.0	8.1
449 UN METHODIST..	1	174	174	3.0	23.8
453 UN PRES CH USA	1	14	17*	0.3	2.3
SNOHOMISH	155	32,270	64,793*	24.4	100.0

*Total adherents estimated from known number of communicant, confirmed, full members.

—Represents a percent less than 0.1.

Percentages may not total due to rounding.

Table 3. Churches and Church Membership by State, County and Denomination: 1971

County and Denomination	Number of churches	Communicant, confirmed, full members	Total adherents: Number	Total adherents: Percent of total population	Total adherents: Percent of total adherents
019 AMER BAPT CONV	10	2,923	3,685*	1.4	5.7
029 AMER LUTH CH..	15	6,655	10,084	3.8	15.6
081 CATHOLIC......	15	0	19,438	7.3	30.0
093 CR CH (DISC)..	2	425	536*	0.2	0.8
097 CR C AND C CR.	4	251	316*	0.1	0.5
105 CHRISTIAN REF.	4	580	1,112	0.4	1.7
123 CH GOD (ANDER)	3	248	478	0.2	0.7
127 CH GOD (CLEVE)	1	45	57*	-	0.1
165 CH OF NAZARENE	7	460	1,092	0.4	1.7
175 CONG CR CH....	1	102	129*	-	0.2
193 EPISCOPAL.....	8	2,040	2,917	1.1	4.5
201 EVAN COV CH AM	4	419	528*	0.2	0.8
221 FREE METH C NA	5	485	617	0.2	1.0
281 LUTH CH AMER..	6	1,833	2,902	1.1	4.5
283 LUTH--MO SYNOD	9	2,988	4,760	1.8	7.3
285 MENNONITE CH..	1	18	23*	-	-
287 MENN GEN CONF.	1	134	169*	0.1	0.3
313 NO AM BAPT GC.	3	193	243*	0.1	0.4
353 PLY BRETHREN..	2	80	130	-	0.2
371 REF CH IN AM..	2	202	368	0.1	0.6
381 REF PRES-EVAN.	2	364	438	0.2	0.7
403 SALVATION ARMY	1	59	258	0.1	0.4
413 S-D ADVENTISTS	8	777	980*	0.4	1.5
419 SO BAPT CONV..	10	1,452	1,831*	0.7	2.8
435 UNITARIAN-UNIV	2	250	420	0.2	0.6
443 UN C OF CHRIST	4	704	888*	0.3	1.4
449 UN METHODIST..	16	6,035	7,132	2.7	11.0
453 UN PRES CH USA	8	2,458	3,099*	1.2	4.8
469 WISC EVAN LUTH	1	90	163	0.1	0.3
SPOKANE	185	46,060	110,317*	38.4	100.0
019 AMER BAPT CONV	9	1,972	2,384*	0.8	2.2
029 AMER LUTH CH..	13	4,868	6,835	2.4	6.2
081 CATHOLIC......	25	0	49,242	17.1	44.6
093 CR CH (DISC)..	10	2,075	2,509*	0.9	2.3
097 CR C AND C CR.	5	469	567*	0.2	0.5
105 CHRISTIAN REF.	1	61	132	-	0.1
123 CH GOD (ANDER)	3	230	494	0.2	0.4
127 CH GOD (CLEVE)	2	39	47*	-	-
165 CH OF NAZARENE	9	1,291	2,554	0.9	2.3
175 CONG CR CH....	2	789	954*	0.3	0.9
193 EPISCOPAL.....	9	4,258	5,638	2.0	5.1
197 EVAN CH OF NA.	3	226	273*	0.1	0.2
201 EVAN COV CH AM	2	276	334*	0.1	0.3
221 FREE METH C NA	3	201	315	0.1	0.3
226 FRIENDS-USA...	1	80	97*	-	0.1
281 LUTH CH AMER..	9	3,519	5,172	1.8	4.7
283 LUTH--MO SYNOD	8	2,730	3,969	1.4	3.6
313 NO AM BAPT GC.	1	100	121*	-	0.1
349 PENT HOLINESS.	1	22	27*	-	-
353 PLY BRETHREN..	2	75	140	-	0.1
403 SALVATION ARMY	1	142	1,376	0.5	1.2
413 S-D ADVENTISTS	8	1,997	2,414*	0.8	2.2
419 SO BAPT CONV..	13	2,846	3,441*	1.2	3.1
435 UNITARIAN-UNIV	1	205	283	0.1	0.3
443 UN C OF CHRIST	9	2,122	2,565*	0.9	2.3
449 UN METHODIST..	19	6,834	7,958	2.8	7.2
453 UN PRES CH USA	15	8,563	10,352*	3.6	9.4
469 WISC EVAN LUTH	1	70	124	-	0.1
STEVENS	29	1,870	4,444*	25.5	100.0
029 AMER LUTH CH..	2	395	560	3.2	12.6
081 CATHOLIC......	11	0	1,871	10.7	42.1
093 CR CH (DISC)..	1	119	145*	0.8	3.3
123 CH GOD (ANDER)	1	132	282	1.6	6.3
165 CH OF NAZARENE	1	68	110	0.6	2.5
193 EPISCOPAL.....	1	102	126	0.7	2.8
221 FREE METH C NA	2	93	124	0.7	2.8
413 S-D ADVENTISTS	3	167	204*	1.2	4.6
443 UN C OF CHRIST	3	415	506*	2.9	11.4
449 UN METHODIST..	1	317	440	2.5	9.9
453 UN PRES CH USA	3	62	76*	0.4	1.7
THURSTON	37	10,763	20,478*	26.6	100.0
029 AMER LUTH CH..	1	731	1,136	1.5	5.5
081 CATHOLIC......	4	0	5,569	7.2	27.2
093 CR CH (DISC)..	2	559	686*	0.9	3.3
105 CHRISTIAN REF.	1	38	66	0.1	0.3
123 CH GOD (ANDER)	1	335	725	0.9	3.5
127 CH GOD (CLEVE)	3	83	102*	0.1	0.5
157 CH OF BRETHREN	1	294	361*	0.5	1.8
165 CH OF NAZARENE	1	196	526	0.7	2.6
193 EPISCOPAL.....	1	1,009	1,500	2.0	7.3
221 FREE METH C NA	1	116	164	0.2	0.8
281 LUTH CH AMER..	2	1,441	2,118	2.8	10.3
283 LUTH--MO SYNOD	2	711	1,074	1.4	5.2
403 SALVATION ARMY	1	36	240	0.3	1.2
413 S-D ADVENTISTS	2	446	547*	0.7	2.7
419 SO BAPT CONV..	2	355	435*	0.6	2.1
435 UNITARIAN-UNIV	1	55	95	0.1	0.5
443 UN C OF CHRIST	1	360	442*	0.6	2.2
449 UN METHODIST..	6	2,507	2,865	3.7	14.0
453 UN PRES CH USA	3	1,473	1,807*	2.3	8.8
469 WISC EVAN LUTH	1	18	20	-	0.1
WAHKIAKUM	7	440	716*	19.9	100.0
029 AMER LUTH CH..	1	150	215	6.0	30.0
081 CATHOLIC......	1	0	120	3.3	16.8
353 PLY BRETHREN..	1	40	60	1.7	8.4
413 S-D ADVENTISTS	1	30	37*	1.0	5.2
443 UN C OF CHRIST	1	109	133*	3.7	18.6

County and Denomination	Number of churches	Communicant, confirmed, full members	Total adherents: Number	Total adherents: Percent of total population	Total adherents: Percent of total adherents
449 UN METHODIST..	2	111	151	4.2	21.1
WALLA WALLA	33	10,663	18,707*	44.4	100.0
019 AMER BAPT CONV	1	465	547*	1.3	2.9
029 AMER LUTH CH..	2	991	1,358	3.2	7.3
059 BAPT MISS ASSN	1	74	87*	0.2	0.5
081 CATHOLIC......	4	0	4,650	11.0	24.9
093 CR CH (DISC)..	2	744	875*	2.1	4.7
123 CH GOD (ANDER)	1	221	437	1.0	2.3
165 CH OF NAZARENE	3	514	1,255	3.0	6.7
193 EPISCOPAL.....	1	594	939	2.2	5.0
221 FREE METH C NA	1	46	53	0.1	0.3
283 LUTH--MO SYNOD	1	190	250	0.6	1.3
403 SALVATION ARMY	1	49	219	0.5	1.2
413 S-D ADVENTISTS	6	3,278	3,853*	9.1	20.6
419 SO BAPT CONV..	1	88	103*	0.2	0.6
435 UNITARIAN-UNIV	1	15	26	0.1	0.1
443 UN C OF CHRIST	1	654	769*	1.8	4.1
449 UN METHODIST..	2	1,725	2,093	5.0	11.2
453 UN PRES CH USA	4	1,015	1,193*	2.8	6.4
WHATCOM	78	14,122	33,699*	41.1	100.0
019 AMER BAPT CONV	5	899	1,077*	1.3	3.2
029 AMER LUTH CH..	7	1,961	2,705	3.3	8.0
081 CATHOLIC......	9	0	4,727	5.8	14.0
093 CR CH (DISC)..	1	292	350*	0.4	1.0
097 CR C AND C CR.	1	78	93*	0.1	0.3
105 CHRISTIAN REF.	8	2,455	4,658	5.7	13.8
123 CH GOD (ANDER)	1	80	222	0.3	0.7
165 CH OF NAZARENE	3	123	418	0.5	1.2
193 EPISCOPAL.....	2	735	954	1.2	2.8
201 EVAN COV CH AM	1	55	66*	0.1	0.2
221 FREE METH C NA	1	83	104	0.1	0.3
281 LUTH CH AMER..	4	820	1,116	1.4	3.3
283 LUTH--MO SYNOD	2	559	761	0.9	2.3
287 MENN GEN CONF.	1	84	101*	0.1	0.3
353 PLY BRETHREN..	2	70	130	0.2	0.4
371 REF CH IN AM..	3	790	9,724	11.9	28.9
381 REF PRES-EVAN.	1	47	55	0.1	0.2
403 SALVATION ARMY	1	73	346	0.4	1.0
413 S-D ADVENTISTS	2	403	483*	0.6	1.4
419 SO BAPT CONV..	2	191	229*	0.3	0.7
435 UNITARIAN-UNIV	2	72	90	0.1	0.3
443 UN C OF CHRIST	4	777	931*	1.1	2.8
449 UN METHODIST..	9	2,243	2,883	3.5	8.6
453 UN PRES CH USA	6	1,232	1,476*	1.8	4.4
WHITMAN	60	6,755	11,353*	30.0	100.0
019 AMER BAPT CONV	7	511	591*	1.6	5.2
029 AMER LUTH CH..	5	979	1,403	3.7	12.4
081 CATHOLIC......	12	0	2,998	7.9	26.4
093 CR CH (DISC)..	6	439	508*	1.3	4.5
165 CH OF NAZARENE	4	236	383	1.0	3.4
193 EPISCOPAL.....	4	445	501	1.3	4.4
283 LUTH--MO SYNOD	1	124	205	0.5	1.8
313 NO AM BAPT GC.	1	251	290*	0.8	2.6
413 S-D ADVENTISTS	3	198	229*	0.6	2.0
419 SO BAPT CONV..	1	113	131*	0.3	1.2
435 UNITARIAN-UNIV	1	25	25	0.1	0.2
443 UN C OF CHRIST	5	675	781*	2.1	6.9
449 UN METHODIST..	8	1,849	2,255	5.9	19.9
453 UN PRES CH USA	2	910	1,053*	2.8	9.3
YAKIMA	138	26,188	57,066*	39.4	100.0
019 AMER BAPT CONV	6	1,553	1,904*	1.3	3.3
029 AMER LUTH CH..	3	447	622	0.4	1.1
059 BAPT MISS ASSN	1	25	31*	-	0.1
081 CATHOLIC......	14	0	22,114	15.3	38.8
093 CR CH (DISC)..	9	2,069	2,536*	1.7	4.4
097 CR C AND C CR.	7	218	267*	0.2	0.5
105 CHRISTIAN REF.	3	494	972	0.7	1.7
123 CH GOD (ANDER)	4	246	685	0.5	1.2
127 CH GOD (CLEVE)	6	332	407*	0.3	0.7
157 CH OF BRETHREN	2	101	124*	0.1	0.2
165 CH OF NAZARENE	12	1,245	2,390	1.6	4.2
193 EPISCOPAL.....	5	1,673	2,234	1.5	3.9
197 EVAN CH OF NA.	2	218	267*	0.2	0.5
201 EVAN COV CH AM	3	439	538*	0.4	0.9
221 FREE METH C NA	3	164	234	0.2	0.4
281 LUTH CH AMER..	3	1,182	1,751	1.2	3.1
283 LUTH--MO SYNOD	5	1,742	2,452	1.7	4.3
349 PENT HOLINESS.	3	100	123*	0.1	0.2
353 PLY BRETHREN..	1	100	150	0.1	0.3
371 REF CH IN AM..	1	150	192	0.1	0.3
403 SALVATION ARMY	1	66	399	0.3	0.7
413 S-D ADVENTISTS	8	1,373	1,683*	1.2	2.9
419 SO BAPT CONV..	9	1,498	1,836*	1.3	3.2
435 UNITARIAN-UNIV	1	72	72	-	0.1
443 UN C OF CHRIST	2	260	319*	0.2	0.6
449 UN METHODIST..	12	5,904	7,132	4.9	12.5
453 UN PRES CH USA	10	4,048	4,962*	3.4	8.7
469 WISC EVAN LUTH	2	469	670	0.5	1.2
CO DATA NOT AVAIL	17	858	67,533*	N/A	N/A
151 L-D SAINTS....	0	0	66,109	N/A	N/A
193 EPISCOPAL.....	2	378	853	N/A	N/A
223 FREE WILL BAPT	7	265	323*	N/A	N/A
467 WESLEYAN......	8	215	248	N/A	N/A

*Total adherents estimated from known number of communicant, confirmed, full members.

—Represents a percent less than 0.1.

Percentages may not total due to rounding.

Table 3. Churches and Church Membership by State, County and Denomination: 1971

County and Denomination	Number of churches	Communicant, confirmed, full members	Total adherents: Number	Total adherents: Percent of total population	Total adherents: Percent of total adherents
WEST VIRGINIA					
THE STATE.....	3,821	489,430	706,179*	40.5	100.0
BARBOUR	58	4,262	4,940*	35.2	100.0
019 AMER BAPT CONV	9	929	1,104*	7.9	22.3
081 CATHOLIC......	4	C	228	1.6	4.6
157 CH OF BRETHREN	3	182	216*	1.5	4.4
165 CH OF NAZARENE	3	71	157	1.1	3.2
193 EPISCOPAL.....	1	16	18	0.1	0.4
357 PRESB CH US...	2	88	105*	0.7	2.1
449 UN METHODIST..	36	2,976	3,112	22.2	63.0
BERKELEY	55	12,781	16,567*	45.6	100.0
081 CATHOLIC......	1	0	1,371	3.8	8.3
093 CR CH (DISC)..	2	406	498*	1.4	3.0
097 CR C AND C CR.	4	642	787*	2.2	4.8
123 CH GOD (ANDER)	1	7	16	-	0.1
127 CH GOD (CLEVE)	1	76	93*	0.3	0.6
157 CH OF BRETHREN	3	714	875*	2.4	5.3
165 CH OF NAZARENE	1	52	131	0.4	0.8
193 EPISCOPAL.....	2	529	652	1.8	3.9
281 LUTH CH AMER..	2	934	1,271	3.5	7.7
357 PRESB CH US...	10	1,371	1,680*	4.6	10.1
403 SALVATION ARMY	1	63	264	0.7	1.6
413 S-D ADVENTISTS	2	220	270*	0.7	1.6
419 SO BAPT CONV..	3	1,411	1,729*	4.8	10.4
443 UN C OF CHRIST	1	427	523*	1.4	3.2
449 UN METHODIST..	21	5,929	6,407	17.6	38.7
BOONE	45	3,375	4,252*	16.9	100.0
019 AMER BAPT CONV	11	1,457	1,779*	7.1	41.8
081 CATHOLIC......	2	0	122	0.5	2.9
093 CR CH (DISC)..	2	143	175*	0.7	4.1
123 CH GOD (ANDER)	1	21	68	0.3	1.6
127 CH GOD (CLEVE)	6	272	332*	1.3	7.8
165 CH OF NAZARENE	4	137	309	1.2	7.3
357 PRESB CH US...	1	76	93*	0.4	2.2
449 UN METHODIST..	14	1,137	1,213	4.8	28.5
453 UN PRES CH USA	4	132	161*	0.6	3.8
BRAXTON	65	3,842	4,306*	34.0	100.0
019 AMER BAPT CONV	17	1,380	1,652*	13.0	38.4
081 CATHOLIC......	1	0	53	0.4	1.2
127 CH GOD (CLEVE)	1	11	13*	0.1	0.3
165 CH OF NAZARENE	1	15	58	0.5	1.3
357 PRESB CH US...	2	62	74*	0.6	1.7
449 UN METHODIST..	43	2,374	2,456	19.4	57.0
BROOKE	34	6,508	13,669*	46.0	100.0
019 AMER BAPT CONV	1	293	355*	1.2	2.6
081 CATHOLIC......	4	0	5,152	17.4	37.7
093 CR CH (DISC)..	4	1,253	1,520*	5.1	11.1
097 CR C AND C CR.	4	1,600	1,940*	6.5	14.2
123 CH GOD (ANDER)	3	123	395	1.3	2.9
165 CH OF NAZARENE	3	282	513	1.7	3.8
193 EPISCOPAL.....	2	199	277	0.9	2.0
221 FREE METH C NA	2	87	137	0.5	1.0
403 SALVATION ARMY	1	60	255	0.9	1.9
419 SO BAPT CONV..	1	61	74*	0.2	0.5
449 UN METHODIST..	6	1,689	2,007	6.8	14.7
453 UN PRES CH USA	3	861	1,044*	3.5	7.6
CABELL	130	34,818	46,079*	43.1	100.0
019 AMER BAPT CONV	36	10,760	12,723*	11.9	27.6
029 AMER LUTH CH..	1	240	352	0.3	0.8
081 CATHOLIC......	4	0	3,677	3.4	8.0
093 CR CH (DISC)..	3	1,493	1,765*	1.7	3.8
097 CR C AND C CR.	7	1,493	1,765*	1.7	3.8
123 CH GOD (ANDER)	5	437	1,166	1.1	2.5
127 CH GOD (CLEVE)	6	400	473*	0.4	1.0
165 CH OF NAZARENE	3	547	1,029	1.0	2.2
193 EPISCOPAL.....	4	1,976	2,842	2.7	6.2
221 FREE METH C NA	3	50	72	0.1	0.2
281 LUTH CH AMER..	1	572	766	0.7	1.7
283 LUTH--MO SYNOD	1	89	119	0.1	0.3
353 PLY BRETHREN..	1	30	50	-	0.1
357 PRESB CH US...	8	3,648	4,313*	4.0	9.4
403 SALVATION ARMY	1	73	398	0.4	0.9
413 S-D ADVENTISTS	2	129	153*	0.1	0.3
419 SO BAPT CONV..	3	230	272*	0.3	0.6
435 UNITARIAN-UNIV	1	20	20	-	-
443 UN C OF CHRIST	1	222	262*	0.2	0.6
449 UN METHODIST..	39	12,409	13,862	13.0	30.1
CALHOUN	31	2,205	2,497*	35.4	100.0
019 AMER BAPT CONV	9	1,135	1,365*	19.4	54.7
449 UN METHODIST..	22	1,070	1,132	16.1	45.3
CLAY	31	1,925	2,455*	26.3	100.0
019 AMER BAPT CONV	16	1,477	1,843*	19.8	75.1
123 CH GOD (ANDER)	2	51	128	1.4	5.2
165 CH OF NAZARENE	1	39	120	1.3	4.9
413 S-D ADVENTISTS	1	24	30*	0.3	1.2
449 UN METHODIST..	11	334	334	3.6	13.6
DODDRIDGE	32	2,310	2,563*	40.1	100.0
019 AMER BAPT CONV	4	615	737*	11.5	28.8
081 CATHOLIC......	2	0	26	0.4	1.0
093 CR CH (DISC)..	2	79	95*	1.5	3.7
097 CR C AND C CR.	3	100	120*	1.9	4.7
127 CH GOD (CLEVE)	1	14	17*	0.3	0.7
281 LUTH CH AMER..	1	53	78	1.2	3.0
415 S-D BAPTIST GC	2	54	65*	1.0	2.5
449 UN METHODIST..	17	1,395	1,425	22.3	55.6
FAYETTE	134	12,644	17,793*	36.1	100.0
019 AMER BAPT CONV	46	5,757	6,849*	13.9	38.5
081 CATHOLIC......	6	0	1,642	3.3	9.2
093 CR CH (DISC)..	2	150	178*	0.4	1.0
097 CR C AND C CR.	3	225	268*	0.5	1.5
123 CH GOD (ANDER)	13	678	2,125	4.3	11.9
127 CH GOD (CLEVE)	8	456	542*	1.1	3.0
157 CH OF BRETHREN	1	102	121*	0.2	0.7
165 CH OF NAZARENE	1	180	487	1.0	2.7
193 EPISCOPAL.....	2	197	271	0.5	1.5
349 PENT HOLINESS.	1	26	31*	0.1	0.2
357 PRESB CH US...	8	790	940*	1.9	5.3
419 SO BAPT CONV..	1	117	139*	0.3	0.8
449 UN METHODIST..	42	3,966	4,200	8.5	23.6
GILMER	30	2,243	2,522*	32.4	100.0
019 AMER BAPT CONV	8	1,050	1,248*	16.0	49.5
081 CATHOLIC......	1	0	27	0.3	1.1
157 CH OF BRETHREN	1	23	27*	0.3	1.1
357 PRESB CH US...	1	96	114*	1.5	4.5
449 UN METHODIST..	19	1,074	1,106	14.2	43.9
GRANT	35	3,314	3,872*	45.0	100.0
019 AMER BAPT CONV	5	274	341*	4.0	8.8
029 AMER LUTH CH..	1	71	87	1.0	2.2
093 CR CH (DISC)..	1	25	31*	0.4	0.8
127 CH GOD (CLEVE)	2	135	168*	2.0	4.3
157 CH OF BRETHREN	8	1,032	1,283*	14.9	33.1
357 PRESB CH US...	2	337	419*	4.9	10.8
449 UN METHODIST..	16	1,440	1,543	17.9	39.9
GREENBRIER	108	12,496	15,422*	48.1	100.0
019 AMER BAPT CONV	27	3,807	4,576*	14.3	29.7
055 AS REF PRES CH	1	165	198*	0.6	1.3
081 CATHOLIC......	4	0	502	1.6	3.3
097 CR C AND C CR.	1	196	236*	0.7	1.5
123 CH GOD (ANDER)	4	113	359	1.1	2.3
127 CH GOD (CLEVE)	7	496	596*	1.9	3.9
157 CH OF BRETHREN	1	34	41*	0.1	0.3
165 CH OF NAZARENE	1	91	159	0.5	1.0
193 EPISCOPAL.....	4	232	351	1.1	2.3
349 PENT HOLINESS.	6	295	355*	1.1	2.3
357 PRESB CH US...	10	1,885	2,266*	7.1	14.7
413 S-D ADVENTISTS	2	31	37*	0.1	0.2
419 SO BAPT CONV..	3	480	577*	1.8	3.7
449 UN METHODIST..	37	4,671	5,169	16.1	33.5
HAMPSHIRE	49	4,272	5,046*	43.1	100.0
019 AMER BAPT CONV	6	332	404*	3.5	8.0
029 AMER LUTH CH..	1	195	264	2.3	5.2
093 CR CH (DISC)..	4	195	237*	2.0	4.7
097 CR C AND C CR.	6	538	655*	5.6	13.0
157 CH OF BRETHREN	3	245	298*	2.5	5.9
165 CH OF NAZARENE	1	46	145	1.2	2.9
193 EPISCOPAL.....	1	67	104	0.9	2.1
281 LUTH CH AMER..	2	132	176	1.5	3.5
357 PRESB CH US...	5	335	408*	3.5	8.1
443 UN C OF CHRIST	1	199	242*	2.1	4.8
449 UN METHODIST..	19	1,988	2,113	18.0	41.9
HANCOCK	47	9,845	25,253*	63.5	100.0
019 AMER BAPT CONV	2	979	1,193*	3.0	4.7
029 AMER LUTH CH..	2	526	673	1.7	2.7
081 CATHOLIC......	6	0	12,147	30.6	48.1
093 CR CH (DISC)..	1	493	601*	1.5	2.4
097 CR C AND C CR.	4	980	1,194*	3.0	4.7
127 CH GOD (CLEVE)	2	144	175*	0.4	0.7
165 CH OF NAZARENE	8	1,108	2,207	5.6	8.7
193 EPISCOPAL.....	2	193	257	0.6	1.0
221 FREE METH C NA	2	66	102	0.3	0.4
281 LUTH CH AMER..	1	18	18	-	0.1
403 SALVATION ARMY	1	133	469	1.2	1.9
413 S-D ADVENTISTS	1	42	51*	0.1	0.2
419 SO BAPT CONV..	1	298	363*	0.9	1.4
449 UN METHODIST..	7	2,657	3,113	7.8	12.3
453 UN PRES CH USA	7	2,208	2,690*	6.8	10.7
HARDY	31	3,559	4,169*	47.1	100.0
029 AMER LUTH CH..	1	24	28	0.3	0.7
157 CH OF BRETHREN	8	1,287	1,547*	17.5	37.1
193 EPISCOPAL.....	1	20	42	0.5	1.0
281 LUTH CH AMER..	1	125	166	1.9	4.0
285 MENNONITE CH..	3	161	193*	2.2	4.6
357 PRESB CH US...	3	313	376*	4.2	9.0
419 SO BAPT CONV..	1	36	43*	0.5	1.0

*Total adherents estimated from known number of communicant, confirmed, full members.

—Represents a percent less than 0.1.

Percentages may not total due to rounding.

Table 3. Churches and Church Membership by State, County and Denomination: 1971

County and Denomination	Number of churches	Communicant, confirmed, full members	Total adherents: Number	Total adherents: Percent of total population	Total adherents: Percent of total adherents
449 UN METHODIST..	13	1,593	1,774	20.0	42.6
HARRISON	150	25,273	38,015*	52.1	100.0
019 AMER BAPT CONV	44	8,114	9,667*	13.2	25.4
081 CATHOLIC......	10	0	8,264	11.3	21.7
093 CR CH (DISC)..	3	397	473*	0.6	1.2
123 CH GOD (ANDER)	2	52	122	0.2	0.3
127 CH GOD (CLEVE)	3	216	257*	0.4	0.7
165 CH OF NAZARENE	1	92	182	0.2	0.5
193 EPISCOPAL.....	2	620	700	1.0	1.8
199 EVAN CONG CH..	1	434	517*	0.7	1.4
221 FREE METH C NA	1	6	6	-	-
281 LUTH CH AMER..	1	457	592	0.8	1.6
403 SALVATION ARMY	1	111	530	0.7	1.4
413 S-D ADVENTISTS	1	118	141*	0.2	0.4
415 S-D BAPTIST GC	2	233	278*	0.4	0.7
419 SO BAPT CONV..	1	189	225*	0.3	0.6
449 UN METHODIST..	73	13,233	14,868	20.4	39.1
453 UN PRES CH USA	4	1,001	1,193*	1.6	3.1
JACKSON	69	4,847	6,070*	29.0	100.0
019 AMER BAPT CONV	10	1,020	1,260*	6.0	20.8
081 CATHOLIC......	1	0	431	2.1	7.1
093 CR CH (DISC)..	1	39	48*	0.2	0.8
097 CR C AND C CR.	1	20	25*	0.1	0.4
127 CH GOD (CLEVE)	2	47	58*	0.3	1.0
165 CH OF NAZARENE	1	101	327	1.6	5.4
193 EPISCOPAL.....	2	108	132	0.6	2.2
281 LUTH CH AMER..	1	78	102	0.5	1.7
357 PRESB CH US...	3	261	322*	1.5	5.3
449 UN METHODIST..	46	3,050	3,213	15.4	52.9
453 UN PRES CH USA	1	123	152*	0.7	2.5
JEFFERSON	54	7,329	9,737*	45.8	100.0
019 AMER BAPT CONV	3	110	135*	0.6	1.4
081 CATHOLIC......	1	0	310	1.5	3.2
127 CH GOD (CLEVE)	2	125	153*	0.7	1.6
157 CH OF BRETHREN	1	83	102*	0.5	1.0
165 CH OF NAZARENE	1	38	73	0.3	0.7
193 EPISCOPAL.....	7	974	1,680	7.9	17.3
281 LUTH CH AMER..	4	770	1,058	5.0	10.9
285 MENNONITE CH..	1	31	38*	0.2	0.4
357 PRESB CH US...	5	810	995*	4.7	10.2
413 S-D ADVENTISTS	1	67	82*	0.4	0.8
419 SO BAPT CONV..	4	858	1,054*	5.0	10.8
443 UN C OF CHRIST	2	100	123*	0.6	1.3
449 UN METHODIST..	22	3,363	3,934	18.5	40.4
KANAWHA	280	59,437	87,679*	38.2	100.0
019 AMER BAPT CONV	54	17,008	20,340*	8.9	23.2
029 AMER LUTH CH..	2	656	868	0.4	1.0
081 CATHOLIC......	9	0	8,991	3.9	10.3
093 CR CH (DISC)..	4	1,083	1,295*	0.6	1.5
097 CR C AND C CR.	8	650	777*	0.3	0.9
123 CH GOD (ANDER)	24	1,697	4,780	2.1	5.5
127 CH GOD (CLEVE)	10	583	697*	0.3	0.8
165 CH OF NAZARENE	34	3,979	9,609	4.2	11.0
193 EPISCOPAL.....	11	2,618	3,470	1.5	4.0
281 LUTH CH AMER..	2	546	719	0.3	0.8
283 LUTH--MO SYNOD	1	77	109	-	0.1
349 PENT HOLINESS.	3	87	104*	-	0.1
357 PRESB CH US...	31	10,869	12,998*	5.7	14.8
403 SALVATION ARMY	2	135	642	0.3	0.7
413 S-D ADVENTISTS	2	429	513*	0.2	0.6
419 SO BAPT CONV..	7	1,480	1,770*	0.8	2.0
435 UNITARIAN-UNIV	1	29	29	-	-
449 UN METHODIST..	74	16,978	19,331	8.4	22.0
453 UN PRES CH USA	1	533	637*	0.3	0.7
LEWIS	60	5,673	7,574*	42.4	100.0
019 AMER BAPT CONV	9	1,458	1,722*	9.6	22.7
081 CATHOLIC......	4	0	1,047	5.9	13.8
123 CH GOD (ANDER)	1	25	95	0.5	1.3
127 CH GOD (CLEVE)	1	30	35*	0.2	0.5
193 EPISCOPAL.....	2	367	578	3.2	7.6
419 SO BAPT CONV..	1	50	59*	0.3	0.8
449 UN METHODIST..	41	3,631	3,906	21.9	51.6
453 UN PRES CH USA	1	112	132*	0.7	1.7
LINCOLN	36	2,965	3,630*	19.2	100.0
019 AMER BAPT CONV	20	1,984	2,454*	13.0	67.6
093 CR CH (DISC)..	1	39	48*	0.3	1.3
123 CH GOD (ANDER)	1	50	130	0.7	3.6
127 CH GOD (CLEVE)	2	47	58*	0.3	1.6
165 CH OF NAZARENE	1	37	75	0.4	2.1
449 UN METHODIST..	11	808	865	4.6	23.8
LOGAN	56	5,775	8,210*	17.7	100.0
019 AMER BAPT CONV	11	1,398	1,713*	3.7	20.9
081 CATHOLIC......	3	0	766	1.7	9.3
093 CR CH (DISC)..	7	632	774*	1.7	9.4
097 CR C AND C CR.	3	280	343*	0.7	4.2
123 CH GOD (ANDER)	1	15	47	0.1	0.6
127 CH GOD (CLEVE)	13	954	1,169*	2.5	14.2
165 CH OF NAZARENE	2	215	523	1.1	6.4
193 EPISCOPAL.....	1	107	141	0.3	1.7
357 PRESB CH US...	2	416	510*	1.1	6.2
403 SALVATION ARMY	1	26	372	0.8	4.5
413 S-D ADVENTISTS	1	42	51*	0.1	0.6
449 UN METHODIST..	11	1,690	1,801	3.9	21.9
MC DOWELL	95	7,140	10,299*	20.3	100.0
019 AMER BAPT CONV	6	1,169	1,449*	2.9	14.1
081 CATHOLIC......	7	0	1,322	2.6	12.8
093 CR CH (DISC)..	3	93	115*	0.2	1.1
097 CR C AND C CR.	1	100	124*	0.2	1.2
123 CH GOD (ANDER)	4	220	631	1.2	6.1
127 CH GOD (CLEVE)	14	1,024	1,269*	2.5	12.3
165 CH OF NAZARENE	1	59	139	0.3	1.3
193 EPISCOPAL.....	4	163	202	0.4	2.0
349 PENT HOLINESS.	10	352	436*	0.9	4.2
357 PRESB CH US...	3	403	500*	1.0	4.9
403 SALVATION ARMY	1	48	220	0.4	2.1
413 S-D ADVENTISTS	1	35	43*	0.1	0.4
419 SO BAPT CONV..	1	117	145*	0.3	1.4
449 UN METHODIST..	38	3,333	3,674	7.3	35.7
453 UN PRES CH USA	1	24	30*	0.1	0.3
MARION	137	18,266	29,402*	47.9	100.0
019 AMER BAPT CONV	19	4,531	5,359*	8.7	18.2
081 CATHOLIC......	12	0	7,658	12.5	26.0
093 CR CH (DISC)..	3	499	590*	1.0	2.0
123 CH GOD (ANDER)	3	46	136	0.2	0.5
127 CH GOD (CLEVE)	2	90	106*	0.2	0.4
157 CH OF BRETHREN	1	48	57*	0.1	0.2
165 CH OF NAZARENE	2	363	725	1.2	2.5
193 EPISCOPAL.....	2	510	631	1.0	2.1
221 FREE METH C NA	5	116	160	0.3	0.5
281 LUTH CH AMER..	1	560	747	1.2	2.5
403 SALVATION ARMY	2	87	347	0.6	1.2
413 S-D ADVENTISTS	1	45	53*	0.1	0.2
419 SO BAPT CONV..	1	58	69*	0.1	0.2
449 UN METHODIST..	80	9,982	11,190	18.2	38.1
453 UN PRES CH USA	3	1,331	1,574*	2.6	5.4
MARSHALL	53	9,569	17,730*	47.2	100.0
019 AMER BAPT CONV	4	1,266	1,537*	4.1	8.7
081 CATHOLIC......	6	0	5,846	15.5	33.0
093 CR CH (DISC)..	7	1,249	1,517*	4.0	8.6
097 CR C AND C CR.	2	750	911*	2.4	5.1
123 CH GOD (ANDER)	2	227	494	1.3	2.8
165 CH OF NAZARENE	2	146	359	1.0	2.0
193 EPISCOPAL.....	1	148	186	0.5	1.0
403 SALVATION ARMY	1	40	149	0.4	0.8
413 S-D ADVENTISTS	1	40	49*	0.1	0.3
419 SO BAPT CONV..	2	444	539*	1.4	3.0
435 UNITARIAN-UNIV	1	24	39	0.1	0.2
449 UN METHODIST..	19	4,523	5,239	13.9	29.5
453 UN PRES CH USA	5	712	865*	2.3	4.9
MASON	65	6,694	8,298*	34.1	100.0
019 AMER BAPT CONV	14	1,600	1,951*	8.0	23.5
081 CATHOLIC......	2	0	173	0.7	2.1
123 CH GOD (ANDER)	2	151	476	2.0	5.7
127 CH GOD (CLEVE)	2	173	211*	0.9	2.5
165 CH OF NAZARENE	1	123	291	1.2	3.5
193 EPISCOPAL.....	2	204	205	0.8	2.5
281 LUTH CH AMER..	5	350	506	2.1	6.1
357 PRESB CH US...	1	257	313*	1.3	3.8
419 SO BAPT CONV..	1	63	77*	0.3	0.9
449 UN METHODIST..	35	3,773	4,095	16.8	49.3
MERCER	127	23,672	30,059*	47.6	100.0
019 AMER BAPT CONV	11	728	869*	1.4	2.9
081 CATHOLIC......	3	0	1,426	2.3	4.7
093 CR CH (DISC)..	10	1,725	2,060*	3.3	6.9
097 CR C AND C CR.	10	925	1,105*	1.7	3.7
123 CH GOD (ANDER)	6	384	1,019	1.6	3.4
127 CH GOD (CLEVE)	7	892	1,065*	1.7	3.5
157 CH OF BRETHREN	2	151	180*	0.3	0.6
165 CH OF NAZARENE	3	325	797	1.3	2.7
193 EPISCOPAL.....	1	480	537	0.8	1.8
221 FREE METH C NA	1	15	30	-	0.1
281 LUTH CH AMER..	1	305	377	0.6	1.3
349 PENT HOLINESS.	4	342	408*	0.6	1.4
357 PRESB CH US...	7	1,921	2,294*	3.6	7.6
403 SALVATION ARMY	2	119	454	0.7	1.5
413 S-D ADVENTISTS	2	130	155*	0.2	0.5
419 SO BAPT CONV..	19	6,972	8,327*	13.2	27.7
449 UN METHODIST..	37	8,236	8,930	14.1	29.7
453 UN PRES CH USA	1	22	26*	-	0.1
MINERAL	54	8,617	11,031*	47.7	100.0
019 AMER BAPT CONV	1	239	293*	1.3	2.7
075 BRETHREN IN CR	1	6	7*	-	0.1
081 CATHOLIC......	2	0	941	4.1	8.5
127 CH GOD (CLEVE)	3	218	268*	1.2	2.4
157 CH OF BRETHREN	7	1,167	1,432*	6.2	13.0
165 CH OF NAZARENE	1	37	60	0.3	0.5
193 EPISCOPAL.....	1	140	209	0.9	1.9
281 LUTH CH AMER..	1	277	386	1.7	3.5
349 PENT HOLINESS.	1	120	147*	0.6	1.3
357 PRESB CH US...	4	689	846*	3.7	7.7
419 SO BAPT CONV..	2	240	295*	1.3	2.7
449 UN METHODIST..	30	5,484	6,147	26.6	55.7
MINGO	40	5,286	6,931*	21.1	100.0

*Total adherents estimated from known number of communicant, confirmed, full members.

—Represents a percent less than 0.1.

Percentages may not total due to rounding.

Table 3. Churches and Church Membership by State, County and Denomination: 1971

County and Denomination	Number of churches	Communicant, confirmed, full members	Total adherents: Number	Total adherents: Percent of total population	Total adherents: Percent of total adherents
019 AMER BAPT CONV	5	1,454	1,814*	5.5	26.2
081 CATHOLIC......	1	0	263	0.8	3.8
093 CR CH (DISC)..	7	349	435*	1.3	6.3
097 CR C AND C CR.	1	150	187*	0.6	2.7
127 CH GOD (CLEVE)	12	829	1,034*	3.2	14.9
165 CH OF NAZARENE	1	10	10	-	0.1
193 EPISCOPAL.....	1	104	150	0.5	2.2
357 PRESB CH US...	2	366	457*	1.4	6.6
403 SALVATION ARMY	1	40	194	0.6	2.8
413 S-D ADVENTISTS	1	12	15*	-	0.2
419 SO BAPT CONV..	3	1,148	1,432*	4.4	20.7
449 UN METHODIST..	5	824	940	2.9	13.6
MONONGALIA	91	13,236	21,913*	34.4	100.0
019 AMER BAPT CONV	10	1,620	1,890*	3.0	8.6
081 CATHOLIC......	5	0	6,278	9.9	28.6
093 CR CH (DISC)..	3	282	329*	0.5	1.5
123 CH GOD (ANDER)	1	42	97	0.2	0.4
127 CH GOD (CLEVE)	2	112	131*	0.2	0.6
157 CH OF BRETHREN	1	131	153*	0.2	0.7
165 CH OF NAZARENE	1	186	241	0.4	1.1
193 EPISCOPAL.....	1	367	629	1.0	2.9
221 FREE METH C NA	2	33	38	0.1	0.2
226 FRIENDS-USA...	1	6	7*	-	-
281 LUTH CH AMER..	1	309	466	0.7	2.1
353 PLY BRETHREN..	1	70	120	0.2	0.5
403 SALVATION ARMY	1	97	268	0.4	1.2
413 S-D ADVENTISTS	1	56	65*	0.1	0.3
419 SO BAPT CONV..	1	149	174*	0.3	0.8
435 UNITARIAN-UNIV	1	45	45	0.1	0.2
443 UN C OF CHRIST	1	39	46*	0.1	0.2
449 UN METHODIST..	52	8,664	9,736	15.3	44.4
453 UN PRES CH USA	5	1,028	1,200*	1.9	5.5
MONROE	64	5,639	6,542*	58.0	100.0
019 AMER BAPT CONV	20	2,393	2,824*	25.1	43.2
055 AS REF PRES CH	1	74	87*	0.8	1.3
081 CATHOLIC......	1	0	50	0.4	0.8
093 CR CH (DISC)..	2	55	65*	0.6	1.0
097 CR C AND C CR.	4	542	640*	5.7	9.8
127 CH GOD (CLEVE)	2	59	70*	0.6	1.1
157 CH OF BRETHREN	1	118	139*	1.2	2.1
165 CH OF NAZARENE	2	55	134	1.2	2.0
193 EPISCOPAL.....	2	29	33	0.3	0.5
357 PRESB CH US...	6	482	569*	5.0	8.7
449 UN METHODIST..	23	1,832	1,931	17.1	29.5
MORGAN	33	3,073	3,902*	45.7	100.0
081 CATHOLIC......	1	0	231	2.7	5.9
093 CR CH (DISC)..	1	81	99*	1.2	2.5
097 CR C AND C CR.	1	130	159*	1.9	4.1
127 CH GOD (CLEVE)	1	12	15*	0.2	0.4
165 CH OF NAZARENE	1	9	45	0.5	1.2
193 EPISCOPAL.....	1	111	137	1.6	3.5
357 PRESB CH US...	2	257	314*	3.7	8.0
419 SO BAPT CONV..	1	46	56*	0.7	1.4
449 UN METHODIST..	24	2,427	2,846	33.3	72.9
NICHOLAS	76	6,981	9,409*	41.7	100.0
019 AMER BAPT CONV	25	3,650	4,515*	20.0	48.0
081 CATHOLIC......	2	0	426	1.9	4.5
097 CR C AND C CR.	1	60	74*	0.3	0.8
123 CH GOD (ANDER)	2	185	656	2.9	7.0
127 CH GOD (CLEVE)	3	90	111*	0.5	1.2
165 CH OF NAZARENE	4	120	479	2.1	5.1
193 EPISCOPAL.....	1	39	44	0.2	0.5
357 PRESB CH US...	2	204	252*	1.1	2.7
413 S-D ADVENTISTS	1	12	15*	0.1	0.2
449 UN METHODIST..	35	2,621	2,837	12.6	30.2
OHIO	70	16,892	39,013*	60.8	100.0
019 AMER BAPT CONV	1	310	363*	0.6	0.9
029 AMER LUTH CH..	3	1,079	1,575	2.5	4.0
081 CATHOLIC......	14	0	17,972	28.0	46.1
093 CR CH (DISC)..	2	552	646*	1.0	1.7
097 CR C AND C CR.	3	823	963*	1.5	2.5
123 CH GOD (ANDER)	3	171	361	0.6	0.9
127 CH GOD (CLEVE)	1	60	70*	0.1	0.2
165 CH OF NAZARENE	2	123	170	0.3	0.4
193 EPISCOPAL.....	5	1,189	1,804	2.8	4.6
281 LUTH CH AMER..	6	1,855	2,415	3.8	6.2
403 SALVATION ARMY	1	104	214	0.3	0.5
413 S-D ADVENTISTS	1	99	116*	0.2	0.3
443 UN C OF CHRIST	3	818	958*	1.5	2.5
449 UN METHODIST..	16	6,045	7,097	11.1	18.2
453 UN PRES CH USA	9	3,664	4,289*	6.7	11.0
PENDLETON	48	3,702	4,353*	61.9	100.0
029 AMER LUTH CH..	10	726	980	13.9	22.5
093 CR CH (DISC)..	1	34	40*	0.6	0.9
097 CR C AND C CR.	1	125	148*	2.1	3.4
123 CH GOD (ANDER)	1	4	12	0.2	0.3
157 CH OF BRETHREN	7	615	727*	10.3	16.7
285 MENNONITE CH..	4	125	148*	2.1	3.4
357 PRESB CH US...	5	463	547*	7.8	12.6
413 S-D ADVENTISTS	1	22	26*	0.4	0.6
449 UN METHODIST..	18	1,588	1,725	24.5	39.6
PLEASANTS	22	2,527	3,098*	42.6	100.0
019 AMER BAPT CONV	6	960	1,181*	16.2	38.1
081 CATHOLIC......	1	0	160	2.2	5.2
165 CH OF NAZARENE	1	35	36	0.5	1.2
193 EPISCOPAL.....	1	101	119	1.6	3.8
449 UN METHODIST..	12	1,245	1,373	18.9	44.3
453 UN PRES CH USA	1	186	229*	3.1	7.4
POCAHONTAS	49	2,888	3,599*	40.6	100.0
029 AMER LUTH CH..	1	19	34	0.4	0.9
081 CATHOLIC......	1	0	33	0.4	0.9
097 CR C AND C CR.	1	10	12*	0.1	0.3
127 CH GOD (CLEVE)	1	35	42*	0.5	1.2
157 CH OF BRETHREN	1	125	150*	1.7	4.2
165 CH OF NAZARENE	3	94	338	3.8	9.4
193 EPISCOPAL.....	2	17	32	0.4	0.9
285 MENNONITE CH..	1	9	11*	0.1	0.3
357 PRESB CH US...	7	622	744*	8.4	20.7
449 UN METHODIST..	31	1,957	2,203	24.8	61.2
PRESTON	105	8,031	7,628*	30.0	100.0
019 AMER BAPT CONV	9	1,123	1,373*	5.4	18.0
081 CATHOLIC......	7	0	934	3.7	12.2
157 CH OF BRETHREN	4	766	937*	3.7	12.3
165 CH OF NAZARENE	3	149	305	1.2	4.0
193 EPISCOPAL.....	1	56	62	0.2	0.8
221 FREE METH C NA	2	38	65	0.3	0.9
281 LUTH CH AMER..	5	247	337	1.3	4.4
349 PENT HOLINESS.	1	30	37*	0.1	0.5
353 PLY BRETHREN..	1	40	80	0.3	1.0
449 UN METHODIST..	69	5,174	2,999	11.8	39.3
453 UN PRES CH USA	3	408	499*	2.0	6.5
PUTNAM	47	5,952	8,101*	29.3	100.0
019 AMER BAPT CONV	15	3,167	3,904*	14.1	48.2
081 CATHOLIC......	1	0	90	0.3	1.1
093 CR CH (DISC)..	1	17	21*	0.1	0.3
123 CH GOD (ANDER)	5	409	1,088	3.9	13.4
165 CH OF NAZARENE	4	281	538	1.9	6.6
193 EPISCOPAL.....	1	101	180	0.7	2.2
281 LUTH CH AMER..	1	108	159	0.6	2.0
357 PRESB CH US...	5	346	427*	1.5	5.3
449 UN METHODIST..	14	1,523	1,694	6.1	20.9
RALEIGH	107	16,727	22,387*	31.9	100.0
019 AMER BAPT CONV	37	7,593	9,138*	13.0	40.8
081 CATHOLIC......	1	0	1,799	2.6	8.0
093 CR CH (DISC)..	3	833	1,002*	1.4	4.5
097 CR C AND C CR.	4	249	300*	0.4	1.3
123 CH GOD (ANDER)	3	240	613	0.9	2.7
127 CH GOD (CLEVE)	16	1,154	1,389*	2.0	6.2
157 CH OF BRETHREN	1	142	171*	0.2	0.8
165 CH OF NAZARENE	1	116	161	0.2	0.7
193 EPISCOPAL.....	1	383	527	0.8	2.4
221 FREE METH C NA	1	23	24	-	0.1
281 LUTH CH AMER..	1	108	159	0.2	0.7
349 PENT HOLINESS.	3	53	64*	0.1	0.3
353 PLY BRETHREN..	1	21	80	0.1	0.4
357 PRESB CH US...	2	866	1,042*	1.5	4.7
403 SALVATION ARMY	1	58	389	0.6	1.7
413 S-D ADVENTISTS	2	89	107*	0.2	0.5
419 SO BAPT CONV..	2	1,641	1,975*	2.8	8.8
435 UNITARIAN-UNIV	1	12	12	-	0.1
449 UN METHODIST..	22	2,972	3,226	4.6	14.4
453 UN PRES CH USA	4	174	209*	0.3	0.9
RANDOLPH	74	6,751	9,233*	37.5	100.0
019 AMER BAPT CONV	4	611	738*	3.0	8.0
081 CATHOLIC......	4	0	1,283	5.2	13.9
097 CR C AND C CR.	2	172	208*	0.8	2.3
127 CH GOD (CLEVE)	4	337	407*	1.7	4.4
157 CH OF BRETHREN	3	108	130*	0.5	1.4
165 CH OF NAZARENE	1	190	471	1.9	5.1
193 EPISCOPAL.....	1	114	157	0.6	1.7
281 LUTH CH AMER..	1	173	209	0.8	2.3
285 MENNONITE CH..	5	109	132*	0.5	1.4
357 PRESB CH US...	12	1,145	1,383*	5.6	15.0
413 S-D ADVENTISTS	1	41	50*	0.2	0.5
449 UN METHODIST..	36	3,751	4,065	16.5	44.0
RITCHIE	49	3,652	4,025*	39.7	100.0
019 AMER BAPT CONV	7	770	919*	9.1	22.8
081 CATHOLIC......	2	0	90	0.9	2.2
127 CH GOD (CLEVE)	2	122	146*	1.4	3.6
415 S-D BAPTIST GC	1	58	69*	0.7	1.7
449 UN METHODIST..	35	2,662	2,753	27.1	68.4
453 UN PRES CH USA	2	40	48*	0.5	1.2
ROANE	53	3,726	4,476*	31.7	100.0
019 AMER BAPT CONV	24	2,209	2,602*	18.4	58.1
081 CATHOLIC......	1	0	86	0.6	1.9
165 CH OF NAZARENE	2	139	383	2.7	8.6
357 PRESB CH US...	1	38	45*	0.3	1.0
449 UN METHODIST..	25	1,340	1,360	9.6	30.4
SUMMERS	45	4,182	4,969*	37.6	100.0
019 AMER BAPT CONV	21	2,268	2,677*	20.3	53.9
081 CATHOLIC......	1	0	81	0.6	1.6

*Total adherents estimated from known number of communicant, confirmed, full members.

—Represents a percent less than 0.1.

Percentages may not total due to rounding.

Table 3. Churches and Church Membership by State, County and Denomination: 1971

County and Denomination	Number of churches	Communicant, confirmed, full members	Total adherents: Number	Total adherents: Percent of total population	Total adherents: Percent of total adherents
093 CR CH (DISC)..	1	142	168*	1.3	3.4
127 CH GOD (CLEVE)	1	14	17*	0.1	0.3
165 CH OF NAZARENE	1	14	34	0.3	0.7
193 EPISCOPAL.....	1	58	66	0.5	1.3
353 PLY BRETHREN..	2	74	230	1.7	4.6
357 PRESB CH US...	2	215	254*	1.9	5.1
449 UN METHODIST..	15	1,397	1,442	10.9	29.0
TAYLOR	38	5,144	6,833*	49.2	100.0
019 AMER BAPT CONV	7	1,588	1,898*	13.7	27.8
081 CATHOLIC......	2	0	681	4.9	10.0
093 CR CH (DISC)..	1	173	207*	1.5	3.0
097 CR C AND C CR.	1	219	262*	1.9	3.8
157 CH OF BRETHREN	1	21	25*	0.2	0.4
165 CH OF NAZARENE	1	60	190	1.4	2.8
193 EPISCOPAL.....	1	51	82	0.6	1.2
281 LUTH CH AMER..	1	67	83	0.6	1.2
403 SALVATION ARMY	1	70	256	1.8	3.7
413 S-D ADVENTISTS	1	37	44*	0.3	0.6
449 UN METHODIST..	20	2,755	2,982	21.5	43.6
453 UN PRES CH USA	1	103	123*	0.9	1.8
TUCKER	35	2,197	3,082*	41.4	100.0
019 AMER BAPT CONV	1	161	194*	2.6	6.3
081 CATHOLIC......	3	0	470	6.3	15.2
127 CH GOD (CLEVE)	4	149	180*	2.4	5.8
157 CH OF BRETHREN	1	20	24*	0.3	0.8
165 CH OF NAZARENE	1	94	206	2.8	6.7
193 EPISCOPAL.....	1	6	7	0.1	0.2
221 FREE METH C NA	1	21	28	0.4	0.9
281 LUTH CH AMER..	1	82	103	1.4	3.3
357 PRESB CH US...	3	172	208*	2.8	6.7
413 S-D ADVENTISTS	1	37	45*	0.6	1.5
449 UN METHODIST..	18	1,455	1,617	21.7	52.5
TYLER	32	2,507	3,266*	32.9	100.0
019 AMER BAPT CONV	3	679	839*	8.4	25.7
081 CATHOLIC......	1	0	201	2.0	6.2
093 CR CH (DISC)..	1	55	68*	0.7	2.1
097 CR C AND C CR.	3	100	124*	1.2	3.8
127 CH GOD (CLEVE)	1	23	28*	0.3	0.9
165 CH OF NAZARENE	2	192	459	4.6	14.1
193 EPISCOPAL.....	1	102	139	1.4	4.3
449 UN METHODIST..	19	1,140	1,141	11.5	34.9
453 UN PRES CH USA	1	216	267*	2.7	8.2
UPSHUR	56	5,379	6,350*	33.3	100.0
019 AMER BAPT CONV	5	739	879*	4.6	13.8
081 CATHOLIC......	1	0	425	2.2	6.7
097 CR C AND C CR.	1	30	36*	0.2	0.6
127 CH GOD (CLEVE)	1	45	54*	0.3	0.9
157 CH OF BRETHREN	1	23	27*	0.1	0.4
165 CH OF NAZARENE	1	61	90	0.5	1.4
193 EPISCOPAL.....	1	78	101	0.5	1.6
413 S-D ADVENTISTS	1	64	76*	0.4	1.2
449 UN METHODIST..	42	4,155	4,443	23.3	70.0
453 UN PRES CH USA	2	184	219*	1.1	3.4
WAYNE	57	9,138	11,094*	29.5	100.0
019 AMER BAPT CONV	23	3,422	4,210*	11.2	37.9
093 CR CH (DISC)..	4	470	578*	1.5	5.2
123 CH GOD (ANDER)	1	80	205	0.5	1.8
127 CH GOD (CLEVE)	5	284	349*	0.9	3.1
175 CONG CR CH....	1	100	123*	0.3	1.1
357 PRESB CH US...	2	256	315*	0.8	2.8
419 SO BAPT CONV..	4	2,072	2,549*	6.8	23.0
449 UN METHODIST..	17	2,454	2,765	7.4	24.9
WEBSTER	32	3,723	4,360*	44.4	100.0
019 AMER BAPT CONV	7	978	1,196*	12.2	27.4
081 CATHOLIC......	2	0	72	0.7	1.7
123 CH GOD (ANDER)	2	11	53	0.5	1.2
165 CH OF NAZARENE	1	11	11	0.1	0.3
413 S-D ADVENTISTS	1	15	18*	0.2	0.4
419 SO BAPT CONV..	1	112	137*	1.4	3.1
449 UN METHODIST..	18	2,596	2,873	29.3	65.9
WETZEL	25	2,886	5,498*	27.1	100.0
019 AMER BAPT CONV	3	524	650*	3.2	11.8
081 CATHOLIC......	3	0	1,032	5.1	18.8
093 CR CH (DISC)..	4	551	684*	3.4	12.4
097 CR C AND C CR.	4	821	1,018*	5.0	18.5
123 CH GOD (ANDER)	3	146	401	2.0	7.3
127 CH GOD (CLEVE)	2	121	150*	0.7	2.7
165 CH OF NAZARENE	1	102	282	1.4	5.1
193 EPISCOPAL.....	1	119	208	1.0	3.8
281 LUTH CH AMER..	1	95	149	0.7	2.7
449 UN METHODIST..	1	45	475	2.3	8.6
453 UN PRES CH USA	2	362	449*	2.2	8.2
WIRT	33	1,716	1,926*	46.4	100.0
019 AMER BAPT CONV	12	680	833*	20.1	43.3
165 CH OF NAZARENE	1	27	48	1.2	2.5
449 UN METHODIST..	19	946	968	23.3	50.3
453 UN PRES CH USA	1	63	77*	1.9	4.0
WOOD	115	25,878	35,963*	41.4	100.0

County and Denomination	Number of churches	Communicant, confirmed, full members	Total adherents: Number	Total adherents: Percent of total population	Total adherents: Percent of total adherents
019 AMER BAPT CONV	25	7,370	9,097*	10.5	25.3
081 CATHOLIC......	3	0	3,866	4.5	10.7
093 CR CH (DISC)..	2	420	518*	0.6	1.4
097 CR C AND C CR.	2	250	309*	0.4	0.9
123 CH GOD (ANDER)	1	126	277	0.3	0.8
127 CH GOD (CLEVE)	3	370	457*	0.5	1.3
165 CH OF NAZARENE	5	631	1,610	1.9	4.5
193 EPISCOPAL.....	3	1,008	1,364	1.6	3.8
281 LUTH CH AMER..	2	954	1,284	1.5	3.6
283 LUTH--MO SYNOD	1	199	341	0.4	0.9
349 PENT HOLINESS.	1	17	21*	-	0.1
403 SALVATION ARMY	1	126	428	0.5	1.2
413 S-D ADVENTISTS	2	304	375*	0.4	1.0
419 SO BAPT CONV..	2	533	658*	0.8	1.8
449 UN METHODIST..	56	11,754	13,117	15.1	36.5
453 UN PRES CH USA	6	1,816	2,241*	2.6	6.2
WYOMING	60	6,363	8,399*	27.9	100.0
019 AMER BAPT CONV	27	3,454	4,311*	14.3	51.3
081 CATHOLIC......	2	0	163	0.5	1.9
093 CR CH (DISC)..	1	59	74*	0.2	0.9
123 CH GOD (ANDER)	3	217	591	2.0	7.0
127 CH GOD (CLEVE)	8	576	719*	2.4	8.6
165 CH OF NAZARENE	1	115	357	1.2	4.3
193 EPISCOPAL.....	1	29	36	0.1	0.4
349 PENT HOLINESS.	1	147	183*	0.6	2.2
357 PRESB CH US...	3	293	366*	1.2	4.4
419 SO BAPT CONV..	1	43	54*	0.2	0.6
449 UN METHODIST..	12	1,430	1,545	5.1	18.4
CO DATA NOT AVAIL	214	9,598	20,690*	N/A	N/A
151 L-D SAINTS....	0	0	9,222	N/A	N/A
193 EPISCOPAL.....	2	206	258	N/A	N/A
223 FREE WILL BAPT	175	8,347	10,066*	N/A	N/A
349 PENT HOLINESS.	4	273	329*	N/A	N/A
467 WESLEYAN......	33	772	815	N/A	N/A

WISCONSIN

County and Denomination	Number of churches	Communicant, confirmed, full members	Total adherents: Number	Total adherents: Percent of total population	Total adherents: Percent of total adherents
THE STATE.....	4,179	1,087,158	2,972,647*	67.3	100.0
ADAMS	13	1,073	2,852*	30.9	100.0
029 AMER LUTH CH..	3	623	908	9.8	31.8
081 CATHOLIC......	2	0	1,360	14.7	47.7
283 LUTH--MO SYNOD	2	223	312	3.4	10.9
413 S-D ADVENTISTS	1	14	17*	0.2	0.6
443 UN C OF CHRIST	3	72	87*	0.9	3.1
449 UN METHODIST..	2	141	168	1.8	5.9
ASHLAND	28	3,862	12,013*	71.7	100.0
029 AMER LUTH CH..	1	357	471	2.8	3.9
081 CATHOLIC......	11	0	6,574	39.3	54.7
193 EPISCOPAL.....	1	107	154	0.9	1.3
201 EVAN COV CH AM	1	60	73*	0.4	0.6
281 LUTH CH AMER..	1	616	1,011	6.0	8.4
283 LUTH--MO SYNOD	5	1,612	2,379	14.2	19.8
413 S-D ADVENTISTS	1	33	40*	0.2	0.3
443 UN C OF CHRIST	3	315	384*	2.3	3.2
449 UN METHODIST..	3	308	374	2.2	3.1
453 UN PRES CH USA	1	454	553*	3.3	4.6
BARRON	58	12,355	23,663*	69.7	100.0
029 AMER LUTH CH..	16	6,194	8,240	24.3	34.8
081 CATHOLIC......	11	0	7,448	21.9	31.5
123 CH GOD (ANDER)	1	48	100	0.3	0.4
157 CH OF BRETHREN	1	50	60*	0.2	0.3
193 EPISCOPAL.....	2	105	187	0.6	0.8
201 EVAN COV CH AM	1	104	125*	0.4	0.5
221 FREE METH C NA	1	34	38	0.1	0.2
281 LUTH CH AMER..	3	632	849	2.5	3.6
283 LUTH--MO SYNOD	9	2,516	3,435	10.1	14.5
413 S-D ADVENTISTS	2	93	112*	0.3	0.5
449 UN METHODIST..	9	2,094	2,451	7.2	10.4
453 UN PRES CH USA	1	380	458*	1.3	1.9
469 WISC EVAN LUTH	1	105	160	0.5	0.7
BAYFIELD	31	2,096	5,992*	51.3	100.0
029 AMER LUTH CH..	3	665	897	7.7	15.0
081 CATHOLIC......	13	0	3,254	27.9	54.3
193 EPISCOPAL.....	1	2	5	-	0.1
281 LUTH CH AMER..	4	577	745	6.4	12.4
283 LUTH--MO SYNOD	2	201	264	2.3	4.4
443 UN C OF CHRIST	3	196	236*	2.0	3.9
449 UN METHODIST..	2	197	281	2.4	4.7
453 UN PRES CH USA	3	258	310*	2.7	5.2
BROWN	102	25,444	127,299*	80.4	100.0
019 AMER BAPT CONV	1	255	327*	0.2	0.3
029 AMER LUTH CH..	10	7,721	11,125	7.0	8.7

*Total adherents estimated from known number of communicant, confirmed, full members.

—Represents a percent less than 0.1.

Percentages may not total due to rounding.

Table 3. Churches and Church Membership by State, County and Denomination: 1971

County and Denomination	Number of churches	Communicant, confirmed, full members	Total adherents		
			Number	Percent of total population	Percent of total adherents
081 CATHOLIC......	39	0	91,480	57.8	71.9
097 CR C AND C CR.	2	142	182*	0.1	0.1
127 CH GOD (CLEVE)	1	18	23*	-	-
165 CH OF NAZARENE	1	38	84	0.1	0.1
175 CONG CR CH....	1	456	586*	0.4	0.5
193 EPISCOPAL.....	4	967	1,428	0.9	1.1
281 LUTH CH AMER..	3	714	1,162	0.7	0.9
283 LUTH--MO SYNOD	8	3,643	5,378	3.4	4.2
293 MORAV CH-NORTH	2	767	967	0.6	0.8
353 PLY BRETHREN..	1	10	20	-	-
403 SALVATION ARMY	1	56	205	0.1	0.2
413 S-D ADVENTISTS	1	326	419*	0.3	0.3
419 SO BAPT CONV..	1	163	209*	0.1	0.2
443 UN C OF CHRIST	3	1,187	1,524*	1.0	1.2
449 UN METHODIST..	8	3,952	5,429	3.4	4.3
453 UN PRES CH USA	6	1,942	2,494*	1.6	2.0
469 WISC EVAN LUTH	9	3,087	4,257	2.7	3.3
BUFFALO	27	5,481	10,061*	73.2	100.0
029 AMER LUTH CH..	7	2,232	3,081	22.4	30.6
081 CATHOLIC......	4	0	2,915	21.2	29.0
283 LUTH--MO SYNOD	4	942	1,289	9.4	12.8
443 UN C OF CHRIST	3	530	653*	4.8	6.5
449 UN METHODIST..	4	700	771	5.6	7.7
469 WISC EVAN LUTH	5	1,077	1,352	9.8	13.4
BURNETT	19	1,780	3,288*	35.4	100.0
029 AMER LUTH CH..	3	496	665	7.2	20.2
081 CATHOLIC......	4	0	831	9.0	25.3
201 EVAN COV CH AM	2	91	108*	1.2	3.3
281 LUTH CH AMER..	3	456	730	7.9	22.2
283 LUTH--MO SYNOD	2	163	210	2.3	6.4
449 UN METHODIST..	5	574	744	8.0	22.6
CALUMET	32	4,778	18,817*	68.2	100.0
081 CATHOLIC......	13	0	12,431	45.0	66.1
127 CH GOD (CLEVE)	1	25	33*	0.1	0.2
193 EPISCOPAL.....	1	33	41	0.1	0.2
283 LUTH--MO SYNOD	6	1,697	2,399	8.7	12.7
443 UN C OF CHRIST	4	1,311	1,719*	6.2	9.1
449 UN METHODIST..	4	741	942	3.4	5.0
453 UN PRES CH USA	1	51	67*	0.2	0.4
469 WISC EVAN LUTH	2	920	1,185	4.3	6.3
CHIPPEWA	61	10,723	32,570*	68.3	100.0
029 AMER LUTH CH..	11	3,954	5,680	11.9	17.4
081 CATHOLIC......	16	0	17,788	37.3	54.6
097 CR C AND C CR.	4	264	332*	0.7	1.0
123 CH GOD (ANDER)	1	25	63	0.1	0.2
157 CH OF BRETHREN	2	253	318*	0.7	1.0
193 EPISCOPAL.....	2	149	228	0.5	0.7
283 LUTH--MO SYNOD	5	1,743	2,399	5.0	7.4
413 S-D ADVENTISTS	1	18	23*	-	0.1
415 S-D BAPTIST GC	1	101	127*	0.3	0.4
443 UN C OF CHRIST	1	190	239*	0.5	0.7
449 UN METHODIST..	10	2,261	2,875	6.0	8.8
453 UN PRES CH USA	3	801	1,008*	2.1	3.1
469 WISC EVAN LUTH	4	964	1,490	3.1	4.6
CLARK	60	9,304	22,545*	74.3	100.0
029 AMER LUTH CH..	7	1,779	2,480	8.2	11.0
081 CATHOLIC......	12	0	9,907	32.6	43.9
193 EPISCOPAL.....	1	81	94	0.3	0.4
221 FREE METH C NA	1	56	58	0.2	0.3
281 LUTH CH AMER..	3	689	979	3.2	4.3
283 LUTH--MO SYNOD	12	3,051	4,348	14.3	19.3
413 S-D ADVENTISTS	2	37	46*	0.2	0.2
443 UN C OF CHRIST	7	1,291	1,600*	5.3	7.1
449 UN METHODIST..	12	1,415	1,799	5.9	8.0
469 WISC EVAN LUTH	3	905	1,234	4.1	5.5
COLUMBIA	65	17,733	33,488*	83.4	100.0
019 AMER BAPT CONV	4	456	557*	1.4	1.7
029 AMER LUTH CH..	5	1,821	2,591	6.5	7.7
081 CATHOLIC......	9	0	9,322	23.2	27.8
105 CHRISTIAN REF.	2	437	828	2.1	2.5
165 CH OF NAZARENE	1	46	131	0.3	0.4
193 EPISCOPAL.....	3	294	344	0.9	1.0
281 LUTH CH AMER..	3	1,541	2,227	5.5	6.7
283 LUTH--MO SYNOD	3	2,430	3,296	8.2	9.8
371 REF CH IN AM..	2	630	1,027	2.6	3.1
413 S-D ADVENTISTS	2	262	320*	0.8	1.0
443 UN C OF CHRIST	3	758	927*	2.3	2.8
449 UN METHODIST..	10	2,630	3,593	8.9	10.7
453 UN PRES CH USA	10	2,668	3,261*	8.1	9.7
469 WISC EVAN LUTH	9	3,760	5,064	12.6	15.1
CRAWFORD	29	3,608	10,055*	65.9	100.0
029 AMER LUTH CH..	7	2,137	3,120	20.5	31.0
081 CATHOLIC......	8	0	5,350	35.1	53.2
097 CR C AND C CR.	2	250	310*	2.0	3.1
127 CH GOD (CLEVE)	1	52	65*	0.4	0.6
175 CONG CR CH....	1	99	123*	0.8	1.2
193 EPISCOPAL.....	1	45	53	0.3	0.5
443 UN C OF CHRIST	1	36	45*	0.3	0.4
449 UN METHODIST..	8	989	989	6.5	9.8
DANE	175	66,740	170,694*	58.8	100.0
019 AMER BAPT CONV	3	1,032	1,266*	0.4	0.7
029 AMER LUTH CH..	39	28,018	39,169	13.5	22.9
081 CATHOLIC......	37	0	79,992	27.6	46.9
097 CR C AND C CR.	3	364	446*	0.2	0.3
105 CHRISTIAN REF.	1	114	216	0.1	0.1
123 CH GOD (ANDER)	1	38	68	-	-
127 CH GOD (CLEVE)	1	13	16*	-	-
165 CH OF NAZARENE	1	140	225	0.1	0.1
175 CONG CR CH....	1	341	418*	0.1	0.2
193 EPISCOPAL.....	6	1,968	2,506	0.9	1.5
201 EVAN COV CH AM	1	46	56*	-	-
221 FREE METH C NA	1	54	68	-	-
226 FRIENDS-USA...	1	106	130*	-	0.1
281 LUTH CH AMER..	9	5,448	7,604	2.6	4.5
283 LUTH--MO SYNOD	8	3,598	4,999	1.7	2.9
293 MORAV CH-NORTH	3	1,002	1,323	0.5	0.8
353 PLY BRETHREN..	1	10	15	-	-
403 SALVATION ARMY	1	78	329	0.1	0.2
413 S-D ADVENTISTS	1	588	721*	0.2	0.4
415 S-D BAPTIST GC	1	107	131*	-	0.1
419 SO BAPT CONV..	2	358	439*	0.2	0.3
435 UNITARIAN-UNIV	2	546	915	0.3	0.5
443 UN C OF CHRIST	14	6,005	7,364*	2.5	4.3
449 UN METHODIST..	21	9,885	13,393	4.6	7.8
453 UN PRES CH USA	9	4,470	5,481*	1.9	3.2
469 WISC EVAN LUTH	7	2,411	3,404	1.2	2.0
DODGE	86	25,567	51,531*	74.7	100.0
019 AMER BAPT CONV	1	219	270*	0.4	0.5
029 AMER LUTH CH..	9	5,520	7,516	10.9	14.6
081 CATHOLIC......	18	0	17,189	24.9	33.4
193 EPISCOPAL.....	3	177	248	0.4	0.5
221 FREE METH C NA	1	30	40	0.1	0.1
281 LUTH CH AMER..	2	877	1,181	1.7	2.3
283 LUTH--MO SYNOD	13	5,500	7,342	10.6	14.2
443 UN C OF CHRIST	4	497	612*	0.9	1.2
449 UN METHODIST..	9	2,340	3,123	4.5	6.1
453 UN PRES CH USA	4	986	1,214*	1.8	2.4
469 WISC EVAN LUTH	22	9,421	12,796	18.5	24.8
DOOR	45	6,911	16,038*	79.8	100.0
029 AMER LUTH CH..	8	1,624	2,047	10.2	12.8
081 CATHOLIC......	13	0	7,005	34.8	43.7
193 EPISCOPAL.....	3	81	102	0.5	0.6
226 FRIENDS-USA...	1	55	66*	0.3	0.4
281 LUTH CH AMER..	2	356	488	2.4	3.0
283 LUTH--MO SYNOD	1	340	460	2.3	2.9
293 MORAV CH-NORTH	4	959	1,198	6.0	7.5
413 S-D ADVENTISTS	2	23	28*	0.1	0.2
443 UN C OF CHRIST	1	214	257*	1.3	1.6
449 UN METHODIST..	4	724	883	4.4	5.5
469 WISC EVAN LUTH	6	2,535	3,504	17.4	21.8
DOUGLAS	49	8,763	22,049*	49.4	100.0
019 AMER BAPT CONV	1	112	134*	0.3	0.6
029 AMER LUTH CH..	5	2,288	3,235	7.2	14.7
081 CATHOLIC......	16	0	9,963	22.3	45.2
193 EPISCOPAL.....	1	250	270	0.6	1.2
201 EVAN COV CH AM	4	195	234*	0.5	1.1
281 LUTH CH AMER..	4	2,367	3,359	7.5	15.2
283 LUTH--MO SYNOD	2	652	870	1.9	3.9
403 SALVATION ARMY	1	88	509	1.1	2.3
413 S-D ADVENTISTS	2	63	76*	0.2	0.3
449 UN METHODIST..	3	966	1,260	2.8	5.7
453 UN PRES CH USA	10	1,782	2,139*	4.8	9.7
DUNN	56	13,072	21,314*	73.1	100.0
019 AMER BAPT CONV	1	18	21*	0.1	0.1
029 AMER LUTH CH..	20	8,342	11,514	39.5	54.0
081 CATHOLIC......	5	0	3,855	13.2	18.1
121 CH GOD (ABR)..	1	35	41*	0.1	0.2
123 CH GOD (ANDER)	1	15	22	0.1	0.1
157 CH OF BRETHREN	1	15	18*	0.1	0.1
165 CH OF NAZARENE	3	130	209	0.7	1.0
193 EPISCOPAL.....	1	88	130	0.4	0.6
283 LUTH--MO SYNOD	3	522	683	2.3	3.2
413 S-D ADVENTISTS	1	39	46*	0.2	0.2
419 SO BAPT CONV..	1	19	22*	0.1	0.1
443 UN C OF CHRIST	1	252	298*	1.0	1.4
449 UN METHODIST..	12	2,243	2,806	9.6	13.2
469 WISC EVAN LUTH	5	1,354	1,649	5.7	7.7
EAU CLAIRE	62	27,739	50,930*	75.8	100.0
019 AMER BAPT CONV	3	555	668*	1.0	1.3
029 AMER LUTH CH..	12	15,102	20,282	30.2	39.8
081 CATHOLIC......	10	0	13,457	20.0	26.4
097 CR C AND C CR.	1	100	120*	0.2	0.2
165 CH OF NAZARENE	1	55	87	0.1	0.2
193 EPISCOPAL.....	2	857	1,213	1.8	2.4
281 LUTH CH AMER..	1	364	525	0.8	1.0
283 LUTH--MO SYNOD	14	5,568	7,799	11.6	15.3
285 MENNONITE CH..	1	23	28*	-	0.1
403 SALVATION ARMY	1	48	179	0.3	0.4
413 S-D ADVENTISTS	1	157	189*	0.3	0.4
435 UNITARIAN-UNIV	1	16	16	-	-
443 UN C OF CHRIST	4	1,449	1,744*	2.6	3.4
449 UN METHODIST..	6	2,686	3,669	5.5	7.2
453 UN PRES CH USA	2	632	761*	1.1	1.5
469 WISC EVAN LUTH	2	127	193	0.3	0.4

*Total adherents estimated from known number of communicant, confirmed, full members.

—Represents a percent less than 0.1.

Percentages may not total due to rounding.

Table 3. Churches and Church Membership by State, County and Denomination: 1971

County and Denomination	Number of churches	Communicant, confirmed, full members	Total adherents: Number	Percent of total population	Percent of total adherents
FLORENCE	8	294	1,272*	38.6	100.0
081 CATHOLIC......	3	0	887	26.9	69.7
201 EVAN COV CH AM	1	15	18*	0.5	1.4
281 LUTH CH AMER..	1	40	48	1.5	3.8
453 UN PRES CH USA	1	94	116*	3.5	9.1
469 WISC EVAN LUTH	2	145	203	6.2	16.0
FOND DU LAC	94	25,223	74,327*	87.9	100.0
019 AMER BAPT CONV	3	594	735*	0.9	1.0
029 AMER LUTH CH..	6	4,016	5,502	6.5	7.4
081 CATHOLIC......	27	0	39,440	46.6	53.1
105 CHRISTIAN REF.	3	597	1,166	1.4	1.6
127 CH GOD (CLEVE)	1	26	32*	-	-
193 EPISCOPAL.....	4	1,186	1,647	1.9	2.2
281 LUTH CH AMER..	1	1,125	1,533	1.8	2.1
283 LUTH--MO SYNOD	3	1,112	1,725	2.0	2.3
371 REF CH IN AM..	6	2,304	3,631	4.3	4.9
403 SALVATION ARMY	1	62	316	0.4	0.4
413 S-D ADVENTISTS	1	32	40*	-	0.1
443 UN C OF CHRIST	10	3,048	6,248*	7.4	8.4
449 UN METHODIST..	13	3,211	4,298	5.1	5.8
453 UN PRES CH USA	1	844	1,045*	1.2	1.4
469 WISC EVAN LUTH	14	5,066	6,969	8.2	9.4
FOREST	17	1,106	3,813*	49.6	100.0
081 CATHOLIC......	6	0	2,251	29.3	59.0
127 CH GOD (CLEVE)	1	54	67*	0.9	1.8
165 CH OF NAZARENE	1	32	88	1.1	2.3
283 LUTH--MO SYNOD	1	133	170	2.2	4.5
413 S-D ADVENTISTS	1	19	24*	0.3	0.6
449 UN METHODIST..	2	242	398	5.2	10.4
453 UN PRES CH USA	2	186	231*	3.0	6.1
469 WISC EVAN LUTH	3	440	584	7.6	15.3
GRANT	73	10,050	35,846*	74.1	100.0
029 AMER LUTH CH..	5	2,423	3,274	6.8	9.1
081 CATHOLIC......	18	0	22,540	46.6	62.9
097 CR C AND C CR.	1	26	32*	0.1	0.1
127 CH GOD (CLEVE)	1	26	32*	0.1	0.1
165 CH OF NAZARENE	1	15	59	0.1	0.2
175 CONG CR CH....	1	79	98*	0.2	0.3
193 EPISCOPAL.....	2	58	72	0.1	0.2
221 FREE METH C NA	2	85	118	0.2	0.3
281 LUTH CH AMER..	4	514	818	1.7	2.3
283 LUTH--MO SYNOD	1	135	176	0.4	0.5
285 MENNONITE CH..	2	59	73*	0.2	0.2
353 PLY BRETHREN..	2	35	60	0.1	0.2
413 S-D ADVENTISTS	2	56	69*	0.1	0.2
443 UN C OF CHRIST	8	1,427	1,764*	3.6	4.9
449 UN METHODIST..	18	4,433	5,801	12.0	16.2
453 UN PRES CH USA	3	448	554*	1.1	1.5
469 WISC EVAN LUTH	2	231	306	0.6	0.9
GREEN	38	9,575	16,382*	61.3	100.0
019 AMER BAPT CONV	3	265	324*	1.2	2.0
029 AMER LUTH CH..	6	1,405	1,864	7.0	11.4
081 CATHOLIC......	4	0	3,772	14.1	23.0
165 CH OF NAZARENE	2	88	151	0.6	0.9
193 EPISCOPAL.....	1	14	14	0.1	0.1
281 LUTH CH AMER..	1	759	1,316	4.9	8.0
353 PLY BRETHREN..	1	20	30	0.1	0.2
435 UNITARIAN-UNIV	1	39	39	0.1	0.2
443 UN C OF CHRIST	7	4,311	5,267*	19.7	32.2
449 UN METHODIST..	8	2,229	3,003	11.2	18.3
453 UN PRES CH USA	1	166	203*	0.8	1.2
469 WISC EVAN LUTH	3	279	399	1.5	2.4
GREEN LAKE	28	5,748	13,268*	78.6	100.0
019 AMER BAPT CONV	2	209	254*	1.5	1.9
029 AMER LUTH CH..	1	702	954	5.7	7.2
081 CATHOLIC......	7	0	5,775	34.2	43.5
175 CONG CR CH....	1	125	152*	0.9	1.1
283 LUTH--MO SYNOD	1	555	744	4.4	5.6
443 UN C OF CHRIST	1	153	186*	1.1	1.4
449 UN METHODIST..	5	1,339	1,693	10.0	12.8
453 UN PRES CH USA	1	16	19*	0.1	0.1
469 WISC EVAN LUTH	9	2,649	3,491	20.7	26.3
IOWA	40	5,179	13,991*	72.5	100.0
019 AMER BAPT CONV	1	58	73*	0.4	0.5
029 AMER LUTH CH..	9	2,087	2,922	15.1	20.9
081 CATHOLIC......	11	0	7,159	37.1	51.2
193 EPISCOPAL.....	1	64	80	0.4	0.6
283 LUTH--MO SYNOD	1	73	106	0.5	0.8
443 UN C OF CHRIST	3	909	1,140*	5.9	8.1
449 UN METHODIST..	12	1,799	2,274	11.8	16.3
453 UN PRES CH USA	2	189	237*	1.2	1.7
IRON	15	739	4,861*	74.4	100.0
081 CATHOLIC......	7	0	3,920	60.0	80.6
165 CH OF NAZARENE	1	23	48	0.7	1.0
283 LUTH--MO SYNOD	2	215	277	4.2	5.7
449 UN METHODIST..	1	132	164	2.5	3.4
453 UN PRES CH USA	2	200	232*	3.6	4.8
469 WISC EVAN LUTH	2	169	220	3.4	4.5
JACKSON	28	4,903	8,299*	54.2	100.0

County and Denomination	Number of churches	Communicant, confirmed, full members	Total adherents: Number	Percent of total population	Percent of total adherents
029 AMER LUTH CH..	8	2,833	3,770	24.6	45.4
081 CATHOLIC......	5	0	1,806	11.8	21.8
097 CR C AND C CR.	1	18	22*	0.1	0.3
283 LUTH--MO SYNOD	3	418	596	3.9	7.2
443 UN C OF CHRIST	2	74	90*	0.6	1.1
449 UN METHODIST..	7	1,331	1,720	11.2	20.7
453 UN PRES CH USA	1	196	238*	1.6	2.9
469 WISC EVAN LUTH	1	33	57	0.4	0.7
JEFFERSON	64	21,880	44,306*	73.8	100.0
019 AMER BAPT CONV	1	135	165*	0.3	0.4
029 AMER LUTH CH..	6	3,029	4,311	7.2	9.7
081 CATHOLIC......	10	0	15,096	25.1	34.1
193 EPISCOPAL.....	2	372	459	0.8	1.0
281 LUTH CH AMER..	3	2,346	3,286	5.5	7.4
283 LUTH--MO SYNOD	3	976	1,260	2.1	2.8
293 MORAV CH-NORTH	5	1,661	2,154	3.6	4.9
313 NO AM BAPT GC.	1	108	132*	0.2	0.3
413 S-D ADVENTISTS	3	150	183*	0.3	0.4
443 UN C OF CHRIST	4	1,747	2,130*	3.5	4.8
449 UN METHODIST..	12	3,499	4,590	7.6	10.4
469 WISC EVAN LUTH	14	7,857	10,540	17.5	23.8
JUNEAU	39	5,703	11,952*	64.8	100.0
019 AMER BAPT CONV	1	107	131*	0.7	1.1
029 AMER LUTH CH..	8	1,823	2,542	13.8	21.3
081 CATHOLIC......	10	0	4,293	23.3	35.9
165 CH OF NAZARENE	1	52	100	0.5	0.8
193 EPISCOPAL.....	1	35	56	0.3	0.5
226 FRIENDS-USA...	1	97	119*	0.6	1.0
283 LUTH--MO SYNOD	3	336	461	2.5	3.9
413 S-D ADVENTISTS	1	34	42*	0.2	0.4
449 UN METHODIST..	6	1,441	1,829	9.9	15.3
453 UN PRES CH USA	1	134	164*	0.9	1.4
469 WISC EVAN LUTH	6	1,644	2,215	12.0	18.5
KENOSHA	68	20,302	68,997*	58.5	100.0
019 AMER BAPT CONV	2	535	670*	0.6	1.0
029 AMER LUTH CH..	3	1,746	2,731	2.3	4.0
081 CATHOLIC......	17	0	40,270	34.2	58.4
097 CR C AND C CR.	1	540	676*	0.6	1.0
105 CHRISTIAN REF.	1	170	297	0.3	0.4
123 CH GOD (ANDER)	1	40	130	0.1	0.2
127 CH GOD (CLEVE)	2	172	215*	0.2	0.3
165 CH OF NAZARENE	1	92	328	0.3	0.5
175 CONG CR CH....	2	1,222	1,530*	1.3	2.2
193 EPISCOPAL.....	3	978	1,274	1.1	1.8
281 LUTH CH AMER..	5	4,284	6,538	5.5	9.5
283 LUTH--MO SYNOD	2	541	893	0.8	1.3
313 NO AM BAPT GC.	1	161	202*	0.2	0.3
353 PLY BRETHREN..	1	30	50	-	0.1
403 SALVATION ARMY	1	84	252	0.2	0.4
413 S-D ADVENTISTS	1	44	55*	-	0.1
419 SO BAPT CONV..	3	939	1,176*	1.0	1.7
443 UN C OF CHRIST	2	341	427*	0.4	0.6
449 UN METHODIST..	10	3,543	5,083	4.3	7.4
453 UN PRES CH USA	1	516	646*	0.5	0.9
469 WISC EVAN LUTH	8	4,324	5,554	4.7	8.0
KEWAUNEE	28	3,630	15,550*	82.0	100.0
081 CATHOLIC......	17	0	10,855	57.2	69.8
175 CONG CR CH....	1	315	393*	2.1	2.5
193 EPISCOPAL.....	1	78	94	0.5	0.6
283 LUTH--MO SYNOD	3	940	1,257	6.6	8.1
353 PLY BRETHREN..	1	30	40	0.2	0.3
449 UN METHODIST..	2	231	272	1.4	1.7
469 WISC EVAN LUTH	3	2,036	2,639	13.9	17.0
LA CROSSE	62	24,510	53,983*	67.1	100.0
019 AMER BAPT CONV	2	396	480*	0.6	0.9
029 AMER LUTH CH..	13	8,955	12,560	15.6	23.3
081 CATHOLIC......	12	0	20,631	25.6	38.2
097 CR C AND C CR.	2	307	372*	0.5	0.7
165 CH OF NAZARENE	1	36	80	0.1	0.1
281 LUTH CH AMER..	2	2,047	3,106	3.9	5.8
283 LUTH--MO SYNOD	1	224	361	0.4	0.7
313 NO AM BAPT GC.	1	123	149*	0.2	0.3
353 PLY BRETHREN..	2	35	60	0.1	0.1
403 SALVATION ARMY	1	54	280	0.3	0.5
413 S-D ADVENTISTS	1	119	144*	0.2	0.3
419 SO BAPT CONV..	1	64	78*	0.1	0.1
435 UNITARIAN-UNIV	1	36	36	-	0.1
443 UN C OF CHRIST	3	1,200	1,454*	1.8	2.7
449 UN METHODIST..	5	3,211	4,221	5.2	7.8
453 UN PRES CH USA	6	2,153	2,608*	3.2	4.8
469 WISC EVAN LUTH	8	5,550	7,363	9.2	13.6
LAFAYETTE	38	5,484	14,567*	83.4	100.0
019 AMER BAPT CONV	1	146	182*	1.0	1.2
029 AMER LUTH CH..	9	2,441	3,337	19.1	22.9
081 CATHOLIC......	13	0	7,196	41.2	49.4
281 LUTH CH AMER..	1	459	622	3.6	4.3
443 UN C OF CHRIST	2	478	596*	3.4	4.1
449 UN METHODIST..	12	1,960	2,634	15.1	18.1
LANGLADE	30	4,383	14,706*	76.5	100.0
019 AMER BAPT CONV	1	179	221*	1.1	1.5
081 CATHOLIC......	9	0	8,848	46.0	60.2

*Total adherents estimated from known number of communicant, confirmed, full members.

—Represents a percent less than 0.1.

Percentages may not total due to rounding.

Table 3. Churches and Church Membership by State, County and Denomination: 1971

County and Denomination	Number of churches	Communicant, confirmed, full members	Total adherents: Number	Total adherents: Percent of total population	Total adherents: Percent of total adherents
127 CH GOD (CLEVE)	2	34	42*	0.2	0.3
165 CH OF NAZARENE	1	18	49	0.3	0.3
193 EPISCOPAL.....	1	75	94	0.5	0.6
281 LUTH CH AMER..	3	627	885	4.6	6.0
283 LUTH--MO SYNOD	6	2,409	3,245	16.9	22.1
413 S-D ADVENTISTS	2	63	78*	0.4	0.5
443 UN C OF CHRIST	3	606	747*	3.9	5.1
449 UN METHODIST..	1	315	427	2.2	2.9
453 UN PRES CH USA	1	57	70*	0.4	0.5
LINCOLN	38	10,358	20,133*	85.7	100.0
019 AMER BAPT CONV	1	69	85*	0.4	0.4
029 AMER LUTH CH..	3	1,517	2,187	9.3	10.9
081 CATHOLIC......	6	0	6,179	26.3	30.7
175 CONG CR CH....	1	20	25*	0.1	0.1
193 EPISCOPAL.....	2	78	91	0.4	0.5
201 EVAN COV CH AM	2	45	56*	0.2	0.3
281 LUTH CH AMER..	2	288	424	1.8	2.1
283 LUTH--MO SYNOD	9	5,370	7,245	30.8	36.0
381 REF PRES-EVAN.	1	74	92	0.4	0.5
413 S-D ADVENTISTS	1	74	91*	0.4	0.5
443 UN C OF CHRIST	2	1,460	1,801*	7.7	8.9
449 UN METHODIST..	3	635	877	3.7	4.4
453 UN PRES CH USA	2	243	300*	1.3	1.5
469 WISC EVAN LUTH	3	485	680	2.9	3.4
MANITOWOC	72	18,961	65,008*	79.0	100.0
019 AMER BAPT CONV	1	90	112*	0.1	0.2
029 AMER LUTH CH..	3	2,732	3,695	4.5	5.7
081 CATHOLIC......	27	0	39,774	48.3	61.2
193 EPISCOPAL.....	1	234	265	0.3	0.4
281 LUTH CH AMER..	1	354	493	0.6	0.8
283 LUTH--MO SYNOD	2	832	1,190	1.4	1.8
313 NO AM BAPT GC.	1	108	135*	0.2	0.2
403 SALVATION ARMY	1	23	154	0.2	0.2
413 S-D ADVENTISTS	1	14	17*	-	-
443 UN C OF CHRIST	7	2,557	3,184*	3.9	4.9
449 UN METHODIST..	6	1,548	1,977	2.4	3.0
453 UN PRES CH USA	3	1,475	1,837*	2.2	2.8
469 WISC EVAN LUTH	18	8,994	12,175	14.8	18.7
MARATHON	103	28,415	73,921*	75.8	100.0
029 AMER LUTH CH..	16	7,026	9,739	10.0	13.2
081 CATHOLIC......	26	0	35,460	36.4	48.0
127 CH GOD (CLEVE)	2	103	129*	0.1	0.2
165 CH OF NAZARENE	1	61	102	0.1	0.1
193 EPISCOPAL.....	2	499	549	0.6	0.7
283 LUTH--MO SYNOD	18	8,926	12,174	12.5	16.5
285 MENNONITE CH..	1	11	14*	-	-
313 NO AM BAPT GC.	1	397	496*	0.5	0.7
371 REF CH IN AM..	1	200	285	0.3	0.4
403 SALVATION ARMY	1	59	309	0.3	0.4
413 S-D ADVENTISTS	2	89	111*	0.1	0.2
419 SO BAPT CONV..	1	53	66*	0.1	0.1
435 UNITARIAN-UNIV	1	296	369	0.4	0.5
443 UN C OF CHRIST	5	2,800	3,497*	3.6	4.7
449 UN METHODIST..	6	2,299	3,147	3.2	4.3
453 UN PRES CH USA	4	2,225	2,778*	2.9	3.8
469 WISC EVAN LUTH	15	3,371	4,696	4.8	6.4
MARINETTE	51	8,196	24,457*	68.3	100.0
019 AMER BAPT CONV	1	403	490*	1.4	2.0
029 AMER LUTH CH..	4	713	1,034	2.9	4.2
081 CATHOLIC......	15	0	13,419	37.5	54.9
193 EPISCOPAL.....	1	182	227	0.6	0.9
201 EVAN COV CH AM	2	151	183*	0.5	0.7
281 LUTH CH AMER..	5	1,533	2,021	5.6	8.3
283 LUTH--MO SYNOD	1	51	72	0.2	0.3
313 NO AM BAPT GC.	1	155	188*	0.5	0.8
403 SALVATION ARMY	1	51	204	0.6	0.8
413 S-D ADVENTISTS	1	29	35*	0.1	0.1
443 UN C OF CHRIST	2	196	238*	0.7	1.0
449 UN METHODIST..	5	1,313	1,760	4.9	7.2
453 UN PRES CH USA	6	1,057	1,284*	3.6	5.3
469 WISC EVAN LUTH	6	2,362	3,302	9.2	13.5
MARQUETTE	27	3,730	7,366*	83.1	100.0
029 AMER LUTH CH..	2	260	319	3.6	4.3
081 CATHOLIC......	5	0	2,643	29.8	35.9
283 LUTH--MO SYNOD	8	1,537	1,878	21.2	25.5
413 S-D ADVENTISTS	1	50	59*	0.7	0.8
443 UN C OF CHRIST	1	127	150*	1.7	2.0
449 UN METHODIST..	5	747	1,017	11.5	13.8
453 UN PRES CH USA	3	310	367*	4.1	5.0
469 WISC EVAN LUTH	2	699	933	10.5	12.7
MENOMINEE	3	0	2,162	82.9	100.0
081 CATHOLIC......	3	0	2,162	82.9	100.0
MILWAUKEE	405	168,429	604,507*	57.4	100.0
019 AMER BAPT CONV	18	5,184	6,326*	0.6	1.0
029 AMER LUTH CH..	21	18,054	24,691	2.3	4.1
081 CATHOLIC......	112	0	377,604	35.8	62.5
093 CR CH (DISC)..	1	206	251*	-	-
097 CR C AND C CR.	1	125	153*	-	-
105 CHRISTIAN REF.	1	153	305	-	0.1
123 CH GOD (ANDER)	5	444	988	0.1	0.2
127 CH GOD (CLEVE)	4	180	220*	-	-
165 CH OF NAZARENE	2	210	505	-	0.1
175 CONG CR CH....	3	4,115	5,021*	0.5	0.8
193 EPISCOPAL.....	16	5,686	8,112	0.8	1.3
201 EVAN COV CH AM	1	142	173*	-	-
226 FRIENDS-USA...	1	40	49*	-	-
281 LUTH CH AMER..	31	21,735	29,586	2.8	4.9
283 LUTH--MO SYNOD	48	42,405	58,328	5.5	9.6
285 MENNONITE CH..	1	21	26*	-	-
313 NO AM BAPT GC.	4	770	940*	0.1	0.2
353 PLY BRETHREN..	2	215	280	-	-
371 REF CH IN AM..	2	443	534	0.1	0.1
403 SALVATION ARMY	3	317	1,575	0.1	0.3
413 S-D ADVENTISTS	1	471	575*	0.1	0.1
419 SO BAPT CONV..	4	807	985*	0.1	0.2
435 UNITARIAN-UNIV	1	414	568	0.1	0.1
443 UN C OF CHRIST	20	8,150	9,945*	0.9	1.6
449 UN METHODIST..	28	17,428	22,781	2.2	3.8
453 UN PRES CH USA	22	10,873	13,268*	1.3	2.2
469 WISC EVAN LUTH	52	29,841	40,718	3.9	6.7
MONROE	43	6,576	17,452*	55.2	100.0
019 AMER BAPT CONV	2	248	304*	1.0	1.7
029 AMER LUTH CH..	7	2,679	3,622	11.5	20.8
081 CATHOLIC......	9	0	6,127	19.4	35.1
123 CH GOD (ANDER)	1	31	76	0.2	0.4
193 EPISCOPAL.....	2	139	229	0.7	1.3
413 S-D ADVENTISTS	3	129	158*	0.5	0.9
443 UN C OF CHRIST	2	794	972*	3.1	5.6
449 UN METHODIST..	6	1,184	1,388	4.4	8.0
469 WISC EVAN LUTH	11	3,372	4,576	14.5	26.2
OCONTO	51	7,134	18,349*	71.8	100.0
029 AMER LUTH CH..	8	2,628	3,677	14.4	20.0
081 CATHOLIC......	14	0	8,726	34.1	47.6
097 CR C AND C CR.	2	96	118*	0.5	0.6
193 EPISCOPAL.....	1	87	147	0.6	0.8
283 LUTH--MO SYNOD	10	1,957	2,557	10.0	13.9
413 S-D ADVENTISTS	3	137	168*	0.7	0.9
449 UN METHODIST..	7	1,246	1,661	6.5	9.1
453 UN PRES CH USA	2	467	573*	2.2	3.1
469 WISC EVAN LUTH	4	516	722	2.8	3.9
ONEIDA	29	6,668	15,941*	65.3	100.0
019 AMER BAPT CONV	1	98	119*	0.5	0.7
029 AMER LUTH CH..	2	1,310	1,818	7.4	11.4
081 CATHOLIC......	9	0	6,917	28.3	43.4
193 EPISCOPAL.....	1	289	349	1.4	2.2
281 LUTH CH AMER..	1	328	474	1.9	3.0
283 LUTH--MO SYNOD	3	652	934	3.8	5.9
413 S-D ADVENTISTS	2	197	239*	1.0	1.5
443 UN C OF CHRIST	3	925	1,124*	4.6	7.1
449 UN METHODIST..	2	1,199	1,654	6.8	10.4
469 WISC EVAN LUTH	5	1,670	2,313	9.5	14.5
OUTAGAMIE	91	32,330	106,188*	89.0	100.0
019 AMER BAPT CONV	2	306	392*	0.3	0.4
029 AMER LUTH CH..	6	6,364	9,149	7.7	8.6
081 CATHOLIC......	29	0	60,661	50.8	57.1
165 CH OF NAZARENE	1	54	116	0.1	0.1
193 EPISCOPAL.....	2	1,309	1,988	1.7	1.9
281 LUTH CH AMER..	2	1,920	3,094	2.6	2.9
283 LUTH--MO SYNOD	5	2,634	3,888	3.3	3.7
293 MORAV CH-NORTH	1	159	205	0.2	0.2
403 SALVATION ARMY	1	49	151	0.1	0.1
413 S-D ADVENTISTS	1	74	95*	0.1	0.1
419 SO BAPT CONV..	1	94	120*	0.1	0.1
435 UNITARIAN-UNIV	1	44	64	0.1	0.1
443 UN C OF CHRIST	7	3,177	4,071*	3.4	3.8
449 UN METHODIST..	11	3,649	4,999	4.2	4.7
453 UN PRES CH USA	2	646	828*	0.7	0.8
469 WISC EVAN LUTH	19	11,851	16,367	13.7	15.4
OZAUKEE	48	15,537	44,026*	80.9	100.0
019 AMER BAPT CONV	1	84	107*	0.2	0.2
029 AMER LUTH CH..	7	3,830	5,438	10.0	12.4
081 CATHOLIC......	12	0	22,594	41.5	51.3
165 CH OF NAZARENE	1	8	55	0.1	0.1
193 EPISCOPAL.....	2	241	394	0.7	0.9
281 LUTH CH AMER..	3	825	1,131	2.1	2.6
283 LUTH--MO SYNOD	6	5,451	7,557	13.9	17.2
435 UNITARIAN-UNIV	1	70	95	0.2	0.2
443 UN C OF CHRIST	5	1,294	1,650*	3.0	3.7
449 UN METHODIST..	3	1,292	1,651	3.0	3.8
453 UN PRES CH USA	1	1,027	1,310*	2.4	3.0
469 WISC EVAN LUTH	6	1,415	2,044	3.8	4.6
PEPIN	16	1,738	5,560*	76.0	100.0
029 AMER LUTH CH..	3	666	937	12.8	16.9
081 CATHOLIC......	3	0	3,252	44.4	58.5
157 CH OF BRETHREN	1	33	41*	0.6	0.7
201 EVAN COV CH AM	2	154	193*	2.6	3.5
281 LUTH CH AMER..	1	243	311	4.2	5.6
283 LUTH--MO SYNOD	1	130	197	2.7	3.5
293 MORAV CH-NORTH	1	32	52	0.7	0.9
413 S-D ADVENTISTS	1	19	24*	0.3	0.4
443 UN C OF CHRIST	1	29	36*	0.5	0.6
449 UN METHODIST..	2	432	517	7.1	9.3
PIERCE	54	8,590	17,496*	65.6	100.0

*Total adherents estimated from known number of communicant, confirmed, full members.

—Represents a percent less than 0.1.

Percentages may not total due to rounding.

Table 3. Churches and Church Membership by State, County and Denomination: 1971

County and Denomination	Number of churches	Communicant, confirmed, full members	Total adherents: Number	Total adherents: Percent of total population	Total adherents: Percent of total adherents
019 AMER BAPT CONV	1	30	37*	0.1	0.2
029 AMER LUTH CH..	11	3,603	5,117	19.2	29.2
081 CATHOLIC......	9	0	6,006	22.5	34.3
193 EPISCOPAL.....	3	113	125	0.5	0.7
201 EVAN COV CH AM	3	299	368*	1.4	2.1
281 LUTH CH AMER..	2	272	413	1.5	2.4
283 LUTH--MO SYNOD	2	294	420	1.6	2.4
443 UN C OF CHRIST	4	1,185	1,459*	5.5	8.3
449 UN METHODIST..	11	1,652	2,057	7.7	11.8
453 UN PRES CH USA	3	310	382*	1.4	2.2
469 WISC EVAN LUTH	5	832	1,112	4.2	6.4
POLK	69	10,468	18,031*	67.6	100.0
029 AMER LUTH CH..	19	3,504	4,991	18.7	27.7
081 CATHOLIC......	9	0	3,700	13.9	20.5
165 CH OF NAZARENE	1	75	152	0.6	0.8
193 EPISCOPAL.....	1	69	97	0.4	0.5
201 EVAN COV CH AM	1	90	110*	0.4	0.6
281 LUTH CH AMER..	13	2,918	3,929	14.7	21.8
283 LUTH--MO SYNOD	4	573	768	2.9	4.3
413 S-D ADVENTISTS	2	152	186*	0.7	1.0
443 UN C OF CHRIST	1	306	374*	1.4	2.1
449 UN METHODIST..	12	1,439	1,775	6.7	9.8
469 WISC EVAN LUTH	6	1,342	1,949	7.3	10.8
PORTAGE	42	6,753	31,855*	67.0	100.0
019 AMER BAPT CONV	3	354	436*	0.9	1.4
029 AMER LUTH CH..	4	1,818	2,604	5.5	8.2
081 CATHOLIC......	18	0	22,755	47.9	71.4
193 EPISCOPAL.....	1	210	240	0.5	0.8
283 LUTH--MO SYNOD	5	2,202	3,111	6.5	9.8
413 S-D ADVENTISTS	1	64	79*	0.2	0.2
435 UNITARIAN-UNIV	1	40	40	0.1	0.1
443 UN C OF CHRIST	1	96	118*	0.2	0.4
449 UN METHODIST..	6	1,456	1,830	3.8	5.7
453 UN PRES CH USA	1	482	594*	1.2	1.9
469 WISC EVAN LUTH	1	31	48	0.1	0.2
PRICE	29	3,404	9,105*	62.7	100.0
029 AMER LUTH CH..	1	68	91	0.6	1.0
081 CATHOLIC......	6	0	4,699	32.4	51.6
175 CONG CR CH....	1	35	43*	0.3	0.5
193 EPISCOPAL.....	2	49	53	0.4	0.6
201 EVAN COV CH AM	1	28	34*	0.2	0.4
281 LUTH CH AMER..	5	1,114	1,425	9.8	15.7
283 LUTH--MO SYNOD	4	1,066	1,467	10.1	16.1
413 S-D ADVENTISTS	2	51	62*	0.4	0.7
443 UN C OF CHRIST	2	455	554*	3.8	6.1
449 UN METHODIST..	3	314	409	2.8	4.5
453 UN PRES CH USA	1	174	212*	1.5	2.3
469 WISC EVAN LUTH	1	50	56	0.4	0.6
RACINE	109	36,844	105,232*	61.6	100.0
019 AMER BAPT CONV	3	742	937*	0.5	0.9
029 AMER LUTH CH..	11	7,967	11,426	6.7	10.9
081 CATHOLIC......	23	0	52,945	31.0	50.3
097 CR C AND C CR.	1	30	38*	-	-
105 CHRISTIAN REF.	1	283	501	0.3	0.5
123 CH GOD (ANDER)	3	217	511	0.3	0.5
127 CH GOD (CLEVE)	2	63	80*	-	0.1
165 CH OF NAZARENE	2	278	486	0.3	0.5
175 CONG CR CH....	1	617	779*	0.5	0.7
193 EPISCOPAL.....	5	1,150	1,507	0.9	1.4
281 LUTH CH AMER..	7	5,782	8,282	4.8	7.9
283 LUTH--MO SYNOD	12	6,676	9,904	5.8	9.4
313 NO AM BAPT GC.	1	271	342*	0.2	0.3
371 REF CH IN AM..	1	151	231	0.1	0.2
403 SALVATION ARMY	1	58	377	0.2	0.4
413 S-D ADVENTISTS	2	210	265*	0.2	0.3
419 SO BAPT CONV..	2	276	349*	0.2	0.3
435 UNITARIAN-UNIV	1	202	322	0.2	0.3
443 UN C OF CHRIST	6	1,213	1,532*	0.9	1.5
449 UN METHODIST..	15	5,721	7,449	4.4	7.1
453 UN PRES CH USA	3	1,717	2,168*	1.3	2.1
469 WISC EVAN LUTH	6	3,220	4,801	2.8	4.6
RICHLAND	34	4,116	8,118*	47.5	100.0
019 AMER BAPT CONV	2	192	234*	1.4	2.9
029 AMER LUTH CH..	3	886	1,288	7.5	15.9
081 CATHOLIC......	5	0	2,717	15.9	33.5
097 CR C AND C CR.	2	260	317*	1.9	3.9
165 CH OF NAZARENE	1	167	239	1.4	2.9
193 EPISCOPAL.....	1	55	70	0.4	0.9
221 FREE METH C NA	1	88	106	0.6	1.3
283 LUTH--MO SYNOD	3	233	284	1.7	3.5
413 S-D ADVENTISTS	1	89	108*	0.6	1.3
449 UN METHODIST..	14	1,877	2,427	14.2	29.9
453 UN PRES CH USA	1	269	328*	1.9	4.0
ROCK	108	42,783	89,298*	67.7	100.0
019 AMER BAPT CONV	6	2,527	3,185*	2.4	3.6
029 AMER LUTH CH..	15	12,611	18,780	14.2	21.0
081 CATHOLIC......	13	0	29,269	22.2	32.8
093 CR CH (DISC)..	1	220	277*	0.2	0.3
097 CR C AND C CR.	3	899	1,133*	0.9	1.3
127 CH GOD (CLEVE)	2	28	35*	-	-
165 CH OF NAZARENE	2	88	280	0.2	0.3
175 CONG CR CH....	2	1,435	1,809*	1.4	2.0
193 EPISCOPAL.....	2	871	1,303	1.0	1.5
201 EVAN COV CH AM	1	83	105*	0.1	0.1
221 FREE METH C NA	2	147	207	0.2	0.2
281 LUTH CH AMER..	3	1,939	2,692	2.0	3.0
283 LUTH--MO SYNOD	11	7,407	10,356	7.8	11.6
371 REF CH IN AM..	1	158	251	0.2	0.3
403 SALVATION ARMY	2	210	773	0.6	0.9
413 S-D ADVENTISTS	4	382	481*	0.4	0.5
415 S-D BAPTIST GC	2	441	556*	0.4	0.6
419 SO BAPT CONV..	2	262	330*	0.3	0.4
443 UN C OF CHRIST	7	2,213	2,789*	2.1	3.1
449 UN METHODIST..	17	7,534	10,040	7.6	11.2
453 UN PRES CH USA	6	2,251	2,837*	2.1	3.2
469 WISC EVAN LUTH	4	1,077	1,810	1.4	2.0
RUSK	34	3,547	9,481*	66.6	100.0
029 AMER LUTH CH..	5	1,198	1,651	11.6	17.4
081 CATHOLIC......	11	0	4,832	33.9	51.0
097 CR C AND C CR.	2	480	589*	4.1	6.2
283 LUTH--MO SYNOD	2	753	1,043	7.3	11.0
285 MENNONITE CH..	3	142	174*	1.2	1.8
413 S-D ADVENTISTS	1	62	76*	0.5	0.8
443 UN C OF CHRIST	4	301	369*	2.6	3.9
449 UN METHODIST..	6	611	747	5.2	7.9
ST CROIX	47	10,711	26,068*	75.9	100.0
019 AMER BAPT CONV	1	164	209*	0.6	0.8
029 AMER LUTH CH..	12	5,375	7,666	22.3	29.4
081 CATHOLIC......	8	0	10,997	32.0	42.2
105 CHRISTIAN REF.	1	172	271	0.8	1.0
193 EPISCOPAL.....	2	137	228	0.7	0.9
201 EVAN COV CH AM	2	49	62*	0.2	0.2
281 LUTH CH AMER..	1	263	409	1.2	1.6
283 LUTH--MO SYNOD	4	1,257	1,767	5.1	6.8
371 REF CH IN AM..	1	427	665	1.9	2.6
443 UN C OF CHRIST	3	448	570*	1.7	2.2
449 UN METHODIST..	8	1,461	1,990	5.8	7.6
453 UN PRES CH USA	2	745	947*	2.8	3.6
469 WISC EVAN LUTH	2	213	287	0.8	1.1
SAUK	59	13,881	30,744*	78.7	100.0
019 AMER BAPT CONV	1	118	145*	0.4	0.5
029 AMER LUTH CH..	7	2,929	4,084	10.5	13.3
081 CATHOLIC......	9	0	12,368	31.7	40.2
123 CH GOD (ANDER)	2	126	278	0.7	0.9
165 CH OF NAZARENE	1	53	111	0.3	0.4
175 CONG CR CH....	1	179	220*	0.6	0.7
193 EPISCOPAL.....	1	208	301	0.8	1.0
281 LUTH CH AMER..	1	533	765	2.0	2.5
283 LUTH--MO SYNOD	5	1,792	2,286	5.9	7.4
313 NO AM BAPT GC.	2	163	200*	0.5	0.7
413 S-D ADVENTISTS	2	128	157*	0.4	0.5
435 UNITARIAN-UNIV	1	44	44	0.1	0.1
443 UN C OF CHRIST	2	641	787*	2.0	2.6
449 UN METHODIST..	13	3,067	3,825	9.8	12.4
453 UN PRES CH USA	3	934	1,146*	2.9	3.7
469 WISC EVAN LUTH	8	2,966	4,027	10.3	13.1
SAWYER	27	2,002	5,359*	55.4	100.0
029 AMER LUTH CH..	3	759	1,054	10.9	19.7
081 CATHOLIC......	8	0	2,741	28.3	51.1
175 CONG CR CH....	1	290	351*	3.6	6.5
193 EPISCOPAL.....	1	67	89	0.9	1.7
281 LUTH CH AMER..	2	187	243	2.5	4.5
283 LUTH--MO SYNOD	1	214	274	2.8	5.1
285 MENNONITE CH..	3	68	82*	0.8	1.5
413 S-D ADVENTISTS	1	18	22*	0.2	0.4
443 UN C OF CHRIST	2	131	159*	1.6	3.0
449 UN METHODIST..	1	56	87	0.9	1.6
453 UN PRES CH USA	4	212	257*	2.7	4.8
SHAWANO	74	15,004	26,366*	80.8	100.0
029 AMER LUTH CH..	16	3,389	4,463	13.7	16.9
081 CATHOLIC......	13	0	6,675	20.4	25.3
165 CH OF NAZARENE	1	103	184	0.6	0.7
193 EPISCOPAL.....	1	54	73	0.2	0.3
283 LUTH--MO SYNOD	24	8,513	11,178	34.2	42.4
335 ORTH PRESB CH.	1	83	162	0.5	0.6
413 S-D ADVENTISTS	2	41	50*	0.2	0.2
419 SO BAPT CONV..	1	15	18*	0.1	0.1
443 UN C OF CHRIST	3	785	966*	3.0	3.7
449 UN METHODIST..	8	1,204	1,543	4.7	5.9
453 UN PRES CH USA	1	352	433*	1.3	1.6
469 WISC EVAN LUTH	3	465	621	1.9	2.4
SHEBOYGAN	104	34,513	75,278*	77.9	100.0
019 AMER BAPT CONV	2	227	279*	0.3	0.4
029 AMER LUTH CH..	4	1,368	1,919	2.0	2.5
075 BRETHREN IN CR	1	10	12*	-	-
081 CATHOLIC......	18	0	27,907	28.9	37.1
105 CHRISTIAN REF.	3	1,039	1,692	1.8	2.2
123 CH GOD (ANDER)	1	11	25	-	-
127 CH GOD (CLEVE)	1	9	11*	-	-
165 CH OF NAZARENE	1	56	80	0.1	0.1
193 EPISCOPAL.....	3	634	787	0.8	1.0
281 LUTH CH AMER..	2	1,263	1,856	1.9	2.5
283 LUTH--MO SYNOD	25	16,123	21,386	22.1	28.4
313 NO AM BAPT GC.	1	80	98*	0.1	0.1
335 ORTH PRESB CH.	2	707	1,052	1.1	1.4
353 PLY BRETHREN..	1	70	120	0.1	0.2

*Total adherents estimated from known number of communicant, confirmed, full members.

—Represents a percent less than 0.1.

Percentages may not total due to rounding.

Table 3. Churches and Church Membership by State, County and Denomination: 1971

County and Denomination	Number of churches	Communicant, confirmed, full members	Total adherents: Number	Total adherents: Percent of total population	Total adherents: Percent of total adherents
371 REF CH IN AM..	8	3,369	4,931	5.1	6.6
403 SALVATION ARMY	1	74	348	0.4	0.5
413 S-D ADVENTISTS	1	60	74*	0.1	0.1
419 SO BAPT CONV..	1	26	32*	-	-
443 UN C OF CHRIST	21	7,861	9,666*	10.0	12.8
449 UN METHODIST..	2	176	1,198	1.2	1.6
453 UN PRES CH USA	3	805	990*	1.0	1.3
469 WISC EVAN LUTH	2	545	815	0.8	1.1
TAYLOR	27	4,107	11,610*	68.5	100.0
029 AMER LUTH CH..	2	322	524	3.1	4.5
081 CATHOLIC......	9	0	5,829	34.4	50.2
281 LUTH CH AMER..	1	485	687	4.1	5.9
283 LUTH--MO SYNOD	3	486	712	4.2	6.1
443 UN C OF CHRIST	1	225	284*	1.7	2.4
449 UN METHODIST..	2	236	296	1.7	2.5
453 UN PRES CH USA	4	331	417*	2.5	3.6
469 WISC EVAN LUTH	5	2,022	2,861	16.9	24.6
TREMPEALEAU	43	10,310	21,336*	91.4	100.0
029 AMER LUTH CH..	27	9,169	12,310	52.7	57.7
081 CATHOLIC......	10	0	7,547	32.3	35.4
283 LUTH--MO SYNOD	1	110	160	0.7	0.7
443 UN C OF CHRIST	1	267	328*	1.4	1.5
449 UN METHODIST..	3	358	492	2.1	2.3
453 UN PRES CH USA	1	406	499*	2.1	2.3
VERNON	60	12,096	18,546*	75.5	100.0
019 AMER BAPT CONV	1	172	206*	0.8	1.1
029 AMER LUTH CH..	23	7,155	9,411	38.3	50.7
081 CATHOLIC......	8	0	2,747	11.2	14.8
097 CR C AND C CR.	2	475	570*	2.3	3.1
165 CH OF NAZARENE	1	30	48	0.2	0.3
193 EPISCOPAL.....	1	508	675	2.7	3.6
221 FREE METH C NA	1	31	33	0.1	0.2
353 PLY BRETHREN..	1	20	30	0.1	0.2
413 S-D ADVENTISTS	1	40	48*	0.2	0.3
443 UN C OF CHRIST	1	363	435*	1.8	2.3
449 UN METHODIST..	13	1,639	2,106	8.6	11.4
469 WISC EVAN LUTH	7	1,663	2,237	9.1	12.1
VILAS	24	2,737	5,543*	50.6	100.0
029 AMER LUTH CH..	1	951	1,212	11.1	21.9
081 CATHOLIC......	7	0	2,044	18.7	36.9
165 CH OF NAZARENE	3	51	149	1.4	2.7
193 EPISCOPAL.....	1	98	120	1.1	2.2
281 LUTH CH AMER..	2	241	322	2.9	5.8
283 LUTH--MO SYNOD	2	377	464	4.2	8.4
443 UN C OF CHRIST	4	420	501*	4.6	9.0
453 UN PRES CH USA	2	187	223*	2.0	4.0
469 WISC EVAN LUTH	2	412	508	4.6	9.2
WALWORTH	75	16,441	32,002*	50.4	100.0
019 AMER BAPT CONV	9	1,473	1,782*	2.8	5.6
029 AMER LUTH CH..	4	1,705	2,358	3.7	7.4
081 CATHOLIC......	10	0	10,849	17.1	33.9
105 CHRISTIAN REF.	1	287	633	1.0	2.0
175 CONG CR CH....	1	71	86*	0.1	0.3
193 EPISCOPAL.....	4	578	805	1.3	2.5
281 LUTH CH AMER..	7	2,600	3,674	5.8	11.5
283 LUTH--MO SYNOD	5	1,416	2,072	3.3	6.5
371 REF CH IN AM..	1	62	119	0.2	0.4
415 S-D BAPTIST GC	1	9	11*	-	-
435 UNITARIAN-UNIV	1	16	16	-	-
443 UN C OF CHRIST	9	2,268	2,744*	4.3	8.6
449 UN METHODIST..	16	3,757	3,788	6.0	11.8
453 UN PRES CH USA	1	140	169*	0.3	0.5
469 WISC EVAN LUTH	5	2,059	2,896	4.6	9.0
WASHBURN	25	2,627	7,000*	66.0	100.0
029 AMER LUTH CH..	4	833	1,166	11.0	16.7
081 CATHOLIC......	7	0	1,994	18.8	28.5
165 CH OF NAZARENE	2	54	146	1.4	2.1
193 EPISCOPAL.....	3	108	165	1.6	2.4
281 LUTH CH AMER..	1	311	403	3.8	5.8
283 LUTH--MO SYNOD	2	461	587	5.5	8.4
413 S-D ADVENTISTS	1	12	14*	0.1	0.2
443 UN C OF CHRIST	1	67	80*	0.8	1.1
449 UN METHODIST..	4	781	2,445	23.1	34.9
WASHINGTON	69	15,296	48,229*	75.5	100.0
029 AMER LUTH CH..	3	1,072	1,551	2.4	3.2
081 CATHOLIC......	21	0	26,292	41.2	54.5
127 CH GOD (CLEVE)	1	20	26*	-	0.1
165 CH OF NAZARENE	1	22	31	-	0.1
175 CONG CR CH....	1	100	130*	0.2	0.3
193 EPISCOPAL.....	2	226	308	0.5	0.6
281 LUTH CH AMER..	4	2,169	3,511	5.5	7.3
283 LUTH--MO SYNOD	5	2,356	3,480	5.5	7.2
443 UN C OF CHRIST	14	3,278	4,256*	6.7	8.8
449 UN METHODIST..	4	1,923	2,696	4.2	5.6
453 UN PRES CH USA	1	48	62*	0.1	0.1
469 WISC EVAN LUTH	12	4,082	5,886	9.2	12.2
WAUKESHA	155	51,192	160,767*	69.5	100.0
019 AMER BAPT CONV	5	1,337	1,701*	0.7	1.1
029 AMER LUTH CH..	12	6,744	9,831	4.2	6.1

County and Denomination	Number of churches	Communicant, confirmed, full members	Total adherents: Number	Total adherents: Percent of total population	Total adherents: Percent of total adherents
081 CATHOLIC......	29	0	88,344	38.2	55.0
093 CR CH (DISC)..	1	49	62*	-	-
097 CR C AND C CR.	1	38	48*	-	-
127 CH GOD (CLEVE)	1	21	27*	-	-
165 CH OF NAZARENE	2	89	205	0.1	0.1
193 EPISCOPAL.....	12	2,477	3,354	1.4	2.1
221 FREE METH C NA	1	88	113	-	0.1
281 LUTH CH AMER..	14	6,945	11,020	4.8	6.9
283 LUTH--MO SYNOD	15	9,306	12,969	5.6	8.1
313 NO AM BAPT GC.	1	276	351*	0.2	0.2
335 ORTH PRESB CH.	1	60	92	-	0.1
371 REF CH IN AM..	1	149	238	0.1	0.1
403 SALVATION ARMY	1	40	269	0.1	0.2
413 S-D ADVENTISTS	3	629	800*	0.3	0.5
435 UNITARIAN-UNIV	3	372	511	0.2	0.3
443 UN C OF CHRIST	12	5,068	6,449*	2.8	4.0
449 UN METHODIST..	15	7,793	10,791	4.7	6.7
453 UN PRES CH USA	11	3,350	4,263*	1.8	2.7
469 WISC EVAN LUTH	14	6,361	9,329	4.0	5.8
WAUPACA	54	15,935	28,693*	75.9	100.0
029 AMER LUTH CH..	15	5,710	7,920	21.0	27.6
081 CATHOLIC......	8	0	7,605	20.1	26.5
193 EPISCOPAL.....	2	202	213	0.6	0.7
283 LUTH--MO SYNOD	9	4,478	5,838	15.5	20.3
413 S-D ADVENTISTS	3	60	73*	0.2	0.3
443 UN C OF CHRIST	5	781	945*	2.5	3.3
449 UN METHODIST..	8	2,324	2,948	7.8	10.3
453 UN PRES CH USA	1	259	313*	0.8	1.1
469 WISC EVAN LUTH	3	2,121	2,838	7.5	9.9
WAUSHARA	33	4,678	8,161*	55.2	100.0
019 AMER BAPT CONV	2	153	184*	1.2	2.3
029 AMER LUTH CH..	6	1,246	1,829	12.4	22.4
081 CATHOLIC......	4	0	1,907	12.9	23.4
221 FREE METH C NA	1	16	21	0.1	0.3
283 LUTH--MO SYNOD	8	1,347	1,836	12.4	22.5
413 S-D ADVENTISTS	2	83	100*	0.7	1.2
443 UN C OF CHRIST	2	228	274*	1.9	3.4
449 UN METHODIST..	5	1,029	1,267	8.6	15.5
453 UN PRES CH USA	1	94	113*	0.8	1.4
469 WISC EVAN LUTH	2	482	630	4.3	7.7
WINNEBAGO	81	35,014	85,321*	65.7	100.0
019 AMER BAPT CONV	4	499	610*	0.5	0.7
029 AMER LUTH CH..	9	8,833	12,446	9.6	14.6
081 CATHOLIC......	13	0	37,606	28.9	44.1
097 CR C AND C CR.	1	60	73*	0.1	0.1
127 CH GOD (CLEVE)	2	24	29*	-	-
165 CH OF NAZARENE	1	25	68	0.1	0.1
193 EPISCOPAL.....	2	1,548	2,076	1.6	2.4
221 FREE METH C NA	1	18	23	-	-
281 LUTH CH AMER..	6	4,288	5,926	4.6	6.9
283 LUTH--MO SYNOD	6	3,427	4,787	3.7	5.6
403 SALVATION ARMY	1	58	279	0.2	0.3
413 S-D ADVENTISTS	1	28	34*	-	-
435 UNITARIAN-UNIV	1	13	20	-	-
443 UN C OF CHRIST	5	2,664	3,256*	2.5	3.8
449 UN METHODIST..	8	3,701	5,118	3.9	6.0
453 UN PRES CH USA	6	2,978	3,640*	2.8	4.3
469 WISC EVAN LUTH	14	6,850	9,330	7.2	10.9
WOOD	70	16,925	50,018*	76.5	100.0
019 AMER BAPT CONV	1	164	208*	0.3	0.4
029 AMER LUTH CH..	2	1,041	1,457	2.2	2.9
081 CATHOLIC......	22	0	26,806	41.0	53.6
105 CHRISTIAN REF.	1	78	112	0.2	0.2
165 CH OF NAZARENE	1	25	70	0.1	0.1
193 EPISCOPAL.....	2	351	515	0.8	1.0
281 LUTH CH AMER..	2	707	1,078	1.6	2.2
283 LUTH--MO SYNOD	13	7,575	10,481	16.0	21.0
293 MORAV CH-NORTH	5	1,027	1,423	2.2	2.8
371 REF CH IN AM..	1	110	179	0.3	0.4
413 S-D ADVENTISTS	3	291	369*	0.6	0.7
435 UNITARIAN-UNIV	1	21	35	0.1	0.1
443 UN C OF CHRIST	7	1,359	1,724*	2.6	3.4
449 UN METHODIST..	5	2,069	2,717	4.2	5.4
453 UN PRES CH USA	2	815	1,034*	1.6	2.1
469 WISC EVAN LUTH	2	1,292	1,810	2.8	3.6
CO DATA NOT AVAIL	28	1,374	6,601	N/A	N/A
151 L-D SAINTS....	0	0	5,040	N/A	N/A
467 WESLEYAN......	28	1,374	1,561	N/A	N/A

WYOMING

County and Denomination	Number of churches	Communicant, confirmed, full members	Total adherents: Number	Total adherents: Percent of total population	Total adherents: Percent of total adherents
THE STATE.....	361	60,950	158,198*	47.6	100.0
ALBANY	17	4,134	10,384*	39.3	100.0
019 AMER BAPT CONV	1	638	765*	2.9	7.4

*Total adherents estimated from known number of communicant, confirmed, full members.

—Represents a percent less than 0.1.

Percentages may not total due to rounding.

Table 3. Churches and Church Membership by State, County and Denomination: 1971

County and Denomination	Number of churches	Communicant, confirmed, full members	Total adherents: Number	Total adherents: Percent of total population	Total adherents: Percent of total adherents
081 CATHOLIC......	3	0	5,010	19.0	48.2
165 CH OF NAZARENE	1	27	144	0.5	1.4
193 EPISCOPAL.....	1	659	878	3.3	8.5
281 LUTH CH AMER..	1	293	443	1.7	4.3
283 LUTH--MO SYNOD	2	325	450	1.7	4.3
403 SALVATION ARMY	1	27	82	0.3	0.8
413 S-D ADVENTISTS	1	190	228*	0.9	2.2
419 SO BAPT CONV..	2	305	366*	1.4	3.5
435 UNITARIAN-UNIV	1	25	44	0.2	0.4
443 UN C OF CHRIST	1	110	132*	0.5	1.3
449 UN METHODIST..	1	825	991	3.7	9.5
453 UN PRES CH USA	1	710	851*	3.2	8.2
BIG HORN	19	1,694	3,135*	30.7	100.0
019 AMER BAPT CONV	2	176	214*	2.1	6.8
081 CATHOLIC......	3	0	875	8.6	27.9
165 CH OF NAZARENE	1	20	30	0.3	1.0
193 EPISCOPAL.....	2	106	218	2.1	7.0
283 LUTH--MO SYNOD	3	452	638	6.3	20.4
413 S-D ADVENTISTS	1	38	46*	0.5	1.5
419 SO BAPT CONV..	1	105	128*	1.3	4.1
449 UN METHODIST..	5	661	821	8.0	26.2
453 UN PRES CH USA	1	136	165*	1.6	5.3
CAMPBELL	6	1,454	2,871*	22.2	100.0
019 AMER BAPT CONV	1	279	367*	2.8	12.8
081 CATHOLIC......	1	0	930	7.2	32.4
097 CR C AND C CR.	1	300	394*	3.0	13.7
283 LUTH--MO SYNOD	1	219	318	2.5	11.1
413 S-D ADVENTISTS	1	45	59*	0.5	2.1
453 UN PRES CH USA	1	611	803*	6.2	28.0
CARBON	23	1,649	4,990*	37.4	100.0
019 AMER BAPT CONV	2	200	245*	1.8	4.9
081 CATHOLIC......	5	0	2,604	19.5	52.2
165 CH OF NAZARENE	1	22	66	0.5	1.3
193 EPISCOPAL.....	3	220	609	4.6	12.2
283 LUTH--MO SYNOD	4	275	398	3.0	8.0
413 S-D ADVENTISTS	2	53	65*	0.5	1.3
449 UN METHODIST..	3	456	486	3.6	9.7
453 UN PRES CH USA	3	423	517*	3.9	10.4
CONVERSE	11	1,163	2,229*	37.5	100.0
019 AMER BAPT CONV	2	329	397*	6.7	17.8
081 CATHOLIC......	2	0	743	12.5	33.3
165 CH OF NAZARENE	1	2	2	-	0.1
193 EPISCOPAL.....	3	288	452	7.6	20.3
283 LUTH--MO SYNOD	1	58	86	1.4	3.9
443 UN C OF CHRIST	1	132	159*	2.7	7.1
449 UN METHODIST..	1	354	390	6.6	17.5
CROOK	9	754	1,449*	32.0	100.0
019 AMER BAPT CONV	1	211	265*	5.8	18.3
081 CATHOLIC......	3	0	493	10.9	34.0
193 EPISCOPAL.....	1	117	174	3.8	12.0
283 LUTH--MO SYNOD	1	107	152	3.4	10.5
413 S-D ADVENTISTS	1	47	59*	1.3	4.1
449 UN METHODIST..	1	140	140	3.1	9.7
453 UN PRES CH USA	1	132	166*	3.7	11.5
FREMONT	37	4,563	10,822*	38.2	100.0
019 AMER BAPT CONV	1	183	233*	0.8	2.2
029 AMER LUTH CH..	2	249	408	1.4	3.8
081 CATHOLIC......	8	0	3,545	12.5	32.8
097 CR C AND C CR.	2	75	95*	0.3	0.9
165 CH OF NAZARENE	3	193	423	1.5	3.9
193 EPISCOPAL.....	5	735	1,903	6.7	17.6
283 LUTH--MO SYNOD	6	725	1,098	3.9	10.1
353 PLY BRETHREN..	1	2	2	-	-
413 S-D ADVENTISTS	2	123	156*	0.6	1.4
419 SO BAPT CONV..	1	412	524*	1.8	4.8
449 UN METHODIST..	4	1,550	2,033	7.2	18.8
453 UN PRES CH USA	2	316	402*	1.4	3.7
GOSHEN	15	3,141	5,094*	46.8	100.0
019 AMER BAPT CONV	1	266	319*	2.9	6.3
081 CATHOLIC......	2	0	1,150	10.6	22.6
097 CR C AND C CR.	2	100	120*	1.1	2.4
165 CH OF NAZARENE	1	33	115	1.1	2.3
193 EPISCOPAL.....	1	160	216	2.0	4.2
283 LUTH--MO SYNOD	1	331	454	4.2	8.9
413 S-D ADVENTISTS	1	102	123*	1.1	2.4
443 UN C OF CHRIST	1	372	447*	4.1	8.8
449 UN METHODIST..	1	593	728	6.7	14.3
453 UN PRES CH USA	4	1,184	1,422*	13.1	27.9
HOT SPRINGS	6	1,020	1,537*	31.0	100.0
019 AMER BAPT CONV	1	364	429*	8.7	27.9
081 CATHOLIC......	1	0	354	7.1	23.0
283 LUTH--MO SYNOD	1	95	158	3.2	10.3
413 S-D ADVENTISTS	1	34	40*	0.8	2.6
449 UN METHODIST..	1	363	363	7.3	23.6
453 UN PRES CH USA	1	164	193*	3.9	12.6
JOHNSON	7	1,008	2,064*	36.9	100.0
081 CATHOLIC......	1	0	689	12.3	33.4
193 EPISCOPAL.....	1	278	476	8.5	23.1
281 LUTH CH AMER..	1	120	180	3.2	8.7
413 S-D ADVENTISTS	1	70	84*	1.5	4.1
443 UN C OF CHRIST	1	236	284*	5.1	13.8
449 UN METHODIST..	2	304	351	6.3	17.0
LARAMIE	42	12,552	25,684*	45.6	100.0
019 AMER BAPT CONV	3	1,293	1,606*	2.8	6.3
029 AMER LUTH CH..	1	215	353	0.6	1.4
081 CATHOLIC......	7	0	8,583	15.2	33.4
093 CR CH (DISC)..	2	1,207	1,499*	2.7	5.8
097 CR C AND C CR.	1	95	118*	0.2	0.5
127 CH GOD (CLEVE)	1	83	103*	0.2	0.4
165 CH OF NAZARENE	2	216	558	1.0	2.2
175 CONG CR CH....	1	1,277	1,586*	2.8	6.2
193 EPISCOPAL.....	2	1,025	1,579	2.8	6.1
201 EVAN COV CH AM	1	27	34*	0.1	0.1
221 FREE METH C NA	1	16	23	-	0.1
281 LUTH CH AMER..	2	751	1,048	1.9	4.1
283 LUTH--MO SYNOD	4	1,146	1,655	2.9	6.4
403 SALVATION ARMY	1	63	343	0.6	1.3
413 S-D ADVENTISTS	2	179	222*	0.4	0.9
419 SO BAPT CONV..	4	782	971*	1.7	3.8
435 UNITARIAN-UNIV	1	25	25	-	0.1
443 UN C OF CHRIST	1	150	186*	0.3	0.7
449 UN METHODIST..	2	2,302	3,081	5.5	12.0
453 UN PRES CH USA	3	1,700	2,111*	3.7	8.2
LINCOLN	7	235	1,049*	12.1	100.0
019 AMER BAPT CONV	1	15	19*	0.2	1.8
081 CATHOLIC......	2	0	670	7.8	63.9
193 EPISCOPAL.....	2	66	145	1.7	13.8
283 LUTH--MO SYNOD	1	68	111	1.3	10.6
449 UN METHODIST..	1	86	104	1.2	9.9
NATRONA	38	10,767	23,179*	45.2	100.0
019 AMER BAPT CONV	4	914	1,126*	2.2	4.9
029 AMER LUTH CH..	2	839	1,258	2.5	5.4
081 CATHOLIC......	4	0	8,348	16.3	36.0
093 CR CH (DISC)..	1	744	916*	1.8	4.0
097 CR C AND C CR.	3	225	277*	0.5	1.2
123 CH GOD (ANDER)	1	42	117	0.2	0.5
127 CH GOD (CLEVE)	1	54	67*	0.1	0.3
165 CH OF NAZARENE	1	233	477	0.9	2.1
193 EPISCOPAL.....	3	1,040	1,890	3.7	8.2
281 LUTH CH AMER..	1	441	666	1.3	2.9
283 LUTH--MO SYNOD	2	727	1,009	2.0	4.4
403 SALVATION ARMY	1	39	147	0.3	0.6
413 S-D ADVENTISTS	1	218	268*	0.5	1.2
419 SO BAPT CONV..	5	1,646	2,027*	4.0	8.7
435 UNITARIAN-UNIV	1	23	23	-	0.1
443 UN C OF CHRIST	1	132	163*	0.3	0.7
449 UN METHODIST..	2	1,938	2,538	5.0	10.9
453 UN PRES CH USA	4	1,512	1,862*	3.6	8.0
NIOBRARA	6	733	1,277*	43.7	100.0
019 AMER BAPT CONV	1	269	317*	10.8	24.8
081 CATHOLIC......	1	0	380	13.0	29.8
097 CR C AND C CR.	1	40	47*	1.6	3.7
193 EPISCOPAL.....	1	69	92	3.1	7.2
283 LUTH--MO SYNOD	1	147	196	6.7	15.3
443 UN C OF CHRIST	1	208	245*	8.4	19.2
PARK	20	3,797	6,720*	37.9	100.0
029 AMER LUTH CH..	2	428	652	3.7	9.7
081 CATHOLIC......	3	0	1,572	8.9	23.4
123 CH GOD (ANDER)	2	59	134	0.8	2.0
165 CH OF NAZARENE	2	85	131	0.7	1.9
193 EPISCOPAL.....	2	318	517	2.9	7.7
283 LUTH--MO SYNOD	2	309	460	2.6	6.8
413 S-D ADVENTISTS	1	85	104*	0.6	1.5
419 SO BAPT CONV..	2	364	446*	2.5	6.6
449 UN METHODIST..	2	961	1,248	7.0	18.6
453 UN PRES CH USA	2	1,188	1,456*	8.2	21.7
PLATTE	14	1,302	2,319*	35.8	100.0
081 CATHOLIC......	4	0	672	10.4	29.0
097 CR C AND C CR.	1	280	337*	5.2	14.5
165 CH OF NAZARENE	1	51	82	1.3	3.5
193 EPISCOPAL.....	2	123	144	2.2	6.2
283 LUTH--MO SYNOD	1	157	250	3.9	10.8
419 SO BAPT CONV..	1	42	51*	0.8	2.2
443 UN C OF CHRIST	1	244	294*	4.5	12.7
449 UN METHODIST..	2	328	396	6.1	17.1
453 UN PRES CH USA	1	77	93*	1.4	4.0
SHERIDAN	19	4,159	7,722*	43.3	100.0
081 CATHOLIC......	5	0	2,272	12.7	29.4
093 CR CH (DISC)..	1	300	350*	2.0	4.5
097 CR C AND C CR.	1	40	47*	0.3	0.6
165 CH OF NAZARENE	1	49	109	0.6	1.4
175 CONG CR CH....	1	45	52*	0.3	0.7
193 EPISCOPAL.....	1	960	1,402	7.9	18.2
281 LUTH CH AMER..	1	370	549	3.1	7.1
283 LUTH--MO SYNOD	1	448	598	3.3	7.7
403 SALVATION ARMY	1	16	64	0.4	0.8
413 S-D ADVENTISTS	1	158	184*	1.0	2.4
419 SO BAPT CONV..	1	85	99*	0.6	1.3

*Total adherents estimated from known number of communicant, confirmed, full members.

—Represents a percent less than 0.1.

Percentages may not total due to rounding.

Table 3. Churches and Church Membership by State, County and Denomination: 1971

County and Denomination	Number of churches	Communicant, confirmed, full members	Total adherents		
			Number	Percent of total population	Percent of total adherents
443 UN C OF CHRIST	1	260	303*	1.7	3.9
449 UN METHODIST..	2	770	926	5.2	12.0
453 UN PRES CH USA	1	658	767*	4.3	9.9
SUBLETTE	9	562	1,303*	34.7	100.0
081 CATHOLIC......	2	0	535	14.2	41.1
175 CONG CR CH....	1	122	154*	4.1	11.8
193 EPISCOPAL.....	2	147	225	6.0	17.3
283 LUTH--MO SYNOD	1	49	81	2.2	6.2
413 S-D ADVENTISTS	1	27	34*	0.9	2.6
419 SO BAPT CONV..	1	110	139*	3.7	10.7
443 UN C OF CHRIST	1	107	135*	3.6	10.4
SWEETWATER	19	2,213	7,670*	41.7	100.0
019 AMER BAPT CONV	2	292	362*	2.0	4.7
081 CATHOLIC......	4	0	4,437	24.1	57.8
165 CH OF NAZARENE	2	48	152	0.8	2.0
193 EPISCOPAL.....	3	350	741	4.0	9.7
283 LUTH--MO SYNOD	2	213	315	1.7	4.1
413 S-D ADVENTISTS	1	73	90*	0.5	1.2
419 SO BAPT CONV..	2	263	326*	1.8	4.3
443 UN C OF CHRIST	2	732	907*	4.9	11.8
449 UN METHODIST..	1	242	340	1.8	4.4
TETON	4	312	1,022*	21.2	100.0
019 AMER BAPT CONV	1	112	138*	2.9	13.5
081 CATHOLIC......	1	0	300	6.2	29.4
193 EPISCOPAL.....	1	115	390	8.1	38.2
283 LUTH--MO SYNOD	1	85	194	4.0	19.0
UINTA	8	396	1,247*	17.6	100.0
019 AMER BAPT CONV	1	77	94*	1.3	7.5
081 CATHOLIC......	3	0	725	10.2	58.1
193 EPISCOPAL.....	1	76	131	1.8	10.5
419 SO BAPT CONV..	1	54	66*	0.9	5.3
453 UN PRES CH USA	2	189	231*	3.3	18.5
WASHAKIE	15	2,695	4,251*	56.2	100.0
019 AMER BAPT CONV	1	319	395*	5.2	9.3
029 AMER LUTH CH..	1	97	183	2.4	4.3
081 CATHOLIC......	1	0	650	8.6	15.3
097 CR C AND C CR.	1	65	80*	1.1	1.9
123 CH GOD (ANDER)	1	40	110	1.5	2.6
165 CH OF NAZARENE	1	21	55	0.7	1.3
193 EPISCOPAL.....	1	206	300	4.0	7.1
283 LUTH--MO SYNOD	1	125	209	2.8	4.9
413 S-D ADVENTISTS	2	79	98*	1.3	2.3
419 SO BAPT CONV..	1	323	400*	5.3	9.4
443 UN C OF CHRIST	1	350	433*	5.7	10.2
449 UN METHODIST..	2	889	1,114	14.7	26.2
453 UN PRES CH USA	1	181	224*	3.0	5.3
WESTON	9	602	1,171*	18.6	100.0
029 AMER LUTH CH..	1	110	157	2.5	13.4
081 CATHOLIC......	1	0	380	6.0	32.5
097 CR C AND C CR.	1	45	56*	0.9	4.8
123 CH GOD (ANDER)	1	25	50	0.8	4.3
193 EPISCOPAL.....	1	87	87	1.4	7.4
413 S-D ADVENTISTS	2	84	104*	1.6	8.9
419 SO BAPT CONV..	1	84	104*	1.6	8.9
449 UN METHODIST..	1	167	233	3.7	19.9
CO DATA NOT AVAIL	1	45	29,009*	N/A	N/A
151 L-D SAINTS....	0	0	28,954	N/A	N/A
223 FREE WILL BAPT	1	45	55*	N/A	N/A

County and Denomination	Number of churches	Communicant, confirmed, full members	Total adherents		
			Number	Percent of total population	Percent of total adherents

*Total adherents estimated from known number of communicant, confirmed, full members.

—Represents a percent less than 0.1.

Percentages may not total due to rounding.

INSTRUMENTS FOR GATHERING THE DATA

LETTER INVITING DENOMINATIONS TO PARTICIPATE IN THE STUDY, JANUARY 10, 1973

TO: Statisticians of American Religious Bodies
FROM: Constant Jacquet, Jr., National Council of the Churches of Christ in the U. S. A.

A wonderful opportunity has arisen for religious bodies in the United States to cooperate in a truly useful and significant research project leading toward the production of a computerized report entitled "A Study of Churches and Church Membership in the U. S. - 1971."

This report will provide each participant denomination with information on: Number of churches, number of communicant, confirmed, full members; total number of adherents; adherents as a percent of total population and as a percent of total adherents.

The above information will be presented in three sets of tables as follows: (1) Churches and church membership: U. S. summary, (2) churches and church membership in the U. S. by state and denomination, (3) churches and church membership in the U. S. by state and counties. A sample of the projected printout is enclosed in this letter.

In order to become involved in the study, each communion should return the enclosed card indicating a willingness to participate. Upon receipt of the enclosed card, additional information will be sent describing the procedures of the study. I am sure you will find these procedures relatively painless.

Many of you will recall that a similar study using 1952 data was made a number of years ago involving 114 U. S. religious bodies which was entitled "Churches and Church Membership in the United States: An Enumeration and Analysis by Counties, States and Regions." This was published by the National Council of Churches in 1957.

This monumental survey has been very much in demand since its appearance in 1957 and is utilized by religious and secular institutions. However, it is apparent that the new report "A Study of Churches and Church Membership in the U. S. - 1971" is vitally needed since the data now available on the subject are 20 years old!

The Executive Committee for this new study includes representatives from the National Council of Churches, the Roman Catholic Church and the Lutheran Church - Missouri Synod. A number of large denominations have indicated a willingness to cooperate in this project.

Furthermore, a financial grant has been received from Aid Association for Lutherans to carry forward the study. The grant provides that at least five copies of the report will be made available at no cost to participating denominations. In addition, the computerized data will be made available to each denomination at cost.

Therefore, I urge you to send in the enclosed card and to work with others on this significant project for the good of all the churches. The data will be valuable in planning mission and development in each communion and can be used in many other ways.

Your cooperation with the Yearbook of American and Canadian Churches over the years has convinced me of your good will and desire to develop reliable and useful statistics for organized religion. Your cooperation in "A Study of Churches and Church Membership in the U.S. 1971" will, it is hoped, continue this trend.

LETTER REQUESTING PRELIMINARY INFORMATION

TO: Participating Denominations
FROM: Paul Picard, Lutheran Church - Missouri Synod

This past week I received notification from the Office of Research and Planning of the National Council of Churches that your denomination will participate in the Church and Church Membership Distribution Study. We are very happy that your denomination will be included in this study, and we are convinced that you will find the final report and the body of data resulting from this study to be of considerable value to your denomination and to you in your work.

Attached to this letter I am sending you a form which I would as you to complete and return to me as the first step in providing the necessary data for your denomination. On this form I am asking you to indicate those states in which your denomination has congregations located. We will then return to you a complete set of prepunched and preprinted IBM cards for these states, on which you may report the churches and church membership data for your denomination. We are asking for this initial form in order to reduce the cost and inconvenience of preparing and sending to you a large number of IBM cards which you would not need.

We would ask you also to indicate on that form the date of the statistics which you will be reporting to us. We hope to receive statistics as of December 31, 1971; however, we recognize that some denominations collect their statistics in the spring, some in the fall, etc.; and we will of course, use these statistics. Also, if the reporting date for statistics in your denomination is other than December 31, 1971, we hope you could report those statistics which are nearest this date.

While you are awaiting our return supply of IBM cards you might wish to begin compiling the data which you will report for your denomination. We will be asking that you report the number of churches, number of confirmed members, number of other members, and total inclusive membership.

Definition of Data Items:

1. Total number of local churches (congregations, parishes) in religious body.

2. Total confirmed or full members (These are "regular" members with full membership status. They may be referred to as "full," "communicant" or "confirmed" members.)

3. Total other members (includes all whom you class as "members" but who are listed as "baptized," not confirmed, not eligible for communion, etc.).

4. Total inclusive membership in the religious body (2 + 3, or 1 if no "other" category).

As soon as we receive the above mentioned form from you with the listing of states in which you have congregations located, we will send you the appropriate IBM cards. You should receive these cards within approximately ten days.

Again, we are very happy that your denomination will be included in this study.

LETTER ABOUT RECEIPT OF IBM CARDS

TO: Participating Denominations
FROM: Paul Picard, Lutheran Church - Missouri Synod

Thank you for sending us the information on the states for which you will need IBM cards for the reporting of your denomination's statistics in the Church Membership Distribution Study.

Under separate cover you will receive these cards on which you will report your denomination's statistics. Included with these cards will be specific instructions regarding the return of these data to us after these cards have been filled out.

These cards that we are sending to you are sequenced alphabetically according to county for each of the states in which you indicated that you have congregations. We are asking that you indicate the number of churches, number of full members, etc. for each of the counties in which you have one or more congregations. Please return these cards to Center for Social Research in the Church, Concordia Teachers College, River Forest, Illinois 60305.

As you probably know the U. S. Bureau of Census redefined the census units within Alaska, and since you indicated that you have congregations located in Alaska you will receive with the IBM cards special instructions for reporting data for these congregations.

You indicated on your form that your denomination has congregations located in Virginia. Frankly, Virginia has created considerable difficulties for us because of the large number of "city-counties" which they have identified in their statistical reporting to the Census Bureau. For this reason I would call your attention to four "city-counties" in Virginia for which we ask that you report your congregations and memberships according to these separate units, as they have been preprinted on the IBM cards sent to you. (The four "city-counties" are Hampton; Newport News; Virginia Beach; and Norfolk-Chesapeake-Portsmouth.)

Enclosed with the IBM cards sent to you is a small form on which we are asking you to provide the name of a contact person whom we may call upon in case any questions arise regarding your data.

LETTER ABOUT PREPARING IBM CARDS

TO: Participating Denominations
FROM: Victor Streufert, Center for Social Research in the Church

Rev. Paul Picard has informed us of the willingness of your religious body to participate in the Church Membership Distribution Study. Enclosed please find a copy of the form which you submitted to Rev. Picard. In accordance with your selection of states on this form, we are sending you the computer cards enclosed in this package. We consider it a privilege to work with you on this highly worthwhile project and wish to extend our thanks to you for your cooperation in the activities which it entails.

Since the data which is gathered for this study will be processed by a computer, it is probably all the more important that directions for recording your denominational statistics be followed carefully. Please note the "General Instruction" which will apply to all of the participating denominations. Should your church body have churches and/or membership in Alaska or Virginia, it is important for you to observe the "Special Instructions" which apply to recording data for these two states.

GENERAL INSTRUCTIONS FOR PREPARING IBM CARDS

State County

CHURCH DISTRIBUTION STUDY

Data to be recorded on this card applies only to county specified above.

A) Total number of churches: number of congregations or parishes in county.

B) Total confirmed or full members: "regular" members with full membership status - "full," "communicant" or "confirmed" members.

C) Total other members: all others classed as "members" - listed as "baptized," "not confirmed," "not eligible for communion," etc.

D) Total inclusive membership: "total confirmed or full members" plus "total other members." List "total confirmed or full members" if there are no members in the "total other members" category.

Note the name of the state and county imprinted at the top of each card. On the card record the data which applies only to the specific county and state indicated at the top. Your office should have received a separate card for every county in each of the states which were specified on the form sent to Rev. Picard. If you should find that we have failed to send you the appropriate cards for a given state or if you discover membership and/or churches in states other than those requested, please mail us the enclosed request and the additional cards will be sent to you by return mail.

Record the TOTAL NUMBER OF CHURCHES for the county specified on the card in the row of boxes preceded by the letter "A." Please place the numbers as far to the right as possible.

Record the TOTAL CONFIRMED OR FULL MEMBERS for the county specified on the card in the row of boxes preceded by the letter "B." "Confirmed or Full Members" are regular members with full membership status. They may be referred to as "full," "confirmed," or "communicant" members. Please place the numbers as far to the right in the boxes as possible.

Record the TOTAL OTHER MEMBERS for the county specified on the card in the row of boxes preceded by the letter "C." The "Other Members" include all whom you class as "members" but who are listed as "baptized," "not confirmed," "not eligible for communion," etc. Once again, place the numbers as far to the right as possible. In case your denomination does not maintain records of "Other Members," please draw a line through the boxes following letter "C."

Finally, record the TOTAL INCLUSIVE MEMBERSHIP for the county specified on the card in the row of boxes preceded by the letter "D." This statistic is obtained by adding the "Total Confirmed or Full Members" and the "Total Other Members." If your church body records only the "Confirmed or Full Member" data, you would write only the "Confirmed or Full Member" data in the boxes following the letter "D."

You probably will have received some recording cards for counties in which your church body has neither churches nor membership. In this event, please place an "X" through the entire card. Even if you place an "X" through a card, please return the card to us along with the cards upon which you have recorded data. In this way we can be confident that there was no applicable data for that county rather than wondering whether a given county was inadvertently excluded from your report.

If you have churches and/or membership in either Alaska or Virginia, please note the "Special Instructions" which pertain to the recording of data for those two states.

SPECIAL INSTRUCTIONS FOR RECORDING ALASKA AND VIRGINIA DATA

ALASKA. The data of the 1970 U. S. Census for Alaska has been classified by "census divisions." Since Alaska has no counties, the census divisions serve as county equivalents for statistical reporting purposes. A list of census divisions follows:

Aleutian Islands, Anchorage, Angoon, Barrow, Bethel, Bristol Bay Borough, Bristol Bay, Cordova-McCarthy, Fairbanks, Haines, Juneau, Kenai-Cook Inlet, Ketchikan, Kobuk, Kodiak, Kuskokwim, Matanuska-Susitna, Nome, Outer Ketchikan, Prince of Wales, Seward, Sitka, Skagway-Yakutat, Southeast Fairbanks, Upper Yukon, Valdez-Chitina-Whittier, Wade Hampton, Wrangell-Petersburg, Yukon-Koyukuk

VIRGINIA. In Virginia there are 38 "Independent Cities" which are legally separate from the counties of that state. Most denominations probably still record churches by location within the counties from which the cities have separated. For this reason we request that the data of your denomination be so organized as to record the data of the following Independent Cities with the indicated counties:

Independent City	County	Abbreviation
Alexandria city with	Arlington	Arlington-Alexandria
Bedford	Bedford	Bedford-Bedford City
Bristol city with	Washington	Washington-Bristol
Buena Vista city with	Rockbridge	Rockbridge-Bn Vs-Lex
Charlottesville city with	Albermarle	Albemarle-Charlottes
Clifton Forge city with	Alleghany	Alleghany-Clf Fr-Cov
Colonial Heights city with	Dinwiddie	Dinwiddie-Col Ht-Pet
Covington city with	Alleghany	Alleghany-Clf Fr-Cov
Danville city with	Pittsylvania	Pittsylvania-Danvill
Emporia city with	Greensville	Greensville-Emporia
Fairfax city with	Fairfax	Fairfax-Fairfx-Fl Ch
Falls Church city with	Fairfax	Fairfax-Fairfx-Fl Ch
Franklin city with	Southampton	Southampton-Franklin
Fredericksburg city with	Spotsylvania	Spotsylvania-Frederi
Galax city with	Carroll	Carroll-Galax City
Harrisonburg city with	Rockingham	Rockingham-Harrison
Hopewell city with	Prince George	Prince George-Hopewe
Lexington city with	Rockbridge	Rockbridge-Bn Vs-Lex
Lynchburg city with	Campbell	Campbell-Lynchburg
Martinsville city with	Henry	Henry-Martinsville
Norton city with	Wise	Wise-Norton City
Petersburg city with	Dinwiddie	Dinwiddie-Col Ht-Pet
Radford city with	Montgomery	Montgomery-Radford
Richmond city with	Henrico	Henrico-Richmond
Roanoke city with	Roanoke	Roanoke-Roanoke-Salm
Salem city with	Roanoke	Roanoke-Roanoke-Salm
South Boston city with	Halifax	Halifax-South Boston
Staunton city with	Augusta	Augusta-Staun-Waynes
Suffolk city with	Nansemond	Nansemond-Suffolk
Waynesboro city with	Augusta	Augusta-Staun-Waynes
Williamsburg city with	James City	James City-Williams
Winchester city with	Frederick	Frederick-Winchester

The only exceptions to the above pattern occur in the case of Independent Cities which have annexed their parent counties. These are usually treated as separate "city-county" combinations and will be treated as such in the church distribution study.

Independent City	Name on Recording Card
Hampton city	Hampton City
Newport News city	Newport News City
Virginia Beach city	Virginia Beach City
Norfolk city Chesapeake city Portsmouth city	Norfolk-Chesap-Ports

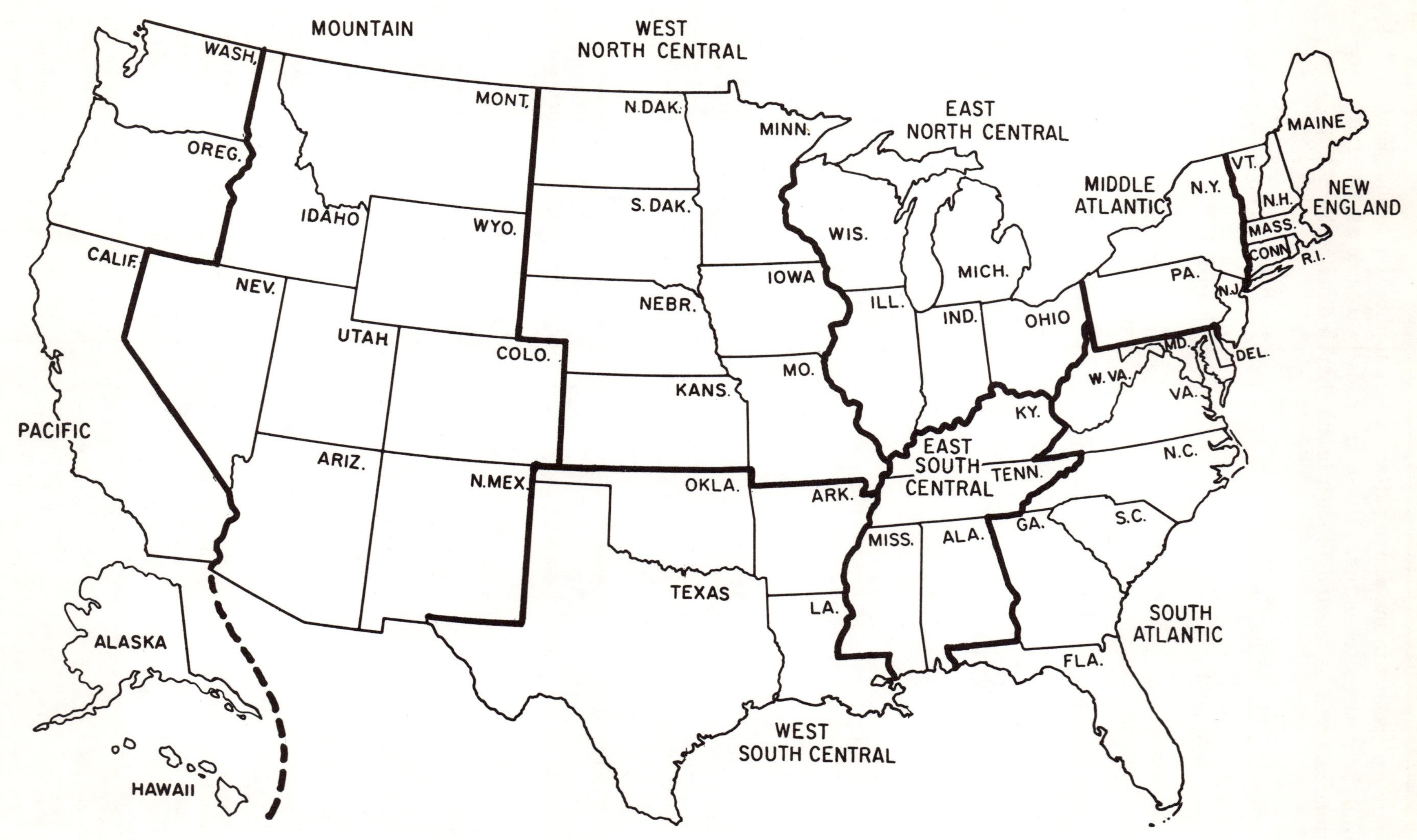

MOUNTAIN
WEST NORTH CENTRAL
EAST NORTH CENTRAL
MIDDLE ATLANTIC
NEW ENGLAND
WASH.
MONT.
N.DAK.
MINN.
MAINE
VT.
N.Y.
N.H.
MASS.
CONN.
R.I.
OREG.
IDAHO
WYO.
S.DAK.
WIS.
MICH.
CALIF.
NEV.
IOWA
PA.
N.J.
NEBR.
ILL.
IND.
OHIO
UTAH
COLO.
MD.
DEL.
MO.
W. VA.
KANS.
VA.
KY.
PACIFIC
EAST SOUTH CENTRAL
TENN.
N.C.
ARIZ.
N.MEX.
OKLA.
ARK.
S.C.
MISS.
ALA.
GA.
TEXAS
LA.
SOUTH ATLANTIC
ALASKA
FLA.
WEST SOUTH CENTRAL
HAWAII

Table 2. Region, State and Denomination

Table 3. State, County and Denomination